THEORY *and* APPLICATION *of the* LINEAR MODEL

THEORY *and* APPLICATION *of the* LINEAR MODEL

FRANKLIN A. GRAYBILL

Colorado State University

DUXBURY PRESS

North Scituate · Massachusetts

Duxbury Press

A DIVISION OF WADSWORTH PUBLISHING COMPANY, INC.

Theory and Application of the Linear Model was edited and prepared for composition by Carol Beal. The interior design was provided by Dorothy Booth. The cover was designed by Oliver Kline.

L. C. Catalog Card No.: 75-41970
ISBN: 0-87872-108-8

PRINTED IN THE UNITED STATES OF AMERICA

1 2 3 4 5 6 7 8 9—80 79 78 77 76

To Jeanne
and
Tonia and Jules

CONTENTS

Preface

A significant portion of the subject called statistics that is used in applied problems is directly or peripherally related to the linear statistical model. There is perhaps no subject within the field of statistics that has been more widely investigated and published. This quantity of publications is ample proof of the usefulness of the linear model in real problems.

There is, of course, no complete agreement by all statisticians about what the content of linear model theory includes. Some would say that it is a part of traditional multivariate analysis, and in most cases it can be viewed this way. However, in this book I consider it to be what is usually referred to as analysis of variance, correlation and regression, and design of experiments.

Since the literature is so vast and the number of users so large, it is impossible to write a book that can cover all the topics or that will be appropriate for all people who are interested in the three areas of statistics referred to above. I have attempted to write a book that will be useful to the following people: (1) students who will obtain a master's degree in statistics and will work as statisticians in industry or government; (2) students who will obtain a Ph.D. degree in statistics and who plan to do teaching, consulting, or research in applied statistics; (3) students who will obtain a master's or Ph.D. degree in a field other than statistics but who plan to work in an area where analysis of variance, regression and correlation, or design of experiments will be required; (4) anyone who is working in a subject area who wants a beginning theory text in linear model theory for self-study or reference.

Background Needed

This is not a book on mathematics nor on theoretical statistics. It is intended to be an introductory book that covers some topics in linear models that will be useful to experimenters, statistical consultants, and those who are training to be statistical consultants. The mathematics courses required for this book include two or three semesters of college-level calculus and one semester of matrix algebra. The statistics requirements are two or three courses in applied statistics, including study of correlation and regression and the design of experiments, and one year of theoretical statistics from books such as [D-13], [F-2], [H-16], [L-10], and [M-7] listed in "References and Further Reading" at the end of this book. For the past several years I have taught a course at Colorado State University from notes which resulted in this book, and some of the students had fewer courses than those listed above, but many students had taken more courses. About twenty-five percent of the students who took this course during those years were graduate students not in statistics; about seventy-five percent of the students were graduate students in statistics. I cover all the material in the book in a two-semester course that meets three times a week.

Approach

In writing the book I have used a definition-theorem-proof procedure, but I have presented the proofs in what I call a "semirigorous" fashion: some proofs are merely sketched and a few are omitted. After Chapter 2, if a proof is omitted, a reference is generally given where a proof can be found. I have attempted to talk to the reader and in many places I have added notes and reminders that some readers may find helpful.

As I stated above, there are so many topics of potential interest in linear models that it is impossible to cover but a few of them. The approach that I take in this book is to discuss principally what is referred to as "normal theory" linear models and "least squares theory" linear models. While it is true that other "theories" of the linear model, often referred to as "distribution free" or "nonparametric" theories of the linear model, have received a great deal of attention, I feel that at the present time the normal and least squares theories are important for a first course. From a knowledge of these, one can study the so-called more robust procedures for the linear model that will certainly become a major part of statistical application in the future.

Emphases and Special Topics

Perhaps the most important chapter in the book is Chapter 6, "The General Linear Model." The chapters following Chapter 6 can be viewed as special cases or generalizations or applications of the material in that chapter. The chapters before Chapter 6 contain material that can be viewed as preparatory.

The word "application" in the title of this book may need some explanation. It refers to the following three methods of presentation: (1) some topics are discussed that are useful in applied problems, such as linear model prediction, tolerance intervals, inverse regression, polynomial and trigonometric models, testing whether models are equivalent, finding maximum (or minimum) of a quadratic model, finding the point of intersection of two models, selection of variables, growth curves, discrimination (classification); (2) in many cases topics are introduced by referring to real situations where they might be useful; (3) computing procedures are discussed for most of the topics covered.

Some of the special topics that are covered are discussed only briefly since a full discussion would require much more space than could possibly be devoted to them. In these cases I have given a setting for understanding the basics of the topic; then I present some elementary theory, followed by references where additional material that is current can be found. This will perhaps allow the reader to find those topics that may be useful and to work through the material in this book, then through some of the current literature on that particular subject.

Examples and Problems

The book contains about 150 examples, many of them involving data. In most cases "real" data are not used since the examples are used mainly to illustrate a point or to help fix an idea for the reader. There is something to be said for using real data, but if sufficient time and space are not devoted to a discussion of the situation that generated the real data, these arguments lose some of their force. I felt that it would not be a good use of space to use real data with all the attending explanations that would be essential. The classroom instructor can enrich the course by using real examples if they seem appropriate.

The book contains a large amount of material about methods for computing the quantities needed in problems where data are involved. Many computing methods are available and some of them are machine dependent. I chose to use the square root (Cholesky) procedure throughout the book. This decision was based on many factors, among which were the following: (1) the normal equations are very useful for the theoretical development of most topics in the linear model and they involve a nonnegative matrix; (2) in most cases (except possibly for high degree polynomial models) the normal equations can be compiled without error from the given data; (3) the square root procedure is one of the "best" all-around methods for obtaining the quantities needed when one starts with the normal equations, where the word "best" means a balance of storage requirements, programming ease, computing time, and accuracy of results. Of course, for very large data sets and poorly conditioned data matrices, a computing procedure that does not start with the normal equations would generally be expected to give more accurate results.

The book contains about 450 problems, and an instructor's solution manual is available that, in addition to answers, includes hints for the more difficult problems. The problems include some that are theoretical and some that require simple computing. Some are quite trivial and some are quite difficult.

Suggested Coverage

The book contains fifteen chapters. Chapters 1 and 2 contain review topics in mathematics (mainly matrix algebra) and statistics and can be read quickly by the reader who has adequate prerequisites for the course. Chapter 3 contains material on the multivariate normal, and Chapter 4 is devoted to quadratic forms of normal random variables. These two chapters can also be covered quite quickly. Chapter 5 discusses various models that are presented in the book and is a reading chapter. Chapter 6 is the first encounter with a detailed presentation of the linear model, and references to material in the first five chapters are made when that material is needed. Chapter 7 is a chapter on computing, and Chapter 8 is devoted to several applications of the general linear model. Chapter 9 contains a brief discussion of inference procedures when sampling from the multivariate normal distribution. Chapter 10 discusses the regression model and relates it to the general linear model, and Chapter 11 is devoted to inference procedures for simple, multiple, and partial correlation. Chapter 12 is devoted to applications of the regression model and includes regression prediction theory, selection of variables, growth curves, and discrimination. Chapter 13 discusses the general theory of the design model and the special case of the one-factor design model. In Chapter 14 there is a detailed discussion of the two-factor design model with and without interaction and with equal and unequal numbers. Chapter 15 is devoted to the subject of variance components.

As was stated previously, the material in this book can be covered in a two-semester course that meets three times per week. For a one-semester course the following is recommended. The material in Chapters 1, 2, 3, 4, and 5 can be covered quite rapidly but not in depth; cover Chapters 6 and 7 in depth; then select other chapters depending on one's interest. For applications of the linear model, cover Chapter 8; for correlation, cover Chapter 9 (but not in depth) and Chapter 11; for applications of the regression model, select Chapters 9, 10, 11, and 12; for design models, cover Chapters 13 and 14 (also Chapter 15 if one is interested in components of variance).

References

The book contains a "References and Further Reading" section where over 200 books and papers are listed. Since the literature on the linear model is so huge, one has to pick and choose to obtain a manageable set that adequately covers the main topics and includes the important publications. All items in this section are not referenced in the book. The intent is to include a list where one can start with a publication on a given topic, examine the referenced papers and others that are included, examine the references listed in these papers, and thereby obtain a set of several papers on the topic of interest. Very few publications dated after 1973 are included.

Acknowledgements

I would like to express appreciation to all who have contributed to this book. However, there have been so many contributors that I hesitate to name them for fear that some will be inadvertently omitted. I must thank my colleagues and the graduate students in the department of statistics at Colorado State University for their assistance which was provided in many ways. Thanks are also due to the administrative officers at Colorado State University for providing resources and an environment in which a project such as this can be accomplished. I am grateful to the Literary Executor of the late Sir Ronald A. Fisher, F.R.S., to Dr. Frank Yates, F.R.S. and to Longman Group Ltd., London, for permission to reprint Table III from their book *Statistical Tables for Biological, Agricultural and Medical Research.* (6th edition, 1974.) I want to thank the many authors and organizations for allowing me to reprint material and these acknowledgements are made in the book where the material appears. Finally, I want to thank my wife Jeanne who has helped me in so many ways, some of which I am sure I am not aware of.

CHAPTER 1

Mathematical Concepts

1.1 Introduction

The theory of the linear statistical model that will be developed in this book will require some knowledge of calculus and matrix algebra. The calculus requirements are taught in conventional college courses given to freshman and sophomore students and it is assumed that the reader is acquainted with this material. It is also assumed that the reader has had one or two college courses in linear or matrix algebra. Since some of the matrix and linear algebra requirements for this book are generally not taught in a first or second year college course, we will review this material here.

In Section 1.2 we state a number of theorems (without proof) that are generally covered in a first course in matrix or linear algebra. In Section 1.3 we discuss partitioned matrices. Section 1.4 contains theorems on nonnegative matrices; some of these theorems are often included in a first course in matrix algebra, but many are not. In Section 1.5 we prove some theorems on generalized and conditional inverses and in Section 1.6 we prove some theorems about the solutions of linear equations. Section 1.7 is devoted to idempotent matrices and Section 1.8 to the trace of matrices. In Section 1.9 some theorems are given for differentiation and integration, and in Section 1.10 we discuss an integral that will be useful in many sections of this book.

Most of the topics to be discussed in this chapter will be used later, and it is not essential for the reader to understand all of them now. When the topics are encountered in later chapters, reference will be made to them and they can be read again at that time. So if desired, the reader can check the topics covered and return to read them in more detail when they are referred to later.

1.2 Elementary Theorems on Linear and Matrix Algebra

In this book matrices are denoted by boldface uppercase letters, for example, **A**, **B**, **U**, **X**. We define a matrix to be a *rectangular array* of elements, called scalars, from a field F. Rather than making specific reference to the field F, we shall assume it is the field of real numbers unless explicitly stated otherwise. Thus a scalar will always be a real number unless otherwise stated. The set of real numbers is denoted by R or E_1.

The matrix **A** has elements denoted by a_{ij}, where j refers to the column and i to the row. We sometimes write

$$\mathbf{A} = [a_{ij}]$$

If **A** denotes a matrix, then $\mathbf{A}'$ will denote the transpose of **A**, and if **A** has an inverse, it will be denoted by $\mathbf{A}^{-1}$. The determinant of **A** will be denoted by either $|\mathbf{A}|$ or det(**A**). An identity matrix will be denoted by **I** (to designate the size of the identity, we shall use $\mathbf{I}_n$, which represents the $n \times n$ identity matrix), and **0** will denote a null matrix. The size of a matrix is the number of its rows by the number of its columns. For example, a matrix **A** of size $n \times m$, or an $n \times m$ matrix **A**, will be a matrix with n rows and m columns. If $m = 1$, the matrix will sometimes be called an $n \times 1$ (column) vector.

Given the matrices $\mathbf{A} = [a_{ij}]$ and $\mathbf{B} = [b_{ij}]$, the product $\mathbf{AB} = \mathbf{C} = [c_{ij}]$ is defined as the matrix **C** with the pqth element equal to

$$\sum_{s=1}^{n} a_{ps} b_{sq}$$

For **AB** to be defined, the number of columns in **A** must equal the number of rows in **B**. For $\mathbf{A} + \mathbf{B}$ to be defined, **A** and **B** must have the same size; $\mathbf{A} + \mathbf{B} = \mathbf{C}$ gives $c_{ij} = a_{ij} + b_{ij}$. If k is a scalar and **A** is a matrix, then $k\mathbf{A}$ (and $\mathbf{A}k$) is defined to be a matrix **B** such that each element of **B** is the corresponding element of **A** multiplied by k.

A diagonal matrix **D** is defined as a square matrix whose off-diagonal elements are zero; that is, if $\mathbf{D} = [d_{ij}]$, then $d_{ij} = 0$ if $i \neq j$.

Let **A** be a square matrix. If there exists a matrix **B** such that $\mathbf{AB} = \mathbf{I}$, then **B** is called the inverse of **A**, denoted by $\mathbf{A}^{-1}$. Also, if $\mathbf{AB} = \mathbf{I}$, then it can be shown that $\mathbf{BA} = \mathbf{I}$. If **A** has an inverse, **A** is called a nonsingular matrix; if **A** does not have an inverse, **A** is called a singular matrix.

THEOREM 1.2.1

If a matrix has an inverse, the inverse is unique.

THEOREM 1.2.2

If $\mathbf{A}$ *has an inverse, then* $\mathbf{A}^{-1}$ *has an inverse and* $(\mathbf{A}^{-1})^{-1} = \mathbf{A}$.

THEOREM 1.2.3

If $\mathbf{A}$ *and* $\mathbf{B}$ *are* $n \times n$ *nonsingular matrices, then* $\mathbf{AB}$ *has an inverse and* $(\mathbf{AB})^{-1} = \mathbf{B}^{-1}\mathbf{A}^{-1}$. *This can be extended to a finite number of nonsingular* $n \times n$ *matrices.*

THEOREM 1.2.4

If $\mathbf{A}$ *is a nonsingular matrix and* k *is a nonzero scalar, then*

$$(k\mathbf{A})^{-1} = (\mathbf{A}k)^{-1} = \frac{1}{(k)}\mathbf{A}^{-1}$$

If the rows and columns of a matrix $\mathbf{A}$ are interchanged, the resulting matrix is called the *transpose* of $\mathbf{A}$ and is denoted by $\mathbf{A}'$. If $\mathbf{A}$ has size $m \times n$, then $\mathbf{A}'$ has size $n \times m$.

THEOREM 1.2.5

If $\mathbf{A}$ *and* $\mathbf{B}$ *are* $m \times n$ *matrices, and* a *and* b *are scalars, then*

$$(a\mathbf{A})' = (\mathbf{A}a)' = \mathbf{A}'a = a\mathbf{A}' \qquad \text{and} \qquad (a\mathbf{A} + b\mathbf{B})' = a\mathbf{A}' + b\mathbf{B}'$$

THEOREM 1.2.6

Let $\mathbf{A}$ *and* $\mathbf{B}$ *be any matrices such that* $\mathbf{AB}$ *is defined; then*

$$(\mathbf{AB})' = \mathbf{B}'\mathbf{A}'$$

This can be extended to a finite number of matrices.

If $\mathbf{A} = \mathbf{A}'$, then $\mathbf{A}$ is called a *symmetric matrix.*

THEOREM 1.2.7

If $\mathbf{A}$ *is any matrix, then* $\mathbf{A}'\mathbf{A}$ *and* $\mathbf{AA}'$ *are symmetric.*

Assuming that the reader is acquainted with the definition of the determinant of a square matrix $\mathbf{A}$, we now state some theorems that will be useful in later developments of the topic.

THEOREM 1.2.8

If **A** *and* **B** *are* $n \times n$ *matrices, then*

$$det(\mathbf{AB}) = [det(\mathbf{A})][det(\mathbf{B})]$$

This result can be extended to a finite number of matrices.

THEOREM 1.2.9

Let A_{ij} *be the cofactor of* a_{ij}; *then*

$$det(\mathbf{A}) = \sum_{j=1}^{n} a_{ij}A_{ij}$$

for any i.

THEOREM 1.2.10

Let **A** *be an* $n \times n$ *matrix*; $|\mathbf{A}| = 0$ *if and only if* **A** *is a singular matrix.*

An $n \times m$ matrix **A** is said to be of rank r if the size of the largest nonsingular square submatrix of **A** is r. The next several theorems concern the rank of matrices.

THEOREM 1.2.11

If matrices **A** *and* **B** *are nonsingular, then for any matrix* **C** *the matrices* **C**, **AC**, **CB**, *and* **ACB** *have the same rank (assuming all multiplications are defined).*

THEOREM 1.2.12

If **A** *is an* $m \times n$ *matrix of rank r, then there exist nonsingular matrices* **P** *and* **Q** *such that* **PAQ** *is equal to*

$$\mathbf{I}, \quad [\mathbf{I}, \mathbf{0}], \quad \begin{bmatrix} \mathbf{I} \\ \mathbf{0} \end{bmatrix}, \quad \text{or} \quad \begin{bmatrix} \mathbf{I} & \mathbf{0} \\ \mathbf{0} & \mathbf{0} \end{bmatrix}$$

where $m = n = r$; $m = r < n$; $m > r = n$; *or* $m > r$ *and* $n > r$, *respectively, and where* **I** *is the* $r \times r$ *identity matrix.*

COROLLARY 1.2.12

If **A** *is an* $m \times n$ *matrix of rank* $r > 0$, *then there exist matrices* $\mathbf{A}_L$ *and* $\mathbf{A}_R$ *of sizes* $m \times r$ *and* $r \times n$, *respectively, and of ranks r such that* $\mathbf{A} = \mathbf{A}_L\mathbf{A}_R$.

In Corollary 1.2.12, $\mathbf{A}_L\mathbf{A}_R$ is called a full rank factorization of **A**.

THEOREM 1.2.13

The rank of the product of the matrices **A** *and* **B** *cannot exceed the rank of either* **A** *or* **B**.

THEOREM 1.2.14

A nonsingular matrix **A** *can always be reduced to* **I** *by elementary row (or column) transformations.*

THEOREM 1.2.15

If **A** *is an* $n \times n$ *matrix, then* $\det(\mathbf{A}) = 0$ *if and only if* $\text{rank}(\mathbf{A}) < n$.

DEFINITION 1.2.1

Quadratic Form. *A function* $f(x_1, x_2, \ldots, x_n)$ *of* n *real variables* $x_1, x_2, \ldots, x_n$ *is defined to be a quadratic form if the function is defined by* $f(x_1, x_2, \ldots, x_n) = \sum_{i=1}^{n} \sum_{j=1}^{n} a_{ij} x_i x_j = \mathbf{x}'\mathbf{A}\mathbf{x}$. *The matrix* **A** *is defined to be the matrix of the quadratic form.*

THEOREM 1.2.16

The matrix of a quadratic form can always be chosen to be symmetric.

Because of this theorem, every quadratic form in this book will be considered to have a symmetric matrix unless explicitly stated otherwise.

In a quadratic form, $\mathbf{x}'\mathbf{A}\mathbf{x}$, it is often necessary to change from the variables x_i to the variables y_i by the set of linear equations $\mathbf{y} = \mathbf{C}^{-1}\mathbf{x}$, where $\mathbf{C}^{-1}$ is an $n \times n$ nonsingular matrix. When this is done, the quadratic form $\mathbf{x}'\mathbf{A}\mathbf{x}$ becomes

$$\mathbf{x}'\mathbf{A}\mathbf{x} = \mathbf{y}'\mathbf{C}'\mathbf{A}\mathbf{C}\mathbf{y} = \mathbf{y}'(\mathbf{C}'\mathbf{A}\mathbf{C})\mathbf{y} = \mathbf{y}'\mathbf{B}\mathbf{y}$$

where **B** denotes $\mathbf{C}'\mathbf{A}\mathbf{C}$. In this case we say that **A** and **B** are congruent.

DEFINITION 1.2.2

Congruent Matrices. *Two matrices* **A** *and* **B** *are defined to be congruent if and only if there exists a nonsingular matrix* **C** *such that* $\mathbf{B} = \mathbf{C}'\mathbf{A}\mathbf{C}$, *and we refer to* **C** *as a congruent transformation of the matrix* **A**.

In this book we are generally interested in a congruent transformation of a symmetric matrix **A**.

THEOREM 1.2.17

The matrix **B** *resulting from a congruent transformation on a symmetric matrix* **A** *is symmetric.*

THEOREM 1.2.18

Let $\mathbf{A}$ *be an* $n \times n$ *(real) symmetric matrix of rank* r*; then there exists a nonsingular (real) matrix* $\mathbf{C}$ *such that* $\mathbf{C}'\mathbf{A}\mathbf{C} = \mathbf{D}$*, where* $\mathbf{D}$ *is a diagonal (real) matrix with exactly* r *nonzero diagonal elements.*

This is equivalent to saying that $\mathbf{A}$ is congruent to a diagonal matrix $\mathbf{D}$ with exactly r nonzero diagonal elements.

THEOREM 1.2.19

If $\mathbf{A}$ *and* $\mathbf{B}$ *are congruent matrices, they have the same rank.*

THEOREM 1.2.20

Let $\mathbf{A}$ *be an* $n \times n$ *symmetric (real) matrix of rank* r*. There exists a nonsingular (real) matrix* $\mathbf{C}$ *such that* $\mathbf{C}'\mathbf{A}\mathbf{C} = \mathbf{D}$*, where*

$$\mathbf{D} = \begin{bmatrix} \mathbf{I}_p & \mathbf{0} & \mathbf{0} \\ \mathbf{0} & -\mathbf{I}_{r-p} & \mathbf{0} \\ \mathbf{0} & \mathbf{0} & \mathbf{0} \end{bmatrix}$$

In other words, $\mathbf{A}$ is congruent to a diagonal matrix $\mathbf{D}$ with $p \geq 0$ diagonal elements equal to $+1$ and $r - p \geq 0$ diagonal elements equal to -1. For a given symmetric matrix $\mathbf{A}$, there may be many nonsingular matrices $\mathbf{C}$ such that $\mathbf{C}'\mathbf{A}\mathbf{C}$ is a diagonal matrix with only $+1$, -1, and 0 on the diagonal, but for any such matrix the integers r and p remain the same. The integer p is called the *index* of the symmetric matrix $\mathbf{A}$.

If the above ideas are applied to a quadratic form $\mathbf{x}'\mathbf{A}\mathbf{x}$ through the change of variables from x_i to y_i by $\mathbf{x} = \mathbf{C}\mathbf{y}$, we get

$$\mathbf{x}'\mathbf{A}\mathbf{x} = \mathbf{y}'(\mathbf{C}'\mathbf{A}\mathbf{C})\mathbf{y} = \mathbf{y}'\mathbf{D}\mathbf{y} = y_1^2 + y_2^2 + \cdots + y_p^2 - y_{p+1}^2 - \cdots - y_r^2$$

and p is called the index and r the rank of the quadratic form $\mathbf{x}'\mathbf{A}\mathbf{x}$. When $r = p = n$, the quadratic form (and also the matrix $\mathbf{A}$) is called *positive definite.* When $r = p < n$, the quadratic form (and also the matrix $\mathbf{A}$) is called *positive semidefinite.* These ideas, which are extremely important in statistics, are elaborated on in other sections of this chapter.

THEOREM 1.2.21

Let $\mathbf{C}$ *be an* $m \times n$ *matrix of rank* r*. The rank of* $\mathbf{C}\mathbf{C}'$ *is* r*, and the rank of* $\mathbf{C}'\mathbf{C}$ *is* r*.*

THEOREM 1.2.22

Let $\mathbf{C}$ *be an* $m \times n$ *matrix of rank* r*;* $\mathbf{C}'\mathbf{C}$ *and* $\mathbf{C}\mathbf{C}'$ *are either positive definite or* *positive semidefinite. If the rank of* $\mathbf{C'C}$ *or* $\mathbf{CC'}$ *is equal to its size, then the matrix is positive definite; otherwise it is positive semidefinite.*

DEFINITION 1.2.3

Orthogonal Matrices. *Let* $\mathbf{P}$ *be an* $n \times n$ *matrix.* $\mathbf{P}$ *is defined to be an orthogonal matrix if and only if* $\mathbf{P}^{-1} = \mathbf{P}'$.

> *Note 1.* In this book we use the term *orthogonal matrix* to mean *real orthogonal matrix.*

THEOREM 1.2.23

If p_{ii} *is the ith diagonal element of an orthogonal matrix, then* $-1 \le p_{ii} \le 1$.

THEOREM 1.2.24

Let the $n \times n$ *matrix* $\mathbf{P}$ *be partitioned as* $[\mathbf{p}_1, \mathbf{p}_2, \ldots, \mathbf{p}_n]$, *where* $\mathbf{p}_i$ *is an* $n \times 1$ *matrix (vector) consisting of the elements in the ith column of* $\mathbf{P}$. *A necessary and sufficient condition that* $\mathbf{P}$ *is an orthogonal matrix is given by the following:*

(1) $\mathbf{p}_i'\mathbf{p}_i = 1$ *for* $i = 1, 2, \ldots, n$;

(2) $\mathbf{p}_i'\mathbf{p}_j = 0$ *for* $i = 1, 2, \ldots, n; j = 1, 2, \ldots, n; i \neq j$.

THEOREM 1.2.25

A necessary and sufficient condition that an $n \times n$ *matrix* $\mathbf{P}$ *is an orthogonal matrix is* $\mathbf{P'P} = \mathbf{I}$.

THEOREM 1.2.26

The determinant of an orthogonal matrix is equal to either $+1$ *or* -1.

THEOREM 1.2.27

The product of a finite number of $n \times n$ *orthogonal matrices is an orthogonal matrix.*

THEOREM 1.2.28

The inverse (and hence the transpose) of an orthogonal matrix is an orthogonal matrix.

THEOREM 1.2.29

Let **A** *be an* $n \times n$ *matrix and let* **P** *be an* $n \times n$ *orthogonal matrix; then det*(**A**) = *det*(**P**′**AP**).

THEOREM 1.2.30

Let **A** *be any (real)* $n \times n$ *matrix. There exists a (real) orthogonal matrix* **P** *such that* **P**′**AP** = **D**, *where* **D** *is a (real) diagonal matrix, if and only if* **A** *is symmetric.*

Vectors play a very important role in many branches of science and especially in statistics. Thus we next define vectors, vector spaces, and subspaces, and state some theorems that are generally discussed in a first course in linear algebra.

We shall use the following definition of a vector in this book, although it certainly is not the most general definition.

DEFINITION 1.2.4

(n-component) Vector. *Let n be a positive integer and let* $a_1, a_2, \ldots, a_n$ *be any elements from a field F. The ordered n-tuple*

$$\mathbf{a} = \begin{bmatrix} a_1 \\ a_2 \\ \vdots \\ a_n \end{bmatrix}$$

is defined as an n-component vector, sometimes called an $n \times 1$ *vector.*

We generally denote vectors by lowercase boldface letters. *Unless explicitly stated otherwise, the field F will be the field of real numbers.* Strictly speaking, **a** is a column vector, but we shall omit the word column. The symbol **a**′ (transpose of **a**) is used for a row vector. Note that an $n \times 1$ vector is a special case of a matrix, and all the rules for addition, subtraction, multiplication, and transposition for matrices also hold for vectors. The rule for multiplication of a matrix by a scalar also holds.for multiplication of a vector by a scalar.

We are interested not only in a single vector but also in a certain collection or set of vectors which we call a *vector space.*

DEFINITION 1.2.5

Vector Space. *Let* V_n *be a set of n-component vectors such that for every two vectors in* V_n, *the sum of the two vectors is also in* V_n, *and for each vector in* V_n *and each scalar, the product is in* V_n. *This set* V_n *is called a vector space.*

Note 2. This definition states that if a collection of $n \times 1$ vectors is "closed" with respect to addition and with respect to multiplication by a scalar, then the set is a vector space V_n.

THEOREM 1.2.31

Let E_n be the set of all $n \times 1$ vectors for a fixed positive integer n; that is, define E_n by

$$E_n = \{\mathbf{a} : \mathbf{a}' = [a_1, a_2, \ldots, a_n]; -\infty < a_i < \infty, i = 1, 2, \ldots, n\}$$

then E_n is a vector space.

Thus the collection of *all* ordered n-tuples of real numbers is a vector space. Geometrically, the $n \times 1$ vector $\mathbf{a}$ can be viewed as a point in n-dimensional Euclidean space. In statistics our interest is generally centered around certain subsets of the vectors in E_n.

By E_n, we shall hereafter always mean the vector space in Theorem 1.2.31.

In this book we generally take E_n for a given positive integer n to be the basic vector space, and every n-component vector will be a member of this set. However, when we want the basic vector space under discussion to consist of a set of n-component vectors that is not the vector space E_n, we shall use some other symbol, such as V_n, S_n, and so forth.

We are generally interested in a subset of a vector space V_n if this subset is itself a vector space. These are called *subspaces* of V_n.

DEFINITION 1.2.6

Subspace. *Let S_n be a subset of vectors in the vector space V_n. If the set S_n is itself a vector space, then S_n is called a vector subspace of the vector space V_n.*

To determine whether or not S_n, a subset of vectors in the vector space V_n, is itself a vector space, the following theorem is useful.

THEOREM 1.2.32

If S_n is a subset of the vectors in the vector space V_n such that, for every two vectors $\mathbf{s}_1$ and $\mathbf{s}_2$ in S_n, the vector $a_1\mathbf{s}_1 + a_2\mathbf{s}_2$ is also in S_n for all real numbers a_1 and a_2, then S_n is a subspace of V_n.

Example 1.2.1

The set of vectors defined by $a\mathbf{a}'$ for $\mathbf{a}' = [1, -1, 1]$ and for every real number a is a subspace of E_3. Also, the set of vectors $\mathbf{a}' = [a_1, a_2, 0]$ for all real numbers a_1 and a_2 is a subspace of E_3. But the set of vectors defined by $b\mathbf{b}'$ for $\mathbf{b}' = [1, 2]$ and all real b is not a subspace of E_3, because $\mathbf{b}'$ is not a member of E_3; it is, however, a subspace of E_2.

The set of vectors

$$V_3 = \{\mathbf{v} : \mathbf{v}' = [a_1, a_2, 0];\ a_i \in R, \text{ where } R \text{ is the set of all real numbers}\}$$

is a vector space, and $V_3 \subset E_3$; that is to say, V_3 is a subspace of E_3. Also, the set of vectors

$$S_3 = \{\mathbf{s} : \mathbf{s}' = [0, a, 0];\ a \in R\}$$

is a vector space, and $S_3 \subset V_3$; that is, S_3 is a subspace of V_3.

The set $\{\mathbf{0}\}$ consisting of the single vector $\mathbf{0}$ is a vector space. Hence we have $\{\mathbf{0}\} \subset S_3 \subset V_3 \subset E_3$. Also,

$$S_3^* = \{\mathbf{s}^* : \mathbf{s}^{*\prime} = [a, 0, 0];\ a \in R\}$$

is a vector space, and it is a subspace of V_3 and of E_3; but S_3^* is not a subspace of S_3. The set of two vectors $U = \{\mathbf{u}_1, \mathbf{u}_2\}$, where $\mathbf{u}_1' = [0, 1, 0]$ and $\mathbf{u}_2' = [0, 2, 0]$, is a *subset* of V_3, of S_3, and of E_3, but U is *not* a subspace.

THEOREM 1.2.33

The set $\{\mathbf{0}\}$, where $\mathbf{0}$ is the $n \times 1$ null vector, is a subspace of every vector space V_n. Every vector space V_n is a subspace of itself.

When a set of n-component vectors is under study, it is important to be able to determine whether some of the vectors can be obtained as linear combinations of other vectors. To be able to do this, we need a definition and some theorems on linear dependence and independence of a set of vectors.

DEFINITION 1.2.7

Linear Dependence and Independence. *Let $\{\mathbf{v}_1, \mathbf{v}_2, \ldots, \mathbf{v}_m\}$ be a set of m vectors each with n components, so that $\mathbf{v}_i \in E_n$ and $i = 1, 2, \ldots, m$. This set of m vectors is defined to be a linearly dependent set if and only if there exists a set of scalars $\{c_1, c_2, \ldots, c_m\}$, at least one of which is not equal to zero, such that*

$$\sum_{i=1}^{m} c_i \mathbf{v}_i = \mathbf{0} \tag{1.2.1}$$

If the only set of scalars $\{c_1, c_2, \ldots, c_m\}$ such that $\sum_{i=1}^{m} c_i \mathbf{v}_i = \mathbf{0}$ is the set $\{0, 0, \ldots, 0\}$, then the set of vectors is defined to be linearly independent.

THEOREM 1.2.34

If the vector $\mathbf{0}$ is included in a set of n-component vectors, the set is linearly dependent.

THEOREM 1.2.35

If $m > 1$ vectors are linearly dependent, it is always possible to express at least one of them as a linear combination of the others.

THEOREM 1.2.36

In the set of m vectors $\{\mathbf{v}_1, \mathbf{v}_2, \ldots, \mathbf{v}_m\}$, if there are s vectors, $s \leq m$, that are linearly dependent, then the entire set of m vectors is linearly dependent.

THEOREM 1.2.37

If the set of m vectors $\{\mathbf{v}_1, \mathbf{v}_2, \ldots, \mathbf{v}_m\}$ is a linearly independent set, while the set of $m + 1$ vectors $\{\mathbf{v}_1, \mathbf{v}_2, \ldots, \mathbf{v}_m, \mathbf{v}_{m+1}\}$ is a linearly dependent set, then $\mathbf{v}_{m+1}$ is expressible as a linear combination of $\mathbf{v}_1, \mathbf{v}_2, \ldots, \mathbf{v}_m$.

We shall have occasion to write the m vectors $\mathbf{v}_1, \mathbf{v}_2, \ldots, \mathbf{v}_m$ as follows:

$$\mathbf{V} = [\mathbf{v}_1, \mathbf{v}_2, \ldots, \mathbf{v}_m] = \left[\begin{bmatrix} v_{11} \\ v_{21} \\ \vdots \\ v_{n1} \end{bmatrix} \begin{bmatrix} v_{12} \\ v_{22} \\ \vdots \\ v_{n2} \end{bmatrix} \cdots \begin{bmatrix} v_{1m} \\ v_{2m} \\ \vdots \\ v_{nm} \end{bmatrix} \right] \tag{1.2.2}$$

which we shall write as

$$\mathbf{V} = \begin{bmatrix} v_{11} & v_{12} & \cdots & v_{1m} \\ v_{21} & v_{22} & \cdots & v_{2m} \\ \vdots & \vdots & & \vdots \\ v_{n1} & v_{n2} & \cdots & v_{nm} \end{bmatrix} \tag{1.2.3}$$

Thus we have an $n \times m$ matrix whose columns consist of m vectors, each with n components. On the other hand, we could view $\mathbf{V}'$ as a matrix whose columns consist of n vectors, each with m elements. We shall call $\mathbf{V}$ a matrix of m column vectors, each with n components, or simply a matrix of vectors.

> ***Note 3.*** In this book when we refer to a matrix of vectors, we mean the set of vectors formed by the *columns* of the matrix, unless explicitly stated otherwise.

THEOREM 1.2.38

A necessary and sufficient condition for the set of $n \times 1$ vectors $\{\mathbf{v}_1, \mathbf{v}_2, \ldots, \mathbf{v}_m\}$ to be a linearly dependent set is that the rank r of the matrix of the vectors be less than the number of vectors m, that is, $r < m$.

THEOREM 1.2.39

If the rank of the matrix of the set of $n \times 1$ vectors $\{\mathbf{v}_1, \mathbf{v}_2, \ldots, \mathbf{v}_m\}$ is r, then r must be less than or equal to m, and if $r > 0$, there exist exactly r of these vectors that are linearly independent, while each of the remaining $m - r$ (if $m - r > 0$) vectors is expressible as a linear combination of these r vectors.

THEOREM 1.2.40

The set of $n \times 1$ vectors $\{\mathbf{v}_1, \mathbf{v}_2, \ldots, \mathbf{v}_m\}$ is always a linearly dependent set if $m > n$.

It is useful to be able to determine a subset of vectors in a vector space V_n such that each vector in V_n can be derived as a linear combination of the vectors in this subset. Such a set is said to generate, or span, the vector space V_n.

THEOREM 1.2.41

Let $\{\mathbf{v}_1, \mathbf{v}_2, \ldots, \mathbf{v}_m\}$ be a set of vectors in V_n, and let the set of vectors V be defined

$$V = \left\{ \mathbf{v} : \mathbf{v} = \sum_{i=1}^{m} c_i \mathbf{v}_i ; c_i \in R \right\}$$

Then V is a subspace of V_n.

This theorem asserts that if we start with any set of vectors in V_n, then the set V, obtained by every possible linear combination of these vectors, is itself a vector space and is a subspace of V_n.

DEFINITION 1.2.8

Generating (or Spanning) Vectors. *Let V_n be a vector space. If each vector in V_n can be obtained by a linear combination of the vectors in the set $\{\mathbf{v}_1, \mathbf{v}_2, \ldots, \mathbf{v}_m\}$, then the set of vectors $\{\mathbf{v}_1, \mathbf{v}_2, \ldots, \mathbf{v}_m\}$ is said to generate (or span) V_n.*

We say that the space V_n is generated, or spanned, by the vectors $\mathbf{v}_1, \mathbf{v}_2, \ldots, \mathbf{v}_m$. We note that the set $\{\mathbf{0}\}$, the set consisting of the zero vector only, is a vector space. We also note that every vector space must include a zero vector and, for any vector space V except the space consisting only of $\mathbf{0}$, there are many sets that span the space V. Nothing was stated as to whether the vectors that span a space are linearly dependent or linearly independent. However, when the set is linearly independent, we give it a special name, a *basis* (set).

DEFINITION 1.2.9

Basis. *Let $\{\mathbf{v}_1, \mathbf{v}_2, \ldots, \mathbf{v}_m\}$ be a set of linearly independent vectors in V_n that span V_n. Then the set is called a basis for V_n. For the special vector space $\{\mathbf{0}\}$, we shall say that $\mathbf{0}$ is a basis (even though it is not linearly independent).*

In general, a basis for a vector space V_n is not unique, and hence there are many different bases for V_n. However, the *number* of vectors in any basis for V_n is unique.

A special name, *dimension*, is applied to the number of vectors in a basis.

DEFINITION 1.2.10

Dimension. *Let V_n be any vector space except $\{\mathbf{0}\}$. Let the number of vectors in a basis of V_n be m. Then m is defined to be the dimension of V_n. The dimension of the vector space $\{\mathbf{0}\}$ is defined to be zero.*

THEOREM 1.2.42

If $r > 0$ is the rank of the matrix of the vectors $\mathbf{v}_1, \mathbf{v}_2, \ldots, \mathbf{v}_m$ that span the vector space V_n, then there are exactly r linearly independent vectors in the set and every vector in V_n can be expressed uniquely as a linear combination of these r vectors.

THEOREM 1.2.43

Let $\{\mathbf{v}_1, \mathbf{v}_2, \ldots, \mathbf{v}_q\}$ be a set of linearly independent vectors in V_n for $q < n$. Then this set is a subset of a basis for V_n.

> ***Note 4.*** If the dimension of V_n is q, then this set is a basis for V_n. This theorem implies that any linearly independent set of vectors that is not a basis can be extended to be a basis by including additional vectors in the set.

DEFINITION 1.2.11

Orthogonal Vectors. *Let $\mathbf{x}$ and $\mathbf{y}$ be two vectors in V_n. Then $\mathbf{x}$ and $\mathbf{y}$ are defined to be orthogonal if and only if $\mathbf{x}'\mathbf{y}$ is equal to the 1×1 zero matrix.*

> ***Note 5.*** The zero vector in V_n is orthogonal to each vector in V_n.

> ***Notation.*** Since the zero matrix of size 1×1 and the real number zero have the same algebraic properties, we generally use the number zero for the zero 1×1 matrix.

Linear transformations and characteristic roots are important in the linear model, so we present a short discussion of these topics.

Let $\mathbf{A}$ be an $m \times n$ matrix, let $\mathbf{x}$ be any vector in E_n, and define the $m \times 1$ vector $\mathbf{y}$ by the equation

$$\mathbf{y} = \mathbf{A}\mathbf{x} \tag{1.2.4}$$

$\mathbf{y}$ is a vector in E_m, and we say, "the vector $\mathbf{x}$ is transformed to the vector $\mathbf{y}$ by the transformation $\mathbf{A}$." We can view Equation (1.2.4) as moving the vector $\mathbf{x}$ in E_n to the vector $\mathbf{y}$ in E_m (or as moving the point $\mathbf{x}$ to the point $\mathbf{y}$). Let $\mathbf{x}_1$ and $\mathbf{x}_2$ be any two vectors in E_n; then $\mathbf{x}_1$ is transformed to $\mathbf{y}_1$ and $\mathbf{x}_2$ is transformed to $\mathbf{y}_2$ by the transformation $\mathbf{A}$ if $\mathbf{y}_1$ and $\mathbf{y}_2$ are defined by

$$\mathbf{y}_1 = \mathbf{A}\mathbf{x}_1 \qquad \mathbf{y}_2 = \mathbf{A}\mathbf{x}_2$$

Also, if we define the vector $\mathbf{x}_3$ to be equal to $c_1\mathbf{x}_1 + c_2\mathbf{x}_2$, where c_1 and c_2 are any two real numbers, then by the transformation $\mathbf{A}$ the vector $\mathbf{x}_3$ is transformed to the vector $\mathbf{y}_3$, where

$$\begin{aligned}\mathbf{y}_3 &= \mathbf{A}\mathbf{x}_3 = \mathbf{A}(c_1\mathbf{x}_1 + c_2\mathbf{x}_2) = \mathbf{A}c_1\mathbf{x}_1 + \mathbf{A}c_2\mathbf{x}_2\\ &= c_1\mathbf{A}\mathbf{x}_1 + c_2\mathbf{A}\mathbf{x}_2 = c_1\mathbf{y}_1 + c_2\mathbf{y}_2\end{aligned}$$

That is,

$$\mathbf{y}_3 = c_1\mathbf{y}_1 + c_2\mathbf{y}_2$$

Thus if we know that by the transformation $\mathbf{A}$, the vector $\mathbf{x}_1$ is transformed to $\mathbf{y}_1$ and $\mathbf{x}_2$ is transformed to $\mathbf{y}_2$, then we know that the vector $c_1\mathbf{x}_1 + c_2\mathbf{x}_2$ is transformed to $c_1\mathbf{y}_1 + c_2\mathbf{y}_2$.

The transformation of vectors in E_n defined by Equation (1.2.4) is called a *linear homogeneous transformation* and is generally referred to as simply a *linear transformation.* Note that $\mathbf{0} = \mathbf{A}\mathbf{0}$; that is, a zero vector is transformed to a zero vector, and for this reason the transformation is called *homogeneous.* It is called *linear* because, for any two vectors $\mathbf{x}_1$ and $\mathbf{x}_2$ in E_n and any two scalars c_1 and c_2, we obtain

$$\mathbf{A}(c_1\mathbf{x}_1 + c_2\mathbf{x}_2) = c_1(\mathbf{A}\mathbf{x}_1) + c_2(\mathbf{A}\mathbf{x}_2)$$

In other words, the transformation $\mathbf{A}$ of a linear combination of two vectors is obtained by taking the same linear combination of the two transformed vectors.

Suppose that

$$\mathbf{y} = \mathbf{A}\mathbf{x}$$

is a transformation of $\mathbf{x}$ to $\mathbf{y}$ and

$$\mathbf{z} = \mathbf{B}\mathbf{y}$$

is a transformation of $\mathbf{y}$ to $\mathbf{z}$. Then by substitution we obtain

$$\mathbf{z} = \mathbf{B}\mathbf{y} = \mathbf{B}(\mathbf{A}\mathbf{x}) = (\mathbf{B}\mathbf{A})\mathbf{x}$$

and **BA** is the transformation that "moves **x** directly to **z**." This can be extended to any finite number of transformations.

We are interested in questions such as the following: If each vector **x** in the vector space E_n is transformed by the equation $\mathbf{y} = \mathbf{A}\mathbf{x}$, does the resulting set of transformed vectors form a vector space? Or, more specifically, if each vector **x** in any vector space V_n is transformed by the equation $\mathbf{y} = \mathbf{A}\mathbf{x}$, does the resulting set of vectors form a vector space? The answer is in the next theorem.

THEOREM 1.2.44

Let S be a set of vectors that results from transforming each vector in a vector space V_n by the transformation **A**, *so that*

$$S = \{\mathbf{y} : \mathbf{y} = \mathbf{A}\mathbf{x}; \mathbf{x} \in V_n\}$$

Then S is a vector space.

Among the questions that are important in considering transformations of vectors is one that concerns the transformation of a vector into a multiple of itself. That is to say, suppose we are discussing the transformation described by the $n \times n$ matrix **A**. For this transformation does there exist a vector **x** in E_n such that

$$\mathbf{A}\mathbf{x} = \lambda\mathbf{x} \tag{1.2.5}$$

for some real number λ? If such a vector **x** and a real number λ do exist, then, since $\lambda\mathbf{x}$ is a multiple of **x**, the vector **x** is transformed to a multiple of itself. Assuming that Equation (1.2.5) holds, we can write it as

$$(\mathbf{A} - \lambda\mathbf{I})\mathbf{x} = \mathbf{0} \tag{1.2.6}$$

and clearly $\mathbf{x} = \mathbf{0}$ satisfies Equation (1.2.6) for any scalar λ. But this merely states that in a linear homogeneous transformation, the origin (vector **0**) is transformed into itself. Therefore, we pose this question: Is there any *nonzero* vector **x** and a scalar λ such that Equation (1.2.5) is satisfied?

We know from the elementary theory of the solutions of linear equations that a nonzero solution to Equation (1.2.6) exists if and only if the determinant of the matrix $\mathbf{A} - \lambda\mathbf{I}$ is equal to zero, that is, if and only if $|\mathbf{A} - \lambda\mathbf{I}| = 0$. But the determinant of $\mathbf{A} - \lambda\mathbf{I}$ is an nth degree polynomial in λ, and in place of $|\mathbf{A} - \lambda\mathbf{I}| = 0$, we can write

$$a_n\lambda^n + a_{n-1}\lambda^{n-1} + \cdots + a_1\lambda + a_0 = 0 \tag{1.2.7}$$

This equation is called the *characteristic equation* of the $n \times n$ matrix **A**. We know from elementary algebra that this equation has exactly n roots; in other words, there are exactly n values of λ (not necessarily all distinct) such that $|\mathbf{A} - \lambda\mathbf{I}| = 0$. These n roots are called the *characteristic roots* (sometimes called eigenvalues), or simply the *roots*, of the $n \times n$ matrix $\mathbf{A}$. However, some of these roots may not be real numbers but may be complex numbers even if $\mathbf{A}$ is a real matrix. If λ_1 is a root of $\mathbf{A}$, and if $\mathbf{x}_1$ is a vector corresponding to this root, that is, if

$$\mathbf{A}\mathbf{x}_1 = \lambda_1\mathbf{x}_1 \qquad \mathbf{x}_1 \neq \mathbf{0}$$

then $\mathbf{x}_1$ is defined to be a *characteristic vector* of the $n \times n$ matrix $\mathbf{A}$ corresponding to the root λ_1. If λ_1 is a complex number, then the elements of $\mathbf{x}_1$ may not be real numbers. The following theorem answers the question presented above.

THEOREM 1.2.45

Let $\mathbf{A}$ *be an* $n \times n$ *(real) matrix. There always exist n complex numbers* $\lambda_1, \lambda_2, \ldots,$ λ_n *(called characteristic roots of matrix* $\mathbf{A}$*) that satisfy the polynomial equation* $|\mathbf{A} - \lambda\mathbf{I}| = 0$*. Some or all of these roots may not be real numbers.*

Characteristic roots, vectors, and polynomials are important in statistics and we now state some theorems usually proved in a first course in matrix algebra.

THEOREM 1.2.46

Let $\mathbf{A}$ *be an* $n \times n$ *(real) matrix. A necessary and sufficient condition that there exists a nonzero vector* $\mathbf{x}$ *that satisfies*

$$\mathbf{A}\mathbf{x} = \lambda\mathbf{x}$$

is that λ *is a characteristic root of* $\mathbf{A}$*. The characteristic vector* $\mathbf{x}$ *has elements which are complex numbers (they may not be real numbers).*

THEOREM 1.2.47

The $n \times n$ *matrix* $\mathbf{A}$ *has at least one characteristic root equal to zero if and only if* $\mathbf{A}$ *is singular.*

THEOREM 1.2.48

Let $\mathbf{A}$ *be an* $n \times n$ *matrix, and let* $\mathbf{C}$ *be any* $n \times n$ *nonsingular matrix. The three matrices* $\mathbf{A}$, $\mathbf{C}^{-1}\mathbf{A}\mathbf{C}$, *and* $\mathbf{C}\mathbf{A}\mathbf{C}^{-1}$ *have the same set of characteristic roots.*

Since quadratic forms play such an important role in statistics, we are led to a discussion of real symmetric matrices.

DEFINITION 1.2.12

Real Symmetric Matrix. *An* $n \times n$ *matrix* $\mathbf{A}$ *is defined to be a real symmetric matrix if and only if* (1) *the elements of* $\mathbf{A}$ *are real, and* (2) $\mathbf{A} = \mathbf{A}'$.

> ***Reminder.*** We shall generally omit the word "real" and say "$\mathbf{A}$ is an $n \times n$ symmetric matrix" to mean that $\mathbf{A}$ is an $n \times n$ real symmetric matrix.

THEOREM 1.2.49

Let $\mathbf{A}$ *be an* $n \times n$ *symmetric matrix. The characteristic roots of* $\mathbf{A}$ *are real.*

The next theorem is used extensively in transforming a real quadratic form to a sum of squares.

THEOREM 1.2.50

Let $\mathbf{A}$ *be an* $n \times n$ *symmetric matrix. There exists an orthogonal matrix* $\mathbf{P}$ *such that* $\mathbf{P}'\mathbf{A}\mathbf{P} = \mathbf{D}$, *where* $\mathbf{D}$ *is a diagonal matrix with the characteristic roots of* $\mathbf{A}$ *displayed on the diagonal of* $\mathbf{D}$.

COROLLARY 1.2.50

Let $\mathbf{A}$ *be an* $n \times n$ *matrix. There exists a nonsingular matrix* $\mathbf{P}$ *such that* $\mathbf{P}^{-1}\mathbf{A}\mathbf{P} = \mathbf{T}$, *where* $\mathbf{T}$ *is an upper triangular matrix.* $\mathbf{P}$ *and* $\mathbf{T}$ *may not be real matrices. The characteristic roots of* $\mathbf{A}$ *are the diagonal elements of* $\mathbf{T}$.

We have used the fact that a matrix can be viewed as a collection of vectors. More specifically, if $\mathbf{A}$ is an $n \times m$ matrix, then we can view the columns of $\mathbf{A}$ as m vectors in E_n. We now define a vector space associated with a matrix $\mathbf{A}$.

DEFINITION 1.2.13

Column Space of a Matrix. *Let* $\mathbf{A}$ *be an* $n \times m$ *matrix; we denote the m columns of* $\mathbf{A}$ *as vectors in* E_n, *so that* $\mathbf{A} = [\mathbf{a}_1, \mathbf{a}_2, \ldots, \mathbf{a}_m]$. *The vector space spanned by these m column vectors of* $\mathbf{A}$ *is defined as the column space of* $\mathbf{A}$.

> ***Note 6.*** The column space of $\mathbf{A}$ is also called the *range space* of $\mathbf{A}$.

Clearly, the dimension of the column space of $\mathbf{A}$ is equal to the number of linearly independent columns of $\mathbf{A}$, which is equal to the rank of $\mathbf{A}$.

Another way to define the column space of an $n \times m$ matrix $\mathbf{A}$ is as the set S of vectors, where

$$S = \left\{\mathbf{y} : \mathbf{y} = \sum_{i=1}^{m} b_i \mathbf{a}_i ; b_i \in R\right\}$$

and S is clearly the vector space spanned by the columns of $\mathbf{A}$.

Still another way to define the column space of $\mathbf{A}$ is as the set S of vectors, where

$$S = \{\mathbf{y} : \mathbf{y} = \mathbf{Ab}; \mathbf{b} \in E_m\}$$

and S is clearly the vector space spanned by the columns of $\mathbf{A}$. By using the last definition, we notice that $\mathbf{y} \in S$ if and only if there exists a vector $\mathbf{b}$ in E_m such that $\mathbf{Ab} = \mathbf{y}$.

THEOREM 1.2.51

Let $\mathbf{A}$ *be an* $n \times n$ *nonsingular matrix. The column space of* $\mathbf{A}$ *is* E_n.

THEOREM 1.2.52

Let $\mathbf{A}$ *be an* $n \times m$ *matrix and* $\mathbf{B}$ *an* $m \times k$ *matrix. The column space of* $\mathbf{AB}$ *is a subspace of the column space of* $\mathbf{A}$.

COROLLARY 1.2.52

In Theorem 1.2.52, *if the rank of* $\mathbf{AB}$ *is equal to the rank of* $\mathbf{A}$, *then the column space of* $\mathbf{A}$ *is the same as the column space of* $\mathbf{AB}$ (*in particular,* $\mathbf{A}$ *and* $\mathbf{AA}'$ *have the same column space*).

THEOREM 1.2.53

Let $\mathbf{A}$ *and* $\mathbf{B}$ *be* $n \times m$ *matrices. There exists a nonsingular* $m \times m$ *matrix* $\mathbf{C}$ *such that* $\mathbf{AC} = \mathbf{B}$ *if and only if* $\mathbf{A}$ *and* $\mathbf{B}$ *have the same column space.*

THEOREM 1.2.54

Let $\mathbf{A}$ *and* $\mathbf{B}$ *be* $n \times m$ *matrices. A necessary and sufficient condition that there exists an* $m \times m$ *matrix* $\mathbf{C}$ *such that* $\mathbf{AC} = \mathbf{B}$ *is that the column space of* $\mathbf{B}$ *is a subspace of the column space of* $\mathbf{A}$.

> *Note 7.* Instead of discussing the column space of matrices, we could just as well have discussed the row space (the vector space spanned by the rows of a matrix $\mathbf{A}$). In fact, the row space of $\mathbf{A}'$ is the same as the column space of $\mathbf{A}$; hence for each of the last four theorems there is an analogous theorem for the row space of the matrix.

1.3 Partitioned Matrices

It is sometimes convenient to describe determinants and inverses of matrices in terms of submatrices, so this section is devoted to the topic of partitioned matrices.

THEOREM 1.3.1

Let $\mathbf{B}$ *be an* $n \times n$ *nonsingular matrix that is partitioned as follows:*

$$\mathbf{B} = \begin{bmatrix} \mathbf{B}_{11} & \mathbf{B}_{12} \\ \mathbf{B}_{21} & \mathbf{B}_{22} \end{bmatrix} \tag{1.3.1}$$

where $\mathbf{B}_{ij}$ *has size* $n_i \times n_j$ *for* $i, j = 1, 2$, *where* $n_1 + n_2 = n$ *and* $0 < n_1 < n$. *Denote* $\mathbf{B}^{-1}$ *by* $\mathbf{A}$, *and partition* $\mathbf{A}$ *as*

$$\mathbf{A} = \begin{bmatrix} \mathbf{A}_{11} & \mathbf{A}_{12} \\ \mathbf{A}_{21} & \mathbf{A}_{22} \end{bmatrix} \tag{1.3.2}$$

where $\mathbf{A}_{ij}$ *has size* $n_i \times n_j$ *for* $i, j = 1, 2$. *If* $|\mathbf{B}_{11}| \neq 0$, *and* $|\mathbf{B}_{22}| \neq 0$, *the results* (1) *through* (3) *follow:*

(1) $\mathbf{A}_{11}^{-1}$ *and* $\mathbf{A}_{22}^{-1}$ *exist;*

(2) $[\mathbf{B}_{11} - \mathbf{B}_{12}\mathbf{B}_{22}^{-1}\mathbf{B}_{21}]^{-1}$ *and* $[\mathbf{B}_{22} - \mathbf{B}_{21}\mathbf{B}_{11}^{-1}\mathbf{B}_{12}]^{-1}$ *exist;*

(3) $\mathbf{B}^{-1}$ *can be written as*

$$\mathbf{B}^{-1} = \begin{bmatrix} [\mathbf{B}_{11} - \mathbf{B}_{12}\mathbf{B}_{22}^{-1}\mathbf{B}_{21}]^{-1} & -\mathbf{B}_{11}^{-1}\mathbf{B}_{12}[\mathbf{B}_{22} - \mathbf{B}_{21}\mathbf{B}_{11}^{-1}\mathbf{B}_{12}]^{-1} \\ -\mathbf{B}_{22}^{-1}\mathbf{B}_{21}[\mathbf{B}_{11} - \mathbf{B}_{12}\mathbf{B}_{22}^{-1}\mathbf{B}_{21}]^{-1} & [\mathbf{B}_{22} - \mathbf{B}_{21}\mathbf{B}_{11}^{-1}\mathbf{B}_{12}]^{-1} \end{bmatrix} \tag{1.3.3}$$

Proof

To prove (2) multiply $\mathbf{B}$ on the left by the nonsingular matrix $\mathbf{B}_1^*$, where

$$\mathbf{B}_1^* = \begin{bmatrix} \mathbf{B}_{11}^{-1} & \mathbf{0} \\ -\mathbf{B}_{21}\mathbf{B}_{11}^{-1} & \mathbf{I} \end{bmatrix} \tag{1.3.4}$$

and get, say,

$$\mathbf{B}_1^*\mathbf{B} = \begin{bmatrix} \mathbf{I} & \mathbf{B}_{11}^{-1}\mathbf{B}_{12} \\ \mathbf{0} & \mathbf{B}_{22} - \mathbf{B}_{21}\mathbf{B}_{11}^{-1}\mathbf{B}_{12} \end{bmatrix} = \mathbf{C}$$

But we also have that

$$|\mathbf{C}| = |\mathbf{I}|\,|\mathbf{B}_{22} - \mathbf{B}_{21}\mathbf{B}_{11}^{-1}\mathbf{B}_{12}| = |\mathbf{B}_1^*\mathbf{B}| = |\mathbf{B}_1^*|\,|\mathbf{B}| \neq 0$$

so (1.3.5)

$$\mathbf{B}_{22} - \mathbf{B}_{21}\mathbf{B}_{11}^{-1}\mathbf{B}_{12}$$

is nonsingular.

Multiply $\mathbf{B}$ on the left by $\mathbf{B}_2^*$ to prove the rest of (2), where

$$\mathbf{B}_2^* = \begin{bmatrix} \mathbf{I} & -\mathbf{B}_{12}\mathbf{B}_{22}^{-1} \\ \mathbf{0} & \mathbf{B}_{22}^{-1} \end{bmatrix}$$

From the result $\mathbf{AB} = \mathbf{I}$ we get

$$\begin{bmatrix} \mathbf{A}_{11} & \mathbf{A}_{12} \\ \mathbf{A}_{21} & \mathbf{A}_{22} \end{bmatrix} \begin{bmatrix} \mathbf{B}_{11} & \mathbf{B}_{12} \\ \mathbf{B}_{21} & \mathbf{B}_{22} \end{bmatrix} = \begin{bmatrix} \mathbf{I} & \mathbf{0} \\ \mathbf{0} & \mathbf{I} \end{bmatrix} \tag{1.3.6}$$

and from this we obtain the following four matrix equations:

$$\begin{aligned} \mathbf{A}_{11}\mathbf{B}_{11} + \mathbf{A}_{12}\mathbf{B}_{21} &= \mathbf{I} \qquad & \mathbf{A}_{21}\mathbf{B}_{11} + \mathbf{A}_{22}\mathbf{B}_{21} &= \mathbf{0} \\ \mathbf{A}_{11}\mathbf{B}_{12} + \mathbf{A}_{12}\mathbf{B}_{22} &= \mathbf{0} \qquad & \mathbf{A}_{21}\mathbf{B}_{12} + \mathbf{A}_{22}\mathbf{B}_{22} &= \mathbf{I} \end{aligned} \tag{1.3.7}$$

Multiply the second equation by $\mathbf{B}_{22}^{-1}$ on the right to get $-\mathbf{A}_{11}\mathbf{B}_{12}\mathbf{B}_{22}^{-1} = \mathbf{A}_{12}$. Substitute this for $\mathbf{A}_{12}$ in the first equation, simplify, and obtain $\mathbf{A}_{11}(\mathbf{B}_{11} - \mathbf{B}_{12}\mathbf{B}_{22}^{-1}\mathbf{B}_{21}) = \mathbf{I}$; so $\mathbf{A}_{11}^{-1}$ exists and is equal to $\mathbf{B}_{11} - \mathbf{B}_{12}\mathbf{B}_{22}^{-1}\mathbf{B}_{21}$. By using the last two equations in Equation (1.3.7), one can show that $\mathbf{A}_{22}^{-1}$ exists and is equal to $\mathbf{B}_{22} - \mathbf{B}_{21}\mathbf{B}_{11}^{-1}\mathbf{B}_{12}$. This proves (1).

By solving for $\mathbf{A}_{12}$ and $\mathbf{A}_{21}$ in Equation (1.3.7), it is straightforward to prove (3).

THEOREM 1.3.2

If $\mathbf{B}_{22}$ is a nonsingular matrix, then the determinant of $\mathbf{B}$ can be written as

$$|\mathbf{B}| = |\mathbf{B}_{22}| \cdot |\mathbf{B}_{11} - \mathbf{B}_{12}\mathbf{B}_{22}^{-1}\mathbf{B}_{21}|$$

If $\mathbf{B}_{11}$ is a nonsingular matrix, the determinant of $\mathbf{B}$ can be written as

$$|\mathbf{B}| = |\mathbf{B}_{11}| \cdot |\mathbf{B}_{22} - \mathbf{B}_{21}\mathbf{B}_{11}^{-1}\mathbf{B}_{12}|$$

Proof

Use Equation (1.3.5).

Note 1. We will use the following notation throughout this book:

$$\mathbf{B}_{11.2} = \mathbf{B}_{11} - \mathbf{B}_{12}\mathbf{B}_{22}^{-1}\mathbf{B}_{21} \qquad \mathbf{B}_{22.1} = \mathbf{B}_{22} - \mathbf{B}_{21}\mathbf{B}_{11}^{-1}\mathbf{B}_{12}$$

for any matrix partitioned as in Equation (1.3.1).

1.4 Nonnegative Matrices

DEFINITION 1.4.1

Positive Semidefinite Matrix. *An $n \times n$ matrix $\mathbf{A}$ is defined to be positive semidefinite if and only if the following conditions are satisfied:*

(1) $\mathbf{A} = \mathbf{A}'$;

(2) $\mathbf{y}'\mathbf{A}\mathbf{y} \geq 0$ *for each vector* $\mathbf{y}$ *in* E_n;

(3) $\mathbf{y}'\mathbf{A}\mathbf{y} = 0$ *for at least one nonzero vector in* E_n.

DEFINITION 1.4.2

Positive Definite Matrix. *An $n \times n$ matrix $\mathbf{A}$ is defined to be positive definite if and only if the following conditions are met:*

(1) $\mathbf{A} = \mathbf{A}'$;

(2) $\mathbf{y}'\mathbf{A}\mathbf{y} > 0$ *for each nonzero vector* $\mathbf{y}$ *in* E_n.

DEFINITION 1.4.3

Nonnegative Matrix. *A matrix is defined to be nonnegative if and only if it is either positive definite or positive semidefinite.*

THEOREM 1.4.1

The results (1a), (2a), *and* (3a) *follow if* $\mathbf{A}$ *is an $n \times n$ positive semidefinite matrix, and the results* (1b), (2b), *and* (3b) *follow if* $\mathbf{A}$ *is an $n \times n$ positive definite matrix.*

(1a) *The rank of* $\mathbf{A}$ *is less than n.* (1b) *The rank of* $\mathbf{A}$ *is equal to n.*

(2a) $a_{ii} \geq 0$ *for all* $i = 1, 2, \ldots, n$; *if* $a_{tt} = 0$, *then each element in the* tth *row and the* tth *column of* **A** *is equal to zero.*

(3a) **P′AP** *is a positive semidefinite matrix for any* $n \times n$ *matrix* **P**.

(2b) $a_{ii} > 0$ *for all* $i = 1, 2, \ldots, n$.

(3b) **P′AP** *is a positive definite matrix for any nonsingular* $n \times n$ *matrix* **P** *(in particular,* $\mathbf{A}^{-1}$ *is positive definite).*

The next theorem states some necessary and sufficient conditions for a matrix to be positive semidefinite or positive definite.

THEOREM 1.4.2

Let **A** *be an* $n \times n$ *symmetric matrix. Each of the conditions* (1a) *and* (2a) *is necessary and sufficient for* **A** *to be a positive semidefinite matrix. Each condition* (1b), (2b), *and* (3b) *is necessary and sufficient for* **A** *to be a positive definite matrix.*

(1a) *There exists an* $n \times n$ *matrix* **B** *of rank less than* n *such that* **B′B** = **A**.

(2a) *The characteristic roots of* **A** *are nonnegative and at least one root is equal to zero.*

(1b) *There exists an* $n \times n$ *matrix* **B** *of rank* n *such that* **B′B** = **A**.

(2b) *The characteristic roots of* **A** *are all positive.*

(3b) $a_{11} > 0, \begin{vmatrix} a_{11} & a_{12} \\ a_{21} & a_{22} \end{vmatrix} > 0, \ldots, |\mathbf{A}| > 0.$

COROLLARY 1.4.2

If **B** *is a* $p \times n$ *matrix of rank* r, *then the following result:*

(1) **B′B** *and* **BB′** *are nonnegative matrices;*

(2) **B′B** *is a positive semidefinite matrix if* $r < n$;

(3) **B′B** *is a positive definite matrix if* $r = n$.

THEOREM 1.4.3

Let **A** *and* **B** *be symmetric* $n \times n$ *matrices.*

(1) *The characteristic roots of* **AB** *are real if either* **A** *or* **B** *is nonnegative.*

(2) *If* **B** *is positive definite, the values of* λ *that satisfy* $|\mathbf{A} - \lambda\mathbf{B}| = 0$ *are real.*

THEOREM 1.4.4

Let $\mathbf{A}$ *and* $\mathbf{B}$ *be* $n \times n$ *symmetric matrices. A necessary and sufficient condition that an orthogonal matrix* $\mathbf{P}$ *exists such that* $\mathbf{P}'\mathbf{A}\mathbf{P}$ *and* $\mathbf{P}'\mathbf{B}\mathbf{P}$ *are each diagonal is that* $\mathbf{AB} = \mathbf{BA}$ *(or* $\mathbf{AB}$ *is a symmetric matrix).*

COROLLARY 1.4.4.1

Let $\mathbf{A}_1, \mathbf{A}_2, \ldots, \mathbf{A}_k$ *be symmetric* $n \times n$ *matrices. A necessary and sufficient condition that there exists an orthogonal matrix* $\mathbf{P}$ *such that* $\mathbf{P}'\mathbf{A}_i\mathbf{P}$ *is a diagonal matrix for each* $i = 1, 2, \ldots, k$ *is* $\mathbf{A}_i\mathbf{A}_j = \mathbf{A}_j\mathbf{A}_i$ *(or* $\mathbf{A}_i\mathbf{A}_j$ *is symmetric) for all* i *and* j.

COROLLARY 1.4.4.2

In Corollary 1.4.4.1, *if* $\mathbf{A}_i\mathbf{A}_j = \mathbf{D}_{ij}$ *for* $i = 1, 2, \ldots, k$, $j = 1, 2, \ldots, k$, *and* $i \neq j$, *where* $\mathbf{D}_{ij}$ *is a diagonal matrix, then there exists an orthogonal matrix* $\mathbf{P}$ *such that* $\mathbf{P}'\mathbf{A}_i\mathbf{P}$ *is a diagonal matrix for each* $i = 1, 2, \ldots, k$.

THEOREM 1.4.5

Let $\mathbf{A}$ *and* $\mathbf{B}$ *be* $n \times n$ *symmetric matrices.*

(1) *If* $\mathbf{A}$ *is positive definite, there exists a nonsingular matrix* $\mathbf{Q}$ *such that* $\mathbf{Q}'\mathbf{A}\mathbf{Q} = \mathbf{I}$ *and* $\mathbf{Q}'\mathbf{B}\mathbf{Q} = \mathbf{D}$, *where* $\mathbf{D}$ *is a diagonal matrix and the diagonal elements of* $\mathbf{D}$ *are the roots* λ *of the polynomial equation* $|\mathbf{B} - \lambda\mathbf{A}| = 0$.

(2) *If* $\mathbf{A}$ *and* $\mathbf{B}$ *are both nonnegative (neither has to be positive definite), there exists a nonsingular matrix* $\mathbf{Q}$ *such that* $\mathbf{Q}'\mathbf{A}\mathbf{Q}$ *and* $\mathbf{Q}'\mathbf{B}\mathbf{Q}$ *are each diagonal.*

1.5 Generalized and Conditional Inverses

In Section 1.2 the inverse of a matrix was defined and various properties were discussed. It was stated that if a matrix $\mathbf{A}$ has an inverse, the matrix must be square and the determinant must be nonzero. The theory of linear models, which includes a large part of theoretical and applied statistics, involves the solutions of a system of linear equations

$$\mathbf{Ax} = \mathbf{g} \tag{1.5.1}$$

and functions of the solutions.

If $\mathbf{A}$ is an $n \times n$ nonsingular matrix, the solution to the system in Equation (1.5.1) exists, is unique, and is given by $\mathbf{x} = \mathbf{A}^{-1}\mathbf{g}$. However, there are cases where $\mathbf{A}$ is not a square matrix and also situations where $\mathbf{A}$ is a square matrix but is singular. In these situations there may still be a solution to the system, and a unified theory to treat all situations may be desirable. One such theory involves the use of "generalized" and "conditional" inverses of matrices, which are discussed in this section. Since these inverses are generally not discussed in a first course in matrix algebra, we shall prove most of the theorems in this section.

Let $\mathbf{A}$ be an $m \times n$ matrix of rank r. We investigate a matrix, denoted by $\mathbf{A}^-$, which has many of the properties that the inverse of the matrix $\mathbf{A}$ would have if the inverse existed.

DEFINITION 1.5.1

Generalized Inverse. *Let* $\mathbf{A}$ *be an* $m \times n$ *matrix. If a matrix denoted by* $\mathbf{A}^-$ *exists that satisfies the four conditions below, it will be defined as a generalized inverse of* $\mathbf{A}$.

(1) $\mathbf{AA}^-$ *is symmetric*;

(2) $\mathbf{A}^-\mathbf{A}$ *is symmetric*;

(3) $\mathbf{AA}^-\mathbf{A} = \mathbf{A}$;

(4) $\mathbf{A}^-\mathbf{AA}^- = \mathbf{A}^-$. (1.5.2)

We use the terminology "g-inverse" for generalized inverse.

If $\mathbf{A}$ is nonsingular, it is clear that $\mathbf{A}^{-1}$ satisfies the conditions of a g-inverse. However, if $\mathbf{A}$ is a square matrix and singular, or if $\mathbf{A}$ is not a square matrix, then the problem remains as to whether a matrix $\mathbf{A}^-$ exists that satisfies Equation (1.5.2). We shall show that for each matrix $\mathbf{A}$, a g-inverse matrix $\mathbf{A}^-$ exists and is unique. We shall also state and prove various properties of this g-inverse.

THEOREM 1.5.1

If a g-inverse of an $m \times n$ *matrix* $\mathbf{A}$ *exists, it has size* $n \times m$.

Proof

The proof follows from the fact that $\mathbf{AA}^-$ is symmetric and hence square.

THEOREM 1.5.2

If $\mathbf{A}$ *is the null matrix of size* $m \times n$, *then* $\mathbf{A}^-$ *is the null matrix of size* $n \times m$.

Proof

Clearly $\mathbf{A}^- = \mathbf{0}$ satisfies the conditions in Equation (1.5.2) if $\mathbf{A} = \mathbf{0}$.

THEOREM 1.5.3

For each matrix $\mathbf{A}$ *there is a matrix* $\mathbf{A}^-$ *satisfying the conditions of Equation* (1.5.2): *that is, each matrix has a g-inverse.*

Proof

If $\mathbf{A} = \mathbf{0}$, then by Theorem 1.5.2, $\mathbf{A}^- = \mathbf{0}$. Assume $\mathbf{A} \neq \mathbf{0}$. By using Corollary 1.2.12, if $\mathbf{A}$ has rank $r > 0$, it can be factored as, say,

$$\mathbf{A} = \mathbf{A}_L\mathbf{A}_R = \mathbf{BC} \tag{1.5.3}$$

where $\mathbf{B}$ is $m \times r$ of rank r and $\mathbf{C}$ is $r \times n$ of rank r. Note that $\mathbf{B}'\mathbf{B}$ and $\mathbf{CC}'$ are both nonsingular. If we define $\mathbf{A}^-$ as

$$\mathbf{A}^- = \mathbf{C}'(\mathbf{CC}')^{-1}(\mathbf{B}'\mathbf{B})^{-1}\mathbf{B}' \tag{1.5.4}$$

then it is easily shown that it satisfies the conditions of Equation (1.5.2). Note also that if $\mathbf{A}$ is real, then $\mathbf{A}^-$ is real.

The factorization of $\mathbf{A}$ in Equation (1.5.3) is not unique; however, the g-inverse $\mathbf{A}^-$ is unique. This is the context of the next theorem.

THEOREM 1.5.4

For each matrix $\mathbf{A}$ *there exists a unique matrix* $\mathbf{A}^-$ *that satisfies the conditions of Equation* (1.5.2); *that is, each matrix* $\mathbf{A}$ *has a unique g-inverse.*

Proof

Assume that $\mathbf{A}_1^-$ and $\mathbf{A}_2^-$ are two g-inverses of a matrix $\mathbf{A}$. This means that $\mathbf{A}_1^-$ and $\mathbf{A}_2^-$ each satisfy the four conditions of Equation (1.5.2). We show that when this is the case, it follows that $\mathbf{A}_1^- = \mathbf{A}_2^-$. First we show that $\mathbf{AA}_1^- = \mathbf{AA}_2^-$. Multiply $\mathbf{A} = \mathbf{AA}_1^-\mathbf{A}$ on the right by $\mathbf{A}_2^-$ and obtain

$$\mathbf{AA}_2^- = \mathbf{AA}_1^-\mathbf{AA}_2^-$$

By Equation (1.5.2), the left-hand side, and hence also the right-hand side, is symmetric; that is,

$$\mathbf{AA}_1^-\mathbf{AA}_2^- = (\mathbf{AA}_1^-\mathbf{AA}_2^-)'$$

From this we get

$$\begin{aligned} \mathbf{AA}_2^- &= \mathbf{AA}_1^-\mathbf{AA}_2^- = [(\mathbf{AA}_1^-)(\mathbf{AA}_2^-)]' = (\mathbf{AA}_2^-)'(\mathbf{AA}_1^-)' \\ &= (\mathbf{AA}_2^-)(\mathbf{AA}_1^-) = \mathbf{AA}_1^- \end{aligned} \tag{1.5.5}$$

since, by Equation (1.5.2), $\mathbf{AA}_1^-$ and $\mathbf{AA}_2^-$ are each symmetric.

By a similar procedure (multiplying $\mathbf{A} = \mathbf{AA}_1^-\mathbf{A}$ by $\mathbf{A}_2^-$ on the left instead of on the right), we obtain

$$\mathbf{A}_1^-\mathbf{A} = \mathbf{A}_2^-\mathbf{A} \tag{1.5.6}$$

By using the results of Equation (1.5.5) and Equation (1.5.6), we get

$$\begin{aligned} \mathbf{A}_1^- &= \mathbf{A}_1^-\mathbf{AA}_1^- = (\mathbf{A}_1^-\mathbf{A})\mathbf{A}_1^- = (\mathbf{A}_2^-\mathbf{A})\mathbf{A}_1^- = \mathbf{A}_2^-(\mathbf{AA}_1^-) \\ &= \mathbf{A}_2^-\mathbf{AA}_2^- = \mathbf{A}_2^- \end{aligned} \tag{1.5.7}$$

and the proof is complete.

In the next several theorems, you will note a resemblance between the properties of the *g*-inverse and a regular inverse.

THEOREM 1.5.5

The g-inverse of the transpose of $\mathbf{A}$ *is the transpose of the g-inverse of* $\mathbf{A}$, *that is,* $(\mathbf{A}')^- = (\mathbf{A}^-)'$.

Proof

The proof consists of showing that $(\mathbf{A}^-)'$ is the *g*-inverse of $\mathbf{A}'$, and since the *g*-inverse of $\mathbf{A}'$ is unique, it follows that $(\mathbf{A}')^- = (\mathbf{A}^-)'$.

Write

$$\mathbf{A} = \mathbf{BC}$$

as in Equation (1.5.3), and get

$$\mathbf{A}^- = \mathbf{C}'(\mathbf{CC}')^{-1}(\mathbf{B}'\mathbf{B})^{-1}\mathbf{B}' \tag{1.5.8}$$

Also

$$\mathbf{A}' = \mathbf{C}'\mathbf{B}'$$

and

$$(\mathbf{A}')^- = \mathbf{B}(\mathbf{B}'\mathbf{B})^{-1}(\mathbf{CC}')^{-1}\mathbf{C}$$

Take the transpose of $\mathbf{A}^-$ in Equation (1.5.8) and get

$$(\mathbf{A}^-)' = \mathbf{B}(\mathbf{B}'\mathbf{B})^{-1}(\mathbf{C}\mathbf{C}')^{-1}\mathbf{C}$$

Hence

$$(\mathbf{A}^-)' = (\mathbf{A}')^-$$

and since the g-inverse of a matrix $\mathbf{A}'$ is unique, the theorem is proved.

THEOREM 1.5.6

The g-inverse of $\mathbf{A}^-$ *is equal to* $\mathbf{A}$*; that is,* $(\mathbf{A}^-)^- = \mathbf{A}$.

Proof

By Definition 1.5.1, the g-inverse of $\mathbf{A}^-$ satisfies the following results:

1. $\mathbf{A}^-(\mathbf{A}^-)^- = [\mathbf{A}^-(\mathbf{A}^-)^-]'$
2. $(\mathbf{A}^-)^-\mathbf{A}^- = [(\mathbf{A}^-)^-\mathbf{A}^-]'$
3. $\mathbf{A}^-(\mathbf{A}^-)^-\mathbf{A}^- = \mathbf{A}^-$
4. $(\mathbf{A}^-)^-\mathbf{A}^-(\mathbf{A}^-)^- = (\mathbf{A}^-)^-$.

But if we substitute $\mathbf{A}$ for $(\mathbf{A}^-)^-$, the four equations above are exactly those in Definition 1.5.1, so $\mathbf{A}$ is the unique g-inverse of $\mathbf{A}^-$; that is, $(\mathbf{A}^-)^- = \mathbf{A}$.

THEOREM 1.5.7

The rank of the g-inverse of $\mathbf{A}$ *is equal to the rank of* $\mathbf{A}$.

Proof

If we apply Theorem 1.2.13 to $\mathbf{A}\mathbf{A}^-\mathbf{A} = \mathbf{A}$, we get $\text{rank}(\mathbf{A}) = \text{rank}(\mathbf{A}\mathbf{A}^-\mathbf{A}) \le \text{rank}(\mathbf{A}^-)$; but from $\mathbf{A}^-\mathbf{A}\mathbf{A}^- = \mathbf{A}^-$, we get $\text{rank}(\mathbf{A}^-) = \text{rank}(\mathbf{A}^-\mathbf{A}\mathbf{A}^-) \le \text{rank}(\mathbf{A})$; hence $\text{rank}(\mathbf{A}) = \text{rank}(\mathbf{A}^-)$.

An extension of this theorem is given in the following corollary.

COROLLARY 1.5.7

If the rank of the matrix $\mathbf{A}$ *is equal to r, the rank of each of the following matrices is also equal to r:* $\mathbf{A}^-$, $\mathbf{A}\mathbf{A}^-$, $\mathbf{A}^-\mathbf{A}$, $\mathbf{A}\mathbf{A}^-\mathbf{A}$, $\mathbf{A}^-\mathbf{A}\mathbf{A}^-$.

THEOREM 1.5.8

If $\mathbf{A}$ *is a symmetric matrix, the g-inverse of* $\mathbf{A}$ *is also symmetric; that is, if* $\mathbf{A} = \mathbf{A}'$, *then* $\mathbf{A}^- = (\mathbf{A}^-)'$.

Proof

By Theorem 1.5.5, we obtain $(\mathbf{A}')^- = (\mathbf{A}^-)'$, but since $\mathbf{A} = \mathbf{A}'$, we obtain $\mathbf{A}^- = (\mathbf{A}^-)'$.

The next several theorems give the form of the *g*-inverses of special matrices.

THEOREM 1.5.9

If the matrix $\mathbf{A}$ *is nonsingular, then* $\mathbf{A}^{-1} = \mathbf{A}^-$.

Proof

The proof is done by showing that $\mathbf{A}^{-1}$ satisfies Equation (1.5.2).

THEOREM 1.5.10

If $\mathbf{A}$ *is symmetric idempotent, then* $\mathbf{A}^- = \mathbf{A}$; *that is, if* $\mathbf{A} = \mathbf{A}'$ *and* $\mathbf{A} = \mathbf{A}^2$, *then* $\mathbf{A}^- = \mathbf{A}$.

Proof

The theorem can be proved by showing that $\mathbf{A}$ satisfies Equation (1.5.2).

THEOREM 1.5.11

Let $\mathbf{D}$ *be an* $n \times n$ *diagonal matrix with diagonal elements* d_{ii} *for* $i = 1, 2, \ldots, n$. *The g-inverse* $\mathbf{D}^-$ *of* $\mathbf{D}$ *is a diagonal matrix with ith diagonal element of* $\mathbf{D}^-$ *equal to* d_{ii}^{-1} *if* $d_{ii} \neq 0$ *and equal to zero if* $d_{ii} = 0$.

Proof

The theorem can be proved by showing that $\mathbf{D}^-$ satisfies Equation (1.5.2).

THEOREM 1.5.12

If $\mathbf{A}$ *is an* $m \times n$ *matrix of rank m, then* $\mathbf{A}^- = \mathbf{A}'(\mathbf{A}\mathbf{A}')^{-1}$ *and* $\mathbf{A}\mathbf{A}^- = \mathbf{I}$. *If the rank of* $\mathbf{A}$ *is n, then* $\mathbf{A}^- = (\mathbf{A}'\mathbf{A})^{-1}\mathbf{A}'$ *and* $\mathbf{A}^-\mathbf{A} = \mathbf{I}$.

The proofs of this theorem and the next theorem are left for the reader.

THEOREM 1.5.13

The matrices $\mathbf{A}\mathbf{A}^-$, $\mathbf{A}^-\mathbf{A}$, $\mathbf{I} - \mathbf{A}\mathbf{A}^-$, *and* $\mathbf{I} - \mathbf{A}^-\mathbf{A}$ *are all symmetric idempotent.*

Note 1. It is not always true that $(\mathbf{GH})^- = \mathbf{H}^-\mathbf{G}^-$ for all matrices $\mathbf{G}$ and $\mathbf{H}$. However, for certain matrices this equation is correct. We now state some theorems related to this problem.

THEOREM 1.5.14

Let $\mathbf{B}$ *be an* $m \times r$ *matrix of rank* r $(r > 0)$, *and let* $\mathbf{C}$ *be an* $r \times m$ *matrix of rank* r; *then* $(\mathbf{BC})^- = \mathbf{C}^-\mathbf{B}^-$.

Proof

By Theorem 1.5.12, we obtain

$$\mathbf{C}^- = \mathbf{C}'(\mathbf{CC}')^{-1} \qquad \mathbf{B}^- = (\mathbf{B}'\mathbf{B})^{-1}\mathbf{B}'$$

and hence $\mathbf{C}^-\mathbf{B}^- = \mathbf{C}'(\mathbf{CC}')^{-1}(\mathbf{B}'\mathbf{B})^{-1}\mathbf{B}'$; but this is $(\mathbf{BC})^-$ (see Equation (1.5.4) where $\mathbf{A} = \mathbf{BC}$).

THEOREM 1.5.15

$(\mathbf{A}'\mathbf{A})^- = \mathbf{A}^-(\mathbf{A}')^-$ *for any matrix* $\mathbf{A}$.

Proof

The g-inverse of $\mathbf{A}'\mathbf{A}$, which is denoted by $(\mathbf{A}'\mathbf{A})^-$, must satisfy the following results:

1. $(\mathbf{A}'\mathbf{A})(\mathbf{A}'\mathbf{A})^- = [(\mathbf{A}'\mathbf{A})(\mathbf{A}'\mathbf{A})^-]'$
2. $(\mathbf{A}'\mathbf{A})^-(\mathbf{A}'\mathbf{A}) = [(\mathbf{A}'\mathbf{A})^-(\mathbf{A}'\mathbf{A})]'$
3. $(\mathbf{A}'\mathbf{A})(\mathbf{A}'\mathbf{A})^-(\mathbf{A}'\mathbf{A}) = \mathbf{A}'\mathbf{A}$
4. $(\mathbf{A}'\mathbf{A})^-(\mathbf{A}'\mathbf{A})(\mathbf{A}'\mathbf{A})^- = (\mathbf{A}'\mathbf{A})^-$.

It can be shown by straightforward multiplication that if $\mathbf{A}^-(\mathbf{A}')^-$ is substituted for $(\mathbf{A}'\mathbf{A})^-$, the equations above are those in Definition 1.5.1. For example, if we substitute $\mathbf{A}^-(\mathbf{A}')^-$ for $(\mathbf{A}'\mathbf{A})^-$ in the third equation above, we get

$$(\mathbf{A}'\mathbf{A})\mathbf{A}^-(\mathbf{A}')^-(\mathbf{A}'\mathbf{A}) = \mathbf{A}'[\mathbf{AA}^-](\mathbf{A}')^-\mathbf{A}'\mathbf{A}$$

We can replace the quantity in the brackets by $(\mathbf{A}')^-\mathbf{A}'$, since by Definition 1.5.1, the g-inverse of $\mathbf{A}$ is such that $\mathbf{AA}^- = (\mathbf{AA}^-)' = (\mathbf{A}^-)'\mathbf{A}'$, and by Theorem 1.5.5, this is equal to $(\mathbf{A}')^-\mathbf{A}'$. So if we substitute this for $\mathbf{AA}^-$ in the above, we get

$$\mathbf{A}'[\mathbf{AA}^-](\mathbf{A}')^-\mathbf{A}'\mathbf{A} = \mathbf{A}'(\mathbf{A}')^-\mathbf{A}'(\mathbf{A}')^-\mathbf{A}'\mathbf{A} = \mathbf{A}'(\mathbf{A}')^-\mathbf{A}'\mathbf{A} = \mathbf{A}'\mathbf{A}$$

We have shown that if we replace $(\mathbf{A}'\mathbf{A})^-$ by $\mathbf{A}^-(\mathbf{A}')^-$, the third equation in Definition 1.5.1 is satisfied. By a similar procedure we can show that the remaining three equations satisfy those in Definition 1.5.1. Hence $\mathbf{A}^-(\mathbf{A}')^-$ is the unique *g*-inverse of $\mathbf{A}'\mathbf{A}$; that is, $(\mathbf{A}'\mathbf{A})^- = \mathbf{A}^-(\mathbf{A}')^-$, and the theorem is proved.

THEOREM 1.5.16

$(\mathbf{AA}^-)^- = \mathbf{AA}^-$ *and* $(\mathbf{A}^-\mathbf{A})^- = \mathbf{A}^-\mathbf{A}$ *for any matrix* $\mathbf{A}$.

This theorem can be proved by a procedure almost identical with the method used to prove Theorem 1.5.15. The details are left for the reader. Also see Theorem 1.5.10.

THEOREM 1.5.17

Let $\mathbf{P}$ *be an* $m \times m$ *orthogonal matrix,* $\mathbf{Q}$ *be an* $n \times n$ *orthogonal matrix, and* $\mathbf{A}$ *be any* $m \times n$ *matrix. Then* $(\mathbf{PAQ})^- = \mathbf{Q}'\mathbf{A}^-\mathbf{P}'$.

Let $\mathbf{B} = \mathbf{PAQ}$. We must show that $\mathbf{B}^- = \mathbf{Q}'\mathbf{A}^-\mathbf{P}'$ satisfies the four conditions of Equation (1.5.2). We get the following results:

1. $\mathbf{BB}^- = \mathbf{PAQQ}'\mathbf{A}^-\mathbf{P}' = \mathbf{PAA}^-\mathbf{P}'$. But $\mathbf{PAA}^-\mathbf{P}'$ is symmetric since $\mathbf{AA}^-$ is symmetric. Hence $\mathbf{BB}^-$ is symmetric.
2. $\mathbf{B}^-\mathbf{B} = (\mathbf{Q}'\mathbf{A}^-\mathbf{P}')(\mathbf{PAQ}) = \mathbf{Q}'\mathbf{A}^-\mathbf{AQ}$ which is symmetric, and so $\mathbf{B}^-\mathbf{B}$ is symmetric.
3. $(\mathbf{PAQ})(\mathbf{Q}'\mathbf{A}^-\mathbf{P}')(\mathbf{PAQ}) = \mathbf{PAA}^-\mathbf{AQ} = \mathbf{PAQ}$, or $\mathbf{BB}^-\mathbf{B} = \mathbf{B}$.
4. $(\mathbf{Q}'\mathbf{A}^-\mathbf{P}')(\mathbf{PAQ})(\mathbf{Q}'\mathbf{A}^-\mathbf{P}') = \mathbf{Q}'\mathbf{A}^-\mathbf{AA}^-\mathbf{P}' = \mathbf{Q}'\mathbf{A}^-\mathbf{P}'$, or $\mathbf{B}^-\mathbf{BB}^- = \mathbf{B}^-$.

Hence $\mathbf{Q}'\mathbf{A}^-\mathbf{P}'$ satisfies the conditions in Equation (1.5.2), and so $\mathbf{Q}'\mathbf{A}^-\mathbf{P}'$ is the *g*-inverse of $\mathbf{PAQ}$.

Note 2. If the two matrices $\mathbf{G}$ and $\mathbf{H}$ are nonsingular, then by Theorem 1.2.3, we get $(\mathbf{GH})^{-1} = \mathbf{H}^{-1}\mathbf{G}^{-1}$. Theorems 1.5.14, 1.5.15, and 1.5.17 state a similar result, that is, $(\mathbf{GH})^- = \mathbf{H}^-\mathbf{G}^-$ if $\mathbf{G}$ and $\mathbf{H}$ are *certain* matrices. However, as we stated above, it is *not* true that $(\mathbf{GH})^- = \mathbf{H}^-\mathbf{G}^-$ for all matrices $\mathbf{G}$ and $\mathbf{H}$.

In the linear model we shall sometimes be interested in $\mathbf{AA}^-$ so we state some theorems about this matrix.

THEOREM 1.5.18

Let $\mathbf{A}$ *be any* $m \times n$ *matrix; then* $\mathbf{AB} = \mathbf{AA}^-$ *if and only if* $\mathbf{B}$ *is such that* $\mathbf{ABA} = \mathbf{A}$ *and* $\mathbf{AB}$ *is symmetric.*

Proof

$\mathbf{AB} = \mathbf{AA}^-\mathbf{AB} = (\mathbf{AA}^-)'(\mathbf{AB})' = \mathbf{A}'^-\mathbf{A}'\mathbf{B}'\mathbf{A}' = \mathbf{A}'^-\mathbf{A}' = \mathbf{AA}^-$. The proof of the "only if" part is left for the reader.

THEOREM 1.5.19

Let an $m \times n$ *matrix* $\mathbf{A}$ *be partitioned as* $\mathbf{A} = [\mathbf{A}_1, \mathbf{A}_2]$, *where* $\mathbf{A}_1$ *has size* $m \times r$ *(where* $r > 0$*). Then*

$$\mathbf{AA}^- = \mathbf{A}_1\mathbf{A}_1^- + [(\mathbf{I} - \mathbf{A}_1\mathbf{A}_1^-)\mathbf{A}_2][(\mathbf{I} - \mathbf{A}_1\mathbf{A}_1^-)\mathbf{A}_2]^-$$

Proof

The proof can be obtained by exhibiting a matrix $\mathbf{B}$ in Theorem 1.5.18 such that $\mathbf{AB} = \mathbf{A}_1\mathbf{A}_1^- + [(\mathbf{I} - \mathbf{A}_1\mathbf{A}_1^-)\mathbf{A}_2][(\mathbf{I} - \mathbf{A}_1\mathbf{A}_1^-)\mathbf{A}_2]^-$ and showing that $\mathbf{ABA} = \mathbf{A}$ and $\mathbf{AB}$ is symmetric. The details will be left for the reader.

In this section we have shown that the generalized inverse of a matrix possesses many of the properties that the inverse of a nonsingular matrix possesses. These properties can be very useful in many areas of statistics, especially in solving systems of linear equations. Since the theory of systems of linear equations plays such an extremely important role in statistics as well as in many other scientific fields, we shall discuss another type of inverse, which we call a *conditional inverse*, that is often useful in these situations.

A conditional inverse of a matrix is generally easier to compute than the generalized inverse, and if the end result of some theoretical work is to do computation that involves solutions of systems of linear equations, then it may be desirable to use a conditional inverse rather than the generalized inverse.

DEFINITION 1.5.2

Conditional Inverse. *Let* $\mathbf{A}$ *be an* $m \times n$ *matrix. A matrix* $\mathbf{A}^c$ *is defined to be a conditional inverse of* $\mathbf{A}$ *if and only if it satisfies*

$$\mathbf{AA}^c\mathbf{A} = \mathbf{A} \tag{1.5.9}$$

We now state some theorems that are obvious consequences of this definition.

THEOREM 1.5.20

The generalized inverse of a matrix $\mathbf{A}$ *is also a conditional inverse of* $\mathbf{A}$*, but a conditional inverse of* $\mathbf{A}$ *may not necessarily be the generalized inverse of* $\mathbf{A}$.

THEOREM 1.5.21

A conditional inverse exists for each matrix, but it may not be unique.

THEOREM 1.5.22

If $\mathbf{A}$ *is an* $m \times n$ *matrix, a conditional inverse is an* $n \times m$ *matrix.*

> ***Note 3.*** A conditional inverse must satisfy only condition (3) of Definition 1.5.1 of a generalized inverse. Hence any theorem concerning generalized inverses that involves only condition (3) of Definition 1.5.1 in the proof is also true for conditional inverses. We sometimes abbreviate conditional inverse as "*c*-inverse."

THEOREM 1.5.23

Let $\mathbf{X}$ *be an* $m \times n$ *matrix of rank* $r > 0$. *The results below follow.*

(1) *The rank of* $\mathbf{X}^c$ *is not less than* r, *the rank of* $\mathbf{X}$.

(2) $\mathbf{X}^c\mathbf{X}$ *and* $\mathbf{X}\mathbf{X}^c$ *are idempotent matrices.*

(3) $Rank[\mathbf{X}^c\mathbf{X}] = rank[\mathbf{X}\mathbf{X}^c] = r$, *the rank of* $\mathbf{X}$.

(4) $\mathbf{X}^c\mathbf{X} = \mathbf{I}$ *if and only if the rank of* $\mathbf{X}$ *is* n (*that is, the rank of* $\mathbf{X}$ *is equal to the number of its columns*).

(5) $\mathbf{X}\mathbf{X}^c = \mathbf{I}$ *if and only if the rank of* $\mathbf{X}$ *is* m (*that is, the rank of* $\mathbf{X}$ *is equal to the number of its rows*).

(6) $tr[\mathbf{X}^c\mathbf{X}] = tr[\mathbf{X}\mathbf{X}^c] = r$, *the rank of* $\mathbf{X}$. $tr[\mathbf{A}]$ *is trace of* $\mathbf{A} = \sum_{i=1}^{K} a_{ii}$, *where* $\mathbf{A}$ *has size* $K \times K$.

(7) *If* $\mathbf{X}^c$ *is any c-inverse of* $\mathbf{X}$, *then* $(\mathbf{X}^c)'$ *is a c-inverse of* $\mathbf{X}'$.

Proof

The proof is a simple application of the definition of a *c*-inverse and will be left for the reader.

THEOREM 1.5.24

For any $m \times n$ *matrix* $\mathbf{X}$ *of rank* $r > 0$, *define* $\mathbf{K}$ *by*

$$\mathbf{K} = \mathbf{X}(\mathbf{X}'\mathbf{X})^c\mathbf{X}'$$

Then **K** *is invariant for any c-inverse of* $\mathbf{X}'\mathbf{X}$.

Proof

Let **A** and **B** be any two c-inverses of $\mathbf{X}'\mathbf{X}$. Then $\mathbf{X}'\mathbf{X}\mathbf{A}\mathbf{X}'\mathbf{X} = \mathbf{X}'\mathbf{X}\mathbf{B}\mathbf{X}'\mathbf{X}$, or we can write this as (since $\mathbf{X} = \mathbf{X}_L\mathbf{X}_R$ by Corollary 1.2.12, where $\mathbf{X}_L$ and $\mathbf{X}_R$ have rank r)

$$\mathbf{X}_R'\mathbf{X}_L'\mathbf{X}_L\mathbf{X}_R\mathbf{A}\mathbf{X}_R'\mathbf{X}_L'\mathbf{X}_L\mathbf{X}_R = \mathbf{X}_R'\mathbf{X}_L'\mathbf{X}_L\mathbf{X}_R\mathbf{B}\mathbf{X}_R'\mathbf{X}_L'\mathbf{X}_L\mathbf{X}_R$$

Multiply both sides of the equation on the left by $(\mathbf{X}_R')^c$ and on the right by $\mathbf{X}_R^c$. Note by (4) and (5) of Theorem 1.5.23 that $(\mathbf{X}_R')^c(\mathbf{X}_R') = \mathbf{I}$ and $\mathbf{X}_R\mathbf{X}_R^c = \mathbf{I}$. The result is

$$\mathbf{X}_L'\mathbf{X}_L\mathbf{X}_R\mathbf{A}\mathbf{X}_R'\mathbf{X}_L'\mathbf{X}_L = \mathbf{X}_L'\mathbf{X}_L\mathbf{X}_R\mathbf{B}\mathbf{X}_R'\mathbf{X}_L'\mathbf{X}_L$$

Multiply both sides of the equation on the left and right by $(\mathbf{X}_L'\mathbf{X}_L)^{-1}$. The result of these operations is

$$\mathbf{X}_R\mathbf{A}\mathbf{X}_R' = \mathbf{X}_R\mathbf{B}\mathbf{X}_R'$$

Now multiply both sides of this equation on the left by $\mathbf{X}_L$ and on the right by $\mathbf{X}_L'$. The result is

$$\mathbf{X}\mathbf{A}\mathbf{X}' = \mathbf{X}\mathbf{B}\mathbf{X}'$$

Since **A** and **B** are any c-inverses of $\mathbf{X}'\mathbf{X}$, the theorem is proved.

THEOREM 1.5.25

$\mathbf{X}(\mathbf{X}'\mathbf{X})^c\mathbf{X}' = \mathbf{X}\mathbf{X}^-$, *where* $(\mathbf{X}'\mathbf{X})^c$ *is any c-inverse of* $\mathbf{X}'\mathbf{X}$.

Proof

By the previous theorem, $\mathbf{X}(\mathbf{X}'\mathbf{X})^c\mathbf{X}'$ is invariant for any c-inverse of $\mathbf{X}'\mathbf{X}$. Since $(\mathbf{X}'\mathbf{X})^-$ is a c-inverse of $\mathbf{X}'\mathbf{X}$, we get

$$\mathbf{X}(\mathbf{X}'\mathbf{X})^c\mathbf{X}' = \mathbf{X}(\mathbf{X}'\mathbf{X})^-\mathbf{X}' = \mathbf{X}(\mathbf{X}^-\mathbf{X}'^-)\mathbf{X}' = \mathbf{X}\mathbf{X}^-\mathbf{X}\mathbf{X}^- = \mathbf{X}\mathbf{X}^-$$

THEOREM 1.5.26

Below are some results involving the matrix **K**, *where* $\mathbf{K} = \mathbf{X}(\mathbf{X}'\mathbf{X})^c\mathbf{X}'$.

(1) $\mathbf{K} = \mathbf{K}'$ *and* $\mathbf{K} = \mathbf{K}^2$, *that is,* **K** *is a symmetric idempotent matrix.*

(2) $rank[\mathbf{K}] = tr[\mathbf{K}] = rank[\mathbf{X}] = r$.

(3) $\mathbf{KX} = \mathbf{X}$; $\mathbf{X}'\mathbf{K} = \mathbf{X}'$.

(4) $(\mathbf{X}'\mathbf{X})^c\mathbf{X}'$ *is a c-inverse of* $\mathbf{X}$ *for any c-inverse of* $\mathbf{X}'\mathbf{X}$.

(5) $\mathbf{X}(\mathbf{X}'\mathbf{X})^c$ *is a c-inverse of* $\mathbf{X}'$ *for any c-inverse of* $\mathbf{X}'\mathbf{X}$.

Proof

The results are easily obtained by using Theorem 1.5.25 and writing $\mathbf{X}(\mathbf{X}'\mathbf{X})^c\mathbf{X} = \mathbf{X}\mathbf{X}^-$.

1.6 Solutions of Linear Equations

There is perhaps no field of mathematical inquiry in which systems of linear equations do not play an important role, and the field of statistics is certainly no exception. This section assumes that the reader is acquainted with some of the elementary theorems for solving systems of linear equations and we review and extend these ideas.

We write a system of m equations in n unknowns as

$$\mathbf{A}\mathbf{x} = \mathbf{g} \tag{1.6.1}$$

where $\mathbf{A}$ is an $m \times n$ real matrix, $\mathbf{g}$ is an $m \times 1$ real vector, and $\mathbf{x}$ is an $n \times 1$ vector. The important problems for our concern are the following:

1. For a given $m \times n$ real matrix $\mathbf{A}$ and a given $m \times 1$ real vector $\mathbf{g}$, does there exist an $n \times 1$ real vector $\mathbf{x}$ that satisfies Equation (1.6.1)?
2. If the answer to part 1 is "yes," the next question is, "How many solution vectors $\mathbf{x}$ are there, and how do they depend on $\mathbf{A}$ and $\mathbf{g}$?"

If the answer to part 1 is "yes," the system is said to be *consistent*; if the answer is "no," the system is said to be *inconsistent*. We defer until Chapter 7 computing methods for solving the system.

Reminder. As usual, we shall consider that every matrix and vector has real elements unless explicitly stated otherwise; however, in some cases the word "real" will be included for emphasis.

In this section we state and prove a number of theorems concerning the existence of a solution vector $\mathbf{x}$ to the system of equations $\mathbf{A}\mathbf{x} = \mathbf{g}$.

THEOREM 1.6.1

If $\mathbf{A}$ *is an* $n \times n$ *nonsingular matrix, then the system* $\mathbf{A}\mathbf{x} = \mathbf{g}$ *has a unique solution.*

Proof

Since $\mathbf{A}^{-1}$ exists, $\mathbf{x} = \mathbf{A}^{-1}\mathbf{g}$ is clearly the unique solution. It is evident that if $\mathbf{A}$ is real, then $\mathbf{A}^{-1}$ is real, and since $\mathbf{g}$ is real, it follows that $\mathbf{x}$ is real.

In the system of equations $\mathbf{Ax} = \mathbf{g}$, the matrix $\mathbf{A}$ is called the *coefficient matrix*, and the matrix $\mathbf{B}$ is called the *augmented matrix*, where $\mathbf{B} = [\mathbf{A}, \mathbf{g}]$; that is, if the vector $\mathbf{g}$ is appended to the matrix $\mathbf{A}$ as the $(n + 1)$st column, the resulting matrix has size $m \times (n + 1)$ and is called the augmented matrix.

Example 1.6.1

Consider the system of equations

$$\begin{aligned} 2x_1 + 3x_2 + x_3 &= 1 \\ 2x_1 - x_2 &= 1 \end{aligned}$$

We obtain

$$\mathbf{A} = \begin{bmatrix} 2 & 3 & 1 \\ 2 & -1 & 0 \end{bmatrix} \qquad \mathbf{g} = \begin{bmatrix} 1 \\ 1 \end{bmatrix}$$

The coefficient matrix is

$$\mathbf{A} = \begin{bmatrix} 2 & 3 & 1 \\ 2 & -1 & 0 \end{bmatrix}$$

and the augmented matrix is

$$\mathbf{B} = [\mathbf{A}, \mathbf{g}] = \begin{bmatrix} 2 & 3 & 1 & 1 \\ 2 & -1 & 0 & 1 \end{bmatrix}$$

The augmented and coefficient matrices can be used to determine whether or not a solution to the system exists.

THEOREM 1.6.2

A solution to the system $\mathbf{Ax} = \mathbf{g}$ *exists if and only if the rank of the coefficient matrix* $\mathbf{A}$ *is equal to the rank of the augmented matrix* $[\mathbf{A}, \mathbf{g}]$.

COROLLARY 1.6.2

The system $\mathbf{Ax} = \mathbf{g}$ *has a solution if and only if the vector* $\mathbf{g}$ *is in the column space of* $\mathbf{A}$.

Next we show how the g-inverse and a c-inverse of $\mathbf{A}$ can be used to determine whether a solution to $\mathbf{Ax} = \mathbf{g}$ exists.

THEOREM 1.6.3

A necessary and sufficient condition for a solution to exist to the system $\mathbf{Ax} = \mathbf{g}$ *is that for any c-inverse* $\mathbf{A}^c$ *of* $\mathbf{A}$, *it follows that* $\mathbf{AA}^c\mathbf{g} = \mathbf{g}$.

Proof

First we assume that $\mathbf{Ax} = \mathbf{g}$ has a solution denoted by $\mathbf{x}_0$; hence $\mathbf{g} = \mathbf{Ax}_0$. Let $\mathbf{A}^c$ be any c-inverse of $\mathbf{A}$. Multiply both sides of $\mathbf{g} = \mathbf{Ax}_0$ by $\mathbf{AA}^c$ on the left and obtain

$$\mathbf{AA}^c\mathbf{g} = \mathbf{AA}^c\mathbf{Ax}_0 = \mathbf{Ax}_0 = \mathbf{g}$$

and thus $\mathbf{AA}^c\mathbf{g} = \mathbf{g}$. Next we assume that $\mathbf{AA}^c\mathbf{g} = \mathbf{g}$. Let $\mathbf{x}_0 = \mathbf{A}^c\mathbf{g}$; then $\mathbf{Ax}_0 = \mathbf{AA}^c\mathbf{g} = \mathbf{g}$ so $\mathbf{Ax}_0 = \mathbf{g}$, and hence a solution exists. This completes the proof.

COROLLARY 1.6.3

The system $\mathbf{Ax} = \mathbf{g}$ *has a solution if and only if* $\mathbf{AA}^-\mathbf{g} = \mathbf{g}$.

THEOREM 1.6.4

If $\mathbf{A}$ *is an* $m \times n$ *matrix of rank* m, *then the system* $\mathbf{Ax} = \mathbf{g}$ *has a solution.*

Proof

By Theorem 1.5.12, if $\mathbf{A}$ is $m \times n$ of rank m, then $\mathbf{AA}^- = \mathbf{I}$, and hence $\mathbf{AA}^-\mathbf{g} = \mathbf{g}$, so a solution exists by Corollary 1.6.3.

If $\mathbf{A}$ is an $m \times n$ matrix, the system $\mathbf{Ax} = \mathbf{0}$ is called a *linear homogeneous system*. Clearly $\mathbf{x} = \mathbf{0}$ is always a solution to this system. We now state and prove a theorem about other solutions of a homogeneous system.

THEOREM 1.6.5

Let $\mathbf{A}$ *be an* $m \times n$ *matrix. The linear homogeneous system* $\mathbf{Ax} = \mathbf{0}$ *has a solution other than* $\mathbf{x} = \mathbf{0}$ *if and only if rank*($\mathbf{A}$) $< n$.

Proof

If $\mathbf{x} \neq \mathbf{0}$ is a solution, then rank($\mathbf{A}$) must be less than n, for if it were not, then we could multiply $\mathbf{Ax} = \mathbf{0}$ on the left by $\mathbf{A}^-$ to obtain $\mathbf{x} = \mathbf{A}^-\mathbf{0} = \mathbf{0}$, which is a contradiction. Next assume rank($\mathbf{A}$) $< n$; this implies that the columns of $\mathbf{A}$ are linearly dependent. If we let $\mathbf{a}_i$ denote the ith column of $\mathbf{A}$, we can write $\mathbf{A} = [\mathbf{a}_1, \mathbf{a}_2, \ldots, \mathbf{a}_n]$. Since the $\mathbf{a}_i$ are linearly dependent, there exists a set of constants $\{x_1, x_2, \ldots, x_n\}$, not all equal to zero, such that $\sum_{i=1}^{n} x_i\mathbf{a}_i = \mathbf{0}$. We can write this as $\mathbf{0} = \sum_{i=1}^{n} \mathbf{a}_i x_i = \mathbf{Ax}$ and the proof is complete.

If the system of equations $\mathbf{Ax} = \mathbf{g}$ has at least one solution, it may be important to determine the "number" of solutions and find the form of the general solution. The following theorem is extremely useful in the theory of systems of linear equations, since it gives a method for determining every solution to the system.

THEOREM 1.6.6

Let $\mathbf{A}$ be an $m \times n$ matrix, let $\mathbf{A}^c$ be any c-inverse of $\mathbf{A}$, and suppose a solution exists to the system $\mathbf{Ax} = \mathbf{g}$. For each $n \times 1$ vector $\mathbf{h}$, the vector $\mathbf{x}_0$ is a solution, where

$$\mathbf{x}_0 = \mathbf{A}^c\mathbf{g} + (\mathbf{I} - \mathbf{A}^c\mathbf{A})\mathbf{h} \tag{1.6.2}$$

Also, every solution to the system can be written in the form of Equation (1.6.2) *for some $n \times 1$ vector $\mathbf{h}$.*

Proof

Since we assume that there is a solution to the system, Theorem 1.6.3 tells us that $\mathbf{AA}^c\mathbf{g} = \mathbf{g}$. Hence to prove that $\mathbf{x}_0$ in Equation (1.6.2) is a solution, we multiply it on the left by $\mathbf{A}$ and obtain

$$\mathbf{Ax}_0 = \mathbf{AA}^c\mathbf{g} + \mathbf{A}(\mathbf{I} - \mathbf{A}^c\mathbf{A})\mathbf{h}$$

But since $\mathbf{A}(\mathbf{I} - \mathbf{A}^c\mathbf{A}) = \mathbf{0}$ and $\mathbf{AA}^c\mathbf{g} = \mathbf{g}$, this reduces to $\mathbf{Ax}_0 = \mathbf{g}$, and hence $\mathbf{x}_0$ in Equation (1.6.2) is a solution.

Next we assume that $\mathbf{x}_0$ is any solution to $\mathbf{Ax} = \mathbf{g}$, and show that there exists a vector $\mathbf{h}$ such that $\mathbf{x}_0$ can be written in the form of Equation (1.6.2). Since $\mathbf{x}_0$ is a solution, we have $\mathbf{Ax}_0 = \mathbf{g}$, and multiplying on the left by $\mathbf{A}^c$ gives

$$\mathbf{A}^c\mathbf{Ax}_0 = \mathbf{A}^c\mathbf{g} \qquad \text{or} \qquad \mathbf{0} = \mathbf{A}^c\mathbf{g} - \mathbf{A}^c\mathbf{Ax}_0$$

If we add $\mathbf{x}_0$ to both sides, we get

$$\mathbf{x}_0 = \mathbf{A}^c\mathbf{g} + \mathbf{x}_0 - \mathbf{A}^c\mathbf{Ax}_0 = \mathbf{A}^c\mathbf{g} + (\mathbf{I} - \mathbf{A}^c\mathbf{A})\mathbf{x}_0$$

which is of the form of Equation (1.6.2) with $\mathbf{h} = \mathbf{x}_0$, and the theorem is proved.

From this theorem we get a number of useful corollaries.

COROLLARY 1.6.6.1

Let the system of equations $\mathbf{Ax} = \mathbf{g}$ *have a solution, where* $\mathbf{A}$ *is an* $m \times n$ *matrix. For each* $n \times 1$ *vector* $\mathbf{h}$, *the vector* $\mathbf{x}_0$ *is a solution, where*

$$\mathbf{x}_0 = \mathbf{A}^-\mathbf{g} + (\mathbf{I} - \mathbf{A}^-\mathbf{A})\mathbf{h} \tag{1.6.3}$$

Also, every solution to the system can be written in the form of Equation (1.6.3) *for some* $n \times 1$ *vector* $\mathbf{h}$.

COROLLARY 1.6.6.2

If the system $\mathbf{Ax} = \mathbf{g}$ *is consistent, the vector* $\mathbf{x}_0 = \mathbf{A}^-\mathbf{g}$ *and the vector* $\mathbf{x}_1 = \mathbf{A}^c\mathbf{g}$ *are solutions.*

Proof

The proof of this corollary is obtained by putting $\mathbf{h} = \mathbf{0}$ in Equations (1.6.3) and (1.6.2), respectively.

COROLLARY 1.6.6.3

If the system $\mathbf{Ax} = \mathbf{g}$ *is consistent, then the solution* $\mathbf{x}_0 = \mathbf{A}^-\mathbf{g}$ *is unique if and only if* $\mathbf{A}^-\mathbf{A} = \mathbf{I}$.

Proof

The proof of this corollary follows from the fact that for every $n \times 1$ vector $\mathbf{h}$,

$$\mathbf{x}_0 = \mathbf{A}^-\mathbf{g} + (\mathbf{I} - \mathbf{A}^-\mathbf{A})\mathbf{h}$$

is a solution to $\mathbf{Ax} = \mathbf{g}$, and clearly this is equal to $\mathbf{A}^-\mathbf{g}$ for every vector $\mathbf{h}$ if and only if $\mathbf{I} - \mathbf{A}^-\mathbf{A} = \mathbf{0}$.

Note 1. $\mathbf{A}^-\mathbf{A} = \mathbf{I}$ if and only if $\mathbf{A}^c\mathbf{A} = \mathbf{I}$ for any c-inverse, $\mathbf{A}^c$, of $\mathbf{A}$, so Corollary 1.6.6.3 is valid if $\mathbf{A}^-$ is replaced throughout by $\mathbf{A}^c$.

COROLLARY 1.6.6.4

If the system $\mathbf{Ax} = \mathbf{g}$ *is consistent (where* $\mathbf{A}$ *is an* $m \times n$ *matrix), then the system has a unique solution if and only if the rank of* $\mathbf{A}$ *is equal to* n.

Proof

Clearly the solution is unique if and only if $\mathbf{A}^-\mathbf{A} = \mathbf{I}$, but in this case the rank of $\mathbf{I}$, and hence of $\mathbf{A}^-\mathbf{A}$, is n. But rank($\mathbf{A}$) = rank($\mathbf{A}^-\mathbf{A}$) = n, so the rank must equal n. Also, if $\mathbf{A}$ is $m \times n$ of rank n, then $\mathbf{A}^-\mathbf{A} = \mathbf{I}$, by Theorem 1.5.12.

COROLLARY 1.6.6.5

If a unique solution exists to the system $\mathbf{Ax} = \mathbf{g}$, *then it is* $\mathbf{A}^-\mathbf{g}$. *In this case* $\mathbf{A}^-\mathbf{g} = \mathbf{A}^c\mathbf{g}$ *for any c-inverse* $\mathbf{A}^c$.

1.7 Idempotent Matrices

Quadratic forms with idempotent matrices are used extensively in statistical theory, and in this section we discuss this topic.

DEFINITION 1.7.1

Idempotent Matrices. *Let an* $n \times n$ *matrix* $\mathbf{B}$ *be such that* (1) $\mathbf{B} = \mathbf{B}'$, *and* (2) $\mathbf{B} = \mathbf{B}^2$. *Then* $\mathbf{B}$ *is defined to be an idempotent matrix if* (2) *is satisfied and a symmetric idempotent matrix if* (1) *and* (2) *are both satisfied.*

THEOREM 1.7.1

If $\mathbf{B}$ *is an* $n \times n$ *idempotent matrix of rank n, then* $\mathbf{B} = \mathbf{I}$. *If* $\mathbf{B}$ *is a symmetric idempotent matrix of rank less than n, then* $\mathbf{B}$ *is a positive semidefinite matrix.*

Proof

If $\mathbf{B}$ has rank n, then $\mathbf{B}^{-1}$ exists and we can multiply $\mathbf{B}^2 = \mathbf{B}$ on the left by $\mathbf{B}^{-1}$ and obtain $\mathbf{B} = \mathbf{I}$. If $\mathbf{B}$ has rank less than n, then we can use part (1a) of Theorem 1.4.2.

THEOREM 1.7.2

Let $\mathbf{B}$ *be any* $n \times n$ *matrix of rank p.*

(1) *If* $\mathbf{B}$ *is idempotent, then* $\mathbf{B}$ *has p nonzero characteristic roots and they are each equal to* $+1$.

(2) *If* $\mathbf{B}$ *is symmetric, then a necessary and sufficient condition that* $\mathbf{B}$ *is idempotent is that it has p nonzero characteristic roots and each is* $+1$.

Proof

First we shall prove part (1). By Equation (1.2.5), if λ is a characteristic root of a matrix $\mathbf{B}$, then for some nonzero vector $\mathbf{x}$ we have

$$\mathbf{Bx} = \lambda\mathbf{x}$$

Multiply on the left by $\mathbf{B}$ and obtain

$$\mathbf{B}(\mathbf{Bx}) = \mathbf{B}^2\mathbf{x} = \lambda(\mathbf{Bx}) = \lambda(\lambda\mathbf{x}) = \lambda^2\mathbf{x}$$

But since $\mathbf{B}$ is idempotent, $\mathbf{B} = \mathbf{B}^2$, and we get

$$\lambda^2\mathbf{x} = \mathbf{B}^2\mathbf{x} = \mathbf{Bx} = \lambda\mathbf{x}$$

or

$$\lambda(\lambda - 1)\mathbf{x} = \mathbf{0}$$

So, since $\mathbf{x}$ is nonzero, we must have either $\lambda = 1$ or $\lambda = 0$. Thus the characteristic roots of an idempotent matrix must be equal to either zero or one. But since the rank was assumed to be p and (see Theorem 1.8.5) $\text{rank}(\mathbf{B}) = \text{tr}(\mathbf{B}) = \sum \lambda_i = p$, there are exactly p nonzero roots and they are each equal to $+1$.

To prove part (2), let $\mathbf{P}$ be an orthogonal matrix such that $\mathbf{P'BP} = \mathbf{D}$, where $\mathbf{D}$ is a diagonal matrix with the characteristic roots of $\mathbf{B}$ on the diagonal. Clearly $\mathbf{D} = \mathbf{D}^2$ if and only if the nonzero diagonal elements are equal to $+1$; and $\mathbf{D} = \mathbf{D}^2$ if and only if $\mathbf{B} = \mathbf{B}^2$. The remaining details of the proof are left for the reader.

THEOREM 1.7.3

Let $\mathbf{A}$ be an $n \times n$ (symmetric) idempotent matrix. Then

(1) $\mathbf{A}'$ *is a (symmetric) idempotent matrix.*

(2) $\mathbf{P'AP}$ *is a (symmetric) idempotent matrix if* $\mathbf{P}$ *is an $n \times n$ orthogonal matrix.*

(3) $\mathbf{PAP}^{-1}$ *is an idempotent matrix, where* $\mathbf{P}$ *is an $n \times n$ nonsingular matrix.*

(4) $\mathbf{I} - \mathbf{A}$ *is a (symmetric) idempotent matrix.*

Proof

In each case the proof is obtained by multiplying the appropriate matrices and simplifying the results.

The next four theorems can be used in the analysis of variance.

THEOREM 1.7.4

Let $\mathbf{A}_0 = \sum_{i=1}^{k} \mathbf{A}_i$, *where each* $\mathbf{A}_i$ *is an* $n \times n$ *symmetric matrix. Any two of the conditions* (1), (2), *and* (3) *below imply the remaining condition.*

(1) $\mathbf{A}_0 = \mathbf{A}_0^2$;

(2) $\mathbf{A}_i = \mathbf{A}_i^2$, $i = 1, 2, \ldots, k$;

(3) $\mathbf{A}_i\mathbf{A}_j = \mathbf{0}$, $i \neq j$, $i = 1, 2, \ldots, k$, *and* $j = 1, 2, \ldots, k$.

Proof

The proof is left for the reader.

A variation of Theorem 1.7.4 is given below.

THEOREM 1.7.5

Let $\mathbf{A}_i$, *for* $i = 1, 2, \ldots, k$, *be* $n \times n$ *symmetric matrices of rank* n_i *such that* $\sum_{i=1}^{k} \mathbf{A}_i = \mathbf{I}$. *If* $\sum_{i=1}^{k} n_i = n$, *then the results below follow:*

(1) $\mathbf{A}_i\mathbf{A}_j = \mathbf{0}$, $i \neq j$, $i = 1, 2, \ldots, k$, *and* $j = 1, 2, \ldots, k$;

(2) $\mathbf{A}_i = \mathbf{A}_i^2$, $i = 1, 2, \ldots, k$.

This theorem states that if the sum of the ranks of the $\mathbf{A}_i$ is equal to the rank of the sum of the $\mathbf{A}_i$, then the $\mathbf{A}_i$ are disjoint and idempotent. The proof is left for the reader.

THEOREM 1.7.6

Let $\mathbf{A}_i$, *for* $i = 1, 2, \ldots, k$, *be* $n \times n$ *symmetric idempotent matrices of rank* n_i, *and let* $\mathbf{A}_{k+1}$ *be an* $n \times n$ *nonnegative matrix. Further, suppose* $\mathbf{I} = \sum_{i=1}^{k+1} \mathbf{A}_i$. *Then* $\mathbf{A}_{k+1}$ *is symmetric idempotent of rank* $n - \sum_{i=1}^{k} n_i$, *and* $\mathbf{A}_i\mathbf{A}_j = \mathbf{0}$ *for all* $i \neq j$, $i = 1, 2, \ldots, k+1$, *and* $j = 1, 2, \ldots, k+1$.

Proof

This theorem follows directly from Theorem 1.7.4.

THEOREM 1.7.7

Let $\mathbf{A}$ *be an* $n \times n$ *symmetric idempotent matrix, let* $\mathbf{B}_i$, *for* $i = 1, 2, \ldots, k$, *be* $n \times n$ *nonnegative matrices, and suppose*

$$\mathbf{I} = \mathbf{A} + \sum_{i=1}^{k} \mathbf{B}_i$$

Then $\mathbf{AB}_i = \mathbf{B}_i\mathbf{A} = \mathbf{0}$ *for* $i = 1, 2, \ldots, k$.

Proof

The proof will be left for the reader.

1.8 Trace of Matrices

This section is devoted to the many applications in which the sum of the diagonal elements (trace) of a matrix plays an important role.

DEFINITION 1.8.1

Trace. *The trace of an* $n \times n$ *matrix* $\mathbf{A}$, *which we write as* $tr(\mathbf{A})$, *is defined to be the sum of the diagonal elements of* $\mathbf{A}$, *that is,*

$$tr(\mathbf{A}) = \sum_{i=1}^{n} a_{ii} \tag{1.8.1}$$

THEOREM 1.8.1

Let $\mathbf{A}$ *and* $\mathbf{B}$ *be* $m \times n$ *and* $n \times m$ *matrices, respectively; then*

$$tr(\mathbf{AB}) = tr(\mathbf{BA}) \tag{1.8.2}$$

Proof

Let $\mathbf{AB} = \mathbf{C}$; then $c_{pq} = \sum_{j=1}^{n} a_{pj}b_{jq}$. Let $\mathbf{G} = \mathbf{BA}$; then

$$g_{rs} = \sum_{i=1}^{m} b_{ri}a_{is}$$

But

$$\text{tr}(\mathbf{AB}) = \text{tr}(\mathbf{C}) = \sum_{p=1}^{m} c_{pp} = \sum_{p=1}^{m} \sum_{j=1}^{n} a_{pj}b_{jp}$$

Also

$$\text{tr}(\mathbf{BA}) = \text{tr}(\mathbf{G}) = \sum_{r=1}^{n} g_{rr} = \sum_{r=1}^{n} \sum_{i=1}^{m} b_{ri}a_{ir}$$

Thus $\text{tr}(\mathbf{AB}) = \text{tr}(\mathbf{BA})$.

THEOREM 1.8.2

Let **A** *be any* $n \times n$ *matrix and let* **P** *be any nonsingular* $n \times n$ *matrix; then*

$$tr(\mathbf{A}) = tr(\mathbf{P}^{-1}\mathbf{A}\mathbf{P}) \tag{1.8.3}$$

If **P** *is an orthogonal matrix, then*

$$tr(\mathbf{A}) = tr(\mathbf{P}'\mathbf{A}\mathbf{P}) \tag{1.8.4}$$

Proof

By the previous theorem,

$$\text{tr}[\mathbf{P}^{-1}\mathbf{A}\mathbf{P}] = \text{tr}[\mathbf{P}^{-1}(\mathbf{A}\mathbf{P})] = \text{tr}[(\mathbf{A}\mathbf{P})\mathbf{P}^{-1}] = \text{tr}(\mathbf{A}\mathbf{I}) = \text{tr}(\mathbf{A})$$

THEOREM 1.8.3

Let **A** *be an* $n \times n$ *matrix with characteristic roots* $\lambda_1, \lambda_2, \ldots, \lambda_n$*; then* $tr(\mathbf{A}) = \sum_{i=1}^{n} \lambda_i$*; that is, the sum of the diagonal elements of an* $n \times n$ *matrix is equal to the sum of the characteristic roots of the matrix.*

Proof

Let **P** be a nonsingular matrix such that $\mathbf{P}^{-1}\mathbf{A}\mathbf{P} = \mathbf{T}$ where **T** is a triangular matrix with characteristic roots λ_i on the diagonal (**P** and **T** may not be real matrices). Then

$$\text{tr}(\mathbf{A}) = \text{tr}(\mathbf{P}^{-1}\mathbf{A}\mathbf{P}) = \text{tr}(\mathbf{T}) = \sum_{i=1}^{n} \lambda_i \tag{1.8.5}$$

The proofs of the remaining theorems in this section are left for the reader. In most cases the proof involves an application of one or more of the first three theorems in the section.

THEOREM 1.8.4

If **A** *and* **B** *are* $n \times n$ *matrices and* a *and* b *are scalars, then*

$$tr(a\mathbf{A} + b\mathbf{B}) = a\, tr(\mathbf{A}) + b\, tr(\mathbf{B}) \tag{1.8.6}$$

THEOREM 1.8.5

If **A** *is an* $n \times n$ *matrix and* $\mathbf{A}^2 = m\mathbf{A}$*, then*

$$tr(\mathbf{A}) = m\, rank(\mathbf{A}) \tag{1.8.7}$$

Note 1. If $\mathbf{A}$ is idempotent, then $m = 1$ and $\text{tr}(\mathbf{A}) = \text{rank}(\mathbf{A})$.

THEOREM 1.8.6

Let $\mathbf{A}$ be an $m \times n$ matrix; then $tr(\mathbf{A}'\mathbf{A}) = tr(\mathbf{A}\mathbf{A}') = \sum_{j=1}^{n} \sum_{i=1}^{m} a_{ij}^2$ and $tr(\mathbf{A}'\mathbf{A}) = tr(\mathbf{A}\mathbf{A}') = \mathbf{0}$ if and only if $\mathbf{A} = \mathbf{0}$.

THEOREM 1.8.7

If $\mathbf{A}$ is an $n \times n$ matrix, then

$$tr(\mathbf{A}') = tr(\mathbf{A}) \tag{1.8.8}$$

THEOREM 1.8.8

If $\mathbf{A}$ is an $n \times m$ matrix, $\mathbf{A}^c$ is any c-inverse of $\mathbf{A}$, and $\mathbf{A}^-$ is the g-inverse of $\mathbf{A}$, then

$$tr(\mathbf{A}^c\mathbf{A}) = tr(\mathbf{A}\mathbf{A}^c) = tr(\mathbf{A}^-\mathbf{A}) = tr(\mathbf{A}\mathbf{A}^-) = rank(\mathbf{A}) \tag{1.8.9}$$

1.9 Derivatives of Quadratic and Linear Forms; Expectation of a Matrix

In many situations it is necessary to obtain the (partial) derivatives of a function with respect to a number of variables. For example, consider a function of the real variables x_1, x_2, and x_3 given by

$$f(\mathbf{x}) = f(x_1, x_2, x_3) = 6x_1^2 - 2x_1x_2 + 2x_3^2 \qquad -\infty < x_i < \infty \qquad i = 1, 2, 3 \tag{1.9.1}$$

and suppose that it is necessary to obtain the three partial derivatives

$$\frac{\partial f(\mathbf{x})}{\partial x_1} \qquad \frac{\partial f(\mathbf{x})}{\partial x_2} \qquad \frac{\partial f(\mathbf{x})}{\partial x_3}$$

Since $f(\mathbf{x})$ can be written as a function of the vector $\mathbf{x}$, it may be desirable to express the three partial derivatives as a vector. We define $\partial f(\mathbf{x})/\partial \mathbf{x}$ by

$$\frac{\partial f(\mathbf{x})}{\partial \mathbf{x}} = \begin{bmatrix} \dfrac{\partial f(\mathbf{x})}{\partial x_1} \\ \dfrac{\partial f(\mathbf{x})}{\partial x_2} \\ \dfrac{\partial f(\mathbf{x})}{\partial x_3} \end{bmatrix}$$

and obtain the expression

$$\frac{\partial f(\mathbf{x})}{\partial \mathbf{x}} = \begin{bmatrix} 12x_1 - 2x_2 \\ -2x_1 \\ 4x_3 \end{bmatrix}$$

from Equation (1.9.1). This leads to the next definition.

DEFINITION 1.9.1

Derivative of a Function with Respect to a Vector. *Let $f(\mathbf{x})$ be a function of n independent real variables $x_1, x_2, \ldots, x_n$. The derivative of $f(\mathbf{x})$ with respect to the vector $\mathbf{x}$, where*

$$\mathbf{x} = \begin{bmatrix} x_1 \\ x_2 \\ \vdots \\ x_n \end{bmatrix}$$

is denoted by $\partial f(\mathbf{x})/\partial \mathbf{x}$ and is defined by

$$\frac{\partial f(\mathbf{x})}{\partial \mathbf{x}} = \begin{bmatrix} \dfrac{\partial f(\mathbf{x})}{\partial x_1} \\ \dfrac{\partial f(\mathbf{x})}{\partial x_2} \\ \vdots \\ \dfrac{\partial f(\mathbf{x})}{\partial x_n} \end{bmatrix}$$

We now state and prove some theorems that are useful in statistical applications.

THEOREM 1.9.1

Let $\ell(\mathbf{x})$ be a linear function of n independent variables defined by $\ell(\mathbf{x}) = \sum_{i=1}^{n} a_i x_i = \mathbf{a}'\mathbf{x} = \mathbf{x}'\mathbf{a}$, where $\mathbf{a}' = [a_1, a_2, \ldots, a_n]$ and the a_i are any constants. Then

$$\frac{\partial \ell(\mathbf{x})}{\partial \mathbf{x}} = \mathbf{a}$$

Proof

The tth element of $\partial\ell(\mathbf{x})/\partial\mathbf{x}$ is, by definition, equal to $\partial\ell(\mathbf{x})/\partial x_t$ and it is clearly a_t.

THEOREM 1.9.2

Let $q(\mathbf{x})$ be a quadratic form in the n independent real variables $x_1, x_2, \ldots, x_n$ defined by

$$q(\mathbf{x}) = \mathbf{x}'\mathbf{A}\mathbf{x}$$

where $\mathbf{A} = [a_{ij}]$ is an $n \times n$ symmetric matrix of constants. Then

$$\frac{\partial q(\mathbf{x})}{\partial \mathbf{x}} = 2\mathbf{A}\mathbf{x}$$

Proof

We can write

$$q(\mathbf{x}) = \sum_{j=1}^{n} \sum_{i=1}^{n} x_i x_j a_{ij}$$

The tth element of $\partial q(\mathbf{x})/\partial\mathbf{x}$ is $\partial q(\mathbf{x})/\partial x_t$, and clearly

$$\left[\frac{\partial q(\mathbf{x})}{\partial x_t}\right] = \left[\sum_{j=1}^{n} x_j a_{tj} + \sum_{i=1}^{n} x_i a_{it}\right] = 2\left[\sum_{j=1}^{n} x_j a_{tj}\right] = 2\mathbf{A}\mathbf{x}$$

since $\mathbf{A}$ is symmetric.

DEFINITION 1.9.2

Expected Value of a Random Matrix. *Let $\mathcal{W}$ be a $k_1 \times k_2$ random matrix (a matrix of functions of the n random variables $X_1, X_2, \ldots, X_n$); that is, let $W_{ij} = t_{ij}(X_1, X_2, \ldots, X_n)$; then the expected value of the matrix $\mathcal{W}$ is denoted by $\mathcal{E}[\mathcal{W}]$ and is defined by the $k_1 \times k_2$ matrix $\mathbf{A}$, where*

$$a_{ij} = \mathcal{E}[t_{ij}(X_1, X_2, \ldots, X_n)]$$

For example, if

$$\mathcal{W} = \begin{bmatrix} X_1 & X_2 \\ X_2 & X_3 \end{bmatrix}$$

then

$$\mathcal{E}[\mathcal{W}] = \begin{bmatrix} \mathcal{E}[X_1] & \mathcal{E}[X_2] \\ \mathcal{E}[X_2] & \mathcal{E}[X_3] \end{bmatrix}$$

THEOREM 1.9.3

If $\mathcal{W}$ is a $k_1 \times k_2$ random matrix, $\mathcal{V}$ is a $k_1 \times k_2$ random matrix, $\mathbf{A}_1$ is an $m_1 \times k_1$ matrix of constants, and $\mathbf{A}_2$ is a $k_2 \times m_2$ matrix of constants, then the following relationships hold:

(1) $\mathcal{E}[\mathbf{A}_1] = \mathbf{A}_1$;

(2) $\mathcal{E}[\mathbf{A}_1 \mathcal{W}] = \mathbf{A}_1(\mathcal{E}[\mathcal{W}])$;

(3) $\mathcal{E}[\mathcal{W}\mathbf{A}_2] = (\mathcal{E}[\mathcal{W}])\mathbf{A}_2$;

(4) $\mathcal{E}[\mathbf{A}_1 \mathcal{W} \mathbf{A}_2] = \mathbf{A}_1(\mathcal{E}[\mathcal{W}])\mathbf{A}_2$;

(5) $\mathcal{E}[\mathcal{V} + \mathcal{W}] = \mathcal{E}[\mathcal{V}] + \mathcal{E}[\mathcal{W}]$;

if all expectations involved exist.

Proof

We shall prove relationship (4); relationships (2) and (3) will follow by setting $\mathbf{A}_1$ or $\mathbf{A}_2$ equal to the identity matrix.

Let $\mathcal{E}[W_{pq}] = c_{pq}$ and hence $\mathcal{E}[\mathcal{W}] = \mathbf{C}$. Now if we set $\mathbf{A}_1 \mathcal{W} \mathbf{A}_2 = \mathcal{U}$, then

$$U_{ij} = \sum_{p=1}^{k_1} \sum_{q=1}^{k_2} a_{ip}^{(1)} W_{pq} a_{qj}^{(2)}$$

where $\mathbf{A}_i = [a_{pq}^{(i)}]$. We get

$$\mathcal{E}[U_{ij}] = \sum_{p=1}^{k_1} \sum_{q=1}^{k_2} a_{ip}^{(1)} c_{pq} a_{qj}^{(2)}$$

and hence

$$\mathcal{E}[\mathcal{U}] = \mathbf{A}_1 \mathbf{C} \mathbf{A}_2 = \mathbf{A}_1(\mathcal{E}[\mathcal{W}])\mathbf{A}_2$$

Relationship (5) follows from the fact that

$$\mathcal{E}[V_{ij} + W_{ij}] = \mathcal{E}[V_{ij}] + \mathcal{E}[W_{ij}]$$

1.10 Evaluation of an Integral

There are many places in this book where the evaluation of an integral related to the integral $\int_{-\infty}^{\infty} e^{-a^2x^2}\,dx$ is required. In this section we state one major result from which many special cases can be obtained.

THEOREM 1.10.1

Let a_0 and b_0 be scalar constants, let **a** *be an $n \times 1$ vector of constants, let* **b** *be an $n \times 1$ vector of constants, let* **A** *be an $n \times n$ symmetric matrix of constants, and let* **B** *be a positive definite matrix of constants. The value of the multiple integral in Equation* (1.10.1) *is given in Equation* (1.10.2).

$$I = \int_{-\infty}^{\infty}\int_{-\infty}^{\infty}\cdots\int_{-\infty}^{\infty}(\mathbf{x}'\mathbf{A}\mathbf{x} + \mathbf{x}'\mathbf{a} + a_0)e^{-(\mathbf{x}'\mathbf{B}\mathbf{x}+\mathbf{x}'\mathbf{b}+b_0)}\,dx_1\,dx_2\cdots dx_n \quad (1.10.1)$$

$$I = \tfrac{1}{2}\pi^{n/2}|\mathbf{B}|^{-1/2}e^{(1/4)\mathbf{b}'\mathbf{B}^{-1}\mathbf{b}-b_0}[tr(\mathbf{A}\mathbf{B}^{-1}) - \mathbf{b}'\mathbf{B}^{-1}\mathbf{a} + \tfrac{1}{2}\mathbf{b}'\mathbf{B}^{-1}\mathbf{A}\mathbf{B}^{-1}\mathbf{b} + 2a_0] \quad (1.10.2)$$

The $n \times 1$ vector **x** *has components $x_1, x_2, \ldots, x_n$.*

Proof

First we shall examine the exponent of Equation (1.10.1). It is easily shown that the exponent can be written as

$$\mathbf{x}'\mathbf{B}\mathbf{x} + \mathbf{x}'\mathbf{b} + b_0 = \tfrac{1}{2}(\mathbf{x} + \tfrac{1}{2}\mathbf{B}^{-1}\mathbf{b})'(2\mathbf{B})(\mathbf{x} + \tfrac{1}{2}\mathbf{B}^{-1}\mathbf{b}) - \tfrac{1}{4}\mathbf{b}'\mathbf{B}^{-1}\mathbf{b} + b_0 \quad (1.10.3)$$

Also, the terms in the integrand that are not part of the exponential term can be written as

$$\mathbf{x}'\mathbf{A}\mathbf{x} + \mathbf{x}'\mathbf{a} + a_0 = (\mathbf{x} + \tfrac{1}{2}\mathbf{B}^{-1}\mathbf{b})'\mathbf{A}(\mathbf{x} + \tfrac{1}{2}\mathbf{B}^{-1}\mathbf{b}) + \mathbf{x}'(\mathbf{a} - \mathbf{A}\mathbf{B}^{-1}\mathbf{b}) - \tfrac{1}{4}\mathbf{b}'\mathbf{B}^{-1}\mathbf{A}\mathbf{B}^{-1}\mathbf{b} + a_0 \quad (1.10.4)$$

Equations (1.10.3) and (1.10.4) can be verified by simply expanding the right-hand member in each case and showing that it reduces to the left-hand member. If we use Equations (1.10.3) and (1.10.4) and substitute into the integrand, we get

$$\begin{aligned} I = {} & [\exp(\tfrac{1}{4}\mathbf{b}'\mathbf{B}^{-1}\mathbf{b} - b_0)]\Bigg[\int_{-\infty}^{\infty}\cdots \\ & \times \int_{-\infty}^{\infty}(\mathbf{x} - \mathbf{c})'\mathbf{A}(\mathbf{x} - \mathbf{c})\exp[-\tfrac{1}{2}(\mathbf{x} - \mathbf{c})'\mathbf{R}(\mathbf{x} - \mathbf{c})]\,dx_1\,dx_2\cdots dx_n \\ & + \int_{-\infty}^{\infty}\cdots\int_{-\infty}^{\infty}\mathbf{x}'\mathbf{d}\exp[-\tfrac{1}{2}(\mathbf{x} - \mathbf{c})'\mathbf{R}(\mathbf{x} - \mathbf{c})]\,dx_1\,dx_2\cdots dx_n \\ & + \int_{-\infty}^{\infty}\cdots\int_{-\infty}^{\infty}(-\tfrac{1}{4}\mathbf{b}'\mathbf{B}^{-1}\mathbf{A}\mathbf{B}^{-1}\mathbf{b} + a_0) \\ & \times \exp[-\tfrac{1}{2}(\mathbf{x} - \mathbf{c})'\mathbf{R}(\mathbf{x} - \mathbf{c})]\,dx_1\,dx_2\cdots dx_n\Bigg] \\ = {} & [\exp(\tfrac{1}{4}\mathbf{b}'\mathbf{B}^{-1}\mathbf{b} - b_0)][I_1 + I_2 + I_3] \end{aligned} \quad (1.10.5)$$

written as a sum of three integrals for brevity.

In Equation (1.10.5) we used the following notation:

$$\mathbf{c} = -\tfrac{1}{2}\mathbf{B}^{-1}\mathbf{b} \qquad \mathbf{d} = \mathbf{a} - \mathbf{A}\mathbf{B}^{-1}\mathbf{b} \qquad \mathbf{R} = 2\mathbf{B} \tag{1.10.6}$$

Notice that $\mathbf{R}$ is positive definite since we assumed in the statement of the theorem that $\mathbf{B}$ is positive definite. Notice also that $\mathbf{c}$, $\mathbf{d}$, and $\mathbf{R}$ are constant vectors and a constant matrix, respectively. Also, the quantity $\frac{1}{4}\mathbf{b}'\mathbf{B}^{-1}\mathbf{b} - b_0$ in the exponent is a constant; hence

$$\exp(\tfrac{1}{4}\mathbf{b}'\mathbf{B}^{-1}\mathbf{b} - b_0) \tag{1.10.7}$$

can be taken outside the integral signs. We get

$$I_1 = (2\pi)^{n/2}|\mathbf{R}|^{-1/2}\operatorname{tr}(\mathbf{A}\mathbf{R}^{-1})$$

and by substituting for $\mathbf{R}$ in Equation (1.10.6), we get

$$I_1 = \tfrac{1}{2}\pi^{n/2}|\mathbf{B}|^{-1/2}\operatorname{tr}(\mathbf{A}\mathbf{B}^{-1}) \tag{1.10.8}$$

Since we can write $\mathbf{x}'\mathbf{d}$ as $\sum_{i=1}^{n} x_i d_i$, the integral represented by I_2 is a sum of n integrals; thus we get

$$(2\pi)^{n/2}|\mathbf{R}|^{-1/2}c_p d_p$$

for the pth integral. Therefore,

$$I_2 = \sum_{i=1}^{n} (2\pi)^{n/2}|\mathbf{R}|^{-1/2}c_i d_i = (2\pi)^{n/2}|\mathbf{R}|^{-1/2}\mathbf{c}'\mathbf{d}$$

If we substitute the pertinent quantities from Equation (1.10.6), we get

$$I_2 = \tfrac{1}{2}\pi^{n/2}|\mathbf{B}|^{-1/2}\mathbf{b}'\mathbf{B}^{-1}(\mathbf{A}\mathbf{B}^{-1}\mathbf{b} - \mathbf{a}) \tag{1.10.9}$$

The integral denoted by I_3 in Equation (1.10.5) can be written as

$$I_3 = (-\tfrac{1}{4}\mathbf{b}'\mathbf{B}^{-1}\mathbf{A}\mathbf{B}^{-1}\mathbf{b} + a_0)\int_{-\infty}^{\infty} \cdots \times \int_{-\infty}^{\infty} \exp[-\tfrac{1}{2}(\mathbf{x} - \mathbf{c})'\mathbf{R}(\mathbf{x} - \mathbf{c})]\, dx_1\, dx_2 \cdots dx_n$$

and we get

$$I_3 = (-\tfrac{1}{4}\mathbf{b}'\mathbf{B}^{-1}\mathbf{A}\mathbf{B}^{-1}\mathbf{b} + a_0)(2\pi)^{n/2}|\mathbf{R}|^{-1/2}$$

If we substitute the pertinent quantities from Equation (1.10.6), we get

$$I_3 = \pi^{n/2}|\mathbf{B}|^{-1/2}(a_0 - \tfrac{1}{4}\mathbf{b}'\mathbf{B}^{-1}\mathbf{A}\mathbf{B}^{-1}\mathbf{b}) \qquad (1.10.10)$$

If we now substitute the quantities for I_1, I_2, and I_3 of Equations (1.10.8), (1.10.9), and (1.10.10), we obtain the result in Equation (1.10.2).

Problems

1.1. Show that the vector $\mathbf{v}$ is in the vector space spanned by $\mathbf{v}_1$ and $\mathbf{v}_2$, where

$$\mathbf{v}_1 = \begin{bmatrix} 1 \\ 1 \\ 0 \\ 1 \end{bmatrix} \quad \mathbf{v}_2 = \begin{bmatrix} -1 \\ 1 \\ 1 \\ 0 \end{bmatrix} \quad \mathbf{v} = \begin{bmatrix} 5 \\ 1 \\ -2 \\ 3 \end{bmatrix}$$

1.2. Show that the four vectors below are linearly dependent.

$$\mathbf{v}_1 = \begin{bmatrix} 1 \\ -1 \\ 1 \\ 0 \end{bmatrix} \quad \mathbf{v}_2 = \begin{bmatrix} 2 \\ 1 \\ 1 \\ 0 \end{bmatrix} \quad \mathbf{v}_3 = \begin{bmatrix} 0 \\ -6 \\ 2 \\ 0 \end{bmatrix} \quad \mathbf{v}_4 = \begin{bmatrix} 0 \\ -3 \\ 1 \\ 0 \end{bmatrix}$$

1.3. In Problem 1.2, find a set of two linearly independent vectors.

1.4. Is the vector $\mathbf{v}$ in the vector space spanned by the four vectors in Problem 1.2, where $\mathbf{v}' = [1, 1, 0, 1]$?

1.5. In Problem 1.2, show that $\mathbf{v}_2$ can be expressed as a linear combination of the other three vectors.

1.6. In Problem 1.2, find two different bases for the vector space spanned by the four vectors.

1.7. Find the roots of the matrix $\mathbf{A}$, where

$$\mathbf{A} = \begin{bmatrix} 4 & 1 \\ 1 & 2 \end{bmatrix}$$

1.8. In Problem 1.7, find a 2×2 matrix $\mathbf{P}$ such that $\mathbf{P}'\mathbf{A}\mathbf{P} = \mathbf{I}$.

1.9. Find the dimension of the column space of **A**, where

$$\mathbf{A} = \begin{bmatrix} 1 & 1 & 1 \\ 2 & 2 & 2 \\ -1 & 1 & -3 \\ 1 & 2 & 0 \end{bmatrix}$$

1.10. For the matrix **A** in Problem 1.9, find two matrices $\mathbf{A}_L$ and $\mathbf{A}_R$ such that $\mathbf{A} = \mathbf{A}_L\mathbf{A}_R$ and where $\mathbf{A}_L$, $\mathbf{A}_R$, and **A** have the same rank.

1.11. Let **A** and **B** be defined by

$$\mathbf{A} = \begin{bmatrix} 1 & 1 & 1 \\ 2 & 2 & 2 \\ -1 & 1 & -3 \end{bmatrix} \qquad \mathbf{B} = \begin{bmatrix} 0 & 2 & 1 \\ 0 & 4 & 2 \\ 0 & -2 & -1 \end{bmatrix}$$

Show that the column space of **B** is a subspace of the column space of **A**.

1.12. For any $n \times 1$ vector $\mathbf{a} \neq \mathbf{0}$, show that $\mathbf{a}^- = \mathbf{a}'/\mathbf{a}'\mathbf{a}$.

1.13. Find the g-inverse of the vector **a** where $\mathbf{a}' = [1, 3, 1, 5, 2]$.

1.14. Show that the system of equations given below is consistent and find a solution.

$$\begin{aligned} 3x_1 - 2x_2 + x_3 &= 3 \\ 3x_1 + x_2 + 2x_3 &= 5 \\ 3x_1 + 10x_2 + 5x_3 &= 11 \end{aligned}$$

1.15. Find the g-inverse of the matrix **A**, where

$$\mathbf{A} = \begin{bmatrix} 1 & 1 & 1 & 0 & 0 \\ 1 & 1 & 1 & 0 & 0 \\ 1 & 1 & 1 & 0 & 0 \\ 0 & 0 & 0 & 2 & 2 \\ 0 & 0 & 0 & 2 & 2 \end{bmatrix}$$

1.16. Let **A** be an $m \times m$ symmetric matrix and **P** be an orthogonal matrix such that $\mathbf{P}'\mathbf{A}\mathbf{P} = \mathbf{D}$, where **D** is a diagonal matrix with the characteristic roots of **A** on the diagonal. Show that $\mathbf{P}'\mathbf{A}^-\mathbf{P}$ is also a diagonal matrix.

1.17. Let λ_i $(i = 1, 2, \ldots, r)$ be the nonzero characteristic roots of an $m \times m$ symmetric matrix **A**. Show that λ_i^{-1} $(i = 1, 2, \ldots, r)$ are the nonzero characteristic roots of $\mathbf{A}^-$.

1.18. If $\mathbf{A}$ is an $m \times m$ symmetric matrix such that $\mathbf{a}'\mathbf{A} = \mathbf{0}$, show that $\mathbf{a}'\mathbf{A}^{-} = \mathbf{0}$ ($\mathbf{a}$ is an $m \times 1$ vector).

1.19. If $\mathbf{A}$ is an $m \times m$ symmetric matrix such that $\mathbf{1}'\mathbf{A} = \mathbf{0}$, show that

$$\begin{bmatrix} \mathbf{A} \\ \mathbf{1}' \end{bmatrix}^{-} = \left[\mathbf{A}^{-}, \left(\frac{1}{m}\right)\mathbf{1}\right]$$

1.20. If $\mathbf{A}$ is an $m \times n$ matrix, $\mathbf{B}$ is an $m \times n$ matrix, $\mathbf{AB}' = \mathbf{0}$, and $\mathbf{B}'\mathbf{A} = \mathbf{0}$, show that

(a) $\mathbf{A}^{-}\mathbf{B} = \mathbf{0}$ (b) $\mathbf{B}^{-}\mathbf{A} = \mathbf{0}$ (c) $\mathbf{AB}^{-} = \mathbf{0}$
(d) $\mathbf{BA}^{-} = \mathbf{0}$ (e) $\mathbf{B}'^{-}\mathbf{A}^{-} = \mathbf{0}$ (f) $\mathbf{A}'^{-}\mathbf{B}^{-} = \mathbf{0}$.

1.21. If $\mathbf{A}$ is a positive semidefinite matrix, show that $\mathbf{A}^{-}$ is also a positive semidefinite matrix.

1.22. Let $\mathbf{A}_1^c$ and $\mathbf{A}_2^c$ be any two c-inverses of the $m \times n$ matrix $\mathbf{A}$, and let $\mathbf{g}$ be any $n \times 1$ vector such that $\mathbf{AA}_1^c\mathbf{g} = \mathbf{g}$. Show that $\mathbf{AA}_2^c\mathbf{g} = \mathbf{g}$.

1.23. For the matrix

$$\mathbf{A} = \begin{bmatrix} 1 & 2 \\ 1 & 1 \\ -1 & 0 \end{bmatrix}$$

find a c-inverse.

1.24. Does $(\mathbf{A}^c)^c = \mathbf{A}$ for all matrices $\mathbf{A}$? For any matrix $\mathbf{A}$? Prove.

1.25. If $\mathbf{A}$ is nonsingular, show that a c-inverse of $\mathbf{A}$ is unique and $\mathbf{A}^c = \mathbf{A}^{-1}$.

1.26. If $\mathbf{A}$ is defined by

$$\mathbf{A} = \begin{bmatrix} \mathbf{B} & \mathbf{0} \\ \mathbf{0} & \mathbf{C} \end{bmatrix}$$

show that $\mathbf{A}^c$ is a c-inverse of $\mathbf{A}$ where

$$\mathbf{A}^c = \begin{bmatrix} \mathbf{B}^c & \mathbf{0} \\ \mathbf{0} & \mathbf{C}^c \end{bmatrix}$$

where $\mathbf{B}^c$ and $\mathbf{C}^c$ are any c-inverses of $\mathbf{B}$ and $\mathbf{C}$, respectively.

1.27. Show that a c-inverse of a singular diagonal matrix is not unique.

1.28. Show that the system of equations $\mathbf{Ax} = \mathbf{g}$ below is consistent.

$$\begin{aligned} x_1 - 2x_2 + 3x_3 + 2x_4 &= 2 \\ x_1 + x_3 - 3x_4 &= -4 \\ x_1 + 2x_2 - 3x_3 &= -4 \end{aligned}$$

1.29. In Problem 1.28, find $\mathbf{A}^c$, a conditional inverse of $\mathbf{A}$.

1.30. In Problem 1.28, find two distinct solution vectors.

1.31. In Problem 1.28, find a linearly independent set of solution vectors.

1.32. Prove that for any matrix $\mathbf{A}$ if there is a c-inverse $\mathbf{A}^c$, such that $\mathbf{AA}^c = \mathbf{I}$, then $\mathbf{AA}^- = \mathbf{I}$.

1.33. Prove that for any matrix $\mathbf{A}$ if $\mathbf{AA}^- = \mathbf{I}$, then $\mathbf{AA}^c = \mathbf{I}$ for each c-inverse of $\mathbf{A}$.

1.34. Show that the system below is inconsistent.

$$\begin{aligned} x_1 + x_2 + x_3 &= 3 \\ x_1 - x_2 + 2x_3 &= -3 \\ 3x_1 - x_2 + 5x_3 &= -2 \\ 2x_1 + x_2 + x_3 &= 4 \end{aligned}$$

1.35. If

$$\mathbf{B} = \begin{bmatrix} a\mathbf{I} & b\mathbf{I} \\ b\mathbf{I} & d\mathbf{I} \end{bmatrix}$$

where each identity matrix is of size $m \times m$, find the determinant of $\mathbf{B}$.

1.36. In Problem 1.35, if $ad - b^2 \neq 0$, find $\mathbf{B}^{-1}$.

1.37. Find the inverse of the triangular matrix $\mathbf{T}$, where

$$\mathbf{T} = \begin{bmatrix} \mathbf{I} & \mathbf{J} & \mathbf{J} \\ \mathbf{0} & \mathbf{I} & \mathbf{J} \\ \mathbf{0} & \mathbf{0} & \mathbf{I} \end{bmatrix}$$

and each submatrix is of order $k \times k$, and $\mathbf{J}$ is a matrix with each element equal to $+1$.

1.38. Find the inverse of the 5×5 lower triangular matrix $\mathbf{T}$, where

$$\mathbf{T} = \begin{bmatrix} 1 & 0 & 0 & 0 & 0 \\ 1 & 1 & 0 & 0 & 0 \\ 1 & 1 & 1 & 0 & 0 \\ 1 & 1 & 1 & 1 & 0 \\ 1 & 1 & 1 & 1 & 1 \end{bmatrix}$$

1.39. Let $\mathbf{A}$ be an $n \times n$ matrix that is partitioned as follows (where $\det(\mathbf{A}_{11}) \neq 0$):

$$\mathbf{A} = \begin{bmatrix} \mathbf{A}_{11} & \mathbf{A}_{12} \\ \mathbf{A}_{21} & \mathbf{A}_{22} \end{bmatrix}$$

If $\operatorname{rank}(\mathbf{A}) = \operatorname{rank}(\mathbf{A}_{11})$, show that $\mathbf{A}_{22} = \mathbf{A}_{21}\mathbf{A}_{11}^{-1}\mathbf{A}_{12}$.

1.40. Let $\mathbf{A}$ be partitioned as in Problem 1.39, where $\mathbf{A}_{12} = \mathbf{0}$ and suppose $\det(\mathbf{A}_{11}) \neq 0$ and $\det(\mathbf{A}_{22}) \neq 0$. Find $\mathbf{A}^{-1}$ in terms of $\mathbf{A}_{11}, \mathbf{A}_{21}, \mathbf{A}_{22}$.

1.41. If $\mathbf{T}$ is an upper (lower) triangular $n \times n$ matrix and $\mathbf{D}$ is a diagonal $n \times n$ matrix, show that $\mathbf{DT}$ and $\mathbf{TD}$ are upper (lower) triangular matrices.

1.42. Show that $\operatorname{tr}(a\mathbf{I}) = na$, where $\mathbf{I}$ is the $n \times n$ identity matrix.

1.43. If $\mathbf{x}_i$ is an $n \times 1$ vector for each $i = 1, 2, \ldots, k$, and $\mathbf{A}$ is an $n \times n$ symmetric matrix, show that

$$\operatorname{tr}\left[\mathbf{A} \sum_{i=1}^{k} \mathbf{x}_i\mathbf{x}_i'\right] = \sum_{i=1}^{k} \mathbf{x}_i'\mathbf{A}\mathbf{x}_i$$

1.44. If $\mathbf{A}$ is an $n \times n$ symmetric idempotent matrix and $\mathbf{V}$ is an $n \times n$ positive definite matrix, show that

$$\operatorname{rank}(\mathbf{A}\mathbf{V}^{-1}\mathbf{A}) = \operatorname{tr}(\mathbf{A})$$

1.45. Let $\mathbf{X}$ be an $n \times p$ matrix of rank p. Partition $\mathbf{X}$ such that $\mathbf{X} = [\mathbf{X}_1, \mathbf{X}_2]$, where $\mathbf{X}_1$ has size $n \times p_1$ and $\mathbf{X}_2$ has size $n \times p_2$, where $p_1 + p_2 = p$. Show that the rank of $\mathbf{B}$ is p_2, where $\mathbf{B}$ is defined by

$$\mathbf{B} = \mathbf{X}(\mathbf{X}'\mathbf{X})^{-1}\mathbf{X}' - \mathbf{X}_1(\mathbf{X}_1'\mathbf{X}_1)^{-1}\mathbf{X}_1'$$

1.46. Evaluate

$$\int_{-\infty}^{\infty}\int_{-\infty}^{\infty}\int_{-\infty}^{\infty}\int_{-\infty}^{\infty} (x_1^2 - 2x_1x_4)\, e^{-(1/2)Q}\, dx_1\, dx_2\, dx_3\, dx_4$$

where

$$Q = 3x_1^2 + 2x_2^2 + 2x_3^2 + x_4^2 + 2x_1x_2 + 2x_3x_4 - 6x_1 - 2x_2 - 6x_3 - 2x_4 + 8$$

1.47. If **x**, **a**, and **b** are $n \times 1$ vectors, and **A** and **B** are symmetric $n \times n$ matrices such that $\mathbf{A} + \mathbf{B}$ is nonsingular, show

$$(\mathbf{x} - \mathbf{a})'\mathbf{A}(\mathbf{x} - \mathbf{a}) + (\mathbf{x} - \mathbf{b})'\mathbf{B}(\mathbf{x} - \mathbf{b})$$

$$= (\mathbf{x} - \mathbf{c})'(\mathbf{A} + \mathbf{B})(\mathbf{x} - \mathbf{c}) + (\mathbf{a} - \mathbf{b})'\mathbf{A}(\mathbf{A} + \mathbf{B})^{-1}\mathbf{B}(\mathbf{a} - \mathbf{b})$$

where $\mathbf{c} = (\mathbf{A} + \mathbf{B})^{-1}(\mathbf{A}\mathbf{a} + \mathbf{B}\mathbf{b})$.

1.48. If **A** is an $n \times n$ positive definite matrix and **B** is a symmetric matrix, show that the expression

$$\int_{-\infty}^{\infty} \cdots \int_{-\infty}^{\infty} \exp[-(\mathbf{x}'\mathbf{A}\mathbf{x}' + \theta\mathbf{x}\mathbf{B}\mathbf{x})]\, dx_1\, dx_2 \cdots dx_n$$

exists for all θ such that $|\theta| < \theta_0$ for a suitable positive number θ_0.

1.49. Let **A**, **B**, and **AB** be symmetric $n \times n$ matrices and let **A** and **B** be positive definite. Show that

$$\int_{-\infty}^{\infty} \cdots \int_{-\infty}^{\infty} e^{-\mathbf{x}'\mathbf{A}\mathbf{B}\mathbf{x}}\, dx_1\, dx_2 \cdots dx_n = \pi^{n/2}|\mathbf{A}\mathbf{B}|^{-1/2}$$

1.50. For the matrices below, determine whether each is positive definite, positive semidefinite, or neither.

$$\mathbf{A} = \begin{bmatrix} 1 & 2 & -1 \\ 2 & 4 & -2 \\ -1 & -2 & 8 \end{bmatrix} \qquad \mathbf{B} = \begin{bmatrix} 2 & 1 & 1 \\ 1 & 1 & -1 \\ 1 & -1 & 5 \end{bmatrix} \qquad \mathbf{C} = \begin{bmatrix} 1 & 2 & 3 \\ 2 & 5 & 2 \\ 3 & 2 & 24 \end{bmatrix}$$

1.51. Show that the matrix **A** below is positive definite, and find a matrix **P** such that $\mathbf{P}'\mathbf{P} = \mathbf{A}$.

$$\mathbf{A} = \begin{bmatrix} 1 & 0 & -1 \\ 0 & 2 & 1 \\ -1 & 1 & 2 \end{bmatrix}$$

1.52. If **A** and **B** are $k \times k$ nonsingular matrices that commute, show that $\mathbf{A}^{-1}$ and $\mathbf{B}^{-1}$ also commute.

1.53. If **A**, **B**, and **AB** are symmetric $k \times k$ matrices and **AB** is nonsingular, show that there exists an orthogonal matrix **P** such that $\mathbf{P}'\mathbf{A}\mathbf{B}\mathbf{P}$, $\mathbf{P}'\mathbf{A}^{-1}\mathbf{B}\mathbf{P}$, $\mathbf{P}'\mathbf{A}\mathbf{B}^{-1}\mathbf{P}$, and $\mathbf{P}'\mathbf{A}^{-1}\mathbf{B}^{-1}\mathbf{P}$ are diagonal matrices.

1.54. Let **A** be a $k \times k$ positive definite matrix, **a** be a $k \times 1$ vector, and a be a scalar such that $a > \mathbf{a}'\mathbf{A}^{-1}\mathbf{a}$; show that $\mathbf{A}^*$ is a positive definite matrix, where $\mathbf{A}^*$ is defined by the following matrix:

$$\mathbf{A}^* = \begin{bmatrix} \mathbf{A} & \mathbf{a} \\ \mathbf{a}' & a \end{bmatrix}$$

1.55. Let $\mathbf{A}$ be a $k \times k$ nonsingular matrix, let $\mathbf{a}$ be a $k \times 1$ vector, and let a be a scalar such that $a > \mathbf{a}'\mathbf{A}^{-1}\mathbf{a} \geq 0$. Show that the matrix $\mathbf{B}$ is nonsingular, where $\mathbf{B}$ is defined by

$$\mathbf{B} = \mathbf{A} - \left(\frac{1}{a}\right)\mathbf{a}\mathbf{a}'$$

1.56. Show that the diagonal elements of a symmetric idempotent matrix $\mathbf{B}$ satisfy $b_{ii} \leq 1$.

1.57. Let

$$\mathbf{P} = \begin{bmatrix} \mathbf{P}_1 \\ \mathbf{P}_2 \end{bmatrix}$$

where $\mathbf{P}$ is orthogonal. Show that $\mathbf{P}_1'\mathbf{P}_1$ is idempotent.

1.58. Show that $\mathbf{a}\mathbf{a}'/\sum a_i^2$ is symmetric idempotent, where $\mathbf{a} = [a_i]$ is an $n \times 1$ nonzero vector.

1.59. Find an orthogonal matrix $\mathbf{P}$ such that $\mathbf{P}'(1/n)\mathbf{J}\mathbf{P} = \mathbf{D}$, where $\mathbf{D}$ is diagonal; $\mathbf{J}$ is a matrix with each element unity.

1.60. If $\mathbf{A}$ is an $n \times n$ symmetric idempotent matrix, show that

$$\sum_{i=1}^{n} \sum_{j=1}^{n} a_{ij}^2 = \text{rank}(\mathbf{A})$$

1.61. Let $\mathbf{A}$ be a symmetric $n \times n$ matrix of rank $n - 1$ such that $\mathbf{1}'\mathbf{A} = \mathbf{0}$; that is, every column of $\mathbf{A}$ adds to zero. Show that $\mathbf{B} = \mathbf{A} + (1/n)\mathbf{1}\mathbf{1}'$ is nonsingular and the inverse is $\mathbf{A}^- + (1/n)\mathbf{J}$.

1.62. Show that $\mathbf{C}$ is nonsingular where $\mathbf{C}$ is defined by

$$\mathbf{C} = \begin{bmatrix} \mathbf{A} & \mathbf{1} \\ \mathbf{1}' & 0 \end{bmatrix}$$

and $\mathbf{A}$ is defined in Problem 1.61.

1.63. In Problem 1.62, let $\mathbf{B} = \mathbf{C}^{-1}$ and partition $\mathbf{B}$ as

$$\mathbf{B} = \begin{bmatrix} \mathbf{B}_{11} & \mathbf{b}_{12} \\ \mathbf{b}_{21} & b \end{bmatrix}$$

where $\mathbf{B}_{11}$ is an $n \times n$ submatrix. Show that
(a) $b = 0$
(b) $\mathbf{b}_{12} = (1/n)\mathbf{1}$
(c) $\mathbf{1}'\mathbf{B}_{11} = \mathbf{0}$
(d) $\mathbf{AB}_{11}$ and $\mathbf{B}_{11}\mathbf{A}$ are idempotent.

1.64. Let $\mathbf{A}$ be a $k \times k$ symmetric matrix, and define δ_i by

$$\delta_1 = a_{11}, \quad \delta_2 = \begin{vmatrix} a_{11} & a_{12} \\ a_{21} & a_{22} \end{vmatrix}, \quad \ldots, \quad \delta_k = |\mathbf{A}|$$

Show that $\delta_i \geq 0$ for $i = 1, 2, \ldots, k$ is not a sufficient condition for $\mathbf{A}$ to be nonnegative.

1.65. Let $\mathbf{A}$ be a symmetric matrix. Show that if a c-inverse of $\mathbf{A}$ exists that is nonnegative, then $\mathbf{A}$ must be nonnegative.

1.66. Let $\mathbf{A}$ be any $n \times n$ nonnegative matrix such that $\mathbf{A} = \mathbf{C}'\mathbf{C}$, where $\mathbf{C}$ has size $n \times n$ and let $\mathbf{B}$ be any c-inverse of $\mathbf{A}$. Show that $(\mathbf{CB})'(\mathbf{CB})$ is also a c-inverse of $\mathbf{A}$.

1.67. If an $n \times n$ matrix $\mathbf{T}$ is an upper triangular, idempotent matrix with the first k diagonal elements equal to unity and the remaining diagonal elements equal to zero, and $\mathbf{T}$ is partitioned so that

$$\mathbf{T} = \begin{bmatrix} \mathbf{T}_{11} & \mathbf{T}_{12} \\ \mathbf{0} & \mathbf{T}_{22} \end{bmatrix}$$

where $\mathbf{T}_{11}$ is a $k \times k$ matrix, show that $\mathbf{T}_{11} = \mathbf{I}$, $\mathbf{T}_{22} = \mathbf{0}$, and $\mathbf{T}_{12}$ is arbitrary.

1.68. If $\mathbf{T}$ is an $n \times n$ upper triangular matrix, show that the n diagonal elements are the characteristic roots of $\mathbf{T}$.

1.69. Let $\mathbf{H}$ and $\mathbf{G}$ be of sizes $q \times p$ and $(p - q) \times p$, respectively, where $0 < q < p$. Let $[\mathbf{H}', \mathbf{G}'] = \mathbf{K}'$ be nonsingular, and also suppose that $\mathbf{HG}^- = \mathbf{0}$. Show that $[\mathbf{H}^-, \mathbf{G}^-]$ is the g-inverse of $\mathbf{K}$.

1.70. If $[\mathbf{X}'\mathbf{X}, \mathbf{V}]$ has rank p, where $\mathbf{X}'\mathbf{X}$ is $p \times p$ of rank q, where $0 < q < p$, and $\mathbf{V}$ is $p \times (p - q)$ of rank $p - q$, show that $\mathbf{W}$ is nonsingular where $\mathbf{W}$ is defined by

$$\mathbf{W} = \begin{bmatrix} \mathbf{X}'\mathbf{X} & \mathbf{V} \\ \mathbf{V}' & \mathbf{0} \end{bmatrix}$$

1.71. In Problem 1.70, if

$$\mathbf{W}^{-1} = \begin{bmatrix} \mathbf{A} & \mathbf{B} \\ \mathbf{B}' & \mathbf{C} \end{bmatrix}$$

where $\mathbf{A}$ has size $p \times p$, show that $\mathbf{C} = \mathbf{0}$ and $\mathbf{A}$ is a c-inverse of $\mathbf{X}'\mathbf{X}$.

CHAPTER 2

Statistical Concepts

2.1 Introduction

In this chapter we shall review some topics in theoretical statistics including random variables, distribution functions, moment generating functions, the normal distribution, derived distributions, point estimation, confidence interval estimation, and hypothesis testing. We assume that the reader is acquainted with material in [D-13], [F-4], [H-13], [H-16], [L-10], [M-7], [R-2], and [S-15]. The purpose of this chapter is to review the basic concepts that will be used in this book, to state a number of theorems for later reference, and to adopt a notation for further chapters. Since this chapter is a review, few proofs will be given.

It is not essential for the reader to understand all of the material in this chapter in order to understand material in subsequent chapters. Most of the material in this chapter will be used later, but it will be discussed again at that time. The reader can quickly survey this chapter and reread the pertinent material when it is referred to later.

2.2 Random Variables and Distribution Functions

One way to obtain knowledge is to observe the outcome of planned or unplanned investigations. Since these observations are generally subject to unpredictable factors, it may be desirable to incorporate them into a probability model. The model we build will contain unknown quantities that remain constant during the investigation (these are called parameters), and it will contain other quantities that vary in an unpredictable (random) fashion during the course of the investigation.

In this book the set of possible outcomes of an investigation will be a set of numbers which is the set of values of a random variable. Associated with a random variable Y is a cumulative distribution function (c.d.f.) denoted by $F_Y(y)$ (some prefer to write this as $F_Y(\cdot)$, F_Y, or $F(y)$; we use these symbols when convenient). $F_Y(y)$ can be used to find the probability that the random variable Y is less than or equal to y for all y from $-\infty$ to ∞, that is, $F_Y(y) = P[Y \le y]$, $-\infty < y < \infty$. In most cases in this book $F_Y(\cdot)$ is a continuous function (in a few cases Y is a degenerate random variable). Also, in most cases that we discuss there is another function, the probability density function (p.d.f.), denoted by $f_Y(y)$, associated with Y and related to $F_Y(y)$ by

$$F_Y(y) = \int_{-\infty}^{y} f_Y(u)\, du$$

and $F'_Y(y) = f_Y(y)$ at all points y where $f_Y(y)$ is continuous. Not all random variables Y have a p.d.f. but each always has a c.d.f.

In many real-world examples the set of all conceivable values that the outcome of an investigation can assume under all circumstances can be described by a histogram idealized by a p.d.f. $f_Y(y)$. The probability that the random variable Y is in the set A is

$$P[Y \in A] = \int_A f_Y(y)\, dy$$

The p.d.f. under discussion will generally contain an unknown parameter (or set of parameters) θ. To indicate that the p.d.f. of a random variable Y depends on θ, we write $f_Y(y : \theta)$, $\theta \in \Omega$ to denote a family (set) of p.d.f.'s, one for each value of θ in Ω, where Ω is called the parameter space. In many statistical investigations the functional form of the p.d.f. is known and the set Ω is known but the particular value that θ assumes in Ω is unknown. An important objective in a study is to observe n values from $f_Y(y : \theta)$, denoted by $y_1, y_2, \ldots, y_n$, and on the basis of these to say something (make inferences) about the unknown value of θ.

Example 2.2.1

An investigation is made to determine the average I.Q. of all 5th grade pupils in a large city. The set of pupils is called a population, and the set of I.Q.'s is the set of values of a random variable Y with p.d.f. $f_Y(y)$. We might assume that this p.d.f. is normal with unknown mean μ and variance σ^2, and that μ can be any positive number, as can σ^2; so $\Omega = \{(\mu, \sigma^2) : \mu > 0, \sigma^2 > 0\}$. Of course, we may have additional information about these parameters; we may know, for example, that μ is less than 150. In this case Ω would be modified to $\Omega = \{(\mu, \sigma^2):$

$0 \leq \mu < 150, \sigma^2 > 0\}$. The problem may be to select 100 observations from this p.d.f., denoted by $y_1, y_2, \ldots, y_{100}$, and use the observed values to "estimate" μ.

In general, we use lowercase letters, say $y_1, y_2, \ldots, y_n$, to denote *observed* values of random variables $Y_1, Y_2, \ldots, Y_n$, and we call $Y_1, Y_2, \ldots, Y_n$ "observable random variables." The joint p.d.f. of $Y_1, Y_2, \ldots, Y_n$ is denoted by $f_{Y_1, Y_2, \ldots, Y_n}(y_1, y_2, \ldots, y_n : \theta_1, \theta_2, \ldots, \theta_K)$, $[\theta_1, \theta_2, \ldots, \theta_K]' \in \Omega$, or equivalently by $f_{\mathbf{Y}}(\mathbf{y} : \boldsymbol{\theta})$, $\boldsymbol{\theta} \in \Omega$, where the vector $\mathbf{Y}$ denotes $[Y_1, Y_2, \ldots, Y_n]'$ and the vector $\boldsymbol{\theta}$ denotes $\boldsymbol{\theta} = [\theta_1, \theta_2, \ldots, \theta_K]'$.

Terminology. We use the word "distribution" to denote a p.d.f. and a c.d.f.

Notation. Generally we shall use a capital letter to represent a random variable (univariate) and a lowercase letter to represent the value of that random variable. However, a random *vector* will sometimes be written as a lowercase bold letter since we have reserved capital bold letters for matrices. Two exceptions to this will be the capital bold letters $\mathbf{Y}$ and $\mathbf{Z}$ which will *always* represent random vectors.

We make extensive use of marginal and conditional distributions so we discuss them briefly.

Let $\mathbf{Y}$ be an $n \times 1$ random vector with p.d.f. denoted by $f_{\mathbf{Y}}(\mathbf{y})$. Let $\mathbf{Y}$ be partitioned into two random vectors $\mathbf{Y}_1$ and $\mathbf{Y}_2$, where $\mathbf{Y}' = [\mathbf{Y}_1', \mathbf{Y}_2']$, where $\mathbf{Y}_1$ has n_1 elements and $\mathbf{Y}_2$ has n_2 elements, and where $n_1 + n_2 = n$ and $0 < n_1 < n$. The marginal p.d.f. of $\mathbf{Y}_2$ is denoted by $f_{\mathbf{Y}_2}(\mathbf{y}_2)$ and defined by

$$f_{\mathbf{Y}_2}(\mathbf{y}_2) = \int_{-\infty}^{\infty} \cdots \int_{-\infty}^{\infty} f_{\mathbf{Y}}(\mathbf{y})\, d\mathbf{y}_1 \tag{2.2.1}$$

where the symbol $d\mathbf{y}_1$ is $dy_1\, dy_2 \cdots dy_{n_1}$. The conditional p.d.f. of a random vector $\mathbf{Y}_1$, given that the value of the random vector $\mathbf{Y}_2$ is $\mathbf{c}$, is often denoted by $f_{\mathbf{Y}_1|\mathbf{Y}_2=\mathbf{c}}(\cdot \mid \mathbf{c})$, but we choose to use a simpler notation in some cases. We use a single letter such as $\mathbf{Z}$, or some other suitable letter, to denote the symbol $\mathbf{Y}_1 \mid \mathbf{Y}_2 = \mathbf{c}$. For clarification we sometimes enclose this in parentheses and write

$$\mathbf{Z} \equiv (\mathbf{Y}_1 \mid \mathbf{Y}_2 = \mathbf{c}) \equiv \mathbf{Y}_1 \mid \mathbf{Y}_2 = \mathbf{c} \tag{2.2.2}$$

Let $f_{\mathbf{Z}}(\mathbf{z} : \mathbf{c})$ denote the p.d.f. of the random vector $\mathbf{Y}_1$, given that the value of the random vector $\mathbf{Y}_2$ is $\mathbf{c}$. If the p.d.f. of $\mathbf{Y}$ is $f_{\mathbf{Y}}(\mathbf{y})$, which can also be written as $f_{\mathbf{Y}}(\mathbf{y}_1, \mathbf{y}_2)$, then the conditional p.d.f. of $\mathbf{Y}_1$ given $\mathbf{Y}_2 = \mathbf{c}$ is defined by

$$f_{\mathbf{Z}}(\mathbf{z} : \mathbf{c}) = \begin{cases} f_{\mathbf{Y}}(\mathbf{z}, \mathbf{c})/f_{\mathbf{Y}_2}(\mathbf{c}) & \text{for the values of } \mathbf{c} \text{ where } f_{\mathbf{Y}_2}(\mathbf{c}) > 0 \\ \text{undefined} & \text{for the values of } \mathbf{c} \text{ where } f_{\mathbf{Y}_2}(\mathbf{c}) = 0 \end{cases} \tag{2.2.3}$$

In this notation $f_{\mathbf{Y}}(\mathbf{z}, \mathbf{c})$ means that $\mathbf{z}$ and $\mathbf{c}$ are substituted for $\mathbf{y}_1$ and $\mathbf{y}_2$, respectively, in $f_{\mathbf{Y}}(\mathbf{y})$; and $f_{\mathbf{Y}_2}(\mathbf{c})$ is the marginal p.d.f. of $\mathbf{Y}_2$ evaluated at $\mathbf{c}$.

2.3 Moment Generating Function

While the p.d.f. and c.d.f. can be used to study and evaluate probabilities of random vectors, there is another function, the moment generating function (m.g.f.), that is sometimes useful for finding the distribution of a specified *function* of a random vector from a knowledge of the distribution of the random vector itself. For example, if the distribution of $\mathbf{Y}' = [Y_1, Y_2, \ldots, Y_n]$ is known, then it may be necessary to find the distribution of Z, where $Z = \mathbf{1}'\mathbf{Y} = \sum_{i=1}^{n} Y_i$. The m.g.f. can often be helpful with these problems.

The m.g.f. derives some of its usefulness from the fact that if *two random vectors have the same m.g.f., they have the same c.d.f.*, and in many situations encountered in the linear model, the m.g.f. is very easy to find. We now formally define the m.g.f. of a random vector and state a theorem that will be used often in this book.

DEFINITION 2.3.1

Moment Generating Function. *Consider the $n \times 1$ random vector $\mathbf{Y}$. The moment generating function of $\mathbf{Y}$, which is denoted by $m_{\mathbf{Y}}(\cdot)$, is defined by*

$$m_{\mathbf{Y}}(\mathbf{t}) = \mathscr{E}[e^{\mathbf{t}'\mathbf{Y}}] \tag{2.3.1}$$

if and only if the expectation exists for $-h < t_i < h$, $i = 1, 2, \ldots, n$, for some number $h > 0$. If this expectation does not exist, then $\mathbf{Y}$ has no m.g.f.

THEOREM 2.3.1

Consider two random $n \times 1$ vectors $\mathbf{Y}_1$ and $\mathbf{Y}_2$ and assume the m.g.f. of each exists. The c.d.f.'s of $\mathbf{Y}_1$ and $\mathbf{Y}_2$ are equal if and only if the m.g.f.'s of $\mathbf{Y}_1$ and $\mathbf{Y}_2$ are equal for all values of $\mathbf{t}$ in an open rectangle that includes the origin.

Note 1. This theorem states that $F_{\mathbf{Y}_1}(\mathbf{u}) \equiv F_{\mathbf{Y}_2}(\mathbf{u})$ for all values of $\mathbf{u}$ in E_n if and only if $m_{\mathbf{Y}_1}(\mathbf{t}) \equiv m_{\mathbf{Y}_2}(\mathbf{t})$ for all t_i satisfying $-h < t_i < h$, $i = 1, 2, \ldots, n$, for some $h > 0$.

2.4 Independence of Random Vectors

In statistical theory it is often necessary to be able to determine if random vectors are mutually independent. We define independence of random vectors in terms of c.d.f.'s, p.d.f.'s, and m.g.f.'s.

DEFINITION 2.4.1

Let the $n \times 1$ random vector $\mathbf{Y}$ be partitioned into M random vectors by

$$\mathbf{Y}' = [\mathbf{Y}'_1, \mathbf{Y}'_2, \ldots, \mathbf{Y}'_M] = [Y_1, Y_2, \ldots, Y_{n_1}, Y_{n_1+1}, \ldots, Y_{n_2}, \ldots, Y_{n_{M-1}+1}, \ldots, Y_n]$$

where $\mathbf{Y}'_i = [Y_{n_{i-1}+1}, \ldots, Y_{n_i}]$. *(Let* $n_0 = 0$.)

(1) *The random vectors $\mathbf{Y}_1, \mathbf{Y}_2, \ldots, \mathbf{Y}_M$ are mutually independent if and only if the c.d.f.'s satisfy*

$$F_{\mathbf{Y}}(\mathbf{u}) \equiv F_{\mathbf{Y}_1}(\mathbf{u}_1)F_{\mathbf{Y}_2}(\mathbf{u}_2) \cdots F_{\mathbf{Y}_M}(\mathbf{u}_M) \tag{2.4.1}$$

for all values of $\mathbf{u}$ in E_n, where $F_{\mathbf{Y}}(\cdot)$ is the c.d.f. of $\mathbf{Y}$ and $F_{\mathbf{Y}_i}(\cdot)$ is the c.d.f. of $\mathbf{Y}_i$, $i = 1, 2, \ldots, M$; and where $\mathbf{u}' = [\mathbf{u}'_1, \mathbf{u}'_2, \ldots, \mathbf{u}'_M]$.

(2) *If $\mathbf{Y}$, $\mathbf{Y}_1, \ldots, \mathbf{Y}_M$ have p.d.f.'s denoted by $f_{\mathbf{Y}}(\cdot)$, $f_{\mathbf{Y}_1}(\cdot), \ldots, f_{\mathbf{Y}_M}(\cdot)$, then the random vectors $\mathbf{Y}_1, \mathbf{Y}_2, \ldots, \mathbf{Y}_M$ are mutually independent if and only if the p.d.f.'s satisfy*

$$f_{\mathbf{Y}}(\mathbf{u}) \equiv f_{\mathbf{Y}_1}(\mathbf{u}_1)\, f_{\mathbf{Y}_2}(\mathbf{u}_2) \cdots f_{\mathbf{Y}_M}(\mathbf{u}_M) \tag{2.4.2}$$

for all values of $\mathbf{u}$ in E_n.

(3) *If $\mathbf{Y}, \mathbf{Y}_1, \ldots, \mathbf{Y}_M$ have m.g.f.'s denoted by $m_{\mathbf{Y}}(\cdot)$, $m_{\mathbf{Y}_1}(\cdot), \ldots, m_{\mathbf{Y}_M}(\cdot)$, then the random vectors $\mathbf{Y}_1, \mathbf{Y}_2, \ldots, \mathbf{Y}_M$ are mutually independent if and only if the m.g.f.'s satisfy*

$$m_{\mathbf{Y}}(\mathbf{t}) \equiv m_{\mathbf{Y}_1}(\mathbf{t}_1)\, m_{\mathbf{Y}_2}(\mathbf{t}_2) \cdots m_{\mathbf{Y}_M}(\mathbf{t}_M) \tag{2.4.3}$$

for all values of $\mathbf{t}$ in an open rectangle that includes the origin, where $\mathbf{t}' = [\mathbf{t}'_1, \mathbf{t}'_2, \ldots, \mathbf{t}'_M]$.

An important result on independence of random vectors is contained in the next theorem.

THEOREM 2.4.1

Let the p vectors $\mathbf{Y}_1, \mathbf{Y}_2, \ldots, \mathbf{Y}_p$ be mutually independent and let Z_i be any function of $\mathbf{Y}_i$, that is, $Z_i = t_i(\mathbf{Y}_i)$, $i = 1, 2, \ldots, p$, then $Z_1, Z_2, \ldots, Z_p$ are also mutually independent.*

---

* Strictly speaking, when we say "any function" we shall mean any function such that the Z_i are jointly distributed random variables; for example, a Borel function. For applications the reader need not be concerned with this. The interested reader can consult [L-8].

This theorem states that functions of independent random vectors are also independent.

2.5 Special Distributions and Some Important Formulas

In the linear model the normal distribution plays a very important role. From this basic distribution useful "derived" distributions can be obtained. We assume that the reader is acquainted with the basic normal distribution and some of the distributions derived from it, such as Student's t distribution, the chi-square distribution, and Snedecor's F distribution. We shall, however, state these here to describe the notation we shall use and for later reference.

2.5.1 The Normal Distribution

The p.d.f., c.d.f., and m.g.f. of a random variable Y that has a normal distribution with mean μ and variance σ^2 are given in Equations (2.5.1), (2.5.2), and (2.5.3), respectively.

$$n(y:\mu,\sigma^2) \equiv \frac{1}{\sqrt{2\pi\sigma^2}} \exp\left[-\frac{(y-\mu)^2}{2\sigma^2}\right] \qquad -\infty < y < \infty \tag{2.5.1}$$

$$N(y:\mu,\sigma^2) \equiv \int_{-\infty}^{y} n(u:\mu,\sigma^2)\,du \qquad -\infty < y < \infty \tag{2.5.2}$$

$$m_Y(t) = \mathscr{E}[e^{tY}] = \exp(t\mu + \tfrac{1}{2}t^2\sigma^2) \qquad -\infty < t < \infty \tag{2.5.3}$$

Notice the symbols $n(y:\mu,\sigma^2)$ and $N(y:\mu,\sigma^2)$ used for the expressions that define the p.d.f. and c.d.f., respectively, of the normal distribution with mean μ and variance σ^2. These symbols will be used throughout the book.

> ***Note 1.*** The *upper* α probability point of a normal p.d.f. with mean zero and variance one is denoted by N_α and is defined by
>
> $$\int_{N_\alpha}^{\infty} n(z:0,1)\,dz = \alpha \tag{2.5.4}$$
>
> Table T.2 contains values of $1-\alpha$ for various values of N_α.

2.5.2 The Chi-Square Distribution

Let $Z_1, Z_2, \ldots, Z_n$ be n independent random variables each distributed normally with mean zero and variance one, that is, for $i = 1, 2, \ldots, n$, the Z_i are distributed

$NID(z:0,1)$. The random variable $U = \sum_{i=1}^{n} Z_i^2$ is distributed as a chi-square random variable with n degrees of freedom. The notation and functional form of the p.d.f. and m.g.f. of U, a chi-square random variable, are, respectively,

$$\chi^2(u:n) \equiv \left(\frac{1}{\Gamma(n/2)2^{n/2}}\right) u^{(n-2)/2} e^{-u/2} \qquad 0 < u < \infty \tag{2.5.5}$$

$$m_U(t) = (1-2t)^{-n/2} \qquad t < \tfrac{1}{2} \tag{2.5.6}$$

The number n, which is generally a positive integer, is called "the degrees of freedom." A notation for the c.d.f. of a chi-square random variable will not be needed in this book. We will make some use of the expectation of certain functions of a chi-square random variable which are given below.

$$\begin{aligned}
\mathscr{E}[U] &= n \\
\mathscr{E}[U^2] &= n(n+2) \\
\mathscr{E}[U^{1/2}] &= \frac{2^{1/2}\Gamma((n+1)/2)}{\Gamma(n/2)} \\
\text{var}[U] &= 2n \\
\mathscr{E}\left[\frac{1}{U}\right] &= \frac{1}{(n-2)} \qquad n > 2 \\
\mathscr{E}\left[\frac{1}{U^2}\right] &= \frac{1}{(n-2)(n-4)} \qquad n > 4 \\
\mathscr{E}[U^{-1/2}] &= \frac{\Gamma((n-1)/2)}{\sqrt{2}\,\Gamma(n/2)}
\end{aligned} \tag{2.5.7}$$

THEOREM 2.5.1

Let $Y_1, Y_2, \ldots, Y_n$ be a random sample from the c.d.f. $N(y:\mu,\sigma^2)$; then

(1) *U_0 is distributed $\chi^2(u:n)$, where $U_0 = \sum_{i=1}^{n} (Y_i-\mu)^2/\sigma^2$;*

(2) *U_1 is distributed $\chi^2(u:n-1)$, where $U_1 = \sum_{i=1}^{n} (Y_i-\bar{Y})^2/\sigma^2$;*

(3) *U_1 and $\bar{Y}$ are independent.* (2.5.8)

Note 2. The *upper* α probability point of a chi-square p.d.f. with n degrees of freedom is denoted by $\chi^2_{\alpha:n}$ and is defined by

$$\int_{\chi^2_{\alpha:n}}^{\infty} \chi^2(u:n)\,du = \alpha \tag{2.5.9}$$

Table T.4 contains values of $\chi^2_{\alpha:n}$ for various values of $1 - \alpha$ and n.

Notation. Throughout this book we use the words "**Z** is distributed" to mean "the c.d.f. (or p.d.f.) of Z is." For example, in Theorem 2.5.1, part (1), the expression "U_0 is distributed $\chi^2(u_0 : n)$" means "the p.d.f. of U_0 is $[\Gamma(n/2)2^{n/2}]^{-1}u_0^{(n/2)-1}\, e^{-u_0/2}$, $0 < u_0 < \infty$.

2.5.3 Student's *t* Distribution

Consider the following:

1. Z is distributed $N(z : 0, 1)$;
2. U is distributed $\chi^2(u : n)$;
3. Z and U are independent. (2.5.10)

Then the random variable T defined by

4. $T = Z/\sqrt{U/n}$

is distributed as Student's t with n degrees of freedom.

The p.d.f. is given by

$$s(t : n) \equiv \frac{\Gamma\left(\frac{n+1}{2}\right)}{\Gamma\left(\frac{n}{2}\right)\sqrt{n\pi}}\left(1 + \frac{t^2}{n}\right)^{-(n+1)/2} \qquad -\infty < t < \infty \qquad (2.5.11)$$

The m.g.f. of this p.d.f. does not exist.

THEOREM 2.5.2

If $Y_1, Y_2, \ldots, Y_n$ is a random sample from $N(y : \mu, \sigma^2)$, then T is distributed $s(t : n - 1)$, where T is defined by

$$T = \frac{(\bar{Y} - \mu)\sqrt{n}}{\hat{\sigma}}$$

where $\hat{\sigma}^2 = [1/(n-1)]\sum_{i=1}^{n}(Y_i - \bar{Y})^2$.

Note 3. The upper α probability point of the t distribution with n degrees of freedom is denoted by $t_{\alpha:n}$ and is defined by

$$\int_{t_{\alpha:n}}^{\infty} s(t : n)\, dt = \alpha \qquad (2.5.12)$$

Table T.3 contains values of $t_{\alpha:n}$ for various values of $1 - \alpha$ and n.

2.5.4 Snedecor's *F* Distribution

Consider the following:

1. U_1 is distributed $\chi^2(u_1 : m_1)$;
2. U_2 is distributed $\chi^2(u_2 : m_2)$;
3. U_1 and U_2 are independent. (2.5.13)

Then the random variable W, defined by

4. $W = (U_1/m_1)/(U_2/m_2)$

is distributed as Snedecor's F.

The p.d.f. of W is denoted by $F(w : m_1, m_2)$, where

$$F(w : m_1, m_2) \equiv \left(\frac{\Gamma\left(\dfrac{m_1 + m_2}{2}\right)\left(\dfrac{m_1}{m_2}\right)^{m_1/2}}{\Gamma\left(\dfrac{m_1}{2}\right)\Gamma\left(\dfrac{m_2}{2}\right)} \right) w^{(m_1 - 2)/2}\left(1 + \left(\frac{m_1}{m_2}\right) w\right)^{-(m_1 + m_2)/2} \qquad 0 < w < \infty$$

This is referred to as an F distribution with m_1 degrees of freedom in the numerator and m_2 degrees of freedom in the denominator.

Note 4. The m.g.f. of the F distribution does not exist.

Note 5. If T is distributed $s(t : m_2)$, then $T^2 = W$ is distributed $F(w : 1, m_2)$.

Note 6. If W is distributed $F(w : m_1, m_2)$, then

$$\mathscr{E}[W] = \frac{m_2}{m_2 - 2} \qquad m_2 > 2$$

$$\mathscr{E}[W^2] = \frac{m_2^2(m_1 + 2)}{m_1(m_2 - 2)(m_2 - 4)} \qquad m_2 > 4 \tag{2.5.14}$$

Note 7. The upper α probability point of $F(w : m_1, m_2)$ is denoted by $F_{\alpha:m_1,m_2}$, and is defined by

$$\int_{F_{\alpha:m_1,m_2}}^{\infty} F(w : m_1, m_2)\, dw = \alpha \tag{2.5.15}$$

Note 8. If W_1 is distributed $F(w_1 : m_1, m_2)$, then $W_2 = 1/W_1$ is distributed $F(w_2 : m_2, m_1)$ and $F_{\alpha:m_1,m_2} = 1/F_{1-\alpha:m_2,m_1}$.

Table T.5 contains values of $F_{\alpha:m_1,m_2}$ for various values of $1-\alpha, m_1$, and m_2.

2.5.5 Some Useful Formulas

In the theory of the linear model, we shall have occasion to use the expectation and variance in conditional p.d.f.'s, so in this subsection we state some definitions and theorems on this subject.

DEFINITION 2.5.1

Let $\mathbf{Y}' = [\mathbf{Y}_1', \mathbf{Y}_2']$ be a $(p+q)\times 1$ random vector, where $\mathbf{Y}_1$ is a $p\times 1$ random vector. Let $g(\mathbf{Y})$, which we also write as $g(\mathbf{Y}_1, \mathbf{Y}_2)$, be a function of $\mathbf{Y}$. The conditional expectation of $g(\mathbf{Y}_1, \mathbf{Y}_2)$ given $\mathbf{Y}_2 = \mathbf{c}$ is denoted by $\mathscr{E}_{\mathbf{Y}_1|\mathbf{Y}_2=\mathbf{c}}[g(\mathbf{Y})]$, or by $\mathscr{E}[(g(\mathbf{Y}) \mid \mathbf{Y}_2 = \mathbf{c})]$, and is defined by

$$\mathscr{E}[(g(\mathbf{Y}) \mid \mathbf{Y}_2 = \mathbf{c})] = \mathscr{E}[(g(\mathbf{Y}_1, \mathbf{Y}_2) \mid \mathbf{Y}_2 = \mathbf{c})] = \int_{-\infty}^{\infty} \cdots \int_{-\infty}^{\infty} g(\mathbf{z}, \mathbf{c}) f_{\mathbf{Z}}(\mathbf{z} : \mathbf{c})\, d\mathbf{z}$$

where $\mathbf{Z}$ is a symbol defined by $\mathbf{Z} = (\mathbf{Y}_1 \mid \mathbf{Y}_2 = \mathbf{c})$, and $f_{\mathbf{Z}}(\mathbf{z} : \mathbf{c})$ is the p.d.f. of $\mathbf{Z}$, which in general depends on $\mathbf{c}$ as the notation indicates. See Equations (2.2.2) *and* (2.2.3).

From this definition we obtain a number of useful results.

THEOREM 2.5.3

Let $\mathbf{Y}, \mathbf{Y}_1, \mathbf{Y}_2$, and $g(\mathbf{Y}_1, \mathbf{Y}_2)$ be as in Definition 2.5.1. The results below follow:

(1) $\mathscr{E}_{\mathbf{Y}_1|\mathbf{Y}_2=\mathbf{c}}[g(\mathbf{Y}_1, \mathbf{Y}_2)]$ *is a function of* $\mathbf{c}$, *say* $h(\mathbf{c})$;

(2) $\mathscr{E}[h(\mathbf{Y}_2)] = \mathscr{E}[g(\mathbf{Y})]$ *which is the same as* $\mathscr{E}[g(\mathbf{Y})] = \mathscr{E}_{\mathbf{Y}_2}[\mathscr{E}_{\mathbf{Y}_1|\mathbf{Y}_2} g(\mathbf{Y})]$, *where* $h(\mathbf{Y}_2)$ *is defined in* (1) *with* $\mathbf{Y}_2$ *replacing* $\mathbf{c}$;

(3) $\mathscr{E}_{\mathbf{Y}_1|\mathbf{Y}_2=\mathbf{c}}[g(\mathbf{Y}_1, \mathbf{Y}_2)] = \mathscr{E}_{\mathbf{Y}_1|\mathbf{Y}_2=\mathbf{c}}[g(\mathbf{Y}_1, \mathbf{c})]$;

(4) $\mathscr{E}_{\mathbf{Y}_1|\mathbf{Y}_2=\mathbf{c}}[q_1(\mathbf{Y}_1)q_2(\mathbf{Y}_2)] = q_2(\mathbf{c})\mathscr{E}_{\mathbf{Y}_1|\mathbf{Y}_2=\mathbf{c}}[q_1(\mathbf{Y}_1)]$, *where* $q_1(\mathbf{Y}_1)$ *is a function of* $\mathbf{Y}_1$ *and* $q_2(\mathbf{Y}_2)$ *is a function of* $\mathbf{Y}_2$;

(5) $\mathscr{E}[\mathbf{Y}] = \mathscr{E}_{\mathbf{Y}_2}[\mathscr{E}_{\mathbf{Y}_1|\mathbf{Y}_2}[\mathbf{Y}]]$;

(6) *let* $p = q = 1$; *then* $var[Y_1] = var_{Y_2}[\mathscr{E}[Z]] + \mathscr{E}_{Y_2}[var[Z]]$, *where* $\mathscr{E}[Z]$ *and* $var[Z]$ *are defined to be the mean and variance in the conditional p.d.f. of* Z *in Definition* 2.5.1.

Proof

For a proof and discussion of this theorem, see [M-7].

Often a conditional argument can be used to find the distribution of a function of random vectors. This is discussed in the next theorem.

THEOREM 2.5.4

Let $\mathbf{Y}$, $\mathbf{Y}_1, \mathbf{Y}_2$, *and* $g(\mathbf{Y}) = g(\mathbf{Y}_1, \mathbf{Y}_2)$ *be as given in Definition* 2.5.1. *Let* $W = g(\mathbf{Y}_1, \mathbf{Y}_2)$, *and suppose that the p.d.f. of* W *is desired. If the conditional p.d.f. of* W *given* $\mathbf{Y}_2 = \mathbf{c}$ *does not depend on* $\mathbf{c}$, *for any vector* $\mathbf{c}$ *such that* $f_{\mathbf{Y}_2}(\mathbf{c}) > 0$, *then this conditional p.d.f. is also the marginal p.d.f. of* W, *or in other words, it is the p.d.f. of* $g(\mathbf{Y}_1, \mathbf{Y}_2)$ *that was sought.*

This theorem is useful because sometimes in linear model theory it is quite *easy* to find the conditional p.d.f. of W given that the value of $\mathbf{Y}_2$ is $\mathbf{c}$, and as the theorem states, if this conditional p.d.f. does not depend on what the conditioned value $\mathbf{c}$ assumes, then this conditional p.d.f. of W is the same as the marginal p.d.f. of W, and hence this is the p.d.f. of $g(\mathbf{Y}_1, \mathbf{Y}_2)$ that was sought.

2.6 Statistical Inference

In conducting investigations the investigator often knows or is willing to assume that the p.d.f. from which he takes observations is of a certain functional form $f(y : \boldsymbol{\theta})$, where the parameter $\boldsymbol{\theta}$ is not known but is the quantity that the investigation is attempting to determine. For example, it might be known from theoretical considerations or from previous investigations that the relative frequency of weights of the 100,000 inhabitants of a given city, as an approximation, has the functional form

$$n(y : \mu, \sigma^2) \equiv \left(\frac{1}{\sigma\sqrt{2\pi}}\right) \exp\left[-\frac{(y-\mu)^2}{2\sigma^2}\right] \qquad -\infty < y < \infty$$

where μ and σ^2 are unknown. In general, when we say that $\mathbf{Y}$ is distributed as $f_{\mathbf{Y}}(\mathbf{y} : \boldsymbol{\theta})$, we shall mean that the p.d.f. of $\mathbf{Y}$ is $f_{\mathbf{Y}}(\mathbf{y} : \boldsymbol{\theta})$, $\boldsymbol{\theta} \in \Omega$, and $\boldsymbol{\theta}$ is an unknown parameter in Ω.

An investigator selects observations from the p.d.f., say $f_{\mathbf{Y}}(\mathbf{y} : \boldsymbol{\theta})$, under study, and on the basis of these observations he tries (1) to ascertain the value of the unknown parameter $\boldsymbol{\theta}$ or of some specified function of $\boldsymbol{\theta}$; or (2) to decide whether some function of $\boldsymbol{\theta}$ is equal to a specified value, say, θ_0. The first procedure is known as *estimating the parameter* $\boldsymbol{\theta}$ and the second as *testing a hypothesis* about the parameter $\boldsymbol{\theta}$. We consider two types of estimation: *point estimation* and *interval estimation.*

The general procedure is to obtain a sample from the p.d.f.'s under study, where the joint p.d.f. of the observable sample, $Y_1, Y_2, \ldots, Y_n$, is denoted by $f_{\mathbf{Y}}(\mathbf{y} : \boldsymbol{\theta})$. The investigator determines a set of r statistics, denoted by $T_1, T_2, \ldots,$

T_r, where $T_i = t_i(Y_1, Y_2, \ldots, Y_n) = t_i(\mathbf{Y})$, which are functions of the observable sample *only* (they are not functions of unknown parameters), and on the basis of *these* r observable random variables (statistics), $T_1, T_2, \ldots, T_r$, inferences are made about the parameters $\theta_1, \theta_2, \ldots, \theta_K$ (that is, about $\boldsymbol{\theta}$). The problem of determining r statistics that have desirable properties is generally quite difficult. A procedure that is often helpful is to reduce the complexity of the problem by first determining a set of *sufficient* or *minimal sufficient statistics*. These concepts are defined below.

DEFINITION 2.6.1

Sufficient Statistics. *Let $Y_1, Y_2, \ldots, Y_n$ be an observable sample with joint p.d.f. $f(y_1, y_2, \ldots, y_n : \theta_1, \theta_2, \ldots, \theta_K)$. Let $S_1 = s_1(Y_1, Y_2, \ldots, Y_n)$, $S_2 = s_2(Y_1, Y_2, \ldots, Y_n), \ldots, S_r = s_r(Y_1, Y_2, \ldots, Y_n)$ be r statistics. The r statistics are defined to be sufficient statistics if and only if the conditional distribution of $Y_1, Y_2, \ldots, Y_n$ given $S_1, S_2, \ldots, S_r$ does not depend on the parameters $\theta_1, \theta_2, \ldots, \theta_K$.*

The use that we make of sufficient statistics is to reduce the n observations to these r statistics (where $r \leq n$), since these r statistics contain all the "information" about $\boldsymbol{\theta}$ that the n observations contain. If r is appreciably less than n, as it will be for many problems in this book, then the very fact that we have to consider only r, rather than n, random variables and their distributions leads to a simplification of many problems. There are many sets of sufficient statistics (the set of original observations is one set), and we would like to use a "smallest" or "minimal" set, which we now define.

DEFINITION 2.6.2

Minimal Sufficient Statistics. *A set of sufficient statistics is defined to be a set of minimal sufficient statistics if and only if it is a function of every set of sufficient statistics.*

In statistical inference we often try to find the "smallest" (minimal) set of sufficient statistics and base our procedures of point estimation, interval estimation, and hypothesis testing on these statistics.

We now state a theorem that can be used to determine if a given set of statistics is a sufficient set. The theorem is often referred to as the factorization theorem. The proof is a direct application of the definition. See [M-7].

THEOREM 2.6.1

Let $f_{\mathbf{Y}}(\mathbf{y} : \boldsymbol{\theta})$ be the p.d.f. of an observable sample $Y_1, Y_2, \ldots, Y_n$. The statistics $S_1, S_2, \ldots, S_r$ are sufficient statistics if and only if the p.d.f. can be factored as

$$f_{\mathbf{Y}}(\mathbf{y} : \boldsymbol{\theta}) = g(S_1, S_2, \ldots, S_r : \boldsymbol{\theta}) \cdot h(\mathbf{y})$$

where $g(S_1, S_2, \ldots, S_r : \boldsymbol{\theta})$ *is a (nonnegative) function of only the statistics* $S_1, S_2, \ldots, S_r$ *and the parameter* $\boldsymbol{\theta}$, *and* $h(\mathbf{y})$ *is not a function of* $\boldsymbol{\theta}$.

Reference [L-10] contains a theorem that can be used to determine if a set of sufficient statistics is a minimal set. However, this is a somewhat advanced theorem and we shall not make use of it in this book since it will be more convenient in linear model theory to use a theorem that relates to an exponential family of densities. For many situations we shall be able to exhibit a set of minimal sufficient statistics by examining the functional form of the joint p.d.f. of the observations and showing that the p.d.f. can be written in a certain form. From this form of the p.d.f., the (minimal) sufficient statistics are easily identified.

DEFINITION 2.6.3

Exponential Family of Densities. *Let* $f_{\mathbf{Y}}(\mathbf{y} : \boldsymbol{\theta})$, $\boldsymbol{\theta} \in \Omega$, *be the joint p.d.f. of the observable sample* $Y_1, Y_2, \ldots, Y_n$, *where* $\boldsymbol{\theta}' = [\theta_1, \theta_2, \ldots, \theta_K]$. *The p.d.f.* $f_{\mathbf{Y}}(\mathbf{y} : \boldsymbol{\theta})$ *is defined to belong to an exponential family of densities if it can be written as*

$$f_{\mathbf{Y}}(\mathbf{y} : \boldsymbol{\theta}) = \begin{cases} h(\boldsymbol{\theta}) g(\mathbf{y}) \, exp\left[\sum_{j=1}^{K} s_j(\mathbf{y}) p_j(\boldsymbol{\theta}) \right], & a_i < y_i < b_i; \quad i = 1, 2, \ldots, n \\ 0 \quad elsewhere \end{cases} \tag{2.6.1}$$

where

(1) a_i *and* b_i *do not depend on the* θ_j; a_i *can be* $-\infty$ *and* b_i *can be* $+\infty$;

(2) Ω, *the parameter space, contains a nondegenerate K-dimensional interval (rectangle)*;

(3) $h(\boldsymbol{\theta})$ *and the* $p_j(\boldsymbol{\theta})$ *do not depend on the* y_i;

(4) $g(\mathbf{y})$ *and the* $s_j(\mathbf{y})$ *do not depend on the* θ_i; $g(\mathbf{y})$ *is nonnegative.* (2.6.2)

Note 1. It is important to note that K in the exponent of the function in Equation (2.6.1) is the same positive integer as K, the number of elements of $\boldsymbol{\theta}$.

We now state a theorem that can often be used to find a set of minimal sufficient statistics from an exponential family. A discussion of this theorem can be found in [H-14].

THEOREM 2.6.2

Let $Y_1, Y_2, \ldots, Y_n$ *be an observable sample with p.d.f.* $f_{\mathbf{Y}}(\mathbf{y} : \boldsymbol{\theta})$, $\boldsymbol{\theta} \in \Omega$. *Suppose that* $f_{\mathbf{Y}}(\mathbf{y} : \boldsymbol{\theta})$ *belongs to an exponential family, that is,* $f_{\mathbf{Y}}(\mathbf{y} : \boldsymbol{\theta})$ *can be written in the form given in Equation* (2.6.1) *and satisfies* (1), (2), (3), *and* (4) *in Equation* (2.6.2). *Suppose further that* (1), (2), (3), *and* (4) *below are satisfied.*

(1) *The* $s_j(\mathbf{y})$ *are functionally independent for* $j = 1, 2, \ldots, K$.

(2) $\partial[s_j(\mathbf{y})]/\partial y_i$ *exists and is continuous for all* $j = 1, 2, \ldots, K$ *and* $i = 1, 2, \ldots, n$.

(3) $p_j(\boldsymbol{\theta})$ *is a continuous function of* $\boldsymbol{\theta}$ *for* $j = 1, 2, \ldots, K$.

(4) *If we set* $\boldsymbol{\gamma}' = [p_1(\boldsymbol{\theta}), p_2(\boldsymbol{\theta}), \ldots, p_K(\boldsymbol{\theta})]$, *then the set of values of* $\boldsymbol{\gamma}$ *(as* $\boldsymbol{\theta}$ *varies over* Ω*) contains a nondegenerate* K*-dimensional rectangle.*

Then the set of K *statistics* $s_1(\mathbf{Y}), s_2(\mathbf{Y}), \ldots, s_K(\mathbf{Y})$ *is a set of minimal sufficient statistics.*

Thus in statistical inference it is generally desirable to simplify the problem by finding a set of sufficient statistics and use these statistics for estimation and hypothesis testing. Theorem 2.6.1 can be used to determine if a given set of statistics is a sufficient set, and Theorem 2.6.2 can often be used (if the p.d.f. belongs to an exponential family) to determine if the set is a minimal sufficient set.

> ***Note 2.*** Often if one can determine a set of K sufficient statistics, where K is the number of parameters, then this set is a minimal set.

In the next three sections we discuss point estimation, hypothesis testing, and confidence intervals, respectively.

2.7 Point Estimation

The problem of point estimation is this: The p.d.f. of an observable sample contains the unknown parameter $\boldsymbol{\theta}$, and one wants to use observed sample values to determine (estimate) the value of $c(\boldsymbol{\theta})$, a known function of $\boldsymbol{\theta}$. An observable sample of size n is denoted by $Y_1, Y_2, \ldots, Y_n$, and the joint p.d.f. of the sample is $f_{\mathbf{Y}}(\mathbf{y} : \boldsymbol{\theta}), \boldsymbol{\theta} \in \Omega$. The parameter space Ω is known and $f_{\mathbf{Y}}(\mathbf{y} : \boldsymbol{\theta}), \boldsymbol{\theta} \in \Omega$, represents a family of p.d.f.'s—one for each value of $\boldsymbol{\theta}$ in Ω. The procedure is to use appropriate statistics to estimate a known function of $\boldsymbol{\theta}$, say $c(\boldsymbol{\theta})$, or to estimate several known functions of $\boldsymbol{\theta}$, say $c_1(\boldsymbol{\theta}), c_2(\boldsymbol{\theta}), \ldots, c_q(\boldsymbol{\theta})$.

A question that immediately arises is, "*Which* statistic should be used to estimate $c(\boldsymbol{\theta})$?" We want to use an estimate that is "close" to $c(\boldsymbol{\theta})$, but $c(\boldsymbol{\theta})$ is fixed and the estimator is a random variable, so even though we decide to use $t(\mathbf{Y})$ as the estimator, the value of the estimator depends on the observed sample and may be close to $c(\boldsymbol{\theta})$ for some samples and not close for others.

The quantity $t(\mathbf{Y}) - c(\boldsymbol{\theta})$ is the error of estimating $c(\boldsymbol{\theta})$ by using $t(\mathbf{Y}) = T$, and $[t(\mathbf{Y}) - c(\boldsymbol{\theta})]^2$ is the squared error. We want the squared error of estimating $c(\boldsymbol{\theta})$ by using $t(\mathbf{Y})$ to be small, but since $\mathbf{Y}$ is a random vector, this squared error will be small for some values of $\mathbf{Y}$ and large for other values. Thus we want this squared error to be small "on the average," so the criterion we shall use for the quality of an estimator is the average (mean) of the square of the error, that is,

$$\mathscr{E}[t(\mathbf{Y}) - c(\boldsymbol{\theta})]^2$$

and, of course,

$$\begin{aligned}\mathscr{E}[t(\mathbf{Y}) - c(\boldsymbol{\theta})]^2 &= \int_{-\infty}^{\infty} \cdots \int_{-\infty}^{\infty} [t(\mathbf{y}) - c(\boldsymbol{\theta})]^2 f_{\mathbf{Y}}(\mathbf{y} : \boldsymbol{\theta})\, d\mathbf{y} \\ &= \int_{-\infty}^{\infty} [t - c(\boldsymbol{\theta})]^2 f_T(t : \boldsymbol{\theta})\, dt\end{aligned}$$

For us an optimum estimator will be one that minimizes the mean-squared-error. However, an estimator $t(\mathbf{Y})$ will almost never exist that will minimize $\mathscr{E}[t(\mathbf{Y}) - c(\boldsymbol{\theta})]^2$ for *all* values of $\boldsymbol{\theta}$ in Ω, so what we do is restrict the class of estimating functions and see if there exists a minimum mean-squared-error estimator in the restricted class.

There are two distinct situations: (1) the functional form of the p.d.f. of the observable random variables is *known*; (2) the functional form of the p.d.f. is *not known.* We shall discuss these in the next two subsections.

2.7.1 Point Estimation When the Functional Form of $f_{\mathbf{Y}}(\mathbf{y} : \boldsymbol{\theta})$ Is Known

We use the mean-squared-error as our guide in defining an optimal estimator. First we state a theorem which shows how a mean-squared-error estimator is related to the bias and the variance of an estimator.

THEOREM 2.7.1

Let $Y_1, Y_2, \ldots, Y_n$ be an observable sample with a p.d.f. $f_{\mathbf{Y}}(\mathbf{y} : \boldsymbol{\theta})$ and let $t(\mathbf{Y})$ be an estimator of $c(\boldsymbol{\theta})$. Then

$$\mathscr{E}[t(\mathbf{Y}) - c(\boldsymbol{\theta})]^2 = var[t(\mathbf{Y})] + \{\mathscr{E}[t(\mathbf{Y})] - c(\boldsymbol{\theta})\}^2 \qquad (2.7.1)$$

We define $\{\mathscr{E}[t(\mathbf{Y})] - c(\boldsymbol{\theta})\}$ to be the bias of $t(\mathbf{Y})$ for estimating $c(\boldsymbol{\theta})$, and it can be positive, negative, or zero. So Equation (2.7.1) states that the mean-squared-error of $t(\mathbf{Y})$ as an estimator of $c(\boldsymbol{\theta})$ is equal to the variance of $t(\mathbf{Y})$ plus the square of the bias of $t(\mathbf{Y})$. Thus a "good" estimator (one that has small mean-squared-error) is one that has small variance and small bias.

It is sometimes reasonable to restrict the estimators of $c(\boldsymbol{\theta})$ to those that are unbiased; then $\{\mathscr{E}[t(\mathbf{Y})] - c(\boldsymbol{\theta})\}^2 = 0$ in Equation (2.7.1). If this is done, then the estimator of $c(\boldsymbol{\theta})$ with minimum mean-squared-error will be the (unbiased) estimator with minimum variance. If there exists an estimator for $c(\boldsymbol{\theta})$ that is unbiased and has minimum variance for *each* value of $\boldsymbol{\theta}$ in Ω, then it will be called a *uniformly* minimum variance unbiased (UMVU) estimator of $\boldsymbol{\theta}$. We shall formalize this in the definition that follows.

DEFINITION 2.7.1

Uniformly Minimum Variance Unbiased Estimator. *Let $Y_1, Y_2, \ldots, Y_n$ be an observable sample with p.d.f. $f_{\mathbf{Y}}(\mathbf{y} : \boldsymbol{\theta})$, $\boldsymbol{\theta} \in \Omega$. Let $t(\mathbf{Y})$ be an estimator of $c(\boldsymbol{\theta})$; then $t(\mathbf{Y})$ is defined to be a uniformly minimum variance unbiased (UMVU) estimator for $c(\boldsymbol{\theta})$ if and only if $t(\mathbf{Y})$ satisfies (1) and (2) below for all $\boldsymbol{\theta}$ in Ω.*

(1) $\mathscr{E}[t(\mathbf{Y})] = c(\boldsymbol{\theta})$, *that is, $t(\mathbf{Y})$ is an unbiased estimator of $c(\boldsymbol{\theta})$.*

(2) $var[t(\mathbf{Y})] \leq var[t^*(\mathbf{Y})]$, *where $t^*(\mathbf{Y})$ is any other unbiased estimator of $c(\boldsymbol{\theta})$.*

We shall use UMVU as the criterion for "best" point estimators. The problem that confronts us now is this: How do we find UMVU estimators? The method of maximum likelihood will be helpful, as will sufficient statistics, the Rao-Blackwell theorem, and the Lehmann-Scheffé theorem. After we discuss the Rao-Blackwell theorem and some theorems on UMVU estimators, we shall define maximum likelihood. We then state explicitly how to find UMVU estimators for most situations in the linear model. We point out here that UMVU estimators do not always exist.

Now we state the Rao-Blackwell theorem and discuss its use in finding UMVU estimators; then we state some additional results on UMVU estimators.

THEOREM 2.7.2

Let $\mathbf{Y}$ be an $n \times 1$ observable random vector with p.d.f. $f_{\mathbf{Y}}(\mathbf{y} : \boldsymbol{\theta})$, $\boldsymbol{\theta} \in \Omega$. Let $S_1, S_2, \ldots, S_r$ be sufficient statistics, where $S_i = s_i(Y_1, Y_2, \ldots, Y_n)$ for $i = 1, 2, \ldots, r$. Let the statistic $T = t(\mathbf{Y})$ be an unbiased estimator of $c(\boldsymbol{\theta})$, and define T^* by $T^* = \mathscr{E}[(T \mid S_1, S_2, \ldots, S_r)]$. Then

(1) *T^* is a statistic;*

(2) *T^* is a function of the sufficient statistics $S_1, S_2, \ldots, S_r$;*

(3) *T^* is an unbiased estimator of $c(\boldsymbol{\theta})$, that is, $\mathscr{E}[T^*] = c(\boldsymbol{\theta})$;*

(4) *$var[T^*] \leq var[T]$ for all $\boldsymbol{\theta}$ in Ω and $var[T^*] < var[T]$ for at least one value of $\boldsymbol{\theta}$ in Ω unless $T \equiv T^*$ (with probability one).*

Proof

A proof of this theorem can be found in [M-7].

The importance of this theorem in UMVU estimation is as follows:

1. If a statistic T is an unbiased estimator of $c(\boldsymbol{\theta})$, then T^* is a statistic and is also an unbiased estimator of $c(\boldsymbol{\theta})$.
2. Either T is the same statistic as T^*, or else the variance of T^* is *smaller* than the variance of T and hence T^* is a "better" estimator of $c(\boldsymbol{\theta})$ than T is (if we use UMVU as the criterion of best).
3. If an UMVU estimator of $c(\boldsymbol{\theta})$ exists, then it must be a function of a minimal set (a function of *every* set) of sufficient statistics.
4. By part 3, an UMVU estimator of $c(\boldsymbol{\theta})$ is a function of *every* set of sufficient statistics so we should use the "simplest" set.

THEOREM 2.7.3

If an UMVU estimator exists for a function of $\boldsymbol{\theta}$, *say* $c(\boldsymbol{\theta})$, *then the UMVU estimator is unique.*

THEOREM 2.7.4

Consider the observable random variables $Y_1, Y_2, \ldots, Y_n$ *with p.d.f.* $f_{\mathbf{Y}}(\mathbf{y} : \boldsymbol{\theta})$. *The statistic* $T = t(\mathbf{Y})$ *is the UMVU estimator of* $c(\boldsymbol{\theta})$ *if and only if*

(1) $\mathscr{E}[t(\mathbf{Y})] = c(\boldsymbol{\theta})$ *for all* $\boldsymbol{\theta}$ *in* Ω; *and*

(2) $\mathscr{E}[t(\mathbf{Y})u_0(\mathbf{Y})] = 0$ *for all statistics* $u_0(\mathbf{Y})$ *such that* $\mathscr{E}[u_0(\mathbf{Y})] = 0$ *for all* $\boldsymbol{\theta}$ *in* Ω. *(We assume all expectations exist.)*

Proof

We sketch the proof and ask the reader to supply the details. Assume $T = t(\mathbf{Y})$ is the UMVU estimator of $c(\boldsymbol{\theta})$. Let $u_0(\mathbf{Y})$ be any unbiased estimator of zero, that is, $u_0(\mathbf{Y})$ is any statistic such that $\mathscr{E}[u_0(\mathbf{Y})] = 0$ for all $\boldsymbol{\theta}$ in Ω. Define a statistic $M(\mathbf{Y})$ by $M(\mathbf{Y}) = t(\mathbf{Y}) + \lambda u_0(\mathbf{Y})$ where λ is any nonzero constant; hence $\mathscr{E}[M(\mathbf{Y})] = c(\boldsymbol{\theta})$. Then $\text{var}[M(\mathbf{Y})] = \text{var}[t(\mathbf{Y})] + 2\lambda\, \text{cov}[u_0(\mathbf{Y}), t(\mathbf{Y})] + \lambda^2\, \text{var}[u_0(\mathbf{Y})]$. But by hypothesis, $t(\mathbf{Y})$ is the UMVU estimator of $c(\boldsymbol{\theta})$, so, $\text{var}[M(\mathbf{Y})] \geq \text{var}[t(\mathbf{Y})]$. Thus $2\lambda\, \text{cov}[u_0(\mathbf{Y}), t(\mathbf{Y})] + \lambda^2\, \text{var}[u_0(\mathbf{Y})]$ must be greater than or equal to zero. But since $\text{cov}[u_0(\mathbf{Y}), t(\mathbf{Y})]$ and $\text{var}[u_0(\mathbf{Y})]$ are constants, there exists a nonzero value of λ such that $2\lambda\, \text{cov}[u_0(\mathbf{Y}), t(\mathbf{Y})] + \lambda^2\, \text{var}[u_0(\mathbf{Y})]$ is negative unless $\text{cov}[u_0(\mathbf{Y}), t(\mathbf{Y})] = 0$. This proves that $\text{cov}[u_0(\mathbf{Y}), t(\mathbf{Y})] = 0$ if $t(\mathbf{Y})$ is the UMVU estimator of $c(\boldsymbol{\theta})$.

Next assume $\text{cov}[u_0(\mathbf{Y}), t(\mathbf{Y})] = 0$ for all statistics $u_0(\mathbf{Y})$ such that $\mathscr{E}[u_0(\mathbf{Y})] = 0$, and assume $\mathscr{E}[t(\mathbf{Y})] = c(\boldsymbol{\theta})$. Define $Q(\mathbf{Y})$ by $Q(\mathbf{Y}) =$

$t(\mathbf{Y}) + u_0(\mathbf{Y})$. Thus $\mathscr{E}[Q(\mathbf{Y})] = c(\boldsymbol{\theta})$ and

$$\begin{aligned}\text{var}[Q(\mathbf{Y})] &= \text{var}[t(\mathbf{Y})] + 2\,\text{cov}[u_0(\mathbf{Y}), t(\mathbf{Y})] + \text{var}[u_0(\mathbf{Y})] \\ &= \text{var}[t(\mathbf{Y})] + \text{var}[u_0(\mathbf{Y})] \geq \text{var}[t(\mathbf{Y})]\end{aligned}$$

Thus for all statistics $Q(\mathbf{Y})$ which are unbiased estimators of $c(\boldsymbol{\theta})$, none can have smaller variance than $t(\mathbf{Y})$, which is also an unbiased estimator of $c(\boldsymbol{\theta})$. Thus $t(\mathbf{Y})$ is the UMVU estimator of $c(\boldsymbol{\theta})$, and this completes the proof.

Note 1. Theorem 2.7.4 states that $Y_1, Y_2, \ldots, Y_n$ are observable random variables, so they could be the original observations or any set of sufficient statistics.

Note 2. Another way of stating this theorem is as follows: $t(\mathbf{Y})$ is the UMVU estimator of $c(\boldsymbol{\theta})$ if and only if $t(\mathbf{Y})$ is unbiased and is uncorrelated with each and every unbiased estimator of zero.

The method of maximum likelihood (M.L.) is a very useful method of estimation and can often be helpful in finding UMVU estimators. First we define the likelihood function and maximum likelihood estimators, then we state a procedure that can often be used in linear model theory to find UMVU estimators for functions of the parameters of interest.

DEFINITION 2.7.2

Likelihood Function. *Let $Y_1, Y_2, \ldots, Y_n$ be n observable random variables with p.d.f. $f_{\mathbf{Y}}(\mathbf{y} : \boldsymbol{\theta})$, $\boldsymbol{\theta} \in \Omega$. The likelihood function of these random variables is denoted by $L(\boldsymbol{\theta} : \mathbf{y})$ and is defined by*

$$L(\boldsymbol{\theta} : \mathbf{y}) = f_{\mathbf{Y}}(\mathbf{y} : \boldsymbol{\theta}) \qquad \boldsymbol{\theta} \in \Omega \tag{2.7.2}$$

Note 3. The likelihood function is simply the p.d.f. of the random variables considered as a function of $\boldsymbol{\theta}$.

DEFINITION 2.7.3

Maximum Likelihood (M.L.) Estimates and Estimators. *Let $L(\boldsymbol{\theta} : \mathbf{y})$ be the likelihood function of the random variables $Y_1, Y_2, \ldots, Y_n$. If $\theta_i^* = t_i(\mathbf{y})$, for $i = 1, 2, \ldots, K$, are the values of the K elements of $\boldsymbol{\theta}$ which maximize $L(\boldsymbol{\theta} : \mathbf{y})$, then these θ_i^* are defined to be the M.L. estimates of the corresponding θ_i; and $\tilde{\theta}_i = t_i(\mathbf{Y})$, for $i = 1, 2, \ldots, K$, are defined to be the M.L. estimators of the corresponding θ_i.*

Note 4. Actually we should use a lowercase letter for an M.L. estimate and the corresponding capital letter for the M.L. estimator. However, we will generally not do this. We often use symbols such as $\hat{\theta}$, $\tilde{\theta}$, $\hat{\gamma}$, $\tilde{\gamma}$, and so on to denote both M.L. estimates and M.L. estimators.

Two important properties of maximum likelihood estimators are stated in the next theorem. The first result is often referred to as the invariance property of M.L. estimators, and the second relates M.L. estimators and sufficient statistics.

THEOREM 2.7.5

Let $\tilde{\theta}_1, \tilde{\theta}_2, \ldots, \tilde{\theta}_K$ be maximum likelihood estimators of $\theta_1, \theta_2, \ldots, \theta_K$ in the p.d.f. $f_{\mathbf{Y}}(\mathbf{y} : \boldsymbol{\theta})$, and let $c(\boldsymbol{\theta})$ be any function of $\boldsymbol{\theta}$. Then

(1) *the M.L. estimator of $c(\boldsymbol{\theta})$ is $c(\tilde{\boldsymbol{\theta}})$;*

(2) *$\tilde{\theta}_1, \tilde{\theta}_2, \ldots, \tilde{\theta}_K$ are functions of every set of sufficient statistics.*

Since, by this theorem, M.L. estimators are functions of *every* set of sufficient statistics, M.L. estimators are functions of *minimal* sufficient statistics and hence are good candidates for UMVU estimators. Here we shall demonstrate how the M.L. procedure can often be used to find UMVU estimators.

Find the M.L. estimator of $c(\boldsymbol{\theta})$, the function of $\boldsymbol{\theta}$ to be estimated (use Theorem 2.7.5). Adjust this if necessary so it is unbiased and denote this unbiased estimator by $K(\tilde{\boldsymbol{\theta}})$, a known function of the M.L. estimator of $\boldsymbol{\theta}$. Thus $\mathscr{E}[K(\tilde{\boldsymbol{\theta}})] = c(\boldsymbol{\theta})$. Let $M(\tilde{\boldsymbol{\theta}})$ be the symbol for the UMVU estimator of $c(\boldsymbol{\theta})$. $M(\tilde{\boldsymbol{\theta}})$ is of course unknown but one hopes that it is $K(\tilde{\boldsymbol{\theta}})$, a known estimator. The reasons that $K(\tilde{\boldsymbol{\theta}})$ is a good candidate for the UMVU estimator of $c(\boldsymbol{\theta})$ are twofold: (1) it is a function of the M.L. estimator $\tilde{\boldsymbol{\theta}}$ and hence is a function of minimal sufficient statistics (by the Rao-Blackwell theorem, UMVU estimators must also be functions of minimal sufficient statistics); and (2) it is unbiased. We examine

$$M(\tilde{\boldsymbol{\theta}}) = K(\tilde{\boldsymbol{\theta}}) + u(\tilde{\boldsymbol{\theta}})$$

where $u(\tilde{\boldsymbol{\theta}})$ is an unknown function to be determined; so the UMVU estimator of $c(\boldsymbol{\theta})$ (if it exists) is the sum of two functions. If $M(\tilde{\boldsymbol{\theta}})$ is the UMVU estimator of $c(\boldsymbol{\theta})$, then $\mathscr{E}[M(\tilde{\boldsymbol{\theta}})] = c(\boldsymbol{\theta})$, and this implies $\mathscr{E}[u(\tilde{\boldsymbol{\theta}})] = 0$ for all $\boldsymbol{\theta}$ in Ω. Also

$$\operatorname{var}[M(\tilde{\boldsymbol{\theta}})] = \operatorname{var}[K(\tilde{\boldsymbol{\theta}})] + \operatorname{var}[u(\tilde{\boldsymbol{\theta}})] + 2\operatorname{cov}[K(\tilde{\boldsymbol{\theta}}), u(\tilde{\boldsymbol{\theta}})]$$

But $\operatorname{cov}[K(\tilde{\boldsymbol{\theta}}), u(\tilde{\boldsymbol{\theta}})] = \mathscr{E}[K(\tilde{\boldsymbol{\theta}}), u(\tilde{\boldsymbol{\theta}})]$, and often various methods can be used to show that this expectation is zero and then Theorem 2.7.4 can be employed. One method that can sometimes be used to show $\mathscr{E}[K(\tilde{\boldsymbol{\theta}}), u(\tilde{\boldsymbol{\theta}})] = 0$ is to differentiate under the integral sign, as we demonstrate in Example 2.7.1.

Example 2.7.1

Let $Y_1, Y_2, \ldots, Y_n$ be a random sample from the p.d.f. $n(y : \mu, \sigma^2)$, where

$\Omega = \{(\mu, \sigma^2): -\infty < \mu < \infty, 0 < \sigma^2 < \infty\}$. We want to determine the UMVU estimator of μ if it exists. The likelihood function is

$$L(\mu, \sigma^2 : \mathbf{y}) = \prod_{i=1}^{n} n(y_i : \mu, \sigma^2) = (2\pi\sigma^2)^{-n/2} \exp\left\{\left(-\frac{1}{2\sigma^2}\right) \sum (y_i - \mu)^2\right\}$$

$$= (2\pi\sigma^2)^{-n/2} \exp\left\{\left(-\frac{1}{2\sigma^2}\right) \sum (y_i - \bar{y})^2 - \frac{n}{2\sigma^2}(\bar{y} - \mu)^2\right\}$$

By Theorem 2.6.1, $(1/n) \sum (Y_i - \bar{Y})^2 = S^2/n$ and $\bar{Y}$ are sufficient statistics. They are also M.L. estimators of σ^2 and μ, respectively. Also $\mathscr{E}[\bar{Y}] = \mu$, so $\bar{Y}$ is a candidate for the UMVU estimator of μ. Let $M(\mathbf{Y})$ denote the UMVU estimator of μ, and let $M(\mathbf{Y}) = \bar{Y} + u(\mathbf{Y})$. We must determine $u(\mathbf{Y})$ so that $M(\mathbf{Y})$ is indeed the UMVU estimator of μ (if μ has an UMVU estimator). Since $\mathscr{E}[M(\mathbf{Y})]$ must equal μ, this implies $\mathscr{E}[u(\mathbf{Y})] = 0$ for all (μ, σ^2) in Ω. This gives us

$$\mathscr{E}[u(\mathbf{Y})] = \int_{-\infty}^{\infty} \cdots \int_{-\infty}^{\infty} u(\mathbf{y})(2\pi\sigma^2)^{-n/2} \exp\left[\frac{-\sum (y_i - \mu)^2}{2\sigma^2}\right]$$

$$\times\, dy_1 dy_2 \cdots dy_n = 0$$

Differentiate with respect to μ and obtain (integration and differentiation can be interchanged here)

$$\frac{\partial\{\mathscr{E}[u(\mathbf{Y})]\}}{\partial \mu} = \int_{-\infty}^{\infty} \cdots \int_{-\infty}^{\infty} \left(\frac{1}{\sigma^2}\right) \sum (y_i - \mu)\, u(\mathbf{y})(2\pi\sigma^2)^{-n/2}$$

$$\times \exp\left[-\frac{1}{2\sigma^2} \sum (y_i - \mu)^2\right] dy_1 dy_2 \cdots dy_n = 0$$

This can be simplified to $\mathscr{E}[u(\mathbf{Y}) \sum (Y_i - \mu)] = 0$, but since $\mathscr{E}[u(\mathbf{Y})] = 0$, we obtain $\mathscr{E}[u(\mathbf{Y})(\sum Y_i)] = 0$, that is, $\mathscr{E}[\bar{Y}u(\mathbf{Y})] = \text{cov}[\bar{Y}, u(\mathbf{Y})] = 0$. Thus we get

$$\text{var}[M(\mathbf{Y})] = \text{var}[\bar{Y} + u(\mathbf{Y})] = \text{var}[\bar{Y}] + \text{var}[u(\mathbf{Y})] + 2\,\text{cov}[\bar{Y}, u(\mathbf{Y})]$$

$$= \frac{\sigma^2}{n} + \text{var}[u(\mathbf{Y})] + 0$$

Hence $\text{var}[M(\mathbf{Y})] \geq \sigma^2/n$ and equality holds if and only if $\text{var}[u(\mathbf{Y})] = 0$. But $\text{var}[u(\mathbf{Y})] = 0$ and $\mathscr{E}[u(\mathbf{Y})] = 0$ imply $u(\mathbf{Y}) = 0$ with probability one. This says that $M(\mathbf{Y})$, the UMVU estimator of μ, is $\bar{Y} + 0 = \bar{Y}$.

Note 5. Instead of using $M(\mathbf{Y})$ to find the UMVU estimator, we could have used $M_1(\bar{Y}, S^2) = \bar{Y} + u(\bar{Y}, S^2)$ since $\bar{Y}$ and S^2 is a set of sufficient statistics and the Rao-Blackwell theorem states that the UMVU estimator (if it exists) must be a function of *every* set of sufficient statistics.

Another method that can be used to find UMVU estimators is to use complete sufficient statistics.

DEFINITION 2.7.4

Complete Statistics. *Let $Y_1, Y_2, \ldots, Y_n$ be an observable sample with joint p.d.f. $f_{\mathbf{Y}}(\mathbf{y} : \boldsymbol{\theta}), \boldsymbol{\theta} \in \Omega$, and let $S_1, S_2, \ldots, S_K$ be a set of K statistics, that is, $S_i = s_i(Y_1, Y_2, \ldots, Y_n)$, $i = 1, 2, \ldots, K$. The set of statistics $S_1, S_2, \ldots, S_K$ is defined to be complete if and only if for every function $t(S_1, S_2, \ldots, S_K)$ of $S_1, S_2, \ldots, S_K$ for which (1) is true, it follows that (2) is also true.*

(1) $\mathscr{E}[t(S_1, S_2, \ldots, S_K)] = 0$ *for all* $\boldsymbol{\theta}$ *in* Ω;

(2) $P[t(S_1, S_2, \ldots, S_K) = 0] = 1$.

Note 6. This definition states that if the only function of the statistics $S_1, S_2, \ldots, S_K$, whose expectation is equal to zero for all $\boldsymbol{\theta} \in \Omega$, is the zero function (that is, the function that is equal to zero with probability one), then the set of statistics is complete.

THEOREM 2.7.6

If $S_1, S_2, \ldots, S_K$ is a set of complete sufficient statistics, and if $T_1, T_2, \ldots, T_K$ is a one-to-one transformation of $S_1, S_2, \ldots, S_K$, then $T_1, T_2, \ldots, T_K$ is also a set of complete sufficient statistics.

One way to find the UMVU estimator (if it exists) of a known function of $\boldsymbol{\theta}$, say $c(\boldsymbol{\theta})$, is as follows:

1. Find a set of complete sufficient statistics; denote them by $S_1, S_2, \ldots, S_K$.
2. Find a function of the complete sufficient statistics that is an unbiased estimator of $c(\boldsymbol{\theta})$, that is, suppose $\mathscr{E}[t(S_1, S_2, \ldots, S_K)] = c(\boldsymbol{\theta})$; then $T = t(S_1, S_2, \ldots, S_K)$ is the UMVU estimator of $c(\boldsymbol{\theta})$.

This result is known as the Lehmann-Scheffé theorem and we now state it formally.

THEOREM 2.7.7

Let $Y_1, Y_2, \ldots, Y_n$ be an observable sample whose joint p.d.f. is $f_{\mathbf{Y}}(\mathbf{y} : \boldsymbol{\theta}), \boldsymbol{\theta} \in \Omega$. Let $S_1 = s_1(Y_1, Y_2, \ldots, Y_n), \ldots, S_K = s_K(Y_1, Y_2, \ldots, Y_n)$ be a set of complete *sufficient statistics. Let* $c(\boldsymbol{\theta})$ *be any known function of* $\boldsymbol{\theta}$, *and suppose* $T = t(S_1, S_2, \ldots, S_K)$ *is an unbiased estimator of* $c(\boldsymbol{\theta})$. *Then* T *is the (unique) UMVU estimator of* $c(\boldsymbol{\theta})$.

> ***Note 7.*** We may want to obtain UMVU estimators of many functions, say $c_1(\boldsymbol{\theta}), c_2(\boldsymbol{\theta}), \ldots, c_m(\boldsymbol{\theta})$, of the parameter $\boldsymbol{\theta}$. All we need to do is find the complete sufficient statistics and then find an unbiased estimator of each $c_i(\boldsymbol{\theta})$ that is a function of only these statistics; these estimators of $c_i(\boldsymbol{\theta})$ are the UMVU estimators of $c_i(\boldsymbol{\theta})$ for $i = 1, 2, \ldots, m$.

The main problem that still confronts us is that of finding the complete sufficient statistics and this is often not an easy task. We remark that many sets of sufficient statistics always exist for a problem, and in fact a set of minimal sufficient statistics always exists, but a set of *complete* sufficient statistics may or may not exist. In the theory of the linear model, when the basic random variables are normally distributed, as we often assume, Theorem 2.7.8 can often be used to find a set of complete sufficient statistics when they exist.

THEOREM 2.7.8

Let $Y_1, Y_2, \ldots, Y_n$ *be an observable sample with p.d.f.* $f_{\mathbf{Y}}(\mathbf{y} : \boldsymbol{\theta}), \boldsymbol{\theta} \in \Omega$. *If* $f_{\mathbf{Y}}(\mathbf{y} : \boldsymbol{\theta})$ *belongs to an exponential family as defined in Definition* 2.6.3, *and if conditions* (1), (2), (3), *and* (4) *of Theorem* 2.6.2 *are satisfied, then the* K *statistics* $s_1(\mathbf{Y}), s_2(\mathbf{Y}), \ldots, s_K(\mathbf{Y})$ *are complete sufficient statistics.*

We are using mean-squared-error as a standard for an estimator, but since minimum mean-squared-error estimators seldom exist, we restrict the class of estimators to the class of unbiased estimators and define minimum mean-squared-error estimators within this class (of course, these are UMVU estimators). However, UMVU estimators do not always exist; thus restricting the class of estimators to be unbiased will not always lead to "best" mean-squared-error estimators. In these situations we may want to restrict our class of estimators in other ways, such as requiring them to be invariant under certain transformations and determining if a minimum mean-squared-error estimator exists in *this* restricted class. (For a discussion of this, see [L-8] and [S-4].) Another procedure is to see how certain estimators behave when the number of observations is large. This is referred to as "asymptotic" properties of estimators (or, more accurately, the asymptotic properties of a sequence of estimators).

To examine this let $Y_1, Y_2, \ldots, Y_n, \ldots$ denote a sequence of observable random variables, and let $T_1 = t_1(Y_1), T_2 = t_2(Y_1, Y_2), \ldots, T_n = t_n(Y_1, Y_2, \ldots, Y_n), \ldots$ denote a sequence of statistics to be considered as estimators of $c(\boldsymbol{\theta})$, where $t_i(Y_1, Y_2, \ldots, Y_i)$ is a function of the first i observable random variables. Generally the functions are all the same "kind" but based on a different "number" of observations. For example, T_1 might be Y_1, T_2 might be $(Y_1 + Y_2)/2 = \bar{Y}_2, \ldots, T_n$ might be $(Y_1 + Y_2 + \cdots + Y_n)/n = \bar{Y}_n$, and so forth. If these estimators get "close" to $c(\boldsymbol{\theta})$ as n gets large, then this could be taken as a measure of the quality of the estimators; in fact, if we use mean-squared-error as our standard, we get a sequence of mean-squared-errors, $\{M_n(\boldsymbol{\theta})\}$, where

$$M_n(\boldsymbol{\theta}) = \mathscr{E}[T_n - c(\boldsymbol{\theta})]^2 = \mathscr{E}[t_n(Y_1, Y_2, \ldots, Y_n) - c(\boldsymbol{\theta})]^2$$

If $\lim_{n\to\infty} [M_n(\boldsymbol{\theta})] = 0$, then we state: For "large" n the estimator T_n gets very "close" to $c(\boldsymbol{\theta})$, the function of the parameter $\boldsymbol{\theta}$ we want to estimate. A sequence of estimators for which the mean-squared-error is zero in the limit as $n \to \infty$ is called a *mean-squared-error consistent estimator* of $c(\boldsymbol{\theta})$, and, for convenience, we call $T_n = t_n(Y_1, Y_2, \ldots, Y_n)$ a mean-squared-error consistent estimator of $c(\boldsymbol{\theta})$. We now define this formally.

DEFINITION 2.7.5

Mean-Squared-Error Consistent Estimator. *Let $T_1, T_2, \ldots, T_n, \ldots$ (also denoted by $\{T_n\}$) be a sequence of estimators, where $T_n = t_n(Y_1, Y_2, \ldots, Y_n)$ is a function of the n observable random variables $Y_1, Y_2, \ldots, Y_n$. The estimator T_n (more accurately, the sequence of estimators $T_1, T_2, \ldots, T_n, \ldots$) is defined to be a mean-squared-error consistent estimator of $c(\boldsymbol{\theta})$ if and only if*

$$\lim_{n\to\infty} \mathscr{E}[t_n(Y_1, Y_2, \ldots, Y_n) - c(\boldsymbol{\theta})]^2 = 0 \qquad \text{for all } \boldsymbol{\theta} \text{ in } \Omega$$

Some important results follow immediately from this definition.

THEOREM 2.7.9

Let $T_n = t_n(Y_1, Y_2, \ldots, Y_n)$, where $\{T_n\}$ is a sequence of estimators of $c(\boldsymbol{\theta})$. Then T_n is a mean-squared-error consistent estimator of $c(\boldsymbol{\theta})$ if and only if

$$\lim_{n\to\infty} \mathscr{E}[T_n] = c(\boldsymbol{\theta}) \qquad \text{for all } \boldsymbol{\theta} \text{ in } \Omega$$

and

$$\lim_{n\to\infty} \mathrm{var}[T_n] = 0 \qquad \text{for all } \boldsymbol{\theta} \text{ in } \Omega$$

Note 8. The theorem states that $\{T_n\}$ is a mean-squared-error consistent estimator of $c(\boldsymbol{\theta})$ if and only if T_n is unbiased in the limit and the variance of T_n is zero in the limit.

COROLLARY 2.7.9

Let $T_n = t_n(Y_1, Y_2, \ldots, Y_n)$, where $\{T_n\}$ is a mean-squared-error consistent estimator *of $c(\boldsymbol{\theta})$. Then for any real number $\varepsilon > 0$,*

$$\lim_{n \to \infty} P[T_n - \varepsilon \le c(\boldsymbol{\theta}) \le T_n + \varepsilon] = 1$$

and another way of writing this is

$$\lim_{n \to \infty} P[c(\boldsymbol{\theta}) - \varepsilon \le T_n \le c(\boldsymbol{\theta}) + \varepsilon] = 1$$

Note 9. A sequence of estimators that satisfies the results of Corollary 2.7.9 is called a *simple consistent estimator* of $c(\boldsymbol{\theta})$.

Example 2.7.2

Let $Y_1, Y_2, \ldots, Y_n$ be a random sample from a normal p.d.f. with unknown mean μ and unknown variance σ^2. The p.d.f. of the sample is

$$f_{\mathbf{Y}}(\mathbf{y} : \boldsymbol{\theta}) = \left(\frac{1}{2\pi\sigma^2}\right)^{n/2} \exp\left[-\frac{1}{2\sigma^2}\sum (y_i - \mu)^2\right]$$

$$\Omega = \{(\mu, \sigma^2) : -\infty < \mu < \infty, 0 < \sigma^2 < \infty\}$$

The maximum likelihood estimators of μ and σ^2 are $\overline{Y}$ and S^2/n, respectively, where $\overline{Y} = (1/n)\sum_{i=1}^{n} Y_i$, and $S^2/n = (1/n)\sum_{i=1}^{n} (Y_i - \overline{Y})^2$.

We can write $f_{\mathbf{Y}}(\mathbf{y} : \boldsymbol{\theta})$ (let $\boldsymbol{\theta}' = [\mu, \sigma^2]$, so $K = 2$) as

$$f_{\mathbf{Y}}(\mathbf{y} : \boldsymbol{\theta}) = \left(\frac{1}{2\pi\sigma^2}\right)^{n/2} \exp\left[-\frac{1}{2\sigma^2}\left(\sum y_i^2 - 2\mu \sum y_i + n\mu^2\right)\right]$$

$$= \left(\frac{1}{2\pi\sigma^2}\right)^{n/2} e^{-n\mu^2/2\sigma^2} \exp\left[-\frac{\sum y_i^2}{2\sigma^2} + \left(\frac{\mu}{\sigma^2}\right)\sum y_i\right]$$

and comparing this with Equation (2.6.1), we get

$$h(\boldsymbol{\theta}) = \left(\frac{1}{2\pi\sigma^2}\right)^{n/2} e^{-n\mu^2/2\sigma^2} \qquad g(\mathbf{y}) = 1$$

$$s_1(\mathbf{y}) = \sum y_i^2 \qquad s_2(\mathbf{y}) = \sum y_i$$

$$p_1(\boldsymbol{\theta}) = \frac{-1}{2\sigma^2} \qquad p_2(\boldsymbol{\theta}) = \frac{\mu}{\sigma^2}$$

Clearly, (1), (2), (3), and (4) of Definition 2.6.3, and (1), (2), (3), and (4) of Theorem 2.6.2 are satisfied, so $\sum Y_i^2$ and $\sum Y_i$ are complete sufficient statistics. Also, $\overline{Y}$ and S^2/n (as well as $\overline{Y}$ and $\hat{\sigma}_n^2$, where $\hat{\sigma}_n^2 = S^2/(n-1)$) are the result of a one-to-one transformation of $\sum Y_i^2$ and $\sum Y_i$, so they are also complete sufficient statistics. Suppose we want UMVU estimators of the following $c_i(\boldsymbol{\theta})$:

1. μ	3. σ^2	5. $\mu + \sigma^2$
2. $3\mu + 6$	4. σ	6. μ/σ^2

If we can find unbiased estimators for each of the functions of μ and σ^2 in parts 1 through 6, and if these unbiased estimators are functions of the complete sufficient statistics *only*, then by Theorem 2.7.7 these estimators are UMVU estimators. The reader can verify that the estimators given below are indeed unbiased and hence UMVU estimators.

1. $\bar{Y}$	3. $\hat{\sigma}_n^2$	5. $\bar{Y} + \hat{\sigma}_n^2$
2. $3\bar{Y} + 6$	4. $\dfrac{\sqrt{\dfrac{n-1}{2}}\,\Gamma\left(\dfrac{n-1}{2}\right)}{\Gamma\left(\dfrac{n}{2}\right)}\hat{\sigma}_n$	6. $\dfrac{\bar{Y}(n-3)}{\hat{\sigma}_n^2(n-1)}, \quad n > 1$

Example 2.7.3

In Example 2.7.2 we showed that $\bar{Y}$ is an UMVU estimator of μ. We will now show that $\bar{Y}_n$ is a mean-squared-error consistent estimator of μ. We must determine if $\lim_{n\to\infty} \mathscr{E}[\bar{Y}_n] = \mu$ and $\lim_{n\to\infty} \text{var}[\bar{Y}_n] = 0$. Since $\mathscr{E}[\bar{Y}_n] = \mu$ for $n = 1, 2, \ldots,$ then $\lim_{n\to\infty} \mathscr{E}[\bar{Y}_n] = \mu$. Also, $\text{var}[\bar{Y}_n] = \sigma^2/n$, so clearly $\lim_{n\to\infty} \text{var}[\bar{Y}_n] = \lim_{n\to\infty} \sigma^2/n = 0$. So $\bar{Y}_n$ is a mean-squared-error consistent estimator (and hence also a simple consistent estimator) of μ.

2.7.2 Point Estimation When the Functional Form of $f(y : \boldsymbol{\theta})$ Is Not Known

In some situations it is not possible to determine whether UMVU estimators exist. One such case is when the functional form of the p.d.f. of the sample is *not* known. We recall that UMVU estimators possess the optimum property of being unbiased with minimum variance within the class of *all* estimating functions (that is, *all* functions of the observable sample $Y_1, Y_2, \ldots, Y_n$). In the linear model, when the functional form of the p.d.f. $f_{\mathbf{Y}}(\mathbf{y} : \boldsymbol{\theta})$ is *not* known, we restrict the class of estimating functions to certain types of functions. The functional forms that we consider in the linear model are generally *linear functions* or *quadratic functions* of the observations, and we attempt to find UMVU estimators in the restricted class. These are called best (minimum variance) *linear* unbiased (BLU) estimators, and best (minimum variance) *quadratic* unbiased (BQU) estimators, respectively. They are defined and discussed in Section 6.10.

In the general linear model, the method of least squares is often used to obtain estimators when the functional form of the p.d.f. of the sample is unknown, and sometimes this method of estimation leads to estimators that are optimum in a certain sense. This method of estimation will be discussed in Chapter 6.

2.8 Hypothesis Testing

In statistical investigations it is sometimes necessary to decide if the parameter $\boldsymbol{\theta}$ in the p.d.f. $f_{\mathbf{Y}}(\mathbf{y}:\boldsymbol{\theta})$ under study is in a specified subspace ω of the parameter space Ω. A procedure is to use sample values from the p.d.f. $f_{\mathbf{Y}}(\mathbf{y}:\boldsymbol{\theta})$ to decide if $\boldsymbol{\theta}$ is indeed in ω or in $\Omega - \omega$. This introduces the subject of hypothesis testing, which can be used to solve these types of problems.

A hypothesis denoted by $H_0 : \boldsymbol{\theta} \in \omega$ is called *the* hypothesis (sometimes called "the null hypothesis") and the alternative hypothesis is denoted by $H_a : \boldsymbol{\theta} \in \bar{\omega}$, where $\bar{\omega} = \Omega - \omega$. A test of H_0 versus H_a, which we often write as $H_0 : \boldsymbol{\theta} \in \omega$ *vs.* $H_a : \boldsymbol{\theta} \in \bar{\omega}$, can be viewed as a rule for deciding whether to reject H_0 (and accept H_a), or to accept H_0 (and reject H_a). The sample (observation) space is partitioned into two sets, R and A, where R is called the rejection (or critical) region and A is called the acceptance region. That is, if $\mathbf{y}$ is observed to be in R, then H_0 is rejected, and if $\mathbf{y}$ is observed to be in A, then H_0 is accepted. Two kinds of errors are possible:

1. Type I error: $\boldsymbol{\theta}$ is in ω but $\mathbf{y}$ falls in R, so H_0 is rejected when it is in fact true;
2. Type II error: $\boldsymbol{\theta}$ is in $\Omega - \omega$ but $\mathbf{y}$ falls in A, so H_0 is accepted when it is in fact false.

It would be desirable to partition the sample space into R and A such that the probability of making these two types of errors is very small for all values of $\boldsymbol{\theta}$ in Ω, but this generally is not possible for a fixed sample size n. Thus the conventional procedure is to specify that the maximum probability of a Type I error will be α, say, and then find an R (and A) that minimizes the probability of a Type II error.

We shall use the power of a test as a measure of how "good" the test is. The power function of a test T, denoted by $\Pi_T(\boldsymbol{\theta})$, is defined to be "the probability of rejecting H_0 as a function of $\boldsymbol{\theta}$." Thus when $\boldsymbol{\theta}$ is in ω (and hence H_0 is true), we want $\Pi_T(\boldsymbol{\theta})$ to be small, and when $\boldsymbol{\theta}$ is in $\Omega - \omega$ (and hence H_0 is false), we want $\Pi_T(\boldsymbol{\theta})$ to be large. Since we fix the probability of a Type I error to be less than or equal to a specified number α (usually α is small; for example, 0.001,

0.005, 0.01, 0.02, 0.025, 0.05, 0.10), we note that $\Pi_T(\boldsymbol{\theta}) \le \alpha$ for $\boldsymbol{\theta} \in \omega$. The "size of a test T" is defined to be $\max_{\boldsymbol{\theta} \in \omega} \Pi_T(\boldsymbol{\theta})$.

The problem is to find R (and A) such that the size of the test is α and the power is as large as possible when $\boldsymbol{\theta}$ is in $\Omega - \omega$.

DEFINITION 2.8.1

Uniformly Most Powerful* (UMP) *Test. *A test T of $H_0 : \boldsymbol{\theta} \in \omega$ vs. $H_a : \boldsymbol{\theta} \in \bar{\omega}$ is defined to be a UMP test of size α if and only if for any other test T^* of H_0 vs. H_a of size $\le \alpha$, the power of T is as large or larger than the power of T^*, that is, if and only if*

(1) $max_{\boldsymbol{\theta} \in \omega} \Pi_T(\boldsymbol{\theta}) = \alpha$;

(2) $\Pi_{T^*}(\boldsymbol{\theta}) \le \Pi_T(\boldsymbol{\theta})$ *for all* $\boldsymbol{\theta}$ *in* $\bar{\omega}$, *where* T^* *is any test of size* $\le \alpha$.

The optimum property we would like a test of size α to satisfy is to be UMP. However, tests seldom exist with this optimum property, so what is done is to restrict the tests to a class with specified desirable properties and find an UMP test (if one exists) within this class. For example, it seems quite desirable for a test to have the property that the probability of rejecting H_0 is larger when H_0 is false than when H_0 is true. This is the property of an unbiased test which we now define.

DEFINITION 2.8.2

Unbiased Test. *Consider tests of H_0 vs. H_a of size α. A test T is defined to be an unbiased test of size α if and only if it satisfies*

(1) $max_{\boldsymbol{\theta} \in \omega} \Pi_T(\boldsymbol{\theta}) = \alpha$, *that is, T has size α*;

(2) $\Pi_T(\boldsymbol{\theta}) \ge \alpha$ *for all* $\boldsymbol{\theta}$ *in* $\bar{\omega}$.

A uniformly most powerful unbiased (UMPU) test of size α is a UMP test among the class of all unbiased tests of size α. We now state this definition formally.

DEFINITION 2.8.3

Uniformly Most Powerful Unbiased* (UMPU) *Test. *Consider tests of H_0 vs. H_a of size α. A test T is a UMPU test of size α if and only if it satisfies*

(1) $max_{\boldsymbol{\theta} \in \omega} \Pi_T(\boldsymbol{\theta}) = \alpha$, *that is, T has size α*;

(2) $\Pi_T(\boldsymbol{\theta}) \ge \alpha$ *for all* $\boldsymbol{\theta}$ *in* $\bar{\omega}$, *that is, T is unbiased of size α*;

(3) $\Pi_T(\boldsymbol{\theta}) \geq \Pi_{T^*}(\boldsymbol{\theta})$ *for all* $\boldsymbol{\theta}$ *in* $\bar{\omega}$ *and for all tests* T^* *that satisfy* (1) *and* (2).

In the important applied problems that fit into the theory of the linear model, UMPU tests do sometimes exist, but often they do not. Thus we may want to restrict the class of tests in *another* way and see if UMP tests exist within *this* restricted class. One such class is the set of tests that is invariant for certain types of transformations. We shall not discuss these tests but the interested reader can consult [L-8], [S-4], and [Z-1].

Note 1. In point estimation we can always use a set of sufficient statistics instead of the original sample observations and no "information" about the unknown parameter $\boldsymbol{\theta}$ is lost in doing so. This result is in Section 2.7. A similar result holds for hypothesis testing.

A problem that still remains is that of actually *finding* a test of a given hypothesis that has some desirable properties. A useful method for finding a test in the linear model is the "generalized likelihood ratio" method, which we now define.

DEFINITION 2.8.4

Generalized Likelihood Ratio Test. *Let* $L(\boldsymbol{\theta} : \mathbf{y})$, $\boldsymbol{\theta} \in \Omega$, *be the likelihood function of the sample observations* $y_1, y_2, \ldots, y_n$. *The generalized likelihood ratio test "statistic" for testing* $H_0 : \boldsymbol{\theta} \in \omega$ *vs.* $H_a : \boldsymbol{\theta} \in \bar{\omega}$ *is* $V = v(\mathbf{Y})$, *where* $v(\mathbf{y})$ *is defined by*

$$v(\mathbf{y}) = \frac{\max\limits_{\boldsymbol{\theta} \in \omega}[L(\boldsymbol{\theta} : \mathbf{y})]}{\max\limits_{\boldsymbol{\theta} \in \Omega}[L(\boldsymbol{\theta} : \mathbf{y})]}$$

The generalized likelihood ratio test of size α *is this: Reject* H_0 *if and only if* $v(\mathbf{y}) \leq v_\alpha$, *where* $\max_{\boldsymbol{\theta} \in \omega}\{P[v(\mathbf{Y}) \leq v_\alpha]\} = \alpha$. $V = v(\mathbf{Y})$ *is the generalized likelihood ratio test statistic when the observed vector* $\mathbf{y}$ *is replaced by the corresponding random vector* $\mathbf{Y}$.

Note 2. $v(\mathbf{y})$ varies between 0 and 1, inclusive.

Note 3. The denominator of $v(\mathbf{y})$ is the likelihood function evaluated at the maximum likelihood estimate of $\boldsymbol{\theta}$.

Note 4. Instead of using "the" generalized likelihood ratio test statistic $V = v(\mathbf{Y})$ with critical region R, it is often more convenient to use a test statistic that is some function of V, say $T = t(V)$, with a corresponding rejection region, such that the resulting test based on

T has the same power function as the likelihood ratio test statistic V. In such a case T is called "a" generalized likelihood ratio test statistic.

Note 5. The generalized likelihood ratio test is often a good test but sometimes it is not. One desirable property of the generalized likelihood ratio test is that it is a function of every set of sufficient statistics.

2.9 Confidence Intervals

In point estimation the procedure is to select a function of the sample random variables that will "best" represent the parameter being estimated. In most studies it is generally not essential to obtain the *exact* value of a parameter under investigation. For example, in ascertaining the average tensile strength of wire, it may well be that a knowledge of the exact average tensile strength is not necessary but that a value within, say, a half pound of the true average tensile strength will be adequate. It is desirable, however, to have some confidence that the value obtained is within the specified limits. A point estimate will not do this. This suggests using an interval estimate, called a confidence interval.

A *confidence interval* is a random interval whose end points $\ell(\mathbf{Y})$ and $u(\mathbf{Y})$, where $\ell(\mathbf{Y}) \leq u(\mathbf{Y})$, are functions of the observable random variables such that the probability that the inequalities $\ell(\mathbf{Y}) \leq \theta_\tau \leq u(\mathbf{Y})$ are satisfied is a predetermined number $1 - \alpha$. In the above formulation θ_τ is the true (unknown) value of the parameter and $1 - \alpha$ is generally taken as 0.80, 0.90, 0.95, and so forth.

In order to examine this in more detail, we denote the observable random variables by $Y_1, Y_2, \ldots, Y_n$ and their joint p.d.f. by $f_{\mathbf{Y}}(\mathbf{y} : \boldsymbol{\theta})$. Let the $K \times 1$ parameter vector $\boldsymbol{\theta}$ be partitioned as $\boldsymbol{\theta}' = [\theta, \boldsymbol{\gamma}']$. We want a confidence interval on θ_τ, the true value of θ, the first element in $\boldsymbol{\theta}$. Also, θ can represent $c(\boldsymbol{\theta})$, a known function of $\boldsymbol{\theta}$. Two statistics, $L = \ell(\mathbf{Y})$ and $U = u(\mathbf{Y})$, are determined such that (we omit the subscript τ on θ when there is no chance for confusion)

$$P[\ell(\mathbf{Y}) \leq \theta_\tau \leq u(\mathbf{Y})] = 1 - \alpha \tag{2.9.1}$$

The quantity $1 - \alpha$ is called the confidence coefficient or confidence level. The interval is called a $1 - \alpha$ confidence interval. Any of the following will be called confidence intervals: $[L, U]$, $[\ell(\mathbf{Y}), u(\mathbf{Y})]$, $\ell(\mathbf{Y}) \leq \theta_\tau \leq u(\mathbf{Y})$, $L \leq \theta_\tau \leq U$, $[\ell, u]$, $[\ell(\mathbf{y}), u(\mathbf{y})]$, $\ell(\mathbf{y}) \leq \theta_\tau \leq u(\mathbf{y})$, $\ell \leq \theta_\tau \leq u$, where $\mathbf{y}$ is the observed value of $\mathbf{Y}$.

Sometimes functions $\ell(\mathbf{Y})$ and $u(\mathbf{Y})$ do not exist such that the confidence interval probability in Equation (2.9.1) is *equal* to $1 - \alpha$ and in these cases it may be possible to find functions $\ell(\mathbf{Y})$ and $u(\mathbf{Y})$ such that

$$P[\ell(\mathbf{Y}) \leq \theta_\tau \leq u(\mathbf{Y})] \geq 1 - \alpha$$

whatever the true value of $\boldsymbol{\theta}$ is in Ω. Generally, however, in linear model theory the equal sign is applicable, so we discuss only that situation here.

The frequency interpretation is this: if for each observed random vector $\mathbf{y}$ the same functions $\ell(\mathbf{y})$ and $u(\mathbf{y})$ are used, then in the long run the proportion of the intervals that will cover the true unknown parameter θ_τ is $1 - \alpha$. Even though we observe only one interval, we have a confidence of $1 - \alpha$ that *this* interval covers the true unknown parameter θ_τ.

There may be many pairs of functions that will give rise to a confidence interval on θ_τ with coefficient $1 - \alpha$. The question is, of all pairs of functions that satisfy Equation (2.9.1), which pair of functions gives "good" (or the "best") intervals?

In determining attributes for "good" confidence intervals, two things are intuitively important: (1) the probability should be small that the interval contains *false* values of θ; (2) the "length" of the interval should be small. We formalize (1) in the next definition and discuss (2) later.

DEFINITION 2.9.1

Uniformly Most Accurate (UMA) Confidence Interval. *A confidence interval* $[L, U]$ *for* θ_τ, *with confidence coefficient* $1 - \alpha$, *is defined to be a uniformly most accurate* $1 - \alpha$ *confidence interval for* θ_τ *if and only if*

$$P[[L, U] \text{ contains } \theta] \leq P[[L^*, U^*] \text{ contains } \theta] \tag{2.9.2}$$

for all other $1 - \alpha$ *confidence intervals* $[L^*, U^*]$ *and all* $\boldsymbol{\theta}$ *in* Ω.

> ***Note 1.*** If $\theta = \theta_\tau$, where θ_τ is the correct value of θ, equality holds in Equation (2.9.2) for all values of $\boldsymbol{\gamma}$ since both $[L, U]$ and $[L^*, U^*]$ are $1 - \alpha$ confidence intervals. For all other possible values of $\boldsymbol{\theta}$, that is, of $[\theta, \boldsymbol{\gamma}']'$, the probability that $[L, U]$ contains θ_I (an incorrect value of θ) is less than or equal to the probability that $[L^*, U^*]$ contains θ_I.

UMA confidence intervals rarely exist, and when they do not, a procedure is to consider only confidence intervals in some restricted class and look for UMA confidence intervals in this class. Two such classes are unbiased confidence intervals and invariant confidence intervals. Invariant confidence intervals will not be discussed in this book, but the interested reader can consult [F-2], [L-8], and [Z-1]. We now define unbiased confidence intervals and uniformly most accurate unbiased (UMAU) confidence intervals.

DEFINITION 2.9.2

Unbiased Confidence Intervals. *A* $1 - \alpha$ *confidence interval on* θ_τ *is defined to be an unbiased confidence interval if and only if the probability of covering false values of* θ *is less than or equal to* $1 - \alpha$.

Note 2. This definition states that an unbiased confidence interval has a lower probability of covering false values of θ than of covering the true value of θ.

DEFINITION 2.9.3

Uniformly Most Accurate Unbiased (UMAU) Confidence Intervals. Let $Y_1, Y_2, \ldots, Y_n$ *be an observable sample with p.d.f.* $f_{\mathbf{Y}}(\mathbf{y} : \boldsymbol{\theta})$, $\boldsymbol{\theta} \in \Omega$. *A confidence interval* $\ell(\mathbf{Y}) \le \theta_\tau \le u(\mathbf{Y})$ *with confidence coefficient* $1 - \alpha$ *is defined to be a UMAU* $1 - \alpha$ *confidence interval if and only if*

(1) $\ell(\mathbf{Y}) \le \theta_\tau \le u(\mathbf{Y})$ *is an unbiased* $1 - \alpha$ *confidence interval;*

(2) *in the class of unbiased* $1 - \alpha$ *confidence intervals,* $\ell(\mathbf{Y}) \le \theta_\tau \le u(\mathbf{Y})$ *is uniformly most accurate.*

There is a relationship between tests of hypotheses and confidence intervals such that if a test of size α about θ is obtained for each possible value of θ in the parameter space, then this family of tests gives rise to a $1 - \alpha$ confidence interval on θ. Typically in linear model theory the tests referred to above lead to an interval $[\ell(\mathbf{Y}), u(\mathbf{Y})]$ such that H_0 is *accepted* if and only if θ is in the interval (that is, H_0 is rejected if and only if θ is *not* in the interval). This interval can also be viewed as a $1 - \alpha$ confidence interval on θ. It can also be shown that if the test is UMP (or UMPU) of size α, then the corresponding confidence interval is a UMA (or UMAU) $1 - \alpha$ confidence interval. The advantage of this is that an optimum property (such as UMAU or UMA) of a *confidence interval* on θ can be inferred by showing that the corresponding *test* has an optimum property (such as UMPU or UMP).

It seems intuitively reasonable that "good" confidence intervals should be such that the width of the confidence interval is "small." Generally, if a two-sided confidence interval is UMA (UMAU), then the expected width, $\mathscr{E}[U - L]$, is a minimum in the class of all (unbiased) confidence intervals. For further information on this subject see [M-1] and [P-6].

Also, to obtain confidence intervals with optimum properties, one need only consider sufficient statistics.

Example 2.9.1

Consider Example 2.7.1. Suppose we want a test of size α of $H_0 : \mu = \mu_0$ *vs.* $H_a : \mu \ne \mu_0$. Here $\theta = \mu$. If we formulate this test in terms of Ω and ω, then

$$\Omega = \{(\mu, \sigma^2) : \sigma^2 > 0, \ -\infty < \mu < \infty\}$$
$$\omega = \{(\mu, \sigma^2) : \sigma^2 > 0, \ \mu = \mu_0\}$$

The likelihood function is

$$L(\boldsymbol{\theta} : \mathbf{y}) = \left(\frac{1}{2\pi\sigma^2}\right)^{n/2} \exp\left[-\frac{1}{2\sigma^2}\sum (y_i - \mu)^2\right]$$

and the generalized likelihood ratio statistic is

$$\frac{\max\limits_{\boldsymbol{\theta}\in\omega} L(\boldsymbol{\theta} : \mathbf{Y})}{\max\limits_{\boldsymbol{\theta}\in\Omega} L(\boldsymbol{\theta} : \mathbf{Y})} = \frac{\left[\dfrac{1}{2\pi(1/n)\sum (Y_i - \mu_0)^2}\right]^{n/2} e^{-n/2}}{\left[\dfrac{1}{2\pi(1/n)\sum (Y_i - \bar{Y})^2}\right]^{n/2} e^{-n/2}} = \left[\frac{\sum (Y_i - \bar{Y})^2}{\sum (Y_i - \mu_0)^2}\right]^{n/2}$$

$$= \left[\frac{\sum (Y_i - \bar{Y})^2}{\sum (Y_i - \bar{Y})^2 + n(\bar{Y} - \mu_0)^2}\right]^{n/2} = \frac{1}{\left[1 + \dfrac{n(\bar{Y} - \mu_0)^2}{\sum (Y_i - \bar{Y})^2}\right]^{n/2}}$$

This test statistic is a monotonic function of T^2, where

$$T = \frac{\sqrt{n}(\bar{Y} - \mu_0)}{\sqrt{[1/(n-1)]\sum (Y_i - \bar{Y})^2}}$$

is distributed $s(t : n - 1)$ when H_0 is true. So the acceptance interval for this test is

$$[\bar{Y} - t_{\alpha/2:n-1}S_{\bar{Y}},\ \bar{Y} + t_{\alpha/2:n-1}S_{\bar{Y}}]$$

where $S_{\bar{Y}}^2 = [1/n(n-1)]\sum (Y_i - \bar{Y})^2$. This is also a $1 - \alpha$ confidence interval on μ. It can be shown that this is a UMPU size α test and hence a UMAU $1 - \alpha$ confidence interval. Hence this interval has the smallest expected width of all unbiased $1 - \alpha$ confidence intervals on μ.

2.10 Comments on Statistical Inference

Progress towards obtaining knowledge about the world in which we live is often made by defining a specific problem that is to be solved and obtaining observations that relate to this problem.

Example 2.10.1

Suppose Company A has 1,000,000 headache tablets that it plans to sell to Company B. However, Company B wants to determine how many (or what percent) of the pills contain the specified amount of aspirin before they purchase them. One way to be certain that the 1,000,000 pills meet the standard is to have a chemist analyze each pill. Of course, if this method were used, not only would an unrealistic amount of time be spent, but each tablet would be destroyed. A procedure that comes to mind is to select a sample from the one million tablets, analyze the pills in the sample, and from this information infer what percentage of the one million pills is satisfactory. Of course, the pills in the sample may not be "representative" of the one million pills so one cannot be *certain* that the results of the sample will accurately reflect the true state of the one million pills. The inference from a "few" pills to "all" the one million pills is called *inductive* inference.

We abstract the essential elements from this simple example and define the following populations:

1. *Target population.* The set of elements (real or hypothetical) that are under discussion and about which information is desired.
2. *Sampled population.* A set of elements from which a subset (sample) of elements can be observed.

The *sampled* and *target* populations should be identical, but this is not always possible. In the example referred to above, they are identical, but often they are not. Consider the following example.

Example 2.10.2

Suppose that a new drug has been found that is thought to be effective in controlling a certain disease in chickens. It is decided to administer the drug to 100 chickens selected at random from the 10,000 chickens on a given farm. The sampled population is the 10,000 chickens on this particular farm. From the results of the 100 chickens that were selected at random from this population, one can make inferences about the sampled population and measure the uncertainty of the inference in a relative frequency probability sense. However, suppose that the target population is defined to be *all* chickens in a certain geographical region where the disease is known to exist. The inference from the sampled population to the target population must be a subject matter consideration, and the uncertainty of the inference cannot be measured in a relative frequency probability sense.

Statistical inference plays a major role as a procedure in helping to determine how to select the sample from the sampled population, how to draw "valid" inductive inferences from the sample to the sampled population, and how to attach the proper measure of uncertainty to the inferences. In the remainder of this book, when we use the word population, we will mean the *sampled* population unless specifically stated otherwise. We often use "population" and "p.d.f. of the population" interchangeably.

The three main procedures for making statistical inferences are point estimation, confidence interval estimation, and hypothesis testing. When point estimation is used, there is no probability statement about the uncertainty of the inference. When testing hypotheses the uncertainty of the inference is reflected in the power of the test procedure. However, often a size of the test, say α, is specified in *advance* and the null hypothesis is rejected or accepted. This is, indeed, the method that is used to derive test statistics in this book. However, it should not be used this way in practice.

To illustrate what we mean we return to Example 2.9.1. If the computed value of T^2, denoted by t^2, is greater than or equal to $F_{\alpha:1,n-1}$, then $H_0 : \mu = \mu_0$ is rejected since we are testing $H_0 : \mu = \mu_0$ *vs.* $H_a : \mu \neq \mu_0$ with a test of size α. However, what one should actually do in practice is to find the smallest number α^* such that $t^2 = F_{\alpha^*:1,n-1}$. Then this statement can be made: "If H_0 is true, the probability of obtaining a value of T^2 that is greater than or equal to $F_{\alpha^*:1,n-1}$ is α^*." Or, stated another way, we can say: "If H_0 is true, the probability of obtaining a value of T^2 that is greater than or equal to the observed t^2 is equal to α^*."

If α^* is quite small, then the investigator feels quite comfortable in rejecting H_0. To illustrate with artificial numbers, suppose one wanted to test $H_0 : \mu = \mu_0$ with a test of size $\alpha = 0.05$ and $n = 10$. Suppose further that the sample was selected, T^2 computed, and the value turned out to be $t^2 = 10.6$. Then the data suggest that H_0 should be rejected. But by examining the F table (Table T.5), one notices that the smallest α^* such that $10.6 = F_{\alpha^*:1,9}$ is $\alpha^* = 0.01$. So instead of the statement, "H_0 is rejected with a size $\alpha = 0.05$ test," one can make the statement, "If H_0 is true, the probability of obtaining a value of T^2 that is greater than or equal to the observed value (which was $t^2 = 10.6$) is 0.01." Thus if one had used a test of size $\alpha = 0.01$ instead of $\alpha = 0.05$, H_0 would be rejected, and it would seem that an investigator would have more evidence that indeed $H_0 : \mu = \mu_0$ is not true.

Thus while the mathematical formulation of hypothesis testing in this book is for a size α test, where α is fixed in advance, the investigator should *always* use the procedure explained above to determine the smallest α^* for which the null hypothesis would be rejected and use this number as "the strength of evidence" for rejecting H_0. For further information on this subject, see [K-4].

Similar comments can be made about confidence interval estimation. In this book the mathematical formulation of the problem will be for a specified confidence coefficient $1 - \alpha$. However, in practice, a set of confidence intervals should always be computed. For instance, in Example 2.9.1 one should compute confidence intervals on μ with confidence coefficients 0.50, 0.75, 0.80, 0.90, 0.95, 0.99, and any other values that might be useful. These intervals are easily computed from $\bar{y}$ and $s_{\bar{y}}$ by simply finding $t_{\alpha/2:n-1}$ for $1 - \alpha = 0.50, 0.75, 0.80,$ $0.90, 0.95, 0.99$ and substituting into the formula $\bar{y} \mp t_{\alpha/2:n-1} s_{\bar{y}}$. These various confidence intervals give the investigator more complete information about what the data imply about the value of μ. In this book we will formulate the problems in terms of a specified confidence coefficient; however, it should be kept in mind that in applications a set of confidence intervals (for various values of $1 - \alpha$) should always be computed and displayed for the investigator. For further information on this subject, see [B-5].

We have discussed tests of hypotheses and confidence intervals as methods for making inferences and attaching measures of uncertainty to the inferences. It is almost always the case, however, when making inferences about parameters of a distribution, that confidence interval procedures are "uniformly more informative" than hypotheses tests, and hence hypotheses tests should seldom be used if confidence intervals are available. For example, in Example 2.9.1 when testing $H_0 : \mu = 0$ *vs.* $H_a : \mu \neq 0$, the data could give a test statistic such that H_0 is rejected with size α. The corresponding $1 - \alpha$ confidence interval could be any interval that does *not* include zero. For example, it could be $0.06 \leq \mu \leq 0.07$, or it could be $50.1 \leq \mu \leq 63.2$. In the first case the investigator would undoubtedly conclude that for practical purposes μ is indeed zero (of no practical importance); in the second case he would undoubtedly conclude that μ is not zero. So the confidence intervals could lead to *opposite* practical conclusions when a test suggests rejection of H_0.

Next suppose the data gave a result such that H_0 was *not* rejected when a size α test was used. The corresponding $1 - \alpha$ confidence interval could be any interval that includes zero. It could be $-0.06 \leq \mu \leq 0.02$, in which case the investigator would undoubtedly conclude that for practical purposes μ is indeed zero (not of practical importance); however, the confidence interval could be $-38.2 \leq \mu \leq 20.6$, and the investigator would decide that the investigation was inconclusive about μ and that additional data are necessary. So even though H_0 is *not* rejected, the confidence interval gives more useful information.

Problems

2.1. Let $Y_1, Y_2, \ldots, Y_n$ be a random sample from a p.d.f. that is normal with unknown mean μ and unknown variance σ^2, where μ can be any real number and σ^2 can be any positive number. Exhibit the joint p.d.f. of $Y_1, Y_2, \ldots, Y_n$.

2.2. In Problem 2.1 find the m.g.f. of the random variable $\overline{Y}$.

2.3. In Problem 2.2 find the p.d.f. of $\overline{Y}$.

2.4. In Problem 2.1 find the generalized likelihood ratio test of size α for $H_0 : \sigma^2 = \sigma_0^2$ (specified) *vs.* $H_a : \sigma^2 > \sigma_0^2$.

2.5. In Problem 2.4 find the corresponding $1 - \alpha$ confidence interval and the power function.

2.6. In Problem 2.1 find the generalized likelihood ratio test of size α for $H_0 : \mu = \mu_0$ (specified) *vs.* $H_a : \mu \neq \mu_0$.

2.7. In Problem 2.6 find the corresponding $1 - \alpha$ confidence interval.

2.8. Let $Y_1, Y_2, \ldots, Y_n$ be a random sample from $N(y : \mu_1, \sigma_1^2)$, and let $X_1, X_2, \ldots, X_m$ be a random sample from $N(x : \mu_2, \sigma_2^2)$, where μ_1, μ_2, σ_1^2, σ_2^2 are unknown and the parameter space is Ω, where $\Omega = \{(\mu_1, \mu_2, \sigma_1^2, \sigma_2^2) : -\infty < \mu_i < \infty, 0 < \sigma_i^2, i = 1, 2\}$. Find the M.L. estimators of the four parameters. Assume the Y's and X's are independent.

2.9. In Problem 2.8 find the M.L. estimator of $\mu_1 + \mu_2$.

2.10. Assume $Y_1, Y_2, \ldots, Y_m$ is a random sample from $N(y : \mu_1, \sigma^2)$, $X_1, X_2, \ldots, X_n$ is a random sample from $N(x : \mu_2, \sigma^2)$, and the Y's and X's are independent. Assume the parameter space Ω is defined by $\Omega = \{(\mu_1, \mu_2, \sigma^2) : -\infty < \mu_1 < \infty, -\infty < \mu_2 < \infty, \sigma^2 > 0\}$. Show that the joint p.d.f. of $Y_1, Y_2, \ldots, Y_m, X_1, X_2, \ldots, X_n$ belongs to an exponential family of densities.

2.11. In Problem 2.10 find the M.L. estimators of μ_1, μ_2, σ^2.

2.12. In Problem 2.11 find the joint p.d.f. of the M.L. estimators of μ_1, μ_2, σ^2.

2.13. In Problem 2.12 show that the joint p.d.f. belongs to an exponential family of densities.

2.14. In Problem 2.11 show that the M.L. estimators are complete sufficient statistics.

2.15. In Problem 2.10 show that UMVU estimator of μ_1 exists and find it.

2.16. In Problem 2.10 find the UMVU estimator of $\mu_1 + 3\mu_2$.

2.17. In Problem 2.10 find the UMVU estimator of $\mu_1/\sigma^2 + \mu_2$.

2.18. In Problem 2.10, for the generalized likelihood ratio test of $H_0 : \mu_1 = \mu_2$ *vs.* $H_a : \mu_1 \neq \mu_2$, define ω and Ω.

2.19. In Problem 2.18 find the generalized likelihood ratio test statistic.

2.20. In Problem 2.10 find a $1 - \alpha$ confidence interval on $\mu_1 - \mu_2$.

2.21. In Equation (2.5.8) are U_0 and $\bar{Y}$ independent? Prove your answer.

2.22. In Problem 2.1 define $\hat{\sigma}^2$ by $\hat{\sigma}^2 = (n - 1)^{-1} \sum_{i=1}^{n} (Y_i - \bar{Y})^2$. Find $\mathscr{E}[\hat{\sigma}]$.

2.23. In Theorem 2.5.3 prove parts (4) and (5) when $p = q = 1$, that is, when Y_1 and Y_2 are scalar random variables.

CHAPTER 3

The Multidimensional Normal Distribution

3.1 Introduction

The normal distribution plays a central role in the theory of the linear model and in this chapter we define and discuss the multidimensional analogue of the univariate normal distribution. We shall discuss only the c.d.f., the p.d.f., and the m.g.f. and defer to later chapters a discussion of sampling from the multidimensional normal distribution.

3.2 The Univariate Normal Distribution

First we define the standard univariate normal distribution, and from this we define the multivariate normal distribution.

DEFINITION 3.2.1

Standard Univariate Normal Distribution. *A univariate random variable Z is defined to have a standard univariate normal distribution if and only if the p.d.f. of Z is given by*

$$n(z:0,1) = \left(\frac{1}{\sqrt{2\pi}}\right) exp\left(-\frac{z^2}{2}\right) \qquad -\infty < z < \infty \qquad (3.2.1)$$

We assume that the reader is acquainted with this p.d.f. The mean of this distribution is zero and the variance is unity. Since the univariate normal p.d.f. is completely determined by its mean and variance, we include them in the functional notation $n(z : 0, 1)$.

THEOREM 3.2.1

The c.d.f. and m.g.f. of a random variable Z that has a standard univariate normal distribution are given by, respectively,

$$N(z : 0, 1) = \int_{-\infty}^{z} n(u : 0, 1)\, du \qquad -\infty < z < \infty \tag{3.2.2}$$

and

$$m_Z(t) = e^{t^2/2} \qquad -\infty < t < \infty \tag{3.2.3}$$

Proof

We assume that the reader is acquainted with these results so we omit the proof.

Notation. We use $n(\cdot)$ for the functional notation of the normal p.d.f. and $N(\cdot)$ for the c.d.f. We use capital letters, X, Z, Y, and so on, to denote scalar random variables and lowercase letters, x, z, y, and so on, to denote values of the random variables. We use capital boldface letters to denote matrices and lowercase boldface letters to denote vectors. However, we deviate from this notation slightly to denote random vectors; we shall use upper boldface $\mathbf{Y}$ and $\mathbf{Z}$ to denote random vectors with elements Y_i and Z_i respectively. We shall use $\boldsymbol{\chi}$ (boldface Greek "chi") rather than $\mathbf{X}$ to denote a random vector with elements X_i and use $\mathbf{X}$ for a nonrandom matrix. We use greek letters to denote unknown parameters.

We now define a univariate normal distribution with *general* mean and variance.

DEFINITION 3.2.2

Univariate Normal Distribution. *The random variable X is defined to have a univariate normal distribution with mean μ and variance σ^2 if and only if the p.d.f. of X is given by*

$$n(x : \mu, \sigma^2) = \left(\frac{1}{\sigma\sqrt{2\pi}}\right) e^{-(x-\mu)^2/2\sigma^2} \qquad -\infty < x < \infty \tag{3.2.4}$$

Note 1. The parameter space for the univariate normal p.d.f. that will generally be used in this book is Ω where $\Omega = \{(\mu, \sigma^2) : a < \mu < b, 0 < \sigma^2 < c, a < b, c > 0\}$. Of course the p.d.f. in Equation (3.2.1) is a special case of the p.d.f. in Equation (3.2.4).

THEOREM 3.2.2

The c.d.f. and m.g.f. of the univariate normal random variable X defined in Definition 3.2.2 are given by, respectively,

$$N(x : \mu, \sigma^2) = \int_{-\infty}^{x} n(u : \mu, \sigma^2)\, du \qquad -\infty < x < \infty \tag{3.2.5}$$

and

$$m_X(t) = e^{t\mu + t^2\sigma^2/2} \qquad -\infty < t < \infty \tag{3.2.6}$$

Proof

We assume that the reader is acquainted with these results so we omit the proof.

3.3 Multivariate Normal Distribution

Now we discuss the joint distribution of K *mutually independent* random variables Z_i, where each is distributed $N(z : 0, 1)$. Since the random variables are mutually independent, the joint p.d.f. is given by

$$\prod_{i=1}^{K} \left(\frac{1}{\sqrt{2\pi}}\right) e^{-z_i^2/2} = \left(\frac{1}{(2\pi)^{K/2}}\right) \exp\left[-\frac{1}{2}\sum_{i=1}^{K} z_i^2\right]$$
$$-\infty < z_i < \infty, \quad i = 1, 2, \ldots, K \tag{3.3.1}$$

Let Z_i be the ith element in the $K \times 1$ vector $\mathbf{Z}$ and write Equation (3.3.1) as

$$\mathbf{n}(\mathbf{z} : \mathbf{0}, \mathbf{I}) = \left(\frac{1}{(2\pi)^{K/2}}\right) e^{-(1/2)\mathbf{z}'\mathbf{z}} \qquad \mathbf{z} \in E_K \tag{3.3.2}$$

where the symbol $\mathbf{n}(\mathbf{z} : \mathbf{0}, \mathbf{I})$ indicates the p.d.f. of the random vector $\mathbf{Z}$. Later we shall indicate why we use $\mathbf{0}, \mathbf{I}$ instead of 0, 1. This p.d.f. can clearly be viewed as a multidimensional generalization of the p.d.f. of the univariate standard normal given in Equation (3.2.1). Hence we call the p.d.f. in Equation (3.3.2) the K-variate *standard* normal p.d.f.; we give the formal definition below.

DEFINITION 3.3.1

K-Variate Standard Normal Distribution. *The* $K \times 1$ *random vector* $\mathbf{Z}$ *is defined to have a K-variate standard normal distribution if and only if the p.d.f. of* $\mathbf{Z}$ *is* $\mathbf{n}(\mathbf{z}:\mathbf{0},\mathbf{I})$ *given in Equation* (3.3.2).

Now we shall find the m.g.f. of $\mathbf{Z}$.

THEOREM 3.3.1

Let $\mathbf{Z}$ *be distributed* $\mathbf{N}(\mathbf{z}:\mathbf{0},\mathbf{I})$, *where* $\mathbf{Z}$ *is a* $K \times 1$ *random vector. The m.g.f. of* $\mathbf{Z}$ *is*

$$m_{\mathbf{Z}}(\mathbf{t}) = e^{\mathbf{t}'\mathbf{t}/2} \qquad \mathbf{t} \in E_K$$

Proof

By Definition 2.3.1 the m.g.f. of $\mathbf{Z}$ exists if the integral shown below exists for all $\mathbf{t}$ in a neighborhood of $\mathbf{0}$ in E_K.

$$m_{\mathbf{Z}}(\mathbf{t}) = \mathscr{E}[e^{\mathbf{t}'\mathbf{Z}}] = \int_{-\infty}^{\infty} \cdots \int_{-\infty}^{\infty} e^{\mathbf{t}'\mathbf{z}} \left(\frac{1}{(2\pi)^{K/2}} \right) e^{-\mathbf{z}'\mathbf{z}/2} \, d\mathbf{z}$$

By Theorem 1.10.1 this integral exists for all $\mathbf{t} \in E_K$ and is equal to $e^{\mathbf{t}'\mathbf{t}/2}$, and the theorem is proved.

Linear functions $\boldsymbol{\gamma}'\mathbf{Z} + \gamma_0$ of univariate random variables Z_i play a significant role in all of statistics and they are especially important in linear model theory. In this linear function, which we can write as $\sum_{i=1}^{K} \gamma_i Z_i + \gamma_0$, the quantities $\gamma_0, \gamma_1, \gamma_2, \ldots, \gamma_K$ are constants. In the next theorem we find the distribution of $\boldsymbol{\gamma}'\mathbf{Z} + \gamma_0$.

THEOREM 3.3.2

Let $\mathbf{Z}$ *be distributed* $\mathbf{N}(\mathbf{z}:\mathbf{0},\mathbf{I})$, *where* $\mathbf{Z}$ *is a* $K \times 1$ *random vector. Let* $\boldsymbol{\gamma}$ *be any nonzero* $K \times 1$ *vector of constants and let* γ_0 *be any constant scalar. The univariate random variable* X, *where* $X = \boldsymbol{\gamma}'\mathbf{Z} + \gamma_0$, *is distributed* $N(x:\gamma_0, \boldsymbol{\gamma}'\boldsymbol{\gamma})$.

Proof

We find the m.g.f. of $\boldsymbol{\gamma}'\mathbf{Z} + \gamma_0$, recognize it as the m.g.f. of a random variable whose distribution is $N(x:\gamma_0, \boldsymbol{\gamma}'\boldsymbol{\gamma})$, and use Theorem 2.3.1. The m.g.f. of $X = \boldsymbol{\gamma}'\mathbf{Z} + \gamma_0$ is, by definition,

$$\begin{aligned} m_X(t) &= \mathscr{E}[e^{t(\boldsymbol{\gamma}'\mathbf{Z} + \gamma_0)}] \\ &= e^{t\gamma_0} \int_{-\infty}^{\infty} \cdots \int_{-\infty}^{\infty} e^{t(\boldsymbol{\gamma}'\mathbf{z})} \left(\frac{1}{(2\pi)^{K/2}} \right) e^{-\mathbf{z}'\mathbf{z}/2} \, d\mathbf{z} \end{aligned}$$

By Theorem 1.10.1 this integral exists, and the m.g.f. is

$$m_X(t) = \exp\left[\gamma_0 t + \frac{(\boldsymbol{\gamma}'\boldsymbol{\gamma})t^2}{2}\right] \qquad t \in E_1$$

But by Equation (3.2.6) this is the m.g.f. of a univariate random variable whose distribution is $N(x : \gamma_0, \boldsymbol{\gamma}'\boldsymbol{\gamma})$, and the theorem is proved.

Example 3.3.1

Let $\mathbf{Z}$ be a 3×1 standard normal random vector, that is, $\mathbf{Z}$ is distributed $\mathbf{N}(\mathbf{z} : \mathbf{0}, \mathbf{I}_3)$. To find the distribution of X, where $X = Z_1 - 2Z_2 + 4Z_3 + 6$, we get $\boldsymbol{\gamma}' = [1, -2, 4]$, $\gamma_0 = 6$, so by Theorem 3.3.2, X is distributed $N(x : 6, 21)$.

Theorem 3.3.2 states that any linear function of a standard normal random vector is normally distributed. We use this fact to define a general multivariate normal distribution, but first we define the first and second moments of a p-variate random vector $\boldsymbol{\chi}$ whose ith element is X_i. The mean of a random vector $\boldsymbol{\chi}$, which we denote by $\boldsymbol{\mu}_{\chi}$, or simply $\boldsymbol{\mu}$, is defined by $\mathscr{E}[\boldsymbol{\chi}] = \boldsymbol{\mu}$, that is, $\boldsymbol{\mu} = [\mu_i]$, where $\mu_i = \mathscr{E}[X_i]$. The variance of each X_i and the covariance of each X_i and X_j for $i \neq j$ are of particular interest. If we denote the variance of X_i by σ_{ii} and the covariance of X_i and X_j by σ_{ij}, then these quantities can be arranged in a $p \times p$ matrix $\boldsymbol{\Sigma}$, where the ijth element of $\boldsymbol{\Sigma}$ is σ_{ij}, the covariance of X_i and X_j. We note that the ith diagonal element of $\boldsymbol{\Sigma}$ is σ_{ii}, the variance of X_i. $\boldsymbol{\Sigma}$ is symmetric since the covariance of X_i and X_j is the same as the covariance of X_j and X_i. Thus we obtain

$$\operatorname{cov}[X_i, X_j] = \sigma_{ij} = \mathscr{E}\{[X_i - \mathscr{E}[X_i]][X_j - \mathscr{E}[X_j]]\} \qquad i = 1, 2, \ldots, p; \quad j = 1, 2, \ldots, p; \quad i \neq j$$

$$\operatorname{var}[X_i] = \sigma_{ii} = \mathscr{E}\{[X_i - \mathscr{E}(X_i)]^2\} \qquad i = 1, 2, \ldots, p$$

Thus it is evident that $\boldsymbol{\Sigma}$ is defined by

$$\boldsymbol{\Sigma} = \mathscr{E}\{[\boldsymbol{\chi} - \mathscr{E}[\boldsymbol{\chi}]][\boldsymbol{\chi} - \mathscr{E}[\boldsymbol{\chi}]]'\} \tag{3.3.3}$$

We generally call $\boldsymbol{\Sigma}$ the covariance (matrix) of the random vector $\boldsymbol{\chi}$ and write $\mathbf{cov}[\boldsymbol{\chi}] = \boldsymbol{\Sigma}$. We remark that a covariance matrix is a nonnegative matrix.

Next we discuss a p-variate normal distribution of rank K.

DEFINITION 3.3.2

p-Variate Normal Distribution of Rank K. *Let $\boldsymbol{\chi}$ be a $p \times 1$ random vector with mean $\boldsymbol{\mu}$ and covariance matrix $\boldsymbol{\Sigma}$, where rank $\boldsymbol{\Sigma} = K > 0$. Let $\boldsymbol{\Gamma}'\boldsymbol{\Gamma} = \boldsymbol{\Sigma}$, that is, $\boldsymbol{\Gamma}'\boldsymbol{\Gamma}$ is a factorization of $\boldsymbol{\Sigma}$, where $\boldsymbol{\Gamma}'$ is a $p \times K$ matrix of rank K. $\boldsymbol{\chi}$ is defined to* *have a p-variate normal distribution of rank K if and only if the c.d.f. of* χ *is the same as the c.d.f. of the random vector* $\mathbf{\Gamma}'\mathbf{Z} + \boldsymbol{\mu}$, *where the distribution of the* $K \times 1$ *random vector* $\mathbf{Z}$ *is* $N(\mathbf{z}:\mathbf{0},\mathbf{I})$, *that is,* $\mathbf{Z}$ *has the K-variate standard normal distribution.*

Note 1. An important point in this definition is that the joint c.d.f. of p random variables (the p elements of χ) has a covariance matrix $\boldsymbol{\Sigma}$ of rank K. Of course $K \le p$.

In the definition we have stated $\mathscr{E}[\chi] = \boldsymbol{\mu}$ and $\mathbf{cov}[\chi] = \boldsymbol{\Sigma}$. Thus if χ is to have the same c.d.f. as $\mathbf{\Gamma}'\mathbf{Z} + \boldsymbol{\mu}$, then $\mathscr{E}[\mathbf{\Gamma}'\mathbf{Z} + \boldsymbol{\mu}]$ must be the same as $\mathscr{E}[\chi]$, and $\mathbf{cov}[\mathbf{\Gamma}'\mathbf{Z} + \boldsymbol{\mu}]$ must be the same as $\mathbf{cov}[\chi]$. These relationships hold as shown below.

$$\mathscr{E}[\mathbf{\Gamma}'\mathbf{Z} + \boldsymbol{\mu}] = \mathbf{\Gamma}'\mathscr{E}[\mathbf{Z}] + \boldsymbol{\mu} = \boldsymbol{\mu}$$

which is the same as $\mathscr{E}[\chi]$.

$$\begin{aligned}\mathbf{cov}[\mathbf{\Gamma}'\mathbf{Z} + \boldsymbol{\mu}] &= \mathscr{E}[\mathbf{\Gamma}'\mathbf{Z} + \boldsymbol{\mu} - \mathscr{E}(\mathbf{\Gamma}'\mathbf{Z} + \boldsymbol{\mu})][\mathbf{\Gamma}'\mathbf{Z} + \boldsymbol{\mu} - \mathscr{E}(\mathbf{\Gamma}'\mathbf{Z} + \boldsymbol{\mu})]' \\ &= \mathscr{E}[(\mathbf{\Gamma}'\mathbf{Z})(\mathbf{\Gamma}'\mathbf{Z})'] = \mathbf{\Gamma}'[\mathscr{E}(\mathbf{Z}\mathbf{Z}')]\mathbf{\Gamma} = \mathbf{\Gamma}'\mathbf{\Gamma} = \boldsymbol{\Sigma}\end{aligned}$$

which is the same as $\mathbf{cov}[\chi]$.

Note 2. Since χ and $\mathbf{\Gamma}'\mathbf{Z} + \boldsymbol{\mu}$ have the same c.d.f., and since the m.g.f. of $\mathbf{\Gamma}'\mathbf{Z} + \boldsymbol{\mu}$ exists, this implies that the m.g.f. of χ also exists and that the two m.g.f.'s are equal.

We shall now find the m.g.f. of a p-variate normal distribution of rank K.

THEOREM 3.3.3

Let the $p \times 1$ *random vector* χ *have a p-variate normal distribution of rank K with mean* $\boldsymbol{\mu}$ *and covariance* $\boldsymbol{\Sigma}$. *The m.g.f. of* χ *is given by*

$$m_\chi(\mathbf{t}) = exp[\mathbf{t}'\boldsymbol{\mu} + \tfrac{1}{2}\mathbf{t}'\boldsymbol{\Sigma}\mathbf{t}] \qquad \mathbf{t} \in E_p \tag{3.3.4}$$

Proof

By Definition 3.3.2, χ and $\mathbf{\Gamma}'\mathbf{Z} + \boldsymbol{\mu}$ have the same c.d.f., and hence they have the same m.g.f. (where $\mathbf{\Gamma}'\mathbf{\Gamma} = \boldsymbol{\Sigma}$). We get

$$\begin{aligned}m_\chi(\mathbf{t}) &= m_{\mathbf{\Gamma}'\mathbf{Z}+\boldsymbol{\mu}}(\mathbf{t}) = \mathscr{E}[\exp\{\mathbf{t}'(\mathbf{\Gamma}'\mathbf{Z} + \boldsymbol{\mu})\}] \\ &= \int_{-\infty}^{\infty} \cdots \int_{-\infty}^{\infty} e^{\mathbf{t}'\boldsymbol{\mu}} \left(\frac{1}{(2\pi)^{K/2}}\right) \exp[\mathbf{t}'\mathbf{\Gamma}'\mathbf{z} - \tfrac{1}{2}\mathbf{z}'\mathbf{z}]\, d\mathbf{z}\end{aligned}$$

By Theorem 1.10.1 we obtain the following, and the theorem is proved.

$$m_{\chi}(\mathbf{t}) = \exp[\mathbf{t}'\boldsymbol{\mu} + \tfrac{1}{2}\mathbf{t}'(\boldsymbol{\Gamma}'\boldsymbol{\Gamma})\mathbf{t}] = \exp[\mathbf{t}'\boldsymbol{\mu} + \tfrac{1}{2}\mathbf{t}'\boldsymbol{\Sigma}\mathbf{t}] \qquad \mathbf{t} \in E_p$$

By this theorem the c.d.f. of χ is completely determined by the mean vector $\boldsymbol{\mu}$ and covariance matrix $\boldsymbol{\Sigma}$. We state: "χ is distributed $\mathbf{N}(\mathbf{x} : \boldsymbol{\mu}, \boldsymbol{\Sigma})$, $\boldsymbol{\Sigma}$ has rank K," to denote that χ is distributed as the p-variate normal distribution of rank K. If the rank of $\boldsymbol{\Sigma}$ is not important in the discussion, it will sometimes be omitted.

If $\boldsymbol{\mu} = \mathbf{0}$ and $\boldsymbol{\Sigma} = \mathbf{I}$, then χ is distributed $\mathbf{N}(\mathbf{x} : \mathbf{0}, \mathbf{I})$ and χ is a standard p-variate normal random vector, thus justifying the use of $\mathbf{0}, \mathbf{I}$ in Equation (3.3.2). Note that if $p = K$, then $\boldsymbol{\Sigma}$ is positive definite; if $K < p$, then $\boldsymbol{\Sigma}$ is positive semidefinite. Also note that the factorization $\boldsymbol{\Sigma} = \boldsymbol{\Gamma}'\boldsymbol{\Gamma}$ is not unique.

THEOREM 3.3.4

If χ is distributed $\mathbf{N}(\mathbf{x} : \boldsymbol{\mu}, \boldsymbol{\Sigma})$, where χ is a $p \times 1$ vector, and if the rank of $\boldsymbol{\Sigma}$ is p, then χ has a p.d.f. and it is given by

$$\mathbf{n}(\mathbf{x} : \boldsymbol{\mu}, \boldsymbol{\Sigma}) = \left(\frac{1}{(2\pi)^{p/2}|\boldsymbol{\Sigma}|^{1/2}}\right) exp[-\tfrac{1}{2}(\mathbf{x} - \boldsymbol{\mu})'\boldsymbol{\Sigma}^{-1}(\mathbf{x} - \boldsymbol{\mu})] \qquad \mathbf{x} \in E_p \qquad (3.3.5)$$

Proof

If $p = K$, then $\boldsymbol{\Sigma}^{-1}$ exists, and clearly $\mathbf{n}(\mathbf{x} : \boldsymbol{\mu}, \boldsymbol{\Sigma})$ is a p.d.f. since $\mathbf{n}(\mathbf{x} : \boldsymbol{\mu}, \boldsymbol{\Sigma}) \geq 0$ for all $\mathbf{x}$ in E_p, and it can be shown that $\int_{-\infty}^{\infty} \cdots \int_{-\infty}^{\infty} \times \mathbf{n}(\mathbf{x} : \boldsymbol{\mu}, \boldsymbol{\Sigma})\, d\mathbf{x} = 1$ by using Theorem 1.10.1. We shall find the m.g.f. of a random vector χ with p.d.f. given by Equation (3.3.5). We get $m_{\chi}(\mathbf{t}) = \mathscr{E}[e^{\mathbf{t}'\chi}] = \int_{-\infty}^{\infty} \cdots \int_{-\infty}^{\infty} e^{\mathbf{t}'\mathbf{x}}\, \mathbf{n}(\mathbf{x} : \boldsymbol{\mu}, \boldsymbol{\Sigma})\, d\mathbf{x}$, which, after substituting for $\mathbf{n}(\mathbf{x} : \boldsymbol{\mu}, \boldsymbol{\Sigma})$ and simplifying, is

$$m_{\chi}(\mathbf{t}) = \int_{-\infty}^{\infty} \cdots \int_{-\infty}^{\infty} \frac{\exp[-\tfrac{1}{2}\mathbf{x}'\boldsymbol{\Sigma}^{-1}\mathbf{x} + (\boldsymbol{\Sigma}^{-1}\boldsymbol{\mu} + \mathbf{t})'\mathbf{x} - \tfrac{1}{2}\boldsymbol{\mu}'\boldsymbol{\Sigma}^{-1}\boldsymbol{\mu}]}{(2\pi)^{p/2}|\boldsymbol{\Sigma}|^{1/2}}\, d\mathbf{x}$$

We evaluate the integral by using Theorem 1.10.1 and obtain

$$m_{\chi}(\mathbf{t}) = \exp(\mathbf{t}'\boldsymbol{\mu} + \tfrac{1}{2}\mathbf{t}'\boldsymbol{\Sigma}\mathbf{t}) \qquad \mathbf{t} \in E_p$$

But this is the m.g.f. of a p-variate normal random vector with c.d.f. $\mathbf{N}(\mathbf{x} : \boldsymbol{\mu}, \boldsymbol{\Sigma})$, where $\boldsymbol{\Sigma}$ has rank p. This completes the proof.

Note 3. In Definition 3.3.2, if $K < p$, then χ does not have a p.d.f.

We stated that linear functions of multivariate normal random variables are of particular significance in the theory of the linear model, and in fact a p-variate normal random vector was defined in terms of linear functions of *independent standard* normal random variables Z_i. Next we examine linear functions of the p-variate normal random vector.

THEOREM 3.3.5

Let the $p \times 1$ random vector $\boldsymbol{\chi}$ be distributed $N(\mathbf{x} : \boldsymbol{\mu}, \boldsymbol{\Sigma})$, where $\boldsymbol{\Sigma}$ has rank K, let $\mathbf{B}$ be any $q \times p$ matrix of constants, and let $\mathbf{b}$ be any $q \times 1$ vector of constants. Then the $q \times 1$ vector $\mathbf{Y}$ defined by $\mathbf{Y} = \mathbf{B}\boldsymbol{\chi} + \mathbf{b}$ is distributed $N(\mathbf{y} : \mathbf{B}\boldsymbol{\mu} + \mathbf{b}, \mathbf{B}\boldsymbol{\Sigma}\mathbf{B}')$.

Proof

We shall find the m.g.f. of $\mathbf{Y}$ and use Theorem 2.3.1. We obtain

$$m_{\mathbf{Y}}(\mathbf{t}) = \mathscr{E}[e^{\mathbf{t}'\mathbf{Y}}] = \mathscr{E}[e^{\mathbf{t}'(\mathbf{B}\boldsymbol{\chi}+\mathbf{b})}] = e^{\mathbf{t}'\mathbf{b}}\,\mathscr{E}[e^{(\mathbf{t}'\mathbf{B})\boldsymbol{\chi}}] = e^{\mathbf{t}'\mathbf{b}} m_{\boldsymbol{\chi}}(\mathbf{B}'\mathbf{t})$$

and by Equation (3.3.4) we obtain

$$m_{\mathbf{Y}}(\mathbf{t}) = \exp[\mathbf{t}'(\mathbf{B}\boldsymbol{\mu} + \mathbf{b}) + \tfrac{1}{2}\mathbf{t}'(\mathbf{B}\boldsymbol{\Sigma}\mathbf{B}')\mathbf{t}] \qquad \mathbf{t} \in E_q$$

But this is the m.g.f. of a normal random vector with mean $\mathbf{B}\boldsymbol{\mu} + \mathbf{b}$ and covariance matrix $\mathbf{B}\boldsymbol{\Sigma}\mathbf{B}'$, and the theorem is proved.

COROLLARY 3.3.5

Let $\boldsymbol{\chi}$ have a p-variate normal distribution of rank K with mean $\boldsymbol{\mu}$ and covariance $\boldsymbol{\Sigma}$. There exists a $K \times p$ matrix $\mathbf{B}$ and a $K \times 1$ vector $\mathbf{b}$ such that the $K \times 1$ vector $\mathbf{Z}$ defined by $\mathbf{Z} = \mathbf{B}\boldsymbol{\chi} + \mathbf{b}$ has the standard K-variate normal distribution, that is, $\mathbf{Z}$ is distributed $N(\mathbf{z} : \mathbf{0}, \mathbf{I})$.

Proof

Since the hypothesis states that $\boldsymbol{\chi}$ has a normal distribution of rank K, this means $\boldsymbol{\Sigma}$ has rank K and $\boldsymbol{\Sigma} = \boldsymbol{\Gamma}'\boldsymbol{\Gamma}$ where $\boldsymbol{\Gamma}$ is $K \times p$ of rank K. Hence $\boldsymbol{\Gamma}\boldsymbol{\Gamma}'$ is nonsingular. Note that $\boldsymbol{\Gamma}'(\boldsymbol{\Gamma}\boldsymbol{\Gamma}')^{-1} = \boldsymbol{\Gamma}^{-}$. Define $\mathbf{B}$ to be $\boldsymbol{\Gamma}'^{-}$ and $\mathbf{b}$ to be $-\boldsymbol{\Gamma}'^{-}\boldsymbol{\mu}$. $\mathbf{Z} = \mathbf{B}\boldsymbol{\chi} + \mathbf{b} = \boldsymbol{\Gamma}'^{-}\boldsymbol{\chi} - \boldsymbol{\Gamma}'^{-}\boldsymbol{\mu} = \boldsymbol{\Gamma}'^{-}(\boldsymbol{\chi} - \boldsymbol{\mu})$, and we can use the results of Theorem 3.3.5. Note that $\mathbf{B}\boldsymbol{\Sigma}\mathbf{B}' = \boldsymbol{\Gamma}'^{-}\boldsymbol{\Sigma}\boldsymbol{\Gamma}^{-} = \mathbf{I}$, since $\boldsymbol{\Gamma}\boldsymbol{\Gamma}^{-} = \mathbf{I}$. Also, $\mathbf{B}\boldsymbol{\mu} + \mathbf{b} = \boldsymbol{\Gamma}'^{-}\boldsymbol{\mu} - \boldsymbol{\Gamma}'^{-}\boldsymbol{\mu} = \mathbf{0}$.

Summary. We have defined a multivariate normal random vector in terms of linear functions of *independent univariate standard normal* random variables. Thus if $\boldsymbol{\chi}_1$ has a p-variate normal distribution of rank K with mean $\boldsymbol{\mu}$ and covariance $\boldsymbol{\Sigma}$ (where $\boldsymbol{\Sigma} = \boldsymbol{\Gamma}'\boldsymbol{\Gamma}$), then we can use $\boldsymbol{\chi}_1 = \boldsymbol{\Gamma}'\mathbf{Z}_1 + \boldsymbol{\mu}$ to transform from $\mathbf{Z}_1$, which is distributed $N(\mathbf{z}_1 : \mathbf{0}, \mathbf{I})$, to $\boldsymbol{\chi}_1$, which is distributed $N(\mathbf{x}_1 : \boldsymbol{\mu}, \boldsymbol{\Sigma})$; and we can use $\mathbf{Z}_0 = \boldsymbol{\Gamma}'^{-}\boldsymbol{\chi}_0 - \boldsymbol{\Gamma}'^{-}\boldsymbol{\mu}$ to transform from $\boldsymbol{\chi}_0$, which is distributed

$N(\mathbf{x}_0 : \boldsymbol{\mu}, \boldsymbol{\Sigma})$, to $\mathbf{Z}_0$, which is distributed $N(\mathbf{z}_0 : \mathbf{0}, \mathbf{I})$. Also, the c.d.f., the m.g.f., and the p.d.f. (if it exists) are completely specified by $\boldsymbol{\mu}$ and $\boldsymbol{\Sigma}$ (or by $\boldsymbol{\mu}$ and $\boldsymbol{\Gamma}$). We end this section with an important theorem.

THEOREM 3.3.6

Let the $p \times 1$ random vector $\boldsymbol{\chi}$ be distributed $N(\mathbf{x} : \mathbf{0}, \sigma^2\mathbf{I})$, and define the $p \times 1$ vector $\mathbf{Y}$ by $\mathbf{Y} = \mathbf{P}\boldsymbol{\chi}$, where $\mathbf{P}$ is a $p \times p$ orthogonal matrix. Then $\mathbf{Y}$ is distributed $N(\mathbf{y} : \mathbf{0}, \sigma^2\mathbf{I})$.

Proof

The proof is obtained by using Theorem 3.3.5 with $\boldsymbol{\mu} = \mathbf{0}$, $\boldsymbol{\Sigma} = \sigma^2\mathbf{I}$, $\mathbf{b} = \mathbf{0}$, and $\mathbf{B} = \mathbf{P}$.

This theorem states that if X_i are independent normal random variables with means zero and variances σ^2, and if $\boldsymbol{\chi}$ is transformed to $\mathbf{Y}$ by an orthogonal transformation, then the Y_i have the same distribution as the X_i.

3.4 Marginal Distributions

When the distribution of a random vector, say $\boldsymbol{\chi}$, is considered, it is also often necessary to consider the joint distribution of any subset of the elements in $\boldsymbol{\chi}$. For example, if $\boldsymbol{\chi}$ is a $p \times 1$ random vector with c.d.f. $N(\mathbf{x} : \boldsymbol{\mu}, \boldsymbol{\Sigma})$, it may be desirable to find the joint distribution of the first q, $0 < q < p$, elements of $\boldsymbol{\chi}$. If we partition $\boldsymbol{\chi}$ as

$$\boldsymbol{\chi} = \begin{bmatrix} \boldsymbol{\chi}_1 \\ \boldsymbol{\chi}_2 \end{bmatrix}$$

where $\boldsymbol{\chi}_1$ has size $q \times 1$, then the distribution of $\boldsymbol{\chi}_1$ is sometimes called the *marginal* distribution of $\boldsymbol{\chi}_1$. We remark that the word marginal is not needed but it is often used and refers to the fact that $\boldsymbol{\chi}_1$ is a subset of another vector $\boldsymbol{\chi}$. We shall derive the distribution of $\boldsymbol{\chi}_1$ from a knowledge of the distribution of $\boldsymbol{\chi}$.

THEOREM 3.4.1

Let the $p \times 1$ random vector $\boldsymbol{\chi}$ be distributed $N(\mathbf{x} : \boldsymbol{\mu}, \boldsymbol{\Sigma})$, and partition $\boldsymbol{\chi}$, $\boldsymbol{\mu}$, and $\boldsymbol{\Sigma}$ as

$$\boldsymbol{\chi} = \begin{bmatrix} \boldsymbol{\chi}_1 \\ \boldsymbol{\chi}_2 \end{bmatrix} \qquad \boldsymbol{\mu} = \begin{bmatrix} \boldsymbol{\mu}_1 \\ \boldsymbol{\mu}_2 \end{bmatrix} \qquad \boldsymbol{\Sigma} = \begin{bmatrix} \boldsymbol{\Sigma}_{11} & \boldsymbol{\Sigma}_{12} \\ \boldsymbol{\Sigma}_{21} & \boldsymbol{\Sigma}_{22} \end{bmatrix} \tag{3.4.1}$$

where $\boldsymbol{\chi}_1$ and $\boldsymbol{\mu}_1$ are $q \times 1$ vectors, $\boldsymbol{\Sigma}_{11}$ is a $q \times q$ matrix ($0 < q < p$), and the size *of the remaining vectors and matrices are thus determined. The random vector $\boldsymbol{\chi}_1$ is normally distributed with mean $\boldsymbol{\mu}_1$ and covariance matrix $\boldsymbol{\Sigma}_{11}$, that is, $\boldsymbol{\chi}_1$ is distributed* $\mathbf{N}(\mathbf{x}_1 : \boldsymbol{\mu}_1, \boldsymbol{\Sigma}_{11})$.

Proof

Let the $q \times p$ matrix $\mathbf{B}$ be defined by $\mathbf{B} = [\mathbf{I}, \mathbf{0}]$, where $\mathbf{I}$ is the $q \times q$ identity matrix. Clearly we can obtain $\boldsymbol{\chi}_1$ from the equation $\boldsymbol{\chi}_1 = \mathbf{B}\boldsymbol{\chi}$. We can then use Theorem 3.3.5 with $\mathbf{b} = \mathbf{0}$ to find the distribution of $\boldsymbol{\chi}_1$. We obtain the result that $\boldsymbol{\chi}_1$ is distributed $\mathbf{N}(\mathbf{x}_1 : \mathbf{B}\boldsymbol{\mu}, \mathbf{B\Sigma B}')$, but $\mathbf{B}\boldsymbol{\mu} = \boldsymbol{\mu}_1$ and $\mathbf{B\Sigma B}' = \boldsymbol{\Sigma}_{11}$, and the theorem is proved.

Clearly if we want the joint distribution of *any* subset of the elements in $\boldsymbol{\chi}$, then a similar result holds. In fact, let $\boldsymbol{\chi}_0$ be any vector obtained from $\boldsymbol{\chi}$ by striking out any $p - q$ variables, $0 < p - q < p$. Then $\boldsymbol{\chi}_0$ is distributed $\mathbf{N}(\mathbf{x}_0 : \boldsymbol{\mu}_0, \boldsymbol{\Sigma}_0)$, where $\boldsymbol{\mu}_0$ is obtained from $\boldsymbol{\mu}$ by striking out the same rows that were struck from $\boldsymbol{\chi}$ to obtain $\boldsymbol{\chi}_0$, and $\boldsymbol{\Sigma}_0$ is obtained by striking the same rows (and columns) from $\boldsymbol{\Sigma}$ that were struck from $\boldsymbol{\chi}$.

Example 3.4.1

Suppose $\boldsymbol{\chi}$ is distributed $\mathbf{N}(\mathbf{x} : \boldsymbol{\mu}, \boldsymbol{\Sigma})$, where

$$\boldsymbol{\mu} = \begin{bmatrix} 1 \\ 2 \\ 0 \\ -1 \end{bmatrix} \qquad \boldsymbol{\Sigma} = \begin{bmatrix} 2 & 2 & 3 & 0 \\ 2 & 2 & 3 & 0 \\ 3 & 3 & 5 & -1 \\ 0 & 0 & -1 & 2 \end{bmatrix}$$

The distribution of

$$\boldsymbol{\chi}_0 = \begin{bmatrix} X_1 \\ X_3 \end{bmatrix}$$

is $\mathbf{N}(\mathbf{x}_0 : \boldsymbol{\mu}_0, \boldsymbol{\Sigma}_0)$, where

$$\boldsymbol{\mu}_0 = \begin{bmatrix} 1 \\ 0 \end{bmatrix} \qquad \boldsymbol{\Sigma}_0 = \begin{bmatrix} 2 & 3 \\ 3 & 5 \end{bmatrix}$$

$\boldsymbol{\chi}_0$ is obtained by striking rows 2 and 4 from $\boldsymbol{\chi}$; hence $\boldsymbol{\mu}_0$ is obtained by striking rows 2 and 4 from $\boldsymbol{\mu}$, and $\boldsymbol{\Sigma}_0$ is obtained by striking rows 2 and 4 and columns 2 and 4 from $\boldsymbol{\Sigma}$.

3.5 Independent and Uncorrelated Random Vectors

In this section we define uncorrelated random vectors and derive methods to determine if random vectors are independent when they have a normal distribution. Let $\boldsymbol{\chi}$ be a $p \times 1$ random vector that is partitioned into M subvectors as follows:

$$\boldsymbol{\chi} = \begin{bmatrix} \boldsymbol{\chi}_1 \\ \boldsymbol{\chi}_2 \\ \vdots \\ \boldsymbol{\chi}_M \end{bmatrix} \tag{3.5.1}$$

where the subvector $\boldsymbol{\chi}_i$ has size $q_i \times 1$, where $q_i > 0$ and $\sum_{i=1}^{M} q_i = p$. We partition $\boldsymbol{\mu}$ and $\boldsymbol{\Sigma}$ similarly, where $\mathscr{E}[\boldsymbol{\chi}] = \boldsymbol{\mu}$ and $\mathbf{cov}[\boldsymbol{\chi}] = \boldsymbol{\Sigma}$. We obtain

$$\boldsymbol{\mu} = \begin{bmatrix} \boldsymbol{\mu}_1 \\ \boldsymbol{\mu}_2 \\ \vdots \\ \boldsymbol{\mu}_M \end{bmatrix} \qquad \boldsymbol{\Sigma} = \begin{bmatrix} \boldsymbol{\Sigma}_{11} & \boldsymbol{\Sigma}_{12} & \cdots & \boldsymbol{\Sigma}_{1M} \\ \boldsymbol{\Sigma}_{21} & \boldsymbol{\Sigma}_{22} & \cdots & \boldsymbol{\Sigma}_{2M} \\ \vdots & \vdots & & \vdots \\ \boldsymbol{\Sigma}_{M1} & \boldsymbol{\Sigma}_{M2} & \cdots & \boldsymbol{\Sigma}_{MM} \end{bmatrix} \tag{3.5.2}$$

where $\boldsymbol{\mu}_i$ has size $q_i \times 1$, $\boldsymbol{\Sigma}_{ij}$ has size $q_i \times q_j$. Clearly $\mathscr{E}[\boldsymbol{\chi}_i] = \boldsymbol{\mu}_i$, and we denote $\mathbf{cov}[\boldsymbol{\chi}_i, \boldsymbol{\chi}_j]$ by $\boldsymbol{\Sigma}_{ij}$, and define $\boldsymbol{\Sigma}_{ij}$ by

$$\boldsymbol{\Sigma}_{ij} = \mathscr{E}\{[\boldsymbol{\chi}_i - \mathscr{E}(\boldsymbol{\chi}_i)][\boldsymbol{\chi}_j - \mathscr{E}(\boldsymbol{\chi}_j)]'\}$$

The rsth element of $\boldsymbol{\Sigma}_{ij}$ is

$$\mathscr{E}\{[X_{ir} - \mathscr{E}(X_{ir})][X_{js} - \mathscr{E}(X_{js})]\}$$

where X_{ir} represents the rth element in the vector $\boldsymbol{\chi}_i$, and so on. Note that the above partitioning is defined for any random vector $\boldsymbol{\chi}$ whose mean and covariance matrix exist; it does not require $\boldsymbol{\chi}$ to be normally distributed. Now we state what is meant by two random vectors being uncorrelated.

DEFINITION 3.5.1

Uncorrelated Random Vectors. *Let $\boldsymbol{\chi}_i$ and $\boldsymbol{\chi}_j$ be two distinct random vectors that have any joint distribution (not necessarily normal) such that the joint covariance matrix exists. The two vectors are defined to be uncorrelated if and only if* $\mathbf{cov}[\boldsymbol{\chi}_i, \boldsymbol{\chi}_j] = \mathbf{0}$.

It is often necessary to determine if random vectors are jointly independent, but it is usually much easier to determine if they are *pairwise uncorrelated.* However, if the vectors have a *normal* distribution and are *pairwise uncorrelated,* they are also *jointly independent*; this is an important result which we now state as a theorem.

THEOREM 3.5.1

Let the $p \times 1$ *random vector* χ *be distributed* $\mathbf{N}(\mathbf{x} : \boldsymbol{\mu}, \boldsymbol{\Sigma})$, *and let* χ, $\boldsymbol{\mu}$, *and* $\boldsymbol{\Sigma}$ *be partitioned as in Equation* (3.5.1) *and Equation* (3.5.2). *The vectors* $\chi_1, \chi_2, \ldots, \chi_M$ *are jointly independent if and only if* $\boldsymbol{\Sigma}_{ij} = \mathbf{0}$ *for all* $i \neq j$.

Proof

(*If*) The m.g.f. of χ is

$$m_\chi(\mathbf{t}) = \mathscr{E}[e^{\mathbf{t}'\chi}] = \exp(\mathbf{t}'\boldsymbol{\mu} + \tfrac{1}{2}\mathbf{t}'\boldsymbol{\Sigma}\mathbf{t}) = \exp\left(\sum_{i=1}^{M} \mathbf{t}_i'\boldsymbol{\mu}_i + \tfrac{1}{2}\sum_{i=1}^{M}\sum_{j=1}^{M} \mathbf{t}_i'\boldsymbol{\Sigma}_{ij}\mathbf{t}_j\right)$$

Since $\boldsymbol{\Sigma}_{ij} = \mathbf{0}$ for all $i \neq j$, we get

$$\begin{aligned} m_\chi(\mathbf{t}) &= \exp(\mathbf{t}_1'\boldsymbol{\mu}_1 + \tfrac{1}{2}\mathbf{t}_1'\boldsymbol{\Sigma}_{11}\mathbf{t}_1) \\ &\quad \times \exp(\mathbf{t}_2'\boldsymbol{\mu}_2 + \tfrac{1}{2}\mathbf{t}_2'\boldsymbol{\Sigma}_{22}\mathbf{t}_2)\cdots\exp(\mathbf{t}_M'\boldsymbol{\mu}_M + \tfrac{1}{2}\mathbf{t}_M'\boldsymbol{\Sigma}_{MM}\mathbf{t}_M) \\ &= m_{\chi_1}(\mathbf{t}_1)m_{\chi_2}(\mathbf{t}_2)\cdots m_{\chi_M}(\mathbf{t}_M) \end{aligned}$$

since by Theorem 3.4.1, χ_i is distributed $\mathbf{N}(\mathbf{x}_i : \boldsymbol{\mu}_i, \boldsymbol{\Sigma}_{ii})$, and by Theorem 3.3.3 the m.g.f. of χ_i is $\exp(\mathbf{t}_i'\boldsymbol{\mu}_i + \tfrac{1}{2}\mathbf{t}_i'\boldsymbol{\Sigma}_{ii}\mathbf{t}_i)$. Thus by Equation (2.4.3) in Definition 2.4.1, the vectors $\chi_1, \chi_2, \ldots, \chi_M$ are jointly independent.

(*Only if*) Assume the vectors are jointly independent. For any $i \neq j$ we obtain

$$\begin{aligned} \boldsymbol{\Sigma}_{ij} &= \mathbf{cov}[\chi_i, \chi_j] = \mathscr{E}[(\chi_i - \boldsymbol{\mu}_i)(\chi_j - \boldsymbol{\mu}_j)'] \\ &= \mathscr{E}[(\chi_i - \boldsymbol{\mu}_i)]\mathscr{E}[(\chi_j - \boldsymbol{\mu}_j)'] = \mathbf{0} \end{aligned}$$

and the theorem is proved.

Note 1. If χ has a normal distribution, this is a relatively easy way to check independence. Also we note that any subvector can consist of a single element, so Theorem 3.5.1 can be used to determine whether the elements within a vector are independent. If the *ij*th element, $i \neq j$, in $\boldsymbol{\Sigma}$ is zero, then X_i and X_j are independent. For instance, in Example 3.4.1, X_1 and X_4 are independent, as are X_2 and X_4, but no other two random variables in χ are independent.

3.6 Conditional Distribution

When the distribution of a random vector is under consideration, it may be desirable to evaluate the conditional distribution of a subset of the elements of the vector given that other elements are held fixed. We shall consider only the case where $\boldsymbol{\chi}$ has a p.d.f.

THEOREM 3.6.1

Let the $p \times 1$ vector $\boldsymbol{\chi}$ be distributed $\mathbf{N}(\mathbf{x} : \boldsymbol{\mu}, \boldsymbol{\Sigma})$, where $\boldsymbol{\Sigma}$ has rank p. Let $\boldsymbol{\chi}$, $\boldsymbol{\mu}$, and $\boldsymbol{\Sigma}$ be partitioned as in Equation (3.4.1), where $\boldsymbol{\chi}_1$ has size $q \times 1$, where $0 < q < p$. The conditional distribution of $\boldsymbol{\chi}_1$ given $\boldsymbol{\chi}_2 = \mathbf{c}_2$, where $\mathbf{c}_2$ is a vector of constants, is normal with mean $\boldsymbol{\mu}_1 + \boldsymbol{\Sigma}_{12}\boldsymbol{\Sigma}_{22}^{-1}(\mathbf{c}_2 - \boldsymbol{\mu}_2)$ and covariance matrix $\boldsymbol{\Sigma}_{11.2}$, where $\boldsymbol{\Sigma}_{11.2} = \boldsymbol{\Sigma}_{11} - \boldsymbol{\Sigma}_{12}\boldsymbol{\Sigma}_{22}^{-1}\boldsymbol{\Sigma}_{21}$.

Proof

Let $f(\mathbf{x}_1, \mathbf{x}_2)$ represent the p.d.f. of $\boldsymbol{\chi}$, and let $f_2(\mathbf{x}_2)$ represent the marginal p.d.f. of $\boldsymbol{\chi}_2$. If $(\boldsymbol{\chi}_1 \mid \boldsymbol{\chi}_2 = \mathbf{c}_2)$ is denoted by $\mathbf{Y}$, and if the conditional p.d.f. of $\boldsymbol{\chi}_1$ given $\boldsymbol{\chi}_2 = \mathbf{c}_2$ is denoted by $g_{\boldsymbol{\chi}_1|\mathbf{c}_2}(\mathbf{y})$, or by $g_{\mathbf{Y}}(\mathbf{y} : \mathbf{c}_2)$, then

$$g_{\mathbf{Y}}(\mathbf{y} : \mathbf{c}_2) = g_{\boldsymbol{\chi}_1|\mathbf{c}_2}(\mathbf{y}) = \frac{f(\mathbf{y}, \mathbf{c}_2)}{f_2(\mathbf{c}_2)} \qquad \text{when } f_2(\mathbf{c}_2) > 0$$

The p.d.f. of $\boldsymbol{\chi}$ is normal with mean $\boldsymbol{\mu}$ and covariance $\boldsymbol{\Sigma}$; the p.d.f. of $\boldsymbol{\chi}_2$ is normal with mean $\boldsymbol{\mu}_2$ and covariance $\boldsymbol{\Sigma}_{22}$. Hence we obtain

$$g_{\mathbf{Y}}(\mathbf{y} : \mathbf{c}_2) = \frac{(2\pi)^{-p/2}|\boldsymbol{\Sigma}|^{-1/2}\exp\left(-\frac{1}{2}\begin{bmatrix}\mathbf{y} - \boldsymbol{\mu}_1 \\ \mathbf{c}_2 - \boldsymbol{\mu}_2\end{bmatrix}'\begin{bmatrix}\boldsymbol{\Sigma}_{11} & \boldsymbol{\Sigma}_{12} \\ \boldsymbol{\Sigma}_{21} & \boldsymbol{\Sigma}_{22}\end{bmatrix}^{-1}\begin{bmatrix}\mathbf{y} - \boldsymbol{\mu}_1 \\ \mathbf{c}_2 - \boldsymbol{\mu}_2\end{bmatrix}\right)}{(2\pi)^{-(p-q)/2}|\boldsymbol{\Sigma}_{22}|^{-1/2}\exp[-\frac{1}{2}(\mathbf{c}_2 - \boldsymbol{\mu}_2)'\boldsymbol{\Sigma}_{22}^{-1}(\mathbf{c}_2 - \boldsymbol{\mu}_2)]}$$

If we use Theorem 1.3.1 and substitute for $\boldsymbol{\Sigma}^{-1}$, we get

$$\begin{bmatrix}\boldsymbol{\Sigma}_{11} & \boldsymbol{\Sigma}_{12} \\ \boldsymbol{\Sigma}_{21} & \boldsymbol{\Sigma}_{22}\end{bmatrix}^{-1} = \begin{bmatrix}\boldsymbol{\Sigma}_{11.2}^{-1} & -\boldsymbol{\Sigma}_{11.2}^{-1}\boldsymbol{\Sigma}_{12}\boldsymbol{\Sigma}_{22}^{-1} \\ -\boldsymbol{\Sigma}_{22}^{-1}\boldsymbol{\Sigma}_{21}\boldsymbol{\Sigma}_{11.2}^{-1} & \boldsymbol{\Sigma}_{22.1}^{-1}\end{bmatrix} = \begin{bmatrix}\boldsymbol{\Sigma}_{11.2}^{-1} & -\boldsymbol{\Sigma}_{11}^{-1}\boldsymbol{\Sigma}_{12}\boldsymbol{\Sigma}_{22.1}^{-1} \\ -\boldsymbol{\Sigma}_{22.1}^{-1}\boldsymbol{\Sigma}_{21}\boldsymbol{\Sigma}_{11}^{-1} & \boldsymbol{\Sigma}_{22.1}^{-1}\end{bmatrix}$$

where $\boldsymbol{\Sigma}_{11.2} = \boldsymbol{\Sigma}_{11} - \boldsymbol{\Sigma}_{12}\boldsymbol{\Sigma}_{22}^{-1}\boldsymbol{\Sigma}_{21}$ and $\boldsymbol{\Sigma}_{22.1} = \boldsymbol{\Sigma}_{22} - \boldsymbol{\Sigma}_{21}\boldsymbol{\Sigma}_{11}^{-1}\boldsymbol{\Sigma}_{12}$. Finally,

$$g_{\mathbf{Y}}(\mathbf{y} : \mathbf{c}_2) = \left(\frac{1}{(2\pi)^{q/2}}\right)\left(\frac{|\boldsymbol{\Sigma}_{22}|^{1/2}}{|\boldsymbol{\Sigma}|^{1/2}}\right) e^{-(1/2)Q+(1/2)Q_2}$$

where

$$Q = (\mathbf{y} - \boldsymbol{\mu}_1)'\boldsymbol{\Sigma}_{11.2}^{-1}(\mathbf{y} - \boldsymbol{\mu}_1) - (\mathbf{y} - \boldsymbol{\mu}_1)'\boldsymbol{\Sigma}_{11.2}^{-1}\boldsymbol{\Sigma}_{12}\boldsymbol{\Sigma}_{22}^{-1}(\mathbf{c}_2 - \boldsymbol{\mu}_2)$$
$$- (\mathbf{c}_2 - \boldsymbol{\mu}_2)'\boldsymbol{\Sigma}_{22}^{-1}\boldsymbol{\Sigma}_{21}\boldsymbol{\Sigma}_{11.2}^{-1}(\mathbf{y} - \boldsymbol{\mu}_1) + (\mathbf{c}_2 - \boldsymbol{\mu}_2)'\boldsymbol{\Sigma}_{22.1}^{-1}(\mathbf{c}_2 - \boldsymbol{\mu}_2)$$

and $Q_2 = (\mathbf{c}_2 - \boldsymbol{\mu}_2)'\boldsymbol{\Sigma}_{22}^{-1}(\mathbf{c}_2 - \boldsymbol{\mu}_2)$.

Now use Theorem 1.3.2 and substitute $|\boldsymbol{\Sigma}_{22}|\,|\boldsymbol{\Sigma}_{11.2}|$ for $|\boldsymbol{\Sigma}|$. We obtain

$$g_{\mathbf{Y}}(\mathbf{y} : \mathbf{c}_2) = \left(\frac{1}{(2\pi)^{q/2}}\right)\left(\frac{|\boldsymbol{\Sigma}_{22}|^{1/2}}{|\boldsymbol{\Sigma}_{22}|^{1/2}|\boldsymbol{\Sigma}_{11.2}|^{1/2}}\right) e^{-(1/2)Q_1}$$

where $Q_1 = Q - Q_2 = [(\mathbf{y} - \boldsymbol{\mu}_1) - \boldsymbol{\Sigma}_{12}\boldsymbol{\Sigma}_{22}^{-1}(\mathbf{c}_2 - \boldsymbol{\mu}_2)]'\boldsymbol{\Sigma}_{11.2}^{-1}[(\mathbf{y} - \boldsymbol{\mu}_1) - \boldsymbol{\Sigma}_{12}\boldsymbol{\Sigma}_{22}^{-1}(\mathbf{c}_2 - \boldsymbol{\mu}_2)]$. Clearly for $\boldsymbol{\chi}_2$ fixed at $\mathbf{c}_2$, the quantity $\boldsymbol{\mu}_1 + \boldsymbol{\Sigma}_{12}\boldsymbol{\Sigma}_{22}^{-1}(\mathbf{c}_2 - \boldsymbol{\mu}_2) = \mathbf{h}$, say, is a fixed $q \times 1$ vector, and we obtain

$$g_{\mathbf{Y}}(\mathbf{y} : \mathbf{c}_2) = \left(\frac{1}{(2\pi)^{q/2}|\boldsymbol{\Sigma}_{11.2}|^{1/2}}\right) \exp[-\tfrac{1}{2}(\mathbf{y} - \mathbf{h})'\boldsymbol{\Sigma}_{11.2}^{-1}(\mathbf{y} - \mathbf{h})] \qquad \mathbf{y} \in E_q$$

but by Theorem 3.3.4 this is the p.d.f. of a normal distribution with mean $\mathbf{h} = \boldsymbol{\mu}_1 + \boldsymbol{\Sigma}_{12}\boldsymbol{\Sigma}_{22}^{-1}(\mathbf{c}_2 - \boldsymbol{\mu}_2)$ and covariance $\boldsymbol{\Sigma}_{11.2}$, and the theorem is proved.

Notation. For convenience we sometimes use the notation $(\boldsymbol{\chi}_1 \mid \mathbf{c}_2)$ for a random variable that has a conditional c.d.f. (or p.d.f.) of $\boldsymbol{\chi}_1$ given $\boldsymbol{\chi}_2 = \mathbf{c}_2$.

COROLLARY 3.6.1

Let the $p \times 1$ random vector $\boldsymbol{\chi}$ be distributed $\mathbf{N}(\mathbf{x} : \boldsymbol{\mu}, \boldsymbol{\Sigma})$, and partition $\boldsymbol{\chi}$ as in Equation (3.4.1). The covariance matrix $\boldsymbol{\Sigma}_{11.2}$ of the c.d.f. of $(\boldsymbol{\chi}_1 \mid \mathbf{c}_2)$, which we denote by $\mathbf{cov}[(\boldsymbol{\chi}_1 \mid \mathbf{c}_2)]$, does not depend on the value of $\mathbf{c}_2$. The mean of the c.d.f. of $(\boldsymbol{\chi}_1 \mid \mathbf{c}_2)$, which we denote by $\mathscr{E}[(\boldsymbol{\chi}_1 \mid \mathbf{c}_2)]$, depends on the value of $\mathbf{c}_2$ unless $\boldsymbol{\Sigma}_{12} = \mathbf{0}$, which is a necessary and sufficient condition for $\boldsymbol{\chi}_1$ and $\boldsymbol{\chi}_2$ to be independent.

The equation $\mathscr{E}[(\boldsymbol{\chi}_1 \mid \mathbf{c}_2)] = \boldsymbol{\mu}_1 + \boldsymbol{\Sigma}_{12}\boldsymbol{\Sigma}_{22}^{-1}(\mathbf{c}_2 - \boldsymbol{\mu}_2)$ is very useful in predicting $\boldsymbol{\chi}_1$ by using the variables in $\boldsymbol{\chi}_2$. This theory of prediction is especially useful when $q = 1$ and $\boldsymbol{\chi}_1$ can then be viewed as a scalar. The theory is known as normal regression theory, and the equation $\mathscr{E}[(X_1 \mid \mathbf{c}_2)] = \mu_1 + \boldsymbol{\Sigma}_{12}\boldsymbol{\Sigma}_{22}^{-1}(\mathbf{c}_2 - \boldsymbol{\mu}_2)$ is called the regression equation of X_1 on the variables in $\boldsymbol{\chi}_2$. In the next section we discuss regression theory when the basic vectors are normally distributed, and in a later chapter we consider regression theory for the case when $\boldsymbol{\chi}$ is not necessarily normally distributed.

Note 1. The covariance matrix of the conditional normal p.d.f. which we denote by $\mathbf{\Sigma}_{11.2}$ can be obtained from the covariance matrix $\mathbf{\Sigma}$ in two ways:

1. by the formula $\mathbf{\Sigma}_{11.2} = \mathbf{\Sigma}_{11} - \mathbf{\Sigma}_{12}\mathbf{\Sigma}_{22}^{-1}\mathbf{\Sigma}_{21}$;

2. by crossing out the rows and columns in $\mathbf{\Sigma}^{-1}$ that correspond to the elements in $\boldsymbol{\chi}_2$ and inverting the resulting matrix, that is, if we let $\mathbf{\Delta} = \mathbf{\Sigma}^{-1}$ and partition $\mathbf{\Delta}$ into the same size submatrices as we partitioned $\mathbf{\Sigma}$, then $\mathbf{\Sigma}_{11.2} = \mathbf{\Delta}_{11}^{-1}$; see Theorem 1.3.1. (3.6.1)

Notation. Let $\boldsymbol{\chi}$ be a $p \times 1$ vector which is partitioned as in Equation (3.4.1). The symbol $\sigma_{ij|(q+1,\ldots,p)}$ will be used to mean the covariance of X_i and X_j in the conditional p.d.f. of $(\boldsymbol{\chi}_1 \mid \boldsymbol{\chi}_2 = \mathbf{c}_2)$. In this symbol i and j can be any two variables in $\boldsymbol{\chi}_1$ and the integers after the vertical line must include the subscripts of *all* random variables in $\boldsymbol{\chi}_2$, that is, $X_{q+1}, X_{q+2}, \ldots, X_p$. Thus by definition $\sigma_{ij|(q+1,\ldots,p)}$ is the ijth element of $\mathbf{\Sigma}_{11.2}$.

3.7 Regression

In this section we define and discuss some aspects of regression theory for the multivariate normal distribution. In later chapters we discuss statistical inference and generalize many of these topics to distributions that are not necessarily normal. Throughout this section we shall use the following definitions and notations.

Let $\boldsymbol{\chi}^*$ be a $(p + 1) \times 1$ random vector with distribution $N(\mathbf{x}^* : \boldsymbol{\mu}^*, \mathbf{\Sigma}^*)$ and partition $\boldsymbol{\chi}^*$, $\boldsymbol{\mu}^*$, and $\mathbf{\Sigma}^*$ as indicated below.

$$\boldsymbol{\chi}^* = \begin{bmatrix} X_0 \\ \boldsymbol{\chi} \end{bmatrix} = \begin{bmatrix} X_0 \\ X_1 \\ \vdots \\ X_p \end{bmatrix} \qquad \boldsymbol{\mu}^* = \begin{bmatrix} \mu_0 \\ \boldsymbol{\mu} \end{bmatrix} \tag{3.7.1}$$

$$\mathbf{\Sigma}^* = \begin{bmatrix} \sigma_{00} & \boldsymbol{\sigma}_{01} \\ \boldsymbol{\sigma}_{10} & \mathbf{\Sigma} \end{bmatrix} \qquad \mathbf{\Delta}^* = (\mathbf{\Sigma}^*)^{-1} = \begin{bmatrix} \delta_{00} & \boldsymbol{\delta}_{01} \\ \boldsymbol{\delta}_{10} & \mathbf{\Delta} \end{bmatrix}$$

where X_0, μ_0, and σ_{00} are scalars, $\boldsymbol{\chi}$ and $\boldsymbol{\mu}$ are $p \times 1$ vectors, $\mathbf{\Sigma}^*$ is a $(p + 1) \times (p + 1)$ positive definite matrix, $\boldsymbol{\sigma}_{01}$ is a $1 \times p$ vector, and $\boldsymbol{\sigma}_{01} = \boldsymbol{\sigma}'_{10}$.

We are interested in the conditional p.d.f. of the random variable X_0 given that $X_1 = x_1, X_2 = x_2, \ldots, X_p = x_p$, which we write as $(X_0 | X_1 = x_1, X_2 =$

$x_2, \ldots, X_p = x_p$), or sometimes as $Y_{\mathbf{x}}$, and when there is no chance for ambiguity we write it as Y.

Note 1. In vector notation we can write $Y_{\mathbf{x}}$ as $(X_0 \mid \boldsymbol{\chi} = \mathbf{x})$, where we use the symbol $\boldsymbol{\chi}$ ("chi") to represent a $p \times 1$ vector of random variables $X_1, X_2, \ldots, X_p$, and we use $\mathbf{x}$ to represent a vector of fixed values of $\boldsymbol{\chi}$, that is, x_i is a fixed value of X_i. In the previous section we used $(\boldsymbol{\chi}_1 \mid \boldsymbol{\chi}_2 = \mathbf{c}_2)$ where we now use $(X_0 \mid X_1 = x_1, X_2 = x_2, \ldots, X_p = x_p)$, that is, $(X_0 \mid \boldsymbol{\chi} = \mathbf{x})$ since this notation is more conventional. By Theorem 3.6.1, $Y_{\mathbf{x}}$ has a normal distribution with mean $\mu_0 + \boldsymbol{\sigma}_{01} \times \boldsymbol{\Sigma}^{-1}(\mathbf{x} - \boldsymbol{\mu})$ and variance $\sigma_{00} - \boldsymbol{\sigma}_{01}\boldsymbol{\Sigma}^{-1}\boldsymbol{\sigma}_{10}$, which we denote by σ^2. An equivalent way to denote this is as follows:

$$Y_{\mathbf{x}} = \mu_0 - \boldsymbol{\sigma}_{01}\boldsymbol{\Sigma}^{-1}\boldsymbol{\mu} + \boldsymbol{\sigma}_{01}\boldsymbol{\Sigma}^{-1}\mathbf{x} + \varepsilon \qquad \varepsilon \text{ is distributed } N(\varepsilon : 0, \sigma^2) \tag{3.7.2}$$

or by

$$Y_{\mathbf{x}} = \beta_0 + \boldsymbol{\beta}'\mathbf{x} + \varepsilon \qquad \varepsilon \text{ is distributed } N(\varepsilon : 0, \sigma^2) \tag{3.7.3}$$

or by

$$Y_{\mathbf{x}} = \beta_0 + \sum_{i=1}^{p} \beta_i x_i + \varepsilon \qquad \varepsilon \text{ is distributed } N(\varepsilon : 0, \sigma^2)$$

where we define β_0 and $\boldsymbol{\beta}'$ by, respectively,

$$\beta_0 = \mu_0 - \boldsymbol{\sigma}_{01}\boldsymbol{\Sigma}^{-1}\boldsymbol{\mu} \qquad \text{and} \qquad \boldsymbol{\beta}' = \boldsymbol{\sigma}_{01}\boldsymbol{\Sigma}^{-1} \tag{3.7.4}$$

We have the following definition.

DEFINITION 3.7.1

Normal Regression. *Let $\boldsymbol{\chi}^*$ be distributed $\mathbf{N}(\mathbf{x}^* : \boldsymbol{\mu}^*, \boldsymbol{\Sigma}^*)$, let $\boldsymbol{\chi}^*$, $\boldsymbol{\mu}^*$, and $\boldsymbol{\Sigma}^*$ be partitioned as in Equation* (3.7.1), *and let β_0 and $\boldsymbol{\beta}$ be defined by Equation* (3.7.4). *The equation $\mathscr{E}[Y_{\mathbf{x}}] = \beta_0 + \boldsymbol{\beta}'\mathbf{x}$ is defined to be the normal regression equation of X_0 on $\boldsymbol{\chi}$. We sometimes refer to Equation* (3.7.3), *including the distribution of ε, as the normal regression model. The β_i, $i = 1, 2, \ldots, p$, are defined to be* (*partial*) *regression coefficients.*

We shall make use of the regression equation to predict a value of X_0 from a knowledge of values of $X_1, X_2, \ldots, X_p$. In other words, an important use for regression models is to predict what a sampled value from $f_{X_0}(x_0)$ would be by sampling, not from $f_{X_0}(x_0)$, but rather from the conditional p.d.f. of $(X_0 \mid \boldsymbol{\chi} = \mathbf{x})$, that is, from $f_{Y_{\mathbf{x}}}(y)$. A fundamental reason for sampling from $f_{Y_{\mathbf{x}}}(y)$

rather than from $f_{X_0}(x_0)$ is that var$[Y_{\mathbf{x}}]$ is less than or equal to var$[X_0]$ (and in some cases may be much smaller). This is the context of the next theorem and is discussed in detail in a later chapter.

THEOREM 3.7.1

Let $\boldsymbol{\chi}^*$ *be distributed* $\mathbf{N}(\mathbf{x}^* : \boldsymbol{\mu}^*, \boldsymbol{\Sigma}^*)$ *and partitioned as in Equation* (3.7.1). *Then* (1) $var[X_0] \geq var[Y_{\mathbf{x}}]$; *and* (2) $var[Y_{\mathbf{x}}] = \delta_{00}^{-1}$.

Proof

var$[X_0] = \sigma_{00}$ and var$[Y_{\mathbf{x}}] = \sigma_{00} - \boldsymbol{\sigma}_{01}\boldsymbol{\Sigma}^{-1}\boldsymbol{\sigma}_{10}$. But $\boldsymbol{\Sigma}$ and $\boldsymbol{\Sigma}^{-1}$ are positive definite; thus $\boldsymbol{\sigma}_{01}\boldsymbol{\Sigma}^{-1}\boldsymbol{\sigma}_{10}$, a quadratic form in the elements of $\boldsymbol{\sigma}_{01}$, is nonnegative; this proves (1). var$[Y_{\mathbf{x}}] = \delta_{00}^{-1}$ by Theorem 1.3.1; this proves (2).

When $p = 1$, the regression is called *simple* linear regression of X_0 on X_1. In that case $\beta_0 = \mu_0 - (\sigma_{01}/\sigma_{11})\mu_1$ and $\beta_1 = \sigma_{01}/\sigma_{11} = \text{cov}[X_0, X_1]/\text{var}[X_1]$.

Notation. In the case when $p > 1$, we defined $\beta_1, \beta_2, \ldots, \beta_p$ to be *partial* regression coefficients, and the word *partial* in correlation and regression implies that *conditional* distributions are involved.

We now state a theorem that demonstrates why the regression coefficients in Equation (3.7.4) are called "partial" regression coefficients.

THEOREM 3.7.2

Let the $(p + 1) \times 1$ *random vector* $\boldsymbol{\chi}^*$ *be distributed* $\mathbf{N}(\mathbf{x}^* : \boldsymbol{\mu}^*, \boldsymbol{\Sigma}^*)$, *where* $\boldsymbol{\chi}^*$, $\boldsymbol{\mu}^*$, *and* $\boldsymbol{\Sigma}^*$ *are partitioned as in Equation* (3.7.1), *and let* $\boldsymbol{\beta}$ *be defined as in Equation* (3.7.4). *Then* β_j, $j = 1, 2, \ldots, p$, *the (partial) regression coefficient corresponding to* X_j *in the regression of* X_0 *on* $X_1, X_2, \ldots, X_p$, *is (assume* $p > 1$)

$$\beta_j = \frac{cov[(X_0, X_j \mid X_1, X_2, \ldots, X_{j-1}, X_{j+1}, \ldots, X_p)]}{var[(X_j \mid X_1, X_2, \ldots, X_{j-1}, X_{j+1}, \ldots, X_p)]}$$

Proof

Using the notation $\sigma_{ij|(q+1,\ldots,p)}$ given on page 108 for covariance in conditional p.d.f.'s, we must prove

$$\beta_j = \frac{\sigma_{0j|(1,\ldots,j-1,j+1,\ldots,p)}}{\sigma_{jj|(1,\ldots,j-1,j+1,\ldots,p)}}$$

The definition of $\boldsymbol{\beta}$ in Equation (3.7.4) is $\boldsymbol{\beta} = \boldsymbol{\Sigma}^{-1}\boldsymbol{\sigma}_{10}$. We can write

$$\mathbf{I} = \boldsymbol{\Sigma}^*\boldsymbol{\Sigma}^{*-1} = \boldsymbol{\Sigma}^*\boldsymbol{\Delta}^* = \begin{bmatrix} \sigma_{00} & \boldsymbol{\sigma}_{01} \\ \boldsymbol{\sigma}_{10} & \boldsymbol{\Sigma} \end{bmatrix} \begin{bmatrix} \delta_{00} & \boldsymbol{\delta}_{01} \\ \boldsymbol{\delta}_{10} & \boldsymbol{\Delta} \end{bmatrix} = \begin{bmatrix} 1 & \mathbf{0} \\ \mathbf{0} & \mathbf{I} \end{bmatrix}$$

If we multiply the second partitioned row of $\boldsymbol{\Sigma}^*$ by the first column of $\boldsymbol{\Delta}^*$, we get $\boldsymbol{\sigma}_{10}\delta_{00} + \boldsymbol{\Sigma}\boldsymbol{\delta}_{10} = \mathbf{0}$, or $-\boldsymbol{\delta}_{10}\delta_{00}^{-1} = \boldsymbol{\Sigma}^{-1}\boldsymbol{\sigma}_{10} = \boldsymbol{\beta}$. Thus $\beta_j = -\delta_{j0}\delta_{00}^{-1}$, and the covariance matrix of the p.d.f. of

$$\left(\begin{matrix} X_0 \\ X_j \end{matrix} \,\middle|\, X_1, X_2, \ldots, X_{j-1}, X_{j+1}, \ldots, X_p\right)$$

is obtained by using part 2 of Equation (3.6.1), that is, by striking all rows and columns from $\boldsymbol{\Sigma}^{*-1}$ (from $\boldsymbol{\Delta}^*$), except the ones corresponding to X_0 and X_j, and inverting the resulting 2×2 matrix. The result is

$$\begin{bmatrix} \sigma_{00|(1,2,\ldots,j-1,j+1,\ldots,p)} & \sigma_{0j|(1,2,\ldots,j-1,j+1,\ldots,p)} \\ \sigma_{j0|(1,2,\ldots,j-1,j+1,\ldots,p)} & \sigma_{jj|(1,2,\ldots,j-1,j+1,\ldots,p)} \end{bmatrix}$$

$$= \mathbf{cov}\left[\left(\begin{matrix} X_0 \\ X_j \end{matrix} \,\middle|\, X_1, X_2, \ldots, X_{j-1}, X_{j+1}, \ldots, X_p\right)\right]$$

$$= \begin{bmatrix} \delta_{00} & \delta_{0j} \\ \delta_{j0} & \delta_{jj} \end{bmatrix}^{-1} = \begin{bmatrix} \delta_{jj} & -\delta_{j0} \\ -\delta_{0j} & \delta_{00} \end{bmatrix} (\delta_{00}\delta_{jj} - \delta_{0j}^2)^{-1}$$

Thus

$$\beta_j = -\delta_{j0}\delta_{00}^{-1} = \frac{\sigma_{0j|(1,2,\ldots,j-1,j+1,\ldots,p)}}{\sigma_{jj|(1,2,\ldots,j-1,j+1,\ldots,p)}}$$

and the theorem is proved.

Note 2. To be accurate we should write β_j as $\beta_{0j|(1,2,\ldots,j-1,j+1,\ldots,p)}$, but for convenience it is written as β_j by most authors. Also, β_j should be called "the *partial* regression coefficient of X_j in the multiple regression equation of X_0 on $X_1, X_2, \ldots, X_p$." However, since the random variables under discussion are generally known, it is more common to call β_j "the jth regression coefficient."

3.8 Correlation

An important concept that will be of interest in studying regression theory and in studying relationships among random variables is correlation. Here we shall define simple correlation, multiple correlation, and partial correlation when the underlying random variables are normal.

DEFINITION 3.8.1

Simple Correlation (Coefficient). *Let the $(p+1) \times 1$ random vector $\boldsymbol{\chi}^*$ have a multivariate normal distribution with mean $\boldsymbol{\mu}^*$ and covariance matrix $\boldsymbol{\Sigma}^*$. The simple correlation coefficient of any two random variables X_i and X_j in $\boldsymbol{\chi}^*$ is denoted by ρ_{ij} and defined by*

$$\rho_{ij} = \frac{cov[X_i, X_j]}{\sqrt{var[X_i]\,var[X_j]}} = \frac{\sigma_{ij}}{\sqrt{\sigma_{ii}\sigma_{jj}}} \tag{3.8.1}$$

if $\sigma_{ii} > 0$ and $\sigma_{jj} > 0$. If $\sigma_{ii} = 0$ or $\sigma_{jj} = 0$, we do not define ρ_{ij}.

Throughout this section we assume that $\sigma_{ii} > 0$ for the basic random variables $X_0, X_1, \ldots, X_p$ in $\boldsymbol{\chi}^*$. We often omit the words "simple" and "coefficient" and call ρ_{ij} the correlation of X_i and X_j. Since correlation is defined for every pair of random variables in $\boldsymbol{\chi}^*$, we can arrange these correlations into a $(p+1) \times (p+1)$ matrix denoted by $\mathbf{R}^*$, whose ijth element is ρ_{ij}.

DEFINITION 3.8.2

Correlation Matrix $\mathbf{R}^*$. *Let the ijth element of the $(p+1) \times (p+1)$ matrix $\mathbf{R}^*$ be ρ_{ij}, the correlation of X_i and X_j in $\boldsymbol{\chi}^*$. Then $\mathbf{R}^*$ is defined to be the correlation matrix of the random vector $\boldsymbol{\chi}^*$. $\mathbf{R}$ is defined to be the correlation matrix of the random vector $\boldsymbol{\chi}$.*

Next we prove some theorems about correlation and correlation matrices.

THEOREM 3.8.1

The ith diagonal element in $\mathbf{R}^*$ (namely ρ_{ii}) is equal to unity.

Proof

This is a direct result of Definition 3.8.1.

THEOREM 3.8.2

A correlation matrix $\mathbf{R}^*$ is nonnegative.

Proof

$\mathbf{R}^*$ can be obtained from the covariance matrix $\boldsymbol{\Sigma}^*$ by

$$\mathbf{R}^* = \mathbf{D}'\boldsymbol{\Sigma}^*\mathbf{D} \tag{3.8.2}$$

where $\mathbf{D}$ is a $(p+1) \times (p+1)$ diagonal matrix with ith diagonal element equal to $\sigma_{ii}^{-1/2}$. Thus since a covariance matrix is nonnegative, $\mathbf{R}^*$ is also nonnegative.

Note 1. The rank of $\mathbf{R}^*$ is the same as the rank of $\boldsymbol{\Sigma}^*$.

THEOREM 3.8.3

For any two scalar random variables X_i and X_j in $\boldsymbol{\chi}^*$, ρ_{ij} satisfies the inequalities

$$-1 \leq \rho_{ij} \leq 1 \tag{3.8.3}$$

Proof

For every real constant c the following holds: $\mathscr{E}[(X_i - \mu_i) - c(X_j - \mu_j)]^2 \geq 0$, which implies that $c^2\sigma_{jj} - 2c\sigma_{ij} + \sigma_{ii} \geq 0$. Since this quadratic function is nonnegative, the discriminant must be nonpositive, that is, $4\sigma_{ij}^2 - 4\sigma_{ii}\sigma_{jj} \leq 0$, which in turn implies $\sigma_{ij}^2/\sigma_{ii}\sigma_{jj} \leq 1$, or $\rho_{ij}^2 \leq 1$, and hence the result.

If $\boldsymbol{\chi}^*$ is distributed $N(\mathbf{x}^* : \boldsymbol{\mu}^*, \boldsymbol{\Sigma}^*)$ and partitioned as in Equation (3.7.1), we will have occasion to consider the simple correlation of X_0 and W, where the scalar random variable W is defined by $W = \mu_0 + \boldsymbol{\sigma}_{01}\boldsymbol{\Sigma}^{-1}(\boldsymbol{\chi} - \boldsymbol{\mu})$. Notice that W is a random variable since $\boldsymbol{\chi}$ is a random vector. The random variable W is a linear combination of the random variables in $\boldsymbol{\chi}$, and the coefficients of the linear combination are the regression coefficients in the regression of X_0 on $\boldsymbol{\chi}$, that is, $W = \beta_0 + \boldsymbol{\beta}'\boldsymbol{\chi}$. This correlation of X_0 and W is defined to be the *multiple* correlation of X_0 and $X_1, X_2, \ldots, X_p$ (or X_0 and $\boldsymbol{\chi}$). We now state the definition formally.

DEFINITION 3.8.3

Multiple Correlation (Coefficient). *Let $\boldsymbol{\chi}^*$ be a $(p + 1) \times 1$ multivariate normal random vector with mean $\boldsymbol{\mu}^*$ and covariance matrix $\boldsymbol{\Sigma}^*$. Let $\boldsymbol{\chi}^*$, $\boldsymbol{\mu}^*$, and $\boldsymbol{\Sigma}^*$ be partitioned as in Equation (3.7.1). The multiple correlation coefficient of X_0 and $\boldsymbol{\chi}$ is denoted by $\rho_{0(1,2,\ldots,p)}$ and defined by*

$$\rho_{0(1,2,\ldots,p)} = cor[W, X_0] = \frac{cov[W, X_0]}{\sqrt{var[W]\, var[X_0]}} \tag{3.8.4}$$

where $W = \mu_0 + \boldsymbol{\sigma}_{01}\boldsymbol{\Sigma}^{-1}(\boldsymbol{\chi} - \boldsymbol{\mu}) = \beta_0 + \boldsymbol{\beta}'\boldsymbol{\chi}$.

THEOREM 3.8.4

The multiple correlation coefficient of X_0 and $\boldsymbol{\chi}$, where $\boldsymbol{\chi}^*$ is defined and partitioned as in Equation (3.7.1), is given by any of the following six formulas.

$$\rho_{0(1,2,\ldots,p)} = \sqrt{\frac{\boldsymbol{\sigma}_{01}\boldsymbol{\Sigma}^{-1}\boldsymbol{\sigma}_{10}}{\sigma_{00}}}$$

$$= \sqrt{\frac{var[X_0] - var[(X_0 \mid X_1 = x_1, X_2 = x_2, \ldots, X_p = x_p)]}{var[X_0]}}$$

$$= \sqrt{\frac{\sigma_{00} - \sigma^2}{\sigma_{00}}} = \sqrt{1 - \frac{\sigma^2}{\sigma_{00}}} = \sqrt{1 - \delta_{00}^{-1}\sigma_{00}^{-1}} = \sqrt{1 - \frac{|\boldsymbol{\Sigma}^*|}{\sigma_{00}|\boldsymbol{\Sigma}|}} \tag{3.8.5}$$

where σ^2, the variance in the p.d.f. of $(X_0 \mid X_1 = x_1, X_2 = x_2, \ldots, X_p = x_p)$, is $\sigma_{00} - \boldsymbol{\sigma}_{01}\boldsymbol{\Sigma}^{-1}\boldsymbol{\sigma}_{10}$.

Proof

$$\begin{aligned}
\text{var}[X_0] &= \mathscr{E}[(X_0 - \mu_0)^2] = \sigma_{00} \\
\text{cov}[X_0, W] &= \mathscr{E}[[X_0 - \mu_0][\mu_0 + \boldsymbol{\beta}'(\boldsymbol{\chi} - \boldsymbol{\mu}) - \mu_0]] \\
&= \mathscr{E}[(X_0 - \mu_0)\boldsymbol{\sigma}_{01}\boldsymbol{\Sigma}^{-1}(\boldsymbol{\chi} - \boldsymbol{\mu})] \\
&= \mathscr{E}[(X_0 - \mu_0)(\boldsymbol{\chi} - \boldsymbol{\mu})'\boldsymbol{\Sigma}^{-1}\boldsymbol{\sigma}_{10}] = \boldsymbol{\sigma}_{01}\boldsymbol{\Sigma}^{-1}\boldsymbol{\sigma}_{10} \\
\text{var}[W] &= \mathscr{E}[\boldsymbol{\sigma}_{01}\boldsymbol{\Sigma}^{-1}(\boldsymbol{\chi} - \boldsymbol{\mu})]^2 \\
&= \boldsymbol{\sigma}_{01}\boldsymbol{\Sigma}^{-1}[\mathscr{E}(\boldsymbol{\chi} - \boldsymbol{\mu})(\boldsymbol{\chi} - \boldsymbol{\mu})']\boldsymbol{\Sigma}^{-1}\boldsymbol{\sigma}_{10} = \boldsymbol{\sigma}_{01}\boldsymbol{\Sigma}^{-1}\boldsymbol{\sigma}_{10}
\end{aligned}$$

Substitution into Equation (3.8.4) proves the first four formulas of the theorem.

Let $\boldsymbol{\Delta}^*$ denote $(\boldsymbol{\Sigma}^*)^{-1}$ and by the proof above, $\rho_{0(1,2,\ldots,p)}^2$ is equal to $1 - \sigma^2/\sigma_{00}$, where σ_{00} is the first diagonal element in $\boldsymbol{\Sigma}^*$, whereas σ^2 is the reciprocal of the first diagonal element in $\boldsymbol{\Delta}^*$, that is, $\sigma^2 = \delta_{00}^{-1}$. (This result follows from Theorem 3.7.1.) This proves the fifth formula. Also, $|\boldsymbol{\Sigma}^*| = |\boldsymbol{\Sigma}| \cdot |\sigma_{00} - \boldsymbol{\sigma}_{01}\boldsymbol{\Sigma}^{-1}\boldsymbol{\sigma}_{01}| = |\boldsymbol{\Sigma}| \cdot \sigma^2$; solve for σ^2 and substitute into the fourth formula to prove formula six. This theorem is now proved.

THEOREM 3.8.5

The inequalities $0 \leq \rho_{0(1,2,\ldots,p)} \leq 1$ hold for the multiple correlation coefficient of X_0 and $\boldsymbol{\chi}$.

Proof

$\rho_{0(1,2,\ldots,p)}$ is nonnegative since $\text{cov}[W, X_0] \geq 0$ from Equation (3.8.5); also, we get the result $\rho_{0(1,2,\ldots,p)} \leq 1$ since $\sigma^2 \leq \sigma_{00}$ by Theorem 3.7.1.

Note 2. If $p = 1$, then $\rho_{0(1)}^2 = \rho_{01}^2$, that is, the squares of the simple and multiple correlation coefficients are the same.

Next we define and briefly discuss partial correlation. Consider a $p \times 1$ random vector $\boldsymbol{\chi}$ which is distributed $N(\mathbf{x} : \boldsymbol{\mu}, \boldsymbol{\Sigma})$, where $\boldsymbol{\chi}$, $\boldsymbol{\mu}$, and $\boldsymbol{\Sigma}$ are partitioned as in Equation (3.4.1). By Theorem 3.6.1 the distribution of $\boldsymbol{\chi}_1$ given $\boldsymbol{\chi}_2 = \mathbf{c}_2$ is normal with mean $\boldsymbol{\mu}_1 + \boldsymbol{\Sigma}_{12}\boldsymbol{\Sigma}_{22}^{-1}(\mathbf{c}_2 - \boldsymbol{\mu}_2)$ and covariance matrix $\boldsymbol{\Sigma}_{11.2}$, where $\boldsymbol{\Sigma}_{11.2} = \boldsymbol{\Sigma}_{11} - \boldsymbol{\Sigma}_{12}\boldsymbol{\Sigma}_{22}^{-1}\boldsymbol{\Sigma}_{21}$. We shall have occasion to determine the correlation between random variables that have a joint conditional p.d.f., the p.d.f. of $(\boldsymbol{\chi}_1 \mid \boldsymbol{\chi}_2 = \mathbf{c}_2)$. For example, if X_i and X_j are elements in $\boldsymbol{\chi}_1$, then we want to determine the correlation between X_i and X_j in the p.d.f. of $\boldsymbol{\chi}_1$ given $\boldsymbol{\chi}_2 = \mathbf{c}_2$. This is determined from the covariance matrix $\boldsymbol{\Sigma}_{11.2}$, and the correlation is called the partial correlation of X_i and X_j given $\boldsymbol{\chi}_2 = \mathbf{c}_2$. It is denoted by $\rho_{ij|(q+1,\ldots,p)}$, where the subscripts to the right of the vertical bar are all of the subscripts of the random variables in $\boldsymbol{\chi}_2$, and the subscripts to the left of the vertical bar are the subscripts of any two random variables in $\boldsymbol{\chi}_1$.

DEFINITION 3.8.4

Partial Correlation (Coefficient). *Let the $p \times 1$ random vector $\boldsymbol{\chi}$ be distributed $N(\mathbf{x} : \boldsymbol{\mu}, \boldsymbol{\Sigma})$, where $\boldsymbol{\Sigma}$ is a positive definite covariance matrix. Partition $\boldsymbol{\chi}$, $\boldsymbol{\mu}$, and $\boldsymbol{\Sigma}$ as shown below.*

$$\boldsymbol{\chi} = \begin{bmatrix} \boldsymbol{\chi}_1 \\ \boldsymbol{\chi}_2 \end{bmatrix} \qquad \boldsymbol{\mu} = \begin{bmatrix} \boldsymbol{\mu}_1 \\ \boldsymbol{\mu}_2 \end{bmatrix} \qquad \boldsymbol{\Sigma} = \begin{bmatrix} \boldsymbol{\Sigma}_{11} & \boldsymbol{\Sigma}_{12} \\ \boldsymbol{\Sigma}_{21} & \boldsymbol{\Sigma}_{22} \end{bmatrix} \tag{3.8.6}$$

where $\boldsymbol{\chi}_1$ and $\boldsymbol{\mu}_1$ have sizes $q \times 1$ and $\boldsymbol{\Sigma}_{11}$ has size $q \times q$. The partial correlation coefficient of X_i and X_j (which are in $\boldsymbol{\chi}_1$) given $\boldsymbol{\chi}_2 = \mathbf{c}_2$ is denoted by $\rho_{ij|(q+1,\ldots,p)}$ and defined by

$$\rho_{ij|(q+1,\ldots,p)} = \frac{\sigma_{ij|(q+1,\ldots,p)}}{\sqrt{\sigma_{ii|(q+1,\ldots,p)}\sigma_{jj|(q+1,\ldots,p)}}} \tag{3.8.7}$$

where $\sigma_{rs|(q+1,\ldots,p)}$ is the rsth element in the covariance matrix $\boldsymbol{\Sigma}_{11.2} = \boldsymbol{\Sigma}_{11} - \boldsymbol{\Sigma}_{12}\boldsymbol{\Sigma}_{22}^{-1}\boldsymbol{\Sigma}_{21}$. If either $\sigma_{ii|(q+1,\ldots,p)}$ or $\sigma_{jj|(q+1,\ldots,p)}$ is zero, then the partial correlation of X_i and X_j given $\boldsymbol{\chi}_2 = \mathbf{c}_2$ is not defined.

Notation. Sometimes in the discussion of correlation and regression we use a $p \times 1$ random vector $\boldsymbol{\chi}$ and sometimes we use a $(p + 1) \times 1$ random vector $\boldsymbol{\chi}^*$. We use $\boldsymbol{\chi}^*$ in those situations where the random variable X_0 plays a special role, that is, in multiple regression and multiple correlation when we are interested in the p.d.f. of $(X_0 \mid X_1 = x_1, X_2 = x_2, \ldots, X_p = x_p)$. In other situations (general multivariate normal random vector, and so on), when X_0 does not play a special role, we use the $p \times 1$ random vector $\boldsymbol{\chi}$.

In Definition 3.8.1 a simple correlation coefficient was defined as a certain operation on the elements of the covariance matrix of two random variables that are normally distributed. In Definition 3.8.4 the partial correlation coefficient was defined as the same operation on the elements of the covariance matrix of a conditional p.d.f. Essentially the two definitions are the same except one involves a conditional p.d.f. and the other does not.

THEOREM 3.8.6

Any partial correlation coefficient defined as in Definition 3.8.4 satisfies the inequalities

$$-1 \leq \rho_{ij|(q+1,\dots,p)} \leq 1 \tag{3.8.8}$$

Proof

The proof is essentially the same as the proof for Theorem 3.8.3.

THEOREM 3.8.7

Let the $(p + 1) \times 1$ *random vector* $\mathbf{Y}$ *be distributed* $N(\mathbf{y} : \boldsymbol{\mu}_{\mathbf{Y}}, \boldsymbol{\Sigma}_{\mathbf{Y}})$, *where* $\boldsymbol{\Sigma}_{\mathbf{Y}}$ *is positive definite (p.d.). Then the following relationship holds for* $K = 2, 3, \dots, p$.

$$\rho^2_{0(1,2,\dots,K)} = \rho^2_{0(1,2,\dots,K-1)} + [1 - \rho^2_{0(1,2,\dots,K-1)}]\rho^2_{0K|(1,2,\dots,K-1)} \tag{3.8.9}$$

Proof

Let $\boldsymbol{\chi}^*$ be any subset of $K + 1$ of the random variables in $\mathbf{Y}$, which we denote by $\boldsymbol{\chi}^* = [X_0, X_1, \dots, X_K]'$. Then $\boldsymbol{\chi}^*$ is distributed $N(\mathbf{x}^* : \boldsymbol{\mu}^*, \boldsymbol{\Sigma}^*)$, where $\boldsymbol{\mu}^*$ and $\boldsymbol{\Sigma}^*$ are obtained from $\boldsymbol{\mu}_{\mathbf{Y}}$ and $\boldsymbol{\Sigma}_{\mathbf{Y}}$ by Theorem 3.4.1. Partition $\boldsymbol{\Sigma}^*$ and its inverse $\boldsymbol{\Delta}^*$ as

$$\boldsymbol{\Sigma}^* = \begin{bmatrix} \sigma_{00} & \boldsymbol{\sigma}_{01} & \sigma_{0K} \\ \boldsymbol{\sigma}_{10} & \boldsymbol{\Sigma} & \boldsymbol{\sigma}_{1K} \\ \sigma_{K0} & \boldsymbol{\sigma}_{K1} & \sigma_{KK} \end{bmatrix} \qquad \boldsymbol{\Sigma}^{*-1} = \boldsymbol{\Delta}^* = \begin{bmatrix} \delta_{00} & \boldsymbol{\delta}_{01} & \delta_{0K} \\ \boldsymbol{\delta}_{10} & \boldsymbol{\Delta} & \boldsymbol{\delta}_{1K} \\ \delta_{K0} & \boldsymbol{\delta}_{K1} & \delta_{KK} \end{bmatrix}$$

where σ_{00}, σ_{0K}, σ_{KK}, δ_{00}, δ_{0K}, and δ_{KK} are scalars. Thus the size of the remaining matrices and vectors are determined. We consider the joint conditional distribution of X_0 and X_K given $X_1, X_2, \dots, X_{K-1}$. We write

$$\mathbf{Z} = \left[\begin{pmatrix} X_0 \\ X_K \end{pmatrix} \middle| \; X_1 = x_1, X_2 = x_2, \dots, X_{K-1} = x_{K-1} \right]$$

and by Theorem 3.6.1 $\mathbf{Z}$ is distributed $N(\mathbf{z} : \boldsymbol{\mu}_{\mathbf{Z}}, \boldsymbol{\Sigma}_{\mathbf{Z}})$, where $\boldsymbol{\Sigma}_{\mathbf{Z}}$ is obtained by eliminating the rows and columns from $\boldsymbol{\Sigma}^{*-1}$ (that is, from $\boldsymbol{\Delta}^{*}$) corresponding to the conditioned variables $X_1, X_2, \ldots, X_{K-1}$ and inverting the resulting matrix. We get

$$\boldsymbol{\Sigma}_{\mathbf{Z}} = \begin{bmatrix} \delta_{00} & \delta_{0K} \\ \delta_{K0} & \delta_{KK} \end{bmatrix}^{-1} = \begin{bmatrix} \delta_{KK} & -\delta_{K0} \\ -\delta_{0K} & \delta_{00} \end{bmatrix} (\delta_{00}\delta_{KK} - \delta_{0K}^2)^{-1}$$

The notation for the conditional covariance matrix $\boldsymbol{\Sigma}_{\mathbf{Z}}$ is

$$\boldsymbol{\Sigma}_{\mathbf{Z}} = \begin{bmatrix} \sigma_{00|(1,2,\ldots,K-1)} & \sigma_{0K|(1,2,\ldots,K-1)} \\ \sigma_{K0|(1,2,\ldots,K-1)} & \sigma_{KK|(1,2,\ldots,K-1)} \end{bmatrix}$$

Thus by definition

$$\rho_{0K|(1,2,\ldots,K-1)}^2 = \frac{\sigma_{0K|(1,2,\ldots,K-1)}^2}{\sigma_{00|(1,2,\ldots,K-1)}\sigma_{KK|(1,2,\ldots,K-1)}} = \frac{(-\delta_{0K})^2}{\delta_{00}\delta_{KK}}$$

By Theorem 3.8.4 we know that

$$\rho_{0(1,2,\ldots,K)}^2 = \frac{\text{var}[X_0] - \text{var}[(X_0 \mid X_1 = x_1, X_2 = x_2, \ldots, X_K = x_K)]}{\text{var}[X_0]}$$

$$= \frac{\sigma_{00} - \delta_{00}^{-1}}{\sigma_{00}}$$

and that

$$\rho_{0(1,2,\ldots,K-1)}^2$$

$$= \frac{\text{var}[X_0] - \text{var}[(X_0 \mid X_1 = x_1, X_2 = x_2, \ldots, X_{K-1} = x_{K-1})]}{\text{var}[X_0]}$$

$$= \frac{\sigma_{00} - \sigma_{00|(1,2,\ldots,K-1)}}{\sigma_{00}} = \frac{\sigma_{00} - \delta_{KK}(\delta_{00}\delta_{KK} - \delta_{0K}^2)^{-1}}{\sigma_{00}}$$

Now let us examine the quantity $[1 - \rho_{0(1,2,\ldots,K-1)}^2][1 - \rho_{0K|(1,2,\ldots,K-1)}^2]$. We get $[1 - \rho_{0(1,2,\ldots,K-1)}^2][1 - \rho_{0K|(1,2,\ldots,K-1)}^2] = [\sigma_{00}^{-1}\delta_{KK}(\delta_{00}\delta_{KK} - \delta_{0K}^2)^{-1}][1 - (\delta_{0K}^2/\delta_{00}\delta_{KK})] = \sigma_{00}^{-1}\delta_{00}^{-1}$, but this is equal to $1 - \rho_{0(1,2,\ldots,K)}^2$. So we get

$$1 - \rho_{0(1,2,\ldots,K)}^2 = [1 - \rho_{0(1,2,\ldots,K-1)}^2][1 - \rho_{0K|(1,2,\ldots,K-1)}^2]$$

which, after simplifying, gives Equation (3.8.9), and the theorem is proved.

COROLLARY 3.8.7

For any positive integer N, $1 \leq N \leq p$, *we get*

$$\rho_{0(1)}^2 \leq \rho_{0(1,2)}^2 \leq \cdots \leq \rho_{0(1,2,\ldots,N)}^2 \tag{3.8.10}$$

Proof

The result follows from Equation (3.8.9) since $1 - \rho_{0(1,2,\ldots,K-1)}^2$ and $\rho_{0K|(1,2,\ldots,K-1)}^2$ are both nonnegative. Hence $\rho_{0(1,2,\ldots,K)}^2 \geq \rho_{0(1,2,\ldots,K-1)}^2$. Let $K = 2$, $K = 3, \ldots$, and finally $K = N$.

Note 3. Regression and correlation were defined in terms of a conditional *normal* distribution, but the regression equation and the correlations involve only elements of the mean vector $\boldsymbol{\mu}^*$ and of the covariance matrix $\boldsymbol{\Sigma}^*$, so we could therefore define regression and correlation in terms of these quantities even when the basic random variables are not normal. This we shall do in a later chapter.

3.9 Examples

In this section we shall discuss some examples to illustrate the theory in this chapter.

Example 3.9.1

Let $\boldsymbol{\chi}$ be distributed $\mathbf{N}(\mathbf{x} : \boldsymbol{\mu}, \boldsymbol{\Sigma})$, where

$$\boldsymbol{\mu} = \begin{bmatrix} 1 \\ -1 \\ 2 \\ 0 \end{bmatrix} \qquad \boldsymbol{\Sigma} = \begin{bmatrix} 2 & 0 & 1 & 0 \\ 0 & 3 & 0 & 2 \\ 1 & 0 & 5 & 0 \\ 0 & 2 & 0 & 3 \end{bmatrix}$$

Find the marginal distribution of $\boldsymbol{\chi}_1$, where $\boldsymbol{\chi}_1' = [X_1, X_3]$.

From Theorem 3.4.1, $\boldsymbol{\chi}_1$ is distributed $\mathbf{N}(\mathbf{x}_1 : \boldsymbol{\mu}_1, \boldsymbol{\Sigma}_{11})$, where $\boldsymbol{\mu}_1$ is obtained from $\boldsymbol{\mu}$ by crossing out rows 2 and 4; $\boldsymbol{\Sigma}_{11}$ is obtained from $\boldsymbol{\Sigma}$ by crossing out rows 2 and 4 and columns 2 and 4. We get

$$\boldsymbol{\mu}_1 = \begin{bmatrix} 1 \\ 2 \end{bmatrix} \qquad \boldsymbol{\Sigma}_{11} = \begin{bmatrix} 2 & 1 \\ 1 & 5 \end{bmatrix}$$

Example 3.9.2

In Example 3.9.1 find the conditional p.d.f. of $(X_1, X_2 \mid X_3 = x_3, X_4 = x_4)$.

Let $\chi_1' = [X_1, X_2]$; $\chi_2' = [X_3, X_4]$. Then we obtain

$$\boldsymbol{\mu}_1 = \begin{bmatrix} 1 \\ -1 \end{bmatrix} \quad \boldsymbol{\mu}_2 = \begin{bmatrix} 2 \\ 0 \end{bmatrix} \quad \boldsymbol{\Sigma}_{11} = \begin{bmatrix} 2 & 0 \\ 0 & 3 \end{bmatrix} \quad \boldsymbol{\Sigma}_{12} = \begin{bmatrix} 1 & 0 \\ 0 & 2 \end{bmatrix}$$

$$\boldsymbol{\Sigma}_{22} = \begin{bmatrix} 5 & 0 \\ 0 & 3 \end{bmatrix} \quad \boldsymbol{\Sigma}_{22}^{-1} = \begin{bmatrix} \frac{1}{5} & 0 \\ 0 & \frac{1}{3} \end{bmatrix}$$

Hence by Theorem 3.6.1 the p.d.f. of $(X_1, X_2 \mid X_3 = x_3, X_4 = x_4)$ is normal with mean

$$\begin{bmatrix} 1 \\ -1 \end{bmatrix} + \begin{bmatrix} 1 & 0 \\ 0 & 2 \end{bmatrix} \begin{bmatrix} \frac{1}{5} & 0 \\ 0 & \frac{1}{3} \end{bmatrix} \begin{bmatrix} x_3 - 2 \\ x_4 \end{bmatrix} = \begin{bmatrix} \frac{1}{5}(x_3 + 3) \\ \frac{2}{3}x_4 - 1 \end{bmatrix}$$

and covariance matrix $\boldsymbol{\Sigma}_{11.2}$, where

$$\boldsymbol{\Sigma}_{11.2} = \begin{bmatrix} 2 & 0 \\ 0 & 3 \end{bmatrix} - \begin{bmatrix} 1 & 0 \\ 0 & 2 \end{bmatrix} \begin{bmatrix} \frac{1}{5} & 0 \\ 0 & \frac{1}{3} \end{bmatrix} \begin{bmatrix} 1 & 0 \\ 0 & 2 \end{bmatrix} = \begin{bmatrix} \frac{9}{5} & 0 \\ 0 & \frac{5}{3} \end{bmatrix}$$

Another way to find $\boldsymbol{\Sigma}_{11.2}$ is to find $\boldsymbol{\Sigma}^{-1}$, eliminate rows and columns 3 and 4, and invert the resulting matrix. We get

$$\boldsymbol{\Sigma}^{-1} = \begin{bmatrix} \frac{5}{9} & 0 & -\frac{1}{9} & 0 \\ 0 & \frac{3}{5} & 0 & -\frac{2}{5} \\ -\frac{1}{9} & 0 & \frac{2}{9} & 0 \\ 0 & -\frac{2}{5} & 0 & \frac{3}{5} \end{bmatrix}$$

After eliminating rows and columns 3 and 4, we get

$$\begin{bmatrix} \frac{5}{9} & 0 \\ 0 & \frac{3}{5} \end{bmatrix}$$

and

$$\boldsymbol{\Sigma}_{11.2} = \begin{bmatrix} \frac{5}{9} & 0 \\ 0 & \frac{3}{5} \end{bmatrix}^{-1} = \begin{bmatrix} \frac{9}{5} & 0 \\ 0 & \frac{5}{3} \end{bmatrix}$$

Example 3.9.3

Let the 4×1 random vector χ^* be distributed $N(\mathbf{x}^* : \boldsymbol{\mu}^*, \boldsymbol{\Sigma}^*)$, where

$$\chi^* = \begin{bmatrix} X_0 \\ X_1 \\ X_2 \\ X_3 \end{bmatrix} \quad \boldsymbol{\mu}^* = \begin{bmatrix} 1 \\ 0 \\ 2 \\ -1 \end{bmatrix} \quad \boldsymbol{\Sigma}^* = \begin{bmatrix} 3 & 1 & 0 & 0 \\ 1 & 2 & 0 & \frac{1}{2} \\ 0 & 0 & 2 & 1 \\ 0 & \frac{1}{2} & 1 & 1 \end{bmatrix}$$

Find $\rho_{0(1,2)}$, the multiple correlation of X_0 and X_1, X_2.

First we find the marginal distribution of X_0, X_1, X_2. The distribution is normal with mean $\boldsymbol{\mu}$ and covariance matrix $\boldsymbol{\Sigma}$, where

$$\boldsymbol{\mu} = \begin{bmatrix} 1 \\ 0 \\ 2 \end{bmatrix} \qquad \boldsymbol{\Sigma} = \begin{bmatrix} 3 & 1 & 0 \\ 1 & 2 & 0 \\ 0 & 0 & 2 \end{bmatrix}$$

Also, $\sigma_{00} = 3$, $\boldsymbol{\sigma}_{01} = [1, 0]$,

$$\boldsymbol{\Sigma}_{22} = \begin{bmatrix} 2 & 0 \\ 0 & 2 \end{bmatrix}$$

so

$$\sigma^2 = 3 - [1, 0] \begin{bmatrix} \frac{1}{2} & 0 \\ 0 & \frac{1}{2} \end{bmatrix} \begin{bmatrix} 1 \\ 0 \end{bmatrix} = \tfrac{5}{2}$$

Thus by Theorem 3.8.4, $\rho_{0(1,2)} = \sqrt{(3 - \frac{5}{2})/3} = \sqrt{\frac{1}{6}}$.

Another way to find $\rho_{0(1,2)}$ is to find σ^2, which is δ_{00}^{-1}, by finding $\boldsymbol{\Sigma}^{-1}$ (denoted by $\boldsymbol{\Delta}$) and use Theorem 3.8.4 to compute $\rho_{0(1,2)}$. We get

$$\boldsymbol{\Delta} = \begin{bmatrix} \frac{2}{5} & -\frac{1}{5} & 0 \\ -\frac{1}{5} & \frac{3}{5} & 0 \\ 0 & 0 & \frac{1}{2} \end{bmatrix} \qquad \delta_{00} = \tfrac{2}{5} \qquad \delta_{00}^{-1} = \sigma^2 = \tfrac{5}{2}$$

$$\rho_{0(1,2)} = \sqrt{1 - \tfrac{5}{2} \cdot \tfrac{1}{3}} = \sqrt{\tfrac{1}{6}}$$

Example 3.9.4

In Example 3.9.3 find $\rho_{12|(3)}$.

We can solve the problem in two ways: from the covariance matrix of the random variable (X_1, X_2, X_3), or from the covariance matrix of the random variable (X_0, X_1, X_2, X_3). The covariance matrix of (X_1, X_2, X_3) is

$$\begin{bmatrix} 2 & 0 & \frac{1}{2} \\ 0 & 2 & 1 \\ \frac{1}{2} & 1 & 1 \end{bmatrix}$$

From this we compute the covariance matrix of $(X_1, X_2 \mid X_3 = x_3)$ and obtain

$$\begin{bmatrix} 2 & 0 \\ 0 & 2 \end{bmatrix} - \begin{bmatrix} \frac{1}{2} \\ 1 \end{bmatrix} 1^{-1} [\tfrac{1}{2}, 1] = \begin{bmatrix} \frac{7}{4} & -\frac{1}{2} \\ -\frac{1}{2} & 1 \end{bmatrix}$$

So $\rho_{12|(3)} = -(\frac{1}{2})/\sqrt{(\frac{7}{4}) \cdot 1} = -1/\sqrt{7}$.

To obtain the answer by starting with the covariance matrix of the random variable (X_0, X_1, X_2, X_3), we first compute the covariance matrix of $(X_0, X_1, X_2 \mid X_3 = x_3)$, which is

$$\begin{bmatrix} 3 & 1 & 0 \\ 1 & 2 & 0 \\ 0 & 0 & 2 \end{bmatrix} - \begin{bmatrix} 0 \\ \frac{1}{2} \\ 1 \end{bmatrix} 1^{-1}[0, \tfrac{1}{2}, 1] = \begin{bmatrix} 3 & 1 & 0 \\ 1 & \frac{7}{4} & -\frac{1}{2} \\ 0 & -\frac{1}{2} & 1 \end{bmatrix}$$

and $\rho_{12|(3)} = -(\frac{1}{2})/\sqrt{(\frac{7}{4}) \cdot 1} = -1/\sqrt{7}$, as was obtained by using X_1, X_2, X_3.

Problems

Problems 3.1 through 3.11 refer to the 3×1 random vector χ, where $\chi' = [X_0, X_1, X_2]$, which is distributed $\mathbf{N}(\mathbf{x} : \mathbf{0}, \Sigma)$, where

$$\Sigma = \begin{bmatrix} 4 & 1 & 0 \\ 1 & 2 & 1 \\ 0 & 1 & 3 \end{bmatrix}$$

(When the answer to a problem is the multivariate normal distribution, just exhibit the vector mean and covariance matrix.)

3.1. Find the marginal distribution of X_1.

3.2. Find the joint distribution of X_1, X_2.

3.3. Find the conditional distribution of X_0 given $X_1 = x_1$ and $X_2 = x_2$.

3.4. Find $\rho_{12}, \rho_{01}, \rho_{02}$.

3.5. Find $\rho_{01|(2)}$.

3.6. Find the distribution of Z, where $Z = 4X_0 - 6X_1 + X_2 - 18$.

3.7. Find $\rho_{0(1,2)}$.

3.8. Find $\sigma_{11|(2)}$.

3.9. Find $\sigma_{02|(1)}$.

3.10. In Problem 3.3 find $\beta_0, \beta_1, \beta_2$.

3.11. Find the covariance of Z_1, Z_2, where

$$Z_1 = X_0 - X_1 + 2X_2 - 6$$
$$Z_2 = 2X_1 + 4$$

3.12. The m.g.f. of a 3×1 random vector $\boldsymbol{\chi}$ is

$$m_{\boldsymbol{\chi}}(\mathbf{t}) = \exp[t_1 - t_2 + 2t_3 + t_1^2 + \tfrac{1}{2}t_2^2 + 2t_3^2 - \tfrac{1}{2}t_1t_2 - t_1t_3]$$

Find a constant c such that

$$P[2X_1 - 3X_2 + X_3 > c] = 0.95$$

3.13. Let the 3×1 vector $\boldsymbol{\chi}' = [X_1, X_2, X_3]$ be distributed $\mathbf{N}(\mathbf{x} : \boldsymbol{\mu}, \boldsymbol{\Sigma})$. Show that

$$\rho_{12|(3)} = \frac{\rho_{12} - \rho_{13}\rho_{23}}{[(1 - \rho_{13}^2)(1 - \rho_{23}^2)]^{1/2}}$$

3.14. The $p \times 1$ vector $\boldsymbol{\chi}$ is distributed $\mathbf{N}(\mathbf{x} : \boldsymbol{\mu}, \boldsymbol{\Sigma})$. Let $\mathbf{Y} = \boldsymbol{\chi} - \boldsymbol{\mu}$. Find the m.g.f. of $\mathbf{Y}$.

3.15. In Problem 3.12 find the distribution of $(X_1 | \bar{X} = 6)$.

3.16. Let the $p \times 1$ vector $\boldsymbol{\chi}$ be distributed $\mathbf{N}(\mathbf{x} : \boldsymbol{\mu}, \boldsymbol{\Sigma})$ and partitioned as in Equation (3.4.1). Use the regression equation $\mathscr{E}[\boldsymbol{\chi}_1 | \boldsymbol{\chi}_2 = \mathbf{c}_2] = \boldsymbol{\mu}_1 + \boldsymbol{\Sigma}_{12}\boldsymbol{\Sigma}_{22}^{-1}(\mathbf{c}_2 - \boldsymbol{\mu}_2)$ to define a random vector $\mathbf{Y}$, where

$$\mathbf{Y} = \boldsymbol{\chi}_1 - \mathscr{E}[\boldsymbol{\chi}_1 | \boldsymbol{\chi}_2] = (\boldsymbol{\chi}_1 - \boldsymbol{\mu}_1) - \boldsymbol{\Sigma}_{12}\boldsymbol{\Sigma}_{22}^{-1}(\boldsymbol{\chi}_2 - \boldsymbol{\mu}_2)$$

Show that $\mathbf{Y}$ and $\boldsymbol{\chi}_2$ are independent vectors.

3.17. Let the $p \times 1$ vector $\boldsymbol{\chi}$ be distributed $\mathbf{N}(\mathbf{x} : \boldsymbol{\mu}, \sigma^2\mathbf{I})$. Show that a necessary and sufficient condition for $\mathbf{a}'\boldsymbol{\chi}$ and $\mathbf{b}'\boldsymbol{\chi}$ to be independent (where $\mathbf{a} \neq \mathbf{0}$, $\mathbf{b} \neq \mathbf{0}$) is $\mathbf{a}'\mathbf{b} = 0$.

3.18. If the $p \times 1$ vector $\boldsymbol{\chi}$ is distributed $\mathbf{N}(\mathbf{x} : \boldsymbol{\mu}, \boldsymbol{\Sigma})$, where $\boldsymbol{\Sigma}$ is positive definite, the p.d.f. is given by

$$\mathbf{n}(\mathbf{x} : \boldsymbol{\mu}, \boldsymbol{\Sigma}) = (2\pi)^{-p/2}|\boldsymbol{\Sigma}|^{-1/2} e^{-Q/2}$$

where $Q = (\mathbf{x} - \boldsymbol{\mu})'\boldsymbol{\Sigma}^{-1}(\mathbf{x} - \boldsymbol{\mu})$. Show that the mean vector $\boldsymbol{\mu}$ is the solution for $\mathbf{x}$ to $\partial\mathbf{n}(\mathbf{x} : \boldsymbol{\mu}, \boldsymbol{\Sigma})/\partial\mathbf{x} = \mathbf{0}$.

3.19. In Problem 3.18 show that the mean vector $\boldsymbol{\mu}$ is the solution for $\mathbf{x}$ to $\partial Q/\partial\mathbf{x} = \mathbf{0}$.

3.20. The 3×1 vector χ is distributed $\mathbf{N}(\mathbf{x} : \boldsymbol{\mu}, \boldsymbol{\Sigma})$ and the p.d.f. is

$$\mathbf{n}(\mathbf{x} : \boldsymbol{\mu}, \boldsymbol{\Sigma}) = (2\pi)^{-3/2}|\boldsymbol{\Sigma}|^{-1/2}e^{-Q/2}$$

where $Q = \frac{3}{2}x_1^2 + 2x_2^2 + x_3^2 - 3x_1x_2 + 2x_1x_3 - 2x_2x_3 + 10x_1 - 14x_2 + 8x_3 + 26$. Find $\boldsymbol{\Sigma}^{-1}$.

3.21. In Problem 3.20 find $\boldsymbol{\Sigma}$.

3.22. In Problem 3.20 find $\boldsymbol{\mu}$.

3.23. In Problem 3.20 find the distribution of $(X_1|X_2 = x_2, X_3 = x_3)$.

3.24. In the p.d.f. of the normal distribution represented in Problem 3.18, let $\chi' = [\chi_1', \chi_2']$, where χ_1' is a $q \times 1$ random vector, $0 < q < p$. Show that $\mathscr{E}(\chi_1|\chi_2 = \mathbf{x}_2)$ is the solution for $\mathbf{x}_1$ to $\partial\mathbf{n}(\mathbf{x} : \boldsymbol{\mu}, \boldsymbol{\Sigma})/\partial\mathbf{x}_1 = \mathbf{0}$.

3.25. In Problem 3.24 show that $\mathscr{E}(\chi_1|\chi_2 = \mathbf{x}_2)$ is the solution for $\mathbf{x}_1$ to $\partial Q/\partial\mathbf{x}_1 = \mathbf{0}$.

3.26. In Problem 3.20 find $\mathscr{E}[(X_1|X_2 = x_2, X_3 = x_3)]$.

3.27. In Problem 3.20 find $\mathscr{E}[(X_1 \mid X_2 = x_2)]$.

3.28. In Problem 3.18 let $\mathbf{T}$ be an upper triangular matrix such that $\boldsymbol{\Sigma} = \mathbf{T}'\mathbf{T}$. Define the $p \times 1$ random vector $\mathbf{Y}$ by $\mathbf{Y} = \mathbf{T}'^{-1}\chi$. Show that $Y_1, Y_2, \ldots, Y_p$ are jointly independent.

3.29. In Example 3.9.3 demonstrate Equation (3.8.9) by showing

$$\rho^2_{0(1,2,3)} = \rho^2_{0(1,2)} + [1 - \rho^2_{0(1,2)}]\rho^2_{03|(1,2)}$$

3.30. In Example 3.9.3 demonstrate Equation (3.8.10) by showing

$$\rho^2_{0(1)} \leq \rho^2_{0(1,2)} \leq \rho^2_{0(1,2,3)}$$

CHAPTER 4

Distributions of Quadratic Forms

4.1 Introduction

In Chapter 2 we stated that if Y_i is distributed $N(y:0,1)$, for $i = 1, 2, \ldots, n$, and if the Y_i are jointly independent, then $U = \sum_{i=1}^{n} Y_i^2$ is distributed as a chi-square random variable with n degrees of freedom. The p.d.f. of U is given in Equation (2.5.5). This result is stated in vector terminology in the next theorem.

THEOREM 4.1.1

Let the $n \times 1$ random vector $\mathbf{Y}$ be distributed $\mathbf{N}(\mathbf{y}:\mathbf{0},\mathbf{I})$, and let $U = \mathbf{Y}'\mathbf{Y}$. Then U has a chi-square distribution with n degrees of freedom.

Proof

There are a number of ways to prove this theorem, and even though we assume that the reader is well acquainted with the result, we shall give the proof by using the m.g.f. and employing Theorem 2.3.1. The m.g.f. of U is, by definition,

$$\begin{aligned} m_U(t) &= \mathscr{E}[e^{tU}] = \mathscr{E}\left[\exp\left(t \sum_{i=1}^{n} Y_i^2\right)\right] \\ &= (2\pi)^{-n/2} \int_{-\infty}^{\infty} \cdots \int_{-\infty}^{\infty} \exp(t\Sigma y_i^2 - \tfrac{1}{2}\Sigma y_i^2)\, d\mathbf{y} \\ &= (2\pi)^{-n/2} \int_{-\infty}^{\infty} \cdots \int_{-\infty}^{\infty} \exp[-\tfrac{1}{2}(1-2t)\Sigma y_i^2]\, d\mathbf{y} \end{aligned}$$

If $1 - 2t > 0$ (that is, if $t < \frac{1}{2}$), then the integral and hence the m.g.f. exist. We evaluate the integral by using Theorem 1.10.1 and obtain $m_U(t) = (1 - 2t)^{-n/2}$. By Theorem 2.3.1 and Equation (2.5.6), U is distributed as a chi-square random variable with n degrees of freedom.

4.2 Noncentral Chi-Square Distribution

In this section we shall generalize Theorem 4.1.1 and find the distribution of the random variable U when the mean of $\mathbf{Y}$ is not $\mathbf{0}$. This is the context of the next theorem.

THEOREM 4.2.1

Let the $n \times 1$ *random vector* $\mathbf{Y}$ *be distributed* $\mathbf{N}(\mathbf{y} : \boldsymbol{\mu}, \mathbf{I})$ *and define* U *by* $U = \mathbf{Y}'\mathbf{Y}$. *Then* U *has a p.d.f. given by*

$$\chi^2(u : n ; \lambda) = \begin{cases} \displaystyle\sum_{j=0}^{\infty} \left(\frac{e^{-\lambda}\lambda^j}{j!}\right)\left(\frac{u^{(n+2j-2)/2}\, e^{-u/2}}{\Gamma\left(\dfrac{n+2j}{2}\right) 2^{j+(n/2)}}\right) & \text{for } u > 0 \\ 0 & \text{for } u \le 0 \end{cases} \tag{4.2.1}$$

where $\lambda = \frac{1}{2}\boldsymbol{\mu}'\boldsymbol{\mu}$ *(hence* $\lambda \ge 0$*), and we define* $\lambda^j = 1$ *when* $\lambda = 0$, $j = 0$.

Proof

To prove the theorem we shall find the m.g.f. of $\mathbf{Y}'\mathbf{Y}$ and then find the m.g.f. of a random variable with p.d.f. as given in Equation (4.2.1). We will recognize that the two m.g.f.'s are identical and use Theorem 2.3.1. The m.g.f. of $\mathbf{Y}'\mathbf{Y}$ is

$$m_{\mathbf{Y}'\mathbf{Y}}(t) = \mathscr{E}[e^{t(\mathbf{Y}'\mathbf{Y})}] = (2\pi)^{-(n/2)} \int_{-\infty}^{\infty} \cdots \int_{-\infty}^{\infty} e^{t(\mathbf{y}'\mathbf{y})}$$

$$\times \exp[-\tfrac{1}{2}(\mathbf{y} - \boldsymbol{\mu})'(\mathbf{y} - \boldsymbol{\mu})]\, d\mathbf{y}$$

$$= (2\pi)^{-n/2} \int_{-\infty}^{\infty} \cdots \int_{-\infty}^{\infty}$$

$$\times \exp(-\tfrac{1}{2}[(1 - 2t)\mathbf{y}'\mathbf{y} - 2\mathbf{y}'\boldsymbol{\mu} + \boldsymbol{\mu}'\boldsymbol{\mu}])\, d\mathbf{y}$$

The integral exists for all t such that $t < \frac{1}{2}$, and we use Theorem 1.10.1 to evaluate it. We obtain

$$m_{\mathbf{Y}'\mathbf{Y}}(t) = (1 - 2t)^{-n/2} \exp\left(\frac{2t\lambda}{1 - 2t}\right) \qquad t < \tfrac{1}{2}$$

To find the m.g.f. of a random variable with p.d.f. given by Equation (4.2.1), we obtain

$$m_U(t) = \mathscr{E}[e^{Ut}] = \int_0^\infty e^{ut} \sum_{j=0}^{\infty} \left(\frac{e^{-\lambda}\lambda^j}{j!}\right)\left(\frac{u^{(n+2j-2)/2}e^{-u/2}}{\Gamma\left(\frac{n+2j}{2}\right)2^{j+n/2}}\right) du$$

$$= \sum_{j=0}^{\infty}\left(\frac{e^{-\lambda}\lambda^j}{j!\,\Gamma\left(\frac{n+2j}{2}\right)2^{j+n/2}}\right)\int_0^\infty u^{(n+2j-2)/2}e^{-(1-2t)u/2}\,du$$

If $t < \frac{1}{2}$, the integral exists for each j and is equal to $\Gamma((n + 2j)/2)2^{j+n/2} \times (1 - 2t)^{-(n+2j)/2}$. The value of $m_U(t)$ is

$$(1 - 2t)^{-n/2} \exp\left(\frac{2t\lambda}{1 - 2t}\right) \qquad t < \tfrac{1}{2}$$

Thus the m.g.f. of $\mathbf{Y}'\mathbf{Y}$ is the same as the m.g.f. of a random variable U with p.d.f. given in Equation (4.2.1). By Theorem 2.3.1 it follows that $\mathbf{Y}'\mathbf{Y}$ has a p.d.f. given by Equation (4.2.1), and the theorem is proved.

Notation. The distribution defined by the p.d.f. in Equation (4.2.1) will be called the noncentral chi-square distribution. The quantity n (a positive integer) will be called the degrees of freedom, and λ will be called the noncentrality parameter. We use the symbol $\chi^2(u : n; \lambda)$ to denote the p.d.f. Clearly $\lambda = 0$ if and only if $\boldsymbol{\mu} = \mathbf{0}$, and in that case the p.d.f. reduces to the "central" chi-square given in Equation (2.5.5). We will write this as either $\chi^2(u : n; 0)$ or as $\chi^2(u : n)$. Some authors use a prime to denote the noncentral chi-square; they write $\chi'^2(u : n; \lambda)$, or simply $\chi'^2(n; \lambda)$.

Note 1. The jth term in the summation in Equation (4.2.1) is the product of the jth term of a Poisson density with parameter λ (that is, $(e^{-\lambda}\lambda^j)/j!$) times a central chi-square density with $n + 2j$ degrees of freedom. It can be shown that all moments of the p.d.f. exist, and to evaluate the qth moment, $\mathscr{E}[U^q]$, summation and integration can be interchanged.

COROLLARY 4.2.1.1

Let the random variable U be distributed $\chi^2(u : n; \lambda)$. The mean of U is $n + 2\lambda$ and the variance of U is $2(n + 4\lambda)$.

COROLLARY 4.2.1.2

Let the two independent random variables U_1 and U_2 be distributed as $\chi^2(u_1 : n_1; \lambda_1)$ and $\chi^2(u_2 : n_2; \lambda_2)$, respectively. The random variable $U = U_1 + U_2$ is distributed as $\chi^2(u : n; \lambda)$, where $n = n_1 + n_2$, $\lambda = \lambda_1 + \lambda_2$.

COROLLARY 4.2.1.3

Let the $n \times 1$ random vector $\mathbf{Y}$ be distributed $\mathbf{N}(\mathbf{y} : \boldsymbol{\mu}, \boldsymbol{\sigma}^2\mathbf{I})$; then $U = \mathbf{Y}'\mathbf{Y}/\sigma^2$ is distributed $\chi^2(u : n; \lambda)$, where $\lambda = \boldsymbol{\mu}'\boldsymbol{\mu}/2\sigma^2$.

COROLLARY 4.2.1.4

Let the $n \times 1$ random vector $\mathbf{Y}$ be distributed $\mathbf{N}(\mathbf{y} : \boldsymbol{\mu}, \boldsymbol{\Sigma})$, where $\boldsymbol{\Sigma}$ has rank n. The random variable $U = \mathbf{Y}'\boldsymbol{\Sigma}^{-1}\mathbf{Y}$ is distributed $\chi^2(u : n; \lambda)$, where $\lambda = \frac{1}{2}\boldsymbol{\mu}'\boldsymbol{\Sigma}^{-1}\boldsymbol{\mu}$.

We shall prove Corollary 4.2.1.4 and leave the proofs of the remaining corollaries for the reader.

Proof

Factor $\boldsymbol{\Sigma}$ as $\boldsymbol{\Sigma} = \boldsymbol{\Gamma}'\boldsymbol{\Gamma}$, where $\boldsymbol{\Gamma}'$ is $n \times n$ of rank n. If we define $\mathbf{Z}$ by $\mathbf{Z} = \boldsymbol{\Gamma}'^{-1}\mathbf{Y}$, then by Theorem 3.3.5, $\mathbf{Z}$ is distributed $\mathbf{N}(\mathbf{z} : \boldsymbol{\Gamma}'^{-1}\boldsymbol{\mu}, \mathbf{I}_n)$. Thus

$$U = \mathbf{Y}'\boldsymbol{\Sigma}^{-1}\mathbf{Y} = \mathbf{Y}'(\boldsymbol{\Gamma}'\boldsymbol{\Gamma})^{-1}\mathbf{Y} = \mathbf{Y}'\boldsymbol{\Gamma}^{-1}\boldsymbol{\Gamma}'^{-1}\mathbf{Y} = \mathbf{Z}'\mathbf{Z}$$

and by Theorem 4.2.1 the random variable $\mathbf{Z}'\mathbf{Z}$ (and hence U) is distributed $\chi^2(u : n; \lambda)$, where

$$\lambda = \tfrac{1}{2}\boldsymbol{\mu}'\boldsymbol{\Gamma}^{-1}\boldsymbol{\Gamma}'^{-1}\boldsymbol{\mu} = \tfrac{1}{2}\boldsymbol{\mu}'\boldsymbol{\Sigma}^{-1}\boldsymbol{\mu}$$

and the corollary is proved.

4.3 Noncentral *F* and Noncentral *t* Distributions

In the previous section we noted that the noncentral chi-square distribution is an extension of the central chi-square distribution. We also know that the ratio of two independent central chi-square random variables (divided by their degrees of freedom) is distributed as the F distribution given in Section 2.5.4. In this section we shall generalize this distribution by considering the ratio V_1/V_2 of two independent random variables, where V_1 is a *noncentral chi-square* random variable divided by its degrees of freedom and V_2 is a *central chi-square* random variable divided by its degrees of freedom. The resulting random variable is known as a noncentral F random variable and we shall now find its p.d.f.

THEOREM 4.3.1

Let U_1 be distributed $\chi^2(u_1 : n_1; \lambda)$ and U_2 be distributed $\chi^2(u_2 : n_2; 0)$, where U_1 and U_2 are independent random variables. The random variable W, defined by $W = (U_1/n_1)/(U_2/n_2)$, has a p.d.f. given by

$$F(w : n_1, n_2; \lambda) = \begin{cases} \displaystyle\sum_{j=0}^{\infty} \frac{\lambda^j e^{-\lambda} \Gamma\left(\frac{2j + n_1 + n_2}{2}\right)\left(\frac{n_1}{n_2}\right)^{(n_1+2j)/2} w^{(n_1+2j-2)/2}}{j!\,\Gamma\left(\frac{n_2}{2}\right)\Gamma\left(\frac{2j+n_1}{2}\right)\left(1 + \frac{n_1 w}{n_2}\right)^{(n_1+n_2+2j)/2}} & w > 0 \\ 0 & w \le 0 \end{cases} \tag{4.3.1}$$

Proof

The joint p.d.f. of U_1 and U_2 is the product of the individual p.d.f.'s and hence is given by

$$\begin{cases} \left(\dfrac{u_2^{(n_2-2)/2} e^{-u_2/2}}{\Gamma\left(\frac{n_2}{2}\right) 2^{n_2/2}}\right) \displaystyle\sum_{j=0}^{\infty} \frac{e^{-\lambda}\lambda^j u_1^{(n_1+2j-2)/2} e^{-u_1/2}}{j!\,\Gamma\left(\frac{2j+n_1}{2}\right) 2^{j+n_1/2}} & u_1 > 0, \quad u_2 > 0 \\ 0 & \text{otherwise} \end{cases}$$

Make the change of variables from u_1 and u_2 to w and z, respectively, by the equations

$$w = \left(\frac{n_2}{n_1}\right)\left(\frac{u_1}{u_2}\right) \qquad z = u_1$$

The Jacobian of the transformation is $(z/w^2)(n_2/n_1)$. After substitution we get for the p.d.f. of W and Z:

$$\begin{cases} \displaystyle\sum_{j=0}^{\infty} C_j \left(\frac{z}{w}\right)^{(n_2-2)/2} z^{(n_1+2j-2)/2}\left(\frac{z}{w^2}\right) \exp\left[-\frac{n_2 z}{2n_1 w} - \frac{z}{2}\right] & z > 0,\ w > 0, \\ 0 & \text{otherwise} \end{cases}$$

where we define C_j as

$$C_j = \frac{e^{-\lambda}\lambda^j\left(\dfrac{n_2}{n_1}\right)^{n_2/2}}{j!\,2^{n_2/2+n_1/2+j}\,\Gamma\left(\dfrac{n_2}{2}\right)\Gamma\left(\dfrac{2j+n_1}{2}\right)}$$

Integrate with respect to z and the result is the p.d.f. of W given in Equation (4.3.1).

Notation. We denote the p.d.f. of the noncentral F distribution by $F(w : n_1, n_2 ; \lambda)$, where n_1 is the degrees of freedom and λ is the noncentrality parameter of the p.d.f. of the noncentral chi-square random variable in the numerator of W; n_2 is the degrees of freedom of the p.d.f. of the central chi-square random variable in the denominator of W. It is clear from Equation (4.3.1) that if $\lambda = 0$, then the p.d.f. is the "central" F and the symbol will be $F(w : n_1, n_2; 0)$, or simply $F(w : n_1, n_2)$. Some authors use $F'(w : n_1, n_2; \lambda)$ for a noncentral F distribution.

The principal use that we make of the noncentral F distribution in this book is to evaluate the power of tests of hypotheses, and this requires us to evaluate

$$\Pi(\lambda) = \int_{F\alpha:n_1,n_2}^{\infty} F(w : n_1, n_2 ; \lambda)\, dw \tag{4.3.2}$$

as a function of λ when n_1 and n_2, the degrees of freedom, and α, the probability of a Type I error, are fixed. The quantity $F_{\alpha:n_1,n_2}$ is the upper α probability point ($1 - \alpha$ percentile) of a central F distribution. Thus $F_{\alpha:n_1,n_2}$ is obtained from

$$\alpha = \int_{F\alpha:n_1,n_2}^{\infty} F(w : n_1, n_2 ; 0)\, dw \tag{4.3.3}$$

for given values of n_1, n_2, and α. The quantity $F_{\alpha:n_1,n_2}$ is tabulated in Table T.5, and Table T.11 can be used to evaluate $1 - \Pi(\lambda)$ for fixed α, n_1, n_2, and various values of λ. Actually instead of λ, the table involves ϕ, where

$$\phi = \sqrt{\frac{2\lambda}{n_1 + 1}} \tag{4.3.4}$$

We illustrate the use of the table with some examples.

Example 4.3.1

Evaluate $1 - \Pi(\lambda)$ for $n_1 = 2$, $n_2 = 8$, $\alpha = 0.01$, $\lambda = 6$.

Compute ϕ by Equation (4.3.4) and obtain $\phi = 2$. Enter Table T.11 for $\alpha = 0.01$, the numerator degrees of freedom $n_1 = 2$, the denominator degrees of freedom $n_2 = 8$, and $\phi = 2$. The quantity $1 - \Pi(\lambda)$ is found equal to 0.6110.

Note 1. The lower limit, $F_{\alpha:n_1,n_2}$, of the integral is not needed to obtain the value of the integral from the table. However, the critical (rejection) region of a test is often the interval $F_{\alpha:n_1,n_2}$ to ∞ and must be evaluated when making a test of hypothesis. This will be discussed in Chapter 6.

Example 4.3.2

Evaluate $1 - \Pi(\lambda)$ for $\lambda = 3$ and for $\lambda = 12$, when $\alpha = 0.05$, $n_1 = 5$, $n_2 = 14$.

The corresponding values of ϕ for the given values of λ, computed by Equation (4.3.4), are $\phi = 1$ and $\phi = 2$. From Table T.11 we obtain $1 - \Pi(3) = 0.6956$, $1 - \Pi(12) = 0.1033$.

Example 4.3.3

In Example 4.3.2 find the lower limit of the integral in Equation (4.3.2), that is, find $F_{0.05:5,14}$. This is the upper 0.05 probability point. (95 percentile) of the central F distribution with 5 degrees of freedom in the numerator and 14 degrees of freedom in the denominator. The value is obtained from Table T.5 and is 2.96.

To evaluate the integral in Equation (4.3.2) for values of ϕ larger than those included in Table T.11 a useful approximation is given in [T-5].

For a more detailed analysis of Equation (4.3.2) that will be useful when considering the power of certain tests of hypotheses in the linear model, we consider the integral as a function of n_1, n_2, λ, and α. We can write this as

$$q(n_1, n_2, \lambda, \alpha) = \int_{F\alpha:n_1,n_2}^{\infty} F(w : n_1, n_2 ; \lambda)\, dw \tag{4.3.5}$$

In discussing the power of some tests of hypotheses it will be important to know that the value of the integral is monotonic decreasing or increasing in certain of the arguments n_1, n_2, λ, or α. This is the context of the next theorem.

THEOREM 4.3.2

$q(n_1, n_2, \lambda, \alpha)$ in Equation (4.3.5) has the following properties:

(1) *monotonic increasing in λ for fixed values of n_1, n_2, and α;*

(2) *monotonic increasing in α for fixed values of n_1, n_2, and λ;*

(3) *monotonic increasing in n_2 for fixed values of α, n_1, and λ;*

(4) *monotonic decreasing in n_1 for fixed values of n_2, α, and λ.*

Proof

The proof of this theorem will be omitted but a discussion of the results can be found in [G-2].

4.3.1 Noncentral *t* Distribution

By Equation (2.5.10), if a random variable Z is distributed $N(z:0, 1)$, if U is distributed $\chi^2(u:\nu)$, and if U and Z are independent, then the random variable $T = Z/\sqrt{U/\nu}$ is distributed $s(t:\nu)$. The p.d.f. of T is given in Equation (2.5.11). In Section 2.5.4 we noted that the random variable T^2 is distributed as an F random variable with 1 and ν degrees of freedom.

In this section we discuss the distribution of a random variable called the "noncentral t."

DEFINITION 4.3.1

Let Z be distributed $N(z:0, 1)$, U be distributed $\chi^2(u:\nu)$, δ be a constant, $-\infty < \delta < \infty$, and let Z and U be independent. Then $T = (Z + \delta)/\sqrt{U/\nu}$ has a noncentral t distribution with ν degrees of freedom and noncentrality parameter δ.

We will not derive the p.d.f. of this distribution here. The interested reader can find a great deal of information about the noncentral t in [O-3].

Notation. The p.d.f. of the noncentral t with ν degrees of freedom and noncentrality parameter δ will be denoted by $s(t:\nu;\delta)$.

Some additional information about the noncentral t distribution is given in the next two theorems.

THEOREM 4.3.3

Let Y be distributed $N(y:\mu, \sigma^2)$, let $V = U/\sigma^2$ be distributed $\chi^2(v:\nu)$, and let Y and V be independent. Then $T = Y/\sqrt{U/\nu}$ is distributed $s(t:\nu;\delta)$ where $\delta = \mu/\sigma$.

Note 2. We use the symbol $t_{\alpha:\nu:(\delta)}$ to denote the upper α probability point of a noncentral t distribution with ν degrees of freedom and noncentrality parameter δ, that is,

$$\int_{t_{\alpha:\nu;(\delta)}}^{\infty} s(t:\nu;\delta)\,dt = \alpha = P[T > t_{\alpha:\nu:(\delta)}]$$

THEOREM 4.3.4

Let T be distributed $s(t:v;\delta)$; *then*

$$1-\alpha = P[T \le t_{\alpha:v;(\delta)}] = 1 - P[T \le -t_{\alpha:v;(-\delta)}] = P[T > -t_{\alpha:v;(-\delta)}] \quad (4.3.6)$$

$$t_{1-\alpha:v;(\delta)} = -t_{\alpha:v;(-\delta)} \quad (4.3.7)$$

$$\alpha = P[T \le t_{1-\alpha:v;(\delta)}] = P[T \le -t_{\alpha:v;(-\delta)}] = P[T > t_{\alpha:v;(\delta)}] \quad (4.3.8)$$

For further discussion of the noncentral t distribution, see [O-3]. See especially Table 5.1 and page 450.

Some applications in this book will require that the quantity $t_{\alpha:v;(\delta)}$ be evaluated. A comprehensive set of tables is available in [R-8]. For illustrative purposes Table 4.3.1 is a table reproduced from [J-6] with instructions for computing $t_{\alpha:v;(\delta)}$.

To evaluate $t_{\alpha:v:(\delta)}$, where $\alpha = P[T \ge t_{\alpha:v;(\delta)}]$, proceed as follows:

1. α, v, and δ are specified;

Table 4.3.1

Noncentral t Distribution; Values of λ as a Function of δ and $\alpha = 0.05$

ξ \ v	4	5	6	7	8	9	16	36	144	∞
1.0	1.636	1.648	1.655	1.660	1.662	1.6638	1.6665	1.6634	1.6559	1.6449
0.9	1.643	1.655	1.662	1.666	1.668	1.6695	1.6711	1.6667	1.6576	1.6449
0.8	1.650	1.662	1.668	1.672	1.674	1.6747	1.6751	1.6691	1.6586	1.6449
0.7	1.657	1.668	1.674	1.677	1.679	1.6796	1.6782	1.6707	1.6589	1.6449
0.6	1.664	1.675	1.680	1.682	1.684	1.6838	1.6804	1.6714	1.6587	1.6449
0.5	1.671	1.681	1.686	1.687	1.687	1.6871	1.6817	1.6709	1.6580	1.6449
0.4	1.679	1.687	1.690	1.691	1.691	1.6896	1.6816	1.6698	1.6568	1.6449
0.3	1.687	1.693	1.694	1.693	1.692	1.6902	1.6804	1.6677	1.6550	1.6449
0.2	1.693	1.697	1.696	1.694	1.692	1.6898	1.6779	1.6646	1.6529	1.6449
0.1	1.698	1.699	1.697	1.693	1.690	1.6874	1.6738	1.6606	1.6504	1.6449
0.0	1.703	1.699	1.695	1.690	1.686	1.6827	1.6682	1.6558	1.6477	1.6449
−0.1	1.702	1.695	1.689	1.684	1.679	1.6756	1.6611	1.6503	1.6447	1.6449
−0.2	1.698	1.688	1.680	1.674	1.669	1.6657	1.6525	1.6442	1.6417	1.6449
−0.3	1.687	1.676	1.667	1.661	1.657	1.6535	1.6427	1.6378	1.6388	1.6449
−0.4	1.670	1.658	1.650	1.645	1.642	1.6391	1.6322	1.6314	1.6359	1.6449
−0.5	1.646	1.636	1.630	1.627	1.624	1.6231	1.6213	1.6252	1.6334	1.6449
−0.6	1.615	1.610	1.607	1.606	1.606	1.6066	1.6108	1.6195	1.6313	1.6449
−0.7	1.582	1.583	1.585	1.587	1.589	1.5911	1.6019	1.6150	1.6299	1.6449
−0.8	1.551	1.559	1.565	1.571	1.575	1.5792	1.5954	1.6122	1.6291	1.6449
−0.9	1.531	1.544	1.553	1.561	1.567	1.5722	1.5925	1.6116	1.6292	1.6449
−1.0	1.528	1.543	1.554	1.563	1.569	1.5744	1.5952	1.6141	1.6307	1.6449

2. compute ξ by the formula

$$\xi = \delta(2\nu + \delta^2)^{-1/2}$$

3. for the computed value of ξ and for the specified values of α and ν in part 1, look up the value of λ in Table 4.3.1;

4. compute $t_{\alpha:\nu;(\delta)}$ by the formula

$$t_{\alpha:\nu;(\delta)} = \frac{\delta + \lambda[1 + (\delta^2 - \lambda^2)/(2\nu)]^{1/2}}{1 - \lambda^2/2\nu} \tag{4.3.9}$$

Example 4.3.4

For $\nu = 16$, $\alpha = 0.05$, $\delta = 2.47$, find $t_{\alpha:\nu;(\delta)}$.

We get

$$\xi = \delta[2\nu + \delta^2]^{-1/2} = 2.47[2(16) + (2.47)^2]^{-1/2} = 0.40$$

For $\nu = 16$, $\alpha = 0.05$, and $\xi = 0.40$, $\lambda = 1.6816$ is obtained from the table, and

$$t_{0.05:16;(2.47)} = \frac{2.47 + 1.6816[1 + \{(2.47)^2 - (1.6816)^2\}/2(16)]^{1/2}}{1 - (1.6816)^2/32}$$

$$= 4.65$$

Example 4.3.5

Evaluate $t_{1-\alpha:\nu;(\delta)}$ when $\delta = -3.2431$, $\nu = 16$, $\alpha = 0.05$.

By Equation (4.3.9) we must compute $-t_{\alpha:\nu;(-\delta)} = -t_{0.05:16;(3.2431)}$ from Table 4.3.1, then use Equation (4.3.7) to get $t_{0.95:16;(-3.2431)}$. To compute $t_{0.05:16;(3.2431)}$ we have $\nu = 16$, $\delta = 3.2431$, and $\xi = 3.2431 \times [2(16) + (3.2431)^2]^{-1/2} = 0.497 \approx 0.50$. From the table for $\nu = 16$, $\xi = 0.50$, we get $\lambda = 1.6817$. Thus

$$t_{0.05:16;(3.2431)} = \frac{3.2431 + 1.6817\left[1 + \dfrac{(3.2431)^2 - (1.6817)^2}{2(16)}\right]^{1/2}}{1 - (1.6817)^2/2(16)}$$

$$= 5.61$$

and by Equation (4.3.7) we get $t_{0.95:16;(-3.2431)} = -5.61$.

4.4 Distribution of Quadratic Forms in Normal Variables

Quadratic forms play a significant role in the theory of the linear model when the basic variables are normally distributed. We shall prove some theorems that will enable us to determine the distribution of quadratic forms by examining only the covariance matrix, mean vector of the normal random variables, and the matrix of the quadratic forms.

In Theorems 4.1.1 and 4.2.1 we proved that $\mathbf{Y}'\mathbf{Y}$ is distributed as central and noncentral chi-square random variables when $\mathbf{Y}$ is distributed $N(\mathbf{y}:\mathbf{0},\mathbf{I})$ and $N(\mathbf{y}:\boldsymbol{\mu},\mathbf{I})$, respectively. In this section we extend these theorems and study the distribution of more general quadratic forms. The next theorem is a generalization of Theorem 4.1.1.

THEOREM 4.4.1

Let the $n \times 1$ random vector $\mathbf{Y}$ be distributed $N(\mathbf{y}:\mathbf{0},\mathbf{I})$. The quadratic form $\mathbf{Y}'\mathbf{A}\mathbf{Y}$ has a central chi-square distribution with K degrees of freedom if and only if $\mathbf{A}$ is a symmetric idempotent matrix of rank K.

Proof

We shall prove the "if" part of the theorem and sketch the "only if" part. We assume that $\mathbf{A}$ is symmetric idempotent of rank K. Hence there exists an orthogonal $n \times n$ matrix $\mathbf{P}$ such that

$$\mathbf{P}'\mathbf{A}\mathbf{P} = \begin{bmatrix} \mathbf{I} & \mathbf{0} \\ \mathbf{0} & \mathbf{0} \end{bmatrix}$$

where $\mathbf{I}$ has size $K \times K$. Partition the matrix $\mathbf{P}$ so that

$$\mathbf{P} = [\mathbf{P}_1, \mathbf{P}_2]$$

where $\mathbf{P}_1$ is the first K columns of $\mathbf{P}$ (note that $\mathbf{P}_1'\mathbf{P}_1 = \mathbf{I}_K$). Define the $n \times 1$ random vector $\mathbf{Z}$ by $\mathbf{Z} = \mathbf{P}'\mathbf{Y}$, and partition $\mathbf{Z}$ so that

$$\mathbf{Z} = \begin{bmatrix} \mathbf{Z}_1 \\ \mathbf{Z}_2 \end{bmatrix}$$

where $\mathbf{Z}_1$ is a $K \times 1$ vector. Then $\mathbf{Z}_1 = \mathbf{P}_1'\mathbf{Y}$, and $\mathbf{Z}_1$ is distributed $N(\mathbf{z}_1:\mathbf{0},\mathbf{I}_K)$. Hence

$$\mathbf{Y}'\mathbf{A}\mathbf{Y} = (\mathbf{P}\mathbf{Z})'\mathbf{A}(\mathbf{P}\mathbf{Z}) = \mathbf{Z}'(\mathbf{P}'\mathbf{A}\mathbf{P})\mathbf{Z} = [\mathbf{Z}_1', \mathbf{Z}_2']\begin{bmatrix} \mathbf{I} & \mathbf{0} \\ \mathbf{0} & \mathbf{0} \end{bmatrix}\begin{bmatrix} \mathbf{Z}_1 \\ \mathbf{Z}_2 \end{bmatrix} = \mathbf{Z}_1'\mathbf{Z}_1$$

and by Theorem 4.1.1, $\mathbf{Z}_1'\mathbf{Z}_1$ is distributed $\chi^2(u : K; 0)$, so the "if" part of the theorem is proved.

To prove the "only if" part, we assume that $\mathbf{Y}'\mathbf{A}\mathbf{Y}$ is distributed as $\chi^2(u : K; 0)$, and we must show that this implies that $\mathbf{A}$ is idempotent of rank K. Since $\mathbf{Y}'\mathbf{A}\mathbf{Y}$ is distributed as $\chi^2(u : K; 0)$, the m.g.f. of $\mathbf{Y}'\mathbf{A}\mathbf{Y}$ is $(1 - 2t)^{-K/2}$. But since $\mathbf{Y}$ is distributed $N(\mathbf{y} : \mathbf{0}, \mathbf{I})$, the m.g.f. of $\mathbf{Y}'\mathbf{A}\mathbf{Y}$ can also be obtained by using the p.d.f. of $\mathbf{Y}$. We get

$$\mathscr{E}[e^{t(\mathbf{Y}'\mathbf{A}\mathbf{Y})}] = (2\pi)^{-n/2} \int_{-\infty}^{\infty} \cdots \int_{-\infty}^{\infty} \exp[t(\mathbf{y}'\mathbf{A}\mathbf{y}) - \tfrac{1}{2}\mathbf{y}'\mathbf{y}]\, d\mathbf{y}$$

and this can be evaluated by Theorem 1.10.1. The value is $\prod_{i=1}^{n} \times (1 - 2t\lambda_{ii})^{-1/2}$, where the λ_{ii} are the characteristic roots of $\mathbf{A}$. These two representations of the m.g.f. must be equal for all t in some neighborhood of the origin. We equate them and obtain

$$\prod_{i=1}^{n} (1 - 2t\lambda_{ii})^{-1/2} = (1 - 2t)^{-K/2}$$

for all t in some neighborhood of zero. It can be shown that this equation implies that K of the λ_{ii} are equal to $+1$ and the remaining λ_{ii} are equal to zero. But λ_{ii} are the characteristic roots of a symmetric matrix $\mathbf{A}$, and hence by Theorem 1.7.2, $\mathbf{A}$ is idempotent of rank K.

Next we generalize this theorem to the case in which the mean is not zero. The proof follows along the lines of the proof of Theorem 4.4.1 and will not be given.

THEOREM 4.4.2

Let the $n \times 1$ random vector $\mathbf{Y}$ be distributed $N(\mathbf{y} : \boldsymbol{\mu}, \mathbf{I})$. The random variable $U = \mathbf{Y}'\mathbf{A}\mathbf{Y}$ is distributed as $\chi^2\,(u : K; \lambda)$, where $\lambda = \frac{1}{2}\boldsymbol{\mu}'\mathbf{A}\boldsymbol{\mu}$, if and only if $\mathbf{A}$ is an idempotent matrix of rank K.

It is quite clear that Theorem 4.4.1 is a special case of Theorem 4.4.2. These two theorems can also be generalized to the situation when the covariance matrix of $\mathbf{Y}$ is a positive definite matrix $\boldsymbol{\Sigma}$ rather than the special covariance matrix $\mathbf{I}$. We generalize Theorem 4.4.2 and point out some special cases.

THEOREM 4.4.3

Let the $n \times 1$ random vector $\mathbf{Y}$ be distributed $N(\mathbf{y} : \boldsymbol{\mu}, \boldsymbol{\Sigma})$, where $\boldsymbol{\Sigma}$ has rank n. Then the quadratic form $U = \mathbf{Y}'\mathbf{A}\mathbf{Y}$ is distributed $\chi^2(u : p; \lambda)$, where $\lambda = \frac{1}{2}\boldsymbol{\mu}'\mathbf{A}\boldsymbol{\mu}$, if and only if any of the following three conditions are satisfied: (1) $\mathbf{A}\boldsymbol{\Sigma}$ is an *idempotent matrix of rank p; (2) $\mathbf{\Sigma A}$ is an idempotent matrix of rank p; (3) $\mathbf{\Sigma}$ is a c-inverse of $\mathbf{A}$ and $\mathbf{A}$ has rank p.*

Proof

To prove (1) define the random vector $\mathbf{Z}$ by $\mathbf{Z} = \mathbf{\Gamma}'^{-1}(\mathbf{Y} - \boldsymbol{\mu})$, where $\mathbf{\Sigma} = \mathbf{\Gamma}'\mathbf{\Gamma}$. Then $\mathbf{Z}$ is distributed $N(\mathbf{z} : \mathbf{0}, \mathbf{I})$. Thus $\mathbf{Y} = \mathbf{\Gamma}'\mathbf{Z} + \boldsymbol{\mu}$, and

$$\begin{aligned} \mathbf{Y}'\mathbf{A}\mathbf{Y} &= (\mathbf{\Gamma}'\mathbf{Z} + \boldsymbol{\mu})'\mathbf{A}(\mathbf{\Gamma}'\mathbf{Z} + \boldsymbol{\mu}) = (\mathbf{Z} + \mathbf{\Gamma}'^{-1}\boldsymbol{\mu})'(\mathbf{\Gamma}\mathbf{A}\mathbf{\Gamma}')(\mathbf{Z} + \mathbf{\Gamma}'^{-1}\boldsymbol{\mu}) \\ &= \mathbf{V}'\mathbf{B}\mathbf{V} \end{aligned}$$

where $\mathbf{B} = \mathbf{\Gamma}\mathbf{A}\mathbf{\Gamma}'$ and $\mathbf{V}$ is distributed $N(\mathbf{v} : \mathbf{\Gamma}'^{-1}\boldsymbol{\mu}, \mathbf{I})$. By Theorem 4.4.2, $U = \mathbf{V}'\mathbf{B}\mathbf{V}$ is distributed $\chi^2(u : p; \lambda)$ if and only if $\mathbf{B}$ is idempotent of rank p. But $\mathbf{B}$ is idempotent of rank p if and only if $(\mathbf{\Gamma}\mathbf{A}\mathbf{\Gamma}')(\mathbf{\Gamma}\mathbf{A}\mathbf{\Gamma}') = \mathbf{\Gamma}\mathbf{A}\mathbf{\Gamma}'$, that is, if and only if $\mathbf{A\Sigma A\Sigma} = \mathbf{A\Sigma}$, that is, if and only if $\mathbf{A\Sigma}$ is idempotent. Also $\text{rank}[\mathbf{A\Sigma}] = \text{rank}[\mathbf{A}] = p$. We use Theorem 4.4.2 to obtain the noncentrality parameter $\lambda = \frac{1}{2}(\mathbf{\Gamma}'^{-1}\boldsymbol{\mu})'\mathbf{B}(\mathbf{\Gamma}'^{-1}\boldsymbol{\mu}) = \frac{1}{2}\boldsymbol{\mu}'\mathbf{\Gamma}^{-1}\mathbf{\Gamma}\mathbf{A}\mathbf{\Gamma}'\mathbf{\Gamma}'^{-1}\boldsymbol{\mu} = \frac{1}{2}\boldsymbol{\mu}'\mathbf{A}\boldsymbol{\mu}$. This proves (1). To show that each condition (2) and (3) is equivalent to (1) is straightforward and will be left for the reader.

Note 1. To obtain the noncentrality parameter λ in the distribution of $\mathbf{Y}'\mathbf{A}\mathbf{Y}$ in previous theorems when $\mathbf{Y}$ is distributed $N(\mathbf{y} : \boldsymbol{\mu}, \mathbf{\Sigma})$, one merely replaces $\mathbf{Y}$ in $\mathbf{Y}'\mathbf{A}\mathbf{Y}$ with the mean of $\mathbf{Y}$ and multiplies by $\frac{1}{2}$, that is, in Theorem 4.4.3, $\lambda = \frac{1}{2}\boldsymbol{\mu}'\mathbf{A}\boldsymbol{\mu} = \frac{1}{2}(\mathscr{E}[\mathbf{Y}])'\mathbf{A}(\mathscr{E}[\mathbf{Y}])$. It may appear at first that the covariance matrix of $\mathbf{Y}$ (namely $\mathbf{\Sigma}$) does not enter into the noncentrality parameter. However, it does, since for $\mathbf{Y}'\mathbf{A}\mathbf{Y}$ to be a chi-square random variable requires $\mathbf{A\Sigma A} = \mathbf{A}$.

In Theorem 4.7.1 we present some additional sufficient conditions for $\mathbf{Y}'\mathbf{A}\mathbf{Y}$ to be distributed as a noncentral chi-square random variable.

Note 2. We point out the fact that $\mathbf{Y}'\mathbf{A}\mathbf{Y}$ may be a *central* chi-square random variable even if $\boldsymbol{\mu} \neq \mathbf{0}$ since we have made no assumptions concerning $\mathbf{A}$ (except, of course, that $\mathbf{A}$ is symmetric), and $\mathbf{A}\boldsymbol{\mu}$ could be $\mathbf{0}$ and hence $\lambda = 0$ for certain nonzero values of $\boldsymbol{\mu}$. Of course, if $\mathbf{A}$ is positive definite, then $\lambda = 0$ if and only if $\boldsymbol{\mu} = \mathbf{0}$.

THEOREM 4.4.4

Let the $n \times 1$ random vector $\mathbf{Y}$ be distributed $N(\mathbf{y} : \boldsymbol{\mu}, \mathbf{\Sigma})$ where $\mathbf{\Sigma}$ has rank n. The random variable $\mathbf{Y}'\mathbf{A}\mathbf{Y}$ has the same distribution as the random variable U, where $U = \sum_{i=1}^{n} d_{ii}U_i$, where d_{ii} are the characteristic roots of the matrix $\mathbf{A\Sigma}$, and where $U_1, U_2, \ldots, U_n$ are n independent noncentral chi-square random variables, each with one degree of freedom.

Proof

The proof will be left for the reader.

Note 3. In Theorem 4.4.4, U is a chi-square random variable with K degrees of freedom if and only if K of the d_{ii} are 1's and $n - K$ of the d_{ii} are 0's.

THEOREM 4.4.5

Let the $n \times 1$ random vector $\mathbf{Y}$ be distributed $\mathbf{N}(\mathbf{y} : \boldsymbol{\mu}, \mathbf{D})$, where $\mathbf{D}$ is a diagonal matrix of rank n. Then $U = \mathbf{Y}'\mathbf{A}\mathbf{Y}$ is distributed $\chi^2(u : n - 1 ; \lambda)$, where $\lambda = \frac{1}{2}\boldsymbol{\mu}'\mathbf{A}\boldsymbol{\mu}$, if $\mathbf{A} = \mathbf{D}^{-1} - (\mathbf{D}^{-1}\mathbf{1}\mathbf{1}'\mathbf{D}^{-1})/(\mathbf{1}'\mathbf{D}^{-1}\mathbf{1})$. Also, $\lambda = 0$ if $\boldsymbol{\mu} = \mathbf{1}\mu$, that is, if $\mu_1 = \mu_2 = \cdots = \mu_n = \mu$ for any scalar μ.

Proof

The proof is an application of Theorem 4.4.3. The details will be left for the reader.

4.5 Independence of Linear Forms and Quadratic Forms

In Chapter 3 we discussed methods for determining when sets of linear functions of normal random variables are jointly independent. In this section we discuss methods for determining when linear functions of normal random variables are independent of a quadratic form of normal random variables. We also discuss methods for determining when two quadratic forms of normal random variables are independent.

THEOREM 4.5.1

Let the $n \times 1$ random vector $\mathbf{Y}$ be distributed $\mathbf{N}(\mathbf{y} : \boldsymbol{\mu}, \mathbf{I})$, and let $\mathbf{B}$ be a $q \times n$ matrix. The $q \times 1$ vector $\mathbf{BY}$ is independent of the quadratic form $\mathbf{Y}'\mathbf{A}\mathbf{Y}$ if $\mathbf{BA} = \mathbf{0}$.

Proof

Since $\mathbf{A}$ is a symmetric matrix, there exists an orthogonal matrix $\mathbf{P}$ such that

$$\mathbf{P}'\mathbf{A}\mathbf{P} = \begin{bmatrix} \mathbf{D} & \mathbf{0} \\ \mathbf{0} & \mathbf{0} \end{bmatrix}$$

where $\mathbf{D}$ is a nonsingular $p \times p$ diagonal matrix and p is the rank of $\mathbf{A}$.

The condition $\mathbf{BA} = \mathbf{0}$ implies $\mathbf{BPP'AP} = \mathbf{0}$. If we let $\mathbf{C}$ denote $\mathbf{BP}$, this becomes

$$\begin{bmatrix} \mathbf{C}_{11} & \mathbf{C}_{12} \\ \mathbf{C}_{21} & \mathbf{C}_{22} \end{bmatrix} \begin{bmatrix} \mathbf{D} & \mathbf{0} \\ \mathbf{0} & \mathbf{0} \end{bmatrix} = \mathbf{0}$$

which in turn implies $\mathbf{C}_{11}\mathbf{D} = \mathbf{0}$ and $\mathbf{C}_{21}\mathbf{D} = \mathbf{0}$; but since $\mathbf{D}$ is nonsingular, it follows that $\mathbf{C}_{11} = \mathbf{0}$ and $\mathbf{C}_{21} = \mathbf{0}$. So we can write $\mathbf{C}$ as $\mathbf{C} = [\mathbf{0}, \mathbf{C}_2]$. Let $\mathbf{Z} = \mathbf{P'Y}$; so $\mathbf{Z}$ is distributed $N(\mathbf{z} : \boldsymbol{\gamma}, \mathbf{I})$, where $\boldsymbol{\gamma} = \mathbf{P'}\boldsymbol{\mu}$, and hence the $\mathbf{Z}_i$ are independent random variables. But

$$\mathbf{Y'AY} = \mathbf{Z'P'APZ} = \mathbf{Z'}\begin{bmatrix} \mathbf{D} & \mathbf{0} \\ \mathbf{0} & \mathbf{0} \end{bmatrix}\mathbf{Z} = \mathbf{Z}_1'\mathbf{D}\mathbf{Z}_1 = \sum_{i=1}^{p} d_{ii} Z_i^2.$$

Also,

$$\mathbf{BY} = \mathbf{BPZ} = \mathbf{CZ} = [\mathbf{0}, \mathbf{C}_2]\begin{bmatrix} \mathbf{Z}_1 \\ \mathbf{Z}_2 \end{bmatrix} = \mathbf{C}_2\mathbf{Z}_2$$

So $\mathbf{Y'AY}$ is a function of only the first p elements in $\mathbf{Z}$, and $\mathbf{BY}$ is a function of only the last $n - p$ elements in $\mathbf{Z}$. But the elements in $\mathbf{Z}$ are mutually independent, hence $\mathbf{Y'AY}$ is independent of the linear forms $\mathbf{BY}$.

We now generalize this to the situation where $\mathbf{Y}$ has a positive definite covariance $\boldsymbol{\Sigma}$.

THEOREM 4.5.2

Let the $n \times 1$ random vector $\mathbf{Y}$ be distributed $N(\mathbf{y} : \boldsymbol{\mu}, \boldsymbol{\Sigma})$, where $\boldsymbol{\Sigma}$ has rank n. If $\mathbf{B\Sigma A} = \mathbf{0}$, the quadratic form $\mathbf{Y'AY}$ is independent of the linear forms $\mathbf{BY}$, where $\mathbf{B}$ is a $q \times n$ matrix.

Proof

Since $\boldsymbol{\Sigma}$ is positive definite and hence nonsingular, it can be written as $\boldsymbol{\Sigma} = \boldsymbol{\Gamma'\Gamma}$, where $\boldsymbol{\Gamma}$ is $n \times n$ of rank n. Define the $n \times 1$ vector $\boldsymbol{\chi}$ by $\boldsymbol{\chi} = \boldsymbol{\Gamma}'^{-1}\mathbf{Y}$; $\boldsymbol{\chi}$ is distributed $N(\mathbf{x} : \boldsymbol{\Gamma}'^{-1}\boldsymbol{\mu}, \mathbf{I})$. Also $\mathbf{Y'AY} = \boldsymbol{\chi}'\boldsymbol{\Gamma}\mathbf{A}\boldsymbol{\Gamma}'\boldsymbol{\chi}$, and $\mathbf{BY} = \mathbf{B}\boldsymbol{\Gamma}'\boldsymbol{\chi}$, so by Theorem 4.5.1, $\mathbf{B}\boldsymbol{\Gamma}'\boldsymbol{\chi}$ is independent of $\boldsymbol{\chi}'\boldsymbol{\Gamma}\mathbf{A}\boldsymbol{\Gamma}'\boldsymbol{\chi}$ if $(\mathbf{B}\boldsymbol{\Gamma}')(\boldsymbol{\Gamma}\mathbf{A}\boldsymbol{\Gamma}') = \mathbf{0}$, or in other words, if $\mathbf{B\Sigma A}\boldsymbol{\Gamma}' = \mathbf{0}$. But since $\boldsymbol{\Gamma}'$ is nonsingular, $\mathbf{B\Sigma A}\boldsymbol{\Gamma}' = \mathbf{0}$ if and only if $\mathbf{B\Sigma A} = \mathbf{0}$, and the theorem is proved.

Now we prove a theorem that will help us determine when two quadratic forms in normal random variables are independent.

THEOREM 4.5.3

Let the $n \times 1$ *random vector* $\mathbf{Y}$ *be distributed* $N(\mathbf{y} : \boldsymbol{\mu}, \boldsymbol{\Sigma})$, *where* $\boldsymbol{\Sigma}$ *has rank* n. *If* $\mathbf{A\Sigma B} = \mathbf{0}$, *then the two quadratic forms* $\mathbf{Y'AY}$ *and* $\mathbf{Y'BY}$ *are independent.*

Proof

Since $\mathbf{A\Sigma B} = \mathbf{0}$, it follows that $\mathbf{A\Gamma'\Gamma B} = \mathbf{0}$ and $(\mathbf{\Gamma A \Gamma'})(\mathbf{\Gamma B \Gamma'}) = \mathbf{0}$, where $\boldsymbol{\Sigma} = \mathbf{\Gamma'\Gamma}$ and $\mathbf{\Gamma}$ is $n \times n$ of rank n. Let $\mathbf{\Gamma A \Gamma'} = \mathbf{C}$ and $\mathbf{\Gamma B \Gamma'} = \mathbf{K}$; then $\mathbf{CK} = \mathbf{0}$, $(\mathbf{CK})' = \mathbf{0}$, and hence $\mathbf{KC} = \mathbf{0}$. Thus $\mathbf{CK} = \mathbf{KC}$, and by Theorem 1.4.4 there exists an orthogonal matrix $\mathbf{P}$ such that

$$\mathbf{P'CP} = \begin{bmatrix} \mathbf{D}_1 & \mathbf{0} \\ \mathbf{0} & \mathbf{0} \end{bmatrix} \quad \text{and} \quad \mathbf{P'KP} = \begin{bmatrix} \mathbf{0} & \mathbf{0} \\ \mathbf{0} & \mathbf{D}_2 \end{bmatrix}$$

where $\mathbf{D}_1$ is an $n_1 \times n_1$ diagonal matrix and $\mathbf{D}_2$ is an $(n - n_1) \times (n - n_1)$ diagonal matrix. If we define $\mathbf{Z}$ by $\mathbf{Z} = \mathbf{P'\Gamma'^{-1}Y}$, then $\mathbf{Z}$ is distributed $N(\mathbf{z} : \mathbf{P'\Gamma'^{-1}}\boldsymbol{\mu}, \mathbf{I})$ and the Z_i are independent random variables. Also, $\mathbf{Y'AY} = \mathbf{Z'P'CPZ} = \mathbf{Z}_1'\mathbf{D}_1\mathbf{Z}_1$, and $\mathbf{Y'BY} = \mathbf{Z'P'KPZ} = \mathbf{Z}_2'\mathbf{D}_2\mathbf{Z}_2$, where $\mathbf{Z}_1$ and $\mathbf{Z}_2$ are defined by $\mathbf{Z}' = [\mathbf{Z}_1', \mathbf{Z}_2']$, where $\mathbf{Z}_1$ has size $n_1 \times 1$. Thus $\mathbf{Y'AY}$ depends only on the first n_1 elements of $\mathbf{Z}$, and $\mathbf{Y'BY}$ depends only on the last $n - n_1$ elements of $\mathbf{Z}$. But the elements of $\mathbf{Z}$ are independent, and hence $\mathbf{Y'AY}$ and $\mathbf{Y'BY}$ are independent.

Example 4.5.1

Let the $n \times 1$ random vector $\mathbf{Y}$ be distributed $N(\mathbf{y} : \boldsymbol{\mu}, \mathbf{I})$, and consider the mean $\bar{Y}$ and the sum of squares $\sum_{i=1}^{n} (Y_i - \bar{Y})^2$. Clearly $\boldsymbol{\Sigma} = \mathbf{I}$, $\bar{Y} = (1/n)\mathbf{1}'\mathbf{Y}$, and $\sum_{i=1}^{n} (Y_i - \bar{Y})^2 = \mathbf{Y}'[\mathbf{I} - (1/n)\mathbf{J}]\mathbf{Y}$. So by Theorem 4.5.1, $\bar{Y}$ is independent of $\sum_{i=1}^{n} (Y_i - \bar{Y})^2$ since $[(1/n)\mathbf{1}'][\mathbf{I} - (1/n)\mathbf{J}] = \mathbf{0}$.

4.6 Expected Value of a Quadratic Form

We are sometimes interested in finding the expected value of a quadratic form and in this section we prove some theorems that will be of help.

THEOREM 4.6.1

Let $\mathbf{Y}$ *be an* $n \times 1$ *random vector and let* $\mathscr{E}[\mathbf{Y}] = \boldsymbol{\mu}$, $\mathbf{cov}[\mathbf{Y}] = \boldsymbol{\Sigma}$. *Then*

$$\mathscr{E}[\mathbf{Y'AY}] = tr(\mathbf{A\Sigma}) + \boldsymbol{\mu}'\mathbf{A}\boldsymbol{\mu}$$

Proof

Clearly $\mathscr{E}[Y_i Y_j] = \sigma_{ij} + \mu_i \mu_j$, so

$$\mathscr{E}[\mathbf{Y}'\mathbf{A}\mathbf{Y}] = \mathscr{E}\left[\sum_{j=1}^{n} \sum_{i=1}^{n} Y_i Y_j a_{ij}\right] = \sum_{j=1}^{n} \sum_{i=1}^{n} a_{ij}(\sigma_{ij} + \mu_i \mu_j)$$

$$= \operatorname{tr}(\mathbf{A}\boldsymbol{\Sigma}) + \boldsymbol{\mu}'\mathbf{A}\boldsymbol{\mu}$$

COROLLARY 4.6.1

In Theorem 4.6.1 *if* $\boldsymbol{\Sigma} = \sigma^2\mathbf{I}$, $\boldsymbol{\mu} = \mathbf{0}$, *and* $\mathbf{A}$ *is idempotent of rank* K, *then*

$$\mathscr{E}[\mathbf{Y}'\mathbf{A}\mathbf{Y}] = \sigma^2 K$$

4.7 Additional Theorems

In this section we shall state some additional theorems and ask the reader to supply the proofs, or we give references where proofs can be found.

THEOREM 4.7.1

Let the $n \times 1$ *random vector* $\mathbf{Y}$ *be distributed* $\mathbf{N}(\mathbf{y} : \boldsymbol{\mu}, \boldsymbol{\Sigma})$ *where* $\boldsymbol{\Sigma}$ *has rank* K. *Also assume there exists an* $n \times 1$ *constant vector* $\mathbf{c}$ *such that* $\boldsymbol{\mu} = \boldsymbol{\Sigma}\mathbf{c}$. *Then any of the following three conditions are sufficient (they may not be necessary) for* $\mathbf{Y}'\mathbf{A}\mathbf{Y}$ *to be distributed as* $\chi^2(u : p; \lambda)$, *where* $\lambda = \frac{1}{2}\boldsymbol{\mu}'\mathbf{A}\boldsymbol{\mu}$:

(1) $\boldsymbol{\Sigma}\mathbf{A}$ *is idempotent of rank* p;

(2) $\mathbf{A}\boldsymbol{\Sigma}$ *is idempotent of rank* p;

(3) $\boldsymbol{\Sigma}$ *is a conditional inverse of* $\mathbf{A}$, *and* $\mathbf{A}$ *has rank* p.

Next we state a theorem proved by Patnaik [P-1] that enables one to use the central F tables to approximate integrals that involve the noncentral F distributions. For other similar approximations see [T-5].

THEOREM 4.7.2

Suppose that the random variable U *is distributed* $F(u : n_1, n_2; \lambda)$. *Then the random variable* V, *defined by* $V = U/c$, *is approximately distributed* $F(v : n_0, n_2; 0)$, *where* $c = (n_1 + 2\lambda)/n_1$ *and* $n_0 = (n_1 + 2\lambda)^2/(n_1 + 4\lambda)$.

Example 4.7.1

Use the approximation in Theorem 4.7.2 to evaluate $\Pi(\lambda)$ when

$\alpha = 0.05$, $n_1 = 6$, $n_2 = 10$, and $\lambda = 14$. We get $c = (6 + 28)/6 = 5.67$, and $n_0 = (6 + 28)^2/(6 + 56) = 18.65 \cong 19$. So

$$\Pi(14) = \int_{F_{0.05:6,10}}^{\infty} F(u : 6, 10; 14)\, du \cong \int_{(1/5.67)F_{0.05:6,10}}^{\infty} F(v : n_0, n_2; 0)\, dv$$

$$= \int_{0.568}^{\infty} F(v : 19, 10; 0) \cong 0.84$$

Using Table T.11 gives the value 0.8583.

Problems

4.1. Prove Corollary 4.2.1.1.

4.2. Prove Corollary 4.2.1.2.

4.3. Find the mean of a random variable W which is distributed $F(w : n_1, n_2; \lambda)$.

4.4. Evaluate the following integral by using Table T.11.

$$\Pi(\lambda) = \int_{F_{0.05:n_1,n_2}}^{\infty} F(w : n_1, n_2; \lambda)\, dw$$

for the following values:

n_1	4	6	7
n_2	2	30	4
λ	10	15	36

4.5. Find $t_{\alpha:v;(\delta)}$ for the following values: $\alpha = 0.05$, $v = 4$, $\delta = 1$.

4.6. If the $n \times 1$ random vector $\mathbf{Y}$ is distributed $\mathbf{N}(\mathbf{y} : \boldsymbol{\mu}, \boldsymbol{\Sigma})$, where $\boldsymbol{\Sigma}$ has rank n, show that U is distributed $\chi^2(u : n; 0)$, where U is defined by $U = (\mathbf{Y} - \boldsymbol{\mu})'\boldsymbol{\Sigma}^{-1}(\mathbf{Y} - \boldsymbol{\mu})$.

4.7. In Problem 4.6 find the distribution of $U = \mathbf{Y}'\boldsymbol{\Sigma}^{-1}\mathbf{Y}$.

4.8. Prove Theorem 4.4.4.

4.9. Prove Theorem 4.4.5.

4.10. Let $\mathbf{X}$ be an $n \times p$ matrix of constants of rank K. Partition $\mathbf{X}$ so that $\mathbf{X} = [\mathbf{X}_1, \mathbf{X}_2]$, where $\mathbf{X}_1$ is of size $n \times p_1$, $0 < p_1 < p$. Show that $(\mathbf{I} - \mathbf{X}\mathbf{X}^c)\mathbf{X}_1 = \mathbf{0}$ and $(\mathbf{I} - \mathbf{X}\mathbf{X}^c)\mathbf{X}_2 = \mathbf{0}$.

4.11. In Problem 4.10 show that $\mathbf{XX}^c - \mathbf{X}_2\mathbf{X}_2^c$ is idempotent if $\mathbf{XX}^c$ and $\mathbf{X}_2\mathbf{X}_2^c$ are symmetric.

4.12. In Problem 4.10 show that $(\mathbf{XX}^c - \mathbf{X}_2\mathbf{X}_2^c)(\mathbf{I} - \mathbf{XX}^c) = \mathbf{0}$ if $\mathbf{XX}^c$ and $\mathbf{X}_2\mathbf{X}_2^c$ are symmetric.

4.13. Let the $n \times 1$ random vector $\mathbf{Y}$ be distributed $N(\mathbf{y} : \mathbf{0}, \mathbf{I})$, and consider the following equation ($\mathbf{XX}^c$, $\mathbf{X}_2\mathbf{X}_2^c$ are assumed to be symmetric):

$$\mathbf{Y}'\mathbf{Y} = \mathbf{Y}'(\mathbf{I} - \mathbf{XX}^c)\mathbf{Y} + \mathbf{Y}'(\mathbf{XX}^c - \mathbf{X}_2\mathbf{X}_2^c)\mathbf{Y} + \mathbf{Y}'(\mathbf{X}_2\mathbf{X}_2^c)\mathbf{Y} = Q_1 + Q_2 + Q_3$$

(a) Prove Q_1 is distributed $\chi^2(u : n - K; 0)$.
(b) Prove Q_2 is distributed $\chi^2(u : K - K_2; 0)$.
(c) Prove Q_3 is distributed $\chi^2(u : K_2; 0)$.
For parts (a), (b), and (c), K_2 is the rank of $\mathbf{X}_2$, which is defined in Problem 4.10.

4.14. In Problem 4.13 show that Q_1, Q_2, Q_3 are pairwise independent.

4.15. Let $\mathbf{A}$ and $\mathbf{B}$ be $n \times n$ symmetric matrices such that $\mathbf{A} + \mathbf{B} = \mathbf{I}$. If $\mathbf{A} = \mathbf{A}^2$, show that $\mathbf{B} = \mathbf{B}^2$ and $\mathbf{AB} = \mathbf{0}$.

4.16. In Problem 4.15 show that $\text{rank}(\mathbf{A}) + \text{rank}(\mathbf{B}) = n$ if $\mathbf{A} = \mathbf{A}^2$.

4.17. Let $\mathbf{A}, \mathbf{B}, \mathbf{C}$ be $n \times n$ symmetric matrices such that $\mathbf{A} + \mathbf{B} + \mathbf{C} = \mathbf{I}$. If $\mathbf{A} = \mathbf{A}^2$, $\mathbf{B} = \mathbf{B}^2$, and $\mathbf{C}$ is nonnegative, show that $\mathbf{C} = \mathbf{C}^2$, $\mathbf{AB} = \mathbf{AC} = \mathbf{BC} = \mathbf{0}$.

4.18. Prove Theorem 4.7.1.

4.19. Use Theorem 4.7.2 to find an approximate value of $\Pi(\lambda)$ for values of n_1, n_2, λ, and α given in Problem 4.4.

CHAPTER 5

Models

5.1 Introduction

One of the aims of science is to find, to describe, and to predict relationships among events in the world in which we live. One way that this is accomplished is by finding a formula or equation that relates quantities in the real world. We may be interested, for example, in the relationship between temperature and pressure in a chemical process; or in the relationship between the number of apples on trees in an orchard and the amount of fertilizer the trees receive; or we may be interested in the relationship of supply, demand, and price of certain commodities; or in how a certain vaccine affects a disease; or in the relationship of rainfall, temperature, and humidity; or in the yields of various varieties of wheat.

To study these types of problems we shall define four models that are very rich in the number of real-world situations that they can be used to represent. Two of these models are classified as quantitative and two as qualitative.

Quantitative Models	*Qualitative Models*
1. General Linear Model	3. Design Model
2. Linear Regression Model	4. Components-of-Variance Model

These models are closely related and procedures for drawing inferences will reveal a great deal of similarity among them. To take advantage of this similarity, we shall first define and discuss the general linear model since the other models can be viewed as variations of this one.

5.2 General Linear Model

A *general linear (statistical) model* that is to be used to determine y from a knowledge of x is usually written in the form

$$Y = \mu(x) + \varepsilon \tag{5.2.1}$$

where Y and ε are random variables, $\mu(x)$ is a function of x, defined in a domain D, and x is a nonrandom variable. The function $\mu(x)$ is defined to be the deterministic portion of the model, Y and ε the random (or stochastic) portions. Also, Y is referred to as the dependent or response variable and x is referred to as the independent or predictor variable. If Y represents, say, the blood pressure of an individual, and if x represents, say, the age of an individual, then $\mu(x)$ is the predicted value of the individual's blood pressure from a knowledge of his age x. Also, $y - \mu(x)$ is the deviation of his measured blood pressure y from his predicted blood pressure $\mu(x)$, and this deviation is denoted by e and defined as the *error*. The random variable ε is not observable, but something about the distribution of ε is often stated as part of the model. In general, the "functional form" of $\mu(x)$ is known but it contains unknown parameters. The word "linear" implies that $\mu(x)$ is a *linear* function of the unknown *parameters*. In the simple case $\mu(x)$ is defined by $\mu(x) = \beta_0 + \beta x$ for x in the set D, the domain of $\mu(x)$; β_0 and β are unknown parameters defined in a parameter space $\Omega_{\boldsymbol{\beta}}$. Often β_0 and β can be any real numbers. Thus we can write this model as

$$Y = \beta_0 + \beta x + \varepsilon \tag{5.2.2}$$

In its most general form, $\mu(x)$ is a linear function of $k + 1$ unknown parameters $\beta_0, \beta_1, \beta_2, \ldots, \beta_k$ and can be written as

$$\mu(x) = \beta_0 + \beta_1 q_1(x) + \beta_2 q_2(x) + \cdots + \beta_k q_k(x)$$

where $q_i(x)$ is a *known* function of x and contains no unknown parameters.

Some examples of a general linear model are given below.

$$
\begin{aligned}
&Y = \beta_0 + \beta_1 x + \beta_2 x^2 + \beta_3 x^3 + \varepsilon && \mathscr{E}[\varepsilon] = 0 && \text{var}[\varepsilon] = \sigma^2 \text{ (unknown)}\\
&Y = \beta x + \varepsilon && \mathscr{E}[\varepsilon] = 0 && \text{var}[\varepsilon] = \sigma^2 \text{ (unknown)}\\
&Y = \beta_0 + \beta_1 x + \beta_2 e^x + \varepsilon && \varepsilon \text{ is distributed } N(\varepsilon : 0, \sigma^2), && \sigma^2 \text{ unknown}
\end{aligned}
\tag{5.2.3}
$$

In each model the reader can identify $q_i(x)$. For example, in the first case $q_1(x) = x$, $q_2(x) = x^2$, and $q_3(x) = x^3$.

The deterministic portion of the model can be a function of more than one x variable. For example, the model could be

$$Y = \mu(x_1, x_2, \ldots, x_{p-1}) + \varepsilon \qquad \mathscr{E}[\varepsilon] = 0 \tag{5.2.4}$$

where $\mu(x_1, x_2, \ldots, x_{p-1}) = \beta_0 + \sum_{i=1}^{p-1} x_i\beta_i$, or more generally,

$$\mu(x_1, x_2, \ldots, x_{p-1}) = \beta_0 + \sum_{i=1}^{k} q_i(x_1, x_2, \ldots, x_{p-1})\beta_i \tag{5.2.5}$$

where each $q_i(x_1, x_2, \ldots, x_{p-1})$ is a known function and contains no unknown parameters. As an example, if $p = 4$, we could have $\mu(x_1, x_2, x_3) = \beta_0 + \beta_1 x_1 + \beta_2 x_2 + \beta_3 x_3$, and this model is

$$Y = \beta_0 + \beta_1 x_1 + \beta_2 x_2 + \beta_3 x_3 + \varepsilon \qquad \mathscr{E}[\varepsilon] = 0$$

These are "population" models and the objective is, in part, to estimate the unknown parameters. To do this it is necessary to obtain some observations from populations represented by these models. For instance, if the model in Equation (5.2.2) is to be used to predict an indiviual's blood pressure y from a knowledge of his age x, then we must first obtain estimates of β_0 and β. To do this we define a population of individuals for each age to which the model applies, and from some of these populations we observe a sample of blood pressures of individuals. For example, if we assume that the model holds only for ages $x = 20, 25, 30, 35, \ldots, 75$ years, then this set of integers is the domain D of $\mu(x)$. Also, there is a population of blood pressures of individuals at each of these ages. Suppose we decide to observe one individual's blood pressure at random from each population defined by the ages $x_1 = 20$, $x_2 = 35$, $x_3 = 50$, $x_4 = 60$, $x_5 = 70$, $x_6 = 75$. Let Y_i denote the observable blood pressure of the person that will be selected at random from the population of blood pressures at age x_i for $i = 1, 2, \ldots, 6$. The sample to be observed is denoted by $(x_1, Y_1), (x_2, Y_2), \ldots, (x_6, Y_6)$, and by Equation (5.2.2) these are related by

$$\left.\begin{aligned} Y_i &= \beta_0 + \beta x_i + \varepsilon_i \\ \mathscr{E}[\varepsilon_i] &= 0 \end{aligned}\right\} \quad \text{for } i = 1, 2, \ldots, 6 \tag{5.2.6}$$

This set of relationships is called a "sample" model. From the six pairs of observations $(x_1, y_1), (x_2, y_2), \ldots, (x_6, y_6)$ which are related by Equation (5.2.6), we compute estimates of β_0, β, and any other quantities of interest. The point we make here is that the models in Equations (5.2.3) and (5.2.5) are population models in that they define a relationship over a set D, the domain of $\mu(x)$, and Y is a random variable for each x in D. From this setup we must obtain a sample of n values $(x_1, y_1), (x_2, y_2), \ldots, (x_n, y_n)$, and we use these observations to make inferences about the unknown parameters in the model.

Since $\mathscr{E}[Y] = \mu(x)$, it is clear that the random variable Y depends on the nonrandom variable x, and hence it would be more revealing to write Equation (5.2.1) as

$$Y_{(x)} = \mu(x) + \varepsilon_{(x)} \qquad \mathscr{E}[\varepsilon_{(x)}] = 0 \qquad \text{for each } x \text{ in } D$$

and when more than a single x is involved, to write Equation (5.2.4) as

$$Y_{(\mathbf{x})} = \mu(\mathbf{x}) + \varepsilon_{(\mathbf{x})} \qquad \mathscr{E}[\varepsilon_{(\mathbf{x})}] = 0 \qquad \text{for each } \mathbf{x} \text{ in } D \tag{5.2.7}$$

or more specifically,

$$Y_{(\mathbf{x})} = \beta_0 + \sum_{i=1}^{p-1} x_i\beta_i + \varepsilon_{(\mathbf{x})} \qquad \mathscr{E}[\varepsilon_{(\mathbf{x})}] = 0 \qquad \text{for each } \mathbf{x} \text{ in } D$$

Equation (5.2.7) states the following:

1. $\mu(\mathbf{x})$ is a function of $p - 1$ (nonrandom) real variables $x_1, x_2, \ldots, x_{p-1}$ and the domain of the function is denoted by D. Clearly D is a subset of E_{p-1};
2. for each $\mathbf{x}$ in D, $Y_{(\mathbf{x})}$ and $\varepsilon_{(\mathbf{x})}$ are random variables with a structure as given in Equation (5.2.7), that is, that $\mu(\mathbf{x})$ is the mean of $Y_{(\mathbf{x})}$ for each $\mathbf{x}$ in D;
3. the function $\mu(\mathbf{x})$ is a linear function of p unknown parameters β_i, that is, $\mu(\mathbf{x})$ is defined by

$$\mu(\mathbf{x}) = \beta_0 + \sum_{i=1}^{p-1} x_i\beta_i$$

for $\boldsymbol{\beta}$ in a parameter space $\Omega_{\boldsymbol{\beta}}$ and each $\mathbf{x}$ in D (or more generally, by $\mu(\mathbf{x})$ as defined in Equation (5.2.5)).

Equation (5.2.7) with the specifications 1, 2, and 3 defines a general linear *population* model.

Summary. In using statistical procedures to draw inferences to real-world situations, it is necessary to first define a conceptual population model that represents the real-world situation that is under investigation. From this conceptual population model, a sample model is defined, and using this model, data are collected and inferences are made. For example, Equation (5.2.7) with conditions 1, 2, and 3 defines a general linear *population* model. This model includes a random variable $Y_{(\mathbf{x})}$, and hence a c.d.f. $F_{Y_{(\mathbf{x})}}(y)$, for each $\mathbf{x}$ in the domain D. To draw inferences to the unknown parameters in the model we must obtain samples, and it may not be possible or desirable to sample each of these c.d.f.'s. Thus we must define the method of sampling to be used and the structure of sample observations.

Since the special case when there is only one x variable is important both in real-world problems and in illustrative examples, we term this a *simple* linear model and define it first. We then extend this to $(p - 1)$ x variables and define a *general* linear model.

DEFINITION 5.2.1

Simple Linear (Sample) Model. *Consider the n equations*

$$\left.\begin{aligned} Y_i &= \beta_0 + \beta x_i + \varepsilon_i \\ \mathscr{E}[\varepsilon_i] &= 0 \end{aligned}\right\} \quad i = 1, 2, \ldots, n \tag{5.2.8}$$

where

(1) *the Y_i are observable random variables;*

(2) *the x_i are observable nonrandom variables from a domain D;*

(3) *β_0 and β are unknown parameters defined in a parameter space $\Omega_{\boldsymbol{\beta}}$;*

(4) *the ε_i are unobservable random variables such that $cov[\varepsilon_i, \varepsilon_j] = \sigma_{ij}$.*

These specifications define a simple linear model.

Before we extend this to a *general linear model*, we discuss some implications of this definition.

Note 1. The n values of x are observed, and each observed x determines a c.d.f., that is, x_1 determines a c.d.f. which we denote by $F_1(\cdot)$. This c.d.f. has a mean $\beta_0 + \beta x_1$ and a variance σ_{11}. From this c.d.f. a random sample of size one will be selected and denoted by Y_1; this is repeated for $x_2, x_3, \ldots,$ and x_n. Thus the observable data are represented by (x_1, Y_1), $(x_2, Y_2), \ldots, (x_n, Y_n)$, and these values are related by Equation (5.2.8).

Note 2. Throughout the discussion the x variable is considered to be fixed at the values $x_1, x_2, \ldots, x_n$, and the long-run relative frequency interpretation of the probabilities involved in the inferences is related to repeated sampling of Y values from the n c.d.f.'s $F_i(\cdot)$, $i = 1, 2, \ldots, n$.

The thing to remember here is that once these n values of x are determined, they specify n c.d.f.'s $F_i(\cdot)$, $i = 1, 2, \ldots, n$, *and these are the only c.d.f.'s that are sampled*! Thus y_1 represents a sample value from $F_1(\cdot)$, y_2 represents a sample value from $F_2(\cdot)$, and so forth. Hence the inference is to the unknown parameters in *these* n c.d.f.'s only. It seems, however, that we may want to use the data to make inferences about parameters in a c.d.f. $F_0(\cdot)$ determined by x_0, where x_0 is not one of our selected x values. We may be able to make this inference since, if x_0 is in the domain D, then the population model may tell us that some of the unknown parameters in the c.d.f. $F_0(\cdot)$ which we *did not sample* are the same parameters in the c.d.f.'s which we *did sample*. These ideas will be amplified in some of the examples.

Note 3. Condition (4) merely indicates the existence of the covariance of Y_i and Y_j. Often additional assumptions on the random errors ε_i will be made. For example, in most cases it will be assumed that the ε_i are independent and normally distributed with constant variance σ^2.

Note 4. In each problem it is essential to define D and $\Omega_{\boldsymbol{\beta}}$, the domain of the function $\mu(\cdot)$ and the parameter space of the β's, respectively. Actually, in many problems the parameter space is E_2 since β_0 and β can be any real numbers. However, in some models it may be realistic to assume $\beta_0 = 0$, or perhaps to assume $\beta > 0$, or to assume other conditions on the β's. The domain D will often be an interval on the x-axis, or perhaps a set of integers, and so on. The reason that it is important to define D is that $\mu(x) = \beta_0 + \beta x$ may be a good model for the real-world situation under investigation for only certain values of x; it may not be a good model for all values of x.

Note 5. It is important that the values of x be observed without error. When this is not the case, the inference situation changes drastically, and in fact there is no optimum inference procedure unless additional assumptions are made about the model. When x is a continuous variable such as height or weight, it is, of course, impossible to observe these quantities without measurement error. This points up a difficulty in trying to model the real world with a conceptual model. We merely state here that if the general linear model is to be used, then in the real-world situation that it represents, the variance of any measurement error on the x's must be "small" relative to the values of the x's observed; so we assume that the x's are fixed numbers and measured without error.

We could write the n equations in the model in Definition 5.2.1 as a single matrix equation

$$\mathbf{Y} = \mathbf{X}\boldsymbol{\beta} + \boldsymbol{\varepsilon} \qquad \mathscr{E}[\boldsymbol{\varepsilon}] = \mathbf{0} \qquad \mathbf{cov}[\boldsymbol{\varepsilon}] = \boldsymbol{\Sigma}$$

where the matrices and vectors are

$$\mathbf{Y} = \begin{bmatrix} Y_1 \\ Y_2 \\ \vdots \\ Y_n \end{bmatrix} \qquad \mathbf{X} = \begin{bmatrix} 1 & x_1 \\ 1 & x_2 \\ \vdots & \vdots \\ 1 & x_n \end{bmatrix} \qquad \boldsymbol{\beta} = \begin{bmatrix} \beta_0 \\ \beta \end{bmatrix} \qquad \boldsymbol{\varepsilon} = \begin{bmatrix} \varepsilon_1 \\ \varepsilon_2 \\ \vdots \\ \varepsilon_n \end{bmatrix}$$

For this simple case the matrix equation method of writing the model is not too advantageous. However, when there are two or more x variables, the matrix model is very useful.

We now extend these concepts and define the *general* linear model.

DEFINITION 5.2.2

General Linear (Sample) Model. *Consider the n equations*

$$\left.\begin{aligned} Y_i &= \sum_{j=1}^{p} x_{ij}\beta_j + \varepsilon_i \\ \mathscr{E}[\varepsilon_i] &= 0 \end{aligned}\right\} \quad i = 1, 2, \ldots, n \tag{5.2.9}$$

where

(1) *the Y_i are observable random variables;*

(2) *the x_{ij} are observable nonrandom variables from a domain D;*

(3) *the β_j are unknown parameters defined in a parameter space $\Omega_{\boldsymbol{\beta}}$;*

(4) *the ε_i are unobservable random variables such that $\operatorname{cov}[\varepsilon_i, \varepsilon_{i'}] = \sigma_{ii'}$.*

These specifications define a general linear model.

Since we use vector and matrix methods throughout this book, we shall state Definition 5.2.2 in these terms.

DEFINITION 5.2.3

General Linear Model. *Consider the matrix equation*

$$\mathbf{Y} = \mathbf{X}\boldsymbol{\beta} + \boldsymbol{\varepsilon} \tag{5.2.10}$$

where

(1) $\mathbf{Y}$ *is an $n \times 1$ observable random vector;*

(2) $\mathbf{X}$ *is an $n \times p$ matrix of fixed observable numbers (the elements of* $\mathbf{X}$ *are not random variables);*

(3) $\boldsymbol{\beta}$ *is a* $p \times 1$ *vector of unobservable parameters defined in a parameter space* $\Omega_{\boldsymbol{\beta}}$;

(4) $\boldsymbol{\varepsilon}$ *is an* $n \times 1$ *unobservable random vector such that* $\mathscr{E}[\boldsymbol{\varepsilon}] = \mathbf{0}$ *and* $\mathbf{cov}[\boldsymbol{\varepsilon}] = \boldsymbol{\Sigma}$.

These specifications define a general linear model.

From here on, when we talk about a general linear model, we will mean a general linear *sample* model given in Definition 5.2.3. However, we should keep in mind the population model that is in the background.

Note 6. In specification (4) the statement $\mathbf{cov}[\boldsymbol{\varepsilon}] = \boldsymbol{\Sigma}$ implies only that $\mathbf{cov}[\boldsymbol{\varepsilon}]$, and hence $\mathbf{cov}[\mathbf{Y}]$, exists and that $\boldsymbol{\Sigma}$ is the symbol we use.

Note 7. In many cases further assumptions about the distributional properties of $\boldsymbol{\varepsilon}$ (or $\mathbf{Y}$) or further assumptions about the structure of $\boldsymbol{\Sigma}$ will be stated as part of the model.

Note 8. If we write the matrices and vectors in Equation (5.2.10) in detail, we get

$$\mathbf{Y} = \begin{bmatrix} Y_1 \\ Y_2 \\ \vdots \\ Y_n \end{bmatrix} \qquad \mathbf{X} = \begin{bmatrix} x_{11} & x_{12} & \cdots & x_{1p} \\ x_{21} & x_{22} & \cdots & x_{2p} \\ \vdots & \vdots & & \vdots \\ x_{n1} & x_{n2} & \cdots & x_{np} \end{bmatrix}$$
$$\boldsymbol{\beta} = \begin{bmatrix} \beta_1 \\ \beta_2 \\ \vdots \\ \beta_p \end{bmatrix} \qquad \boldsymbol{\varepsilon} = \begin{bmatrix} \varepsilon_1 \\ \varepsilon_2 \\ \vdots \\ \varepsilon_n \end{bmatrix} \tag{5.2.11}$$

Notice the slight change in notation—the subscripts on the β_j run from 1 to p instead of 0 to $p - 1$. The same is true for the second subscript on the x_{ij}. Since our theoretical work will be almost exclusively with the matrix model, this notation will be more symmetrical and natural. When special cases are presented and the model is written in detail, the reader should have no difficulty in identifying the various elements. For example, if a constant term β_0 is in the model, then the first column of the $\mathbf{X}$ matrix has each element equal to unity and the $\boldsymbol{\beta}$ vector will have elements $\beta_0, \beta_1, \ldots, \beta_{p-1}$.

In the remainder of this section, we discuss how this model can be generated from real-world situations and give guidelines to help in developing the model.

Suppose two nonrandom variables x and z represent the measurements of quantities in the real world and they are functionally related by $q(x, z) = 0$. Some may argue that $q(x, z) = 0$ is simply a mathematical abstraction and that no such functional relationship *can* exist in the real world. It is nevertheless true that the *concept* of a functional relationship in the real world is important. And although the relationship may not be exact, it may be so close that the approximation is very useful. For example, a circle (or a triangle, or rectangle) is an idealized geometrical figure; a physical circle does not exist. Nevertheless, it is the model for the wheel as well as for many other physical quantities and very precise predictions in the real world can be made by using the geometrical circle as a model. Similarly, a geometric point, line, and plane are useful models for certain quantities in the real world. Therefore, when we say that a functional relationship exists among the measurements of a set of variables in the real world, we mean that the function describes a relationship to a very close approximation.

Instead of representing the relationship by $q(x, z) = 0$, it is sometimes more useful to represent it by

$$z = \mu(x)$$

where z is the value of the quantity that is to be determined from the value x of another quantity.

For example, consider the relationship between time t and the distance s that a particle in a vacuum falls under the influence of the earth's gravity, that is, $s = \frac{1}{2}gt^2$. For many practical purposes we consider this a functional relationship, and from a knowledge of t we can determine the distance quite accurately in a real-world experience.

In many fields of scientific endeavor, for example, in physics, relationships are often so exact that they can indeed be expressed by a function such as $z = \mu(x)$, or more generally by $z = \mu(x_1, x_2, \ldots, x_k)$. For instance, Ohm's law states that the electromotive force z is equal to the resistance x_1 of the conductor times the current x_2, that is, $z = x_1 x_2$. The law of gravitation states that the force of attraction z between two unit mass points is inversely proportional to the square of the distance x between the points, that is, $z = \beta/x^2$. There are many other such relationships: Boyle's gas law, Kirchhoff's law in electricity, Newton's laws of force and acceleration, Newton's law of cooling, and so forth.

If there is a functional relationship between x and z which is represented by $z = \mu(x)$, then the model $z = \mu(x)$ is a very special case of the model in Equation (5.2.1), that is, the mean and variance of ε are equal to zero. Thus the model has no stochastic component, and hence it is not a statistical model but it is a mathematical model. There are situations, however, when this model becomes a statistical model. Suppose, as is sometimes the case, that z is not observable, and instead of observing z one observes Y, where $Y = z + \varepsilon$, that is, the random variable Y is equal to the correct value z plus a random measurement error ε. If we replace z by $Y - \varepsilon$ in the equation $z = \mu(x)$, we obtain

$$Y = \mu(x) + \varepsilon$$

What we have shown here is that even though there is a functional relationship between two variables z and x, it may be necessasy to cast this in the form of the statistical model in Equation (5.2.1) if there is measurement error involved in the *dependent* variable. The reason there is no functional relationship between x and Y is due to *measurement error* in the *dependent* variable.

Although functional relationships are assumed in many fields of science such as physics, there are many scientific areas such as biology, economics, and meteorology where quantities are related *not* functionally but in a much more obscure manner.

For example, it is known that the yield of wheat in a given plot of ground cannot be predicted exactly. Many of the factors affecting this yield are known, but the equation relating the quantities is obscure. It is known that the amount of fertilizer applied x, temperature x_1, rainfall x_2, amount of sunshine x_3, fertility of the soil x_4, and *many* other factors influence the yield z. Although *all* of the factors that affect this yield are not known, and although the relationship is not known, it may nevertheless be useful in model building to assume as a working hypothesis that if the investigator knew all of the variables that are involved, could measure all of them, and knew the correct function, then he could exactly determine z by a formula $z = g(x, x_1, \ldots, x_k)$. In most studies it is not possible to identify all of the variables, but it is often possible to isolate a few that dominate in determining z. Suppose, for example, that one nonrandom variable x, that can be observed without error, has been identified as intuitively important in determining z. The model $z = g(x, x_1, \ldots, x_k)$ would then be separated as follows:

$$z = \mu(x) + h(x, x_1, \ldots, x_k) \tag{5.2.12}$$

where the function $\mu(x)$ is assumed to be known (except for unknown parameters), and the function $h(x, x_1, \ldots, x_k)$ is not known. The values of $h(x, x_1, \ldots, x_k)$ are assumed to be small relative to the values of $\mu(x)$ for all values of $x, x_1, \ldots, x_k$ in the domain of interest. If this is not the case, then the model may not be useful. Although it is recognized by the investigator that the x variable dominates in determining z, he also realizes that there are other variables $x_1, x_2, \ldots, x_k$ (some random, some nonrandom) which are necessary to include if z is to be determined exactly. It is assumed that these variables are of secondary importance but that they vary in unknown ways as the main variable x changes. That is, for a fixed value of x there is an unpredictability in z due to the influence of the remaining x_i. These remaining variables thus contribute "noise" to the model, where "noise" is defined as a seemingly random component of variation that still remains in z after the effect of the known variable is accounted for.

One way to consider the problem is to assume that $h(x, x_1, \ldots, x_k)$ acts as a random component and write the model in Equation (5.2.12) as

$$Y = \mu(x) + \varepsilon \tag{5.2.13}$$

where $h(x, x_1, \ldots, x_k)$ has been replaced by the random variable ε. Note that z is now replaced by the random variable Y, and if $\mathscr{E}[\varepsilon] = 0$, this implies that $\mathscr{E}[Y] = \mu(x)$. The model is now a statistical model as given in Equation (5.2.1).

It is important to note here that $\mu(x)$ would be used to determine z from a knowledge of x, but that for a given x the value $\mu(x)$ is not the "true" value of z since there are possibly many different values of z that correspond to the one value of x. To make this more explicit, if $x = a$, then the formula in Equation (5.2.12) is

$$z = \mu(a) + h(a, x_1, \ldots, x_k)$$

and z will depend on the values of $x_1, x_2, \ldots, x_k$, which can take on different values for a fixed $x = a$. If, however, we write this as

$$Y = \mu(a) + \varepsilon$$

and if the values of $h(a, x_1, \ldots, x_k)$ vary in a small range (that is, if $\text{var}[\varepsilon]$ is small), then for many practical purposes $\mu(a)$ may be satisfactorily used to represent the value of z at the value $x = a$. The random component is due to the wrong equation in determining z, that is, we use $\mu(x)$ to determine z instead of the correct value $\mu(x) + h(x, x_1, \ldots, x_k)$. The reason there is no functional relationship between x and z is not due to measurement error in z, as was the case in the functional relationship model referred to above, but is due to *equation error* (due to the wrong equation).

It should be pointed out that if Y is not observable but there is a measurement error and Y^* is observable, where $Y^* = Y + \varepsilon^*$, then we substitute this into Equation (5.2.13) and get

$$Y^* = \mu(x) + \varepsilon^{**}$$

where $\varepsilon^{**} = \varepsilon + \varepsilon^*$, and this is also in the form of Equation (5.2.1).

We note that the function $h(x, x_1, \ldots, x_k)$, that we replace by ε, includes the variable x. This allows for the distribution of ε to depend on the dominant variable x as it does in some models. For example, in some models it may be realistic to assume that $\text{var}[\varepsilon]$ depends on x. However, we will always assume as a part of our model that $\mathscr{E}[\varepsilon] = 0$ for each value of x, since if $\mathscr{E}[\varepsilon]$ depends on x, we can incorporate this as a part of $\mu(x)$.

When modeling a real world problem it is extremely important to *state* the values that the variable x can assume. For instance, the function $\mu(x)$ may be a realistic model only for x in a certain interval, or it may be realistic to define $\mu(x)$ only for certain positive integers. The importance of stating the values that x can assume will be brought out in the examples of this section.

Now we give some examples of real-world problems that can be represented by a *general linear statistical model*, such as Equation (5.2.1) or Equation (5.2.4).

Example 5.2.1

Suppose the distance s that a mass-particle moves from a point of reference in time t is given by the formula

$$s = \beta_0 + \beta t \tag{5.2.14}$$

In this problem t is a nonrandom variable and we assume it can be observed without error. However, suppose that s cannot be measured accurately, but instead of observing s, one can observe values of Y, where $Y = s + \varepsilon$, that is, the observable variable Y is equal to the true distance s plus a measurement error ε. If we substitute, we get

$$Y = \beta_0 + \beta t + \varepsilon \qquad \mathscr{E}[\varepsilon] = 0 \qquad \text{var}[\varepsilon] = \sigma^2 \text{ (unknown)} \tag{5.2.15}$$

Suppose that this model is assumed to hold only for t in the interval $0 \leq t \leq 100$. This is a functional relationship model with measurement error in the dependent variable. To obtain sample values the investigator would preselect n values of time, say $t_1, t_2, \ldots, t_n$, and observe the corresponding distances $y_1, y_2, \ldots, y_n$. Thus the sample model is

$$\left.\begin{aligned} Y_i &= \beta_0 + \beta t_i + \varepsilon_i \\ \mathscr{E}[\varepsilon_i] &= 0 \end{aligned}\right\} \quad i = 1, 2, \ldots, n$$

and this fits the simple linear model in Definition 5.2.1.

Example 5.2.2

It is known that as a river moves downstream and carries small rocks along its path, the rocks tend to become smooth and round in shape. The shape of these rocks can possibly be used to determine how far they have been transported, and hence the source of the rocks can be determined. A geologist is therefore interested in the relationship between the shape (a measure of this is called sphericity) of granite pebbles in a certain stream and the distance from a source point that the pebbles have been transported by the stream. The linear model is

$$Y = \beta_0 + \beta x + \varepsilon \qquad \mathscr{E}[\varepsilon] = 0 \qquad \text{var}[\varepsilon] = \sigma^2 \text{ (unknown)} \tag{5.2.16}$$

This is a model with *equation* error since there are factors that determine the sphericity Y other than the distance the pebble is transported by the water in the stream. Suppose that this model is assumed to hold only for x in the interval $50 \leq x \leq 300$ miles. Hence the set D is defined by $D = \{x : 50 \leq x \leq 300\}$. Thus we are discussing a collection of a nondenumerable number of random variables $\{Y_{(x)} : x \in D\}$. Suppose we assume that for each $x \in D$, $Y_{(x)}$ is distributed normally with mean $\mu(x)$ and variance σ^2, where $\mu(x) = \beta_0 + \beta x$ and where β_0, β, σ^2 are unknown. *It is important to note that nothing has been stated about the joint distribution of the random variables but only about the marginal distribution of the random variable $Y_{(x)}$ for each x in D.*

One of the objectives in this model is to estimate the unknown parameters β_0, β, and σ^2 from sample observations from the model. Another objective may be to estimate x_0, the distance a pebble has been transported by observing y_0, the sphericity of the pebble. This is sometimes referred to as inverse regression since a value of the dependent variable is used to estimate the value of the independent variable.

Suppose the investigator decides to measure the sphericity of a pebble (or more realistically, a handful of pebbles) every 50 miles along the stream. Thus he selects a set of six x's from D, denoted by $x_1 = 50$, $x_2 = 100$, $x_3 = 150$, $x_4 = 200$, $x_5 = 250$, $x_6 = 300$, and these determine the c.d.f.'s that will be sampled. The sphericity observations are obtained from the c.d.f.'s of the six random variables $Y_{(50)}$, $Y_{(100)}$, $Y_{(150)}$, $Y_{(200)}$, $Y_{(250)}$, $Y_{(300)}$. For the random variables in the sample, we shall use the symbol Y_1 to denote the sample random variable with $x = x_1$, that is, Y_1 denotes a random observation from the c.d.f. of the random variable $Y_{(x_1)}$; $Y_2, Y_3, \ldots, Y_6$ have similar meanings. For instance, in this example if a pebble is selected at random from the stream at $x_1 = 50$ miles from the point of reference, then Y_1 will represent a random sphericity observation. If this process is repeated at $x_2 = 100, \ldots, x_6 = 300$, and if the pebbles are selected in a manner so that the observations can be assumed to be independent, the *sample* model can be written

$$\left.\begin{array}{l} Y_i = \beta_0 + \beta x_i + \varepsilon_i \\ \varepsilon_i \text{ are independent with } \mathscr{E}[\varepsilon_i] = 0 \end{array}\right\} \quad i = 1, 2, \ldots, 6 \qquad (5.2.17)$$

On the basis of the six pairs of observations $(x_1, y_1), \ldots, (x_6, y_6)$, we develop an inference for β_0, β, σ^2 and functions of these parameters.

Note 9. As a general rule, no inference can be made about any of the c.d.f.'s from which we did not sample. For instance, we did not observe any pebbles at the distance $x = 235$ miles, hence we did not sample the c.d.f. $F_{Y_{(235)}}(\cdot)$, and, in general, we cannot make an inference about parameters in a c.d.f. when we have no observations from that particular c.d.f. However, since by the "population" model the random variable $Y_{(235)}$ is distributed normally with mean $\beta_0 + 235\beta$ and variance σ^2, we can estimate the mean and variance of $Y_{(235)}$ without sampling from that c.d.f. This, of course, is due to the fact that we can estimate the parameters β_0, β, and σ^2 by sampling from the c.d.f.'s of the random variables $Y_{(50)}, \ldots, Y_{(300)}$. It should be noted that we *cannot* estimate the parameters in the c.d.f. of $Y_{(350)}$, say, since we know *nothing* about these parameters. We *do not know* whether or not the mean of $Y_{(350)}$ is $\beta_0 + 350\beta$ or whether the variance is σ^2. Our "population model" tells us nothing about any random variables, and hence about any c.d.f.'s, except those c.d.f.'s in the collection $\{F_{Y_{(x)}}(\cdot) : 50 \leq x \leq 300\}$, and $F_{Y_{(350)}}(\cdot)$ is not in the collection. Perhaps the investigator included only the x values from 50 to 300 in the "population model" because he was not interested in other values, or perhaps he did not have enough information to model the real world for other values of x. For example, a function other than $\mu(x) = \beta_0 + \beta x$ may be appropriate when $x > 300$ or $x < 50$.

Example 5.2.3

For another example, consider a company that produces a certain chemical. Each day the company makes x batches of the chemical, where $x = 1, 2, 3, \ldots, 10$ and is determined by the production superintendent. The quality control section of the company notices that the percentage of impurities Y in a day's production is approximately linearly related to the number of batches made that day. The following model is used: $Y = \mu(x) + \varepsilon = \beta_0 + \beta x + \varepsilon$, where Y is the percentage of impurities in a day's production and $\mu(x)$ is the average percentage of impurities, averaged over those days in which x batches were produced. For example, $\mu(4)$ is the average (percentage of impurities) over all those days for which four batches were produced. One thing to notice here is that the domain of the function $\mu(x)$ is $1, 2, \ldots, 10$. Thus while $\mu(x)$ is a function of x, it is indeed true that x is defined only for certain positive integers. Suppose that the company has never made more than seven batches in any one day, but it wants to increase production to ten batches per day. The objective will be to estimate $\mu(10)$, the average percentage of impurities in a day's production when ten batches are made in one day. The domain D is defined by $D = \{x : x = 1, 2, \ldots, 10\}$. There are ten points in D and hence there are only ten c.d.f.'s under discussion, namely $\{F_{Y_{(1)}}(\cdot), F_{Y_{(2)}}(\cdot), \ldots, F_{Y_{(10)}}(\cdot)\}$. We assume that $\mu(x) = \beta_0 + \beta x$, and that $Y_{(x)}$ is a normal random variable with mean $\mu(x)$ and variance equal to σ^2 for each x in D. Only the first seven of the c.d.f.'s are available for sampling since the company has never made more than seven batches in a single day. Nevertheless, it is assumed that the model represents the physical situation for 1, 2, ..., 10 batches. Since the objective is to estimate the impurities when ten batches are produced in one day, we want to estimate a function of parameters in a c.d.f. without sampling from that particular c.d.f. We can do this since the model states that $\mathscr{E}[Y_{(10)}] = \mu(10) = \beta_0 + 10\beta$, and we can estimate β_0 and β, and hence $\beta_0 + 10\beta$, by sampling from only the c.d.f.'s $F_{Y_{(1)}}(\cdot), \ldots, F_{Y_{(7)}}(\cdot)$, that is, by sampling from days when one through seven batches are produced.

Suppose we decide to sample impurities Y for days when one, three, five, and seven batches are produced. Thus we select a sample of size one from the c.d.f. of the random variable $Y_{(1)}$ and denote this observation by y_1; similarly for $x_2 = 3, x_3 = 5$, and $x_4 = 7$. The set of observations is denoted by (x_1, y_1), (x_2, y_2), (x_3, y_3), (x_4, y_4), where $x_1 = 1$, $x_2 = 3$, $x_3 = 5$, $x_4 = 7$, and they are related by the model

$$\left.\begin{array}{l} Y_i = \beta_0 + \beta x_i + \varepsilon_i \\ \varepsilon_i \text{ are independent with } \mathscr{E}[\varepsilon_i] = 0 \end{array}\right\} \quad i = 1, 2, 3, 4$$

We assume that the sampling is done in a manner so that the ε_i (and hence the Y_i) are independent.

Example 5.2.4

Suppose it is desired to examine the relationship of temperature x_1 and pressure x_2 during production to the strength Y of a certain material. One objective is to estimate what the strength of the material will be as a function of the temperature and pressure at which the material is made. As a first approximation the population model is assumed to be

$$Y_{(x_1, x_2)} = \beta_0 + \beta_1 x_1 + \beta_2 x_2 + \beta_3 x_1 x_2 + \varepsilon \qquad \mathscr{E}[\varepsilon] = 0$$

where the domain D is

$$D = \{(x_1, x_2): 500 \le x_1 \le 1500;\ 1000 \le x_2 \le 2000\}$$

where x_1 is degrees centigrade, x_2 is pounds per square inch, and Y is in pounds per square inch. It is desired to obtain a picture of the response Y over the domain D, so a sample of one Y value is selected at every 100 degrees centigrade and every 100 pounds per square inch pressure. We assume that for each (x_1, x_2) value in the domain, the random variable is normally distributed with mean $\beta_0 + \beta_1 x_1 + \beta_2 x_2 + \beta_3 x_1 x_2$ and variance σ^2. We select a sample of one Y value from the c.d.f. of each of the random variables $Y_{(500,1000)}, Y_{(600,1000)}, \ldots, Y_{(1500,2000)}$ and denote these sample values by $y_1, y_2, \ldots, y_{121}$, since there are 121 distinct (x_1, x_2) values. One of the objectives here may be to find the value of (x_1, x_2) that maximizes $\mu(\cdot, \cdot)$, that is, to find the value of temperature and pressure that gives a maximum strength of the material.

These examples will perhaps help you understand how the general linear model can be used to model real-world situations.

Next we discuss the general linear regression model.

5.3 Linear Regression Model

As we develop this model, the reader will notice a close similarity with the general linear model; the main thing that distinguishes a linear regression model from a general linear model is that in a general linear model the independent variable is nonrandom while in a regression model it is a random variable. Thus in a linear regression model, Z and X have a joint distribution, and one of the objectives is to estimate parameters in the conditional c.d.f. of $(Z \mid X = x)$. We will see that when a regression model applies, it will allow for a more complete analysis of many problems by the use of correlation.

To introduce the problem we will assume that Z and X have a bivariate *normal* distribution with mean $\boldsymbol{\mu}$ and covariance $\boldsymbol{\Sigma}$ defined by

$$\boldsymbol{\mu} = \begin{bmatrix} \mu_Z \\ \mu_X \end{bmatrix} \qquad \boldsymbol{\Sigma} = \begin{bmatrix} \sigma_Z^2 & \sigma_{XZ} \\ \sigma_{ZX} & \sigma_X^2 \end{bmatrix} \qquad \rho = \frac{\sigma_{XZ}}{\sqrt{\sigma_X^2 \sigma_Z^2}}$$

We consider the conditional c.d.f. of $(Z \mid X = x)$. By Theorem 3.6.1 we know that this conditional c.d.f. is normal with mean

$$\mathscr{E}[Z \mid X = x] = \mu_Z + \left(\frac{\sigma_{XZ}}{\sigma_X^2}\right)(x - \mu_X) = \beta_0 + \beta x$$

and variance

$$\operatorname{var}[Z \mid X = x] = \sigma_Z^2(1 - \rho^2) = \sigma^2$$

We use the notation $Y = (Z \mid X = x)$ to represent a random variable with p.d.f. $f_{Z|X=x}(y)$. We use $\mu_Y(x)$ to represent the mean of $(Z \mid X = x)$, that is, $\mu_Y(x) = \beta_0 + \beta x$; and σ_Y^2 (or σ^2) to represent the variance of $(Z \mid X = x)$, that is, $\sigma_Y^2 = \sigma_Z^2(1 - \rho^2)$. We can write

$$Y = (Z \mid X = x) = \mu_Y(x) + \varepsilon(x) \qquad \varepsilon(x) \text{ distributed } N(\varepsilon(x) : 0, \sigma^2)$$
$$-\infty < x < \infty$$

From this we see the similarity of the general linear model and the regression model. In fact, many of the inference procedures for the general linear model can be used for this model.

Before we discuss sampling for this model, we shall explain with an example how the model can be used.

Example 5.3.1

Suppose it is desired to determine the height z that an individual male of a certain large city will be at age 18 from a knowledge of his height x at age 10. We assume that the heights at age 18, Z, and at age 10, X, for all males in the city form a bivariate normal distribution, that is,

$$\begin{bmatrix} Z \\ X \end{bmatrix}$$

is distributed normally with mean and covariance matrix given by, respectively,

$$\begin{bmatrix} \mu_Z \\ \mu_X \end{bmatrix} \qquad \begin{bmatrix} \sigma_Z^2 & \sigma_{XZ} \\ \sigma_{ZX} & \sigma_X^2 \end{bmatrix}$$

Suppose we want to predict how tall a certain individual, who is 10 years old, will be when he reaches the age of 18. One useful predictor is μ_Z. The quantity μ_Z can be used to predict his height at 18 years of age because the distribution of the heights that all males in the city were (or will be) at age 18 is normally distributed with mean μ_Z and variance σ_Z^2. So μ_Z is a predicted value using the marginal distribution of Z, heights at age 18. However, there is another predicted value that may be "better," that is, have smaller variance. This is obtained by using the mean of a conditional distribution. That is, since we know x_0, the height at age 10 of the individual whose height we want to predict at age 18, we know that *his* height belongs to the conditional distribution of $Y = (Z \mid X = x_0)$. We also know that this distribution has mean $\mu_Z + (\sigma_{ZX}/\sigma_X^2)(x_0 - \mu_X) = \mu_Y(x_0)$, say, and variance $\sigma_Z^2 \times (1 - \rho^2) = \sigma^2$, say. Since ρ^2 is less than or equal to one, but might be quite close to one, it follows that $\sigma^2 \leq \sigma_Z^2$ and hence the variance using the conditional distribution of Z given $X = x_0$ may be considerably less that the variance using the marginal distribution of Z.

In summary, if (Z, X) has a bivariate normal distribution, we can use either μ_Z or $\mu_Y(x_0)$ to predict a person's height at age 18 from a knowledge of x_0, his height at age 10. If σ^2 is less than σ_Z^2, then we prefer to use $\mu_Y(x_0)$ rather than μ_Z to estimate the height that an individual will be at age 18 who is x_0 inches tall at age 10. This preference is due to the fact that at age 18 the individual who is x_0 inches tall at age 10 has a higher probability of having a height "close" to $\mu_Y(x_0)$ than to μ_Z (that is, smaller variance). Of course, since μ_Z is an unknown parameter and $\mu_Y(x_0)$ contains unknown parameters, neither of them can be used directly as predictors of height at age 18; we must select a sample from the bivariate distribution of (Z, X), estimate μ_Z or $\mu_Y(x_0)$, and use this estimator to predict. That is, we select a random sample from the bivariate normal distribution and represent it by (X_1, Z_1), $(X_2, Z_2), \ldots, (X_n, Z_n)$. This means that we select a random sample of n males over eighteen years of age, and for the ith person selected, his heights at age 10, X_i, and at age 18, Z_i, are obtained. From this sample we estimate $\mu_Z, \mu_X, \sigma_X^2, \sigma_Z^2, \sigma_{XZ}$, the parameters in the bivariate normal distribution. From these we estimate β_0, β, and σ^2, the parameters in the conditional distribution of $Y = (Z \mid X = x)$, and, ultimately, we estimate $\mu_Y(x)$ for any x.

Sampling from the general linear *regression* model should be contrasted with the sampling in the general linear model, where a set of x values is obtained first (either by design or at random) and this determines the c.d.f.'s in the population model from which random Y values are obtained. Another way to view the differences is this: (1) in the general linear model there is a c.d.f. for every x in a domain D, the mean of the c.d.f. is $\beta_0 + \beta x$ and the variance is σ^2; (2) in the linear regression model there is a bivariate distribution, and it is assumed that the bivariate c.d.f. is such that the mean of the conditional c.d.f. of $(Z \mid X = x)$ is $\beta_0 + \beta x$ and the variance is σ^2. In the general linear model, we had to distinguish the population and the sample model since every c.d.f. may not be sampled. In the linear regression model, no such distinction is made since there is only one distribution, the joint distribution of (Z, X), and a sample of n values is selected from it.

We have been discussing only a bivariate distribution of two normal random variables (Z, X). The ideas are readily generalized to a $K + 1$ variate random variable $(X_0, X_1, \ldots, X_K)$ that is not necessarily normal (for symmetry we now replace Z with X_0).

We now define a general linear regression model.

DEFINITION 5.3.1

General Linear Regression Model. *Let the $K + 1$ random variables X_0, X_1, $X_2, \ldots, X_K$ have a joint distribution with mean $\boldsymbol{\mu}^*$ and covariance matrix $\boldsymbol{\Sigma}^*$ and such that the conditional c.d.f. of $Y = (X_0 \mid X_1 = x_1, X_2 = x_2, \ldots, X_K = x_K)$ satisfies*

(1) $\mathscr{E}[(X_0 \mid X_1 = x_1, X_2 = x_2, \ldots, X_K = x_K)] = \mu_Y(x_1, x_2, \ldots, x_K) = \beta_0 + \sum_{i=1}^K \beta_i x_i$, *that is, the expectation of* $Y = (X_0 \mid X_1 = x_1, X_2 =$

$x_2, \ldots, X_K = x_K$) is the linear function (given above) which is linear in x_i and linear in unknown parameters β_i;

(2) $var[(X_0 \mid X_1 = x_1, X_2 = x_2, \ldots, X_K = x_K)] = \sigma_Y^2 = \sigma^2$.

These specifications define a general linear regression model.

Note 1. Specification (2) merely states that σ^2 is finite and does not depend on the conditioned values $x_1, x_2, \ldots, x_K$.

Note 2. In certain cases some assumptions (such as normality) will be made concerning the joint distribution of the random variables as part of the model.

This model will be discussed in detail in Chapter 10, and we conclude this section with some examples of real-world situations where it is appropriate.

Example 5.3.2

It is known that the yield of wheat in a given plot of land cannot be predicted exactly. Many, but not all, of the factors affecting this yield are known, and the equation relating the quantities is obscure. It is known that average daily temperature X_1, total rainfall X_2, amount of sunshine X_3, fertility of the soil X_4, and many other factors influence the yield X_0. As a first approximation it will be assumed that the random variables X_0, X_1, X_2, X_3, X_4 form a five-variate normal distribution, and hence this is a general linear regression model defined in Definition 5.3.1. To sample this model one might assume that these five measurements on all farms in a well-defined large area form a five-variate normal population. The investigator may decide to select 30 of these farms and measure the five variables for each farm. The observable random sample is denoted by

	Sample number
$[X_{10}, X_{11}, X_{12}, X_{13}, X_{14}]$	1
$[X_{20}, X_{21}, X_{22}, X_{23}, X_{24}]$	2
$\vdots$	$\vdots$
$[X_{30,0}, X_{30,1}, X_{30,2}, X_{30,3}, X_{30,4}]$	30

If we assume that the sampling is done such that the observations from farm to farm are independent, then we have a random sample of size 30 from a five-variate normal distribution, and we want to estimate $\mu_{X_0}, \mu_{X_1}, \ldots, \mu_{X_4}, \sigma_{X_0}^2, \sigma_{X_1}^2, \ldots, \sigma_{X_4}^2, \rho_{X_0,X_1}, \rho_{X_1,X_2}, \ldots, \rho_{X_3,X_4}$ and hence estimate $\mu_Y(x_1, x_2, x_3, x_4)$, the mean of $Y = (X_0 \mid X_1 = x_1, X_2 = x_2,$

$X_3 = x_3, X_4 = x_4$). For a new geographical location for which an investigator observes the values of x_1, x_2, x_3, x_4, he may want to use $\mu_Y(x_1, x_2, x_3, x_4)$ to predict the yield of wheat to determine if it is profitable to grow it there.

Example 5.3.3

A study was made to determine how age X_1 and cholesterol X_2 affect (systolic) blood pressure X_0 of women over 35 years of age. We assume that age X_1, cholesterol X_2, and blood pressure X_0 of all the women over 35 years old in the state of New York form a three-variate distribution that satisfies Definition 5.3.1. To sample this model a random sample of n women over 35 years of age in New York state is selected, and for each person sampled the age, cholesterol, and blood pressure are recorded. The observable random sample is denoted by

	Sample number
$[X_{10}, X_{11}, X_{12}]$	1
$[X_{20}, X_{21}, X_{22}]$	2
$\vdots$	$\vdots$
$[X_{n0}, X_{n1}, X_{n2}]$	n

Suppose we assume that this is a random sample of n values from a three-variate normal distribution, and rather than determine a function $\mu_Y(x_1, x_2) = \beta_0 + \beta_1 x_1 + \beta_2 x_2$ to predict a woman's blood pressure from a knowledge of her age and cholesterol, the objectives may be to estimate β_2, the change in blood pressure per unit change in cholesterol. From this, one can determine if it may be possible for women with high blood pressure and high cholesterol to reduce blood pressure by reducing cholesterol (by proper diet).

5.4 Design Models

In this section and the next we shall discuss two qualitative models, namely, design models and components-of-variance models. The terms qualitative and quantitative refer to the predicator or independent variable x used in the previous sections. A model is generally called quantitative if the independent variables x are measurable variables such as time, weight, height, and pressure. If they are attributes such as colors, varieties, types of machines, makes of automobiles, and methods of production, the model is called qualitative. However, we will not adhere strictly to this terminology since our qualitative model will allow for quantitative variables if they are used in a qualitative fashion. This will be explained in more detail in Example 5.4.2.

Before we define the design model, we illustrate it with some examples.

Example 5.4.1

Suppose that a company wants to determine if there is any difference in the strength of $\frac{3}{4}$-inch steel bolts made by two different methods. There are two populations involved. Population i consists of a year's output of $\frac{3}{4}$-inch bolts made by method i, for $i = 1, 2$. The mean and variance of the two c.d.f.'s are denoted respectively by (μ_1, σ_1^2), (μ_2, σ_2^2). A sample of three bolts is selected from each population and the strengths are measured. We denote the six observable values by Y_{11}, Y_{12}, Y_{13}, Y_{21}, Y_{22}, Y_{23}, where the first subscript refers to the population and the second refers to the sample within the population. The model can be written in detail as

$$\begin{aligned} Y_{11} &= \mu_1 + \varepsilon_{11} \\ Y_{12} &= \mu_1 + \varepsilon_{12} \\ Y_{13} &= \mu_1 + \varepsilon_{13} \\ Y_{21} &= \mu_2 + \varepsilon_{21} \\ Y_{22} &= \mu_2 + \varepsilon_{22} \\ Y_{23} &= \mu_2 + \varepsilon_{23} \end{aligned} \tag{5.4.1}$$

or as

$$\mathbf{Y} = \mathbf{X}\boldsymbol{\beta} + \boldsymbol{\varepsilon} \tag{5.4.2}$$

where

$$\mathbf{Y} = \begin{bmatrix} Y_{11} \\ Y_{12} \\ Y_{13} \\ Y_{21} \\ Y_{22} \\ Y_{23} \end{bmatrix} \quad \mathbf{X} = \begin{bmatrix} 1 & 0 \\ 1 & 0 \\ 1 & 0 \\ 0 & 1 \\ 0 & 1 \\ 0 & 1 \end{bmatrix} \quad \boldsymbol{\beta} = \begin{bmatrix} \mu_1 \\ \mu_2 \end{bmatrix} \quad \boldsymbol{\varepsilon} = \begin{bmatrix} \varepsilon_{11} \\ \varepsilon_{12} \\ \varepsilon_{13} \\ \varepsilon_{21} \\ \varepsilon_{22} \\ \varepsilon_{23} \end{bmatrix} \tag{5.4.3}$$

The **X** matrix consists of zeros and ones only, and essentially it is an indicator matrix, that is, each x_{ij} value indicates whether μ_i is present in that particular equation. However, the model in Equation (5.4.2) is similar to the general linear model and most of the inference procedures are applicable.

Example 5.4.2

In this example we illustrate how quantitative variables can be used in what we term a qualitative model. Suppose an experiment is conducted to determine how various temperatures of water in which a fabric is laundered affect the strength of the fabric after 100 launderings. It is decided to use two different water temperatures, 150° F and 180° F, and 3 similar pieces of fabric which will receive 100 launderings at each temperature; each piece of fabric will then be tested for strength. Let Y_{ij} be the strength measurement of the jth piece of fabric that will be laundered in water at the ith temperature, where $i = 1$ refers to 150° F temperature and $i = 2$ refers to 180° F temperature. The model can be written

$$Y_{ij} = \mu_i + \varepsilon_{ij} \qquad i = 1, 2; \quad j = 1, 2, 3 \tag{5.4.4}$$

In matrix notation we write this model as

$$\mathbf{Y} = \mathbf{X}\boldsymbol{\beta} + \boldsymbol{\varepsilon}$$

or in detail as

$$\begin{bmatrix} Y_{11} \\ Y_{12} \\ Y_{13} \\ Y_{21} \\ Y_{22} \\ Y_{23} \end{bmatrix} = \begin{bmatrix} 1 & 0 \\ 1 & 0 \\ 1 & 0 \\ 0 & 1 \\ 0 & 1 \\ 0 & 1 \end{bmatrix} \begin{bmatrix} \mu_1 \\ \mu_2 \end{bmatrix} + \begin{bmatrix} \varepsilon_{11} \\ \varepsilon_{12} \\ \varepsilon_{13} \\ \varepsilon_{21} \\ \varepsilon_{22} \\ \varepsilon_{23} \end{bmatrix} \tag{5.4.5}$$

In this case the μ_i are quantitative variables (temperature), but since we are interested in only two distinct temperatures, they are used in what we call a qualitative sense. $\mathbf{X}$ is an indicator matrix consisting of only zeros and ones to indicate whether μ_1 or μ_2 is present or absent in each equation. In this model Y_{11}, Y_{12}, Y_{13} is assumed to be a random sample from a population with mean μ_1 and variance σ^2 (we assume $\mathscr{E}[\varepsilon_{ij}] = 0$, $\text{var}[\varepsilon_{ij}] = \sigma^2$, and the ε_{ij} are independent). Y_{21}, Y_{22}, Y_{23} is a random sample from a population with mean μ_2 and variance σ^2. The objective here may be to estimate the population means μ_1, μ_2 and the difference between the population means $\mu_1 - \mu_2$. It may be somewhat instructive to write μ_i as $\mu_i = \mu + \tau_i$, where μ is the average strength of all the fabric before laundering and τ_i is the added strength (the τ_i may be negative) due to laundering in water at the ith temperature. This model is

$$Y_{ij} = \mu + \tau_i + \varepsilon_{ij} \qquad \mathscr{E}[\varepsilon_{ij}] = 0 \qquad i = 1, 2; \quad j = 1, 2, 3 \tag{5.4.6}$$

In matrix notation this is

$$\begin{bmatrix} Y_{11} \\ Y_{12} \\ Y_{13} \\ Y_{21} \\ Y_{22} \\ Y_{23} \end{bmatrix} = \begin{bmatrix} 1 & 1 & 0 \\ 1 & 1 & 0 \\ 1 & 1 & 0 \\ 1 & 0 & 1 \\ 1 & 0 & 1 \\ 1 & 0 & 1 \end{bmatrix} \begin{bmatrix} \mu \\ \tau_1 \\ \tau_2 \end{bmatrix} + \begin{bmatrix} \varepsilon_{11} \\ \varepsilon_{12} \\ \varepsilon_{13} \\ \varepsilon_{21} \\ \varepsilon_{22} \\ \varepsilon_{23} \end{bmatrix} \tag{5.4.7}$$

In Equation (5.4.4) and Equation (5.4.6) are two models that describe the same physical setup. Clearly $\mu + \tau_i$ is another way of writing μ_i, and we notice that the $\boldsymbol{\beta}$ vector consists of two subvectors $\boldsymbol{\mu}$ and $\boldsymbol{\tau}$, so we can write $\boldsymbol{\beta}' = [\boldsymbol{\mu}, \boldsymbol{\tau}']$, where $\boldsymbol{\mu} = [\mu]$, $\boldsymbol{\tau}' = [\tau_1, \tau_2]$. In this example there seems to be no reason to write the model in the form of Equation (5.4.6). However, we shall see that in more complex cases it will be useful to write the model so that it appears similar to Equation (5.4.6). One important thing to notice is that in the matrix model in Equation (5.4.7), the matrix $\mathbf{X}$ has size 6×3 and rank 2, whereas in Equation (5.4.5) $\mathbf{X}$ has size 6×2 and rank 2. When the rank of the $\mathbf{X}$ matrix is equal to the number of columns, we call it full rank, and in the contrary case we call it less than full rank. We often distinguish the two cases when we apply statistical procedures.

Example 5.4.3

An investigator wants to measure the effect on the yield of a certain variety of corn of two different chemical compounds and four different methods of applying these compounds. Suppose α_i is the effect of the ith chemical ($i = 1, 2$) and τ_j is the effect of the jth method of applying the compounds ($j = 1, 2, 3, 4$). If the investigator assumes that the effects are additive, he might assume the following model:

$$\begin{aligned} Y_{11} &= \mu + \alpha_1 + \tau_1 + \varepsilon_{11} \\ Y_{12} &= \mu + \alpha_1 + \tau_2 + \varepsilon_{12} \\ Y_{13} &= \mu + \alpha_1 + \tau_3 + \varepsilon_{13} \\ Y_{14} &= \mu + \alpha_1 + \tau_4 + \varepsilon_{14} \\ Y_{21} &= \mu + \alpha_2 + \tau_1 + \varepsilon_{21} \\ Y_{22} &= \mu + \alpha_2 + \tau_2 + \varepsilon_{22} \\ Y_{23} &= \mu + \alpha_2 + \tau_3 + \varepsilon_{23} \\ Y_{24} &= \mu + \alpha_2 + \tau_4 + \varepsilon_{24} \end{aligned} \tag{5.4.8}$$

or, written in shorter form,

$$Y_{ij} = \mu + \alpha_i + \tau_j + \varepsilon_{ij} \qquad i = 1, 2; \quad j = 1, 2, 3, 4 \tag{5.4.9}$$

where Y_{ij} is the observable yield of corn on a plot of ground that received the ith chemical applied by the jth method. The investigator is assuming that the observable random variable Y_{ij} is equal to a constant μ, the average yield when no chemical is applied and hence no method of application is used, plus α_i, the effect due to the ith chemical, plus τ_j, the effect due to the jth method of application, plus a random error ε_{ij} due to all the uncontrolled factors, such as differences of fertility among the plots. The experimenter may desire to test or estimate a function of the parameters μ, α_i, τ_j. In matrix notation this model is

$$\mathbf{Y} = \mathbf{X}\boldsymbol{\beta} + \boldsymbol{\varepsilon}$$

which when written in detail is

$$\begin{bmatrix} Y_{11} \\ Y_{12} \\ Y_{13} \\ Y_{14} \\ Y_{21} \\ Y_{22} \\ Y_{23} \\ Y_{24} \end{bmatrix} = \begin{bmatrix} 1 & 1 & 0 & 1 & 0 & 0 & 0 \\ 1 & 1 & 0 & 0 & 1 & 0 & 0 \\ 1 & 1 & 0 & 0 & 0 & 1 & 0 \\ 1 & 1 & 0 & 0 & 0 & 0 & 1 \\ 1 & 0 & 1 & 1 & 0 & 0 & 0 \\ 1 & 0 & 1 & 0 & 1 & 0 & 0 \\ 1 & 0 & 1 & 0 & 0 & 1 & 0 \\ 1 & 0 & 1 & 0 & 0 & 0 & 1 \end{bmatrix} \begin{bmatrix} \mu \\ \alpha_1 \\ \alpha_2 \\ \tau_1 \\ \tau_2 \\ \tau_3 \\ \tau_4 \end{bmatrix} + \begin{bmatrix} \varepsilon_{11} \\ \varepsilon_{12} \\ \varepsilon_{13} \\ \varepsilon_{14} \\ \varepsilon_{21} \\ \varepsilon_{22} \\ \varepsilon_{23} \\ \varepsilon_{24} \end{bmatrix} \tag{5.4.10}$$

We notice a number of things here.

1. The $\mathbf{X}$ matrix consists of only 0's and 1's.
2. The $\boldsymbol{\beta}$ vector can be partitioned into 3 subvectors, that is,

$$\boldsymbol{\beta} = \begin{bmatrix} \boldsymbol{\mu} \\ \boldsymbol{\alpha} \\ \boldsymbol{\tau} \end{bmatrix} \tag{5.4.11}$$

where $\boldsymbol{\mu} = [\mu]$ consists of the general mean, $\boldsymbol{\alpha}' = [\alpha_1, \alpha_2]$ consists of the two parameters that refer to the two chemicals, and $\boldsymbol{\tau}' = [\tau_1, \tau_2, \tau_3, \tau_4]$ consists of the four parameters that refer to the four methods of application.

3. Each equation in the model contains exactly one element from each of the subvectors and this forces the **X** matrix to assume a certain pattern.

In Chapter 13 we discuss the design model in detail and explain how it is used. Here we merely state that when the design model is written in matrix form, it is defined to be a special case of the general linear model and we give the definition below.

DEFINITION 5.4.1

Design Model. *The design model satisfies the definition of the general linear model except that the rank of the* $n \times p$ *matrix* $\mathbf{X}$ *is* K, *where* $n > p \geq K$. *In addition, the* $\mathbf{X}$ *matrix of the design model consists of only the numbers* 0 *and* 1, *and the* $\mathbf{X}$ *matrix assumes a certain pattern depending on the particular design.*

In Chapter 13 this definition is expanded to include the details of the distribution of the error term and the pattern of the **X** matrix.

5.5 Components-of-Variance Model

The form of this model is similar to the design model since the x_{ij} variables are the values 0 and 1 only. The model in the simplest case can be written $Y_{ij} = \mu + \tau_i + \varepsilon_{ij}$. In the components-of-variance model, the τ_i and ε_{ij} are unobservable random variables from distributions with variances σ_τ^2 and σ_ε^2, respectively. The objective in this model is to observe the Y_{ij} and estimate σ_τ^2 and σ_ε^2. We illustrate with an example.

Example 5.5.1

In examining the nitrogen content of the foliage in a large orchard, leaves from trees are collected, and the nitrogen content of the leaves is measured. There are two major sources of variation: the variation of the leaves on a tree, and the variation of trees in the orchard. The objective is to measure the two variances. However, it is impossible to measure the "true" nitrogen content of the foliage of a tree without stripping all the leaves from the tree. That is, each tree in the orchard has a "true" nitrogen content of its leaves (this true value can be obtained only by measuring the nitrogen content of every leaf on the tree).

Let the distribution of "true" nitrogen contents of all trees in the orchard be represented by a p.d.f. $f_T(\cdot)$ of a random variable T, the "true" nitrogen content of a tree. Theoretically, $f_T(\cdot)$ could be found by determining the "true" nitrogen content of each tree in the orchard (by measuring each leaf on each tree), and the collection of the "true" nitrogen contents of the trees could be used to construct a histogram (the p.d.f. $f_T(\cdot)$ referred to above). One problem is to determine σ_T^2, the variance of the "true" nitrogen contents of the trees. The difficulty is that we cannot observe the "true" nitrogen content of any tree (since it is, in a practical sense, impossible to strip all the leaves from any tree). Thus we are in the position of wanting to determine (estimate) the variance of a random variable T and not being able to observe any values of the random variable. To accomplish our objective we will build a theoretical model, select some trees at random from the orchard, select some leaves at random from each of these trees, measure the nitrogen content of the selected leaves, and use these observed values with the theoretical model to estimate σ_T^2.

We consider two basic random variables. One random variable T is the set of numbers represented by the "true" nitrogen content of trees, and let μ and σ_T^2 be the mean and variance of T. Another population (actually a family of populations) is obtained by considering the leaves on each tree as a population. For a given tree the nitrogen content of the leaves is a random variable with mean equal to t_0, say, and this value is the "true" nitrogen content of that tree, and hence t_0 is a value of the first random variable referred to above. We assume that the variance of the nitrogen content of the leaves on the given tree is σ_L^2 and is the same for all trees. The sampling scheme we use is as follows:

1. a tree is selected at random from the orchard, and we assume the "true" nitrogen content is T_1^* (this is an unobservable random variable);

2. J leaves are selected at random from this tree, and we measure the nitrogen content of each leaf and denote the J observable values by $Y_{11}, Y_{12}, \ldots, Y_{1J}$ (these are observable random variables);

3. we write the model for the first tree selected as

$$Y_{1j} = \mu + (T_1^* - \mu) + (Y_{1j} - T_1^*) \qquad j = 1, 2, \ldots, J$$

   where μ is the mean of the "true" nitrogen content of all leaves of all trees in the orchard;

4. in all, we draw I trees at random and assume that the "true" nitrogen contents are respectively $T_1^*, T_2^*, \ldots, T_I^*$; we draw J leaves at random from each tree and denote the observable nitrogen content of the jth leaf from the ith tree by Y_{ij}. We write the model as

$$Y_{ij} = \mu + (T_i^* - \mu) + (Y_{ij} - T_i^*)$$

   or as

$$Y_{ij} = \mu + T_i + L_{ij} \qquad i = 1, 2, \ldots, I; \quad j = 1, 2, \ldots, J$$

The term T_i is the effect of the ith tree, and $\mathscr{E}[T_i] = 0$, $\text{var}[T_i] = \sigma_T^2$. The term L_{ij} is the effect of the jth leaf from the ith tree, and for each i, it is clear that $\mathscr{E}[L_{ij}] = 0$, $\text{var}[L_{ij}] = \sigma_L^2$, and hence $\mathscr{E}[L_{ij}] = 0$, $\text{var}[L_{ij}] = \sigma_L^2$ for each i and j. We also assume that $T_{i'}$ and L_{ij} are uncorrelated for all i, i', and j. With the properties mentioned, it follows that

$$\text{var}[Y] = \text{var}[T] + \text{var}[L]$$

or

$$\sigma_Y^2 = \sigma_T^2 + \sigma_L^2$$

and σ_T^2, σ_L^2 are "components" of the variance of the observable random variable Y. We may also want to assume distributional properties (such as normality) for the T_i and L_{ij}, and in Chapter 15 we will show that it is possible to find "good" estimators of σ_T^2 and σ_L^2.

Now we will abstract the important concepts of the above discussion and define this variance components model.

Let Y_{ij}, for $i = 1, 2, \ldots, I$ and $j = 1, 2, \ldots, J$, be observable random variables with a structure

$$Y_{ij} = \mu + A_i + \varepsilon_{ij} \tag{5.5.1}$$

where A_i and ε_{ij} are uncorrelated and unobservable random variables with $\mathscr{E}[A_i] = \mathscr{E}[\varepsilon_{ij}] = 0$, $\text{var}[A_i] = \sigma_A^2$, $\text{var}[\varepsilon_{ij}] = \sigma_\varepsilon^2$, and where μ is an unknown parameter. These specifications define a variance component (or components-of-variance) model. Sometimes there will be additional distributional assumptions assumed for the random variables A_i, ε_{ij} as part of the model.

We notice that the design model can be written in matrix form as in Equation (5.4.7), or in more detail as in Equation (5.4.6). This is the case for the components-of-variance model also. For example, the model in Equation (5.5.1) can be written in matrix form (assume for a special case that $I = 2$ and $J = 3$) as

$$\mathbf{Y} = \mathbf{X}\boldsymbol{\beta} + \boldsymbol{\varepsilon}$$

where

$$\mathbf{Y} = \begin{bmatrix} Y_{11} \\ Y_{12} \\ Y_{13} \\ Y_{21} \\ Y_{22} \\ Y_{23} \end{bmatrix} \qquad \mathbf{X} = \begin{bmatrix} 1 & 1 & 0 \\ 1 & 1 & 0 \\ 1 & 1 & 0 \\ 1 & 0 & 1 \\ 1 & 0 & 1 \\ 1 & 0 & 1 \end{bmatrix} \qquad \boldsymbol{\beta} = \begin{bmatrix} \boldsymbol{\mu} \\ \mathbf{a} \end{bmatrix} = \begin{bmatrix} \mu \\ A_1 \\ A_2 \end{bmatrix} \qquad \boldsymbol{\varepsilon} = \begin{bmatrix} \varepsilon_{11} \\ \varepsilon_{12} \\ \varepsilon_{13} \\ \varepsilon_{21} \\ \varepsilon_{22} \\ \varepsilon_{23} \end{bmatrix}$$

μ is an unknown constant, the A_i are random variables with means zero and variances σ_A^2, and the ε_{ij} are random variables with means zero and variances σ_ε^2.

We now define the components-of-variance model (in Chapter 15 we define it in matrix form and discuss it in detail).

DEFINITION 5.5.1

Components-of-Variance Model. *Let an observable random variable* $Y_{ij\ldots m}$ *be such that*

$$Y_{ij\ldots m} = \mu + A_i + B_{ij} + \cdots + \varepsilon_{ij\ldots m}$$

where μ *is a constant,* A_i *is a random variable with mean* 0 *and variance* σ_A^2, B_{ij} *is a random variable with mean* 0 *and variance* $\sigma_B^2, \ldots,$ *and* $\varepsilon_{ij\ldots m}$ *is a random variable with mean* 0 *and variance* σ_ε^2. *Let all the random variables* $A_i, B_{ij}, \ldots, \varepsilon_{ij\ldots m}$ *be uncorrelated. These specifications define a components-of-variance model.*

> ***Note 1.*** In many cases we will assume certain distributional properties (such as normality) for the random variables $A_i, B_{ij}, \ldots, \varepsilon_{ij\ldots m}$.

This concludes the general discussion of the various models that will be the subject of the remainder of this book. Each model will be discussed in some detail in succeeding chapters.

CHAPTER 6

General Linear Model

6.1 Introduction

In this chapter we discuss inference for the general linear model defined in Definition 5.2.2. This will include point estimation, interval estimation, and testing hypotheses.

We redefine the sample model here, but in applications it is important to keep in mind the population model that is in the background (see Equation (5.2.7)).

DEFINITION 6.1.1

General Linear Model. *Let* $\mathbf{Y}$ *be an* $n \times 1$ *observable vector of random variables; let* $\mathbf{X}$ *be an* $n \times p$ *matrix* ($n > p$) *of known fixed numbers; let* $\boldsymbol{\beta}$ *be a* $p \times 1$ *vector of unknown parameters; let* $\boldsymbol{\varepsilon}$ *be an* $n \times 1$ *unobservable vector of random variables, where* $\mathscr{E}[\boldsymbol{\varepsilon}] = \mathbf{0}$ *and* $\mathbf{cov}[\boldsymbol{\varepsilon}] = \boldsymbol{\Sigma}$; *let these quantities be related by*

$$\mathbf{Y} = \mathbf{X}\boldsymbol{\beta} + \boldsymbol{\varepsilon} \tag{6.1.1}$$

These specifications define a general linear model.

Note 1. This model has many special cases depending on (1) the distribution of $\boldsymbol{\varepsilon}$, (2) the structure of the covariance matrix $\boldsymbol{\Sigma}$, and (3) the rank and structure of $\mathbf{X}$. In this chapter we assume that the rank of $\mathbf{X}$ is p, and we consider two cases for the distribution of $\boldsymbol{\varepsilon}$.

Case 1. $\boldsymbol{\varepsilon}$ is distributed normally with mean zero and covariance matrix $\sigma^2\mathbf{I}$, where $\sigma^2 > 0$ is unknown, that is, $\boldsymbol{\varepsilon}$ is distributed $N(\boldsymbol{\varepsilon} : \mathbf{0}, \sigma^2\mathbf{I})$.

Case 2. $\boldsymbol{\varepsilon}$ has an unknown distribution with mean vector and covariance matrix of $\boldsymbol{\varepsilon}$ equal to $\mathscr{E}[\boldsymbol{\varepsilon}] = \mathbf{0}$ and $\mathbf{cov}[\boldsymbol{\varepsilon}] = \sigma^2\mathbf{I}$, respectively, where $\sigma^2 > 0$ is unknown.

Unless stated otherwise, the parameter space for Cases 1 and 2 is Ω, where $\Omega = \{(\boldsymbol{\beta}, \sigma^2) : \boldsymbol{\beta} \text{ in } E_p, \sigma^2 > 0\}$.

For Case 1, which is referred to as the normal theory case, we sometimes generalize slightly and consider the situation when $\boldsymbol{\varepsilon}$ is distributed $\mathbf{N}(\boldsymbol{\varepsilon} : \mathbf{0}, \sigma^2\mathbf{V})$, where $\sigma^2 > 0$ is unknown and $\mathbf{V}$ is a *known* matrix. For Case 2 more stringent assumptions are sometimes required such as that the Y_i are independent and identically distributed with a continuous c.d.f.

The definition for Case 1 is equivalent to saying that each ε_i is normally distributed with mean 0 and unknown variance σ^2 and that the ε_i are jointly independent. Case 2 is equivalent to saying that the expected value of each ε_i is zero, the ε_i are uncorrelated, and the ε_i have a common unknown variance σ^2.

Below is a list of topics that are discussed in this chapter.

I. Point estimation is discussed for Cases 1 and 2 for the following:
   1. σ^2;
   2. $\ell'\boldsymbol{\beta}$, linear functions of the β_i, and specifically each β_i;
   3. $\mu(\mathbf{x}_0)$ for a *given* vector $\mathbf{x}_0$.

II. Tests of hypotheses are discussed for Case 1 for the following:
   1. $\sigma^2 = \sigma_0^2$, where σ_0^2 is a given constant;
   2. $\ell'\boldsymbol{\beta} = \ell_0$, where ℓ is a given $p \times 1$ vector and ℓ_0 is a given constant; this is a test of the hypothesis that a given linear combination of the β_i is equal to a given constant;
   3. $\beta_1 = b_1, \beta_2 = b_2, \ldots, \beta_p = b_p$ (that is, $\boldsymbol{\beta} = \mathbf{b}$), where each b_i is a given constant;
   4. $\beta_1 = b_1, \beta_2 = b_2, \ldots, \beta_r = b_r; r < p$, where $b_1, b_2, \ldots, b_r$ is a set of given constants; this is a test that elements in a subset of $\boldsymbol{\beta}$ are equal to given constants;
   5. $\mathbf{H}\boldsymbol{\beta} = \mathbf{h}$, where $\mathbf{H}$ is a given $q \times p$ matrix of rank q and $\mathbf{h}$ is a given $q \times 1$ vector; this is a test about q linear functions of $\boldsymbol{\beta}$.

III. Confidence intervals for Case 1 are discussed for the following:
   1. σ^2;
   2. $\ell'\boldsymbol{\beta}$, linear functions of the β_i, specifically each β_i;
   3. $\mu(\mathbf{x}_0)$ for a *given* vector $\mathbf{x}_0$.

Note 2. The tests in 2, 3, and 4 of part II are special cases of the test in 5. In Chapter 8 we consider some special applications of this model.

6.2 Point Estimation of σ^2 and Linear Functions of β_i: Case 1

First we find maximum likelihood estimators of σ^2 and linear functions of the β_i, and then we consider UMVU estimators. Since **Y** is distributed $N(\mathbf{y} : \mathbf{X}\boldsymbol{\beta}, \sigma^2\mathbf{I})$, the likelihood function is

$$L(\boldsymbol{\beta}, \sigma^2 : y_1, y_2, \ldots, y_n; x_{11}, x_{12}, \ldots, x_{np}) = L(\boldsymbol{\beta}, \sigma^2 : \mathbf{y}; \mathbf{X}) = \left(\frac{1}{2\pi\sigma^2}\right)^{n/2} \times \exp\left[-\frac{1}{2\sigma^2}(\mathbf{y} - \mathbf{X}\boldsymbol{\beta})'(\mathbf{y} - \mathbf{X}\boldsymbol{\beta})\right] \tag{6.2.1}$$

Using logarithms we get

$$\begin{aligned}\log L(\boldsymbol{\beta}, \sigma^2 : \mathbf{y}; \mathbf{X}) &= -\frac{n}{2}\log 2\pi - \frac{n}{2}\log\sigma^2 - \frac{1}{2\sigma^2}(\mathbf{y} - \mathbf{X}\boldsymbol{\beta})'(\mathbf{y} - \mathbf{X}\boldsymbol{\beta}) \\ &= -\frac{n}{2}\log 2\pi - \frac{n}{2}\log\sigma^2 - \frac{1}{2\sigma^2}(\mathbf{y}'\mathbf{y} - 2\mathbf{y}'\mathbf{X}\boldsymbol{\beta} + \boldsymbol{\beta}'\mathbf{X}'\mathbf{X}\boldsymbol{\beta})\end{aligned} \tag{6.2.2}$$

The parameter space Ω is

$$\Omega = \{(\boldsymbol{\beta}, \sigma^2) : \sigma^2 > 0, -\infty < \beta_i < \infty, i = 1, 2, \ldots, p\} \tag{6.2.3}$$

To find the values of $\boldsymbol{\beta}$ and σ^2 in Ω that maximize the likelihood function, we set to zero the partial derivatives with respect to $\boldsymbol{\beta}$ and σ^2. These are given below.

$$\begin{aligned}\frac{\partial}{\partial\boldsymbol{\beta}}\log L(\boldsymbol{\beta}, \sigma^2 : \mathbf{y}; \mathbf{X}) &= \frac{2}{2\sigma^2}(\mathbf{X}'\mathbf{y} - \mathbf{X}'\mathbf{X}\boldsymbol{\beta}) \\ \frac{\partial}{\partial\sigma^2}\log L(\boldsymbol{\beta}, \sigma^2 : \mathbf{y}; \mathbf{X}) &= -\frac{n}{2\sigma^2} + \frac{1}{2\sigma^4}(\mathbf{y} - \mathbf{X}\boldsymbol{\beta})'(\mathbf{y} - \mathbf{X}\boldsymbol{\beta})\end{aligned}$$

Let $\tilde{\boldsymbol{\beta}}$ and $\tilde{\sigma}^2$ denote the solution of the equations for $\boldsymbol{\beta}$ and σ^2 when the derivatives are set equal to zero. We get

$$\begin{aligned}\mathbf{X}'\mathbf{X}\tilde{\boldsymbol{\beta}} &= \mathbf{X}'\mathbf{y} \\ \tilde{\sigma}^2 &= \frac{1}{n}(\mathbf{y} - \mathbf{X}\tilde{\boldsymbol{\beta}})'(\mathbf{y} - \mathbf{X}\tilde{\boldsymbol{\beta}})\end{aligned} \tag{6.2.4}$$

and ($\mathbf{X}'\mathbf{X}$ is nonsingular since $\mathbf{X}$ and hence $\mathbf{X}'\mathbf{X}$ have rank p) the M.L. estimators are

$$\begin{aligned}\tilde{\boldsymbol{\beta}} &= (\mathbf{X}'\mathbf{X})^{-1}\mathbf{X}'\mathbf{Y} = \mathbf{X}^{-}\mathbf{Y} \\ \tilde{\sigma}^2 &= \left(\frac{1}{n}\right)\mathbf{Y}'[\mathbf{I} - \mathbf{X}(\mathbf{X}'\mathbf{X})^{-1}\mathbf{X}']\mathbf{Y} = \left(\frac{1}{n}\right)\mathbf{Y}'(\mathbf{I} - \mathbf{X}\mathbf{X}^{-})\mathbf{Y} \\ &= \left(\frac{1}{n}\right)\mathbf{Y}'(\mathbf{I} - \mathbf{K})\mathbf{Y} = \left(\frac{1}{n}\right)\mathbf{Y}'\mathbf{M}\mathbf{Y}\end{aligned} \tag{6.2.5}$$

where we denote $\mathbf{X}(\mathbf{X}'\mathbf{X})^{-1}\mathbf{X}'$ by $\mathbf{K}$, $\mathbf{I} - \mathbf{K}$ by $\mathbf{M}$, and $(\mathbf{X}'\mathbf{X})^{-1}\mathbf{X}'$ by $\mathbf{X}^{-}$ (see Theorem 1.5.12). The quantity $\tilde{\sigma}^2$ is obtained by noting that $\mathbf{Y} - \mathbf{X}\tilde{\boldsymbol{\beta}} = [\mathbf{I} - \mathbf{X}(\mathbf{X}'\mathbf{X})^{-1}\mathbf{X}']\mathbf{Y}$ and that $\mathbf{I} - \mathbf{X}(\mathbf{X}'\mathbf{X})^{-1}\mathbf{X}'$ is symmetric and idempotent. To demonstrate that $\tilde{\boldsymbol{\beta}}$ and $\tilde{\sigma}^2$ are maximum likelihood estimators of $\boldsymbol{\beta}$ and σ^2, we must show that they do indeed maximize the likelihood function. This proof is given in Section 9.3.

Next we examine the properties of the estimators $\tilde{\boldsymbol{\beta}}$ and $\tilde{\sigma}^2$ and determine their distributions. First we show that the $p + 1$ estimators $\tilde{\beta}_1, \tilde{\beta}_2, \ldots, \tilde{\beta}_p$, and $\tilde{\sigma}^2$ are sufficient statistics. To do this we use Theorem 2.6.1. This requires us to show that the p.d.f. of $\mathbf{Y}$, namely $f(\mathbf{y} : \mathbf{X}; \boldsymbol{\beta}, \sigma^2)$, factors as $g(\tilde{\boldsymbol{\beta}}, \tilde{\sigma}^2 : \boldsymbol{\beta}, \sigma^2) \cdot h(\mathbf{y})$, where $g(\tilde{\boldsymbol{\beta}}, \tilde{\sigma}^2 : \boldsymbol{\beta}, \sigma^2)$ contains the observation $\mathbf{y}$ in the form of $\tilde{\boldsymbol{\beta}}$ and $\tilde{\sigma}^2$ only, and $h(\mathbf{y})$ does not contain the parameters $\boldsymbol{\beta}$ and σ^2.

The p.d.f. of $\mathbf{Y}$ is

$$f(\mathbf{y} : \mathbf{X}; \boldsymbol{\beta}, \sigma^2) = \left(\frac{1}{(2\pi\sigma^2)^{n/2}}\right)\exp\left[-\frac{1}{2\sigma^2}(\mathbf{y} - \mathbf{X}\boldsymbol{\beta})'(\mathbf{y} - \mathbf{X}\boldsymbol{\beta})\right] \tag{6.2.6}$$

We work with a portion of the exponent and get

$$\begin{aligned}(\mathbf{y} - \mathbf{X}\boldsymbol{\beta})'(\mathbf{y} - \mathbf{X}\boldsymbol{\beta}) &= [(\mathbf{y} - \mathbf{X}\tilde{\boldsymbol{\beta}}) - \mathbf{X}(\boldsymbol{\beta} - \tilde{\boldsymbol{\beta}})]'[(\mathbf{y} - \mathbf{X}\tilde{\boldsymbol{\beta}}) - \mathbf{X}(\boldsymbol{\beta} - \tilde{\boldsymbol{\beta}})] \\ &= (\mathbf{y} - \mathbf{X}\tilde{\boldsymbol{\beta}})'(\mathbf{y} - \mathbf{X}\tilde{\boldsymbol{\beta}}) + (\boldsymbol{\beta} - \tilde{\boldsymbol{\beta}})'\mathbf{X}'\mathbf{X}(\boldsymbol{\beta} - \tilde{\boldsymbol{\beta}}) \\ &= n\tilde{\sigma}^2 + (\boldsymbol{\beta} - \tilde{\boldsymbol{\beta}})'\mathbf{X}'\mathbf{X}(\boldsymbol{\beta} - \tilde{\boldsymbol{\beta}})\end{aligned}$$

since $\mathbf{X}'(\mathbf{y} - \mathbf{X}\tilde{\boldsymbol{\beta}}) = \mathbf{X}'\mathbf{y} - \mathbf{X}'\mathbf{X}(\mathbf{X}'\mathbf{X})^{-1}\mathbf{X}'\mathbf{y} = \mathbf{0}$.

If we substitute into Equation (6.2.6), we get

$$\begin{aligned}f(\mathbf{y} : \mathbf{X}; \boldsymbol{\beta}, \sigma^2) &= \left(\frac{1}{(2\pi\sigma^2)^{n/2}}\right)\exp\left(-\frac{1}{2\sigma^2}[(n\tilde{\sigma}^2) + (\boldsymbol{\beta} - \tilde{\boldsymbol{\beta}})'\mathbf{X}'\mathbf{X}(\boldsymbol{\beta} - \tilde{\boldsymbol{\beta}})]\right) \\ &= g(\tilde{\boldsymbol{\beta}}, \tilde{\sigma}^2 : \boldsymbol{\beta}, \sigma^2) \cdot h(\mathbf{y})\end{aligned}$$

where $h(\mathbf{y}) \equiv 1$. Hence $\tilde{\boldsymbol{\beta}}$ and $\tilde{\sigma}^2$ are sufficient statistics. It can be shown by using Theorem 2.7.8 that they are *complete* sufficient statistics.

Next we find the distribution of $\tilde{\boldsymbol{\beta}}$ and $\tilde{\sigma}^2$. Since $\tilde{\boldsymbol{\beta}} = \mathbf{X}^-\mathbf{Y}$, we can use Theorem 3.3.5 to state that $\tilde{\boldsymbol{\beta}}$ has a p-variate normal distribution; to specify the distribution completely, we must find the vector mean and covariance matrix of $\tilde{\boldsymbol{\beta}}$. We get for the mean

$$\mathscr{E}[\tilde{\boldsymbol{\beta}}] = \mathscr{E}[\mathbf{X}^-\mathbf{Y}] = \mathbf{X}^-[\mathscr{E}(\mathbf{Y})] = \mathbf{X}^-\mathbf{X}\boldsymbol{\beta} = \boldsymbol{\beta} \tag{6.2.7}$$

since $\mathbf{X}^-\mathbf{X} = \mathbf{I}$. For the covariance of $\tilde{\boldsymbol{\beta}}$ we obtain

$$\begin{aligned}\text{cov}(\tilde{\boldsymbol{\beta}}) &= \mathscr{E}\{[\tilde{\boldsymbol{\beta}} - \mathscr{E}(\tilde{\boldsymbol{\beta}})][\tilde{\boldsymbol{\beta}} - \mathscr{E}(\tilde{\boldsymbol{\beta}})]'\} = \mathscr{E}\{[\mathbf{X}^-(\mathbf{X}\boldsymbol{\beta} + \boldsymbol{\varepsilon}) - \boldsymbol{\beta}][\mathbf{X}^-(\mathbf{X}\boldsymbol{\beta} + \boldsymbol{\varepsilon}) - \boldsymbol{\beta}]'\} \\ &= \mathscr{E}\{[\mathbf{X}^-\boldsymbol{\varepsilon}][\mathbf{X}^-\boldsymbol{\varepsilon}]'\} = \mathscr{E}[\mathbf{X}^-\boldsymbol{\varepsilon}\boldsymbol{\varepsilon}'\mathbf{X}'^-] \\ &= \mathbf{X}^-[\mathscr{E}(\boldsymbol{\varepsilon}\boldsymbol{\varepsilon}')]\mathbf{X}'^- = \sigma^2(\mathbf{X}'\mathbf{X})^{-1}\end{aligned} \tag{6.2.8}$$

Thus we have the result

$$\tilde{\boldsymbol{\beta}} \text{ is distributed } N(\tilde{\boldsymbol{\beta}} : \boldsymbol{\beta}, \sigma^2(\mathbf{X}'\mathbf{X})^{-1})$$

To find the distribution of $\tilde{\sigma}^2$ we note that we can write

$$\begin{aligned}(\mathbf{Y} - \mathbf{X}\tilde{\boldsymbol{\beta}})'(\mathbf{Y} - \mathbf{X}\tilde{\boldsymbol{\beta}}) &= [\mathbf{Y} - \mathbf{X}(\mathbf{X}'\mathbf{X})^{-1}\mathbf{X}'\mathbf{Y}]'[\mathbf{Y} - \mathbf{X}(\mathbf{X}'\mathbf{X})^{-1}\mathbf{X}'\mathbf{Y}] \\ &= \mathbf{Y}'(\mathbf{I} - \mathbf{K})\mathbf{Y} = \mathbf{Y}'\mathbf{M}\mathbf{Y}\end{aligned}$$

since $\mathbf{I} - \mathbf{K}$ is a symmetric idempotent $n \times n$ matrix. By Theorem 4.4.3 we obtain the fact that

$$U = \left(\frac{1}{\sigma^2}\right)\mathbf{Y}'(\mathbf{I} - \mathbf{K})\mathbf{Y}$$

has a noncentral chi-square p.d.f. with degrees of freedom equal to $n - p$ since $\text{tr}(\mathbf{I} - \mathbf{K}) = \text{tr}(\mathbf{I}) - \text{tr}(\mathbf{K}) = n - p$. The noncentrality parameter λ is given by

$$\lambda = \frac{1}{2\sigma^2}(\mathscr{E}[\mathbf{Y}])'[\mathbf{I} - \mathbf{K}](\mathscr{E}[\mathbf{Y}]) = \left(\frac{1}{2\sigma^2}\right)\boldsymbol{\beta}'\mathbf{X}'(\mathbf{I} - \mathbf{K})\mathbf{X}\boldsymbol{\beta}$$

But we note that $(\mathbf{I} - \mathbf{K})\mathbf{X} = \mathbf{0}$ and hence $\lambda = 0$, so U is distributed as $\chi^2(u : n - p)$. We notice that $\mathscr{E}[U] = n - p$; so it follows that $n\tilde{\sigma}^2/(n - p)$ is an unbiased estimator of σ^2. Thus we shall use the symbol $\hat{\sigma}^2$ to represent $[1/(n - p)]\mathbf{Y}'(\mathbf{I} - \mathbf{K})\mathbf{Y}$, and to be consistent we shall use the symbol $\hat{\boldsymbol{\beta}}$ instead of $\tilde{\boldsymbol{\beta}}$.

Now we show that the random vector $\hat{\boldsymbol{\beta}}$ is independent of $\hat{\sigma}^2$. To show this we use Equation (6.2.5) and Theorem 4.5.2 with $\mathbf{B} = \mathbf{X}^-$ and $\mathbf{A} = \mathbf{I} - \mathbf{X}\mathbf{X}^-$. But $\mathbf{B}\boldsymbol{\Sigma}\mathbf{A} = \mathbf{X}^-(\sigma^2\mathbf{I})(\mathbf{I} - \mathbf{X}\mathbf{X}^-) = \mathbf{0}$, and hence the result.

Note 1. There are a number of formulas for $\hat{\sigma}^2$ which we summarize here:

$$(n-p)\hat{\sigma}^2 = (\mathbf{Y} - \mathbf{X}\hat{\boldsymbol{\beta}})'(\mathbf{Y} - \mathbf{X}\hat{\boldsymbol{\beta}}) \quad \text{where} \quad \hat{\boldsymbol{\beta}} = (\mathbf{X}'\mathbf{X})^{-1}\mathbf{X}'\mathbf{Y} = \mathbf{X}^{-}\mathbf{Y}$$

$$\begin{aligned}(n-p)\hat{\sigma}^2 &= \mathbf{Y}'(\mathbf{I} - \mathbf{X}\mathbf{X}^{-})\mathbf{Y} = \mathbf{Y}'\mathbf{Y} - \mathbf{Y}'\mathbf{X}\mathbf{X}^{-}\mathbf{Y} \\ &= \mathbf{Y}'(\mathbf{I} - \mathbf{K})\mathbf{Y} = \mathbf{Y}'\mathbf{M}\mathbf{Y}\end{aligned} \tag{6.2.9}$$

$$(n-p)\hat{\sigma}^2 = \mathbf{Y}'\mathbf{Y} - \hat{\boldsymbol{\beta}}'\mathbf{X}'\mathbf{Y} \quad \text{where} \quad \hat{\boldsymbol{\beta}} = (\mathbf{X}'\mathbf{X})^{-1}\mathbf{X}'\mathbf{Y} = \mathbf{X}^{-}\mathbf{Y}$$

We summarize many of the results proved above in the following theorem.

THEOREM 6.2.1

Let $\mathbf{Y} = \mathbf{X}\boldsymbol{\beta} + \boldsymbol{\varepsilon}$, *where* $\boldsymbol{\varepsilon}$ *is distributed* $N(\boldsymbol{\varepsilon} : \mathbf{0}, \sigma^2\mathbf{I})$, *be given by Definition* 6.1.1. *The results below follow:*

(1) $\hat{\boldsymbol{\beta}} = \mathbf{X}^{-}\mathbf{Y}$ *is the maximum likelihood estimator for* $\boldsymbol{\beta}$;

(2) $\hat{\sigma}^2 = [1/(n-p)]\mathbf{Y}'(\mathbf{I} - \mathbf{K})\mathbf{Y}$ *is the maximum likelihood estimator for* σ^2 *(it has been adjusted so it is unbiased)*;

(3) $\hat{\boldsymbol{\beta}}$ *is distributed* $N(\hat{\boldsymbol{\beta}} : \boldsymbol{\beta}, \sigma^2\mathbf{C})$, *where* $\mathbf{C} = (\mathbf{X}'\mathbf{X})^{-1}$;

(4) $(n-p)\hat{\sigma}^2/\sigma^2 = U$ *is distributed* $\chi^2(u : n-p)$;

(5) $\hat{\boldsymbol{\beta}}$ *and* $\hat{\sigma}^2$ *are independent*;

(6) $\hat{\boldsymbol{\beta}}$ *and* $\hat{\sigma}^2$ *are sufficient statistics for* $\boldsymbol{\beta}$ *and* σ^2;

(7) $\hat{\boldsymbol{\beta}}$ *and* $\hat{\sigma}^2$ *are complete statistics.*

Result (7) will not be proved, but it is important and can be proved by showing that the joint p.d.f. of $\hat{\boldsymbol{\beta}}$ and $\hat{\sigma}^2$, a set of sufficient statistics, is a member of the exponential family. Then use Theorem 2.7.8. By using (6) and (7) and Theorem 2.7.7, we can state a strong result about optimum properties of estimators of $\boldsymbol{\beta}$ and σ^2 for Case 1 of the general linear model. The result is given in the next theorem.

THEOREM 6.2.2

Let $\mathbf{Y} = \mathbf{X}\boldsymbol{\beta} + \boldsymbol{\varepsilon}$, *where* $\boldsymbol{\varepsilon}$ *is distributed* $N(\boldsymbol{\varepsilon} : \mathbf{0}, \sigma^2\mathbf{I})$, *be given by Definition* 6.1.1. *Let* $t(\boldsymbol{\beta}, \sigma^2)$ *be any function of the parameters* $\boldsymbol{\beta}$ *and* σ^2 *for which an unbiased estimator exists. Then there exists a function of the sufficient statistics* $\hat{\boldsymbol{\beta}}$ *and* $\hat{\sigma}^2$, *say* $q(\hat{\boldsymbol{\beta}}, \hat{\sigma}^2)$, *that is also an unbiased estimator of* $t(\boldsymbol{\beta}, \sigma^2)$. *In addition,* $q(\hat{\boldsymbol{\beta}}, \hat{\sigma}^2)$ *is the uniformly minimum variance unbiased (UMVU) estimator for* $t(\boldsymbol{\beta}, \sigma^2)$.

We illustrate some of the above results.

Example 6.2.1

Consider the simple linear model

$$\left.\begin{aligned}
&Y_i = \beta_0 + \beta x_i + \varepsilon_i \\
&\varepsilon_i \text{ are distributed } NID(\varepsilon : 0, \sigma^2) \qquad i = 1, 2, \dots, n, \quad n > 2 \\
&\Omega = \{(\beta_0, \beta, \sigma^2) : \beta_0 \in E_1, \beta \in E_1, \sigma^2 > 0\}
\end{aligned}\right\} \tag{6.2.10}$$

We rewrite this in vector and matrix form as

$$\mathbf{Y} = \begin{bmatrix} Y_1 \\ Y_2 \\ \vdots \\ Y_n \end{bmatrix} \qquad \mathbf{X} = \begin{bmatrix} 1 & x_1 \\ 1 & x_2 \\ \vdots & \vdots \\ 1 & x_n \end{bmatrix} \qquad \boldsymbol{\beta} = \begin{bmatrix} \beta_0 \\ \beta \end{bmatrix} \qquad \boldsymbol{\varepsilon} = \begin{bmatrix} \varepsilon_1 \\ \varepsilon_2 \\ \vdots \\ \varepsilon_n \end{bmatrix}$$

$$\mathbf{X'X} = \begin{bmatrix} n & \sum_{i=1}^n x_i \\ \sum_{i=1}^n x_i & \sum_{i=1}^n x_i^2 \end{bmatrix} \qquad \mathbf{X'Y} = \begin{bmatrix} \sum_{i=1}^n Y_i \\ \sum_{i=1}^n x_i Y_i \end{bmatrix}$$

$$(\mathbf{X'X})^{-1} = \left(\frac{1}{n \sum_{i=1}^n x_i^2 - \left(\sum_{i=1}^n x_i \right)^2} \right) \begin{bmatrix} \sum_{i=1}^n x_i^2 & -\sum_{i=1}^n x_i \\ -\sum_{i=1}^n x_i & n \end{bmatrix}$$

$$\begin{aligned}
\hat{\boldsymbol{\beta}} &= \mathbf{X^- Y} = (\mathbf{X'X})^{-1}\mathbf{X'Y} \\
&= \left(\frac{1}{n \sum (x_i - \bar{x})^2} \right) \begin{bmatrix} \left(\sum Y_i\right)\left(\sum x_i^2\right) - (\sum x_j)(\sum x_i Y_i) \\ n \sum x_i Y_i - (\sum x_j)(\sum Y_i) \end{bmatrix}
\end{aligned}$$

Thus

$$\hat{\boldsymbol{\beta}} = \begin{bmatrix} \bar{Y} - \hat{\beta}\bar{x} \\ \dfrac{\sum (x_i - \bar{x})(Y_i - \bar{Y})}{\sum (x_i - \bar{x})^2} \end{bmatrix}$$

so

$$\begin{aligned}
\hat{\beta}_0 &= \bar{Y} - \hat{\beta}\bar{x} \\
\hat{\beta} &= \frac{\sum (x_i - \bar{x})(Y_i - \bar{Y})}{\sum (x_i - \bar{x})^2}
\end{aligned} \tag{6.2.11}$$

Also, for $\hat{\sigma}^2$ we would have the following:

$$\begin{aligned}\hat{\sigma}^2 &= \frac{1}{n-2}[\mathbf{Y}'\mathbf{Y} - \hat{\boldsymbol{\beta}}'\mathbf{X}'\mathbf{Y}] \\ &= \frac{1}{n-2}[\sum Y_i^2 - \bar{Y}(\sum Y_i) + \hat{\beta}\bar{x}(\sum Y_i) - \hat{\beta}\sum x_i Y_i] \\ &= \frac{1}{n-2}\left\{\sum (Y_i - \bar{Y})^2 - \frac{[\sum (x_i - \bar{x})(Y_i - \bar{Y})]^2}{\sum (x_i - \bar{x})^2}\right\} \qquad (6.2.12)\end{aligned}$$

Suppose we wish to estimate the following:

1. β
2. β_0
3. σ^2
4. $2\beta - 3\beta_0$
5. $5\sigma^2 + 8\beta$
6. $\beta_0 + 1.94\sigma$
7. β_0/σ^2
8. $\log^3 |\beta|$

By Theorem 6.2.2, if we can find unbiased estimators for these functions of the parameters, and if these unbiased estimators are based on $\hat{\beta}_0$, $\hat{\beta}$, and $\hat{\sigma}^2$, then these estimators are the uniformly minimum variance unbiased estimators of the respective functions of the parameters. By parts (1) and (2) of Theorem 6.2.1, we know that $\hat{\beta}$, $\hat{\beta}_0$, and $\hat{\sigma}^2$ are unbiased estimators of β, β_0, and σ^2, respectively. Also, $2\hat{\beta} - 3\hat{\beta}_0$ is an unbiased estimator of $2\beta - 3\beta_0$ and $5\hat{\sigma}^2 + 8\hat{\beta}$ is an unbiased estimator of $5\sigma^2 + 8\beta$. Since these estimators are all based on (a function of) the complete sufficient statistics $\hat{\beta}$, $\hat{\beta}_0$, $\hat{\sigma}^2$, we use Theorem 6.2.2 and state: The uniformly minimum variance unbiased estimators of the function of the parameters in the preceding parts 1 through 5 are given below.

1. $\hat{\beta} = \dfrac{\sum(x_i - \bar{x})(Y_i - \bar{Y})}{\sum(x_i - \bar{x})^2}$

2. $\hat{\beta}_0 = \bar{Y} - \hat{\beta}\bar{x}$

3. $\hat{\sigma}^2 = \dfrac{1}{n-2}\left\{\sum(Y_i - \bar{Y})^2 - \dfrac{[\sum(x_i - \bar{x})(Y_i - \bar{Y})]^2}{\sum(x_i - \bar{x})^2}\right\}$

4. $2\left[\dfrac{\sum(x_i - \bar{x})(Y_i - \bar{Y})}{\sum(x_i - \bar{x})^2}\right] - 3[\bar{Y} - \hat{\beta}\bar{x}]$

5. $5\left(\dfrac{1}{n-2}\right)\left(\sum(Y_i - \bar{Y})^2 - \dfrac{[\sum(x_i - \bar{x})(Y_i - \bar{Y})]^2}{\sum(x_i - \bar{x})^2}\right) + 8\left[\dfrac{\sum(x_i - \bar{x})(Y_i - \bar{Y})}{\sum(x_i - \bar{x})^2}\right]$

6. To find the uniformly minimum variance unbiased estimator of $\beta_0 + 1.94\sigma$, we must find an unbiased estimator of σ. Since $(n-2)\hat{\sigma}^2/\sigma^2 = U$ is a central chi-square random variable, we use

a result in Equation (2.5.7) to obtain

$$\mathscr{E}[U^{1/2}] = \frac{\sqrt{2}\,\Gamma\left(\frac{n-1}{2}\right)}{\Gamma\left(\frac{n-2}{2}\right)}$$

and hence

$$\mathscr{E}\left[\frac{\Gamma\left(\frac{n-2}{2}\right)(n-2)^{1/2}}{\sqrt{2}\,\Gamma\left(\frac{n-1}{2}\right)}\hat{\sigma}\right] = \sigma$$

Thus

$$\hat{\beta}_0 + 1.94\left[\frac{(n-2)^{1/2}\,\Gamma\left(\frac{n-2}{2}\right)}{\sqrt{2}\,\Gamma\left(\frac{n-1}{2}\right)}\hat{\sigma}\right]$$

(which is an unbiased estimator based on the sufficient complete statistics $\hat{\beta}_0$, $\hat{\beta}$, and $\hat{\sigma}^2$) is the uniformly minimum variance unbiased estimator of $\beta_0 + 1.94\sigma$, where $\hat{\beta}_0$ and $\hat{\sigma}$ are obtained from Equations (6.2.11) and (6.2.12).

7. To obtain the uniformly minimum variance unbiased estimator of β_0/σ^2, we must obtain an unbiased estimator of β_0/σ^2 based on the complete sufficient statistics $\hat{\beta}_0$, $\hat{\beta}$, $\hat{\sigma}^2$. From Equation (2.5.7) we note that $(n-4)/(n-2)\hat{\sigma}^2$ is an unbiased estimator of $1/\sigma^2$. Also by part (5) of Theorem 6.2.1, we note that $\hat{\beta}_0$ and $\hat{\sigma}^2$ are independent. We get

$$\mathscr{E}\left[\frac{(n-4)\hat{\beta}_0}{(n-2)\hat{\sigma}^2}\right] = \mathscr{E}\left[\frac{(n-4)}{(n-2)\hat{\sigma}^2}\right]\mathscr{E}[\hat{\beta}_0] = \frac{\beta_0}{\sigma^2}$$

and thus $[(n-4)/(n-2)](\hat{\beta}_0/\hat{\sigma}^2)$ is the uniformly minimum variance unbiased estimator of β_0/σ^2, where $\hat{\beta}_0$ and $\hat{\sigma}^2$ are given by Equations (6.2.11) and (6.2.12).

8. An unbiased estimator is not known for $\log^3|\beta|$ and hence no minimum variance unbiased estimator is known.

Note 2. By condition (6) of Theorem 6.2.1 we know that we do not need the **Y** vector nor the **X** matrix except to obtain the sufficient statistics $\hat{\boldsymbol{\beta}}$ and $\hat{\sigma}^2$. Since the $p + 1$ random variables $\hat{\beta}_1, \hat{\beta}_2, \ldots, \hat{\beta}_p, \hat{\sigma}^2$ are sufficient statistics, they contain all the "information" about the model (for Case 1) that is contained in the $n + np$ elements of $\mathbf{Y}$ and $\mathbf{X}$. Since we know the joint distribution of the $p + 1$ random variables $\hat{\beta}_1, \hat{\beta}_2, \ldots, \hat{\beta}_p, \hat{\sigma}^2$, we can use this distribution for point estimation, interval estimation, and tests of hypotheses without sacrificing "information" by not using the original observations $\mathbf{Y}$ and $\mathbf{X}$.

Next we discuss "large" sample properties of $\hat{\boldsymbol{\beta}}$ and $\hat{\sigma}^2$. For this situation we use a sequence of models defined by

$$\mathbf{Y}_n = \mathbf{X}_n\boldsymbol{\beta} + \boldsymbol{\varepsilon}_n \qquad \boldsymbol{\varepsilon}_n \text{ is distributed } \mathbf{N}(\boldsymbol{\varepsilon}_n : \mathbf{0}_n, \sigma^2\mathbf{I}_n) \qquad n = p + 1, p + 2, \ldots$$

where $\mathbf{Y}_n$ is an $n \times 1$ random vector of observations and $\mathbf{X}_n$ is an $n \times p$ matrix of constants. This model illustrates the fact that the number of observations increases, but for each set of n observations, the model is a general linear model.

THEOREM 6.2.3

Consider the sequence of general linear models

$$\mathbf{Y}_n = \mathbf{X}_n\boldsymbol{\beta} + \boldsymbol{\varepsilon}_n \qquad \boldsymbol{\varepsilon}_n \text{ is distributed } \mathbf{N}(\boldsymbol{\varepsilon}_n : \mathbf{0}_n, \sigma^2\mathbf{I}_n) \qquad n = p + 1, p + 2, \ldots$$

where $\mathbf{Y}_n$ is an $n \times 1$ vector of observable random variables, $\mathbf{X}_n$ is an $n \times p$ matrix of rank p (for each n) of observable nonrandom variables, $\boldsymbol{\beta}$ is a $p \times 1$ vector of nonobservable constants, and $\boldsymbol{\varepsilon}_n$ is an $n \times 1$ vector of nonobservable random variables. Let $\hat{\boldsymbol{\beta}}_n$ and $\hat{\sigma}_n^2$ denote, respectively, the maximum likelihood ($\hat{\sigma}_n^2$ is adjusted for bias) estimators of $\boldsymbol{\beta}$ and σ^2 in the nth model. Hence

$$\hat{\boldsymbol{\beta}}_n = (\mathbf{X}_n'\mathbf{X}_n)^{-1}\mathbf{X}_n'\mathbf{Y}_n$$
$$\hat{\sigma}_n^2 = (n - p)^{-1}\mathbf{Y}_n'[\mathbf{I}_n - \mathbf{X}_n(\mathbf{X}_n'\mathbf{X}_n)^{-1}\mathbf{X}_n']\mathbf{Y}_n \qquad n = p + 1, p + 2, \ldots$$

(1) *If $\lim_{n \to \infty} (\mathbf{X}_n'\mathbf{X}_n)^{-1} = \mathbf{0}$, then the sequence of estimators $\{\ell'\hat{\boldsymbol{\beta}}_n\}$ is a mean-squared-error (and simple) consistent estimator of $\ell'\boldsymbol{\beta}$ (where ℓ is any $p \times 1$ vector of constants).*

(2) *The sequence of estimators $\{\hat{\sigma}_n^2\}$ is a mean-squared-error (and simple) consistent estimator of σ^2.*

Proof

The proof is a direct application of Theorem 2.7.9 (and Corollary 2.7.9) after it is shown that $\hat{\sigma}_n^2$ and $\ell'\hat{\boldsymbol{\beta}}_n$ are unbiased in the limit and that the variances of $\hat{\sigma}_n^2$ and $\ell'\hat{\boldsymbol{\beta}}_n$ are zero in the limit. We leave the details for the reader.

COROLLARY 6.2.3

Under the conditions of Theorem 6.2.3, each element of $\hat{\boldsymbol{\beta}}_n$ is a mean-squared-error (and simple) consistent estimator of the corresponding element in $\boldsymbol{\beta}$.

6.2.1 Point Estimation of $\ell'\boldsymbol{\beta}$ and $\mu(\mathbf{x})$ for Case 1

For a given vector $\mathbf{x}$ in domain D, it follows that

$$\mu(\mathbf{x}) = \boldsymbol{\beta}'\mathbf{x} = \sum_{i=1}^{p} \beta_i x_i$$

and this is a given linear combination of the β_i. Hence by parts (6) and (7) of Theorem 6.2.1, and more specifically by Theorem 6.2.2, we can let the function $t(\boldsymbol{\beta}, \sigma^2)$ be $\boldsymbol{\beta}'\mathbf{x}$, and it follows that the uniformly minimum variance unbiased estimator of $\mu(\mathbf{x})$ is $\hat{\mu}(\mathbf{x}) = \hat{\boldsymbol{\beta}}'\mathbf{x}$ for any vector $\mathbf{x}$ in domain D, where $\hat{\boldsymbol{\beta}}$ is as given in part (1) of Theorem 6.2.1.

For *any* constant $p \times 1$ vector ℓ, the uniformly minimum variance unbiased estimator of $\ell'\boldsymbol{\beta}$, any linear combination of $\boldsymbol{\beta}$, is given by $\ell'\hat{\boldsymbol{\beta}}$. That is,

$$\widehat{\ell'\boldsymbol{\beta}} = \ell'\hat{\boldsymbol{\beta}}$$

Of course, $\mu(\mathbf{x})$ is a special case of $\ell'\boldsymbol{\beta}$, as will be pointed out in the following example.

Example 6.2.2

Consider Example 5.2.2, where $\mu(x) = \beta_0 + \beta x$ for x in the interval $50 \leq x \leq 300$ miles. If we collect data and use the formulas in Example 6.2.1, we can estimate β_0 and β. Suppose we want to estimate the mean of the random variable $Y_{(60)}$, that is, $\mu(60)$. Since $\mu(60) = \beta_0 + 60\beta$, the UMVU estimator of $\mu(60)$ is

$$\hat{\mu}(60) = \hat{\beta}_0 + 60\hat{\beta}$$

On the other hand, suppose an investigator wants to estimate $30\beta_0 - 80\beta$, which we denote by $\ell'\boldsymbol{\beta}$ where $\ell' = [30, -80]$. According to the model of the real-world situation, $30\beta_0 - 80\beta$ is not the mean $\mu(x)$ of any of the pebble distributions. However, we can estimate $\ell'\boldsymbol{\beta}$, and by Theorem 6.2.2 the UMVU estimator is $\ell'\hat{\boldsymbol{\beta}} = 30\hat{\beta}_0 - 80\hat{\beta}$.

Example 6.2.3

In this example we demonstrate how Theorem 2.7.4 can be used to find the UMVU estimator of $\ell'\boldsymbol{\beta}$, a specified linear function of $\boldsymbol{\beta}$, for Case 1 of the general linear model. First we note that $\hat{\boldsymbol{\beta}}$ and $\hat{\sigma}^2$ are *sufficient* statistics; hence by the Rao-Blackwell theorem we need only consider the distribution of these $p + 1$ statistics in our search for UMVU estimators. $\ell'\hat{\boldsymbol{\beta}}$ is an unbiased estimator of $\ell'\boldsymbol{\beta}$ (it is also the M.L. estimator). Thus $\ell'\hat{\boldsymbol{\beta}}$ is an unbiased estimator of $\ell'\boldsymbol{\beta}$ that is based on sufficient statistics, so it is a good candidate to consider for the UMVU estimator of $\ell'\boldsymbol{\beta}$ (if one exists).

Let $M(\hat{\boldsymbol{\beta}}, \hat{\sigma}^2)$ be a general unbiased estimator of $\ell'\boldsymbol{\beta}$, where $M(\hat{\boldsymbol{\beta}}, \hat{\sigma}^2)$ is unknown, and define $u(\hat{\boldsymbol{\beta}}, \hat{\sigma}^2)$ by

$$M(\hat{\boldsymbol{\beta}}, \hat{\sigma}^2) = \ell'\hat{\boldsymbol{\beta}} + u(\hat{\boldsymbol{\beta}}, \hat{\sigma}^2)$$

Since $\ell'\hat{\boldsymbol{\beta}}$ is known (a known statistic), in order to determine $M(\hat{\boldsymbol{\beta}}, \hat{\sigma}^2)$, we must determine $u(\hat{\boldsymbol{\beta}}, \hat{\sigma}^2)$. Since $M(\hat{\boldsymbol{\beta}}, \hat{\sigma}^2)$ is an unbiased estimator of $\ell'\boldsymbol{\beta}$, this implies

$$\ell'\boldsymbol{\beta} = \mathscr{E}[M(\hat{\boldsymbol{\beta}}, \hat{\sigma}^2)] = \mathscr{E}[\ell'\hat{\boldsymbol{\beta}}] + \mathscr{E}[u(\hat{\boldsymbol{\beta}}, \hat{\sigma}^2)] = \ell'\boldsymbol{\beta} + \mathscr{E}[u(\hat{\boldsymbol{\beta}}, \hat{\sigma}^2)]$$

or

$$\mathscr{E}[u(\hat{\boldsymbol{\beta}}, \hat{\sigma}^2)] = 0 \qquad \text{for all } (\boldsymbol{\beta}, \sigma^2) \text{ in } \Omega$$

If we can show $\mathscr{E}[\ell'\hat{\boldsymbol{\beta}} \cdot u(\hat{\boldsymbol{\beta}}, \hat{\sigma}^2)] = 0$ for all $(\boldsymbol{\beta}, \sigma^2)$ in Ω, then we would have

$$\text{var}[M(\hat{\boldsymbol{\beta}}, \hat{\sigma}^2)] = \text{var}[\ell'\hat{\boldsymbol{\beta}}] + \text{var}[u(\hat{\boldsymbol{\beta}}, \hat{\sigma}^2)]$$

since $\mathscr{E}[\ell'\hat{\boldsymbol{\beta}} \cdot u(\hat{\boldsymbol{\beta}}, \hat{\sigma}^2)] = 0$ and $\mathscr{E}[u(\hat{\boldsymbol{\beta}}, \hat{\sigma}^2)] = 0$ together imply $\text{cov}[\ell'\hat{\boldsymbol{\beta}}, u(\hat{\boldsymbol{\beta}}, \hat{\sigma}^2)] = 0$. Hence $\text{var}[M(\hat{\boldsymbol{\beta}}, \hat{\sigma}^2)] \geq \text{var}[\ell'\hat{\boldsymbol{\beta}}]$, and $\text{var}[\ell'\hat{\boldsymbol{\beta}}]$ is a lower bound for the variance of *all* unbiased estimators of $\ell'\boldsymbol{\beta}$. The lower bound is attained, and $M(\hat{\boldsymbol{\beta}}, \hat{\sigma}^2)$ is the UMVU estimator of $\ell'\boldsymbol{\beta}$ if and only if $\text{var}[u(\hat{\boldsymbol{\beta}}, \hat{\sigma}^2)] = 0$. But $\text{var}[u(\hat{\boldsymbol{\beta}}, \hat{\sigma}^2)] = 0$ along with $\mathscr{E}[u(\hat{\boldsymbol{\beta}}, \hat{\sigma}^2)] = 0$ implies that $u(\hat{\boldsymbol{\beta}}, \hat{\sigma}^2) = 0$ with probability one, and this implies that $M(\hat{\boldsymbol{\beta}}, \hat{\sigma}^2) = \ell'\hat{\boldsymbol{\beta}}$ is the UMVU estimator of $\ell'\boldsymbol{\beta}$.

We now show that $\mathscr{E}[\ell'\hat{\boldsymbol{\beta}} \cdot u(\hat{\boldsymbol{\beta}}, \hat{\sigma}^2)] = 0$. We start with $\mathscr{E}[u(\hat{\boldsymbol{\beta}}, \hat{\sigma}^2)] = 0$. This gives

$$0 = \mathscr{E}[u(\hat{\boldsymbol{\beta}}, \hat{\sigma}^2)] = \int_0^{\infty} \int_{-\infty}^{\infty} \cdots \int_{-\infty}^{\infty} u(\hat{\boldsymbol{\beta}}, \hat{\sigma}^2) f_1(\hat{\boldsymbol{\beta}} : \boldsymbol{\beta}, \sigma^2) f_2(\hat{\sigma}^2 : \sigma^2) \, d\hat{\boldsymbol{\beta}} \, d\hat{\sigma}^2 \tag{6.2.13}$$

where $f_2(\hat{\sigma}^2 : \sigma^2)$ is the p.d.f. of $\hat{\sigma}^2$ (it does not depend on $\boldsymbol{\beta}$). $f_1(\hat{\boldsymbol{\beta}} : \boldsymbol{\beta}, \sigma^2)$, which is $\mathbf{n}(\hat{\boldsymbol{\beta}} : \boldsymbol{\beta}, \sigma^2\mathbf{C})$, is the p.d.f. of $\hat{\boldsymbol{\beta}}$; hence since $\hat{\sigma}^2$ and $\hat{\boldsymbol{\beta}}$ are independent, $f_2(\hat{\sigma}^2 : \sigma^2) f_1(\hat{\boldsymbol{\beta}} : \boldsymbol{\beta}, \sigma^2)$ is the joint p.d.f. of $\hat{\sigma}^2$ and $\hat{\boldsymbol{\beta}}$.

Differentiate both sides of Equation (6.2.13) with respect to $\boldsymbol{\beta}$ and get (we can interchange integration and differentiation in this problem)

$$\mathbf{0} = \int_0^\infty \left\{ \int_{-\infty}^\infty \cdots \int_{-\infty}^\infty u(\hat{\boldsymbol{\beta}}, \hat{\sigma}^2) \left(\frac{\partial f_1(\hat{\boldsymbol{\beta}} : \boldsymbol{\beta}, \sigma^2)}{\partial \boldsymbol{\beta}} \right) d\hat{\boldsymbol{\beta}} \right\} f_2(\hat{\sigma}^2 : \sigma^2)\, d\hat{\sigma}^2$$

But

$$\frac{\partial f_1(\hat{\boldsymbol{\beta}} : \boldsymbol{\beta}, \sigma^2)}{\partial \boldsymbol{\beta}} = f_1(\hat{\boldsymbol{\beta}} : \boldsymbol{\beta}, \sigma^2) \left[\frac{1}{2\sigma^2} (-2\mathbf{X}'\mathbf{X}\boldsymbol{\beta} + 2\mathbf{X}'\mathbf{X}\hat{\boldsymbol{\beta}}) \right]$$

so we get

$$\mathbf{0} = \int_0^\infty \left\{ \int_{-\infty}^\infty \cdots \int_{-\infty}^\infty u(\hat{\boldsymbol{\beta}}, \hat{\sigma}^2) [\mathbf{X}'\mathbf{X}\boldsymbol{\beta} - \mathbf{X}'\mathbf{X}\hat{\boldsymbol{\beta}}] f_1(\hat{\boldsymbol{\beta}} : \boldsymbol{\beta}, \sigma^2)\, d\hat{\boldsymbol{\beta}} \right\} \times f_2(\hat{\sigma}^2 : \sigma^2)\, d\hat{\sigma}^2$$

Another way of writing this is as follows:

$$\begin{aligned} \mathbf{0} &= \mathscr{E}[u(\hat{\boldsymbol{\beta}}, \hat{\sigma}^2)\{\mathbf{X}'\mathbf{X}\boldsymbol{\beta} - \mathbf{X}'\mathbf{X}\hat{\boldsymbol{\beta}}\}] \\ &= \mathscr{E}[u(\hat{\boldsymbol{\beta}}, \hat{\sigma}^2)\{\mathbf{X}'\mathbf{X}\boldsymbol{\beta}\}] - \mathscr{E}[u(\hat{\boldsymbol{\beta}}, \hat{\sigma}^2)\{\mathbf{X}'\mathbf{X}\hat{\boldsymbol{\beta}}\}] \\ &= \mathbf{X}'\mathbf{X}\boldsymbol{\beta}\{\mathscr{E}[u(\hat{\boldsymbol{\beta}}, \hat{\sigma}^2)]\} - \mathbf{X}'\mathbf{X}\{\mathscr{E}[\hat{\boldsymbol{\beta}} \cdot u(\hat{\boldsymbol{\beta}}, \hat{\sigma}^2)]\} \end{aligned}$$

This gives us

$$\mathscr{E}[\hat{\boldsymbol{\beta}} \cdot u(\hat{\boldsymbol{\beta}}, \hat{\sigma}^2)] = \mathbf{0} \qquad \text{for all } (\boldsymbol{\beta}, \sigma^2) \text{ in } \Omega$$

If we multiply both sides by $\boldsymbol{\ell}'$, we get the result we want, namely,

$$\mathscr{E}[(\boldsymbol{\ell}'\hat{\boldsymbol{\beta}}) \cdot u(\hat{\boldsymbol{\beta}}, \hat{\sigma}^2)] = 0 \qquad \text{for all } (\boldsymbol{\beta}, \sigma^2) \text{ in } \Omega$$

6.3 Test of the Hypothesis $\mathbf{H\beta = h}$: Case 1

In this section we derive and discuss a test of the hypothesis $\mathbf{H\beta = h}$ for the general linear model for Case 1. In succeeding sections we discuss various special cases of this test.

The tests that are generally of interest are those involving linear functions of the unknown β_i. We illustrate some of these with examples.

Example 6.3.1

Consider a simple linear model

$$Y_i = \beta_0 + \beta x_i + \varepsilon_i \qquad i = 1, 2, \ldots, n$$

The following are examples of tests that may be of interest:

1. $\beta_0 = 0$ (or $\beta_0 = b_0$, where b_0 is a given constant); this is a test that the intercept is zero (or equal to a given constant b_0);
2. $\beta = 1$ (or $\beta = b$, where b is a given constant); this is a test that the slope is equal to unity (or equal to a given constant b).

Example 6.3.2

Consider a linear model

$$Y_i = \beta_0 + \beta_1 x_{i1} + \beta_2 x_{i2} + \beta_3 x_{i3} + \beta_4 x_{i4} + \varepsilon_i \qquad i = 1, 2, \ldots, n$$

The following are examples of tests that may be of interest:

1. $\beta_1 = \beta_2$; a test that β_1 is equal to β_2 ignoring the values of the remaining β_j;
2. $\beta_1 = \beta_2$ and $\beta_3 = \beta_4$; a test that β_1 is equal to β_2 and β_3 is equal to β_4 ignoring the value of β_0;
3. $\beta_1 = \beta_2 = 6$; this is a different test than in part 1; here the test is that β_1 and β_2 are both equal to six; in part 1 the test is that β_1 is equal to β_2 without stating what the common value is;
4. $\beta_0 = \beta_1 = \beta_2 = \beta_3 = \beta_4 = 0$; a test that the β_j are simultaneously equal to zero;
5. $\beta_1 = \beta_2 = \beta_3 = \beta_4$; a test that all the β_j (except β_0) are equal, but not stating what the common value is;
6. $$\left.\begin{aligned} \beta_1 - 2\beta_2 &= 4\beta_3 \\ \beta_1 + 2\beta_2 &= 6 \end{aligned}\right\}$$

   a test of two specific linear relationships among the β_j.

One thing to notice is that each hypothesis above is a special case of

$$\mathbf{H}\boldsymbol{\beta} = \mathbf{h}$$

where $\mathbf{H}$ is a given $q \times p$ matrix and $\mathbf{h}$ is a given $q \times 1$ vector. We shall exhibit $\mathbf{H}$ and $\mathbf{h}$ for each hypothesis in Example 6.3.2. The $\boldsymbol{\beta}$ vector is $\boldsymbol{\beta}' = [\beta_0, \beta_1, \beta_2, \beta_3, \beta_4]$.

1. $\mathbf{H} = [0, 1, -1, 0, 0]$, $\mathbf{h} = \mathbf{0}$;

2. $\mathbf{H} = \begin{bmatrix} 0 & 1 & -1 & 0 & 0 \\ 0 & 0 & 0 & 1 & -1 \end{bmatrix}$, $\mathbf{h} = \begin{bmatrix} 0 \\ 0 \end{bmatrix}$;

3. $\mathbf{H} = \begin{bmatrix} 0 & 1 & 0 & 0 & 0 \\ 0 & 0 & 1 & 0 & 0 \end{bmatrix}$, $\mathbf{h} = \begin{bmatrix} 6 \\ 6 \end{bmatrix}$;

4. $\mathbf{H} = \mathbf{I}_5$, $\mathbf{h} = \mathbf{0}$;

5. $\mathbf{H} = \begin{bmatrix} 0 & 1 & -1 & 0 & 0 \\ 0 & 1 & 0 & -1 & 0 \\ 0 & 1 & 0 & 0 & -1 \end{bmatrix}$, $\mathbf{h} = \begin{bmatrix} 0 \\ 0 \\ 0 \end{bmatrix}$;

6. $\mathbf{H} = \begin{bmatrix} 0 & 1 & -2 & -4 & 0 \\ 0 & 1 & 2 & 0 & 0 \end{bmatrix}$, $\mathbf{h} = \begin{bmatrix} 0 \\ 6 \end{bmatrix}$.

The reader can verify each hypothesis by simply performing the multiplication and evaluating $\mathbf{H}\boldsymbol{\beta} = \mathbf{h}$ for each case.

Note 1. The matrices $\mathbf{H}$ and $\mathbf{h}$ are not necessarily unique. For example, consider part 5. We could write this as $\mathbf{H}_1\boldsymbol{\beta} = \mathbf{h}_1$ or $\mathbf{H}_2\boldsymbol{\beta} = \mathbf{h}_2$, where $\mathbf{H}_1$ and $\mathbf{H}_2$ are given below and $\mathbf{h}_1 = \mathbf{h}_2 = \mathbf{0}$.

$$\mathbf{H}_1 = \begin{bmatrix} 0 & 1 & -1 & 0 & 0 \\ 0 & 1 & 1 & -2 & 0 \\ 0 & 1 & 1 & 1 & -3 \end{bmatrix} \qquad \mathbf{H}_2 = \begin{bmatrix} 0 & -1 & 0 & 0 & 1 \\ 0 & 0 & -1 & 0 & 1 \\ 0 & 0 & 0 & -1 & 1 \end{bmatrix}$$

The reader can easily verify that the hypothesis in part 5 of Example 6.3.2 is true if and only if $\mathbf{H}_1\boldsymbol{\beta} = \mathbf{h}_1$ and if and only if $\mathbf{H}_2\boldsymbol{\beta} = \mathbf{h}_2$.

In view of the above discussion, we now derive a test of $H_0 : \mathbf{H}\boldsymbol{\beta} = \mathbf{h}$ *vs.* $H_a : \mathbf{H}\boldsymbol{\beta} \neq \mathbf{h}$ for the general linear model $\mathbf{Y} = \mathbf{X}\boldsymbol{\beta} + \boldsymbol{\varepsilon}$, $\boldsymbol{\varepsilon}$ is distributed $N(\boldsymbol{\varepsilon} : \mathbf{0}, \sigma^2\mathbf{I})$. We place the following restrictions on $\mathbf{H}$ and $\mathbf{h}$:

1. $\mathbf{H}\boldsymbol{\beta} = \mathbf{h}$ is a consistent set of equations;
2. the $q \times p$ matrix $\mathbf{H}$ has rank q (this is just for convenience so that $\mathbf{H}\mathbf{H}'$ is full rank). (6.3.1)

We shall use the generalized likelihood ratio test. Recall that the generalized likelihood ratio is

$$v(\mathbf{y}) = \frac{\max\limits_{(\boldsymbol{\beta},\sigma^2)\text{ in }\omega} [L(\boldsymbol{\beta}, \sigma^2 : \mathbf{y})]}{\max\limits_{(\boldsymbol{\beta},\sigma^2)\text{ in }\Omega} [L(\boldsymbol{\beta}, \sigma^2 : \mathbf{y})]} = \frac{L(\hat{\omega})}{L(\hat{\Omega})} \tag{6.3.2}$$

where the sample spaces Ω and ω are given by

$$\begin{aligned} \Omega &= \{(\boldsymbol{\beta}, \sigma^2) : \boldsymbol{\beta} \in E_p, \sigma^2 > 0\} \\ \omega &= \{(\boldsymbol{\beta}, \sigma^2) : \boldsymbol{\beta} \in E_p, \mathbf{H}\boldsymbol{\beta} = \mathbf{h}, \sigma^2 > 0\} \end{aligned} \tag{6.3.3}$$

The denominator is obtained in a straightforward manner; it is the likelihood function evaluated at the maximum likelihood value of the parameters $\boldsymbol{\beta}$ and σ^2. The numerator can be found by either of two methods: (1) by solving $\mathbf{H}\boldsymbol{\beta} = \mathbf{h}$ for $\boldsymbol{\beta}$, substituting the constraints into the likelihood function, and maximizing the resulting function; (2) by using Lagrange multipliers and maximizing the likelihood function subject to the constraints $\mathbf{H}\boldsymbol{\beta} = \mathbf{h}$. We discuss each method since in applications there is sometimes an advantage to one method and sometimes to the other.

To demonstrate the first method, substitute the constraints $\mathbf{H}\boldsymbol{\beta} = \mathbf{h}$ into the model $\mathbf{Y} = \mathbf{X}\boldsymbol{\beta} + \boldsymbol{\varepsilon}$ and get a new model, a model reduced by the hypothesis. To do this let $\mathbf{G}$ be a $(p - q) \times p$ matrix of rank $p - q$, $0 < q < p$, such that (later we let $p = q$) $\mathbf{HG}' = \mathbf{0}$ ($\mathbf{G}$ is an orthogonal completion of $\mathbf{H}$). The $p \times p$ matrix

$$\begin{bmatrix} \mathbf{H} \\ \mathbf{G} \end{bmatrix}$$

is full rank, and by Problem 1.20, $\mathbf{HG}^- = \mathbf{0}$. Note that $\mathbf{G}^- = \mathbf{G}'(\mathbf{GG}')^{-1}$ since $\text{rank}[\mathbf{G}] = p - q$. Hence

$$\begin{bmatrix} \mathbf{H} \\ \mathbf{G} \end{bmatrix}^{-1} = [\mathbf{H}^-, \mathbf{G}^-] \qquad \text{and} \qquad \mathbf{I} = \begin{bmatrix} \mathbf{H} \\ \mathbf{G} \end{bmatrix}^{-1} \begin{bmatrix} \mathbf{H} \\ \mathbf{G} \end{bmatrix} = \mathbf{H}^-\mathbf{H} + \mathbf{G}^-\mathbf{G}$$

The rank of $\mathbf{XG}^-$ is $p - q$; this can be shown by noting that $\mathbf{X}^-\mathbf{XG}^- = \mathbf{G}^-$, since $\mathbf{X}^-\mathbf{X} = \mathbf{I}$. Then $p - q = \text{rank}[\mathbf{G}^-] = \text{rank}[\mathbf{X}^-\mathbf{XG}^-] \leq \text{rank}[\mathbf{XG}^-] \leq \text{rank}[\mathbf{G}^-] = p - q$; so $\text{rank}[\mathbf{XG}^-] = p - q$. We write

$$\mathbf{Y} = \mathbf{X}\boldsymbol{\beta} + \boldsymbol{\varepsilon} = \mathbf{X}\begin{bmatrix} \mathbf{H} \\ \mathbf{G} \end{bmatrix}^{-1} \begin{bmatrix} \mathbf{H} \\ \mathbf{G} \end{bmatrix} \boldsymbol{\beta} + \boldsymbol{\varepsilon} = \mathbf{XH}^-\mathbf{H}\boldsymbol{\beta} + \mathbf{XG}^-\mathbf{G}\boldsymbol{\beta} + \boldsymbol{\varepsilon}$$

When $H_0 : \mathbf{H}\boldsymbol{\beta} = \mathbf{h}$ obtains, the model becomes

$$\mathbf{Y} = \mathbf{XH}^-\mathbf{h} + (\mathbf{XG}^-)(\mathbf{G}\boldsymbol{\beta}) + \boldsymbol{\varepsilon}$$

If we let $\mathbf{Z}$ represent $\mathbf{Y} - \mathbf{XH}^-\mathbf{h}$, $\mathbf{B}$ represent $\mathbf{XG}^-$, and $\boldsymbol{\gamma}$ represent $\mathbf{G}\boldsymbol{\beta}$, we can write $\mathbf{Z} = \mathbf{B}\boldsymbol{\gamma} + \boldsymbol{\varepsilon}$ for the model $\mathbf{Y} = \mathbf{X}\boldsymbol{\beta} + \boldsymbol{\varepsilon}$ with the restrictions imposed by H_0. This is a general linear model since $\mathbf{Z}$ is an observable $n \times 1$ random vector, $\mathbf{B}$ is an observable $n \times (p - q)$ nonrandom matrix of rank $p - q$,

$\boldsymbol{\gamma}$ is a $(p - q) \times 1$ vector of unknown parameters and can be any vector in E_{p-q}, $\boldsymbol{\varepsilon}$ is distributed $\mathbf{N}(\boldsymbol{\varepsilon} : \mathbf{0}, \sigma^2\mathbf{I})$.

Hence we consider two models which we define as follows:

1. The full model: $\mathbf{Y} = \mathbf{X}\boldsymbol{\beta} + \boldsymbol{\varepsilon}$, $\Omega = \{(\boldsymbol{\beta}, \sigma^2) : \sigma^2 > 0, \boldsymbol{\beta} \in E_p\}$, $\boldsymbol{\varepsilon}$ is distributed $\mathbf{N}(\boldsymbol{\varepsilon} : \mathbf{0}, \sigma^2\mathbf{I})$;
2. the reduced model: $\mathbf{Z} = \mathbf{B}\boldsymbol{\gamma} + \boldsymbol{\varepsilon}$, $\omega = \{(\boldsymbol{\gamma}, \sigma^2) : \sigma^2 > 0, \boldsymbol{\gamma} \in E_{p-q}\}$, $\boldsymbol{\varepsilon}$ is distributed $\mathbf{N}(\boldsymbol{\varepsilon} : \mathbf{0}, \sigma^2\mathbf{I})$. (6.3.4)

The reduced model means "the full model reduced by the restrictions of the hypothesis H_0." Each model is a general linear model and satisfies the assumptions of Case 1.

To find the generalized likelihood ratio test of $H_0 : \mathbf{H}\boldsymbol{\beta} = \mathbf{h}$ with the alternative $H_a : \mathbf{H}\boldsymbol{\beta} \neq \mathbf{h}$, we substitute the maximum likelihood estimators of $\boldsymbol{\beta}$ and σ^2 (when allowed to vary in Ω) into the likelihood function given in Equation (6.2.1). In Equation (6.2.5) we have obtained the maximum likelihood estimators of $\boldsymbol{\beta}$ and σ^2 in Ω, which we now denote by $\hat{\boldsymbol{\beta}}_\Omega$ and $\hat{\sigma}^2_\Omega$, respectively. We obtain

$$\hat{\boldsymbol{\beta}}_\Omega = \mathbf{X}^-\mathbf{Y} \qquad \hat{\sigma}^2_\Omega = \frac{1}{n}\mathbf{Y}'(\mathbf{I} - \mathbf{X}\mathbf{X}^-)\mathbf{Y}$$
$$L(\hat{\Omega}) = (2\pi)^{-n/2}(\hat{\sigma}^2_\Omega)^{-n/2}e^{-n/2} \tag{6.3.5}$$

To find $L(\hat{\omega})$ we must find the maximum of the likelihood function $L(\boldsymbol{\beta}, \sigma^2 : \mathbf{y}; \mathbf{X})$ with respect to $\boldsymbol{\beta}$ and σ^2 when these parameters are allowed to vary in ω. We substitute the restrictions $\mathbf{H}\boldsymbol{\beta} = \mathbf{h}$ into the model $\mathbf{Y} = \mathbf{X}\boldsymbol{\beta} + \boldsymbol{\varepsilon}$ to get a new model that includes the restrictions. But this is exactly the reduced model given in Equation (6.3.4). Therefore using this model, the maximum likelihood estimators of $\boldsymbol{\gamma}$ and σ^2 are also given by Equation (6.2.5) with $\mathbf{B}$ replacing $\mathbf{X}$ and $\mathbf{Z}$ replacing $\mathbf{Y}$. They are denoted by $\hat{\boldsymbol{\gamma}}_\omega$ and $\hat{\sigma}^2_\omega$, and given by

$$\hat{\boldsymbol{\gamma}}_\omega = \mathbf{B}^-\mathbf{Z} \qquad \hat{\sigma}^2_\omega = \left(\frac{1}{n}\right)\mathbf{Z}'(\mathbf{I} - \mathbf{B}\mathbf{B}^-)\mathbf{Z} \tag{6.3.6}$$

and

$$L(\hat{\omega}) = (2\pi)^{-n/2}(\hat{\sigma}^2_\omega)^{-n/2}e^{-n/2} \tag{6.3.7}$$

The generalized likelihood ratio statistic $v(\mathbf{Y})$ is

$$v(\mathbf{Y}) = V = \left(\frac{\hat{\sigma}^2_\Omega}{\hat{\sigma}^2_\omega}\right)^{n/2}$$

Note 2. If $q = p$, then $\mathbf{B} = \mathbf{0}$ and the reduced model is $\mathbf{Z} = \boldsymbol{\varepsilon}$, where $\mathbf{Z} = \mathbf{Y} - \mathbf{X}\mathbf{H}^{-1}\mathbf{h}$ and the parameter space ω is $\omega = \{(\boldsymbol{\beta}, \sigma^2) : \boldsymbol{\beta} = \mathbf{H}^{-1}\mathbf{h} = \mathbf{b}$ (say), $\sigma^2 > 0\}$; also $L(\hat{\omega}) = (2\pi)^{-n/2}(\hat{\sigma}^2_\omega)^{-n/2}e^{-n/2}$, where $\hat{\sigma}^2_\omega = (1/n)\mathbf{Z}'\mathbf{Z} = (1/n)(\mathbf{Y} - \mathbf{X}\mathbf{b})'(\mathbf{Y} - \mathbf{X}\mathbf{b})$.

In place of V we use a statistic that is a monotonic function of V, that is, we use W, where $W = (V^{-2/n} - 1)(n - p)/q$, which is

$$W = \left(\frac{n-p}{q}\right)\left(\frac{\hat{\sigma}_\omega^2 - \hat{\sigma}_\Omega^2}{\hat{\sigma}_\Omega^2}\right) = \left(\frac{\mathbf{Z}'(\mathbf{I} - \mathbf{BB}^-)\mathbf{Z} - \mathbf{Y}'(\mathbf{I} - \mathbf{XX}^-)\mathbf{Y}}{\mathbf{Y}'(\mathbf{I} - \mathbf{XX}^-)\mathbf{Y}}\right)\left(\frac{n-p}{q}\right) \tag{6.3.8}$$

Terminology. We call W a generalized likelihood ratio test statistic (strictly speaking we should call W a "function of the" generalized likelihood ratio test statistic).

To obtain the distribution of W, we note first that

$$\mathbf{Y}'(\mathbf{I} - \mathbf{XX}^-)\mathbf{Y} = \mathbf{Z}'(\mathbf{I} - \mathbf{XX}^-)\mathbf{Z}$$

since

$$\mathbf{Z} = \mathbf{Y} - \mathbf{XH}^-\mathbf{h}$$

and

$$(\mathbf{I} - \mathbf{XX}^-)\mathbf{Z} = (\mathbf{I} - \mathbf{XX}^-)(\mathbf{Y} - \mathbf{XH}^-\mathbf{h}) = (\mathbf{I} - \mathbf{XX}^-)\mathbf{Y}$$

Thus we can write

$$W = \frac{\left(\frac{1}{q}\right)\mathbf{Z}'\left[\frac{\mathbf{XX}^- - \mathbf{BB}^-}{\sigma^2}\right]\mathbf{Z}}{\left(\frac{1}{n-p}\right)\mathbf{Z}'\left[\frac{\mathbf{I} - \mathbf{XX}^-}{\sigma^2}\right]\mathbf{Z}} = \frac{\left(\frac{1}{q}\right)\mathbf{Z}'\mathbf{A}_1\mathbf{Z}}{\left(\frac{1}{n-p}\right)\mathbf{Z}'\mathbf{A}_2\mathbf{Z}} = \frac{\left(\frac{1}{q}\right)U_1}{\left(\frac{1}{n-p}\right)U_2}$$

and $\mathbf{Z}$ is distributed $N(\mathbf{z} : \mathbf{X\beta} - \mathbf{XH}^-\mathbf{h}, \sigma^2\mathbf{I})$.

From these facts the results below follow.

1. $\mathbf{A}_1(\sigma^2\mathbf{I}) = \mathbf{XX}^- - \mathbf{BB}^-$ is idempotent of rank q, so by Theorem 4.4.3, U_1 is distributed $\chi^2(u_1 : q; \lambda)$, where λ will be determined later.

2. $\mathbf{A}_2(\sigma^2\mathbf{I}) = \mathbf{I} - \mathbf{XX}^-$ is idempotent of rank $n - p$, so by Theorem 4.4.3, U_2 is distributed $\chi^2(u_2 : n - p; 0)$. Clearly the noncentrality λ_2 for the distribution of U_2 is zero since

$$\begin{aligned}\lambda_2 &= \frac{1}{2\sigma^2}(\mathscr{E}[\mathbf{Z}])'(\mathbf{I} - \mathbf{XX}^-)(\mathscr{E}[\mathbf{Z}]) \\ &= \frac{1}{2\sigma^2}[\mathbf{X\beta} - \mathbf{XH}^-\mathbf{h}]'(\mathbf{I} - \mathbf{XX}^-)[\mathbf{X\beta} - \mathbf{XH}^-\mathbf{h}] \\ &= \frac{1}{2\sigma^2}[\mathbf{X}(\mathbf{\beta} - \mathbf{H}^-\mathbf{h})]'(\mathbf{I} - \mathbf{XX}^-)[\mathbf{X}(\mathbf{\beta} - \mathbf{H}^-\mathbf{h})] = 0\end{aligned}$$

since $(\mathbf{I} - \mathbf{XX}^-)\mathbf{X} = \mathbf{0}$.

3. By Theorem 4.5.3, U_1 and U_2 are independent since

$$\mathbf{A}_1(\sigma^2\mathbf{I})\mathbf{A}_2 = \frac{1}{\sigma^2}(\mathbf{XX}^- - \mathbf{BB}^-)(\mathbf{I} - \mathbf{XX}^-) = \mathbf{0}$$

4. W is distributed $F(w : q, n - p; \lambda)$, where (λ is derived below)

$$\lambda = \frac{1}{2\sigma^2}(\mathbf{H\beta} - \mathbf{h})'[\mathbf{H}(\mathbf{X}'\mathbf{X})^{-1}\mathbf{H}']^{-1}(\mathbf{H\beta} - \mathbf{h})$$

and $\lambda = 0$ if and only if $\mathbf{H\beta} = \mathbf{h}$, that is, if and only if H_0 is true since $\mathbf{H}(\mathbf{X}'\mathbf{X})^{-1}\mathbf{H}'$ is a positive definite matrix.

In Section 6.11.1 we show by the Lagrange multiplier technique that the test statistic W in Equation (6.3.8) can also be written as

$$W = \left(\frac{(\mathbf{H}\hat{\boldsymbol{\beta}} - \mathbf{h})'[\mathbf{H}(\mathbf{X}'\mathbf{X})^{-1}\mathbf{H}']^{-1}(\mathbf{H}\hat{\boldsymbol{\beta}} - \mathbf{h})}{\mathbf{Y}'(\mathbf{I} - \mathbf{XX}^-)\mathbf{Y}}\right)\left(\frac{n - p}{q}\right) \tag{6.3.9}$$

Here we look further into this alternate expression for W.

Define $\boldsymbol{\theta}$ by $\boldsymbol{\theta} = \mathbf{H\beta} - \mathbf{h}$. Then the problem is to test $H_0 : \boldsymbol{\theta} = \mathbf{0}$ *vs.* $H_a : \boldsymbol{\theta} \neq \mathbf{0}$. By Theorem 6.2.1 the maximum likelihood (and UMVU) estimator of $\boldsymbol{\theta}$ is $\hat{\boldsymbol{\theta}} = \mathbf{H}\hat{\boldsymbol{\beta}} - \mathbf{h}$. Also $\hat{\boldsymbol{\theta}}$ is distributed $N(\hat{\boldsymbol{\theta}} : \boldsymbol{\theta}, \sigma^2\mathbf{H}(\mathbf{X}'\mathbf{X})^{-1}\mathbf{H}')$, and by Theorem 4.4.3,

$$\frac{U_1}{\sigma^2} = \left(\frac{1}{\sigma^2}\right)\hat{\boldsymbol{\theta}}'[\mathbf{H}(\mathbf{X}'\mathbf{X})^{-1}\mathbf{H}']^{-1}\hat{\boldsymbol{\theta}} = \frac{1}{\sigma^2}(\mathbf{H}\hat{\boldsymbol{\beta}} - \mathbf{h})'[\mathbf{H}(\mathbf{X}'\mathbf{X})^{-1}\mathbf{H}']^{-1}(\mathbf{H}\hat{\boldsymbol{\beta}} - \mathbf{h})$$

is distributed $\chi^2(u_1 : q; \lambda)$, where

$$\lambda = \frac{1}{2\sigma^2}(\mathbf{H\beta} - \mathbf{h})'[\mathbf{H}(\mathbf{X}'\mathbf{X})^{-1}\mathbf{H}']^{-1}(\mathbf{H\beta} - \mathbf{h})$$

Also, $\lambda = 0$ if and only if H_0 is true (that is, $\mathbf{H\beta} = \mathbf{h}$) since $\mathbf{H}(\mathbf{X}'\mathbf{X})^{-1}\mathbf{H}'$ is a positive definite matrix.

By Theorem 6.2.1 the two quantities $\hat{\boldsymbol{\beta}}$ and $\hat{\sigma}^2$ are independent, so $(\mathbf{H}\hat{\boldsymbol{\beta}} - \mathbf{h})' \times [\mathbf{H}(\mathbf{X}'\mathbf{X})^{-1}\mathbf{H}']^{-1}(\mathbf{H}\hat{\boldsymbol{\beta}} - \mathbf{h})$ and $\mathbf{Y}'(\mathbf{I} - \mathbf{XX}^-)\mathbf{Y}$ are independent. Thus since W in Equations (6.3.8) and (6.3.9) have the same distribution, W is a function of the sufficient statistics $\hat{\sigma}^2$ and $\hat{\boldsymbol{\beta}}$. We summarize these results in the following theorem.

THEOREM 6.3.1

In the general linear model, $\mathbf{Y} = \mathbf{X\beta} + \boldsymbol{\varepsilon}$, *where* $\boldsymbol{\varepsilon}$ *is distributed* $N(\boldsymbol{\varepsilon} : \mathbf{0}, \sigma^2\mathbf{I})$, *$W$ is a (function of the) generalized likelihood ratio test statistic for testing the* *hypothesis given below, where* $\mathbf{H}$ *is a* $q \times p$ *matrix of rank* q.

$$H_0 : \mathbf{H}\boldsymbol{\beta} = \mathbf{h} \ vs. \ H_a : \mathbf{H}\boldsymbol{\beta} \neq \mathbf{h}$$

W is given in two forms below:

(1)
$$W = \frac{\frac{1}{q}(\mathbf{H}\hat{\boldsymbol{\beta}} - \mathbf{h})'[\mathrm{cov}(\mathbf{H}\hat{\boldsymbol{\beta}} - \mathbf{h})]^{-1}(\mathbf{H}\hat{\boldsymbol{\beta}} - \mathbf{h})}{\hat{\sigma}^2/\sigma^2}$$
$$= \left(\frac{n-p}{q}\right)\left(\frac{(\mathbf{H}\hat{\boldsymbol{\beta}} - \mathbf{h})'[\mathbf{H}(\mathbf{X}'\mathbf{X})^{-1}\mathbf{H}']^{-1}(\mathbf{H}\hat{\boldsymbol{\beta}} - \mathbf{h})}{\mathbf{Y}'(\mathbf{I} - \mathbf{X}\mathbf{X}^-)\mathbf{Y}}\right)$$
$$= \frac{1}{q}(\mathbf{H}\hat{\boldsymbol{\beta}} - \mathbf{h})'[\widehat{\mathrm{cov}}(\mathbf{H}\hat{\boldsymbol{\beta}} - \mathbf{h})]^{-1}(\mathbf{H}\hat{\boldsymbol{\beta}} - \mathbf{h}) \tag{6.3.10}$$

where $\hat{\boldsymbol{\beta}} = \mathbf{X}^-\mathbf{Y}$ *and* $\hat{\sigma}^2 = (1/(n-p))\mathbf{Y}'(\mathbf{I} - \mathbf{X}\mathbf{X}^-)\mathbf{Y}$ *are UMVU estimators of* $\boldsymbol{\beta}$ *and* σ^2*, respectively.*

(2)
$$W = \left(\frac{\hat{\sigma}_\omega^2 - \hat{\sigma}_\Omega^2}{\hat{\sigma}_\Omega^2}\right)\left(\frac{n-p}{q}\right) \tag{6.3.11}$$

where

$$\hat{\sigma}_\Omega^2 = \left(\frac{1}{n}\right)\mathbf{Y}'(\mathbf{I} - \mathbf{X}\mathbf{X}^-)\mathbf{Y} = \frac{1}{n}(\mathbf{Y}'\mathbf{Y} - \hat{\boldsymbol{\beta}}'\mathbf{X}'\mathbf{Y})$$

is the maximum likelihood estimator of σ^2 *in the full model* $\mathbf{Y} = \mathbf{X}\boldsymbol{\beta} + \boldsymbol{\varepsilon}$*, and where*

$$\hat{\sigma}_\omega^2 = \left(\frac{1}{n}\right)\mathbf{Z}'(\mathbf{I} - \mathbf{B}\mathbf{B}^-)\mathbf{Z} = \frac{1}{n}(\mathbf{Z}'\mathbf{Z} - \hat{\boldsymbol{\gamma}}'\mathbf{B}'\mathbf{Z})$$

is the maximum likelihood estimator of σ^2 *in the reduced model* $\mathbf{Z} = \mathbf{B}\boldsymbol{\gamma} + \boldsymbol{\varepsilon}$ *(where* $\mathbf{Z} = \mathbf{B}\boldsymbol{\gamma} + \boldsymbol{\varepsilon}$ *is the full model reduced by the hypothesis* H_0*).*

Further, W *is distributed* $F(w : q, n-p; \lambda)$*, where*

$$\lambda = \frac{1}{2\sigma^2}(\mathbf{H}\boldsymbol{\beta} - \mathbf{h})'[\mathbf{H}(\mathbf{X}'\mathbf{X})^{-1}\mathbf{H}']^{-1}(\mathbf{H}\boldsymbol{\beta} - \mathbf{h})$$

The generalized likelihood ratio test of size α *is as follows: Reject* H_0 *if and only if* w *satisfies* $w \geq F_{\alpha:q,n-p}$*, where* $F_{\alpha:q,n-p}$ *is the upper* α *probability point of the central F distribution with* q *and* $n - p$ *degrees of freedom;* w *is the computed* *value of W. The power of the test is* $\Pi(\lambda)$, *where* $\Pi(\lambda)$ *is*

$$\Pi(\lambda) = \int_{F_{\alpha:q,n-p}}^{\infty} F(w : q, n - p; \lambda)\, dw$$

Equation (6.3.10) and Equation (6.3.11) will be used repeatedly in this book. They are the basic formulas for finding test statistics, and what is more important, for finding confidence intervals on linear functions of the β_i. Another way to look at the formulas is as follows:

$$\begin{aligned} n\hat{\sigma}_\Omega^2 &= \min_{\boldsymbol{\beta} \text{ in } \Omega} [(\mathbf{Y} - \mathbf{X}\boldsymbol{\beta})'(\mathbf{Y} - \mathbf{X}\boldsymbol{\beta})] = \min_{\boldsymbol{\beta} \text{ in } E_p} [(\mathbf{Y} - \mathbf{X}\boldsymbol{\beta})'(\mathbf{Y} - \mathbf{X}\boldsymbol{\beta})] \\ n\hat{\sigma}_\omega^2 &= \min_{\boldsymbol{\beta} \text{ in } \omega} [(\mathbf{Y} - \mathbf{X}\boldsymbol{\beta})'(\mathbf{Y} - \mathbf{X}\boldsymbol{\beta})] = \min_{\boldsymbol{\gamma} \text{ in } E_{p-q}} [(\mathbf{Z} - \mathbf{B}\boldsymbol{\gamma})'(\mathbf{Z} - \mathbf{B}\boldsymbol{\gamma})] \end{aligned} \qquad (6.3.12)$$

Note 3. The hypothesis $H_0 : \mathbf{H}\boldsymbol{\beta} = \mathbf{h}$ *vs.* $H_a : \mathbf{H}\boldsymbol{\beta} \neq \mathbf{h}$ is a statement about $\boldsymbol{\beta}$ (all allowable values of σ^2 are the same in both Ω and ω). In Ω the vector $\boldsymbol{\beta}$ is known to be in E_p. In ω the vector $\boldsymbol{\beta}$ is stated to be in a subset of E_p, that is, in ω, where $\omega = \{(\boldsymbol{\beta}, \sigma^2) : \mathbf{H}\boldsymbol{\beta} = \mathbf{h}, \boldsymbol{\beta} \text{ in } E_p, \sigma^2 > 0\}$. But for any nonsingular $q \times q$ matrix $\mathbf{Q}$, the set of $\boldsymbol{\beta}$ satisfying $\mathbf{H}\boldsymbol{\beta} = \mathbf{h}$ is the same as the set of $\boldsymbol{\beta}$ satisfying $\mathbf{QH}\boldsymbol{\beta} = \mathbf{Qh}$. Hence ω can be written as shown below, and ω is the same set of points for all $q \times q$ nonsingular matrices $\mathbf{Q}$.

$$\omega = \{(\boldsymbol{\beta}, \sigma^2) : \mathbf{QH}\boldsymbol{\beta} = \mathbf{Qh}, \boldsymbol{\beta} \text{ in } E_p, \sigma^2 > 0\}$$

Thus it appears that the test statistic W and its distribution will be the same if $\mathbf{H}$ and $\mathbf{h}$ are replaced by $\mathbf{QH}$ and $\mathbf{Qh}$, respectively. If these replacements are made in W in Equation (6.3.10), it is noted that W is unchanged; it is easy to show that λ is also unchanged.

For any $q \times p$ matrix $\mathbf{H}$ of rank q there exists a nonsingular matrix $\mathbf{Q}$ such that $\mathbf{P} = \mathbf{QH}$, where $\mathbf{PP}' = \mathbf{I}$, that is, $\mathbf{P}$ is the first q rows of an orthogonal matrix. Thus $H_0 : \mathbf{H}\boldsymbol{\beta} = \mathbf{h}$ can be written $H_0 : \mathbf{P}\boldsymbol{\beta} = \mathbf{Qh} = \mathbf{k}$, say, and $\mathbf{PP}' = \mathbf{I}$. We have proved the following theorem and corollary.

THEOREM 6.3.2

Consider the general linear model $\mathbf{Y} = \mathbf{X}\boldsymbol{\beta} + \boldsymbol{\varepsilon}$, *where* $\Omega = \{(\boldsymbol{\beta}, \sigma^2) : \boldsymbol{\beta} \in E_p, \sigma^2 > 0\}$, *and where* $\boldsymbol{\varepsilon}$ *is distributed* $\mathbf{N}(\boldsymbol{\varepsilon} : \mathbf{0}, \sigma^2\mathbf{I})$. *The generalized likelihood ratio test for testing* $H_0 : \mathbf{H}\boldsymbol{\beta} = \mathbf{h}$ *vs.* $H_a : \mathbf{H}\boldsymbol{\beta} \neq \mathbf{h}$, *where* $\mathbf{H}$ *is a* $q \times p$ *matrix of rank* q, *is the same as the generalized likelihood ratio test for testing* $H_0 : \mathbf{QH}\boldsymbol{\beta} = \mathbf{Qh}$ *vs.* $H_a : \mathbf{QH}\boldsymbol{\beta} \neq \mathbf{Qh}$ *for any nonsingular* $q \times q$ *matrix* $\mathbf{Q}$.

COROLLARY 6.3.2

Under the conditions of Theorem 6.3.2 there exists a nonsingular matrix $\mathbf{Q}$ *such that* $\mathbf{QH} = \mathbf{P}$; *where* $\mathbf{PP}' = \mathbf{I}$, *and hence the generalized likelihood ratio test of*

$H_0 : \mathbf{H\beta} = \mathbf{h}$ vs. $H_a : \mathbf{H\beta} \neq \mathbf{h}$ is equivalent to the generalized likelihood ratio test of $H_0 : \mathbf{P\beta} = \mathbf{k}$ vs. $H_a : \mathbf{P\beta} \neq \mathbf{k}$, where $\mathbf{Qh} = \mathbf{k}$ and $\mathbf{PP}' = \mathbf{I}$.

6.4 Special Cases for Hypothesis Testing

In this section we discuss two special cases of hypothesis testing and determine how the test statistic W in Equations (6.3.10) and (6.3.11) is modified in each case. We also give some computing instructions, although it is not our purpose to discuss computing in depth since there are many special innovations depending on which type of computer is used, the particular quantities to be computed, and the amount of data. There are, however, some basic ideas of computing for the general linear model that we discuss in Chapter 7.

The two special cases that will be considered here are as follows:

1. $H_0 : \ell'\boldsymbol{\beta} = \ell_0$ *vs.* $H_a : \ell'\boldsymbol{\beta} \neq \ell_0$; ℓ' is a given vector and ℓ_0 is a given constant. This is a test that *one* linear combination of $\boldsymbol{\beta}$ is equal to a constant ℓ_0.
2. $H_0 : \boldsymbol{\beta}_2 = \mathbf{b}_2$ *vs.* $H_a : \boldsymbol{\beta}_2 \neq \mathbf{b}_2$; $\boldsymbol{\beta}_2$ is a $q \times 1$ vector of parameters that contains the last q elements of $\boldsymbol{\beta}$, and $\mathbf{b}_2$ is a known $q \times 1$ vector. This is equivalent to testing

$$\beta_{p-q+1} = b_{p-q+1}, \beta_{p-q+2} = b_{p-q+2}, \ldots, \beta_p = b_p$$

   that is, that the last q elements of $\boldsymbol{\beta}$ are equal to given constants.

We discuss these in turn.

Case 1. $H_0 : \ell'\boldsymbol{\beta} = \ell_0$ *vs.* $H_a : \ell'\boldsymbol{\beta} \neq \ell_0$. Use Equation (6.3.10) and make the following identifications: $\mathbf{H} = \ell'$, $\mathbf{h} = \ell_0$, $q = 1$; we get

$$W = \frac{(\ell'\hat{\boldsymbol{\beta}} - \ell_0)'(\ell'\mathbf{C}\ell)^{-1}(\ell'\hat{\boldsymbol{\beta}} - \ell_0)}{\hat{\sigma}^2} = \frac{(\ell'\hat{\boldsymbol{\beta}} - \ell_0)^2}{\hat{\sigma}^2(\ell'\mathbf{C}\ell)} = \frac{(\ell'\hat{\boldsymbol{\beta}} - \ell_0)^2}{\widehat{\text{var}}[\ell'\hat{\boldsymbol{\beta}}]}$$

H_0 is rejected if and only if $w \geq F_{\alpha:1,n-p}$. Since $F_{\alpha:1,n-p} = t^2_{\alpha/2:n-p}$, this test is equivalent to the following: Reject H_0 if and only if

$$\frac{(\ell'\hat{\boldsymbol{\beta}} - \ell_0)^2}{\hat{\sigma}^2(\ell'\mathbf{C}\ell)} \geq t^2_{\alpha/2:n-p} \tag{6.4.1}$$

This is equivalent to the following: Accept H_0 if and only if ℓ_0 is in the interval

$$[\ell'\hat{\boldsymbol{\beta}} - t_{\alpha/2:n-p}\sqrt{\hat{\sigma}^2\ell'\mathbf{C}\ell}, \ell'\hat{\boldsymbol{\beta}} + t_{\alpha/2:n-p}\sqrt{\hat{\sigma}^2(\ell'\mathbf{C}\ell)}] \tag{6.4.2}$$

This interval is a $1 - \alpha$ confidence interval on $\ell'\boldsymbol{\beta}$. We write this confidence interval as

$$\ell'\hat{\boldsymbol{\beta}} \mp t_{\alpha/2:n-p}\sqrt{\hat{\sigma}^2 \ell' \mathbf{C} \ell} \tag{6.4.3}$$

or as

$$\ell'\hat{\boldsymbol{\beta}} \mp t_{\alpha/2:n-p}\sqrt{\widehat{\text{var}}[\ell'\hat{\boldsymbol{\beta}}]} \tag{6.4.4}$$

It can be shown that this test is a UMPU test of size α of $H_0 : \ell'\boldsymbol{\beta} = \ell_0$ *vs.* $H_a : \ell'\boldsymbol{\beta} \neq \ell_0$, and hence the confidence interval is a UMAU $1 - \alpha$ confidence interval on $\ell'\boldsymbol{\beta}$. The expected length of the confidence interval is

$$\mathscr{E}\left[2t_{\alpha/2:n-p}\sqrt{\hat{\sigma}^2 \ell' \mathbf{C} \ell}\right] = 2t_{\alpha/2:n-p}(\sigma\sqrt{\ell' \mathbf{C} \ell}) \frac{\Gamma\left(\frac{n-p+1}{2}\right)}{\left(\sqrt{\frac{n-p}{2}}\right)\Gamma\left(\frac{n-p}{2}\right)}$$

and this has the smallest expected length of any unbiased confidence interval for $\ell'\boldsymbol{\beta}$ with confidence coefficient $1 - \alpha$.

Case 2. $H_0 : \boldsymbol{\beta}_2 = \mathbf{b}_2$ *vs.* $H_a : \boldsymbol{\beta}_2 \neq \mathbf{b}_2$. We assume here that $\boldsymbol{\beta}$ and $\mathbf{X}$ are partitioned as

$$\boldsymbol{\beta} = \begin{bmatrix} \boldsymbol{\beta}_1 \\ \boldsymbol{\beta}_2 \end{bmatrix} \qquad \mathbf{X} = [\mathbf{X}_1, \mathbf{X}_2]$$

and we obtain

$$\mathbf{Y} = \mathbf{X}\boldsymbol{\beta} + \boldsymbol{\varepsilon} = [\mathbf{X}_1, \mathbf{X}_2]\begin{bmatrix} \boldsymbol{\beta}_1 \\ \boldsymbol{\beta}_2 \end{bmatrix} + \boldsymbol{\varepsilon} = \mathbf{X}_1\boldsymbol{\beta}_1 + \mathbf{X}_2\boldsymbol{\beta}_2 + \boldsymbol{\varepsilon}$$

where $\boldsymbol{\beta}_1$ contains the first $p - q$ elements of $\boldsymbol{\beta}$, where $0 < q < p$, and $\mathbf{X}_1$ contains the first $p - q$ columns of $\mathbf{X}$. If $q = p$, then H_0 is $\boldsymbol{\beta} = \mathbf{b}$ and the vector $\boldsymbol{\beta}$ and matrix $\mathbf{X}$ are not partitioned in this case.

If we desire to test any q, rather than the *last* q, elements of $\boldsymbol{\beta}$ equal to given constants, we simply permute the elements of $\boldsymbol{\beta}$ until the desired elements are the last q. We make the following identifications with the quantities in W in Equation (6.3.10): $C = (X'X)^{-1}$

$$\mathbf{H} = [\mathbf{0}, \mathbf{I}_q] \qquad \mathbf{h} = \mathbf{b}_2 \qquad \mathbf{H}\mathbf{C}\mathbf{H}' = [\mathbf{0}, \mathbf{I}_q]\begin{bmatrix} \mathbf{C}_{11} & \mathbf{C}_{12} \\ \mathbf{C}_{21} & \mathbf{C}_{22} \end{bmatrix}\begin{bmatrix} \mathbf{0} \\ \mathbf{I}_q \end{bmatrix} = \mathbf{C}_{22}$$

$$W = \frac{(\hat{\boldsymbol{\beta}}_2 - \mathbf{b}_2)'\mathbf{C}_{22}^{-1}(\hat{\boldsymbol{\beta}}_2 - \mathbf{b}_2)}{q\hat{\sigma}^2} \qquad \lambda = \frac{(\boldsymbol{\beta}_2 - \mathbf{b}_2)'\mathbf{C}_{22}^{-1}(\boldsymbol{\beta}_2 - \mathbf{b}_2)}{2\sigma^2} \tag{6.4.5}$$

Note that the elements of $\hat{\boldsymbol{\beta}}_2$ are the last q elements of $\hat{\boldsymbol{\beta}} = \mathbf{X}^{-}\mathbf{Y}$.

We note from Theorem 1.3.1 that $\mathbf{C}_{22}^{-1}$ can be written as (we use $\mathbf{X}'\mathbf{X} = \mathbf{S} = \mathbf{C}^{-1}$)

$$\mathbf{C}_{22}^{-1} = \mathbf{S}_{22} - \mathbf{S}_{21}\mathbf{S}_{11}^{-1}\mathbf{S}_{12} = \mathbf{X}_2'\mathbf{X}_2 - \mathbf{X}_2'\mathbf{X}_1(\mathbf{X}_1'\mathbf{X}_1)^{-1}\mathbf{X}_1'\mathbf{X}_2$$

We now discuss this test when we use Equation (6.3.11) and the normal equations of the full and reduced models since there are often computing advantages in doing it this way. We discuss only the case when $\mathbf{b}_2 = \mathbf{0}$, that is, $H_0 : \boldsymbol{\beta}_2 = \mathbf{0}$ *vs.* $H_a : \boldsymbol{\beta}_2 \neq \mathbf{0}$.

We must obtain $\hat{\sigma}_\Omega^2$ and $\hat{\sigma}_\omega^2$. To find $\hat{\sigma}_\omega^2$ we use the reduced model, which is $\mathbf{Y} = \mathbf{X}_1\boldsymbol{\beta}_1 + \boldsymbol{\varepsilon}$, which is obtained by substituting $\boldsymbol{\beta}_2 = \mathbf{0}$. We can write this as $\mathbf{Y} = \mathbf{B}\boldsymbol{\gamma} + \boldsymbol{\varepsilon}$, where $\mathbf{B} = \mathbf{X}_1$ and $\boldsymbol{\gamma} = \boldsymbol{\beta}_2$. The normal equations are

$$\mathbf{X}_1'\mathbf{X}_1\hat{\boldsymbol{\gamma}} = \mathbf{X}_1'\mathbf{Y}$$

and we obtain

$$\hat{\boldsymbol{\gamma}} = \mathbf{X}_1^-\mathbf{Y} \qquad \text{and} \qquad n\hat{\sigma}_\omega^2 = \mathbf{Y}'\mathbf{Y} - \hat{\boldsymbol{\gamma}}'\mathbf{X}_1'\mathbf{Y} = \mathbf{Y}'\mathbf{Y} - \mathbf{Y}'\mathbf{X}_1\mathbf{X}_1^-\mathbf{Y}$$

To find $\hat{\sigma}_\Omega^2$ we use the full model $\mathbf{Y} = \mathbf{X}\boldsymbol{\beta} + \boldsymbol{\varepsilon}$. The normal equations are

$$\mathbf{X}'\mathbf{X}\hat{\boldsymbol{\beta}} = \mathbf{X}'\mathbf{Y}$$

and we obtain

$$n\hat{\sigma}_\Omega^2 = \mathbf{Y}'\mathbf{Y} - \hat{\boldsymbol{\beta}}'\mathbf{X}'\mathbf{Y} = \mathbf{Y}'\mathbf{Y} - \mathbf{Y}'\mathbf{X}\mathbf{X}^-\mathbf{Y}$$

If we substitute into Equation (6.3.11) we get

$$W = \left(\frac{\hat{\boldsymbol{\beta}}'\mathbf{X}'\mathbf{Y} - \hat{\boldsymbol{\gamma}}'\mathbf{X}_1'\mathbf{Y}}{\mathbf{Y}'\mathbf{Y} - \hat{\boldsymbol{\beta}}'\mathbf{X}'\mathbf{Y}}\right)\left(\frac{n-p}{q}\right) = \left(\frac{\mathbf{Y}'(\mathbf{X}\mathbf{X}^- - \mathbf{X}_1\mathbf{X}_1^-)\mathbf{Y}}{\mathbf{Y}'(\mathbf{I} - \mathbf{X}\mathbf{X}^-)\mathbf{Y}}\right)\left(\frac{n-p}{q}\right) \tag{6.4.6}$$

Note 1. There are two sets of normal equations:

From the full model: $\mathbf{X}'\mathbf{X}\hat{\boldsymbol{\beta}} = \mathbf{X}'\mathbf{Y}$

From the reduced model: $\mathbf{X}_1'\mathbf{X}_1\hat{\boldsymbol{\gamma}} = \mathbf{X}_1'\mathbf{Y}$

From the first set we obtain $\hat{\boldsymbol{\beta}}'\mathbf{X}'\mathbf{Y}$, and from the second set we obtain $\hat{\boldsymbol{\gamma}}'\mathbf{X}_1'\mathbf{Y}$. Along with $\mathbf{Y}'\mathbf{Y}$, these two quantities are all that are needed to obtain W. In Chapter 7 we discuss the details for computing this test statistic.

6.5 Confidence Intervals Associated with the Test $H_0: \mathbf{H\beta} = \mathbf{h}$

To discuss the test $H_0: \mathbf{H\beta} = \mathbf{h}$ *vs.* $H_a: \mathbf{H\beta} \neq \mathbf{h}$, we now use the test statistic in Equation (6.3.10). For convenience we use the notation $\boldsymbol{\theta} = \mathbf{H\beta} - \mathbf{h}$, and H_0 *vs.* H_a can be written

$$H_0: \boldsymbol{\theta} = \mathbf{0} \qquad vs. \qquad H_a: \boldsymbol{\theta} \neq \mathbf{0}$$

The test statistic W is

$$W = \frac{\frac{1}{q}(\hat{\boldsymbol{\theta}}'\mathbf{V}^{-1}\hat{\boldsymbol{\theta}})}{\hat{\sigma}^2} \tag{6.5.1}$$

where

$$\hat{\boldsymbol{\theta}} = \mathbf{H}\hat{\boldsymbol{\beta}} - \mathbf{h} = \mathbf{HX^-Y} - \mathbf{h} \qquad \mathbf{V} = \mathbf{H}(\mathbf{X}'\mathbf{X})^{-1}\mathbf{H}'$$
$$\hat{\sigma}^2 = (n - p)^{-1}\mathbf{Y}'(\mathbf{I} - \mathbf{XX}^-)\mathbf{Y}$$

H_0 is rejected if and only if $w \geq F_{\alpha:q,n-p}$. Confidence intervals for the case for $q = 1$ were discussed in Section 6.4, and now we consider the case $q > 1$. We remark again that in making statistical inferences from data, confidence intervals are the important procedures, and hypothesis testing is discussed mainly as a method to find and evaluate confidence intervals. Thus in discussing the test of $H_0: \boldsymbol{\theta} = \mathbf{0}$ *vs.* $H_a: \boldsymbol{\theta} \neq \mathbf{0}$, what we really want are confidence intervals on $\theta_1, \theta_2, \ldots, \theta_q$, each element in $\boldsymbol{\theta}$, and perhaps on linear combinations of the θ_i. There are two distinct situations:

1. *One-at-a-time confidence intervals.* This means that each θ_i is treated individually, and a $1 - \alpha$ confidence interval is determined separately for each θ_i. The formula given in Equation (6.4.3) for each $\theta_i = \mathbf{k}_i'\boldsymbol{\beta}$ is

$$\mathbf{k}_i'\hat{\boldsymbol{\beta}} \mp t_{\alpha/2:n-p}\sqrt{\widehat{\text{var}}[\mathbf{k}_i'\hat{\boldsymbol{\beta}}]} \qquad i = 1, 2, \ldots, q \tag{6.5.2}$$

   where $\mathbf{k}_i'$ is the ith row of $\mathbf{H}$.

2. *Simultaneous confidence intervals.* This means that all of the θ_i are treated simultaneously, and confidence intervals are determined for each θ_i such that the probability is equal to $1 - \alpha$ that the q intervals simultaneously cover their respective θ_i.

For each problem the investigator must decide which method to use. As a general rule, *simultaneous confidence intervals* should be used in situations when an investigator will take a certain action that depends on his "knowing" (high probability) the approximate values (confidence intervals) of *all* the θ_i simultaneously. Some examples may help distinguish between the two situations.

Example 6.5.1

In evaluating the performance of a rocket during a certain 30-second interval, $15 \leq t \leq 45$, the linear model $Y_i = \beta_0 + \beta t_i + \varepsilon_i$ is assumed, where Y is velocity in feet per second and t is in seconds. It is also assumed that the ε_i are distributed $NID(\varepsilon : 0, \sigma^2)$. Data are collected from test firings of small models and $\hat{\beta}_0$, $\hat{\beta}$, and $\hat{\sigma}^2$ are evaluated by the formulas in Theorem 6.2.1. A decision must be made about a piece of equipment that is to be installed on the rocket, and the correct decision depends on knowing the velocities at both times $t = 15$ and $t = 45$. Therefore, confidence intervals on $\beta_0 + 15\beta$ and on $\beta_0 + 45\beta$ are needed so that there is a high probability (say, $1 - \alpha = 0.95$) that both of the intervals cover their respective true values. Thus one is interested in simultaneous confidence intervals.

On the other hand, suppose the results are going to be published and a number of different investigators will use the results. One investigator may want to know the velocity at $t = 20$; he will compute a confidence interval on $\beta_0 + 20\beta$. Another investigator may want to know the velocity at $t = 30$; he will compute a confidence interval on $\beta_0 + 30\beta$. But there is no single action or decision based on both of these confidence intervals being simultaneously correct, so each investigator will perhaps use a one-at-a-time $1 - \alpha$ confidence interval. The probability that both intervals are simultaneously correct is of no interest and not computed in this case.

Example 6.5.2

For another example, consider a store manager who is interested in the demand for a certain commodity over a twelve-month period. He assumes as a first approximation that the demand Y is given by $Y_t = \mu(t) + \varepsilon_t = \beta_0 + \beta_1 t + \beta_2 t^2 + \varepsilon_t$, where t is the time in months of the year ($t = 1, 2, \ldots, 12$) and the ε_t are distributed $NID(\varepsilon : 0, \sigma^2)$. At the beginning of the year, the manager must determine how much of the commodity will be sold each month and place the order with the manufacturer so the proper amount can be delivered the first day of each month. To determine the amount of commodity to order, he uses sales data for the past several years and computes confidence intervals on $\mu(1), \mu(2), \ldots, \mu(12)$. He wants to be quite certain ($1 - \alpha = 0.95$, say) that *all* of his confidence intervals are correct, so he is interested in simultaneous confidence intervals.

In the previous section we determined a $1 - \alpha$ confidence interval on the single parametric function $\ell'\boldsymbol{\beta}$ from a size α test of a hypothesis on the *same* parametric function, $\ell'\boldsymbol{\beta}$. For the hypothesis $H_0 : \boldsymbol{\theta} = \mathbf{0}$ *vs.* $H_a : \boldsymbol{\theta} \neq \mathbf{0}$, which is a test that q linear functions of $\boldsymbol{\beta}$ are simultaneously equal to zero, we might expect that the test will lead to *simultaneous confidence* intervals on each θ_i. However, the generalized likelihood ratio test does more than this—it provides simultaneous confidence intervals not only on all θ_i but on *every* linear function of the θ_i, that is, it provides confidence intervals on $\ell'\boldsymbol{\theta}$ for all $q \times 1$ vectors ℓ, and the probability is $1 - \alpha$ that these intervals (infinite in number) *simultaneously* cover their true parameters. This might be expected from the fact that the generalized likelihood ratio test of $H_0 : \boldsymbol{\theta} = \mathbf{0}$ *vs.* $H_a : \boldsymbol{\theta} \neq \mathbf{0}$ is exactly the same as the test of $H_0 : \mathbf{Q}\boldsymbol{\theta} = \mathbf{0}$ *vs.* $H_a : \mathbf{Q}\boldsymbol{\theta} \neq \mathbf{0}$ for any $q \times q$ nonsingular matrix $\mathbf{Q}$; see Theorem 6.3.2. Thus the test is actually a test that *every* linear combination of $\boldsymbol{\theta}$ is zero versus the alternative that at least one linear combination of $\boldsymbol{\theta}$ is not zero. So we might expect that the confidence intervals obtained from this test will be confidence intervals on *every* linear combination of $\boldsymbol{\theta}$.

We now derive confidence intervals from the generalized likelihood ratio test in Section 6.3. First we derive another formula for W given in Equation (6.3.10) and Equation (6.3.11).

THEOREM 6.5.1

The test statistic W in Equation (6.3.10) *is equal to W^*, where W^* is defined by*

$$W^* = \frac{1}{q\hat{\sigma}^2} \max_{\ell \text{ in } E_q^*} \left[\frac{[\ell'(\mathbf{H}\hat{\boldsymbol{\beta}} - \mathbf{h})]^2}{\ell'[\mathbf{H}(\mathbf{X}'\mathbf{X})^{-1}\mathbf{H}']\ell} \right] \tag{6.5.3}$$

The symbol E_q^* stands for the q-dimensional vector space E_q with $\mathbf{0}$ *removed (since W^* is undefined for $\ell = \mathbf{0}$), that is, E_q^* is the set of all $q \times 1$ vectors except* $\mathbf{0}$, *the $q \times 1$ zero vector.*

Proof

To simplify the notation we write W^* as

$$W^* = \max_{\ell \text{ in } E_q^*} \left[\frac{(\ell'\hat{\boldsymbol{\theta}})^2}{q\hat{\sigma}^2(\ell'\mathbf{V}\ell)} \right] = \left(\frac{1}{q\hat{\sigma}^2} \right) \max_{\ell \text{ in } E_q^*} \left\{ \frac{(\ell'\hat{\boldsymbol{\theta}})^2}{(\ell'\mathbf{V}\ell)} \right\} \tag{6.5.4}$$

where $\hat{\boldsymbol{\theta}}$ and $\mathbf{V}$ are defined at the beginning of Section 6.5 and do not involve ℓ. In Section 6.11.2 it is shown that the maximum of the expression $(\ell'\hat{\boldsymbol{\theta}})^2/\ell'\mathbf{V}\ell$ (for fixed $\mathbf{V}$ and $\hat{\boldsymbol{\theta}}$) as ℓ varies over E_q^* is $\hat{\boldsymbol{\theta}}'\mathbf{V}^{-1}\hat{\boldsymbol{\theta}}$, so

$$W^* = \frac{\hat{\boldsymbol{\theta}}'\mathbf{V}^{-1}\hat{\boldsymbol{\theta}}}{q\hat{\sigma}^2} = \frac{(\mathbf{H}\hat{\boldsymbol{\beta}} - \mathbf{h})'[\mathbf{H}(\mathbf{X}'\mathbf{X})^{-1}\mathbf{H}']^{-1}(\mathbf{H}\hat{\boldsymbol{\beta}} - \mathbf{h})}{q\hat{\sigma}^2} = W \tag{6.5.5}$$

which is the formula for W in Equation (6.3.10), and the theorem is proved.

Next we state a theorem that shows how the test statistic W leads to confidence intervals.

THEOREM 6.5.2

Consider the linear model $\mathbf{Y} = \mathbf{X}\boldsymbol{\beta} + \boldsymbol{\varepsilon}$, $\boldsymbol{\varepsilon}$ *is distributed* $\mathbf{N}(\boldsymbol{\varepsilon} : \mathbf{0}, \sigma^2\mathbf{I})$. *Consider the totality of confidence intervals on* $\ell'(\mathbf{H}\boldsymbol{\beta})$, *one for each* $q \times 1$ *vector* ℓ, *where* $\mathbf{H}$ *is a fixed* $q \times p$ *matrix of rank* q.

$$\ell'(\mathbf{H}\hat{\boldsymbol{\beta}}) - \sqrt{qF_{\alpha:q,n-p}}\sqrt{\hat{\sigma}^2\ell'[\mathbf{H}(\mathbf{X}'\mathbf{X})^{-1}\mathbf{H}']\ell} \le \ell'(\mathbf{H}\boldsymbol{\beta}) \le \ell'(\mathbf{H}\hat{\boldsymbol{\beta}}) + \sqrt{qF_{\alpha:q,n-p}}\sqrt{\hat{\sigma}^2\ell'[\mathbf{H}(\mathbf{X}'\mathbf{X})^{-1}\mathbf{H}']\ell} \quad (6.5.6)$$

These confidence intervals (infinite in number) are simultaneously correct with probability $1 - \alpha$.

Proof

In Equation (6.3.10) the random variable W has a central F distribution if $\mathbf{h} = \mathbf{H}\boldsymbol{\beta}$ is the true but unknown value of $\mathbf{H}\boldsymbol{\beta}$. If we substitute $\mathbf{H}\boldsymbol{\beta}$ for $\mathbf{h}$, we get

$$1 - \alpha = P\left[\frac{(\hat{\boldsymbol{\beta}} - \boldsymbol{\beta})'\mathbf{H}'[\mathbf{H}(\mathbf{X}'\mathbf{X})^{-1}\mathbf{H}']^{-1}\mathbf{H}(\hat{\boldsymbol{\beta}} - \boldsymbol{\beta})}{q\hat{\sigma}^2} \le F_{\alpha:q,n-p}\right]$$

and using the equivalent expression for W in Equation (6.5.3), this is

$$1 - \alpha = P\left[\max_{\ell \text{ in } E_q^*}\left\{\left(\frac{[\ell'\mathbf{H}(\hat{\boldsymbol{\beta}} - \boldsymbol{\beta})]^2}{\ell'[\mathbf{H}(\mathbf{X}'\mathbf{X})^{-1}\mathbf{H}']\ell}\right)\left(\frac{1}{q\hat{\sigma}^2}\right)\right\} \le F_{\alpha:q,n-p}\right] \quad (6.5.7)$$

$$= P\left[\left(\frac{[\ell'\mathbf{H}(\hat{\boldsymbol{\beta}} - \boldsymbol{\beta})]^2}{\ell'[\mathbf{H}(\mathbf{X}'\mathbf{X})^{-1}\mathbf{H}']\ell}\right)\left(\frac{1}{q\hat{\sigma}^2}\right) \le F_{\alpha:q,n-p} \quad \text{for all } \ell \text{ in } E_q^*\right] \quad (6.5.8)$$

$$= P\left[\ell'(\mathbf{H}\hat{\boldsymbol{\beta}}) - S\sqrt{\hat{\sigma}^2\ell'[\mathbf{H}(\mathbf{X}'\mathbf{X})^{-1}\mathbf{H}']\ell} \le \ell'(\mathbf{H}\boldsymbol{\beta}) \le \ell'(\mathbf{H}\hat{\boldsymbol{\beta}}) + S\sqrt{\hat{\sigma}^2\ell'[\mathbf{H}(\mathbf{X}'\mathbf{X})^{-1}\mathbf{H}']\ell} \quad \text{for all } q \times 1 \text{ vectors } \ell\right]$$

where $S = \sqrt{qF_{\alpha:q,n-p}}$, and the theorem is proved.

Note 1. To show that the probability in Equation (6.5.7) is equal to the probability in Equation (6.5.8), define $q(\ell)$, a function of ℓ, by

$$q(\ell) = \frac{[\ell'\mathbf{H}(\hat{\boldsymbol{\beta}} - \boldsymbol{\beta})]^2}{(q\hat{\sigma}^2)(\ell'[\mathbf{H}(\mathbf{X}'\mathbf{X})^{-1}\mathbf{H}']\ell)}$$

ℓ is any vector in E_q^*. Then clearly $\{\max_{\ell \text{ in } E_q^*} [q(\ell)] \le F_{\alpha:q,n-p}\}$ if and only if $\{q(\ell) \le F_{\alpha:q,n-p}$ for all ℓ in $E_q^*\}$, so since the statements in the two sets of braces are equivalent, the probabilities are equal that the two statements are true.

Note 2. The confidence intervals can be written

$$\ell'(\mathbf{H}\hat{\boldsymbol{\beta}}) \mp S\sqrt{\widehat{\text{var}}[\ell'(\mathbf{H}\hat{\boldsymbol{\beta}})]} \tag{6.5.9}$$

for all $q \times 1$ vectors ℓ. When $q = 1$ this is, of course, the same as the confidence interval on the single parametric function $\ell'\mathbf{H}\boldsymbol{\beta}$.

Note 3. The (infinite) set of confidence intervals in Equation (6.5.9) is not the set of confidence intervals on $\ell'\boldsymbol{\beta}$ for *all* $p \times 1$ vectors ℓ unless $\mathbf{H}$ is a full rank $p \times p$ matrix. If $\mathbf{H}$ is a $p \times p$ nonsingular matrix, then $\mathbf{H}$ is not needed in the problem since, by Theorem 6.3.2, we can let $\mathbf{Q} = \mathbf{H}^{-1}$, and the result is a test (and hence confidence intervals) that in no way involves $\mathbf{H}$.

Note 4. The reason for using $\mathbf{H}$ in setting simultaneous confidence intervals by the formula in Equation (6.5.9) is that this restricts the set of all confidence intervals to the set, not of *all* linear combinations of $\boldsymbol{\beta}$, but rather to the set of *all* linear combinations of the rows of $\mathbf{H}\boldsymbol{\beta}$.

Note 5. The formula in Equation (6.5.6) for the method of simultaneous confidence intervals explained in this section was first stated by Scheffé (see [M-4] and [S-4]) and will be referred to as "Scheffé's method of simultaneous confidence intervals."

Discussion. In any applied problem it is impossible to compute an infinite number of confidence intervals, but an investigator can make as many as he desires, and the probability that they are simultaneously correct is greater than or equal to $1 - \alpha$, that is,

$$P[\ell'\mathbf{H}\hat{\boldsymbol{\beta}} - S\sqrt{\widehat{\text{var}}[\ell'\mathbf{H}\hat{\boldsymbol{\beta}}]} \le \ell'\mathbf{H}\boldsymbol{\beta} \le \ell'\mathbf{H}\hat{\boldsymbol{\beta}} + S\sqrt{\widehat{\text{var}}[\ell'\mathbf{H}\hat{\boldsymbol{\beta}}]} \text{ for any set of } q \times 1 \text{ vectors } \ell] \ge 1 - \alpha \tag{6.5.10}$$

In making these confidence statements, the investigator can even look at the data and set confidence intervals on any parametric functions that the data suggest are interesting.

Example 6.5.3

Consider Example 6.3.2 and suppose we are interested in confidence intervals on all linear combinations of β_1 and β_2. Then we can choose the matrix **H** such that

$$\mathbf{H} = \begin{bmatrix} 0 & 1 & 0 & 0 & 0 \\ 0 & 0 & 1 & 0 & 0 \end{bmatrix} \quad \text{thus} \quad \mathbf{H\beta} = \begin{bmatrix} \beta_1 \\ \beta_2 \end{bmatrix}$$

and $\ell'(\mathbf{H\beta}) = \ell_1\beta_1 + \ell_2\beta_2$. If ℓ assumes every value in E_2, then every linear combination of β_1 and β_2 is included.

Example 6.5.4

Consider Example 6.3.2 and suppose we are interested in confidence intervals on all linear combinations of $\beta_1, \beta_2, \beta_3, \beta_4$. Then choose **H** such that

$$\mathbf{H} = \begin{bmatrix} 0 & 1 & 0 & 0 & 0 \\ 0 & 0 & 1 & 0 & 0 \\ 0 & 0 & 0 & 1 & 0 \\ 0 & 0 & 0 & 0 & 1 \end{bmatrix} = [\mathbf{0}, \mathbf{I}_4] \quad \text{thus} \quad \mathbf{H\beta} = \begin{bmatrix} \beta_1 \\ \beta_2 \\ \beta_3 \\ \beta_4 \end{bmatrix}$$

and $\ell'(\mathbf{H\beta}) = \sum_{i=1}^{4} \ell_i\beta_i$, every linear combination of $\beta_1, \beta_2, \beta_3$, and β_4 as ℓ varies over E_4.

6.5.1 Confidence Intervals on $\mu(\mathbf{x}) = \beta_0 + \beta_1 x_1 + \cdots + \beta_{p-1} x_{p-1}$

Sometimes it may be desirable to set simultaneous confidence intervals on $\mu(\mathbf{x}) = \beta_0 + \beta_1 x_1 + \cdots + \beta_{p-1} x_{p-1}$ for a large number of different **x** values, or it may be desirable to set confidence limits on $\mu(\mathbf{x})$ for *all possible* values of **x** in E_{p-1}. Simultaneous confidence bands (intervals) on $\mu(\mathbf{x})$ for *all* **x** (with confidence coefficient equal to $1 - \alpha$) are given by

$$\hat{\mu}(\mathbf{x}) \mp \sqrt{pF_{\alpha:p,n-p}\,\widehat{\text{var}}[\hat{\mu}(\mathbf{x})]} \qquad \text{for all } (p-1) \times 1 \text{ vectors } \mathbf{x} \qquad (6.5.11)$$

For the *simple* linear model, the bands are

$$\hat{\beta}_0 + \hat{\beta}x \mp \sqrt{2F_{\alpha:2,n-2}\left[\frac{1}{n} + \frac{(\bar{x} - x)^2}{\sum (x_i - \bar{x})^2}\right]^{1/2}}\;\hat{\sigma} \qquad \text{for all } x \text{ in } E_1 \qquad (6.5.12)$$

The formulas are derived by noting that the maximum of the function in Equation (6.5.3) when ℓ varies over E_p^* is exactly the same as when ℓ varies over E_p^* with the added restriction $\ell_0 = 1$ (the first element in ℓ is equal to one).

6.6 Further Discussion of Confidence Intervals Associated with the Test H_0: $\mathbf{H\beta} = \mathbf{h}$

For further discussion of the test $\mathbf{H\beta} = \mathbf{h}$, we use the notation in Equation (6.5.1) and test $H_0 : \boldsymbol{\theta} = \mathbf{0}$ *vs.* $H_a : \boldsymbol{\theta} \neq \mathbf{0}$. We saw that the generalized likelihood ratio test (which is based on the F distribution) treats all linear combinations of $\boldsymbol{\theta}$ equally, that is, the test $H_0 : \boldsymbol{\theta} = \mathbf{0}$ *vs.* $H_a : \boldsymbol{\theta} \neq \mathbf{0}$ is equivalent to the test $H_0 : \mathbf{Q}\boldsymbol{\theta} = \mathbf{0}$ *vs.* $H_a : \mathbf{Q}\boldsymbol{\theta} \neq \mathbf{0}$ for all nonsingular $q \times q$ matrices $\mathbf{Q}$. We saw also that the confidence intervals associated with this test are simultaneous confidence intervals on *all* linear combinations of $\boldsymbol{\theta}$. These confidence intervals may sometimes be useful, but there may be situations when one is interested *mainly* in simultaneous confidence intervals on the θ_i only and not on *all* linear combinations of the θ_i. This problem will be discussed in this section. First we shall derive the distribution of the "multivariate t" random variable and then show how it will be used in the problem of simultaneous confidence intervals.

THEOREM 6.6.1

Let the $q \times 1$ random vector $\hat{\boldsymbol{\theta}}$ be distributed $\mathbf{N}(\hat{\boldsymbol{\theta}} : \boldsymbol{\theta}, \sigma^2\mathbf{V})$, where $\mathbf{V}$ is a known positive definite matrix; let $U = (n - p)\hat{\sigma}^2/\sigma^2$ be distributed $\chi^2(u : n - p)$; and let $\hat{\boldsymbol{\theta}}$ be independent of U. Define the $q \times 1$ random vector $\boldsymbol{t}$ by

$$\boldsymbol{t}' = [T_1, T_2, \ldots, T_q] \tag{6.6.1}$$

where

$$T_i = \frac{(\hat{\theta}_i - \theta_i)}{\sqrt{\hat{\sigma}^2 v_{ii}}} \qquad i = 1, 2, \ldots, q$$

The p.d.f. of $\boldsymbol{t}$ is called the multivariate t distribution and is given by

$$\mathbf{S}(\mathbf{t} : q, n - p; \mathbf{R}) = \left(\frac{\Gamma\left(\dfrac{q + n - p}{2}\right) |\mathbf{R}|^{-1/2}}{(n - p)^{q/2}(\pi)^{q/2}\,\Gamma\left(\dfrac{n - p}{2}\right)} \right) \left(1 + \left(\frac{1}{n - p}\right)\mathbf{t}'\mathbf{R}^{-1}\mathbf{t}\right)^{-(q+n-p)/2}$$

$$-\infty < t_i < \infty, \quad i = 1, 2, \ldots, q \tag{6.6.2}$$

where

$$\mathbf{R} = [r_{ij}] \qquad r_{ij} = \frac{v_{ij}}{\sqrt{v_{ii}v_{jj}}}$$

Proof

The proof of this theorem is obtained by starting with the joint p.d.f. of $U = (n-p)\hat{\sigma}^2/\sigma^2$, which is $\chi^2(u:n-p)$, and the $(\hat{\theta}_i - \theta_i)/\sqrt{v_{ii}}$, $i = 1, 2, \ldots, q$. Let $\mathbf{Z}' = [Z_1, Z_2, \ldots, Z_q]$, where $Z_i = (\hat{\theta}_i - \theta_i)/\sqrt{v_{ii}}$; then $\mathbf{Z}$ is distributed $\mathbf{N}(\mathbf{z}:\mathbf{0}, \sigma^2\mathbf{R})$, where $\mathbf{R} = [r_{ij}]$ and $r_{ij} = v_{ij}/\sqrt{v_{ii}v_{jj}}$. Also, U is independent of $\mathbf{Z}$. We get

$$f_{\mathbf{Z},U}(\mathbf{z}, u) = (2\pi)^{-q/2}(\sigma^2)^{-q/2}|\mathbf{R}|^{-1/2}\, e^{-(1/2\sigma^2)\mathbf{z}'\mathbf{R}^{-1}\mathbf{z}} \times \left(\frac{1}{\Gamma\left(\frac{n-p}{2}\right)(2^{(n-p)/2})}\right) u^{[(n-p)/2]-1}\, e^{-u/2}$$

Let $t_i = z_i/\hat{\sigma} = z_i/\sqrt{u\sigma^2/(n-p)}$, which gives $z_i = t_i\sqrt{\sigma^2 u/(n-p)}$, $i = 1, 2, \ldots, q$; the Jacobian is obtained from $\partial z_i/\partial t_j = \delta_{ij}\sqrt{u\sigma^2/(n-p)}$ where $\delta_{ij} = 0$ if $i \neq j$ and $\delta_{ii} = 1$, and is $[u\sigma^2/(n-p)]^{q/2}$.

For the joint p.d.f. of $T_1, T_2, \ldots, T_q$ and U, we get

$$f_{\ell,U}(\mathbf{t}, u) = \left(\frac{(2\pi)^{-q/2}|\mathbf{R}|^{-1/2}}{(n-p)^{q/2}\,\Gamma\left(\frac{n-p}{2}\right)(2^{(n-p)/2})}\right) u^{[(n-p+q)/2]-1} \times \exp\left[\left(-\frac{u}{2(n-p)}\right)\mathbf{t}'\mathbf{R}^{-1}\mathbf{t} - \frac{u}{2}\right]$$

and the p.d.f. of ℓ is obtained by integrating this with respect to u from 0 to ∞.

We note that the p.d.f. of ℓ, denoted by $\mathbf{S}(\mathbf{t}:q, n-p; \mathbf{R})$, contains no unknown parameters; so to set simultaneous confidence intervals on $\theta_1, \theta_2, \ldots, \theta_q$, the quantity $t_{\alpha/2:q,n-p;\mathbf{R}}$ is determined such that (for a specified $1-\alpha$)

$$1 - \alpha = P[-t_{\alpha/2:q,n-p;\mathbf{R}} \leq T_1 \leq t_{\alpha/2:q,n-p;\mathbf{R}}, \ldots, -t_{\alpha/2:q,n-p;\mathbf{R}} \leq T_q \leq t_{\alpha/2:q,n-p;\mathbf{R}}] \quad (6.6.3)$$

which can also be written as

$$P[\max_{i=1,2,\ldots,q} |T_i| \leq t_{\alpha/2:q,n-p;\mathbf{R}}] = 1 - \alpha$$

In this probability statement we substitute for $T_1, T_2, \ldots, T_q$ and obtain

$$P\left[-t_{\alpha/2:q,n-p;\mathbf{R}} \leq \frac{\hat{\theta}_i - \theta_i}{\sqrt{\hat{\sigma}^2 v_{ii}}} \leq t_{\alpha/2:q,n-p;\mathbf{R}} \quad \text{for } i = 1, 2, \ldots, q\right] = 1 - \alpha \quad (6.6.4)$$

and finally we obtain the statement

$$P[\hat{\theta}_i - t_{\alpha/2:q,n-p;\mathbf{R}}\sqrt{\widehat{\text{var}}[\hat{\theta}_i]} \le \theta_i \le \hat{\theta}_i + t_{\alpha/2:q,n-p;\mathbf{R}}\sqrt{\widehat{\text{var}}[\hat{\theta}_i]} \quad \text{for } i = 1, 2, \ldots, q] = 1 - \alpha \qquad (6.6.5)$$

Then the ith rows of $\mathbf{H}\hat{\boldsymbol{\beta}} - \mathbf{h}$ and $\mathbf{H}\boldsymbol{\beta} - \mathbf{h}$ are substituted for $\hat{\theta}_i$ and θ_i, respectively. Also, $\widehat{\text{var}}[\hat{\theta}_i] = \hat{\sigma}^2 v_{ii}$, where v_{ii} is the ith diagonal element of $\mathbf{V} = \mathbf{H}(\mathbf{X}'\mathbf{X})^{-1}\mathbf{H}'$.

The value of $t_{\alpha/2:q,n-p;\mathbf{R}}$ in Equation (6.6.5) is found by solving

$$\int_{-t_{\alpha/2:q,n-p;\mathbf{R}}}^{t_{\alpha/2:q,n-p;\mathbf{R}}} \cdots \int_{-t_{\alpha/2:q,n-p;\mathbf{R}}}^{t_{\alpha/2:q,n-p;\mathbf{R}}} S(\mathbf{t} : q, n - p; \mathbf{R})\, d\mathbf{t} = 1 - \alpha \qquad (6.6.6)$$

The matrix $\mathbf{R}$ is known, but to determine $t_{\alpha/2:n,p-q;\mathbf{R}}$ for all possible matrices $\mathbf{R}$ would require an impossibly large set of tables. A table of values has been computed [H-3] for various values of α, q, $n - p$, and $r_{ij} = r$ for $i \neq j$, that is, for all r_{ij} that are equal when $i \neq j$. To utilize the intervals in Equation (6.6.5), we can use the following theorem.

THEOREM 6.6.2

If the $q \times 1$ vector $\mathbf{t}$ is distributed $S(\mathbf{t} : q, n - p; \mathbf{R})$, then $t_{\alpha/2:q,n-p;\mathbf{R}} \le t_{\alpha/2:q,n-p;\mathbf{I}}$, and hence

$$P[\max_{i=1,2,\ldots,q} |T_i| \le t_{\alpha/2:q,n-p;\mathbf{I}}] \begin{cases} \ge 1 - \alpha \text{ for any matrix } \mathbf{R} \text{ defined in Equation (6.6.2)} \\ = 1 - \alpha \text{ if } \mathbf{R} = \mathbf{I} \end{cases} \qquad (6.6.7)$$

where T_i is defined in Equation (6.6.1).

Proof

The proof can be found in [S-12] and will not be given here.

This theorem states that even though the p.d.f. of $\mathbf{t}$ involves the matrix $\mathbf{R}$, the values $t_{\alpha/2:q,n-p;\mathbf{I}}$ can be used in place of $t_{\alpha/2:q,n-p;\mathbf{R}}$ (that is, we use "t values" that are computed using $\mathbf{I}$ instead of $\mathbf{R}$), and the probability is greater than or equal to $1 - \alpha$ instead of equal to $1 - \alpha$.

Thus the confidence intervals in Equation (6.6.5) are

$$P[\hat{\theta}_i - t_{\alpha/2:q,n-p}\sqrt{\widehat{\text{var}}[\hat{\theta}_i]} \le \theta_i \le \hat{\theta}_i + t_{\alpha/2:q,n-p}\sqrt{\widehat{\text{var}}[\hat{\theta}_i]} \quad \text{for } i = 1, 2, \ldots, q] \ge 1 - \alpha \qquad (6.6.8)$$

where $t_{\alpha/2:q,n-p}$ is computed from Equation (6.6.6) with $\mathbf{R} = \mathbf{I}$ (we use the symbol $t_{\alpha/2:q,n-p}$ instead of $t_{\alpha/2:q,n-p;\mathbf{I}}$). Thus whatever the matrix **R** is in any applied problem, it follows that the joint confidence intervals on θ_i in Equation (6.6.5) are simultaneously correct with probability *greater* than or equal to $1 - \alpha$. Table T.6 from [H-3] has values of $t_{\alpha/2:q,m}$ for a few values of $1-\alpha$, q, and m.

The distribution $\mathbf{S}(\mathbf{t}:q, n-p;\mathbf{R})$ is a Student's t distribution $s(t:n-p)$ when $q = 1$, and hence the value of $t_{\alpha/2:1,n-p}$ is the upper $\alpha/2$ point of the Student's t distribution (that is, $t_{\alpha/2:n-p}$). Also, it can be shown that

$$t_{\alpha/2:n-p} \leq t_{\alpha/2:q,n-p} \leq \sqrt{qF_{\alpha:q,n-p}} \tag{6.6.9}$$

for all α, q, and $n-p$ values ($0 < \alpha < 1$, q, and $n-p$ are positive integers).

Example 6.6.1

Consider Example 6.5.3. If we want simultaneous $1-\alpha$ confidence intervals on β_1 and β_2, we use the **H** in the example and get the intervals

$$\hat{\beta}_1 \mp t_{\alpha/2:2,n-p}\sqrt{\widehat{\text{var}}[\hat{\beta}_1]} \qquad \hat{\beta}_2 \mp t_{\alpha/2:2,n-p}\sqrt{\widehat{\text{var}}[\hat{\beta}_2]}$$

which are simultaneously correct with the probability greater than or equal to $1-\alpha$.

Note 1. It is important to remember that the confidence intervals in Equation (6.6.8) require **H** to have rank q. If **H** does not have rank q, the number of rows of **H**, then the confidence intervals in Equation (6.6.8) may not be correct.

Note 2. Due to the inequalities in Equation (6.6.9), the lengths of one-at-a-time $1-\alpha$ confidence intervals on $\theta_1, \theta_2, \ldots, \theta_q$ in Equation (6.5.2) are respectively less than the corresponding lengths using Equation (6.5.6).

Note 3. When $q = 2$, we can use the computed t values, $t_{\alpha/2:2,n-p;\mathbf{R}}$ instead of $t_{\alpha/2:2,n-p;\mathbf{I}}$ in Equation (6.6.7) and get exact $1-\alpha$ confidence intervals rather than greater than or equal to $1-\alpha$ confidence intervals. Tables for these values are found in [H-3].

6.6.1 Confidence Interval on σ^2: Case 1

We use the fact that $U = (n-p)\hat{\sigma}^2/\sigma^2$ is distributed $\chi^2(u:n-p)$ and obtain

$$P[\chi^2_{1-\alpha_2:n-p} \leq U \leq \chi^2_{\alpha_1:n-p}] = 1-\alpha$$

where $\alpha_1 + \alpha_2 = \alpha$. If we substitute for U and solve the inequalities for σ^2, we get

$$P\left[\frac{(n-p)\hat{\sigma}^2}{\chi^2_{\alpha_1:n-p}} \le \sigma^2 \le \frac{(n-p)\hat{\sigma}^2}{\chi^2_{1-\alpha_2:n-p}}\right] = 1 - \alpha \tag{6.6.10}$$

which is a $1 - \alpha$ confidence interval on σ^2.

The quantities α_1 and α_2 can be chosen to minimize the length of the interval in Equation (6.6.10), or α_1 and α_2 can be chosen ($\alpha_1 > 0$, $\alpha_2 > 0$) so that the interval is UMAU and hence has the shortest expected width of any unbiased $1 - \alpha$ confidence interval on σ^2; see [P-2] and [T-3] for tables; also see [G-15] and [J-2]. If $\alpha_1 = 0$ and $\alpha_2 = \alpha$, then the interval in Equation (6.6.10) is UMA; if $\alpha_1 = \alpha$ and $\alpha_2 = 0$, then the interval in Equation (6.6.10) is UMAU. Tests of $H_0 : \sigma^2 = \sigma_0^2$ *vs.* $H_a : \sigma^2 \ne \sigma_0^2$, or $\sigma^2 \ge \sigma_0^2$ *vs.* $\sigma^2 < \sigma_0^2$, and so forth, can be obtained by using the confidence interval in Equation (6.6.10) as the acceptance region when α_1 and α_2 are chosen properly.

6.7 Example

In this section we present an example of a simple linear model to illustrate various procedures and formulas in this chapter. We assume that the data below satisfy a simple linear model $Y_j = \beta_0 + \beta x_j + \varepsilon_j$, ε_j are distributed $NID(\varepsilon : 0, \sigma^2)$, $j = 1, 2, \ldots, 10$. (The data are from [K-12], page 231.)

x_j	550	200	280	340	410	475	160	380	510	510
y_j	200	50	60	140	130	180	20	120	190	160

The elements in the last row of the table are the elements in $\mathbf{y}$.

$$\mathbf{X}' = \begin{bmatrix} 1 & 1 & 1 & 1 & 1 & 1 & 1 & 1 & 1 & 1 \\ 550 & 200 & 280 & 340 & 410 & 475 & 160 & 380 & 510 & 510 \end{bmatrix}$$

$\mathbf{X}'\mathbf{X}\hat{\boldsymbol{\beta}} = \mathbf{X}'\mathbf{y}$ is

$$\begin{bmatrix} 10 & 3{,}815 \\ 3{,}815 & 1{,}620{,}425 \end{bmatrix} \begin{bmatrix} \hat{\beta}_0 \\ \hat{\beta} \end{bmatrix} = \begin{bmatrix} 1{,}250 \\ 550{,}500 \end{bmatrix}$$

$\mathbf{y}'\mathbf{y} = 191{,}500$, $n = 10$, $p = 2$. The solution is $\hat{\beta}_0 = -45.227$, $\hat{\beta} = 0.446$; so $\hat{\mu}(x) = -45.227 + 0.446x$, and $\hat{\sigma}^2 = (1/(n-2))[\mathbf{y}'\mathbf{y} - \hat{\boldsymbol{\beta}}'\mathbf{X}'\mathbf{y}] = 299.766$.

Suppose we want a size $\alpha = 0.05$ test of $H_0 : \beta_0 = 0, \beta = 0$ *vs.* $H_a : \beta_0 \neq 0$ or $\beta \neq 0$. The full model is $Y_j = \beta_0 + \beta x_j + \varepsilon_j$ and $\hat{\sigma}^2_\Omega = (1/n)[\mathbf{y}'\mathbf{y} - \hat{\boldsymbol{\beta}}'\mathbf{X}'\mathbf{y}] = 239.813$. The reduced model is $Y_j = \varepsilon_j$ and $\hat{\sigma}^2_\omega = (1/n)\mathbf{y}'\mathbf{y} = 19{,}150$.

$$w = \left(\frac{8}{2}\right)\left(\frac{19{,}150 - 239.813}{239.813}\right) = 315.416$$

and $F_{0.05:2,8} = 4.46$, so H_0 is rejected.

Suppose we want 95 percent confidence intervals on β_0 and β. In this case $\mathbf{H} = \mathbf{I}$, $\ell'_1 = [1, 0]$, $\ell'_2 = [0, 1]$.

1. One-at-a-time confidence intervals on β_0, β with $1 - \alpha = 0.95$ are

$$\beta_0 : -45.227 \mp 2.306\sqrt{294.389} \quad \text{or} \quad -84.793 \leq \beta_0 \leq -5.661$$

$$\beta : 0.446 \mp 2.306\sqrt{0.00182} \quad \text{or} \quad 0.348 \leq \beta \leq 0.544$$

2. Simultaneous confidence intervals on β_0, β with probability greater than or equal to 0.95 are, by Equation (6.6.8),

$$\beta_0 : -45.227 \mp 2.718\sqrt{294.389} \quad \text{or} \quad -91.862 \leq \beta_0 \leq 1.408$$

$$\beta : 0.446 \mp 2.718\sqrt{0.00182} \quad \text{or} \quad 0.330 \leq \beta \leq 0.562$$

   Since $q = 2$ in this problem, the tables in [H-3] can be used to obtain simultaneous confidence intervals on β_0 and β with probability equal to 0.95.

3. If we want 0.95 simultaneous confidence intervals on all (or a large number) of linear combinations of β_0 and β, we use Equation (6.5.9); if we use this formula on only β_0 and β, we get the following confidence intervals with probability greater than 0.95:

$$\beta_0 : -45.227 \mp 2.987\sqrt{294.389} \quad \text{or} \quad -96.477 \leq \beta_0 \leq 6.023$$

$$\beta : 0.446 \mp 2.987\sqrt{0.00182} \quad \text{or} \quad 0.319 \leq \beta \leq 0.573$$

Note 1. The reader should keep the following in mind:

1. If the generalized likelihood ratio test (the F test in Theorem 6.3.1) of size α of $H_0 : \mathbf{H}\boldsymbol{\beta} = \mathbf{h}$ *vs.* $H_a : \mathbf{H}\boldsymbol{\beta} \neq \mathbf{h}$ is rejected, and if Scheffé simultaneous $1 - \alpha$ confidence intervals are computed for the q linear combinations of $\boldsymbol{\beta}$ represented by $\mathbf{H}\boldsymbol{\beta}$, they can *all* include the corresponding values of $\mathbf{h}$. For instance, in testing $H_0 : \beta_0 = \beta_1 = 0$ in the example in Section 6.7, it is possible to reject H_0 at the 0.05 level and still have 0.95 confidence intervals on β_0 and β,

obtained by using Equation (6.5.9), which possibly both include zero. However there must be *some* linear combination of β_0 and β whose confidence interval does *not* include zero.

2. If the generalized likelihood ratio size α test referred to in part 1 is *not* rejected, then *all* simultaneous $1 - \alpha$ confidence intervals computed by using Equation (6.5.9) *must* include the corresponding values, that is, the confidence interval on $\ell'\mathbf{H\beta}$ *must* include $\ell'\mathbf{h}$ for *all* $q \times 1$ vectors ℓ.

6.8 The General Linear Model, Case 1, and $\Sigma \neq \sigma^2 I$

In this section we briefly discuss the general linear model when the covariance matrix $\mathbf{\Sigma}$ is not necessarily $\sigma^2\mathbf{I}$. Two cases are considered. The first case is when $\mathbf{\Sigma} = \sigma^2\mathbf{V}$, where $\mathbf{V}$ is a known p.d. matrix. This case presents no difficulty except for additional computing. The second case is when $\mathbf{\Sigma}$ is a general positive definite unknown matrix, and this presents very difficult problems.

6.8.1 The General Linear Model, Case 1, $\Sigma = \sigma^2 V$, V Known

In this section we consider the model $\mathbf{Y} = \mathbf{X\beta} + \boldsymbol{\varepsilon}$, $\boldsymbol{\varepsilon}$ is distributed $N(\boldsymbol{\varepsilon} : \mathbf{0}, \sigma^2\mathbf{V})$, $\mathbf{V}$ is a *known* positive definite matrix.

Let $\mathbf{G}$ be an $n \times n$ matrix of rank n such that $\mathbf{V} = \mathbf{G'G}$. Consider the random vector $\mathbf{Z}$ defined by $\mathbf{Z} = \mathbf{G}'^{-1}\mathbf{Y}$. Then $\mathbf{Z}$ is distributed $N(\mathbf{z} : \mathbf{G}'^{-1}\mathbf{X\beta}, \sigma^2\mathbf{I})$. Let $\mathbf{A} = \mathbf{G}'^{-1}\mathbf{X}$ and let $\boldsymbol{\eta} = \mathbf{G}'^{-1}\boldsymbol{\varepsilon}$. Then the model $\mathbf{Y} = \mathbf{X\beta} + \boldsymbol{\varepsilon}$, $\boldsymbol{\varepsilon}$ is distributed $N(\boldsymbol{\varepsilon} : \mathbf{0}, \sigma^2\mathbf{V})$, has been transformed to the model $\mathbf{Z} = \mathbf{A\beta} + \boldsymbol{\eta}$, $\boldsymbol{\eta}$ is distributed $N(\boldsymbol{\eta} : \mathbf{0}, \sigma^2\mathbf{I})$, and this model satisfies the definition of the general linear model Case 1, so all the results of previous sections of this chapter are applicable. For example,

$$\hat{\boldsymbol{\beta}} = (\mathbf{A'A})^{-1}\mathbf{A'Z} = (\mathbf{X'V}^{-1}\mathbf{X})^{-1}\mathbf{X'V}^{-1}\mathbf{Y} \tag{6.8.1}$$

$$\hat{\sigma}^2 = \left(\frac{1}{n-p}\right)[\mathbf{Z'Z} - \hat{\boldsymbol{\beta}}'\mathbf{A'Z}]$$
$$= \left(\frac{1}{n-p}\right)\mathbf{Y}'[\mathbf{V}^{-1} - \mathbf{V}^{-1}\mathbf{X}(\mathbf{X'V}^{-1}\mathbf{X})^{-1}\mathbf{X'V}^{-1}]\mathbf{Y} \tag{6.8.2}$$

$$\mathrm{cov}[\hat{\boldsymbol{\beta}}] = \sigma^2(\mathbf{X'V}^{-1}\mathbf{X})^{-1} \tag{6.8.3}$$

and these are the quantities that are needed for point estimation, tests of hypotheses, and confidence intervals. Thus under the model considered in this section, $\hat{\boldsymbol{\beta}}$ and $\hat{\sigma}^2$ given above are complete sufficient statistics for $\boldsymbol{\beta}$ and σ^2. Thus they can be used in Theorem 6.2.2 to find UMVU estimators.

The quantities $\hat{\boldsymbol{\beta}}$, $\hat{\sigma}^2$, and $\mathbf{cov}[\hat{\boldsymbol{\beta}}]$ above can be substituted into Equation (6.3.10) to obtain the generalized likelihood ratio test of $H_0 : \mathbf{H}\boldsymbol{\beta} = \mathbf{h}$ *vs.* $H_a : \mathbf{H}\boldsymbol{\beta} \neq \mathbf{h}$. These quantities can also be substituted into the formulas for confidence intervals to obtain confidence intervals for parameters in the model considered in this chapter.

> *Note 1.* In this section we have assumed that $\mathbf{V}$ is known. If $\mathbf{V}$ is not known, then $\hat{\boldsymbol{\beta}}$ and $\hat{\sigma}^2$ given in Equations (6.8.1) and (6.8.2) cannot be used and the situation is much more complicated. We briefly discuss some special cases in the next two sections.

6.8.2 The General Linear Model: Point Estimation When Σ Is Unknown

When the covariance matrix of $\boldsymbol{\varepsilon}$ in the model $\mathbf{Y} = \mathbf{X}\boldsymbol{\beta} + \boldsymbol{\varepsilon}$ is $\boldsymbol{\Sigma}$, the point estimator of $\ell'\boldsymbol{\beta}$ is

$$\ell'(\mathbf{X}'\boldsymbol{\Sigma}^{-1}\mathbf{X})^{-1}\mathbf{X}'\boldsymbol{\Sigma}^{-1}\mathbf{Y} \tag{6.8.4}$$

If $\boldsymbol{\Sigma}$ is not known, this is not an estimator because it is not observable. A question that comes to mind is this: Suppose the fact that $\mathbf{cov}[\boldsymbol{\varepsilon}] = \boldsymbol{\Sigma}$ is ignored, and one assumes instead that $\mathbf{cov}[\boldsymbol{\varepsilon}] = \sigma^2\mathbf{I}$ (under this assumption, the UMVU estimate of $\ell'\boldsymbol{\beta}$ is $\ell'(\mathbf{X}'\mathbf{X})^{-1}\mathbf{X}'\mathbf{y}$ and can be computed from observed data), then are there any values of $\boldsymbol{\Sigma}$ for which these two estimates are the same, that is, are there any values of $\boldsymbol{\Sigma}$ for which $(\mathbf{X}'\boldsymbol{\Sigma}^{-1}\mathbf{X})^{-1}\mathbf{X}'\boldsymbol{\Sigma}^{-1}\mathbf{y} = (\mathbf{X}'\mathbf{X})^{-1}\mathbf{X}'\mathbf{y}$ for all values of $\mathbf{y}$ in E_n? We answer this question in the next theorem. First we state a definition that will be used.

DEFINITION 6.8.1

Ordinary Least Squares (OLS) Estimators. *Consider the model* $\mathbf{Y} = \mathbf{X}\boldsymbol{\beta} + \boldsymbol{\varepsilon}$, *where* $\boldsymbol{\varepsilon}$ *is distributed* $\mathbf{N}(\boldsymbol{\varepsilon} : \mathbf{0}, \boldsymbol{\Sigma})$. *For this model* $(\mathbf{X}'\mathbf{X})^{-1}\mathbf{X}'\mathbf{Y}$ *is defined to be the ordinary least squares (OLS) estimator of* $\boldsymbol{\beta}$, *and for any constant* $p \times 1$ *vector* ℓ, *the OLS estimator of* $\ell'\boldsymbol{\beta}$ *is defined to be* $\ell'(\mathbf{X}'\mathbf{X})^{-1}\mathbf{X}'\mathbf{Y}$.

In Section 6.10 ordinary least squares are discussed in some detail.

Of course, if $\boldsymbol{\varepsilon}$ is distributed $\mathbf{N}(\boldsymbol{\varepsilon} : \mathbf{0}, \sigma^2\mathbf{I})$, then the OLS estimator of $\ell'\boldsymbol{\beta}$ is the UMVU estimator of $\ell'\boldsymbol{\beta}$. We now state and prove some results that relate OLS estimators to UMVU estimators.

THEOREM 6.8.1

Consider the general linear model $\mathbf{Y} = \mathbf{X}\boldsymbol{\beta} + \boldsymbol{\varepsilon}$, $\boldsymbol{\varepsilon}$ *is distributed* $\mathbf{N}(\boldsymbol{\varepsilon} : \mathbf{0}, \boldsymbol{\Sigma})$. *The UMVU estimator of* $\boldsymbol{\beta}$ *is given by* $(\mathbf{X}'\mathbf{X})^{-1}\mathbf{X}'\mathbf{Y}$ (*the OLS estimator*) *if and only if there exists a* $p \times p$ *nonsingular matrix* $\mathbf{F}$ *such that*

$$\boldsymbol{\Sigma}\mathbf{X} = \mathbf{X}\mathbf{F} \tag{6.8.5}$$

Proof

We must show that $(\mathbf{X}'\boldsymbol{\Sigma}^{-1}\mathbf{X})^{-1}\mathbf{X}'\boldsymbol{\Sigma}^{-1}\mathbf{y} \equiv (\mathbf{X}'\mathbf{X})^{-1}\mathbf{X}'\mathbf{y}$ if and only if Equation (6.8.5) is satisfied. These two quantities must be equal for all $\mathbf{y}$ in E_n and this means that they are equal if and only if $(\mathbf{X}'\boldsymbol{\Sigma}^{-1}\mathbf{X})^{-1}\mathbf{X}'\boldsymbol{\Sigma}^{-1} = (\mathbf{X}'\mathbf{X})^{-1}\mathbf{X}'$; simplifying this expression gives us $\boldsymbol{\Sigma}\mathbf{X} = \mathbf{X}(\mathbf{X}'\boldsymbol{\Sigma}^{-1}\mathbf{X})^{-1}(\mathbf{X}'\mathbf{X}) = \mathbf{X}\mathbf{F}$, say, where $\mathbf{F}$ is nonsingular.

Next assume $\boldsymbol{\Sigma}\mathbf{X} = \mathbf{X}\mathbf{F}$, where $\mathbf{F}$ is a nonsingular matrix. Then

$$\begin{aligned}(\mathbf{X}'\mathbf{X})^{-1}\mathbf{X}' &= (\mathbf{X}'\mathbf{X})^{-1}\mathbf{F}'\mathbf{F}'^{-1}\mathbf{X}' = (\mathbf{F}'^{-1}\mathbf{X}'\mathbf{X})^{-1}\mathbf{F}'^{-1}\mathbf{X}' \\ &= (\mathbf{X}'\boldsymbol{\Sigma}^{-1}\mathbf{X})^{-1}\mathbf{X}'\boldsymbol{\Sigma}^{-1}\end{aligned}$$

and this proves the theorem.

COROLLARY 6.8.1.1

Consider the general linear model in Theorem 6.8.1 *and let* $\boldsymbol{\Sigma}$ *be defined by* $\boldsymbol{\Sigma} = \mathbf{X}\boldsymbol{\Delta}_1\mathbf{X}' + (\mathbf{I} - \mathbf{X}\mathbf{X}^-)(\boldsymbol{\Delta}_2)(\mathbf{I} - \mathbf{X}\mathbf{X}^-) + \theta\mathbf{I}$, *where* $\boldsymbol{\Delta}_1, \boldsymbol{\Delta}_2$, *and* θ *are restricted only so that* $\boldsymbol{\Sigma}$ *is p.d. and* $\boldsymbol{\Delta}_1\mathbf{X}'\mathbf{X} + \theta\mathbf{I}$ *is nonsingular. Then the UMVU estimator of* $\boldsymbol{\ell}'\boldsymbol{\beta}$ *is equal to the OLS estimator of* $\boldsymbol{\ell}'\boldsymbol{\beta}$ *for any* $p \times 1$ *constant vector* $\boldsymbol{\ell}$.

Proof

Simply show that $\boldsymbol{\Sigma}\mathbf{X} = \mathbf{X}\mathbf{F}$, for a nonsingular matrix $\mathbf{F}$, and use Theorem 6.8.1.

COROLLARY 6.8.1.2

Consider the linear model $\mathbf{Y} = \mathbf{X}\boldsymbol{\beta} + \boldsymbol{\varepsilon}$, $\boldsymbol{\varepsilon}$ *is distributed* $\mathbf{N}(\boldsymbol{\varepsilon} : \mathbf{0}, \boldsymbol{\Sigma})$, *where* $\mathbf{X} = [\mathbf{1}, \mathbf{x}_2, \ldots, \mathbf{x}_p]$, *that is, the model has an intercept term, say* β_0. *If* $\boldsymbol{\Sigma}$ *is defined by* $\boldsymbol{\Sigma} = \sigma^2(1 - \rho)\mathbf{I} + \sigma^2\rho\mathbf{J}$, *for* $-1/(n-1) < \rho < 1$, *then* $\boldsymbol{\ell}'\hat{\boldsymbol{\beta}} = \boldsymbol{\ell}'(\mathbf{X}'\mathbf{X})^{-1}\mathbf{X}'\mathbf{Y}$ *is the UMVU estimator of* $\boldsymbol{\ell}'\boldsymbol{\beta}$ *for any* $p \times 1$ *constant vector* $\boldsymbol{\ell}$.

Proof

In Corollary 6.8.1.1, let $\boldsymbol{\Delta}_2 = \mathbf{0}$, $\boldsymbol{\Delta}_1$ be a $p \times p$ matrix with each element equal to zero except the $(1, 1)$ element, which is $\sigma^2\rho$, and let θ be $\sigma^2(1 - \rho)$. The details are left for the reader.

Note 2. The restriction on ρ, namely, $-1/(n-1) < \rho < 1$, is required so that $\mathbf{\Sigma}$ is p.d. and $\mathbf{\Delta}_1\mathbf{X}'\mathbf{X} + \theta\mathbf{I}$ is nonsingular.

Note 3. When the model has an intercept term, this corollary states that if the variance of ε_i is an unknown constant σ^2, and if the correlation of ε_i with ε_j (for all $i \neq j$) is an unknown constant ρ, then the UMVU estimator of $\ell'\boldsymbol{\beta}$ is the same as when the ε_i and ε_j are uncorrelated with constant variance σ^2. In other words, when $\mathbf{\Sigma} = \sigma^2(1-\rho)\mathbf{I} + \sigma^2\rho\mathbf{J}$, the OLS and UMVU estimators of $\ell'\boldsymbol{\beta}$ are the same.

6.8.3 The General Linear Model: Tests of Hypotheses and Confidence Intervals When Σ Is Unknown

In Section 6.8.2 we discussed point estimation of $\ell'\boldsymbol{\beta}$ when the covariance matrix of the error term $\boldsymbol{\varepsilon}$ is $\mathbf{\Sigma}$, where $\mathbf{\Sigma}$ is unknown except for some relationship with the known matrix $\mathbf{X}$. In this section we examine the test of the hypothesis $H_0 : \boldsymbol{\beta}_2 = \mathbf{0}$ given in Section 6.4. The test statistic given in Equation (6.4.6) is

$$W = \left(\frac{\mathbf{Y}'(\mathbf{X}\mathbf{X}^- - \mathbf{X}_1\mathbf{X}_1^-)\mathbf{Y}}{\mathbf{Y}'(\mathbf{I} - \mathbf{X}\mathbf{X}^-)\mathbf{Y}}\right)\left(\frac{n-p}{q}\right) \tag{6.8.6}$$

and if $\boldsymbol{\varepsilon}$ is distributed $\mathbf{N}(\boldsymbol{\varepsilon} : \mathbf{0}, \sigma^2\mathbf{I})$, W is distributed as $F(w : q, n-p; \lambda)$, where

$$\lambda = \frac{\boldsymbol{\beta}_2'[\mathbf{X}_2'\mathbf{X}_2 - \mathbf{X}_2'\mathbf{X}_1(\mathbf{X}_1'\mathbf{X}_1)^{-1}\mathbf{X}_1'\mathbf{X}_2]\boldsymbol{\beta}_2}{2\sigma^2}$$

and $\lambda = 0$ if and only if H_0 is true.

We now state a theorem on the distribution of W if the covariance matrix of $\boldsymbol{\varepsilon}$ is not $\sigma^2\mathbf{I}$.

THEOREM 6.8.2

Consider the general linear model $\mathbf{Y} = \mathbf{X}\boldsymbol{\beta} + \boldsymbol{\varepsilon}$, where $\mathbf{X} = [\mathbf{X}_1, \mathbf{X}_2]$ and where $\mathbf{X}_1 = [\mathbf{x}_1, \mathbf{x}_2, \ldots, \mathbf{x}_{p-q}]$, $\mathbf{X}_2 = [\mathbf{x}_{p-q+1}, \ldots, \mathbf{x}_p]$, that is, $\mathbf{x}_i$ is the ith column of $\mathbf{X}$. Also, assume $\boldsymbol{\varepsilon}$ is distributed $\mathbf{N}(\boldsymbol{\varepsilon} : \mathbf{0}, \mathbf{\Sigma})$, where

$$\mathbf{\Sigma} = \sum_{i=1}^{p-q} \theta_i\mathbf{x}_i\mathbf{x}_i^- + \theta_0\left(\mathbf{I} - \sum_{i=1}^{p-q} \theta_i\mathbf{x}_i\mathbf{x}_i^-\right) \tag{6.8.7}$$

and where the θ_i are unknown constants such that $\mathbf{\Sigma}$ is p.d. Then W in Equation (6.8.6) is distributed $F(w : q, n-p; \lambda^*)$, where $\lambda^* = [\boldsymbol{\beta}_2'\mathbf{X}_2'(\mathbf{I} - \mathbf{X}_1\mathbf{X}_1^-)\mathbf{X}_2\boldsymbol{\beta}_2]/2\theta_0$.

Proof

Let $\mathbf{A}_1 = (\mathbf{XX}^- - \mathbf{X}_1\mathbf{X}_1^-)/\theta_0$ and $\mathbf{A}_2 = (\mathbf{I} - \mathbf{XX}^-)/\theta_0$, and note that $\theta_0\mathbf{A}_1 = (\mathbf{I} - \mathbf{X}_1\mathbf{X}_1^-) - (\mathbf{I} - \mathbf{XX}^-)$. Also, since $(\mathbf{I} - \mathbf{X}_1\mathbf{X}_1^-)\mathbf{X}_1 = \mathbf{0}$ and $(\mathbf{I} - \mathbf{XX}^-)\mathbf{X} = \mathbf{0}$, these imply

$$(\mathbf{I} - \mathbf{X}_1\mathbf{X}_1^-)\left(\sum_{i=1}^{p-q} \theta_i\mathbf{x}_i\mathbf{x}_i^-\right) = \mathbf{0} \qquad \text{and} \qquad (\mathbf{I} - \mathbf{XX}^-)\left(\sum_{i=1}^{p-q} \theta_i\mathbf{x}_i\mathbf{x}_i^-\right) = \mathbf{0}$$

We can write Equation (6.8.6) as

$$W = \left(\frac{\mathbf{Y}'\mathbf{A}_1\mathbf{Y}}{\mathbf{Y}'\mathbf{A}_2\mathbf{Y}}\right)\left(\frac{n-p}{q}\right)$$

Clearly, $\mathbf{A}_1\mathbf{\Sigma} = \mathbf{XX}^- - \mathbf{X}_1\mathbf{X}_1^-$ and is idempotent of rank q. Also, $\frac{1}{2}(\mathscr{E}[\mathbf{Y}])'(\mathbf{A}_1)(\mathscr{E}[\mathbf{Y}]) = \lambda^* = \boldsymbol{\beta}_2'\mathbf{X}_2'(\mathbf{I} - \mathbf{X}_1\mathbf{X}_1^-)\mathbf{X}_2\boldsymbol{\beta}_2/2\theta_0$, so by Theorem 4.4.3, $U_1 = \mathbf{Y}'\mathbf{A}_1\mathbf{Y}$ is distributed $\chi^2(u_1 : q; \lambda^*)$. Clearly, $\mathbf{A}_2\mathbf{\Sigma} = \mathbf{I} - \mathbf{XX}^-$ and is idempotent of rank $n - p$; also, $(\mathscr{E}[\mathbf{Y}])'(\mathbf{A}_2)(\mathscr{E}[\mathbf{Y}]) = 0$, so $U_2 = \mathbf{Y}'\mathbf{A}_2\mathbf{Y}$ is distributed $\chi^2(u_2 : n - p)$. It is straightforward to show $\mathbf{A}_1\mathbf{\Sigma}\mathbf{A}_2 = \mathbf{0}$, so by Theorem 4.5.3, U_1 and U_2 are independent. This proves the theorem.

Example 6.8.1

We shall demonstrate one useful application of this theorem. Consider the model $\mathbf{Y} = \mathbf{X}\boldsymbol{\beta} + \boldsymbol{\varepsilon}$, where $\mathbf{X} = [\mathbf{1}, \mathbf{X}_2]$ and $\boldsymbol{\varepsilon}$ is distributed $\mathrm{N}(\boldsymbol{\varepsilon} : \mathbf{0}, \mathbf{\Sigma})$, that is, $\mathbf{X}_1$ in Theorem 6.8.2 is the vector $\mathbf{1}$. Let $\theta_0 = \sigma^2(1 - \rho)$; let $\theta_1 = n\sigma^2\rho/[1 - \sigma^2(1 - \rho)]$; let $\theta_2 = \theta_3 = \cdots = \theta_{p-q} = 0$. Then we get

$$\mathbf{\Sigma} = \sigma^2(1 - \rho)\mathbf{I} + \sigma^2\rho\mathbf{J} \tag{6.8.8}$$

and ρ must satisfy $-1/(n - 1) < \rho < 1$ so $\mathbf{\Sigma}$ will be p.d. Thus when $\mathbf{\Sigma}$ has the structure $\mathrm{var}[\varepsilon_i] = \sigma^2$, $\mathrm{cor}[\varepsilon_i, \varepsilon_j] = \rho$, for all $i \neq j$, the test statistic W for $H_0 : \boldsymbol{\beta}_2 = \mathbf{0}$ *vs.* $H_a : \boldsymbol{\beta}_2 \neq \mathbf{0}$ in Equation (6.8.6) is distributed $F(w : p - 1, n - p; \lambda)$, where

$$\lambda = \frac{\boldsymbol{\beta}_2'\mathbf{X}_2'(\mathbf{I} - \mathbf{X}_1\mathbf{X}_1^-)\mathbf{X}_2\boldsymbol{\beta}_2}{2\sigma^2(1 - \rho)}$$

The test is this: Reject H_0 if and only if $w \geq F_{\alpha:p-1,n-p}$. Since $\mathbf{X}_1 = \mathbf{1}$ in this example, the model has an intercept term β_0.

Note 4. To test any hypothesis concerning $\boldsymbol{\beta}_2$, for example, $\mathbf{H}_2\boldsymbol{\beta}_2 = \mathbf{h}_2$, the test in Theorem 6.3.1 can be used when $\mathbf{\Sigma}$ has the structure in

Equation (6.8.7), where the θ_i are unknown parameters. Also, one-at-a-time or simultaneous confidence intervals on linear functions of $\boldsymbol{\beta}_2$ are exact when $\boldsymbol{\Sigma}$ has the structure in Equation (6.8.7).

Note 5. If the model has an intercept term (if $\mathbf{X}_1 = \mathbf{1}$), then the test in Theorem 6.3.1 or corresponding confidence interval statements about all the parameters of $\boldsymbol{\beta}_2$ are exact when $\boldsymbol{\Sigma}$ has the structure given in Equation (6.8.8).

For further information about the general linear model when the covariance matrix is a general p.d. matrix $\boldsymbol{\Sigma}$, see [Z-2].

6.9 Examination of Assumptions

In the general linear model, some basic assumptions are made, data are collected, and from these data inferences are made about the parameters in the model. For example, in the simple linear model (similar assumptions are made in the *general* linear model),

$$Y_i = \beta_0 + \beta x_i + \varepsilon_i \qquad \varepsilon_i \text{ are distributed } NID(\varepsilon : 0, \sigma^2) \qquad i = 1, 2, \ldots, n$$

the assumptions are as follows:

1. $\mathscr{E}[\varepsilon_i] = 0$, that is, the expected values of the ε_i's are zero;
2. the errors ε_i are independent;
3. the errors ε_i have a constant variance σ^2;
4. the errors ε_i are normally distributed (for Case 1). (6.9.1)

Data (x_i, y_i), $i = 1, 2, \ldots, n$, are collected, and these data are used to draw inferences (point estimators, confidence intervals, and tests of hypotheses) about the parameters β_0, β, and σ^2 in the model. Strictly speaking, these inferences are correct in a relative frequency probability sense if the assumptions 1, 2, 3, and 4 are correct. However, these assumptions are conceptual and can never be exactly satisfied in a real-world situation, that is, in a real-world model there can be no random variable ε whose distribution is exactly normal, and so on. Nevertheless, if the assumptions are "satisfied reasonably well," then the inferences are accurate enough to be useful.

In this section we shall give a brief discussion of how the data can be used to examine these basic assumptions. The problem is a difficult one since in order to draw inferences about the assumptions in a model, "other assumptions" must be made, and, of course, it may not be known whether these "other assumptions" are correct.

There are two aspects to this problem. One aspect is to determine if the assumptions are or are not correct, and if they are correct, the procedures discussed in previous sections of this chapter can be used to make inferences about the parameters. If the assumptions are *not* correct, then one must decide what procedures to use to draw *valid* inferences about the unknown parameters. A second aspect of the problem is that of deciding which of the *valid* procedures for making correct inferences is the "best" procedure, that is, if there are two correct methods for setting a 0.95 confidence interval on β, then one would want to use the method that gives the "shortest" interval since this extracts the "most" information from the data.

If one decides that some of the assumptions in Equation (6.9.1) are violated, then it may be possible to proceed in one of the following ways.

1. Ignore the violations of the assumptions and proceed as if all assumptions are satisfied.

2. If possible, decide what is the correct assumption for the one (or ones) that is violated and use a valid procedure that takes into consideration the new assumption. For example, if it is determined that the ε_i have a gamma distribution rather than a normal distribution, then use an inference procedure that is valid when the ε_i have a gamma distribution. For another example, if it is determined that the ε_i are not independent but have a constant unknown covariance matrix $\mathbf{\Sigma}$, then use a valid inference procedure that includes this new assumption. In many cases when the assumptions in Equation (6.9.1) are violated and other assumptions are known to hold (for example, suppose the ε_i have an unknown covariance matrix), then "valid" inference procedures that are applicable to these new assumptions may not be known.

3. If possible, devise a new model that has the important aspects of the original model and satisfies all the assumptions in Equation (6.9.1). For example, this may sometimes be accomplished by (1) making an appropriate transformation of the data (x_i, y_i); (2) eliminating some of the observations (outliers) if these are clearly incorrect measurements.

4. Use a distribution-free procedure that is valid even if various assumptions in Equation (6.9.1) are violated, if it is not known what assumptions to use for the ones violated. For example, if there is evidence that the Y_i are not normally distributed, and if it is not known what the distributions of the Y_i are (except perhaps that they are continuous random variables), then a distribution-free procedure that is valid under these assumptions can be used. (6.9.2)

A considerable amount of literature is available on this subject, but there seems to be very few "best" procedures available for handling the various situations. Most of the procedures are either asymptotic results or "intuitive." We shall proceed by first giving some methods for examining the assumptions and then make some recommendations on how to cope with the model when some assumptions are violated.

6.9.1 Residual Analysis

Since the assumptions that we are discussing are assumptions on the unobservable errors ε_i, we will "estimate" these and then draw some conclusions based on these "estimates." We have put estimates in quotation marks since, in general, we only discuss the estimation of fixed parameters, but here we are attempting to determine the value of an unobservable random variable ε_i on the basis of data (x_i, y_i). We estimate the ε_i by residuals which we now define.

DEFINITION 6.9.1

Residuals. *Consider the linear model* $\mathbf{Y} = \mathbf{X}\boldsymbol{\beta} + \boldsymbol{\varepsilon}$, *where no assumptions are made about the random error vector* $\boldsymbol{\varepsilon}$. *The vector* $\mathbf{r}$, *given by* $\mathbf{r} = \mathbf{Y} - \mathbf{X}\hat{\boldsymbol{\beta}}$, *where* $\hat{\boldsymbol{\beta}} = \mathbf{X}^{-}\mathbf{Y}$, *is defined to be the vector of residuals.*

Note 1. We sometimes use $\hat{\mathbf{Y}}$ for $\mathbf{X}\hat{\boldsymbol{\beta}}$ and write $\mathbf{r} = \mathbf{Y} - \hat{\mathbf{Y}}$.

We now state and prove some results about the random vector $\mathbf{r}$.

THEOREM 6.9.1

The vector of residuals can be written as

$$\mathbf{r} = (\mathbf{I} - \mathbf{X}\mathbf{X}^{-})\mathbf{Y} = (\mathbf{I} - \mathbf{X}\mathbf{X}^{-})\boldsymbol{\varepsilon}$$

Proof

The proof is obtained by substituting for $\hat{\boldsymbol{\beta}}$.

THEOREM 6.9.2

Under the assumptions of Equation (6.9.1),

(1) $\mathbf{r}$ *is distributed* $N(\mathbf{r} : \mathbf{0}, \mathbf{M}\sigma^2)$, *where* $\mathbf{M} = \mathbf{I} - \mathbf{X}\mathbf{X}^{-}$;

(2) $\mathbf{r}$ *and* $\hat{\boldsymbol{\beta}}$ *are independent.*

Proof

The proof is a straightforward application of Theorems 3.3.5 and 4.5.2.

Note 2. To examine the various assumptions in Equation (6.9.1), one can assume that the r_i, which are defined by $r_i = Y_i - \hat{Y}_i$, for $i = 1, 2, \ldots, n$, are normally distributed with means zero. Also, under quite general conditions, and if n is large compared to $p + 1$, one can assume as a first approximation that the r_i are independent random variables with variances $\hat{\sigma}^2$. Under these conditions one assumes (approximately) that $\mathbf{r}$ is distributed $\mathbf{N}(\mathbf{r} : \mathbf{0}, \hat{\sigma}^2\mathbf{I})$.

While there are various test statistics that are functions of $\mathbf{r}$ that could be used to test the various assumptions, very little is known about the operating characteristics of these tests. Consequently, in many cases it is adequate to use graphical procedures and make decisions based on these results.

6.9.2 Plots of Residuals to Examine Assumption 1 in Equation (6.9.1)

Suppose we *assume* that the model is $\mathbf{Y} = \mathbf{X}\boldsymbol{\beta} + \boldsymbol{\varepsilon}$, $\mathscr{E}[\boldsymbol{\varepsilon}] = \mathbf{0}$, but that the model is *really* $\mathbf{Y} = \mathbf{X}\boldsymbol{\beta} + \mathbf{B}\boldsymbol{\gamma} + \boldsymbol{\eta}$, $\mathscr{E}[\boldsymbol{\eta}] = \mathbf{0}$, where $\boldsymbol{\gamma}$ is a set of q unknown parameters and $\mathbf{B}$ is an $n \times q$ matrix of nonrandom variables, that is, the random error $\boldsymbol{\varepsilon}$ does not have expectation equal to zero but instead $\mathscr{E}[\boldsymbol{\varepsilon}] = \mathscr{E}[\mathbf{B}\boldsymbol{\gamma} + \boldsymbol{\eta}]$, where $\mathscr{E}[\boldsymbol{\eta}] = \mathbf{0}$. A plot of residuals as ordinates and the corresponding elements of each column of $\mathbf{X}$ (one column at a time) as abcissas might reveal this. We illustrate with an example.

Example 6.9.1

Suppose an investigator *assumes* a model $Y_i = \beta_0 + \beta_1 x_i + \varepsilon_i$, where $\mathscr{E}[\varepsilon_i] = 0$, but suppose the model is *really* $Y_i = \beta_0 + \beta_1 x_i + \beta_2 x_i^2 + \eta_i$, where $\mathscr{E}[\eta_i] = 0$. Then in the assumed model, $Y_i = \beta_0 + \beta_1 x_i + \varepsilon_i$, the expectation of ε_i is not zero (that is, $\mathscr{E}[\varepsilon_i] \neq 0$), but instead $\mathscr{E}[\varepsilon_i] = \beta_2 x_i^2$. A plot of the residuals versus x_i would perhaps reveal not a haphazard scattering of the residuals but a curvilinear pattern due to the term $\beta_2 x_i^2$ being in the residuals.

If we examine the general model $\mathbf{Y} = \mathbf{X}\boldsymbol{\beta} + \boldsymbol{\varepsilon}$, which we *assume* to be correct, we compute $\hat{\boldsymbol{\beta}} = \mathbf{X}^-\mathbf{Y}$ and the residual vector $\mathbf{r} = (\mathbf{I} - \mathbf{X}\mathbf{X}^-)\mathbf{Y}$. Thus we have the following:

1. If the correct model is in fact $\mathbf{Y} = \mathbf{X}\boldsymbol{\beta} + \mathbf{B}\boldsymbol{\gamma} + \boldsymbol{\eta}$, $\mathscr{E}[\boldsymbol{\eta}] = \mathbf{0}$, instead of $\mathbf{Y} = \mathbf{X}\boldsymbol{\beta} + \boldsymbol{\varepsilon}$, $\mathscr{E}[\boldsymbol{\varepsilon}] = \mathbf{0}$, then the residual vector is
$$\mathbf{r}_1 = (\mathbf{I} - \mathbf{X}\mathbf{X}^-)\mathbf{B}\boldsymbol{\gamma} + (\mathbf{I} - \mathbf{X}\mathbf{X}^-)\boldsymbol{\eta}$$
2. If the correct model is really $\mathbf{Y} = \mathbf{X}\boldsymbol{\beta} + \boldsymbol{\varepsilon}$, $\mathscr{E}[\boldsymbol{\varepsilon}] = \mathbf{0}$, then the residual vector is $\mathbf{r}_2 = (\mathbf{I} - \mathbf{X}\mathbf{X}^-)\mathbf{Y} = (\mathbf{I} - \mathbf{X}\mathbf{X}^-)\boldsymbol{\varepsilon}$.

Under certain conditions on the $\mathbf{X}'\mathbf{X}$ matrix and for large n, $\mathbf{X}\mathbf{X}^-$ is approximately $\mathbf{0}$, so $\mathbf{r}_1 \approx \mathbf{B}\boldsymbol{\gamma} + \boldsymbol{\eta}$, $\mathscr{E}[\boldsymbol{\eta}] = \mathbf{0}$, and $\mathbf{r}_2 \approx \boldsymbol{\varepsilon}$, $\mathscr{E}[\boldsymbol{\varepsilon}] = \mathbf{0}$.

Thus if we assume the correct model is $\mathbf{Y} = \mathbf{X}\boldsymbol{\beta} + \boldsymbol{\varepsilon}$, $\mathscr{E}[\boldsymbol{\varepsilon}] = \mathbf{0}$, and if indeed it is the correct model, then a plot of the residuals in $\mathbf{r}$ (which is really $\mathbf{r}_2$) versus each column in $\mathbf{X}$ results in a haphazard scattering. If, however, the true model is in fact $\mathbf{Y} = \mathbf{X}\boldsymbol{\beta} + \mathbf{B}\boldsymbol{\gamma} + \boldsymbol{\eta}$, $\mathscr{E}[\boldsymbol{\eta}] = \mathbf{0}$, then a plot of the residuals in $\mathbf{r}$ (which is really $\mathbf{r}_1$) versus each column of $\mathbf{X}$ would *not* indicate a haphazard scattering but would reflect a dependence on the parameter $\boldsymbol{\gamma}$.

Example 6.9.2

In Example 6.9.1 we would obtain (approximately) $\mathbf{r}_1 = \mathbf{B}\boldsymbol{\gamma} + \boldsymbol{\eta} = [\beta_2 x_i^2 + \eta_i]$, where $\mathscr{E}[\eta_i] = 0$. So a plot of the residuals versus x_i would indicate that a quadratic term should be included in the model.

If a plot of residuals indicates that $\mathbf{B}\boldsymbol{\gamma}$ should be included in the model, where $\mathbf{B}$ is known, then one can write the model as

$$\mathbf{Y} = [\mathbf{X}, \mathbf{B}]\begin{bmatrix} \boldsymbol{\beta} \\ \boldsymbol{\gamma} \end{bmatrix} + \boldsymbol{\varepsilon}$$

and use the methods of this chapter to test $H_0 : \boldsymbol{\gamma} = \mathbf{0}$. Special cases will be considered in various sections in Chapters 8 and 12.

To check the error ε_i for independence, an overall technique that seems to be satisfactory is the run test described in [D-9]. To use this we would assume that the $r_i = \varepsilon_i$ (approximately, for large n) and test for independence of the r_i and hence of the ε_i.

To check that the errors have constant variance, one could assume that $r_i = \varepsilon_i$ (approximately, for large n) and use one of the tests described in [G-1]. We must assume the error vector $\boldsymbol{\varepsilon}$ has a normal p.d.f. to use this test.

To check for normality of the ε_i, a technique that seems to be satisfactory is described in [D-1], [S-9], [S-10], [W-5], and [W-6]. Assume that $r_i = \varepsilon_i$ (approximately, for large n) and test for normality of the r_i and hence of the ε_i.

We emphasize again that these are very approximate procedures for checking the assumptions in Equation (6.9.1), but we also emphasize that in any practical problem the residuals should *always* be examined by these and other procedures. For further reading, see [B-3], [C-7], and [C-8].

6.10 Inference in the Linear Model: Case 2

In this section we assume the general linear model of Definition 6.1.1, where the error vector $\boldsymbol{\varepsilon}$ has mean $\mathbf{0}$ and covariance matrix $\sigma^2\mathbf{I}$. The form of the c.d.f. of $\boldsymbol{\varepsilon}$ will be unspecified and so the principle of maximum likelihood cannot be used to obtain the estimators of the unknown parameters. Instead we shall use the method of least squares; that is, we find the value of $\boldsymbol{\beta}$, say $\hat{\boldsymbol{\beta}}$, that minimizes the sum of squares $\sum_{i=1}^{n} \varepsilon_i^2$. This value of $\hat{\boldsymbol{\beta}}$ is defined as the *least squares* estimator of $\boldsymbol{\beta}$. The sum of squares $\sum_{i=1}^{n} \varepsilon_i^2$ is $\boldsymbol{\varepsilon}'\boldsymbol{\varepsilon} = (\mathbf{Y} - \mathbf{X}\boldsymbol{\beta})'(\mathbf{Y} - \mathbf{X}\boldsymbol{\beta})$, and the value of $\boldsymbol{\beta}$ that minimizes $\boldsymbol{\varepsilon}'\boldsymbol{\varepsilon}$ is given by the solution to $\partial(\boldsymbol{\varepsilon}'\boldsymbol{\varepsilon})/\partial\boldsymbol{\beta} = \mathbf{0}$. We get $\partial(\boldsymbol{\varepsilon}'\boldsymbol{\varepsilon})/\partial\boldsymbol{\beta} = -2\mathbf{X}'\mathbf{Y} + 2\mathbf{X}'\mathbf{X}\hat{\boldsymbol{\beta}} = \mathbf{0}$. The least squares estimator of $\boldsymbol{\beta}$ is therefore

$$\hat{\boldsymbol{\beta}} = (\mathbf{X}'\mathbf{X})^{-1}\mathbf{X}'\mathbf{Y} = \mathbf{X}^{-}\mathbf{Y} \tag{6.10.1}$$

which is the same as the maximum likelihood estimator when $\boldsymbol{\varepsilon}$ satisfies the conditions of Case 1.

Minimizing the sum of squares $\boldsymbol{\varepsilon}'\boldsymbol{\varepsilon}$ does not provide an estimator of σ^2; however, an unbiased estimator of σ^2 based on the least squares estimator of $\boldsymbol{\beta}$ is given by

$$\hat{\sigma}^2 = \left(\frac{1}{n-p}\right)(\mathbf{Y} - \mathbf{X}\hat{\boldsymbol{\beta}})'(\mathbf{Y} - \mathbf{X}\hat{\boldsymbol{\beta}}) = \left(\frac{1}{n-p}\right)\mathbf{Y}'(\mathbf{I} - \mathbf{X}\mathbf{X}^{-})\mathbf{Y} \tag{6.10.2}$$

This is the same as the maximum likelihood estimator (adjusted for bias) of σ^2 when $\boldsymbol{\varepsilon}$ satisfies the conditions of Case 1, and we call it the least squares estimator of σ^2.

The discussion above leads to the following theorem.

THEOREM 6.10.1

In the general linear model $\mathbf{Y} = \mathbf{X}\boldsymbol{\beta} + \boldsymbol{\varepsilon}$, *where* $\mathscr{E}[\boldsymbol{\varepsilon}] = \mathbf{0}$ *and* $\mathbf{cov}[\boldsymbol{\varepsilon}] = \sigma^2\mathbf{I}$, *the least squares estimators of* $\boldsymbol{\beta}$ *and* σ^2 *are given by*

$$\hat{\boldsymbol{\beta}} = \mathbf{C}\mathbf{X}'\mathbf{Y} = \mathbf{X}^{-}\mathbf{Y}$$

$$\hat{\sigma}^2 = \left(\frac{1}{n-p}\right)(\mathbf{Y} - \mathbf{X}\hat{\boldsymbol{\beta}})'(\mathbf{Y} - \mathbf{X}\hat{\boldsymbol{\beta}}) = \left(\frac{1}{n-p}\right)\mathbf{Y}'(\mathbf{I} - \mathbf{X}\mathbf{X}^{-})\mathbf{Y}$$

Next we investigate the properties of the least squares estimators of $\boldsymbol{\beta}$ and σ^2 given in Equations (6.10.1) and (6.10.2).

Since the functional form of the c.d.f. of the random vector $\boldsymbol{\varepsilon}$ (and $\mathbf{Y}$) is unspecified, it is not possible, in general, to state optimal properties of the least squares estimators relative to *all* estimating functions as it is when the random vector $\boldsymbol{\varepsilon}$ satisfies Case 1. For example, Theorem 6.2.2 tells us that if $\boldsymbol{\varepsilon}$ is distributed $N(\boldsymbol{\varepsilon} : \mathbf{0}, \sigma^2\mathbf{I})$, then of *all* functions of the observations $\mathbf{Y}$ that could be used as estimators of $\boldsymbol{\ell}'\boldsymbol{\beta}$, the particular function $\boldsymbol{\ell}'\mathbf{X}^{-}\mathbf{Y}$ is the uniformly minimum variance unbiased estimator. For Case 2 we have much less information about the random variables contained in $\mathbf{Y}$, and hence we would not expect to be able to make so strong a statement about the properties of the estimators.

We still want to use "minimum variance unbiased" as an optimum property of estimators, but we will limit the class of functions of $\mathbf{Y}$ that will be allowable as estimating functions. We note that $\mathcal{E}[\mathbf{Y}] = \mathbf{X}\boldsymbol{\beta}$, and hence for a given vector $\boldsymbol{\ell}$, $\mathcal{E}[\boldsymbol{\ell}'\mathbf{X}^{-}\mathbf{Y}] = \boldsymbol{\ell}'\boldsymbol{\beta}$. Thus $\boldsymbol{\ell}'\boldsymbol{\beta}$, any linear function of $\boldsymbol{\beta}$, can be estimated unbiasedly by a linear function $\boldsymbol{\ell}'\mathbf{X}^{-}\mathbf{Y}$ of the elements in $\mathbf{Y}$. It therefore seems reasonable to restrict the class of estimating functions to the class of *linear* functions and see if uniformly minimum variance unbiased estimators of $\boldsymbol{\ell}'\boldsymbol{\beta}$ exist within this restricted class.

Another justification for restricting the class of estimating functions for $\boldsymbol{\ell}'\boldsymbol{\beta}$ to linear functions of $\mathbf{Y}$ is the following: Suppose we consider a "general" function $t(\mathbf{Y})$ as an estimator for $\boldsymbol{\ell}'\boldsymbol{\beta}$. Under quite general conditions the function can be expanded into a Taylor series with a linear term plus a remainder. If the remainder is ignored, then the linear term in $\mathbf{Y}$ can be used as a first approximation to the "general" estimating function $t(\mathbf{Y})$.

On the basis of this discussion we shall now define uniformly minimum variance unbiased *linear* estimators.

DEFINITION 6.10.1

Uniformly Minimum Variance Unbiased Linear Estimator. *Let $Y_1, Y_2, \ldots, Y_n$ be n observable random variables with joint c.d.f. $F_{\mathbf{Y}}(\cdot : \boldsymbol{\gamma})$, $\boldsymbol{\gamma} \in \Omega$. Let $s(\boldsymbol{\gamma})$, a known function of $\boldsymbol{\gamma}$, be denoted by θ, that is, $\theta = s(\boldsymbol{\gamma})$. If $\hat{\theta}$ is a linear function of the Y_i's, and if, in the class of all linear functions of the Y_i's (and for all values of $\boldsymbol{\gamma}$ in Ω), $\hat{\theta}$ is unbiased and has the smallest variance of any unbiased estimator in the class of linear functions of the Y_i's, then $\hat{\theta}$ is defined to be the uniformly best (minimum variance) linear unbiased estimator of θ (of $s(\boldsymbol{\gamma})$).*

> ***Note 1.*** We call these estimators "Best Linear Unbiased" (BLU) estimators.
>
> ***Note 2.*** To find BLU estimators we first examine $\mathbf{a}'\mathbf{Y} + a_0$, a general linear function of the Y_i's. We must determine the constant a_0 and the elements of the vector $\mathbf{a}$. For the unbiased property we note that $\mathcal{E}[\mathbf{a}'\mathbf{Y} + a_0] = \theta$ for all possible values of θ, and this will put some restrictions on the a_i. Next we look at the variance, that is, $\text{var}[\mathbf{a}'\mathbf{Y} + a_0]$, and find the values of a_i, subject to the restrictions of unbiasedness, that make the variance a minimum for all values of θ. If these restrictions imply a unique value of $\mathbf{a}$ and a_0, say $\mathbf{a}^*$ and a_0^*, then $(\mathbf{a}^*)'\mathbf{Y} + a_0^*$ is the BLU estimator of θ.

Now we shall prove a theorem about optimum properties of least square estimators. It tells us that in the general linear model when the errors satisfy Case 2, the estimator of $\boldsymbol{\ell}'\boldsymbol{\beta}$ given by least squares is the BLU estimator of $\boldsymbol{\ell}'\boldsymbol{\beta}$. This theorem was first proved by Gauss and rediscovered by Markov and is generally referred to as the Gauss-Markov theorem.

THEOREM 6.10.2

Consider the general linear model $\mathbf{Y} = \mathbf{X}\boldsymbol{\beta} + \boldsymbol{\varepsilon}$, *where* $\mathscr{E}[\boldsymbol{\varepsilon}] = \mathbf{0}$, $\mathbf{cov}[\boldsymbol{\varepsilon}] = \sigma^2\mathbf{I}$, *and* $\Omega = \{(\boldsymbol{\beta}, \sigma^2) : \boldsymbol{\beta} \in E_p, \sigma^2 > 0\}$. *The least squares estimator of* $\ell'\boldsymbol{\beta}$ (*where* ℓ *is any given constant* $p \times 1$ *vector*) *is given by* $\ell'\hat{\boldsymbol{\beta}}$ (*that is,* $\ell'\hat{\boldsymbol{\beta}} = \ell'\mathbf{X}^-\mathbf{Y}$) *and this is the uniformly minimum variance linear unbiased (BLU) estimator of* $\ell'\boldsymbol{\beta}$.

Proof

First we show that the least squares estimator of $\ell'\boldsymbol{\beta}$, which we denote by $\widehat{\ell'\boldsymbol{\beta}}$, is $\ell'\mathbf{X}^-\mathbf{Y}$. To do this let $\mathbf{L}'$ be any $p \times p$ nonsingular matrix whose first row is ℓ', that is, $\mathbf{L} = [\ell, \mathbf{L}_0]$. Let $\mathbf{K} = (\mathbf{L}')^{-1}$. Then we can write

$$\mathbf{Y} = \mathbf{X}\boldsymbol{\beta} + \boldsymbol{\varepsilon} = (\mathbf{XK})(\mathbf{L}'\boldsymbol{\beta}) + \boldsymbol{\varepsilon} = \mathbf{W}\boldsymbol{\theta} + \boldsymbol{\varepsilon}$$

where $\mathbf{XK}$ is denoted by $\mathbf{W}$ and $\mathbf{L}'\boldsymbol{\beta}$ by $\boldsymbol{\theta}$ (note $\theta_1 = \ell'\boldsymbol{\beta}$). By Theorem 6.10.1 the least squares estimator of $\boldsymbol{\theta}$ is given by $\hat{\boldsymbol{\theta}} = (\mathbf{W}'\mathbf{W})^{-1}\mathbf{W}'\mathbf{Y}$. We substitute for $\mathbf{W}$ and get

$$\begin{aligned}\hat{\boldsymbol{\theta}} &= (\mathbf{K}'\mathbf{X}'\mathbf{X}\mathbf{K})^{-1}\mathbf{K}'\mathbf{X}'\mathbf{Y} = \mathbf{K}^{-1}(\mathbf{X}'\mathbf{X})^{-1}(\mathbf{K}')^{-1}\mathbf{K}'\mathbf{X}'\mathbf{Y} \\ &= \mathbf{K}^{-1}(\mathbf{X}'\mathbf{X})^{-1}\mathbf{X}'\mathbf{Y} = \mathbf{K}^{-1}\mathbf{X}^-\mathbf{Y} = \mathbf{L}'\hat{\boldsymbol{\beta}} = \begin{bmatrix}\ell' \\ \mathbf{L}_0'\end{bmatrix}\hat{\boldsymbol{\beta}}\end{aligned}$$

Thus $\hat{\theta}_1 = \ell'\hat{\boldsymbol{\beta}}$, and this demonstrates that $\ell'\hat{\boldsymbol{\beta}}$ (that is, $\ell'\mathbf{X}^-\mathbf{Y}$) is the least squares estimator of $\ell'\boldsymbol{\beta}$.

Next we want to show that $\ell'\mathbf{X}^-\mathbf{Y}$ is the BLU estimator of $\ell'\boldsymbol{\beta}$. First, for the estimator to be a linear function of the observations, we write it as $\mathbf{a}'\mathbf{Y} + a_0$, where $\mathbf{a}$ and a_0 are to be determined so that $\mathbf{a}'\mathbf{Y} + a_0$ is an unbiased estimator of $\ell'\boldsymbol{\beta}$ and has minimum variance of all unbiased estimators. We will let $\mathbf{a}' = \ell'\mathbf{X}^- + \mathbf{b}'$, and since $\ell'\mathbf{X}^-$ is known, we will determine $\mathbf{b}$ (and hence $\mathbf{a}$) and a_0. For unbiasedness we obtain

$$\begin{aligned}\ell'\boldsymbol{\beta} &= \mathscr{E}[\mathbf{a}'\mathbf{Y} + a_0] = \mathscr{E}[(\ell'\mathbf{X}^- + \mathbf{b}')\mathbf{Y} + a_0] \\ &= \ell'\mathbf{X}^-\mathbf{X}\boldsymbol{\beta} + \mathbf{b}'\mathbf{X}\boldsymbol{\beta} + a_0 = \ell'\boldsymbol{\beta} + \mathbf{b}'\mathbf{X}\boldsymbol{\beta} + a_0\end{aligned}$$

Thus $\mathbf{b}'\mathbf{X}\boldsymbol{\beta} + a_0 = 0$ for all values of $\boldsymbol{\beta}$ in E_p. This implies that $\mathbf{b}'\mathbf{X} = \mathbf{0}$ and $a_0 = 0$.

For the variance of $\mathbf{a}'\mathbf{Y} + a_0$, we obtain

$$\begin{aligned}\text{var}[\mathbf{a}'\mathbf{Y} + a_0] &= \text{var}[\mathbf{a}'\mathbf{Y}] = \text{var}[(\ell'\mathbf{X}^- + \mathbf{b}')\mathbf{Y}] \\ &= \text{var}[(\ell'\mathbf{X}^- + \mathbf{b}')(\mathbf{X}\boldsymbol{\beta} + \boldsymbol{\varepsilon})] = \text{var}[\ell'\boldsymbol{\beta} + (\ell'\mathbf{X}^- + \mathbf{b}')\boldsymbol{\varepsilon}] \\ &= \text{var}[\ell'\mathbf{X}^-\boldsymbol{\varepsilon} + \mathbf{b}'\boldsymbol{\varepsilon}] = \sigma^2\ell'(\mathbf{X}'\mathbf{X})^{-1}\ell + \sigma^2\mathbf{b}'\mathbf{b}\end{aligned}$$

by noting that $\mathbf{b}'\mathbf{X} = \mathbf{0}$ and $\mathbf{b}'\mathbf{X}'^- = \mathbf{0}$ from the unbiased condition.

But σ^2 and $\ell'(\mathbf{X}'\mathbf{X})^{-1}\ell$ are constants, so to minimize var[$\mathbf{a}'\mathbf{Y}$] we must minimize $\mathbf{b}'\mathbf{b} = \sum_{i=1}^{n} b_i^2$. But the minimum value of $\mathbf{b}'\mathbf{b}$ is zero and occurs when $\mathbf{b} = \mathbf{0}$; this is consistent with the restriction of unbiasedness $\mathbf{b}'\mathbf{X} = \mathbf{0}$. Hence the minimum of var[$\mathbf{a}'\mathbf{Y} + a_0$], subject to $\mathscr{E}[\mathbf{a}'\mathbf{Y} + a_0] = \ell'\boldsymbol{\beta}$, is $\sigma^2\ell'(\mathbf{X}'\mathbf{X})^{-1}\ell$ and occurs when $\mathbf{a}' = \ell'\mathbf{X}^-$ and $a_0 = 0$. Thus the BLU estimator of $\ell'\boldsymbol{\beta}$ is $\mathbf{a}'\mathbf{Y} = \ell'\mathbf{X}^-\mathbf{Y} = \ell'\hat{\boldsymbol{\beta}}$, and the proof is complete.

To find optimum properties that the least squares estimator of σ^2 satisfies, we restrict the estimating functions similarly to what we did for $\ell'\boldsymbol{\beta}$. We note that $\mathscr{E}[Y_i - \mathscr{E}(Y_i)]^2 = \sigma^2$ for $i = 1, 2, \ldots, p$, and hence in the model $\mathbf{Y} = \mathbf{X}\boldsymbol{\beta} + \boldsymbol{\varepsilon}$ for Case 2, it seems reasonable to restrict the class of estimating functions for σ^2 to quadratic functions of $\mathbf{Y}$ and attempt to find minimum variance unbiased estimators in this restricted class. These will be called *uniformly minimum variance unbiased quadratic* estimators, and the formal definition is below.

DEFINITION 6.10.2

Uniformly Minimum Variance Quadratic Unbiased Estimators. *Let $Y_1, Y_2, \ldots, Y_n$ be n observable random variables with joint c.d.f. $F_{\mathbf{Y}}(\cdot : \boldsymbol{\gamma})$, $\boldsymbol{\gamma} \in \Omega$. Let $\tau = r(\boldsymbol{\gamma})$ denote a known function of the unknown parameter $\boldsymbol{\gamma}$, and let $\hat{\tau} = q(\mathbf{Y})$ denote an estimator of τ, where $q(\mathbf{Y})$ is a quadratic form in the observable random vector $\mathbf{Y}$. If in this class of quadratic forms of the Y_i's (and for all possible values of $\boldsymbol{\gamma}$ in Ω), $\hat{\tau}$ is unbiased and has the smallest variance of any unbiased estimator in this class of quadratic forms of Y_i's, then $\hat{\tau}$ is defined to be the uniformly best (minimum variance) unbiased quadratic estimator of τ (of $r(\boldsymbol{\gamma})$).*

Note 3. We shall call these estimators "Best Quadratic Unbiased" (BQU) estimators.

Note 4. To find BQU estimators we follow the procedure outlined in Note 2 except the word "linear" is replaced by "homogeneous quadratic" throughout.

We now state a theorem about optimum properties of the least squares estimator of σ^2.

THEOREM 6.10.3

Consider the general linear model $\mathbf{Y} = \mathbf{X}\boldsymbol{\beta} + \boldsymbol{\varepsilon}$ with the following conditions on the random error vector $\boldsymbol{\varepsilon}$.

(1) $\mathscr{E}[\boldsymbol{\varepsilon}] = \mathbf{0}$;

(2) $var[\varepsilon_i] = \sigma^2$;

(3) $\mathscr{E}[\varepsilon_i^4] = 3\sigma^4$;

(4) $\varepsilon_1, \varepsilon_2, \ldots, \varepsilon_n$ *are jointly independent.* (6.10.3)

Then the BQU estimator of σ^2 is given by least squares, that is, is given by $\hat{\sigma}^2$ in Equation (6.10.2). *We assume* $\Omega = \{(\boldsymbol{\beta}, \sigma^2) : \boldsymbol{\beta} \in E_p, \sigma^2 > 0\}$.

Proof

The proof involves tedious algebra and will be omitted. A proof can be found in [G-6] and [H-20].

When the error vector $\boldsymbol{\varepsilon}$ satisfies Case 2, there are two methods that can be used to set confidence intervals and hence test hypotheses about the β_i. One method is to use asymptotic theory, and the other method is to use a distribution-free technique. For a distribution-free procedure see [S-8] and references contained in that paper.

For asymptotic methods, consider the sequence of general linear models, where the nth model is given by

$$\mathbf{Y}_n = \mathbf{X}_n\boldsymbol{\beta} + \boldsymbol{\varepsilon}_n \qquad n = p + 1, p + 2, \ldots$$

where $\mathbf{Y}_n$ is an $n \times 1$ vector of random observations, $\mathbf{X}_n$ is an $n \times p$ matrix of nonrandom observations of rank p, $\boldsymbol{\beta}$ is a $p \times 1$ vector of unknown parameters, and $\boldsymbol{\varepsilon}_n$ is an $n \times 1$ vector of unobservable random errors. We are interested in the asymptotic properties of the least squares estimator of $\boldsymbol{\beta}$ and σ^2. For any $n > p$, the least squares estimators are

$$\left.\begin{aligned} \hat{\boldsymbol{\beta}}_n &= (\mathbf{X}_n'\mathbf{X}_n)^{-1}\mathbf{X}_n'\mathbf{Y}_n \\ \hat{\sigma}_n^2 &= \left(\frac{1}{n - p}\right)\mathbf{Y}_n'[\mathbf{I} - \mathbf{X}_n(\mathbf{X}_n'\mathbf{X}_n)^{-1}\mathbf{X}_n']\mathbf{Y}_n \end{aligned}\right\} \quad n = p + 1, p + 2, \ldots \qquad (6.10.4)$$

Under quite general conditions on the sequence of errors $\{\boldsymbol{\varepsilon}_n\}$ and on the sequence of matrices $\{\mathbf{X}_n\}$, it can be proved that for large n the estimator $\hat{\boldsymbol{\beta}}_n$ is approximately normally distributed with vector mean $\boldsymbol{\beta}$ and covariance matrix $\hat{\sigma}_n^2(\mathbf{X}_n'\mathbf{X}_n)^{-1}$. When these assumptions are satisfied and when n is large, all the theorems for Case 1 of the linear model can be utilized and the results are approximately correct.

For details see [A-4] and [E-1].

6.11 Further Discussion of the Test $\mathbf{H\beta} = \mathbf{h}$

In this section we discuss the Lagrange multiplier method for deriving the test statistic W in Equation (6.3.9) and show that the expressions in Equations (6.3.10) and (6.3.11) are the same. We then derive the formula for W^* in Equation (6.5.5). If the reader is not interested in these proofs, this section and Problems 6.35 through 6.38 can be omitted.

6.11.1 The Lagrange Method

To demonstrate that the Lagrange multiplier technique can be used to obtain W in Equation (6.3.9), we must determine $L(\hat{\omega})$ by using Lagrange multipliers where

$$L(\hat{\omega}) = \max[L(\boldsymbol{\beta}, \sigma^2 : \mathbf{y}; \mathbf{X})] \qquad \text{for } (\boldsymbol{\beta}, \sigma^2) \text{ in } \omega$$

The value of $\boldsymbol{\beta}$ and σ^2 in ω, such that $L(\boldsymbol{\beta}, \sigma^2 : \mathbf{y}; \mathbf{X})$ is maximized, is obtained by setting to zero the partial derivatives with respect to $\boldsymbol{\beta}$, σ^2, and $\boldsymbol{\lambda}$ of $L = L(\boldsymbol{\beta}, \sigma^2 : \mathbf{y}; \mathbf{X}) - \boldsymbol{\lambda}'(\mathbf{H}\boldsymbol{\beta} - \mathbf{h})$ and solving the resulting equations. We get

$$\frac{\partial L}{\partial \boldsymbol{\beta}} = -(2\sigma^2)^{-1}(2\mathbf{X}'\mathbf{X}\boldsymbol{\beta} - 2\mathbf{X}'\mathbf{y})L(\boldsymbol{\beta}, \sigma^2 : \mathbf{y}; \mathbf{X}) - \mathbf{H}'\boldsymbol{\lambda}$$

$$\frac{\partial L}{\partial \sigma^2} = -\left(\frac{n}{2}\right)(\sigma^2)^{-1}L(\boldsymbol{\beta}, \sigma^2 : \mathbf{y}; \mathbf{X}) + \left(\frac{1}{2\sigma^4}\right)(\mathbf{y} - \mathbf{X}\boldsymbol{\beta})'(\mathbf{y} - \mathbf{X}\boldsymbol{\beta})L(\boldsymbol{\beta}, \sigma^2 : \mathbf{y}; \mathbf{X})$$

$$\frac{\partial L}{\partial \boldsymbol{\lambda}} = -(\mathbf{H}\boldsymbol{\beta} - \mathbf{h})$$

If we equate these derivatives to zero and let $\tilde{\boldsymbol{\beta}}_\omega$, $\tilde{\sigma}^2_\omega$, and $\tilde{\boldsymbol{\lambda}}$ denote the solution to the resulting equations, we get the expressions below (let $\boldsymbol{\lambda}^* = \tilde{\sigma}^2_\omega \tilde{\boldsymbol{\lambda}}/L(\tilde{\boldsymbol{\beta}}_\omega, \tilde{\sigma}^2_\omega : \mathbf{y}; \mathbf{X})$, and note that $L(\boldsymbol{\beta}, \sigma^2 : \mathbf{y}; \mathbf{X}) > 0$).

$$\begin{bmatrix} \mathbf{X}'\mathbf{X} & \mathbf{H}' \\ \mathbf{H} & \mathbf{0} \end{bmatrix} \begin{bmatrix} \tilde{\boldsymbol{\beta}}_\omega \\ \boldsymbol{\lambda}^* \end{bmatrix} = \begin{bmatrix} \mathbf{X}'\mathbf{y} \\ \mathbf{h} \end{bmatrix}$$
$$\tilde{\sigma}^2_\omega = \left(\frac{1}{n}\right)(\mathbf{y} - \mathbf{X}\tilde{\boldsymbol{\beta}}_\omega)'(\mathbf{y} - \mathbf{X}\tilde{\boldsymbol{\beta}}_\omega) \tag{6.11.1}$$

From these we get the solutions

$$\tilde{\boldsymbol{\beta}}_\omega = \mathbf{X}^-\mathbf{Y} - (\mathbf{X}'\mathbf{X})^{-1}\mathbf{H}'[\mathbf{H}(\mathbf{X}'\mathbf{X})^{-1}\mathbf{H}']^{-1}(\mathbf{H}\mathbf{X}^-\mathbf{Y} - \mathbf{h})$$
$$= \tilde{\boldsymbol{\beta}}_\Omega - (\mathbf{X}'\mathbf{X})^{-1}\mathbf{H}'[\mathbf{H}(\mathbf{X}'\mathbf{X})^{-1}\mathbf{H}']^{-1}(\mathbf{H}\tilde{\boldsymbol{\beta}}_\Omega - \mathbf{h}) \tag{6.11.2}$$
$$\tilde{\sigma}^2_\omega = \left(\frac{1}{n}\right)\{(\mathbf{Y} - \mathbf{X}\tilde{\boldsymbol{\beta}}_\Omega)'(\mathbf{Y} - \mathbf{X}\tilde{\boldsymbol{\beta}}_\Omega) + (\mathbf{H}\tilde{\boldsymbol{\beta}}_\Omega - \mathbf{h})'[\mathbf{H}(\mathbf{X}'\mathbf{X})^{-1}\mathbf{H}']^{-1}(\mathbf{H}\tilde{\boldsymbol{\beta}}_\Omega - \mathbf{h})\}$$
$$= \tilde{\sigma}^2_\Omega + \left(\frac{1}{n}\right)(\mathbf{H}\tilde{\boldsymbol{\beta}}_\Omega - \mathbf{h})'[\mathbf{H}(\mathbf{X}'\mathbf{X})^{-1}\mathbf{H}']^{-1}(\mathbf{H}\tilde{\boldsymbol{\beta}}_\Omega - \mathbf{h})$$

where $\tilde{\boldsymbol{\beta}}_\Omega = \mathbf{X}^-\mathbf{Y}$ is the M.L. estimator of $\boldsymbol{\beta}$ in the full model, $\tilde{\sigma}^2_\Omega$ is the M.L. estimator of σ^2 in the full model. If we substitute into Equation (6.3.8) and simplify, we get the test statistic W in Equation (6.3.9).

We now show by algebraic methods that the formula for the test statistic in Equation (6.3.8) is identical to the formula in Equation (6.3.9). We must show that

$$(\mathbf{H}\hat{\boldsymbol{\beta}} - \mathbf{h})'[\mathbf{H}(\mathbf{X}'\mathbf{X})^{-1}\mathbf{H}']^{-1}(\mathbf{H}\hat{\boldsymbol{\beta}} - \mathbf{h}) \tag{6.11.3}$$

in Equation (6.3.9) is equal to

$$\mathbf{Z}'(\mathbf{I} - \mathbf{B}\mathbf{B}^{-})\mathbf{Z} - \mathbf{Y}'(\mathbf{I} - \mathbf{X}\mathbf{X}^{-})\mathbf{Y} \tag{6.11.4}$$

in Equation (6.3.8), where $\hat{\boldsymbol{\beta}} = \mathbf{X}^{-}\mathbf{Y}$, $\mathbf{Z} = \mathbf{Y} - \mathbf{X}\mathbf{H}^{-}\mathbf{h}$, $\mathbf{B} = \mathbf{X}\mathbf{G}^{-}$, and $\mathbf{H}$ and $\mathbf{G}$ are defined in Section 6.3. First we note the following, which are easily proved.

1. $\mathbf{X}^{-}\mathbf{X} = \mathbf{I}$
2. $(\mathbf{H}\mathbf{X}^{-})(\mathbf{X}\mathbf{H}^{-}) = \mathbf{H}(\mathbf{X}^{-}\mathbf{X})\mathbf{H}^{-} = \mathbf{H}\mathbf{H}^{-} = \mathbf{I}$
3. $(\mathbf{H}\mathbf{X}^{-}\mathbf{Y} - \mathbf{h}) = \mathbf{H}\mathbf{X}^{-}(\mathbf{Y} - \mathbf{X}\mathbf{H}^{-}\mathbf{h})$
4. $[\mathbf{H}(\mathbf{X}'\mathbf{X})^{-1}\mathbf{H}']^{-1} = (\mathbf{H}\mathbf{X}^{-})'^{-}(\mathbf{H}\mathbf{X}^{-})^{-}$
5. $\mathbf{H}\hat{\boldsymbol{\beta}} = \mathbf{H}\mathbf{X}^{-}\mathbf{Y}$
6. $(\mathbf{H}\hat{\boldsymbol{\beta}} - \mathbf{h}) = \mathbf{H}\mathbf{X}^{-}(\mathbf{Y} - \mathbf{X}\mathbf{H}^{-}\mathbf{h})$ (6.11.5)

If we substitute into Equation (6.11.3) and simplify, we get

$$\begin{aligned}
&(\mathbf{H}\hat{\boldsymbol{\beta}} - \mathbf{h})'[\mathbf{H}(\mathbf{X}'\mathbf{X})^{-1}\mathbf{H}']^{-1}(\mathbf{H}\hat{\boldsymbol{\beta}} - \mathbf{h}) \\
&\quad = [(\mathbf{H}\mathbf{X}^{-})(\mathbf{Y} - \mathbf{X}\mathbf{H}^{-}\mathbf{h})]'[(\mathbf{H}\mathbf{X}^{-})'^{-}(\mathbf{H}\mathbf{X}^{-})^{-}](\mathbf{H}\mathbf{X}^{-})(\mathbf{Y} - \mathbf{X}\mathbf{H}^{-}\mathbf{h}) \\
&\quad = \mathbf{Z}'(\mathbf{H}\mathbf{X}^{-})^{-}(\mathbf{H}\mathbf{X}^{-})\mathbf{Z}
\end{aligned} \tag{6.11.6}$$

If we substitute for $\mathbf{B}$, $\mathbf{B}^{-}$, and $\mathbf{Z}$ in Equation (6.11.4) and simplify, we get

$$\begin{aligned}
\mathbf{Z}'(\mathbf{I} - \mathbf{B}\mathbf{B}^{-})\mathbf{Z} - \mathbf{Y}'(\mathbf{I} - \mathbf{X}\mathbf{X}^{-})\mathbf{Y} &= \mathbf{Z}'(\mathbf{X}\mathbf{X}^{-} - \mathbf{B}\mathbf{B}^{-})\mathbf{Z} \\
&= \mathbf{Z}'[\mathbf{X}\mathbf{X}^{-} - (\mathbf{X}\mathbf{G}^{-})(\mathbf{X}\mathbf{G}^{-})^{-}]\mathbf{Z}
\end{aligned} \tag{6.11.7}$$

So to prove the test statistics in Equations (6.3.8) and (6.3.9) are the same, we must show that Equations (6.11.6) and (6.11.7) are the same, and this means that we must prove

$$\mathbf{X}\mathbf{X}^{-} = (\mathbf{X}\mathbf{G}^{-})(\mathbf{X}\mathbf{G}^{-})^{-} + (\mathbf{H}\mathbf{X}^{-})^{-}(\mathbf{H}\mathbf{X}^{-}) \tag{6.11.8}$$

To do this we define the $n \times n$ matrix $\mathbf{N}$ by

$$\mathbf{N} = (\mathbf{X}\mathbf{G}^{-})(\mathbf{X}\mathbf{G}^{-})^{-} + (\mathbf{H}\mathbf{X}^{-})^{-}(\mathbf{H}\mathbf{X}^{-})$$

and we must prove that $\mathbf{N} = \mathbf{XX}^-$. It can be easily shown that

1. $(\mathbf{XG}^-)(\mathbf{XG}^-)^-$ is a symmetric idempotent matrix of rank $p - q$;
2. $(\mathbf{HX}^-)^-(\mathbf{HX}^-)$ is a symmetric idempotent matrix of rank q;
3. $[(\mathbf{HX}^-)^-(\mathbf{HX}^-)][(\mathbf{XG}^-)(\mathbf{XG}^-)^-] = \mathbf{0}$. (6.11.9)

Conditions 1, 2, and 3 imply

4. $\mathbf{N}$ is a symmetric idempotent matrix of rank p.

If we define a $p \times n$ matrix $\mathbf{A}$ by

$$\mathbf{A} = (\mathbf{X}'\mathbf{X})^{-1}\mathbf{H}'(\mathbf{HX}^-)'^- + \mathbf{G}^-(\mathbf{XG}^-)^- \tag{6.11.10}$$

then it is straightforward to show that

1. $\mathbf{XA} = \mathbf{N}$;
2. $\mathbf{A}$ has rank p;
3. $\mathbf{XAX} = \mathbf{X}$. (6.11.11)

We can now prove that $\mathbf{N} = \mathbf{XX}^-$ by the following:

$$\begin{aligned}\mathbf{XX}^- &= (\mathbf{XX}^-)' = [(\mathbf{XAX})\mathbf{X}^-]' = [(\mathbf{XA})(\mathbf{XX}^-)]' = (\mathbf{XX}^-)'(\mathbf{XA})' \\ &= \mathbf{XX}^-\mathbf{N}' = \mathbf{XX}^-\mathbf{N} = \mathbf{XX}^-\mathbf{XA} = \mathbf{XA} = \mathbf{N}\end{aligned}$$

This proves that W in Equation (6.3.8) is the same as W in Equation (6.3.9).

6.11.2 $\max[(\ell'\hat{\boldsymbol{\theta}})^2/\ell'\mathbf{V}\ell]$

In this section we prove the following theorem.

THEOREM 6.11.1

If $\hat{\boldsymbol{\theta}}$ is a given $q \times 1$ vector and $\mathbf{V}$ is a given positive definite $q \times q$ matrix, then

$$\max_{\ell \in E_q^*}\left[\frac{(\ell'\hat{\boldsymbol{\theta}})^2}{\ell'\mathbf{V}\ell}\right] = \hat{\boldsymbol{\theta}}'\mathbf{V}^{-1}\hat{\boldsymbol{\theta}}$$

where E_q^* is the set of all $q \times 1$ vectors except $\mathbf{0}$.

Proof

If $\hat{\boldsymbol{\theta}} = \mathbf{0}$, the proof is obvious; so assume $\hat{\boldsymbol{\theta}} \neq \mathbf{0}$. Denote $\hat{\boldsymbol{\theta}}\hat{\boldsymbol{\theta}}'$ by $\mathbf{A}$, which is a nonnegative matrix of rank 1, so $(\ell'\hat{\boldsymbol{\theta}})^2/\ell'\mathbf{V}\ell$ can be written as

$\ell'\hat{\boldsymbol{\theta}}\hat{\boldsymbol{\theta}}'\ell/\ell'\mathbf{V}\ell = \ell'\mathbf{A}\ell/\ell'\mathbf{V}\ell$. Since $\mathbf{V}$ is a positive definite matrix, there exists a nonsingular matrix $\mathbf{P}$ such that $\mathbf{P}'\mathbf{V}\mathbf{P} = \mathbf{I}$ and $\mathbf{P}'\mathbf{A}\mathbf{P} = \mathbf{D}$, where $\mathbf{D}$ is a diagonal matrix (of rank 1) with $d_{ii} = 0$ for $i > 1$ and $d_{11} > 0$. Let $\mathbf{k} = \mathbf{P}^{-1}\ell$; then $\mathbf{k}$ takes on every value in E_q^* as ℓ takes on every value in E_q^*. Substituting we get

$$\frac{\ell'\hat{\boldsymbol{\theta}}\hat{\boldsymbol{\theta}}'\ell}{\ell'\mathbf{V}\ell} = \frac{\ell'\mathbf{A}\ell}{\ell'\mathbf{V}\ell} = \frac{\mathbf{k}'\mathbf{P}'\mathbf{A}\mathbf{P}\mathbf{k}}{\mathbf{k}'\mathbf{P}'\mathbf{V}\mathbf{P}\mathbf{k}} = \frac{\mathbf{k}'\mathbf{D}\mathbf{k}}{\mathbf{k}'\mathbf{k}} = \frac{k_1^2 d_{11}}{\sum k_i^2} \le d_{11}$$

So d_{11} is an upper bound for $\ell'\hat{\boldsymbol{\theta}}\hat{\boldsymbol{\theta}}'\ell/\ell'\mathbf{V}\ell$ as ℓ varies over E_q^*. If we can show that for some values of ℓ in E_q^* this upper bound is attained, then d_{11} is the maximum we desire. Let $\ell = \mathbf{V}^{-1}\hat{\boldsymbol{\theta}}$; then

$$\frac{(\ell'\hat{\boldsymbol{\theta}})^2}{\ell'\mathbf{V}\ell} = \frac{(\hat{\boldsymbol{\theta}}'\mathbf{V}^{-1}\hat{\boldsymbol{\theta}})^2}{\hat{\boldsymbol{\theta}}'\mathbf{V}^{-1}\mathbf{V}\mathbf{V}^{-1}\hat{\boldsymbol{\theta}}} = \hat{\boldsymbol{\theta}}'\mathbf{V}^{-1}\hat{\boldsymbol{\theta}} = \mathrm{tr}\{\hat{\boldsymbol{\theta}}'\mathbf{V}^{-1}\hat{\boldsymbol{\theta}}\} = \mathrm{tr}\{\hat{\boldsymbol{\theta}}\hat{\boldsymbol{\theta}}'\mathbf{V}^{-1}\}$$

$$= \mathrm{tr}\{\mathbf{A}\mathbf{V}^{-1}\} = \mathrm{tr}\{\mathbf{A}\mathbf{P}\mathbf{P}'\} = \mathrm{tr}\{\mathbf{P}'\mathbf{A}\mathbf{P}\} = \mathrm{tr}\{\mathbf{D}\} = d_{11}$$

So

$$\max_{\ell \in E_q^*}\left\{\frac{(\ell'\hat{\boldsymbol{\theta}})^2}{\ell'\mathbf{V}^{-1}\ell}\right\} = \hat{\boldsymbol{\theta}}'\mathbf{V}^{-1}\hat{\boldsymbol{\theta}}$$

and this completes the proof.

Problems

6.1. In the model $\mathbf{Y} = \mathbf{X}\boldsymbol{\beta} + \boldsymbol{\varepsilon}$, $\boldsymbol{\varepsilon}$ is distributed $N(\boldsymbol{\varepsilon} : \mathbf{0}, \sigma^2\mathbf{I})$, where $n = 10$ and $p = 3$, the following normal equations were computed ($\mathbf{y}'\mathbf{y} = 58$).

$$\begin{aligned} 4\hat{\beta}_1 + 2\hat{\beta}_2 - 2\hat{\beta}_3 &= 4 \\ 2\hat{\beta}_1 + 2\hat{\beta}_2 + \hat{\beta}_3 &= 7 \\ -2\hat{\beta}_1 + \hat{\beta}_2 + 6\hat{\beta}_3 &= 9 \end{aligned}$$

(a) Find $\hat{\boldsymbol{\beta}}$ and $\hat{\sigma}^2$.
(b) Set 95 percent one-at-a-time confidence limits on β_1, β_2, β_3, $\beta_1 - \beta_2$, and $\beta_1 + \beta_3$.

6.2. In Problem 6.1 test $H_0 : 2\beta_1 + \beta_2 = 0,\ \beta_2 + 3\beta_3 = 0$ *vs.* $H_a : 2\beta_1 + \beta_2 \neq 0$ or $\beta_2 + 3\beta_3 \neq 0$. Use a Type I error probability of 0.05. Set 95 percent simultaneous confidence intervals on the two linear functions by the multivariate t method with $\mathbf{R} = \mathbf{I}$ in Equation (6.6.8).

6.3. In Problem 6.1 set 95 percent simultaneous confidence intervals on β_1, β_2, β_3, $\beta_1 - \beta_2$, and $\beta_1 + \beta_3$ by the method in Equation (6.5.10).

6.4. In storing ice cream at low temperatures, the average volume loss $\mathscr{E}[Y]$ of the ice cream (in 100-cubic-centimeter containers) is related to the storage time by the linear model $Y = \beta t + \varepsilon$. An experiment is conducted and the volume loss of ice cream over an extended period is measured. The results (t in weeks, y in cubic centimeters) are given below.

t_i	1	2	3	4	5	6	7	8
y_i	2.10	2.81	3.04	3.10	6.24	8.01	5.79	8.38

Estimate β and σ^2. Compute 95 percent one-at-a-time confidence intervals on β and σ^2. Assume the ε_i are $NID(\varepsilon : 0, \sigma^2)$.

6.5. In Problem 6.4 test $H_0 : \beta = 0$ *vs.* $H_a : \beta \neq 0$. Use $\alpha = 0.05$.

6.6. In Problem 6.5 find the power of the test when $\beta/\sigma = 0.2$.

6.7. Fill in the details of the proof of Theorem 6.2.3.

6.8. Consider the simple linear model $Y_i = \beta_0 + \beta x_i + \varepsilon_i$, where the ε_i are distributed $NID(\varepsilon : 0, \sigma^2)$ and the x_i values are $1, 2, 3, \ldots$, that is, $X_i = i$. Are $\hat{\sigma}_n^2$, $\ell_1'\hat{\boldsymbol{\beta}}_n$, and $\ell_2'\hat{\boldsymbol{\beta}}_n$ mean-squared-error consistent estimators of σ^2, β_0, and β, respectively, where $\ell_1' = [1, 0]$ and $\ell_2' = [0, 1]$? Prove your answers by finding the limits of the appropriate expectations and variances.

6.9. In Problem 6.4 if $\hat{\sigma}^2$ is assumed to be the true value σ^2, determine n so that the expected width squared of the confidence interval on β is equal to 0.1.

6.10. In Problem 6.4 set 95 percent bands on the entire line.

6.11. In the simple linear model $Y_i = \beta_0 + \beta x_i + \varepsilon_i$, $i = 1, 2, \ldots, n > 2$, prove that $\text{var}[\hat{\beta}_0]$ is a minimum if the x_i are chosen so that $\bar{x} = 0$.

6.12. In Problem 6.11 prove the following: If the x_i can be selected anywhere in the interval $[a, b]$, and if n is an even integer, then the variance of $\hat{\beta}$ is minimized if $n/2$ values of x_i are selected equal to a and $n/2$ values equal to b.

6.13. Show that the test statistic W in Equation (6.3.10) is unchanged if $H_0 : \mathbf{H}\boldsymbol{\beta} = \mathbf{h}$ *vs.* $H_a : \mathbf{H}\boldsymbol{\beta} \neq \mathbf{h}$ is replaced by $H_0 : \mathbf{QH}\boldsymbol{\beta} = \mathbf{Qh}$ *vs.* $H_a : \mathbf{QH}\boldsymbol{\beta} \neq \mathbf{Qh}$, where $\mathbf{Q}$ is any $q \times q$ nonsingular matrix.

6.14. If $\mathbf{X}$ is an $n \times p$ matrix of rank p and if $\mathbf{H}$ is a $q \times p$ matrix of rank q, prove that $\mathbf{H}(\mathbf{X}'\mathbf{X})^{-1}\mathbf{H}'$ has an inverse. Is $\mathbf{H}(\mathbf{X}'\mathbf{X})^{-1}\mathbf{H}'$ positive definite? Prove your answer.

6.15. In Equation (6.4.2) find the distribution of L^2, the square of the length of the confidence interval.

6.16. In Problem 6.15 find var[L].

6.17. In Problem 6.15 find the distribution of L.

6.18. In Example 6.5.3 exhibit two distinct **H** matrices, say $\mathbf{H}_1$ and $\mathbf{H}_2$, that could be used if one was interested in simultaneous confidence intervals on all linear combinations of β_0 and $\beta_1 + \beta_2$.

6.19. Exhibit two vectors ℓ_{11} and ℓ_{12} for confidence intervals on β_0 and $\beta_1 + \beta_2$ when using the matrix $\mathbf{H}_1$ in Problem 6.18. Exhibit two vectors when the matrix $\mathbf{H}_2$ is used.

6.20. Prove the confidence interval statement in Equation (6.5.11).

6.21. Prove the confidence interval statement in Equation (6.5.12).

6.22. In the proof of Theorem 6.6.1, complete the proof by performing the integration of $f_{\mathbf{t},U}(\mathbf{t}, u)$ with respect to u from 0 to ∞ to show that $f_{\mathbf{t}}(\mathbf{t})$ is given by Equation (6.6.2).

6.23. In the example in Section 6.7, find simultaneous 0.95 confidence intervals on β_0 and $\beta_0 + \beta$ by using the method described in Section 6.5, that is, use Equation (6.5.10).

6.24. In Problem 6.2 find *exact* 95 percent simultaneous confidence limits on $\theta_1 = 2\beta_1 + \beta_2$ and $\theta_2 = \beta_2 + 3\beta_3$ by using the tables in *Biometrika*, vol. 58, page 323, if they are available.

6.25. For the general linear model $\mathbf{Y} = \mathbf{X}\boldsymbol{\beta} + \boldsymbol{\varepsilon}$, $\boldsymbol{\varepsilon}$ is distributed $N(\boldsymbol{\varepsilon} : \mathbf{0}, \sigma^2\mathbf{V})$, where $\mathbf{V}$ is a known positive definite matrix, show how the test statistic W in Equation (6.3.10) is modified to test $H_0 : \mathbf{H}\boldsymbol{\beta} = \mathbf{h}$ *vs*. $H_a : \mathbf{H}\boldsymbol{\beta} \neq \mathbf{h}$.

6.26. Prove Equation (6.6.9).

6.27. Find the expected width of the confidence interval on β in terms of σ^2 in the example in Section 6.7.

6.28. Consider the following data that are assumed to come from the model $Y_i = \beta_0 + \beta_1 x_{i1} + \beta_2 x_{i2} + \varepsilon_i$, ε_i are distributed $NID(\varepsilon : 0, \sigma^2)$.

y	12.1	5.5	4.6	4.5	10.8	4.9	6.0	4.2	5.3	6.7	4.0	6.1
x_1	0.870	0.202	0.203	0.198	0.730	0.510	0.205	0.670	0.205	0.271	0.203	0.264
x_2	1.69	1.17	1.17	1.21	1.63	1.59	1.14	1.92	1.22	1.71	1.16	1.37

(a) Compute the normal equations.

(b) Find $\hat{\boldsymbol{\beta}}$, $\hat{\sigma}^2$, and $\hat{\mu}(\mathbf{x})$.

(c) Find the point estimates of $\ell_1'\boldsymbol{\beta}$ and $\ell_2'\boldsymbol{\beta}$, where $\ell_1' = [0, 1, -1]$ and $\ell_2' = [0, 1, 2]$.

(d) Test $H_0 : \beta_0 - 2\beta_2 = 0$, $\beta_0 = 8.00$ *vs.* $H_a : \beta_0 - 2\beta_2 \neq 0$ or $\beta_0 \neq 8.00$ with $\alpha = 0.05$.

(e) Set one-at-a-time 0.95 confidence intervals on β_0, β_1, and β_2.

(f) Set simultaneous 0.95 confidence intervals on β_0, β_1, and β_2. Use Equation (6.5.10).

(g) Set simultaneous 0.95 confidence intervals on β_0, β_1, and β_2. Use Equation (6.6.8).

6.29. Consider the model $Y_i = \mu(x) + \varepsilon = \beta_0 + \beta_1 x_i + \varepsilon_i$, ε_i are distributed $NID(\varepsilon : 0, \sigma^2)$. Use the data for y and x_1 in Problem 6.28. Find the equations for 0.95 confidence bands on the entire line $\mu(x)$. Plot the bands.

6.30. Work through the details of the proof of Corollary 6.8.1.1.

6.31. Work through the details of the proof of Corollary 6.8.1.2.

6.32. In Note 2 in Section 6.8, prove that $\boldsymbol{\Sigma}$ is p.d. if and only if $-1/(n-1) < \rho < 1$.

6.33. In Problem 6.28 compute the residual vector.

6.34. In Problem 6.33 plot the residuals versus x_1; versus x_2; versus y.

6.35. Prove the six statements in Equation (6.11.5).

6.36. Prove the four statements in Equation (6.11.9).

6.37. Prove the statements in Equation (6.11.11). Hint: Show that $\mathbf{N} = \mathbf{N}^2$ and $\mathbf{A}$ is $p \times n$ of rank p; hence $\mathbf{AA}^- = \mathbf{I}$.

6.38. Prove that $\tilde{\boldsymbol{\beta}}_\omega$ in Equation (6.11.2) is the solution to the matrix equation in Equation (6.11.1). Find $\boldsymbol{\lambda}^*$.

CHAPTER 7

Computing Techniques

7.1 Introduction

To obtain the values of point estimators of $\boldsymbol{\beta}$ and σ^2, or to obtain the values of test statistics or confidence intervals in the general linear model, often requires a significant amount of computing of the basic data in the $\mathbf{X}$ matrix and $\mathbf{y}$ vector. In this chapter computing techniques are discussed that will enable one to perform most of the computations needed for statistical procedures considered in this book.

There are a number of methods available to perform the computations required in the general linear model, and the decision as to which method to use depends on several factors: (1) the amount of data (the values of n and p); (2) how "ill-conditioned" the $\mathbf{X}$ matrix is; (3) what statistics are needed; (4) the type of computing equipment that is available. The problem of computation in the linear model is not a statistical problem, but rather a problem in numerical analysis and computing science. However, statisticians who apply linear model theory to real problems should be aware of some of the important aspects of the required computations and understand some of the computing techniques.

One basic point of departure is the normal equations

$$\mathbf{X}'\mathbf{X}\hat{\boldsymbol{\beta}} = \mathbf{X}'\mathbf{y} \tag{7.1.1}$$

which we write as

$$\mathbf{S}\hat{\boldsymbol{\beta}} = \mathbf{s}$$

where S is a positive definite matrix. From this system we compute point estimates $\ell'\hat{\boldsymbol{\beta}}$ and $\hat{\sigma}^2$ and the estimated covariance matrix of $\ell'\hat{\boldsymbol{\beta}}$, namely $\hat{\sigma}^2\ell'(\mathbf{X}'\mathbf{X})^{-1}\ell$.

The method we shall use for solving Equation (7.1.1) uses the fact that **S** can be factored into the product of two matrices, that is, $\mathbf{S} = \mathbf{AB}$, where **B** is an upper triangular matrix and **A** is a lower triangular matrix. Thus the original system can be written as

$$\mathbf{AB}\hat{\boldsymbol{\beta}} = \mathbf{s}$$

and we perform row operations on the system that are equivalent to multiplying on the left by $\mathbf{A}^{-1}$. The result is

$$\mathbf{B}\hat{\boldsymbol{\beta}} = \mathbf{A}^{-1}\mathbf{s}$$

and since **B** is a triangular matrix, the resulting system is easily solved for $\hat{\boldsymbol{\beta}}$.

Several procedures for factoring **S** are available; three of these are the following:

1. Gaussian elimination;
2. Doolittle;
3. square root (Cholesky).

Another point of departure is to start directly with the **X** matrix and **y** vector and not compute the normal equations. Two computing procedures that can be used are the following:

1. Gram-Schmidt orthogonalization;
2. orthogonal Householder transformation.

All these methods are called *exact* methods since the desired computations are performed using a finite number of arithmetic operations. However, the exact solutions are generally not obtained; it is usually impossible to perform the exact arithmetic operations since decimal approximations must be used in place of the actual numbers and since round-off error may be impossible to avoid.

In solving linear equations or in inverting matrices, the round-off error can be a most troublesome factor. In fact, for an "ill-conditioned" matrix, the round-off error can virtually prevent one from obtaining a solution that is "close" to the true value $\hat{\boldsymbol{\beta}}$ or $\mathbf{S}^{-1}$. A matrix is called "ill-conditioned" if the entries are such that a "very small" change in one or more elements in **S** produces a "significantly large" change in the solution vector $\hat{\boldsymbol{\beta}}$ or $\mathbf{S}^{-1}$ (see [F-1] for a discussion of ill-conditioned matrices).

It is a fact that if the matrix **X** is ill-conditioned, then $\mathbf{X}'\mathbf{X}$ is apt to be "more" ill-conditioned. Hence, since $\hat{\boldsymbol{\beta}}$ is equal to $\mathbf{X}^{-}\mathbf{y}$, a good method for computing

$\hat{\boldsymbol{\beta}}$ is to compute $\mathbf{X}^-$ directly rather than to compute $\hat{\boldsymbol{\beta}}$ from the normal equations (since they involve $\mathbf{X}'\mathbf{X}$). We shall not use this method but we briefly discuss it in Section 7.7.

We shall describe the *square root method* in detail and show how it can be used to compute the quantities necessary for point estimates, test statistics, and confidence intervals from the normal equations of the general linear model. The reasons we choose the square root method are threefold:

1. It is one of the best methods (small number of computations and storage requirements balanced with good accuracy) for factoring positive definite and semidefinite matrices (for solving the normal equations).
2. The square root method is very easy to describe and use. The method can be used with large computers, or with mechanical, electric, or programmable desk calculators when they have a square root device (most calculators do have this device), or with small hand-held calculators.
3. If the data matrix $\mathbf{X}$ is very large or ill-conditioned, one of the best methods for use with large computers is the orthogonal Householder transformation method. When this method is used, the normal equations are not computed (that is, $\mathbf{X}'\mathbf{X}$ is not computed), but the computations are performed directly on the data matrix $\mathbf{X}$, and this is related to the square root method, as we shall show in Section 7.7.

7.2 Square Root Method of Factoring a Positive Definite Matrix

We state a theorem that will allow us to write $\mathbf{S}$ as $\mathbf{T}'\mathbf{T}$, where $\mathbf{T}$ is a unique $p \times p$ upper triangular matrix.

THEOREM 7.2.1

Let $\mathbf{S} = \mathbf{X}'\mathbf{X}$ *be a* $p \times p$ *positive definite matrix. There exists an upper triangular matrix* $\mathbf{T}$ *of rank* p *such that*

$$\mathbf{S} = \mathbf{T}'\mathbf{T} \tag{7.2.1}$$

and such that $t_{ii} > 0$ *for* $i = 1, 2, \ldots, p$. *Also, the matrix* $\mathbf{T}$ *is unique*

Proof

The proof is found in Section 7.7.

To find the formulas to evaluate **T** from a knowledge of **S**, we write $\mathbf{S} = \mathbf{T}'\mathbf{T}$ in detail and get

$$\begin{bmatrix} s_{11} & s_{12} & s_{13} & \cdots & s_{1p} \\ s_{21} & s_{22} & s_{23} & \cdots & s_{2p} \\ s_{31} & s_{32} & s_{33} & \cdots & s_{3p} \\ \vdots & \vdots & \vdots & & \vdots \\ s_{p1} & s_{p2} & s_{p3} & \cdots & s_{pp} \end{bmatrix} = \begin{bmatrix} t_{11} & 0 & 0 & \cdots & 0 \\ t_{12} & t_{22} & 0 & \cdots & 0 \\ t_{13} & t_{23} & t_{33} & \cdots & 0 \\ \vdots & \vdots & \vdots & & \vdots \\ t_{1p} & t_{2p} & t_{3p} & \cdots & t_{pp} \end{bmatrix} \begin{bmatrix} t_{11} & t_{12} & t_{13} & \cdots & t_{1p} \\ 0 & t_{22} & t_{23} & \cdots & t_{2p} \\ 0 & 0 & t_{33} & \cdots & t_{3p} \\ \vdots & \vdots & \vdots & & \vdots \\ 0 & 0 & 0 & \cdots & t_{pp} \end{bmatrix} \tag{7.2.2}$$

where $s_{ij} = s_{ji}$.

If we equate the (i, j)th elements on the left and right sides of Equation (7.2.2) in a certain order, we get formulas for t_{ij} in terms of s_{ij}. We get

1. $t_{11} = \sqrt{s_{11}}$;
2. $t_{1j} = \dfrac{s_{1j}}{t_{11}} = \dfrac{s_{1j}}{\sqrt{s_{11}}}, \; j = 2, 3, \ldots, p$;
3. $t_{ii} = \sqrt{s_{ii} - \sum_{k=1}^{i-1} t_{ki}^2}, \; i = 2, 3, \ldots, p$;
4. $t_{ij} = \dfrac{1}{t_{ii}}\left[s_{ij} - \sum_{k=1}^{i-1} t_{ki}t_{kj}\right], \; j > i$ and $i = 2, 3, \ldots, p - 1$;
5. $t_{ij} = 0, \; j < i$ and $i = 2, 3, \ldots, p.$ (7.2.3)

The computations are done in the following order.

1. Compute the (1, 1) element in **T** as the square root of s_{11} by formula 1.
2. Next compute the elements in the first row of **T** by formula 2.
3. Each element below the diagonal in **T** is zero by formula 5, so they need not be computed.
4. Compute t_{22} by formula 3. Only the element s_{22} and the element t_{12} in the first row of **T** that is already computed are needed in the formula.
5. Compute the remaining elements in row two of **T** by formula 4.
6. Proceed by computing a diagonal element of **T** by formula 3 and then compute all remaining elements in that *row* by formula 4.

We will illustrate with a simple example.

Example 7.2.1

Find $\mathbf{T}$ such that $\mathbf{T'T} = \mathbf{S}$, where $\mathbf{S}$ is the positive definite matrix below.

$$\mathbf{S} = \begin{bmatrix} 16 & 8 & 12 & -4 \\ 8 & 5 & 11 & -4 \\ 12 & 11 & 70 & -31 \\ -4 & -4 & -31 & 63 \end{bmatrix}$$

1. By formula 1 we get $t_{11} = \sqrt{s_{11}} = 4$.
2. By formula 2 we get $t_{12} = \dfrac{s_{12}}{t_{11}} = \dfrac{8}{4} = 2$; $t_{13} = \dfrac{s_{13}}{t_{11}} = \dfrac{12}{4} = 3$;

$$t_{14} = \frac{s_{14}}{t_{11}} = \frac{-4}{4} = -1.$$

3. By formula 5 we get $t_{21} = t_{31} = t_{32} = t_{41} = t_{42} = t_{43} = 0$.
4. By formula 3 we get $t_{22} = \sqrt{s_{22} - t_{12}^2} = \sqrt{5 - 2^2} = 1$.
5. By formula 4 we get $t_{23} = \dfrac{1}{t_{22}}[s_{23} - t_{12}t_{13}] = \dfrac{1}{1}[11 - 6] = 5$;

$$t_{24} = \frac{1}{t_{22}}[s_{24} - t_{12}t_{14}] = \frac{1}{1}[-4 - (2)(-1)] = -2.$$

6. By formula 3 we get $t_{33} = \sqrt{s_{33} - t_{13}^2 - t_{23}^2} = \sqrt{70 - 3^2 - 5^2} = 6$.
7. By formula 4 we get $t_{34} = \dfrac{1}{t_{33}}[s_{34} - t_{13}t_{14} - t_{23}t_{24}]$

$$= \frac{1}{6}[-31 - (3)(-1) - (5)(-2)] = -3.$$

8. By formula 3 we get $t_{44} = \sqrt{s_{44} - t_{14}^2 - t_{24}^2 - t_{34}^2}$

$$= \sqrt{63 - (-1)^2 - (-2)^2 - (-3)^2} = 7.$$

Thus

$$\mathbf{T} = \begin{bmatrix} 4 & 2 & 3 & -1 \\ 0 & 1 & 5 & -2 \\ 0 & 0 & 6 & -3 \\ 0 & 0 & 0 & 7 \end{bmatrix}$$

and it is easily verified that $\mathbf{T'T} = \mathbf{S}$.

For hand-held calculators or desk calculators that have no printing device, or for illustrative purposes, a useful procedure is to write **S** with elements below the main diagonal omitted (they are not needed) and write the elements of **T** below **S** as they are computed. For the example above we get

$$\begin{bmatrix} 16 & 8 & 12 & -4 \\ & 5 & 11 & -4 \\ & & 70 & -31 \\ & & & 63 \\ \hline 4 & 2 & 3 & -1 \\ & 1 & 5 & -2 \\ & & 6 & -3 \\ & & & 7 \end{bmatrix} = \begin{bmatrix} \mathbf{S} \\ \hline \mathbf{T} \end{bmatrix}$$

To compute any *diagonal* element of **T** (say t_{33}), use s_{33} (the corresponding diagonal element of **S**) minus the sum of the squares of all elements in column three of **T** that have been computed so far; then take the square root of the result. For example, $t_{33} = \sqrt{70 - 3^2 - 5^2} = 6$. To compute any t_{ij} with $j > i$ (any off-diagonal element in **T** above the diagonal), we must have already computed the diagonal element in that row, that is, t_{ii}. Then t_{ij} is s_{ij} (the corresponding element in **S**) minus the cumulative products of all elements in the ith column and jth column of **T** that have been computed so far. Then divide the result by the diagonal element t_{ii}. For example,

$$t_{34} = \frac{[s_{34} - t_{13}t_{14} - t_{23}t_{24}]}{t_{33}} = \frac{[-31 - (3)(-1) - (5)(-2)]}{6} = -3$$

Since by row operations on **S**, the matrix **S** is reduced to an upper triangular matrix **T**, and since $\mathbf{S} = \mathbf{T}'\mathbf{T}$, these row operations are equivalent to multiplying **S** on the left by the matrix $\mathbf{T}'^{-1}$. Suppose that **S** is augmented by a column vector $\mathbf{s} = \mathbf{X}'\mathbf{y}$; if we reduce this column by formula 4 in Equation (7.2.3), we obtain a $p \times 1$ vector **t**, where

$$\begin{aligned} t_1 &= \frac{s_1}{\sqrt{s_{11}}} = \frac{s_1}{t_{11}} \\ t_i &= \frac{1}{t_{ii}}\left[s_i - \sum_{k=1}^{i-1} t_k t_{ki}\right] \qquad i = 2, 3, \ldots, p \end{aligned} \tag{7.2.4}$$

Thus the matrix $[\mathbf{S} \mid \mathbf{s}]$ becomes $[\mathbf{T} \mid \mathbf{t}]$ by the operations in Equation (7.2.3) and Equation (7.2.4). We will illustrate with a simple example.

Example 7.2.2

Consider the normal equations $\mathbf{S}\hat{\boldsymbol{\beta}} = \mathbf{s}$, where the format $[\mathbf{S} \mid \mathbf{s}]$ is given below.

$$\left[\begin{array}{ccc|c} 4 & 2 & -4 & 12 \\ 2 & 10 & 4 & 6 \\ -4 & 4 & 9 & -15 \end{array}\right]$$

After reducing the system by the square root method, we get $[\mathbf{T} \mid \mathbf{t}]$, which is

$$\left[\begin{array}{ccc|c} 2 & 1 & -2 & 6 \\ & 3 & 2 & 0 \\ & & 1 & -3 \end{array}\right] \tag{7.2.5}$$

For example, $t_1 = s_1/t_{11} = 12/2 = 6$; $t_2 = [s_2 - t_1 t_{12}]/t_{22} = [6 - (6)(1)]/3 = 0$; $t_3 = [s_3 - t_1 t_{13} - t_2 t_{23}]/t_{33} = [-15 - (6)(-2) - (0)(2)]/1 = -3$.

The principal reason for reducing a matrix $\mathbf{S} = \mathbf{X}'\mathbf{X} = \mathbf{T}'\mathbf{T}$ to a triangular matrix is that a system of equations with a triangular coefficient matrix is very easy to solve. For example, from the system $\mathbf{X}'\mathbf{X}\hat{\boldsymbol{\beta}} = \mathbf{X}'\mathbf{y}$, we can write $\mathbf{T}'\mathbf{T}\hat{\boldsymbol{\beta}} = \mathbf{X}'\mathbf{y}$, and reducing this by the square root method is equivalent to multiplying on the left by $\mathbf{T}'^{-1}$. This gives us $\mathbf{T}\hat{\boldsymbol{\beta}} = \mathbf{T}'^{-1}\mathbf{X}'\mathbf{y}$, or $\mathbf{T}\hat{\boldsymbol{\beta}} = \mathbf{t}$. From this it is easy to solve for $\hat{\boldsymbol{\beta}}$. If we write this in detail, we get

$$\begin{aligned} t_{11}\hat{\beta}_1 + t_{12}\hat{\beta}_2 + t_{13}\hat{\beta}_3 + \cdots + t_{1p}\hat{\beta}_p &= t_1 \\ t_{22}\hat{\beta}_2 + t_{23}\hat{\beta}_3 + \cdots + t_{2p}\hat{\beta}_p &= t_2 \\ &\vdots \\ t_{p-1,p-1}\hat{\beta}_{p-1} + t_{p-1,p}\hat{\beta}_p &= t_{p-1} \\ t_{pp}\hat{\beta}_p &= t_p \end{aligned}$$

The solution is

$$\begin{aligned} \hat{\beta}_p &= \frac{t_p}{t_{pp}} \\ \hat{\beta}_{p-1} &= \frac{[t_{p-1} - t_{p-1,p}\hat{\beta}_p]}{t_{p-1,p-1}} \\ &\vdots \\ \hat{\beta}_1 &= \frac{[t_1 - t_{1p}\hat{\beta}_p - t_{1,p-1}\hat{\beta}_{p-1} - \cdots - t_{12}\hat{\beta}_2]}{t_{11}} \end{aligned}$$

From the triangular system in Equation (7.2.5), we get

$$\hat{\beta}_3 = \frac{-3}{1} = -3$$

$$\hat{\beta}_2 = \frac{0 - 2(-3)}{3} = 2$$

$$\hat{\beta}_1 = \frac{6 - (-2)(-3) - (1)(2)}{2} = -1$$

If one is using a calculator with no printing device, the quantities in $\hat{\boldsymbol{\beta}}$ can conveniently be written below the matrix **T** as they are computed. They are computed in reverse order, $\hat{\beta}_p, \hat{\beta}_{p-1}, \ldots, \hat{\beta}_1$. For example, from Equation (7.2.5), suppose $\hat{\beta}_3$ and $\hat{\beta}_2$ have been computed; the result at this stage is

$$\begin{array}{rrr|r} 2 & 1 & -2 & 6 \\ & 3 & 2 & 0 \\ & & 1 & -3 \\ \hline \end{array}$$

$$\hat{\boldsymbol{\beta}}' = [\quad 2 \quad -3]$$

and to compute $\hat{\beta}_1$ we write $[6 - (-2)(-3) - (1)(2)]/2 = -1$, that is, $\hat{\beta}_1 = [t_1 - t_{13}\hat{\beta}_3 - t_{12}\hat{\beta}_2]/t_{11}$.

Up to now we have concentrated on computing $\hat{\boldsymbol{\beta}}$ only. However, in the next section we show how a solution to the normal equations can be used to advantage to compute other quantities needed in the general linear model.

7.3 Computing Point Estimates, Test Statistics, and Confidence Intervals

The quantities we need for point estimates, test statistics, and confidence intervals are the following:

Point Estimates

1. $\hat{\boldsymbol{\beta}}, \boldsymbol{\ell}'\hat{\boldsymbol{\beta}}$.

2. $\hat{\sigma}^2 = \dfrac{1}{n-p}[\mathbf{y}'\mathbf{y} - \hat{\boldsymbol{\beta}}'\mathbf{X}'\mathbf{y}] = \dfrac{1}{n-p}[\mathbf{y}'\mathbf{y} - \mathbf{y}'\mathbf{X}\mathbf{X}^{-}\mathbf{y}]$.

Test Statistics and Confidence Intervals

3. $\hat{\sigma}^2$, $\boldsymbol{\ell}_i'\hat{\boldsymbol{\beta}}$, and $\boldsymbol{\ell}_i'(\mathbf{X}'\mathbf{X})^{-1}\boldsymbol{\ell}_i$, $i = 1, 2, \ldots, q$, for one-at-a-time and simultaneous confidence intervals.
4. $\mathbf{H}\hat{\boldsymbol{\beta}} - \mathbf{h}$, $[\mathbf{H}(\mathbf{X}'\mathbf{X})^{-1}\mathbf{H}']^{-1}$, $\hat{\sigma}^2$, and w in Equation (6.3.10) to test $H_0 : \mathbf{H}\boldsymbol{\beta} = \mathbf{h}$. (7.3.1)

We shall discuss these in turn.

1. $\hat{\boldsymbol{\beta}}$ is computed by the methods described in Section 7.2.
2. To compute $\hat{\sigma}^2$, the quantity $\mathbf{y}'\mathbf{y}$ is easily computed from the $\mathbf{y}$ vector. If $\hat{\boldsymbol{\beta}}$ is computed, then $\hat{\boldsymbol{\beta}}'\mathbf{X}'\mathbf{y}$ is merely the sum of p cross products and is easily computed. However, $\hat{\boldsymbol{\beta}}'\mathbf{X}'\mathbf{y}$ can be computed very easily without evaluating $\hat{\boldsymbol{\beta}}$. From the normal equations $[\mathbf{S} \mid \mathbf{s}]$, we reduce $\mathbf{S}$ to the triangular matrix $\mathbf{T}$ and we get

$$[\mathbf{T} \mid \mathbf{t}] = \mathbf{T}'^{-1}[\mathbf{S} \mid \mathbf{s}] = \mathbf{T}'^{-1}[\mathbf{X}'\mathbf{X} \mid \mathbf{X}'\mathbf{y}]$$

and

$$\begin{aligned} \mathbf{t}'\mathbf{t} &= [\mathbf{T}'^{-1}\mathbf{s}]'[\mathbf{T}'^{-1}\mathbf{s}] = \mathbf{s}'\mathbf{T}^{-1}\mathbf{T}'^{-1}\mathbf{s} = \mathbf{y}'\mathbf{X}(\mathbf{X}'\mathbf{X})^{-1}\mathbf{X}'\mathbf{y} \\ &= \mathbf{y}'\mathbf{X}\mathbf{X}^{-}\mathbf{y} = \hat{\boldsymbol{\beta}}'\mathbf{X}'\mathbf{y} \end{aligned} \tag{7.3.2}$$

Thus

$$\hat{\sigma}^2 = \frac{1}{n - p}[\mathbf{y}'\mathbf{y} - \mathbf{t}'\mathbf{t}] \tag{7.3.3}$$

Even if $\hat{\boldsymbol{\beta}}$ is computed, the quantity $\mathbf{t}'\mathbf{t}$ may be easier to compute and more accurate than $\hat{\boldsymbol{\beta}}'\mathbf{X}'\mathbf{y}$; $\mathbf{t}'\mathbf{t}$ can also be used as a check on $\hat{\boldsymbol{\beta}}'\mathbf{X}'\mathbf{y}$.

3. In general, it is a relatively large task to compute $(\mathbf{X}'\mathbf{X})^{-1}$ and $\boldsymbol{\ell}_i'(\mathbf{X}'\mathbf{X})^{-1}\boldsymbol{\ell}_i$. We present a method for computing $\boldsymbol{\ell}_i'(\mathbf{X}'\mathbf{X})^{-1}\boldsymbol{\ell}_i$, $i = 1, 2, \ldots, q$, without actually computing $(\mathbf{X}'\mathbf{X})^{-1}$. Use the format

$$[\mathbf{S} \mid \mathbf{s} \mid \boldsymbol{\ell}_1, \boldsymbol{\ell}_2, \ldots, \boldsymbol{\ell}_q] \tag{7.3.4}$$

and reduce $\mathbf{S}$ to an upper triangular matrix. The result is

$$\mathbf{T}'^{-1}[\mathbf{S} \mid \mathbf{s} \mid \boldsymbol{\ell}_1, \boldsymbol{\ell}_2, \ldots, \boldsymbol{\ell}_q] = [\mathbf{T} \mid \mathbf{t} \mid \mathbf{a}_1, \mathbf{a}_2, \ldots, \mathbf{a}_q] \tag{7.3.5}$$

where $\mathbf{a}_i = \mathbf{T}'^{-1}\boldsymbol{\ell}_i$, $\mathbf{t} = \mathbf{T}'^{-1}\mathbf{X}'\mathbf{y}$. Now we have the following:

(a) $\mathbf{t}'\mathbf{t} = \hat{\boldsymbol{\beta}}'\mathbf{X}'\mathbf{y} = \mathbf{y}'(\mathbf{X}\mathbf{X}^{-})\mathbf{y}$;

(b) $\mathbf{a}_i'\mathbf{a}_i = \ell_i'\mathbf{T}^{-1}\mathbf{T}'^{-1}\ell_i = \ell_i'(\mathbf{X}'\mathbf{X})^{-1}\ell_i = \ell_i'\mathbf{C}\ell_i$;

(c) $\mathbf{a}_i'\mathbf{t} = \ell_i'\mathbf{T}^{-1}\mathbf{T}'^{-1}\mathbf{X}'\mathbf{y} = \ell_i'(\mathbf{X}'\mathbf{X})^{-1}\mathbf{X}'\mathbf{y} = \ell_i'\mathbf{X}^{-}\mathbf{y} = \ell_i'\hat{\boldsymbol{\beta}}$;

(d) $\hat{\sigma}^2 = \dfrac{1}{n-p}[\mathbf{y}'\mathbf{y} - \mathbf{t}'\mathbf{t}]$.

So all the quantities needed for one-at-a-time and simultaneous confidence intervals can be computed by a simple sum of squares or a sum of cross products of the columns of the matrix in Equation (7.3.5), which is obtained by reducing the matrix in Equation (7.3.4) by the square root method.

Before discussing part 4 of Equation (7.3.1), we will illustrate parts 1, 2, and 3 with a simple example.

Example 7.3.1

Consider the model

$$Y_i = \beta_1 x_{i1} + \beta_2 x_{i2} + \beta_3 x_{i3} + \beta_4 x_{i4} + \varepsilon_i$$
$$\varepsilon_i \text{ are distributed } NID(\varepsilon : 0, \sigma^2) \qquad i = 1, 2, \ldots, 36$$

We want the following:

1. point estimates of β_1, β_2, β_3, and β_4;
2. point estimate of σ^2;
3. 95 percent one-at-a-time confidence intervals on $2\beta_1 + \beta_2 + 3\beta_3 - \beta_4$ and on $2\beta_1 + 2\beta_2 + \beta_3$.

The sum of squares $\mathbf{y}'\mathbf{y}$ has been computed and is $\mathbf{y}'\mathbf{y} = 581$. The normal equations have been computed and are as follows:

$$\begin{aligned} 4\hat{\beta}_1 + 2\hat{\beta}_2 + 2\hat{\beta}_3 + 2\hat{\beta}_4 &= 14 \\ 2\hat{\beta}_1 + 2\hat{\beta}_2 + 2\hat{\beta}_3 + 3\hat{\beta}_4 &= 11 \\ 2\hat{\beta}_1 + 2\hat{\beta}_2 + 3\hat{\beta}_3 + 4\hat{\beta}_4 &= 11 \\ 2\hat{\beta}_1 + 3\hat{\beta}_2 + 4\hat{\beta}_3 + 10\hat{\beta}_4 &= 19 \end{aligned} \tag{7.3.6}$$

We will first do the computing by finding $(\mathbf{X}'\mathbf{X})^{-1}$ and using

$$\hat{\boldsymbol{\beta}} = (\mathbf{X}'\mathbf{X})^{-1}\mathbf{X}'\mathbf{y}$$
$$\hat{\sigma}^2 = \frac{1}{n-p}[\mathbf{y}'\mathbf{y} - \mathbf{y}'\mathbf{X}(\mathbf{X}'\mathbf{X})^{-1}\mathbf{X}'\mathbf{y}]$$
$$\ell_1'(\mathbf{X}'\mathbf{X})^{-1}\ell_1 \qquad \ell_2'(\mathbf{X}'\mathbf{X})^{-1}\ell_2$$

We can compute $(\mathbf{X}'\mathbf{X})^{-1}$ with the format $[\mathbf{S} \mid \mathbf{X}'\mathbf{y} \mid \mathbf{I}]$ and the square root method (in Section 7.3.1 another method for computing $(\mathbf{X}'\mathbf{X})^{-1}$ is given). We get

$$\mathbf{T}'^{-1}[\mathbf{S} \mid \mathbf{X}'\mathbf{y} \mid \mathbf{I}] = [\mathbf{T} \mid \mathbf{T}'^{-1}\mathbf{X}'\mathbf{y} \mid \mathbf{T}'^{-1}]$$

and $(\mathbf{X}'\mathbf{X})^{-1} = (\mathbf{T}'\mathbf{T})^{-1} = \mathbf{T}^{-1}\mathbf{T}'^{-1}$. Thus we have

$$\frac{[\mathbf{S} \mid \mathbf{X}'\mathbf{y} \mid \ \mathbf{I}\ ]}{[\mathbf{T} \mid \ \mathbf{t}\ \mid \mathbf{T}'^{-1}]} = \frac{\left[\begin{array}{cccc|c|cccc} 4 & 2 & 2 & 2 & 14 & 1 & 0 & 0 & 0 \\ & 2 & 2 & 3 & 11 & 0 & 1 & 0 & 0 \\ & & 3 & 4 & 11 & 0 & 0 & 1 & 0 \\ & & & 10 & 19 & 0 & 0 & 0 & 1 \end{array}\right]}{\left[\begin{array}{cccc|c|cccc} 2 & 1 & 1 & 1 & 7 & \frac{1}{2} & 0 & 0 & 0 \\ & 1 & 1 & 2 & 4 & -\frac{1}{2} & 1 & 0 & 0 \\ & & 1 & 1 & 0 & 0 & -1 & 1 & 0 \\ & & & 2 & 2 & \frac{1}{4} & -\frac{1}{2} & -\frac{1}{2} & \frac{1}{2} \end{array}\right]} \tag{7.3.7}$$

$\mathbf{T}^{-1}\mathbf{T}'^{-1}$ can be found directly from the lower right-hand matrix (which is $\mathbf{T}'^{-1}$) by multiplying column by column. We get

$$\mathbf{C} = (\mathbf{X}'\mathbf{X})^{-1} = \frac{1}{16}\begin{bmatrix} 9 & -10 & -2 & 2 \\ -10 & 36 & -12 & -4 \\ -2 & -12 & 20 & -4 \\ 2 & -4 & -4 & 4 \end{bmatrix}$$

It can easily be checked that $\mathbf{C}(\mathbf{X}'\mathbf{X}) = \mathbf{I}$. We note that since $\mathbf{T}$ is upper triangular, $\mathbf{T}^{-1}$ is also upper triangular and $\mathbf{T}'^{-1}$ is lower triangular; thus each element above the diagonal is zero and need not be computed in the lower right-hand matrix of Equation (7.3.7). Also, the diagonal elements of this matrix are the inverses of the respective diagonal elements of $\mathbf{T}$ and can be written down immediately.

We now compute the three items we wanted initially.

1. $\hat{\boldsymbol{\beta}}' = [(\mathbf{X}'\mathbf{X})^{-1}\mathbf{X}'\mathbf{y}]' = [2, 3, -1, 1]$.

2. $\hat{\sigma}^2 = \dfrac{1}{36 - 4}[581 - (2)(14) - (3)(11) - (-1)(11) - (1)(19)] = 16.$

3. Let $\ell_1' = [2, 1, 3, -1]$; then

$$\ell_1'\hat{\boldsymbol{\beta}} = 3 \qquad \ell_1'(\mathbf{X}'\mathbf{X})^{-1}\ell_1 = 9$$
$$\widehat{\text{var}}(\ell_1'\hat{\boldsymbol{\beta}}) = \hat{\sigma}^2\ell_1'(\mathbf{X}'\mathbf{X})^{-1}\ell_1 = (16)(9) = 144$$

Substituting into Equation (6.5.2) gives the 95 percent confidence interval

$$3 - 2.04(12) \leq \ell_1'\boldsymbol{\beta} \leq 3 + 2.04(12)$$

or

$$-21.48 \leq 2\beta_1 + \beta_2 + 3\beta_3 - \beta_4 \leq 27.48$$

Let $\ell_2' = [2, 2, 1, 0]$; then

$$\ell_2'\hat{\boldsymbol{\beta}} = 9 \qquad \ell_2'(\mathbf{X}'\mathbf{X})^{-1}\ell_2 = 4$$
$$\widehat{\text{var}}(\ell_2'\hat{\boldsymbol{\beta}}) = \hat{\sigma}^2\ell_2'(\mathbf{X}'\mathbf{X})^{-1}\ell_2 = (16)(4) = 64$$

The 95 percent confidence interval is

$$9 - 2.04(8) \leq 2\beta_1 + 2\beta_2 + \beta_3 \leq 9 + 2.04(8)$$

or

$$-7.32 \leq 2\beta_1 + 2\beta_2 + \beta_3 \leq 25.32$$

Note 1. The quantities $\ell_1'\hat{\boldsymbol{\beta}}, \ell_2'\hat{\boldsymbol{\beta}}, \hat{\sigma}^2, \ell_1'(\mathbf{X}'\mathbf{X})^{-1}\ell_1$, and $\ell_2'(\mathbf{X}'\mathbf{X})^{-1}\ell_2$ are also all that are needed to compute simultaneous confidence intervals on $\ell_1'\boldsymbol{\beta}$ and $\ell_2'\boldsymbol{\beta}$ using Equation (6.6.8). If we use $t_{0.025:2,32;\mathbf{I}} = 2.35$, the intervals (with confidence coefficient greater than or equal to 0.95) are as follows:

$$3 - 2.35(12) \leq \ell_1'\boldsymbol{\beta} \leq 3 + 2.35(12)$$

and

$$9 - 2.35(8) \leq \ell_2'\boldsymbol{\beta} \leq 9 + 2.35(8)$$

or

$$-25.20 \leq 2\beta_1 + \beta_2 + 3\beta_3 - \beta_4 \leq 31.20$$
$$-9.80 \leq 2\beta_1 + 2\beta_2 + \beta_3 \leq 27.80$$

Now we will compute $\hat{\sigma}^2$, $\ell_1'\hat{\boldsymbol{\beta}}$, $\ell_1'(\mathbf{X}'\mathbf{X})^{-1}\ell_1$, $\ell_2'\hat{\boldsymbol{\beta}}$, and $\ell_2'(\mathbf{X}'\mathbf{X})^{-1}\ell_2$ without computing $\hat{\boldsymbol{\beta}}$ or $(\mathbf{X}'\mathbf{X})^{-1}$. The format is as follows:

$$\frac{[\mathbf{X}'\mathbf{X} \mid \mathbf{X}'\mathbf{y} \mid \ell_1, \ell_2]}{[\;\mathbf{T}\;\mid\;\mathbf{t}\;\mid \mathbf{a}_1, \mathbf{a}_2]} = \frac{\left[\begin{array}{cccc|c|cc} 4 & 2 & 2 & 2 & 14 & 2 & 2 \\ & 2 & 2 & 3 & 11 & 1 & 2 \\ & & 3 & 4 & 11 & 3 & 1 \\ & & & 10 & 19 & -1 & 0 \end{array}\right]}{\left[\begin{array}{cccc|c|cc} 2 & 1 & 1 & 1 & 7 & 1 & 1 \\ & 1 & 1 & 2 & 4 & 0 & 1 \\ & & 1 & 1 & 0 & 2 & -1 \\ & & & 2 & 2 & -2 & -1 \end{array}\right]}$$

Now $\hat{\boldsymbol{\beta}}'\mathbf{X}'\mathbf{y} = \mathbf{t}'\mathbf{t} = 69$; $\ell_1'\hat{\boldsymbol{\beta}} = \mathbf{t}'\mathbf{a}_1 = 3$; $\ell_1'(\mathbf{X}'\mathbf{X})^{-1}\ell_1 = \mathbf{a}_1'\mathbf{a}_1 = 9$; $\ell_2'\hat{\boldsymbol{\beta}} = \mathbf{t}'\mathbf{a}_2 = 9$; $\ell_2'(\mathbf{X}'\mathbf{X})^{-1}\ell_2 = \mathbf{a}_2'\mathbf{a}_2 = 4$; and these are, of course, the same values we obtained above by computing $(\mathbf{X}'\mathbf{X})^{-1}$.

Now we discuss part 4 of Equation (7.3.1). We show that to test the hypothesis $\mathbf{H}\boldsymbol{\beta} = \mathbf{h}$ by the formula in Equation (6.3.10), the quantity in the numerator of w can be computed by two applications of the square root method without computing $(\mathbf{X}'\mathbf{X})^{-1}$ or $[\mathbf{H}(\mathbf{X}'\mathbf{X})^{-1}\mathbf{H}']^{-1}$ directly. The format is as follows:

$$[\mathbf{X}'\mathbf{X} \mid \mathbf{X}'\mathbf{y} \mid \mathbf{H}'] = [\mathbf{T}'\mathbf{T} \mid \mathbf{X}'\mathbf{y} \mid \mathbf{H}']$$

$$\text{and applying the square root method gives} \tag{7.3.8}$$

$$\mathbf{T}'^{-1}[\mathbf{X}'\mathbf{X} \mid \mathbf{X}'\mathbf{y} \mid \mathbf{H}'] = [\mathbf{T} \mid \mathbf{T}'^{-1}\mathbf{X}'\mathbf{y} \mid \mathbf{T}'^{-1}\mathbf{H}'] = [\mathbf{T} \mid \mathbf{t} \mid \mathbf{G}']$$

Next compute $\mathbf{G}\mathbf{G}'$ and $\mathbf{G}\mathbf{t} - \mathbf{h} = \mathbf{g}$ and put these into a format

$$[\mathbf{G}\mathbf{G}' \mid \mathbf{g}]$$

Note that $\mathbf{G}' = \mathbf{T}'^{-1}\mathbf{H}'$ and $\mathbf{t} = \mathbf{T}'^{-1}\mathbf{X}'\mathbf{y}$. Hence $\mathbf{G}\mathbf{G}' = \mathbf{H}\mathbf{T}^{-1}\mathbf{T}'^{-1}\mathbf{H}' = \mathbf{H}(\mathbf{X}'\mathbf{X})^{-1}\mathbf{H}'$, which is a $q \times q$ positive definite matrix and can be written $\mathbf{T}_0'\mathbf{T}_0$, where $\mathbf{T}_0$ is an upper triangular matrix. Thus

$$\mathbf{g} + \mathbf{h} = \mathbf{G}\mathbf{t} = \mathbf{H}\mathbf{T}^{-1}\mathbf{T}'^{-1}\mathbf{X}'\mathbf{y} = \mathbf{H}(\mathbf{X}'\mathbf{X})^{-1}\mathbf{X}'\mathbf{y} = \mathbf{H}\hat{\boldsymbol{\beta}}$$

and the format in Equation (7.3.8) is

$$[\mathbf{G}\mathbf{G}' \mid \mathbf{g}] = [\mathbf{T}_0'\mathbf{T}_0 \mid \mathbf{g}]$$

and reducing this by the square root method is equivalent to multiplying on the left by $\mathbf{T}_0'^{-1}$. We get

$$\mathbf{T}_0'^{-1}[\mathbf{GG}' \mid \mathbf{g}] = [\mathbf{T}_0 \mid \mathbf{T}_0'^{-1}\mathbf{g}] = [\mathbf{T}_0 \mid \mathbf{t}_0]$$

and $\mathbf{t}_0'\mathbf{t}_0 = \mathbf{g}'\mathbf{T}_0^{-1}\mathbf{T}_0'^{-1}\mathbf{g} = \mathbf{g}'(\mathbf{GG}')^{-1}\mathbf{g} = (\mathbf{H}\hat{\boldsymbol{\beta}} - \mathbf{h})'[\mathbf{H}(\mathbf{X}'\mathbf{X})^{-1}\mathbf{H}']^{-1}(\mathbf{H}\hat{\boldsymbol{\beta}} - \mathbf{h})$.
For w, the computed value of W, we get

$$w = \left(\frac{\mathbf{t}_0'\mathbf{t}_0}{\mathbf{y}'\mathbf{y} - \mathbf{t}'\mathbf{t}}\right)\left(\frac{n - p}{q}\right)$$

Example 7.3.2

With the $\mathbf{X}'\mathbf{X}$, $\mathbf{X}'\mathbf{y}$, $\mathbf{y}'\mathbf{y}$, n, and p of Example 7.3.1, test the hypothesis (with $\alpha = 0.05$)

$$H_0: \begin{cases} 2\beta_1 + \beta_2 + 3\beta_3 - \beta_4 = 15 \\ -2\beta_1 - \beta_2 + \beta_3 + \beta_4 = -17 \end{cases}$$

We get

$$\mathbf{H} = \begin{bmatrix} 2 & 1 & 3 & -1 \\ -2 & -1 & 1 & 1 \end{bmatrix} \qquad \mathbf{h} = \begin{bmatrix} 15 \\ -17 \end{bmatrix}$$

and the format

$$\frac{[\mathbf{X}'\mathbf{X} \mid \mathbf{X}'\mathbf{y} \mid \mathbf{H}']}{[\ \mathbf{T} \mid \mathbf{t} \mid \mathbf{G}']} = \frac{\left[\begin{array}{cccc|c|cc} 4 & 2 & 2 & 2 & 14 & 2 & -2 \\ & 2 & 2 & 3 & 11 & 1 & -1 \\ & & 3 & 4 & 11 & 3 & 1 \\ & & & 10 & 19 & -1 & 1 \end{array}\right]}{\left[\begin{array}{cccc|c|cc} 2 & 1 & 1 & 1 & 7 & 1 & -1 \\ & 1 & 1 & 2 & 4 & 0 & 0 \\ & & 1 & 1 & 0 & 2 & 2 \\ & & & 2 & 2 & -2 & 0 \end{array}\right]}$$

$$\frac{[\mathbf{GG}' \mid \mathbf{g}]}{[\ \mathbf{T}_0 \mid \mathbf{t}_0]} = \frac{\left[\begin{array}{cc|c} 9 & 3 & -12 \\ 3 & 5 & 10 \end{array}\right]}{\left[\begin{array}{cc|c} 3 & 1 & -4 \\ & 2 & 7 \end{array}\right]}$$

$$w = \left(\frac{(-4)^2 + (7)^2}{581 - 69}\right)\left(\frac{32}{2}\right) = 2.03$$

$F_{0.05:2,32} = 3.31$, so H_0 is not rejected.

The test $H_0 : \boldsymbol{\beta}_2 = \mathbf{b}_2$ *vs.* $H_a : \boldsymbol{\beta}_2 \neq \mathbf{b}_2$ is a test that is used a great deal in applications of statistics, and the square root method is a very easy procedure for computing the test statistic w for this situation. First we consider the case when $\mathbf{b}_2 = \mathbf{0}$, that is, we will find the test statistic for the hypothesis $H_0 : \boldsymbol{\beta}_2 = \mathbf{0}$, where $\boldsymbol{\beta}_2$ contains the last q elements of $\boldsymbol{\beta}$, $0 < q < p$.

The test statistic formula is given in Equation (6.4.5) except $\mathbf{b}_2$ is replaced by zero, that is,

$$w = \left(\frac{\hat{\boldsymbol{\beta}}_2' \mathbf{C}_{22}^{-1} \hat{\boldsymbol{\beta}}_2}{\mathbf{y}'\mathbf{y} - \hat{\boldsymbol{\beta}}'\mathbf{X}'\mathbf{y}}\right)\left(\frac{n-p}{q}\right) \tag{7.3.9}$$

The quantity $\mathbf{y}'\mathbf{y} - \hat{\boldsymbol{\beta}}'\mathbf{X}'\mathbf{y}$ can be written as $\mathbf{y}'\mathbf{y} - \mathbf{t}'\mathbf{t}$, and we show that $\hat{\boldsymbol{\beta}}_2' \mathbf{C}_{22}^{-1} \hat{\boldsymbol{\beta}}_2$ is the quantity $\mathbf{t}_2'\mathbf{t}_2$, where $\mathbf{t}' = [\mathbf{t}_1', \mathbf{t}_2']$, that is, $\mathbf{t}_2$ is the last q elements of $\mathbf{t}$. To show this, write the format $\mathbf{T}'^{-1}[\mathbf{X}'\mathbf{X} \mid \mathbf{X}'\mathbf{y}] = [\mathbf{T} \mid \mathbf{t}]$ in partitioned form and obtain

$$[\mathbf{T} \mid \mathbf{t}] = \left[\begin{array}{cc|c} \mathbf{T}_{11} & \mathbf{T}_{12} & \mathbf{t}_1 \\ \mathbf{0} & \mathbf{T}_{22} & \mathbf{t}_2 \end{array}\right] \tag{7.3.10}$$

from which we obtain $\mathbf{T}_{22}\hat{\boldsymbol{\beta}}_2 = \mathbf{t}_2$, or $\hat{\boldsymbol{\beta}}_2 = \mathbf{T}_{22}^{-1}\mathbf{t}_2$, and thus

$$\hat{\boldsymbol{\beta}}_2' \mathbf{C}_{22}^{-1} \hat{\boldsymbol{\beta}}_2 = \mathbf{t}_2'\mathbf{T}_{22}'^{-1}\mathbf{C}_{22}^{-1}\mathbf{T}_{22}^{-1}\mathbf{t}_2 = \mathbf{t}_2'\mathbf{t}_2$$

since

$$\mathbf{T}_{22}'^{-1}\mathbf{C}_{22}^{-1}\mathbf{T}_{22}^{-1} = \mathbf{I} \tag{7.3.11}$$

Thus to test the hypothesis $H_0 : \boldsymbol{\beta}_2 = \mathbf{0}$ (the last q elements of $\boldsymbol{\beta}$ are zero), the test statistic w is computed from the quantities in Equation (7.3.10):

$$w = \left(\frac{\mathbf{t}_2'\mathbf{t}_2}{\mathbf{y}'\mathbf{y} - \mathbf{t}'\mathbf{t}}\right)\left(\frac{n-p}{q}\right) \tag{7.3.12}$$

Example 7.3.3

Consider the model $\mathbf{Y} = \mathbf{X}\boldsymbol{\beta} + \boldsymbol{\varepsilon}$, which we write in detail as $Y_i = \beta_0 + \beta_1 x_{i1} + \beta_2 x_{i2} + \beta_3 x_{i3} + \beta_4 x_{i4} + \varepsilon_i$, ε_i are distributed $NID(\varepsilon : 0, \sigma^2)$, for $i = 1, 2, \ldots, 25$. We want to test the hypothesis $(\alpha = 0.05)$ $H_0 : \beta_3 = \beta_4 = 0$ *vs.* $H_a : \beta_3 \neq 0$ or $\beta_4 \neq 0$. There are 25 observations y_i, so $\mathbf{y}$ is a 25×1 vector, $\mathbf{X}$ is a 25×5 matrix, also $\boldsymbol{\beta}' = [\beta_0, \beta_1, \beta_2, \beta_3, \beta_4]$.

The $\mathbf{X'X}$ matrix, the $\mathbf{X'y}$ vector, and $\mathbf{y'y}$ have been computed and are given below.

$$\mathbf{X'X} = \begin{bmatrix} 25 & 5 & -10 & -15 & -5 \\ 5 & 2 & -1 & -2 & 1 \\ -10 & -1 & 9 & 3 & 6 \\ -15 & -2 & 3 & 23 & -3 \\ -5 & 1 & 6 & -3 & 14 \end{bmatrix} \quad \mathbf{X'y} = \begin{bmatrix} 10 \\ 1 \\ -15 \\ 39 \\ -45 \end{bmatrix} \quad \mathbf{y'y} = 810$$

The reduction by the square root method gives

$$[\mathbf{T} \mid \mathbf{t}] = \left[\begin{array}{ccccc|c} 5 & 1 & -2 & -3 & -1 & 2 \\ 0 & 1 & 1 & 1 & 2 & -1 \\ 0 & 0 & 2 & -2 & 1 & -5 \\ 0 & 0 & 0 & 3 & -2 & 12 \\ 0 & 0 & 0 & 0 & 2 & -6 \end{array}\right]$$

and w can be computed very easily from $\mathbf{y'y}$ and the $\mathbf{t}$ vector. We get

$$w = \left(\frac{\mathbf{t}_2'\mathbf{t}_2}{\mathbf{y'y} - \mathbf{t't}}\right)\left(\frac{n-p}{q}\right) = \left(\frac{180}{600}\right)\left(\frac{20}{2}\right) = 3.0 < F_{0.05:2,20} = 3.49$$

so H_0 is not rejected.

To obtain the test statistic w to test $H_0 : \boldsymbol{\beta}_2 = \mathbf{b}_2$ *vs.* $H_a : \boldsymbol{\beta}_2 \neq \mathbf{b}_2$ (where $\mathbf{b}_2$ may not be $\mathbf{0}$), compute $\mathbf{X'(y - X_2b_2) = X'z}$, say, and reduce the format $[\mathbf{X'X} \mid \mathbf{X'z}]$ to $[\mathbf{T} \mid \mathbf{t}]$ by the square root method. Then

$$w = \left(\frac{\mathbf{t}_2'\mathbf{t}_2}{\mathbf{z'z} - \mathbf{t't}}\right)\left(\frac{n-p}{q}\right)$$

Note 2. The test $H_0 : \boldsymbol{\beta}_2 = \mathbf{b}_2$ is a special case of part 4 in Equation (7.3.1), with $\mathbf{H} = [\mathbf{0}, \mathbf{I}_q]$, $\mathbf{h} = \mathbf{b}_2$. We notice that $\mathbf{y} - \mathbf{X}_2\mathbf{b}_2$ above is $\mathbf{y} - \mathbf{XH}^-\mathbf{h}$.

7.3.1 Computing the Inverse of X'X

In Example 7.3.1 the inverse of $\mathbf{X'X}$ was computed by using $\mathbf{T}^{-1}\mathbf{T}'^{-1}$, where $\mathbf{T}'^{-1}$ was computed by using the format $[\mathbf{X'X} \mid \mathbf{I}]$ and reducing $\mathbf{X'X} = \mathbf{T'T}$ by the square root procedure to obtain $\mathbf{T}'^{-1}[\mathbf{X'X} \mid \mathbf{I}] = \mathbf{T}'^{-1}[\mathbf{T'T} \mid \mathbf{I}] = [\mathbf{T} \mid \mathbf{T}'^{-1}]$. This method of computing $(\mathbf{X'X})^{-1}$ was presented mainly for illustrative purposes, and we now briefly discuss a method for computing this inverse.

One distinct *advantage* of the square root procedure is the storage requirement. To illustrate this we notice that since $\mathbf{X}'\mathbf{X}$ is symmetric, only the elements on and above the diagonal need be used to compute $\mathbf{T}$. To compute an element in $\mathbf{T}$, say t_{ij} for $j > i$, the only element in $\mathbf{S} = \mathbf{X}'\mathbf{X}$ that is needed is s_{ij}. Also, after t_{ij} is computed, the element s_{ij} is not needed to compute other elements in $\mathbf{T}$; hence s_{ij} can be replaced by t_{ij}. So the elements on and above the diagonal of $\mathbf{S}$ are replaced by the elements on and above the diagonal of $\mathbf{T}$ as they are computed; the elements below the diagonal of $\mathbf{T}$ are zero.

If an element of $\mathbf{S}$, say s_{ij}, is needed after $\mathbf{T}$ is computed, it can be evaluated by $s_{ij} = \sum_{k=1}^{i} t_{ki}t_{kj}$ for $j \geq i$ (and $s_{ij} = s_{ji}$ for $j < i$). So the total storage requirements are $p(p+1)/2$ elements of $\mathbf{S}$, which are replaced by $p(p+1)/2$ elements of $\mathbf{T}$ as $\mathbf{T}$ is computed. Of course, p elements of storage are required for $\mathbf{X}'\mathbf{y}$ and for each vector $\boldsymbol{\ell}_i$ that is used.

After the format $[\mathbf{X}'\mathbf{X} \mid \mathbf{X}'\mathbf{y} \mid \boldsymbol{\ell}_1, \boldsymbol{\ell}_2, \ldots, \boldsymbol{\ell}_q]$ is reduced to $[\mathbf{T} \mid \mathbf{t} \mid \mathbf{a}_1, \mathbf{a}_2, \ldots, \mathbf{a}_q]$, and the necessary statistics are computed, such as $\mathbf{t}'\mathbf{t}$, $\mathbf{a}_i'\mathbf{a}_i$, and $\mathbf{a}_i'\mathbf{t}$ for $i = 1, 2, \ldots, q$, then one can compute $\mathbf{T}^{-1}$ and obtain $(\mathbf{X}'\mathbf{X})^{-1}$ if desired. No additional storage is required (unless, as may be the case, more significant digits are required for an element of $\mathbf{T}^{-1}$ than were required for an element of $\mathbf{T}$) since as each element in $\mathbf{T}^{-1}$ is computed, it can replace the corresponding element in $\mathbf{T}$.

The formulas for computing $\mathbf{T}^{-1}$ (which we denote by $\mathbf{R}$, which is an upper triangular matrix) are given in Equation (7.3.13). These formulas can be obtained by writing $\mathbf{TR} = \mathbf{I}$ in detail. We get

$$\begin{bmatrix} t_{11} & t_{12} & \cdots & t_{1p} \\ 0 & t_{22} & \cdots & t_{2p} \\ \vdots & \vdots & & \vdots \\ 0 & 0 & \cdots & t_{pp} \end{bmatrix} \begin{bmatrix} r_{11} & r_{12} & \cdots & r_{1p} \\ 0 & r_{22} & \cdots & r_{2p} \\ \vdots & \vdots & & \vdots \\ 0 & 0 & \cdots & r_{pp} \end{bmatrix} = \begin{bmatrix} 1 & 0 & \cdots & 0 \\ 0 & 1 & \cdots & 0 \\ \vdots & \vdots & & \vdots \\ 0 & 0 & \cdots & 1 \end{bmatrix}$$

which we write as $\mathbf{T}[\mathbf{r}_1, \mathbf{r}_2, \ldots, \mathbf{r}_p] = [\mathbf{e}_1, \mathbf{e}_2, \ldots, \mathbf{e}_p]$. We can solve the p equations $\mathbf{Tr}_i = \mathbf{e}_i$ for $\mathbf{r}_i$, $i = 1, 2, \ldots, p$. Clearly the formulas are

1. $r_{ii} = t_{ii}^{-1}$ for $i = 1, 2, \ldots, p$;
2. $r_{ij} = 0$ for $i > j$;
3. $r_{ij} = -\sum_{k=i+1}^{j} t_{ik}r_{kj}/t_{ii}$ for $j = i+1, i+2, \ldots, p$ and

$$i = p-1, p-2, \ldots, 1. \tag{7.3.13}$$

The r_{ij} must be computed in a certain order. First compute r_{pp}; next $r_{p-1,p-1}$; then $r_{p-1,p}$. After a row of $\mathbf{R}$ is computed, say the $(i+1)$st, move up to the next row, the ith, and compute r_{ii}; then compute all elements in the ith row in the order $r_{i,i+1}, r_{i,i+2}, \ldots, r_{i,p}$. Then move up to the $(i-1)$st row and repeat the same process.

After $\mathbf{T}^{-1}$ is computed, one can compute $(\mathbf{X}'\mathbf{X})^{-1} = \mathbf{T}^{-1}\mathbf{T}'^{-1}$ by multiplying the rows of $\mathbf{T}^{-1}$; that is, if $\mathbf{C} = (\mathbf{X}'\mathbf{X})^{-1}$, then $c_{ij} = \mathbf{q}_i'\mathbf{q}_j$, where $\mathbf{q}_s$ is the sth row of $\mathbf{T}^{-1}$. Hence, $\mathbf{T}^{-1}$ can be replaced by the corresponding elements of $(\mathbf{X}'\mathbf{X})^{-1}$ as they are computed, so storage for only $p(p+1)/2$ elements are needed.

In summary, the storage requirement for $\mathbf{X}'\mathbf{X}$ is for $p(p+1)/2$ elements; these can be replaced by the $p(p+1)/2$ elements of $\mathbf{T}$; these can be replaced by the $p(p+1)/2$ elements of $\mathbf{T}^{-1}$; finally, these can be replaced by $p(p+1)/2$ elements of $(\mathbf{X}'\mathbf{X})^{-1}$, the elements on and above the diagonal.

However, if $\mathbf{T}^{-1}$ is not needed, but one wants to compute $(\mathbf{X}'\mathbf{X})^{-1}$, which we denote by $\mathbf{C}$, then the following procedure can be used after $\mathbf{T}$ is obtained by reducing $\mathbf{X}'\mathbf{X}$ by the square root method. Note that $\mathbf{T}'^{-1} = \mathbf{T}\mathbf{T}^{-1}\mathbf{T}'^{-1} = \mathbf{T}(\mathbf{T}'\mathbf{T})^{-1} = \mathbf{T}(\mathbf{X}'\mathbf{X})^{-1} = \mathbf{TC}$. We can use the equation $\mathbf{TC} = \mathbf{T}'^{-1}$ to compute $\mathbf{C}$ from a knowledge of $\mathbf{T}$ without computing $\mathbf{T}'^{-1}$. We utilize the fact that the ith diagonal element of $\mathbf{T}'^{-1}$ is t_{ii}^{-1}. If we write $\mathbf{TC} = \mathbf{T}'^{-1}$ in detail, we get (let $\mathbf{A} = \mathbf{T}'^{-1}$)

$$\begin{bmatrix} t_{11} & t_{12} & t_{13} & \cdots & t_{1p} \\ 0 & t_{22} & t_{23} & \cdots & t_{2p} \\ 0 & 0 & t_{33} & \cdots & t_{3p} \\ \vdots & \vdots & \vdots & & \vdots \\ 0 & 0 & 0 & \cdots & t_{pp} \end{bmatrix} \begin{bmatrix} c_{11} & c_{12} & c_{13} & \cdots & c_{1p} \\ c_{21} & c_{22} & c_{23} & \cdots & c_{2p} \\ c_{31} & c_{32} & c_{33} & \cdots & c_{3p} \\ \vdots & \vdots & \vdots & & \vdots \\ c_{p1} & c_{p2} & c_{p3} & \cdots & c_{pp} \end{bmatrix} = \begin{bmatrix} t_{11}^{-1} & 0 & 0 & \cdots & 0 \\ a_{21} & t_{22}^{-1} & 0 & \cdots & 0 \\ a_{31} & a_{32} & t_{33}^{-1} & \cdots & 0 \\ \vdots & \vdots & \vdots & & \vdots \\ a_{p1} & a_{p2} & a_{p3} & \cdots & t_{pp}^{-1} \end{bmatrix} \tag{7.3.14}$$

Since $\mathbf{C} = \mathbf{C}'$, we have $c_{ij} = c_{ji}$, and we need only compute the elements on and above the diagonal of $\mathbf{C}$. If we equate terms on the left and right sides of Equation (7.3.14) in a certain order, we get formulas for c_{ij} in terms of t_{ij}.

1. $c_{pp} = 1/t_{pp}^2$.
2. $c_{ii} = [t_{ii}^{-1} - \sum_{k=i+1}^{p} t_{ik}c_{ki}]t_{ii}^{-1}$ for $i = p-1, p-2, \ldots, 1$.
3. $c_{ij} = -[\sum_{k=i+1}^{p} t_{ik}c_{kj}]t_{ii}^{-1}$ for $i = j-1, j-2, \ldots, 1$

   and $j = p, p-1, \ldots, 2$.
4. $c_{ij} = c_{ji}$. (7.3.15)

The computations are done in the following order.

1. Compute the (p, p) element by formula 1.
2. Compute the elements in the pth column by formula 3 and in the following order: $c_{p-1,p}, c_{p-2,p}, \ldots, c_{1p}$.
3. Compute $c_{p-1,p-1}$ by formula 2.

4. Compute the elements above the diagonal in column $p-1$ by formula 3 in the following order: $c_{p-2,p-1}, c_{p-3,p-1}, \ldots, c_{1,p-1}$.
5. Proceed by computing a diagonal element in a column by formula 2 and then compute the elements above the diagonal in that column by formula 3.
6. Compute all elements below the diagonal by formula 4.

7.4 Analysis of Variance

A procedure that is useful in organizing quantities for computing in the general linear model is called the *analysis of variance*, and sometimes abbreviated to AOV or ANOVA. The procedure consists of partitioning the total sum of squares of the observations, $\mathbf{y}'\mathbf{y}$, into a sum of k quadratic forms, that is, $\mathbf{y}'\mathbf{y} = \sum_{i=1}^{k} \mathbf{y}'\mathbf{A}_i\mathbf{y}$. For example, in testing $H_0 : \boldsymbol{\beta}_2 = \mathbf{0}$ in the previous section, we need the quantities

$$\mathbf{y}'\mathbf{y} \qquad \hat{\boldsymbol{\beta}}'\mathbf{X}'\mathbf{y} = \mathbf{y}'\mathbf{X}\mathbf{X}^{-}\mathbf{y} \qquad \hat{\boldsymbol{\gamma}}'\mathbf{X}_1'\mathbf{y} = \mathbf{y}'\mathbf{X}_1\mathbf{X}_1^{-}\mathbf{y} \qquad \hat{\sigma}^2 = \left(\frac{1}{n-p}\right)\mathbf{y}'(\mathbf{I} - \mathbf{X}\mathbf{X}^{-})\mathbf{y}$$

We can include these quantities in an identity in $\mathbf{y}$ that partitions $\mathbf{y}'\mathbf{y}$ into a sum of quadratic forms and such that the elements needed in the test statistic w are available. The identity is

$$\mathbf{y}'\mathbf{y} \equiv \mathbf{y}'(\mathbf{X}_1\mathbf{X}_1^{-})\mathbf{y} + \mathbf{y}'(\mathbf{X}\mathbf{X}^{-} - \mathbf{X}_1\mathbf{X}_1^{-})\mathbf{y} + \mathbf{y}'(\mathbf{I} - \mathbf{X}\mathbf{X}^{-})\mathbf{y}$$

and clearly the last two quadratic forms and the degrees of freedom are all that are needed to compute the test statistic w. These quantities are usually exhibited in a table which is called an "Analysis of Variance Table." Each row in the table represents a quadratic form that is useful in computing or exhibiting quantities that are needed in the test statistic w or for point or interval estimation. One quantity that is almost always displayed in an ANOVA table is $\hat{\sigma}^2$, the "best" estimate of σ^2. Each column of the table contains a useful description of the quadratic forms. Although all investigators do not include identical entries in an ANOVA table, the one given in Table 7.4.1 would be typical to test $H_0 : \mathbf{H}\boldsymbol{\beta} = \mathbf{0}$.

The two models (full and reduced) and respective normal equations are represented by

$$\text{Full model:} \quad \mathbf{y} = \mathbf{X}\boldsymbol{\beta} + \boldsymbol{\varepsilon} \qquad \mathbf{X}'\mathbf{X}\hat{\boldsymbol{\beta}} = \mathbf{X}'\mathbf{y}$$

$$\text{Reduced model:} \quad \mathbf{y} = \mathbf{B}\boldsymbol{\gamma} + \boldsymbol{\varepsilon} \qquad \mathbf{B}'\mathbf{B}\hat{\boldsymbol{\gamma}} = \mathbf{B}'\mathbf{y}$$

The quantities needed for the test statistic w in Equation (6.3.11) are

$$\hat{\boldsymbol{\beta}}'\mathbf{X}'\mathbf{y} = \mathbf{y}'\mathbf{X}\mathbf{X}^{-}\mathbf{y} \qquad \hat{\boldsymbol{\gamma}}'\mathbf{B}'\mathbf{y} = \mathbf{y}'\mathbf{B}\mathbf{B}^{-}\mathbf{y} \qquad \text{and} \qquad \mathbf{y}'\mathbf{y}$$

Table 7.4.1

ANOVA for Testing $\mathbf{H\beta} = \mathbf{0}$

Source of Variation	*Degrees of Freedom*	*Sum of Squares*	*Mean Square*	*F Value*
Total	n	$\mathbf{y'y}$		
Reduction due to $\boldsymbol{\beta}$	p	$\hat{\boldsymbol{\beta}}'\mathbf{X'y} = \mathbf{y}'(\mathbf{XX}^-)\mathbf{y}$		
Reduction due to $\boldsymbol{\gamma}$	$p - q$	$\hat{\boldsymbol{\gamma}}'\mathbf{B'y} = \mathbf{y}'(\mathbf{BB}^-)\mathbf{y}$		
Reduction due to H_0	q	$\hat{\boldsymbol{\beta}}'\mathbf{X'y} - \hat{\boldsymbol{\gamma}}'\mathbf{B'y}$	$\left(\frac{1}{q}\right)(\hat{\boldsymbol{\beta}}'\mathbf{X'y} - \hat{\boldsymbol{\gamma}}'\mathbf{B'y})$	$\left(\frac{\hat{\boldsymbol{\beta}}'\mathbf{X'y} - \hat{\boldsymbol{\gamma}}'\mathbf{B'y}}{\mathbf{y'y} - \hat{\boldsymbol{\beta}}'\mathbf{X'y}}\right) \times \left(\frac{n-p}{q}\right) = w$
Error Variance	$n - p$	$\mathbf{y'y} - \hat{\boldsymbol{\beta}}'\mathbf{X'y}$	$\left(\frac{1}{n-p}\right)(\mathbf{y'y} - \hat{\boldsymbol{\beta}}'\mathbf{X'y})$	

The identity in $\mathbf{y'y}$ for this situation is

$$\mathbf{y'y} \equiv \mathbf{y}'(\mathbf{BB}^-)\mathbf{y} + \mathbf{y}'(\mathbf{XX}^- - \mathbf{BB}^-)\mathbf{y} + \mathbf{y}'(\mathbf{I} - \mathbf{XX}^-)\mathbf{y}$$

In Table 7.4.1 the "Source of Variation" column lists every quadratic form that the user wants in the table. In the next column is listed the degrees of freedom associated with each quadratic form. The next column exhibits the computation of the sum of squares for each quadratic form in the "Source of Variation" column. The "sum of squares" of a quadratic form is defined here by the following: If $\mathbf{y'Ay}/\sigma^2$ is a chi-square random variable with M degrees of freedom, then $\mathbf{y'Ay}$ is the "sum of squares." The "mean square" of a quadratic form is defined to be the "sum of squares" divided by the respective degrees of freedom. A mean square will not always be computed for each row of the table because it will not be used. The "F Value" column is the ratio of two elements in the mean square column, and it is the computed value of a test statistic w (this column is not always computed).

The identification of the various quadratic forms in the table under the "Source of Variation" column will always include the two quantities "Total" and "Error Variance." The other elements will depend on the investigator (or the computer output) and what he wants to list. The identification "Reduction due to $\boldsymbol{\beta}$" is used by many authors and will be used in this book. It will always mean reduction due to the parameters in $\boldsymbol{\beta}$. The words "Reduction due to $\boldsymbol{\beta}$"

can be thought of in the following way (we consider Case 1 of various models):

1. if $\boldsymbol{\beta}$ is not in the model, the model is simply $\mathbf{Y} = \boldsymbol{\varepsilon}$;
2. in this case $(1/\sigma^2)\mathbf{Y}'\mathbf{Y}$ is a chi-square random variable, and the mean square, $(1/n)\mathbf{Y}'\mathbf{Y}$, is an *unbiased* estimator of the error variance σ^2;
3. thus in the model $\mathbf{Y} = \boldsymbol{\varepsilon}$, $\mathbf{Y}'\mathbf{Y}$ is the *sum of squares* used in estimating σ^2;
4. when $\boldsymbol{\beta}$ *is* in the model, the model is $\mathbf{Y} = \mathbf{X}\boldsymbol{\beta} + \boldsymbol{\varepsilon}$, and $(1/\sigma^2)(\mathbf{Y} - \mathbf{X}\hat{\boldsymbol{\beta}})'(\mathbf{Y} - \mathbf{X}\hat{\boldsymbol{\beta}})$ is a chi-square random variable, and the mean square, $(1/(n-p))(\mathbf{Y}'\mathbf{Y} - \hat{\boldsymbol{\beta}}'\mathbf{X}'\mathbf{Y})$, is now an *unbiased* estimator of σ^2;
5. thus in the model $\mathbf{Y} = \mathbf{X}\boldsymbol{\beta} + \boldsymbol{\varepsilon}$, the quantity $\mathbf{Y}'\mathbf{Y} - \hat{\boldsymbol{\beta}}'\mathbf{X}'\mathbf{Y}$ is the *sum of squares* used in estimating σ^2;
6. hence, the sum of squares for estimating σ^2 is $\mathbf{Y}'\mathbf{Y}$ when the model is $\mathbf{Y} = \boldsymbol{\varepsilon}$ and is $\mathbf{Y}'\mathbf{Y} - \hat{\boldsymbol{\beta}}'\mathbf{X}'\mathbf{Y}$ when the model is $\mathbf{Y} = \mathbf{X}\boldsymbol{\beta} + \boldsymbol{\varepsilon}$; thus "the *reduction* in the sum of squares for estimating σ^2 *due to* $\boldsymbol{\beta}$ being in the model" is $\hat{\boldsymbol{\beta}}'\mathbf{X}'\mathbf{Y}$.

In general, "Reduction due to $\boldsymbol{\gamma}$" means the model is $\mathbf{Y} = \mathbf{B}\boldsymbol{\gamma} + \boldsymbol{\varepsilon}$, the normal equations are $\mathbf{B}'\mathbf{B}\hat{\boldsymbol{\gamma}} = \mathbf{B}'\mathbf{Y}$, and reduction due to $\boldsymbol{\gamma}$ is $\hat{\boldsymbol{\gamma}}'\mathbf{B}'\mathbf{Y} = \mathbf{Y}'\mathbf{B}\mathbf{B}^-\mathbf{Y}$. The words "reduction due to" will often be abbreviated to "due to," and sometimes the words will be replaced by the symbols $R(\boldsymbol{\beta})$, $R(\boldsymbol{\gamma})$, and so forth.

In summary, to test $H_0: \mathbf{H}\boldsymbol{\beta} = \mathbf{0}$, we use the following identifications and sum of squares.

1. Reduction due to $\boldsymbol{\beta} = R(\boldsymbol{\beta}) = \hat{\boldsymbol{\beta}}'\mathbf{X}'\mathbf{Y} = \mathbf{Y}'\mathbf{X}\mathbf{X}^-\mathbf{Y}$ and is obtained from the normal equations of the full model $\mathbf{Y} = \mathbf{X}\boldsymbol{\beta} + \boldsymbol{\varepsilon}$.
2. Reduction due to $\boldsymbol{\gamma} = R(\boldsymbol{\gamma}) = \hat{\boldsymbol{\gamma}}'\mathbf{B}'\mathbf{Y} = \mathbf{Y}'\mathbf{B}\mathbf{B}^-\mathbf{Y}$ and is obtained from the normal equations of the reduced model $\mathbf{Y} = \mathbf{B}\boldsymbol{\gamma} + \boldsymbol{\varepsilon}$.
3. Reduction due to $H_0 = R(H_0) = R(\boldsymbol{\beta}) - R(\boldsymbol{\gamma}) = \hat{\boldsymbol{\beta}}'\mathbf{X}'\mathbf{Y} - \hat{\boldsymbol{\gamma}}\mathbf{B}'\mathbf{Y}$.
4. Error sum of squares is $\mathbf{Y}'\mathbf{Y} - R(\boldsymbol{\beta})$.

To test the more general hypothesis $\mathbf{H}\boldsymbol{\beta} = \mathbf{h}$ instead of $\mathbf{H}\boldsymbol{\beta} = \mathbf{0}$, all quantities in Table 7.4.1 and in the summary are the same as above except $\mathbf{y}$ is replaced by $\mathbf{z} = \mathbf{y} - \mathbf{X}\mathbf{H}^-\mathbf{h}$ in all normal equations, and consequently $\hat{\boldsymbol{\beta}}$ and $\hat{\boldsymbol{\gamma}}$ are respectively replaced by $\hat{\boldsymbol{\beta}} = \mathbf{X}^-\mathbf{z}$ and $\hat{\boldsymbol{\gamma}} = \mathbf{B}^-\mathbf{z}$.

Example 7.4.1

Exhibit an ANOVA table for Example 7.3.3. We get Table 7.4.2 where d.f., S.S., and M.S. are abbreviations for degrees of freedom, sum of squares, and mean square, respectively.

Table 7.4.2

ANOVA for Testing $\beta_3 = \beta_4 = 0$

Source	*d.f.*	*S.S.*	*M.S.*	*F*
Total	25	810		
$R(\boldsymbol{\beta})$	5	210		
$R(\boldsymbol{\gamma})$	3	30		
$R(H_0)$	2	180	90	3
Error	20	600	30	

7.4.1 Further Discussion of the Notation $R(\boldsymbol{\beta})$

In Table 7.4.2 we used the notation $R(\boldsymbol{\beta})$ which was referred to as "Reduction due to $\boldsymbol{\beta}$," and in this section we discuss this further. To formalize this we shall state the meaning of the notation $R(\boldsymbol{\beta})$ and $R(\boldsymbol{\beta} \mid \boldsymbol{\gamma})$.

Notation $R(\boldsymbol{\beta})$. When the notation $R(\boldsymbol{\beta})$ is used, it will mean the following:

1. the linear model is $\mathbf{Y} = \mathbf{X}\boldsymbol{\beta} + \boldsymbol{\varepsilon}$;
2. the normal equations are $\mathbf{X}'\mathbf{X}\hat{\boldsymbol{\beta}} = \mathbf{X}'\mathbf{Y}$;
3. $R(\boldsymbol{\beta})$ is defined by $R(\boldsymbol{\beta}) = \hat{\boldsymbol{\beta}}'\mathbf{X}'\mathbf{Y} = \mathbf{Y}'\mathbf{X}\mathbf{X}^{-}\mathbf{Y}$. (7.4.1)

In Table 7.4.2 the sum of squares in the numerator of the W statistic, which we denoted by $R(H_0)$, is, by our notation, equal to $R(\boldsymbol{\beta}) - R(\boldsymbol{\gamma})$. We will use a special notation for this quantity.

Notation $R(\boldsymbol{\beta} \mid \boldsymbol{\gamma})$. The notation $R(\boldsymbol{\beta} \mid \boldsymbol{\gamma})$ is defined as $R(\boldsymbol{\beta}) - R(\boldsymbol{\gamma})$ and by Equation (7.4.1) it will mean the following:

1. there are two models: the full model, $\mathbf{Y} = \mathbf{X}\boldsymbol{\beta} + \boldsymbol{\varepsilon}$, and the reduced model, $\mathbf{Z} = \mathbf{B}\boldsymbol{\gamma} + \boldsymbol{\varepsilon}$;
2. the corresponding normal equations are

$$\text{full model:} \quad \mathbf{X}'\mathbf{X}\hat{\boldsymbol{\beta}} = \mathbf{X}'\mathbf{Y}$$

$$\text{reduced model:} \quad \mathbf{B}'\mathbf{B}\hat{\boldsymbol{\gamma}} = \mathbf{B}'\mathbf{Z}$$

3. $R(\boldsymbol{\beta}) = \hat{\boldsymbol{\beta}}'\mathbf{X}'\mathbf{Y} = \mathbf{Y}'\mathbf{X}\mathbf{X}^{-}\mathbf{Y}$ and $R(\boldsymbol{\gamma}) = \hat{\boldsymbol{\gamma}}'\mathbf{B}'\mathbf{Z} = \mathbf{Z}'\mathbf{B}\mathbf{B}^{-}\mathbf{Z}$;
4. $R(\boldsymbol{\beta} \mid \boldsymbol{\gamma}) = R(\boldsymbol{\beta}) - R(\boldsymbol{\gamma}) = \hat{\boldsymbol{\beta}}'\mathbf{X}'\mathbf{Y} - \hat{\boldsymbol{\gamma}}'\mathbf{B}'\mathbf{Z} = \mathbf{Z}'(\mathbf{X}\mathbf{X}^{-} - \mathbf{B}\mathbf{B}^{-})\mathbf{Z}$.

Note 1. The notation $R(\boldsymbol{\beta} \mid \boldsymbol{\gamma})$ in words is "reduction due to $\boldsymbol{\beta}$ adjusted for $\boldsymbol{\gamma}$," or another way of saying it is "reduction due to $\boldsymbol{\beta}$ after reduction in $\boldsymbol{\gamma}$ has been accounted for," or still another way is "reduction due to $\boldsymbol{\beta}$ over and above the reduction due to $\boldsymbol{\gamma}$."

In Table 7.4.2 the term $R(H_0)$ is equal to $R(\boldsymbol{\beta} \mid \boldsymbol{\gamma}) = R(\boldsymbol{\beta}) - R(\boldsymbol{\gamma}) = \hat{\boldsymbol{\beta}}'\mathbf{X}'\mathbf{y} - \hat{\boldsymbol{\gamma}}'\mathbf{B}'\mathbf{y}$. In most cases throughout this book, this notation will be useful in the model $Y_i = \beta_0 + \beta_1 x_{i1} + \beta_2 x_{i2} + \cdots + \beta_{p-1} x_{ip-1} + \varepsilon_i$, $i = 1, 2, \ldots, n$, where we want to test various sets of the β_i simultaneously equal to zero. We write the full model as (we assume an intercept model, otherwise $\beta_0 = 0$)

$$\mathbf{Y} = \beta_0 \mathbf{1} + \beta_1 \mathbf{x}_1 + \beta_2 \mathbf{x}_2 + \cdots + \beta_{p-1} \mathbf{x}_{p-1} + \boldsymbol{\varepsilon}$$

Some tests that might be of interest (and the corresponding sum of squares in the numerator of W) are

1. $H_0: \beta_0 = 0$; $R(\beta_0 \mid \beta_1, \beta_2, \ldots, \beta_{p-1}) = R(\beta_0, \beta_1, \ldots, \beta_{p-1}) - R(\beta_1, \beta_2, \ldots, \beta_{p-1})$;
2. $H_0: \beta_1 = \beta_2 = 0$; $R(\beta_1, \beta_2 \mid \beta_0, \beta_3, \ldots, \beta_{p-1}) = R(\beta_0, \beta_1, \ldots, \beta_{p-1}) - R(\beta_0, \beta_3, \ldots, \beta_{p-1})$;
3. $H_0: \beta_{p-1} = 0$; $R(\beta_{p-1} \mid \beta_0, \ldots, \beta_{p-2}) = R(\beta_0, \ldots, \beta_{p-1}) - R(\beta_0, \ldots, \beta_{p-2})$.

Note 2. In the model $\mathbf{Y} = \mathbf{X}\boldsymbol{\beta} + \boldsymbol{\varepsilon}$, the error sum of squares in an analysis of variance table is $\mathbf{y}'\mathbf{y} - R(\boldsymbol{\beta})$.

We now state two theorems that will be useful when applying the notation $R(\boldsymbol{\beta})$ and $R(\boldsymbol{\beta} \mid \boldsymbol{\gamma})$ in an ANOVA table.

THEOREM 7.4.1

Consider the model $\mathbf{Y} = \mathbf{X}\boldsymbol{\beta} + \boldsymbol{\varepsilon}$, *which we write as* $\mathbf{Y} = \mathbf{X}_1\boldsymbol{\beta}_1 + \mathbf{X}_2\boldsymbol{\beta}_2 + \mathbf{X}_3\boldsymbol{\beta}_3 + \boldsymbol{\varepsilon}$; *then* $R(\boldsymbol{\beta}_2, \boldsymbol{\beta}_3 \mid \boldsymbol{\beta}_1) - R(\boldsymbol{\beta}_2 \mid \boldsymbol{\beta}_1) = R(\boldsymbol{\beta}_3 \mid \boldsymbol{\beta}_1, \boldsymbol{\beta}_2)$.

Proof

The proof will be asked for in the problems.

THEOREM 7.4.2

Consider the model $\mathbf{Y} = \mathbf{X}\boldsymbol{\beta} + \boldsymbol{\varepsilon}$, *which we write as* $\mathbf{Y} = \mathbf{X}_1\boldsymbol{\beta}_1 + \mathbf{X}_2\boldsymbol{\beta}_2 + \boldsymbol{\varepsilon}$; *then* $R(\boldsymbol{\beta}_1 \mid \boldsymbol{\beta}_2) = R(\boldsymbol{\beta}_1)$ *if and only if* $\mathbf{X}_1'\mathbf{X}_2 = \mathbf{0}$.

Proof

The proof will be asked for in the problems.

Note 3. When $\mathbf{X}_1'\mathbf{X}_2 = \mathbf{0}$, we say "$\boldsymbol{\beta}_1$ and $\boldsymbol{\beta}_2$ are orthogonal."

7.5 The Normal Equations Using Deviations from Means

When the model $\mathbf{Y} = \mathbf{X}\boldsymbol{\beta} + \boldsymbol{\varepsilon}$ has a constant term β_0, the normal equations can easily be reduced from a $p \times p$ system to a $(p-1) \times (p-1)$ system. In this case we write the model as

$$\mathbf{Y} = [\mathbf{1}, \mathbf{X}_2]\begin{bmatrix} \beta_0 \\ \boldsymbol{\beta}_2 \end{bmatrix} + \boldsymbol{\varepsilon} = \mathbf{1}\beta_0 + \mathbf{X}_2\boldsymbol{\beta}_2 + \boldsymbol{\varepsilon}$$

where $\boldsymbol{\beta}_2' = [\beta_1, \beta_2, \ldots, \beta_{p-1}]$ and $\mathbf{X}_2$ is an $n \times (p-1)$ matrix. The normal equations are

$$\mathbf{X}'\mathbf{X}\hat{\boldsymbol{\beta}} = \mathbf{X}'\mathbf{Y} \qquad \text{or} \qquad [\mathbf{1}, \mathbf{X}_2]'[\mathbf{1}, \mathbf{X}_2]\begin{bmatrix} \hat{\beta}_0 \\ \hat{\boldsymbol{\beta}}_2 \end{bmatrix} = [\mathbf{1}, \mathbf{X}_2]'\mathbf{Y}$$

or

$$\begin{bmatrix} n & \mathbf{1}'\mathbf{X}_2 \\ \mathbf{X}_2'\mathbf{1} & \mathbf{X}_2'\mathbf{X}_2 \end{bmatrix}\begin{bmatrix} \hat{\beta}_0 \\ \hat{\boldsymbol{\beta}}_2 \end{bmatrix} = \begin{bmatrix} \mathbf{1}'\mathbf{Y} \\ \mathbf{X}_2'\mathbf{Y} \end{bmatrix} \tag{7.5.1}$$

We write $\mathbf{X}_2 = [\mathbf{x}_1, \mathbf{x}_2, \ldots, \mathbf{x}_{p-1}]$ and $\mathbf{1}'\mathbf{X}_2 = [n\bar{x}_1, n\bar{x}_2, \ldots, n\bar{x}_{p-1}] = n\bar{\mathbf{x}}'$, where $\bar{x}_j = (1/n)\sum_{i=1}^{n} x_{ij}$ for $j = 1, 2, \ldots, p-1$. If we substitute $n\bar{\mathbf{x}}'$ for $\mathbf{1}'\mathbf{X}_2$ in the normal equations of Equation (7.5.1) and multiply on the left by the matrix

$$\begin{bmatrix} 1 & \mathbf{0} \\ -\bar{\mathbf{x}} & \mathbf{I} \end{bmatrix}$$

we get

$$\begin{bmatrix} 1 & \mathbf{0} \\ -\bar{\mathbf{x}} & \mathbf{I} \end{bmatrix}\begin{bmatrix} n & n\bar{\mathbf{x}}' \\ n\bar{\mathbf{x}} & \mathbf{X}_2'\mathbf{X}_2 \end{bmatrix}\begin{bmatrix} \hat{\beta}_0 \\ \hat{\boldsymbol{\beta}}_2 \end{bmatrix} = \begin{bmatrix} 1 & \mathbf{0} \\ -\bar{\mathbf{x}} & \mathbf{I} \end{bmatrix}\begin{bmatrix} \mathbf{1}'\mathbf{Y} \\ \mathbf{X}_2'\mathbf{Y} \end{bmatrix} \tag{7.5.2}$$

which becomes

$$\begin{bmatrix} n & n\bar{\mathbf{x}}' \\ \mathbf{0} & \mathbf{X}_2'\mathbf{X}_2 - n\bar{\mathbf{x}}\bar{\mathbf{x}}' \end{bmatrix}\begin{bmatrix} \hat{\beta}_0 \\ \hat{\boldsymbol{\beta}}_2 \end{bmatrix} = \begin{bmatrix} \sum Y_i \\ \mathbf{X}_2'\mathbf{Y} - n\bar{\mathbf{x}}\bar{Y} \end{bmatrix} \tag{7.5.3}$$

The equations for $\hat{\boldsymbol{\beta}}_2$ give us

$$(\mathbf{X}_2'\mathbf{X}_2 - n\bar{\mathbf{x}}\bar{\mathbf{x}}')\hat{\boldsymbol{\beta}}_2 = \mathbf{X}_2'\mathbf{Y} - n\bar{\mathbf{x}}\bar{Y}$$

which we write as

$$\mathbf{X}_D'\mathbf{X}_D\hat{\boldsymbol{\beta}}_2 = \mathbf{X}_D'\mathbf{Y}_D \qquad \text{or} \qquad \mathbf{S}_D\hat{\boldsymbol{\beta}}_2 = \mathbf{s}_D \tag{7.5.4}$$

where $\mathbf{X}_D$, $\mathbf{Y}_D$, $\mathbf{S}_D$, and $\mathbf{s}_D$ refer to deviations from the means. Written in detail the deviation normal equations $\mathbf{S}_D\hat{\boldsymbol{\beta}}_2 = \mathbf{s}_D$ are

$$\begin{bmatrix} \sum (x_{i1} - \bar{x}_1)^2 & \sum (x_{i1} - \bar{x}_1)(x_{i2} - \bar{x}_2) & \cdots \sum (x_{i1} - \bar{x}_1)(x_{i,p-1} - \bar{x}_{p-1}) \\ \sum (x_{i2} - \bar{x}_2)(x_{i1} - \bar{x}_1) & \sum (x_{i2} - \bar{x}_2)^2 & \cdots \sum (x_{i2} - \bar{x}_2)(x_{i,p-1} - \bar{x}_{p-1}) \\ \vdots & \vdots & \vdots \\ \sum (x_{i,p-1} - \bar{x}_{p-1})(x_{i1} - \bar{x}_1) & \sum (x_{i,p-1} - \bar{x}_{p-1})(x_{i2} - \bar{x}_2) & \cdots \sum (x_{i,p-1} - \bar{x}_{p-1})^2 \end{bmatrix} \begin{bmatrix} \hat{\beta}_1 \\ \hat{\beta}_2 \\ \vdots \\ \hat{\beta}_{p-1} \end{bmatrix}$$

$$= \begin{bmatrix} \sum (x_{i1} - \bar{x}_1)(Y_i - \bar{Y}) \\ \sum (x_{i2} - \bar{x}_2)(Y_i - \bar{Y}) \\ \vdots \\ \sum (x_{i,p-1} - \bar{x}_{p-1})(Y_i - \bar{Y}) \end{bmatrix} \tag{7.5.5}$$

We call the $(p - 1) \times (p - 1)$ system in Equation (7.5.5) the "deviation" normal equations (using deviations from the means). After solving for $\hat{\boldsymbol{\beta}}_2$, we use Equation (7.5.3) and get

$$\hat{\beta}_0 = \bar{Y} - \hat{\boldsymbol{\beta}}_2'\bar{\mathbf{x}} \tag{7.5.6}$$

Note 1. $\mathbf{X}_D = (\mathbf{I} - (1/n)\mathbf{J})\mathbf{X}_2$; $\mathbf{Y}_D = (\mathbf{I} - (1/n)\mathbf{J})\mathbf{Y}$.

We now state and prove a theorem to show that in the general linear model with an intercept (β_0 term), only the deviation normal equations and $\mathbf{Y}_D'\mathbf{Y}_D$ are needed to test $\mathbf{H}_2\boldsymbol{\beta}_2 = \mathbf{h}_2$, that is, any hypothesis that involves *only* the elements in $\boldsymbol{\beta}_2$ (does not involve β_0), or to set a confidence interval on $\ell_2'\boldsymbol{\beta}_2$, that is, any linear combination of the elements in $\boldsymbol{\beta}_2$.

THEOREM 7.5.1

In the general linear model $\mathbf{Y} = \mathbf{1}\beta_0 + \mathbf{X}_2\boldsymbol{\beta}_2 + \boldsymbol{\varepsilon}$, *where* $\boldsymbol{\varepsilon}$ *is distributed* $N(\boldsymbol{\varepsilon} : \mathbf{0}, \sigma^2\mathbf{I})$, *to test* $H_0 : \mathbf{H}_2\boldsymbol{\beta}_2 = \mathbf{h}_2$ *vs.* $H_a : \mathbf{H}_2\boldsymbol{\beta}_2 \neq \mathbf{h}_2$, *the test statistic W in Equation* (6.3.10) *is (we assume* $\mathbf{H}_2$ *is a* $q \times (p - 1)$ *known matrix of rank* q, $0 < q < p$)

$$W = \left(\frac{(\mathbf{H}_2\hat{\boldsymbol{\beta}}_2 - \mathbf{h}_2)'(\mathbf{H}_2\mathbf{S}_D^{-1}\mathbf{H}_2')^{-1}(\mathbf{H}_2\hat{\boldsymbol{\beta}}_2 - \mathbf{h}_2)}{\mathbf{Y}_D'\mathbf{Y}_D - \hat{\boldsymbol{\beta}}_2'\mathbf{X}_D'\mathbf{Y}_D}\right)\left(\frac{n - p}{q}\right) \tag{7.5.7}$$

where $\hat{\boldsymbol{\beta}}_2$ *is obtained from the deviation normal equations in Equation* (7.5.4), *that is,*

Equation (7.5.5). Hence W is obtained from a knowledge of only the deviation normal equations and $\mathbf{Y}_D'\mathbf{Y}_D$.

Proof

To obtain W in Equation (6.3.10), we must obtain $\mathbf{H}\hat{\boldsymbol{\beta}}$, $\mathbf{H}(\mathbf{X}'\mathbf{X})^{-1}\mathbf{H}'$, and $\hat{\sigma}^2$. Clearly for $\mathbf{H}_2\boldsymbol{\beta}_2 = \mathbf{h}_2$, it follows that

$$\mathbf{H} = [\mathbf{0}, \mathbf{H}_2] \qquad \mathbf{h} = \mathbf{h}_2$$

From Equation (7.5.4) we get $\hat{\boldsymbol{\beta}}' = [\hat{\beta}_0, \mathbf{S}_D^{-1}\mathbf{X}_D'\mathbf{Y}_D]$, so $\mathbf{H}\hat{\boldsymbol{\beta}} - \mathbf{h} = \mathbf{H}_2\hat{\boldsymbol{\beta}}_2 - \mathbf{h}_2 = \mathbf{H}_2\mathbf{S}_D^{-1}\mathbf{X}_D'\mathbf{Y}_D - \mathbf{h}_2$; thus $\mathbf{H}\hat{\boldsymbol{\beta}} - \mathbf{h}$ is obtained from the *deviation* normal equations. Also,

$$\mathbf{H}(\mathbf{X}'\mathbf{X})^{-1}\mathbf{H}' = \mathbf{HCH}' = [\mathbf{0}, \mathbf{H}_2]\begin{bmatrix} c_{11} & \mathbf{C}_{12} \\ \mathbf{C}_{21} & \mathbf{C}_{22} \end{bmatrix}\begin{bmatrix} \mathbf{0} \\ \mathbf{H}_2' \end{bmatrix} = \mathbf{H}_2\mathbf{C}_{22}\mathbf{H}_2'$$

where $\mathbf{C}_{22}$ is obtained from

$$(\mathbf{X}'\mathbf{X})^{-1} = \mathbf{C} = \begin{bmatrix} c_{11} & \mathbf{C}_{12} \\ \mathbf{C}_{21} & \mathbf{C}_{22} \end{bmatrix} = \begin{bmatrix} n & n\bar{\mathbf{x}}' \\ n\bar{\mathbf{x}} & \mathbf{X}_2'\mathbf{X}_2 \end{bmatrix}^{-1}$$

and by Theorem 1.3.1, $\mathbf{C}_{22}^{-1} = \mathbf{X}_2'\mathbf{X}_2 - n\bar{\mathbf{x}}\bar{\mathbf{x}}' = \mathbf{X}_D'\mathbf{X}_D = \mathbf{S}_D$. Hence $\mathbf{H}(\mathbf{X}'\mathbf{X})^{-1}\mathbf{H}' = \mathbf{H}_2\mathbf{S}_D^{-1}\mathbf{H}_2'$ is obtained from the deviation normal equations.

Finally,

$$\hat{\sigma}^2 = \frac{1}{n-p}(\mathbf{Y}'\mathbf{Y} - \hat{\boldsymbol{\beta}}'\mathbf{X}'\mathbf{Y}) = \frac{1}{n-p}[\mathbf{Y}_D'\mathbf{Y}_D + n\bar{Y}^2 - \hat{\boldsymbol{\beta}}'\mathbf{X}'\mathbf{Y}]$$

but

$$\hat{\boldsymbol{\beta}}'\mathbf{X}'\mathbf{Y} = \begin{bmatrix} \hat{\beta}_0 \\ \hat{\boldsymbol{\beta}}_2 \end{bmatrix}'\begin{bmatrix} \sum Y_i \\ \mathbf{X}_2'\mathbf{Y} \end{bmatrix} = \hat{\beta}_0 \sum Y_i + \hat{\boldsymbol{\beta}}_2'\mathbf{X}_2'\mathbf{Y} = (\bar{Y} - \hat{\boldsymbol{\beta}}_2'\bar{\mathbf{x}})\sum Y_i + \hat{\boldsymbol{\beta}}_2'\mathbf{X}_2'\mathbf{Y}$$

$$= n\bar{Y}^2 + \hat{\boldsymbol{\beta}}_2'(\mathbf{X}_2'\mathbf{Y} - \bar{\mathbf{x}}\sum Y_i) = n\bar{Y}^2 + \hat{\boldsymbol{\beta}}_2'\mathbf{X}_D'\mathbf{Y}_D$$

so

$$\hat{\sigma}^2 = \frac{1}{n-p}(\mathbf{Y}_D'\mathbf{Y}_D - \hat{\boldsymbol{\beta}}_2'\mathbf{X}_D'\mathbf{Y}_D) = \left(\frac{1}{n-p}\right)\mathbf{Y}_D'(\mathbf{I} - \mathbf{X}_D\mathbf{X}_D^{-})\mathbf{Y}_D$$

and $\hat{\sigma}^2$ can be obtained from the deviation normal equations and $\mathbf{Y}_D'\mathbf{Y}_D$. This completes the proof.

The following theorem is an obvious consequence of Theorem 7.5.1.

THEOREM 7.5.2

Consider the general linear model $\mathbf{Y} = \mathbf{1}\beta_0 + \mathbf{X}_2\boldsymbol{\beta}_2 + \boldsymbol{\varepsilon}$, *where* $\boldsymbol{\varepsilon}$ *is distributed* $N(\boldsymbol{\varepsilon} : \mathbf{0}, \sigma^2\mathbf{I})$, *that is, Case* 1 *of a linear model with a constant term* β_0. *Consider the deviation normal equations in Equation* (7.5.5), *which we denote by*

$$\mathbf{X}'_D\mathbf{X}_D\hat{\boldsymbol{\beta}}_2 = \mathbf{X}'_D\mathbf{Y}_D$$

All of the results in Section 7.3 *apply (with* $\mathbf{S}$, $\mathbf{Y}'\mathbf{Y}$, *and* $\mathbf{X}'\mathbf{Y}$ *replaced by* $\mathbf{S}_D$, $\mathbf{Y}'_D\mathbf{Y}_D$, *and* $\mathbf{X}'_D\mathbf{Y}_D$, *respectively) to accomplish the following: To test* $\mathbf{H}_2\boldsymbol{\beta}_2 = \mathbf{h}_2$ *(any linear hypothesis that involves only* $\boldsymbol{\beta}_2$*); to set one-at-a-time or simultaneous confidence intervals on any linear functions of* $\boldsymbol{\beta}_2$, *say,* $\boldsymbol{\ell}'_1\boldsymbol{\beta}_2, \boldsymbol{\ell}'_2\boldsymbol{\beta}_2, \ldots, \boldsymbol{\ell}'_q\boldsymbol{\beta}_2$; *to obtain UMVU estimators of* $\boldsymbol{\ell}'_1\boldsymbol{\beta}_2, \boldsymbol{\ell}'_2\boldsymbol{\beta}_2, \ldots, \boldsymbol{\ell}'_q\boldsymbol{\beta}_2$.

We next state a theorem to show how the deviation model relates to $R(\boldsymbol{\beta})$, $R(\boldsymbol{\beta}_2)$, and $R(\beta_0)$.

THEOREM 7.5.3

Consider the general linear model $\mathbf{Y} = \mathbf{1}\beta_0 + \mathbf{X}_2\boldsymbol{\beta}_2 + \boldsymbol{\varepsilon}$, *where* $\boldsymbol{\varepsilon}$ *is distributed* $N(\boldsymbol{\varepsilon} : \mathbf{0}, \sigma^2\mathbf{I})$, *that is, Case* 1 *of a linear model with a constant term* β_0. *To test* $H_0 : \boldsymbol{\beta}_2 = \mathbf{0}$ *vs.* $H_a : \boldsymbol{\beta}_2 \neq \mathbf{0}$, *the quantity* $R(\boldsymbol{\beta}_2 \mid \beta_0)$, *which is the numerator sum of squares in the test statistic* W *in Equation* (6.3.11), *can be written as*

$$R(\boldsymbol{\beta}_2 \mid \beta_0) = R(\beta_0, \boldsymbol{\beta}_2) - R(\beta_0) = R(\boldsymbol{\beta}) - R(\beta_0) = \mathbf{Y}'_D\mathbf{X}_D\mathbf{X}_D^-\mathbf{Y}_D$$

Proof

The proof will be left for the reader.

THEOREM 7.5.4

Let the model be as given in Theorem 7.5.3. *Consider a partition of the total sum of squares* $\mathbf{Y}'\mathbf{Y} = n\bar{Y}^2 + \sum_{i=1}^{q} \mathbf{Y}'\mathbf{A}_i\mathbf{Y}$, *where* $\mathbf{Y}'\mathbf{A}_i\mathbf{Y}$ *for* $i = 1, 2, \ldots, q$ *are nonnegative quadratic forms. Then* $n\bar{Y}^2$ *is independent of each sum of squares* $\mathbf{Y}'\mathbf{A}_i\mathbf{Y}$ *for* $i = 1, 2, \ldots, q$.

Proof

The proof will be asked for in the problems.

Example 7.5.1

Consider the model $Y_i = \beta_0 + \beta_1 x_{i1} + \beta_2 x_{i2} + \varepsilon_i$, $i = 1, 2, \ldots, 9$, the ε_i are distributed $NID(\varepsilon : 0, \sigma^2)$. Find the estimates of $\boldsymbol{\beta}$ and σ^2; set a 95 percent confidence interval on $6\beta_1 + \beta_2$, and test the hypothesis $\beta_2 = 0$ with a Type I error of 10 percent.

Some data for easy calculation are given below.

$$\mathbf{X} = \begin{bmatrix} 1 & 13 & 20 \\ 1 & 6 & 17 \\ 1 & 10 & 17 \\ 1 & 9 & 16 \\ 1 & 9 & 21 \\ 1 & 6 & 19 \\ 1 & 9 & 19 \\ 1 & 10 & 17 \\ 1 & 9 & 16 \end{bmatrix} \qquad \mathbf{y} = \begin{bmatrix} 24 \\ 26 \\ 28 \\ 27 \\ 27 \\ 29 \\ 26 \\ 29 \\ 27 \end{bmatrix}$$

We will solve this problem first by using the regular normal equations and then by using the deviations from the means. First, $\mathbf{y}'\mathbf{y} = 6581$ and from the regular normal equations $\mathbf{X}'\mathbf{X}\hat{\boldsymbol{\beta}} = \mathbf{X}'\mathbf{y}$, we get the format ($\ell' = [0, 6, 1]$)

$$\frac{[\mathbf{X}'\mathbf{X} \mid \mathbf{X}'\mathbf{y} \mid \ell]}{[\;\mathbf{T} \mid \mathbf{t} \mid \mathbf{a}]} = \left[\begin{array}{ccc|c|c} 9 & 81 & 162 & 243 & 0 \\ 81 & 765 & 1464 & 2175 & 6 \\ 162 & 1464 & 2942 & 4367 & 1 \\ \hline 3 & 27 & 54 & 81 & 0 \\ & 6 & 1 & -2 & 1 \\ & & 5 & -1 & 0 \end{array}\right]$$

This gives

$$\hat{\boldsymbol{\beta}}' = \left[\frac{333}{10}, -\frac{3}{10}, -\frac{2}{10}\right] \qquad \hat{\sigma}^2 = \frac{1}{n-p}[\mathbf{y}'\mathbf{y} - \mathbf{t}'\mathbf{t}] = \frac{1}{6}(6581 - 6566) = 2.5$$

$$\hat{\sigma} = 1.58 \qquad \ell'\hat{\boldsymbol{\beta}} = -2 \qquad \ell'(\mathbf{X}'\mathbf{X})^{-1}\ell = 1$$

A 95 percent confidence interval on $6\beta_1 + \beta_2$ is given by $\ell'\hat{\boldsymbol{\beta}} \mp t_{0.025:6}\sqrt{\hat{\sigma}^2\ell'(\mathbf{X}'\mathbf{X})^{-1}\ell}$, or

$$-5.87 \le 6\beta_1 + \beta_2 \le 1.87 \tag{7.5.8}$$

To test $H_0 : \beta_2 = 0$, we use the formula in Equation (7.3.12) and get

$$w = \left(\frac{\mathbf{t}_2'\mathbf{t}_2}{\mathbf{y}'\mathbf{y} - \mathbf{t}'\mathbf{t}}\right)\left(\frac{n-p}{q}\right) = \left(\frac{1}{6581 - 6566}\right)\left(\frac{6}{1}\right) = \frac{1}{2.5} \tag{7.5.9}$$

Table 7.5.1

ANOVA for Testing $\beta_2 = 0$

Source	*d.f.*	*S.S.*	*M.S.*	*F*
Total	9	6581		
$R(\boldsymbol{\beta}) = R(\beta_0, \beta_1, \beta_2)$	3	6566		
$R(\boldsymbol{\gamma}) = R(\beta_0, \beta_1)$	2	6565		
$R(H_0) = R(\beta_2 \mid \beta_0, \beta_1)$	1	1	1	1/2.5
Error	6	15	2.5	

The ANOVA table is shown in Table 7.5.1. The hypothesis is not rejected.

Now we work the problem by using the deviation normal equations (the deviations from the means). We get

$$\mathbf{X}'_D\mathbf{X}_D = \begin{bmatrix} \sum (x_{i1} - \bar{x}_1)^2 & \sum (x_{i1} - \bar{x}_1)(x_{i2} - \bar{x}_2) \\ \sum (x_{i2} - \bar{x}_2)(x_{i1} - \bar{x}_1) & \sum (x_{i2} - \bar{x}_2)^2 \end{bmatrix}$$

$$= \begin{bmatrix} 36 & 6 \\ 6 & 26 \end{bmatrix}$$

$$\mathbf{X}'_D\mathbf{y}_D = \begin{bmatrix} \sum (x_{i1} - \bar{x}_1)(y_i - \bar{y}) \\ \sum (x_{i2} - \bar{x}_2)(y_i - \bar{y}) \end{bmatrix} = \begin{bmatrix} -12 \\ -7 \end{bmatrix} \qquad \mathbf{y}'_D\mathbf{y}_D = \sum (y_i - \bar{y})^2 = 20$$

From the normal equations $\mathbf{X}'_D\mathbf{X}_D\hat{\boldsymbol{\beta}}_2 = \mathbf{X}'_D\mathbf{y}_D$ and the linear function $\ell'_2\boldsymbol{\beta}_2 = 6\beta_1 + \beta_2$ we get the format

$$\frac{[\mathbf{X}'_D\mathbf{X}_D \mid \mathbf{X}'_D\mathbf{y}_D \mid \ell_2]}{[\ \mathbf{T}_D \mid \mathbf{t}_D \mid \mathbf{a}_2]} = \frac{\left[\begin{array}{cc|c|c} 36 & 6 & -12 & 6 \\ 6 & 26 & -7 & 1 \end{array}\right]}{\left[\begin{array}{cc|c|c} 6 & 1 & -2 & 1 \\ & 5 & -1 & 0 \end{array}\right]} \tag{7.5.10}$$

Thus

$$\hat{\beta}_1 = -\frac{3}{10} \qquad \hat{\beta}_2 = -\frac{2}{10} \qquad \hat{\sigma}^2 = \left(\frac{1}{6}\right)[20 - (-2)^2 - (-1)^2] = 2.5$$

$$\ell'\hat{\boldsymbol{\beta}} = \ell'_2\hat{\boldsymbol{\beta}}_2 = \mathbf{t}'_D\mathbf{a}_2 = -2 \qquad \ell'(\mathbf{X}'\mathbf{X})^{-1}\ell = \ell'_2(\mathbf{X}'_D\mathbf{X}_D)^{-1}\ell_2 = \mathbf{a}'_2\mathbf{a}_2 = 1$$

and the confidence interval on $6\beta_1 + \beta_2$ is, of course, the same as given in Equation (7.5.8).

Table 7.5.2

ANOVA for Testing $\beta_2 = 0$

Source	*d.f.*	*S.S.*	*M.S.*	*F*
Total (deviation)	8	20		
$R(\beta_1, \beta_2 \mid \beta_0)$	2	5		
$R(\beta_1 \mid \beta_0)$	1	4		
$R(H_0) = R(\beta_2 \mid \beta_0, \beta_1)$	1	1	1	1/2.5
Error	6	15	2.5	

To test $H_0 : \beta_2 = 0$, we use the format in Equation (7.5.10) and the formula in Equation (7.3.12). We get

$$w = \left(\frac{\mathbf{t}_2'\mathbf{t}_2}{\mathbf{y}_D'\mathbf{y}_D - \mathbf{t}_D'\mathbf{t}_D}\right)\left(\frac{n-p}{q}\right) = \left(\frac{1}{20-5}\right)\left(\frac{6}{1}\right) = \frac{1}{2.5}$$

the same as in Equation (7.5.9) when the regular normal equations were used.

The ANOVA table is given in Table 7.5.2. Note that the M.S. column of $R(H_0)$ and error are the same in Table 7.5.1 and Table 7.5.2. Also note that "total (deviation)" can be written $\mathbf{y}'\mathbf{y} - R(\beta_0)$, which is sometimes called "the total *corrected* sum of squares."

While it is true that the "deviation" normal equations give a smaller system to solve than the regular normal equations, it does require more work to construct the system of "deviation" normal equations. In general, however, it is better from a computing standpoint to use the "deviation" normal equations when there is an "intercept" term in the model. In fact, it is generally advisable to use the "correlation" normal equations. See Problem 7.22.

7.6 Some Computing Procedures When cov[Y] = σ^2V

When the model is $\mathbf{Y} = \mathbf{X}\boldsymbol{\beta} + \boldsymbol{\varepsilon}$ and $\boldsymbol{\varepsilon}$ is distributed $N(\boldsymbol{\varepsilon} : \mathbf{0}, \sigma^2\mathbf{V})$, where $\mathbf{V}$ is a *known* positive definite matrix, the square root method can be used to compute the quantities necessary for point estimates, confidence intervals, and tests of hypotheses. These results are summarized in the following theorem.

THEOREM 7.6.1

Consider the general linear model $\mathbf{Y} = \mathbf{X}\boldsymbol{\beta} + \boldsymbol{\varepsilon}$, $\boldsymbol{\varepsilon}$ *is distributed* $N(\boldsymbol{\varepsilon} : \mathbf{0}, \sigma^2\mathbf{V})$, *where* $\mathbf{V}$ *is a known positive definite matrix. To find point and interval estimates and tests of hypotheses about* $\boldsymbol{\beta}$, *the quantities in Equations* (6.8.1), (6.8.2), *and* (6.8.3) *are needed. They can be computed by the square root method as follows. Let* $\mathbf{V} = \mathbf{T}_V'\mathbf{T}_V$, *where* $\mathbf{T}_V$ *is an upper triangular matrix. The format below is formed*:

$$[\mathbf{V} \mid \mathbf{X} \mid \mathbf{y}] \tag{7.6.1}$$

Reduce this by the square root method on $\mathbf{V}$ *and represent the resulting format by*

$$[\mathbf{T}_V \mid \mathbf{X}_V \mid \mathbf{y}_V] \tag{7.6.2}$$

Then

$$\begin{aligned} \mathbf{X}_V'\mathbf{X}_V &= \mathbf{X}'\mathbf{V}^{-1}\mathbf{X} \\ \mathbf{y}_V'\mathbf{y}_V &= \mathbf{y}'\mathbf{V}^{-1}\mathbf{y} \\ \mathbf{X}_V'\mathbf{y}_V &= \mathbf{X}'\mathbf{V}^{-1}\mathbf{y} \end{aligned} \tag{7.6.3}$$

Proof

The proof will be asked for in the problems.

We next state a theorem to show how the quantities $\mathbf{X}_V$ and $\mathbf{y}_V$ can be used to obtain point and interval estimates of $\ell_1'\boldsymbol{\beta}, \ell_2'\boldsymbol{\beta}, \ldots, \ell_q'\boldsymbol{\beta}$ and a test of the hypothesis $\mathbf{H}\boldsymbol{\beta} = \mathbf{h}$.

THEOREM 7.6.2

Consider the general linear model $\mathbf{Y} = \mathbf{X}\boldsymbol{\beta} + \boldsymbol{\varepsilon}$, $\boldsymbol{\varepsilon}$ *is distributed* $N(\boldsymbol{\varepsilon} : \mathbf{0}, \sigma^2\mathbf{V})$, *where* $\mathbf{V}$ *is a known positive definite matrix. Reduce the data* $[\mathbf{V} \mid \mathbf{X} \mid \mathbf{y}]$ *by the square root method and obtain* $\mathbf{X}_V$ *and* $\mathbf{y}_V$. *Consider the new model* $\mathbf{Y}_V = \mathbf{X}_V\boldsymbol{\beta} + \boldsymbol{\varepsilon}_V$. *Then* $\boldsymbol{\varepsilon}_V$ *is distributed* $N(\boldsymbol{\varepsilon}_V : \mathbf{0}, \sigma^2\mathbf{I})$, *and all the computing procedures and formulas in Sections* 7.3, 7.4, *and* 7.5 *apply for computing point estimates, interval estimates, and tests on* $\boldsymbol{\beta}$, *except* $\mathbf{X}$ *is replaced by* $\mathbf{X}_V$ *and* $\mathbf{y}$ *is replaced by* $\mathbf{y}_V$.

Proof

The proof will be asked for in the problems.

Note 1. To compute $\hat{\sigma}^2; \ell_1'\hat{\boldsymbol{\beta}}, \ell_2'\hat{\boldsymbol{\beta}}, \ldots, \ell_q'\hat{\boldsymbol{\beta}}$; $\text{cov}[\ell_1'\hat{\boldsymbol{\beta}}]$, $\text{cov}[\ell_2'\hat{\boldsymbol{\beta}}], \ldots$, $\text{cov}[\ell_q'\hat{\boldsymbol{\beta}}]$ (the quantities needed for confidence intervals on $\ell_1'\boldsymbol{\beta}, \ell_2'\boldsymbol{\beta}, \ldots, \ell_q'\boldsymbol{\beta}$), it is necessary to perform the square root method twice, once to obtain the new data matrix $[\mathbf{X}_V \mid \mathbf{y}_V]$ and then once to reduce $[\mathbf{X}_V'\mathbf{X}_V \mid \mathbf{X}_V'\mathbf{y}_V \mid \ell_1, \ell_2, \ldots, \ell_q]$.

7.7 Appendix

This section is devoted to a discussion of triangular matrices and factoring positive definite (and positive semidefinite) matrices. First we restate and prove Theorem 7.2.1.

THEOREM 7.7.1

Let $\mathbf{S}$ *be a* $p \times p$ *positive definite (real) matrix. There exists a (real) upper triangular matrix* $\mathbf{T}$ *of rank* p, *with* $t_{ii} > 0$ *for* $i = 1, 2, \ldots, p$, *such that* $\mathbf{S} = \mathbf{T}'\mathbf{T}$. *Also,* $\mathbf{T}$ *is unique.*

Proof

The proof will be by mathematical induction. First, let $p = 1$; then since $\mathbf{S}$ is positive definite (and real) we can write $\mathbf{S} = [s_{11}^2]$. Clearly $t_{11} = |s_{11}|$, and hence $\mathbf{T} = [t_{11}]$ is an upper triangular (real) matrix with $t_{11} > 0$. Also, t_{11} is unique.

Now suppose the theorem is true for $p = k$. We must show it is also true for $p = k + 1$. By the theorem being true for $p = k$, we mean that for *any* positive definite (real) $k \times k$ matrix $\mathbf{S}_{11}$, there exists a unique upper triangular (real) matrix $\mathbf{T}_{11}$, with $t_{ii} > 0$ for $i = 1, 2, \ldots, k$, such that $\mathbf{S}_{11} = \mathbf{T}'_{11}\mathbf{T}_{11}$. Let $\mathbf{S}$ be any known $(k + 1) \times (k + 1)$ positive definite (real) matrix. Since $\mathbf{S}$ is positive definite, we can write $\mathbf{S}$ as

$$\mathbf{S} = \begin{bmatrix} \mathbf{S}_{11} & \mathbf{s}_{12} \\ \mathbf{s}_{21} & s_{22} \end{bmatrix}$$

where $\mathbf{S}_{11}$ is a $k \times k$ positive definite matrix. But by the induction hypothesis, we can write $\mathbf{S}_{11} = \mathbf{T}'_{11}\mathbf{T}_{11}$, where $\mathbf{T}_{11}$ is a unique upper triangular matrix with positive diagonal elements. Thus ($\mathbf{s}_{12} = \mathbf{s}'_{21}$ since $\mathbf{S}$ is symmetric)

$$\mathbf{S} = \begin{bmatrix} \mathbf{S}_{11} & \mathbf{s}_{12} \\ \mathbf{s}_{21} & s_{22} \end{bmatrix} = \begin{bmatrix} \mathbf{T}'_{11}\mathbf{T}_{11} & \mathbf{s}_{12} \\ \mathbf{s}_{21} & s_{22} \end{bmatrix} = \begin{bmatrix} \mathbf{T}'_{11} & \mathbf{0} \\ \mathbf{s}'_{12}\mathbf{T}_{11}^{-1} & b \end{bmatrix} \begin{bmatrix} \mathbf{T}_{11} & \mathbf{T}'^{-1}_{11}\mathbf{s}_{12} \\ \mathbf{0} & b \end{bmatrix}$$

$$= \mathbf{T}'\mathbf{T} \tag{7.7.1}$$

where $b = (s_{22} - \mathbf{s}_{21}\mathbf{S}_{11}^{-1}\mathbf{s}_{12})^{1/2}$. If we can show that $s_{22} - \mathbf{s}_{21}\mathbf{S}_{11}^{-1}\mathbf{s}_{12}$ is positive, so that b is real, then $\mathbf{T}$ is upper triangular with positive diagonal elements and $\mathbf{T}$ is unique. To show this we write $|\mathbf{S}| = |\mathbf{S}_{11}| \cdot |s_{22} - \mathbf{s}_{21}\mathbf{S}_{11}^{-1}\mathbf{s}_{12}|$. But $\mathbf{S}$ and $\mathbf{S}_{11}$ are positive definite, so $|\mathbf{S}| > 0$, $|\mathbf{S}_{11}| > 0$. This means that $|s_{22} - \mathbf{s}_{21}\mathbf{S}_{11}^{-1}\mathbf{s}_{12}| > 0$, but $s_{22} - \mathbf{s}_{21}\mathbf{S}_{11}^{-1}\mathbf{s}_{12}$ is a scalar and hence is equal to its determinant. This implies $s_{22} - \mathbf{s}_{21}\mathbf{S}_{11}^{-1}\mathbf{s}_{12} > 0$, and the theorem is proved.

In Section 7.1 we stated that in some cases it might be advantageous to perform calculations directly from the $\mathbf{X}$ matrix rather than from the normal equations $\mathbf{X}'\mathbf{X}\hat{\boldsymbol{\beta}} = \mathbf{X}'\mathbf{y}$. The reason for this is that if $\mathbf{X}$ is an ill-conditioned matrix, then $\mathbf{X}'\mathbf{X}$ is apt to be more ill-conditioned. For additional information see [F-1], [G-5], [H-17], [K-9], [W-12]. The next theorem states the main result.

THEOREM 7.7.2

Let $\mathbf{X}$ *be an* $n \times p$ *(real) matrix (where* $n > p$*) of rank* p*. There exists an orthogonal matrix* $\mathbf{P}$ *such that*

$$\mathbf{P}'\mathbf{X} = \begin{bmatrix} \mathbf{T} \\ \mathbf{0} \end{bmatrix}$$

where $\mathbf{T}$ *is a* $p \times p$ *upper triangular matrix with positive diagonal elements. Also,* $\mathbf{T}$ *is unique.*

Proof

The theorem can be proved by induction.

Note 1. Since $\mathbf{X}'\mathbf{X} = \mathbf{X}'\mathbf{P}\mathbf{P}'\mathbf{X} = \mathbf{T}'\mathbf{T}$, the upper triangular matrix $\mathbf{T}$ in Theorem 7.7.2 is the same matrix as the upper triangular matrix $\mathbf{T}$ in Theorem 7.7.1. We will not discuss this method for computing $\mathbf{T}$ but the interested reader can consult [G-5].

Since upper triangular matrices will be encountered extensively in this book, we state several results about them in the next theorem.

THEOREM 7.7.3

If $\mathbf{T}$ *is an upper triangular* $p \times p$ *matrix, then*

(1) $\mathbf{T}^{-1}$, *if it exists, is an upper triangular matrix;*

(2) *if* $\mathbf{T}^{-1}$ *exists, the ith diagonal element is* t_{ii}^{-1};

(3) $\mathbf{T}'$ *is a lower triangular matrix;*

(4) *the product of two* $p \times p$ *upper triangular matrices is a* $p \times p$ *upper triangular matrix;*

(5) *if* $\mathbf{S} = \mathbf{T}'\mathbf{T}$, *then* $det(\mathbf{S}) = \left[\prod_{i=1}^{p} t_{ii}\right]^2$.

Proof

The proof will be left for the reader.

In the next theorem we state a result for positive semidefinite matrices. The proof can be found in [G-8].

THEOREM 7.7.4

Let **S** *be a* $p \times p$ *positive semidefinite matrix of rank k. There exists an upper triangular matrix* **T** *(of rank k) with* $p - k$ *zero rows such that* $\mathbf{S} = \mathbf{T}'\mathbf{T}$.

> *Note 2.* A positive semidefinite matrix **S** can be reduced by the square root method described in Section 7.2, with the modification that whenever a zero diagonal element is encountered, that entire row of **T** is set to zero.

Problems

7.1. The positive definite matrix **S** is defined by

$$\mathbf{S} = \begin{bmatrix} 4 & -2 & 6 & 0 \\ -2 & 2 & -1 & -1 \\ 6 & -1 & 17 & 0 \\ 0 & -1 & 0 & 6 \end{bmatrix}$$

Use the square root method to find the upper triangular matrix **T** such that $\mathbf{T}'\mathbf{T} = \mathbf{S}$.

7.2. In Problem 7.1 find det[**S**].

7.3. In Problem 7.1 find $\mathbf{T}^{-1}$.

7.4. In Problem 7.1 find $\mathbf{S}^{-1}$.

7.5. By using the results of Problem 7.1, find an upper triangular matrix $\mathbf{T}_1$ such that $\mathbf{T}_1'\mathbf{T}_1 = \mathbf{S}_1$, where $\mathbf{S}_1$ is defined by

$$\mathbf{S}_1 = \begin{bmatrix} 4 & -2 & 6 \\ -2 & 2 & -1 \\ 6 & -1 & 17 \end{bmatrix}$$

Note

$$\mathbf{S} = \begin{bmatrix} \mathbf{S}_1 & \mathbf{s}_{12} \\ \mathbf{s}_{21} & s_{22} \end{bmatrix} \quad \text{and} \quad \mathbf{T} = \begin{bmatrix} \mathbf{T}_1 & \mathbf{t}_{12} \\ \mathbf{0} & t_{22} \end{bmatrix}$$

7.6. In Problem 7.1 find an upper triangular matrix $\mathbf{T}$ with $t_{11} < 0$ and all other $t_{ii} > 0$ such that $\mathbf{T}'\mathbf{T} = \mathbf{S}$.

7.7. Give an example of a 2×2 symmetric matrix $\mathbf{S}$ for which there exists no upper triangular matrix $\mathbf{T}$ such that $\mathbf{S} = \mathbf{T}'\mathbf{T}$.

7.8. In Problem 7.1 show that $\det[\mathbf{S}] = [\prod_{i=1}^{p} t_{ii}]^2$.

7.9. Consider the general linear model $\mathbf{Y} = \mathbf{X}\boldsymbol{\beta} + \boldsymbol{\varepsilon}$, $\boldsymbol{\varepsilon}$ is distributed $N(\boldsymbol{\varepsilon} : \mathbf{0}, \sigma^2\mathbf{I})$, $\mathbf{Y}$ is a 16×1 random vector, and $\boldsymbol{\beta}' = [\beta_0, \beta_1, \beta_2, \beta_3]$. The normal equations are

$$
\begin{aligned}
16\hat{\beta}_0 + 8\hat{\beta}_1 + 4\hat{\beta}_2 - 4\hat{\beta}_3 &= 4 \\
8\hat{\beta}_0 + 5\hat{\beta}_1 + 3\hat{\beta}_2 &= 5 \\
4\hat{\beta}_0 + 3\hat{\beta}_1 + 6\hat{\beta}_2 + 3\hat{\beta}_3 &= 0 \\
-4\hat{\beta}_0 + 3\hat{\beta}_2 + 7\hat{\beta}_3 &= 5
\end{aligned}
$$

and $\mathbf{y}'\mathbf{y} = 54$. Use the square root procedures described in Section 7.3 to find point estimates of the following:

(a) $\boldsymbol{\beta}$ (b) σ^2 (c) $4\beta_0 + 5\beta_1 + \beta_2 + 5\beta_3$ (d) $8\beta_0 + 5\beta_1 + 9\beta_2 + 4\beta_3$
(e) test the hypothesis

$$
H_0 : \begin{cases} 2\beta_1 + 4\beta_3 = 0 \\ 2\beta_2 + \beta_3 = 0 \end{cases} \quad vs. \quad H_a : \begin{cases} 2\beta_1 + 4\beta_3 \neq 0 \\ 2\beta_2 + \beta_3 \neq 0 \end{cases}
$$

Use $\alpha = 0.05$.

7.10. In Problem 7.9 test $H_0 : \beta_2 = -3$, $\beta_3 = 3$ *vs.* $H_a : \beta_2 \neq -3$ or $\beta_3 \neq 3$; use $\alpha = 0.05$.

7.11. In Problem 7.9 set 0.95 one-at-a-time confidence intervals on $\beta_0, \beta_1, \beta_2$, and β_3.

7.12. In Problem 7.9 set simultaneous 0.95 confidence intervals on $\beta_0, \beta_1, \beta_2$, and β_3 by using the multivariate t method.

7.13. In the general linear model $\mathbf{Y} = \mathbf{X}\boldsymbol{\beta} + \boldsymbol{\varepsilon}$, let $\mathbf{X}$ be an $n \times p$ matrix and let the data matrix $[\mathbf{X} \mid \mathbf{y}]$ have rank $p + 1$. Let $\mathbf{S}^*$ be defined by

$$
\mathbf{S}^* = [\mathbf{X} \mid \mathbf{y}]'[\mathbf{X} \mid \mathbf{y}] = (\mathbf{T}^*)'(\mathbf{T}^*)
$$

where $\mathbf{T}^*$ is an upper triangular matrix. Prove that

$$
\mathbf{T}^* = \begin{bmatrix} \mathbf{T} & \mathbf{a} \\ \mathbf{0} & b \end{bmatrix}
$$

where $\mathbf{T}$ is an upper triangular matrix such that $\mathbf{T}'\mathbf{T} = \mathbf{X}'\mathbf{X}$ and $b^2 = (n - p)\hat{\sigma}^2$.

7.14. In Problem 7.13 find $\mathbf{a}$ in terms of $\mathbf{X}$, $\mathbf{y}$, and $\mathbf{T}$.

7.15. In Problem 7.9 write the normal equation as $\mathbf{S}\hat{\boldsymbol{\beta}} = \mathbf{s}$ and let $\mathbf{D}^{-1/2}$ be a 4×4 diagonal matrix whose ith diagonal element is $s_{ii}^{-1/2}$, where $\mathbf{S} = [s_{ij}]$. Find $\mathbf{R}$ defined by $\mathbf{D}^{-1/2}\mathbf{S}\mathbf{D}^{-1/2}$.

7.16. In Problem 7.15 transform the system of normal equations to $\mathbf{R}\hat{\boldsymbol{\gamma}} = \mathbf{r}$ by $\mathbf{D}^{-1/2}\mathbf{S}\mathbf{D}^{-1/2}\mathbf{D}^{1/2}\hat{\boldsymbol{\beta}} = \mathbf{D}^{-1/2}\mathbf{s}$, that is, $\mathbf{D}^{1/2}\hat{\boldsymbol{\beta}} = \hat{\boldsymbol{\gamma}}$, $\mathbf{D}^{-1/2}\mathbf{s} = \mathbf{r}$. Solve the system $[\mathbf{R} \mid \mathbf{r}]$ by the square root method to get $[\mathbf{T}_0 \mid \mathbf{t}_0]$, where $\mathbf{T}_0'\mathbf{T}_0 = \mathbf{R}$.

7.17. From Problem 7.16 show that $\mathbf{t}_0'\mathbf{t}_0 = \mathbf{t}'\mathbf{t}$ given in Equation (7.3.2).

7.18. In Problem 7.16 find $\hat{\boldsymbol{\gamma}}$.

7.19. In Problem 7.18 find $\hat{\boldsymbol{\beta}} = \mathbf{D}^{-1/2}\hat{\boldsymbol{\gamma}}$ and compare it with part (a) in Problem 7.9.

7.20. In Problem 7.16 find $\hat{\sigma}^2 = [1/(n - p)](\mathbf{y}'\mathbf{y} - \mathbf{t}_0'\mathbf{t}_0)$ and compare it with part (b) in Problem 7.9.

7.21. Solve parts (c) and (d) in Problem 7.9 by using the normal equations $\mathbf{R}\hat{\boldsymbol{\gamma}} = \mathbf{r}$ in Problem 7.16. The format is $[\mathbf{R} \mid \mathbf{r} \mid \mathbf{r}_1 \mid \mathbf{r}_2]$, where $\mathbf{r}_i = \mathbf{D}^{-1/2}\ell_i$, $i = 1, 2$. Reduce by the square root method. Compare your answer with parts (c) and (d) in Problem 7.9.

7.22. Generalize Problem 7.17 as follows: In the general linear model $\mathbf{Y} = \mathbf{X}\boldsymbol{\beta} + \boldsymbol{\varepsilon}$, let the set of $p \times p$ normal equations be $\mathbf{X}'\mathbf{X}\hat{\boldsymbol{\beta}} = \mathbf{X}'\mathbf{y}$, that is, $\mathbf{S}\hat{\boldsymbol{\beta}} = \mathbf{s}$. Define $\mathbf{R}$ by $\mathbf{D}^{-1/2}\mathbf{S}\mathbf{D}^{-1/2}$, $\mathbf{r}$ by $\mathbf{D}^{-1/2}\mathbf{X}'\mathbf{y}$, and $\hat{\boldsymbol{\gamma}} = \mathbf{D}^{1/2}\hat{\boldsymbol{\beta}}$, where $\mathbf{D}^{-1/2}$ is a diagonal matrix whose ith diagonal element is $s_{ii}^{-1/2}$. Then the normal equations can be written as $\mathbf{R}\hat{\boldsymbol{\gamma}} = \mathbf{r}$. Reduce the system $[\mathbf{R} \mid \mathbf{r}]$ by the square root method and obtain $[\mathbf{T}_\mathbf{R} \mid \mathbf{t}_\mathbf{r}]$. Prove that $\mathbf{t}_\mathbf{r}'\mathbf{t}_\mathbf{r} = \mathbf{t}'\mathbf{t}$, where $\mathbf{t}$ is obtained by reducing $[\mathbf{S} \mid \mathbf{s}]$ by the square root method to obtain $[\mathbf{T} \mid \mathbf{t}]$. $\mathbf{R}\hat{\boldsymbol{\gamma}} = \mathbf{r}$ are called "correlation" normal equations.

7.23. Prove that if the $p \times p$ matrix

$$\mathbf{B} = \begin{bmatrix} 1 & -\bar{x}_1 & -\bar{x}_2 & \cdots & -\bar{x}_{p-1} \\ 0 & 1 & 0 & \cdots & 0 \\ 0 & 0 & 1 & \cdots & 0 \\ \vdots & \vdots & \vdots & & \vdots \\ 0 & 0 & 0 & \cdots & 1 \end{bmatrix}$$

then

$$\mathbf{B}^{-1} = \begin{bmatrix} 1 & \bar{x}_1 & \bar{x}_2 & \cdots & \bar{x}_{p-1} \\ 0 & 1 & 0 & \cdots & 0 \\ 0 & 0 & 1 & \cdots & 0 \\ \vdots & \vdots & \vdots & & \vdots \\ 0 & 0 & 0 & \cdots & 1 \end{bmatrix}$$

7.24. Let $\mathbf{Y} = \mathbf{X}\boldsymbol{\beta} + \boldsymbol{\varepsilon}$ be a general linear model, where $\mathbf{X} = [\mathbf{1}, \mathbf{X}_2]$ has size $n \times p$, and let $\mathbf{X}'\mathbf{X}\hat{\boldsymbol{\beta}} = \mathbf{X}'\mathbf{Y}$ be the normal equations. Prove the following.

$$\mathbf{B}'\mathbf{X}'\mathbf{X}\mathbf{B} = \begin{bmatrix} n & \mathbf{0} \\ \mathbf{0} & \mathbf{X}_D'\mathbf{X}_D \end{bmatrix}$$

where $\mathbf{B}$ is defined in Problem 7.23 and $\mathbf{X}_D'\mathbf{X}_D$ are the "deviation" sum of squares and cross products defined in Equation (7.5.5).

7.25. In Problem 7.24 prove that

$$\mathbf{B}'\mathbf{X}'\mathbf{Y} = \begin{bmatrix} n\bar{Y} \\ \mathbf{X}_D'\mathbf{Y}_D \end{bmatrix}$$

7.26. In measuring the various constituents of cow's milk, it is of interest to determine how protein Y is related to fat x_1 and solids-nonfat x_2. The following linear model was assumed:

$$Y_i = \mu(\mathbf{x}_i) + \varepsilon_i = \beta_0 + \beta_1 x_{i1} + \beta_2 x_{i2} + \varepsilon_i$$

ε_i are distributed $NID(\varepsilon : 0, \sigma^2)$, $i = 1, 2, \ldots, 16$. Samples from 16 cows were taken and the data that were obtained are given in the table below.

Protein y	*Fat* x_1	*Solid Nonfat* x_2	*Protein* y	*Fat* x_1	*Solid Nonfat* x_2
3.75	4.74	9.50	3.16	3.36	8.86
3.19	3.66	8.56	3.65	3.64	9.21
2.99	4.27	8.54	3.36	3.92	8.93
3.46	4.03	8.62	3.60	2.99	9.16
3.27	3.51	9.35	3.87	3.28	8.45
3.27	3.97	8.39	3.14	3.23	9.09
2.78	3.23	7.87	3.00	3.65	8.36
3.59	3.79	9.33	3.18	4.23	9.28

(a) Find the normal equations.
(b) By the square root method find $\hat{\boldsymbol{\beta}}$, $\hat{\sigma}^2$, and $\hat{\mu}(\mathbf{x})$.
(c) We are interested in testing whether $\beta_1 = \beta_2 = 0$ (only). We are not interested in whether linear combinations of β_1 and β_2 are zero. Test this hypothesis with $\alpha = 0.05$.

7.27. In Problem 7.26 set simultaneous 0.95 confidence intervals on β_1 and β_2.

7.28. In Problem 7.26 set 0.95 one-at-a-time confidence intervals on β_1 and β_2.

7.29. Solve Problem 7.26 by using the deviation normal equations $\mathbf{X}_D'\mathbf{X}_D\hat{\boldsymbol{\beta}}_2 = \mathbf{X}_D'\mathbf{y}_D$ and then by using correlation normal equations.

7.30. In Problem 7.26 suppose we want to determine if *any* linear combination of β_1 and β_2 is zero. Test this hypothesis with $\alpha = 0.05$. Exhibit an ANOVA table.

7.31. Find 0.95 confidence bands on the entire line $\mu(\mathbf{x})$ in Problem 7.26.

7.32. In Problem 7.30 find the power of the test when $\beta_1/\sigma = \beta_2/\sigma = 1$.

7.33. In the general linear model $\mathbf{Y} = \mathbf{X}\boldsymbol{\beta} + \boldsymbol{\varepsilon}$, show that

$$\frac{\det\begin{bmatrix} \mathbf{X}'\mathbf{X} & \mathbf{X}'\mathbf{Y} \\ \mathbf{Y}'\mathbf{X} & \mathbf{Y}'\mathbf{Y} \end{bmatrix}}{\det[\mathbf{X}'\mathbf{X}]} = \mathbf{Y}'(\mathbf{I} - \mathbf{X}\mathbf{X}^{-})\mathbf{Y} = (n-p)\hat{\sigma}^2$$

7.34. Prove Theorem 7.4.1.

7.35. Prove Theorem 7.4.2.

7.36. For the data in Section 6.7, assume the model $\mathbf{Y} = \mathbf{X}\boldsymbol{\beta} + \boldsymbol{\varepsilon}$, $\boldsymbol{\varepsilon}$ is distributed $N(\boldsymbol{\varepsilon} : \mathbf{0}, \sigma^2\mathbf{V})$, where

$$\mathbf{V} = \begin{bmatrix} \mathbf{V}_{11} & \mathbf{0} \\ \mathbf{0} & \mathbf{I} \end{bmatrix} \quad \text{and} \quad \mathbf{V}_{11} = \begin{bmatrix} 4 & 2 \\ 2 & 2 \end{bmatrix}$$

Find the following by using the square root computing procedures discussed in Theorems 7.6.1 and 7.6.2.

(a) $\hat{\boldsymbol{\beta}}$ (b) $\hat{\sigma}^2$ (c) $\hat{\beta}_0 - \hat{\beta}$ (d) $\widehat{\text{var}}[\hat{\beta}_0]$ (e) $\widehat{\text{var}}[\hat{\beta}]$ (f) $\widehat{\text{cov}}[\hat{\beta}_0, \hat{\beta}]$

7.37. Prove Theorem 7.5.4.

7.38. Prove Theorem 7.6.1.

7.39. Prove Theorem 7.6.2.

7.40. Compute $\mathbf{S}^{-1}$ for the matrix $\mathbf{S}$ in Example 7.2.2 by computing $\mathbf{T}^{-1}$ by the formulas in Equation (7.3.13); then use $\mathbf{S}^{-1} = (\mathbf{X}'\mathbf{X})^{-1} = \mathbf{T}^{-1}\mathbf{T}'^{-1}$.

7.41. In Problem 7.40 compute $\mathbf{S}^{-1}$ by using $\mathbf{T}$ and the formulas in Equation (7.3.15). Do not compute $\mathbf{T}^{-1}$.

7.42. Consider the general linear model with an intercept term, that is, consider $\mathbf{Y} = \mathbf{X}\boldsymbol{\beta} + \boldsymbol{\varepsilon} = \mathbf{1}\beta_0 + \mathbf{X}_2\boldsymbol{\beta}_2 + \boldsymbol{\varepsilon}$, and the normal equations $\mathbf{X}'\mathbf{X}\hat{\boldsymbol{\beta}} = \mathbf{X}'\mathbf{y}$. If the normal equations are reduced by the square root method, we obtain

$$\left[\begin{array}{c|c} \mathbf{X}'\mathbf{X} & \mathbf{X}'\mathbf{y} \\ \hline \mathbf{T} & \mathbf{t} \end{array}\right] = \left[\begin{array}{cc|c} n & n\bar{\mathbf{x}}' & \mathbf{1}'\mathbf{y} \\ n\bar{\mathbf{x}} & \mathbf{X}_2'\mathbf{X}_2 & \mathbf{X}_2'\mathbf{y} \\ \hline t_{11} & \mathbf{t}_{12} & t_1 \\ \mathbf{0} & \mathbf{T}_{22} & \mathbf{t}_2 \end{array}\right]$$

Show that $\mathbf{T}_{22}'\mathbf{T}_{22}\hat{\boldsymbol{\beta}}_2 = \mathbf{T}_{22}'\mathbf{t}_2$ are the deviation normal equations given in Equation (7.5.4).

CHAPTER 8

Applications of the General Linear Model

8.1 Introduction

In this chapter we will illustrate how the general linear model can be used to solve a number of problems that are useful in real-world applications.

In Section 8.2 we will discuss prediction intervals. Section 8.3 and Section 8.4 will be devoted to tolerance intervals. Section 8.5 will be devoted to the calibration problem. Testing the equality of a set of lines will be the subject of Section 8.6; Sections 8.7 and 8.8 will be devoted to polynomial and trigonometric models, respectively. In Section 8.9 we discuss briefly the "design" problem for the general linear model and in Section 8.10 we discuss "the maximum and minimum" of a quadratic function. In Section 8.11 we determine a method for setting a confidence interval on the point of intersection of two lines.

8.2 Prediction Intervals

We use an example to introduce the problem to be discussed in this section.

Example 8.2.1

Suppose when firing a missile the maximum speed Y, a critical factor in the operation, is linearly related to the size x of the opening of the fuel valve. The relationship is given by $Y = \beta_0 + \beta x + \varepsilon$. Suppose n missiles, with different sizes of fuel valves (denoted by x_i), are fired and the speed Y_i at a certain time after firing is observable. The data

(x_i, y_i), $i = 1, 2, \ldots, n$, are obtained and used to estimate β_0, β, and σ^2. With these values it is possible to estimate $\mu(x_0)$, the *average* speed of all missiles when the fuel valve opening is x_0 units. However, what is wanted here is *not* the mean $\mu(x_0)$ of *all* missiles with valve opening x_0 but rather an estimate of the speed of *this particular* missile that is to be fired. If we view the speed of *this* missile as a random observation from the population of the speeds of all missiles that could be fired with fuel valve size x_0, then we want to determine in advance an interval for the random observation, which we will denote by Y_0.

In other words, we determine an interval (L, U) such that if an observation Y_0 is to be selected at random from a normal distribution with mean $\mu(x_0) = \beta_0 + \beta x_0$ and variance σ^2, then the probability is equal to $1 - \alpha$ that Y_0 will fall in the interval. Clearly if β_0, β, and σ are known, then the interval (ℓ, u) is $(\beta_0 + \beta x_0 - N_{\alpha/2}\sigma, \beta_0 + \beta x_0 + N_{\alpha/2}\sigma)$ and, referring to the example above, if a new missile is fired, we can state that, with probability $1 - \alpha$, the speed will be between $\beta_0 + \beta x_0 - N_{\alpha/2}\sigma$ and $\beta_0 + \beta x_0 + N_{\alpha/2}\sigma$.

Since β_0, β, and σ^2 are unknown, we must obtain estimates of these parameters from data (in the example we use the data from missiles that have been fired with various fuel valve openings x_i and speeds y_i). From these data we will construct an interval of a form similar to that above, except the unknown parameters will be replaced by their estimates and a constant $h_{\alpha/2}$, different from $N_{\alpha/2}$, will have to be determined. The lower and upper limits are

$$L = \hat{\beta}_0 + \hat{\beta}x_0 - h_{\alpha/2}\hat{\sigma} \qquad U = \hat{\beta}_0 + \hat{\beta}x_0 + h_{\alpha/2}\hat{\sigma}$$

The interval for this problem is similar to a confidence interval, but whereas a confidence interval is concerned with an unknown parameter, this interval is concerned with the unknown value of a random variable. We label the interval for this problem a prediction interval—an interval that predicts (with probability $1 - \alpha$) that the value of a random variable is contained in it. We now formulate and give a solution to this problem. We will slightly generalize the formulation of the discussion above from a prediction interval on Y_0, a future observation, to a prediction interval on $\bar{Y}_0$, the mean of k future observations, and from a simple linear model to a general linear model.

THEOREM 8.2.1

Consider the general linear model given in Definition 6.1.1 *for Case* 1, *and let* $\hat{\boldsymbol{\beta}}$ *and* $\hat{\sigma}^2$ *be the UMVU estimators of* $\boldsymbol{\beta}$ *and* σ^2, *respectively. Let* $\mathbf{x}_0$ *be a vector in domain D of* $\mu(\mathbf{x}_0)$. *In Equation* (8.2.1) *a* $1 - \alpha$ *prediction interval is given for* $\bar{Y}_0$, *the mean of k future observations selected at random from the normal distribution with mean* $\mu(\mathbf{x}_0) = \boldsymbol{\beta}'\mathbf{x}_0$ *and variance* σ^2.

$$\hat{\boldsymbol{\beta}}'\mathbf{x}_0 - h_{\alpha/2}\hat{\sigma} \le \bar{Y}_0 \le \hat{\boldsymbol{\beta}}'\mathbf{x}_0 + h_{\alpha/2}\hat{\sigma} \tag{8.2.1}$$

where

$$h_{\alpha/2} = t_{\alpha/2:n-p}\left(\frac{1}{k} + \mathbf{x}_0'\mathbf{S}^{-1}\mathbf{x}_0\right)^{1/2}$$

Proof

We must show

$$P[\hat{\boldsymbol{\beta}}'\mathbf{x}_0 - h_{\alpha/2}\hat{\sigma} \le \bar{Y}_0 \le \hat{\boldsymbol{\beta}}'\mathbf{x}_0 + h_{\alpha/2}\hat{\sigma}] = 1 - \alpha$$

where $\hat{\boldsymbol{\beta}} = \mathbf{X}^-\mathbf{Y}$ and $\hat{\sigma}^2 = [1/(n-p)]\mathbf{Y}'(\mathbf{I} - \mathbf{X}\mathbf{X}^-)\mathbf{Y}$ are obtained from the linear model $\mathbf{Y} = \mathbf{X}\boldsymbol{\beta} + \boldsymbol{\varepsilon}$ and where $\bar{Y}_0 = (1/k)\sum_{i=1}^{k} Y_{0i}$, where $Y_{01}, Y_{02}, \ldots, Y_{0k}$ represent k future observations. The three random variables $\hat{\boldsymbol{\beta}}'\mathbf{x}_0$, $\hat{\sigma}^2$, and $\bar{Y}_0$ are clearly jointly independent. We obtain

1. $V = \bar{Y}_0 - \hat{\boldsymbol{\beta}}'\mathbf{x}_0$ is distributed $N(v:0, \sigma^2A^2)$, where $\sigma^2A^2 = \text{var}[V] = \text{var}[\bar{Y}_0] + \text{var}[\hat{\boldsymbol{\beta}}'\mathbf{x}_0] = \sigma^2[(1/k) + \mathbf{x}_0'\mathbf{S}^{-1}\mathbf{x}_0]$;
2. $Z = (\bar{Y}_0 - \hat{\boldsymbol{\beta}}'\mathbf{x}_0)/\sigma A$ is distributed $N(z:0, 1)$;
3. $U = (n-p)\hat{\sigma}^2/\sigma^2$ is distributed $\chi^2(u:n-p)$;
4. U and Z are independent;
5. $T = Z/\sqrt{U/(n-p)}$ is distributed as Student's t with $n - p$ degrees of freedom;
6. $P[-t_{\alpha/2:n-p} \le T \le t_{\alpha/2:n-p}] = 1 - \alpha$.

Substitute for T, simplify, and the proof is complete.

The quantities needed to evaluate the prediction intervals in Equation (8.2.1) can be computed from $\mathbf{y}'\mathbf{y}$ and the results of reducing the format $[\mathbf{X}'\mathbf{X} \mid \mathbf{X}'\mathbf{y} \mid \mathbf{x}_0]$ by the square root method.

COROLLARY 8.2.1

For the simple linear model given in Example 6.2.1, *a* $1 - \alpha$ *prediction interval on* $\bar{Y}_0$, *the mean of k future observations from a normal distribution with mean* $\mu(x_0) = \beta_0 + \beta x_0$ *and variance* σ^2, *is given by*

$$\hat{\beta}_0 + \hat{\beta}x_0 - t_{\alpha/2:n-2}\hat{\sigma}A_1 \le \bar{Y}_0 \le \hat{\beta}_0 + \hat{\beta}x_0 + t_{\alpha/2:n-2}\hat{\sigma}A_1 \tag{8.2.2}$$

where A_1^2 is defined as follows:

$$A_1^2 = \left[\frac{1}{k} + \frac{1}{n} + \frac{(\bar{x} - x_0)^2}{\sum (x_i - \bar{x})^2}\right]$$

Proof

It is straightforward to compute $\mathbf{x}_0'\mathbf{S}^{-1}\mathbf{x}_0$ for the simple linear model, where $\mathbf{x}_0' = [1, x_0]$.

Note 1. The data for this problem consist of $\mathbf{y}$, $\mathbf{X}$ for the general linear model and a vector $\mathbf{x}_0$. These data are used to compute the prediction interval in Equation (8.2.1). $\bar{Y}_0$ is not observed but is the mean of k future observations, and the prediction interval in Equation (8.2.1) tells us something about what the value of $\bar{Y}_0$ would be if we did observe it. For further information on this subject, see [H-2] and [L-9].

8.3 Tolerance Intervals

In many of the problems that we have discussed, we have been interested in confidence intervals on parameters (or on the mean of k future observations discussed in the previous section). Another very important problem in applications is that of determining a number γ_P such that a $1 - P$ proportion of the distribution under study is below it (a $1 - P$ proportion of the distribution is in the interval $-\infty$ to γ_P); or a similar problem of determining two numbers $\gamma_{1-P/2}, \gamma_{P/2}$ such that a $1 - P$ proportion of the distribution is between the two numbers (a $1 - P$ proportion of the distribution is in the interval $\gamma_{1-P/2}$ to $\gamma_{P/2}$). The intervals referred to above are known as tolerance intervals and we shall discuss them in this section.

Example 8.3.1

Consider Example 5.2.3. Generally the main concern of the superintendent is not what the *average* percentage of impurities is as a function of the number of batches produced; rather he may want to know that a large proportion of the batches produced have a small percentage of impurities in them. In other words, suppose he plans to increase production and produce 10 batches every day. He predicts that the average percentage of impurities is $\hat{\mu}(10)$, but this could mean that on some days the percentage of impurities is very low and some days very high. When it is very high, he can't sell the material, so he doesn't want this to happen very often. He knows that in the long run (when 10 batches are produced) a $1 - P$ proportion of the batches have a percentage of impurities that will be below $\mu(10) + N_P\sigma$; so he may want to find point and interval estimates of this number.

We will first consider the *simple* linear model $Y_i = \beta_0 + \beta x_i + \varepsilon_i$ under Case 1. For a given value x_0 of x, it is desired to find the following:

1. the point γ_P such that a $1 - P$ proportion of the distribution at x_0 is below γ_P (is in the interval $-\infty$ to γ_P); γ_P is called the upper Pth tolerance point (also called the $(1 - P)$th quantile);
2. the point γ_{1-P} such that a $1 - P$ proportion of the distribution at x_0 is above γ_{1-P} (is in the interval γ_{1-P} to ∞); γ_{1-P} is called the lower Pth tolerance point (also called the Pth quantile);
3. the two points $\gamma_{1-P/2}$, $\gamma_{P/2}$ such that a $P/2$ proportion of the distribution at x_0 is below $\gamma_{1-P/2}$ and a $P/2$ proportion is above $\gamma_{P/2}$ (hence a $1 - P$ proportion is in the interval $\gamma_{1-P/2}$ to $\gamma_{P/2}$); this defines a *symmetric* two-sided tolerance interval.

Clearly the values of γ for the three parts are, respectively,

1. $\gamma_P = \beta_0 + \beta x_0 + N_P\sigma$;
2. $\gamma_{1-P} = \beta_0 + \beta x_0 - N_P\sigma$;
3. the interval $(\gamma_{1-P/2}, \gamma_{P/2})$ is $(\beta_0 + \beta x_0 - N_{P/2}\sigma, \beta_0 + \beta x_0 + N_{P/2}\sigma)$. (8.3.1)

In part 1, the number γ_P is such that a $1 - P$ proportion of the distribution at x_0 is below it, but since γ_P contains unknown parameters we cannot compute it. We can, however, obtain a UMVU estimator of γ_P by substituting UMVU estimators of β_0, β, and σ into the equation $\gamma_P = \beta_0 + \beta x_0 + N_P\sigma$. Since γ_P cannot be known, in applied problems it may be useful to determine a random variable $\tilde{\gamma}_P$ such that $P[\gamma_P < \tilde{\gamma}_P] = 1 - \alpha$; see Example 8.3.1. To do this we determine a constant g_P such that $P[\beta_0 + \beta x_0 + N_P\sigma < \hat{\beta}_0 + \hat{\beta} x_0 + g_P\hat{\sigma}] = 1 - \alpha$, which is P[at least a $1 - P$ proportion of the distribution at x_0 is less than $\hat{\beta}_0 + \hat{\beta} x_0 + g_P\hat{\sigma}] = 1 - \alpha$, and $\hat{\beta}_0 + \hat{\beta} x_0 + g_P\hat{\sigma}$ is called an *upper P tolerance point with confidence coefficient* $1 - \alpha$.

Parts 2 and 3 have similar interpretations. Part 3 will not be discussed in this book.

8.3.1 Upper and Lower Tolerance Intervals

We now state and prove a theorem for Part 1 for the general linear model.

THEOREM 8.3.1

Consider the general linear model $\mathbf{Y} = \mathbf{X}\boldsymbol{\beta} + \boldsymbol{\varepsilon}$ *under Case* 1. *The upper Pth tolerance point at the point* $\mathbf{x}_0$ *and with confidence coefficient* $1 - \alpha$ *is*

$$\hat{\boldsymbol{\beta}}'\mathbf{x}_0 + g_P\hat{\sigma} \tag{8.3.2}$$

where g_P *is given by*

$$g_P = -At_{1-\alpha:n-p;(\delta)} \tag{8.3.3}$$

where $A^2 = \mathbf{x}_0'\mathbf{S}^{-1}\mathbf{x}_0$ *and* $t_{1-\alpha:n-p;(\delta)}$ *is the upper* $1 - \alpha$ *probability point of the noncentral t distribution with* $n - p$ *degrees of freedom and noncentrality* $\delta = -N_P/A$.

Note 1. N_P and A are positive and hence δ is negative; thus $t_{1-\alpha:n-p;(\delta)}$ is negative and g_P is positive (we assume here that $1 - \alpha > 0.50$).

Proof

We must prove that g_P is such that $P[\boldsymbol{\beta}'\mathbf{x}_0 + N_P\sigma < \hat{\boldsymbol{\beta}}'\mathbf{x}_0 + g_P\hat{\sigma}] = 1 - \alpha$. Let

$$V = \frac{\hat{\boldsymbol{\beta}}'\mathbf{x}_0 - \boldsymbol{\beta}'\mathbf{x}_0}{\sigma A} - \frac{N_P}{A}$$

where $A^2 = \mathbf{x}_0'\mathbf{S}^{-1}\mathbf{x}_0$, and let $U = (n - p)\hat{\sigma}^2/\sigma^2$; then

1. V is distributed $N(v : -N_P/A, 1)$;
2. U is distributed $\chi^2(u : n - p)$;
3. U and V are independent;
4. $T = V/\sqrt{U/(n - p)}$ is distributed $s(t : n - p; -N_P/A)$.

For a given $1 - \alpha$ and $\delta = -N_P/A$, evaluate $t_{1-\alpha:n-p;(\delta)}$ from

$$P[T < t_{1-\alpha:n-p;(\delta)}] = \int_{-\infty}^{t_{1-\alpha:n-p;(\delta)}} s(t : n - p; \delta)\, dt = \alpha$$

by Table 4.3.1. Then compute g_P from $g_P = -At_{1-\alpha:n-p;(\delta)}$. From this we get the following probability statement:

$$1 - \alpha = P[T > t_{1-\alpha:n-p;(\delta)}] = P\left[\frac{V}{\sqrt{U/(n-p)}} > -\frac{g_P}{A}\right]$$

$$= P\left[\frac{\dfrac{\hat{\boldsymbol{\beta}}'\mathbf{x}_0 - \boldsymbol{\beta}'\mathbf{x}_0}{\sigma A} - \dfrac{N_P}{A}}{\hat{\sigma}/\sigma} + \frac{g_P}{A} > 0\right]$$

$$= P[\boldsymbol{\beta}'\mathbf{x}_0 + N_P\sigma < \hat{\boldsymbol{\beta}}'\mathbf{x}_0 + g_P\hat{\sigma}]$$

and this completes the proof.

Next the case for the lower tolerance point is considered.

THEOREM 8.3.2

Under the conditions of Theorem 8.3.1, *the lower Pth tolerance point at the point* $\mathbf{x}_0$ *and with coefficient* $1 - \alpha$ *is*

$$\hat{\boldsymbol{\beta}}'\mathbf{x}_0 - g_P\hat{\sigma} \tag{8.3.4}$$

where g_P *is given by*

$$g_P = At_{\alpha:n-p;(\delta)} \tag{8.3.5}$$

where $t_{\alpha:n-p;(\delta)}$ *is the upper* α *probability point of the noncentral t distribution with* $n - p$ *degrees of freedom and noncentrality* $\delta = N_P/A$.

THEOREM 8.3.3

For the simple linear model under Case 1, *the upper Pth tolerance point in Equation* (8.3.2) *is*

$$\hat{\beta}_0 + \hat{\beta}x_0 + g_P\hat{\sigma}$$

where

$$g_P = -At_{1-\alpha:n-2;(\delta)} \qquad A^2 = \frac{1}{n} + \frac{(\bar{x} - x_0)^2}{\sum (x_i - \bar{x})^2} \qquad \delta = -\frac{N_P}{A}$$

The lower Pth tolerance point in Equation (8.3.4) *is* $\hat{\beta}_0 + \hat{\beta}x_0 - g_P\hat{\sigma}$, *where*

$$g_P = At_{\alpha:n-2;(\delta)} \qquad A^2 = \frac{1}{n} + \frac{(\bar{x} - x_0)^2}{\sum (x_i - \bar{x})^2} \qquad \delta = \frac{N_P}{A}$$

Note 2. The computed quantity g_P in Equation (8.3.5) has the same value as g_P in Equation (8.3.3).

The quantities needed to evaluate the tolerance intervals in Equations (8.3.2) and (8.3.4) are $\mathbf{A}^2 = \mathbf{x}_0'\mathbf{S}^{-1}\mathbf{x}_0$, $\hat{\sigma}^2$, and $\mathbf{x}_0'\hat{\boldsymbol{\beta}}$. These quantities can be computed from $\mathbf{y}'\mathbf{y}$ and the results of reducing the format $[\mathbf{X}'\mathbf{X} \mid \mathbf{X}'\mathbf{y} \mid \mathbf{x}_0]$ by the square root method.

Example 8.3.2

The data below are assumed to come from the model $Y_i = \beta_0 + \beta x_i + \varepsilon_i$, ε_i are distributed $NID(\varepsilon : 0, \sigma^2)$ for $i = 1, 2, \ldots, 18$. Find the upper 20 percent tolerance point with confidence coefficient equal to 95 percent at the point $x_0 = 3.0$.

x	1.0	1.1	1.3	1.6	1.8	1.8	1.8	2.1	2.4	2.6
y	4.81	3.60	4.90	3.05	3.44	3.17	3.34	1.61	1.22	0.20

x	2.6	2.7	2.9	3.0	3.5	3.6	4.1	5.2
y	1.56	0.55	−2.56	−0.34	−2.56	−2.96	−1.04	−4.64

From this we compute

$$\left[\frac{\mathbf{X}'\mathbf{X} \mid \mathbf{X}'\mathbf{y} \mid \mathbf{x}_0}{\mathbf{T} \mid \mathbf{t} \mid \mathbf{a}}\right] = \left[\begin{array}{cc|c|c} 18 & 45.10 & 17.350 & 1 \\ 45.10 & 133.63 & -6.152 & 3 \\ \hline 4.24264 & 10.63017 & 4.08943 & 0.23570 \\ & 4.54196 & -10.92553 & 0.10886 \end{array}\right]$$

We get

$$\mathbf{y}'\mathbf{y} = \sum_{i=1}^{18} y_i^2 = 153.8989 \qquad \mathbf{t}'\mathbf{t} = 136.09075 \qquad \hat{\sigma}^2 = 1.11301$$

$$\hat{\sigma} = 1.055 \qquad A^2 = \mathbf{a}'\mathbf{a} = 0.06741 = (0.25963)^2$$

$$\hat{\boldsymbol{\beta}}' = [6.99, -2.41] \qquad \hat{\mu}(3) = -0.225 = \mathbf{a}'\mathbf{t}$$

To compute the upper 20 percent tolerance point with 95 percent confidence coefficient we obtain $P = 0.20$, $N_{0.20} = 0.842$. From Theorem 8.3.3 we compute δ by $\delta = -N_P/A = -0.842/0.2596 = -3.2431$. We must evaluate $t_{1-\alpha:\nu;(\delta)}$ for $\alpha = 0.05$, $\nu = 16$, $\delta = -3.2431$. But by Equation (4.3.7) we get $t_{1-\alpha:\nu;(\delta)} = -t_{\alpha:\nu;(-\delta)}$ and we can compute $t_{\alpha:\nu;(-\delta)}$ from Table 4.3.1. First we compute ξ by the formula in Equation (4.3.9) and get $\xi \approx 0.50$. The value of λ from the table for $\nu = 16$ and $\xi = 0.50$ is $\lambda = 1.6817$. Substituting into the formula in Equation

(4.3.9) gives $t_{0.05:16;(3.2431)} = 5.61$, so from Equation (4.3.7) we get $t_{0.95:16;(-3.2431)} = -5.61$, and thus $g_P = g_{0.20} = -(0.25963)(-5.61) = 1.46$. The upper 20 percent tolerance point with confidence coefficient 0.95 is $\hat{\gamma}_{0.20} = \hat{\mu}(3) + g_{0.20}\hat{\sigma} = -0.225 + (1.46)(1.055) = 1.31$.

8.4 Other Tolerance and Associated Intervals

Information about similar types of problems, which we shall not discuss, can be found in the references below.

1. Symmetric two-sided tolerance intervals: [O-2].
2. Nonsymmetric two-sided tolerance intervals: [D-8] and [W-2].
3. Expected coverage tolerance intervals: [G-12], [G-19], [G-20], [G-21], and [G-22].
4. Confidence intervals on a quantile: [O-3].
5. Simultaneous tolerance intervals: [M-4] and [W-13].

8.5 Determining x for a Given Value of Y (the Calibration Problem)

Next we turn our attention to a somewhat different kind of problem; namely, it is observed that a random Y value is equal to y_0, and it is desired to determine the x value (say x_0) corresponding to this. We shall illustrate this problem with some examples.

Example 8.5.1

Consider Example 5.2.1. Suppose it is observed that the particle has moved a distance of y_0 units and it is desired to ascertain how long it took the particle to move this distance. We want to determine t_0.

Example 8.5.2

Suppose that the linear model $Y = \beta_0 + \beta t + \varepsilon$ relates the weight Y in grams of a certain breed of chickens and the time t in weeks that they have been fed a new ration. It is assumed that the model holds for $0 \le t \le 20$ weeks. Thus β_0 is the initial weight of the chickens when the feeding of the new ration started and β is the growth rate. A farmer receives a group of k chickens that have been fed this new ration for t_0

(unknown to him) weeks. The farmer observes the weights of the chickens and wants to estimate t_0, the number of weeks they have been fed the new ration.

Example 8.5.3

In calibrating an instrument, say a new type of thermometer, n readings Y_i are taken at predetermined known temperatures x_i (known by using a standard temperature gauge). The relationship between the readings Y_i on the new thermometer and the readings x_i on the standard gauge is assumed to be a simple linear model $Y_i = \beta_0 + \beta x_i + \varepsilon_i, i = 1, 2, \ldots, n$. Then a reading (say y_0) is observed on the new thermometer and it is desired to estimate the correct temperature (the reading x_0 on the standard gauge when the new thermometer reading is y_0).

Since the procedure described in this section can be used in calibrating instruments, the procedure is sometimes referred to as the *calibration problem.*

Example 8.5.4

A certain drug is being tried for lowering blood pressure. It is observed that the number of units Y that the blood pressure is reduced is a linear function of the quantity of the drug x administered in one week. Over a period of time, n patients are treated with different levels x_i of the drug and the decrease y_i in blood pressure is observed. The pairs of observations are assumed to fit the simple linear model

$$Y_i = \beta_0 + \beta x_i + \varepsilon_i \qquad i = 1, 2, \ldots, n$$

In applying the treatment a doctor measures a patient's blood pressure and determines that it should be reduced by y_0 units. The problem is how many units x_0 of the drug should be administered? In other words, one wants to estimate the x_0 value for an observed Y value equal to y_0.

In summary, the problem is this: Y and x are related by the simple linear model (assume for the moment the β_0 and β are known)

$$Y = \mu(x) + \varepsilon = \beta_0 + \beta x + \varepsilon$$

For a given value of x, say x_0 (x_0 unknown), a Y value (or random sample of k values of Y) is observed from the p.d.f. determined by the x_0 value. The problem is to estimate x_0.

At first it might appear that we would use the model

$$X = \gamma_0 + \gamma y + \varepsilon \qquad \text{where} \qquad \mu(y) = \gamma_0 + \gamma y \tag{8.5.1}$$

as defined in Definition 5.2.1 with X and y interchanged; that is, we would let

X be the dependent variable and y the predictor or independent variable. In fact, if X is an observable random variable for each fixed value of y, and hence if the model does indeed satisfy the assumptions in Definition 5.2.1, then the model in Equation (8.5.1) is appropriate and we use Theorem 6.2.1 to obtain the prediction equation of X for a given y equal to y_0.

If the model in Equation (8.5.1) is the appropriate one to use for this problem, we note that $\mu(y)$, the mean of the random variable X for each fixed value of y, *must have meaning*. Hence if X is *not* a *random* variable, then the conventional model in Definition 5.2.1 is *not* appropriate for this problem. For instance, in the illustrations at the beginning of this section, the variable t (time) in Example 8.5.1 is *not* a random variable. In other examples cited it does not seem realistic to assume that the independent variable x is a random variable. Therefore, for these types of problems we shall take another approach.

We consider a simple linear model given in Definition 5.2.1:

$$Y = \mu(x) + \varepsilon = \beta_0 + \beta x + \varepsilon \tag{8.5.2}$$

We assume $\beta \neq 0$ and solve the equation $\mu(x) = \beta_0 + \beta x$ for x. We get

$$x = \frac{\mu(x) - \beta_0}{\beta} \tag{8.5.3}$$

If Y_0 denotes a random observation from the c.d.f. with mean $\mu(x_0)$, then since $\mathscr{E}[Y_0] = \mu(x_0) = \beta_0 + \beta x_0$, we use Y_0 to estimate $\mu(x_0)$ in Equation (8.5.3) and get

$$X_0 = \frac{Y_0 - \beta_0}{\beta} \tag{8.5.4}$$

To utilize this equation we take a random sample of size n, say $(x_1, Y_1), (x_2, Y_2), \ldots, (x_n, Y_n)$, use Theorem 6.2.1 to estimate β_0 and β, put these estimators into Equation (8.5.4) and obtain

$$\hat{x}_0 = \frac{Y_0 - \hat{\beta}_0}{\hat{\beta}} \tag{8.5.5}$$

We show that this is the maximum likelihood estimator of x_0 for an observed Y_0 in the model given in Equation (8.5.2). We generalize this slightly by assuming that instead of observing one value of Y at an unknown x_0, we observe k values of Y at x_0.

We assume the model $Y = \beta_0 + \beta x + \varepsilon$, ε is distributed $N(\varepsilon : 0, \sigma^2)$. A sample of $n + k$ values is selected and denoted by

$$(x_1, Y_1), (x_2, Y_2), \ldots, (x_n, Y_n) \qquad (x_0, Y_{n+1}), (x_0, Y_{n+2}), \ldots, (x_0, Y_{n+k})$$

where x_0 is unknown. Note in the notation of the sample that the k values of Y, denoted by $Y_{n+1}, Y_{n+2}, \ldots, Y_{n+k}$, are all selected from the same distribution, namely a normal distribution with mean $\beta_0 + \beta x_0$ and variance σ^2, where x_0, σ^2, β_0, and β are unknown. The sample values are related by

$$\left.\begin{array}{ll} Y_i = \beta_0 + \beta x_i + \varepsilon_i & i = 1, 2, \ldots, n \\ Y_i = \beta_0 + \beta x_0 + \varepsilon_i & i = n+1, n+2, \ldots, n+k \end{array}\right\} \begin{array}{l} \varepsilon_i \text{ are distributed} \\ NID(\varepsilon : 0, \sigma^2) \end{array}$$

The likelihood function is

$$L(\beta_0, \beta, \sigma^2, x_0 : y_1, x_1, \ldots, y_n, x_n; y_{n+1}, y_{n+2}, \ldots, y_{n+k})$$
$$= \left(\frac{1}{(2\pi\sigma^2)^{(n+k)/2}}\right) \exp\left\{-\frac{1}{2\sigma^2}\left[\sum_{i=1}^{n} (y_i - \beta_0 - \beta x_i)^2 + \sum_{i=n+1}^{n+k} (y_i - \beta_0 - \beta x_0)^2\right]\right\}$$

If we take partial derivatives with respect to β_0, β, σ^2, and x_0, set them equal to zero, and solve, we get (we have corrected $\hat{\sigma}^2$ for bias) the M.L. estimators

$$\hat{\beta} = \frac{\sum_{i=1}^{n} (Y_i - \bar{Y})(x_i - \bar{x})}{\sum_{i=1}^{n} (x_i - \bar{x})^2}$$

$$\hat{\beta}_0 = \bar{Y} - \hat{\beta}\bar{x}$$

$$\hat{x}_0 = \frac{\bar{Y}_0 - \hat{\beta}_0}{\hat{\beta}} \qquad \text{if } \hat{\beta} \neq 0 \text{ (which has probability one)}$$

$$\hat{\sigma}^2 = \frac{1}{n+k-3}\left[\sum_{i=1}^{n} (Y_i - \hat{\beta}_0 - \hat{\beta}x_i)^2 + \sum_{i=n+1}^{n+k} (Y_i - \bar{Y}_0)^2\right]$$

$$\text{where } \bar{Y} = \frac{1}{n}\sum_{i=1}^{n} Y_i \qquad \bar{x} = \frac{1}{n}\sum_{i=1}^{n} x_i \qquad \bar{Y}_0 = \frac{1}{k}\sum_{i=n+1}^{n+k} Y_i \qquad (8.5.6)$$

This is summarized in the following theorem.

THEOREM 8.5.1

Let (x_i, Y_i), $i = 1, 2, \ldots, n$, be related by the simple linear model $Y_i = \beta_0 + \beta x_i + \varepsilon_i$, ε_i are distributed $NID(\varepsilon : 0, \sigma^2)$. Further let Y_{n+i}, $i = 1, 2, \ldots, k$, $k \geq 1$, be an observable random sample from a normal distribution with mean $\beta_0 + \beta x_0$ (x_0 unknown) and variance σ^2. Let all random variables Y_i be independent. The maximum likelihood estimators of x_0, β_0, β, and σ^2 (corrected for bias) are given in Equation (8.5.6).

Note 1. $\hat{\beta}_0$ and $\hat{\beta}$ are obtained from the first n values of (x_i, Y_i) by using the formulas in Theorem 6.2.1, or, more specifically, in Equation (6.2.11). Hence they have the optimum properties given in Theorems 6.2.1 and 6.2.2. The quantity $\hat{\sigma}^2$ is not obtained by the formulas in Theorem 6.2.1.

We shall now prove a theorem about the distributional properties of the estimators in Equation (8.5.6).

THEOREM 8.5.2

Consider the model given in Theorem 8.5.1 *and the estimators given in Equation* (8.5.6).

(1) *The quantities* $\hat{\beta}_0$ *and* $\hat{\beta}$ *have the joint distribution given in Theorem* 6.2.1.

(2) $U = (n + k - 3)(\hat{\sigma}^2/\sigma^2)$ *is distributed as* $\chi^2(u : n + k - 3)$.

(3) $\hat{\sigma}^2$ *is independent of* $(\hat{\beta}_0, \hat{\beta}, \hat{x}_0)$.

Proof

Part (1) is a direct result of Theorem 6.2.1. To prove parts (2) and (3), we will denote S_1^2 and S_2^2, respectively, by

$$S_1^2 = \sum_{i=1}^{n} (Y_i - \hat{\beta}_0 - \hat{\beta}x_i)^2 \qquad S_2^2 = \sum_{i=n+1}^{n+k} (Y_i - \bar{Y}_0)^2$$

hence $\hat{\sigma}^2 = (1/(n + k - 3))(S_1^2 + S_2^2)$. It follows by Theorem 6.2.1 that $U_1 = S_1^2/\sigma^2$ is distributed as $\chi^2(u_1 : n - 2)$, and by Theorem 2.5.1 that $U_2 = S_2^2/\sigma^2$ is distributed as $\chi^2(u_2 : k - 1)$. But U_1 depends only on $Y_1, Y_2, \ldots, Y_n$, and U_2 depends only on $Y_{n+1}, Y_{n+2}, \ldots, Y_{n+k}$. Since the Y_i are mutually independent, it follows that U_1 and U_2 (and hence S_1^2 and S_2^2) are independent. Thus $U_1 + U_2$ is distributed as a chi-square random variable with $n + k - 3$ degrees of freedom. But $U_1 + U_2 = (S_1^2/\sigma^2) + (S_2^2/\sigma^2) = (n + k - 3)(\hat{\sigma}^2/\sigma^2)$, and part (2) is proved.

To prove part (3) we note that by Theorem 6.2.1, S_1^2 is independent of $\hat{\beta}_0$ and $\hat{\beta}$. But since S_2^2 depends only on the last k Y_i's, it is clear that the four random variables $(\hat{\beta}_0, \hat{\beta})$, $\bar{Y}_0$, S_1^2, and S_2^2 are mutually independent. Thus $(\hat{\beta}_0, \hat{\beta})$ and $\bar{Y}_0$ are also independent of $S_1^2 + S_2^2$ and hence of $\hat{\sigma}^2$. But $\hat{x}_0$ depends only on $(\hat{\beta}_0, \hat{\beta})$ and $\bar{Y}_0$; hence the result of part (3).

Note 2. We have not stated the distribution of $\hat{x}_0$. This distribution is quite complicated and is not needed to set a confidence interval on x_0.

8.5.1 Confidence Interval on x_0 for a Given Value of Y_0 in Simple Linear Models: Case 1

In this section we discuss one-at-a-time confidence intervals on x_0 for a given Y_0. For simultaneous confidence intervals and additional information about this problem the reader can refer to [M-4], [S-5], [S-11], and [W-9].

From Theorem 8.5.2 we obtain the following:

1. $$Z = \frac{\bar{Y}_0 - \hat{\beta}_0 - \hat{\beta}x_0}{\sqrt{\text{var}[\bar{Y}_0 - \hat{\beta}_0 - \hat{\beta}x_0]}}$$

   is distributed $N(z : 0, 1)$, where

$$\text{var}[\bar{Y}_0 - \hat{\beta}_0 - \hat{\beta}x_0] = \sigma^2\left[\frac{1}{k} + \frac{1}{n} + \frac{(x_0 - \bar{x})^2}{\sum_{i=1}^{n}(x_i - \bar{x})^2}\right] = \sigma^2 A^2$$

2. $$U = \frac{(n + k - 3)\hat{\sigma}^2}{\sigma^2} = \frac{\sum_{i=1}^{n}(Y_i - \hat{\beta}_0 - \hat{\beta}x_i)^2 + \sum_{i=n+1}^{n+k}(Y_i - \bar{Y}_0)^2}{\sigma^2}$$

   is distributed $\chi^2(u : n + k - 3)$;

3. Z and U are independent;

4. $$T = \frac{Z}{\sqrt{U/(n + k - 3)}}$$

   is distributed $s(t : n + k - 3)$;

5. $P[-t_{\alpha/2:n+k-3} \le T \le t_{\alpha/2:n+k-3}] = 1 - \alpha$.

To solve the inequalities for x_0 we proceed as follows.

The quantity in the brackets is equivalent to $T^2 \le t^2_{\alpha/2:n+k-3}$ or

$$\frac{(\bar{Y}_0 - \hat{\beta}_0 - \hat{\beta}x_0)^2}{\hat{\sigma}^2 A^2} \le t^2_{\alpha/2:n+k-3} \quad \text{or} \quad (\bar{Y}_0 - \hat{\beta}_0 - \hat{\beta}x_0)^2 - \hat{\sigma}^2 A^2 t^2_{\alpha/2:n+k-3} \le 0$$

The only unknown in this inequality is x_0. If we expand this we get

$$q(x_0) = \left[\hat{\beta}^2 - \frac{\hat{\sigma}^2 t^2_{\alpha/2:n+k-3}}{\sum_{i=1}^{n}(x_i - \bar{x})^2}\right]x_0^2 + 2\left[\frac{\bar{x}\hat{\sigma}^2 t^2_{\alpha/2:n+k-3}}{\sum_{i=1}^{n}(x_i - \bar{x})^2} - \hat{\beta}(\bar{Y}_0 - \bar{Y}) - \hat{\beta}^2\bar{x}\right]x_0$$
$$+ \left[(\bar{Y}_0 - \hat{\beta}_0)^2 - \hat{\sigma}^2 t^2_{\alpha/2:n+k-3}\left(\frac{1}{k} + \frac{1}{n} + \frac{\bar{x}^2}{\sum_{i=1}^{n}(x_i - \bar{x})^2}\right)\right] \leq 0 \quad (8.5.7)$$

We write this as $q(x_0) = ax_0^2 + 2bx_0 + c \leq 0$, where a, b, and c are easily identified above and are computed from the data of a problem. If the values of x_0 that satisfy this inequality are an interval, then these values form a $1 - \alpha$ confidence interval on x_0. We will examine this quadratic inequality.

The discriminant is $b^2 - ac$, and if this quantity is negative, the quadratic function $q(x_0)$ cannot be zero. In this case either $q(x_0) < 0$ for *all* x_0 and the confidence interval is $-\infty < x_0 < \infty$ (if $b^2 - ac < 0$, then $q(x_0) < 0$ for all x_0 if and only if $a < 0$), or $q(x_0) > 0$ for *all* x_0 and there is no confidence interval on x_0 (if $b^2 - ac < 0$, then $q(x_0) > 0$ if and only if $a > 0$). Hence the quadratic inequality $q(x_0) \leq 0$ is of no use for obtaining a confidence interval on x_0 if the discriminant is negative, so we examine the inequality for positive values of the discriminant.

If the discriminant is positive and $a < 0$, the graph is as displayed in Figure 8.5.1, and the values of x_0 for which $q(x_0) \leq 0$ form two infinite intervals. In

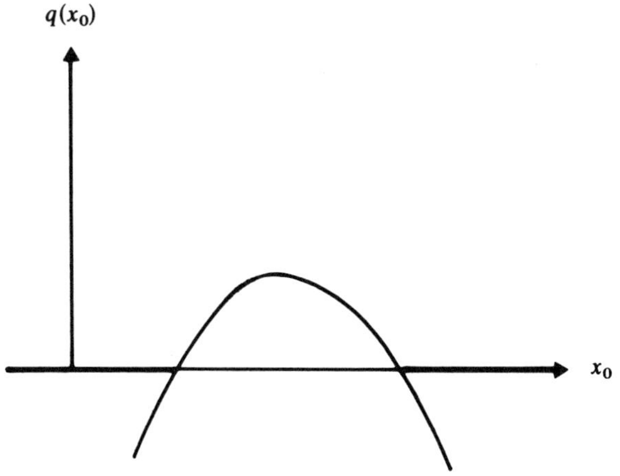

Figure 8.5.1

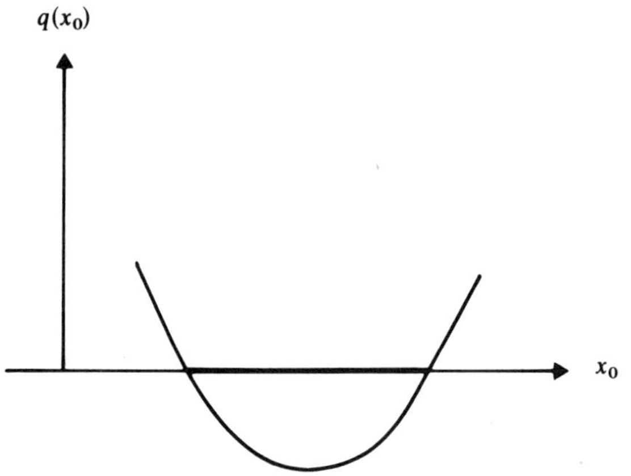

Figure 8.5.2

this case the inequality $q(x_0) \leq 0$ does not lead to a confidence interval (nor to a useful confidence region). If the discriminant is positive and $a > 0$, the graph is as displayed in Figure 8.5.2, and clearly, for this case, the values of x_0 for which $q(x_0) \leq 0$ form an interval; hence it is a confidence interval on x_0.

The above discussion leads us to the conclusion that the inequality $q(x_0) \leq 0$ results in a confidence interval for x_0 if and only if $a > 0$ and $b^2 - ac > 0$. If we evaluate $b^2 - ac$, we get

$$b^2 - ac = \hat{\sigma}^2 t^2_{\alpha/2:n+k-3} \left[\left(\frac{1}{n} + \frac{1}{k} \right) a + \frac{(\hat{\beta}\bar{x} - \bar{Y}_0 + \hat{\beta}_0)^2}{\sum_{i=1}^{n} (x_i - \bar{x})^2} \right]$$

and note that if $a \geq 0$, then the discriminant $b^2 - ac \geq 0$. So the inequality $q(x_0) \leq 0$ gives a confidence interval on x_0 if and only if $a \geq 0$, or, in other words, if and only if $(\hat{\beta}^2 - \hat{\sigma}^2 t^2_{\alpha/2:n+k-3})/\sum (x_i - \bar{x})^2 \geq 0$. If we simplify the inequality $a \geq 0$, we get $\hat{\beta}^2/(\hat{\sigma}^2/\sum_{i=1}^{n} (x_i - \bar{x})^2) \geq t^2_{\alpha/2:n+k-3} = F_{\alpha:1,n+k-3}$, which is a size α test of $H_0: \beta = 0$ *vs.* $H_a: \beta \neq 0$.

In view of the above discussion, a reasonable procedure for determining the value of x_0 for a given value of $\bar{Y}_0$ is as follows:

1. Use the statistics in Equation (8.5.6) and obtain the M.L. estimator of x_0, which is $(\bar{Y}_0 - \hat{\beta}_0)/\hat{\beta}$.

If one wants a confidence interval on x_0, then proceed to parts 2, 3, and 4.

2. Test $H_0 : \beta = 0$ *vs.* $H_a : \beta \neq 0$ with a size α test; reject H_0 if and only if

$$\frac{\hat{\beta}^2}{\hat{\sigma}^2 \Big/ \sum_{i=1}^{n} (x_i - \bar{x})^2} \geq t^2_{\alpha/2:n+k-3}$$

3. If H_0 is *not* rejected, assume that the model is $Y_i = \beta_0 + \varepsilon_i$, and hence assume that x_0 is not in the model, so no confidence interval exists.

4. If H_0 *is* rejected, set a $1 - \alpha$ confidence interval on x_0. This confidence interval always exists if H_0 is rejected, and it is

$$x_0 = \bar{x} + \frac{\hat{\beta}(\bar{Y}_0 - \bar{Y})}{a} \mp \frac{t_{\alpha/2:n+k-3}\hat{\sigma}}{a} \times \sqrt{a\left(\frac{1}{n} + \frac{1}{k}\right) + \frac{(\bar{Y}_0 - \bar{Y})^2}{\sum_{i=1}^{n} (x_i - \bar{x})^2}} \qquad (8.5.8)$$

where

$$a = \hat{\beta}^2 - \frac{\hat{\sigma}^2 t^2_{\alpha/2:n+k-3}}{\sum_{i=1}^{n} (x_i - \bar{x})^2}$$

This is not a $1 - \alpha$ confidence interval on x_0 but it has confidence coefficient less than $1 - \alpha$. This is easily seen by noticing that the probability is equal to $1 - \alpha$ that x_0 satisfies the inequality in Equation (8.5.7). The method explained above, however, seems to be a reasonable way to proceed in an applied problem.

8.6 Parallel, Intersecting, and Identical Models

Some problems that have important applications are the following: determine if all lines in a set intersect in one specified point; determine if all lines in a set are "parallel"; or determine if all lines in a set are identical.

For instance, an investigator is studying three different experimental situations and assumes a linear model for each. He wants to determine if these three linear models are identical, or he *may* want to determine if some of the parameters of the models are the same from model to model. We illustrate with two examples.

Example 8.6.1

Commercial fertilizer is applied to wheat to determine how it affects the yield. Three varieties of wheat are used, and for each variety the relationship between yield in bushels per acre Y and amount of fertilizer applied in tons per acre x is given by

$$Y_{1j} = \alpha_1 + \beta_1 x_{1j} + \varepsilon_{1j} \qquad Y_{2j} = \alpha_2 + \beta_2 x_{2j} + \varepsilon_{2j} \qquad Y_{3j} = \alpha_3 + \beta_3 x_{3j} + \varepsilon_{3j}$$

The investigator may want to determine if the lines are parallel, that is, if $\beta_1 = \beta_2 = \beta_3$ (if the increase in average yield per unit of fertilizer is the same for all varieties). Or he may want to determine if the intercepts are the same, that is, if $\alpha_1 = \alpha_2 = \alpha_3$ (if the yield of each variety is the same when no fertilizer is applied).

Example 8.6.2

A study is made to determine the relationship of age x and blood pressure Y of individuals between 50 and 75 years of age. A simple linear model was assumed, but the study included both males and females, so it was decided that a separate model for each was appropriate. The models are $Y_{1j} = \alpha_1 + \beta_1 x_{1j} + \varepsilon_{1j}$ for females and $Y_{2j} = \alpha_2 + \beta_2 x_{2j} + \varepsilon_{2j}$ for males. The interest was in studying the models separately and together. In looking at the two models together, interest was centered on testing $\beta_1 = \beta_2$ and $\alpha_1 = \alpha_2$ simultaneously; that is, are the models the same for males and females?

In Section 8.6.1 we derive test statistics for the following hypotheses: (1) H *simple* linear models are parallel; (2) H *simple* linear models have a common intercept; (3) all H of the lines intersect in exactly one *specified* point. In Section 8.6.2 we derive a test statistic to test the hypothesis that H *general* linear models are identical, and in Section 8.6.3 we extend Section 8.6.1 to H *general* linear models.

8.6.1 Tests about H Simple Linear Models

Before we derive test statistics for the hypotheses referred to above, we will discuss the models in some detail, describe some notation, and state some general theorems.

Consider H *simple* linear models (to keep the use of double subscripts to a minimum, we will use the symbol α for the intercept and β for the slope).

$$\left.\begin{array}{ll} Y_{1j} = \alpha_1 + \beta_1 x_{1j} + \varepsilon_{1j} & j = 1, 2, \ldots, n_1 \\ Y_{2j} = \alpha_2 + \beta_2 x_{2j} + \varepsilon_{2j} & j = 1, 2, \ldots, n_2 \\ \vdots & \vdots \\ Y_{Hj} = \alpha_H + \beta_H x_{Hj} + \varepsilon_{Hj} & j = 1, 2, \ldots, n_H \end{array}\right\} \begin{array}{l} \sum_{h=1}^{H} n_h = N \\ n_h > 2 \text{ for all } h \\ \varepsilon_{ij} \text{ are distributed} \\ NID(\varepsilon : 0, \sigma^2) \end{array} \tag{8.6.1}$$

The various hypotheses that we consider in this section are the following:

1. $H_0 : \beta_1 = \beta_2 = \cdots = \beta_H$, that is, the lines are parallel;
2. $H_0 : \alpha_1 = \alpha_2 = \cdots = \alpha_H$, that is, the lines have a common intercept;
3. $H_0 : \alpha_1 + \beta_1 x_0 = \alpha_2 + \beta_2 x_0 = \cdots = \alpha_H + \beta_H x_0$ (x_0 known), that is, the lines intersect at the x value x_0 which is specified in advance. (8.6.2)

The H simple linear models can be cast in the framework of the general linear model $\mathbf{Y} = \mathbf{X\beta} + \boldsymbol{\varepsilon}$. We first note that the hth simple linear model can be written

$$\mathbf{Y}_h = \mathbf{X}_h \boldsymbol{\beta}_h + \boldsymbol{\varepsilon}_h \tag{8.6.3}$$

where

$$\mathbf{Y}_h = \begin{bmatrix} Y_{h1} \\ Y_{h2} \\ \vdots \\ Y_{hn_h} \end{bmatrix} \quad \mathbf{X}_h = \begin{bmatrix} 1 & x_{h1} \\ 1 & x_{h2} \\ \vdots & \vdots \\ 1 & x_{hn_h} \end{bmatrix} \quad \boldsymbol{\beta}_h = \begin{bmatrix} \alpha_h \\ \beta_h \end{bmatrix} \quad \boldsymbol{\varepsilon}_h = \begin{bmatrix} \varepsilon_{h1} \\ \varepsilon_{h2} \\ \vdots \\ \varepsilon_{hn_h} \end{bmatrix} \tag{8.6.4}$$

We can then write the H models in the form of the general linear model $\mathbf{Y} = \mathbf{X\beta} + \boldsymbol{\varepsilon}$ with the following identifications:

$$\mathbf{Y} = \begin{bmatrix} \mathbf{Y}_1 \\ \mathbf{Y}_2 \\ \vdots \\ \mathbf{Y}_H \end{bmatrix} \quad \mathbf{X} = \begin{bmatrix} \mathbf{X}_1 & \mathbf{0} & \cdots & \mathbf{0} \\ \mathbf{0} & \mathbf{X}_2 & \cdots & \mathbf{0} \\ \vdots & \vdots & & \vdots \\ \mathbf{0} & \mathbf{0} & \cdots & \mathbf{X}_H \end{bmatrix} \quad \boldsymbol{\beta} = \begin{bmatrix} \boldsymbol{\beta}_1 \\ \boldsymbol{\beta}_2 \\ \vdots \\ \boldsymbol{\beta}_H \end{bmatrix} \quad \boldsymbol{\varepsilon} = \begin{bmatrix} \boldsymbol{\varepsilon}_1 \\ \boldsymbol{\varepsilon}_2 \\ \vdots \\ \boldsymbol{\varepsilon}_H \end{bmatrix} \tag{8.6.5}$$

Clearly $\boldsymbol{\varepsilon}$ is distributed $\mathbf{N}(\boldsymbol{\varepsilon} : \mathbf{0}, \sigma^2\mathbf{I})$. Also,

$$\mathbf{X}'\mathbf{X} = \begin{bmatrix} \mathbf{X}_1'\mathbf{X}_1 & \mathbf{0} & \cdots & \mathbf{0} \\ \mathbf{0} & \mathbf{X}_2'\mathbf{X}_2 & \cdots & \mathbf{0} \\ \vdots & \vdots & & \vdots \\ \mathbf{0} & \mathbf{0} & \cdots & \mathbf{X}_H'\mathbf{Y}_H \end{bmatrix} \qquad \mathbf{X}'\mathbf{Y} = \begin{bmatrix} \mathbf{X}_1'\mathbf{Y}_1 \\ \mathbf{X}_2'\mathbf{Y}_2 \\ \vdots \\ \mathbf{X}_H'\mathbf{Y}_H \end{bmatrix}$$

$$\boldsymbol{\beta} = \mathbf{X}^-\mathbf{Y} = \begin{bmatrix} \mathbf{X}_1^-\mathbf{Y}_1 \\ \mathbf{X}_2^-\mathbf{Y}_2 \\ \vdots \\ \mathbf{X}_H^-\mathbf{Y}_H \end{bmatrix} \tag{8.6.6}$$

that is, $\hat{\boldsymbol{\beta}}_h = \mathbf{X}_h^-\mathbf{Y}_h$;

$$\hat{\sigma}^2 = \left(\frac{1}{N-2H}\right)(\mathbf{Y}'\mathbf{Y} - \hat{\boldsymbol{\beta}}'\mathbf{X}'\mathbf{Y}) = \left(\frac{1}{N-2H}\right)\left(\sum_{h=1}^{H} \mathbf{Y}_h'\mathbf{Y}_h - \sum_{h=1}^{H} \hat{\boldsymbol{\beta}}_h'\mathbf{X}_h'\mathbf{Y}_h\right)$$

$$= \left(\frac{1}{N-2H}\right)\left(\sum_{h=1}^{H} \mathbf{Y}_h'(\mathbf{I} - \mathbf{X}_h\mathbf{X}_h^-)\mathbf{Y}_h\right) \tag{8.6.7}$$

By Theorem 6.2.1 the complete sufficient statistics for this problem are $\hat{\boldsymbol{\beta}}_1, \hat{\boldsymbol{\beta}}_2, \ldots, \hat{\boldsymbol{\beta}}_H, \hat{\sigma}^2$. This essentially states that $\hat{\alpha}_h$ and $\hat{\beta}_h$ are computed from the data for the hth model and that $\hat{\sigma}^2$ is computed by pooling the estimators of $\hat{\sigma}^2$ from each model.

Before we consider hypotheses 1, 2, and 3 in Equation (8.6.2), we will discuss a somewhat more general situation. The complete sufficient statistics for the H models in Equation (8.6.1) are $\hat{\boldsymbol{\beta}}_1, \hat{\boldsymbol{\beta}}_2, \ldots, \hat{\boldsymbol{\beta}}_H, \hat{\sigma}^2$, where

$$\hat{\boldsymbol{\beta}}_h = \begin{bmatrix} \hat{\alpha}_h \\ \hat{\beta}_h \end{bmatrix} = \begin{bmatrix} \bar{Y}_h - \hat{\beta}_h\bar{x}_h \\ \dfrac{\sum_{j=1}^{n_h} (Y_{hj} - \bar{Y}_h)(x_{hj} - \bar{x}_h)}{\sum_{j=1}^{n_h} (x_{hj} - \bar{x}_h)^2} \end{bmatrix} \qquad h = 1, 2, \ldots, H \tag{8.6.8}$$

$$\hat{\sigma}^2 = \frac{\sum_{h=1}^{H} (n_h - 2)\hat{\sigma}_h^2}{\sum_{h=1}^{H} (n_h - 2)} \tag{8.6.9}$$

where

$$\hat{\sigma}_h^2 = \left(\frac{1}{n_h - 2}\right)\left\{\sum_{j=1}^{n_h} (Y_{hj} - \bar{Y}_h)^2 - \frac{\left[\sum_{j=1}^{n_h} (Y_{hj} - \bar{Y}_h)(x_{hj} - \bar{x}_h)\right]^2}{\sum_{j=1}^{n_h} (x_{hj} - \bar{x}_h)^2}\right\}$$

So a test of the various hypotheses in Equation (8.6.2) will be a function of these $H + 1$ complete sufficient statistics.

Consider the distribution of Z_h, where $Z_h = a\hat{\alpha}_h + b\hat{\beta}_h$ and a and b are known constants to be determined later. We have that Z_h is distributed $NID(z_h : \mu_h, d_{hh}^{-1}\sigma^2)$, where $\mu_h = \mathscr{E}[Z_h] = a\alpha_h + b\beta_h$ and

$$d_{hh}^{-1}\sigma^2 = \text{var}[Z_h] = [a, b](\mathbf{X}_h'\mathbf{X}_h)^{-1}\begin{bmatrix} a \\ b \end{bmatrix}\sigma^2$$

$$= \frac{\sigma^2\left(a^2 \sum_{j=1}^{n_h} x_{hj}^2 - 2ab \sum_{j=1}^{n_h} x_{hj} + b^2 n_h\right)}{n_h \sum_{i=1}^{n_h} (x_{hi} - \bar{x}_h)^2} = \frac{\sum_{j=1}^{n_h} (ax_{hj} - b)^2}{n_h \sum_{i=1}^{n_h} (x_{hi} - \bar{x}_h)^2}(\sigma^2)$$

Next consider the random variable W defined by

$$W = \frac{\sum_{h=1}^{H} (Z_h - \bar{Z}^*)^2 d_{hh}}{(H - 1)\hat{\sigma}^2} \qquad \text{where} \qquad \bar{Z}^* = \frac{\sum_{h=1}^{H} Z_h d_{hh}}{\sum_{i=1}^{H} d_{ii}} \tag{8.6.10}$$

By Theorem 4.4.5

$$U_1 = \frac{\sum_{h=1}^{H} (Z_h - \bar{Z}^*)^2 d_{hh}}{\sigma^2}$$

is distributed $\chi^2(u_1 : H - 1; \lambda)$, where

$$\lambda = \left(\frac{1}{2\sigma^2}\right) \sum_{h=1}^{H} (\mu_h - \bar{\mu}^*)^2 d_{hh} \qquad \text{and} \qquad \bar{\mu}^* = \frac{\sum_{h=1}^{H} \mu_h d_{hh}}{\sum_{i=1}^{H} d_{ii}}$$

Define U_2 by $U_2 = (N - 2H)\hat{\sigma}^2/\sigma^2$; U_2 is distributed $\chi^2(u_2 : N - 2H)$. Also, U_1 and U_2 are independent. Thus W is distributed $F(w : H - 1, N - 2H; \lambda)$; also, $\lambda = 0$ if and only if $\mu_1 = \mu_2 = \cdots = \mu_H$. We will now substitute $a\alpha_h + b\beta_h$ for μ_h and summarize the above in a theorem.

THEOREM 8.6.1

Consider the H simple linear models for Case 1 given in Equation (8.6.1). The statistic W given by

$$W = \frac{\displaystyle\sum_{h=1}^{H} \left[(a\hat{\alpha}_h + b\hat{\beta}_h) - \frac{\sum_{i=1}^{H} (a\hat{\alpha}_i + b\hat{\beta}_i)d_{ii}}{\sum_{j=1}^{H} d_{jj}} \right]^2 d_{hh}}{(H-1)\hat{\sigma}^2} \tag{8.6.11}$$

is distributed $F(w : H-1, N-2H; \lambda)$;

$$\lambda = \left(\frac{1}{2\sigma^2}\right) \sum_{h=1}^{H} \left[(a\alpha_h + b\beta_h) - \frac{\sum_{i=1}^{H} (a\alpha_i + b\beta_i)d_{ii}}{\sum_{j=1}^{H} d_{jj}} \right]^2 d_{hh}$$

where

$$d_{hh} = \frac{n_h \sum_{j=1}^{n_h} (x_{hj} - \bar{x}_h)^2}{\sum_{i=1}^{n_h} (ax_{hi} - b)^2}$$

Note 1. $\lambda = 0$ if and only if $a\alpha_1 + b\beta_1 = a\alpha_2 + b\beta_2 = \cdots = a\alpha_H + b\beta_H$.

Next we state a theorem to show how Theorem 8.6.1 can be used to test a hypothesis that includes parts 1, 2, and 3 of Equation (8.6.2) as special cases.

THEOREM 8.6.2

Consider the H simple linear models for Case 1 given in Equation (8.6.1). The likelihood ratio test of size α of H_0 vs. H_a is as follows: Reject H_0 if and only if

$$w \geq F_{\alpha:H-1,N-2H}$$

where w is the computed value of W given in Equation (8.6.11) and H_0 and H_a are

$$\begin{aligned} &H_0 : a\alpha_1 + b\beta_1 = a\alpha_2 + b\beta_2 = \cdots = a\alpha_H + b\beta_H \\ &H_a : \text{at least one equality is an inequality} \end{aligned} \tag{8.6.12}$$

Proof

This theorem is a special case of Theorem 6.3.1 and can be proved by selecting the proper **H** matrix and substituting into Equation (6.3.10).

Another way to prove this theorem is to use the fact that the likelihood ratio test is a function of the sufficient statistics $\hat{\boldsymbol{\beta}}_1, \hat{\boldsymbol{\beta}}_2, \ldots, \hat{\boldsymbol{\beta}}_H, \hat{\sigma}^2$, and from the joint distribution of these $H + 1$ jointly independent statistics, show that W in Equation (8.6.11) is the likelihood ratio test statistic. We leave the details of the proof to the reader and will ask for them in the problems.

We will now demonstrate how this theorem can be used to test the hypotheses 1, 2, and 3 of Equation (8.6.2).

THEOREM 8.6.3

Consider the H simple linear models for Case 1 given in Equation (8.6.1). The tests of hypotheses 1, 2, and 3 of Equation (8.6.2) are given below.

(1) $H_0: \beta_1 = \beta_2 = \cdots = \beta_H$ *(H lines are parallel) vs.* $H_a: \beta_i \neq \beta_j$ *for at least one* $i \neq j$ *(the H lines are not all parallel). The test of* H_0 *vs.* H_a *is this: Reject* H_0 *if and only if* $w_P \geq F_{\alpha:H-1,N-2H}$, *where*

$$W_P = \frac{\sum_{h=1}^{H} \left[\hat{\beta}_h - \frac{\sum_{j=1}^{H} \hat{\beta}_j b_{jj}}{\sum_{i=1}^{H} b_{ii}} \right]^2 b_{hh}}{(H-1)\hat{\sigma}^2} \quad \textit{where} \quad b_{hh} = \sum_{t=1}^{n_h} (x_{ht} - \bar{x}_h)^2$$

(2) $H_0: \alpha_1 = \alpha_2 = \cdots = \alpha_H$ *(H lines have the same intercept) vs.* $H_a: \alpha_i \neq \alpha_j$ *for at least one* $i \neq j$.

$$W_I = \frac{\sum_{h=1}^{H} \left[\hat{\alpha}_h - \frac{\sum_{j=1}^{H} \hat{\alpha}_j a_{jj}}{\sum_{i=1}^{H} a_{ii}} \right]^2 a_{hh}}{(H-1)\hat{\sigma}^2}$$

where

$$a_{hh} = \frac{n_h \sum_{t=1}^{n_h} (x_{ht} - \bar{x}_h)^2}{\sum_{s=1}^{n_h} x_{hs}^2}$$

The size α *test of* H_0 *vs.* H_a *is this: Reject* H_0 *if and only if* $w_I \geq F_{\alpha:H-1,N-2H}$.

(3) $H_0: \alpha_1 + \beta_1 x_0 = \alpha_2 + \beta_2 x_0 = \cdots = \alpha_H + \beta_H x_0$ *(all H lines intersect at* $x = x_0$*, known) vs.* H_a *: at least one equality is an inequality (all H lines do not intersect at* $x = x_0$*). The size* α *test of* H_0 *vs.* H_a *is this: Reject* H_0 *if and only if* $w_0 \geq F_{\alpha:H-1,N-2H}$*, where*

$$W_0 = \frac{\sum_{h=1}^{H}\left[(\hat{\alpha}_h + \hat{\beta}_h x_0) - \frac{\sum_{j=1}^{H}(\hat{\alpha}_j + \hat{\beta}_j x_0)c_{jj}}{\sum_{i=1}^{H} c_{ii}}\right]^2 c_{hh}}{(H-1)\hat{\sigma}^2}$$

where

$$c_{hh} = \frac{n_h \sum_{t=1}^{n_h}(x_{ht} - \bar{x}_h)^2}{\sum_{s=1}^{n_h}(x_{hs} - x_0)^2}$$

Proof

These hypotheses are special cases of the hypothesis in Theorem 8.6.2 and especially Equation (8.6.12). To test whether H lines are parallel, we set $a = 0$ and $b = 1$; to test that H lines intersect at $x = x_0$, we set $a = 1$ and $b = x_0$; to test that H lines have the same *intercept* (all lines intersect at $x = x_0 = 0$), set $a = 1$ and $b = 0$.

We can perform the computations for these tests by the square root method. To illustrate this we return to Theorem 8.6.2, but first we simplify the test statistic W in Equation (8.6.10). We consider the numerator of W and get

$$\sum_{h=1}^{H}\left[Z_h - \frac{\sum_{i=1}^{H} Z_i d_{ii}}{\sum_{j=1}^{H} d_{jj}}\right]^2 d_{hh} = \sum_{h=1}^{H} Z_h^2 d_{hh} - \frac{\left[\sum_{h=1}^{H} Z_h d_{hh}\right]^2}{\sum_{j=1}^{H} d_{jj}}$$

Thus W can be written

$$W = \frac{\dfrac{\sum_{h=1}^{H} Z_h^2 d_{hh} - \left(\sum_{h=1}^{H} Z_h d_{hh}\right)^2}{\sum_{j=1}^{H} d_{jj}}}{\dfrac{\sum_{h=1}^{H}(n_h - 2)\hat{\sigma}_h^2}{\sum_{i=1}^{H}(n_i - 2)}}\left(\frac{1}{H-1}\right)$$

Now consider the normal equations for the hth model and the format for reducing it to a triangular system by the square root method:

$$\left[\begin{array}{c|c|c} \mathbf{X}_h'\mathbf{X}_h & \mathbf{X}_h'\mathbf{y}_h & \ell \\ \hline \mathbf{T}_h & \mathbf{t}_h & \mathbf{a}_h \end{array}\right] \qquad \text{where} \qquad \ell' = [a, b]$$

We get (z_h is the computed value of Z_h)

$$\begin{aligned}
\mathbf{a}_h'\mathbf{t}_h &= \ell'\mathbf{T}_h^{-1}\mathbf{T}_h'^{-1}\mathbf{X}_h'\mathbf{y}_h = \ell'\mathbf{X}_h^-\mathbf{y}_h = \ell'\hat{\boldsymbol{\beta}}_h = a\hat{\alpha}_h + b\hat{\beta}_h = z_h \\
\mathbf{a}_h'\mathbf{a}_h &= \ell'\mathbf{T}_h^{-1}\mathbf{T}_h'^{-1}\ell = \ell'(\mathbf{X}_h'\mathbf{X}_h)^{-1}\ell = d_{hh}^{-1} \\
\mathbf{y}_h'\mathbf{y}_h - \mathbf{t}_h'\mathbf{t}_h &= \mathbf{y}_h'(\mathbf{I} - \mathbf{X}_h\mathbf{X}_h^-)\mathbf{y}_h = (n_h - 2)\hat{\sigma}_h^2
\end{aligned}$$

Thus from the square root method on each model we can compute $\hat{\alpha}_1, \hat{\beta}_1, \hat{\sigma}_1^2$; $\hat{\alpha}_2, \hat{\beta}_2, \hat{\sigma}_2^2; \ldots; \hat{\alpha}_H, \hat{\beta}_H, \hat{\sigma}_H^2$, the pertinent statistics for each model, and z_1, d_{11}; $z_2, d_{22}; \ldots; z_H, d_{HH}$, the ingredients for the test statistic w above (and in Theorem 8.6.2) to test $a\alpha_1 + b\beta_1 = a\alpha_2 + b\beta_2 = \cdots = a\alpha_H + b\beta_H$.

For appropriate values of a and b (of ℓ), we get test statistics for any of the three hypotheses in Equation (8.6.2). From these results, one-at-a-time and simultaneous confidence intervals can be constructed for any set of the parameters α_i, β_i, or on any set of linear combinations of the α_i, β_i, or on σ^2. If an investigator questions whether the σ^2's are the same from model to model, it can be assumed that $\mathbf{cov}[\boldsymbol{\varepsilon}_h] = \sigma_h^2\mathbf{I}$ and $\hat{\sigma}_h^2$ can be computed for $h = 1, 2, \ldots, H$. These statistics can be used in one of the tests described in [G-1] to test $H_0 : \sigma_1^2 = \sigma_2^2 = \cdots = \sigma_H^2$.

8.6.2 Testing the Equality of a Set of Linear Models

In this section we derive a test statistic for the hypothesis that H *general* linear models are identical.

THEOREM 8.6.4

Let $\mathbf{Y}_h = \mathbf{X}_h\boldsymbol{\beta}_h + \boldsymbol{\varepsilon}_h$, where $\mathbf{X}_h$ is an $n_h \times p$ matrix, $h = 1, 2, \ldots, H$, be a set of H general linear models where the $\boldsymbol{\varepsilon}_h$ are distributed $\mathbf{NID}(\boldsymbol{\varepsilon}_h : \mathbf{0}, \sigma^2\mathbf{I})$. A size α test of $H_0 : \boldsymbol{\beta}_1 = \boldsymbol{\beta}_2 = \cdots = \boldsymbol{\beta}_H$ vs. H_a : at least one equality is an inequality is this: Reject H_0 if and only if $w \geq F_{\alpha:(H-1)p, N-Hp}$, where (let $N = \sum_{h=1}^H n_h$)

$$W = \left(\frac{\sum_{h=1}^{H} \mathbf{Y}_h'(\mathbf{X}_h\mathbf{X}_h^-)\mathbf{Y}_h - \left(\sum_{i=1}^{H} \mathbf{Y}_i'\mathbf{X}_i\right)\left(\sum_{h=1}^{H} \mathbf{X}_h'\mathbf{X}_h\right)^{-1}\left(\sum_{j=1}^{H} \mathbf{X}_j'\mathbf{Y}_j\right)}{\sum_{h=1}^{H} \mathbf{Y}_h'\mathbf{Y}_h - \sum_{h=1}^{H} \mathbf{Y}_h'(\mathbf{X}_h\mathbf{X}_h^-)\mathbf{Y}_h}\right)\left(\frac{N - Hp}{(H-1)p}\right) \tag{8.6.13}$$

Proof

We form the following matrices and vectors:

$$\mathbf{Y}' = [\mathbf{Y}_1', \mathbf{Y}_2', \ldots, \mathbf{Y}_H'] \qquad \mathbf{X} = \begin{bmatrix} \mathbf{X}_1 & \mathbf{0} & \cdots & \mathbf{0} \\ \mathbf{0} & \mathbf{X}_2 & \cdots & \mathbf{0} \\ \vdots & \vdots & & \vdots \\ \mathbf{0} & \mathbf{0} & \cdots & \mathbf{X}_H \end{bmatrix}$$

$$\boldsymbol{\beta}' = [\boldsymbol{\beta}_1', \boldsymbol{\beta}_2', \ldots, \boldsymbol{\beta}_H'] \qquad \boldsymbol{\varepsilon}' = [\boldsymbol{\varepsilon}_1', \boldsymbol{\varepsilon}_2', \ldots, \boldsymbol{\varepsilon}_H']$$

Since the $\boldsymbol{\varepsilon}_h$ are normal and independent, it follows that $\boldsymbol{\varepsilon}$ is an $N \times 1$ vector that is distributed $\mathbf{N}(\boldsymbol{\varepsilon} : \mathbf{0}, \sigma^2\mathbf{I})$, $\mathbf{X}$ is an $N \times Hp$ matrix, $\mathbf{Y}$ is an $N \times 1$ vector, and $\boldsymbol{\beta}$ is an $Hp \times 1$ vector. We put these into the model

$$\mathbf{Y} = \mathbf{X}\boldsymbol{\beta} + \boldsymbol{\varepsilon} \qquad \boldsymbol{\varepsilon} \text{ is distributed } \mathbf{N}(\boldsymbol{\varepsilon} : \mathbf{0}, \sigma^2\mathbf{I}) \tag{8.6.14}$$

and this is equivalent to the H models

$$\begin{aligned} \mathbf{Y}_1 &= \mathbf{X}_1\boldsymbol{\beta}_1 + \boldsymbol{\varepsilon}_1 \\ \mathbf{Y}_2 &= \mathbf{X}_2\boldsymbol{\beta}_2 + \boldsymbol{\varepsilon}_2 \\ &\vdots \\ \mathbf{Y}_H &= \mathbf{X}_H\boldsymbol{\beta}_H + \boldsymbol{\varepsilon}_H \end{aligned}$$

Thus in the general linear model in Equation (8.6.14), we want to test $H_0 : \boldsymbol{\beta}_1 = \boldsymbol{\beta}_2 = \cdots = \boldsymbol{\beta}_H$. We use the test statistic in Equation (6.3.11), so we must determine $\hat{\sigma}_\Omega^2$ and $\hat{\sigma}_\omega^2$. The normal equations are $\mathbf{X}'\mathbf{X}\hat{\boldsymbol{\beta}} = \mathbf{X}'\mathbf{Y}$, and the solution is $\hat{\boldsymbol{\beta}} = (\mathbf{X}'\mathbf{X})^{-1}\mathbf{X}'\mathbf{Y}$, which is, (see Equations (8.6.5), (8.6.6), and (8.6.7))

$$\hat{\boldsymbol{\beta}} = \begin{bmatrix} \hat{\boldsymbol{\beta}}_1 \\ \hat{\boldsymbol{\beta}}_2 \\ \vdots \\ \hat{\boldsymbol{\beta}}_H \end{bmatrix} = \begin{bmatrix} (\mathbf{X}_1'\mathbf{X}_1)^{-1} & \mathbf{0} & \cdots & \mathbf{0} \\ \mathbf{0} & (\mathbf{X}_2'\mathbf{X}_2)^{-1} & \cdots & \mathbf{0} \\ \vdots & \vdots & & \vdots \\ \mathbf{0} & \mathbf{0} & \cdots & (\mathbf{X}_H'\mathbf{X}_H)^{-1} \end{bmatrix} \begin{bmatrix} \mathbf{X}_1'\mathbf{Y}_1 \\ \mathbf{X}_2'\mathbf{Y}_2 \\ \vdots \\ \mathbf{X}_H'\mathbf{Y}_H \end{bmatrix}$$

So $\hat{\boldsymbol{\beta}}_h = (\mathbf{X}_h'\mathbf{X}_h)^{-1}\mathbf{X}_h'\mathbf{Y}_h = \mathbf{X}_h^-\mathbf{Y}_h$, $h = 1, 2, \ldots, H$. Thus $\hat{\boldsymbol{\beta}}_h$ is the same as if it was obtained from the hth model $\mathbf{Y}_h = \mathbf{X}_h\boldsymbol{\beta}_h + \boldsymbol{\varepsilon}_h$. Now

$$\hat{\boldsymbol{\beta}}'\mathbf{X}'\mathbf{Y} = \sum_{h=1}^{H} \hat{\boldsymbol{\beta}}_h'\mathbf{X}_h'\mathbf{Y}_h = \sum_{h=1}^{H} \mathbf{Y}_h'\mathbf{X}_h\mathbf{X}_h^-\mathbf{Y}_h$$

so we get the following for $\hat{\sigma}_\Omega^2$:

$$\hat{\sigma}_\Omega^2 = \left(\frac{1}{N}\right)\left(\mathbf{Y}'\mathbf{Y} - \sum_{h=1}^{H} \mathbf{Y}_h'\mathbf{X}_h\mathbf{X}_h^- \mathbf{Y}_h\right) = \left(\frac{1}{N}\right) \sum_{h=1}^{H} \mathbf{Y}_h'(\mathbf{I} - \mathbf{X}_h\mathbf{X}_h^-)\mathbf{Y}_h$$

The reduced model is $\mathbf{Y} = \mathbf{X}\boldsymbol{\gamma} + \boldsymbol{\varepsilon}$, where $\boldsymbol{\gamma}' = [\boldsymbol{\xi}', \boldsymbol{\xi}', \ldots, \boldsymbol{\xi}']$ and $\boldsymbol{\xi}$ is the common *unknown* parameter vector $\boldsymbol{\xi} = \boldsymbol{\beta}_1 = \boldsymbol{\beta}_2 = \cdots = \boldsymbol{\beta}_H$. We get

$$\begin{aligned}
N\hat{\sigma}_\omega^2 &= \min_{\gamma}(\boldsymbol{\varepsilon}'\boldsymbol{\varepsilon}) = \min_{\gamma}\left[\sum_{h=1}^{H} (\boldsymbol{\varepsilon}_h'\boldsymbol{\varepsilon}_h)\right] \\
&= \min_{\boldsymbol{\xi} \text{ in } E_p}\left[\sum_{h=1}^{H} (\mathbf{Y}_h - \mathbf{X}_h\boldsymbol{\xi})'(\mathbf{Y}_h - \mathbf{X}_h\boldsymbol{\xi})\right] \\
&= \min_{\boldsymbol{\xi} \text{ in } E_p}\left[\sum_{h=1}^{H} \mathbf{Y}_h'\mathbf{Y}_h - 2\boldsymbol{\xi}'\left(\sum_{h=1}^{H} \mathbf{X}_h'\mathbf{Y}_h\right) + \boldsymbol{\xi}'\left(\sum_{h=1}^{H} \mathbf{X}_h'\mathbf{X}_h\right)\boldsymbol{\xi}\right]
\end{aligned}$$

and thus

$$\hat{\boldsymbol{\xi}} = \left(\sum_{h=1}^{H} \mathbf{X}_h'\mathbf{X}_h\right)^{-1}\left(\sum_{i=1}^{H} \mathbf{X}_i'\mathbf{Y}_i\right)$$

Thus

$$N\hat{\sigma}_\omega^2 = \sum_{h=1}^{H} \mathbf{Y}_h'\mathbf{Y}_h - \left(\sum_{i=1}^{H} \mathbf{Y}_i'\mathbf{X}_i\right)\left(\sum_{h=1}^{H} \mathbf{X}_h'\mathbf{X}_h\right)^{-1}\left(\sum_{j=1}^{H} \mathbf{X}_j'\mathbf{Y}_j\right)$$

We obtain

$$W = \left(\frac{\sum_{h=1}^{H} \mathbf{Y}_h'(\mathbf{X}_h\mathbf{X}_h^-)\mathbf{Y}_h - \left(\sum_{i=1}^{H} \mathbf{Y}_i'\mathbf{X}_i\right)\left(\sum_{h=1}^{H} \mathbf{X}_h'\mathbf{X}_h\right)^{-1}\left(\sum_{j=1}^{H} \mathbf{X}_j'\mathbf{Y}_j\right)}{\sum_{h=1}^{H} \mathbf{Y}_h'\mathbf{Y}_h - \sum_{h=1}^{H} \mathbf{Y}_h'(\mathbf{X}_h\mathbf{X}_h^-)\mathbf{Y}_h}\right) \times \left(\frac{N - Hp}{(H-1)p}\right)$$

and this is the likelihood ratio test statistic for $H_0 : \boldsymbol{\beta}_1 = \boldsymbol{\beta}_2 = \cdots = \boldsymbol{\beta}_H$. Of course, W is distributed $F(w : (H-1)p, N - Hp; \lambda)$, where

$$\lambda = \left(\frac{1}{2\sigma^2}\right)\left[\sum_{h=1}^{H} \boldsymbol{\beta}_h'(\mathbf{X}_h'\mathbf{X}_h)\boldsymbol{\beta}_h - \left(\sum_{i=1}^{H} \boldsymbol{\beta}_i'\mathbf{X}_i'\mathbf{X}_i\right)\left(\sum_{h=1}^{H} \mathbf{X}_h'\mathbf{X}_h\right)^{-1}\left(\sum_{j=1}^{H} \mathbf{X}_j'\mathbf{X}_j\boldsymbol{\beta}_j\right)\right]$$

This completes the proof.

The square root method can be used to compute w. We have $H + 1$ sets of normal equations and hence $H + 1$ formats to reduce as follows:

$$\left[\begin{array}{c|c} \mathbf{X}_1'\mathbf{X}_1 & \mathbf{X}_1'\mathbf{y}_1 \\ \hline \mathbf{T}_1 & \mathbf{t}_1 \end{array}\right];\ \left[\begin{array}{c|c} \mathbf{X}_2'\mathbf{X}_2 & \mathbf{X}_2'\mathbf{y}_2 \\ \hline \mathbf{T}_2 & \mathbf{t}_2 \end{array}\right];\ \cdots;\ \left[\begin{array}{c|c} \mathbf{X}_H'\mathbf{X}_H & \mathbf{X}_H'\mathbf{y}_H \\ \hline \mathbf{T}_H & \mathbf{t}_H \end{array}\right];\ \left[\begin{array}{c|c} \sum \mathbf{X}_h'\mathbf{X}_h & \sum \mathbf{X}_h'\mathbf{y}_h \\ \hline \mathbf{T} & \mathbf{t} \end{array}\right] \tag{8.6.15}$$

and w, the computed value of the test statistic W, is given by

$$w = \left(\frac{\sum_{h=1}^{H} \mathbf{t}_h'\mathbf{t}_h - \mathbf{t}'\mathbf{t}}{\sum_{h=1}^{H} \mathbf{y}_h'\mathbf{y}_h - \sum_{h=1}^{H} \mathbf{t}_h'\mathbf{t}_h} \right) \left(\frac{N - Hp}{(H-1)p} \right) \tag{8.6.16}$$

For a set of H *simple* linear models, the formula for w simplifies and can be computed by the format of Table 8.6.1. We compute w by

$$w = \left(\frac{[S_{yy} - S_y^2/N] - \dfrac{[S_{xy} - S_x S_y/N]^2}{S_{xx} - S_x^2/N} - S_{\hat{\sigma}^2}}{S_{\hat{\sigma}^2}} \right) \left(\frac{N - 2H}{2(H-1)} \right) \tag{8.6.17}$$

Table 8.6.1

Format for Testing the Equality of H Simple Linear Models

Model	n	$\sum_{j=1}^{n_h} y_{hj}$	$\sum_{j=1}^{n_h} y_{hj}^2$	$\sum_{j=1}^{n_h} x_{hj}$	$\sum_{j=1}^{n_h} x_{hj}^2$	$\sum_{j=1}^{n_h} y_{hj}x_{hj}$	$(n_h - 2)\hat{\sigma}_h^2$
1	n_1	$\sum y_{1j}$	$\sum y_{1j}^2$	$\sum x_{1j}$	$\sum x_{1j}^2$	$\sum y_{1j}x_{1j}$	$\sum (y_{1j} - \bar{y}_1)^2 - \dfrac{[\sum (y_{1j} - \bar{y}_1)(x_{1j} - \bar{x}_1)]^2}{\sum (x_{1j} - \bar{x}_1)^2}$
2	n_2	$\sum y_{2j}$	$\sum y_{2j}^2$	$\sum x_{2j}$	$\sum x_{2j}^2$	$\sum y_{2j}x_{2j}$	$\sum (y_{2j} - \bar{y}_2)^2 - \dfrac{[\sum (y_{2j} - \bar{y}_2)(x_{2j} - \bar{x}_2)]^2}{\sum (x_{2j} - \bar{x}_2)^2}$
⋮	⋮	⋮	⋮	⋮	⋮	⋮	⋮
H	n_H	$\sum y_{Hj}$	$\sum y_{Hj}^2$	$\sum x_{Hj}$	$\sum x_{Hj}^2$	$\sum y_{Hj}x_{Hj}$	$\sum (y_{Hj} - \bar{y}_H)^2 - \dfrac{[\sum (y_{Hj} - \bar{y}_H)(x_{Hj} - \bar{x}_H)]^2}{\sum (x_{Hj} - \bar{x}_H)^2}$
Total	N	S_y	S_{yy}	S_x	S_{xx}	S_{xy}	$S_{\hat{\sigma}^2}$

Example 8.6.3

A new food supplement (x units) was fed to three different breeds of chickens for six weeks to determine the effect on hardness Y of the egg shells. A simple linear model was assumed for each breed.

$$\left.\begin{array}{ll} Y_{1j} = \alpha_1 + \beta_1 x_{1j} + \varepsilon_{1j} & j = 1, 2, \ldots, n_1 \text{ for breed } 1 \\ Y_{2j} = \alpha_2 + \beta_2 x_{2j} + \varepsilon_{2j} & j = 1, 2, \ldots, n_2 \text{ for breed } 2 \\ Y_{3j} = \alpha_3 + \beta_3 x_{3j} + \varepsilon_{3j} & j = 1, 2, \ldots, n_3 \text{ for breed } 3 \end{array}\right\}$$

$$\varepsilon_{ij} \text{ distributed } NID(\varepsilon : 0, \sigma^2)$$

The problem is to determine if the models are the same for all breeds, that is, to test the hypothesis

$$H_0 : \alpha_1 = \alpha_2 = \alpha_3 \qquad \beta_1 = \beta_2 = \beta_3$$

with a Type I error of 5 percent. The data are given in Table 8.6.2.

We will solve this problem two ways: by using the formula in Equation (8.6.17), and then by the square root method in Equation (8.6.15) and Equation (8.6.16). To use the formula in Equation (8.6.17), we compute the quantities needed in Table 8.6.1. These are given in Table 8.6.3.

Table 8.6.2

Data for Example 8.6.3

Breed 1		*Breed 2*		*Breed 3*	
x	y	x	y	x	y
1	8.42	3	9.86	2	6.52
3	14.68	3	9.54	5	5.11
5	21.42	4	11.96	7	7.75
6	25.45	5	12.46	8	6.84
7	27.14	6	11.38	10	7.65
8	30.53	8	14.69	15	9.49
9	34.51	9	16.48	16	7.03
9	34.52	12	20.11	18	9.41
10	33.24			20	12.01
11	39.63				
12	43.98				
14	47.77				

Substituting the appropriate quantities into Equation (8.6.17), we get

$$w = \frac{[14{,}449.8862 - (539.58)^2/29] - \dfrac{[4964.8700 - (246)(539.58)/29]^2}{2738 - (246)^2/29} - 34.0978}{34.0978} \times \left(\frac{29 - (3)(2)}{(2)(2)}\right)$$

$$= 699.05$$

and clearly the hypothesis is rejected.

We will demonstrate the square root method in Equations (8.6.15) and (8.6.16). From the data in Table 8.6.2, we get $[\mathbf{X}_h'\mathbf{X}_h \mid \mathbf{X}_h'\mathbf{y}_h]$ for each model and for the total of the three models; we then reduce these by the square root method. The formats are illustrated in Equation (8.6.15). We get

$$\left[\begin{array}{cc|c} 12 & 95 & 361.29 \\ 95 & 907 & 3332.6200 \\ \hline 3.4641 & 27.4241 & 104.2954 \\ & 12.4466 & 37.9549 \end{array}\right]$$

$$\left[\begin{array}{cc|c} 8 & 50 & 106.48 \\ 50 & 384 & 743.7800 \\ \hline 2.8284 & 17.6777 & 37.6464 \\ & 8.4558 & 9.2576 \end{array}\right] \qquad \left[\begin{array}{cc|c} 9 & 101 & 71.81 \\ 101 & 1447 & 888.4700 \\ \hline 3.0 & 33.6667 & 23.9367 \\ & 17.7075 & 4.6648 \end{array}\right]$$

$$\left[\begin{array}{cc|c} 29 & 246 & 539.58 \\ 246 & 2738 & 4964.8700 \\ \hline 5.3852 & 45.6811 & 100.1975 \\ & 25.5194 & 15.1940 \end{array}\right]$$

We get $\sum_{h=1}^{3} \mathbf{t}_h'\mathbf{t}_h = 14{,}415.7884$; $\mathbf{t}'\mathbf{t} = 10{,}270.3958$. By the formula in Equation (8.6.16), we get

$$w = \left(\frac{14{,}415.7884 - 10{,}270.3958}{14{,}449.8862 - 14{,}415.7884}\right)\left(\frac{29 - (3)(2)}{(2)(2)}\right) = 699.05$$

Computations for this example were done with 10 significant figures.

Table 8.6.3

Summary for Data in Table 8.6.2

Model	n_h	$\sum_{j=1}^{n_h} y_{hj}$	$\sum_{j=1}^{n_h} y_{hj}^2$	$\sum_{j=1}^{n_h} x_{hj}$	$\sum_{j=1}^{n_h} x_{hj}^2$	$\sum_{j=1}^{n_h} y_{hj}x_{hj}$	$(n_h - 2)\hat{\sigma}_h^2$
1	12	361.29	12335.7965	95	907	3332.6200	17.6843
2	8	106.48	1507.8274	50	384	743.7800	4.8757
3	9	71.81	606.2623	101	1447	888.4700	11.5378
Total	29 N	539.58 S_y	14449.8862 S_{yy}	246 S_x	2738 S_{xx}	4964.8700 S_{xy}	34.0978 $S_{\hat{\sigma}^2}$

Also, from the first three formats above (in Equation (8.6.15)), we can obtain point estimates of α_1, α_2, α_3, β_1, β_2, and β_3; also point estimates of σ^2 (or σ_1^2, σ_2^2, and σ_3^2, if each model is assumed to have a different variance) can be obtained. From these results, confidence intervals can be computed.

8.6.3 An Extension of the Test That *H* Simple Linear Models Are Parallel

We will extend the test of the hypothesis that *H simple* linear models are "parallel" to the case of *general* linear models. First we will illustrate with an example.

Example 8.6.4

Consider *H* polynomial models of third degree given by

$$Y_{hj} = \beta_{h0} + \beta_{h1}x_j + \beta_{h2}x_j^2 + \beta_{h3}x_j^3 + \varepsilon_{hj}$$
$$j = 1, 2, \ldots, n_h > 4 \qquad h = 1, 2, \ldots, H > 1$$

Suppose we want to test

$$H_0 : \beta_{10} = \beta_{20} = \cdots = \beta_{H0}$$

(all *H* intercepts are equal). Or suppose we want to test

$$H_0 : \beta_{12} = \beta_{22} = \cdots = \beta_{H2} \qquad \text{and} \qquad \beta_{13} = \beta_{23} = \cdots = \beta_{H3}$$

(the coefficients of the second and third degree terms are respectively equal).

Consider the H general linear models

$$\mathbf{Y}_h = \mathbf{X}_h\boldsymbol{\beta}_h + \boldsymbol{\varepsilon}_h \qquad h = 1, 2, \ldots, H$$

where $\boldsymbol{\beta}_h$ is partitioned as

$$\boldsymbol{\beta}_h = \begin{bmatrix} \boldsymbol{\alpha}_h \\ \boldsymbol{\delta}_h \end{bmatrix}$$

and $\boldsymbol{\beta}_h$ is a $p \times 1$ vector of unknown parameters, $\boldsymbol{\alpha}_h$ is a $p_1 \times 1$ $(0 < p_1 < p)$ vector of unknown parameters. In Theorem 8.6.5 we give a test statistic for a test of the hypothesis

$$H_0 : \boldsymbol{\delta}_1 = \boldsymbol{\delta}_2 = \cdots = \boldsymbol{\delta}_H = \boldsymbol{\delta} \quad \text{(unknown)}$$

THEOREM 8.6.5

Consider the H general linear models

$$\mathbf{Y}_h = \mathbf{X}_h\boldsymbol{\beta}_h + \boldsymbol{\varepsilon}_h$$

$\boldsymbol{\varepsilon}_h$ *distributed* $\mathbf{NID}(\boldsymbol{\varepsilon} : \mathbf{0}, \sigma^2\mathbf{I})$, $h = 1, 2, \ldots, H$, *where* $\mathbf{X}_h$ *has size* $n_h \times p$, *and let* $N = \sum_{h=1}^{H} n_h$. *Partition* $\boldsymbol{\beta}_h$ *and* $\mathbf{X}_h$ *as*

$$\boldsymbol{\beta}_h = \begin{bmatrix} \boldsymbol{\alpha}_h \\ \boldsymbol{\delta}_h \end{bmatrix} \qquad \mathbf{X}_h = [\mathbf{U}_h, \mathbf{V}_h]$$

where $\boldsymbol{\alpha}_h$ *is* $p_1 \times 1$, $\boldsymbol{\delta}_h$ *is* $p_2 \times 1$, *and so on. The likelihood ratio test statistic is W for testing* $H_0 : \boldsymbol{\delta}_1 = \boldsymbol{\delta}_2 = \cdots = \boldsymbol{\delta}_H = \boldsymbol{\delta}$ *(unknown) vs.* $H_a : \boldsymbol{\delta}_h \neq \boldsymbol{\delta}_{h'}$ *for at least one* $h \neq h' = 1, 2, \ldots, H$, *where W is given by*

$$\begin{aligned} W = \Bigg(\Bigg\{ & \sum_{h=1}^{H} \mathbf{Y}_h'\mathbf{X}_h\mathbf{X}_h^-\mathbf{Y}_h \\ & - \sum_{i=1}^{H} \mathbf{Y}_i'\mathbf{U}_i\mathbf{U}_i^-\mathbf{Y}_i - \left[\sum_{h=1}^{H} \mathbf{Y}_h'(\mathbf{I} - \mathbf{U}_h\mathbf{U}_h^-)\mathbf{V}_h\right]\left[\sum_{i=1}^{H} \mathbf{V}_i'(\mathbf{I} - \mathbf{U}_i\mathbf{U}_i^-)\mathbf{V}_i\right]^{-1} \\ & \times \left[\sum_{j=1}^{H} \mathbf{V}_j'(\mathbf{I} - \mathbf{U}_j\mathbf{U}_j^-)\mathbf{Y}_j\right]\Bigg\} \Bigg/ \Bigg\{\sum_{h=1}^{H} \mathbf{Y}_h'\mathbf{Y}_h - \sum_{j=1}^{H} \mathbf{Y}_j'\mathbf{X}_j\mathbf{X}_j^-\mathbf{Y}_j\Bigg\}\Bigg) \\ & \times \left(\frac{N - Hp}{(H - 1)p_2}\right) \end{aligned}$$

Proof

We use Theorem 6.3.1 and specifically Equation (6.3.11). Clearly

$$\hat{\sigma}_\Omega^2 = \frac{1}{N}(\mathbf{Y}'\mathbf{Y} - \hat{\boldsymbol{\beta}}'\mathbf{X}'\mathbf{Y}) = \frac{1}{N}\left(\sum_{h=1}^{H} \mathbf{Y}_h'\mathbf{Y}_h - \sum_{h=1}^{H} \mathbf{Y}_h'\mathbf{X}_h\mathbf{X}_h^-\mathbf{Y}_h\right)$$

which was obtained for the full model in the previous section.

To obtain $\hat{\sigma}_\omega^2$ we use the reduced model $\mathbf{Z} = \mathbf{B}\boldsymbol{\gamma} + \boldsymbol{\varepsilon}$. The model reduced by H_0 is the set of H general linear models

$$\mathbf{Y}_h = [\mathbf{U}_h, \mathbf{V}_h]\begin{bmatrix} \boldsymbol{\alpha}_h \\ \boldsymbol{\delta} \end{bmatrix} + \boldsymbol{\varepsilon}_h \qquad h = 1, 2, \ldots, H$$

which, when put into one model, is (here $\mathbf{Z} = \mathbf{Y}$)

$$\mathbf{Y} = \mathbf{B}\boldsymbol{\gamma} + \boldsymbol{\varepsilon} \qquad \text{where } \mathbf{Y}' = [\mathbf{Y}_1', \mathbf{Y}_2', \ldots, \mathbf{Y}_H']$$

$$\boldsymbol{\gamma}' = [\boldsymbol{\delta}', \boldsymbol{\alpha}_1', \boldsymbol{\alpha}_2', \ldots, \boldsymbol{\alpha}_H']$$

$$\mathbf{B} = \begin{bmatrix} \mathbf{V}_1 & \mathbf{U}_1 & \mathbf{0} & \cdots & \mathbf{0} \\ \mathbf{V}_2 & \mathbf{0} & \mathbf{U}_2 & \cdots & \mathbf{0} \\ \vdots & \vdots & \vdots & & \vdots \\ \mathbf{V}_H & \mathbf{0} & \mathbf{0} & \cdots & \mathbf{U}_H \end{bmatrix}$$

$$\mathbf{B}'\mathbf{B} = \begin{bmatrix} \sum_{i=1}^{H} \mathbf{V}_i'\mathbf{V}_i & \mathbf{V}_1'\mathbf{U}_1 & \mathbf{V}_2'\mathbf{U}_2 & \cdots & \mathbf{V}_H'\mathbf{U}_H \\ \mathbf{U}_1'\mathbf{V}_1 & \mathbf{U}_1'\mathbf{U}_1 & \mathbf{0} & \cdots & \mathbf{0} \\ \mathbf{U}_2'\mathbf{V}_2 & \mathbf{0} & \mathbf{U}_2'\mathbf{U}_2 & \cdots & \mathbf{0} \\ \vdots & \vdots & \vdots & & \vdots \\ \mathbf{U}_H'\mathbf{V}_H & \mathbf{0} & \mathbf{0} & \cdots & \mathbf{U}_H'\mathbf{U}_H \end{bmatrix}$$

$$\mathbf{B}'\mathbf{Y} = \begin{bmatrix} \sum_{i=1}^{H} \mathbf{V}_i'\mathbf{Y}_i \\ \mathbf{U}_1'\mathbf{Y}_1 \\ \vdots \\ \mathbf{U}_H'\mathbf{Y}_H \end{bmatrix}$$

$\hat{\sigma}_\omega^2$ is the maximum likelihood estimator of σ^2 in the reduced model, which is

$$\hat{\sigma}_\omega^2 = \frac{1}{N}(\mathbf{Y} - \mathbf{B}\tilde{\boldsymbol{\gamma}})'(\mathbf{Y} - \mathbf{B}\tilde{\boldsymbol{\gamma}}) = \frac{1}{N}(\mathbf{Y}'\mathbf{Y} - \tilde{\boldsymbol{\gamma}}'\mathbf{B}'\mathbf{Y})$$

$$= \frac{1}{N}\left(\sum_{h=1}^{H} \mathbf{Y}_h'\mathbf{Y}_h - \tilde{\boldsymbol{\gamma}}'\mathbf{B}'\mathbf{Y}\right)$$

where $\tilde{\boldsymbol{\gamma}}$ is the solution of the reduced normal equations

$$\mathbf{B}'\mathbf{B}\tilde{\boldsymbol{\gamma}} = \mathbf{B}'\mathbf{Y}$$

It is easy to show by direct substitution that the solution $\tilde{\boldsymbol{\gamma}}$ to these normal equations is

$$\tilde{\boldsymbol{\delta}} = \left[\sum_{i=1}^{H} \mathbf{V}_i'(\mathbf{I} - \mathbf{U}_i\mathbf{U}_i^-)\mathbf{V}_i\right]^{-1}\left[\sum_{j=1}^{H} \mathbf{V}_j'(\mathbf{I} - \mathbf{U}_j\mathbf{U}_j^-)\mathbf{Y}_j\right]$$

and

$$\tilde{\boldsymbol{\alpha}}_h = \mathbf{U}_h^-\mathbf{Y}_h - \mathbf{U}_h^-\mathbf{V}_h\tilde{\boldsymbol{\delta}} \qquad h = 1, 2, \ldots, H$$

Hence

$$\hat{\sigma}_\omega^2 = \frac{1}{N}\left[\sum_{h=1}^{H} \mathbf{Y}_h'\mathbf{Y}_h - \tilde{\boldsymbol{\delta}}'\left(\sum_{i=1}^{H} \mathbf{V}_i'\mathbf{Y}_i\right) - \sum_{i=1}^{H} \tilde{\boldsymbol{\alpha}}_i'\mathbf{U}_i'\mathbf{Y}_i\right]$$

$$= \frac{1}{N}\left[\sum_{h=1}^{H} \mathbf{Y}_h'\mathbf{Y}_h - \tilde{\boldsymbol{\delta}}'\left(\sum_{i=1}^{H} \mathbf{V}_i'\mathbf{Y}_i\right) - \sum_{i=1}^{H} (\mathbf{Y}_i' - \tilde{\boldsymbol{\delta}}'\mathbf{V}_i')\mathbf{U}_i'^-\mathbf{U}_i'\mathbf{Y}_i\right]$$

$$= \frac{1}{N}\left[\sum_{h=1}^{H} \mathbf{Y}_h'\mathbf{Y}_h - \tilde{\boldsymbol{\delta}}'\sum_{i=1}^{H} \mathbf{V}_i'(\mathbf{I} - \mathbf{U}_i\mathbf{U}_i^-)\mathbf{Y}_i - \sum_{i=1}^{H} \mathbf{Y}_i'\mathbf{U}_i\mathbf{U}_i^-\mathbf{Y}_i\right]$$

Now by Equation (6.3.11)

$$W = \left(\frac{N - Hp}{(H-1)p_2}\right)\left(\frac{\hat{\sigma}_\omega^2 - \hat{\sigma}_\Omega^2}{\hat{\sigma}_\Omega^2}\right)$$

$$= \left(\frac{N - Hp}{(H-1)p_2}\right)\left\{\sum_{h=1}^{H} \mathbf{Y}_h'\mathbf{X}_h\mathbf{X}_h^-\mathbf{Y}_h - \left[\sum_{j=1}^{H} \mathbf{Y}_j'(\mathbf{I} - \mathbf{U}_j\mathbf{U}_j^-)\mathbf{V}_j\right]\right.$$

$$\times \left[\sum_{h=1}^{H} \mathbf{V}_h'(\mathbf{I} - \mathbf{U}_h\mathbf{U}_h^-)\mathbf{V}_h\right]^{-1}\left[\sum_{i=1}^{H} \mathbf{V}_i'(\mathbf{I} - \mathbf{U}_i\mathbf{U}_i^-)\mathbf{Y}_i\right]$$

$$\left. - \sum_{i=1}^{H} \mathbf{Y}_i'\mathbf{U}_i\mathbf{U}_i^-\mathbf{Y}_i\right\} \Big/ \left[\sum_{h=1}^{H} \mathbf{Y}_h'\mathbf{Y}_h - \sum_{h=1}^{H} \mathbf{Y}_h'\mathbf{X}_h\mathbf{X}_h^-\mathbf{Y}_h\right]$$

and this completes the proof.

The formula for W appears to be very complicated, but we will now show that it can be obtained by computing the normal equations for each of the models, solving each of these normal equations by the square root method, and then solving one additional $p_2 \times p_2$ system of equations also by the square root method.

The H sets of normal equations and the reduction of each by the square root method is given in the format below.

$$\left[\frac{\mathbf{X}_1'\mathbf{X}_1 \mid \mathbf{X}_1'\mathbf{y}_1}{\mathbf{T}_1 \mid \mathbf{t}_1}\right]; \quad \left[\frac{\mathbf{X}_2'\mathbf{X}_2 \mid \mathbf{X}_2'\mathbf{y}_2}{\mathbf{T}_2 \mid \mathbf{t}_2}\right]; \quad \ldots; \quad \left[\frac{\mathbf{X}_H'\mathbf{X}_H \mid \mathbf{X}_H'\mathbf{y}_H}{\mathbf{T}_H \mid \mathbf{t}_H}\right] \tag{8.6.18}$$

but we note that since $\mathbf{X}_h = [\mathbf{U}_h, \mathbf{V}_h]$, we get for the hth set

$$\frac{[\mathbf{X}_h'\mathbf{X}_h \mid \mathbf{X}_h'\mathbf{y}_h]}{[\mathbf{T}_h \mid \mathbf{t}_h]} = \frac{\begin{bmatrix} \mathbf{U}_h'\mathbf{U}_h & \mathbf{U}_h'\mathbf{V}_h & \mathbf{U}_h'\mathbf{y}_h \\ \mathbf{V}_h'\mathbf{U}_h & \mathbf{V}_h'\mathbf{V}_h & \mathbf{V}_h'\mathbf{y}_h \end{bmatrix}}{\begin{bmatrix} \mathbf{T}_{11(h)} & \mathbf{T}_{12(h)} & \mathbf{t}_{1(h)} \\ \mathbf{0} & \mathbf{T}_{22(h)} & \mathbf{t}_{2(h)} \end{bmatrix}} \qquad h = 1, 2, \ldots, H$$

We note the following:

$$\sum_{h=1}^{H} \mathbf{y}_h'\mathbf{X}_h\mathbf{X}_h^{-}\mathbf{y}_h = \sum_{h=1}^{H} \mathbf{t}_h'\mathbf{t}_h = \sum_{h=1}^{H} (\mathbf{t}_{1(h)}'\mathbf{t}_{1(h)} + \mathbf{t}_{2(h)}'\mathbf{t}_{2(h)})$$

and

$$\sum_{h=1}^{H} \mathbf{y}_h'\mathbf{U}_h\mathbf{U}_h^{-}\mathbf{y}_h = \sum_{h=1}^{H} \mathbf{t}_{1(h)}'\mathbf{t}_{1(h)}$$

Also, consider the format $[\mathbf{A} \mid \mathbf{a}]$, where

$$\mathbf{A} = \sum_{h=1}^{H} \mathbf{T}_{22(h)}'\mathbf{T}_{22(h)} = \sum_{h=1}^{H} \mathbf{V}_h'(\mathbf{I} - \mathbf{U}_h\mathbf{U}_h^{-})\mathbf{V}_h$$

$$\mathbf{a} = \sum_{h=1}^{H} \mathbf{T}_{22(h)}'\mathbf{t}_{2(h)} = \sum_{h=1}^{H} \mathbf{V}_h'(\mathbf{I} - \mathbf{U}_h\mathbf{U}_h^{-})\mathbf{y}_h$$

If we solve the system $[\mathbf{A} \mid \mathbf{a}]$ by the square root method, we get

$$\left[\frac{\mathbf{A} \mid \mathbf{a}}{\mathbf{T} \mid \mathbf{t}}\right]$$

and

$$\mathbf{t}'\mathbf{t} = \mathbf{a}'\mathbf{A}^{-1}\mathbf{a} = \left[\sum_{j=1}^{H} \mathbf{y}_j'(\mathbf{I} - \mathbf{U}_j\mathbf{U}_j^{-})\mathbf{V}_j\right]\left[\sum_{h=1}^{H} \mathbf{V}_h'(\mathbf{I} - \mathbf{U}_h\mathbf{U}_h^{-})\mathbf{V}_h\right]^{-1} \times \left[\sum_{i=1}^{H} \mathbf{V}_i'(\mathbf{I} - \mathbf{U}_i\mathbf{U}_i^{-})\mathbf{y}_i\right]$$

If we substitute into Theorem 8.6.5, we get w (the computed value of W):

$$w = \left(\frac{\sum_{h=1}^{H} \mathbf{t}'_{2(h)}\mathbf{t}_{2(h)} - \mathbf{t}'\mathbf{t}}{\sum_{h=1}^{H} \mathbf{y}'_h\mathbf{y}_h - \sum_{h=1}^{H} \mathbf{t}'_h\mathbf{t}_h} \right) \left(\frac{N - Hp}{(H-1)p_2} \right)$$

8.7 Polynomial Models

As we pointed out in Section 5.2, $Y = \mu(x) + \varepsilon$ is a *linear* model if $\mu(x)$ is given by

$$\mu(x) = \beta_0 + \beta_1 q_1(x) + \beta_2 q_2(x) + \cdots + \beta_H q_H(x)$$

where the $q_i(x)$ are known functions of x and contain no unknown parameters. In this section we will study the special case where $\mu(x)$ is a polynomial.

8.7.1 Polynomial Model

The model is

$$Y_i = \beta_0 + \beta_1 x_i + \beta_2 x_i^2 + \cdots + \beta_H x_i^H + \varepsilon_i \qquad i = 1, 2, \ldots, n > H + 1$$

H is a *known* positive integer. We can put this into the form of the general linear model $\mathbf{Y} = \mathbf{X}\boldsymbol{\beta} + \boldsymbol{\varepsilon}$; we get

$$\mathbf{X} = \begin{bmatrix} 1 & x_1 & x_1^2 & \cdots & x_1^H \\ 1 & x_2 & x_2^2 & \cdots & x_2^H \\ \vdots & \vdots & \vdots & & \vdots \\ 1 & x_n & x_n^2 & \cdots & x_n^H \end{bmatrix} \qquad \boldsymbol{\beta} = \begin{bmatrix} \beta_0 \\ \beta_1 \\ \vdots \\ \beta_H \end{bmatrix} \tag{8.7.1}$$

$$\mathbf{X}'\mathbf{X} = \begin{bmatrix} n & \sum x_i & \sum x_i^2 & \cdots & \sum x_i^H \\ \sum x_i & \sum x_i^2 & \sum x_i^3 & \cdots & \sum x_i^{H+1} \\ \vdots & \vdots & \vdots & & \vdots \\ \sum x_i^H & \sum x_i^{H+1} & \sum x_i^{H+2} & \cdots & \sum x_i^{2H} \end{bmatrix} \qquad \mathbf{X}'\mathbf{Y} = \begin{bmatrix} \sum Y_i \\ \sum x_i Y_i \\ \sum x_i^2 Y_i \\ \vdots \\ \sum x_i^H Y_i \end{bmatrix}$$

where all summations are from 1 to n. This is exactly the general linear model, so all the appropriate theorems in Chapter 6 apply for point estimation, confidence interval estimation, and testing hypotheses of the parameters. If H is large, the $\mathbf{X}'\mathbf{X}$ matrix may be poorly conditioned and a method of computing which uses $\mathbf{X}$ directly rather than $\mathbf{X}'\mathbf{X}$ should be considered (see Theorem 7.7.2 and reference [G-5]). This remark also applies to Section 8.7.2.

8.7.2 Determining the Degree of a Polynomial Model

A problem that sometimes arises when a polynomial model is under consideration is that of determining the degree of the polynomial. Consider the polynomial model $Y_j = \mu(x_j) + \varepsilon_j$, where $\mu(x_j)$ is a polynomial of degree K. We write this in detail as

$$Y_j = \beta_0 + \beta_1 x_j + \beta_2 x_j^2 + \cdots + \beta_K x_j^K + \varepsilon_j \qquad j = 1, 2, \ldots, n > K + 1$$

where K is a *specified* positive integer. We assume that the degree of the polynomial $\mu(x)$ is *less than or equal to* K (given), and the problem is to determine the exact degree. The procedure is to test the hypothesis $H_0 : \beta_K = 0$, then test $\beta_{K-1} = 0$, then test $\beta_{K-2} = 0$, and so on, until a hypothesis is rejected. Suppose $\beta_M = 0$ is the first hypothesis that is rejected; the conclusion is that the polynomial is of degree M.

We write the procedure in more detail below.

1. K degree model: $Y_j = \beta_0 + \beta_1 x_j + \cdots + \beta_K x_j^K + \varepsilon_j$.
   Test $H_0 : \beta_K = 0$ *vs.* $H_a : \beta_K \neq 0$.
   If H_0 is rejected, declare Kth degree model correct.
   If H_0 is not rejected, examine $K - 1$ degree model.
2. $K - 1$ degree model: $Y_j = \beta_0 + \beta_1 x_j + \cdots + \beta_{K-1} x_j^{K-1} + \varepsilon_j$.
   Test $H_0 : \beta_{K-1} = 0$ *vs.* $H_a : \beta_{K-1} \neq 0$.
   If H_0 is rejected, declare $K - 1$ degree model correct.
   If H_0 is not rejected, examine, $K - 2$ degree model.
3. Continue until H_0 is rejected, say for the model of degree M.
   Declare the M degree model correct.
   If no H_0 is rejected, declare $Y_j = \beta_0 + \varepsilon_j$ the correct model. (8.7.2)

It has been shown [A-4] that this procedure for determining the degree of a polynomial model has some desirable optimum properties. We will show how the square root method can be used to compute the statistics to test these various hypotheses.

Consider the model of degree K:

$$Y_j = \beta_0 + \beta_1 x_j + \cdots + \beta_K x_j^K + \varepsilon_j \qquad \varepsilon_j \text{ are distributed } NID(\varepsilon : 0, \sigma^2)$$

Denote the normal equations by $\mathbf{X}_K'\mathbf{X}_K\hat{\boldsymbol{\beta}}_K = \mathbf{X}_K'\mathbf{Y}$ and reduce these to triangular form by the square root method. The format is

$$\left[\frac{\mathbf{X}_K'\mathbf{X}_K \mid \mathbf{X}_K'\mathbf{Y}}{\mathbf{T}_K \quad \mid \ell_K}\right] \tag{8.7.3}$$

note $\mathbf{X}_K'\mathbf{X}_K$ is a $(K + 1) \times (K + 1)$ matrix. To test $H_0 : \beta_K = 0$ *vs.* $H_a : \beta_K \neq 0$ the test statistic is

$$W_K = \frac{(n - K - 1)T_K^2}{\mathbf{Y}'\mathbf{Y} - \ell_K'\ell_K} \tag{8.7.4}$$

where $\ell_K = [T_0, T_1, \ldots, T_K]$.

By Theorem 6.3.1, W_K is distributed $F(w : 1, n - K - 1; \lambda)$, and $\lambda = 0$ if and only if $\beta_K = 0$, that is, H_0 is true. Thus the likelihood ratio test of size α is to reject H_0 if and only if $w_K \geq F_{\alpha:1,n-K-1}$. If H_0 is rejected, declare that the correct model is a K degree model. If H_0 is not rejected, examine the $K - 1$ degree model

$$Y_j = \beta_0 + \beta_1 x_j + \cdots + \beta_{K-1}x_j^{K-1} + \varepsilon_j \qquad \varepsilon_j \text{ are distributed } NID(\varepsilon : 0, \sigma^2) \tag{8.7.5}$$

Denote the normal equations of this model by $\mathbf{X}_{K-1}'\mathbf{X}_{K-1}\hat{\boldsymbol{\beta}}_{K-1} = \mathbf{X}_{K-1}'\mathbf{Y}$, and reduce these to triangular form by the square root method.

$$\left[\frac{\mathbf{X}_{K-1}'\mathbf{X}_{K-1} \mid \mathbf{X}_{K-1}'\mathbf{Y}}{\mathbf{T}_{K-1}^* \quad \mid \ell_{K-1}^*}\right] \tag{8.7.6}$$

Note that $\hat{\boldsymbol{\beta}}_{K-1}$ is not generally the first K elements of $\hat{\boldsymbol{\beta}}_K$ obtained from Equation (8.7.3).

The test statistic for the hypothesis $H_0 : \beta_{K-1} = 0$ *vs.* $H_a : \beta_{K-1} \neq 0$ for the model in Equation (8.7.5) is

$$W_{K-1} = \frac{(n - K)T_{K-1}^{*2}}{\mathbf{Y}'\mathbf{Y} - \ell_{K-1}^{*\prime}\ell_{K-1}^*} \tag{8.7.7}$$

and by Theorem 6.3.1, W_{K-1} is distributed $F(w : 1, n - K; \lambda)$, and $\lambda = 0$ if and only if $\beta_{K-1} = 0$, that is, H_0 is true. So the likelihood ratio test of size α is to reject H_0 if and only if $w_{K-1} \geq F_{\alpha:1,n-K}$. But $\mathbf{X}_{K-1}'\mathbf{X}_{K-1}$ is a matrix that is the first K rows and columns of the matrix $\mathbf{X}_K'\mathbf{X}_K$ in the Kth degree model. Also, the vector $\mathbf{X}_{K-1}'\mathbf{Y}$ is the first K elements of the vector $\mathbf{X}_K'\mathbf{Y}$ in the Kth degree model. Thus ℓ_{K-1}^* is a $K \times 1$ vector whose elements are the first K elements of the vector ℓ_K in Equation (8.7.3). So referring to Equation (8.7.3), W_{K-1} is given by the expressions shown below.

$$W_{K-1} = \frac{(n-K)T_{K-1}^2}{\mathbf{Y}'\mathbf{Y} - \ell_K'\ell_K + T_K^2} = \frac{(n-K)T_{K-1}^2}{\mathbf{Y}'\mathbf{Y} - \sum_{k=0}^{K-1} T_K^2} \tag{8.7.8}$$

Now suppose we are examining the Mth degree model, that is, we have not rejected $H_0 : \beta_K = 0, H_0 : \beta_{K-1} = 0, \ldots, H_0 : \beta_{M+1} = 0$. The Mth degree model is

$$Y_j = \beta_0 + \beta_1 x_j + \cdots + \beta_M x_j^M + \varepsilon_j \qquad \varepsilon_j \text{ are distributed } NID(\varepsilon : 0, \sigma^2) \tag{8.7.9}$$

Denote the normal equations by $\mathbf{X}_M'\mathbf{X}_M\hat{\boldsymbol{\beta}}_M = \mathbf{X}_M'\mathbf{Y}$, and reduce these to triangular form by the square root method. The format is

$$\left[\begin{array}{c|c} \mathbf{X}_M'\mathbf{X}_M & \mathbf{X}_M'\mathbf{Y} \\ \hline \mathbf{T}_M^{**} & \ell_M^{**} \end{array}\right] \tag{8.7.10}$$

The test statistic for the hypothesis $H_0 : \beta_M = 0$ *vs.* $H_a : \beta_M \neq 0$ is W_M, where

$$W_M = \frac{(n - M - 1)(T_M^{**})^2}{\mathbf{Y}'\mathbf{Y} - (\ell_M^{**})'(\ell_M^{**})} \tag{8.7.11}$$

By Theorem 6.3.1, W_M is distributed $F(w : 1, n - M - 1; \lambda)$, and $\lambda = 0$ if and only if $\beta_M = 0$, that is, if and only if H_0 is true. The likelihood ratio test of size α is to reject $H_0 : \beta_M = 0$ if and only if $w_M \geq F_{\alpha:1,n-M-1}$.

Clearly the matrix $\mathbf{X}_M'\mathbf{X}_M$ is the first $M + 1$ rows and columns of the matrix $\mathbf{X}_K'\mathbf{X}_K$ for the Kth degree model, and the vector $\mathbf{X}_M'\mathbf{Y}$ is the first $M + 1$ elements in the vector $\mathbf{X}_K'\mathbf{Y}$ for the Kth degree model. Hence the vector ℓ_M^{**} consists of the first $M + 1$ elements of the vector ℓ_K in Equation (8.7.3). Thus W_M can be obtained from Equation (8.7.3). We get

$$W_M = \frac{(n - M - 1)T_M^2}{\mathbf{Y}'\mathbf{Y} - \sum_{k=0}^{M} T_K^2}$$

The computing procedure can be summarized as follows:

1. Specify K, compute the normal equations $\mathbf{X}'\mathbf{X}\hat{\boldsymbol{\beta}} = \mathbf{X}'\mathbf{y}$ for the Kth degree model, and reduce the normal equations to triangular form by the square root method. The format is

$$\left[\begin{array}{c|c} \mathbf{X}'\mathbf{X} & \mathbf{X}'\mathbf{y} \\ \hline \mathbf{T} & \mathbf{t} \end{array}\right]$$

2. Compute $w_K, w_{K-1}, \ldots,$ in turn, until $w_M \geq F_{\alpha:1,n-M-1}$ and stop.
3. Declare that the correct model is of Mth degree. (If there is no M for which $w_M \geq F_{\alpha:1,n-M-1}$, declare that the model is $Y_j = \beta_0 + \varepsilon_j$.)
4. w_M is given by

$$w_M = \frac{(n - M - 1)t_M^2}{\mathbf{y}'\mathbf{y} - \sum_{k=0}^{M} t_K^2}$$

for $M = K, K - 1, \ldots, 1.$ (8.7.12)

Before we discuss the theoretical aspects of this procedure, we will illustrate with a numerical example.

Example 8.7.1

Suppose it is to be assumed that the following data came from a polynomial model with degree less than or equal to 5, and an investigator wants to determine the correct degree of the model. $\alpha = 0.10$ is used.

y	48.574	52.346	54.846	68.379	81.861	89.876	112.238
x	1.1	1.3	1.4	1.8	2.1	2.2	2.5

y	119.315	139.673	161.095	203.079	233.938	329.386
x	2.6	2.8	3.0	3.3	3.5	4.0

In this problem $K = 5$, $n = 13$, and we compile $\mathbf{X}'\mathbf{X}$ and $\mathbf{X}'\mathbf{y}$ by Equation (8.7.1). The format in Equation (8.7.3) is

$$\left[\begin{array}{c|c} \mathbf{X}_K'\mathbf{X}_K & \mathbf{X}_K'\mathbf{y} \\ \hline \mathbf{T}_K & \mathbf{t}_K \end{array}\right] = \left[\begin{array}{c|c} \mathbf{X}_5'\mathbf{X}_5 & \mathbf{X}_5'\mathbf{y} \\ \hline \mathbf{T}_5 & \mathbf{t}_5 \end{array}\right]$$

$$= \left[\begin{array}{cccccc|c}
13.00 & 31.60 & 86.34 & 256.978 & 813.4134 & 2694.12106 & 1694.60600 \\
 & 86.34 & 256.978 & 813.4134 & 2694.12106 & 9236.96645 & 4962.65420 \\
 & & 813.4134 & 2694.12106 & 9236.96654 & 32539.13098 & 15672.68728 \\
 & & & 9236.96645 & 32539.13098 & 117134.2553 & 52119.36594 \\
 & & & & 117134.2553 & 429110.3120 & 179828.76250 \\
 & & & & & 1594637.0950 & 637791.77380 \\
\hline
3.60555 & 8.76426 & 23.94641 & 71.27287 & 225.60029 & 747.21474 & 469.99914 \\
 & 3.08670 & 15.26078 & 61.15250 & 232.25507 & 870.89233 & 273.25596 \\
 & & 2.66301 & 20.33678 & 108.99593 & 509.02137 & 93.05184 \\
 & & & 1.98259 & 20.34971 & 135.68674 & 9.33930 \\
 & & & & 1.45828 & 18.41493 & -0.39952 \\
 & & & & & 1.01460 & -0.26031
\end{array}\right]$$

(8.7.13)

From the data we compute $\sum_{i=1}^{13} y_i^2 = 304{,}319.0162$. From the result of reducing the normal equations, we get $\mathbf{t}_K'\mathbf{t}_K = 304{,}314.1062$. To test $H_0 : \beta_5 = 0$ *vs.* $H_a : \beta_5 \neq 0$, we use Equation (8.7.12) and get $w_5 = 7(-0.26031)^2/4.9100 = 0.097$ and $F_{0.10:1,7} = 3.59$. So we declare $\beta_5 = 0$, and test $H_0 : \beta_4 = 0$ *vs.* $H_a : \beta_4 \neq 0$. We get

$$w_4 = \frac{8(-0.39952)^2}{4.9100 + (-0.26031)^2} = 0.2565 \qquad \text{and} \qquad F_{0.10:1,8} = 3.46$$

So we declare $\beta_4 = 0$, and test $H_0 : \beta_3 = 0$ *vs.* $H_a : \beta_3 \neq 0$. We get

$$w_3 = \frac{9(9.3393)^2}{4.9100 + (-0.26031)^2 + (-0.39952)^2} = 152.7840$$

and

$$F_{0.10:1,9} = 3.36$$

So we declare $\beta_3 \neq 0$ and that the degree of the polynomial that fits the data is three. We write the model

$$Y_j = \beta_0 + \beta_1 x_j + \beta_2 x_j^2 + \beta_3 x_j^3 + \varepsilon_j$$
$$\varepsilon_j \text{ are distributed } NID(\varepsilon : 0, \sigma^2) \qquad j = 1, 2, \ldots, 13$$

We now may want point and interval estimators of the β_i. These can be obtained directly from the format in Equation (8.7.13). Just eliminate the last two rows and columns from the $\mathbf{X}_K'\mathbf{X}_K$ and $\mathbf{T}_K$ matrices and the last two rows from the $\mathbf{X}_K'\mathbf{y}_K$ and $\mathbf{t}_K$ vector (eliminate those rows and columns corresponding to β_5 and β_4). The resulting format is the first four rows and four columns of $\mathbf{X}_K'\mathbf{X}_K$ and the first four elements of $\mathbf{X}_K'\mathbf{y}$ in Equation (8.7.13) and of the corresponding $\mathbf{T}_K$ and $\mathbf{t}_K$. From this format we get $\hat{\beta}_0 = 43.3537$, $\hat{\beta}_1 = 0.3036$, $\hat{\beta}_2 = -1.0322$, and $\hat{\beta}_3 = 4.7107$. $(\mathbf{X}_3'\mathbf{X}_3)^{-1}$ and hence confidence intervals on the β_i, $i = 0, 1, 2, 3$, can be obtained from Equation (8.7.13). All the results of Section 7.3 apply.

One problem that concerns us is the overall "protection" level of the above procedure for determining the correct degree of a polynomial model. We shall first state two theorems on the distributional properties of the elements in the various tests described above. (The reader not interested in this can go directly to Section 8.8.)

THEOREM 8.7.1

Consider the following polynomial model whose degree is assumed to be less than or equal to K (specified)

$$Y_j = \beta_0 + \beta_1 x_j + \beta_2 x_j^2 + \cdots + \beta_K x_j^K + \varepsilon_j \qquad j = 1, 2, \ldots, n > K + 1$$
$$\varepsilon_j \text{ are distributed } NID(\varepsilon : 0, \sigma^2) \qquad (8.7.14)$$

Consider the normal equations denoted by

$$\mathbf{X}'\mathbf{X}\hat{\boldsymbol{\beta}} = \mathbf{X}'\mathbf{Y}$$

and reduce them by the square root method. We get

$$\left[\begin{array}{c|c} \mathbf{X}'\mathbf{X} & \mathbf{X}'\mathbf{Y} \\ \hline \mathbf{T} & \boldsymbol{\ell} \end{array}\right]$$

Then the random vector $\boldsymbol{\ell}$ *is distributed* $\mathbf{N}(\mathbf{t} : \mathbf{T}\boldsymbol{\beta}, \sigma^2\mathbf{I})$, *that is, the elements* $T_0, T_1, \ldots, T_K$ *are normal and independent random variables.*

Proof

The proof is obtained by noting that $\boldsymbol{\ell} = \mathbf{T}'^{-1}\mathbf{X}'\mathbf{Y}$ and using Theorem 3.3.5.

THEOREM 8.7.2

Let the model be given by Equation (8.7.14). Let M be a specified integer, $0 < M \leq K - 1$, *and assume* $\beta_K = \beta_{K-1} = \cdots = \beta_{M+1} = 0$. *The random variables* $W_K, W_{K-1}, \ldots, W_M$ *are jointly independent and* W_m *is distributed* $F(w_m : 1, n - m - 1; \lambda_m)$, $m = K, K - 1, \ldots, M$, *where* W_m *is defined by*

$$W_m = \frac{(n - m - 1)T_m^2}{\mathbf{Y}'\mathbf{Y} - \sum_{j=0}^{m} T_j^2} \qquad m = K, K - 1, \ldots, M$$

Also, $\lambda_K = \lambda_{K-1} = \cdots = \lambda_{M+1} = 0$; $\lambda_M = t_{MM}^2 \beta_M^2 / 2\sigma^2$, *where* t_{MM} *is the* $(M + 1)$*st diagonal element of* $\mathbf{T}$ *(corresponding to* β_M*).*

Proof

The proof will be asked for in the problems.

Now we shall examine the probability of making an error in determining the degree of the polynomial model by using the procedure given above. Of course, the error will depend on the value of the particular β under examination and on σ^2.

For example, recall that to test whether the degree of the polynomial is K or less, we test the hypothesis that $\beta_K = 0$ with a test of size α. There are two kinds of errors: (1) the error of declaring $\beta_K \neq 0$ when in fact $\beta_K = 0$ (the probability of making this error is equal to α, the size of the test); (2) the error of declaring $\beta_K = 0$ when in fact $\beta_K \neq 0$ (this is the Type II error and the probability of making this error depends on what the actual value of β_K is). Thus the operating characteristic of the procedure can be determined as in Table 8.7.1, where a hypothesis H_N is $\beta_N = 0$. $\Pi(\beta_K/\sigma)$, and so on, is the power of the test and depends on σ and the β parameter specified.

For example, suppose that the correct degree of the model is $K - 2$. Then an error is made if and only if $\{\beta_K = 0$ is rejected$\}$ or $\{\beta_K = 0$ is accepted and

Table 8.7.1

If the Correct Degree of the Model Is:	*An Error Is Made If and Only If:*	*Probability of an Error*
K	H_K accepted	$1 - \Pi(\beta_K/\sigma)$
$K - 1$	1. H_K rejected or 2. H_K and H_{K-1} accepted	1. α plus 2. $(1 - \alpha)[1 - \Pi(\beta_{K-1}/\sigma)]$
$K - 2$	1. H_K rejected or 2. H_K accepted and H_{K-1} rejected or 3. H_K, H_{K-1}, and H_{K-2} accepted	1. α plus 2. $\alpha(1 - \alpha)$ plus 3. $[(1 - \alpha)^2][1 - \Pi(\beta_{K-2}/\sigma)]$
⋮	⋮	⋮
0	$H_K, H_{K-1}, \ldots,$ or H_1 rejected	$1 - (1 - \alpha)^K$

$\beta_{K-1} = 0$ is rejected} or {$\beta_K = 0$ is accepted and $\beta_{K-1} = 0$ is accepted and $\beta_{K-2} = 0$ is accepted}. This is equivalent to $\{W_K \geq F_{\alpha:1,n-K-1}\}$ or $\{W_K \leq F_{\alpha:1,n-K-1}$ and $W_{K-1} \geq F_{\alpha:1,n-K}\}$ or $\{W_K \leq F_{\alpha:1,n-K-1}$ and $W_{K-1} \leq F_{\alpha:1,n-K}$ and $W_{K-2} \leq F_{\alpha:1,n-K+1}\}$. But these three events are mutually disjoint, so the probability of an error is the sum of the probabilities of the three events. By Theorem 8.7.2 the random variables W_K, W_{K-1}, and W_{K-2} are independent (since $\beta_K = \beta_{K-1} = 0$), so the probability of an error is

$$\begin{aligned} P[W_K \geq F_{\alpha:1,n-K-1}] &+ P[W_K \leq F_{\alpha:1,n-K-1}]P[W_{K-1} \geq F_{\alpha:1,n-K}] \\ &+ P[W_K \leq F_{\alpha:1,n-K-1}]P[W_{K-1} \leq F_{\alpha:1,n-K}]P[W_{K-2} \leq F_{\alpha:1,n-K+1}] \\ &= \alpha + (1 - \alpha)\alpha + (1 - \alpha)(1 - \alpha)[1 - \Pi(\beta_{K-2}/\sigma)] \end{aligned}$$

8.8 Trigonometric Models

In this section we discuss the model $Y = \mu(x) + \varepsilon$, where $\mu(x)$ is given by

$$\mu(x) = \beta_0 + [\alpha_1 \cos x + \gamma_1 \sin x] + [\alpha_2 \cos 2x + \gamma_2 \sin 2x] + \cdots + [\alpha_H \cos Hx + \gamma_H \sin Hx]$$

This is defined to be a trigonometric model where β_0, the α_i, and the γ_i are unknown parameters.

In Section 8.8.1 we discuss a *simple* trigonometric model, and in Section 8.8.2 we discuss a more *general* trigonometric model.

First we review some ideas from trigonometry that will be used in discussing the model.

A function $f(x)$ defined for all x on the real line is said to be *periodic* with *period* (of length) P if for some $P > 0$, $f(x + P) = f(x)$ for all x. The smallest positive number, say P_0, for which $f(x + P_0) = f(x)$ for all x is called the *fundamental* period of $f(x)$. If $f(x + P) = f(x)$, then clearly $f(x + 2P) = f(x)$, $f(x + 3P) = f(x), \ldots, f(x + kP) = f(x)$ for any integer k. Hence kP is also a period. This means that for every P units on the x-axis, the graph of the function repeats itself.

If P is a period of a function $f(x)$, then $F = 1/P$ is called a *frequency* of the function, and $F_0 = 1/P_0$ is called the fundamental frequency of $f(x)$ if P_0 is the fundamental period. The frequency F means the number of cycles (or repetitions) that $f(x)$ goes through per unit of x.

Two well-known periodic functions are sine and cosine. For example, if

$$f(x) = \cos\left(\frac{2\pi}{P}\right)x$$

then clearly we have that

$$f(x + P) = \cos\left(\frac{2\pi}{P}\right)(x + P) = \cos\left(\frac{2\pi}{P}x + 2\pi\right)$$

$$= \cos\left(\frac{2\pi}{P}\right)x \cos 2\pi - \sin\left(\frac{2\pi}{P}\right)x \sin 2\pi = \cos\left(\frac{2\pi}{P}\right)x = f(x)$$

So $\cos(2\pi/P)x$ is periodic with fundamental period P. Similarly, $\sin(2\pi/P)x$ is periodic with fundamental period P.

If we define $\mu(x)$ by

$$\mu(x) = \beta + \alpha \cos\left(\frac{2\pi}{P}\right)x + \gamma \sin\left(\frac{2\pi}{P}\right)x \qquad -\infty < x < \infty$$

then it is easy to show $\mu(x + P) = \mu(x)$; hence $\mu(x)$ is a periodic function with fundamental period P.

The maximum that the periodic function $f(x) = \alpha \cos(2\pi/P)x + \gamma \sin(2\pi/P)x$ can attain is called the *amplitude* of $f(x)$ and this value is clearly equal to $\sqrt{\alpha^2 + \gamma^2}$.

There are many natural phenomena that exhibit a periodic (cyclic) or approximate periodic character, such as prices of certain commodities (the period may be one year), voltage at an outlet (the period may be one-sixtieth of a second), rainfall at a certain locality (the period may be one year), pressure inside the cylinder of a reciprocating engine (the period may be one-three hundredth of a second), daily temperature during the month of July at a certain location (the period may be one day), and so on.

8.8.1 Simple Trigonometric Models

In each of the examples given above, the model to describe the physical situation might be given by

$$Y = \beta + \alpha \cos\left(\frac{2\pi}{P}\right)x + \gamma \sin\left(\frac{2\pi}{P}\right)x + \varepsilon \tag{8.8.1}$$

where β, α, and γ are unknown parameters and P is a known number. Since we assume P is known, this is a special case of the general linear model given in Section 5.2, with $q_1(x) = \cos(2\pi/P)x$, $q_2(x) = \sin(2\pi/P)x$, and all the appropriate theorems in Chapter 6 apply. However, under certain conditions the computations for this model are very easy. These conditions are the following:

1. the observed x_t are the integers $1, 2, \ldots, n$, that is, $x_t = t$, $t = 1, 2, \ldots, n$;

2. the length of the fundamental period P is a known positive integer such that $P \geq 3$;

3. $n = CP$, where C is a known positive integer. (8.8.2)

We will briefly discuss these assumptions.

1. This assumption merely states that the x values are equally spaced, and in many applications where this model is useful, they can be considered positive integers, that is, *hourly* temperature, *monthly* price, *yearly* rainfall, and so on.

2. 3. These assumptions imply that the observed x's take on the values $1, 2, \ldots, P, P + 1, \ldots, 2P, 2P + 1, \ldots, CP = n$. Thus C fundamental periods are sampled and the observed x's are equally spaced within each period. The restriction $P \geq 3$ insures that the sine term is in the model, since if $P = 1$ or $P = 2$, the term $\alpha \sin(2\pi/P)x = 0$ for all $x = 1, 2, \ldots, n$.

The usefulness of the assumptions will become clear as the theory develops. Since this model fits the general linear model $\mathbf{Y} = \mathbf{X\beta} + \boldsymbol{\varepsilon}$, we make the following identifications.

$$\mathbf{X} = \begin{bmatrix} 1 & \cos\left(\frac{2\pi}{P}\right) & \sin\left(\frac{2\pi}{P}\right) \\ 1 & \cos\left(\frac{2\pi}{P}\right)2 & \sin\left(\frac{2\pi}{P}\right)2 \\ \vdots & \vdots & \vdots \\ 1 & \cos\left(\frac{2\pi}{P}\right)n & \sin\left(\frac{2\pi}{P}\right)n \end{bmatrix} \quad \boldsymbol{\beta} = \begin{bmatrix} \beta \\ \alpha \\ \gamma \end{bmatrix} \quad \mathbf{X'Y} = \begin{bmatrix} \sum Y_t \\ \sum Y_t \cos\left(\frac{2\pi}{P}\right)t \\ \sum Y_t \sin\left(\frac{2\pi}{P}\right)t \end{bmatrix}$$

$$\mathbf{X'X} = \begin{bmatrix} n & \sum \cos\left(\frac{2\pi}{P}\right)t & \sum \sin\left(\frac{2\pi}{P}\right)t \\ \sum \cos\left(\frac{2\pi}{P}\right)t & \sum \cos^2\left(\frac{2\pi}{P}\right)t & \sum \cos\left(\frac{2\pi}{P}\right)t \sin\left(\frac{2\pi}{P}\right)t \\ \sum \sin\left(\frac{2\pi}{P}\right)t & \sum \cos\left(\frac{2\pi}{P}\right)t \sin\left(\frac{2\pi}{P}\right)t & \sum \sin^2\left(\frac{2\pi}{P}\right)t \end{bmatrix}$$

where all summations are for $t = 1, 2, \ldots, n$.

The following relationships can be established, where $n = CP$, C and P are positive integers, and $P \geq 3$.

1. $\sum_{t=1}^{n} \cos\left(\frac{2\pi}{P}\right)t = 0 \quad \sum_{t=1}^{n} \sin\left(\frac{2\pi}{P}\right)t = 0 \quad \sum_{t=1}^{n} \cos\left(\frac{2\pi}{P}\right)t \sin\left(\frac{2\pi}{P}\right)t = 0$

2. $\sum_{t=1}^{n} \cos^2\left(\frac{2\pi}{P}\right)t = \frac{n}{2} \quad \sum_{t=1}^{n} \sin^2\left(\frac{2\pi}{P}\right)t = \frac{n}{2}$

Hence

$$\mathbf{X'X} = \begin{bmatrix} n & 0 & 0 \\ 0 & \frac{n}{2} & 0 \\ 0 & 0 & \frac{n}{2} \end{bmatrix}$$

Since $\mathbf{X'X}$ is a diagonal matrix, the computations for $\hat{\boldsymbol{\beta}}$ and $\hat{\sigma}^2$ are very simple. We note here that conditions 1 and 2 may not hold if n is not a multiple of P; hence these are some consequences of the assumptions in Equation (8.8.2). The solution of the normal equations gives the following results.

$$\hat{\boldsymbol{\beta}} = \begin{bmatrix} \hat{\beta} \\ \hat{\alpha} \\ \hat{\gamma} \end{bmatrix} = \begin{bmatrix} \bar{Y} \\ \frac{2}{n}\sum_{t=1}^{n} Y_t \cos\left(\frac{2\pi}{P}\right)t \\ \frac{2}{n}\sum_{t=1}^{n} Y_t \sin\left(\frac{2\pi}{P}\right)t \end{bmatrix} \tag{8.8.3}$$

and

$$\begin{aligned} \hat{\sigma}^2 &= \left(\frac{1}{n-3}\right)(\mathbf{Y'Y} - \hat{\boldsymbol{\beta}}'\mathbf{X'Y}) \\ &= \frac{1}{n-3}\left(\sum_{t=1}^{n} Y_t^2 - \bar{Y}\sum_{t=1}^{n} Y_t - \frac{2}{n}\left[\sum_{t=1}^{n} Y_t \cos\left(\frac{2\pi}{P}\right)t\right]^2 - \frac{2}{n}\left[\sum_{t=1}^{n} Y_t \sin\left(\frac{2\pi}{P}\right)t\right]^2\right) \\ &= \frac{1}{n-3}\left[\sum_{t=1}^{n} (Y_t - \bar{Y})^2 - \frac{n}{2}(\hat{\alpha}^2 + \hat{\gamma}^2)\right] \end{aligned} \tag{8.8.4}$$

The formulas for $\hat{\alpha}$ and $\hat{\gamma}$ can be further simplified. For example, consider $\hat{\alpha}$; we get

$$\begin{aligned} \hat{\alpha} &= \left(\frac{2}{n}\right)\sum_{t=1}^{n} Y_t \cos\left(\frac{2\pi}{P}\right)t = \left(\frac{2}{CP}\right)\sum_{t=1}^{CP} Y_t \cos\left(\frac{2\pi}{P}\right)t \\ &= \frac{2}{CP}\left[\sum_{t=1}^{P} Y_t \cos\left(\frac{2\pi}{P}\right)t + \sum_{t=P+1}^{2P} Y_t \cos\left(\frac{2\pi}{P}\right)t + \cdots + \sum_{t=(C-1)P+1}^{CP} Y_t \cos\left(\frac{2\pi}{P}\right)t\right] \end{aligned} \tag{8.8.5}$$

but we know that, for $t = 1, 2, \ldots, P$

$$\cos\left(\frac{2\pi}{P}\right)t = \cos\left(\frac{2\pi}{P}\right)(P + t) = \cos\left(\frac{2\pi}{P}\right)(2P + t) = \cdots = \cos\left(\frac{2\pi}{P}\right)(\{C - 1\}P + t)$$

So Equation (8.8.5) becomes

$$\hat{\alpha} = \left(\frac{2}{CP}\right) \sum_{j=1}^{P} \left(\sum_{i=0}^{C-1} Y_{j+iP}\right) \cos\left(\frac{2\pi}{P}\right) j = \left(\frac{2}{CP}\right) \sum_{j=1}^{P} T_j \cos\left(\frac{2\pi}{P}\right) j$$

where $T_j = \sum_{i=0}^{C-1} Y_{j+iP}$. Thus we get

$$\hat{\alpha} = \left(\frac{2}{CP}\right) \sum_{j=1}^{P} T_j \cos\left(\frac{2\pi}{P}\right) j$$

Similarly for $\hat{\gamma}$ we get

$$\hat{\gamma} = \left(\frac{2}{CP}\right) \sum_{j=1}^{P} T_j \sin\left(\frac{2\pi}{P}\right) j$$

For $\hat{\sigma}^2$ we get

$$\hat{\sigma}^2 = \left(\frac{1}{n - 3}\right)\left[\sum_{i=1}^{n} (Y_t - \bar{Y})^2 - \left(\frac{n}{2}\right)\hat{\alpha}^2 - \left(\frac{n}{2}\right)\hat{\gamma}^2\right]$$

The observable data (x_t, Y_t) are $(1, Y_1), (2, Y_2), \ldots, (n, Y_n)$, and we can arrange these in a $C \times P$ table and compute the row of totals T_j and the grand total $\sum T_j$. The cosine and sine rows can be obtained from a trigonometric table; then the computations are quite simple for $\hat{\alpha}$, $\hat{\gamma}$, and $\hat{\sigma}^2$. This is illustrated in Table 8.8.1.

We will illustrate the discussion above with an example.

Example 8.8.1

A piece of mechanical equipment is cyclic in nature and the pressure on a certain part as a function of time is represented by

$$Y_t = \beta + \alpha \cos\left(\frac{2\pi}{P}\right)t + \gamma \sin\left(\frac{2\pi}{P}\right)t + \varepsilon_t$$

$$\varepsilon_t \text{ are distributed } NID(\varepsilon : 0, \sigma^2) \quad t = 1, 2, \ldots, 12$$

Table 8.8.1

Number of Period					*Total*
1	Y_1	Y_2	Y_3	$\cdots$ Y_P	
2	Y_{P+1}	Y_{P+2}	Y_{P+3}	$\cdots$ Y_{2P}	
3	Y_{2P+1}	Y_{2P+2}	Y_{2P+3}	$\cdots$ Y_{3P}	
$\vdots$	$\vdots$	$\vdots$	$\vdots$	$\vdots$	
C	$Y_{(C-1)P+1}$	$Y_{(C-1)P+2}$	$Y_{(C-1)P+3}$	$\cdots$ Y_{CP}	
Total T_j	T_1	T_2	T_3	$\cdots$ T_P	$\sum_{j=1}^{P} T_j$
cosine	$\cos\left(\frac{2\pi}{P}\right)$	$\cos\left(\frac{4\pi}{P}\right)$	$\cos\left(\frac{6\pi}{P}\right)$	$\cdots$ $\cos(2\pi)$	$\sum_{j=1}^{P} T_j \cos\left(\frac{2\pi}{P}\right)j$
sine	$\sin\left(\frac{2\pi}{P}\right)$	$\sin\left(\frac{4\pi}{P}\right)$	$\sin\left(\frac{6\pi}{P}\right)$	$\cdots$ $\sin(2\pi)$	$\sum_{j=1}^{P} T_j \sin\left(\frac{2\pi}{P}\right)j$

The length P of the period of the equipment is 4 seconds, and 12 observations are taken at one-second intervals. The data are given below.

t, time in seconds	1	2	3	4	5	6	7	8	9	10	11	12
y, pressure	7.53	3.85	3.22	6.40	7.42	3.43	1.60	7.26	7.33	3.20	2.67	6.74

Find point estimates of β, α, γ, and σ^2.

For this problem, $n = 12$, $P = 4$, and $C = 3$. We organize the data into a table, shown below, similar to Table 8.8.1.

	Seconds				
Period	1	2	3	4	*Total*
1 2 3	7.53 7.42 7.33	3.85 3.43 3.20	3.22 1.60 2.67	6.40 7.26 6.74	
Total t_j	22.28	10.48	7.49	20.40	60.65
cosine	0.0	−1.0	0.0	1.0	9.92
sine	1.0	0.0	−1.0	0.0	14.79

$$\mathbf{X}'\mathbf{y} = \begin{bmatrix} 60.65 \\ 9.92 \\ 14.79 \end{bmatrix} \qquad \mathbf{X}'\mathbf{X} = \begin{bmatrix} 12 & 0 & 0 \\ 0 & 6 & 0 \\ 0 & 0 & 6 \end{bmatrix} \qquad \hat{\boldsymbol{\beta}} = \begin{bmatrix} \hat{\beta} \\ \hat{\alpha} \\ \hat{\gamma} \end{bmatrix} = \begin{bmatrix} 5.05 \\ 1.65 \\ 2.47 \end{bmatrix}$$

$$\mathbf{y}'\mathbf{y} = 361.4661 \qquad \hat{\sigma}^2 = \frac{1}{9}(361.4661 - 359.3936) = 0.2303$$

$$\hat{\mu}(t) = 5.05 + 1.65\cos\left(\frac{2\pi}{4}\right)t + 2.47\sin\left(\frac{2\pi}{4}\right)t$$

Confidence intervals and tests of hypotheses can be obtained by using the results in Chapter 6.

8.8.2 General Trigonometric Model

In the simple trigonometric model, $\mu(x)$ consists of a constant β, one sine term, and one cosine term. In more complicated situations that are cyclic in nature, a more complex model is required. By using a theorem in mathematics, we know that under certain conditions a "very complicated" periodic function can be "closely approximated" by the sum of a finite number of sine and cosine terms. Thus to model real-world situations that are periodic, we will investigate a model that has H sine and cosine terms in it, that is, the model we consider is

$$Y = \beta + \sum_{h=1}^{H}\left[\alpha_h \cos\left(\frac{2\pi}{P_h}\right)x + \gamma_h \sin\left(\frac{2\pi}{P_h}\right)x\right] + \varepsilon \qquad -\infty < x < \infty \qquad (8.8.6)$$

where β, α_h, and γ_h are unknown parameters, and H and the P_h are specified (known) constants. Thus $\cos(2\pi/P_h)x$ and $\sin(2\pi/P_h)x$ are known; they are the $q_h(x)$ of Section 5.2. This is a general linear model for which all the appropriate theorems in Chapter 6 apply. However, when certain restrictions are put on this model, similar to the restrictions in Equation (8.8.2) for the simple trigonometric model, the computations are simplified considerably. In the remaining portion of this section, the general trigonometric model is discussed when these restrictions are assumed. The term $\alpha_h \cos(2\pi/P_h)t + \gamma_h \sin(2\pi/P_h)t$ is defined to be the hth component of the model with period P_h (or frequency F_h). Hence the model is the sum of H periodic components with respective periods P_1, $P_2, \ldots, P_H$ (or respective frequencies $F_1, F_2, \ldots, F_H$).

To sample the populations represented by this model, we observe n values of x. We assume that these x values are the integers $1, 2, \ldots, n$. The sample model can be written

$$Y_t = \beta + \sum_{h=1}^{H}\left[\alpha_h \cos\left(\frac{2\pi}{P_h}\right)t + \gamma_h \sin\left(\frac{2\pi}{P_h}\right)t\right] + \varepsilon_t$$

$$\varepsilon_t \text{ are distributed } NID(\varepsilon : 0, \sigma^2) \qquad t = 1, 2, \ldots, n$$

The model contains the known constants H, $P_1, P_2, \ldots, P_H$ and the unknown parameters β, the α_h, the γ_h and σ^2. There are $2H + 2$ unknown parameters in the model, and if n is an odd integer (say $n = 2M + 1$), we require the restriction $H < M$, or else there will be more unknown parameters than observations and we cannot hope to obtain satisfactory estimators for the parameters. If n is an even integer (say $n = 2M$), we also require the restriction $H < M$, or else there will be more parameters than observations.

We shall consider only a very special case of the trigonometric model and this will be reflected in the allowable values for $P_1, P_2, \ldots, P_H$. We assume that the trigonometric model is to be used to investigate only a subset of H of the periods $P, P/2, \ldots, P/(M-1)$, where P is a positive integer equal to n, the sample size. Thus the model in Equation (8.8.6) is periodic and is the sum of H periodic components. The period of the hth component, $\alpha_h \cos(2\pi/P_h)t + \gamma_h \sin(2\pi/P_h)t$, is P_h, which is a member of the set $\{P, P/2, \ldots, P/(M-1)\}$.

Example 8.8.2

The pressure on a certain piece of mechanical equipment is periodic in nature. An observer notices that the piece of equipment makes a complete cycle every 19 seconds. He decides to measure the pressure every second during one complete cycle and investigate a trigonometric model. Thus $n = 19 = 2M + 1$, so $M = 9$. Suppose he is interested in including periodic terms in his model with the following periods: 19, 19/2, 19/3, ..., 19/8. Then the model is

$$Y_t = \beta + \sum_{h=1}^{8} \left[\alpha_h \cos\left(\frac{2\pi h}{n}\right)t + \gamma_h \sin\left(\frac{2\pi h}{n}\right)t \right] + \varepsilon_t$$

$$\varepsilon_t \text{ are distributed } NID(\varepsilon : 0, \sigma^2) \qquad t = 1, 2, \ldots, 19$$

In this case $P_h = n/h = 19/h$, $h = 1, 2, \ldots, H = M - 1 = 8$. There are 18 unknown parameters, $\beta, \alpha_1, \gamma_1, \ldots, \alpha_8, \gamma_8, \sigma^2$, and 19 observations.

Example 8.8.3

In the previous example suppose the investigator is interested only in the periods 19, 19/2, 19/5. We let $P_1 = 19$, $P_2 = 19/2$, $P_3 = 19/5$; H is equal to 3. The model is

$$Y_t = \beta + \sum_{h=1}^{3} \left[\alpha_h \cos\left(\frac{2\pi}{P_h}\right)t + \gamma_h \sin\left(\frac{2\pi}{P_h}\right)t \right] + \varepsilon_t$$

$$\varepsilon_t \text{ are distributed } NID(\varepsilon : 0, \sigma^2) \qquad t = 1, 2, \ldots, 19$$

In this case there are 8 unknown parameters and 19 observations.

Thus the only periodic terms that we consider for a trigonometric model are those with periods $n, n/2, n/3, \ldots, n/(M-1)$. Hence the P_h are a selection of H

of these numbers. We shall now summarize the previous discussion and define a "special" trigonometric model.

DEFINITION 8.8.1

A "Special" Trigonometric Model. *The following model is defined to be a trigonometric model with H components with periods $P_1, P_2, \ldots, P_H$, respectively.*

$$Y_t = \beta + \sum_{h=1}^{H} \left[\alpha_h \cos\left(\frac{2\pi}{P_h}\right)t + \gamma_h \sin\left(\frac{2\pi}{P_h}\right)t \right] + \varepsilon_t$$

$$\varepsilon_t \text{ are distributed } NID(\varepsilon : 0, \sigma^2) \qquad t = 1, 2, \ldots, n$$

$$n = 2M \text{ or } 2M + 1 \qquad H \leq M - 1 \quad (8.8.7)$$

P_h are H distinct numbers from the set $\{n, n/2, n/3, \ldots, n/(M-1)\}$, and M is a positive integer greater than one.

We shall now continue to investigate the model in Equation (8.8.7). This is a general linear model $\mathbf{Y} = \mathbf{X\beta} + \boldsymbol{\varepsilon}$, where we have the following:

$$\mathbf{X} = \begin{bmatrix} 1 & \cos\left(\frac{2\pi}{P_1}\right)\cdot 1 & \sin\left(\frac{2\pi}{P_1}\right)\cdot 1 & \cos\left(\frac{2\pi}{P_2}\right)\cdot 1 & \sin\left(\frac{2\pi}{P_2}\right)\cdot 1 & \cdots & \cos\left(\frac{2\pi}{P_H}\right)\cdot 1 & \sin\left(\frac{2\pi}{P_H}\right)\cdot 1 \\ 1 & \cos\left(\frac{2\pi}{P_1}\right)\cdot 2 & \sin\left(\frac{2\pi}{P_1}\right)\cdot 2 & \cos\left(\frac{2\pi}{P_2}\right)\cdot 2 & \sin\left(\frac{2\pi}{P_2}\right)\cdot 2 & \cdots & \cos\left(\frac{2\pi}{P_H}\right)\cdot 2 & \sin\left(\frac{2\pi}{P_H}\right)\cdot 2 \\ \vdots & \vdots & \vdots & \vdots & \vdots & & \vdots & \vdots \\ 1 & \cos\left(\frac{2\pi}{P_1}\right)\cdot n & \sin\left(\frac{2\pi}{P_1}\right)\cdot n & \cos\left(\frac{2\pi}{P_2}\right)\cdot n & \sin\left(\frac{2\pi}{P_2}\right)\cdot n & \cdots & \cos\left(\frac{2\pi}{P_H}\right)\cdot n & \sin\left(\frac{2\pi}{P_H}\right)\cdot n \end{bmatrix}$$

$$\boldsymbol{\beta}' = [\beta, \alpha_1, \gamma_1, \alpha_2, \gamma_2, \ldots, \alpha_H, \gamma_H] \qquad \mathbf{Y}' = [Y_1, Y_2, \ldots, Y_n]$$

To obtain the normal equations we compute **X′X** and **X′Y**. We get

$$\mathbf{X'X} = \begin{bmatrix} n & \sum C_{1t} & \sum S_{1t} & \cdots & \sum C_{Ht} & \sum S_{Ht} \\ \sum C_{1t} & \sum C_{1t}^2 & \sum C_{1t}S_{1t} & \cdots & \sum C_{1t}C_{Ht} & \sum C_{1t}S_{Ht} \\ \sum S_{1t} & \sum S_{1t}C_{1t} & \sum S_{1t}^2 & \cdots & \sum S_{1t}C_{Ht} & \sum S_{1t}S_{Ht} \\ \vdots & \vdots & \vdots & & \vdots & \vdots \\ \sum C_{Ht} & \sum C_{Ht}C_{1t} & \sum C_{Ht}S_{1t} & \cdots & \sum C_{Ht}^2 & \sum C_{Ht}S_{Ht} \\ \sum S_{Ht} & \sum S_{Ht}C_{1t} & \sum S_{Ht}S_{1t} & \cdots & \sum S_{Ht}C_{Ht} & \sum S_{Ht}^2 \end{bmatrix}$$

where all summations are for $t = 1, 2, \ldots, n$, and where $C_{ht} = \cos(2\pi/P_h)t$, $S_{ht} = \sin(2\pi/P_h)t$.

The following relationships can be shown to hold:

$$\sum_{t=1}^{n} \cos\left(\frac{2\pi}{P_h}\right)t \sin\left(\frac{2\pi}{P_k}\right)t = 0 \qquad h = 1, 2, \ldots, H \qquad k = 1, 2, \ldots, H$$

$$\sum_{t=1}^{n} \cos\left(\frac{2\pi}{P_h}\right)t \cos\left(\frac{2\pi}{P_k}\right)t = 0 \qquad h = 1, 2, \ldots, H \qquad k = 1, 2, \ldots, H \quad h \neq k$$

$$\sum_{t=1}^{n} \sin\left(\frac{2\pi}{P_h}\right)t \sin\left(\frac{2\pi}{P_k}\right)t = 0 \qquad h = 1, 2, \ldots, H \qquad k = 1, 2, \ldots, H \quad h \neq k$$

$$\sum_{t=1}^{n} \cos\left(\frac{2\pi}{P_h}\right)t = \sum_{t=1}^{n} \sin\left(\frac{2\pi}{P_h}\right)t = 0 \qquad h = 1, 2, \ldots, H$$

$$\sum_{t=1}^{n} \cos^2\left(\frac{2\pi}{P_h}\right)t = \sum_{t=1}^{n} \sin^2\left(\frac{2\pi}{P_h}\right)t = \frac{n}{2} \qquad h = 1, 2, \ldots, H$$

Note 1. Remember P_h are H distinct numbers from the set $\{n, n/2, n/3, \ldots, n/(M-1)\}$.

Thus

$$\mathbf{X'X} = \begin{bmatrix} n & 0 & 0 & \cdots & 0 \\ 0 & \frac{n}{2} & 0 & \cdots & 0 \\ 0 & 0 & \frac{n}{2} & \cdots & 0 \\ \vdots & \vdots & \vdots & & \vdots \\ 0 & 0 & 0 & \cdots & \frac{n}{2} \end{bmatrix} \qquad \mathbf{X'Y} = \begin{bmatrix} \sum Y_t \\ \sum Y_t \cos\left(\frac{2\pi}{P_1}\right)t \\ \sum Y_t \sin\left(\frac{2\pi}{P_1}\right)t \\ \vdots \\ \sum Y_t \cos\left(\frac{2\pi}{P_H}\right)t \\ \sum Y_t \sin\left(\frac{2\pi}{P_H}\right)t \end{bmatrix} \tag{8.8.8}$$

Thus $\hat{\boldsymbol{\beta}} = (\mathbf{X}'\mathbf{X})^{-1}\mathbf{X}'\mathbf{Y}$ and $\hat{\sigma}^2 = (n - 2H - 1)^{-1}(\mathbf{Y}'\mathbf{Y} - \hat{\boldsymbol{\beta}}'\mathbf{X}'\mathbf{Y})$. We get

$$\begin{aligned}
\hat{\beta} &= \bar{Y} \\
\hat{\alpha}_h &= \left(\frac{2}{n}\right)\sum_{t=1}^{n} Y_t \cos\left(\frac{2\pi}{P_h}\right)t \qquad h = 1, 2, \ldots, H \\
\hat{\gamma}_h &= \left(\frac{2}{n}\right)\sum_{t=1}^{n} Y_t \sin\left(\frac{2\pi}{P_h}\right)t \qquad h = 1, 2, \ldots, H \qquad (8.8.9)\\
\hat{\sigma}^2 &= (n - 2H - 1)^{-1}\left[\sum_{t=1}^{n} Y_t^2 - \bar{Y}\sum_{t=1}^{n} Y_t - \left(\frac{n}{2}\right)\sum_{h=1}^{H} (\hat{\alpha}_h^2 + \hat{\gamma}_h^2)\right] \\
&= (n - 2H - 1)^{-1}\left[\sum_{t=1}^{n} (Y_t - \bar{Y})^2 - \left(\frac{n}{2}\right)\sum_{h=1}^{H} (\hat{\alpha}_h^2 + \hat{\gamma}_h^2)\right]
\end{aligned}$$

All the theory in Chapter 6 applies for estimating and testing hypotheses about the parameters. We note particularly that since $\mathbf{X}'\mathbf{X}$ is a diagonal matrix, the estimators $\hat{\beta}, \hat{\alpha}_1, \hat{\gamma}_1, \ldots, \hat{\alpha}_H, \hat{\gamma}_H$, and $\hat{\sigma}^2$ are jointly independent.

The above results are summarized in the following theorems.

THEOREM 8.8.1

Consider the "special" trigonometric model given in Definition 8.8.1.

$$Y_t = \beta + \sum_{h=1}^{H}\left[\alpha_h \cos\left(\frac{2\pi}{P_h}\right)t + \gamma_h \sin\left(\frac{2\pi}{P_h}\right)t\right] + \varepsilon_t$$

$$\varepsilon_t \text{ are distributed } NID(\varepsilon : 0, \sigma^2) \qquad t = 1, 2, \ldots, n = 2M \text{ or } 2M + 1 \qquad (8.8.10)$$

where $H, P_1, P_2, \ldots, P_H$ are specified numbers such that $H \leq M - 1$ and M is a positive integer greater than one. $P_1, P_2, \ldots, P_H$ are H distinct and specified numbers from the set $\{n, n/2, n/3, \ldots, n/(M - 1)\}$. The maximum likelihood estimators of $\beta, \alpha_1, \gamma_1, \ldots, \alpha_H, \gamma_H$, and σ^2 (corrected for bias) are

$$\hat{\beta} = \bar{Y} \qquad \hat{\sigma}^2 = (n - 2H - 1)^{-1}\left[\sum_{t=1}^{n} (Y_t - \bar{Y})^2 - \left(\frac{n}{2}\right)\sum_{h=1}^{H} (\hat{\alpha}_h^2 + \hat{\gamma}_h^2)\right]$$

$$\hat{\alpha}_h = \left(\frac{2}{n}\right)\sum_{t=1}^{n} Y_t \cos\left(\frac{2\pi}{P_h}\right)t$$

$$\hat{\gamma}_h = \left(\frac{2}{n}\right)\sum_{t=1}^{n} Y_t \sin\left(\frac{2\pi}{P_h}\right)t \qquad h = 1, 2, \ldots, H$$

These estimators satisfy the optimal properties stated in Theorem 6.2.3.

Next we state a theorem about the distributions of these estimators.

THEOREM 8.8.2

The estimators $\hat{\beta}, \hat{\alpha}_1, \hat{\gamma}_1, \ldots, \hat{\alpha}_H, \hat{\gamma}_H$, and $\hat{\sigma}^2$ in Theorem 8.8.1 are jointly independent random variables which have the following distributions: $\hat{\beta}$ is distributed $N(\hat{\beta} : \beta, \sigma^2/n)$, $U = (n - 2H - 1)\hat{\sigma}^2/\sigma^2$ is distributed $\chi^2(u : n - 2H - 1)$, $\hat{\alpha}_h$ is distributed $N(\hat{\alpha}_h : \alpha_h, 2\sigma^2/n)$, $\hat{\gamma}_h$ is distributed $N(\hat{\gamma}_h : \gamma_h, 2\sigma^2/n)$, $h = 1, 2, \ldots, H$.

Example 8.8.4

In attempting to understand the mechanism involved in the price of eggs an investigator decided to use the following model:

$$Y_t = \beta + \sum_{h=1}^{H} \left[\alpha_h \cos\left(\frac{2\pi}{P_h}\right)t + \gamma_h \sin\left(\frac{2\pi}{P_h}\right)t \right] + \varepsilon_t$$

$$\varepsilon_t \text{ are distributed } NID(\varepsilon : 0, \sigma^2) \quad t = 1, 2, \ldots, n$$

Three years of monthly prices were collected ($n = 36$); since $n = 36 = 2M, M = 18$, and the periodic terms P_h can be selected from the numbers 36, 36/2, 36/3, ..., 36/17. The investigator assumed that egg prices are cyclic with a fundamental period of one year. He decides to include terms in the model that are periodic with periods 12 months, 6 months, 4 months, and 3 months, that is, $P_1 = 36/3$, $P_2 = 36/6$, $P_3 = 36/9$, and $P_4 = 36/12$. The data are given in Table 8.8.2.

We want to evaluate $\hat{\beta}, \hat{\alpha}_1, \hat{\gamma}_1, \ldots, \hat{\alpha}_4, \hat{\gamma}_4, \hat{\sigma}^2$, and $\hat{\mu}(t)$. To compute $\hat{\alpha}_h$ and $\hat{\gamma}_h$, we note that (since $P_h = 12, 6, 4, 3$) $\cos[(2\pi/P_h)(t + 12j)] = \cos(2\pi/P_h)t$ for $j = 0, 1, 2$; also, $\sin(2\pi/P_h)(t + 12j) = \sin(2\pi/P_h)t$ for

Table 8.8.2

t	1	2	3	4	5	6	7	8	9	10	11	12
y_t	7.36	7.51	7.53	6.30	5.37	3.85	2.51	2.62	3.22	3.61	4.59	6.40
t	13	14	15	16	17	18	19	20	21	22	23	24
y_t	7.27	8.08	7.42	6.07	5.34	3.43	2.19	2.15	1.60	4.19	5.93	7.26
t	25	26	27	28	29	30	31	32	33	34	35	36
y_t	8.00	8.43	7.33	6.40	4.66	3.20	1.50	1.80	2.67	3.38	5.25	6.74
$\sum_{j=0}^{2} y_{t+12j}$	22.63	24.02	22.28	18.77	15.37	10.48	6.20	6.57	7.49	11.18	15.77	20.40

$j = 0, 1, 2$. Hence

$$\hat{\alpha}_h = \left(\frac{2}{n}\right) \sum_{t=1}^{36} y_t \cos\left(\frac{2\pi}{P_h}\right)t = \left(\frac{2}{n}\right) \sum_{t=1}^{12} \sum_{j=0}^{2} y_{t+12j} \cos\left(\frac{2\pi}{P_h}\right)t$$

$$\hat{\gamma}_h = \left(\frac{2}{n}\right) \sum_{t=1}^{36} y_t \sin\left(\frac{2\pi}{P_h}\right)t = \left(\frac{2}{n}\right) \sum_{t=1}^{12} \sum_{j=0}^{2} y_{t+12j} \sin\left(\frac{2\pi}{P_h}\right)t$$

for $P_h = 12, 6, 4, 3$. Thus we can simplify the computations by first computing $\sum_{j=0}^{2} y_{t+12j}$ for $t = 1, 2, \ldots, 12$. This is the reason that the row labeled $\sum_{j=0}^{2} y_{t+12j}$ is computed in Table 8.8.2. This row is used in Table 8.8.3. The column to the extreme right in Table 8.8.3 contains the elements in the vector $\mathbf{X}'\mathbf{y}$. From this column it is easy to compute the desired quantities. We get $\sum y_t = 181.16$, $\sum y_t^2 = 1075.6842$, $\sum (y_t - \bar{y})^2 = 164.0468$, and the following:

$$\begin{array}{lll} \hat{\alpha}_1 = 1.635 & \hat{\gamma}_1 = 2.472 & \hat{\beta} = 5.032 \\ \hat{\alpha}_2 = 0.046 & \hat{\gamma}_2 = -0.080 & \hat{\sigma}^2 = 0.199 \\ \hat{\alpha}_3 = 0.003 & \hat{\gamma}_3 = 0.069 & \\ \hat{\alpha}_4 = 0.022 & \hat{\gamma}_4 = -0.142 & \end{array}$$

$$\begin{aligned} \hat{\mu}(t) = 5.032 &+ 1.635 \cos\left(\frac{2\pi}{12}\right)t + 2.472 \sin\left(\frac{2\pi}{12}\right)t \\ &+ 0.046 \cos\left(\frac{2\pi}{6}\right)t - 0.080 \sin\left(\frac{2\pi}{6}\right)t + 0.003 \cos\left(\frac{2\pi}{4}\right)t \\ &+ 0.069 \sin\left(\frac{2\pi}{4}\right)t + 0.022 \cos\left(\frac{2\pi}{3}\right)t - 0.142 \sin\left(\frac{2\pi}{3}\right)t \end{aligned}$$

An important problem in the trigonometric model is to determine which periodic terms are to be included in the model. To illustrate we consider Example 8.8.4 in which the investigator decided that the basic model must include terms with periods of 12, 6, 4, and 3 months. He may want to determine on the basis of the data if any of the following are zero: (α_1, γ_1), (α_2, γ_2), (α_3, γ_3), (α_4, γ_4). If, for instance, $\alpha_2 = \gamma_2 = 0$, then the term with a 6-month period is not needed in the model. Clearly the qth component is or is not in the model given in Equation (8.8.10) if and only if $\alpha_q^2 + \gamma_q^2$ is or is not zero. Also, $\alpha_q^2 + \gamma_q^2 = 0$ if and only if $\alpha_q = \gamma_q = 0$, so a procedure to determine whether or not the qth component is in the model is to test $H_0: \alpha_q = \gamma_q = 0$ *vs.* H_a: at least one of the quantities α_q, γ_q is not zero. This is the context of the next theorem.

THEOREM 8.8.3

Let the model be given in Definition 8.8.1. *A size* α *test of* $H_0: \alpha_q = \gamma_q = 0$ *vs.* H_a: *at least one of the quantities* α_q, γ_q *is not zero is this: Reject* H_0 *if and only if*

Table 8.8.3

t	1	2	3	4	5	6	7	8	9	10	11	12	$X'y$
$\sum_{j=0}^{2} y_{t+12j}$	22.630	24.020	22.280	18.770	15.370	10.480	6.200	6.570	7.490	11.180	15.770	20.400	181.160
$\cos\left(\frac{2\pi}{12}\right)t$	0.866	0.500	0.000	−0.500	−0.866	−1.000	−0.866	−0.500	0.000	0.500	0.866	1.000	29.425
$\sin\left(\frac{2\pi}{12}\right)t$	0.500	0.866	1.000	0.866	0.500	0.000	−0.500	−0.866	−1.000	−0.866	−0.500	0.000	44.490
$\cos\left(\frac{2\pi}{6}\right)t$	0.500	−0.500	−1.000	−0.500	0.500	1.000	0.500	−0.500	−1.000	−0.500	0.500	1.000	0.825
$\sin\left(\frac{2\pi}{6}\right)t$	0.866	0.866	0.000	−0.866	−0.866	0.000	0.866	0.866	0.000	−0.866	−0.866	0.000	−1.446
$\cos\left(\frac{2\pi}{4}\right)t$	0.000	−1.000	0.000	1.000	0.000	−1.000	0.000	1.000	0.000	−1.000	0.000	1.000	0.060
$\sin\left(\frac{2\pi}{4}\right)t$	1.000	0.000	−1.000	0.000	1.000	0.000	−1.000	0.000	1.000	0.000	−1.000	0.000	1.240
$\cos\left(\frac{2\pi}{3}\right)t$	−0.500	−0.500	1.000	−0.500	−0.500	1.000	−0.500	−0.500	1.000	−0.500	−0.500	1.000	0.395
$\sin\left(\frac{2\pi}{3}\right)t$	0.866	−0.866	0.000	0.866	−0.866	0.000	0.866	−0.866	0.000	0.866	−0.866	0.000	−2.555

$w \geq F_{\alpha:2,m}$, where $W = n(\hat{\alpha}_q^2 + \hat{\gamma}_q^2)/4\hat{\sigma}^2$ is distributed $F(w:2,m;\lambda)$, where $m = n - 2H - 1$ and $\lambda = n(\alpha_q^2 + \gamma_q^2)/4\sigma^2$. The power of the test is

$$\Pi(\lambda) = \int_{F_{\alpha:2,m}}^{\infty} F(w:2,m;\lambda)\,dw$$

Proof

Clearly $Z_1 = \hat{\alpha}_q\sqrt{n/2\sigma^2}$ is distributed $N(z_1 : \alpha_q\sqrt{n/2\sigma^2}, 1)$, $Z_2 = \hat{\gamma}_q\sqrt{n/2\sigma^2}$ is distributed $N(z_2 : \gamma_q\sqrt{n/2\sigma^2}, 1)$, $U = m\hat{\sigma}^2/\sigma^2$ is distributed $\chi^2(u:m)$, and Z_1, Z_2, and U are mutually independent. So $U_1 = Z_1^2 + Z_2^2$ is distributed $\chi^2(u_2 : 2; \lambda)$, where $\lambda = n(\alpha_q^2 + \gamma_q^2)/4\sigma^2$, and $W = n(\hat{\alpha}_q^2 + \hat{\gamma}_q^2)/4\hat{\sigma}^2$ is distributed $F(w:2,m;\lambda)$. Hence the result. Also the multivariate t distribution can be used to set simultaneous confidence intervals on $\alpha_1, \gamma_1, \alpha_2, \gamma_2, \alpha_3, \gamma_3, \alpha_4, \gamma_4$.

8.8.3 Combined Polynomial and Trigonometric Models

A model that finds useful application in real-world situations is a combination of the polynomial and trigonometric models given by

$$Y_j = \beta_0 + \sum_{k=1}^{K} \beta_k x_j^k + \sum_{h=1}^{H} (\alpha_h \cos hx_j + \gamma_h \sin hx_j) + \varepsilon_j \qquad j = 1, 2, \ldots, n$$

This is a general linear model where the $q_i(x)$ can be easily identified. All of the appropriate theorems of Chapter 6 apply.

8.9 Designing Investigations

In this section we briefly discuss the subject that is often referred to as design, by which we mean "choosing the elements of the **X** matrix" so that point estimators, confidence intervals, and hypotheses tests will be optimum in some sense, or so that some special property (such as some of the assumptions) can be investigated. In the general linear model, the elements in the **X** matrix are assumed to be nonrandom variables, and the investigator can often specify the values of these variables. When this is the case, they should be chosen so the investigation is as informative as possible. However, sometimes it may be desirable to select values in the **X** matrix that optimize one characteristic (say one parameter), but this may in turn tend to give less information about another characteristic (another parameter). Much has been written on this subject and we shall discuss it very briefly in the following two sections.

8.9.1 Optimum Designs for the General Linear Model

In the general linear model for Case 1, suppose that our interest is in $\ell'\boldsymbol{\beta}$, a specified linear function of $\boldsymbol{\beta}$. We know the following:

1. the variance of $\ell'\hat{\boldsymbol{\beta}}$, the UMVU estimator of $\ell'\boldsymbol{\beta}$, is given by $\text{var}[\ell'\hat{\boldsymbol{\beta}}] = \sigma^2\ell'(\mathbf{X}'\mathbf{X})^{-1}\ell$;

2. the expected width of a $1 - \alpha$ confidence interval on $\ell'\boldsymbol{\beta}$ is $\mathscr{E}[\text{width}] = C_n t_{\alpha/2:n-p}\sigma\sqrt{\ell'(\mathbf{X}'\mathbf{X})^{-1}\ell}$, where

$$C_n = 2^{3/2}\Gamma\left(\frac{n-p+1}{2}\right)\Big/\sqrt{n-p}\,\Gamma\left(\frac{n-p}{2}\right)$$

3. the power of a size α test of $H_0 : \ell'\boldsymbol{\beta} = \ell_0$ *vs.* $H_a : \ell'\boldsymbol{\beta} \neq \ell_0$ is a monotonic increasing function of $\lambda = (\ell'\boldsymbol{\beta} - \ell_0)^2/2\sigma^2 \times \ell'(\mathbf{X}'\mathbf{X})^{-1}\ell$. (8.9.1)

So for given values of the parameters σ^2 and $\boldsymbol{\beta}$ and for fixed values for ℓ, n, and α, it is evident that, if possible, an investigator should choose the $\mathbf{X}$ matrix so that $\ell'(\mathbf{X}'\mathbf{X})^{-1}\ell$ is a minimum. However, it is generally the case that an investigator is interested not only in one linear function of $\boldsymbol{\beta}$, say $\ell'\boldsymbol{\beta}$, but in many linear functions of $\boldsymbol{\beta}$, say $\ell'_1\boldsymbol{\beta}, \ell'_2\boldsymbol{\beta}, \ldots, \ell'_q\boldsymbol{\beta}$. In this case it is generally not possible to choose an $\mathbf{X}$ matrix that simultaneously minimizes $\ell'_i(\mathbf{X}'\mathbf{X})^{-1}\ell_i$ for $i = 1, 2, \ldots, q$. What is generally done is to concentrate on the $\mathbf{X}$ matrix and choose it to minimize some function of its elements that in some general sense optimizes estimators and tests. We discuss three situations for Cases 1 and 2 of the general linear model where $\hat{\boldsymbol{\beta}}$ is the best estimator of $\boldsymbol{\beta}$.

1. The mean-squared-error of $\hat{\boldsymbol{\beta}}$, the M.L. estimator of $\boldsymbol{\beta}$, is

$$\begin{aligned}\mathscr{E}[(\hat{\boldsymbol{\beta}} - \boldsymbol{\beta})'(\hat{\boldsymbol{\beta}} - \boldsymbol{\beta})] &= \mathscr{E}[(\mathbf{X}^-\mathbf{Y} - \boldsymbol{\beta})'(\mathbf{X}^-\mathbf{Y} - \boldsymbol{\beta})] \\ &= \mathscr{E}[(\mathbf{X}^-\mathbf{X}\boldsymbol{\beta} + \mathbf{X}^-\boldsymbol{\varepsilon} - \boldsymbol{\beta})'(\mathbf{X}^-\mathbf{X}\boldsymbol{\beta} + \mathbf{X}^-\boldsymbol{\varepsilon} - \boldsymbol{\beta})] \\ &= \mathscr{E}[\boldsymbol{\varepsilon}'\mathbf{X}'^-\mathbf{X}^-\boldsymbol{\varepsilon}] = \sigma^2\,\text{tr}[\mathbf{X}'^-\mathbf{X}^-] \\ &= \sigma^2\,\text{tr}[\mathbf{X}^-\mathbf{X}'^-] = \sigma^2\,\text{tr}[(\mathbf{X}'\mathbf{X})^{-1}]\end{aligned}$$

   So the $\mathbf{X}$ matrix that minimizes $\text{tr}[(\mathbf{X}'\mathbf{X})^{-1}]$ will be the $\mathbf{X}$ matrix that minimizes the mean-squared-error of the M.L. estimator of $\boldsymbol{\beta}$.

2. The "generalized variance" of a random vector, say $\mathbf{Z}$, is defined to be the determinant of $\textbf{cov}[\mathbf{Z}]$. Thus the generalized variance of $\hat{\boldsymbol{\beta}}$ is $\det[\sigma^2(\mathbf{X}'\mathbf{X})^{-1}]$. So choosing the $\mathbf{X}$ matrix that minimizes $\det[(\mathbf{X}'\mathbf{X})^{-1}]$ will also minimize the generalized variance of $\hat{\boldsymbol{\beta}}$.

3. For any $p \times 1$ vector ℓ (where $\ell'\ell = 1$) the maximum of var$[\ell'\hat{\boldsymbol{\beta}}]$ is $\sigma^2\lambda_p$, where λ_p is the largest characteristic root of $(\mathbf{X}'\mathbf{X})^{-1}$. So the $\mathbf{X}$ matrix that *minimizes* the largest characteristic root of $(\mathbf{X}'\mathbf{X})^{-1}$ will be the $\mathbf{X}$ matrix that minimizes the maximum var$[\ell'\hat{\boldsymbol{\beta}}]$ for all $p \times 1$ vectors ℓ such that $\ell'\ell = 1$.

From the above discussion it is clear that it might be desirable to choose an $\mathbf{X}$ matrix so that det$[(\mathbf{X}'\mathbf{X})^{-1}]$ is a minimum, or tr$[(\mathbf{X}'\mathbf{X})^{-1}]$ is a minimum, or λ_p, the largest characteristic root of $(\mathbf{X}'\mathbf{X})^{-1}$, is a minimum. This topic will not be pursued further here, but the interested reader can consult [S-19] and the papers referenced there.

Example 8.9.1

For a simple illustration consider the simple linear model with a zero intercept, $Y_j = \beta x_j + \varepsilon_j$, ε_j are distributed $NID(\varepsilon : 0, \sigma^2), j = 1, 2, \ldots, n$. The UMVU estimator of β is $\hat{\beta} = \sum x_j Y_j / \sum x_i^2$. Also, $\hat{\beta}$ is distributed $N(\hat{\beta} : \beta, \sigma^2/\sum x_i^2)$. Now the $\mathbf{X}$ matrix in this case is a vector, since $p = 1$, and is given by $\mathbf{X}' = [x_1, x_2, \ldots, x_n]$; thus $(\mathbf{X}'\mathbf{X})^{-1} = (\sum x_i^2)^{-1}$. In this simple case det$[(\mathbf{X}'\mathbf{X})^{-1}] = $ tr$[(\mathbf{X}'\mathbf{X})^{-1}] = \lambda_p$, the largest characteristic root of $(\mathbf{X}'\mathbf{X})^{-1}$. Generally these three functions of the elements of the $\mathbf{X}$ matrix are not equal. To minimize $(\sum x_i^2)^{-1}$, the x_j's are selected to be equal and as large as possible in absolute value. For example, if the x_j's can be selected to be any values in the closed interval $[a, b]$, where a and b are any real numbers such that $a < b$, then they should all be equal to max$[|a|, |b|]$.

For the choice of the $\mathbf{X}$ matrix in the simple linear model $Y_j = \beta_0 + \beta x_j + \varepsilon_j$, see Problems 6.11 and 6.12.

8.9.2 General Linear Model with Repeated Observations

In some investigations it is possible to select more than one Y value for a given $\mathbf{x}$ value. When this is the case, it is often desirable to do so, particularly if the Y values for a given $\mathbf{x}$ value represent a random sample from the population to which the inference is to be made. We illustrate by using Example 5.2.2. The populations involved might be considered to be the sphericities of all the pebbles in the river bed down to 3 feet in depth and 100 yards from the points $x = 50$ miles, $x = 51$ miles, $\ldots, x = 300$ miles from some origin point. There are 251 populations involved and each contains tens of thousands of pebbles. The mean of the population of the sphericities of the tens of thousands of pebbles at any point x is $\beta_0 + \beta x$ and the variance is σ^2.

If the investigator decides to sample the populations at $x_1 = 50$ miles, $x_2 = 100$ miles, $\ldots, x_6 = 300$ miles from the point of origin, and if one pebble is selected at random from each of these 6 populations, the data consist of $(50, y_1)$, $(100, y_2), \ldots, (300, y_6)$.

However, instead of selecting one pebble at each x_i point, suppose a random sample of n_i pebbles is selected at point x_i. At each x_i point where $n_i > 1$, the n_i values of Y, denoted by $y_{i1}, y_{i2}, \ldots, y_{in_i}$, can be used to estimate σ^2. In this example the sample of Y values for a fixed x value is selected from a population to which the inference is to be made.

However, suppose at each x_i point a sample of one pebble is selected but n_i measurements are made on this pebble. The important thing to consider here is that even though there are n_i observations (measurements on one pebble) at the point x_i, these n_i values are not a random sample from the population of pebbles (of sphericities of pebbles) but instead they are a random sample from a population of measurements on *one* pebble. If the objective is to say estimate σ^2, the variance of the population of pebble sphericities, then these repeated measurements on *one* pebble cannot be used to do this. The point we make with this illustration is that in the model to be discussed now, a general linear model with repeated Y observations at the **x** points, if the repeated observations are used for inference it is important that the repeated Y observations are samples from populations to which the inference is to be made.

Now we define the general linear model with repeated observations. It is given by

$$Y_{ik} = \beta_0 + \sum_{j=1}^{p-1} \beta_j x_{ij} + \varepsilon_{ik} \qquad \varepsilon_{ik} \text{ are distributed } NID(\varepsilon : 0, \sigma^2)$$

$$k = 1, 2, \ldots, n_i \quad i = 1, 2, \ldots, M \quad n_i > 1 \text{ for at least one } i$$

$$N = \sum_{i=1}^{M} n_i \qquad (8.9.2)$$

Note 1. It follows from the model in Equation (8.9.2) that Y_{ik}, for $k = 1, 2, \ldots, n_i$, are independent and have identical distributions, namely, $N(y_{ik} : \beta_0 + \sum_{j=1}^{p-1} \beta_j x_{ij}, \sigma^2)$.

Note 2. We write $\beta_0 + \sum_{j=1}^{p-1} \beta_j x_{ij}$, for $i = 1, 2, \ldots, M$ as $\mathbf{X\beta}$, where $\mathbf{X}$ has size $M \times p$. From Equation (8.9.2) we obtain $\bar{Y}_{i.} = \beta_0 + \sum_{j=1}^{p-1} \beta_j x_{ij} + \bar{\varepsilon}_{i.}$ where $\bar{Y}_{i.} = (1/n_i) \sum_{k=1}^{n_i} Y_{ik}$ and $\bar{\varepsilon}_{i.} = (1/n_i) \sum_{k=1}^{n_i} \varepsilon_{ik}$.

If we define the vector $\mathbf{Z}$ by $\mathbf{Z} = [\bar{Y}_{1.}, \bar{Y}_{2.}, \ldots, \bar{Y}_{M.}]'$ and the vector $\mathbf{e}$ by $\mathbf{e} = [\bar{\varepsilon}_{1.}, \bar{\varepsilon}_{2.}, \ldots, \bar{\varepsilon}_{M.}]'$, we can write $\mathbf{Z} = \mathbf{X\beta} + \mathbf{e}$, $\mathbf{e}$ is distributed $\mathbf{N}(\mathbf{e} : \mathbf{0}, \sigma^2\mathbf{D})$, where $\mathbf{D} = [d_{ii'}]$ and $d_{ii} = 1/n_i, d_{ii'} = 0$ if $i \neq i'$.

The likelihood function for this model is

$$L = L(\boldsymbol{\beta}, \sigma^2 : y_{11}, y_{22}, \ldots, y_{Mn_M}; \mathbf{X})$$
$$= (2\pi\sigma^2)^{-N/2} \exp\left\{\left(-\frac{1}{2\sigma^2}\right) \sum_{i=1}^{M} \sum_{k=1}^{n_i} \left(y_{ik} - \beta_0 - \sum_{j=1}^{p-1} \beta_j x_{ij}\right)^2\right\}$$
$$= (2\pi\sigma^2)^{-N/2} \exp\left\{\left(-\frac{1}{2\sigma^2}\right) \left[\sum_{i=1}^{M} \sum_{k=1}^{n_i} (y_{ik} - \bar{y}_{i.})^2 + \sum_{i=1}^{M} \sum_{k=1}^{n_i} \left(\bar{y}_{i.} - \beta_0 - \sum_{j=1}^{p-1} \beta_j x_{ij}\right)^2\right]\right\}$$
$$= (2\pi\sigma^2)^{-N/2} \exp\left\{\left(-\frac{1}{2\sigma^2}\right) \left[\sum_{i=1}^{M} \sum_{k=1}^{n_i} (y_{ik} - \bar{y}_{i.})^2 + (\mathbf{z} - \mathbf{X}\boldsymbol{\beta})'\mathbf{D}^{-1}(\mathbf{z} - \mathbf{X}\boldsymbol{\beta})\right]\right\}$$

By using the factorization theorem, it is clear that the following are $M + 1$ sufficient statistics for this model:

$$\sum\sum (Y_{ik} - \bar{Y}_{i.})^2 \qquad \bar{Y}_{1.}, \bar{Y}_{2.}, \ldots, \bar{Y}_{M.}$$

From these results we state the following theorem.

THEOREM 8.9.1

Let the model be given by Equation (8.9.2). *The results below follow.*

(1) $\mathbf{Z}$ *is distributed* $\mathbf{N}(\mathbf{z} : \mathbf{X}\boldsymbol{\beta}, \sigma^2\mathbf{D})$, $d_{ii} = 1/n_i$, $d_{ii'} = 0$ *if* $i \neq i'$;

(2) $\sum_{i=1}^{M} \sum_{k=1}^{n_i} (Y_{ik} - \bar{Y}_{i.})^2$, $\bar{Y}_{1.}, \bar{Y}_{2.}, \ldots, \bar{Y}_{M.}$, *is a set of* $M + 1$ *sufficient statistics*;

(3) $S_W^2, \bar{Y}_{1.}, \bar{Y}_{2.}, \ldots, \bar{Y}_{M.}$ *are jointly independent, where* S_W^2 *is defined by* $S_W^2 = \sum_{i=1}^{M} \sum_{k=1}^{n_i} (Y_{ik} - \bar{Y}_{i.})^2$;

(4) $U_W = S_W^2/\sigma^2$ *is distributed* $\chi^2(u_W : N - M)$.

Proof

The proof is a straightforward application of results in Chapter 6 and will be left for the reader.

The term $(\mathbf{z} - \mathbf{X}\boldsymbol{\beta})'\mathbf{D}^{-1}(\mathbf{z} - \mathbf{X}\boldsymbol{\beta})$ in the exponent of the likelihood function can be written

$$(\mathbf{z} - \mathbf{X}\boldsymbol{\beta})'\mathbf{D}^{-1}(\mathbf{z} - \mathbf{X}\boldsymbol{\beta})$$
$$= [(\mathbf{z} - \mathbf{X}\hat{\boldsymbol{\beta}}_{\mathbf{D}}) - (\mathbf{X}\boldsymbol{\beta} - \mathbf{X}\hat{\boldsymbol{\beta}}_{\mathbf{D}})]'\mathbf{D}^{-1} [(\mathbf{z} - \mathbf{X}\hat{\boldsymbol{\beta}}_{\mathbf{D}}) - (\mathbf{X}\boldsymbol{\beta} - \mathbf{X}\hat{\boldsymbol{\beta}}_{\mathbf{D}})]$$

where $\hat{\boldsymbol{\beta}}_{\mathbf{D}} = (\mathbf{X}'\mathbf{D}^{-1}\mathbf{X})^{-1}\mathbf{X}'\mathbf{D}^{-1}\mathbf{z}$ is the M.L. estimate of $\boldsymbol{\beta}$ in the model $\mathbf{Z} = \mathbf{X}\boldsymbol{\beta} + \mathbf{e}$, where $\mathbf{e}$ is distributed $\mathrm{N}(\mathbf{e}:\mathbf{0}, \sigma^2\mathbf{D})$; see Section 6.8. If we simplify, then we get

$$\begin{aligned}(\mathbf{z} - \mathbf{X}\boldsymbol{\beta})'\mathbf{D}^{-1}(\mathbf{z} - \mathbf{X}\boldsymbol{\beta}) &= (\mathbf{z} - \mathbf{X}\hat{\boldsymbol{\beta}}_{\mathbf{D}})'\mathbf{D}^{-1}(\mathbf{z} - \mathbf{X}\hat{\boldsymbol{\beta}}_{\mathbf{D}}) + (\boldsymbol{\beta} - \hat{\boldsymbol{\beta}}_{\mathbf{D}})'\mathbf{X}'\mathbf{D}^{-1}\mathbf{X}(\boldsymbol{\beta} - \hat{\boldsymbol{\beta}}_{\mathbf{D}})\\ &= S_R^2 + (\boldsymbol{\beta} - \hat{\boldsymbol{\beta}}_{\mathbf{D}})'\mathbf{X}'\mathbf{D}^{-1}\mathbf{X}(\boldsymbol{\beta} - \hat{\boldsymbol{\beta}}_{\mathbf{D}})\end{aligned}$$

where we have denoted S_R^2 by

$$S_R^2 = (\mathbf{z} - \mathbf{X}\hat{\boldsymbol{\beta}}_{\mathbf{D}})'\mathbf{D}^{-1}(\mathbf{z} - \mathbf{X}\hat{\boldsymbol{\beta}}_{\mathbf{D}}) = \mathbf{z}'[\mathbf{D}^{-1} - \mathbf{D}^{-1}\mathbf{X}(\mathbf{X}'\mathbf{D}^{-1}\mathbf{X})^{-1}\mathbf{X}'\mathbf{D}^{-1}]\mathbf{z}$$

The likelihood function can be written as

$$L = (2\pi\sigma^2)^{-N/2} \exp\left\{\left(-\frac{1}{2\sigma^2}\right)[S_W^2 + S_R^2 + (\boldsymbol{\beta} - \hat{\boldsymbol{\beta}}_{\mathbf{D}})'(\mathbf{X}'\mathbf{D}^{-1}\mathbf{X})(\boldsymbol{\beta} - \hat{\boldsymbol{\beta}}_{\mathbf{D}})]\right\}$$

and from this we can state the following theorem.

THEOREM 8.9.2

Let the model be the same as in Theorem 8.9.1. *The results below follow.*

(1) $S_W^2 + S_R^2, \hat{\boldsymbol{\beta}}_{\mathbf{D}} = (\mathbf{X}'\mathbf{D}^{-1}\mathbf{X})^{-1}\mathbf{X}'\mathbf{D}^{-1}\mathbf{Z}$ *is a set of* $p + 1$ *complete sufficient statistics*;

(2) S_W^2, S_R^2, *and* $\hat{\boldsymbol{\beta}}_{\mathbf{D}}$ *are jointly independent (the elements in* $\hat{\boldsymbol{\beta}}_{\mathbf{D}}$ *are not necessarily independent)*;

(3) $U_R = S_R^2/\sigma^2$ *is distributed* $\chi^2(u_R : M - p)$;

(4) $U = (S_R^2 + S_W^2)/\sigma^2$ *is distributed* $\chi^2(u : N - p)$;

(5) $\hat{\boldsymbol{\beta}}_{\mathbf{D}}$ *is distributed* $\mathrm{N}(\hat{\boldsymbol{\beta}}_{\mathbf{D}} : \boldsymbol{\beta}, \sigma^2(\mathbf{X}'\mathbf{D}^{-1}\mathbf{X})^{-1})$;

(6) $\hat{\sigma}_{\mathbf{D}}^2 = (N - p)^{-1}(S_R^2 + S_W^2)$ *is the UMVU estimator of* σ^2;

(7) $\boldsymbol{\ell}'\hat{\boldsymbol{\beta}}_{\mathbf{D}}$ *is the UMVU estimator of* $\boldsymbol{\ell}'\boldsymbol{\beta}$;

(8) *tests and confidence intervals on* $\boldsymbol{\ell}'\boldsymbol{\beta}$ *can be computed by using the procedures in Sections* 6.3, 6.4, *and* 6.5 *with* $\hat{\sigma}_{\mathbf{D}}^2$ *and* $\hat{\boldsymbol{\beta}}_{\mathbf{D}}$ *replacing* $\hat{\sigma}^2$ *and* $\hat{\boldsymbol{\beta}}$.

Proof

The proof is a direct application of results in Chapter 6.

The principal reason for taking repeated Y observations at fixed values of $\mathbf{x}$ is not to use the results for estimating and testing hypotheses about elements in $\boldsymbol{\beta}$, since these can be achieved without repeating Y observations. The chief reason for repeating Y observations is to examine the assumptions of the model. For example, if repeated observations are obtained for a fixed $\mathbf{x}_i$, then we know that these n_i values of Y make up a random sample from a single population. These n_i values can be used to estimate σ^2 for *that* population, and an appropriate test [S-10] can be used to examine the assumption of normality for *that* population. From the estimate of the variance of each population an examination can be made for the equality of the variances [G-1].

Another use that can be made of the model in Equation (8.9.2) is to check for the adequacy of that model, that is, we shall show that by using the two sums of squares S_R^2 and S_W^2, one can test whether additional terms should be included in the model. For example, suppose one wants to test whether the deterministic portion of the model is really $\mathbf{X}\boldsymbol{\beta} + \mathbf{X}^*\boldsymbol{\beta}^*$ rather than $\mathbf{X}\boldsymbol{\beta}$, where $\mathbf{X}^*$ may even consist of unknown parameters and $\boldsymbol{\beta}^*$ is a vector of unknown parameters. If the objective is to test whether $\mathbf{X}\boldsymbol{\beta} + \mathbf{X}^*\boldsymbol{\beta}^*$ or $\mathbf{X}\boldsymbol{\beta}$ is the correct deterministic portion of the model, then one wants to test $H_0 : \boldsymbol{\beta}^* = \mathbf{0}$ *vs.* $H_a : \boldsymbol{\beta}^* \neq \mathbf{0}$. If $\boldsymbol{\beta}^* = \mathbf{0}$, then $U_R = S_R^2/\sigma^2$ is distributed $\chi^2(u_R : M - p)$. Also, regardless of whether H_0 or H_a is true, $U_W = S_W^2/\sigma^2$ is distributed $\chi^2(u_W : N - M)$, and U_W and U_R are independent. Hence when H_0 is true, W is distributed $F(w : M - p, N - M)$, where $W = (S_R^2/S_W^2)[(N - M)/(M - p)]$. A size α test of $H_0 : \boldsymbol{\beta}^* = \mathbf{0}$ *vs.* $H_a : \boldsymbol{\beta}^* \neq \mathbf{0}$ is this: Reject H_0 if and only if $w \geq F_{\alpha:M-p,N-M}$.

This test procedure appears similar to the one described in Section 6.3 where the full model is $\mathbf{Z} = \mathbf{X}\boldsymbol{\beta} + \mathbf{X}^*\boldsymbol{\beta}^* + \boldsymbol{\varepsilon}$ and the reduced model is $\mathbf{Z} = \mathbf{X}\boldsymbol{\beta} + \boldsymbol{\varepsilon}$. There is, however, one very important difference between the two situations. For the model discussed in Section 6.3, the *full* model must be known (the $\mathbf{X}$ and $\mathbf{X}^*$ matrices must be known) in order to compute $\hat{\sigma}^2$ in the test statistic. On the other hand, for the model defined in this section, the matrix $\mathbf{X}^*$ need not be known since it is not used in the test statistic. The reason that $\mathbf{X}^*$ is not required in the computation is that $\hat{\sigma}^2$ is computed from the repeated Y observations and not from the residuals of the full model as it is in Section 6.3. In other words, $\hat{\sigma}^2$, which is given by $S_W^2/(N - M)$, is separate and independent of either the full or the reduced model, and hence does not depend on whether the specified model is correct.

Of course, the power of the test depends on $\mathbf{X}^*$, that is, on which alternative model is being tested. So the test described above is a test of the adequacy of $\mathbf{X}\boldsymbol{\beta}$, the deterministic portion of the model in Equation (8.9.2).

If the hypothesis $H_0 : \boldsymbol{\beta}^* = \mathbf{0}$ is rejected, then an investigator might wish to test a more complete model. For example, if the model under test is $\beta_0 + \beta_1 x$ and it is rejected, then the model $\beta_0 + \beta_1 x + \beta_2 x^2$ might be examined, and so on.

Note 3. The quantity S_R^2 is referred to by some authors as "the lack of fit sum of squares," and S_W^2 is referred to as "the pure error sum of squares." These names are appropriate because S_R^2/σ^2 is a central chi-square random variable if $\mathbf{X}\boldsymbol{\beta}$ is the correct deterministic portion of the model (it is generally *not* a central chi-square random variable if $\mathbf{X\beta} + \mathbf{X^*\beta^*}$ is the correct deterministic portion of the model). So S_R^2 is a sum of squares whose distribution is determined by which model is correct or "fits." On the other hand, S_W^2/σ^2 is a central chi-square random variable regardless of which of the two models is correct, so for both models it is called "pure error."

For further information on a model with repeated Y values, see [D-9].

8.10 Maximum or Minimum of a Quadratic Function

Consider the model $Y = \mu(x) + \varepsilon$, where $\mu(x)$ is $\mu(x) = \beta_0 + \beta_1 x + \beta_2 x^2$ and $-\infty < x < \infty$. Suppose it is desired to find a point and interval estimator of x_M, the point where the maximum (or minimum) of $\mu(x)$ occurs. Let x_M be the point where $d[\mu(x)]/dx = 0$. This gives

$$\frac{d[\mu(x)]}{dx} = \beta_1 + 2\beta_2 x \tag{8.10.1}$$

and the point where this is zero is the point where $\mu(x)$ has a maximum (or minimum) and is $x_M = -\beta_1/2\beta_2$. To find the maximum likelihood estimator of x_M, denoted by $\tilde{x}_M$, we select a sample of size n from the model $Y = \beta_0 + \beta_1 x + \beta_2 x^2 + \varepsilon$. The sample model is

$$Y_i = \beta_0 + \beta_1 x_i + \beta_2 x_i^2 + \varepsilon_i \qquad \varepsilon_i \text{ are distributed } NID(\varepsilon : 0, \sigma^2) \qquad i = 1, 2, \ldots, n \tag{8.10.2}$$

The maximum likelihood estimator of x_M is

$$\tilde{x}_M = -\hat{\beta}_1/2\hat{\beta}_2 \tag{8.10.3}$$

where $\hat{\beta}_1$ and $\hat{\beta}_2$ are the maximum likelihood estimators of β_1 and β_2, respectively.

To set a confidence interval on x_M, consider the random variable $V = \hat{\beta}_1 + 2\hat{\beta}_2 x_M$. Clearly V is distributed $N(v : 0, \sigma_V^2)$, where

$$\sigma_V^2 = \text{var}[\hat{\beta}_1] + 4x_M^2 \text{ var}[\hat{\beta}_2] + 4x_M \text{ cov}[\hat{\beta}_1, \hat{\beta}_2]$$

If we let $\mathbf{C} = (\mathbf{X'X})^{-1}$, then

$$\sigma_V^2 = (c_{22} + 4x_M^2 c_{33} + 4x_M c_{23})\sigma^2 \quad \text{and} \quad \hat{\sigma}_V^2 = (c_{22} + 4x_M^2 c_{33} + 4x_M c_{23})\hat{\sigma}^2$$

where, as usual, $\hat{\sigma}^2 = (n-3)^{-1}\mathbf{Y}'(\mathbf{I} - \mathbf{X}\mathbf{X}^-)\mathbf{Y}$. Also, let $W = V^2/\hat{\sigma}_V^2$; W is distributed $F(w : 1, n-3)$, so $P[W \le F_{\alpha:1,n-3}] = 1 - \alpha$, and substituting for W

$$P[(\hat{\beta}_1 + 2\hat{\beta}_2 x_M)^2 \le F_{\alpha:1,n-3}(c_{22} + 4x_M^2 c_{33} + 4x_M c_{23})\hat{\sigma}^2] = 1 - \alpha \qquad (8.10.4)$$

The inequality in the brackets involves a quadratic function of x_M, the only unknown quantity. We can solve this inequality to obtain a $1-\alpha$ confidence interval on x_M. We get

$$(4\hat{\beta}_2^2 - 4c_{33}\hat{\sigma}^2 F_{\alpha:1,n-3})x_M^2 + 2(2\hat{\beta}_1\hat{\beta}_2 - 2c_{23}\hat{\sigma}^2 F_{\alpha:1,n-3})x_M + (\hat{\beta}_1^2 - c_{22}\hat{\sigma}^2 F_{\alpha:1,n-3}) \le 0 \qquad (8.10.5)$$

which we write as $q(x_M) = ax_M^2 + 2bx_M + c \le 0$, where $q(x_M)$ denotes a quadratic function in x_M. This is similar to the situation in Section 8.5.

The set of x_M that satisfies $q(x_M) \le 0$ is a $1-\alpha$ confidence set. However, this set is not *always* an interval. The solution set is a finite interval if and only if $a \ge 0$ and $b^2 - ac \ge 0$. If $a \ge 0$, and $b^2 - ac \ge 0$, the $1-\alpha$ confidence interval on x_M is

$$\frac{-b - \sqrt{b^2 - ac}}{a} \le x_M \le \frac{-b + \sqrt{b^2 - ac}}{a} \qquad (8.10.6)$$

where a, b, and c are defined in Equation (8.10.5). It can be shown that if $a \ge 0$, then $b^2 - ac \ge 0$, so this means that there does indeed exist a confidence interval on x_M if and only if $a \ge 0$.

Since a is the symbol used for $4\hat{\beta}_2^2 - 4c_{33}\hat{\sigma}^2 F_{\alpha:1,n-3}$, this means that a "$1-\alpha$ confidence interval" on x_M exists (for a given set of data) if and only if

$$\frac{\hat{\beta}_2^2}{c_{33}\hat{\sigma}^2} \ge F_{\alpha:1,n-3} \qquad (8.10.7)$$

or, in other words, if and only if H_0 is rejected at the α level in the test

$$H_0 : \beta_2 = 0 \qquad vs. \qquad H_a : \beta_2 \ne 0$$

If H_0 is accepted, this means that for a size α test, the data imply that $\beta_2 = 0$, so there is no maximum (nor minimum) and a confidence interval has no meaning.

Thus a suggested procedure is the following:

1. Test the hypothesis $H_0 : \beta_2 = 0$ *vs.* $H_a : \beta_2 \ne 0$ with a size α test. the test is this: Reject H_0 if and only if Equation (8.10.7) is satisfied.

2. If H_0 is accepted, assume that the model is $Y = \beta_0 + \beta x + \varepsilon$, and hence no maximum (or minimum) exists.

3. If H_0 is rejected, use the formula in Equation (8.10.6) to set a "$1 - \alpha$ confidence interval" on x_M. If H_0 is rejected at the α level, then a "$1 - \alpha$ confidence interval" will exist.

We have enclosed "$1 - \alpha$ confidence interval" in quotation marks since the so-called $1 - \alpha$ confidence interval that is computed by this procedure has probability less than $1 - \alpha$ of containing x_M. See the remarks at the end of Section 8.5.

8.11 Point of Intersection of Two Lines

In Section 8.6.1 we discussed the problem of whether H simple linear models intersected in a single *specified* point x_0. In this section we discuss a somewhat related problem, namely, estimating the point where *two* simple linear models intersect.

Consider two simple linear models

$$Y = \alpha_1 + \beta_1 x + \varepsilon \qquad \text{and} \qquad Y = \alpha_2 + \beta_2 x + \varepsilon$$

The point on the x-axis which is the intersection point (denoted by x_0) of the deterministic portion of these two models is obtained by equating $\alpha_1 + \beta_1 x$ and $\alpha_2 + \beta_2 x$ and solving for x. If we denote the solution by x_0, we get

$$\alpha_1 + \beta_1 x_0 = \alpha_2 + \beta_2 x_0$$

which gives

$$x_0 = \frac{\alpha_1 - \alpha_2}{\beta_2 - \beta_1}$$

We assume $\beta_1 \neq \beta_2$, otherwise there is no intersection.

Data are collected from each model and used to obtain point and interval estimates of x_0. The two simple linear models are

$$\begin{aligned} Y_{1j} &= \alpha_1 + \beta_1 x_{1j} + \varepsilon_{1j} \qquad j = 1, 2, \ldots, n_1 > 2 \\ Y_{2j} &= \alpha_2 + \beta_2 x_{2j} + \varepsilon_{2j} \qquad j = 1, 2, \ldots, n_2 > 2 \end{aligned}$$

and the ε_{ij} are distributed $NID(\varepsilon : 0, \sigma^2)$. Clearly the M.L. estimators of α_1, β_1,

α_2, β_2, and σ^2 (adjusted for bias) are given by

$$\hat{\beta}_1 = \frac{\sum_{j=1}^{n_1} (Y_{1j} - \bar{Y}_{1.})(x_{1j} - \bar{x}_{1.})}{\sum_{k=1}^{n_1} (x_{1k} - \bar{x}_{1.})^2} \qquad \hat{\alpha}_1 = \bar{Y}_{1.} - \hat{\beta}_1 \bar{x}_{1.}$$

$$\hat{\beta}_2 = \frac{\sum_{j=1}^{n_2} (Y_{2j} - \bar{Y}_{2.})(x_{2j} - \bar{x}_{2.})}{\sum_{k=1}^{n_2} (x_{2k} - \bar{x}_{2.})^2} \qquad \hat{\alpha}_2 = \bar{Y}_{2.} - \hat{\beta}_2 \bar{x}_{2.}$$

$$\hat{\sigma}^2 = (n_1 + n_2 - 4)^{-1} \sum_{i=1}^{2} \sum_{j=1}^{n_i} (Y_{ij} - \hat{\alpha}_i - \hat{\beta}_i \bar{x}_{ij})^2$$

The estimators are UMVU estimators of their respective parameters. Due to the invariance property of M.L. estimators, the M.L. estimator of x_0, denoted by $\tilde{x}_0$, is

$$\tilde{x}_0 = \frac{\hat{\alpha}_1 - \hat{\alpha}_2}{\hat{\beta}_2 - \hat{\beta}_1}$$

The distributional properties of $\hat{\alpha}_1, \hat{\beta}_1, \hat{\alpha}_2, \hat{\beta}_2$, and $\hat{\sigma}^2$ are given in Theorem 6.2.1. Note that the three sets of random variables $\{\hat{\alpha}_1, \hat{\beta}_1\}$, $\{\hat{\alpha}_2, \hat{\beta}_2\}$, and $\{\hat{\sigma}^2\}$ are jointly independent.

To find a $1 - \alpha$ confidence interval on x_0, consider the following:

1. $Z = (\hat{\alpha}_1 - \hat{\alpha}_2) + x_0(\hat{\beta}_1 - \hat{\beta}_2)$ is distributed $N(z : 0, A^2\sigma^2)$ where

$$\begin{aligned} A^2\sigma^2 &= \text{var}[Z] = \text{var}[\hat{\alpha}_1 + x_0\hat{\beta}_1] + \text{var}[\hat{\alpha}_2 + x_0\hat{\beta}_2] \\ &= \sigma^2 \left\{ \frac{\sum x_{1j}^2 - 2x_0 \sum x_{1j} + x_0^2 n_1}{n_1 \sum (x_{1j} - \bar{x}_{1.})^2} \right. \\ &\qquad \left. + \frac{\sum x_{2j}^2 - 2x_0 \sum x_{2j} + x_0^2 n_2}{n_2 \sum (x_{2j} - \bar{x}_{2.})} \right\} \end{aligned}$$

2. $U = N\hat{\sigma}^2/\sigma^2$ is distributed $\chi^2(u : N)$, where $N = n_1 + n_2 - 4$;
3. U and Z are independent;
4. $W = Z^2/A^2\hat{\sigma}^2$ is distributed $F(w : 1, N)$;
5. $P[Z^2/A^2\hat{\sigma}^2 \le F_{\alpha:1,N}] = 1 - \alpha$.

If the values of x_0 that satisfy $Z^2/A^2\hat{\sigma}^2 \le F_{\alpha:1,N}$ are an interval, then this interval is a $1 - \alpha$ confidence interval on x_0. If this expression is simplified, we obtain (let $S_1^2 = \sum (x_{1j} - \bar{x}_{1.})^2$ and $S_2^2 = \sum (x_{2j} - \bar{x}_{2.})^2$)

$$\left[(\hat{\beta}_1 - \hat{\beta}_2)^2 - \left(\frac{1}{S_1^2} + \frac{1}{S_2^2}\right)\hat{\sigma}^2 F_{\alpha:1,N}\right]x_0^2$$
$$+ 2\left[(\hat{\alpha}_1 - \hat{\alpha}_2)(\hat{\beta}_1 - \hat{\beta}_2) + \left(\frac{\bar{x}_{1.}}{S_1^2} + \frac{\bar{x}_{2.}}{S_2^2}\right)\hat{\sigma}^2 F_{\alpha:1,N}\right]x_0$$
$$+ \left[(\hat{\alpha}_1 - \hat{\alpha}_2)^2 - \left(\frac{\sum x_{1j}^2}{n_1 S_1^2} + \frac{\sum x_{2j}^2}{n_2 S_2^2}\right)\hat{\sigma}^2 F_{\alpha:1,N}\right] \leq 0$$

which we write as $q(x_0) = ax_0^2 + 2bx_0 + c \leq 0$.

This is similar to the situation in Sections 8.5 and 8.10. If the set of x_0 values that satisfies $q(x_0) \leq 0$ is a finite interval, then this is a $1 - \alpha$ confidence interval on x_0. The solution set is a finite interval if and only if $a \geq 0$ and $b^2 - ac \geq 0$. If $a \geq 0$ and $b^2 - ac \geq 0$, then a $1 - \alpha$ confidence interval on x_0 is

$$\frac{-b - \sqrt{b^2 - ac}}{a} \leq x_0 \leq \frac{-b + \sqrt{b^2 - ac}}{a}$$

For a discussion of the problem of testing whether three (or more) lines intersect in a single (unspecified) point, see [S-3].

Problems

8.1. Assume that the data given below satisfy the model

$$Y_i = \beta_0 + \beta_1 x_{i1} + \beta_2 x_{i2} + \varepsilon_i \qquad \varepsilon_i \text{ are distributed } NID(\varepsilon : 0, \sigma^2)$$

y	12.0	11.7	9.3	11.9	11.8	9.5	9.3	7.2	8.1	8.3	7.0	6.5	5.9
x_1	3	4	5	6	7	8	9	10	11	12	13	14	15
x_2	6	4	2	1	0	1	2	1	−1	0	−2	−1	−3

(a) Find 80 percent, 90 percent, 95 percent, and 99 percent confidence intervals for Y_0, the mean of one future observation at $x_1 = 9.5$, $x_2 = 2.5$.

(b) Find a 90 percent confidence interval for $\bar{Y}_0$, the mean of six future observations at $x_1 = 9.5$, $x_2 = 2.5$.

8.2. Consider the simple linear model $Y_i = \beta_0 + \beta x_i + \varepsilon_i$, where ε_i are distributed $NID(\varepsilon : 0, \sigma^2)$, $i = 1, 2, \ldots, n$. Find the p.d.f. of the length L of a $1 - \alpha$ confidence interval on $\bar{Y}_0$, the mean of k future observations.

8.3. In Problem 8.2 find $\mathscr{E}[L]$ and $\mathscr{E}[L^2]$.

8.4. In designing an experiment (determining values of $x_1, x_2, \ldots, x_n$) in a simple linear model to set a $1 - \alpha$ confidence interval on $\bar{Y}_0$, the mean of k future observations at x_0, how would you select the x_i's to minimize $\mathscr{E}[L^2]$ for fixed n, k, and $1 - \alpha$ if all x_i's are in the interval $[a, b]$? Assume n is an even integer.

8.5. If you have no control over determining the values of the x_i's in Problem 8.4, how could you reduce $\mathscr{E}[L^2]$ by varying n and k, if $1 - \alpha$ is fixed?

8.6. In a simple linear model $Y_i = \beta_0 + \beta x_i + \varepsilon_i$, ε_i are distributed $NID(\varepsilon : 0, \sigma^2)$, $n = 18$ values of (x_i, y_i) were observed and the following were computed: $\hat{\beta}_0 = -4.0$, $\hat{\beta} = 1.3$, $\hat{\sigma}^2 = 1.4$, and $A = 0.269$. Compute the upper 0.20 tolerance point at $x_0 = 2.3$ with a confidence coefficient of $1 - \alpha = 0.95$.

8.7. In Problem 8.6 compute the lower 0.20 tolerance point.

8.8. From the data in Example 8.3.2, find the lower 0.10 tolerance point with $1 - \alpha = 0.95$.

8.9. In the data in Example 8.3.2, a value of Y_0 is observed to be $y_0 = 2.10$. Obtain the maximum likelihood estimator of x_0.

8.10. In Problem 8.9 find a 0.95 confidence interval on x_0 or show that one doesn't exist.

8.11. Assume that the data in the table on page 337 came from the three models

$$Y_{ij} = \alpha_i + \beta_i x_{ij} + \varepsilon_{ij} \qquad \varepsilon_{ij} \text{ are distributed } NID(\varepsilon : 0, \sigma^2)$$

Use $\alpha = 0.05$ and test $H_0 : \beta_1 = \beta_2 = \beta_3$ *vs.* H_a : at least one equality is an inequality.

8.12. In Problem 8.11 test $H_0 : \alpha_1 = \alpha_2 = \alpha_3$ *vs.* H_a : at least one equality is an inequality.

8.13. In Problem 8.11 test the hypothesis that the three lines intersect at $x = 3.3$. Use $\alpha = 0.05$.

8.14. In Problem 8.11 test the hypothesis that the three lines are identical. Use $\alpha = 0.05$.

8.15. The data in the table on page 338 are assumed to fit the models

$$Y_{hj} = \beta_{h0} + \beta_{h1} x_j + \beta_{h2} x_j^2 + \beta_{h3} x_j^3 + \varepsilon_{hj} \qquad \varepsilon_{hj} \text{ are distributed } NID(\varepsilon : 0, \sigma^2)$$

Test $H_0 : \beta_{13} = \beta_{23} = \beta_{33}$ *vs.* H_a : at least one equality is an inequality.

8.16. In Problem 8.15 test $H_0 : \beta_{12} = \beta_{22} = \beta_{32}$, $\beta_{13} = \beta_{23} = \beta_{33}$ *vs.* H_a : at least one equality is an inequality.

Data for Problem 8.11

y_{1j}	1.2	1.8	1.9	2.1	2.8	2.8	3.1	4.2	4.5	6.2						
x_{1j}	2.94	1.43	0.48	1.42	−0.96	−1.20	0.01	−1.85	−3.26	−6.73						
y_{2j}	1.0	1.8	2.3	2.5	2.6	3.1	3.4	3.6	3.8	4.2	5.3	6.3	6.5	7.1	7.3	7.6
x_{2j}	4.39	5.49	4.03	0.50	2.04	−1.72	−0.04	2.75	−1.52	−2.58	−4.98	−4.53	−7.75	−6.60	−7.15	−8.17
y_{3j}	−2.0	−1.8	−0.6	0.4	0.5	0.6	1.2	1.5	1.9	2.0	3.8	5.2				
x_{3j}	9.61	7.78	6.75	4.39	4.05	1.93	3.88	3.65	2.49	3.71	−1.50	−1.29				

Data for Problem 8.15

Model 1	x_i	1	2	3	4	5	6	7	8	9	10
data	y_i	−44.418	−53.156	−66.006	−71.002	−88.622	−112.170	−125.110	−141.646	−154.386	−170.520
Model 2	x_i	−4	−3	−3	−2	0	1	2	4	4	
data	y_i	−76.618	−60.552	−62.718	−52.112	−46.380	−54.780	−64.182	−89.972	−98.124	
Model 3	x_i	1	3	4	5	6	6	7	7		
data	y_i	−85.280	−73.916	−59.716	−40.068	−12.990	−16.690	−17.168	−20.920		

8.17. The data below are assumed to have come from the model

$$Y_i = \beta_0 + \beta_1 x_i + \beta_2 x_i^2 + \cdots + \beta_K x_i^K + \varepsilon_i \qquad \varepsilon_i \text{ are distributed } NID(\varepsilon : 0, \sigma^2)$$

It is assumed that $K \leq 5$. Use an α value of 0.10 and determine the degree of the polynomial.

x	−1.2	−1.0	−0.6	1.1	1.2	1.2	1.3
y	−14.59	−17.14	−18.93	−21.36	−22.36	−21.50	−25.22

x	1.6	2.1	3.4	3.4	3.6	4.1	4.5
y	−23.50	−22.44	−39.18	−42.23	−39.68	−50.18	−53.31

8.18. In Problem 8.17 if the correct degree of the polynomial is three, determine the probability of making an error if $\beta_3/\sigma = 2.0$.

Problems 8.19 through 8.22 refer to the proof of Theorem 8.7.2.

8.19. Let U_1 be distributed $\chi^2(u_1 : n_1; 0)$, U_2 be distributed $\chi^2(u_2 : n_2; 0)$, and let U_1 and U_2 be independent. Show that $W = (n_2/n_1)(U_1/U_2)$ is distributed $F(w : n_1, n_2; 0)$, $U = U_1 + U_2$ is distributed $\chi^2(u : n_1 + n_2; 0)$, and W and U are independent.

8.20. Let S, U_1, U_2, and U_3 be jointly independent chi-square random variables with n_S, 1, 1, and 1 degrees of freedom, respectively, and with noncentrality parameters $\lambda_S = \lambda_1 = \lambda_2 = 0$, $\lambda_3 \neq 0$.

(a) Prove that U_1/S, $U_1 + S$, U_2, and U_3 are jointly independent random variables.

(b) Prove that U_1/S, $U_2/(U_1 + S)$, $U_1 + U_2 + S$, and U_3 are jointly independent random variables.

(c) Prove U_1/S, $U_2/(U_1 + S)$, and $U_3/(U_1 + U_2 + S)$ are jointly independent random variables.

(d) Let $W_1 = n_S(U_1/S)$, $W_2 = (n_S + 1)U_2/(U_1 + S)$, and $W_3 = (n_S + 2)U_3/(U_1 + U_2 + S)$. Prove that W_1, W_2, and W_3 are jointly independent random variables and

$$W_1 \text{ is distributed } F(w_1 : 1, n_S; 0)$$
$$W_2 \text{ is distributed } F(w_2 : 1, n_S + 1; 0)$$
$$W_3 \text{ is distributed } F(w_3 : 1, n_S + 2; \lambda_3)$$

8.21. To generalize Problem 8.20 let $S, U_1, U_2, \ldots, U_H$ be independent chi-square random variables with degrees of freedom $n_S, 1, 1, \ldots, 1$, respectively, and noncentrality parameters $\lambda_S = \lambda_1 = \cdots = \lambda_{H-1} = 0$, $\lambda_H \neq 0$. Define W_h by

$$W_h = \frac{(n_S + h - 1)U_h}{S + U_1 + \cdots + U_{h-1}} \qquad h = 1, 2, \ldots, H \quad (U_0 = 0)$$

(a) Show that W_h is distributed $F(w_h: 1, n_S + h - 1; \lambda_h)$, where $h = 1, 2, \ldots, H$, and $\lambda_1 = \lambda_2 = \cdots = \lambda_{H-1} = 0$, $\lambda_H \neq 0$.
(b) Show that $W_1, W_2, \ldots, W_H$ are jointly independent.

8.22. Prove Theorem 8.7.2. Hint: Let $S = (\mathbf{Y}'\mathbf{Y} - \ell'\ell)/\sigma^2$, $U_1 = T_K^2/\sigma^2$, $U_2 = T_{K-1}^2/\sigma^2, \ldots, U_H = T_M^2/\sigma^2$. (Note $n_S = n - K - 1$.)

8.23. In Example 8.8.4 use only the first 24 observations. Thus $n = 24$. Assume the model

$$Y_t = \beta + \sum_{h=1}^{3} \left[\alpha_h \cos\left(\frac{2\pi}{P_h}\right)t + \gamma_h \sin\left(\frac{2\pi}{P_h}\right)t \right] + \varepsilon_t$$

where ε_t are distributed $NID(\varepsilon: 0, \sigma^2)$, and where $P_1 = 24/2$, $P_2 = 24/4$, and $P_3 = 24/6$. Find maximum likelihood estimates of $\beta, \alpha_1, \gamma_1, \alpha_2, \gamma_2, \alpha_3, \gamma_3$, and σ^2.

8.24. In Problem 8.23 test whether the model contains the component with period P_1.

8.25. In Problem 8.23 set one-at-a-time 95 percent confidence intervals on $\alpha_1, \gamma_1, \alpha_2, \gamma_2, \alpha_3$, and γ_3.

8.26. In Problem 8.25 set simultaneous 95 percent confidence intervals on the parameters indicated.

8.27. In Problem 8.23 set a confidence interval on $\alpha_1^2 + \gamma_1^2$ with $1 - \alpha \geq 0.90$.

8.28. Assume that the data below satisfy the quadratic model

$$Y_i = \mu(x_i) + \varepsilon_i = \beta_0 + \beta_1 x_i + \beta_2 x_i^2 + \varepsilon_i \qquad \varepsilon_i \text{ are distributed } NID(\varepsilon: 0, \sigma^2)$$

Find the maximum likelihood estimate of the minimum of $\mu(x)$.

y_i	12.1	11.9	10.2	8.0	7.7	5.3	7.9	7.8	9.1	8.7
x_i	0	1	2	3	4	5	6	7	8	9

8.29. In Problem 8.28 set a 95 percent confidence interval on the location of the minimum of $\mu(x)$ or show that one doesn't exist.

8.30. In Problem 8.11 find the M.L. estimate of the point x_0 where the first two lines intersect.

8.31. In Problem 8.30 set a 90 percent confidence interval on the point x_0 or show that the confidence interval does not exist.

8.32. In Equation (8.10.5) prove that $b^2 - ac \geq 0$ if $a \geq 0$, where a and b are, respectively, the coefficients of x_M^2 and x_M and c is the constant term.

CHAPTER 9

Sampling from the Multivariate Normal Distribution

9.1 Introduction

In this book we shall not devote much space to estimating or testing hypotheses about parameters in the multivariate normal distribution. However, it will be necessary to develop some understanding of these procedures since they will be needed in later chapters. In Section 9.2 we give the functional form of the p.d.f. of the multivariate normal and state the notation that will be used throughout this chapter. In Section 9.3 we find point estimators of the parameters in the multivariate normal and state some optimum properties they possess. Sections 9.4 and 9.5 will be devoted to a discussion of tests of hypotheses and confidence intervals, respectively. In Section 9.6 we briefly discuss some computing aspects of the multivariate normal, and in Section 9.7 some additional theorems are proved about the estimators of the mean vector and covariance matrix.

9.2 Notation

Throughout this chapter we assume that the $K \times 1$ vector χ is distributed $\mathbf{N}(\mathbf{x} : \boldsymbol{\mu}, \boldsymbol{\Sigma})$, where $\boldsymbol{\Sigma}$ has rank K; hence by Theorem 3.3.4, χ has a p.d.f. given by

$$f_\chi(\mathbf{x}) = (2\pi)^{-K/2}|\boldsymbol{\Sigma}|^{-1/2} \exp[-\tfrac{1}{2}(\mathbf{x} - \boldsymbol{\mu})'\boldsymbol{\Sigma}^{-1}(\mathbf{x} - \boldsymbol{\mu})] \qquad (9.2.1)$$

where $\mathbf{x} \in E_K$ and $\boldsymbol{\Sigma}$ is positive definite.

We let $\chi_1, \chi_2, \ldots, \chi_n$ represent a random sample of size $n > K$ from this p.d.f. We use the following notation.

$$\chi' = [X_1, X_2, \ldots, X_K] \qquad \chi_i' = [X_{i1}, X_{i2}, \ldots, X_{iK}] \qquad \mathscr{X}' = [\chi_1, \chi_2, \ldots, \chi_n]$$

where $\mathscr{X}$ is script capital **X**. The matrix $\mathscr{X}$ has size $n \times K$ and is a random matrix (matrix of random variables X_{ij}), that is,

$$\mathscr{X} = \begin{bmatrix} X_{11} & X_{12} & \cdots & X_{1K} \\ X_{21} & X_{22} & \cdots & X_{2K} \\ \vdots & \vdots & & \vdots \\ X_{n1} & X_{n2} & \cdots & X_{nK} \end{bmatrix} = \begin{bmatrix} \chi_1' \\ \chi_2' \\ \vdots \\ \chi_n' \end{bmatrix} \qquad \bar{\chi} = \frac{1}{n} \sum_{i=1}^{n} \chi_i$$

$$\mathbf{x}_i' = [x_{i1}, x_{i2}, \ldots, x_{iK}] \qquad \bar{\mathbf{x}} = \frac{1}{n} \sum_{i=1}^{n} \mathbf{x}_i$$

$$\mathbf{X} = \begin{bmatrix} x_{11} & x_{12} & \cdots & x_{1K} \\ x_{21} & x_{22} & \cdots & x_{2K} \\ \vdots & \vdots & & \vdots \\ x_{n1} & x_{n2} & \cdots & x_{nK} \end{bmatrix} = \begin{bmatrix} \mathbf{x}_1' \\ \mathbf{x}_2' \\ \vdots \\ \mathbf{x}_n' \end{bmatrix} \tag{9.2.2}$$

$$\mathscr{A} = \sum_{t=1}^{n} (\chi_t - \bar{\chi})(\chi_t - \bar{\chi})' = [A_{ij}] \qquad A_{ij} = \sum_{t=1}^{n} (X_{ti} - \bar{X}_i)(X_{tj} - \bar{X}_j)$$

$$\mathbf{A} = \sum_{t=1}^{n} (\mathbf{x}_t - \bar{\mathbf{x}})(\mathbf{x}_t - \bar{\mathbf{x}})' = [a_{ij}] \qquad a_{ij} = \sum_{t=1}^{n} (x_{ti} - \bar{x}_i)(x_{tj} - \bar{x}_j)$$

$$\boldsymbol{\Sigma} = [\sigma_{ij}] \qquad \boldsymbol{\mu} = [\mu_i]$$

Note 1. We attempt to maintain the notation that a random variable is denoted by a capital, nonboldface letter, and the corresponding lowercase letter represents the value of the random variable. Where possible we denote a matrix of random variables by *script* capital boldface letters such as $\mathscr{A}$ and $\mathscr{W}$, and the corresponding nonrandom matrix whose elements are values of the random variables by nonscript, capital boldface letters such as **A** and **W**. For example, $\mathscr{A} = [A_{ij}]$ is a matrix of the random variables A_{ij}, and $\mathbf{A} = [a_{ij}]$ is a nonrandom matrix that represents fixed values of $\mathscr{A}$. A similar notation is used for $\mathscr{X}$ and **X**, and so on. The parameter space will be denoted by Ω, and unless otherwise stated, Ω will be defined by $\Omega = \{(\boldsymbol{\mu}, \boldsymbol{\Sigma}) : \boldsymbol{\mu} \in E_K, \boldsymbol{\Sigma} \text{ is positive definite}\}$.

9.3 Point Estimators of μ and Σ

To find point estimators we first find maximum likelihood estimators, then we find sufficient statistics, and finally we find UMVU and consistent estimators of $\boldsymbol{\mu}$ and $\boldsymbol{\Sigma}$.

THEOREM 9.3.1

Let $\chi_1, \chi_2, \ldots, \chi_n$ be a random sample from the multivariate normal distribution $N(\mathbf{x} : \boldsymbol{\mu}, \boldsymbol{\Sigma})$, *where the parameter space is* Ω. *The maximum likelihood estimators of* $\boldsymbol{\mu}$ *and* $\boldsymbol{\Sigma}$, *denoted by* $\tilde{\boldsymbol{\mu}}$ *and* $\tilde{\boldsymbol{\Sigma}}$, *respectively, are given by*

$$\begin{aligned}\tilde{\boldsymbol{\mu}} &= \bar{\chi} = \frac{1}{n}\sum_{i=1}^{n} \chi_i \\ \tilde{\boldsymbol{\Sigma}} &= \frac{1}{n}\sum_{i=1}^{n} (\chi_i - \bar{\chi})(\chi_i - \bar{\chi})' = \frac{1}{n}\mathscr{A}\end{aligned} \tag{9.3.1}$$

Proof

The likelihood function is the joint p.d.f. of $\chi_1, \chi_2, \ldots, \chi_n$, viewed as a function of $\boldsymbol{\mu}$ and $\boldsymbol{\Sigma}$. We get

$$\begin{aligned}L &= L(\boldsymbol{\mu}, \boldsymbol{\Sigma} : \mathbf{x}_1, \mathbf{x}_2, \ldots, \mathbf{x}_n) \\ &= (2\pi)^{-nK/2}|\boldsymbol{\Sigma}|^{-n/2} \exp\left[-\tfrac{1}{2}\sum_{i=1}^{n} (\mathbf{x}_i - \boldsymbol{\mu})'\boldsymbol{\Sigma}^{-1}(\mathbf{x}_i - \boldsymbol{\mu})\right]\end{aligned} \tag{9.3.2}$$

If we examine the exponent, we get

$$\begin{aligned}&-\tfrac{1}{2}\sum_{i=1}^{n} (\mathbf{x}_i - \boldsymbol{\mu})'\boldsymbol{\Sigma}^{-1}(\mathbf{x}_i - \boldsymbol{\mu}) \\ &\quad = -\tfrac{1}{2}\sum_{i=1}^{n} [(\mathbf{x}_i - \bar{\mathbf{x}}) - (\boldsymbol{\mu} - \bar{\mathbf{x}})]'\boldsymbol{\Sigma}^{-1}[(\mathbf{x}_i - \bar{\mathbf{x}}) - (\boldsymbol{\mu} - \bar{\mathbf{x}})] \\ &\quad = -\tfrac{1}{2}\left\{\sum_{i=1}^{n} (\mathbf{x}_i - \bar{\mathbf{x}})'\boldsymbol{\Sigma}^{-1}(\mathbf{x}_i - \bar{\mathbf{x}}) + n(\bar{\mathbf{x}} - \boldsymbol{\mu})'\boldsymbol{\Sigma}^{-1}(\bar{\mathbf{x}} - \boldsymbol{\mu})\right\}\end{aligned}$$

since the cross products terms are zero, that is, $\sum_{i=1}^{n} (\mathbf{x}_i - \bar{\mathbf{x}})'\boldsymbol{\Sigma}^{-1} \times (\boldsymbol{\mu} - \bar{\mathbf{x}}) = 0$ since $\sum_{i=1}^{n} (\mathbf{x}_i - \bar{\mathbf{x}}) = \mathbf{0}$. (Note $\bar{\mathbf{x}} = (1/n)\sum_{i=1}^{n} \mathbf{x}_i$.) Thus the likelihood function can be written

$$\begin{aligned}L &= (2\pi)^{-Kn/2}|\boldsymbol{\Sigma}|^{-n/2} \\ &\quad \times \exp\left[-\tfrac{1}{2}\sum_{i=1}^{n} (\mathbf{x}_i - \bar{\mathbf{x}})'\boldsymbol{\Sigma}^{-1}(\mathbf{x}_i - \bar{\mathbf{x}}) - \tfrac{1}{2}n(\bar{\mathbf{x}} - \boldsymbol{\mu})'\boldsymbol{\Sigma}^{-1}(\bar{\mathbf{x}} - \boldsymbol{\mu})\right] \\ &\le (2\pi)^{-Kn/2}|\boldsymbol{\Sigma}^{-1}|^{n/2} \exp\left[-\tfrac{1}{2}\sum_{i=1}^{n} (\mathbf{x}_i - \bar{\mathbf{x}})'\boldsymbol{\Sigma}^{-1}(\mathbf{x}_i - \bar{\mathbf{x}})\right] = L_1\end{aligned}$$

say, because $n(\bar{\mathbf{x}} - \boldsymbol{\mu})'\boldsymbol{\Sigma}^{-1}(\bar{\mathbf{x}} - \boldsymbol{\mu}) \geq 0$ since $\boldsymbol{\Sigma}$, and hence $\boldsymbol{\Sigma}^{-1}$, are positive definite matrices.

Next we show that $L_1 \leq (2\pi)^{-nK/2}|n\mathbf{A}^{-1}|^{n/2} e^{-nK/2} = L_0$, say. To do this we work with the exponent of L_1 and get (note the exponent is a scalar and hence equal to its trace)

$$\begin{aligned}
-\tfrac{1}{2}\sum_{i=1}^{n}(\mathbf{x}_i - \bar{\mathbf{x}})'\boldsymbol{\Sigma}^{-1}(\mathbf{x}_i - \bar{\mathbf{x}}) &= -\tfrac{1}{2}\operatorname{tr}\left[\sum_{i=1}^{n}(\mathbf{x}_i - \bar{\mathbf{x}})'\boldsymbol{\Sigma}^{-1}(\mathbf{x}_i - \bar{\mathbf{x}})\right] \\
&= -\tfrac{1}{2}\sum_{i=1}^{n}\operatorname{tr}[(\mathbf{x}_i - \bar{\mathbf{x}})'\boldsymbol{\Sigma}^{-1}(\mathbf{x}_i - \bar{\mathbf{x}})] \\
&= -\tfrac{1}{2}\sum_{i=1}^{n}\operatorname{tr}[(\mathbf{x}_i - \bar{\mathbf{x}})(\mathbf{x}_i - \bar{\mathbf{x}})'\boldsymbol{\Sigma}^{-1}] \\
&= -\tfrac{1}{2}\operatorname{tr}\left[\sum_{i=1}^{n}(\mathbf{x}_i - \bar{\mathbf{x}})(\mathbf{x}_i - \bar{\mathbf{x}})'\boldsymbol{\Sigma}^{-1}\right] \\
&= -\tfrac{1}{2}\operatorname{tr}[\mathbf{A}\boldsymbol{\Sigma}^{-1}] \qquad (9.3.3)
\end{aligned}$$

Thus

$$\begin{aligned}
L_1 &= (2\pi)^{-nK/2}|\boldsymbol{\Sigma}^{-1}|^{n/2}\exp\left[-\tfrac{1}{2}\sum_{i=1}^{n}(\mathbf{x}_i - \bar{\mathbf{x}})'\boldsymbol{\Sigma}^{-1}(\mathbf{x}_i - \bar{\mathbf{x}})\right] \\
&= (2\pi)^{-nK/2}|n\mathbf{A}^{-1}|^{n/2}|n^{-1}\mathbf{A}|^{n/2}|\boldsymbol{\Sigma}^{-1}|^{n/2}\exp\{-\tfrac{1}{2}\operatorname{tr}[\mathbf{A}\boldsymbol{\Sigma}^{-1}]\} \\
&= (2\pi)^{-nK/2}|n\mathbf{A}^{-1}|^{n/2}n^{-nK/2}|\mathbf{A}\boldsymbol{\Sigma}^{-1}|^{n/2}\exp\{-\tfrac{1}{2}\operatorname{tr}[\mathbf{A}\boldsymbol{\Sigma}^{-1}]\} \\
&= (2\pi)^{-nK/2}|n\mathbf{A}^{-1}|^{n/2}n^{-nK/2}|\boldsymbol{\Delta}|^{n/2}\exp[-\tfrac{1}{2}\operatorname{tr}\boldsymbol{\Delta}] \\
&= (2\pi)^{-nK/2}|n\mathbf{A}^{-1}|^{n/2}n^{-nK/2}\left[\prod_{i=1}^{K}\lambda_{ii}^{n/2}\right]\exp\left[-\tfrac{1}{2}\sum_{j=1}^{K}\lambda_{jj}\right] \qquad (9.3.4)
\end{aligned}$$

where $\boldsymbol{\Delta} = \mathbf{A}\boldsymbol{\Sigma}^{-1}$ and λ_{jj} are the characteristic roots of $\boldsymbol{\Delta}$, which are nonnegative. Thus

$$L_1 = (2\pi)^{-nK/2}|n\mathbf{A}^{-1}|^{n/2}n^{-nK/2}\prod_{i=1}^{K}\lambda_{ii}^{n/2}e^{-(1/2)\lambda_{ii}}$$

By setting the derivative of $x^{n/2}e^{-x/2}$ equal to zero, we can easily show that $\max_{x \geq 0}[x^{n/2}e^{-x/2}] = n^{n/2}e^{-n/2}$ and occurs at $x = n$. Thus

$$\begin{aligned}
\max_{\lambda_{ii} \geq 0}\left[\prod_{i=1}^{K}\lambda_{ii}^{n/2}e^{-(1/2)\lambda_{ii}}\right] &= \prod_{i=1}^{K}\max_{\lambda_{ii} \geq 0}[\lambda_{ii}^{n/2}e^{-(1/2)\lambda_{ii}}] = \prod_{i=1}^{K}n^{n/2}e^{-n/2} \\
&= n^{Kn/2}e^{-nK/2}
\end{aligned}$$

So $L_1 \leq (2\pi)^{-nK/2}|n\mathbf{A}^{-1}|^{n/2}e^{-nK/2} = L_0$, say, and the value L_0

does not depend on any unknown parameters. So $L \le L_0$, and if we can find values of $\boldsymbol{\mu}$ and $\boldsymbol{\Sigma}$ in Ω in Equation (9.3.2) that depend only on the observations (statistics) such that $L = L_0$, then these values of $\boldsymbol{\mu}$ and $\boldsymbol{\Sigma}$ clearly maximize the likelihood function, and hence they are the maximum likelihood estimators.

Let $\tilde{\boldsymbol{\mu}}$ and $\tilde{\boldsymbol{\Sigma}}$ be defined by $\tilde{\boldsymbol{\mu}} = \bar{\mathbf{x}}$ and $\tilde{\boldsymbol{\Sigma}} = (1/n)\mathbf{A} = (1/n)\sum(\mathbf{x}_i - \bar{\mathbf{x}}) \times (\mathbf{x}_i - \bar{\mathbf{x}})'$. Substitute these values into L in Equation (9.3.2) and get

$$L = (2\pi)^{-nK/2}|\tilde{\boldsymbol{\Sigma}}|^{-n/2}\exp(-\tfrac{1}{2})\{\text{tr}[\mathbf{A}\tilde{\boldsymbol{\Sigma}}^{-1}] + n(\bar{\mathbf{x}} - \tilde{\boldsymbol{\mu}})'\tilde{\boldsymbol{\Sigma}}^{-1}(\bar{\mathbf{x}} - \tilde{\boldsymbol{\mu}})\}$$

We see that for these values $L = L_0$. So $\tilde{\boldsymbol{\mu}}$ and $\tilde{\boldsymbol{\Sigma}}$ are indeed maximum likelihood estimators of $\boldsymbol{\mu}$ and $\boldsymbol{\Sigma}$, respectively. It is easily shown that $\tilde{\boldsymbol{\mu}}$ and $\tilde{\boldsymbol{\Sigma}}$ are unique M.L. estimators. This completes the proof.

We now state a theorem on sufficiency, completeness, and unbiasedness of $\tilde{\boldsymbol{\mu}}$ and $\tilde{\boldsymbol{\Sigma}}$ (we now use the notation $\hat{\boldsymbol{\mu}} = \tilde{\boldsymbol{\mu}}$ and $\hat{\boldsymbol{\Sigma}}$ for $(1/(n-1))\mathscr{A} = (n/(n-1))\tilde{\boldsymbol{\Sigma}}$ and some distributional properties of $\hat{\boldsymbol{\mu}}$ and $\hat{\boldsymbol{\Sigma}}$.

THEOREM 9.3.2

Let the $K \times 1$ vectors $\chi_1, \chi_2, \ldots, \chi_n$ be a random sample from $\mathrm{N}(\mathbf{x} : \boldsymbol{\mu}, \boldsymbol{\Sigma})$. *Define $\hat{\boldsymbol{\mu}}$ by $\bar{\chi}$ and $\hat{\boldsymbol{\Sigma}}$ by $(1/(n-1))\sum(\chi_i - \bar{\chi})(\chi_i - \bar{\chi})' = (1/(n-1))\mathscr{A}$. Then*

(1) $\hat{\boldsymbol{\mu}}, \hat{\boldsymbol{\Sigma}}$ *are complete sufficient statistics*;

(2) $\hat{\boldsymbol{\mu}}$ *is distributed* $\mathrm{N}(\hat{\boldsymbol{\mu}} : \boldsymbol{\mu}, (1/n)\boldsymbol{\Sigma})$;

(3) $\hat{\boldsymbol{\mu}}$ *and* $\hat{\boldsymbol{\Sigma}}$ *are independent*;

(4) $U = \mathbf{c}'\mathscr{A}\mathbf{c}/\mathbf{c}'\boldsymbol{\Sigma}\mathbf{c}$ *is distributed* $\chi^2(u : n-1, 0)$ *for any constant nonzero $K \times 1$ vector* $\mathbf{c}$;

(5) $\hat{\boldsymbol{\Sigma}}$ *is an unbiased estimator of* $\boldsymbol{\Sigma}$.

Proof

To prove that $\hat{\boldsymbol{\mu}}$ and $\hat{\boldsymbol{\Sigma}}$ are sufficient statistics, we use the factorization criterion given in Theorem 2.6.1. The p.d.f. of $X_{11}, X_{21}, \ldots, X_{nK}$ is the product of the p.d.f.'s of $\chi_1, \chi_2, \ldots, \chi_n$. We get

$$\begin{aligned} f &= \prod_{i=1}^{n} f_{\chi_i}(\mathbf{x}_i : \boldsymbol{\mu}, \boldsymbol{\Sigma}) \\ &= (2\pi)^{-nK/2}|\boldsymbol{\Sigma}|^{-n/2}\exp\left(-\tfrac{1}{2}\sum_{i=1}^{n}(\mathbf{x}_i - \boldsymbol{\mu})'\boldsymbol{\Sigma}^{-1}(\mathbf{x}_i - \boldsymbol{\mu})\right) \end{aligned}$$

and by Equation (9.3.3) this can be written as

$$f = (2\pi)^{-nK/2}|\mathbf{\Sigma}|^{-n/2}$$
$$\times \exp\left\{-\tfrac{1}{2}\left(\sum_{i=1}^{n} (\mathbf{x}_i - \bar{\mathbf{x}})'\mathbf{\Sigma}^{-1}(\mathbf{x}_i - \bar{\mathbf{x}}) + n(\bar{\mathbf{x}} - \boldsymbol{\mu})'\mathbf{\Sigma}^{-1}(\bar{\mathbf{x}} - \boldsymbol{\mu})\right)\right\}$$
$$= (2\pi)^{-nK/2}|\mathbf{\Sigma}|^{-n/2} \exp(-\tfrac{1}{2})\{\text{tr}[\mathbf{A}\mathbf{\Sigma}^{-1}] + n(\bar{\mathbf{x}} - \boldsymbol{\mu})'\mathbf{\Sigma}^{-1}(\bar{\mathbf{x}} - \boldsymbol{\mu})\}$$

By Theorem 2.6.1 we get for the $S_1, S_2, \ldots, S_r$, the quantities a_{ij} in $\mathbf{A}$ and $\bar{x}_i$ in $\bar{\mathbf{x}}$; in other words $S_1, S_2, \ldots, S_r$ are identified as $a_{11}, a_{12}, \ldots, a_{KK}, \bar{x}_1, \bar{x}_2, \ldots, \bar{x}_K$. The elements in $\boldsymbol{\theta}$ are identified as $\sigma_{11}, \sigma_{12}, \ldots, \sigma_{KK}, \mu_1, \mu_2, \ldots, \mu_K$. Thus

$$g(S_1, S_2, \ldots, S_r : \boldsymbol{\theta})$$
$$= |\mathbf{\Sigma}|^{-n/2} \exp(-\tfrac{1}{2})\{\text{tr}[\mathbf{A}\mathbf{\Sigma}^{-1}] + n(\bar{\mathbf{x}} - \boldsymbol{\mu})'\mathbf{\Sigma}^{-1}(\bar{\mathbf{x}} - \boldsymbol{\mu})\}$$

and for the function $h(\mathbf{y})$ in Theorem 2.6.1 we use $(2\pi)^{-nK/2}$. Thus $\mathscr{A}$ and $\bar{\boldsymbol{\chi}}$ (or $\hat{\mathbf{\Sigma}}$ and $\hat{\boldsymbol{\mu}}$) are sufficient statistics. We will not prove that they are also complete, but Theorem 2.7.8 can be used. This proves (1).

To prove (2) we note that we can write $\hat{\boldsymbol{\mu}} = \bar{\boldsymbol{\chi}} = (1/n)\sum_{i=1}^{n} \boldsymbol{\chi}_i = (1/n)[\mathbf{I}, \mathbf{I}, \ldots, \mathbf{I}]\boldsymbol{\chi}_0 = \mathbf{B}\boldsymbol{\chi}_0$, say, where $\boldsymbol{\chi}_0 = [\boldsymbol{\chi}_1', \boldsymbol{\chi}_2', \ldots, \boldsymbol{\chi}_n']'$. Since the $\boldsymbol{\chi}_i$ are independent, the p.d.f. of $\boldsymbol{\chi}_0$ is

$$f_{\chi_0}(\mathbf{x}_0) = \prod_{i=1}^{n} \mathbf{n}(\mathbf{x}_i : \boldsymbol{\mu}, \mathbf{\Sigma})$$
$$= (2\pi)^{-nK/2}|\mathbf{\Sigma}|^{-n/2} \exp\left[-\tfrac{1}{2}\sum_{i=1}^{n} (\mathbf{x}_i - \boldsymbol{\mu})'\mathbf{\Sigma}^{-1}(\mathbf{x}_i - \boldsymbol{\mu})\right]$$

which we can write as $(2\pi)^{-nK/2}|\mathbf{\Sigma}_D|^{-1/2} \exp[-\tfrac{1}{2}(\mathbf{x}_0 - \boldsymbol{\mu}_0)'\mathbf{\Sigma}_D^{-1}(\mathbf{x}_0 - \boldsymbol{\mu}_0)]$, where

$$\boldsymbol{\mu}_0 = \begin{bmatrix} \boldsymbol{\mu} \\ \boldsymbol{\mu} \\ \vdots \\ \boldsymbol{\mu} \end{bmatrix} \qquad \mathbf{\Sigma}_D = \begin{bmatrix} \mathbf{\Sigma} & \mathbf{0} & \cdots & \mathbf{0} \\ \mathbf{0} & \mathbf{\Sigma} & \cdots & \mathbf{0} \\ \vdots & \vdots & & \vdots \\ \mathbf{0} & \mathbf{0} & \cdots & \mathbf{\Sigma} \end{bmatrix} \qquad \mathbf{x}_0 = \begin{bmatrix} \mathbf{x}_1 \\ \mathbf{x}_2 \\ \vdots \\ \mathbf{x}_n \end{bmatrix} \tag{9.3.5}$$

Note that $\mathbf{\Sigma}_D$ has size $nK \times nK$. Here $\bar{\boldsymbol{\chi}} = \hat{\boldsymbol{\mu}}$ is distributed $\mathbf{N}(\bar{\mathbf{x}} : \mathbf{B}\boldsymbol{\mu}_0, \mathbf{B}\mathbf{\Sigma}_D\mathbf{B}')$, but $\mathbf{B}\boldsymbol{\mu}_0 = \boldsymbol{\mu}$ and $\mathbf{B}\mathbf{\Sigma}_D\mathbf{B}' = (1/n)\mathbf{\Sigma}$; this proves (2).

To prove (3) we define the vector

$$\mathbf{Z}_0 = \begin{bmatrix} \mathbf{Z}_1 \\ \bar{\boldsymbol{\chi}} \end{bmatrix}$$

where $\mathbf{Z}_0$ can be written as

$$\mathbf{Z}_0 = \mathbf{G}_0\chi_0 = \begin{bmatrix}\mathbf{G}\\ \mathbf{B}\end{bmatrix}\chi_0 = \begin{bmatrix}\mathbf{Z}_1\\ \bar{\chi}\end{bmatrix}$$

$\mathbf{B}$ is defined above, and $\mathbf{Z}_1$ and $\mathbf{G}$ are defined below.

$$\mathbf{Z}_1 = \begin{bmatrix}\chi_1 - \bar{\chi}\\ \chi_2 - \bar{\chi}\\ \vdots\\ \chi_n - \bar{\chi}\end{bmatrix} = \begin{bmatrix}\mathbf{I} - \left(\frac{1}{n}\right)\mathbf{I} & -\left(\frac{1}{n}\right)\mathbf{I} & \cdots & -\left(\frac{1}{n}\right)\mathbf{I}\\ -\left(\frac{1}{n}\right)\mathbf{I} & \mathbf{I} - \left(\frac{1}{n}\right)\mathbf{I} & \cdots & -\left(\frac{1}{n}\right)\mathbf{I}\\ \vdots & \vdots & & \vdots\\ -\left(\frac{1}{n}\right)\mathbf{I} & -\left(\frac{1}{n}\right)\mathbf{I} & \cdots & \mathbf{I} - \left(\frac{1}{n}\right)\mathbf{I}\end{bmatrix}\begin{bmatrix}\chi_1\\ \chi_2\\ \vdots\\ \chi_n\end{bmatrix} = \mathbf{G}\chi_0$$

So $\mathbf{Z}_1$ is distributed $\mathbf{N}(\mathbf{z}_1 : \mathbf{G}\boldsymbol{\mu}_0, \mathbf{G}\boldsymbol{\Sigma}_D\mathbf{G}')$, but $\mathbf{G}\boldsymbol{\mu}_0 = \mathbf{0}$ and $\mathbf{G}\boldsymbol{\Sigma}_D\mathbf{G}' = \boldsymbol{\Sigma}_D - (1/n)\boldsymbol{\Sigma}_\mathbf{J}$, where $\boldsymbol{\Sigma}_\mathbf{J}$ is defined by

$$\boldsymbol{\Sigma}_\mathbf{J} = \begin{bmatrix}\boldsymbol{\Sigma} & \boldsymbol{\Sigma} & \cdots & \boldsymbol{\Sigma}\\ \boldsymbol{\Sigma} & \boldsymbol{\Sigma} & \cdots & \boldsymbol{\Sigma}\\ \vdots & \vdots & & \vdots\\ \boldsymbol{\Sigma} & \boldsymbol{\Sigma} & \cdots & \boldsymbol{\Sigma}\end{bmatrix}$$

By Theorem 3.3.5, $\mathbf{Z}_0$ is distributed $\mathbf{N}(\mathbf{z}_0 : \mathbf{G}_0\boldsymbol{\mu}_0, \mathbf{G}_0\boldsymbol{\Sigma}_D\mathbf{G}_0')$. If we can show $\mathbf{cov}[\bar{\chi}, \mathbf{Z}_1] = \mathbf{0}$, this will imply that $\mathbf{Z}_1$ and $\bar{\chi}$ are independent, which in turn will imply that $\bar{\chi}$ is independent of any function of the elements $\chi_i - \bar{\chi}$ in $\mathbf{Z}_1$. Since

$$\hat{\boldsymbol{\Sigma}} = \left(\frac{1}{n-1}\right)\mathscr{A} = \left(\frac{1}{n-1}\right)\sum_{i=1}^{n}(\chi_i - \bar{\chi})(\chi_i - \bar{\chi})'$$

$\bar{\chi}$ will be independent of $\hat{\boldsymbol{\Sigma}}$, and this will prove (3).

To show $\mathbf{cov}[\bar{\chi}, \mathbf{Z}_1] = \mathbf{0}$, we get (since $\mathscr{E}[\mathbf{Z}_1] = \mathbf{0}$),

$$\begin{aligned}\mathbf{cov}[\bar{\chi}, \mathbf{Z}_1] &= \mathscr{E}[\bar{\chi}\mathbf{Z}_1'] = \mathscr{E}[\mathbf{B}\chi_0\chi_0'\mathbf{G}'] = \mathbf{B}(\mathscr{E}[\chi_0\chi_0'])\mathbf{G}'\\ &= \mathbf{B}(\boldsymbol{\mu}_0\boldsymbol{\mu}_0' + \boldsymbol{\Sigma}_D)\mathbf{G}' = \mathbf{B}\boldsymbol{\Sigma}_D\mathbf{G}'\end{aligned}$$

But $\mathbf{B\Sigma}_D\mathbf{G}'$ is equal to

$$\mathbf{B\Sigma}_D\mathbf{G}' = \left(\frac{1}{n}\right)[\mathbf{I},\mathbf{I},\ldots,\mathbf{I}]\begin{bmatrix} \mathbf{\Sigma} & \mathbf{0} & \cdots & \mathbf{0} \\ \mathbf{0} & \mathbf{\Sigma} & \cdots & \mathbf{0} \\ \vdots & \vdots & & \vdots \\ \mathbf{0} & \mathbf{0} & \cdots & \mathbf{\Sigma} \end{bmatrix}$$

$$\times \begin{bmatrix} \mathbf{I} - \left(\frac{1}{n}\right)\mathbf{I} & -\left(\frac{1}{n}\right)\mathbf{I} & \cdots & -\left(\frac{1}{n}\right)\mathbf{I} \\ -\left(\frac{1}{n}\right)\mathbf{I} & \mathbf{I} - \left(\frac{1}{n}\right)\mathbf{I} & \cdots & -\left(\frac{1}{n}\right)\mathbf{I} \\ \vdots & \vdots & & \vdots \\ -\left(\frac{1}{n}\right)\mathbf{I} & -\left(\frac{1}{n}\right)\mathbf{I} & \cdots & \mathbf{I} - \left(\frac{1}{n}\right)\mathbf{I} \end{bmatrix}$$

which is clearly equal to $\mathbf{0}$. So (3) is proved.

To prove (4) we note

$$\begin{aligned} \mathbf{c}'\mathscr{A}\mathbf{c} &= \mathbf{c}'\left[\sum_{i=1}^{n} (\chi_i - \bar{\chi})(\chi_i - \bar{\chi})'\right]\mathbf{c} \\ &= \sum_{i=1}^{n} [\mathbf{c}'(\chi_i - \bar{\chi})][(\chi_i - \bar{\chi})'\mathbf{c}] = \sum_{i=1}^{n} Y_i^2 \end{aligned}$$

where $Y_i = \mathbf{c}'(\chi_i - \bar{\chi})$ and $i = 1, 2, \ldots, n$. Define $\mathbf{Y}' = [Y_1, Y_2, \ldots, Y_n]$ and

$$\mathbf{C} = \begin{bmatrix} \mathbf{c}' & \mathbf{0} & \cdots & \mathbf{0} \\ \mathbf{0} & \mathbf{c}' & \cdots & \mathbf{0} \\ \vdots & \vdots & & \vdots \\ \mathbf{0} & \mathbf{0} & \cdots & \mathbf{c}' \end{bmatrix}$$

Thus $\mathbf{Y} = \mathbf{CZ}_1 = \mathbf{CG}\chi_0$, so $\mathbf{Y}$ is distributed $N(\mathbf{y}:\mathbf{0},\mathbf{\Sigma}_0)$, where $\mathbf{\Sigma}_0 = \mathbf{CG\Sigma}_D\mathbf{G}'\mathbf{C}'$, which by simple multiplication can be shown to be equal to $\mathbf{c}'\mathbf{\Sigma}\mathbf{c}(\mathbf{I} - (1/n)\mathbf{J})$. Define $\mathbf{Y}_0$ by

$$\mathbf{Y}_0 = \left(\frac{1}{\sqrt{\mathbf{c}'\mathbf{\Sigma}\mathbf{c}}}\right)\mathbf{Y}$$

$\mathbf{Y}_0$ is distributed $N(\mathbf{y}_0:\mathbf{0},\mathbf{I} - (1/n)\mathbf{J})$, and by (1) of Theorem 4.4.3,

$U = \mathbf{Y}_0'\mathbf{Y}_0$ is distributed $\chi^2(u : n - 1; 0)$; but

$$\mathbf{Y}_0'\mathbf{Y}_0 = \frac{\mathbf{Y}'\mathbf{Y}}{\mathbf{c}'\boldsymbol{\Sigma}\mathbf{c}} = \frac{\mathbf{c}'\left[\sum_{i=1}^{n} (\boldsymbol{\chi}_i - \bar{\boldsymbol{\chi}})(\boldsymbol{\chi}_i - \bar{\boldsymbol{\chi}})'\right]\mathbf{c}}{\mathbf{c}'\boldsymbol{\Sigma}\mathbf{c}} = \frac{\mathbf{c}'\mathscr{A}\mathbf{c}}{\mathbf{c}'\boldsymbol{\Sigma}\mathbf{c}}$$

and this proves (4).

Note 1. The distribution of $\mathbf{c}'\mathscr{A}\mathbf{c}/\mathbf{c}'\boldsymbol{\Sigma}\mathbf{c}$ does not depend on $\mathbf{c}$.

The proof of (5), that $\hat{\boldsymbol{\Sigma}}$ is an unbiased estimator of $\boldsymbol{\Sigma}$, will be left for the reader and asked for in the problems.

We could derive the joint distribution of the elements in $\hat{\boldsymbol{\Sigma}}$ (or in $\mathscr{A}$), but we will not make much use of this distribution in this book. However, for further reference we define it here.

DEFINITION 9.3.1

Wishart Distribution. *Let the $K \times 1$ random vectors $\boldsymbol{\chi}_1, \boldsymbol{\chi}_2, \ldots, \boldsymbol{\chi}_n$ $(n > K)$ be independent and each distributed $\mathbf{N}(\mathbf{x} : \boldsymbol{\mu}, \boldsymbol{\Sigma})$. Define $\mathscr{V}$ by $\mathscr{V} = \sum_{i=1}^{n} \boldsymbol{\chi}_i\boldsymbol{\chi}_i'$. Then $\mathscr{V}$ is defined to be a K-variate Wishart matrix with n degrees of freedom, covariance matrix $\boldsymbol{\Sigma}$, and noncentrality $\lambda = \frac{1}{2}\boldsymbol{\mu}'\boldsymbol{\Sigma}^{-1}\boldsymbol{\mu}$. We denote the joint distribution of the elements of $\mathscr{V}$ by $\mathbf{W}_K(\mathbf{V} : n; \boldsymbol{\Sigma}, \lambda)$, and call it the Wishart distribution. If $\lambda = 0$, $\mathscr{V}$ is defined to be a central Wishart matrix and the p.d.f. is denoted by $\mathbf{W}_K(\mathbf{V} : n; \boldsymbol{\Sigma}, 0)$, or more simply by $\mathbf{W}_K(\mathbf{V} : n; \boldsymbol{\Sigma})$; if $\lambda \neq 0$, $\mathscr{V}$ is defined to be a noncentral Wishart matrix.*

Note 2. Since $\boldsymbol{\Sigma}$ is positive definite, $\lambda = 0$ if and only if $\boldsymbol{\mu} = \mathbf{0}$.

The functional form of the Wishart p.d.f. will not be derived or used in this book. The interested reader can consult [A-3]. However, the m.g.f. of the central Wishart p.d.f. will be derived here.

THEOREM 9.3.3

Let the $K \times 1$ vectors $\boldsymbol{\chi}_1, \boldsymbol{\chi}_2, \ldots, \boldsymbol{\chi}_n$ be a random sample of size $n > K$ from the p.d.f. $\mathbf{N}(\mathbf{x} : \mathbf{0}, \boldsymbol{\Sigma})$, where $\boldsymbol{\Sigma}$ has rank K. Define $\mathscr{V}$ by $\mathscr{V} = \sum_{i=1}^{n} \boldsymbol{\chi}_i\boldsymbol{\chi}_i'$. Let $\mathbf{T}$ be a $K \times K$ symmetric matrix of real variables, with diagonal elements t_{ii} and off-diagonal elements t_{ij} such that $\mathbf{I} - 2\boldsymbol{\Sigma}\mathbf{T}$ is p.d. for all t_{ij} that satisfy $-h < t_{ij} < h$ for some positive number h. The m.g.f. of $\mathscr{V}$ is

$$m_{\mathscr{V}}(\mathbf{T}) = |\mathbf{I} - 2\boldsymbol{\Sigma}\mathbf{T}|^{-n/2}$$

and hence this is the m.g.f. of the p.d.f. $\mathbf{W}_K(\mathbf{V} : n; \boldsymbol{\Sigma})$.

Proof

By definition the m.g.f. (if it exists) of $\mathscr{V}$ is the joint m.g.f. of the elements of $\mathscr{V}$, which we shall denote by V_{ij}. Since $V_{ij} = V_{ji}$, the joint m.g.f. of the elements of $\mathscr{V}$ is the m.g.f. of $V_{11}, V_{22}, \ldots, 2V_{12}, \ldots, 2V_{K-1,K}$. The m.g.f. is thus defined by

$$\mathscr{E}\left[\exp\left\{\sum_{i=1}^{K}\sum_{j=1}^{K} t_{ij}V_{ij}\right\}\right]$$

if this exists for all t_{ij} such that $-h < t_{ij} < h$ for some $h > 0$. To simplify notation we define a $K \times K$ symmetric matrix $\mathbf{T}$ of real numbers by $\mathbf{T} = [t_{ij}]$ and write

$$\sum_{i=1}^{K}\sum_{j=1}^{K} t_{ij}V_{ij} = \text{tr}[\mathbf{T}\mathscr{V}] = \text{tr}[\mathscr{V}\mathbf{T}]$$

From $\mathscr{V} = \sum_{i=1}^{n} \boldsymbol{\chi}_i\boldsymbol{\chi}_i'$ we get

$$\begin{aligned}\text{tr}[\mathbf{T}\mathscr{V}] &= \text{tr}\left[\mathbf{T}\sum_{i=1}^{n} \boldsymbol{\chi}_i\boldsymbol{\chi}_i'\right] = \sum_{i=1}^{n} \text{tr}[\mathbf{T}\boldsymbol{\chi}_i\boldsymbol{\chi}_i'] = \sum_{i=1}^{n} \text{tr}[\boldsymbol{\chi}_i'\mathbf{T}\boldsymbol{\chi}_i] \\ &= \sum_{i=1}^{n} \boldsymbol{\chi}_i'\mathbf{T}\boldsymbol{\chi}_i\end{aligned}$$

since $\boldsymbol{\chi}_i'\mathbf{T}\boldsymbol{\chi}_i$ is a scalar. Thus

$$\begin{aligned}m_{\mathscr{V}}(\mathbf{T}) &= \mathscr{E}[e^{\text{tr}[\mathscr{V}\mathbf{T}]}] = \mathscr{E}\left[\exp\left(\sum_{i=1}^{n} \boldsymbol{\chi}_i'\mathbf{T}\boldsymbol{\chi}_i\right)\right] \\ &= \int_{-\infty}^{\infty}\cdots\int_{-\infty}^{\infty} (2\pi)^{-nK/2}|\boldsymbol{\Sigma}|^{-n/2} \\ &\quad \times \exp\left\{-\tfrac{1}{2}\sum_{i=1}^{n} \mathbf{x}_i'\boldsymbol{\Sigma}^{-1}\mathbf{x}_i + \sum_{i=1}^{n} \mathbf{x}_i'\mathbf{T}\mathbf{x}_i\right\} d\mathbf{x}_1\, d\mathbf{x}_2 \cdots d\mathbf{x}_n \\ &= \int_{-\infty}^{\infty}\cdots\int_{-\infty}^{\infty} (2\pi)^{-nK/2}|\boldsymbol{\Sigma}|^{-n/2} \\ &\quad \times \exp\left\{-\tfrac{1}{2}\sum_{i=1}^{n} \mathbf{x}_i'(\boldsymbol{\Sigma}^{-1} - 2\mathbf{T})\mathbf{x}_i\right\} d\mathbf{x}_1\, d\mathbf{x}_2 \cdots d\mathbf{x}_n\end{aligned}$$

By Theorem 1.10.1 this integral exists since $\boldsymbol{\Sigma}^{-1} - 2\mathbf{T}$ is positive definite for all values of t_{ij} that satisfy $-h < t_{ij} < h$ for a small enough positive h. Under these conditions the value of the integral is equal to

$$|\boldsymbol{\Sigma}|^{-n/2}|\boldsymbol{\Sigma}^{-1} - 2\mathbf{T}|^{-n/2} = |\mathbf{I} - 2\boldsymbol{\Sigma}\mathbf{T}|^{-n/2}$$

and the theorem is proved.

COROLLARY 9.3.3

In Theorem 9.3.3 let the matrix $\mathcal{V}^*$ be defined by $\mathcal{V}^* = \mathbf{P}'\mathcal{V}\mathbf{P}$, where $\mathbf{P}$ is a $K \times K$ nonsingular matrix of constants. The matrix $\mathcal{V}^*$ is distributed $\mathbf{W}_K(\mathbf{V}^* : n; \mathbf{P}'\boldsymbol{\Sigma}\mathbf{P})$.

THEOREM 9.3.4

Let $t(\boldsymbol{\mu}, \boldsymbol{\Sigma})$ be any known function of μ_i and σ_{ij} for which an unbiased estimator exists. Then there exists an UMVU estimator of $t(\boldsymbol{\mu}, \boldsymbol{\Sigma})$, and this UMVU estimator is a function of $\hat{\boldsymbol{\mu}}$ and $\hat{\boldsymbol{\Sigma}}$. In particular, $\hat{\boldsymbol{\mu}}$ and $\hat{\boldsymbol{\Sigma}}$ are UMVU estimators of $\boldsymbol{\mu}$ and $\boldsymbol{\Sigma}$, respectively.

Proof

Since the statistics $\hat{\boldsymbol{\mu}}$, $\hat{\boldsymbol{\Sigma}}$ are complete sufficient statistics, the result follows from Theorem 2.7.7.

Example 9.3.1

The UMVU estimator of $\boldsymbol{\ell}'\boldsymbol{\mu}$ for any known $K \times 1$ constant vector $\boldsymbol{\ell}$ is $\boldsymbol{\ell}'\hat{\boldsymbol{\mu}}$.

Example 9.3.2

The UMVU estimator of μ_i is $\bar{X}_i$.

Example 9.3.3

The UMVU estimator of $\sum_{i=1}^n \sum_{j=1}^n \ell_{ij}\sigma_{ij}$ is $\sum_{i=1}^n \sum_{j=1}^n \ell_{ij}\hat{\sigma}_{ij}$ for any constants ℓ_{ij}.

Note 3. If the $\mathcal{V}_i$ have a p.d.f. $\mathbf{W}_K(\mathbf{V}_i : n_i; \Sigma)$ and are independent for $i = 1, 2, \ldots, q$, then $\mathcal{V} = \sum_{i=1}^q \mathcal{V}_i$ has a p.d.f. $\mathbf{W}_K(\mathbf{V} : n; \Sigma)$, where $n = \sum_{i=1}^q n_i$.

THEOREM 9.3.5

For each $n = K + 1, K + 2, \ldots$, let the $K \times 1$ vectors $\boldsymbol{\chi}_1, \boldsymbol{\chi}_2, \ldots, \boldsymbol{\chi}_n$ be a random sample of size n from the distribution $\mathbf{N}(\mathbf{x} : \boldsymbol{\mu}, \boldsymbol{\Sigma})$. Let $\boldsymbol{\ell}$ be any $K \times 1$ vector of constants. Then $\boldsymbol{\ell}'\hat{\boldsymbol{\mu}}_n$ is a mean-squared-error consistent and simple consistent estimator of $\boldsymbol{\ell}'\boldsymbol{\mu}$, where $\hat{\boldsymbol{\mu}}_n = n^{-1}\sum_{i=1}^n \boldsymbol{\chi}_i$.

Proof

We shall prove that $\boldsymbol{\ell}'\hat{\boldsymbol{\mu}}_n$ is a mean-squared-error consistent estimator of $\boldsymbol{\ell}'\boldsymbol{\mu}$, and by Corollary 2.7.9 it will follow that it is also a simple consistent estimator. We have a sequence of estimators, denoted by $\boldsymbol{\ell}'\hat{\boldsymbol{\mu}}_1, \boldsymbol{\ell}'\hat{\boldsymbol{\mu}}_2, \ldots$, where we define $\boldsymbol{\ell}'\hat{\boldsymbol{\mu}}_n = \boldsymbol{\ell}'\bar{\boldsymbol{\chi}}_n$ and where $\bar{\boldsymbol{\chi}}_n = (1/n)\sum_{i=1}^n \bar{\boldsymbol{\chi}}_i$ is based on a sample of size n. Also, by Theorem 9.3.2, $\text{var}[\boldsymbol{\ell}'\hat{\boldsymbol{\mu}}_n] =$

$(1/n)(\ell'\Sigma\ell)$. To show that an estimator is mean-squared-error consistent, we must show

$$\lim_{n\to\infty} \{\mathscr{E}[\ell'\hat{\boldsymbol{\mu}}_n]\} = \ell'\boldsymbol{\mu} \qquad \text{and} \qquad \lim_{n\to\infty} \{\text{var}[\ell'\hat{\boldsymbol{\mu}}_n]\} = 0$$

Since $\mathscr{E}[\ell'\hat{\boldsymbol{\mu}}_n] = \ell'\boldsymbol{\mu}$ for $n = K+1, K+2, \ldots,$ then clearly $\lim_{n\to\infty}\{\mathscr{E}[\ell'\hat{\boldsymbol{\mu}}_n]\} = \ell'\boldsymbol{\mu}$, and $\lim_{n\to\infty} \text{var}[\ell'\hat{\boldsymbol{\mu}}_n] = \lim_{n\to\infty}(1/n)(\ell'\Sigma\ell) = 0$, so $\ell'\hat{\boldsymbol{\mu}}$ is a mean-squared-error (and a simple) consistent estimator of $\ell'\boldsymbol{\mu}$. This proves the theorem.

THEOREM 9.3.6

Under the conditions of Theorem 9.3.5, $\ell'\hat{\Sigma}_n\ell$ is a mean-squared-error and simple consistent estimator of $\ell'\Sigma\ell$, where $\hat{\Sigma}_n = (n-1)^{-1}\sum_{i=1}^{n}(\mathfrak{X}_i - \bar{\mathfrak{X}}_n)(\mathfrak{X}_i - \bar{\mathfrak{X}}_n)'$.

Proof

By Theorem 9.3.2 part (4), the random variable $U = (\ell'\mathscr{A}\ell)/(\ell'\Sigma\ell)$ is distributed $\chi^2(u : n-1)$. Thus

$$2(n-1) = \text{var}[U] = \text{var}\left[\frac{\ell'\mathscr{A}\ell}{\ell'\Sigma\ell}\right] = \text{var}\left[\frac{\ell'(n-1)\hat{\Sigma}\ell}{\ell'\Sigma\ell}\right]$$
$$= (n-1)^2\,\text{var}\left[\frac{\ell'\hat{\Sigma}\ell}{\ell'\Sigma\ell}\right]$$

So

$$\text{var}[\ell'\hat{\Sigma}\ell] = \frac{2(n-1)}{(n-1)^2}(\ell'\Sigma\ell)^2$$

and

$$\lim_{n\to\infty} \text{var}[\ell'\hat{\Sigma}_n\ell] = \lim_{n\to\infty}\frac{(\ell'\Sigma\ell)^2}{(n-1)/2} = 0$$

Also, $\mathscr{E}[\ell'\hat{\Sigma}_n\ell] = \ell'\Sigma\ell$, so $\ell'\hat{\Sigma}_n\ell$ is a mean-squared-error and simple consistent estimator of $\ell'\Sigma\ell$.

9.4 Test of the Hypothesis $H_0 : \boldsymbol{\mu} = \mathbf{h}_0$

First we derive a test of $H_0 : \boldsymbol{\mu} = \mathbf{h}_0$ ($\mathbf{h}_0$ known), and then we generalize this slightly to a test of $H_0 : \mathbf{H}\boldsymbol{\mu} = \mathbf{h}$. Recall that throughout this chapter we assume $K < n$.

THEOREM 9.4.1

Let the $K \times 1$ vectors $\boldsymbol{\chi}_1, \boldsymbol{\chi}_2, \ldots, \boldsymbol{\chi}_n$ be a random sample from the K-variate normal distribution $\mathbf{N}(\mathbf{x} : \boldsymbol{\mu}, \boldsymbol{\Sigma})$, where $\boldsymbol{\Sigma}$ is positive definite. A likelihood ratio test statistic of $H_0 : \boldsymbol{\mu} = \mathbf{h}_0$ vs. $H_a : \boldsymbol{\mu} \neq \mathbf{h}_0$ ($\mathbf{h}_0$ is known) is

$$W = \left[\frac{n(n-K)}{K}\right](\bar{\boldsymbol{\chi}} - \mathbf{h}_0)' \mathscr{A}^{-1}(\bar{\boldsymbol{\chi}} - \mathbf{h}_0) \tag{9.4.1}$$

A size α test is this: Reject H_0 if and only if $w \geq F_{\alpha:K,n-K}$. The power of the test is

$$\Pi(\lambda) = \int_{F_{\alpha:K,n-K}}^{\infty} F(w : K, n-K; \lambda)\, dw \qquad \text{where } \lambda = \tfrac{1}{2}n(\boldsymbol{\mu} - \mathbf{h}_0)'\boldsymbol{\Sigma}^{-1}(\boldsymbol{\mu} - \mathbf{h}_0) \tag{9.4.2}$$

and W is distributed $F(w : K, n-K; \lambda)$.

Before we present a proof of this theorem we make a couple of remarks.

Note 1. This hypothesis is a multivariate analogue of the hypothesis about the mean μ of a univariate normal distribution, and we would expect the test statistic to reduce to Student's t (actually to the square of Student's t since W in Equation (9.4.1) is distributed as Snedecor's F). If we set $K = 1$, $\boldsymbol{\chi}_i = X_i$, and $\mathbf{h}_0 = h_0$, then W in Equation (9.4.1) is $W = n(\bar{X} - h_0)^2/\hat{\sigma}^2$, which is the square of a Student's t statistic.

Note 2. The statistic $T^2 = n(\bar{\boldsymbol{\chi}} - \mathbf{h}_0)'\hat{\boldsymbol{\Sigma}}^{-1}(\bar{\boldsymbol{\chi}} - \mathbf{h}_0)$ is called Hotelling's T^2 since he proposed it and derived its distribution [A-3]. This can be viewed as a multivariate analogue of the square of Student's t, and W in Equation (9.4.1) is related to T^2 by $W = T^2(n-K)/K(n-1)$.

Proof

The generalized likelihood ratio statistic is

$$v = v(\mathbf{X}) = \frac{\max_{\omega}[L(\boldsymbol{\mu}, \boldsymbol{\Sigma} : \mathbf{x}_1, \mathbf{x}_2, \ldots, \mathbf{x}_n)]}{\max_{\Omega}[L(\boldsymbol{\mu}, \boldsymbol{\Sigma} : \mathbf{x}_1, \mathbf{x}_2, \ldots, \mathbf{x}_n)]} = \frac{L(\tilde{\omega})}{L(\tilde{\Omega})}$$

We shall derive $v(\mathbf{X})$ and the distribution of $V = v(\mathscr{X})$ (actually we derive the p.d.f. of a convenient function of V).

The likelihood of the sample is

$$\begin{aligned} L &= L(\boldsymbol{\mu}, \boldsymbol{\Sigma} : \mathbf{x}_1, \mathbf{x}_2, \ldots, \mathbf{x}_n) \\ &= (2\pi)^{-Kn/2}|\boldsymbol{\Sigma}|^{-n/2} \exp\left[-\tfrac{1}{2}\sum_{i=1}^{n}(\mathbf{x}_i - \boldsymbol{\mu})'\boldsymbol{\Sigma}^{-1}(\mathbf{x}_i - \boldsymbol{\mu})\right] \end{aligned}$$

where $\Omega = \{(\boldsymbol{\mu}, \boldsymbol{\Sigma}) : \boldsymbol{\mu} \in E_K,\ \boldsymbol{\Sigma}$ is positive definite$\}$. The maximum likelihood estimates $\tilde{\boldsymbol{\mu}}$ and $\tilde{\boldsymbol{\Sigma}}$ were derived in Section 9.3 and are $\tilde{\boldsymbol{\mu}} = \bar{\mathbf{x}}, \tilde{\boldsymbol{\Sigma}} = (1/n)\mathbf{A}$. Thus

$$L(\tilde{\Omega}) = (2\pi)^{-Kn/2}\left|\left(\frac{1}{n}\right)\mathbf{A}\right|^{-n/2} \exp\left[-\tfrac{1}{2}\sum_{i=1}^{n}(\mathbf{x}_i - \bar{\mathbf{x}})'\left(\left(\frac{1}{n}\right)\mathbf{A}\right)^{-1}(\mathbf{x}_i - \bar{\mathbf{x}})\right]$$

The quantity in the exponent is a scalar and equal to its trace; so the exponent is

$$-\frac{1}{2}\sum_{i=1}^{n}(\mathbf{x}_i - \bar{\mathbf{x}})'\left(\left(\frac{1}{n}\right)\mathbf{A}\right)^{-1}(\mathbf{x}_i - \bar{\mathbf{x}}) = -\frac{1}{2}\operatorname{tr}\left[\mathbf{A}\left(\left(\frac{1}{n}\right)\mathbf{A}\right)^{-1}\right] = -\frac{nK}{2}$$

and

$$L(\tilde{\Omega}) = (2\pi)^{-nK/2} n^{nK/2} |\mathbf{A}|^{-n/2} e^{-nK/2}$$

Since $\omega = \{(\boldsymbol{\mu}, \boldsymbol{\Sigma}) : \boldsymbol{\mu} = \mathbf{h}_0,\ \boldsymbol{\Sigma}$ is positive definite$\}$, we must find the value of $\boldsymbol{\Sigma}$ that maximizes the function

$$L(\boldsymbol{\Sigma} : \mathbf{x}_1, \mathbf{x}_2, \ldots, \mathbf{x}_n) = (2\pi)^{-Kn/2}|\boldsymbol{\Sigma}|^{-1/2} \exp\left[-\tfrac{1}{2}\sum_{i=1}^{n}(\mathbf{x}_i - \mathbf{h}_0)'\boldsymbol{\Sigma}^{-1}(\mathbf{x}_i - \mathbf{h}_0)\right]$$

This is identical to L_1 in Equation (9.3.4) with $\bar{\mathbf{x}}$ replaced by $\mathbf{h}_0$, and the maximum likelihood estimate of $\boldsymbol{\Sigma}$, which we shall denote by $\tilde{\boldsymbol{\Sigma}}_\omega$, is $(1/n)\mathbf{A}_\omega = (1/n)\sum(\mathbf{x}_i - \mathbf{h}_0)(\mathbf{x}_i - \mathbf{h}_0)'$. By the procedure used to find $L(\tilde{\Omega})$, we get

$$L(\tilde{\omega}) = (2\pi)^{-Kn/2} n^{Kn/2} |\mathbf{A}_\omega|^{-n/2} e^{-Kn/2}$$

and the generalized likelihood ratio statistic V is

$$V = \frac{(2\pi)^{-Kn/2} n^{Kn/2} |\mathscr{A}_\omega|^{-n/2} e^{-nK/2}}{(2\pi)^{-Kn/2} n^{Kn/2} |\mathscr{A}|^{-n/2} e^{-nK/2}} = \left(\frac{|\mathscr{A}_\omega|}{|\mathscr{A}|}\right)^{-n/2} \tag{9.4.3}$$

We examine

$$\begin{aligned}
\frac{|\mathscr{A}_\omega|}{|\mathscr{A}|} &= |\mathscr{A}_\omega|\,|\mathscr{A}|^{-1} = |\mathscr{A}_\omega \mathscr{A}^{-1}| \\
&= \left|\left[\sum_{i=1}^{n}(\boldsymbol{\chi}_i - \mathbf{h}_0)(\boldsymbol{\chi}_i - \mathbf{h}_0)'\right]\mathscr{A}^{-1}\right| \\
&= \left|\left[\sum_{i=1}^{n}(\boldsymbol{\chi}_i - \bar{\boldsymbol{\chi}})(\boldsymbol{\chi}_i - \bar{\boldsymbol{\chi}})' + n(\bar{\boldsymbol{\chi}} - \mathbf{h}_0)(\bar{\boldsymbol{\chi}} - \mathbf{h}_0)'\right]\mathscr{A}^{-1}\right| \\
&= |\mathbf{I} + n(\bar{\boldsymbol{\chi}} - \mathbf{h}_0)(\bar{\boldsymbol{\chi}} - \mathbf{h}_0)'\mathscr{A}^{-1}| \\
&= 1 + n(\bar{\boldsymbol{\chi}} - \mathbf{h}_0)'\mathscr{A}^{-1}(\bar{\boldsymbol{\chi}} - \mathbf{h}_0)
\end{aligned} \tag{9.4.4}$$

(See Problem 9.4.) So instead of the likelihood ratio test function V, we will use a monotonic function of V, namely,

$$W = \left(\frac{n-K}{K}\right)[V^{-2/n} - 1] = \left(\frac{n(n-K)}{K}\right)(\bar{\boldsymbol{\chi}} - \mathbf{h}_0)'\mathscr{A}^{-1}(\bar{\boldsymbol{\chi}} - \mathbf{h}_0) \tag{9.4.5}$$

To complete the proof of the theorem, we must show that W is distributed $F(w : K, n - K; \lambda)$, where $\lambda = \frac{1}{2}n(\boldsymbol{\mu} - \mathbf{h}_0)'\boldsymbol{\Sigma}^{-1}(\boldsymbol{\mu} - \mathbf{h}_0)$. This will be done in Theorem 9.7.4.

Now we slightly generalize this theorem.

THEOREM 9.4.2

Let the $K \times 1$ vectors $\boldsymbol{\chi}_1, \boldsymbol{\chi}_2, \ldots, \boldsymbol{\chi}_n$ be a random sample from the distribution $\mathbf{N}(\mathbf{x} : \boldsymbol{\mu}, \boldsymbol{\Sigma})$. To test $H_0 : \mathbf{H}\boldsymbol{\mu} = \mathbf{h}$ vs. $H_a : \mathbf{H}\boldsymbol{\mu} \neq \mathbf{h}$, where $\mathbf{H}$ and $\mathbf{h}$ are known and $\mathbf{H}$ is $q \times K$ of rank q, a likelihood ratio test statistic is W, where

$$W = \left(\frac{n(n-q)}{q}\right)(\mathbf{H}\bar{\boldsymbol{\chi}} - \mathbf{h})'(\mathbf{H}\mathscr{A}\mathbf{H}')^{-1}(\mathbf{H}\bar{\boldsymbol{\chi}} - \mathbf{h}) \tag{9.4.6}$$

W is distributed $F(w : q, n - q; \lambda)$, where $\lambda = \frac{1}{2}n(\mathbf{H}\boldsymbol{\mu} - \mathbf{h})'(\mathbf{H}\boldsymbol{\Sigma}\mathbf{H}')^{-1}(\mathbf{H}\boldsymbol{\mu} - \mathbf{h})$. The generalized likelihood ratio test of H_0 vs. H_a of size α is this: Reject H_0 if and only if $w \geq F_{\alpha:q,n-q}$. The power of the test is

$$\Pi(\lambda) = \int_{F_{\alpha:q,n-q}}^{\infty} F(w : q, n - q; \lambda)\, dw$$

Proof

Let $\mathbf{Y}_i = \mathbf{H}\boldsymbol{\chi}_i$; then $\mathbf{Y}_1, \mathbf{Y}_2, \ldots, \mathbf{Y}_n$ are independent and each is distributed $\mathbf{N}(\mathbf{y} : \mathbf{H}\boldsymbol{\mu}, \mathbf{H}\boldsymbol{\Sigma}\mathbf{H}')$. Let $\mathbf{H}\boldsymbol{\mu} = \boldsymbol{\mu}_\mathbf{Y}$ and $\mathbf{H}\boldsymbol{\Sigma}\mathbf{H}' = \boldsymbol{\Sigma}_\mathbf{Y}$. Then H_0 *vs.* H_a is equivalent to $H_0 : \boldsymbol{\mu}_\mathbf{Y} = \mathbf{h}$ *vs.* $H_a : \boldsymbol{\mu}_\mathbf{Y} \neq \mathbf{h}$, and the results of Theorem 9.4.1 can be applied directly, with $\mathbf{H}\bar{\boldsymbol{\chi}} = \bar{\mathbf{Y}}$, $\mathbf{H}\boldsymbol{\mu} = \boldsymbol{\mu}_\mathbf{Y}$, $\boldsymbol{\Sigma}_\mathbf{Y} = \mathbf{H}\boldsymbol{\Sigma}\mathbf{H}'$, $\mathscr{A}_\mathbf{Y} = \sum_{i=1}^{n} (\mathbf{Y}_i - \bar{\mathbf{Y}})(\mathbf{Y}_i - \bar{\mathbf{Y}})' = \mathbf{H}\mathscr{A}\mathbf{H}'$, and $K = q$. So the test statistic W is

$$\begin{aligned} W &= \left(\frac{n(n-q)}{q}\right)(\bar{\mathbf{Y}} - \mathbf{h})'\mathscr{A}_\mathbf{Y}^{-1}(\bar{\mathbf{Y}} - \mathbf{h}) \\ &= \left(\frac{n(n-q)}{q}\right)(\mathbf{H}\bar{\boldsymbol{\chi}} - \mathbf{h})'(\mathbf{H}\mathscr{A}\mathbf{H}')^{-1}(\mathbf{H}\bar{\boldsymbol{\chi}} - \mathbf{h}) \end{aligned} \tag{9.4.7}$$

and W is distributed $F(w : q, n - q; \lambda)$, where $\lambda = \frac{1}{2}n(\mathbf{H}\boldsymbol{\mu} - \mathbf{h})'(\mathbf{H}\boldsymbol{\Sigma}\mathbf{H}')^{-1} \times (\mathbf{H}\boldsymbol{\mu} - \mathbf{h})$. This completes the proof.

Note 3. If $q = K$, then H is full rank and $H_0 : \mathbf{H}\boldsymbol{\mu} = \mathbf{h}$ is equivalent to $H_0 : \boldsymbol{\mu} = \mathbf{H}^{-1}\mathbf{h}$. If we set $\mathbf{h}_0$ in Theorem 9.4.1 equal to $\mathbf{H}^{-1}\mathbf{h}$ in Theorem 9.4.2, it is easily seen that the two test statistics (and hence the two tests) are identical (as they should be since, in each case, we are testing $H_0 : \boldsymbol{\mu} = \mathbf{h}_0$).

COROLLARY 9.4.2

If $\mathbf{H} = \ell'$, that is, if $q = 1$ in Theorem 9.4.2, then the test is that one linear combination of $\boldsymbol{\mu}$ is equal to a specified constant. The hypothesis is $H_0 : \ell'\boldsymbol{\mu} = \ell_0$ vs. $H_a : \ell'\boldsymbol{\mu} \neq \ell_0$, and the generalized likelihood ratio test of size α is this: Reject H_0 if and only if $w \geq F_{\alpha:1,n-1}$, where

$$W = n(n-1)\frac{(\ell'\bar{\boldsymbol{\chi}} - \ell_0)^2}{\ell'\mathcal{A}\ell} = \frac{(\ell'\hat{\boldsymbol{\mu}} - \ell_0)^2 n}{\ell'\hat{\boldsymbol{\Sigma}}\ell} \tag{9.4.8}$$

Note 4. We can write Equation (9.4.8) as

$$W = \frac{(\ell'\hat{\boldsymbol{\mu}} - \ell_0)^2}{\ell'\left(\left(\frac{1}{n}\right)\hat{\boldsymbol{\Sigma}}\right)\ell} = \frac{(\ell'\hat{\boldsymbol{\mu}} - \ell_0)^2}{\widehat{\operatorname{var}}[\ell'\hat{\boldsymbol{\mu}} - \ell_0]} \tag{9.4.9}$$

Note the similarity to Equation (6.4.1). To demonstrate that Equation (9.4.9) is equivalent to Equation (9.4.8), we note that

$$\operatorname{var}[\ell'\hat{\boldsymbol{\mu}} - \ell_0] = \operatorname{var}[\ell'\hat{\boldsymbol{\mu}}] = \ell'\,\mathbf{cov}[\hat{\boldsymbol{\mu}}]\ell = \ell'\left(\left(\frac{1}{n}\right)\boldsymbol{\Sigma}\right)\ell \tag{9.4.10}$$

and

$$\widehat{\operatorname{var}}[\ell'\hat{\boldsymbol{\mu}} - \ell_0] = \ell'\left(\left(\frac{1}{n}\right)\hat{\boldsymbol{\Sigma}}\right)\ell = \ell'\left(\left(\frac{1}{n}\right)\left(\frac{1}{n-1}\right)\mathcal{A}\right)\ell = \left[\frac{n(n-1)}{\ell'\mathcal{A}\ell}\right]^{-1}$$

9.4.1 Extensions

There are two particular special cases that are of interest and will be discussed in this section: a test that the vector means of two K-variate normal populations are equal; and a test that all of the components in a vector mean are equal, that is, $\mu_1 = \mu_2 = \cdots = \mu_K$. We will state two theorems relating to these problems.

THEOREM 9.4.3

Let the $K \times 1$ vectors $\mathbf{Y}_1, \mathbf{Y}_2, \ldots, \mathbf{Y}_{n_1}$ be a random sample of size n_1 from $\mathbf{N}(\mathbf{y} : \boldsymbol{\mu}_1, \boldsymbol{\Sigma})$. Let the $K \times 1$ vectors $\boldsymbol{\chi}_1, \boldsymbol{\chi}_2, \ldots, \boldsymbol{\chi}_{n_2}$ be a random sample of size n_2

from $N(\mathbf{x} : \boldsymbol{\mu}_2, \boldsymbol{\Sigma})$. *Let the two samples be independent. The generalized likelihood ratio test of size* α *of* $H_0 : \boldsymbol{\mu}_1 = \boldsymbol{\mu}_2$ *vs.* $H_a : \boldsymbol{\mu}_1 \neq \boldsymbol{\mu}_2$ *is this: Reject* H_0 *if and only if*

$$w \geq F_{\alpha:K,n_1+n_2-K-1} \tag{9.4.11}$$

where w *is the observed value of* W *and*

$$W = \left(\frac{n_1 + n_2 - K - 1}{K}\right)\left(\frac{n_1 n_2}{n_1 + n_2}\right)(\overline{\mathbf{Y}} - \overline{\boldsymbol{\chi}})' \mathscr{A}_0^{-1} (\overline{\mathbf{Y}} - \overline{\boldsymbol{\chi}}) \tag{9.4.12}$$

and

$$\mathscr{A}_0 = \sum_{i=1}^{n_1} (\mathbf{Y}_i - \overline{\mathbf{Y}})(\mathbf{Y}_i - \overline{\mathbf{Y}})' + \sum_{i=1}^{n_2} (\boldsymbol{\chi}_i - \overline{\boldsymbol{\chi}})(\boldsymbol{\chi}_i - \overline{\boldsymbol{\chi}})' = \mathscr{A}_1 + \mathscr{A}_2 \tag{9.4.13}$$

say. We assume $n_1 + n_2 - 2 \geq K$.

Proof

We sketch the proof and ask the reader to fill in the details in the problems. Here $\overline{\mathbf{Z}} = \overline{\mathbf{Y}} - \overline{\boldsymbol{\chi}}$ is distributed $N(\mathbf{z} : \boldsymbol{\mu}_1 - \boldsymbol{\mu}_2, ((n_1 + n_2)/n_1 n_2)\boldsymbol{\Sigma})$. The random matrix $\mathscr{A}_i$ is distributed $\mathbf{W}_K(A_i : n_i - 1; \boldsymbol{\Sigma})$ and the $\mathscr{A}_i$ are independent for $i = 1, 2$. Hence the random matrix $\mathscr{A}_0$ is distributed $\mathbf{W}_K(\mathscr{A}_0 : n; \boldsymbol{\Sigma})$, where $n = n_1 + n_2 - 2$. Also, $\mathscr{A}_0$ is independent of $\overline{Y} - \overline{\boldsymbol{\chi}}$. Theorem 9.4.1 can now be used to complete the proof.

THEOREM 9.4.4

Let the $K \times 1$ *vectors* $\boldsymbol{\chi}_1, \boldsymbol{\chi}_2, \ldots, \boldsymbol{\chi}_n$ *be a random sample from* $N(\mathbf{x} : \boldsymbol{\mu}, \boldsymbol{\Sigma})$. *The generalized likelihood ratio test of size* α *of* $H_0 : \mu_1 = \mu_2 = \cdots = \mu_K$ *vs.* $H_a : \mu_i \neq \mu_j$ *for at least one* $i \neq j$ *is this: Reject* H_0 *if and only if*

$$w \geq F_{\alpha:K-1,n-K+1} \tag{9.4.14}$$

where w *is the observed value of* W *and*

$$W = \left(\frac{n(n - K + 1)}{K - 1}\right)(\mathbf{H}\overline{\boldsymbol{\chi}})'(\mathbf{H}\mathscr{A}\mathbf{H}')^{-1}(\mathbf{H}\overline{\boldsymbol{\chi}}) \tag{9.4.15}$$

and $\mathbf{H}$ *is the* $(K - 1) \times K$ *matrix*

$$\mathbf{H} = \begin{bmatrix} 1 & -1 & 0 & \cdots & 0 \\ 1 & 0 & -1 & \cdots & 0 \\ \vdots & \vdots & \vdots & & \vdots \\ 1 & 0 & 0 & \cdots & -1 \end{bmatrix} \tag{9.4.16}$$

Proof

The proof will be asked for in the problems.

COROLLARY 9.4.4

In Theorem 9.4.4, to test $H_0 : \mu_{i_1} = \mu_{i_2} = \cdots = \mu_{i_q}$ vs. H_a : at least one equality is an inequality (that is, to test that any set of q of the K elements in $\boldsymbol{\mu}$ are equal), form a $(q-1) \times K$ matrix $\mathbf{H}$ defined by

$$\begin{array}{r} \text{Column } 1 \quad \cdots \quad i_1 \quad \cdots \quad i_2 \quad \cdots \quad i_q \quad \cdots \quad K \\ \mathbf{H} = \begin{bmatrix} 0 & \cdots & 1 & \cdots & -1 & \cdots & 0 & \cdots & 0 \\ 0 & \cdots & 1 & \cdots & 0 & \cdots & 0 & \cdots & 0 \\ 0 & \cdots & 1 & \cdots & 0 & \cdots & 0 & \cdots & 0 \\ \vdots & & \vdots & & \vdots & & \vdots & & \vdots \\ 0 & \cdots & 1 & \cdots & 0 & \cdots & 0 & \cdots & 0 \\ 0 & \cdots & 1 & \cdots & 0 & \cdots & 0 & \cdots & 0 \\ 0 & \cdots & 1 & \cdots & 0 & \cdots & -1 & \cdots & 0 \end{bmatrix} \end{array} \tag{9.4.17}$$

The i_1 column is a column of 1's; the i_2 column has a -1 in row 1 and 0's elsewhere; the i_3 column has a -1 in row 2 and 0's elsewhere, and so on. The i_q column has a -1 in row $q-1$ and 0's elsewhere; all other columns are composed of zeros. Then use the formula in Equation (9.4.15), with K replaced by q.

Note 5. In Equation (9.4.16), $\mathbf{H}$ can be any $(K-1) \times K$ matrix, say $\mathbf{H}^*$, such that $\mu_1 = \mu_2 = \cdots = \mu_K$ if and only if $\mathbf{H}^*\boldsymbol{\mu} = \mathbf{0}$. The test statistic W in Equation (9.4.15) is invariant for any $\mathbf{H}^*$ that satisfies the condition.

9.5 Confidence Intervals on $\ell_i'\boldsymbol{\mu}$, for $i = 1, 2, \ldots, q$

In Corollary 9.4.2 suppose ℓ_0 is the true (but unknown) value of $\ell'\boldsymbol{\mu}$; then $W = T^2$ in Equation (9.4.8), and the random variable T are distributed as $s(t : n-1)$ when $\ell'\boldsymbol{\mu}$ is substituted for ℓ_0. We get

$$1 - \alpha = P[-t_{\alpha/2:n-1} \leq T \leq t_{\alpha/2:n-1}]$$

and substituting for T and simplifying gives

$$1 - \alpha = P[\ell'\hat{\boldsymbol{\mu}} - t_{\alpha/2:n-1}\sqrt{\widehat{\mathrm{var}}[\ell'\hat{\boldsymbol{\mu}}]} \leq \ell'\boldsymbol{\mu} \leq \ell'\hat{\boldsymbol{\mu}} + t_{\alpha/2:n-1}\sqrt{\widehat{\mathrm{var}}[\ell'\hat{\boldsymbol{\mu}}]}] \tag{9.5.1}$$

The inequalities define a $1 - \alpha$ confidence interval on the true unknown value of $\ell'\boldsymbol{\mu}$.

Note 1. The $\widehat{\mathrm{var}}[\ell'\hat{\boldsymbol{\mu}}]$ in the confidence interval in Equation (9.5.1) is

$$\widehat{\mathrm{var}}[\ell'\hat{\boldsymbol{\mu}}] = \ell'\left(\frac{1}{n}\right)\hat{\boldsymbol{\Sigma}}\ell = \frac{\ell'\mathcal{A}\ell}{n(n-1)}$$

THEOREM 9.5.1

Let the $K \times 1$ vectors $\boldsymbol{\chi}_1, \boldsymbol{\chi}_2, \ldots, \boldsymbol{\chi}_n$ be a random sample from the distribution $\mathrm{N}(\mathbf{x} : \boldsymbol{\mu}, \boldsymbol{\Sigma})$. One-at-a-time $1 - \alpha$ confidence intervals on $\ell_i'\boldsymbol{\mu}$ for $i = 1, 2, \ldots, q$ are given by

$$\ell_i'\hat{\boldsymbol{\mu}} \mp t_{\alpha/2:n-1}\sqrt{\widehat{var}[\ell_i'\hat{\boldsymbol{\mu}}]} \qquad i = 1, 2, \ldots, q \tag{9.5.2}$$

which can be written

$$\ell_i'\bar{\boldsymbol{\chi}} \mp t_{\alpha/2:n-1}\sqrt{\frac{\ell_i'\mathcal{A}\ell_i}{n(n-1)}} \qquad i = 1, 2, \ldots, q$$

or (9.5.3)

$$\ell_i'\bar{\boldsymbol{\chi}} \mp t_{\alpha/2:n-1}\sqrt{\ell_i'\left(\left(\frac{1}{n}\right)\hat{\boldsymbol{\Sigma}}\right)\ell_i} \qquad i = 1, 2, \ldots, q$$

In particular, one-at-a-time $1 - \alpha$ confidence intervals on $\mu_1, \mu_2, \ldots, \mu_K$, the K components of the mean vector $\boldsymbol{\mu}$, are

$$\hat{\mu}_i \mp t_{\alpha/2:n-1}\sqrt{\widehat{var}[\hat{\mu}_i]} \qquad i = 1, 2, \ldots, K \tag{9.5.4}$$

which can be written

$$\bar{X}_i \mp t_{\alpha/2:n-1}\sqrt{\frac{\hat{\sigma}_{ii}}{n}} \tag{9.5.5}$$

where

$$\bar{X}_i = \left(\frac{1}{n}\right)\sum_{j=1}^{n} X_{ji} \qquad \text{and} \qquad \hat{\sigma}_{ii} = \left(\frac{1}{n-1}\right)\sum_{j=1}^{n}(X_{ji} - \bar{X}_i)^2$$

THEOREM 9.5.2

Let the $K \times 1$ *vectors* $\boldsymbol{\chi}_1, \boldsymbol{\chi}_2, \ldots, \boldsymbol{\chi}_n$ *be a random sample from* $\mathbf{N}(\mathbf{x} : \boldsymbol{\mu}, \boldsymbol{\Sigma})$. *Simultaneous confidence intervals on* $\ell'_1\boldsymbol{\mu}, \ell'_2\boldsymbol{\mu}, \ldots, \ell'_q\boldsymbol{\mu}$ *with confidence coefficient at least* $1 - \alpha$ *are given by (assume the* ℓ_i *are linearly independent)*

$$\ell'_i\hat{\boldsymbol{\mu}} \mp t_{\alpha/2q:n-1}\sqrt{\widehat{var}[\ell'_i\hat{\boldsymbol{\mu}}]} \qquad i = 1, 2, \ldots, q \qquad (9.5.6)$$

which can be written

$$\ell'_i\bar{\boldsymbol{\chi}} \mp t_{\alpha/2q:n-1}\sqrt{\frac{\ell'_i\hat{\boldsymbol{\Sigma}}\ell_i}{n}} \qquad i = 1, 2, \ldots, q \qquad (9.5.7)$$

In particular, simultaneous confidence intervals on $\mu_1, \mu_2, \ldots, \mu_q$, *any* q *components of the vector mean* $\boldsymbol{\mu}$, *with confidence coefficient at least* $1 - \alpha$, *are*

$$\hat{\mu}_i \mp t_{\alpha/2q:n-1}\sqrt{\frac{\hat{\sigma}_{ii}}{n}} \qquad i = 1, 2, \ldots, q \qquad (9.5.8)$$

which can also be written

$$\bar{X}_i \mp t_{\alpha/2q:n-1}\sqrt{\frac{\sum_{j=1}^{n}(X_{ji} - \bar{X}_i)^2}{n(n-1)}} \qquad i = 1, 2, \ldots, q \qquad (9.5.9)$$

Proof

Let $E_1, E_2, \ldots, E_q$ be q events and $P[E_1, E_2, \ldots, E_q]$ be the probability that the q events simultaneously occur. Then

$$P[E_1, E_2, \ldots, E_q] \geq 1 - \sum_{i=1}^{q} P[\bar{E}_i] \qquad (9.5.10)$$

where $P[\bar{E}_i]$ is the probability that event E_i does *not* occur. This is sometimes referred to as the Bonferroni inequality. To demonstrate Equation (9.5.10), start with two events E_1 and E_2. Then $\overline{E_1, E_2} = (\bar{E}_1 \cup \bar{E}_2)$ and

$$\begin{aligned} P[E_1, E_2] &= 1 - P[\overline{E_1, E_2}] = 1 - P[\bar{E}_1 \cup \bar{E}_2] \\ &= 1 - \{P[\bar{E}_1] + P[\bar{E}_2] - P[\bar{E}_1, \bar{E}_2]\} \geq 1 - P[\bar{E}_1] - P[\bar{E}_2] \end{aligned}$$

Use induction to go from 2 to q events. Now let E_i be the event that $\ell'_i\boldsymbol{\mu}$ is contained in the interval

$$(\ell'_i\hat{\boldsymbol{\mu}} - t_{\alpha/2q:n-1}\sqrt{\widehat{\text{var}}[\ell'_i\hat{\boldsymbol{\mu}}]}, \ell'_i\hat{\boldsymbol{\mu}} + t_{\alpha/2q:n-1}\sqrt{\widehat{\text{var}}[\ell'_i\hat{\boldsymbol{\mu}}]})$$

Then clearly $P[E_i] = 1 - \alpha/q$ and $P[\bar{E}_i] = \alpha/q$. Thus

$$P[\ell_i'\hat{\boldsymbol{\mu}} - t_{\alpha/2q:n-1}\sqrt{\widehat{\text{var}}[\ell_i'\hat{\boldsymbol{\mu}}]} \le \ell_i'\boldsymbol{\mu} \le \ell_i'\hat{\boldsymbol{\mu}} + t_{\alpha/2q:n-1}\sqrt{\widehat{\text{var}}[\ell_i'\hat{\boldsymbol{\mu}}]}$$
$$i = 1, 2, \ldots, q] \ge 1 - \sum_{i=1}^{q}\left(\frac{\alpha}{q}\right) = 1 - \alpha$$

So the probability is greater than or equal to $1 - \alpha$ that the q confidence intervals in Equation (9.5.6) simultaneously cover their respective parameters, and this completes the proof of Equation (9.5.6). The proofs for the remaining confidence intervals follow directly from these.

9.6 Computations

If we want to utilize the formulas in Chapter 7 to compute the quantities needed for estimates and test statistics in this chapter, we can do so. The data matrix is $\mathbf{X}$, which has size $n \times K$ and is defined by $\mathbf{X}' = [\mathbf{x}_1, \mathbf{x}_2, \ldots, \mathbf{x}_n]$, where $\mathbf{x}_i$ is the observed value of the random $K \times 1$ vector χ_i of the random sample $\chi_1, \chi_2, \ldots, \chi_n$.

To test $H_0: \boldsymbol{\mu} = \mathbf{h}_0$, compute $\mathbf{A}$ and $\bar{\mathbf{x}} - \mathbf{h}_0$, and use the format discussed in Section 7.3 (note $\mathbf{A} = \sum \mathbf{x}_i\mathbf{x}_i' - n\bar{\mathbf{x}}\bar{\mathbf{x}}'$):

$$\left[\begin{array}{c|c} \mathbf{A} & \bar{\mathbf{x}} - \mathbf{h}_0 \\ \hline \mathbf{T} & \mathbf{t} \end{array}\right]$$

where $\mathbf{T}$ is the upper triangular matrix that is obtained from $\mathbf{A}$ by the square root method (that is, $\mathbf{A} = \mathbf{T}'\mathbf{T}$). Then the test statistic w in Equation (9.4.1) is

$$w = \left(\frac{n(n - K)}{K}\right)\mathbf{t}'\mathbf{t}$$

To test $H_0: \mathbf{H}\boldsymbol{\mu} = \mathbf{h}$, compute $\mathbf{HAH}'$ and $\mathbf{H}\bar{\mathbf{x}} - \mathbf{h}$, and use the format

$$\left[\begin{array}{c|c} \mathbf{HAH}' & \mathbf{H}\bar{\mathbf{x}} - \mathbf{h} \\ \hline \mathbf{T} & \mathbf{t} \end{array}\right]$$

The test statistic w in Equation (9.4.6) is

$$w = \left(\frac{n(n - q)}{q}\right)\mathbf{t}'\mathbf{t}$$

Example 9.6.1

The data in the table below are assumed to be values of a random sample from the distribution $\mathbf{N}(\mathbf{x} : \boldsymbol{\mu}, \boldsymbol{\Sigma})$.

1. For $\alpha = 0.05$ test the hypothesis $H_0 : \boldsymbol{\mu} = \mathbf{h}_0$ *vs.* $H_a : \boldsymbol{\mu} \neq \mathbf{h}_0$, where $\mathbf{h}_0' = [5, 5, 4, 4]$.

2. Set one-at-a-time 95 percent confidence intervals on μ_1, μ_2, μ_3, and μ_4.

3. Set simultaneous 80 percent confidence intervals on μ_1, μ_2, μ_3, and μ_4.

We compute

$$\mathbf{A} = \begin{bmatrix} 62.1899 & 29.1456 & -3.4376 & 12.4589 \\ 29.1456 & 25.2010 & 6.2364 & 19.0208 \\ -3.4376 & 6.2364 & 30.4898 & 20.6811 \\ 12.4589 & 19.0208 & 20.6811 & 26.3102 \end{bmatrix} \qquad \bar{\mathbf{x}} = \begin{bmatrix} 5.2465 \\ 5.2970 \\ 4.3248 \\ 3.9637 \end{bmatrix}$$

i	$[x_{i1}$	x_{i2}	x_{i3}	$x_{i4}]$	$= \mathbf{x}_i'$
1	5.285	4.639	1.981	2.672	$\mathbf{x}_1'$
2	5.144	4.191	2.327	1.793	$\mathbf{x}_2'$
3	6.247	5.389	4.334	3.857	$\mathbf{x}_3'$
4	9.221	6.776	4.786	5.117	$\mathbf{x}_4'$
5	3.339	5.596	5.504	4.122	$\mathbf{x}_5'$
6	2.242	5.349	4.651	5.179	$\mathbf{x}_6'$
7	2.221	2.512	3.704	1.801	$\mathbf{x}_7'$
8	4.913	5.000	3.761	3.297	$\mathbf{x}_8'$
9	5.480	5.657	5.630	4.762	$\mathbf{x}_9'$
10	5.312	4.882	3.155	2.754	$\mathbf{x}_{10}'$
11	3.940	4.469	6.895	4.651	$\mathbf{x}_{11}'$
12	5.367	5.963	3.521	4.184	$\mathbf{x}_{12}'$
13	4.026	5.088	5.931	4.891	$\mathbf{x}_{13}'$
14	6.394	4.785	3.680	2.856	$\mathbf{x}_{14}'$
15	5.369	6.149	3.575	4.476	$\mathbf{x}_{15}'$
16	2.894	3.358	4.111	3.181	$\mathbf{x}_{16}'$
17	7.338	6.687	3.596	3.866	$\mathbf{x}_{17}'$
18	6.893	6.675	6.218	6.152	$\mathbf{x}_{18}'$
19	7.719	7.088	4.103	5.029	$\mathbf{x}_{19}'$
20	5.586	5.686	5.032	4.633	$\mathbf{x}_{20}'$

So we get the following:

$$\hat{\boldsymbol{\Sigma}} = \begin{bmatrix} 3.2732 & 1.5340 & -0.1809 & 0.6557 \\ 1.5340 & 1.3264 & 0.3282 & 1.0011 \\ -0.1809 & 0.3282 & 1.6047 & 1.0885 \\ 0.6557 & 1.0011 & 1.0885 & 1.3847 \end{bmatrix} \qquad \hat{\boldsymbol{\mu}} = \begin{bmatrix} 5.2465 \\ 5.2970 \\ 4.3248 \\ 3.9637 \end{bmatrix}$$

To solve part 1 we use the format $[\mathbf{A} \mid \bar{\mathbf{x}} - \mathbf{h}_0]$ and reduce it by the square root method. We get

$$\left[\begin{array}{c|c} \mathbf{A} & \bar{\mathbf{x}} - \mathbf{h}_0 \\ \hline \mathbf{T} & \mathbf{t} \end{array}\right]$$

$$= \left[\begin{array}{cccc|c} 62.1900 & 29.1456 & -3.4376 & 12.4589 & 0.2465 \\ 29.1456 & 25.2010 & 6.2364 & 19.0208 & 0.2970 \\ -3.4376 & 6.2364 & 30.4898 & 20.6811 & 0.3248 \\ 12.4589 & 19.0208 & 20.6811 & 26.3102 & -0.0363 \\ \hline 7.8861 & 3.6958 & -0.4359 & 1.5799 & 0.0313 \\ 0.0 & 3.3973 & 2.3099 & 3.8801 & 0.0534 \\ 0.0 & 0.0 & 4.9964 & 2.4832 & 0.0430 \\ 0.0 & 0.0 & 0.0 & 1.6102 & -0.2483 \end{array}\right]$$

1. $\mathbf{t}'\mathbf{t} = (-0.2483)^2 + (0.0430)^2 + (0.0534)^2 + (0.0313)^2 = 0.0673$. We compute

$$w = \left(\frac{20(20 - 4)}{4}\right)(0.0673) = 5.3863$$

   and the tabulated F is $F_{0.05:4,16} = 3.017$; so H_0 is rejected.

2. $t_{0.025:19} = 2.093$, so by Equation (9.5.2) we get 95 percent one-at-a-time confidence intervals on μ_1, μ_2, μ_3, and μ_4 to be

$$4.3998 \le \mu_1 \le 6.0932 \qquad 4.7580 \le \mu_2 \le 5.8359$$
$$3.7319 \le \mu_3 \le 4.9176 \qquad 3.4129 \le \mu_4 \le 4.5144$$

3. From Equation (9.5.7) we get the t value to be $t_{\alpha/2K:19} = t_{0.025:19} = 2.093$, and the 80 percent simultaneous confidence intervals are the same as the 95 percent one-at-a-time confidence intervals in part 2.

9.7 Additional Theorems about $\hat{\boldsymbol{\mu}}$ and $\hat{\boldsymbol{\Sigma}}$

In this section we state and prove some theorems about $\hat{\boldsymbol{\mu}}$ and $\hat{\boldsymbol{\Sigma}}$ that were used in previous sections. In Theorem 9.7.4 we derive the distribution of the test statistic W in Theorem 9.4.1. This section can be omitted if the reader is not interested in these proofs.

THEOREM 9.7.1

Let the $K \times 1$ random vectors $\boldsymbol{\chi}_1, \boldsymbol{\chi}_2, \ldots, \boldsymbol{\chi}_n$ be a random sample from $\mathbf{N}(\mathbf{x} : \boldsymbol{\mu}, \boldsymbol{\Sigma})$, and define the n random vectors $\mathbf{Z}_1, \mathbf{Z}_2, \ldots, \mathbf{Z}_n$ by

$$\mathbf{Z}_1 = \sum_{j=1}^{n} p_{1j}\boldsymbol{\chi}_j,\ \mathbf{Z}_2 = \sum_{j=1}^{n} p_{2j}\boldsymbol{\chi}_j, \ldots, \mathbf{Z}_n = \sum_{j=1}^{n} p_{nj}\boldsymbol{\chi}_j$$

where $\mathbf{P} = [p_{ij}]$ is an $n \times n$ orthogonal matrix whose first row is

$$\left[\frac{1}{\sqrt{n}}, \frac{1}{\sqrt{n}}, \ldots, \frac{1}{\sqrt{n}}\right]$$

Define $\mathscr{V} = \sum_{i=2}^{n} \mathbf{Z}_1\mathbf{Z}_i'$; then

(1) *$\mathbf{Z}_1, \mathbf{Z}_2, \ldots, \mathbf{Z}_n$ are jointly independent vectors;*

(2) *$(1/\sqrt{n})\mathbf{Z}_1$ is distributed $\mathbf{N}(\mathbf{z} : \boldsymbol{\mu}, (1/n)\boldsymbol{\Sigma})$ (note that $(1/\sqrt{n})\mathbf{Z}_1 = \bar{\boldsymbol{\chi}}$);*

(3) *$\mathbf{Z}_2, \mathbf{Z}_3, \ldots, \mathbf{Z}_n$ are distributed $\mathbf{NID}(\mathbf{z} : \mathbf{0}, \boldsymbol{\Sigma})$;*

(4) *$U = (\mathbf{c}'\mathscr{V}\mathbf{c})/(\mathbf{c}'\boldsymbol{\Sigma}\mathbf{c})$ is distributed $\chi^2(u : n-1)$ for any $K \times 1$ nonzero constant vector $\mathbf{c}$ (note that the p.d.f. of U does not depend on $\mathbf{c}$).*

Proof

First we note that since $\mathbf{P}$ is an orthogonal matrix with first row equal to

$$\left[\frac{1}{\sqrt{n}}, \frac{1}{\sqrt{n}}, \ldots, \frac{1}{\sqrt{n}}\right]$$

we get

1. $\sum_{j=1}^{n} p_{rj}p_{sj} = \delta_{rs}$, where $\delta_{rs} = 0$ if $r \neq s$ and $\delta_{rs} = 1$ if $r = s$;

2. $\sum_{j=1}^{n} p_{ij} = 0$ for $i = 2, 3, \ldots, n$;

3. $$\sum_{r=2}^{n} p_{rj}p_{ri} = \sum_{r=1}^{n} p_{rj}p_{ri} - p_{1j}p_{1i} = \delta_{ij} - 1/n. \tag{9.7.1}$$

By Theorem 3.3.5 the vector $\mathbf{Z}_0$, defined by

$$\mathbf{Z}_0' = [\mathbf{Z}_1', \mathbf{Z}_2', \ldots, \mathbf{Z}_n'] = \left[\sum_{j=1}^{n} p_{1j}\boldsymbol{\chi}_j', \sum_{j=1}^{n} p_{2j}\boldsymbol{\chi}_j', \ldots, \sum_{j=1}^{n} p_{nj}\boldsymbol{\chi}_j'\right]$$

is distributed normally since the joint distribution of the $\boldsymbol{\chi}_1, \boldsymbol{\chi}_2, \ldots, \boldsymbol{\chi}_n$ is normal and each element in $\mathbf{Z}_0$ is clearly just a linear function of each element X_{ij} in the $\boldsymbol{\chi}_j$.

To prove part (1) we note that $\mathbf{Z}_1, \mathbf{Z}_2, \ldots, \mathbf{Z}_n$ are jointly normally distributed, and by Theorem 3.5.1 they are mutually independent vectors if we can show $\mathbf{cov}[\mathbf{Z}_r, \mathbf{Z}_s] = \mathbf{0}$ for all $r \neq s$. To do this we have

$$\begin{aligned}
\mathbf{cov}[\mathbf{Z}_r, \mathbf{Z}_s] &= \mathscr{E}[(\mathbf{Z}_r - \mathscr{E}[\mathbf{Z}_r])(\mathbf{Z}_s - \mathscr{E}[\mathbf{Z}_s])'] \\
&= \mathscr{E}\left[\sum_{j=1}^{n} p_{rj}(\boldsymbol{\chi}_j - \boldsymbol{\mu})\right]\left[\sum_{i=1}^{n} p_{si}(\boldsymbol{\chi}_i - \boldsymbol{\mu})'\right] \\
&= \sum_{j=1}^{n}\sum_{i=1}^{n} p_{rj}p_{si}\,\mathscr{E}[(\boldsymbol{\chi}_j - \boldsymbol{\mu})(\boldsymbol{\chi}_i - \boldsymbol{\mu})'] \\
&= \sum_{j=1}^{n}\sum_{i=1}^{n} p_{rj}p_{si}[\delta_{ij}\boldsymbol{\Sigma}]
\end{aligned}$$

where

$$\delta_{ij} = \begin{cases} 1 & \text{if } i = j \\ 0 & \text{if } i \neq j \end{cases}$$

We obtained $\mathscr{E}[(\boldsymbol{\chi}_j - \boldsymbol{\mu})(\boldsymbol{\chi}_i - \boldsymbol{\mu})'] = \delta_{ij}\boldsymbol{\Sigma}$, since $\boldsymbol{\chi}_i$ and $\boldsymbol{\chi}_j$ are independent if $i \neq j$. Also, $\mathbf{cov}[\boldsymbol{\chi}_i] = \boldsymbol{\Sigma}$. Thus we get

$$\mathbf{cov}[\mathbf{Z}_r, \mathbf{Z}_s] = \left[\sum_{j=1}^{n}\sum_{i=1}^{n} p_{rj}p_{si}\delta_{ij}\right]\boldsymbol{\Sigma} = \left[\sum_{j=1}^{n} p_{rj}p_{sj}\right]\boldsymbol{\Sigma} = \delta_{rs}\boldsymbol{\Sigma} \tag{9.7.2}$$

This tells us that $\mathbf{Z}_r$ and $\mathbf{Z}_s$ are uncorrelated if $r \neq s$, so by Theorem 3.5.1, the set of vectors $\mathbf{Z}_1, \mathbf{Z}_2, \ldots, \mathbf{Z}_n$ are jointly independent, and this proves (1).

To prove part (2) we note

$$\mathbf{Z}_1 = \sum_{j=1}^{n} p_{1j}\boldsymbol{\chi}_j = \left(\frac{1}{\sqrt{n}}\right)\sum_{j=1}^{n}\boldsymbol{\chi}_j = \sqrt{n}\left(\left(\frac{1}{n}\right)\sum_{j=1}^{n}\boldsymbol{\chi}_j\right) = \sqrt{n}\,\bar{\boldsymbol{\chi}}$$

and by Theorem 9.3.2 part (2), the result follows since $\hat{\boldsymbol{\mu}} = (1/\sqrt{n})\mathbf{Z}_1$.

To prove part (3) we must find only the mean and covariance of $\mathbf{Z}_r$, $r = 2, 3, \ldots, n$, since we know from above that each $\mathbf{Z}_i$ is distributed normally and independently. We get

$$\mathscr{E}[\mathbf{Z}_r] = \mathscr{E}\left[\sum_{j=1}^{n} p_{rj}\boldsymbol{\chi}_j\right] = \sum_{j=1}^{n} p_{rj}\mathscr{E}[\boldsymbol{\chi}_j] = \boldsymbol{\mu}\sum_{j=1}^{n} p_{rj} = \mathbf{0} \qquad \text{for } r = 2, 3, \ldots, n$$

since, by Equation (9.7.1), $\sum_{j=1}^{n} p_{rj} = 0$ for $r = 2, 3, \ldots, n$. Also, $\mathbf{cov}[\mathbf{Z}_r] = \boldsymbol{\Sigma}$ by Equation (9.7.2). Thus $\mathbf{Z}_r$ is distributed $\mathbf{NID}(\mathbf{z} : \mathbf{0}, \boldsymbol{\Sigma})$ for $r = 2, 3, \ldots, n$ and this proves (3).

To prove part (4) we note that

$$\begin{aligned}
\mathscr{V} &= \sum_{r=2}^{n} \mathbf{Z}_r\mathbf{Z}_r' = \sum_{r=2}^{n}\left(\sum_{j=1}^{n} p_{rj}\boldsymbol{\chi}_j\right)\left(\sum_{i=1}^{n} p_{ri}\boldsymbol{\chi}_i\right)' = \sum_{j=1}^{n}\sum_{i=1}^{n}\boldsymbol{\chi}_i\boldsymbol{\chi}_j'\sum_{r=2}^{n} p_{rj}p_{ri} \\
&= \sum_{j=1}^{n}\sum_{i=1}^{n}\boldsymbol{\chi}_i\boldsymbol{\chi}_j'\left[\delta_{ij} - \frac{1}{n}\right] = \sum_{i=1}^{n}\boldsymbol{\chi}_i\boldsymbol{\chi}_i' - \frac{1}{n}\left(\sum_{i=1}^{n}\boldsymbol{\chi}_i\right)\left(\sum_{j=1}^{n}\boldsymbol{\chi}_j'\right) \\
&= \sum_{i=1}^{n}(\boldsymbol{\chi}_i - \bar{\boldsymbol{\chi}})(\boldsymbol{\chi}_i - \bar{\boldsymbol{\chi}})'
\end{aligned}$$

This quantity has been defined to be $\mathscr{A}$ in Equation (9.2.2). So $(\mathbf{c}'\mathscr{V}\mathbf{c})/(\mathbf{c}'\boldsymbol{\Sigma}\mathbf{c})$ has the same distribution as $(\mathbf{c}'\mathscr{A}\mathbf{c})/(\mathbf{c}'\boldsymbol{\Sigma}\mathbf{c})$ of part (4) in Theorem 9.3.2. This proves (4).

Note 1. We can write $\mathscr{A}$ as

$$\begin{aligned}
\mathscr{A} &= [\boldsymbol{\chi}_1, \boldsymbol{\chi}_2, \ldots, \boldsymbol{\chi}_n]\left[\mathbf{I} - \left(\frac{1}{n}\right)\mathbf{J}\right][\boldsymbol{\chi}_1, \boldsymbol{\chi}_2, \ldots, \boldsymbol{\chi}_n]' \\
&= \mathscr{X}'\left(\mathbf{I} - \left(\frac{1}{n}\right)\mathbf{J}\right)\mathscr{X} \qquad (9.7.3)
\end{aligned}$$

COROLLARY 9.7.1

Let the $K \times 1$ vectors $\boldsymbol{\chi}_1, \boldsymbol{\chi}_2, \ldots, \boldsymbol{\chi}_n$ be a random sample from $\mathbf{N}(\mathbf{x} : \boldsymbol{\mu}, \boldsymbol{\Sigma})$. Then $\mathscr{A}$ is distributed $\mathbf{W}_K(\mathbf{A} : n - 1; \boldsymbol{\Sigma})$, the central Wishart distribution with $n - 1$ degrees of freedom.

Under the conditions of Theorem 9.3.2 part (4), we proved that $(\mathbf{c}'\mathscr{A}\mathbf{c})/(\mathbf{c}'\boldsymbol{\Sigma}\mathbf{c})$ is a chi-square random variable. We now prove that $(\mathbf{c}'\boldsymbol{\Sigma}^{-1}\mathbf{c})/(\mathbf{c}'\mathscr{A}^{-1}\mathbf{c})$ is also a chi-square random variable. Before we prove this result we will list the notation that will be used.

Let $\mathbf{Z}_1, \mathbf{Z}_2, \ldots, \mathbf{Z}_n$ be a random sample from $\mathbf{N}(\mathbf{z}:\mathbf{0}, \boldsymbol{\Sigma})$, where $\boldsymbol{\Sigma}$ is a $K \times K$ positive definite matrix.

1. Let $\mathscr{V} = \sum_{i=1}^{n} \mathbf{Z}_i\mathbf{Z}_i'$; let $\mathscr{W} = \mathscr{V}^{-1}$; and let $\boldsymbol{\Delta} = \boldsymbol{\Sigma}^{-1}$.

2. Partition $\mathbf{Z}_i$, $\mathscr{V}$, $\mathscr{W}$, $\boldsymbol{\Sigma}$, and $\boldsymbol{\Delta}$ as follows:

$$\mathbf{Z}_i = \begin{bmatrix} Q_i \\ \boldsymbol{\chi}_i \end{bmatrix} \qquad \mathscr{V} = \begin{bmatrix} V_{11} & \mathscr{V}_{12} \\ \mathscr{V}_{21} & \mathscr{V}_{22} \end{bmatrix} \qquad \mathscr{W} = \begin{bmatrix} W_{11} & \mathscr{W}_{12} \\ \mathscr{W}_{21} & \mathscr{W}_{22} \end{bmatrix}$$

$$\boldsymbol{\Sigma} = \begin{bmatrix} \sigma_{11} & \boldsymbol{\sigma}_{12} \\ \boldsymbol{\sigma}_{21} & \boldsymbol{\Sigma}_{22} \end{bmatrix} \qquad \boldsymbol{\Delta} = \begin{bmatrix} \delta_{11} & \boldsymbol{\delta}_{12} \\ \boldsymbol{\delta}_{21} & \boldsymbol{\Delta}_{22} \end{bmatrix}$$

where Q_i, V_{11}, W_{11}, σ_{11}, and δ_{11} are scalars, and the size of the other vectors and matrices are thus determined. (9.7.4)

We are now going to prove that δ_{11}/W_{11} is a chi-square random variable with $n - K + 1$ degrees of freedom.

THEOREM 9.7.2

Let $\mathbf{Z}_1, \mathbf{Z}_2, \ldots, \mathbf{Z}_n$ be a random sample from $\mathbf{N}(\mathbf{z}:\mathbf{0}, \boldsymbol{\Sigma})$. In the notation of Equation (9.7.4), the random variable $U = \delta_{11}/W_{11}$ is distributed $\chi^2(u:n - K + 1)$.

Proof

Notice by Theorem 1.3.1 that $W_{11}^{-1} = V_{11} - \mathscr{V}_{12}\mathscr{V}_{22}^{-1}\mathscr{V}_{21}$, and by the definition of $\mathscr{V}$ this is

$$W_{11}^{-1} = \sum_{i=1}^{n} Q_i^2 - \left(\sum_{i=1}^{n} Q_i\boldsymbol{\chi}_i'\right)\left[\sum_{t=1}^{n} \boldsymbol{\chi}_t\boldsymbol{\chi}_t'\right]^{-1}\left(\sum_{j=1}^{n} \boldsymbol{\chi}_j Q_j\right)$$

If we define the $n \times 1$ vector $\mathbf{Q}$ by $\mathbf{Q}' = [Q_1, Q_2, \ldots, Q_n]$ and use the notation of Equation (9.2.2), we can then write $W_{11}^{-1} = \mathbf{Q}'(\mathbf{I} - \mathscr{X}(\mathscr{X}'\mathscr{X})^{-1}\mathscr{X}']\mathbf{Q}$. By Theorem 1.3.1, $\delta_{11}^{-1} = \sigma_{11} - \boldsymbol{\sigma}_{12}\boldsymbol{\Sigma}_{22}^{-1}\boldsymbol{\sigma}_{21}$. Define $U = W_{11}^{-1}/\delta_{11}^{-1}$.

Now consider the conditional p.d.f. of $Y_1, Y_2, \ldots, Y_n$ defined by $Y_i = (Q_i \mid \boldsymbol{\chi}_i = \mathbf{x}_i)$. Clearly Y_i is distributed $N(y_i:\boldsymbol{\sigma}_{12}\boldsymbol{\Sigma}_{22}^{-1}\mathbf{x}_i, \sigma_{11} - \boldsymbol{\sigma}_{12}\boldsymbol{\Sigma}_{22}^{-1}\boldsymbol{\sigma}_{21})$, and the Y_i are independent. Define the $n \times 1$ vector $\mathbf{Y}$ by $\mathbf{Y}' = [Y_1, Y_2, \ldots, Y_n]$, and $\mathbf{Y}$ is distributed $\mathbf{N}(\mathbf{y}:\mathbf{X}\boldsymbol{\Sigma}_{22}^{-1}\boldsymbol{\sigma}_{21}, \delta_{11}^{-1}\mathbf{I})$.

Define $U_{\mathbf{X}}$ as follows:

$$U_{\mathbf{X}} = (U \mid \mathscr{X} = \mathbf{X}) = \left(\frac{W_{11}^{-1}}{\delta_{11}^{-1}} \,\middle|\, \mathscr{X} = \mathbf{X}\right)$$

which can be written as

$$\frac{\mathbf{Y}'[\mathbf{I} - \mathbf{X}(\mathbf{X}'\mathbf{X})^{-1}\mathbf{X}']\mathbf{Y}}{\delta_{11}^{-1}}$$

and by Theorem 4.4.3, the p.d.f. of $U_{\mathbf{X}}$ is a chi-square p.d.f. with $n - K + 1$ degrees of freedom (note $\mathbf{X}'\mathbf{X}$ has size $(K-1) \times (K-1)$ and rank $K - 1$) and noncentrality

$$\begin{aligned}\lambda &= \left(\frac{1}{2\delta_{11}^{-1}}\right)(\mathscr{E}[\mathbf{Y}])'[\mathbf{I} - \mathbf{X}(\mathbf{X}'\mathbf{X})^{-1}\mathbf{X}'](\mathscr{E}[\mathbf{Y}]) \\ &= \left(\frac{1}{2\delta_{11}^{-1}}\right)\boldsymbol{\sigma}_{12}\boldsymbol{\Sigma}_{22}^{-1}\mathbf{X}'[\mathbf{I} - \mathbf{X}(\mathbf{X}'\mathbf{X})^{-1}\mathbf{X}']\mathbf{X}\boldsymbol{\Sigma}_{22}^{-1}\boldsymbol{\sigma}_{21} = 0\end{aligned}$$

So $U_{\mathbf{X}}$ is distributed $\chi^2(u_{\mathbf{X}} : n - K + 1; 0)$ and hence does not depend on the value $\mathbf{X}$ that the random matrix $\mathscr{X}$ assumes. Since the conditional p.d.f. of $(U \mid \mathscr{X} = \mathbf{X})$ does not depend on the conditioned values, it is equal to the marginal p.d.f. of U. Thus $U = W_{11}^{-1}/\delta_{11}^{-1} = \delta_{11}/W_{11}$ is distributed $\chi^2(u : n - K + 1)$, and this completes the proof.

Note 2. The degrees of freedom $n - K + 1$ are arrived at by the number of independent vectors in $\mathscr{V}$ (or $\mathscr{W}$), which is n, minus $(K - 1)$, one less than the size of $\mathscr{V}$, which is $K \times K$.

THEOREM 9.7.3

Let the $K \times 1$ vectors $\mathbf{Y}_1, \mathbf{Y}_2, \ldots, \mathbf{Y}_n$ be a random sample from $\mathbf{N}(\mathbf{y} : \mathbf{0}, \boldsymbol{\Sigma})$. Define $\mathscr{V}$ by $\mathscr{V} = \sum_{i=1}^{n} \mathbf{Y}_i\mathbf{Y}_i'$. Then for any nonzero $K \times 1$ constant vector $\mathbf{c}$, the random variable U is distributed $\chi^2(u : n - K + 1)$, where $U = (\mathbf{c}'\boldsymbol{\Sigma}^{-1}\mathbf{c})/\mathbf{c}'\mathscr{V}^{-1}\mathbf{c}$.

Proof

Let $\mathbf{P}$ be any orthogonal $K \times K$ matrix such that

$$\mathbf{P}' = \begin{bmatrix} \mathbf{c}_1' \\ \mathbf{C}_2' \end{bmatrix}$$

where $\mathbf{c}_1 = \mathbf{c}/\sqrt{\mathbf{c}'\mathbf{c}}$. Define $\mathbf{Z}_i$ by $\mathbf{Z}_i = \mathbf{P}'\mathbf{Y}_i$; then $\mathbf{Z}_1, \mathbf{Z}_2, \ldots, \mathbf{Z}_n$ are distributed $\mathbf{NID}(\mathbf{z}:\mathbf{0},\boldsymbol{\Sigma}^*)$, where $\mathbf{P}'\boldsymbol{\Sigma}\mathbf{P} = \boldsymbol{\Sigma}^*$. Define $\mathscr{V}^*$ by $\sum_{i=1}^n \mathbf{Z}_i\mathbf{Z}_i'$ and $\mathscr{W}^*$ by $(\mathscr{V}^*)^{-1}$. Define $\boldsymbol{\Delta}^*$ by $(\boldsymbol{\Sigma}^*)^{-1}$. By Theorem 9.7.2, $U = \delta_{11}^*/W_{11}^*$ is distributed $\chi^2(u:n-K+1)$. But

$$\mathscr{V}^* = \mathbf{P}'\mathscr{V}\mathbf{P}$$

$$(\mathscr{V}^*)^{-1} = \mathscr{W}^* = (\mathbf{P}'\mathscr{V}\mathbf{P})^{-1} = \mathbf{P}'\mathscr{V}^{-1}\mathbf{P} = \begin{bmatrix}\mathbf{c}_1' \\ \mathbf{C}_2'\end{bmatrix}\mathscr{V}^{-1}[\mathbf{c}_1, \mathbf{C}_2]$$

$$= \begin{bmatrix}\mathbf{c}_1'\mathscr{V}^{-1}\mathbf{c}_1 & \mathbf{c}_1'\mathscr{V}^{-1}\mathbf{C}_2 \\ \mathbf{C}_2'\mathscr{V}^{-1}\mathbf{c}_1 & \mathbf{C}_2'\mathscr{V}^{-1}\mathbf{C}_2\end{bmatrix}$$

Thus $W_{11}^* = \mathbf{c}_1'\mathscr{V}^{-1}\mathbf{c}_1$. Also, $\boldsymbol{\Sigma}^* = (\mathbf{P}'\boldsymbol{\Sigma}\mathbf{P})$, so $\boldsymbol{\Delta}^* = (\boldsymbol{\Sigma}^*)^{-1} = (\mathbf{P}'\boldsymbol{\Sigma}\mathbf{P})^{-1} = \mathbf{P}'\boldsymbol{\Sigma}^{-1}\mathbf{P}$, and $\delta_{11}^* = \mathbf{c}_1'\boldsymbol{\Sigma}^{-1}\mathbf{c}_1$; then we have $\delta_{11}^*/W_{11}^* = (\mathbf{c}'\boldsymbol{\Sigma}^{-1}\mathbf{c})/\mathbf{c}'\mathscr{V}^{-1}\mathbf{c}$, and the theorem is proved since by Theorem 9.7.2, δ_{11}^*/W_{11}^* is distributed as a chi-square random variable with $n-K+1$ degrees of freedom.

One immediate consequence of this result is in the following corollary.

COROLLARY 9.7.3

Under the conditions of Theorem 9.7.3, the p.d.f. of the random variable $(\mathbf{c}'\boldsymbol{\Sigma}^{-1}\mathbf{c})/(\mathbf{c}'\mathscr{V}^{-1}\mathbf{c})$ *does not depend on* $\mathbf{c}$.

THEOREM 9.7.4

Let the $K \times 1$ *vectors* $\chi_1, \chi_2, \ldots, \chi_n$ *be a random sample from* $\mathbf{N}(\mathbf{x}:\boldsymbol{\mu},\boldsymbol{\Sigma})$. *The random variable* W *defined by*

$$W = \left(\frac{n(n-K)}{K}\right)\bar{\chi}'\left[\sum_{i=1}^n (\chi_i - \bar{\chi})(\chi_i - \bar{\chi})'\right]^{-1}\bar{\chi}$$

is distributed $F(w:K, n-K;\lambda)$, *where*

$$\lambda = \left(\frac{n}{2}\right)\boldsymbol{\mu}'\boldsymbol{\Sigma}^{-1}\boldsymbol{\mu}$$

Proof

Define $\mathbf{Z}_1, \mathbf{Z}_2, \ldots, \mathbf{Z}_n$ as in Theorem 9.7.1. Then $\mathbf{Z}_1(= \mathbf{Y}_1)$ is distributed $\mathbf{N}(\mathbf{z}:\sqrt{n}\boldsymbol{\mu},\boldsymbol{\Sigma})$, and $\boldsymbol{\Sigma}_2, \boldsymbol{\Sigma}_3, \ldots, \boldsymbol{\Sigma}_n$ are distributed $\mathbf{NID}(\mathbf{z}:\mathbf{0},\boldsymbol{\Sigma})$. In Theorem 9.7.3 let the vectors $\mathbf{Z}_i = \mathbf{Y}_i$ for $i = 2, 3, \ldots, n$, and let

$\mathscr{V} = \sum_{i=2}^{n} \mathbf{Y}_i\mathbf{Y}_i' = \sum_{i=2}^{n} \mathbf{Z}_i\mathbf{Z}_i'$. Define U_1^* by

$$U_1^* = (U_1|\mathbf{Y}_1 = \mathbf{c}) = \left(\frac{\mathbf{Y}_1'\mathbf{\Sigma}^{-1}\mathbf{Y}_1}{\mathbf{Y}_1'\mathscr{V}^{-1}\mathbf{Y}_1}\middle|\mathbf{Y}_1 = \mathbf{c}\right)$$

$$= \frac{\mathbf{c}'\mathbf{\Sigma}^{-1}\mathbf{c}}{\mathbf{c}'(\mathscr{V}^{-1}|\mathbf{Y}_1 = \mathbf{c})\mathbf{c}} = \frac{\mathbf{c}'\mathbf{\Sigma}^{-1}\mathbf{c}}{\mathbf{c}'\mathscr{V}_{\mathbf{c}}^{-1}\mathbf{c}}$$

where $\mathscr{V}_{\mathbf{c}}^{-1}$ stands for $\mathscr{V}^{-1} \mid \mathbf{Y}_1 = \mathbf{c}$. But $\mathscr{V}^{-1}$ is independent of $\mathbf{Y}_1$, so by Theorem 9.7.3, $U_1^* = (U_1 \mid \mathbf{Y}_1 = \mathbf{c})$ is distributed $\chi^2(u_1^* : n - K)$. Note the degrees of freedom are $n - K$, the number of independent vectors in $\mathscr{V}$, which is $(n - 1)$, minus $K - 1$, one less than the size of $\mathscr{V}$. But the p.d.f. of U_1^* does not depend on the conditioned values $\mathbf{c}$ of $\mathbf{Y}_1$; so U_1 and $\mathbf{Y}_1$ are independent and thus U_1^* and U_1 have the same distribution, that is, U_1 is distributed $\chi^2(u_1 : n - K)$.

Now define $U_2 = \mathbf{Y}_1'\mathbf{\Sigma}^{-1}\mathbf{Y}_1$ which, by Corollary 4.2.1.4, is distributed $\chi^2(u_2 : K; \lambda)$, where $\lambda = \frac{1}{2}\{\mathscr{E}[\mathbf{Y}_1]\}'\mathbf{\Sigma}^{-1}\{\mathscr{E}[\mathbf{Y}_1]\} = (n/2)\boldsymbol{\mu}'\mathbf{\Sigma}^{-1}\boldsymbol{\mu}$. As we stated above, U_1 and $\mathbf{Y}_1$ (and hence U_1 and U_2) are independent. Thus $W = (U_2/K)/(U_1/(n - K))$ is distributed $F(w : K, n - K; \lambda)$, where $\lambda = (n/2)\boldsymbol{\mu}\mathbf{\Sigma}^{-1}\boldsymbol{\mu}$. But

$$W = \left(\frac{n - K}{K}\right)\left(\frac{U_2}{U_1}\right) = \frac{\left(\dfrac{n - K}{K}\right)\mathbf{Y}_1'\mathbf{\Sigma}^{-1}\mathbf{Y}_1}{\dfrac{\mathbf{Y}_1'\mathbf{\Sigma}^{-1}\mathbf{Y}_1}{\mathbf{Y}_1'\mathscr{V}^{-1}\mathbf{Y}_1}} = \left(\frac{n - K}{K}\right)\mathbf{Y}_1'\mathscr{V}^{-1}\mathbf{Y}_1$$

$$= \left(\frac{n(n - K)}{K}\right)\bar{\chi}'\left[\sum_{i=1}^{n}(\chi_i - \bar{\chi})(\chi_i - \bar{\chi})'\right]^{-1}\bar{\chi} = \left(\frac{n(n - K)}{K}\right)\bar{\chi}'\mathscr{A}^{-1}\bar{\chi}$$

This concludes the proof. We can now complete the proof of Theorem 9.4.1.

We now state a theorem that is a generalization of part (4) of Theorem 9.3.2.

THEOREM 9.7.5

Let the $K \times 1$ vectors $\chi_1, \chi_2, \ldots, \chi_n$ be a random sample of size n from the p.d.f. $\mathbf{N}(\mathbf{x} : \boldsymbol{\mu}, \mathbf{\Sigma})$, where $\mathbf{\Sigma}$ is positive definite. Define $\mathscr{A}_{\mathbf{B}}$ by

$$\mathscr{A}_{\mathbf{B}} = [\chi_1, \chi_2, \ldots, \chi_n]\,\mathbf{B}[\chi_1, \chi_2, \ldots, \chi_n]'$$

If $\mathbf{B}$ is a symmetric idempotent $n \times n$ constant matrix of rank m, and $\mathbf{c}$ is any nonzero $K \times 1$ constant vector, then $U = \mathbf{c}'\mathscr{A}_{\mathbf{B}}\mathbf{c}/\mathbf{c}'\mathbf{\Sigma}\mathbf{c}$ is distributed $\chi^2(u : m; \lambda)$, where $\lambda = \{\mathbf{c}'[\boldsymbol{\mu}, \boldsymbol{\mu}, \ldots, \boldsymbol{\mu}]\,\mathbf{B}[\boldsymbol{\mu}, \boldsymbol{\mu}, \ldots, \boldsymbol{\mu}]'\mathbf{c}\}/2\mathbf{c}'\mathbf{\Sigma}\mathbf{c}$.

Proof

The proof will be asked for in the problems.

Note 3. If $\boldsymbol{\mu} = \mathbf{0}$, of course, U is distributed as a central chi-square random variable, but U *can* be distributed as a central chi-square random variable even if $\boldsymbol{\mu} \neq \mathbf{0}$.

Note 4. The random matrix $\mathscr{A}$ defined in Equation (9.2.2) is $\mathscr{A}_{\mathbf{B}}$ defined above when $\mathbf{B} = \mathbf{I} - (1/n)\mathbf{J}$.

Note 5. If $\lambda = 0$ for all nonzero $K \times 1$ vectors $\mathbf{c}$, then the p.d.f. of U does not depend on $\mathbf{c}$.

Problems

9.1. Prove part (5) of Theorem 9.3.2, that is, prove that $\hat{\boldsymbol{\Sigma}}$ is an unbiased estimator of $\boldsymbol{\Sigma}$.

9.2. In the proof of Theorem 9.3.3, show that there exists a positive number h such that $\boldsymbol{\Sigma}^{-1} - 2\mathbf{T}$ is a positive definite matrix for all values of t_{ij} in the interval $-h < t_{ij} < h$ and for all i and j.

9.3. Prove Corollary 9.3.3.

9.4. Prove $|\mathbf{I} + \mathbf{b}\mathbf{b}'\mathbf{A}^{-1}| = 1 + \mathbf{b}'\mathbf{A}^{-1}\mathbf{b}$, where $\mathbf{b}$ is an $n \times 1$ vector and $\mathbf{A}^{-1}$ is an $n \times n$ symmetric matrix.

9.5. The following data are assumed to be the values of a random sample of size $n = 8$ from a bivariate normal p.d.f. with mean $\boldsymbol{\mu}$ and covariance $\boldsymbol{\Sigma}$.

x	6.8	17.3	15.1	26.7	13.2	5.2	17.1	8.3
y	27.0	35.1	36.2	45.1	32.8	27.1	39.5	30.1

(a) Find the maximum likelihood (and UMVU) estimate of $\boldsymbol{\mu}$.
(b) Find the UMVU estimate of $\boldsymbol{\Sigma}$.

9.6. Refer to Problem 9.5.
(a) Test $H_0 : \boldsymbol{\mu}' = [15, 30]$ *vs* $H_a : \boldsymbol{\mu}' \neq [15, 30]$.
(b) Find the power of the test in part (a) when $\boldsymbol{\mu}' = [10, 35]$, $\sigma_{11} = \sigma_{22} = 1$, and $\sigma_{12} = 0$.

9.7. Refer to Problem 9.5.
(a) Set a 95 percent confidence interval on μ_1.
(b) Set a 95 percent confidence interval on μ_2.

9.8. In Problem 9.5 set simultaneous 95 percent confidence intervals on μ_1 and μ_2 (use Bonferroni's inequality). Compare these answers with those in Problem 9.7.

9.9. In Problem 9.5 test the hypothesis $\mathbf{H\mu} = \mathbf{h}$ *vs.* $\mathbf{H\mu} \neq \mathbf{h}$, where $\mathbf{H\mu} = \mathbf{h}$ is

$$\begin{aligned} \mu_1 - \mu_2 &= -15 \\ \mu_1 + \mu_2 &= \quad 45 \end{aligned}$$

Use $\alpha = 0.05$.

9.10. Is the value of the test statistic in Problem 9.6 the same as the value of the test statistic in Problem 9.9? Why?

9.11. In Problem 9.5 set 95 percent one-at-a-time confidence intervals on $\mu_1 - \mu_2$ and $\mu_1 + 2\mu_2$.

9.12. In Problem 9.11 set 95 percent simultaneous confidence intervals on the two linear combinations of μ_1 and μ_2 (use the Bonferroni inequality).

9.13. In Problem 9.5 set a 95 percent confidence interval on $\sigma_{11} - 4\sigma_{12} + 4\sigma_{22}$.

9.14. Check all computations in the example in Section 9.6.

9.15. In the example in Section 9.6, test $H_0 : \mu_1 = \mu_2 = \mu_3 = \mu_4$ *vs.* H_a : at least one equality is an inequality. Use $\alpha = 0.10$.

9.16. In the example in Section 9.6, set simultaneous 94 percent confidence intervals on μ_1, μ_2, and μ_3.

9.17. Prove Theorem 9.4.4.

9.18. Prove Corollary 9.4.4.

9.19. In Theorem 9.3.3, let $\mathbf{\Sigma} = \mathbf{I}$ and $U = \text{tr}[\mathscr{V}]$. Show that U is distributed $\chi^2(u : nK; \lambda)$.

9.20. Prove Theorem 9.7.5.

9.21. Consider the data in Problem 9.5 to be a random sample of size $n_1 = 8$ from the bivariate distribution $N(\mathbf{x} : \boldsymbol{\mu}_1, \Sigma)$, and the data below to be a random sample of size $n_2 = 6$ from the bivariate distribution $N(\mathbf{u} : \boldsymbol{\mu}_2, \Sigma)$. With $\alpha = 0.10$, test $H_0 : \boldsymbol{\mu}_1 = \boldsymbol{\mu}_2$ *vs.* $H_a : \boldsymbol{\mu}_1 \neq \boldsymbol{\mu}_2$.

u	7.3	16.2	12.5	28.0	12.6	4.3
v	28.0	31.4	35.2	36.4	41.8	29.9

CHAPTER 10

Multiple Regression

10.1 Introduction

In this chapter we discuss the linear regression model defined in Definition 5.3.1. This model is often referred to as a *multiple regression model.* As we stated in Section 5.3, there is a strong similarity between this model and the general linear model, and many of the computing formulas developed for that model are the same for the multiple regression model. Some users do not distinguish between the general linear model and the multiple regression model.

A major difference between the two models is that in the general linear model the x values are *not random* variables, whereas in the regression model they are. For instance, in Example 5.2.1, time t is not a random variable. Also, in Example 5.2.2 it appears that the distance is a nonrandom variable, and for preselected values of the distance, an investigator would select a sample of pebbles.

In the general linear model, the x values are selected by either a random process or by deliberate selection, but once the x values have been selected they determine the p.d.f.'s (or the parameters) to which the inference is made.

In some problems an investigator may want to preselect the x values and then select random Y values from the p.d.f.'s determined by these x values since by preselecting the x values, the investigator can "design" (choose) the x observation to optimize (in some sense) the width of confidence intervals, variance of point estimators, or power of tests. However, it is sometimes difficult to obtain this type of sample. For instance, consider Example 5.3.1. If the investigator decides to preselect the x values, then he must predetermine say n heights, denoted by $x_1, x_2, \ldots, x_n$. It must then be possible to sample a Y value from each of these n populations (for example, one population would be the heights of all males over 18 years old in the city who were x_1 inches tall at age 10, and so on). This sampling procedure may be quite difficult or impossible to carry out. It would require that an investigator have a list of all males in the city over 18 years old who were x_1 inches tall when they were 10 years old; from this population a random sample of size one (or perhaps more than one) would be obtained, and this gives the data (x_1, y_1). Then for a predetermined value x_2, the investigator must have a list of all of the males in the city who are age 18 and over and who were x_2 inches tall when they were 10 years old; from this population a random sample of size one (or more) would be obtained, and this gives the data (x_2, y_2). This procedure would be repeated n times and the data obtained could be denoted by $(x_1, y_1), (x_2, y_2), \ldots, (x_n, y_n)$.

From these data one can estimate β_0, β, and $\mu(x_0) = \beta_0 + \beta x_0$, and one can set confidence intervals on, and test hypotheses about, the parameters of interest. The quality of these inference procedures depends on the preselected x values and, of course, an investigator would want to select x values so that the inference is, in some sense, "optimum."

On the other hand, if the model is assumed to be a 2-variable regression model with variables Y (height at age 18) and X (height at age 10), a random sample of n males in the city who are over 18 years old can be selected and their heights at ages 18 and 10 obtained. The observable sample values can be represented by $(X_1, Y_1), (X_2, Y_2), \ldots, (X_n, Y_n)$, and from these one can make inferences about β_0, β, and $\mu(x_0) = \beta_0 + \beta x_0$. These inferences will depend on the x values that were actually observed, but since they are observed values of random variables, they cannot be controlled by the investigator. The sampling procedure for the latter situation is often, but not always, easier to carry out.

Below is a summary of some of the properties and distinctive features of the general linear model and the multiple regression model.

General Linear Model: (1) x values are nonrandom variables; (2) repeated Y values can often be obtained for some x values and this is often desirable (see Section 8.9.2); (3) the x values can be chosen (designed) to perhaps optimize inference techniques such as width of confidence intervals, and so on (see Section 8.9.1).

Multiple Regression Model: (1) X and Y are jointly distributed random variables; (2) if X has a continuous c.d.f., then repeated Y values for a given X value will not be available in the sample; (3) the X values cannot be "designed" to optimize inference techniques; (4) correlation procedures allow for a more complete analysis of the problem.

Now we define the multiple regression model.

DEFINITION 10.1.1

General (Multiple) Linear Regression Model. *Let the* $K + 1$ *random variables*

$X_0, X_1, X_2, \ldots, X_K$ have a joint distribution with mean $\boldsymbol{\mu}^*$ and covariance matrix $\boldsymbol{\Sigma}^*$ such that

(1) *$\mathscr{E}[(X_0 \mid X_1 = x_1, X_2 = x_2, \ldots, X_K = x_K)] = \mu_Y(x_1, x_2, \ldots, x_K) = \sum_{i=0}^K \beta_i g_i(x_1, x_2, \ldots, x_K)$, where the $g_i(x_i, x_2, \ldots, x_K)$ are known functions of the x_j and contain no unknown parameters. The parameters β_i are functions of the parameters in the p.d.f. of the X_i. Y is a symbol used for $(X_0 \mid X_1 = x_1, X_2 = x_2, \ldots, X_K = x_K)$;*

(2) *$var[(X_0 \mid X_1 = x_1, X_2 = x_2, \ldots, X_K = x_K)] = \sigma^2$.*

These specifications define a multiple regression model denoted by

$$Y = \mu_Y(x_1, x_2, \ldots, x_K) + \varepsilon \qquad \mathscr{E}[\varepsilon] = 0 \qquad var[Y] = \sigma^2$$

If $g_0(x_1, x_2, \ldots, x_K) = 1$ and $g_i(x_1, x_2, \ldots, x_K) = x_i$, for $i = 1, 2, \ldots, K$, then $\mu_Y(x_1, x_2, \ldots, x_K) = \beta_0 + \sum_{i=1}^K \beta_i x_i$ and $Y = \mu_Y(x_1, x_2, \ldots, x_K) + \varepsilon = \beta_0 + \sum_{i=1}^K \beta_i x_i + \varepsilon$ is defined to be a multiple "linear" (linear in the x_i) regression model. Our discussion will be mostly about the multiple "linear" regression model, so we suppress the word "linear" and call it a multiple regression model.

Note 1. Specification (2) merely states that σ^2 is finite and does not depend on the conditioned values $x_1, x_2, \ldots, x_K$.

Note 2. In certain cases some assumptions (such as normality) will be made concerning the joint distribution of the random variables as part of the model.

The objectives for this model will be similar to those stated in Section 6.1 for the general linear model: to estimate σ^2 and linear combinations of the β_i, and to test various hypotheses about σ^2 and linear combinations of the β_i. In addition, an analysis of the model by correlation will be discussed in Chapter 11. Three cases will be considered here.

Case I. The $K + 1$ random variables $X_0, X_1, X_2, \ldots, X_K$ are jointly *normally* distributed.

Case II. The distribution of $(X_0 \mid X_1 = x_1, X_2 = x_2, \ldots, X_K = x_K)$ is *normal* with mean and variance given in Definition 10.1.1, but the marginal distribution of $X_1, X_2, \ldots, X_K$ is not known.

Case III. The distribution-free case, that is, the joint distribution of $X_0, X_1, \ldots, X_K$ is unknown.

10.2 Multiple Regression Model: Case I, Case II, and Point Estimation

First we consider Case I for two random variables (bivariate normal) X_0 and X_1, and then we extend this to $K + 1$ random variables. In Section 10.2.1 we consider Case II. We use the notation outlined in Section 3.7 and specifically in Equation (3.7.1). Here we use K instead of p. Also, it might be useful to reread the paragraph on *notation* on page 115.

Thus $\boldsymbol{\chi}^*$ is a 2×1 random vector with elements X_0 and X_1, and $\boldsymbol{\chi}^*$ is distributed $N(\mathbf{x}^* : \boldsymbol{\mu}^*, \boldsymbol{\Sigma}^*)$, where we assume that $\boldsymbol{\Sigma}^*$ is positive definite. We select a random sample of n vectors from this bivariate normal p.d.f. and denote it by $\boldsymbol{\chi}_1^*, \boldsymbol{\chi}_2^*, \ldots, \boldsymbol{\chi}_n^*$. The likelihood function of this sample is

$$L(\boldsymbol{\mu}^*, \boldsymbol{\Sigma}^* : \mathbf{x}_1^*, \mathbf{x}_2^*, \ldots, \mathbf{x}_n^*) = (2\pi)^{-n}|\boldsymbol{\Sigma}^*|^{-n/2} \exp\left[-\tfrac{1}{2} \sum_{i=1}^{n} (\mathbf{x}_i^* - \boldsymbol{\mu}^*)'\boldsymbol{\Sigma}^{*-1}(\mathbf{x}_i^* - \boldsymbol{\mu}^*)\right] \quad (10.2.1)$$

The parameter space Ω is

$$\Omega = \{(\boldsymbol{\mu}^*, \boldsymbol{\Sigma}^*) : -\infty < \mu_0 < \infty, -\infty < \mu_1 < \infty, 0 < \sigma_{00} < \infty, 0 < \sigma_{11} < \infty, -\infty < \sigma_{01} < \infty, 0 < \sigma_{00}\sigma_{11} - \sigma_{01}^2 < \infty\}$$

By Theorem 9.3.1, the maximum likelihood estimators of $\boldsymbol{\mu}^*$ and $\boldsymbol{\Sigma}^*$ ($\hat{\boldsymbol{\Sigma}}^*$ is corrected for bias) are

$$\hat{\mu}_0 = \bar{X}_0 = \left(\frac{1}{n}\right) \sum_{i=1}^{n} X_{i0} \qquad \hat{\mu}_1 = \bar{X}_1 = \left(\frac{1}{n}\right) \sum_{i=1}^{n} X_{i1}$$

$$\hat{\sigma}_{00} = \left(\frac{1}{n-1}\right) \sum_{i=1}^{n} (X_{i0} - \bar{X}_0)^2 \qquad \hat{\sigma}_{01} = \hat{\sigma}_{10} = \left(\frac{1}{n-1}\right) \sum_{i=1}^{n} (X_{i0} - \bar{X}_0)(X_{i1} - \bar{X}_1)$$

$$\hat{\sigma}_{11} = \left(\frac{1}{n-1}\right) \sum_{i=1}^{n} (X_{i1} - \bar{X}_1)^2 \quad (10.2.2)$$

Define S_{pq} by $S_{pq} = \sum (X_{ip} - \bar{X}_p)(X_{iq} - \bar{X}_q)$, $p, q = 0, 1$. By Equation (3.7.2) and Theorem 3.6.1 we get

$$\mathscr{E}[(X_0 \mid X_1 = x)] = \beta_0 + \beta x \quad \text{and} \quad \text{var}[(X_0 \mid X_1 = x)] = \sigma^2$$

where

$$\beta_0 = \mu_0 - \left(\frac{\sigma_{01}}{\sigma_{11}}\right)\mu_1 \qquad \beta = \frac{\sigma_{01}}{\sigma_{11}} \qquad \sigma^2 = \sigma_{00} - \frac{\sigma_{01}^2}{\sigma_{11}}$$

Hence the maximum likelihood estimators $\hat{\beta}_0$, $\hat{\beta}$, and $\hat{\sigma}^2$ are

$$\hat{\beta}_0 = \hat{\mu}_0 - \left(\frac{\hat{\sigma}_{01}}{\hat{\sigma}_{11}}\right)\hat{\mu}_1 \qquad \hat{\beta} = \frac{\hat{\sigma}_{01}}{\hat{\sigma}_{11}} \qquad \tilde{\sigma}^2 = \frac{S_{00} - S_{01}^2/S_{11}}{n} \qquad \hat{\sigma}^2 = \frac{n\tilde{\sigma}^2}{n-2} \tag{10.2.3}$$

It follows from the results of Theorem 9.3.2 that $\hat{\mu}_0$, $\hat{\mu}_1$, $\hat{\sigma}_{00}$, $\hat{\sigma}_{01}$, and $\hat{\sigma}_{11}$ are complete sufficient statistics and since they are unbiased estimators of their respective parameters (by Theorem 9.3.4), they are UMVU estimators; by Theorems 9.3.5 and 9.3.6 they are mean-squared-error and simple consistent estimators. These results are summed up in the following theorem.

THEOREM 10.2.1

Let $\chi_1^*, \chi_2^*, \ldots, \chi_n^*$ be a random sample of n vectors from a bivariate normal distribution with mean $\boldsymbol{\mu}^*$ and covariance matrix $\boldsymbol{\Sigma}^*$. The UMVU estimators of μ_0, μ_1, σ_{00}, σ_{10}, and σ_{11} are given by the respective quantities in Equation (10.2.2). *These are also mean-squared-error and simple consistent estimators.*

Next we state a theorem about the estimators of β_0, β, and σ^2.

THEOREM 10.2.2

The estimators $\hat{\beta}_0$, $\hat{\beta}$, and $\hat{\sigma}^2$ in Equation (10.2.3) *are the UMVU estimators of their respective parameters. They are also mean-squared-error and simple consistent estimators.*

Proof

Since the estimators are functions of complete sufficient statistics, to prove that they are UMVU estimators we have only to prove that the estimators are unbiased and use Theorem 9.3.4. Consider the distribution of Y_i defined by $Y_i = (X_{i0} \mid X_{i1} = x_i)$. Clearly $Y_1, Y_2, \ldots, Y_n$ have a joint c.d.f. which is a product of the c.d.f.s $N(y_i : \beta_0 + \beta x_i, \sigma^2)$.

Consider a general function $T = t(\chi_1^*, \chi_2^*, \ldots, \chi_n^*)$; this is a function of $X_{10}, X_{11}; X_{20}, X_{21}; \ldots; X_{n0}, X_{n1}$. We can write

$$\begin{aligned}\mathscr{E}[t(\chi_1^*, \chi_2^*, \ldots, \chi_n^*)] &= \mathscr{E}_{X_{11},X_{21},\ldots,X_{n1}}\{\mathscr{E}_{Y_1,Y_2,\ldots,Y_n}[t(\chi_1^*, \chi_2^*, \ldots, \chi_n^*)]\} \\ &= \mathscr{E}_{\tilde{\chi}_1'}\{\mathscr{E}_{\tilde{\chi}_0'|\tilde{\chi}_1'}[T]\}\end{aligned}$$

where $\tilde{\chi}_j' = [X_{1j}, X_{2j}, \ldots, X_{nj}]$, $j = 0, 1$. Define $t(\chi_1^*, \chi_2^*, \ldots, \chi_n^*)$ to be the random variable

$$\frac{\hat{\sigma}_{01}}{\hat{\sigma}_{11}} = \frac{\sum_{i=1}^{n} (X_{i0} - \bar{X}_0)(X_{i1} - \bar{X}_1)}{\sum_{j=1}^{n} (X_{j1} - \bar{X}_1)^2}$$

We note that

$$\mathscr{E}_{\tilde{\chi}_0|\tilde{\chi}_1}[(X_{i0} - \overline{X}_0)] = \mathscr{E}_{\tilde{\chi}_0|\tilde{\chi}_1}[X_{i0}] - \mathscr{E}_{\tilde{\chi}_0|\tilde{\chi}_1}[\overline{X}_0]$$
$$= \beta_0 + \beta X_{i1} - \beta_0 - \beta \overline{X}_1 = \beta(X_{i1} - \overline{X}_1)$$

thus

$$\mathscr{E}\begin{bmatrix}\hat{\sigma}_{10}\\ \hat{\sigma}_{11}\end{bmatrix} = \mathscr{E}_{\tilde{\chi}_1'}\left(\frac{\sum_{i=1}^{n}(X_{i1} - \overline{X}_1)}{\sum_{j=1}^{n}(X_{j1} - \overline{X}_1)^2}\right)\{\mathscr{E}_{\tilde{\chi}_0'|\tilde{\chi}_1'}[X_{i0} - \overline{X}_0]\}$$

$$= \mathscr{E}_{\tilde{\chi}_1'}(\beta)\left(\frac{\sum_{i=1}^{n}(X_{i1} - \overline{X}_1)^2}{\sum_{j=1}^{n}(X_{j1} - \overline{X}_1)^2}\right) = \mathscr{E}_{\tilde{\chi}_1'}[\beta] = \beta$$

Hence $\hat{\beta}$ is an unbiased (and UMVU) estimator of β.

A similar procedure can be used for $\hat{\beta}_0$ and $\hat{\sigma}^2$. The proof that $\hat{\beta}_0$, $\hat{\beta}$, and $\hat{\sigma}^2$ are consistent estimators will be left for the reader.

These results will now be extended to the $K + 1$ variable case. In this case the random variables $X_0, X_1, \ldots, X_K$ are distributed as a $(K + 1)$-variate normal distribution. We let the letter $\boldsymbol{\chi}^*$ represent this $K + 1$ vector of random variables, that is, $\boldsymbol{\chi}^* = [X_0, X_1, \ldots, X_K]'$, and let $\mathbf{x}^*$ represent the vector of the values of these random variables, that is, $\mathbf{x}^* = [x_0, x_1, \ldots, x_K]'$. The p.d.f. of $\boldsymbol{\chi}^*$ is

$$\mathbf{N}(\mathbf{x}^* : \boldsymbol{\mu}^*, \boldsymbol{\Sigma}^*) = \left(\frac{1}{(2\pi)^{(K+1)/2}|\boldsymbol{\Sigma}^*|^{1/2}}\right)\exp\left[-\frac{1}{2}(\mathbf{x}^* - \boldsymbol{\mu}^*)'\boldsymbol{\Sigma}^{*-1}(\mathbf{x}^* - \boldsymbol{\mu}^*)\right]$$

The notation $\boldsymbol{\mu}^*$, $\boldsymbol{\Sigma}^*$, $\boldsymbol{\chi}^*$, and $\mathbf{x}^*$ is the same as Equation (3.7.1), namely,

$$\boldsymbol{\chi}^* = \begin{bmatrix}X_0\\ \boldsymbol{\chi}\end{bmatrix} \qquad \boldsymbol{\Sigma}^* = \begin{bmatrix}\sigma_{00} & \boldsymbol{\sigma}_{01}\\ \boldsymbol{\sigma}_{10} & \boldsymbol{\Sigma}\end{bmatrix} \qquad \boldsymbol{\mu}^* = \begin{bmatrix}\mu_0\\ \boldsymbol{\mu}\end{bmatrix} \qquad \mathbf{x}^* = \begin{bmatrix}x_0\\ \mathbf{x}\end{bmatrix}$$

If we select a sample of size n from this p.d.f. (each sample is a $K + 1$ vector), the sample values are $\mathbf{x}_1^*, \mathbf{x}_2^*, \ldots, \mathbf{x}_n^*$, and the likelihood function is

$$L(\boldsymbol{\mu}^*, \boldsymbol{\Sigma}^* : \mathbf{x}_1^*, \mathbf{x}_2^*, \ldots, \mathbf{x}_n^*)$$
$$= \left(\frac{1}{(2\pi)^{n(K+1)/2}|\boldsymbol{\Sigma}^*|^{n/2}}\right)\exp\left[-\frac{1}{2}\sum_{i=1}^{n}(\mathbf{x}_i^* - \boldsymbol{\mu}^*)'\boldsymbol{\Sigma}^{*-1}(\mathbf{x}_i^* - \boldsymbol{\mu}^*)\right]$$

The maximum likelihood estimators of the parameters $\boldsymbol{\mu}^*$ and $\boldsymbol{\Sigma}^*$ were derived in Section 9.3. They are

$$\tilde{\boldsymbol{\mu}}^* = \left(\frac{1}{n}\right)\sum_{i=1}^{n} \boldsymbol{\chi}_i^* = \bar{\boldsymbol{\chi}}^* \qquad \tilde{\boldsymbol{\Sigma}}^* = \left(\frac{1}{n}\right)\sum_{i=1}^{n} (\boldsymbol{\chi}_i^* - \bar{\boldsymbol{\chi}}^*)(\boldsymbol{\chi}_i^* - \bar{\boldsymbol{\chi}}^*)' = \left(\frac{1}{n}\right)\mathscr{A}^* \tag{10.2.4}$$

From Section 3.7, the quantities $\boldsymbol{\beta}$, β_0, and σ^2 in Definition 10.1.1 are

$$\begin{aligned} \boldsymbol{\beta} &= [\beta_1, \beta_2, \ldots, \beta_K]' = \boldsymbol{\Sigma}^{-1}\boldsymbol{\sigma}_{10} \qquad \beta_0 = \mu_0 - \boldsymbol{\sigma}_{01}\boldsymbol{\Sigma}^{-1}\boldsymbol{\mu} \\ \sigma^2 &= \sigma_{00} - \boldsymbol{\sigma}_{01}\boldsymbol{\Sigma}^{-1}\boldsymbol{\sigma}_{10} \end{aligned} \tag{10.2.5}$$

Let

$$\mathscr{A}^* = \begin{bmatrix} A_{00} & \boldsymbol{a}_{01} \\ \boldsymbol{a}_{10} & \mathscr{A} \end{bmatrix} \tag{10.2.6}$$

then

$$\mathscr{A} = \sum_{i=1}^{n} (\boldsymbol{\chi}_i - \bar{\boldsymbol{\chi}})(\boldsymbol{\chi}_i - \bar{\boldsymbol{\chi}})' \qquad \boldsymbol{a}_{01} = \boldsymbol{a}_{10}' = \sum_{i=1}^{n} (X_{i0} - \bar{X}_0)(\boldsymbol{\chi}_i - \bar{\boldsymbol{\chi}})'$$

Thus

$$\begin{aligned} \hat{\boldsymbol{\Sigma}} &= \left(\frac{1}{n-1}\right)\sum_{i=1}^{n} (\boldsymbol{\chi}_i - \bar{\boldsymbol{\chi}})(\boldsymbol{\chi}_i - \bar{\boldsymbol{\chi}})' = \left(\frac{1}{n-1}\right)\mathscr{A} \qquad \hat{\boldsymbol{\Sigma}}^* = \left(\frac{1}{n-1}\right)\mathscr{A}^* \\ \hat{\boldsymbol{\mu}} &= \left(\frac{1}{n}\right)\sum_{i=1}^{n} \boldsymbol{\chi}_i = \bar{\boldsymbol{\chi}} \qquad \hat{\boldsymbol{\mu}}^* = \left(\frac{1}{n}\right)\sum_{i=1}^{n} \boldsymbol{\chi}_i^* = \bar{\boldsymbol{\chi}}^* \\ \hat{\boldsymbol{\sigma}}_{01} &= \hat{\boldsymbol{\sigma}}_{10}' = \left(\frac{1}{n-1}\right)\boldsymbol{a}_{01} = \left(\frac{1}{n-1}\right)\boldsymbol{a}_{10}' = \left(\frac{1}{n-1}\right)\sum_{i=1}^{n} (X_{i0} - \bar{X}_0)(\boldsymbol{\chi}_i - \bar{\boldsymbol{\chi}})' \end{aligned} \tag{10.2.7}$$

where $\hat{\boldsymbol{\mu}}$, $\hat{\boldsymbol{\mu}}^*$, $\hat{\boldsymbol{\Sigma}}$, $\hat{\boldsymbol{\Sigma}}^*$, and $\hat{\boldsymbol{\sigma}}_{10}$ are maximum likelihood estimators ($\hat{\boldsymbol{\Sigma}}$, $\hat{\boldsymbol{\Sigma}}^*$, and $\hat{\boldsymbol{\sigma}}_{10}$ are corrected for bias) of $\boldsymbol{\mu}$, $\boldsymbol{\mu}^*$, $\boldsymbol{\Sigma}$, $\boldsymbol{\Sigma}^*$, and $\boldsymbol{\sigma}_{10}$, respectively.

By the invariance property of maximum likelihood estimators, we get for the M.L. estimators of β_0, $\boldsymbol{\beta}$, and σ^2 (adjusted to be unbiased if necessary)

$$\begin{aligned} \hat{\beta}_0 &= \bar{X}_0 - \boldsymbol{a}_{01}\mathscr{A}^{-1}\bar{\boldsymbol{\chi}} \\ \hat{\boldsymbol{\beta}} &= \mathscr{A}^{-1}\boldsymbol{a}_{10} \\ \hat{\sigma}^2 &= \left(\frac{1}{n-K-1}\right)(A_{00} - \boldsymbol{a}_{01}\mathscr{A}^{-1}\boldsymbol{a}_{10}) \end{aligned} \tag{10.2.8}$$

These results are an extension of the 2-variate case and an application of Theorem 9.3.2. We summarize the results in the following theorem. (Also see Theorems 9.3.4 and 9.3.5.)

THEOREM 10.2.3

Let the $(K+1) \times 1$ random vector $\boldsymbol{\chi}^*$ be distributed $\mathbf{N}(\mathbf{x}^* : \boldsymbol{\mu}^*, \boldsymbol{\Sigma}^*)$, and let $\boldsymbol{\chi}_1^*, \boldsymbol{\chi}_2^*, \ldots, \boldsymbol{\chi}_n^*$ be a random sample of n vectors from this distribution. The maximum likelihood estimators (adjusted for bias if necessary) of $\boldsymbol{\mu}$, $\boldsymbol{\Sigma}$, $\boldsymbol{\sigma}_{10}$, $\boldsymbol{\mu}^*$, $\boldsymbol{\Sigma}^*$, $\boldsymbol{\beta}$, β_0, and σ^2 are given in Equations (10.2.7) and (10.2.8). The random variables $\hat{\mu}_0, \hat{\mu}_1, \ldots, \hat{\mu}_K$ and $\hat{\sigma}_{00}, \hat{\sigma}_{01}, \ldots, \hat{\sigma}_{KK}$ (that is, $\hat{\boldsymbol{\mu}}^*$ and $\hat{\boldsymbol{\Sigma}}^*$) are complete sufficient statistics. Also, $\hat{\mu}_0, \hat{\mu}_1, \ldots, \hat{\mu}_K, \hat{\sigma}_{00}, \hat{\sigma}_{01}, \ldots, \hat{\sigma}_{KK}, \hat{\beta}_0, \hat{\beta}_1, \ldots, \hat{\beta}_K$, and $\hat{\sigma}^2$ are unbiased estimators of their respective parameters; hence they are UMVU estimators of their respective parameters. They are also mean-squared-error and simple consistent estimators of their respective parameters.

10.2.1 Multiple Regression Model: Case II, Point Estimation

In this case the conditional c.d.f. of $(X_0 \mid X_1 = x_1, X_2 = x_2, \ldots, X_K = x_K)$, which we denote by Y, is $N(y : \beta_0 + \sum_{i=1}^{K} \beta_i x_i, \sigma^2)$, and the joint marginal distribution of $X_1, X_2, \ldots, X_K$ is not known. However, we denote the p.d.f. of $X_1, X_2, \ldots, X_K$ by $f_{\chi}(\mathbf{x} : \boldsymbol{\theta})$, and we assume that the parameters $\boldsymbol{\theta}, \beta_0, \beta_1, \ldots, \beta_K$, and σ^2 are functionally independent. Thus the joint p.d.f. of $X_0, X_1, \ldots, X_K$ can be written as

$$f_{\chi^*}(\mathbf{x}^* : \beta_0, \boldsymbol{\beta}, \sigma^2, \boldsymbol{\theta}) = (2\pi\sigma^2)^{-1/2} \exp\left\{-\left(\frac{1}{2\sigma^2}\right)\left[x_0 - \beta_0 - \sum_{k=1}^{K} \beta_k x_k\right]^2\right\} \cdot f_{\chi}(\mathbf{x} : \boldsymbol{\theta}) \tag{10.2.9}$$

Let $\boldsymbol{\chi}_1^*, \boldsymbol{\chi}_2^*, \ldots, \boldsymbol{\chi}_n^*$ represent a random sample from a population with this p.d.f. The likelihood function is

$$L(\beta_0, \boldsymbol{\beta}, \sigma^2, \boldsymbol{\theta} : \mathbf{x}_1^*, \mathbf{x}_2^*, \ldots, \mathbf{x}_n^*)$$
$$= (2\pi\sigma^2)^{-n/2} \exp\left\{-\left(\frac{1}{2\sigma^2}\right) \sum_{i=1}^{n} \left(x_{i0} - \beta_0 - \sum_{k=1}^{K} \beta_k x_{ik}\right)^2\right\} \prod_{t=1}^{n} f_{\chi_t}(\mathbf{x}_t : \boldsymbol{\theta})$$

Clearly the maximum likelihood estimators of the β_i and σ^2 (adjusted for bias) are the same as those given in Equation (10.2.8). The $\hat{\beta}_0, \hat{\beta}_1, \ldots, \hat{\beta}_K$, and $\hat{\sigma}^2$ in Equation (10.2.8) are *unbiased* estimators of their respective parameters, but they are *not* necessarily UMVU estimators. Whether or not they are UMVU estimators depends on the p.d.f. of $X_1, X_2, \ldots, X_K$, which is unknown. We now summarize these results in the following theorem.

THEOREM 10.2.4

Let $\boldsymbol{\chi}_1^*, \boldsymbol{\chi}_2^*, \ldots, \boldsymbol{\chi}_n^*$ be a random sample from the $(K+1)$-variate population whose p.d.f. is given by Equation (10.2.9). The maximum likelihood estimators of β_0,

$\beta_1, \ldots, \beta_K$ and of σ^2 (corrected for bias) are given in Equation (10.2.8). These estimators are unbiased for the respective parameters.

10.3 Multiple Regression Model: Confidence Intervals and Tests of Hypotheses, Case I and Case II

In this section we discuss confidence intervals and tests of hypotheses when $\chi_1^*, \chi_2^*, \ldots, \chi_n^*$ is a random sample from the p.d.f. given in Equation (10.2.9). We show that the formulas given in Chapter 6 are valid under this more general model which includes Case I and Case II.

10.3.1 Confidence Intervals

First we discuss confidence intervals.

THEOREM 10.3.1

Let the $(K + 1) \times 1$ vectors $\chi_1^*, \chi_2^*, \ldots, \chi_n^*$ be a random sample from $\mathbf{N}(\mathbf{x}^* : \boldsymbol{\mu}^*, \boldsymbol{\Sigma}^*)$. Consider the conditional distribution of Y_i denoted by $Y_i = (X_{i0} \mid \chi_i = \mathbf{x}_i)$, $i = 1, 2, \ldots, n$. Define the $n \times 1$ vector $\mathbf{Y}$ by $\mathbf{Y}' = [Y_1, Y_2, \ldots, Y_n]$. Then $\mathbf{Y}$ is denoted by

$$\mathbf{Y} = \begin{bmatrix} X_{10} \mid \chi_1' = \mathbf{x}_1' \\ X_{20} \mid \chi_2' = \mathbf{x}_2' \\ \vdots \\ X_{n0} \mid \chi_n' = \mathbf{x}_n' \end{bmatrix} = \left[\begin{array}{c} X_{10} \\ X_{20} \\ \vdots \\ X_{n0} \end{array} \middle| \, \mathscr{X} = \mathbf{X} \right] = (\mathbf{X}_0 \mid \mathscr{X} = \mathbf{X}) \tag{10.3.1}$$

where

$$\mathbf{X}_0 = \begin{bmatrix} X_{10} \\ X_{20} \\ \vdots \\ X_{n0} \end{bmatrix}$$

and where $\mathscr{X}$ and $\mathbf{X}$ are defined in Equation (9.2.2). The c.d.f. of $\mathbf{Y}$ is $\mathbf{N}(\mathbf{y} : \beta_0\mathbf{1} + \mathbf{X}\boldsymbol{\beta}, \sigma^2\mathbf{I})$, where $\sigma^2 = \sigma_{00} - \boldsymbol{\sigma}_{01}\boldsymbol{\Sigma}^{-1}\boldsymbol{\sigma}_{10}$, $\beta_0 = \mu_0 - \boldsymbol{\sigma}_{01}\boldsymbol{\Sigma}^{-1}\boldsymbol{\mu}$, and $\boldsymbol{\beta} = \boldsymbol{\Sigma}^{-1}\boldsymbol{\sigma}_{10}$ are defined in Section 3.7.

Proof

Since the χ_i^* are jointly independent and since

$$\chi_i^* = \begin{bmatrix} X_{i0} \\ \chi_i \end{bmatrix}$$

we note by Section 3.7 that $Y_i = (X_{i0} \mid \chi_i = \mathbf{x}_i)$, $i = 1, 2, \ldots, n$, have a joint p.d.f. $\Pi_{i=1}^n n(y_i : \beta_0 + \boldsymbol{\beta}'\mathbf{x}_i, \sigma_{00} - \boldsymbol{\sigma}_{01}\boldsymbol{\Sigma}^{-1}\boldsymbol{\sigma}_{10})$. Let $\mathscr{E}[Y_i] = \beta_0 + \boldsymbol{\beta}'\mathbf{x}_i = \beta_0 + \mathbf{x}_i'\boldsymbol{\beta}$; then $\mathscr{E}[\mathbf{Y}] = \boldsymbol{\mu}_\mathbf{Y} = \beta_0\mathbf{1} + \mathbf{X}\boldsymbol{\beta}$. This completes the proof.

Note 1. If we make the transformation $\boldsymbol{\varepsilon} = \mathbf{Y} - \boldsymbol{\mu}_\mathbf{Y}$, we get $\boldsymbol{\varepsilon}$ is distributed $\mathbf{N}(\boldsymbol{\varepsilon} : \mathbf{0}, \sigma^2\mathbf{I})$. We can write this as $\mathbf{Y} = \boldsymbol{\mu}_\mathbf{Y} + \boldsymbol{\varepsilon}$, or

$$\mathbf{Y} = \mathbf{1}\beta_0 + \mathbf{X}\boldsymbol{\beta} + \boldsymbol{\varepsilon} \qquad \boldsymbol{\varepsilon} \text{ is distributed } \mathbf{N}(\boldsymbol{\varepsilon} : \mathbf{0}, \sigma^2\mathbf{I}) \tag{10.3.2}$$

and this is exactly the general linear model discussed in Chapter 6. *But we must keep in mind that here the p.d.f. of Y is a conditional p.d.f., where the random vectors $\chi_1, \chi_2, \ldots, \chi_n$ are respectively fixed at* $\mathbf{x}_1, \mathbf{x}_2, \ldots, \mathbf{x}_n$, that is, $\mathscr{X} = \mathbf{X}$.

Thus it appears as if all the theorems in Chapter 6 are applicable to the model in Equation (10.3.2), and indeed they are as long as $\mathscr{X}$ is held fixed at $\mathbf{X}$. This means that the long-term relative frequency interpretation of the confidence interval statements and tests of hypotheses in formulas in that chapter is exact if the repeated sampling is done in the conditional distribution with $\mathscr{X}$ fixed at $\mathbf{X}$. However, this does not seem to be as general as we would like for practical applications.

For instance, consider the example in Section 6.7. In that example we assumed that the x_i were selected values of nonrandom variables and these determined $n = 10$ p.d.f.'s and a random sample of size one, denoted by Y_i, was selected from each. From these data a 95 percent one-at-a-time confidence interval was set on β, and the long-run relative frequency interpretation is this: If repeated random samples are selected from the *same* p.d.f.'s (determined by these same x_i values), then in 95 percent of the samples the respective confidence intervals will include the unknown parameter β.

The formula for computing this confidence interval on β is given in Equation (6.4.3) and is $\ell'\hat{\boldsymbol{\beta}} \mp t_{\alpha/2:n-2}\sqrt{\hat{\sigma}^2\ell'(\mathbf{X}'\mathbf{X})^{-1}\ell}$. But $\hat{\boldsymbol{\beta}}$, $\hat{\sigma}^2$ and, of course, $\mathbf{X}'\mathbf{X}$ are functions of the constant values $\mathbf{x}_i$. The quantities $\hat{\boldsymbol{\beta}}$ and $\hat{\sigma}^2$ are also functions of the random quantities Y_i, and this is why the confidence intervals are random. "In the long run" they cover the true unknown $\ell'\boldsymbol{\beta}$ in a fixed proportion, say $1 - \alpha$, of the samples selected at random.

However, suppose the (y_i, x_i) in Section 6.7 are values of random 2×1 vectors from a bivariate normal p.d.f. and we want a 0.95 confidence interval on β. We want a procedure such that, when repeated bivariate samples are selected and 0.95 confidence intervals set on β, "in the long run" 0.95 of the intervals will cover β. Then we have "0.95 confidence" that a particular computed interval covers β. However, in this case the x_i are not preselected but are values of random variables.

We shall now prove that the formulas are valid even if $\mathbf{X}$ is replaced by the random matrix $\mathscr{X}$ throughout Chapter 6, as long as the model in Equation (10.3.2) is the correct model.

THEOREM 10.3.2

Let the model in Equation (10.3.2) *hold for* $\mathscr{X} = \mathbf{X}$, *where* $\mathbf{X}$ *is a matrix of fixed known numbers and* $\mathbf{Y}$, $\mathbf{X}_0$, χ,*and so on, are defined in Theorem* 10.3.1. *Let*

$$P[\ell(\mathbf{Y}, \mathbf{X}) \leq q(\boldsymbol{\beta}, \sigma^2) \leq u(\mathbf{Y}, \mathbf{X})] = 1 - \alpha \tag{10.3.3}$$

be a $1 - \alpha$ *confidence interval on* $q(\boldsymbol{\beta}, \sigma^2)$, *a known function of the unknown parameters* $\boldsymbol{\beta}$ *and* σ^2. *Equation* (10.3.3) *is also valid when* $(\mathbf{Y}, \mathbf{X})$ *is replaced by* $(\mathbf{X}_0, \mathscr{X})$, *where* $\chi_1^*, \chi_2^*, \ldots, \chi_n^*$ *is a random sample from the* $(K + 1)$*-variate p.d.f. defined by Equation* (10.2.9); *that is, the following probability statement is a valid* $1 - \alpha$ *confidence interval on* $q(\boldsymbol{\beta}, \sigma^2)$:

$$P[\ell(\mathbf{X}_0, \mathscr{X}) \leq q(\boldsymbol{\beta}, \sigma^2) \leq u(\mathbf{X}_0, \mathscr{X})] = 1 - \alpha \tag{10.3.4}$$

Proof

We outline the proof. Let A be the event defined by $A = \{\ell(\mathbf{X}_0, \mathscr{X}) \leq q(\boldsymbol{\beta}, \sigma^2) \leq u(\mathbf{X}_0, \mathscr{X})\}$, and let the event $(A \mid \mathscr{X} = \mathbf{X})$ be defined by $(A \mid \mathscr{X} = \mathbf{X}) = \{\ell(\mathbf{Y}, \mathbf{X}) \leq q(\boldsymbol{\beta}, \sigma^2) \leq u(\mathbf{Y}, \mathbf{X})\}$. Then Equation (10.3.3) is equivalent to $P[(A \mid \mathscr{X} = \mathbf{X})] = 1 - \alpha$, where $\mathbf{Y}$ is the symbol for $(\mathbf{X}_0 \mid \mathscr{X} = \mathbf{X})$. Now (see [M-7], page 148)

$$P[A] = \mathscr{E}_{\mathscr{X}}\{P[(A \mid \mathscr{X})]\} = \mathscr{X}_{\mathscr{X}}[1 - \alpha] = 1 - \alpha$$

since $1 - \alpha$ is a constant and $\mathscr{E}_{\mathscr{X}}[\cdot]$ means the expectation with respect to the joint p.d.f. of $\mathscr{X}$, where $\mathscr{X}' = [\chi_1, \chi_2, \ldots, \chi_n]$ is defined in Equation (9.2.2). This completes the proof.

Note 2. Any confidence interval statement in Chapter 6 which is derived from the general linear model for Case 1 (Y_i are normal variables and the x_{ij} in $\mathbf{X}$ are nonrandom variables) is also valid when the $\mathbf{X}_0$ and $\mathscr{X}$ are joint random variables, where $\chi_1^*, \chi_2^*, \ldots, \chi_n^*$ is a random sample from the p.d.f. in Equation (10.2.9).

10.3.2 Tests of Hypotheses

Consider any test of H_0 *vs.* H_a and a test statistic $W = g(\mathbf{Y}, \mathbf{X})$ when the assumptions of the general linear model hold. Suppose H_0 is rejected when w, the value of the random variable W, is in the rejection region R (that is, in Equation (6.3.10), H_0 is rejected if $w \geq F_{\alpha:q,n-p}$ and $P[W \geq F_{\alpha:q,n-p}] = \alpha$ when H_0 is true). In Chapter 6 all of the tests of H_0 *vs.* H_a of size α when the assumptions of the general linear model hold are given in the following form: Reject H_0 if and only if $g(\mathbf{y}, \mathbf{X})$ is in R; also, $P[g(\mathbf{Y}, \mathbf{X})$ is in $R] = \alpha$ when H_0 is true.

Let A be the event $\{g(\mathbf{X}_0, \mathscr{X})$ is in $R\}$ and $(A \mid \mathscr{X} = \mathbf{X})$ be the event $\{g(\mathbf{X}_0, \mathscr{X}) \mid \mathscr{X} = \mathbf{X}$ is in $R\}$; $\mathbf{Y}, \mathbf{X}_0$, and $\mathscr{X}$ are defined in Theorem 10.3.1. Thus $P[(A \mid \mathscr{X} = \mathbf{X})] = \alpha$ when H_0 is true is valid for the general linear model since the X_{ij} values are fixed at x_{ij}, that is, $\mathscr{X} = \mathbf{X}$. But when H_0 is true, $P[A] = \mathscr{E}_{\mathscr{X}}\{P[(A \mid \mathscr{X})]\} = \mathscr{E}_{\mathscr{X}}\{\alpha\} = \alpha$ since α is a constant. Thus let $\chi_1^*, \chi_2^*, \ldots, \chi_n^*$ be a random sample from the p.d.f. given in Equation (10.2.9). Then any size α test procedure in Chapter 6 that is valid under Case 1 of the general linear model when H_0 is true remains valid for a test of size α if $\mathbf{X}$ is replaced by $\mathscr{X}$ and $\mathbf{Y}$ is replaced by $\mathbf{X}_0$.

Example 10.3.1

To illustrate more explicitly, consider the test of $H_0: \mathbf{H}\boldsymbol{\beta} = \mathbf{h}$ *vs.* $H_a: \mathbf{H}\boldsymbol{\beta} \neq \mathbf{h}$ given in Theorem 6.3.1. The test statistic W in Equation (6.3.10) is

$$W = g(\mathbf{Y}, \mathbf{X}) = \left(\frac{n-p}{q}\right)\left(\frac{(\mathbf{H}\mathbf{X}^-\mathbf{Y} - \mathbf{h})'[\mathbf{H}(\mathbf{X}'\mathbf{X})^{-1}\mathbf{H}']^{-1}(\mathbf{H}\mathbf{X}^-\mathbf{Y} - \mathbf{h})}{\mathbf{Y}'(\mathbf{I} - \mathbf{X}\mathbf{X}^-)\mathbf{Y}}\right)$$

If H_0 is true, $P[W \geq F_{\alpha:q,n-p}] = \alpha$, so a size α test is this: Reject H_0 if and only if $w \geq F_{\alpha:q,n-p}$.

Now we will replace $\mathbf{Y}$ by $\mathbf{X}_0$ and $\mathbf{X}$ by $\mathscr{X}$, where $\chi_1^*, \chi_2^*, \ldots, \chi_n^*$ is a random sample from the p.d.f. given in Equation (10.2.9). We get

$$\begin{aligned} W^* &= g(\mathbf{X}_0, \mathscr{X}) \\ &= \left(\frac{n-p}{q}\right)\left(\frac{(\mathbf{H}\mathscr{X}^-\mathbf{X}_0 - \mathbf{h})'[\mathbf{H}(\mathscr{X}'\mathscr{X})^{-1}\mathbf{H}']^{-1}(\mathbf{H}\mathscr{X}^-\mathbf{X}_0 - \mathbf{h})}{\mathbf{X}_0'(\mathbf{I} - \mathscr{X}\mathscr{X}^-)\mathbf{X}_0}\right) \end{aligned}$$

Consider the conditional p.d.f. of $(W^* \mid \mathscr{X} = \mathbf{X}) = (g(\mathbf{X}_0, \mathscr{X}) \mid \mathscr{X} = \mathbf{X})$, which can be written as $g(\mathbf{X}_0 \mid \mathscr{X} = \mathbf{X}, \mathscr{X} \mid \mathscr{X} = \mathbf{X}) \equiv g(\mathbf{Y}, \mathbf{X})$ since $(\mathscr{X} \mid \mathscr{X} = \mathbf{X})$ is the same as $\mathbf{X}$, and $\mathbf{Y}$ is the symbol used for $(\mathbf{X}_0 \mid \mathscr{X} = \mathbf{X})$. Hence $(W^* \mid \mathscr{X} = \mathbf{X})$ is distributed the same as $g(\mathbf{Y}, \mathbf{X})$, which is distributed $F(w: q, n-p; \lambda)$, where $\lambda = (1/2\sigma^2)(\mathbf{H}\boldsymbol{\beta} - \mathbf{h})'[\mathbf{H}(\mathbf{X}'\mathbf{X})^{-1}\mathbf{H}']^{-1} \times (\mathbf{H}\boldsymbol{\beta} - \mathbf{h})$. So this p.d.f. depends on $\mathbf{X}$.

Now if H_0 is true, then $\mathbf{H}\boldsymbol{\beta} = \mathbf{h}$ and hence $\lambda = 0$. Thus under H_0, the test statistic $(W^* \mid \mathscr{X} = \mathbf{X})$ is distributed as $F(w^*: q, n-p; 0)$ and *this* p.d.f. does *not* depend on the conditioned value $\mathbf{X}$. Since the p.d.f. of $(W^* \mid \mathscr{X} = \mathbf{X})$ does not depend on $\mathbf{X}$ when H_0 is true, the conditional p.d.f. of $(W^* \mid \mathscr{X} = \mathbf{X})$ is the same as the marginal p.d.f. of W^*; this says that the p.d.f. of $W^* = g(\mathbf{X}_0, \mathscr{X})$ is the same as the p.d.f. of $W = g(\mathbf{Y}, \mathbf{X})$ *when* H_0 *is true*. Thus $P[W \geq F_{\alpha:q,n-p}] = \alpha$ when H_0 is true, and also, $P[W^* \geq F_{\alpha:q,n-p}] = \alpha$ when H_0 is true.

10.3.3 Additional Comments

Some final comments are in order for the multiple *linear* regression model.

Note 3. We have proved that confidence coefficients and Type I error probabilities are unchanged if the formulas derived for the general linear model are used for Case I or Case II of the multiple regression model. However, the two models *are different* and the difference is evident in the probability of Type II errors and in the widths of confidence intervals. This is clear since, in general, it is seen that these depend on the values of the random variables in $\mathscr{X}$, that is, they depend on $\mathbf{X}$.

Note 4. We have not derived the distributions of $\hat{\beta}_0$, $\hat{\boldsymbol{\beta}}$, or $\hat{\sigma}^2$ for the multiple regression model. We have not done so because the distributions are not needed to compute confidence intervals or tests of hypotheses. Also, it should be noted that the distributions of the estimators can be found for Case I of the multiple regression model, but for Case II a knowledge of the distribution of $\chi_1, \chi_2, \ldots, \chi_n$ is required.

10.4 Multiple Regression Model: Case III

In this case the $(K + 1) \times 1$ vectors $\chi_1^*, \chi_2^*, \ldots, \chi_n^*$ are considered to be a random sample from the p.d.f. $f_{\chi^*}(\cdot)$. Nothing is known about $f_{\chi^*}(\cdot)$ except we denote the mean by $\boldsymbol{\mu}^*$ and the covariance matrix by $\boldsymbol{\Sigma}^*$, and it is positive definite. However, to satisfy (1) and (2) of Definition 10.1.1, the p.d.f. $f_{\chi^*}(\cdot)$ must satisfy certain restrictions, that is, the regression function must be a *linear* function of $x_1, x_2, \ldots, x_K$ and the variance of $(X_0 \mid \chi = \mathbf{x})$ must *not* depend on $\mathbf{x}$. We do not discuss inference procedures for Case III, but we show how the regression parameters are related for Cases I, II, and III. We discuss only the bivariate case but the extension to $(K + 1)$-variates is obvious.

Let X_0 and X_1 be jointly distributed random variables; we use the following notations:

$$
\begin{aligned}
&Y = (X_0 \mid X_1 = x_1) && \\
&f_{X_0,X_1}(\cdot,\cdot) && \text{p.d.f. of } X_0, X_1 \\
&F_{X_0,X_1}(\cdot,\cdot) && \text{c.d.f. of } X_0, X_1 \\
&f_{X_1}(\cdot), F_{X_1}(\cdot) && \text{p.d.f. and c.d.f of } X_1 \\
&f_{X_0}(\cdot), F_{X_0}(\cdot) && \text{p.d.f. and c.d.f. of } X_0 \\
&\boldsymbol{\mu} = \begin{bmatrix} \mu_{X_0} \\ \mu_{X_1} \end{bmatrix} && \boldsymbol{\Sigma} = \begin{bmatrix} \sigma_{X_0X_0} & \sigma_{X_0X_1} \\ \sigma_{X_1X_0} & \sigma_{X_1X_1} \end{bmatrix} \\
&\mu_Y(x) = \mathscr{E}[(X_0 \mid X_1 = x)] && \\
&\sigma_Y^2(x) = \text{var}[(X_0 \mid X_1 = x)] &&
\end{aligned}
\tag{10.4.1}
$$

We first state the definition of the regression function.

DEFINITION 10.4.1

Regression Function of X_0 on X_1. *The function $\mathscr{E}[(X_0 \mid X_1 = x)]$, which we denote by $\mu_Y(x)$, is defined to be the regression function of X_0 on X_1.*

Note 1. We have not indicated it in our notation, but in most cases the function $\mu_Y(x)$ will contain unknown parameters which include some or all of the unknown parameters in $f_{X_0,X_1}(x_0, x_1)$ from which $\mu_Y(x)$ is obtained.

Note 2. There is no reason to expect $\mu_Y(x)$ to be linear in x as it is in Case I and Case II of the multiple linear regression model. In [K-7] is a discussion of conditions on the c.d.f. $F_{X_0,X_1}(x_0, x_1)$ so that the regression function will indeed be linear.

Reminder. The word "linear" in linear regression function means linear in the (domain) variable x. For example, $\mu_Y(x) = \beta_0 + \beta^2 x$ is a linear regression function, $\mu_Y(x) = \beta_0 + \beta x^2$ is not. However, the latter is linear in x^2.

In the next two theorems we show that for *any* jointly distributed random variables X_0 and X_1 for which the regression function is linear, the regression coefficients (and the average of $\text{var}[(X_0 \mid X_1)]$) are the same as when X_0 and X_1 have a bivariate normal p.d.f. (for Case I) or when the p.d.f. of X_0 and X_1 satisfies Case II.

THEOREM 10.4.1

Let X_0 and X_1 be jointly distributed random variables and assume the notation in Equation (10.4.1). If the regression function of X_0 on X_1 is linear in x (that is, if $\mu_Y(x) = \beta_0 + \beta x$), then $\beta_0 = \mu_{X_0} - (\sigma_{X_1X_0}/\sigma_{X_1X_1})\mu_{X_1}$ and $\beta = \sigma_{X_1X_0}/\sigma_{X_1X_1}$.

Proof

First we derive a relationship between μ_{X_0} and μ_{X_1}. The hypothesis of the theorem (the regression is linear) implies $\mu_Y(x) = \beta_0 + \beta x$. Consider

$$\begin{aligned}\mu_{X_0} &= \mathscr{E}[X_0] = \mathscr{E}_{X_1}\mathscr{E}_{X_0|X_1}[X_0] = \mathscr{E}_{X_1}[\mu_Y(X_1)]\\ &= \mathscr{E}_{X_1}[\beta_0 + \beta X_1] = \beta_0 + \beta\mu_{X_1}\end{aligned}$$

hence

$$\mu_{X_0} = \beta_0 + \beta\mu_{X_1} \tag{10.4.2}$$

Next consider $\mathscr{E}_{X_1}[(\mu_Y(X_1) - \mu_{X_1})(X_1 - \mu_{X_1})]$ which is

$$\begin{aligned}&\mathscr{E}_{X_1}[(\mathscr{E}_{X_0|X_1}[X_0] - \mu_{X_1})(X_1 - \mu_{X_1})]\\ &\quad= \mathscr{E}_{X_1}[(\mathscr{E}_{X_0|X_1}[X_0])(X_1 - \mu_{X_1})] - \mathscr{E}_{X_1}[(X_1 - \mu_{X_1})\mu_{X_1}]\\ &\quad= \mathscr{E}_{X_1}[(\mathscr{E}_{X_0|X_1}[X_0])(X_1 - \mu_{X_1})] - \mu_{X_1}\mathscr{E}_{X_1}[X_1 - \mu_{X_1}]\\ &\quad= \mathscr{E}_{X_1}[(\mathscr{E}_{X_0|X_1}[X_0])(X_1 - \mu_{X_1})]\\ &\quad= \mathscr{E}_{X_1}[(\mathscr{E}_{X_0|X_1}[X_0])X_1] - \mathscr{E}_{X_1}[\mathscr{E}_{X_0|X_1}[X_0]\mu_{X_1}]\\ &\quad= \mathscr{E}[X_1X_0] - \mathscr{E}_{X_1}[(\beta_0 + \beta X_1)\mu_{X_1}]\\ &\quad= (\sigma_{X_1X_0} + \mu_{X_0}\mu_{X_1}) - (\beta_0\mu_{X_1} + \beta\mu_{X_1}^2) = \sigma_{X_1X_0}\end{aligned}$$

by using Equation (10.4.2). But $\mathscr{E}_{X_1}[(\mu_Y(X_1) - \mu_{X_1})(X_1 - \mu_{X_1})]$ can also be written as $\mathscr{E}_{X_1}[(\beta_0 + \beta X_1 - \mu_{X_1})(X_1 - \mu_{X_1})] = \beta\sigma_{X_1X_1}$. If we equate the two expressions for $\mathscr{E}_{X_1}[(\mu_Y(X_1) - \mu_{X_1})(X_1 - \mu_{X_1})]$, we get

$$\sigma_{X_1X_0} = \beta\sigma_{X_1X_1}$$

or

$$\beta = \frac{\sigma_{X_1X_0}}{\sigma_{X_1X_1}} \tag{10.4.3}$$

If we substitute Equation (10.4.3) into Equation (10.4.2), we get

$$\beta_0 = \mu_{X_0} - \left(\frac{\sigma_{X_1X_0}}{\sigma_{X_1X_1}}\right)\mu_{X_1} \tag{10.4.4}$$

This completes the proof.

For the (bivariate) normal p.d.f., we have shown in Section 3.6 that $\text{var}[(X_0 \mid X_1 = x_1)]$ is independent of x_1 and is equal to $\sigma_{X_0X_0} - \sigma^2_{X_1X_0}/\sigma_{X_1X_1}$. We now determine the formula for the variance of the p.d.f. of $(X_0 \mid X_1 = x_1)$ when the joint distribution of X_0 and X_1 does not necessarily satisfy Case I or Case II.

THEOREM 10.4.2

Let X_0 and X_1 be jointly distributed random variables and assume the notation in Equation (10.4.1).

(1) *If the regression of X_0 on X_1 is linear, the "average" variance of $(X_0 \mid X_1)$ is $\sigma_{X_0X_0} - \sigma^2_{X_1X_0}/\sigma_{X_1X_1}$, the same as it is when X_0 and X_1 are jointly "normally" distributed.*

(2) *If the regression of X_0 on X_1 is linear and if the variance of $(X_0 \mid X_1)$ is constant (does not depend on the value of X_1), then the variance of $(X_0 \mid X_1)$ is $\sigma_{X_0X_0} - \sigma^2_{X_1X_0}/\sigma_{X_1X_1}$, the same as it is when X_1 and X_0 are jointly "normally" distributed.*

Proof

Consider the formula for the variance of X_0 in terms of conditional expectation and variance;

$$\begin{aligned}\sigma_{X_0X_0} &= \text{var}[X_0] = \text{var}_{X_1}\mathscr{E}[(X_0 \mid X_1)] + \mathscr{E}_{X_1}[\text{var}(X_0 \mid X_1)] \\ &= \text{var}_{X_1}[\beta_0 + \beta X_1] + \mathscr{E}_{X_1}[\text{var}(X_0 \mid X_1)] \\ &= \beta^2\sigma_{X_1X_1} + \mathscr{E}_{X_1}[\text{var}(X_0 \mid X_1)]\end{aligned}$$

so

$$\mathscr{E}_{X_1}[\text{var}[(X_0 \mid X_1)]] = \sigma_{X_0X_0} - \beta^2\sigma_{X_1X_1} = \sigma_{X_0X_0} - \frac{\sigma^2_{X_1X_0}}{\sigma_{X_1X_1}}$$

and (1) is proved since $\mathscr{E}_{X_1}[\text{var}(X_0 \mid X_1)]$ is the "average" (averaged over the X_1 values, that is, averaged with respect to the p.d.f. of X_1) variance of $(X_0 \mid X_1)$. If $\text{var}[(X_0 \mid X_1)]$ does not depend on X_1, then $\mathscr{E}_{X_1}[\text{var}(X_0 \mid X_1)]$ is the same as $\text{var}[(X_0 \mid X_1)]$, and hence by the above, we get

$$\text{var}[(X_0 \mid X_1)] = \sigma_{X_0X_0} - \frac{\sigma^2_{X_1X_0}}{\sigma_{X_1X_1}}$$

which proves (2).

Thus we have shown that for any bivariate distribution, if the regression function is linear, the formulas for β_0 and β turn out to be the same as when the p.d.f. of X_0 and X_1 satisfies Case I or Case II; the variance of $(X_0 \mid X_1)$ is also closely related to the variance of $(X_0 \mid X_1)$ for these two cases. The results can be extended to $K + 1$ random variables $X_0, X_1, \ldots, X_K$.

Problems

10.1. Find $\text{var}[(\hat{\beta}|X_{11} = x_{11}, \ldots, X_{n1} = x_{n1})]$, where $\hat{\beta}$ is defined in Equation (10.2.3).

10.2. In Problem 10.1 find $\text{var}[\hat{\beta}]$.

10.3. Find $\text{var}[(\hat{\sigma}^2 \mid X_{11} = x_{11}, \ldots, X_{n1} = x_{n1})]$, where $\hat{\sigma}^2$ is defined in Equation (10.2.3).

10.4. In Problem 10.3 find $\text{var}[\hat{\sigma}^2]$.

10.5. In Theorem 10.2.2 prove that $\hat{\beta}_0$, given in Equation (10.2.3), is an unbiased estimator and mean-squared-error (and hence also simple) consistent estimator of β_0. Show that $\hat{\sigma}^2$ is a mean-squared-error consistent estimator of σ^2.

10.6. In the p.d.f. given in Equation (10.2.9), suppose $f_\chi(\mathbf{x} : \boldsymbol{\theta})$ is the univariate normal p.d.f. with mean μ_{X_1} and variance $\sigma_{X_1}^2$ (both unknown). Show that in this case the estimators $\hat{\beta}_0$, $\hat{\boldsymbol{\beta}}$, and $\hat{\sigma}^2$ given in Equation (10.2.8) are UMVU estimators of their respective parameters.

10.7. In Problem 10.6 suppose $f_\chi(\mathbf{x} : \boldsymbol{\theta})$ is the univariate normal p.d.f. with mean zero and variance one. Show that the estimators in Equation (10.2.8) are *not* UMVU estimators of their respective parameters.

10.8. In Problem 10.6 if $f_\chi(\mathbf{x} : \boldsymbol{\theta})$ is the univariate normal p.d.f. with mean μ_{X_1} (unknown) and variance one, is $\hat{\beta}_0$, $\hat{\boldsymbol{\beta}}$, or $\hat{\sigma}^2$ in Equation (10.2.8) an UMVU estimator of its respective parameter? Prove your answer.

CHAPTER 11

Correlation

11.1 Introduction

Correlation was defined in Section 3.8 and the usefulness of correlation in studying relationships among random variables was also discussed there. In this chapter we discuss point estimation, interval estimation, and hypotheses tests for correlation coefficients.

In Sections 11.2, 11.3, and 11.4 we discuss simple correlation, partial correlation, and multiple correlation, respectively, when the random vectors are normally distributed.

The notation and distributions for Sections 11.2, 11.3, and 11.4 are given below. $\boldsymbol{\chi}^*$ is a random $K + 1$ vector with elements $X_0, X_1, \ldots, X_K$.

1. $\boldsymbol{\chi}^*$ is distributed $\mathbf{N}(\mathbf{x}^* : \boldsymbol{\mu}^*, \boldsymbol{\Sigma}^*)$.

2. $$\boldsymbol{\chi}^* = \begin{bmatrix} X_0 \\ \boldsymbol{\chi} \end{bmatrix}$$

   where elements of the $K \times 1$ vector $\boldsymbol{\chi}$ are $X_1, X_2, \ldots, X_K$.

3. $$\boldsymbol{\mu}^* = \begin{bmatrix} \mu_0 \\ \boldsymbol{\mu} \end{bmatrix} \qquad \boldsymbol{\Sigma}^* = \begin{bmatrix} \sigma_{00} & \boldsymbol{\sigma}_{01} \\ \boldsymbol{\sigma}_{10} & \boldsymbol{\Sigma} \end{bmatrix}$$

   $\boldsymbol{\Sigma}^*$ is positive definite.

4. $$\mathbf{R}^* = [\rho_{ij}] = \begin{bmatrix} 1 & \boldsymbol{\rho}_{01} \\ \boldsymbol{\rho}_{10} & \mathbf{R} \end{bmatrix}$$

   is a $(K + 1) \times (K + 1)$ matrix of simple correlation coefficients, $\rho_{ij} = \sigma_{ij}/\sqrt{\sigma_{ii}\sigma_{jj}}$.

5. $\chi_1^*, \chi_2^*, \ldots, \chi_n^*$ is a random sample of $n > K + 1$ vectors from the p.d.f. in part 1.

6. $$\mathscr{A}^* = \begin{bmatrix} A_{00} & a_{01} \\ a_{10} & \mathscr{A} \end{bmatrix} = \sum_{i=1}^{n} (\chi_i^* - \bar{\chi}^*)(\chi_i^* - \bar{\chi}^*)' \qquad (11.1.1)$$

In Sections 11.5 and 11.6 we present a brief discussion of correlation when χ^* is not a multivariate *normal* random vector.

11.2 Simple Correlation

For the distributional setup in Equation (11.1.1), a random sample of n vectors is obtained and the likelihood function is given in Section 10.2. The maximum likelihood estimator of $\mathbf{\Sigma}^*$, denoted by $\tilde{\mathbf{\Sigma}}^*$, is

$$\tilde{\mathbf{\Sigma}}^* = \left(\frac{1}{n}\right) \sum_{i=1}^{n} (\chi_i^* - \bar{\chi}^*)(\chi_i^* - \bar{\chi}^*)' \qquad \text{where} \qquad \bar{\chi}^* = \left(\frac{1}{n}\right) \sum_{i=1}^{n} \chi_i^* \qquad (11.2.1)$$

By the invariance property of maximum likelihood estimators, this gives $\tilde{\rho}_{ij}$ for a maximum likelihood estimator of ρ_{ij}, where

$$\tilde{\rho}_{ij} = \frac{\tilde{\sigma}_{ij}}{\sqrt{\tilde{\sigma}_{ii}\tilde{\sigma}_{jj}}} = \frac{\sum_{t=1}^{n} (X_{ti} - \bar{X}_i)(X_{tj} - \bar{X}_j)}{\left[\sum_{s=1}^{n} (X_{si} - \bar{X}_i)^2 \sum_{p=1}^{n} (X_{pj} - \bar{X}_j)^2\right]^{1/2}} \qquad (11.2.2)$$

We notice from Equation (11.2.2) that $\tilde{\rho}_{ij}$ for any fixed i and j depends only on the random variables $X_{1i}, X_{2i}, \ldots, X_{ni}$ and $X_{1j}, X_{2j}, \ldots, X_{nj}$. These can be viewed as a random sample of size n from the p.d.f. of the two random variables X_i and X_j. The p.d.f. of these two random variables is a bivariate normal with mean vector and covariance matrix, respectively,

$$\begin{bmatrix} \mu_i \\ \mu_j \end{bmatrix} \qquad \begin{bmatrix} \sigma_{ii} & \sigma_{ij} \\ \sigma_{ji} & \sigma_{jj} \end{bmatrix}$$

To discuss estimation and hypotheses tests for ρ_{ij}, we need only the p.d.f. of X_i and X_j. We will use the symbols X and Y, respectively, in place of X_i and X_j in the remainder of this section to simplify the notation. Thus X, Y has a joint p.d.f. that is normal with mean vector $\boldsymbol{\mu}$, covariance matrix $\mathbf{\Sigma}$, and (simple) correlation coefficient ρ, where

$$\boldsymbol{\mu} = \begin{bmatrix} \mu_X \\ \mu_Y \end{bmatrix} \qquad \mathbf{\Sigma} = \begin{bmatrix} \sigma_{XX} & \sigma_{XY} \\ \sigma_{YX} & \sigma_{YY} \end{bmatrix} \qquad \rho_{XY} = \rho_{YX} = \rho = \frac{\sigma_{XY}}{\sqrt{\sigma_{XX}\sigma_{YY}}} \qquad (11.2.3)$$

A random sample of n vectors $[X_1, Y_1], [X_2, Y_2], \ldots, [X_n, Y_n]$ is obtained from this p.d.f., and the maximum likelihood estimators are (we use $n-1$ instead of n in $\hat{\sigma}_{XX}$, $\hat{\sigma}_{YY}$, and $\hat{\sigma}_{XY}$ to correct for bias in estimating σ_{XX}, σ_{YY}, and σ_{XY}; $\tilde{\rho}$, however, is biased)

$$\hat{\mu}_X = \left(\frac{1}{n}\right)\sum_{i=1}^{n} X_i = \bar{X} \qquad \hat{\mu}_Y = \left(\frac{1}{n}\right)\sum_{i=1}^{n} Y_i = \bar{Y}$$

$$\hat{\sigma}_{XY} = \left(\frac{1}{n-1}\right)\sum_{i=1}^{n}(X_i - \bar{X})(Y_i - \bar{Y}) \quad \hat{\sigma}_{XX} = \left(\frac{1}{n-1}\right)\sum_{i=1}^{n}(X_i - \bar{X})^2 \tag{11.2.4}$$

$$\hat{\sigma}_{YY} = \left(\frac{1}{n-1}\right)\sum_{i=1}^{n}(Y_i - \bar{Y})^2 \qquad \tilde{\rho} = R = \frac{\sum_{i=1}^{n}(X_i - \bar{X})(Y_i - \bar{Y})}{\sqrt{\sum_{j=1}^{n}(X_j - \bar{X})^2 \sum_{k=1}^{n}(Y_k - \bar{Y})^2}}$$

The p.d.f. of R is

$$f_R(r) = \frac{(n-2)(1-\rho^2)^{(1/2)(n-1)}}{\pi}(1-r^2)^{(1/2)(n-4)}\int_0^{\infty}(\cosh w - \rho r)^{-(n-1)}\,dw$$
$$-1 < r < 1 \quad -1 < \rho < 1 \tag{11.2.5}$$

We shall not derive the p.d.f. of R here, but a derivation can be found in [A-3] and [K-6].

Note 1. A remarkable thing about the p.d.f. of R is that the only parameter it depends on is ρ.

Notation. We shall denote the p.d.f. in Equation (11.2.5) by $c(r:n;\rho)$ and the upper α probability point by $r_{\alpha:n;(\rho)}$, that is, for fixed α, n, and ρ, we can evaluate $r_{\alpha:n;(\rho)}$ from

$$1 - \alpha = \int_{-1}^{r_{\alpha:n;(\rho)}} c(r:n;\rho)\,dr = P[R \leq r_{\alpha:n;(\rho)}] = C(r_{\alpha:n;(\rho)}:n;\rho) \tag{11.2.6}$$

where we denote $C(r:n;\rho)$ as the c.d.f. of R.

Note 2. It can be shown that $r_{\alpha:n;(\rho)}$ is an increasing function of ρ for fixed α and n. For various values of ρ, n, and $r_{\alpha:n;(\rho)} = r$, F. N. David [D-6] has tabulated the integral

$$1 - \alpha = \int_{-1}^{r_{\alpha:n;(\rho)}} c(r:n;\rho)\,dr \tag{11.2.7}$$

for the following values: $r = r_{\alpha:n;(\rho)} = -1.00, -0.95, -0.90, \ldots, 0.90, 0.95, 1.00$; $n = 3, 4, 5, \ldots, 25, 50, 100, 200, 400$; $\rho = 0.0, 0.1, 0.2, \ldots, 0.9$. The entries in the table are $1 - \alpha$.

Note 3. The tables include no negative values of ρ. We notice, however, from the p.d.f. in Equation (11.2.5), that $c(r:n;\rho) = c(-r:n;-\rho)$, which implies

$$r_{\alpha:n;(\rho)} = -r_{1-\alpha:n;(-\rho)} \quad \text{and} \quad r_{\alpha:n;(-\rho)} = -r_{1-\alpha:n;(\rho)} \tag{11.2.8}$$

This relation can be used to evaluate the integral in Equation (11.2.7) for $\rho < 0$. Equation (11.2.7) can be written

$$1 - \alpha = P[R \leq r_{\alpha:n;(\rho)}] = P[R \leq -r_{1-\alpha:n;(-\rho)}] \qquad \text{for } -1 < \rho < 1 \tag{11.2.9}$$

To briefly demonstrate the use of F. N. David's tables, we have reproduced the case for $n = 24$ (see Table 11.2.1).

Example 11.2.1

The random variable R, which is the correlation coefficient of a random sample of size n from a bivariate normal p.d.f., has the p.d.f. given in Equation (11.2.5). From Table 11.2.1 find the following:

1. $r = r_{0.05:24;(0.2)}$;
2. $r = r_{0.95:24;(0)}$;
3. $r = r_{0.01:24;(-0.3)}$.

From the table we get the following.

1. $r_{0.05:24;(0.2)} = r_{\alpha:n;(\rho)}$. This means that in the p.d.f. of R (for $n = 24$ and $\rho = 0.2$), we must find the value such that $1 - \alpha = 0.95$ of the probability (area) is below it. We enter Table 11.2.1 with $n = 24$, and find the entry $0.94198 \approx 0.95$ in the column headed $\rho = 0.2$. The corresponding value of r is $+0.50$ and hence $r_{0.05:24;(0.2)} \approx +0.50$; thus $P[R \leq r_{0.05:24;(0.2)}] = P[R \leq 0.50 \mid n = 24; \rho = 0.2] \approx 0.95$.
2. By the same procedure, $r_{0.95:24;(0)} \approx -0.35$.
3. By Equation (11.2.8) we get $r_{0.01:24;(-0.3)} = -r_{0.99:24;(0.3)} \approx -(-0.19) = 0.19$. For illustrative purposes we use linear interpolation.

Table 11.2.1

David's Tables for $n = 24$

r	$\rho = 0.0$ $1 - \alpha$	$\rho = 0.1$ $1 - \alpha$	$\rho = 0.2$ $1 - \alpha$	$\rho = 0.3$ $1 - \alpha$	$\rho = 0.4$ $1 - \alpha$	r	$\rho = 0.5$ $1 - \alpha$	$\rho = 0.6$ $1 - \alpha$	$\rho = 0.7$ $1 - \alpha$	$\rho = 0.8$ $1 - \alpha$	r	$\rho = 0.9$ $1 - \alpha$
−1.00	0.00 000	0.00 000	0.00 000	0.00 000	0.00 000	−1.00	0.00 000	0.00 000	0.00 000	0.00 000	−1.00	0.00 000
−0.95	0.00 000	0.00 000	0.00 000	0.00 000	0.00 000	−0.95	0.00 000	0.00 000	0.00 000	0.00 000	−0.95	0.00 000
−0.90	0.00 000	0.00 000	0.00 000	0.00 000	0.00 000	−0.90	0.00 000	0.00 000	0.00 000	0.00 000	−0.90	0.00 000
−0.85	0.00 000	0.00 000	0.00 000	0.00 000	0.00 000	−0.85	0.00 000	0.00 000	0.00 000	0.00 000	−0.85	0.00 000
−0.80	0.00 000	0.00 000	0.00 000	0.00 000	0.00 000	−0.80	0.00 000	0.00 000	0.00 000	0.00 000	−0.80	0.00 000
−0.75	0.00 001	0.00 000	0.00 000	0.00 000	0.00 000	−0.75	0.00 000	0.00 000	0.00 000	0.00 000	−0.75	0.00 000
−0.70	0.00 007	0.00 001	0.00 000	0.00 000	0.00 000	−0.70	0.00 000	0.00 000	0.00 000	0.00 000	−0.70	0.00 000
−0.65	0.00 029	0.00 006	0.00 001	0.00 000	0.00 000	−0.65	0.00 000	0.00 000	0.00 000	0.00 000	−0.65	0.00 000
−0.60	0.00 097	0.00 021	0.00 004	0.00 001	0.00 000	−0.60	0.00 000	0.00 000	0.00 000	0.00 000	−0.60	0.00 000
−0.55	0.00 268	0.00 065	0.00 013	0.00 002	0.00 000	−0.55	0.00 000	0.00 000	0.00 000	0.00 000	−0.55	0.00 000
−0.50	0.00 642	0.00 171	0.00 038	0.00 007	0.00 001	−0.50	0.00 000	0.00 000	0.00 000	0.00 000	−0.50	0.00 000
−0.45	0.01 368	0.00 400	0.00 098	0.00 019	0.00 003	−0.45	0.00 000	0.00 000	0.00 000	0.00 000	−0.45	0.00 000
−0.40	0.02 639	0.00 846	0.00 226	0.00 049	0.00 008	−0.40	0.00 001	0.00 000	0.00 000	0.00 000	−0.40	0.00 000
−0.35	0.04 681	0.01 644	0.00 479	0.00 112	0.00 020	−0.35	0.00 003	0.00 000	0.00 000	0.00 000	−0.35	0.00 000
−0.30	0.07 718	0.02 966	0.00 943	0.00 241	0.00 047	−0.30	0.00 007	0.00 001	0.00 000	0.00 000	−0.30	0.00 000
−0.25	0.11 936	0.05 013	0.01 740	0.00 483	0.00 102	−0.25	0.00 015	0.00 001	0.00 000	0.00 000	−0.25	0.00 000
−0.20	0.17 438	0.07 992	0.03 025	0.00 915	0.00 210	−0.20	0.00 034	0.00 003	0.00 000	0.00 000	−0.20	0.00 000
−0.15	0.24 209	0.12 083	0.04 988	0.01 646	0.00 412	−0.15	0.00 072	0.00 008	0.00 000	0.00 000	−0.15	0.00 000
−0.10	0.32 100	0.17 407	0.07 831	0.02 820	0.00 771	−0.10	0.00 147	0.00 017	0.00 001	0.00 000	−0.10	0.00 000
−0.05	0.40 826	0.23 986	0.11 748	0.04 620	0.01 381	−0.05	0.00 279	0.00 036	0.00 002	0.00 000	−0.05	0.00 000
0.00	0.50 000	0.31 718	0.16 890	0.07 256	0.02 378	0.00	0.00 546	0.00 076	0.00 005	0.00 000	0.00	0.00 000
+0.05	0.59 174	0.40 367	0.23 323	0.10 945	0.03 940	+0.05	0.00 998	0.00 154	0.00 011	0.00 000	+0.05	0.00 000
+0.10	0.67 900	0.49 575	0.30 997	0.15 883	0.06 287	+0.10	0.01 760	0.00 301	0.00 024	0.00 001	+0.10	0.00 000
+0.15	0.75 791	0.58 898	0.39 719	0.22 198	0.09 673	+0.15	0.03 005	0.00 575	0.00 051	0.00 001	+0.15	0.00 000
+0.20	0.82 562	0.67 863	0.49 150	0.29 904	0.14 355	+0.20	0.04 964	0.01 067	0.00 108	0.00 003	+0.20	0.00 000
+0.25	0.88 064	0.76 029	0.58 825	0.38 856	0.20 548	+0.25	0.07 931	0.01 925	0.00 223	0.00 007	+0.25	0.00 000
+0.30	0.92 282	0.83 051	0.68 215	0.48 724	0.28 359	+0.30	0.12 247	0.03 378	0.00 452	0.00 016	+0.30	0.00 000
+0.35	0.95 319	0.88 726	0.76 794	0.59 001	0.37 715	+0.35	0.18 254	0.05 754	0.00 897	0.00 038	+0.35	0.00 000
+0.40	0.97 361	0.93 009	0.84 129	0.69 052	0.48 298	+0.40	0.26 211	0.09 495	0.01 744	0.00 088	+0.40	0.00 000
+0.45	0.98 632	0.96 006	0.89 952	0.78 212	0.59 518	+0.45	0.36 179	0.15 130	0.03 311	0.00 206	+0.45	0.00 001
+0.50	0.99 358	0.97 928	0.94 198	0.85 910	0.70 556	+0.50	0.47 872	0.23 191	0.06 120	0.00 480	+0.50	0.00 002

r	$\rho = 0.9$ $1 - \alpha$
+0.800	0.03 395
+0.825	0.06 808
+0.850	0.13 480
+0.875	0.25 814
+0.900	0.46 156
+0.925	0.72 775
+0.950	0.94 161
+0.975	0.99 905
+1.000	1.00 000

r	$\rho = 0.0$ $1-\alpha$	$\rho = 0.1$ $1-\alpha$	$\rho = 0.2$ $1-\alpha$	$\rho = 0.3$ $1-\alpha$	$\rho = 0.4$ $1-\alpha$
+0.55	0.99 732	0.99 042	0.97 004	0.91 794	0.80 497
+0.60	0.99 903	0.99 616	0.98 652	0.95 808	0.88 542
+0.65	0.99 971	0.99 871	0.99 491	0.98 190	0.94 245
+0.70	0.99 993	0.99 966	0.99 847	0.99 373	0.97 658
+0.75	0.99 999	0.99 993	0.99 966	0.99 840	0.99 289
+0.80	1.00 000	0.99 999	0.99 995	0.99 974	0.99 859
+0.85	1.00 000	1.00 000	1.00 000	0.99 998	0.99 985
+0.90	1.00 000	1.00 000	1.00 000	1.00 000	0.99 999
+0.95	1.00 000	1.00 000	1.00 000	1.00 000	1.00 000
+1.00	1.00 000	1.00 000	1.00 000	1.00000	1.00 000

r	$\rho = 0.5$ $1-\alpha$	$\rho = 0.6$ $1-\alpha$	$\rho = 0.7$ $1-\alpha$	$\rho = 0.8$ $1-\alpha$
+0.55	0.60 556	0.34 015	0.10 948	0.01 110
+0.60	0.73 059	0.47 444	0.18 815	0.02 535
+0.625	0.78 802	0.54 864	0.24 212	0.03 805
+0.650	0.83 980	0.62 485	0.30 727	0.05 675
+0.675	0.88 453	0.70 031	0.38 357	0.08 393
+0.700	0.92 134	0.77 187	0.47 009	0.12 279
+0.725	0.94 991	0.83 631	0.56 429	0.17 712
+0.750	0.97 062	0.89 085	0.66 175	0.25 085
+0.775	0.98 442	0.93 360	0.75 641	0.34 704
+0.800	0.99 273	0.96 408	0.84 113	0.46 587
+0.825	0.99 711	0.98 333	0.90 934	0.60 192
+0.850	0.99 908	0.99 370	0.95 697	0.74 177
+0.875	0.99 973	0.99 822	0.98 430	0.86 461
+0.900	0.99 995	0.99 967	0.99 614	0.94 953
+0.925	1.00 000	0.99 997	0.99 949	0.98 956
+0.950	1.00 000	1.00 000	0.99 997	0.99 932
+0.975	1.00 000	1.00 000	1.00 000	1.00 000
+1.0000	1.00 000	1.00 000	1.00 000	1.00 000

r	$\rho = 0.9$ $1-\alpha$
+0.55	0.00 005
+0.60	0.00 017
+0.625	0.00 032
+0.650	0.00 060
+0.675	0.00 114
+0.700	0.00 219
+0.725	0.00 428
+0.750	0.00 848
+0.775	0.01 692
+0.800	0.03 395
+0.810	0.04 488
+0.820	0.05 927
+0.830	0.07 817
+0.840	0.10 284
+0.850	0.13 480
+0.860	0.17 578
+0.870	0.22 761
+0.880	0.29 198
+0.890	0.37 000
+0.900	0.46 156
+0.910	0.56 446
+0.920	0.67 349
+0.930	0.78 004
+0.940	0.87 294
+0.950	0.94 161
+0.955	0.96 500
+0.960	0.98 126
+0.965	0.99 134
+0.970	0.99 671
+0.975	0.99 905
+0.980	0.99 981
+0.985	0.99 997
+0.990	1.00 000
+0.995	1.00 000
+1.000	1.00 000

1. For $\rho \geq 0$, the entries in the table are $1 - \alpha$, where $1 - \alpha = \int_{-1}^{r_{\alpha:n;(\rho)}} c(r : n ; \rho)\, dr$ and r in the table is $r_{\alpha:n;(\rho)}$.
2. For $\rho < 0$, use Equation (11.2.8).

11.2.1 Point Estimation

In this section we state a theorem about the point estimation of ρ.

THEOREM 11.2.1

Under the distributional setup given in Equation (11.1.1), *the results below follow.*

(1) *R, the M.L. estimator of ρ, is a function of complete sufficient statistics;*

(2) *The UMVU estimator of ρ is $\hat{\rho} = G(R)$, where*

$$\hat{\rho} = G(R) = R\left(\frac{\Gamma\left(\frac{n-2}{2}\right)}{\Gamma\left(\frac{1}{2}\right)\Gamma\left(\frac{n-3}{2}\right)}\right)\int_0^1 \frac{t^{-1/2}(1-t)^{(n-5)/2}}{[1-t(1-R^2)]^{1/2}}\,dt$$

Proof

By Section 10.2, $\hat{\mu}_Y$, $\hat{\mu}_X$, $\hat{\sigma}_{YY}$, $\hat{\sigma}_{XY}$, and $\hat{\sigma}_{XX}$ are complete sufficient statistics for the setup in Equation (11.1.1). But $R = \hat{\sigma}_{XY}/\sqrt{\hat{\sigma}_{XX}\hat{\sigma}_{YY}}$ and hence the result (1). In (2) we note that R is a function of complete sufficient statistics, and if we can find an unbiased estimator for ρ based on R, it is the UMVU estimator. The maximum likelihood estimator R is *not* an unbiased estimator of ρ. We will not prove that $G(R)$ is an unbiased estimator of ρ, but a proof can be found in [O-1] where a table for $G(r)$ is given for values of $r = 0, 0.1, 0.2, \ldots, 0.9$ and $n = 3, 5, 7, \ldots, 31, \infty$. An approximation for $G(r)$, where r is a value of R, is given by the following:

$$G(r) \approx r + \frac{r(1-r^2)}{2(n-4)} \tag{11.2.10}$$

11.2.2 Tests of Hypotheses

In previous chapters we have used pivotal quantities to set confidence intervals on (or to test hypotheses about) parameters. To test hypotheses about ρ or set a confidence interval on ρ, the c.d.f. can be used as a pivotal quantity since it is a function of R (the statistic) and ρ (the parameter under discussion) and the distribution of $C(R:n;\rho)$ is the uniform distribution from 0 to 1 and hence contains no unknown parameters.

THEOREM 11.2.2

Let $(X_1, Y_1), (X_2, Y_2), \ldots, (X_n, Y_n)$ be a random sample of size $n > 2$ from a normal distribution with mean $\boldsymbol{\mu}$ and covariance $\boldsymbol{\Sigma}$ defined in Equation (11.2.3).

Let r_c be the computed value of the correlation coefficient given in Equation (11.2.4). *Below are tests of various hypotheses on ρ of size α (r^* is a given constant such that $-1 < r^* < 1$).*

(1) $H_0 : \rho = r^*$ *vs.* $H_a : \rho \neq r^*$. *Reject H_0 if and only if either $r_c \geq r_{\alpha/2:n;(r^*)}$ or $r_c \leq r_{1-\alpha/2:n;(r^*)}$. The power of the test is*

$$\Pi(\rho) = \int_{-1}^{r_{1-\alpha/2:n;(r^*)}} c(r:n;\rho)\,dr + \int_{r_{\alpha/2:n;(r^*)}}^{1} c(r:n;\rho)\,dr \qquad -1 < \rho < 1$$

(2) $H_0 : \rho = r^*$ *vs.* $H_a : \rho > r^*$. *Reject H_0 if and only if $r_c \geq r_{\alpha:n;(r^*)}$. The power of this test is*

$$\Pi(\rho) = \int_{r_{\alpha:n;(r^*)}}^{1} c(r:n;\rho)\,dr \qquad r^* \leq \rho < 1$$

(3) $H_0 : \rho \leq r^*$ *vs.* $H_a : \rho > r^*$. *The same procedure as in part* (2) *except the power function is defined for $-1 < \rho < 1$.*

(4) $H_0 : \rho = r^*$ *vs.* $H_a : \rho < r^*$. *Reject H_0 if and only if $r_c \leq r_{1-\alpha:n;(r^*)}$. The power of this test is*

$$\Pi(\rho) = \int_{-1}^{r_{1-\alpha:n;(r^*)}} c(r:n;\rho)\,dr \qquad -1 < \rho \leq r^*$$

(5) $H_0 : \rho \geq r^*$ *vs.* $H_a : \rho < r^*$. *The same procedure as in part* (4) *except the power function is defined for $-1 < \rho < 1$.*

In the above, $r_{\gamma:n;(r^*)}$ is defined by

$$\int_{-1}^{r_{\gamma:n;(r^*)}} c(r:n;r^*)\,dr = 1 - \gamma \qquad (11.2.11)$$

Note 4. By Equation (11.2.11) it is clear that $r_{\gamma:n;(r^*)}$ is the upper γ probability point of the p.d.f. $c(r:n;\rho)$ when $\rho = r^*$.

Proof

We will prove parts (1) and (2). The proofs of the remaining parts are similar.

To prove (1) we get $\Pi(\rho) = P[\text{rejecting } H_0 \text{ when } \rho \text{ is the true value}]$, but H_0 is rejected if and only if r_c, the computed value of R, is *not* in the interval $(r_{1-\alpha/2:n;(r^*)}, r_{\alpha/2:n;(r^*)})$. So

$$\Pi(\rho) = 1 - P[r_{1-\alpha/2:n;(r^*)} \leq R \leq r_{\alpha/2:n;(r^*)} \mid \rho]$$

$$= \int_{r_{\alpha/2:n;(r^*)}}^{1} c(r:n;\rho)\,dr + \int_{-1}^{r_{1-\alpha/2:n;(r^*)}} c(r:n;\rho)\,dr \qquad \text{for } -1 < \rho < 1$$

and clearly $\Pi(r^*) = \alpha$, the size of the test. Thus (1) is proved.

To prove (2) we get $\Pi(\rho) = P$[rejecting H_0 when ρ is the true value], but H_0 is rejected if and only if r_c, the computed value of R, satisfies $r_c \geq r_{\alpha:n;(r^*)}$. So

$$\Pi(\rho) = P[R \geq r_{\alpha:n;(r^*)} \mid \rho] = \int_{r_{\alpha:n;(r^*)}}^{1} c(r:n;\rho)\,dr$$

but we notice that the parameter space is $r^* \leq \rho < 1$. Clearly $\Pi(r^*) = \alpha$. Thus (2) is proved.

We have not stated the optimum properties of this test, but a discussion can be found in [A-3], [K-7], and [L-8].

Note 5. If r^* in the above theorem is zero, that is, if the hypothesis is $H_0 : \rho = 0$, and so on, then Student's t can be used as a test function. However, David's tables are used to evaluate power. We state this result next.

COROLLARY 11.2.2

Consider the distributional setup given in Theorem 11.2.2. *T is distributed* $s(t:n-2)$, *where* $T = R\sqrt{n-2}/\sqrt{(1-R^2)}$. *The five tests below are of size* α.

(1) *To test* $H_0 : \rho = 0$ *vs.* $H_a : \rho \neq 0$, *reject* H_0 *if and only if* $|t_c| \geq t_{\alpha/2:n-2}$.

(2) *To test* $H_0 : \rho = 0$ *vs.* $H_a : \rho > 0$, *reject* H_0 *if and only if* $t_c \geq t_{\alpha:n-2}$.

(3) *To test* $H_0 : \rho \leq 0$ *vs.* $H_a : \rho > 0$, *reject* H_0 *if and only if* $t_c \geq t_{\alpha:n-2}$.

(4) *To test* $H_0 : \rho = 0$ *vs.* $H_a : \rho < 0$, *reject* H_0 *if and only if* $t_c \leq t_{1-\alpha:n-2}$.

(5) *To test* $H_0 : \rho \geq 0$ *vs.* $H_a : \rho < 0$, *reject* H_0 *if and only if* $t_c \leq t_{1-\alpha:n-2}$.

The quantity t_c *is computed by*

$$t_c = \frac{r_c\sqrt{n-2}}{\sqrt{1-r_c^2}}$$

Proof

We must prove that $T = R\sqrt{n-2}/\sqrt{1-R^2}$ is distributed $s(t:n-2)$ when $\rho = 0$. This can be done in at least two ways: one way is directly from the joint p.d.f. of the random sample $(X_1, Y_1), (X_2, Y_2), \ldots, (X_n, Y_n)$ from the bivariate normal; the second way is by letting $\rho = 0$ in the p.d.f. $c(r:n;\rho)$ in Equation (11.2.5) and making the transformation from R to T. The second method is a simple transformation of variables and will be left for the reader. We will demonstrate the first method.

We note that $(Y_i \mid X_i = x_i)$, $i = 1, 2, \ldots, n$, is distributed normally and that it has a mean $\mu_Y + \rho\sqrt{\sigma_{YY}/\sigma_{XX}}(x_i - \mu_X)$ and a variance $\sigma_{YY}(1 - \rho^2)$. When $\rho = 0$, $(Y_i \mid X_i = x_i)$ is distributed normally and with mean μ_Y and variance σ_{YY} (hence when $\rho = 0$, the random variables $X_1, Y_1, X_2, Y_2, \ldots, X_n, Y_n$ are jointly independent). We want the distribution of

$$T = \frac{R\sqrt{n-2}}{\sqrt{1-R^2}} \qquad \text{when} \qquad \rho = 0 \tag{11.2.12}$$

First we consider the p.d.f. of $(T \mid X_1 = x_1, X_2 = x_2, \ldots, X_n = x_n)$, which we write as

$$\begin{aligned}(T \mid X_1 = x_1, X_2 = x_2, \ldots, X_n = x_n) &= \left(\frac{R\sqrt{n-2}}{\sqrt{1-R^2}}\middle| X_1 = x_1, X_2 = x_2, \ldots, X_n = x_n\right) \\ &= \frac{\left(\sum_{i=1}^{n} Y_i c_i\right)\sqrt{n-2}}{\sqrt{\sum_{i=1}^{n}(Y_i - \bar{Y})^2 - \left(\sum_{i=1}^{n} Y_i c_i\right)^2}}\end{aligned}$$

where we have set

$$c_i = \frac{(x_i - \bar{x})}{\sqrt{\sum_{j=1}^{n}(x_j - \bar{x})^2}} \qquad i = 1, 2, \ldots, n$$

Also, since we assume $\rho = 0$, X_i and Y_i are independent and hence $(Y_i \mid X_i = x_i)$ has the same p.d.f. as Y_i, so in the conditional p.d.f. of T we use the symbol Y_i rather than $(Y_i \mid X_i = x_i)$.

So the $n \times 1$ random vector $\mathbf{Y}$ with elements $Y_1, Y_2, \ldots, Y_n$ is distributed $\mathbf{N}(\mathbf{y} : \mu_Y \mathbf{1}, \sigma_{YY}\mathbf{I})$. Define Z by $Z = \sum Y_i c_i = \mathbf{Y}'\mathbf{c}$ and Z is distributed $N(z : 0, \sigma_{YY})$. Define U by

$$\frac{U}{\sigma_{YY}} = \frac{\sum(Y_i - \bar{Y})^2 - (\sum Y_i c_i)^2}{\sigma_{YY}} = \frac{\mathbf{Y}'\left[\mathbf{I} - \left(\frac{1}{n}\right)\mathbf{J} - \mathbf{cc}'\right]\mathbf{Y}}{\sigma_{YY}} = \mathbf{Y}'\left(\frac{\mathbf{B}}{\sigma_{YY}}\right)\mathbf{Y}$$

Then $\mathbf{Y}'(\mathbf{B}/\sigma_{YY})\mathbf{Y}$ is distributed $\chi^2(u : n - 2)$ since $(\mathbf{B}/\sigma_{YY})(\sigma_{YY}\mathbf{I}) = \mathbf{B} = \mathbf{B}^2$, and $(\mathbf{B}/\sigma_{YY})(\mu_Y \mathbf{1}) = \mathbf{0}$ (then use (1) of Theorem 4.4.3). Also, U and Z are independent since $\mathbf{c}'\mathbf{B} = \mathbf{0}$ (use Theorem 4.5.2). Thus $(T \mid X_1 = x_1, X_2 = x_2, \ldots, X_n = x_n) = Z\sqrt{n-2}/\sqrt{U} = (R\sqrt{n-2}/\sqrt{1-R^2}$

given $X_1 = x_1, X_2 = x_2, \ldots, X_n = x_n$) is distributed $s(t : n - 2)$. But this p.d.f. of $(T \mid X_1 = x_1, X_2 = x_2, \ldots, X_n = x_n)$ does not depend on the values $x_1, x_2, \ldots, x_n$; hence T is independent of $X_1, X_2, \ldots, X_n$ and so T in Equation (11.2.12) is marginally distributed $s(t : n - 2)$. Thus t_c is the observed value of the random variable T and the rejection regions in parts (1) through (5) clearly have size α. Thus the theorem is proved.

11.2.3 Confidence Intervals

To set a confidence interval on ρ, we shall use the p.d.f. of R given in Equation (11.2.5).

THEOREM 11.2.3

Let $(X_1, Y_1), (X_2, Y_2), \ldots, (X_n, Y_n)$ be a random sample of size $n > 2$ from a bivariate normal distribution with mean $\boldsymbol{\mu}$ and covariance $\boldsymbol{\Sigma}$ defined in Equation (11.2.3). Let r_c be the computed value of the correlation coefficient given in Equation (11.2.4). The upper, lower, and two-sided $1 - \alpha$ confidence intervals on ρ are given by the following:

(1) *upper confidence interval*: $\tilde{\rho}_{r_c:\alpha;n} \leq \rho < 1$;

(2) *lower confidence interval*: $-1 < \rho \leq \tilde{\rho}_{r_c:1-\alpha;n}$;

(3) *two-sided confidence interval*: $\tilde{\rho}_{r_c:\alpha/2;n} \leq \rho \leq \tilde{\rho}_{r_c:1-\alpha/2;n}$;

where $\tilde{\rho}_{r_c:\gamma;n}$ is the value of ρ that satisfies

$$\int_{-1}^{r_c} c(r : n; \rho)\, dr = 1 - \gamma \tag{11.2.13}$$

for given values of γ, n, and the observed value r_c.

Proof

The proof is obtained by "inverting" the appropriate test statistic in Theorem 11.2.2. We will demonstate how the upper confidence interval in (1) is obtained by inverting the test (2) in Theorem 11.2.2. We get the following: Accept H_0 if and only if $r_c \leq r_{\alpha:n;(r^*)}$.

Now $1 - \alpha = P[R \leq r_{\alpha:n;(\rho)}]$, and if we denote the solution of $r_c = r_{\alpha:n;(\rho)}$ for ρ by $\tilde{\rho}_{r_c:\alpha;n}$, where r_c is the computed value of R, we have that $r_c \leq r_{\alpha:n;(\rho)}$ if and only if $\tilde{\rho}_{r_c:\alpha;n} \leq \rho$, since $r_{\alpha:n;(\rho)}$ is a monotonic increasing function of ρ. Thus $1 - \alpha = P[R \leq r_{\alpha:n;(\rho)}] = P[\tilde{\rho}_{R:\alpha;n} \leq \rho]$, and if r_c, the computed value of R, is substituted for R, the computed $1 - \alpha$ upper confidence interval on ρ is $\tilde{\rho}_{r_c:\alpha;n} \leq \rho < 1$.

To find the number $\tilde{\rho}_{r_c:\alpha;n}$, one can use David's tables if $n \leq 25$ and solve $r_c = r_{\alpha:n;(\rho)}$ for ρ. For example, if $n = 24$, $1 - \alpha = 0.95$, and $r_c = 0.65$, then $\tilde{\rho}_{r_c:\alpha;n} = \tilde{\rho}_{0.65:0.05;24} \approx 0.4$, so for these data a 95 percent upper confidence interval on ρ is $0.4 \leq \rho < 1$.

The values $\tilde{\rho}_{r_c:\gamma;n}$ for $\gamma = 1 - \alpha, \alpha/2$, and $1 - \alpha/2$ and $n \leq 25$ can be found by using David's tables. Table T.8 contains graphs that can also be used to obtain confidence intervals on ρ for special values of $1 - \alpha$, r_c, and n. The procedure for obtaining confidence intervals from the charts are given below.

1. Select the chart corresponding to the desired $1 - \alpha$.
2. On the horizontal axis find the number corresponding to the computed correlation coefficient r_c.
3. Go vertically up the graph on the line corresponding to r_c until the first curve corresponding to the n value is encountered.
4. Go horizontally to the ρ margin and this value of ρ is $\tilde{\rho}_{r_c:\alpha/2;n}$.
5. In step 3 go vertically up the graph on the line corresponding to r_c until the second curve corresponding to the n value is encountered.
6. Go horizontally to the ρ margin and this value of ρ is $\tilde{\rho}_{r_c:1-\alpha/2;n}$.

For the data above, since we want to determine a 0.95 upper confidence interval, we want to determine $\tilde{\rho}_{0.65:0.05;24}$, so $\alpha/2 = 0.05$, $\alpha = 0.10$, and $1 - \alpha = 0.90$. Use the chart corresponding to $1 - \alpha = 0.90$ and locate $r_c = 0.65$. We go up to the first curve where $n = 24$ and we go horizontally to the ρ-axis and we get $\tilde{\rho}_{0.65:0.05;24} = 0.4$. A two-sided 90 percent confidence interval is $0.4 \leq \rho \leq 0.8$.

We may want to perform tests or set confidence intervals on correlation coefficients for situations other than those discussed in Theorems 11.2.2 and 11.2.3. For instance, if we have M bivariate populations, we may want to test whether all correlation coefficients are equal to each other (or equal to a specified constant). The preceding theory will not serve for all of these problems, but an approximation developed by R. A. Fisher, see [K-7], can be used for many of them. The approximation and some of its uses are discussed below.

THEOREM 11.2.4

Let $(X_1, Y_1), (X_2, Y_2), \ldots, (X_n, Y_n)$ be a random sample of size $n > 2$ from a normal distribution with mean $\boldsymbol{\mu}$ and covariance $\boldsymbol{\Sigma}$ defined in Equation (11.2.3). *Let R be the correlation coefficient obtained by the formula in Equation* (11.2.4).

Define Z, δ, and v by

$$Z = \frac{1}{2}\log_e\left(\frac{1+R}{1-R}\right) = \operatorname{arctanh}[R]$$

$$\delta = \frac{1}{2}\log_e\left(\frac{1+\rho}{1-\rho}\right) = \operatorname{arctanh}[\rho] \tag{11.2.14}$$

$$v^2 = (n-3)^{-1}$$

Then Z is approximately distributed $N(z : \delta, v^2)$.

Proof

A proof of this theorem can be found in [K-7].

Table T.9 can be used to obtain values of z for various values of r.

To test the various hypotheses about ρ in Theorem 11.2.2, or to set confidence intervals on ρ, one can use tables or graphs [D-6] when $n \leq 25$. When $n > 25$, the approximation in Theorem 11.2.4 can be used (to test ρ has the value zero, the t test can be used for any $n > 2$). In the next theorem we demonstrate how "the Z transformation" in Equation (11.2.14) can be used.

THEOREM 11.2.5

Let $(X_1, Y_1), (X_2, Y_2), \ldots, (X_n, Y_n)$ *be a random sample of size* $n > 3$ *from a bivariate normal distribution with mean* $\boldsymbol{\mu}$ *and covariance* $\boldsymbol{\Sigma}$ *defined in Equation* (11.2.3). *Let R be the sample correlation coefficient. Let Z, δ, and v be the quantities in Equation* (11.2.14). *Define V by*

$$V = \frac{(Z-\delta)}{v} = (Z-\delta)\sqrt{n-3}$$

Then V is approximately distributed $N(v : 0, 1)$. *To test the various hypotheses in Theorem* 11.2.2, *let* v_c *denote the computed value of V, that is,* $z_c = \operatorname{arctanh}[r_c]$, $d_0 - \operatorname{arctanh}[r^*]$, *and* $v_c = (z_c - d_0)\sqrt{n-3}$. *The five tests below are of (approximate) size* α; r^* *can be any specified number such that* $-1 < r^* < 1$.

(1) *To test* $H_0 : \rho = r^*$ *vs.* $H_a : \rho \neq r^*$, *reject* H_0 *if and only if* $|v_c| \geq N_{\alpha/2}$. *The power of this test is*

$$\Pi(\rho) = \int_{-\infty}^{\lambda_1} n(y:0,1)\,dy + \int_{\lambda_2}^{\infty} n(y:0,1)\,dy$$

where $\lambda_1 = (\operatorname{arctanh}[r^*] - \operatorname{arctanh}[\rho])\sqrt{n-3} - N_{\alpha/2}$ *and* $\lambda_2 = (\operatorname{arctanh}[r^*] - \operatorname{arctanh}[\rho])\sqrt{n-3} + N_{\alpha/2}$ *for* $-1 < \rho < 1$.

(2) *To test* $H_0 : \rho = r^*$ *vs.* $H_a : \rho > r^*$, *reject* H_0 *if and only if* $v_c \geq N_\alpha$. *The power of this test is*

$$\Pi(\rho) = \int_{\lambda_3}^{\infty} n(y : 0, 1)\, dy$$

where $\lambda_3 = (\text{arctanh}[r^*] - \text{arctanh}[\rho])\sqrt{n-3} + N_\alpha$ *for* $r^* \leq \rho < 1$.

(3) *To test* $H_0 : \rho \leq r^*$ *vs.* $H_a : \rho > r^*$, *the procedure is the same as part* (2) *except* ρ *can vary in the interval* $-1 < \rho < 1$.

(4) *To test* $H_0 : \rho = r^*$ *vs.* $H_a : \rho < r^*$, *reject* H_0 *if and only if* $v_c \leq -N_\alpha$. *The power of this test is*

$$\Pi(\rho) = \int_{-\infty}^{\lambda_4} n(y : 0, 1)\, dy$$

where λ_4 *is* $\lambda_4 = (\text{arctanh}[r^*] - \text{arctanh}[\rho])\sqrt{n-3} - N_\alpha$ *for* $-1 < \rho \leq r^*$.

(5) *To test* $H_0 : \rho \geq r^*$ *vs.* $H_a : \rho < r^*$, *the procedure is the same as part* (4) *except* ρ *can vary in the interval* $-1 < \rho < 1$.

Proof

We shall demonstrate parts (1) and (2) since the other tests are variations of (2).

To demonstrate (1) we note (approximately) $Z = \text{arctanh}[R]$ is distributed $N(z : \delta, v^2)$, where $\delta = \text{arctanh}[\rho]$ and $v^2 = (n-3)^{-1}$. Let $d_0 = \text{arctanh}[r^*]$, and let $V = (Z - d_0)/v$. Then V is a random variable distributed $N(v : (\delta - d_0)/v, 1)$, and when H_0 is true (that is, $\delta = d_0$), then $V = (Z - d_0)\sqrt{n-3}$ is distributed $N(v : 0, 1)$. Hence the rejection region is $-\infty < v < -N_{\alpha/2}$ or $N_{\alpha/2} < v < \infty$, or in terms of z it is $\{z : -\infty < z < d_0 - N_{\alpha/2}/\sqrt{n-3}$ or $d_0 + N_{\alpha/2}/\sqrt{n-3} < z < \infty\}$. The power is

$$\begin{aligned}
&P[\text{rejecting } H_0 \mid \rho] \\
&\quad = P[-\infty < Z < d_0 - N_{\alpha/2}v \mid \rho] + P[d_0 + N_{\alpha/2}v < Z < \infty \mid \rho] \\
&\quad = P\left[-\infty < \frac{Z-\delta}{v} < \frac{d_0 - \delta}{v} - N_{\alpha/2} \mid \rho\right] \\
&\qquad + P\left[\frac{d_0-\delta}{v} + N_{\alpha/2} < \frac{Z-\delta}{v} < \infty \mid \rho\right] \\
&\quad = \int_{-\infty}^{\lambda_1} n(y : 0, 1)\, dy + \int_{\lambda_2}^{\infty} n(y : 0, 1)\, dy = \Pi(\rho)
\end{aligned}$$

where $\lambda_1 = (d_0 - \delta)/v - N_{\alpha/2}$ and $\lambda_2 = (d_0 - \delta)/v + N_{\alpha/2}$. This proves (1).

To prove (2) let $V = (Z - d_0)/v$, let the rejection region be $N_\alpha < v < \infty$, and note that $P[N_\alpha < V < \infty \mid H_0] = \alpha$. The rejection region in terms of z is $d_0 + N_\alpha v < z < \infty$, which we can write as $[(d_0 - \delta)/v] + N_\alpha < (z - \delta)/v < \infty$, where $Y = (Z - \delta)/v$ is distributed $N(y:0, 1)$. The power is

$$P[\text{rejecting } H_0 \mid \rho] = P\left[\frac{d_0 - \delta}{v} + N_\alpha < Y < \infty \mid \rho\right]$$
$$= \int_{\lambda_3}^{\infty} N(y:0, 1)\, dy$$

where

$$\lambda_3 = \frac{d_0 - \delta}{v} + N_\alpha = (\operatorname{arctanh}[r^*] - \operatorname{arctanh}[\rho])\sqrt{n-3} + N_\alpha$$

This completes the proof.

COROLLARY 11.2.5

Approximate $1 - \alpha$ confidence intervals on ρ are as follows.

(1) *upper confidence interval*: $\tanh(\operatorname{arctanh}[r_c] - N_\alpha/\sqrt{n-3}) \le \rho < 1$;

(2) *lower confidence interval*: $-1 < \rho \le \tanh(\operatorname{arctanh}[r_c] + N_\alpha/\sqrt{n-3})$;

(3) *two-sided confidence interval*: $\tanh(\operatorname{arctanh}[r_c] - N_{\alpha/2}/\sqrt{n-3}) \le \rho \le \tanh(\operatorname{arctanh}[r_c] + N_{\alpha/2}/\sqrt{n-3})$.

Next consider M bivariate p.d.f.'s and suppose we want to test that all M correlation coefficients are equal to each other, or are equal to a common specified value r^*. These tests are given in the next theorem.

THEOREM 11.2.6

Let $\rho_1, \rho_2, \ldots, \rho_M$ be the correlation coefficients from M bivariate normal p.d.f.'s, and let $R_1, R_2, \ldots, R_M$ be the respective M.L. estimators based on samples of sizes $n_1, n_2, \ldots, n_M$, respectively. Assume that $R_1, R_2, \ldots, R_M$ are jointly independent. The two tests given below are of (approximate) size α.

(1) *To test $H_0: \rho_1 = \rho_2 = \cdots = \rho_M = r^*$ (specified) vs. H_a: at least one equality is an inequality, reject H_0 if and only if $u_1 \ge \chi^2_{\alpha:M}$, where u_1 is defined by*

$$u_1 = \sum_{m=1}^{M} (z_m - d_0)^2 (n_m - 3)$$

where $d_0 = arctanh[r^*]$, $z_m = arctanh[r_m]$, *and where* r_m *is the computed value of* R_m. *The power of this test is (approximately)*

$$\Pi(\lambda) = \int_{\chi^2_{\alpha:M}}^{\infty} \chi^2(u_1 : M; \lambda)\, du_1$$

where

$$\lambda = \tfrac{1}{2} \sum_{m=1}^{M} (\delta_m - d_0)^2(n_m - 3) \qquad \text{and} \qquad \delta_m = arctanh[\rho_m]$$

(2) *To test* $H_0 : \rho_1 = \rho_2 = \cdots = \rho_M$ *vs.* H_a: *at least one equality is an inequality, reject* H_0 *if and only if* $u_2 \geq \chi^2_{\alpha:M-1}$, *where* u_2 *is defined by*

$$u_2 = \sum_{m=1}^{M} (z_m - \bar{z})^2(n_m - 3)$$

where $z_m = arctanh[r_m]$, r_m *is the computed value of* R_m, *and* $\bar{z} = \sum (n_m - 3)z_m / \sum (n_i - 3)$. *The power of this test is (approximately)*

$$\Pi(\lambda) = \int_{\chi^2_{\alpha:M-1}}^{\infty} \chi^2(u_2 : M - 1; \lambda)\, du_2$$

where

$$\lambda = \tfrac{1}{2} \sum_{m=1}^{M} (\delta_m - \bar{\delta})^2(n_m - 3) \qquad \text{and} \qquad \bar{\delta} = \frac{\sum_{m=1}^{M} (n_m - 3)\delta_m}{\sum_{m=1}^{M} (n_i - 3)}$$

Proof

The proof is a result of the fact that the sum of squares of independent normal random variables has a chi-square distribution. The details are left for the reader.

Suppose it is decided (a priori or on the basis of a test) that the ρ_i are all equal in the setup in Theorem 11.2.6. It may then be desirable to combine the independent estimators to obtain a "best" estimator for ρ, the common value. This is the context of the next theorem.

THEOREM 11.2.7

If $\rho_1 = \rho_2 = \cdots = \rho_M$ *in Theorem* 11.2.6, *then a combined estimator of the common value* ρ *is*

$$R = tanh[\bar{Z}]$$

where $\bar{Z}$ is defined as follows:

$$\bar{Z} = \frac{\sum_{m=1}^{M} (n_m - 3)Z_m}{\sum_{i=1}^{M} (n_i - 3)}$$

Proof

If we assume $Z_m = \text{arctanh}[R_m]$ are independent and distributed normally with mean $\delta = \text{arctanh}[\rho]$ and variance $(n_m - 3)^{-1} = v_m^2 = \omega_m^{-1}$, then the minimum variance unbiased estimator of δ is

$$\hat{\delta} = \frac{\sum_{m=1}^{M} Z_m \omega_m}{\sum_{i=1}^{M} \omega_i} = \frac{\sum_{m=1}^{M} Z_m(n_m - 3)}{\sum_{i=1}^{M} (n_i - 3)} = \bar{Z}$$

Thus transform $\bar{Z}$ and get $R = \tanh[\bar{Z}]$.

COROLLARY 11.2.7

In Theorem 11.2.7 an improved combined estimator is given by

$$R^* = tanh[Z^*]$$

where

$$Z^* = \bar{Z} - \frac{Q\rho^*}{2} \qquad \rho^* = \left(\frac{1}{M}\right) \sum_{m=1}^{M} \hat{\rho}_m \qquad Q = \frac{\sum_{m=1}^{M} \frac{(n_m - 3)}{(n_m - 1)}}{\sum_{i=1}^{M} (n_i - 1)}$$

and $\bar{Z}$ is defined in Theorem 11.2.7.

Example 11.2.2

We shall illustrate some of the previous theorems with an example. Consider the correlation between protein and butterfat content of milk from the milk of four breeds of dairy cattle. Suppose we want to perform the following tests, each with size $\alpha = 0.05$ (let the four breeds be denoted by 1, 2, 3, 4, and let ρ_i denote the simple correlation coefficient of protein and butterfat of milk from breed i):

1. $H_0: \rho_1 = 0$ *vs.* $H_a: \rho_1 > 0$. Calculate the power of this test for $\rho_1 = 0.2$ and 0.3.
2. $H_0: \rho_3 = 0.5$ *vs.* $H_a: \rho_3 \neq 0.5$. Calculate the power of this test for $\rho_3 = 0.2$.
3. $H_0: \rho_1 = \rho_2 = 0$ *vs.* H_a: at least one equality is an inequality.
4. $H_0: \rho_1 = \rho_2 = \rho_3 = \rho_4$ *vs.* H_a: at least one equality is an inequality.
5. $H_0: \rho_1 = 0$ *vs.* $H_a: \rho_1 \neq 0$. Calculate the power for $\rho_1 = 0.2$ and for $\rho_1 = -0.2$.

We assume that the average (for a year) butterfat content and average protein content of the milk of each cow have bivariate normal distributions. A random sample of n_i cows from breed i is selected, and the butterfat content and protein of the milk are measured and the simple correlation coefficients computed. The data are given in the table below.

	Breed 1	*Breed* 2	*Breed* 3	*Breed* 4
r_c	0.028	0.054	0.407	0.381
n_i	24	28	24	20

1. Since the hypothesized value r^* is zero, we can use the T in Equation (11.2.12) and part (2) in Corollary 11.2.2. We get

$$t_c = \frac{0.028\sqrt{22}}{\sqrt{1 - (0.028)^2}} = 0.131$$

Since $t_{\alpha:n_1-2} = t_{0.05:22} = 1.717$, we cannot reject H_0. The power of the test by (2) of Theorem 11.2.2 is, for a value ρ,

$$\Pi(\rho) = \int_{r_{\alpha:n;(r^*)}}^{1} c(r:n;\rho)\,dr$$

where $r_{\alpha:n;(r^*)}$ is such that

$$\int_{r_{\alpha:n;(r^*)}}^{1} c(r:n;r^*)\,dr = 0.05$$

From David's tables for $n = 24$, we get $r_{\alpha:n;(r^*)} = r_{0.05:24;(0)} \approx 0.345$ and $\Pi(0.2) \approx 0.241$, $\Pi(0.3) \approx 0.421$.

We can also solve this problem by using Fisher's Z transformation and (2) of Theorem 11.2.5. We get $z_c = \text{arctanh}[0.028] = 0.028$, $d_0 = \text{arctanh}[0.0] = 0, v_c = 0.028\sqrt{21} = 0.1283$, and $N_\alpha = N_{0.05} = 1.645$; so we cannot reject H_0. For the power $\Pi(0.2)$ we get $\lambda_3 = (0.0 - 0.20)\sqrt{21} + 1.645 = 0.73$ and

$$\Pi(0.2) = \int_{0.73}^{\infty} n(y:0,1) \approx 0.24$$

For the power $\Pi(0.3)$ we get $\lambda_3 = (0.0 - 0.31)\sqrt{21} + 1.645 = 0.22$ and

$$\Pi(0.3) = \int_{0.22}^{\infty} n(y:0,1) \approx 0.41$$

2. We can use David's tables or graphs and have an exact test, or we can use Fisher's Z transformation and (1) of Theorem 11.2.5. If we use the Z transformation, we get (for $n = 24$) $r^* = 0.50$, $r_c = 0.407$, $d_0 = \text{arctanh}[0.50] = 0.549$, $z_c = \text{arctanh}[0.407] = 0.432$, $v_c = (0.432 - 0.549)\sqrt{21} = -0.536$, and $N_{\alpha/2} = 1.96$; so $|v_c| < N_{\alpha/2}$ and H_0 is not rejected at the 5 percent level.

   For the power at $\rho_3 = 0.2$ we get $\lambda_1 = (0.549 - 0.203)\sqrt{21} - 1.96 = -0.374$, $\lambda_2 = (0.549 - 0.203)\sqrt{21} + 1.96 = 3.548$, and $\Pi(0.2) = \int_{-\infty}^{\lambda_1} n(y:0,1)\,dy + \int_{\lambda_2}^{\infty} n(y:0,1)\,dy = 0.36$. The exact test can be obtained by using David's tables and (1) of Theorem 11.2.2. We compute $r_{\alpha/2:n;(r^*)} = r_{0.025:24;(0.5)}$ and $r_{1-\alpha/2:24;(r^*)} = r_{0.975:24;(0.5)}$ from Equation (11.2.9). We get

$$0.025 = \int_{-1}^{r_{0.975:24;(0.5)}} c(r:24;0.5)\,dr \qquad r_{0.975:24;(0.5)} = 0.130$$

   Also

$$0.975 = \int_{-1}^{r_{0.025:24;(0.5)}} c(r:24;0.5)\,dr \qquad r_{0.025:24;(0.5)} = 0.758$$

   Thus the rejection region is the two intervals -1.00 to 0.130 and 0.758 to 1.00. Since the computed value is $r_c = 0.407$, it is not in the rejection region, and hence H_0 is not rejected. The power for $\rho = 0.2$ is

$$\Pi(0.2) = \int_{-1.00}^{0.130} c(r:24;0.2)\,dr + \int_{0.758}^{1.00} c(r:24;0.2)\,dr = 0.36$$

Note 6. We have used an equal-tail test.

3. We use (1) of Theorem 11.2.6. We get $r^* = 0$, $d_0 = 0$, $z_1 = 0.028$, $z_2 = 0.054$, $n_1 - 3 = 21$, $n_2 - 3 = 25$, $K = 2$, and $\alpha = 0.05$. Thus

$$u_1 = (0.028 - 0.000)^2(21) + (0.054 - 0.000)^2(25) = 0.0894$$

and

$$\chi^2_{0.05:2} = 5.99$$

Hence we do not reject H_0.

4. We can use (2) of Theorem 11.2.6, which is applied by computing the entries in Table 11.2.2. From the table we compute

$$\bar{z} = \frac{\sum (n_i - 3)z_i}{\sum (n_i - 3)} = \frac{17.8304}{84} = 0.2123$$

$$u_2 = \sum (n_i - 3)(z_i - \bar{z})^2 = \sum (n_i - 3)z_i^2 - \bar{z}^2 \sum (n_i - 3)$$

$$= 6.7448 - (0.2123)^2(84) = 2.96$$

If we compare this value of u_2 with $\chi^2_{0.05:3} = 7.81$, we conclude that we have no reason to reject the hypothesis that these r_i are all estimates of the same ρ.

5. To find the rejection region we could use (1) of Theorem 11.2.2, (1) of Corollary 11.2.2, or (1) of Theorem 11.2.5. To compute the power we could use (1) of Theorem 11.2.2 or (1) of Theorem 11.2.5. We shall demonstrate the use of the procedures by using (1) of Theorem 11.2.2. We get $r^* = 0.0$, $r_{0.975:24;(0)} \approx -0.41$, and $r_{0.025:24;(0)} \approx 0.41$. So H_0 is *accepted* if and only if r_c is in the interval $(-0.41, 0.41)$, and

Table 11.2.2

Table for Testing $\rho_1 = \rho_2 = \rho_3 = \rho_4$

	1	2	3	4	*Sum*
r_i	0.0280	0.0540	0.4070	0.3810	
z_i	0.0280	0.0540	0.4320	0.4012	
$n_i - 3$	21	25	21	17	84
$z_i(n_i - 3)$	0.5880	1.3500	9.0720	6.8204	17.8304
$z_i^2(n_i - 3)$	0.0165	0.0729	3.9191	2.7363	6.7448

$r_c = 0.028$; so H_0 is accepted. The power at $\rho_1 = -0.2$ is

$$\Pi(-0.2) = \int_{-1}^{-0.41} c(r:24;\ -0.2)\,dr + \int_{0.41}^{1} c(r:24;\ -0.2)\,dr \approx 0.152$$

Also, $\Pi(0.2) \approx 0.152$.

Example 11.2.3

In Example 11.2.2 suppose we want the following:

1. a 95 percent confidence interval on ρ_4;
2. a pooled estimate of ρ assuming $\rho_1 = \rho_2 = \rho_3 = \rho_4 = \rho$.

The solutions to these two problems are given below.

1. We can use David's charts or (3) of Theorem 11.2.3 for an exact confidence interval on ρ_4. This gives $\tilde{\rho}_{r_c:1-\alpha/2;n} = \tilde{\rho}_{0.3810:0.975;20} \approx 0.71$; $\tilde{\rho}_{r_c:\alpha/2;n} = \tilde{\rho}_{0.3810:0.025;20} \approx -0.07$, and the confidence interval is $-0.07 \le \rho_4 \le 0.71$.

   To demonstrate the use of Fisher's Z transformation, we use Corollary 11.2.5. We get

$$\tanh\left[\operatorname{arctanh}(0.381) - \frac{1.96}{\sqrt{17}}\right] \le \rho_4 \le \tanh\left[\operatorname{arctanh}(0.381) + \frac{1.96}{\sqrt{17}}\right]$$

   which gives $-0.07 \le \rho_4 \le 0.70$.

2. We will use Theorem 11.2.7 and get $\bar{z} = 0.2123$ from Table 11.2.2. This gives the combined estimated value $r_c = 0.21$. If we want to use the improved estimator in Corollary 11.2.7, we get $\rho^* = 0.2175$, $Q = 0.0396$, and the improved combined estimate is $0.208 \approx 0.21$.

11.3 Partial Correlation

To gain a better insight into relationships among random variables in a multivariate normal population, it may be desirable to stratify the population into subpopulations in which one or more random variables are held constant and to determine the correlations among the other random variables.

This was the case in trying to determine the relationship among blood pressure X_0, age X_1, and cholesterol X_2 of women over 35 years of age in New York state (see Example 5.3.3). Suppose, for example, $\rho_{01} = 0.41$,

$\rho_{02} = 0.32$, and $\rho_{12} = 0.88$. One of the reasons for the study might be to determine if it is feasible to reduce blood pressure by reducing cholesterol as a result of modifying one's diet. The value of the correlation coefficient ρ_{02} indicates that perhaps this may be the case.

However, there is also a positive correlation between age and cholesterol, and the high value of ρ_{02} may be due to age rather than to cholesterol. So it would be important to determine the correlation of blood pressure and cholesterol when age is held fixed, that is, to determine the value of ρ_{02} in various populations of women of the same age. We could obtain an estimate of ρ_{02} for women of age 50 by selecting a random sample of women 50 years of age, but this sampling procedure might be difficult. It would be easier if we could use a sample from the 3-variate distribution of X_0, X_1, X_2 to estimate ρ_{02} for women of the same age. So we could select n women at random from those under study (say over 35 years of age in New York state) and, on the basis of these data, estimate the correlation of blood pressure and cholesterol, holding age constant. This is defined to be the partial correlation of blood pressure and cholesterol given age, and is denoted by $\rho_{02|(1)}$.

Partial correlation is defined in Chapter 3 for the K-variate normal p.d.f. For example, suppose we know the following population values (of course, in any real situation these would have to be estimated from samples): $\rho_{01} = 0.41$, $\rho_{02} = 0.32$, and $\rho_{12} = 0.88$. From the formula in Problem 3.13, we get $\rho_{02|(1)} = -0.09$. Thus the correlation of 0.32 showing some relationship between blood pressure and cholesterol is reduced to -0.09 when age is held constant, so the conclusion is that blood pressure probably cannot be lowered by reducing cholesterol.

However, suppose the following were the known population values: $\rho_{01} = 0.41$, $\rho_{02} = 0.32$, and $\rho_{12} = 0.09$, that is, all values are the same as before except $\rho_{12} = 0.09$. We compute $\rho_{02|(1)} = 0.31$, so it appears that blood pressure might be lowered by reducing cholesterol.

These data are, of course, artificial, but it is often important to examine partial correlation when investigating the relationship among variables to gain insight into how one might proceed to change one factor by changing another. We discussed the population partial correlation coefficients in Chapter 3. In this section we shall discuss point estimators, confidence interval estimators, and tests of hypotheses.

Throughout this section we use the following notation.

1. χ is a random $K \times 1$ vector with elements $X_1, X_2, \ldots, X_K$.
2. χ is distributed $\mathbf{N}(\mathbf{x} : \boldsymbol{\mu}, \boldsymbol{\Sigma})$.
3. $$\chi = \begin{bmatrix} \chi_1 \\ \chi_2 \end{bmatrix}$$

   where χ_1 has size $M \times 1$ with elements $X_1, X_2, \ldots, X_M$.

4.
$$\boldsymbol{\mu} = \begin{bmatrix} \boldsymbol{\mu}_1 \\ \boldsymbol{\mu}_2 \end{bmatrix}$$

where $\boldsymbol{\mu}_1$ has size $M \times 1$, $0 < M < K$.

5.
$$\boldsymbol{\Sigma} = \begin{bmatrix} \boldsymbol{\Sigma}_{11} & \boldsymbol{\Sigma}_{12} \\ \boldsymbol{\Sigma}_{21} & \boldsymbol{\Sigma}_{22} \end{bmatrix}$$

where $\boldsymbol{\Sigma}_{11}$ has size $M \times M$, and so on.

6. $\boldsymbol{\Sigma}_{11.2} = \boldsymbol{\Sigma}_{11} - \boldsymbol{\Sigma}_{12}\boldsymbol{\Sigma}_{22}^{-1}\boldsymbol{\Sigma}_{21}$.

7. $\sigma_{ij|(M+1,\ldots,K)}$, $i = 1, 2, \ldots, M$, $j = 1, 2, \ldots, M$, is the ijth element of $\boldsymbol{\Sigma}_{11.2}$.

8.
$$\rho_{ij|(M+1,\ldots,K)} = \frac{\sigma_{ij|(M+1,\ldots,K)}}{\sqrt{\sigma_{ii|(M+1,\ldots,K)}\sigma_{jj|(M+1,\ldots,K)}}}$$

$i = 1, 2, \ldots, M$, $j = 1, 2, \ldots, M$, is the partial correlation coefficient between X_i and X_j holding $X_{M+1}, X_{M+2}, \ldots, X_K$ fixed. This follows from part 7.

9. The p.d.f. of $\mathbf{Y}_{1.2} = (\boldsymbol{\chi}_1 | \boldsymbol{\chi}_2 = \mathbf{x}_2)$ is $\mathbf{N}(\mathbf{y}_{1.2} : \boldsymbol{\mu}_{1.2}, \boldsymbol{\Sigma}_{11.2})$, where $\boldsymbol{\mu}_{1.2} = \boldsymbol{\mu}_1 + \boldsymbol{\Sigma}_{12}\boldsymbol{\Sigma}_{22}^{-1}(\mathbf{x}_2 - \boldsymbol{\mu}_2)$ and $\sigma_{ij|(M+1,\ldots,K)}$ is the covariance of the (i, j) element in $\mathbf{Y}_{1.2}$. (11.3.1)

There are two possible ways to estimate $\sigma_{ij|(M+1,\ldots,K)}$ (the elements of $\boldsymbol{\Sigma}_{11.2}$). One way is to stratify the population of the K random variables into subpopulations, one for each value of $X_{M+1}, X_{M+2}, \ldots, X_K$, and sample each of the subpopulations. The resulting sample would be random $M \times 1$ vectors from the conditional density defined in part 9 of Equation (11.3.1).

To illustrate this method, consider again Example 5.3.3. Suppose we are interested in $\rho_{02|(1)}$, the correlation of blood pressure and cholesterol in subpopulations where age X_1 is held fixed. If blood pressure, age, and cholesterol of all women in New York state were listed, they could be sorted into groups by ages, and for each age group the blood pressure and cholesterol is a (conditional) bivariate p.d.f. A sample of size n could be selected from one (or more) of these groups and the simple correlation coefficient computed. This is an estimate of $\rho_{02|(1)}$. All the theorems and procedures in Section 11.2 apply for estimation (point and interval) and hypothesis testing on $\rho_{02|(1)}$.

However, this method of sampling is generally not practical. It is generally easier to sample the entire K-variate population rather than the M-variate conditional population. For instance, in the above example it would undoubtedly be easier to obtain a random sample from *all* women in New York state (rather than by age) and measure blood pressure, cholesterol, and age of each. From these data one could estimate ρ_{01}, ρ_{02}, and ρ_{12} and use the formula in Problem 3.13 to compute an estimate of $\rho_{02|(1)}$.

The problem we now consider is that of estimation (point and interval) and testing of $\rho_{02|(1)}$, or, more generally, we shall estimate and test $\rho_{ij|(M+1,\ldots,K)}$, when the joint p.d.f. rather than the conditional p.d.f. is sampled.

It is a remarkable fact that in estimation (point or interval) and in testing hypotheses on the *partial* correlation coefficients $\rho_{ij|(M+1,\ldots,K)}$, all the theorems and formulas of Section 11.2 on the *simple* correlation coefficients ρ_{ij} apply with one minor modification: n, the sample size in all formulas, is replaced by $n - K + M$, that is, n is replaced by the sample size minus the number of variables in χ that are held fixed. We shall now discuss this in detail.

THEOREM 11.3.1

Consider the setup in Equation (11.3.1), *and let* $\chi_1, \chi_2, \ldots, \chi_n$ *be a random sample of n vectors from the p.d.f. in part* (2). $\bar{\chi}$ *and* $\mathscr{A}$ *are given by*

$$\bar{\chi} = \left(\frac{1}{n}\right) \sum_{i=1}^{n} \chi_i$$

$$\mathscr{A} = \sum_{i=1}^{n} (\chi_i - \bar{\chi})(\chi_i - \bar{\chi})'$$

Partition $\mathscr{A}$ *as*

$$\mathscr{A} = \begin{bmatrix} \mathscr{A}_{11} & \mathscr{A}_{12} \\ \mathscr{A}_{21} & \mathscr{A}_{22} \end{bmatrix}$$

where $\mathscr{A}_{11}$ *has size* $M \times M$, *and so on.*

(1) *The maximum likelihood estimator of* $\boldsymbol{\Sigma}_{11.2}$ *is* $\tilde{\boldsymbol{\Sigma}}_{11.2}$, *where*

$$\tilde{\boldsymbol{\Sigma}}_{11.2} = \left(\frac{1}{n}\right)\mathscr{A}_{11.2} = \left(\frac{1}{n}\right)(\mathscr{A}_{11} - \mathscr{A}_{12}\mathscr{A}_{22}^{-1}\mathscr{A}_{21})$$

(2) *The m.g.f. of* $\mathscr{A}_{11.2}$ *is* $m_{\mathscr{A}_{11.2}}(\mathbf{T})$, *where*

$$m_{\mathscr{A}_{11.2}}(\mathbf{T}) = |\mathbf{I} - 2\mathbf{T}\boldsymbol{\Sigma}_{11.2}|^{-[n-1-(K-M)]/2} \qquad |t_{ij}| < h$$

for some number $h > 0$.

(3) $\mathscr{A}_{11.2}$ *is distributed* $\mathbf{W}_M(\mathbf{A}_{11.2} : n - 1 - K + M; \boldsymbol{\Sigma}_{11.2})$, *see Definition* 9.3.1.

(4) *Define the ijth element of* $\mathscr{A}_{11.2}$ *by* $A_{ij.2}$; *then* $\tilde{\rho}_{ij|(M+1,\ldots,K)} = A_{ij.2}/\sqrt{A_{ii.2}A_{jj.2}}$. *All the theorems in Section* 11.2 *apply with the following replacements*:

(a) $\tilde{\rho}_{ij}$ *replaced by* $\tilde{\rho}_{ij|(M+1,\ldots,K)}$ (*or* $\tilde{\rho}$ *replaced by* $\tilde{\rho}_{ij|(M+1,\ldots,K)}$ *in those theorems where the ij subscripts have been omitted*);

(b) ρ_{ij} (*or* ρ) *replaced by* $\rho_{ij|(M+1,\ldots,K)}$;

(c) n *replaced by* N, *where* $N = n - (K - M)$.

(5) *The elements in* $\tilde{\mathbf{\Sigma}}_{11.2}$, *and hence* $\tilde{\rho}_{ij|(M+1,\ldots,K)}$, *are functions of complete sufficient statistics, so Theorem* 11.2.1 *can be used to obtain the UMVU estimator of* $\rho_{ij|(M+1,\ldots,K)}$. *Equation* (11.2.10) *can also be used with n replaced with N*.

Proof

To prove part (1) we note that $\mathbf{\Sigma}_{11.2} = \mathbf{\Sigma}_{11} - \mathbf{\Sigma}_{12}\mathbf{\Sigma}_{22}^{-1}\mathbf{\Sigma}_{21}$, and by Theorem 9.3.1 the maximum likelihood estimator of $\mathbf{\Sigma}$ is $(1/n)\mathscr{A}$. Hence this means that the maximum likelihood estimator of $\mathbf{\Sigma}_{ij}$ is $(1/n)\mathscr{A}_{ij}$. Then by the invariant property of maximum likelihood estimators, the estimator of $\mathbf{\Sigma}_{11} - \mathbf{\Sigma}_{12}\mathbf{\Sigma}_{22}^{-1}\mathbf{\Sigma}_{21}$ is $\tilde{\mathbf{\Sigma}}_{11} - \tilde{\mathbf{\Sigma}}_{12}\tilde{\mathbf{\Sigma}}_{22}^{-1}\tilde{\mathbf{\Sigma}}_{21} = (1/n)\mathscr{A}_{11.2}$ as was to be shown. We omit the proof for (2).

The proof for part (3) is a direct consequence of (2). The m.g.f. of $\mathscr{A}_{11.2}$, that is, the joint m.g.f. of the elements $A_{ij.2}$ in $\mathscr{A}_{11.2}$, is exactly the same as the m.g.f. of $\mathscr{A}$ in Corollary 9.7.1 with n replaced by $n - (K - M)$ and $\mathbf{\Sigma}$ replaced by $\mathbf{\Sigma}_{11.2}$. Hence by Theorem 2.3.1, $\mathscr{A}_{11.2}$ is distributed $\mathbf{W}_M(\mathbf{A}_{11.2} : n - 1 - K + M; \mathbf{\Sigma}_{11.2})$, and this proves (3).

To prove (4) we note that all of the theorems about ρ (or ρ_{ij}) in Section 11.2 are based on the joint p.d.f. of the random variables A_{ij} in $\mathscr{A}$. In a similar manner, to estimate (point or interval) or test hypotheses about the $\rho_{ij|(M+1,\ldots,K)}$, the elements $A_{ij.2}$ (that is, the elements in $\mathscr{A}_{11.2}$) are used. Hence we must derive the joint p.d.f. of the $A_{ij|(M+1,\ldots,K)}$. But by (3) the joint p.d.f. of $A_{ij|(M+1,\ldots,K)}$ is exactly the same as the p.d.f. of the A_{ij} in $\mathscr{A}$ except n is replaced by $n - (K - M)$ and $\mathbf{\Sigma}$ is replaced by $\mathbf{\Sigma}_{11.2}$, that is, σ_{ij} is replaced by $\sigma_{ij|(M+1,\ldots,K)}$. To simplify notation we use $R_{ij.2}$ for $R_{ij|(M+1,\ldots,K)}$, $r_{ij.2}$ for $r_{ij|(M+1,\ldots,K)}$, and $\rho_{ij.2}$ for $\rho_{ij|(M+1,\ldots,K)}$. Thus the p.d.f. of $R_{ij.2}$ is, by Equation (11.2.5),

$$f_{R_{ij.2}}(r_{ij.2} : n - K + M; \rho_{ij.2}) = \frac{(n - 2 - K + M)(1 - \rho_{ij.2}^2)^{(1/2)(n-K+M-1)}}{\pi} \times (1 - r_{ij.2}^2)^{(1/2)(n-K+M-4)} \int_0^\infty (\cosh w - r_{ij.2}\rho_{ij.2})^{-(n-K+M-1)}\, dw \tag{11.3.2}$$

From this p.d.f. all the theorems in Section 11.2 are derived. Hence all the theorems in Section 11.2 apply with R replaced by $R_{ij|(M+1,\ldots,K)}$, ρ replaced by $\rho_{ij|(M+1,\ldots,K)}$, and n replaced by $n - K + M$. This proves (4).

The proof for (5) will be left for the reader.

11.3.1 Computation of $\tilde{\boldsymbol{\Sigma}}_{11.2}$

In this section we demonstrate how the square root method can be used to compute $\mathbf{A}_{11.2} = \mathbf{A}_{11} - \mathbf{A}_{12}\mathbf{A}_{22}^{-1}\mathbf{A}_{21}$. This quantity divided by n is the M.L. estimate of $\boldsymbol{\Sigma}_{11.2}$, and from this matrix the partial correlation coefficients $\rho_{ij:(M+1,\ldots,K)}$ can be easily obtained. The matrix $\mathbf{A}$ is partitioned as in Theorem 11.3.1, and the matrix $[\mathbf{A}_{22} \mid \mathbf{A}_{21}]$ is reduced by the square root method. The result is

$$\left[\begin{array}{c|c} \mathbf{A}_{22} & \mathbf{A}_{21} \\ \hline \mathbf{T} & \mathbf{B}_{21} \end{array}\right] \qquad (11.3.3)$$

Since $\mathbf{A}_{22}$ is positive definite, we can write it as $\mathbf{T}'\mathbf{T}$ and hence $\mathbf{B}_{21} = \mathbf{T}'^{-1}\mathbf{A}_{21}$. Thus $\mathbf{B}'_{21}\mathbf{B}_{21} = \mathbf{A}_{12}\mathbf{T}^{-1}\mathbf{T}'^{-1}\mathbf{A}_{21} = \mathbf{A}_{12}\mathbf{A}_{22}^{-1}\mathbf{A}_{21}$, and

$$\mathbf{A}_{11.2} = \mathbf{A}_{11} - \mathbf{B}'_{21}\mathbf{B}_{21} \qquad (11.3.4)$$

Another way to compute $\mathbf{A}_{11.2}$ by the square root method is to reduce the matrix $\mathbf{A}_0$, where $\mathbf{A}_0$ is defined by

$$\mathbf{A}_0 = \begin{bmatrix} \mathbf{A}_{22} & \mathbf{A}_{21} \\ \mathbf{A}_{12} & \mathbf{A}_{11} \end{bmatrix} \qquad (11.3.5)$$

We get

$$\left[\begin{array}{c} \mathbf{A}_0 \\ \hline \mathbf{T}_0 \end{array}\right] = \left[\begin{array}{cc} \mathbf{A}_{22} & \mathbf{A}_{21} \\ \mathbf{A}_{12} & \mathbf{A}_{11} \\ \hline \mathbf{T}_{22} & \mathbf{T}_{21} \\ \mathbf{0} & \mathbf{T}_{11} \end{array}\right] \qquad (11.3.6)$$

and

$$\mathbf{T}'_{11}\mathbf{T}_{11} = \mathbf{A}_{11.2} \qquad (11.3.7)$$

since $\mathbf{A}_0 = \mathbf{T}'_0\mathbf{T}_0$, and from this we get $\mathbf{A}_{11} = \mathbf{T}'_{11}\mathbf{T}_{11} + \mathbf{T}'_{21}\mathbf{T}_{21}$; we write this as $\mathbf{T}'_{11}\mathbf{T}_{11} = \mathbf{A}_{11} - \mathbf{T}'_{21}\mathbf{T}_{21}$. But $\mathbf{T}_{21}$ is the same as $\mathbf{B}_{21}$ in Equation (11.3.3); hence $\mathbf{T}'_{11}\mathbf{T}_{11} = \mathbf{A}_{11} - \mathbf{B}'_{21}\mathbf{B}_{21} = \mathbf{A}_{11.2}$ by Equation (11.3.4).

Example 11.3.1

Assume that the 4×1 vector χ is distributed $\mathbf{N}(\mathbf{x} : \boldsymbol{\mu}, \boldsymbol{\Sigma})$ and that a random sample of size $n = 26$ was selected from this p.d.f. and the matrix $\mathbf{A}$ computed, where

$$\mathbf{A} = \begin{bmatrix} 10 & 9 & -1 & -16 \\ 9 & 20 & -3 & -16 \\ -1 & -3 & 5 & 3 \\ -16 & -16 & 3 & 27 \end{bmatrix}$$

Suppose we want the following:

1. a point estimate of $\rho_{12|(34)}$;
2. a test $H_0 : \rho_{12|(34)} = 0$ *vs.* $H_a : \rho_{12|(34)} \neq 0$, with $\alpha = 0.05$;
3. a 95 percent confidence interval on $\rho_{12|(34)}$.

First we compute $\mathbf{A}_{11.2}$ and get

$$\begin{aligned} \mathbf{A}_{11.2} &= \mathbf{A}_{11} - \mathbf{A}_{12}\mathbf{A}_{22}^{-1}\mathbf{A}_{21} \\ &= \begin{bmatrix} 10 & 9 \\ 9 & 20 \end{bmatrix} - \begin{bmatrix} -1 & -16 \\ -3 & -16 \end{bmatrix} \begin{bmatrix} \frac{27}{126} & -\frac{3}{126} \\ -\frac{3}{126} & \frac{5}{126} \end{bmatrix} \begin{bmatrix} -1 & -3 \\ -16 & -16 \end{bmatrix} \\ &= \frac{1}{126} \begin{bmatrix} 49 & -35 \\ -35 & 1285 \end{bmatrix} \end{aligned}$$

If we compute $\mathbf{A}_{11.2}$ by Equation (11.3.4), we use Equation (11.3.3) to obtain $\mathbf{B}_{21}$. We get

$$\left[\begin{array}{c|c} \mathbf{A}_{22} & \mathbf{A}_{21} \\ \hline \mathbf{T} & \mathbf{B}_{21} \end{array}\right] = \left[\begin{array}{cc|cc} 5 & 3 & -1 & -3 \\ 3 & 27 & -16 & -16 \\ \hline \sqrt{5} & \frac{3}{\sqrt{5}} & \frac{-1}{\sqrt{5}} & \frac{-3}{\sqrt{5}} \\ & \frac{\sqrt{126}}{\sqrt{5}} & \frac{-77}{\sqrt{5(126)}} & \frac{-71}{\sqrt{5(126)}} \end{array}\right]$$

Thus

$$\mathbf{B}_{21}'\mathbf{B}_{21} = \begin{bmatrix} \frac{1211}{126} & \frac{1169}{126} \\ \frac{1169}{126} & \frac{1235}{126} \end{bmatrix}$$

and by Equation (11.3.4) we, of course, get the same value for $\mathbf{A}_{11.2}$ as above.

1. From this we get the maximum likelihood estimate of $\rho_{12|(34)}$ as $r_c = -35/\sqrt{(49)(1285)} = -0.139$. By (2) of Theorem 11.2.1 an unbiased (and hence the UMVU) estimate of $\rho_{12|(34)}$ can be found.

2. To solve this problem we can use Student's t and (1) of Corollary 11.2.2. We get $K = 4, M = 2, n - (K - M) = n - 2 = N = 24$, and

$$|t_c| = \left| \frac{-0.139\sqrt{22}}{\sqrt{1 - (-0.139)^2}} \right| = 0.661 \qquad t_{0.025:22} = 2.074$$

   So H_0 is not rejected.

3. To solve this problem we can use (3) of Theorem 11.2.3 with David's tables (or charts), or we can use Corollary 11.2.5 with Fisher's Z transformation. Using David's tables we get the confidence interval $\tilde{\rho}_{r_c:0.025;24} \leq \rho \leq \tilde{\rho}_{r_c:0.975;24}$, where $\tilde{\rho}_{r_c:0.025;24}$ is found by solving the following for ρ ($N = 26 - K + M = 24$):

$$0.975 = \int_{-1}^{-0.139} c(r : N; \rho)\, dr = 1 - \int_{-1}^{0.139} c(r : N; -\rho)\, dr$$

   We get $-\tilde{\rho}_{r_c:0.025;24} \approx 0.51$, so $\tilde{\rho}_{r_c:0.025;24} \approx -0.51$. Then $\tilde{\rho}_{r_c:0.975;24}$ is found by solving

$$0.025 = \int_{-1}^{-0.139} c(r : N; \rho)\, dr$$

   We get $\tilde{\rho}_{r_c:0.975;24} \approx 0.28$. Hence the 0.95 confidence interval on ρ is $-0.51 \leq \rho \leq 0.28$. If we use Fisher's Z transformation, we get (since $\text{arctanh}[-0.139] \approx -0.140$)

$$\tanh\left[-0.140 - \frac{1.96}{\sqrt{21}}\right] \leq \rho \leq \tanh\left[-0.140 + \frac{1.96}{\sqrt{21}}\right]$$

   or $-0.51 \leq \rho \leq 0.28$. The charts in Table T.8 can also be used.

11.4 Multiple Correlation

The utility of the multiple correlation coefficient is explained in Chapter 3 and further information on it can be found in Chapter 12. We assume the distributional setup in Equation (11.1.1). The multiple correlation coefficient of X_0 on $X_1, X_2, \ldots, X_K$ is denoted by $\rho_{0(1,2,\ldots,K)}$ and defined by

$$\rho_{0(1,2,\ldots,K)} = \sqrt{\rho^2_{0(1,2,\ldots,K)}} = \sqrt{\frac{\boldsymbol{\sigma}_{01}\boldsymbol{\Sigma}^{-1}\boldsymbol{\sigma}_{10}}{\sigma_{00}}} \tag{11.4.1}$$

To obtain point estimates, interval estimates, and tests of hypotheses of $\rho^2_{0(1,2,\ldots,K)}$, we select a random sample of size n from the p.d.f. of χ^* and find the maximum likelihood estimator of $\boldsymbol{\Sigma}^*$, which is $\tilde{\boldsymbol{\Sigma}}^* = (1/n)\mathscr{A}^*$. By the invariant property of maximum likelihood estimators, we get

$$\tilde{\rho}^2_{0(1,2,\ldots,K)} = \frac{\boldsymbol{a}_{01}\mathscr{A}^{-1}\boldsymbol{a}_{10}}{A_{00}} \tag{11.4.2}$$

for the maximum likelihood estimator of the square of the multiple correlation coefficient. This estimator is based on complete sufficient statistics but it is not an unbiased estimator and hence not an UMVU estimator. For more information on point estimation the reader is referred to [O-1].

The distribution of $\tilde{\rho}^2_{0(1,2,\ldots,K)}$ is quite complicated unless $\rho^2_{0(1,2,\ldots,K)} = 0$, and we shall derive it for that case only. For the distribution of $\tilde{\rho}^2_{0(1,2,\ldots,K)}$ when $\rho^2_{0(1,2,\ldots,K)} = 0$, we state the following theorem.

THEOREM 11.4.1

Consider the distributional setup in Equation (11.1.1) *and the estimator* $\tilde{\rho}^2_{0(1,2,\ldots,K)}$ *given in Equation* (11.4.2). *The random variable* W *is distributed* $F(w : K, n - K - 1)$ *when* $\rho^2_{0(1,2,\ldots,K)} = 0$, *where*

$$W = \left(\frac{\tilde{\rho}^2_{0(1,2,\ldots,K)}}{1 - \tilde{\rho}^2_{0(1,2,\ldots,K)}}\right)\left(\frac{n - K - 1}{K}\right) \tag{11.4.3}$$

Proof

The proof follows along the lines of the proof that T is distributed $s(t : n - 2)$ in Corollary 11.2.2 and will be asked for in the problems.

The result of this theorem can be used to test $H_0 : \rho_{0(1,2,\ldots,K)} = 0$ *vs.* $H_a : \rho_{0(1,2,\ldots,K)} > 0$.

THEOREM 11.4.2

Consider the distributional setup in Equation (11.1.1) *and the statistic* W *given in Equation* (11.4.3). *A test of size* α *of* $H_0 : \rho_{0(1,2,\ldots,K)} = 0$ *vs.* $H_a : \rho_{0(1,2,\ldots,K)} > 0$ *is this: Reject* H_0 *if and only if* $w \geq F_{\alpha:K,n-K-1}$.

Proof

The proof is a direct consequence of Theorem 11.4.1.

Note 1. The test in Theorem 11.4.2 is a test that X_0 is independent of $X_1, X_2, \ldots, X_K$.

We now discuss a procedure that can be used to obtain confidence intervals on $\rho_{0(1,2,\ldots,K)}$ and hence to obtain corresponding tests of hypotheses other than $\rho_{0(1,2,\ldots,K)}$ is zero.

THEOREM 11.4.3

Consider the distributional setup in Equation (11.1.1). *Let r_c^2 be the computed value of $\tilde{\rho}^2_{0(1,2,\ldots,K)}$ in Equation* (11.4.2) *based on an observed random sample of size $n > K + 1$ of $(K + 1) \times 1$ vectors represented by $\mathbf{x}_1^*, \mathbf{x}_2^*, \ldots, \mathbf{x}_n^*$. Lower, upper, and two-sided (equal-tailed) $1 - \alpha$ confidence intervals on $\rho_{0(1,2,\ldots,K)}$ are given by the following:*

(1) *upper confidence interval: $r_{\alpha:c} \le \rho_{0(1,2,\ldots,K)} < 1$, where $r_{\alpha:c}$ is the value of ρ_0 that satisfies $r_c = r_{\alpha:K,n-K-1;(\rho_0)}$;*

(2) *lower confidence interval: $0 \le \rho_{0(1,2,\ldots,K)} \le r_{1-\alpha:c}$, where $r_{1-\alpha:c}$ is the value of ρ_0 that satisfies $r_c = r_{1-\alpha:K,n-K-1;(\rho_0)}$;*

(3) *two-sided confidence interval: $r_{\alpha/2:c} \le \rho_{0(1,2,\ldots,K)} \le r_{1-\alpha/2:c}$, where $r_{1-\alpha/2:c}$ and $r_{\alpha/2:c}$ are defined above.*

Note 2. The symbol $r_{\gamma:K,n-K-1;(\rho_0)}$ is used to represent the *upper* γ probability point of the p.d.f. of $\tilde{\rho}_{0(1,2,\ldots,K)}$, which is based on a random sample of n vectors $\chi_1^*, \chi_2^*, \ldots, \chi_n^*$ from a $(K + 1)$-variate normal distribution with multiple correlation coefficient of X_0 on $X_1, X_2, \ldots, X_K$ denoted by $\rho_{0(1,2,\ldots,K)}$ (or by ρ_0 when there is no chance for ambiguity).

Proof

We shall demonstrate the upper $1 - \alpha$ confidence interval. The others can be derived by a similar argument. Clearly, $P[\tilde{\rho}_{0(1,2,\ldots,K)} \le r_{\alpha:K,n-K-1;(\rho_0)}] = 1 - \alpha$. Let r_c be the value of $\tilde{\rho}_{0(1,2,\ldots,K)}$ computed from observed data. Then the inequality $r_c \le r_{\alpha:K,n-K-1;(\rho_0)}$ is "correct with probability $1 - \alpha$," and if the solution for ρ_0 of the equation $r_c = r_{\alpha:K,n-K-1;(\rho_0)}$ is denoted by $r_{\alpha:c}$, then $r_{\alpha:c} \le \rho_{0(1,2,\ldots,K)}$ is correct if and only if $r_c \le r_{\alpha:K,n-K-1;(\rho_0)}$. Thus since $r_c \le r_{\alpha:K,n-K-1:(\rho_0)}$ is "correct with probability $1 - \alpha$," it follows that $r_{\alpha:c} \le \rho_{0(1,2,\ldots,K)}$ is also "correct with probability $1 - \alpha$." Thus $(r_{\alpha:c}, 1)$ is an upper $1 - \alpha$ confidence interval on $\rho_{0(1,2,\ldots,K)}$. The arguments for the lower and two-sided confidence intervals are similar.

In Table T.10 the values of $r_{\gamma:K,n-K-1;(\rho_0)}$ are computed, where $r_{\gamma:K,n-K-1;(\rho_0)}$ is given by

$$\gamma = \int_{r_{\gamma:K,n-K-1;(\rho_0)}}^{1} f_R(r : K, n - K - 1; \rho_0)\, dr$$

for $\gamma = 0.01, 0.05, 0.95, 0.99$; $n - K - 1 = 10, 20, 30, 40, 50$; $K = 2, 4, 6, 8, 10, 12, 16, 20, 24, 30, 34, 40$; and $\rho_0 = \rho_{0(1,2,\ldots,K)} = 0.0, 0.1, 0.2, 0.3, 0.4, 0.5, 0.6, 0.7, 0.8, 0.9$. The p.d.f. of $\tilde{\rho}_{0(1,2,\ldots,K)}$ is denoted by $f_R(r : K, n - K - 1; \rho_0)$ above. Thus from these tables one can compute upper 5 percent and 1 percent confidence intervals, lower 5 percent and 1 percent confidence intervals, and 2 percent and 10 percent two-sided (equal-tail) confidence intervals.

Example 11.4.1

A random sample of size 45 (size n) is selected from a 5-variate [$(K + 1)$-variate] normal p.d.f. and the M.L. estimate of the multiple correlation coefficient is computed as $r_c = 0.767$.

1. Set an upper 95 percent confidence interval on $\rho_{0(1,2,\ldots,4)}$.
2. Set a 98 percent two-sided, equal-tail confidence interval on $\rho_{0(1,2,\ldots,4)}$.

The solutions are given below.

1. For the upper 95 percent confidence interval, we must find $r_{0.05:c}$, so enter the table for $\alpha = 0.05$, $n - K - 1 = 40$, and $K = 4$, and in the body of the table solve $r_{0.05:4,40;(\rho_0)} = 0.767$ for ρ_0. The solution is $\rho_0 = \rho_{0(1,2,\ldots,4)} = 0.6$ and $0.60 \le \rho_{0(1,2,\ldots,4)} \le 1$ is the upper 0.95 confidence interval computed from the observed data.
2. For a two-sided (equal-tail) 98 percent confidence interval, we must determine $r_{1-\alpha/2:c} = r_{0.99:c}$ and $r_{\alpha/2:c} = r_{0.01:c}$. We solve $r_c = r_{0.99:4,40;(\rho_0)}$ for ρ_0 to get $r_{0.99:c}$. We enter the table $\alpha = 0.99$ at $K = 4$, $n - K - 1 = 40$, and look for $r_c = 0.767$. The value 0.767 gives a value of ρ_0 between 0.8 and 0.9, and by using linear interpolation, we get $r_{0.99:c} = 0.87$. To determine $r_{0.01:c}$ we solve $r_c = r_{0.01:4,40;(\rho_0)}$ and get $r_{0.01:c} = 0.52$ (by linear interpolation). Hence $0.52 \le \rho_{0(1,2,\ldots,4)} \le 0.87$ is a computed 98 percent two-sided confidence interval on $\rho_{0(1,2,\ldots,4)}$.

11.4.1 Computation of $\tilde{\rho}^2_{0(1,2,\ldots,K)}$

In this section we demonstrate how the M.L. estimate of $\rho^2_{0(1,2,\ldots,K)}$, namely $\tilde{\rho}^2_{0(1,2,\ldots,K)}$, can be computed by the square root method. By Equation (11.4.2) the only computation of any difficulty is $\mathbf{a}_{01}\mathbf{A}^{-1}\mathbf{a}_{10}$, where $\mathbf{A}^*$ is the observed $\mathscr{A}^*$ in Equation (11.1.1) and

$$\mathbf{A}^* = \begin{bmatrix} a_{00} & \mathbf{a}_{01} \\ \mathbf{a}_{10} & \mathbf{A} \end{bmatrix} \tag{11.4.4}$$

To compute $\mathbf{a}_{01}\mathbf{A}^{-1}\mathbf{a}_{10}$ we reduce $[\mathbf{A} \mid \mathbf{a}_{10}]$ by the square root method and obtain

$$\left[\begin{array}{c|c} \mathbf{A} & \mathbf{a}_{10} \\ \hline \mathbf{T} & \mathbf{t} \end{array}\right] \tag{11.4.5}$$

Clearly $\mathbf{t}'\mathbf{t} = \mathbf{a}_{01}\mathbf{A}^{-1}\mathbf{a}_{10}$, and

$$\tilde{\rho}^2_{0(1,2,\ldots,K)} = \frac{\mathbf{t}'\mathbf{t}}{a_{00}} \tag{11.4.6}$$

Also from this format we can obtain $\tilde{\rho}^2_{0(1,2,\ldots,q)}$ by the formula

$$\tilde{\rho}^2_{0(1,2,\ldots,q)} = \sum_{i=1}^{q} \frac{t_i^2}{a_{00}} \qquad \text{for } q = 1, 2, \ldots, K \tag{11.4.7}$$

We note the similarity of this computation with the computation for the regression coefficients in the general linear model. In fact, the matrix $\mathbf{A}$ in Equation (11.4.4) is the matrix $\mathbf{S}_D$ of sum of squares and cross products given in Section 7.5, and the vector $\mathbf{a}_{10}$ in Equation (11.4.4) is the vector $\mathbf{s}_D$ in Section 7.5, where the symbols y_i are used instead of x_{i0} for the ith observation of the dependent variable; also p in Section 7.5 is $K + 1$ in the present section. The format

$$\left[\begin{array}{c|c} \mathbf{S}_D & \mathbf{s}_D \\ \hline \mathbf{T} & \mathbf{t} \end{array}\right] \quad \text{is the same as} \quad \left[\begin{array}{c|c} \mathbf{A} & \mathbf{a}_{10} \\ \hline \mathbf{T} & \mathbf{t} \end{array}\right]$$

An ANOVA table for testing $H_0 : \beta_1 = \beta_2 = \cdots = \beta_{p-1}$ always includes an "error sum of squares" term which for the "deviation from the means" model is $ESS = \mathbf{y}'_D\mathbf{y}_D - \hat{\boldsymbol{\beta}}'_2\mathbf{X}'_D\mathbf{y}_D$; see the proof of Theorem 7.5.1. But from the formats above we obtain $ESS = \mathbf{y}'_D\mathbf{y}_D - \hat{\boldsymbol{\beta}}'_2\mathbf{X}'_D\mathbf{y}_D = a_{00} - \mathbf{t}'\mathbf{t}$, since $a_{00} = \sum_{i=1}^{n}(x_{i0} - \bar{x}_0)^2$, and in the notation of Section 7.5, we get $a_{00} = \sum(x_{i0} - \bar{x}_0)^2 = \sum(y_i - \bar{y})^2 = \mathbf{y}'_D\mathbf{y}_D$. Thus from Equation (11.4.6) we get a relationship between the error sum of squares and the estimate of the multiple correlation coefficient.

The relationship is

$$\tilde{\rho}^2_{0(1,2,\ldots,K)} = \frac{a_{00} - ESS}{a_{00}} = \frac{\sum (y_i - \bar{y})^2 - ESS}{\sum (y_i - \bar{y})^2}$$

$$= \frac{[\text{total deviation sum of squares of } y_i \text{ (of } x_{i0})] \text{ minus [error sum of squares]}}{\text{total deviation sum of squares of } y_i \text{ (or of } x_{i0})}$$

For further information on the multiple correlation coefficient, see [A-3], [K-7], and [R-2]. For further information on tables for percentage points of the p.d.f. of the multiple correlation coefficient, see [K-11], [L-7], and [P-4].

11.5 Correlation for Non-normal p.d.f.'s

In Chapter 3 we defined simple, multiple, and partial correlation coefficients and regression coefficients under the assumption that χ^* (*and* χ) has a $(p + 1)$-variate *normal* distribution. We will now define simple, multiple, and partial correlation coefficients and regression coefficients when the random variables are not necessarily normal.

DEFINITION 11.5.1

Correlation and Regression Coefficients. *Let χ^* be a $(K + 1) \times 1$ random vector with elements $\chi^* = [X_0, X_1, \ldots, X_K]'$, with mean μ^*, and with positive definite covariance matrix Σ^*. We use the notation in Equation* (3.7.1). *The simple, multiple, and partial correlation coefficients, the regression function, and the regression coefficients are defined below.*

Simple Correlation: Definition 3.8.1 (*normality not assumed*);
Multiple Correlation: Definition 3.8.3 (*normality not assumed*);
Partial Correlation: Definition 3.8.4 (*normality not assumed*);
Regression Function: Definition 10.4.1;
Regression Coefficients: Equation (10.4.3) *and Equation* (10.4.4) *if the regression function is linear in x; otherwise the definition depends on the p.d.f. of χ^*.* (11.5.1)

Note 1. It is, of course, clear that the definitions in Equation (11.5.1) are the same as when the random variables are jointly normal. (We sometimes interchange the symbols p and K.)

Note 2. We note that the regression function *defined* by Equation (11.5.1) is the same as given in Equations (3.7.2), (3.7.3), and (3.7.4) without the normality assumption. In Chapter 3 the definition is given by $\mathscr{E}[(X_0 \mid \boldsymbol{\chi} = \mathbf{x})]$, and this is also the definition of the regression function for the non-normal case. In Section 10.4 we discussed the relationship between the regression coefficients for the normal and non-normal case. In the next theorem we show that many of the theorems about correlation in Chapter 3 are valid when the random vector $\boldsymbol{\chi}^*$ is not necessarily normally distributed.

THEOREM 11.5.1

Let the elements of the $(p + 1) \times 1$ *random vector* $\boldsymbol{\chi}^*$ *be jointly distributed with mean* $\boldsymbol{\mu}^*$ *and positive definite covariance matrix* $\boldsymbol{\Sigma}^*$. *Let the correlation coefficients be defined as in Definition* 11.5.1. *The following theorems are valid regardless of whether the joint p.d.f. is normal (the notation in Equation* (3.7.1) *is used): Theorems* 3.8.1, 3.8.2, 3.8.3, 3.8.4, 3.8.5, 3.8.6, 3.8.7, *and Corollary* 3.8.7.

Proof

The results in the theorems listed in Theorem 11.5.1 are results obtained from a positive definite matrix $\boldsymbol{\Sigma}^*$ and do not depend on the p.d.f. of the random vector $\boldsymbol{\chi}^*$. Hence they apply to any p.d.f. with a positive definite covariance matrix $\boldsymbol{\Sigma}^*$.

In Section 11.5.1 we discuss correlation for the case when $(X_0 \mid \boldsymbol{\chi} = \mathbf{x})$ has a univariate normal p.d.f. but the p.d.f. of $\boldsymbol{\chi}$ is not known.

11.5.1 Correlation for a Conditional Normal Distribution

In this section we use the notation and distributional properties of Equation (11.1.1) except condition 1. Instead of condition 1 we assume that the p.d.f. of the $K + 1$ random vector $\boldsymbol{\chi}^*$ is given by Equation (10.2.9), that is, the p.d.f. of $\boldsymbol{\chi}^*$ is

$$\begin{aligned} f_{\boldsymbol{\chi}^*}(\mathbf{x}^* : \beta_0, \boldsymbol{\beta}, \sigma^2, \boldsymbol{\theta}) &= (2\pi\sigma^2)^{-1/2} \exp\left\{-\frac{1}{2\sigma^2}\left[x_0 - \beta_0 - \sum_{j=1}^{K} \beta_j x_j\right]^2\right\} f_{\boldsymbol{\chi}}(\mathbf{x} : \boldsymbol{\theta}) \\ &= f_{X_0|\boldsymbol{\chi}}(y : \beta_0, \boldsymbol{\beta}, \sigma^2) f_{\boldsymbol{\chi}}(\mathbf{x} : \boldsymbol{\theta}) \qquad (11.5.2) \end{aligned}$$

where $\boldsymbol{\chi}$ does not equal a constant c with probability one.

THEOREM 11.5.2

Let the $(K + 1) \times 1$ *vectors* $\boldsymbol{\chi}_1^*, \boldsymbol{\chi}_2^*, \ldots, \boldsymbol{\chi}_n^*$ *be a random sample from the p.d.f. in Equation* (11.5.2). *The p.d.f. of* $\tilde{\rho}^2_{0(1,2,\ldots,K)}$ *in Equation* (11.4.2) *depends on the p.d.f.*

of $\boldsymbol{\chi}$. *A test of size of* $H_0 : \rho^2_{0(1,2,\ldots,K)} = 0$ *vs.* $H_a : \rho^2_{0(1,2,\ldots,K)} > 0$ *is this: Reject* H_0 *if and only if* $w \geq F_{\alpha:K,n-K-1}$, *where* w *is the computed value of* W *and* W *is defined in Equation* (11.4.3).

Proof

The proof is similar to the proof of Corollary 11.2.2.

Note 3. If $K = 1$, that is, if X_0, X_1 has a joint p.d.f. given by Equation (11.5.2), then the test is a test that the simple correlation coefficient of X_0, X_1 is zero.

Note 4. The power of the test depends on the p.d.f. $f_\chi(\mathbf{x} : \boldsymbol{\theta})$.

COROLLARY 11.5.2

The test in Theorem 11.5.2 *is a test of the hypothesis that* X_0 *is independent of* $X_1, X_2, \ldots, X_K$ *for the random variables with joint p.d.f. given in Equation* (11.5.2), *regardless of the p.d.f. of* $X_1, X_2, \ldots, X_K$.

Proof

Generally, the fact that $\rho^2_{0(1,2,\ldots,K)} = 0$ does not imply that X_0 is independent of $X_1, X_2, \ldots, X_K$. But we note that $\rho^2_{0(1,2,\ldots,K)} = \boldsymbol{\sigma}_{01}\boldsymbol{\Sigma}^{-1}\boldsymbol{\sigma}_{10}/\sigma_{00}$. Also, by Definition 11.5.1, since the regression function is linear in Equation (11.5.2), the regression coefficients (that is, $\boldsymbol{\beta}$) are defined by $\boldsymbol{\beta} = \boldsymbol{\Sigma}^{-1}\boldsymbol{\sigma}_{10}$; hence $\rho^2_{0(1,2,\ldots,K)} = 0$ if and only if $\boldsymbol{\beta} = \mathbf{0}$. But if $\boldsymbol{\beta} = \mathbf{0}$, it is clear that the p.d.f. in Equation (11.5.2) factors into the product of the p.d.f. of X_0 and the p.d.f. of $\boldsymbol{\chi}$. Hence X_0 is independent of $\boldsymbol{\chi}$.

For further information concerning tests about correlation coefficients when the p.d.f. is given by Equation (11.5.2), see references [K-7] and [T-2].

11.6 Correlation and Independence of Random Variables

It is often useful to be able to determine from observed data how random variables are "related." If X and Y are two jointly distributed random variables, the two extremes of the "relationship" between them are as follows: (1) X and Y are independent; and (2) X and Y are functionally related. The next theorem concerns these two extreme relationships.

THEOREM 11.6.1

Let X and Y be jointly distributed random variables with mean $\boldsymbol{\mu}$ *and covariance* $\boldsymbol{\Sigma}$.

(1) $\rho^2_{XY} = 1$ *if and only if there is a linear functional relationship between X and Y, that is, if and only if there exist constants* β_0 *and* β *such that* $Y = \beta_0 + \beta X$ *(with probability one).*

(2) *Let* $Z_1 = g_1(X, Y)$, $Z_2 = g_2(X, Y)$. $\rho^2_{Z_1Z_2} = 1$ *if and only if there is a linear functional relationship between* $g_1(X, Y)$ *and* $g_2(X, Y)$*, that is, if and only if there exist constants* β_0^* *and* β^* *such that* $g_1(X, Y) = \beta_0^* + \beta^* g_2(X, Y)$ *(with probability one).*

(3) *If* $\rho_{XY} \neq 0$*, then X and Y are not independent random variables; if X and Y are independent, then* $\rho_{XY} = 0$.

Proof

The result in part (2) is a direct consequence of part (1), so we shall prove (1) and leave it to the reader to supply the details for (2).

Define U_1 and U_2 by $U_1 = (X - \mu_X)/\sigma_X$, $U_2 = (Y - \mu_Y)/\sigma_Y$; then

$$\begin{aligned}\mathscr{E}[(U_1 - U_2)^2] &= \mathscr{E}[U_1^2] + \mathscr{E}[U_2^2] - 2\,\text{cov}[U_1, U_2] \\ &= 1 + 1 - 2\mathscr{E}[U_1U_2] = 0\end{aligned}$$

since $\rho^2_{XY} = \{\mathscr{E}[U_1U_2]\}^2 = 1$ by hypothesis, and we take $\rho_{XY} = +1$. (If we use $\rho_{XY} = -1$, then replace $(U_1 - U_2)^2$ with $(U_1 + U_2)^2$, and we get the same result.) Hence $\mathscr{E}[(U_1 - U_2)^2] = 0$, which implies that $U_1 - U_2 = 0$ (with probability one). So $U_1 = U_2$, or $(X - \mu_X)/\sigma_X = (Y - \mu_Y)/\sigma_Y$, which, when solving for Y, gives

$$Y = \left[\mu_Y - \left(\frac{\sigma_Y}{\sigma_X}\right)\mu_X\right] + \left(\frac{\sigma_Y}{\sigma_X}\right)X = \beta_0 + \beta X$$

This proves (1).

The proof of (3) follows directly from the fact that if X and Y are independent, $\rho_{XY} = 0$; so if $\rho_{XY} \neq 0$, it must imply that X and Y are *not* independent.

Now suppose ρ_{XY} is not equal to 1, but is a number, say 0.18. How does this number measure the "relationship" between X and Y? Does $\rho_{XY} = 0.36$ imply two times the relationship between X and Y as a value $\rho_{XY} = 0.18$ implies? There is no complete answer to this question and we should perhaps not expect to summarize the relationship between two random variables (actually between two p.d.f.'s) by a single number ρ_{XY}. Yet as we have stated in Theorem 11.6.1, there are some situations (the case when $\rho^2_{XY} = 1$) when the one number ρ_{XY}

contains all the information about the "relationship" between X and Y. Also, as we discussed in Section 5.3, the correlation ρ_{XY}^2 measures the proportional decrease in the variance of Y when a related variable X is used to predict Y by a linear regression equation. This is a useful concept of how a correlation coefficient is a measure of the "relationship" between two random variables X and Y. This interpretation of ρ_{XY}^2 may not be correct, however, if the regression function of Y on X is not linear in X (see Theorem 10.4.2).

It is often useful to be able to infer from observed data whether two random variables, say X and Y, are independent. If X and Y are jointly normal random variables, or if the p.d.f. of X, Y is given by Equation (10.2.9), then a test of $\rho = 0$ given in Section 11.5.1 can be used to check for independence. However, there are p.d.f.'s in which $\rho_{XY} = 0$ and yet X and Y are not independent but instead are "functionally" related. For example, define the discrete p.d.f. $f_{X,Y}(\cdot, \cdot)$ by $f_{X,Y}(1, 1) = \frac{1}{4}$, $f_{X,Y}(2, 4) = \frac{1}{4}$, $f_{X,Y}(-1, 1) = \frac{1}{4}$, $f_{X,Y}(-2, 4) = \frac{1}{4}$, and $f_{X,Y}(x, y) = 0$ for all other values x, y. Then $\mathscr{E}[X] = (1)(\frac{1}{4}) + (2)(\frac{1}{4}) + (-1)(\frac{1}{4}) - (2)(\frac{1}{4}) = 0$; $\mathscr{E}[XY] = (1 \cdot 1)(\frac{1}{4}) + (2 \cdot 4)(\frac{1}{4}) + (-1 \cdot 1)(\frac{1}{4}) + (-2 \cdot 4)(\frac{1}{4}) = 0$; hence $\rho_{XY} = 0$. But clearly $y = x^2$, so y is a function of x, that is, y and x are *functionally* related. So if the p.d.f. is not known, and if it is not known whether the regression of Y on X is linear, it is difficult to determine what the value of ρ_{XY} tells about the "relationship" between X and Y (except when $\rho_{XY}^2 = 1$).

Sometimes an investigator has little or no information about the form of the p.d.f., so to examine independence between X and Y, one may feel more comfortable in using a test whose Type I error probability is valid for "any" p.d.f. (a distribution-free procedure). We shall not discuss this, but listed below are three correlation coefficients that are frequently found useful.

1. The permutation correlation coefficient: [K-7];
2. Spearman's correlation coefficient: [K-5];
3. Kendall's tau correlation coefficient: [K-5].

The correlation coefficient discussed in previous sections of this chapter is generally referred to as Pearson's correlation coefficient or the "product-moment" correlation coefficient.

Problems

11.1. The following are M.L. estimates of simple correlation coefficients from random samples of sizes n_i from six bivariate normal p.d.f.'s. (The $\tilde{\rho}_i$ are jointly independent.)

ith p.d.f.	1	2	3	4	5	6
$\tilde{\rho}_i$	0.04	0.05	0.81	0.72	0.75	-0.62
n_i	24	90	24	95	64	24

(a) Use Student's t to test $H_0 : \rho_1 = 0$ *vs.* $H_a : \rho_1 > 0$.
(b) Use Student's t to test $H_0 : \rho_1 = 0$ *vs.* $H_a : \rho_1 < 0$.
(c) Use Student's t to test $H_0 : \rho_1 = 0$ *vs.* $H_a : \rho_1 \neq 0$.

11.2. In Problem 11.1 repeat parts (a), (b), and (c) by using Fisher's Z transformation.

11.3. In Problem 11.1(a) find the power of the test when $\rho_1 = 0.2$ (use Fisher's Z transformation and $\alpha = 0.05$).

11.4. In Problem 11.1(b) find the power of the test when $\rho_1 = -0.2$ (use Fisher's Z transformation and $\alpha = 0.05$).

11.5. In Problem 11.1(c) find the power of the test when $\rho_1 = 0.2$ and $\rho_1 = -0.2$ (use David's tables and $\alpha = 0.05$).

11.6. In Problem 11.1 use Fisher's Z transformation to set a 95 percent confidence interval on ρ_1 (two-sided interval).

11.7. In Problem 11.1 use David's tables to set a 95 percent (two-sided) confidence interval on ρ_1. Check your answer with the charts in Table T.8.

11.8. In Problem 11.1 set a 95 percent confidence interval (two-sided) on

$$\frac{(1 + \rho_1)(1 - \rho_2)}{(1 - \rho_1)(1 + \rho_2)}$$

11.9. In Problem 11.1 find an approximate unbiased estimate of ρ_3 and ρ_4. Use Equation (11.2.10).

11.10. In Problem 11.1 test $H_0 : \rho_3 = \rho_4$ *vs.* $H_a : \rho_3 \neq \rho_4$.

11.11. In Problem 11.1 use David's tables to test $H_0 : \rho_3 \leq 0.60$ *vs* $H_a : \rho_3 > 0.60$, with $\alpha = 0.05$. Find the power of the test when $\rho_3 = 0.90$.

11.12. In Problem 11.1 test $H_0 : \rho_6 = -0.50$ *vs.* $H_a : \rho_6 \neq -0.50$, with $\alpha = 0.05$. Find the power when $\rho_6 = -0.60$ and when $\rho_6 = -0.70$ (use David's tables).

11.13. Repeat Problem 11.12 using Fisher's Z transformation.

11.14. In Problem 11.1 set upper 80 percent, 90 percent, 95 percent, and 99 percent confidence intervals on ρ_6 (use Fisher's Z transformation).

11.15. Work Problem 11.14 by using David's tables.

11.16. In Problem 11.1 test $H_0 : \rho_3 = \rho_4 = \rho_5$ *vs.* H_a : at least one equality is an inequality. Use $\alpha = 0.05$.

11.17. In Problem 11.1 test $H_0 : \rho_3 = \rho_4 = \rho_5 = 0.75$ *vs.* H_a : at least one equality is an inequality. Use $\alpha = 0.05$. How does H_0 in Problem 11.17 differ from H_0 in Problem 11.16?

11.18. For the data in Example 11.3.1, find the M.L. estimate of $\rho_{13|(2,4)}$.

11.19. For the data in Example 11.3.1, find the M.L. estimate of $\rho_{12|(3)}$.

11.20. For the data in Example 11.3.1, set a two-sided 90 percent confidence interval on $\rho_{12|(3,4)}$. Use Fisher's Z transformation, David's tables, and David's charts.

11.21. For the data in Example 11.3.1, test $H_0 : \rho_{23|(1)} = 0$ *vs.* $H_a : \rho_{23|(1)} \neq 0$. Use $\alpha = 0.10$.

11.22. For the data in Example 11.3.1, find the M.L. estimate of $\rho^2_{1(2,3,4)}$.

11.23. For the data in Example 11.3.1, find the M.L. estimate of $\rho^2_{1(2,3)}$.

11.24. A random sample of size $n = 37$ was selected from a 7-variate normal p.d.f. and the computed value of $\tilde{\rho}^2_{0(1,2,\ldots,6)}$ was 0.490. Set 90 percent two-sided confidence limits on $\rho^2_{0(1,2,\ldots,6)}$.

11.25. In Problem 11.24 set a 99 percent upper confidence interval on $\rho^2_{0(1,2,\ldots,6)}$.

CHAPTER 12

Some Applications of the Regression Model

12.1 Introduction

In this chapter we discuss some special cases of the regression model that are useful in applied work. In Section 12.2 we introduce the topic of prediction; in Section 12.3 we briefly discuss the problem of selection of variables. Section 12.4 is devoted to a short discussion of growth curves, and Section 12.5 is devoted to the topic of classification. None of these topics will be discussed in depth, but some introductory material will be presented and references for further reading will be given.

12.2 Prediction

In this section we undertake a brief study of a topic that has many important applications; the topic is prediction. We illustrate first with examples.

Example 12.2.1

The director of admissions of a university wants an objective procedure for determining which students should be admitted as freshmen. He wants to obtain information about each prospective student and, on the basis of this information, to "predict" what a student's grade point average will be at the end of the freshman year. The information to be used for each student might be such things as follows: high school grade point average X_1, I.Q. X_2, the grade on a special entrance examination X_3, the grade on a certain personality test X_4, and so on. If a "prediction function," say $g(X_1, X_2, X_3, X_4)$, is available, this would be used to predict what the student's grade point average Y would be at the end of the freshman year. Of course, if for a certain student the predicted grade point average is high, he would be admitted; if it is low, he would not.

Example 12.2.2

Suppose a drug firm has a new drug that it believes will reduce the blood pressure of patients with high blood pressure. It would be useful to predict the reduction in blood pressure Y as a function of the level of the daily dosage of the drug X_1 and the age of the patient X_2. A prediction function $g(X_1, X_2)$ will be used to predict Y, the reduction in blood pressure.

Example 12.2.3

There are many other examples that could be cited: (1) the prediction of the number of barrels of oil that a new field will produce as a function of some physical properties, such as porosity of the sand, permeability of the rocks, and so on; (2) the prediction of the mature height of a newborn female baby as a function of her length at birth, her father's mature height, her mother's mature height, and so on; (3) the prediction of the price of a certain commodity, such as a gallon of gasoline, five years into the future as a function of the present price, the rate of inflation, the amount of crude oil available at the present time, and so on; (4) the prediction of the supply of a certain commodity, such as wheat, that will be available one year from today as a function of the number of acres of wheat planted this year, the number of bushels of wheat in storage at the present time, the anticipated increase in average income, a cost of living index, and so on.

Two things are necessary to be able to predict: (1) the predictor factors $1, 2, \ldots, K$ and random observations associated with these factors, which we denote by $X_1, X_2, \ldots, X_K$, that will be used to predict; (2) a prediction function $g(X_1, X_2, \ldots, X_K)$. In general, the factors will be a subject matter consideration, and an expert in the subject should determine factors that are candidates for good predictors. There may also be subject matter considerations as to which function will be a good prediction function (this may be derived from more basic considerations in model development that include differential equations, stochastic processes, and so forth).

There are at least two reasons why a prediction function is useful: (1) the user may actually want to predict (or know) the value y of a factor when he cannot observe it (it may be a value that is available only in the future but he wants to know it now so he can plan ahead, or it may be a quantity that is expensive or difficult to measure and he wants to predict, or determine, the value of Y from observations $x_1, x_2, \ldots, x_K$ of factors that are inexpensive or easy to measure); (2) the user may be interested mainly in the prediction function (and not primarily interested in the predicted value) since the function may tell him what factors "drive the system" and how they "drive" it. For example, a drug firm may be interested in a function to predict blood pressure Y from a knowledge of one's age X_1 and the amount of cholesterol in one's blood X_2. Certainly blood pressure can be measured more easily and accurately than one can measure cholesterol, but if a "good" prediction function can be determined, then the *function* is the important quantity. It may be possible to get ideas from this function as to how one's blood pressure is related to cholesterol and age.

In this section we assume that the factors to be used in predicting are given, and we shall discuss methods for determining the prediction function. In the next section we shall briefly discuss some methods for determining whether the factors are important (or useful) in predicting, and the *relative* importance of the various factors.

The basic problem that we consider in this section is this: $K + 1$ jointly distributed random variables $X_0, X_1, \ldots, X_K$ are available for examination and a function $g(X_1, X_2, \ldots, X_K)$ is to be determined that will be defined as a prediction function of X_0.

Let y, where $y = g(x_1, x_2, \ldots, x_K)$, be the predicted value of x_0 for an observation $x_1, x_2, \ldots, x_K$; of course, we want the predicted value to be "close" to the true (unknown) value. The measure that we use for "closeness" is mean-squared-error. We reason as follows:

1. Consider an observation $x_1, x_2, \ldots, x_K$ of some quantity; suppose x_0 is the "true" value of the quantity that one wants to predict and y is the predicted value of x_0 based on this observation. The number $x_0 - y$, which we denote by e, is the error of prediction (the true value x_0 minus the predicted value y); we can write

$$e = x_0 - y = x_0 - g(x_1, x_2, \ldots, x_K)$$

2. The squared-error of prediction e^2 is $[x_0 - g(x_1, x_2, \ldots, x_K)]^2$ and depends on the observed values of the random variables.

3. For a measure of "closeness" we want the squared-error to be small "on the average," so we use average squared-error, that is, mean-squared-error, denoted by

$$\mathscr{E}[\varepsilon^2] = \mathscr{E}[\{X_0 - Y\}^2] = \mathscr{E}[\{X_0 - g(X_1, X_2, \ldots, X_K)\}^2] \quad (12.2.1)$$

We now formalize the definition of a "best" prediction function.

DEFINITION 12.2.1

Best Prediction Function. *$g_0(X_1, X_2, \ldots, X_K)$ is defined to be a best (minimum mean-squared-error) prediction function of X_0 based on $X_1, X_2, \ldots, X_K$ if and only if*

$$\mathscr{E}[\{X_0 - g_0(X_1, X_2, \ldots, X_K)\}^2] \leq \mathscr{E}[\{X_0 - g(X_1, X_2, \ldots, X_K)\}^2] \quad (12.2.2)$$

for all functions $g(X_1, X_2, \ldots, X_K)$.

Note 1. We assume throughout that all expectations exist.

Note 2. This definition states that if no prediction function of X_0, based on $X_1, X_2, \ldots, X_K$, has smaller mean-squared-error than $g_0(X_1, X_2, \ldots, X_K)$, then $g_0(X_1, X_2, \ldots, X_K)$ is defined as the "best" prediction function of X_0.

Note 3. Actually we will have occasion to use the concept of best prediction function "in a class $\mathscr{C}$." This means that only functions in a certain class are considered and the best prediction function in this class is optimum. For example, the class $\mathscr{C}$ could be "all linear functions" or "all quadratic functions" of $X_1, X_2, \ldots, X_K$.

Our first problem is to determine, if possible, a general form for the best prediction function. In the theorem that follows, we prove that the best prediction function can be determined when the joint p.d.f. of $X_0, X_1, \ldots, X_K$ is *known*.

THEOREM 12.2.1

Let $f_{X_0, X_1, \ldots, X_K}(x_0, x_1, \ldots, x_K)$ be the p.d.f. of the $K + 1$ random variables $X_0, X_1, \ldots, X_K$. The best prediction function of X_0 based on the K random variables $X_1, X_2, \ldots, X_K$ is denoted by $g_0(x_1, x_2, \ldots, x_K)$ and is given by $\mathscr{E}[(X_0 \mid X_1 = x_1, X_2 = x_2, \ldots, X_K = x_K)]$; that is, $g_0(x_1, x_2, \ldots, x_K)$ is the best prediction function of X_0, where

$$g_0(x_1, x_2, \ldots, x_K) = \mathscr{E}[(X_0 \mid X_1 = x_1, X_2 = x_2, \ldots, X_K = x_K)] \quad (12.2.3)$$

for each $x_1, x_2, \ldots, x_K$ in E_K.

Proof

Our problem is to find a function $g(X_1, X_2, \ldots, X_K)$ such that $\mathscr{E}[X_0 - g(X_1, X_2, \ldots, X_K)]^2$ is minimized. We have

$$\begin{aligned}
&\mathscr{E}[X_0 - g(X_1, X_2, \ldots, X_K)]^2 \\
&\quad = \mathscr{E}\big[\{X_0 - \mathscr{E}[(X_0 \mid X_1, X_2, \ldots, X_K)] \\
&\qquad + \mathscr{E}[(X_0 \mid X_1, X_2, \ldots, X_K)] - g(X_1, X_2, \ldots, X_K)\}^2\big] \\
&\quad = \mathscr{E}\big[\{X_0 - \mathscr{E}[(X_0 \mid X_1, X_2, \ldots, X_K)]\}^2\big] \\
&\qquad + \mathscr{E}\big[\{\mathscr{E}[(X_0 \mid X_1, X_2, \ldots, X_K)] - g(X_1, X_2, \ldots, X_K)\}^2\big]
\end{aligned} \tag{12.2.4}$$

since the cross product term is zero. To show that the cross product term is zero, we recall that $\mathscr{E}_{X_0 \mid X_1, X_2, \ldots, X_K}[X_0]$ is a symbol for $\mathscr{E}[(X_0 \mid X_1, X_2, \ldots, X_K)]$, and write

$$\begin{aligned}
&\mathscr{E}\big[\{X_0 - \mathscr{E}[(X_0 \mid X_1, X_2, \ldots, X_K)]\}\{\mathscr{E}[(X_0 \mid X_1, X_2, \ldots, X_K)] \\
&\qquad\qquad - g(X_1, X_2, \ldots, X_K)\}\big] \\
&\quad = \mathscr{E}_{X_1, X_2, \ldots, X_K}\big[\mathscr{E}_{X_0 \mid X_1, X_2, \ldots, X_K}\{X_0 - \mathscr{E}[(X_0 \mid X_1, X_2, \ldots, X_K)]\} \\
&\qquad \times \{\mathscr{E}[(X_0 \mid X_1, X_2, \ldots, X_K)] - g(X_1, X_2, \ldots, X_K)\}\big]
\end{aligned} \tag{12.2.5}$$

But the second term in braces, namely $\{\mathscr{E}[(X_0 \mid X_1, X_2, \ldots, X_K)] - g(X_1, X_2, \ldots, X_K)\}$, does not depend on the random variable X_0. Hence if we examine the expectation in the first brackets in Equation (12.2.5), we get

$$\begin{aligned}
&\mathscr{E}_{X_0 \mid X_1, X_2, \ldots, X_K}\{X_0 - \mathscr{E}[(X_0 \mid X_1, X_2, \ldots, X_K)]\} \\
&\qquad \times \{\mathscr{E}[(X_0 \mid X_1, X_2, \ldots, X_K)] - g(X_1, X_2, \ldots, X_K)\} \\
&\quad = \{\mathscr{E}[(X_0 \mid X_1, X_2, \ldots, X_K)] - g(X_1, X_2, \ldots, X_K)\} \\
&\qquad \times \mathscr{E}_{X_0 \mid X_1, X_2, \ldots, X_K}\{X_0 - \mathscr{E}[(X_0 \mid X_1, X_2, \ldots, X_K)]\} = 0
\end{aligned}$$

since

$$\begin{aligned}
&\mathscr{E}_{X_0 \mid X_1, X_2, \ldots, X_K}[X_0 - \mathscr{E}[(X_0 \mid X_1, X_2, \ldots, X_K)]] \\
&\qquad = \mathscr{E}_{X_0 \mid X_1, X_2, \ldots, X_K}[X_0] - \mathscr{E}[(X_0 \mid X_1, X_2, \ldots, X_K)] = 0
\end{aligned}$$

Thus by Equation (12.2.4) we have

$$\mathscr{E}[X_0 - g(X_1, X_2, \ldots, X_K)]^2 \geq \mathscr{E}\{X_0 - \mathscr{E}[(X_0 \mid X_1, X_2, \ldots, X_K)]\}^2$$

and equality holds if and only if $\mathscr{E}\big[\{\mathscr{E}[(X_0 \mid X_1, X_2, \ldots, X_K)] - g(X_1, X_2, \ldots, X_K)\}^2\big] = 0$, or, in other words, if and only if (with probability one)

$$g(X_1, X_2, \ldots, X_K) = \mathscr{E}[(X_0 \mid X_1, X_2, \ldots, X_K)]$$

which we denote by $g_0(X_1, X_2, \ldots, X_K)$. This completes the proof that $\mathscr{E}[(X_0 \mid X_1 = x_1, X_2 = x_2, \ldots, X_K = x_K)]$, which we denote by $g_0(x_1, x_2, \ldots, x_K)$, is the best (minimum mean-squared-error) prediction function of X_0.

We note that $\mathscr{E}[(X_0 \mid X_1 = x_1, X_2 = x_2, \ldots, X_K = x_K)]$ is indeed a function of $x_1, x_2, \ldots, x_K$, and by Theorem 2.5.3,

$$\begin{aligned}\mathscr{E}[X_0] &= \mathscr{E}_{X_1,X_2,\ldots,X_K}\mathscr{E}_{X_0|X_1,X_2,\ldots,X_K}[X_0] \\ &= \mathscr{E}_{X_1,X_2,\ldots,X_K}\{\mathscr{E}[(X_0 \mid X_1, X_2, \ldots, X_K)]\} \\ &= \mathscr{E}_{X_1,X_2,\ldots,X_K}[g_0(X_1, X_2, \ldots, X_K)]\end{aligned}$$

so we have proved the following corollary.

COROLLARY 12.2.1.1

Under the assumptions in Theorem 12.2.1, *it follows that* $g_0(X_1, X_2, \ldots, X_K)$ *has the same expectation as* X_0.

> ***Note 4.*** The best prediction function is the regression function of X_0 on $X_1, X_2, \ldots, X_K$. See Definition 10.4.1.

We shall now exhibit the best prediction function when the joint p.d.f. of $X_0, X_1, \ldots, X_K$ is a normal p.d.f.

COROLLARY 12.2.1.2

Let the $K + 1$ *random vector* $\boldsymbol{\chi}^*$ *be distributed* $\mathbf{N}(\mathbf{x}^* : \boldsymbol{\mu}^*, \boldsymbol{\Sigma}^*)$. *The best prediction function of* X_0 *based on* $X_0, X_1, \ldots, X_K$ *is*

$$\begin{aligned}\mathscr{E}[(X_0 \mid X_1 = x_1, X_2 = x_2, \ldots, X_K = x_K)] &= \mu_0 + \boldsymbol{\sigma}_{01}\boldsymbol{\Sigma}^{-1}(\mathbf{x} - \boldsymbol{\mu}) \\ &= \beta_0 + \sum_{k=1}^{K} \beta_k x_k \qquad (12.2.6)\end{aligned}$$

where the quantities $\boldsymbol{\chi}^*, \mathbf{x}^*, \boldsymbol{\mu}^*, \boldsymbol{\Sigma}^*, \boldsymbol{\sigma}_{01}, \boldsymbol{\Sigma}, \boldsymbol{\mu}$, *and* β_k *are defined in Section* 3.7.

Proof

The proof will be left for the reader.

The following theorem is a direct consequence of this corollary.

THEOREM 12.2.2

If the joint p.d.f. of the X_i*'s is given by Equation* (10.2.9), *then the best prediction function is given by Equation* (12.2.6).

Next, suppose that nothing is known about the p.d.f. of the $K + 1$ random vector χ^* (except that the covariance matrix Σ^* exists). Then we cannot determine the functional form of the best prediction function $\mathscr{E}[(X_0 \mid X_1 = x_1, X_2 = x_2, \ldots, X_K = x_K)]$. Thus, as we often do in these situations (when the joint p.d.f. of the random variable is not known), we restrict the class of prediction functions to a particular class $\mathscr{C}$ and search for the best prediction function in this class. If we consider only those functions that are *linear* in the predictor variables $X_1, X_2, \ldots, X_K$, we have the following definition.

DEFINITION 12.2.2

Best Linear Prediction Function. *Consider the $K + 1$ random vector χ^* with mean μ^* and covariance Σ^*. A function $\ell^*(X_1, X_2, \ldots, X_K)$ will be defined as the "best" linear prediction function of X_0 based on $X_1, X_2, \ldots, X_K$ if and only if $\ell^*(X_1, X_2, \ldots, X_K)$ satisfies the two conditions below.*

(1) *$\ell^*(X_1, X_2, \ldots, X_K)$ is a linear function of $X_1, X_2, \ldots, X_K$, that is,*

$$\ell^*(X_1, X_2, \ldots, X_K) = \gamma_0 + \sum_{i=1}^{K} \gamma_i X_i$$

(2) $\mathscr{E}[X_0 - \ell^*(X_1, X_2, \ldots, X_K)]^2 \le \mathscr{E}[X_0 - \ell(X_1, X_2, \ldots, X_K)]^2$;

where $\ell(X_1, X_2, \ldots, X_K)$ is any linear function of $X_1, X_2, \ldots, X_K$.

Now we state a theorem about a best linear prediction function.

THEOREM 12.2.3

Consider the $K + 1$ random vector χ^* with mean μ^* and covariance matrix Σ^*, where χ^*, μ^*, and Σ^* are defined in Equation (3.7.1). The best linear prediction function of X_0 is $\ell_0(x_1, x_2, \ldots, x_K)$, where $\ell_0(x_1, x_2, \ldots, x_K)$ is defined by

$$\ell_0(x_1, x_2, \ldots, x_K) = \mu_0 + \boldsymbol{\sigma}_{01}\boldsymbol{\Sigma}^{-1}(\mathbf{x} - \boldsymbol{\mu}) = \beta_0 + \sum_{k=1}^{K} \beta_k x_k \qquad \mathbf{x} \in E_K \quad (12.2.7)$$

Proof

Let $\ell(x_1, x_2, \ldots, x_K) = \gamma_0 + \sum_{k=1}^{K} \gamma_k x_k$ be a general linear function of $x_1, x_2, \ldots, x_K$. We must find the γ_i so that part (2) of Definition 12.2.2 is satisfied. We get

$$\begin{aligned}
&\mathscr{E}[\{X_0 - \ell(X_1, X_2, \ldots, X_K)\}^2] \\
&\quad = \mathscr{E}[\{X_0 - \gamma_0 - \boldsymbol{\chi}'\boldsymbol{\gamma}\}^2] \\
&\quad = \mathscr{E}[\{X_0 - \mu_0 - \boldsymbol{\sigma}_{01}\boldsymbol{\Sigma}^{-1}(\boldsymbol{\chi} - \boldsymbol{\mu})\} \\
&\qquad + \{\mu_0 + \boldsymbol{\sigma}_{01}\boldsymbol{\Sigma}^{-1}(\boldsymbol{\chi} - \boldsymbol{\mu}) - \gamma_0 - \boldsymbol{\chi}'\boldsymbol{\gamma}\}]^2 \\
&\quad = \mathscr{E}[\{X_0 - \mu_0 - \boldsymbol{\sigma}_{01}\boldsymbol{\Sigma}^{-1}(\boldsymbol{\chi} - \boldsymbol{\mu})\}^2] \\
&\qquad + \mathscr{E}[\{\mu_0 + \boldsymbol{\sigma}_{01}\boldsymbol{\Sigma}^{-1}(\boldsymbol{\chi} - \boldsymbol{\mu}) - \gamma_0 - \boldsymbol{\chi}'\boldsymbol{\gamma}\}^2] \qquad (12.2.8)
\end{aligned}$$

since the cross product term is zero. Thus by Equation (12.2.8),

$$\mathscr{E}[\{X_0 - \ell(X_1, X_2, \ldots, X_K)\}^2] \geq \mathscr{E}[\{(X_0 - \mu_0) - \boldsymbol{\sigma}_{01}\boldsymbol{\Sigma}^{-1}(\boldsymbol{\chi} - \boldsymbol{\mu})\}^2]$$

and equality holds if and only if (with probability one) $\gamma_0 + \boldsymbol{\chi}'\boldsymbol{\gamma} = \mu_0 + \boldsymbol{\sigma}_{01}\boldsymbol{\Sigma}^{-1}(\boldsymbol{\chi} - \boldsymbol{\mu})$, and this is defined to be $\ell_0(X_1, X_2, \ldots, X_K)$. This completes the proof.

COROLLARY 12.2.3

The best "constant" prediction function of X_0 is μ_0, the expected value of X_0.

Next we examine the "error" of predicting X_0; we state three definitions, and we state some results of these definitions.

DEFINITION 12.2.3

Error of the Best Predictor of X_0 Based on $X_1, X_2, \ldots, X_K$. *The error of the best predictor of X_0 based on $X_1, X_2, \ldots, X_K$ is defined as follows: $\mathscr{E}[\{X_0 - g_0(X_1, X_2, \ldots, X_K)\}^2]$; $g_0(X_1, X_2, \ldots, X_K)$ is given in Theorem* 12.2.1.

DEFINITION 12.2.4

Error of Best Linear Predictor of X_0 Based on $X_1, X_2, \ldots, X_K$. *The error of the best linear predictor of X_0 based on $X_1, X_2, \ldots, X_K$ is defined to be $\mathscr{E}[\{X_0 - \ell_0(X_1, X_2, \ldots, X_K)\}^2]$; $\ell_0(X_1, X_2, \ldots; X_K)$ is given in Theorem* 12.2.3.

DEFINITION 12.2.5

Relative Error of the Best Predictor and Best Linear Predictor of X_0 Based on $X_1, X_2, \ldots, X_K$. *The "relative" error of the best predictor and best linear predictor of X_0 based on the random variables $X_1, X_2, \ldots, X_K$ are defined, respectively, to be*

$$\textit{relative error of the best predictor of } X_0 \textit{ is } \frac{\mathscr{E}[\{X_0 - g_0(X_1, X_2, \ldots, X_K)\}^2]}{\mathscr{E}[(X_0 - \mu_0)^2]}$$

$$\textit{relative error of best linear predictor of } X_0 \textit{ is } \frac{\mathscr{E}[\{X_0 - \ell_0(X_1, X_2, \ldots, X_K)\}^2]}{\mathscr{E}[(X_0 - \mu_0)^2]}$$

where $g_0(X_1, X_2, \ldots, X_K)$ and $\ell_0(X_1, X_2, \ldots, X_K)$ are given in Theorems 12.2.1 *and* 12.2.3, *respectively.*

Note 5. The "relative" error means the error when using the best prediction function of X_0 based on $X_1, X_2, \ldots, X_K$ relative to the error when using the best *constant* prediction function.

THEOREM 12.2.4

If $\chi^* = [X_0, X_1, \ldots, X_K]'$ is distributed $\mathbf{N}(\mathbf{x}^* : \boldsymbol{\mu}^*, \boldsymbol{\Sigma}^*)$, the error of the best predictor of X_0 is $\sigma_{00} - \boldsymbol{\sigma}_{01}\boldsymbol{\Sigma}^{-1}\boldsymbol{\sigma}_{10}$ and the relative error of the best predictor of X_0 is $1 - \rho^2_{0(1,2,\ldots,K)}$, one minus the square of the multiple correlation coefficient of X_0 with $X_1, X_2, \ldots, X_K$. If χ^* has any distribution with mean $\boldsymbol{\mu}^*$ and covariance $\boldsymbol{\Sigma}^*$, the error and relative error of the best "linear" predictor of X_0 are $\sigma_{00} - \boldsymbol{\sigma}_{01}\boldsymbol{\Sigma}^{-1}\boldsymbol{\sigma}_{10}$ and $1 - \rho^2_{0(1,2,\ldots,K)}$, respectively.

Proof

By definition, the error of the best predictor of X_0 is $\mathscr{E}[\{X_0 - g_0(X_1, X_2, \ldots, X_K)\}^2]$, where $g_0(X_1, X_2, \ldots, X_K)$ is the best prediction function (which is $\beta_0 + \sum_{i=1}^K \beta_i X_i$ for both a "linear" prediction function of X_0 for the p.d.f. of any random variable χ^*, and for a "general" prediction function of X_0 when the p.d.f. is normal). Thus for both cases we have the following for the error of the best predictor of X_0.

$$\begin{aligned}
\mathscr{E}[(X_0 - \beta_0 - \textstyle\sum \beta_i X_i)^2] &= \mathscr{E}[\{(X_0 - \mu_0) - \textstyle\sum \beta_i (X_i - \mu_i)\}^2] \\
&= \mathscr{E}[\{(X_0 - \mu_0) - \boldsymbol{\sigma}_{01}\boldsymbol{\Sigma}^{-1}(\boldsymbol{\chi} - \boldsymbol{\mu})\}^2] \\
&= \mathscr{E}[\{(X_0 - \mu_0) - \boldsymbol{\sigma}_{01}\boldsymbol{\Sigma}^{-1}(\boldsymbol{\chi} - \boldsymbol{\mu})\} \\
&\qquad \times \{(X_0 - \mu_0) - \boldsymbol{\sigma}_{01}\boldsymbol{\Sigma}^{-1}(\boldsymbol{\chi} - \boldsymbol{\mu})\}'] \\
&= \sigma_{00} - \boldsymbol{\sigma}_{01}\boldsymbol{\Sigma}^{-1}\boldsymbol{\sigma}_{10}
\end{aligned}$$

The relative error of the best predictor of X_0 for both cases is $(\sigma_{00} - \boldsymbol{\sigma}_{01}\boldsymbol{\Sigma}^{-1}\boldsymbol{\sigma}_{10})/\sigma_{00}$, which, by Equation (3.8.5) in Theorem 3.8.4 is $1 - \rho^2_{0(1,2,\ldots,K)}$, and the proof is complete.

All of the material presented so far in this section has been concerned with a discussion of population models to be used for prediction. The best prediction functions discussed above would generally contain unknown parameters, and values for these unknown parameters must be determined if the prediction function is to be useful. A procedure that comes to mind for point estimation of these parameters is to select a random sample $\chi_1^*, \chi_2^*, \ldots, \chi_n^*$ from the p.d.f. of χ^*, which has mean $\boldsymbol{\mu}^*$ and covariance matrix $\boldsymbol{\Sigma}^*$. Then from this sample compute UMVU (or BLU) estimates of the parameters and use these estimates in the prediction function to obtain an estimated prediction function. Also, the estimated relative error of prediction is $1 - \tilde{\rho}^2_{0(1,2,\ldots,K)}$, where $\tilde{\rho}^2_{0(1,2,\ldots,K)}$ is an estimate of the square of the multiple correlation coefficient given in Section 11.4.

Example 12.2.4

The director of admissions of a university wants to compute a function to be used to predict the grade point average (G.P.A.) that potential students will attain at the end of their freshman year. He will use this function as a basis for admitting students to the university. The three factors that will be used to predict G.P.A. X_0 are the following: (1) the score on a mathematics entrance examination X_1; (2) the verbal score on an entrance examination X_2; (3) the grade point average of all subjects taken in high school X_3. Forty students who completed the freshman year at this university the previous year were selected at random, and for each student the values of X_0, X_1, X_2, and X_3 were observed. Estimate the best linear prediction function and the predicted value for a prospective student whose scores x_1, x_2, and x_3 are 80, 70, and 3.30, respectively.

The data were used to compute $\mathbf{A}^*$ and $\bar{\mathbf{x}}^*$, which are given below.

$$\mathbf{A}^* = \begin{bmatrix} a_{00} & \mathbf{a}_{01} \\ \mathbf{a}_{10} & \mathbf{A} \end{bmatrix} = \begin{bmatrix} 12.636 & 65.286 & 84.630 & 2.379 \\ 65.286 & 785.109 & 676.260 & 13.494 \\ 84.630 & 676.260 & 854.373 & 14.976 \\ 2.379 & 13.494 & 14.976 & 0.858 \end{bmatrix} \qquad \bar{\mathbf{x}}^* = \begin{bmatrix} 2.862 \\ 73.000 \\ 81.000 \\ 2.830 \end{bmatrix}$$

To compute $\hat{\boldsymbol{\beta}}' = [\hat{\beta}_0, \hat{\beta}_1, \hat{\beta}_2, \hat{\beta}_3]$ and $\hat{\sigma}^2$, we use the square root method.

$$\left[\begin{array}{c|c} \mathbf{A} & \mathbf{a}_{10} \\ \hline \mathbf{T} & \mathbf{t} \end{array}\right] = \left[\begin{array}{ccc|c} 785.109 & 676.260 & 13.494 & 65.286 \\ 676.260 & 854.373 & 14.976 & 84.630 \\ 13.494 & 14.976 & 0.858 & 2.379 \\ \hline 28.01979657 & 24.13507886 & 0.48158808 & 2.32999550 \\ & 16.48851019 & 0.20334364 & 1.72213102 \\ & & 0.76467267 & 1.18575907 \end{array}\right]$$

The backward solution gives $\hat{\beta}_3 = 1.551$, $\hat{\beta}_2 = 0.085$, $\hat{\beta}_1 = -0.017$, and $\hat{\beta}_0 = \bar{x}_0 - \hat{\beta}_1\bar{x}_1 - \hat{\beta}_2\bar{x}_2 - \hat{\beta}_3\bar{x}_3 = -7.197$. Thus the estimated best linear prediction function of X_0 based on factors 1, 2, and 3 is

$$\hat{X}_0 = -7.197 - 0.017X_1 + 0.085X_2 + 1.551X_3$$

The estimated predicted value of X_0 at the point $x_1 = 80$, $x_2 = 70$, and $x_3 = 3.30$ is 2.533. Also, the estimate of $\sigma_{00} - \boldsymbol{\sigma}_{01}\boldsymbol{\Sigma}^{-1}\boldsymbol{\sigma}_{10}$ is $[1/(40 - 3 - 1)][a_{00} - \mathbf{t}'\mathbf{t}] = (1/36)(12.636 - 9.801) = 0.07876$, and $\tilde{\rho}^2_{0(1,2,3)} = 9.801/12.636 = 0.776$.

We have given a very brief introduction to prediction theory for a very special case for the distribution of the observable random variables. The literature on prediction theory is vast, and much of it is contained in the subject of Time Series. For further reading see [R-2], [H-2], and references listed there.

12.3 Selecting Variables for a Model

In the previous section we showed that to predict the value of a random variable X_0 by using K random variables $X_1, X_2, \ldots, X_K$, the "best" linear prediction function (or "best" prediction function when $X_0, X_1, \ldots, X_K$ are jointly normal) is the regression function $\beta_0 + \sum \beta_i X_i$, where the β_i are given by Equation (3.7.4). The β_i are unknown but they can be estimated by maximum likelihood from a random sample of size n when $X_0, X_1, \ldots, X_K$ are normal, or by least squares when the joint distribution of $X_0, X_1, \ldots, X_K$ is unknown, and denoted by $\hat{\beta}_i$. The estimated best predictor of X_0 is then $\hat{X}_0 = \hat{\beta}_0 + \sum \hat{\beta}_i X_i$.

A problem that is of considerable interest in some applied work is this: Given a set of K factors (actually a $K \times 1$ random vector with elements $X_1, X_2, \ldots, X_K$), is there a subset of these factors that is "best" or "adequate" in some sense for predicting another factor (the value of a random variable X_0)? We first consider two examples.

Example 12.3.1

In Example 12.2.1 we were interested in predicting the grade point average of a student at the end of his freshman year based on the values of factors observed before he is admitted to the university. Of course, the more factors on which we can base this prediction, the better the predictor will be. This is due to Equation (3.8.10) since the multiple correlation of the variable X_0 with $X_1, X_2, \ldots, X_K$ cannot be smaller than the multiple correlation based on any subset of these variables. However, after, say, four factors are used, the use of more factors may not increase the predictive value appreciably, and hence these additional factors may be of marginal value in improving the prediction. Thus if one is presented with K factors to use in predicting X_0, then one may want to investigate the possibility that fewer than K factors will do almost as good a job as all K factors will do. Hence an investigator may want to find a useful prediction function that is a reasonable balance between the number of factors used and the quality of the prediction function. Also, one must consider the cost and difficulty of measuring certain factors if they don't contribute much to the value of the prediction. Thus the problem of prediction is often as follows: K factors are considered as possibly good candidates for predicting X_0; an investigator makes an analysis of these factors to determine (based on many considerations) which of these K factors are to be used in the prediction function.

Example 12.3.2

In some investigations the main emphasis may be on "which" set of factors perform adequately in predicting X_0. For example, an investigator may not actually be interested in predicting X_0, the amount that blood pressure can be reduced by using various factors such as age, cholesterol in the blood, amount of a certain drug administered, heart rate, and so forth. Rather, he may be interested in "which" factors are useful in reducing blood pressure and how they contribute when other factors are present or absent. Also, in using the prediction function, it is recognized that some factors (such as the amount of drug administered) can be controlled while others (such as age) cannot.

The solution to the problem of selecting variables generally requires a considerable amount of computing, and even with the availability of high-speed computers, this quantity of computing must often be taken into consideration.

A large amount of material has been written on this subject within the past decade, but there are very few rigorous results of an inferential nature; most of the procedures are merely descriptive.

These types of problems are often referred to as problems in "selection of variables," that is, selecting a subset of variables from the set $X_1, X_2, \ldots, X_K$ that will "adequately" predict X_0. There are a number of important considerations involved in this problem: (1) What is the purpose of the study? (2) What will be a measure of whether one set of random variables is better than another set for predicting X_0? (3) What will be a measure of whether a set of variables is "best" for predicting X_0?

We will discuss this problem only briefly and refer the reader to the accompanying bibliography for additional information. We make the following assumptions for Sections 12.3.1, 12.3.2, and 12.3.3. Other assumptions will be made in Section 12.3.4.

1. $\boldsymbol{\chi}^* = \lfloor X_0, X_1, \ldots, X_K \rfloor'$ is distributed $\mathbf{N}(\mathbf{x}^* : \boldsymbol{\mu}^*, \boldsymbol{\Sigma}^*)$.
2. $\boldsymbol{\chi}_1^*, \boldsymbol{\chi}_2^*, \ldots, \boldsymbol{\chi}_n^*$ is a random sample from the distribution $\mathbf{N}(\mathbf{x}^* : \boldsymbol{\mu}^*, \boldsymbol{\Sigma}^*)$.
3. We use the notation in Equation (11.1.1) and in Theorem 11.3.1.
4. $\rho^2_{0(i_1, i_2, \ldots, i_q)}$ will be used as the measure of how good the factors $i_1, i_2, \ldots, i_q$ are in predicting X_0. (12.3.1)

We shall briefly discuss three general procedures that have been suggested to solve these kinds of problems. They are referred to as the following:

1. all regressions procedure;
2. forward selection procedure;
3. backward elimination procedure.

12.3.1 All Regressions Method

To illustrate the idea we first assume $\boldsymbol{\mu}^*$ and $\boldsymbol{\Sigma}^*$ are known, and then we describe the procedure when a random sample is available to estimate these parameters. This procedure is very simple in principle.

From the covariance matrix $\boldsymbol{\Sigma}^*$, all of the multiple correlation coefficients are computed, and the investigator decides, on the basis of values of these correlation coefficients, which subset of variables in $X_1, X_2, \ldots, X_K$ is "best" or "adequate" for the situation under study. From Equation (3.8.10) we know that if $i_1, i_2, \ldots, i_q$ is a subset of integers in the set $1, 2, \ldots, K$, and if $j_1, j_2, \ldots, j_m$ is a subset of the integers $i_1, i_2, \ldots, i_q$, then $\rho^2_{0(j_1,j_2,\ldots,j_m)} \leq \rho^2_{0(i_1,i_2,\ldots,i_q)} \leq \rho^2_{0(1,2,\ldots,K)}$. Thus no subset of factors in $X_1, X_2, \ldots, X_K$ can be a better predictor of X_0 than the predictor when all factors are used.

However, an investigator would generally want a more detailed analysis of the problem than this. For example, in Section 3.8 it is true that $\rho^2_{0(1,2,3,4)} \geq \rho^2_{0(1,2,3)}$, but the difference may be so small that the added predictive "value" of X_4 after using X_1, X_2, and X_3 may not be practically useful.

Furthermore, it may be that $\rho^2_{0(1,2)}$ and $\rho^2_{0(2,3,4)}$ are essentially equal and this may be useful information to an investigator in determining the main "driving force" of X_0. Some factors may be difficult to measure accurately, say factor 1, so if $\rho^2_{0(1,2)}$ is essentially equal to $\rho^2_{0(2,3,4)}$, an investigator may decide to use factors 2, 3, and 4 rather than factors 1 and 2 to predict X_0. Many other reasons could be given for wanting a complete analysis of the problem.

In principle, the solution of the "all regression" method is straightforward. One computes the multiple correlation coefficients (or their squares) of all combinations of the random variables $X_1, X_2, \ldots, X_K$ with X_0, that is, one computes $\rho^2_{0(1)}, \rho^2_{0(2)}, \ldots, \rho^2_{0(K)}; \rho^2_{0(1,2)}, \rho^2_{0(1,3)}, \ldots, \rho^2_{0(K-1,K)}; \cdots; \rho^2_{0(1,2,\ldots,K)}$. There are $2^K - 1$ multiple correlation coefficients to compute, and based on these and knowledge of the subject, an investigator makes an analysis of the problem as to which factors are "useful," "adequate," or "best" for predicting X_0. After it is decided which set (or perhaps more than one set) is to be used for predicting X_0, then the appropriate prediction equation (or equations) is computed. All the (squared) multiple correlation coefficients are functions of the elements of the covariance matrix $\boldsymbol{\Sigma}^*$, and the coefficients in the appropriate prediction function are a function of $\boldsymbol{\mu}^*$ and $\boldsymbol{\Sigma}^*$ only.

We stated above that the solution by the "all regressions" method of selecting variables is straightforward. However, there are two practical difficulties: (1) the parameters in $\boldsymbol{\mu}^*$ and $\boldsymbol{\Sigma}^*$ are unknown; (2) if K is large, the computation of all the ρ^2's is a formidable task even for large computers. For example, there are $2^K - 1$ multiple correlations to compute. (A discussion of procedures to help reduce this task is discussed in [H-11], [M-8], and [L-5].) The problem is to compute the estimate of the square of the multiple correlation coefficient of X_0 with every subset of the random variables $X_1, X_2, \ldots, X_K$. If one wants to spend the time and effort, difficulty (2) above can be overcome, but the fact that $\boldsymbol{\mu}^*$ and $\boldsymbol{\Sigma}^*$ are unknown presents a different kind of problem. To handle this difficulty a random sample of size $n \geq K + 2$ is selected from the distribution $N(\mathbf{x}^* : \boldsymbol{\mu}^*, \boldsymbol{\Sigma}^*)$. On the basis of this sample, estimates of the square of the $2^K - 1$ multiple correlation coefficients are obtained, and the investigator makes a determination as to which set (or sets) of factors is "adequate" for predicting X_0; then an estimated prediction function of X_0 is obtained based on the random sample values. One difficulty that this presents, of course, is that estimates do not present a "true" value of the ρ^2's, and on the basis of these *estimates* of the ρ^2's, one set of variables might be selected when another set might actually be better. For example, $\rho^2_{0(1,2)}$ might be larger than $\rho^2_{0(1,3,4)}$, but the estimate of $\rho^2_{0(1,3,4)}$ might be larger than the estimate of $\rho^2_{0(1,2)}$, so factors 1, 3, and 4 would be used to predict X_0 whereas factors 1 and 2 would be better.

We now formulate the problem of selecting variables by the "all regressions" method. The assumptions are as follows:

1. a $(K + 1) \times 1$ random vector $\boldsymbol{\chi}^*$ is distributed $N(\mathbf{x}^* : \boldsymbol{\mu}^*, \boldsymbol{\Sigma}^*)$;
2. a random sample of n vectors, denoted $\boldsymbol{\chi}_1^*, \boldsymbol{\chi}_2^*, \ldots, \boldsymbol{\chi}_n^*$, is selected from this c.d.f. We use the notation $\mathscr{X}^* = [\boldsymbol{\chi}_1^*, \boldsymbol{\chi}_2^*, \ldots, \boldsymbol{\chi}_n^*]'$; also $\mathbf{x}^*, \boldsymbol{\mu}^*, \boldsymbol{\Sigma}^*$, and so on are as defined in Equation (11.1.1). (12.3.2)

We illustrate with an artificial example in which the computation is easy.

Example 12.3.3

In an artificial example, where $K = 4$ and $n = 20$, suppose $\boldsymbol{\chi}^* = [X_0, X_1, X_2, X_3, X_4]'$ is distributed $N(\mathbf{x}^* : \boldsymbol{\mu}^*, \boldsymbol{\Sigma}^*)$, and $\hat{\boldsymbol{\Sigma}}^*$ is computed and given below.

$$\hat{\boldsymbol{\Sigma}}^* = \begin{bmatrix} 100 & -40 & 90 & 20 & 40 \\ -40 & 400 & 240 & 120 & 40 \\ 90 & 240 & 900 & -120 & 12 \\ 20 & 120 & -120 & 400 & 160 \\ 40 & 40 & 12 & 160 & 1600 \end{bmatrix} \qquad (12.3.3)$$

We get the following:

$$\tilde{\rho}^2_{0(1)} = 0.040 \qquad \tilde{\rho}^2_{0(2)} = 0.090 \qquad \tilde{\rho}^2_{0(3)} = 0.010$$
$$\tilde{\rho}^2_{0(4)} = 0.010 \qquad \tilde{\rho}^2_{0(1,2)} = 0.212 \qquad \tilde{\rho}^2_{0(1,3)} = 0.068$$
$$\tilde{\rho}^2_{0(1,4)} = 0.052 \qquad \tilde{\rho}^2_{0(2,3)} = 0.117 \qquad \tilde{\rho}^2_{0(2,4)} = 0.099$$
$$\tilde{\rho}^2_{0(3,4)} = 0.017 \qquad \tilde{\rho}^2_{0(1,2,3)} = 0.330 \qquad \tilde{\rho}^2_{0(1,2,4)} = 0.225$$
$$\tilde{\rho}^2_{0(1,3,4)} = 0.074 \qquad \tilde{\rho}^2_{0(2,3,4)} = 0.121 \qquad \tilde{\rho}^2_{0(1,2,3,4)} = 0.332$$

From these computed multiple correlation coefficients squared, one can gain insight into how the various combinations of the factors 1, 2, 3, and 4 contribute to the prediction of X_0. It is clear that factors 1, 2, and 3 are essentially as good as factors 1, 2, 3, and 4 for predicting X_0, and no other subset is as good as 1, 2, 3.

12.3.2 Forward Selection Procedure

To explain the "forward selection procedure," we first assume that $\boldsymbol{\mu}^*$ and $\boldsymbol{\Sigma}^*$ are known; then we discuss the procedure when $\boldsymbol{\mu}^*$ and $\boldsymbol{\Sigma}^*$ are *not* known but samples are available to estimate them. The central idea is that an investigator wants to determine the best *single* predictor of X_0 from the set $X_1, X_2, \ldots, X_K$. He then wants to determine the best *two* predictors of X_0 *which include the best single predictor*. He then wants to determine the best *three* predictors of X_0 *which include the best two predictors* and also the best *single* predictor, and so on.

If the largest multiple correlation coefficient squared is the measure of "best" to be used, then the procedure involves computing these quantities. For example, suppose $K = 3$; then the square of the multiple (simple) correlation coefficients $\rho^2_{0(1)}$, $\rho^2_{0(2)}$, and $\rho^2_{0(3)}$ are examined. Suppose $\rho^2_{0(2)}$ is the largest multiple correlation coefficient squared of a *single* variable with X_0; it follows that X_2 is the *best* single predictor of X_0. We must now examine $\rho^2_{0(1,2)}$ and $\rho^2_{0(2,3)}$ to see which is larger, and this will give us the best *two* variables for predicting X_0 which include the best *single* predictor. We needn't examine $\rho^2_{0(1,3)}$ since it does not include X_2, the best single predictor. It should be remarked, however, that $\rho^2_{0(1,3)}$ could be larger than either $\rho^2_{0(1,2)}$ or $\rho^2_{0(2,3)}$. This is a point to remember!

In the "forward selection" procedure, the emphasis is on finding the best *single* predictor, then the best *two* predictors (which include the best *single* predictor), then the best *three* predictors (which include the best *two* predictors, which in turn include the best single predictor), and so forth. The procedure is outlined in detail below.

1. Compute all multiple correlation coefficients (or their squares) of X_0 with X_k for $k = 1, 2, \ldots, K$; that is, compute $\rho^2_{0(1)}, \rho^2_{0(2)}, \ldots, \rho^2_{0(K)}$.

(These are the same as the square of all *simple* correlation coefficients of X_0 with each X_k.) Pick the largest, suppose it is $\rho^2_{0(1)}$; then X_1 is the best *single* predictor of X_0.

2. Compute all multiple correlation coefficients (or their squares) of X_0 with all pairs of variables where one of the variables is X_1; that is, compute $\rho^2_{0(1,2)}, \rho^2_{0(1,3)}, \ldots, \rho^2_{0(1,K)}$ and select the largest. Suppose it is $\rho^2_{0(1,2)}$; then X_1 and X_2 are the best *two* predictors of X_0 which include the best *single* predictor X_1.

3. Compute all multiple correlation coefficients (or their squares) of X_0 with all sets of three variables that include X_1 and X_2; that is, compute $\rho^2_{0(1,2,3)}, \rho^2_{0(1,2,4)}, \ldots, \rho^2_{0(1,2,K)}$ and select the largest.

4. Continue this procedure until it is decided that additional variables are of insignificant importance in predicting X_0 or until all K factors have been arranged in order according to the magnitude of the multiple correlation coefficients squared.

All of these computations can be accomplished by using the quantities in the covariance matrix $\mathbf{\Sigma}^*$ (or the correlation matrix $\mathbf{R}^*$). Of course, in any applied problem these quantities are not known, so a random sample of n vectors $\chi_1^*, \chi_2^*, \ldots, \chi_n^*$ is selected from the c.d.f. $\mathbf{N}(\mathbf{x}^* : \boldsymbol{\mu}^*, \mathbf{\Sigma}^*)$ and the M.L. estimator of $\mathbf{\Sigma}^*$ (or of $\mathbf{R}^*$) is obtained. Steps 1, 2, 3, and 4 above are executed using the estimated quantities, that is, use $\hat{\mathbf{\Sigma}}^*$. After the K factors have been arranged in order, a decision can be made as to which variables are unimportant in predicting X_0, or the decision can be made to terminate the process when it is judged (perhaps by a hypothesis test) that additional variables in the set will not "materially" improve the prediction of X_0. About the only merit this method has over the "all regressions" method is ease of computation.

Example 12.3.4

For the data in Example 12.3.3, use the forward selection procedure to arrange the factors for predicting X_0 in order of importance.

We note from the results of Example 12.3.3 that the best single factor for predicting factor 0 (we use the square of the multiple correlation coefficient as the measure of best) is factor 2, and $\tilde{\rho}^2_{0(2)} = 0.090$. The best *two* factors (for predicting factor 0) which include the best *single* factor (which is factor 2) are factors 2 and 1 since $\tilde{\rho}^2_{0(1,2)} = 0.212$, $\tilde{\rho}^2_{0(2,3)} = 0.117$, and $\tilde{\rho}^2_{0(2,4)} = 0.099$. We do not consider any other pair of factors since they do not include factor 2 (the best single predictor). Next we look for the best *three* factors which include the best *two* factors (1 and 2), which include the best *single* factor. We must examine only $\tilde{\rho}^2_{0(1,2,3)}$ and $\tilde{\rho}^2_{0(1,2,4)}$ since factors 1, 2, and 3 and factors 1, 2, and 4 are the only three factors in the total set of factors 1, 2, 3, and 4 which include the best *two* factors (1 and 2) which include the best *single* factor. Thus the best *three* factors, by the forward selection procedure, are 1, 2, and 3, and $\tilde{\rho}^2_{0(1,2,3)} = 0.330$. Of course, the best *four* factors must be 1, 2, 3, and 4 since these are the only four under consideration.

In summary, we get the following:

Step	1	2	3	4
Factor	2	1	3	4
$\tilde{\rho}^2$	0.090	0.212	0.330	0.332

(12.3.4)

Note 1. If at any step in the forward selection procedure, the q factors, which for notational convenience we shall denote as the first q factors $1, 2, \ldots, q$, are included, then the next factor to include is the jth factor corresponding to the largest of the partial correlation coefficients below.

$$\tilde{\rho}^2_{0j|(1,2,\ldots,q)} \qquad \text{for } j = q + 1, \ldots, K$$

That this is the case is easily seen from the formula in Theorem 3.8.7, with the parameters replaced by M.L. estimates. This gives us

$$\tilde{\rho}^2_{0(1,2,\ldots,q,j)} = \tilde{\rho}^2_{0(1,2,\ldots,q)} + [1 - \tilde{\rho}^2_{0(1,2,\ldots,q)}]\tilde{\rho}^2_{0j|(1,2,\ldots,q)}, \qquad j = q + 1, \ldots, K \tag{12.3.5}$$

From this we can see that the factor j which produces the largest $\tilde{\rho}^2_{0(1,2,\ldots,q,j)}$ is the same factor j that produces the largest estimated partial correlation coefficient squared, $\tilde{\rho}^2_{0j|(1,2,\ldots,q)}$.

At any step (perhaps at *every* step) in the forward selection procedure the investigator may want to determine whether the addition of more variables will "appreciably" improve the estimator of X_0. This decision could be made by graphical techniques or by a hypothesis test. We will describe a hypothesis testing procedure that is often used.

Suppose the q variables $X_1, X_2, \ldots, X_q$ corresponding, respectively, to factors $1, 2, \ldots, q$ have been included in the prediction equation, and the procedure implies that factor $q + 1$ is the next one to be included. This means that

$$\tilde{\rho}^2_{0,q+1|(1,2,\ldots,q)} > \tilde{\rho}^2_{0j|(1,2,\ldots,q)} \qquad \text{for } j = q + 2, \ldots, K$$

We want to determine if factor $q + 1$ contributes "appreciably" to the prediction of X_0 over and above what the factors $1, 2, \ldots, q$ contribute. Another way to state this is as follows: Do factors $1, 2, \ldots, q, q + 1$ do a better job of predicting X_0 than do factors $1, 2, \ldots, q$? Since we are using the multiple correlation coefficient as the measure of the adequacy of a set of factors in predicting X_0, it follows that the test

$$H_0 : \rho^2_{0(1,2,\ldots,q+1)} = \rho^2_{0(1,2,\ldots,q)} \tag{12.3.6}$$

can be used to determine if factor $q + 1$ contributes anything over and above the contribution of factors $1, 2, \ldots, q$. However, H_0 in Equation (12.3.6) is true if and only if $\rho^2_{0,q+1|(1,2,\ldots,q)}$ is zero; see Equation (3.8.9). Hence we can use H_0 in Equation (12.3.7):

$$H_0 : \rho^2_{0,q+1|(1,2,\ldots,q)} = 0 \tag{12.3.7}$$

From a random sample $\chi_1^*, \chi_2^*, \ldots, \chi_n^*$, the t statistic (or the F statistic) is computed; see Theorem 11.3.1, Example 11.3.1, and part (1) of Corollary 11.2.2. The test statistic is W, where

$$W = \frac{(n - q - 2)\tilde{\rho}^2_{0,q+1|(1,2,\ldots,q)}}{1 - \tilde{\rho}^2_{0,q+1|(1,2,\ldots,q)}}$$

If H_0 is true, W is distributed $F(w : 1, n - q - 2)$; the hypothesis H_0 is rejected (for a size α test) if and only if $w \geq F_{\alpha:1,n-q-2}$; w is the computed value of W.

Another way to view the hypothesis $H_0 : \rho^2_{0,q+1|(1,2,\ldots,q)} = 0$ is to use Equation (3.8.7) and notice that H_0 is true if and only if $\sigma_{0,q+1|(1,2,\ldots,q)} = 0$. But by Theorem 3.7.2 and the note following it, H_0 is true if and only if $\beta_{0,q+1|(1,2,\ldots,q)} = 0$. This says that in the regression of X_0 on $X_1, X_2, \ldots, X_q, X_{q+1}$, we can write

$$\begin{aligned} Y &= \mathscr{E}[(X_0 \mid X_1 = x_1, X_2 = x_2, \ldots, X_{q+1} = x_{q+1})] + \varepsilon \\ &= \beta_0 + \sum_{j=1}^{q+1} \beta_j x_j + \varepsilon \end{aligned}$$

where β_j is the "partial regression coefficient of X_0 on $X_1, X_2, \ldots, X_{j-1}, X_{j+1}, \ldots, X_{q+1}$." Thus we can actually consider the data on the variables $X_0, X_1, \ldots, X_{q+1}$ as the general linear model, and by a hypothesis test that $\beta_{q+1} = 0$, one can determine if factor $q + 1$ is important in predicting factor 0 over and above the effects of factors $1, 2, \ldots, q$.

To test $H_0 : \beta_{q+1} = 0$ *vs.* $H_a : \beta_{q+1} \neq 0$ for a model with assumptions given by Equation (12.3.1) with $K = q + 1$, we know that when H_0 is true, $\hat{\beta}^2_{q+1}/\widehat{\text{var}}[\hat{\beta}_{q+1}]$ is distributed as a central F random variable with 1 and $n - q - 2$ degrees of freedom. But clearly

$$\frac{\hat{\beta}^2_{q+1}}{\widehat{\text{var}}[\hat{\beta}_{q+1}]} = \frac{(n - q - 2)\tilde{\rho}^2_{0,q+1|(1,2,\ldots,q)}}{1 - \tilde{\rho}^2_{0,q+1|(1,2,\ldots,q)}} \tag{12.3.8}$$

where we have written $\hat{\beta}_{q+1}$ instead of the more complete notation

$\hat{\beta}_{0,q+1|(1,2,\ldots,q)}$. If at any step, say step $q + 1$, the hypothesis $H_0 : \rho^2_{0,q+1|(1,2,\ldots,q)} = 0$ (that the last variable added contributes nothing) is accepted, then the process is terminated, and the decision is made by the forward selection procedure that factors $1, 2, \ldots, q$ are adequate for predicting X_0. If H_0 is rejected, then one proceeds to the next step.

Note 2. It should be stated that very little is known about the operating characteristics of these tests since they are not independent, and the model used at each step depends on the result of a hypothesis test at the preceding steps.

Note 3. A variation of the forward selection procedure that is widely used is often referred to as "stepwise regression" [B-9] and [D-9].

12.3.3 Backward Elimination Procedure

In this procedure all K of the factors are considered for the prediction of X_0, and then the less important ones are eliminated one at a time. The procedure is stated below (first we assume, as in the other methods, that $\boldsymbol{\mu}^*$ and $\boldsymbol{\Sigma}^*$ are known, and then we discuss the procedure when these parameters are unknown).

1. Compute $\rho^2_{01|(2,3,\ldots,K)}, \rho^2_{02|(1,3,\ldots,K)}, \ldots, \rho^2_{0K|(1,2,\ldots,K-1)}$ and select the smallest. Suppose it is $\rho^2_{01|(2,3,\ldots,K)}$. Then omit factor 1 from the set of predictor factors.
2. Compute $\rho^2_{02|(3,4,\ldots,K)}, \rho^2_{03|(2,4,\ldots,K)}, \ldots, \rho^2_{0K|(2,3,\ldots,K-1)}$ and select the smallest. Suppose it is $\rho^2_{02|(3,4,\ldots,K)}$. Then omit factor 2 from the set of predictor factors (factors 1 and 2 have now been omitted).
3. Continue this procedure until all factors except one have been omitted.
4. Suppose the factors are omitted in the following order: $1, 2, \ldots, K - 1$. The conclusion is this: Factor 1 contributes the least to predicting X_0 of any *single* factor in the set $1, 2, \ldots, K$ after the effect of the other $K - 1$ factors is considered; factor 2 contributes the least to predicting X_0 of any *single* factor in the set $2, 3, \ldots, K$ after the effect of the other $K - 2$ factors is considered, and so forth.

At this point we will briefly discuss what these partial correlation coefficients imply in this problem. Let us consider $K = 3$ and examine $\rho^2_{01|(2,3)}$. In words, this quantity is the proportional "additional" reduction in the variance of the random variable X_0 due to X_1. "Additional" here means in addition to the reduction due to the random variables X_2 and X_3. We also examine $\rho^2_{02|(1,3)}$ and $\rho^2_{03|(1,2)}$, and suppose $0 \leq \rho^2_{01|(2,3)} < \rho^2_{02|(1,3)} < \rho^2_{03|(1,2)}$. Then factor 1 is the least important single factor for predicting X_0 after the effects of the remaining two factors are considered. By Equation (3.8.7) we get

$$\rho^2_{01|(2,3)} = \frac{\sigma^2_{01|(2,3)}}{\sigma_{00|(2,3)}\sigma_{11|(2,3)}} = \frac{\text{var}[(X_0 \mid X_2, X_3)] - \text{var}[(X_0 \mid X_1, X_2, X_3)]}{\text{var}[(X_0 \mid X_2, X_3)]} \tag{12.3.9}$$

The numerator represents the conditional variance of X_0 when X_2 and X_3 are used to predict X_0 minus the variance when X_1, X_2, and X_3 are used. The fraction represents the proportional reduction of the variance.

We have been discussing the situation when the parameters $\boldsymbol{\mu}^*$ and $\boldsymbol{\Sigma}^*$ are known. However, in any real situation these are not known but must be estimated from observed data. As usual, let $\boldsymbol{\chi}_1^*, \boldsymbol{\chi}_2^*, \ldots, \boldsymbol{\chi}_n^*$ be a random sample of size n from the distribution $\mathbf{N}(\mathbf{x}^* : \boldsymbol{\mu}^*, \boldsymbol{\Sigma}^*)$. Compute the M.L. estimates of the partial correlation coefficients referred to in step 1, step 2, and step 3. In step 4 the estimate of the order of importance of the variables is obtained by the definition of the "backward elimination" procedure.

To implement the method when sample data are used, the following procedure is sometimes recommended: At step 1 determine the smallest of the estimated partial correlation coefficients and use this to determine (perhaps by a hypothesis test) whether the corresponding population partial correlation coefficient is zero. If the result of the test is that the population value is zero, eliminate that variable and go to step 2 and repeat the test. If at any step the hypothesis is rejected, then terminate the procedure and declare that the factors which have *not* been eliminated give an "adequate" prediction function of X_0. This function can then be computed if desired.

Example 12.3.5

For the data in Example 12.3.3, compute and order the correlation coefficients by the backward elimination procedure.

First we compute the estimate of the square of the *partial* correlation coefficients of each variable with X_0, holding the other three fixed. We get

$$\tilde{\rho}^2_{01|(2,3,4)} = 0.240 \qquad \tilde{\rho}^2_{02|(1,3,4)} = 0.278$$
$$\tilde{\rho}^2_{03|(1,2,4)} = 0.138 \qquad \tilde{\rho}^2_{04|(1,2,3)} = 0.003$$

Since $\tilde{\rho}^2_{04|(1,2,3)}$ is the smallest, we eliminate factor 4 and repeat the process using only factors 1, 2, and 3. We get

$$\tilde{\rho}^2_{01|(2,3)} = 0.241 \qquad \tilde{\rho}^2_{02|(1,3)} = 0.281 \qquad \tilde{\rho}^2_{03|(1,2)} = 0.150$$

We do not compute $\tilde{\rho}^2_{04|(1,2)}$ and so on, since factor four has been eliminated. The smallest contribution of a single factor among factors 1, 2, and 3 when two factors are given is factor 3 since

$$\tilde{\rho}^2_{03|(1,2)} < \tilde{\rho}^2_{01|(2,3)} < \tilde{\rho}^2_{02|(1,3)}$$

We now repeat the process by using only factors 1 and 2. We get

$$\tilde{\rho}^2_{01|(2)} = 0.134 \qquad \tilde{\rho}^2_{02|(1)} = 0.179$$

So by the backward solution the factors are eliminated in the following order: 4, 3, 1, 2. At any step one could determine, perhaps by a test of hypothesis by using the t or F statistic and Theorem 11.3.1, whether the population partial correlation coefficient, corresponding to the one to be omitted, is zero. If at any step the hypothesis about the population partial correlation coefficient (corresponding to the smallest estimated partial correlation coefficient) is rejected and declared not zero, the process is terminated and all factors not yet eliminated are presumed to be necessary for an "adequate" prediction function for X_0. The prediction function based on these factors can then be estimated from the data.

Note 4. In this example, the forward selection and backward elimination procedures give the same result (the same ordering of the factors). This is not always the case.

Note 5. It should be stressed that the size of the test used is not the correct probability of rejecting H_0 when H_0 is true. One reason is that the data have been examined and the correlation coefficient that is tested is the one for which the estimate is smallest.

12.3.4 All Regressions Method for a General Model

One of the difficulties with the all regressions procedure, in addition to the huge amount of computation that is required if K is large, is the interpretation of the results. If one computes *all possible* multiple correlation coefficients, it is an immense task to interpret them.

If the objective is only to determine the factors that "adequately" predict the factor 0, then perhaps either the forward selection or backward elimination method is satisfactory. If the investigator, however, wants to make a more complete analysis and use all regressions, a method that may reduce the amount of computing is explained in [F-5] and [L-5]. The investigator may be interested in not only selecting a subset of factors that adequately predict factor 0, but he may also be interested in examining models that contain all possible combinations of all K factors to see how well each predicts factor 0. This may give him ideas as to which factors are useful in controlling or changing the factor 0. Hence he is interested in the all regressions method and a procedure for examining the results of all the 2^K models. This is the topic of this section.

To generalize the situation where $\boldsymbol{\chi}^*$ is a random vector, we consider the case where some or all of the assumptions in Equation (12.3.1) may not be valid (or even approximately valid). Some of the variables may not be random variables, or if they are, they may not be normally distributed; or one variable may be X_i, another X_i^2; and another may be $\log |X_i|$; and so on. In these cases an alternative procedure that has been found useful, at least for interpolation within the region of the observed x_{ij} values, is to use the "general linear model" and view *all* x_{ij} values as nonrandom variables. If some or all of the x_{ij} values are observed values of *random* variables, we can still examine them as *fixed* values of random variables as we did in the general linear model in Chapter 6.

The assumptions for this model are the following:

1. K (predetermined) factors are under study; the independent variables x_{ij} are observed measurements of these factors.
2. The observation x_{ij} is a nonrandom variable (it may be an observed value of a random variable) and is the ith observation of the jth factor.
3. The true model is assumed to be $\mathbf{Y} = \mathbf{X}\boldsymbol{\beta} + \boldsymbol{\varepsilon}$, the general linear model defined in Chapter 6, where $\mathbf{X}$, the matrix $[x_{ij}]$ of observed values of the K factors, has size $n \times (K + 1)$ and rank $K + 1$. We assume each model contains an intercept term β_0.
4. The random variable $\boldsymbol{\varepsilon}$ is distributed $(\boldsymbol{\varepsilon} : \mathbf{0}, \sigma^2\mathbf{I})$. (12.3.10)

4a. In some cases we specify that $\boldsymbol{\varepsilon}$ is distributed $N(\boldsymbol{\varepsilon} : \mathbf{0}, \sigma^2\mathbf{I})$. (12.3.10a)

The problem is to determine if a submodel (one that contains a subset of the K factors) is an "adequate" substitute for the true model in a region where the x_{ij} values are observed. This would mean that some of the β_i in the true model are zero (or are very small), and so a submodel, with those β_i that are zero (or small) eliminated, would adequately represent the true model.

To determine the "adequacy" of a submodel that contains a given subset of the β_i, we will use a measure of how "close" the mean of the submodel under consideration is to the mean $\mathbf{X}\boldsymbol{\beta}$ of the true model for the x_{ij} values *actually observed*; that is, how "close" the model under consideration is to $\mathbf{X}\boldsymbol{\beta}$

for the x_{ij} values ($\mathbf{X}$ matrix) actually observed. First we will present a simple example and then formally define this measure and discuss ways to estimate it.

Let the model be given by Equation (12.3.10), and suppose there are K factors under consideration and the model contains an intercept term. The true model can be written as $\mathbf{Y} = \mathbf{X}\boldsymbol{\beta} + \boldsymbol{\varepsilon}$, $\boldsymbol{\varepsilon}$ is distributed $(\boldsymbol{\varepsilon} : \mathbf{0}, \sigma^2\mathbf{I})$. Suppose the investigator is interested in determining if the mean of a model which contains only q factors (say the first q factors) is "adequate" as a substitute for $\mathbf{X}\boldsymbol{\beta}$, the mean of $\mathbf{Y}$ for the true model.

We write the true model as $\mathbf{Y} = \mathbf{X}_1\boldsymbol{\beta}_1 + \mathbf{X}_2\boldsymbol{\beta}_2 + \boldsymbol{\varepsilon}$, where $\mathbf{X} = [\mathbf{X}_1, \mathbf{X}_2]$ and $\mathbf{X}_1$ has $q + 1$ columns; the first column of $\mathbf{X}_1$ is $\mathbf{1}$ and the other q columns of $\mathbf{X}_1$ are the n observations on factors $1, 2, \ldots, q$, respectively; the matrix $\mathbf{X}_2$ contains the n observations on factors $q + 1, \ldots, K$. The problem is to determine if the last $K - q$ factors are of importance in predicting the mean of factor 0, whose observed values are the elements of the vector $\mathbf{y}$.

If only the first q factors are used (that is, if the model used is $\mathbf{Y} = \mathbf{X}_1\boldsymbol{\beta}_1 + \boldsymbol{\varepsilon}$), then for this submodel the estimated values of $\mathbf{X}_1\boldsymbol{\beta}_1$, the mean of the observations, are the elements of $\mathbf{X}_1\hat{\boldsymbol{\beta}}_1$, where $\hat{\boldsymbol{\beta}}_1$ is the solution to the normal equations $\mathbf{X}_1'\mathbf{X}_1\hat{\boldsymbol{\beta}}_1 = \mathbf{X}_1'\mathbf{Y}$. The error of estimating $\mathbf{X}\boldsymbol{\beta}$ by $\mathbf{X}_1\hat{\boldsymbol{\beta}}_1$ is $\mathbf{X}\boldsymbol{\beta} - \mathbf{X}_1\hat{\boldsymbol{\beta}}_1$, and the sum of squares of the error of estimation is $(\mathbf{X}\boldsymbol{\beta} - \mathbf{X}_1\hat{\boldsymbol{\beta}}_1)'(\mathbf{X}\boldsymbol{\beta} - \mathbf{X}_1\hat{\boldsymbol{\beta}}_1)$ (this is an estimate of how "close" $\mathbf{X}_1\boldsymbol{\beta}_1$ is to $\mathbf{X}\boldsymbol{\beta}$ for the x_{ij} values actually observed). The mean-squared-error is

$$\mathscr{E}[(\mathbf{X}\boldsymbol{\beta} - \mathbf{X}_1\hat{\boldsymbol{\beta}}_1)'(\mathbf{X}\boldsymbol{\beta} - \mathbf{X}_1\hat{\boldsymbol{\beta}}_1)] = \boldsymbol{\beta}_2'\mathbf{X}_2'(\mathbf{I} - \mathbf{X}_1\mathbf{X}_1^-)\mathbf{X}_2\boldsymbol{\beta}_2 + (q + 1)\sigma^2$$

If the mean-squared-error is divided by σ^2, we get a measure which is the mean-squared-error as a proportion of the true variance. Thus we shall use

$$\begin{aligned}\left(\frac{1}{\sigma^2}\right)\mathscr{E}[(\mathbf{X}\boldsymbol{\beta} - \mathbf{X}_1\hat{\boldsymbol{\beta}}_1)'(\mathbf{X}\boldsymbol{\beta} - \mathbf{X}_1\hat{\boldsymbol{\beta}}_1)] &= \left(\frac{1}{\sigma^2}\right)\boldsymbol{\beta}_2'\mathbf{X}_2'(\mathbf{I} - \mathbf{X}_1\mathbf{X}_1^-)\mathbf{X}_2\boldsymbol{\beta}_2 + (q + 1)\\ &= \left(\frac{1}{\sigma^2}\right)\boldsymbol{\beta}'\mathbf{X}'(\mathbf{I} - \mathbf{X}_1\mathbf{X}_1^-)\mathbf{X}\boldsymbol{\beta} + (q + 1)\end{aligned}$$

as the measure of the adequacy of the first q factors for estimating $\mathbf{X}\boldsymbol{\beta}$ in the model $\mathbf{Y} = \mathbf{X}\boldsymbol{\beta} + \boldsymbol{\varepsilon}$, $\boldsymbol{\varepsilon}$ is distributed $(\boldsymbol{\varepsilon} : \mathbf{0}, \sigma^2\mathbf{I})$. Here q can be any integer $1, 2, \ldots, K$, and for a given integer q, any subset of q (rather than the first q) of the factors can be used for estimating $\mathbf{X}\boldsymbol{\beta}$.

We now give the notation we shall use and then formally define the measure to be used for assessing the quality of a subset of factors for estimating $\mathbf{X}\boldsymbol{\beta}$.

Notation. Let the model be defined by Equation (12.3.10). The symbol $\boldsymbol{\beta}_{ij}$ will represent an $i \times 1$ vector which includes β_0 and $i - 1$ distinct elements of the other K elements in $\boldsymbol{\beta}$. The second subscript, namely j, refers to a particular subset of the $i - 1$ elements of $\boldsymbol{\beta}$ (other than β_0)

that the vector $\boldsymbol{\beta}_{ij}$ contains. The subscript j can take on the values $1, 2, \ldots, \binom{K}{i-1}$ since there are $\binom{K}{i-1}$ distinct subsets of $i - 1$ elements in K elements. These subsets can be labeled the 1st, 2nd, ..., $\binom{K}{i-1}$th subset by any method of labeling. We present a simple example to illustrate the notation.

Example 12.3.6

Consider the model where $K = 3$ and $\boldsymbol{\beta}' = [\beta_0, \beta_1, \beta_2, \beta_3]$. We get $\boldsymbol{\beta}'_{11} = [\beta_0]$, and this is the only subset that contains no elements of $\boldsymbol{\beta}$ except β_0.

$$\boldsymbol{\beta}'_{21} = [\beta_0, \beta_1] \qquad \boldsymbol{\beta}'_{22} = [\beta_0, \beta_2] \qquad \boldsymbol{\beta}'_{23} = [\beta_0, \beta_3]$$

and these are all the vectors with two elements of $\boldsymbol{\beta}$ including β_0. Thus the second subscript in $\boldsymbol{\beta}_{23}$, namely 3, is equal to $\binom{3}{1}$.

$$\boldsymbol{\beta}'_{31} = [\beta_0, \beta_1, \beta_2] \qquad \boldsymbol{\beta}'_{32} = [\beta_0, \beta_1, \beta_3]$$

$$\boldsymbol{\beta}'_{33} = [\beta_0, \beta_2, \beta_3] \qquad \boldsymbol{\beta}'_{41} = [\beta_0, \beta_1, \beta_2, \beta_3]$$

The symbol $\mathbf{X}_{ij}$ will be used to indicate an $n \times i$ matrix that consists of i columns of the matrix $\mathbf{X}$. The second subscript, namely j, will denote which subset of the i columns of $\mathbf{X}$ is included (the first column is $\mathbf{1}$).

Thus we are considering the 2^K models $\mathbf{Y} = \mathbf{X}_{ij}\boldsymbol{\beta}_{ij} + \boldsymbol{\varepsilon}_{ij}$, $j = 1, 2, \ldots, \binom{K}{i-1}$ and $i = 1, 2, \ldots, K + 1$. This is the set of all models (one for every subset of the K factors and where each model contains β_0).

DEFINITION 12.3.1

Relative Error of Estimating $\mathbf{X}\boldsymbol{\beta}$. *Consider the model* $\mathbf{Y} = \mathbf{X}\boldsymbol{\beta} + \boldsymbol{\varepsilon}$, $\boldsymbol{\varepsilon}$ *is distributed* $(\boldsymbol{\varepsilon} : \mathbf{0}, \sigma^2\mathbf{I})$; *the matrix* $\mathbf{X}$ *is an* $n \times (K + 1)$ *matrix of rank* $K + 1$. *Consider the "submodel"*

$$\mathbf{Y} = \mathbf{X}_{ij}\boldsymbol{\beta}_{ij} + \boldsymbol{\varepsilon}_{ij} \qquad \boldsymbol{\varepsilon}_{ij} \textit{ is distributed } (\boldsymbol{\varepsilon}_{ij} : \mathbf{0}, \sigma^2\mathbf{I})$$

$$\textit{and } \mathbf{X}_{ij} \textit{ and } \boldsymbol{\beta}_{ij} \textit{ are defined above} \qquad (12.3.11)$$

The relative error of estimating $\mathbf{X}\boldsymbol{\beta}$ *by this submodel is denoted by* Γ_{ij} *and is defined by*

$$\Gamma_{ij} = \left(\frac{1}{\sigma^2}\right) \mathscr{E}[(\mathbf{X}\boldsymbol{\beta} - \mathbf{X}_{ij}\hat{\boldsymbol{\beta}}_{ij})'(\mathbf{X}\boldsymbol{\beta} - \mathbf{X}_{ij}\hat{\boldsymbol{\beta}}_{ij})]$$

where $\hat{\boldsymbol{\beta}}_{ij}$ *is the BLU estimator of* $\boldsymbol{\beta}_{ij}$ *in the model in Equation* (12.3.11) *or the UMVU estimator of* $\boldsymbol{\beta}_{ij}$ *if* $\boldsymbol{\varepsilon}_{ij}$ *is distributed* $N(\boldsymbol{\varepsilon}_{ij}:\mathbf{0},\sigma^2\mathbf{I})$. *Thus* $\hat{\boldsymbol{\beta}}_{ij}$ *is the vector that satisfies* $\mathbf{X}'_{ij}\mathbf{X}_{ij}\hat{\boldsymbol{\beta}}_{ij}=\mathbf{X}'_{ij}\mathbf{Y}$.

Clearly if the submodel is the full model $\mathbf{Y}=\mathbf{X}\boldsymbol{\beta}+\boldsymbol{\varepsilon}$, then the relative error of estimating $\mathbf{X}\boldsymbol{\beta}$ is denoted by $\Gamma_{K+1,1}$ and is given by

$$\begin{aligned}\Gamma_{K+1,1} &= \left(\frac{1}{\sigma^2}\right)\mathscr{E}[(\mathbf{X}\boldsymbol{\beta}-\mathbf{X}\hat{\boldsymbol{\beta}})'(\mathbf{X}\boldsymbol{\beta}-\mathbf{X}\hat{\boldsymbol{\beta}})]\\ &= \left(\frac{1}{\sigma^2}\right)\mathscr{E}[(\mathbf{X}\boldsymbol{\beta}-\mathbf{X}\mathbf{X}^-\mathbf{Y})'(\mathbf{X}\boldsymbol{\beta}-\mathbf{X}\mathbf{X}^-\mathbf{Y})]\\ &= \left(\frac{1}{\sigma^2}\right)\mathscr{E}[(\mathbf{X}\mathbf{X}^-\boldsymbol{\varepsilon})'(\mathbf{X}\mathbf{X}^-\boldsymbol{\varepsilon})]\\ &= \left(\frac{1}{\sigma^2}\right)\sigma^2\,\mathrm{tr}[\mathbf{X}\mathbf{X}^-]=K+1 \qquad (12.3.12)\end{aligned}$$

We now state and prove some theorems about Γ_{ij} and a method of estimating it.

THEOREM 12.3.1

Let the model and the submodel be given in Definition 12.3.1. *The relative error of estimating* $\mathbf{X}\boldsymbol{\beta}$, *namely* Γ_{ij}, *is*

$$\Gamma_{ij}=\left(\frac{1}{\sigma^2}\right)\boldsymbol{\beta}'\mathbf{X}'(\mathbf{I}-\mathbf{X}_{ij}\mathbf{X}_{ij}^-)\mathbf{X}\boldsymbol{\beta}+i$$

Proof

By Definition 12.3.1,

$$\Gamma_{ij}=\left(\frac{1}{\sigma^2}\right)\mathscr{E}[(\mathbf{X}\boldsymbol{\beta}-\mathbf{X}_{ij}\mathbf{X}_{ij}^-\mathbf{Y})'(\mathbf{X}\boldsymbol{\beta}-\mathbf{X}_{ij}\mathbf{X}_{ij}^-\mathbf{Y})]$$

From this we get

$$\begin{aligned}\Gamma_{ij} &= \left(\frac{1}{\sigma^2}\right)\mathscr{E}[(\mathbf{X}\boldsymbol{\beta}-\mathbf{X}_{ij}\mathbf{X}_{ij}^-\mathbf{X}\boldsymbol{\beta}-\mathbf{X}_{ij}\mathbf{X}_{ij}^-\boldsymbol{\varepsilon})'(\mathbf{X}\boldsymbol{\beta}-\mathbf{X}_{ij}\mathbf{X}_{ij}^-\mathbf{X}\boldsymbol{\beta}-\mathbf{X}_{ij}\mathbf{X}_{ij}^-\boldsymbol{\varepsilon})]\\ &= \left(\frac{1}{\sigma^2}\right)\{\boldsymbol{\beta}'\mathbf{X}'(\mathbf{I}-\mathbf{X}_{ij}\mathbf{X}_{ij}^-)\mathbf{X}\boldsymbol{\beta}+\sigma^2\,\mathrm{tr}[\mathbf{X}_{ij}\mathbf{X}_{ij}^-]\}\\ &= \left(\frac{1}{\sigma^2}\right)\boldsymbol{\beta}'\mathbf{X}'(\mathbf{I}-\mathbf{X}_{ij}\mathbf{X}_{ij}^-)\mathbf{X}\boldsymbol{\beta}+i\end{aligned}$$

Note 6. The quantity $\boldsymbol{\beta}'\mathbf{X}'(\mathbf{I} - \mathbf{X}_{ij}\mathbf{X}_{ij}^{-})\mathbf{X}\boldsymbol{\beta}$ is called the *bias* and $i\sigma^2$ is called the *variance* of the mean-squared-error of estimating $\mathbf{X}\boldsymbol{\beta}$ in the model $\mathbf{Y} = \mathbf{X}\boldsymbol{\beta} + \boldsymbol{\varepsilon}$ by using the submodel $\mathbf{Y} = \mathbf{X}_{ij}\boldsymbol{\beta}_{ij} + \boldsymbol{\varepsilon}_{ij}$.

To find a suitable estimator of Γ_{ij} we proceed as follows:

1. Using the full model, the BQU estimator of σ^2 is

$$\hat{\sigma}^2 = (n - K - 1)^{-1}\mathbf{Y}'(\mathbf{I} - \mathbf{X}\mathbf{X}^{-})\mathbf{Y}$$

   when the error vector $\boldsymbol{\varepsilon}$ satisfies the conditions of Equation (6.10.3), or $\hat{\sigma}^2$ above is the UMVU estimator of σ^2 when the full model is used and $\boldsymbol{\varepsilon}$ is distributed $N(\boldsymbol{\varepsilon} : \mathbf{0}, \sigma^2\mathbf{I})$.

2. The error sum of squares in the submodel $\mathbf{Y} = \mathbf{X}_{ij}\boldsymbol{\beta}_{ij} + \boldsymbol{\varepsilon}_{ij}$, where $\boldsymbol{\varepsilon}_{ij}$ is distributed $N(\boldsymbol{\varepsilon}_{ij} : \mathbf{0}, \sigma^2\mathbf{I})$, is $\mathbf{Y}'\mathbf{Y} - R(\boldsymbol{\beta}_{ij}) = \mathbf{Y}'(\mathbf{I} - \mathbf{X}_{ij}\mathbf{X}_{ij}^{-})\mathbf{Y}$; we shall denote this sum of squares by *ESS*(*ij*). Under the weaker assumption on the error vector $\boldsymbol{\varepsilon}_{ij}$, namely $\boldsymbol{\varepsilon}_{ij}$ is distributed $(\boldsymbol{\varepsilon}_{ij} : \mathbf{0}, \sigma^2\mathbf{I})$, *ESS*(*ij*) is an unbiased estimator of $\boldsymbol{\beta}'\mathbf{X}'(\mathbf{I} - \mathbf{X}_{ij}\mathbf{X}_{ij}^{-})\mathbf{X}\boldsymbol{\beta} + (n - i)\sigma^2$.

3. If we use C_{ij} defined by

$$C_{ij} = \frac{ESS(ij) - (n - 2i)\hat{\sigma}^2}{\hat{\sigma}^2} \tag{12.3.13}$$

   where $\hat{\sigma}^2$ is defined in step 1, then the expected value of the numerator of C_{ij} is the numerator of Γ_{ij}, and the expected value of the denominator of C_{ij} is the denominator of Γ_{ij}.

4. The quantity C_{ij} can be used as an estimator of Γ_{ij}, the measure of the quality of estimating $\mathbf{X}\boldsymbol{\beta}$ by using the submodel $\mathbf{Y} = \mathbf{X}_{ij}\boldsymbol{\beta}_{ij} + \boldsymbol{\varepsilon}_{ij}$.

Note 7. This estimator of Γ_{ij} does not possess any particularly optimum properties and is used mainly for plotting and graphical analysis. For example, what is often done is to plot C_{ij} versus i for each j and visually examine the results. We illustrate this in the following example.

Example 12.3.7

For the data in Example 12.3.3, compute C_{ij} for all $i = 1, 2, 3, 4, 5$ and $j = 1, 2, \ldots, \binom{4}{i - 1}$. The results are given in the table below.

In Figure 12.3.1, C_{ij} is plotted versus i.

If for any value ij, the plot of C_{ij} is "close" to the line connecting the points $(0, 0)$ and $(K + 1, K + 1)$, the factors represented by the variables involved may be useful for predicting the value of factor 0.

Factors in the Model	$\tilde{\rho}^2_{0(\text{Factors in Model})}$	The i Parameters in the Model	C_{ij}	Factors in the Model	$\tilde{\rho}^2_{0(\text{Factors in Model})}$	The i Parameters in the Model	C_{ij}
none	0.000	β_0	4.45	2, 4	0.099	$\beta_0, \beta_2, \beta_4$	6.22
1	0.040	β_0, β_1	5.55	3, 4	0.017	$\beta_0, \beta_3, \beta_4$	8.08
2	0.090	β_0, β_2	4.43	1, 2, 3	0.330	$\beta_0, \beta_1, \beta_2, \beta_3$	3.05
3	0.010	β_0, β_3	6.23	1, 2, 4	0.225	$\beta_0, \beta_1, \beta_2, \beta_4$	5.40
4	0.010	β_0, β_4	6.23	1, 3, 4	0.074	$\beta_0, \beta_1, \beta_3, \beta_4$	8.78
1, 2	0.212	$\beta_0, \beta_1, \beta_2$	3.69	2, 3, 4	0.121	$\beta_0, \beta_2, \beta_3, \beta_4$	7.74
1, 3	0.068	$\beta_0, \beta_1, \beta_3$	6.92	1, 2, 3, 4	0.332	$\beta_0, \beta_1, \beta_2, \beta_3, \beta_4$	5.00
1, 4	0.052	$\beta_0, \beta_1, \beta_4$	7.28				
2, 3	0.117	$\beta_0, \beta_2, \beta_3$	5.83				

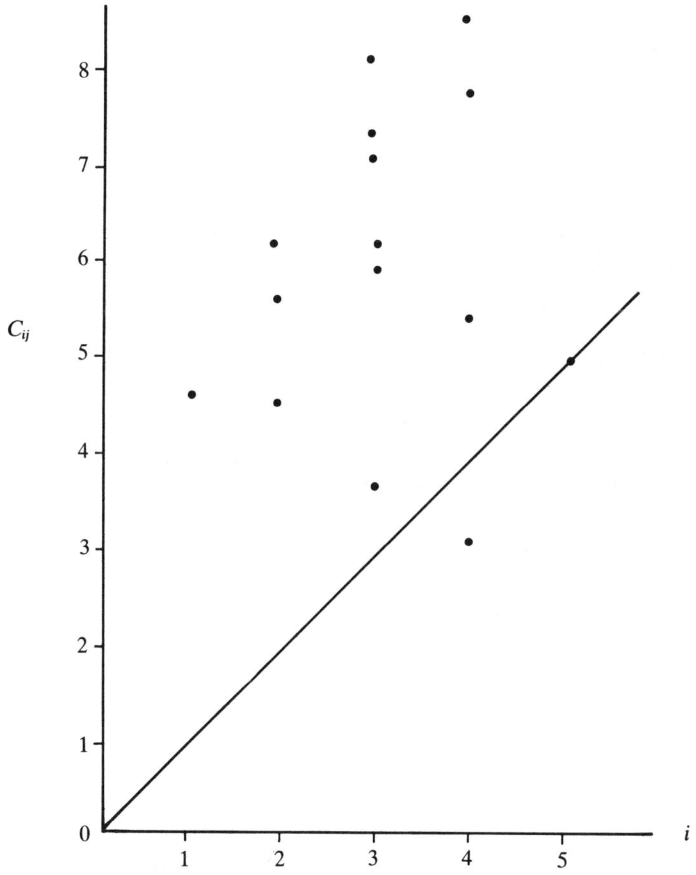

Figure 12.3.1

Note 8. C_{ij} is a simple function of the multiple correlation coefficients. The function is

$$C_{ij} = \left[\frac{1 - \tilde{\rho}^2_{0[i,j]}}{1 - \tilde{\rho}^2_{0(1,2,\ldots,K)}}\right](n - K - 1) - (n - 2i)$$

where $\tilde{\rho}^2_{0[i,j]}$ is the "estimate" of the square of the multiple correlation coefficient of X_0 with the variables in $\mathbf{X}_{ij}$ (where the variables in $\mathbf{X}_{ij}$ are considered as observed values of random variables) and computed by Equation (11.4.6), where $\mathbf{A}^*$ includes only factors 0 and those in $\mathbf{X}_{ij}$ even though they may be nonrandom factors; the first column of $\mathbf{X}_{ij}$ is always a column of ones. Also, n is the sample size and $K + 1$ is the number of parameters including β_0 in the full model (5 in Example 12.3.7).

For additional information on this procedure see [D-2] and [M-2].

12.4 Growth Curves

In this section we discuss an important application which can be viewed as a slight modification of the multiple regression model. This application is called *growth curves* which are sometimes referred to as longitudinal models. We introduce the subject with examples.

Example 12.4.1

Suppose it is desired to study the weight change of pigs as a function of the number of weeks they have been fed a certain supplement in their diet. The weight change is where the word "growth" is used, and an investigator may want to determine a function (curve) that "estimates" this weight change with respect to time.

Example 12.4.2

Suppose an investigator wants to determine the change in blood pressure of individuals as a function of time (each minute for thirty minutes) during which they are placed in a certain stress situation, such as parachuting from an airplane. In this example "change" in blood pressure is used for the word "growth."

Example 12.4.3

It is desired to determine the gas mileage a certain brand of automobile gets as a function of the number of miles it has been driven. In this example "miles per gallon of gasoline" is used for "growth" and miles the auto has been driven is "time."

Example 12.4.4

An agronomist is interested in the height of a new variety of wheat as a function of time. In this example it is clear why the "height" curve is called a "growth" curve.

At first it might appear that a model for these examples is the general linear model or the multiple regression model. However, in some cases a modification may be necessary. The principal modification is in the covariance matrix. In the general linear model, the observable random variables were generally assumed to be independent (random samples), and hence the covariance matrix was generally $\sigma^2\mathbf{I}$. However, in models known as growth models, it may be more realistic to assume that the random observations are not *all* independent.

We will illustrate by considering the simple case discussed in Example 12.4.4. As a first approximation we assume that the set of stalks of wheat in a large field (which would include tens of thousands of stalks) is the population under study. Suppose at each of K times, denoted by $t_1, t_2, \ldots, t_K$, the heights of n stalks of wheat are observed. If the model for this problem is a general linear model, then the distribution of the height observations on the stalks at each of K times has the same variance and the observations are independent (the covariance matrix of the nK observations is $\sigma^2\mathbf{I}$).

This is, perhaps, the correct model if the sampling procedure is as follows: (1) a random sample of n plants is selected and their heights observed at time t_1; (2) another random sample of n plants is selected and their heights observed at time t_2; (3) this process is continued until finally a random sample of n plants is selected and their heights observed at time t_K. Clearly by this method of sampling the nK observations are independent and the general linear model could be appropriate.

However, in these kinds of studies the sampling is often not performed as explained above but is done as follows: n stalks of wheat are selected at random and the height of *each* of *these* n stalks is observed at times $t_1, t_2, \ldots, t_K$. This results in nK observations, but it does not seem appropriate to treat them as independent observations for three reasons: (1) only n stalks are selected at *random*; (2) the height of *each* stalk was observed at times $t_1, t_2, \ldots, t_K$; (3) it seems realistic to assume that if a very short stalk was one of the n selected, then its height measurement at each time t_i would perhaps be less than the average height of the population of all stalks. Hence it appears that any two measurements on the same stalk at different times would be correlated. For example, if the height of a given stalk is low at time t_i relative to the population height at time t_i, it would tend to be low at time t_{i+1}, and so on.

Actually, in this example it would seem more realistic to collect a random sample of n stalks of wheat at each of the time periods $t_1, t_2, \ldots, t_K$, measure the nK heights, and use the general linear model. But suppose the investigation was intended to observe the "growth" of wheat after it was subjected to a certain treatment. It may not be practical (or possible) to subject the entire field of wheat to the treatment, so n stalks may be selected at random from the field and given the treatment. Then at times $t_1, t_2, \ldots, t_K$, the height of each of the n *treated* stalks is measured. Thus the nK measurements are perhaps not independent and a model other than the general linear model may be more appropriate.

We shall discuss two models that have been considered for these kinds of problems. The first model we call "the random coefficient" growth model, the second "the multivariate" growth model.

12.4.1 The "Random Coefficient" Growth Model

To introduce this section we again use Example 12.4.4. The set of stalks of wheat in a large field is the population under study and n of these stalks are selected at random for growth studies. The height of each of these stalks is measured at times $t_1, t_2, \ldots, t_K$ weeks (as an example these times might be 6, 8, 9, 12, and 15 weeks after a certain date is selected as a starting time).

We assume in this example that in the time period under study, the growth is linear. The meaning of this assumption is very crucial. We mean that the growth curve of each of the many thousands of stalks is linear, but each may be a *different linear function* (that is, each may have different slope and intercept coefficients). Thus the slope and intercept coefficients, B_1 and B_0, of the stalks are assumed to be random variables with means β_1 and β_0 and covariance matrix Σ.

The "true" mean or "population" growth curve of the entire field of wheat is $\beta_0 + \beta_1 t$ for t in the time interval under consideration (say from 6 to 15 weeks). A stalk is selected at random and the intercept b_0 and slope b_1 are assumed to be values of a random sample from a population of slopes and intercepts with means β_0 and β_1, respectively, and unknown covariance matrix. Of course, the slope and intercept are not observable for the stalk selected at random, and hence they must be estimated from K height measurements on the stalk at the time periods $t_1, t_2, \ldots, t_K$.

The measurements on the randomly selected stalks are assumed to be mutually independent with mean $\beta_0 + \beta_1 t$ and variance σ^2. See Figure 12.4.1. Clearly the observations (denoted by ○) around the line corresponding to the sample growth curve 1 are correlated; the element selected from the population is larger than the population average, so the observations at each time period tend to be large. On the other hand, the observations (denoted by +) around the line corresponding to sample growth curve 2 are *all* small relative to the population average. The fact that the observations denoted by ○ are correlated is perhaps dramatized in Figure 12.4.2, where the sample line is omitted (similarly for the observations denoted by +).

The observations denoted by ○ in Figure 12.4.1 do not fall on its growth curve for the particular randomly drawn element of the population. That is

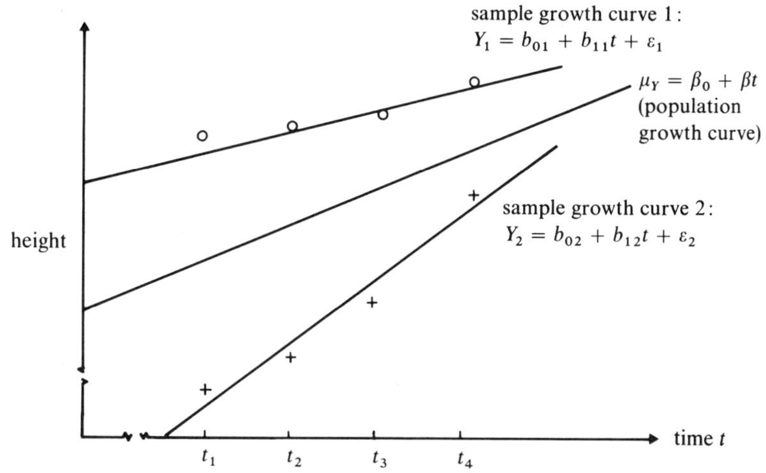

Figure 12.4.1

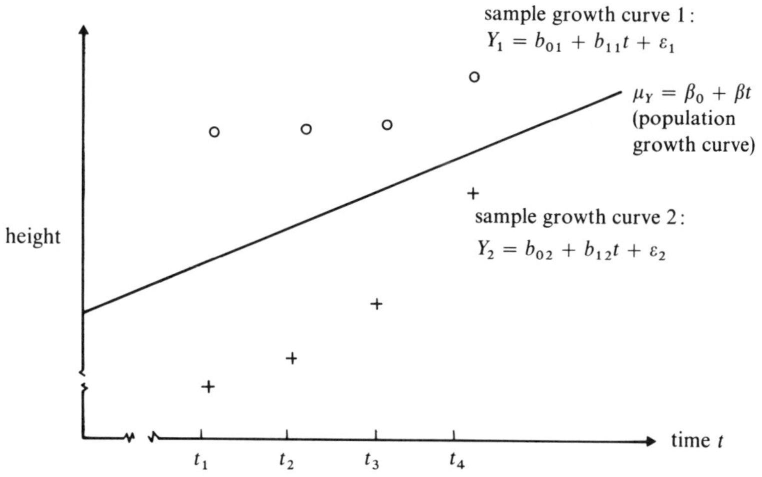

Figure 12.4.2

due to measurement error and equation error (see Section 5.2). We now make the assumptions for a "random coefficient" growth curve model explicit.

In the "random coefficient" growth model as we shall formulate and discuss it, we assume the following:

1. There is a population of *individuals.*

2. Each individual's "growth" curve $\mu(t)$ is a linear (polynomial) model of specified degree $M - 1$ (this assumption can be extended to be any general linear model where each individual's growth curve is of the same functional form).

3. The linear models in step 2 are given by $X = B_0 + \sum_{m=1}^{M-1} B_m t^m + \varepsilon$.

4. The coefficients $[B_0, B_1, \ldots, B_{M-1}] = \mathbf{b}'$ are random variables.

5. n individuals are selected at random and the model for the kth observation on the jth individual is $X_{kj} = B_{0j} + \sum_{m=1}^{M-1} B_{mj} t_k^m + \varepsilon_{kj}$.

6. At specified times $t_1, t_2, \ldots, t_K$, an observation (growth measurement) is made on each of n individuals. The K observations on the jth individual are denoted by the $K \times 1$ random vector $\boldsymbol{\chi}_j$. (12.4.1)

7. The structure of the observable vector χ_j on the jth individual is as follows:

   (a) $\boldsymbol{\chi}_j = \mathbf{T}\mathbf{b}_j + \boldsymbol{\varepsilon}_j$ for $j = 1, 2, \ldots, n$;

   (b) $\{\mathbf{b}_j, \boldsymbol{\varepsilon}_j$ for $j = 1, 2, \ldots, n\}$ is a set of $2n$ (random) independent vectors;

   (c) $\mathbf{b}_j$ for $j = 1, 2, \ldots, n$ are distributed $\mathbf{NID}(\mathbf{b} : \boldsymbol{\beta}, \boldsymbol{\Sigma}_\mathbf{b})$, $\boldsymbol{\Sigma}_\mathbf{b}$ is p.d., and $\boldsymbol{\beta} \in E_M$;

   (d) $\boldsymbol{\varepsilon}_j$ for $j = 1, 2, \ldots, n$ are distributed $\mathbf{NID}(\boldsymbol{\varepsilon} : \mathbf{0}, \sigma^2\mathbf{I})$ and $\sigma^2 > 0$;

   (e) $\mathbf{T}$ is a $K \times M$ matrix of known constants of rank M, where $\mathbf{T} = [t_{km}]$, $t_{km} = t_k^{m-1}$;

   (f) $n > K \geq M$. (12.4.2)

Note 1. From this it follows that

1. $\mathbf{cov}[\boldsymbol{\chi}_j] = \mathbf{T}\boldsymbol{\Sigma}_\mathbf{b}\mathbf{T}' + \sigma^2\mathbf{I} = \boldsymbol{\Sigma}$;

2. $\boldsymbol{\chi}_j$ for $j = 1, 2, \ldots, n$ are distributed $\mathbf{NID}(\mathbf{x} : \mathbf{T}\boldsymbol{\beta}, \boldsymbol{\Sigma})$;

3. $\mathbf{Y}_j = \mathbf{T}^-\boldsymbol{\chi}_j$ for $j = 1, 2, \ldots, n$ are distributed $\mathbf{NID}(\mathbf{y} : \boldsymbol{\beta}, \boldsymbol{\Sigma}_0)$, where $\boldsymbol{\Sigma}_0 = \boldsymbol{\Sigma}_\mathbf{b} + \sigma^2(\mathbf{T}'\mathbf{T})^{-1}$. (12.4.3)

To help relate these assumptions to a real situation we use Example 12.4.4. In this example we assume the growth curve is a linear function of time t in weeks for the time interval under study, so $M = 2$. A stalk of wheat is selected at random and its heights at times 6, 8, 9, 12, and 15 weeks are observed to be as follows ($K = 5$):

t_k	6	8	9	12	15
x_{k1}	14	17	20	27	33

The model for *this* stalk of wheat is $X_{k1} = b_{01} + b_{11}t_k + \varepsilon_{k1}$ for $k = 1, 2, 3, 4, 5$. Thus we identify the following with Equation (12.4.2).

$$\mathbf{x}_1 = \begin{bmatrix} 14 \\ 17 \\ 20 \\ 27 \\ 33 \end{bmatrix} \qquad \mathbf{b}_1 = \begin{bmatrix} b_{01} \\ b_{11} \end{bmatrix} \qquad \mathbf{T} = \begin{bmatrix} 1 & 6 \\ 1 & 8 \\ 1 & 9 \\ 1 & 12 \\ 1 & 15 \end{bmatrix} \qquad \boldsymbol{\varepsilon}_1 = \begin{bmatrix} \varepsilon_{11} \\ \varepsilon_{21} \\ \varepsilon_{31} \\ \varepsilon_{41} \\ \varepsilon_{51} \end{bmatrix}$$

$\boldsymbol{\varepsilon}_1$ is distributed $\mathbf{N}(\boldsymbol{\varepsilon} : \mathbf{0}, \sigma^2\mathbf{I})$

From the data $\mathbf{T}$ and $\mathbf{x}_1$ we estimate b_{01}, b_{11} (these are values of the random variables B_0 and B_1) and σ^2 by the method of maximum likelihood presented in Section 6.2.

Then a second stalk of wheat is selected at random, and the model is $X_{k2} = b_{02} + b_{12}t_k + \varepsilon_{k2}$ for $k = 1, 2, 3, 4, 5$. Suppose the heights at times 6, 8, 9, 12, and 15 weeks are observed to be as follows:

t_k	6	8	9	12	15
x_{k2}	15	18	20	26	35

Then we get

$$\mathbf{x}_2 = \begin{bmatrix} 15 \\ 18 \\ 20 \\ 26 \\ 35 \end{bmatrix} \qquad \mathbf{b}_2 = \begin{bmatrix} b_{02} \\ b_{12} \end{bmatrix} \qquad \mathbf{T} = \begin{bmatrix} 1 & 6 \\ 1 & 8 \\ 1 & 9 \\ 1 & 12 \\ 1 & 15 \end{bmatrix} \qquad \boldsymbol{\varepsilon}_2 = \begin{bmatrix} \varepsilon_{12} \\ \varepsilon_{22} \\ \varepsilon_{32} \\ \varepsilon_{42} \\ \varepsilon_{52} \end{bmatrix}$$

$\boldsymbol{\varepsilon}_2$ is distributed $\mathbf{N}(\boldsymbol{\varepsilon} : \mathbf{0}, \sigma^2\mathbf{I})$

The quantities b_{02} and b_{12} are values of the random variables B_0 and B_1, respectively, and from $\mathbf{T}$ and $\mathbf{x}_2$ we estimate b_{02}, b_{12}, and σ^2 by the method of M.L. presented in Section 6.2.

This procedure can be repeated until n stalks of wheat are examined, where $\mathbf{b}_1, \mathbf{b}_2, \ldots, \mathbf{b}_n$ are the values of a random sample of size n from the distribution

$N(\mathbf{b} : \boldsymbol{\beta}, \boldsymbol{\Sigma}_{\mathbf{b}})$. These vectors are *not* observable but they can be "estimated" by the method of M.L. discussed above. From the observations $\mathbf{x}_1, \mathbf{x}_2, \ldots, \mathbf{x}_n$ and $\mathbf{T}$, we want to obtain tests and estimates of the parameters $\boldsymbol{\beta}$, $\boldsymbol{\Sigma}_{\mathbf{b}}$, and σ^2. Since the growth curve is assumed to be linear, the matrix $\mathbf{T}$ is

$$\mathbf{T} = \begin{bmatrix} 1 & t_1 \\ 1 & t_2 \\ \vdots & \vdots \\ 1 & t_K \end{bmatrix}$$

If the growth curve is assumed to be quadratic, $\mathbf{T}$ would be

$$\mathbf{T} = \begin{bmatrix} 1 & t_1 & t_1^2 \\ 1 & t_2 & t_2^2 \\ \vdots & \vdots & \vdots \\ 1 & t_K & t_K^2 \end{bmatrix}$$

If the growth curve is assumed to be a polynomial of degree $M - 1$, it is then clear how $\mathbf{T}$ is constructed.

We now state and prove a theorem about M.L. estimators of the parameters in this model.

THEOREM 12.4.1

Under the assumptions given in Equation (12.4.1) *and Equation* (12.4.2), *the following are M.L. estimators (adjusted for bias if necessary) of the parameters* $\boldsymbol{\beta}$, $\boldsymbol{\Sigma}_0 = \boldsymbol{\Sigma}_{\mathbf{b}} + \sigma^2(\mathbf{T}'\mathbf{T})^{-1}$, *and* σ^2:

$$\begin{aligned} \hat{\boldsymbol{\beta}} &= (\mathbf{T}'\mathbf{T})^{-1}\mathbf{T}'\bar{\boldsymbol{\chi}} = \mathbf{T}^{-}\bar{\boldsymbol{\chi}} \\ \hat{\boldsymbol{\Sigma}}_0 &= \mathbf{T}^{-}\left[\left(\frac{1}{n-1}\right)\sum_{j=1}^{n}(\boldsymbol{\chi}_j - \bar{\boldsymbol{\chi}})(\boldsymbol{\chi}_j - \bar{\boldsymbol{\chi}})'\right]\mathbf{T}'^{-} \\ \hat{\sigma}^2 &= \left(\frac{1}{n(K-M)}\right)\sum_{j=1}^{n}\boldsymbol{\chi}_j'(\mathbf{I} - \mathbf{T}\mathbf{T}^{-})\boldsymbol{\chi}_j \end{aligned} \tag{12.4.4}$$

Proof

The p.d.f. of $\boldsymbol{\chi}_j$ is $(2\pi)^{-K/2}|\boldsymbol{\Sigma}|^{-1/2}\exp\{-\frac{1}{2}(\mathbf{x}_j - \mathbf{T}\boldsymbol{\beta})'\boldsymbol{\Sigma}^{-1}(\mathbf{x}_j - \mathbf{T}\boldsymbol{\beta})\}$. From the joint p.d.f. of $\boldsymbol{\chi}_1, \boldsymbol{\chi}_2, \ldots, \boldsymbol{\chi}_n$, we get the likelihood function:

$$\begin{aligned} &L(\boldsymbol{\beta}, \boldsymbol{\Sigma}_{\mathbf{b}}, \sigma^2 : \mathbf{x}_1, \mathbf{x}_2, \ldots, \mathbf{x}_n) \\ &= (2\pi)^{-nK/2}|\boldsymbol{\Sigma}|^{-n/2}\exp\left\{-\left(\frac{1}{2}\right)\sum_{j=1}^{n}(\mathbf{x}_j - \mathbf{T}\boldsymbol{\beta})'\boldsymbol{\Sigma}^{-1}(\mathbf{x}_j - \mathbf{T}\boldsymbol{\beta})\right\} \end{aligned} \tag{12.4.5}$$

For $\mathbf{T}$ in Equation (12.4.5) construct a $K \times K$ nonsingular matrix $\mathbf{G}$, where $\mathbf{G}' = [\mathbf{T}'^{-}\mathbf{C}']$, and where $\mathbf{T}^{-}\mathbf{C}' = \mathbf{0}$ and $\mathbf{C}\mathbf{C}' = \mathbf{I}$. (See Problems 1.20 and 1.69.) It follows that

$$\mathbf{T}^{-}\mathbf{T} = \mathbf{I} \qquad \mathbf{C}\mathbf{T} = \mathbf{0} \qquad \mathbf{T}^{-}\mathbf{C}' = \mathbf{0} \qquad \mathbf{C}'\mathbf{C} = \mathbf{I} - \mathbf{T}\mathbf{T}^{-}$$

Since $\mathbf{T}$ is a known matrix, $\mathbf{C}$ can be computed, and thus $\mathbf{G}$ is a known matrix ($\mathbf{C}$ and hence $\mathbf{G}$ may not be unique).

Now consider

$$\mathbf{G}\boldsymbol{\Sigma}\mathbf{G}' = \begin{bmatrix} \mathbf{T}^{-} \\ \mathbf{C} \end{bmatrix} (\mathbf{T}\boldsymbol{\Sigma}_{\mathbf{b}}\mathbf{T}' + \sigma^2\mathbf{I})[\mathbf{T}'^{-}\mathbf{C}'] = \begin{bmatrix} \boldsymbol{\Sigma}_{\mathbf{b}} + (\mathbf{T}'\mathbf{T})^{-1}\sigma^2 & \mathbf{0} \\ \mathbf{0} & \sigma^2\mathbf{I} \end{bmatrix}$$

$$\mathbf{G}\mathbf{T} = \begin{bmatrix} \mathbf{T}^{-}\mathbf{T} \\ \mathbf{C}\mathbf{T} \end{bmatrix} = \begin{bmatrix} \mathbf{I} \\ \mathbf{0} \end{bmatrix} \tag{12.4.6}$$

Consider the exponent of the likelihood function in Equation (12.4.5). We get

$$\begin{aligned}
&-\left(\frac{1}{2}\right)\sum_{j=1}^{n}[(\mathbf{x}_j - \mathbf{T}\boldsymbol{\beta})'\boldsymbol{\Sigma}^{-1}(\mathbf{x}_j - \mathbf{T}\boldsymbol{\beta})] \\
&\quad = -\left(\frac{1}{2}\right)\sum_{j=1}^{n}[(\mathbf{x}_j - \mathbf{T}\boldsymbol{\beta})'\mathbf{G}'\mathbf{G}'^{-1}\boldsymbol{\Sigma}^{-1}\mathbf{G}^{-1}\mathbf{G}(\mathbf{x}_j - \mathbf{T}\boldsymbol{\beta})] \\
&\quad = -\left(\frac{1}{2}\right)\sum_{j=1}^{n}[(\mathbf{G}\mathbf{x}_j - \mathbf{G}\mathbf{T}\boldsymbol{\beta})'(\mathbf{G}\boldsymbol{\Sigma}\mathbf{G}')^{-1}(\mathbf{G}\mathbf{x}_j - \mathbf{G}\mathbf{T}\boldsymbol{\beta})] \\
&\quad = -\left(\frac{1}{2}\right)\sum_{j=1}^{n}\begin{bmatrix} \mathbf{y}_j - \boldsymbol{\beta} \\ \mathbf{v}_j \end{bmatrix}'\begin{bmatrix} [\boldsymbol{\Sigma}_{\mathbf{b}} + (\mathbf{T}'\mathbf{T})^{-1}\sigma^2]^{-1} & \mathbf{0} \\ \mathbf{0} & \sigma^{-2}\mathbf{I} \end{bmatrix}\begin{bmatrix} \mathbf{y}_j - \boldsymbol{\beta} \\ \mathbf{v}_j \end{bmatrix} \\
&\quad = -\left(\frac{1}{2}\right)\sum_{j=1}^{n}(\mathbf{y}_j - \boldsymbol{\beta})'\boldsymbol{\Sigma}_0^{-1}(\mathbf{y}_j - \boldsymbol{\beta}) - \left(\frac{1}{2\sigma^2}\right)\sum_{j=1}^{n}\mathbf{v}_j'\mathbf{v}_j
\end{aligned}$$

where $\mathbf{y}_j = \mathbf{T}^{-}\mathbf{x}_j$, $\mathbf{v}_j = \mathbf{C}\mathbf{x}_j$, and $\boldsymbol{\Sigma}_0 = \boldsymbol{\Sigma}_{\mathbf{b}} + (\mathbf{T}'\mathbf{T})^{-1}\sigma^2$.

So the likelihood function can be written

$$\begin{aligned}
&L(\boldsymbol{\beta}, \boldsymbol{\Sigma}_{\mathbf{b}}, \sigma^2 : \mathbf{x}_1, \mathbf{x}_2, \ldots, \mathbf{x}_n) \\
&\quad = (2\pi)^{-nK/2}|\boldsymbol{\Sigma}|^{-n/2}\exp\left\{-\left(\frac{1}{2}\right)\sum_{j=1}^{n}(\mathbf{x}_j - \mathbf{T}\boldsymbol{\beta})'\boldsymbol{\Sigma}^{-1}(\mathbf{x}_j - \mathbf{T}\boldsymbol{\beta})\right\} \\
&\quad = (2\pi)^{-nK/2}|\mathbf{T}'\mathbf{T}|^{-n/2}|\boldsymbol{\Sigma}_0|^{-n/2} \\
&\qquad \times \exp\left\{-\left(\frac{1}{2}\right)\sum_{j=1}^{n}(\mathbf{y}_j - \boldsymbol{\beta})'\boldsymbol{\Sigma}_0^{-1}(\mathbf{y}_j - \boldsymbol{\beta})\right\}|\sigma^2\mathbf{I}|^{-n/2} \\
&\qquad \times \exp\left\{-\left(\frac{1}{2\sigma^2}\right)\sum_{j=1}^{n}\mathbf{v}_j'\mathbf{v}_j\right\}
\end{aligned} \tag{12.4.7}$$

Thus by utilizing Theorem 9.3.1, we get for M.L. estimates (unbiased)

$$\hat{\boldsymbol{\beta}} = \bar{\mathbf{y}} = \mathbf{T}^{-}\bar{\mathbf{x}}$$

$$\hat{\boldsymbol{\Sigma}}_0 = \left(\frac{1}{n-1}\right)\sum_{j=1}^{n}(\mathbf{y}_j - \bar{\mathbf{y}})(\mathbf{y}_j - \bar{\mathbf{y}})'$$

$$= \mathbf{T}^{-}\left\{\left(\frac{1}{n-1}\right)\sum_{j=1}^{n}(\mathbf{x}_j - \bar{\mathbf{x}})(\mathbf{x}_j - \bar{\mathbf{x}})'\right\}\mathbf{T}'^{-} = \mathbf{T}^{-}\left(\frac{1}{n-1}\right)\mathbf{A}\mathbf{T}'^{-}$$

$$\hat{\sigma}^2 = \left(\frac{1}{n(K-M)}\right)\sum_{j=1}^{n}\mathbf{v}_j'\mathbf{v}_j = \left(\frac{1}{n(K-M)}\right)\sum_{j=1}^{n}\mathbf{x}_j'\mathbf{C}'\mathbf{C}\mathbf{x}_j$$

$$= \left(\frac{1}{n(K-M)}\right)\sum_{j=1}^{n}\mathbf{x}_j'(\mathbf{I} - \mathbf{T}\mathbf{T}^{-})\mathbf{x}_j$$

and the theorem is proved.

We note that we can write the likelihood function in Equation (12.4.7) as

$$(2\pi)^{-nM/2}|\boldsymbol{\Sigma}_0|^{-n/2}\exp\left\{-\frac{1}{2}\left[\sum_{j=1}^{n}(\mathbf{y}_j - \bar{\mathbf{y}})'\boldsymbol{\Sigma}_0^{-1}(\mathbf{y}_j - \bar{\mathbf{y}}) + n(\bar{\mathbf{y}} - \boldsymbol{\beta})'\boldsymbol{\Sigma}_0^{-1}(\bar{\mathbf{y}} - \boldsymbol{\beta})\right]\right\}$$
$$\times (2\pi)^{-n(K-M)/2}(\sigma^2)^{-n(K-M)/2}\exp\left\{-\left(\frac{1}{2\sigma^2}\right)\sum_{j=1}^{n}\mathbf{v}_j'\mathbf{v}_j\right\}|\mathbf{T}'\mathbf{T}|^{-n/2}$$

But

$$\sum_{j=1}^{n}(\mathbf{y}_j - \bar{\mathbf{y}})'\boldsymbol{\Sigma}_0^{-1}(\mathbf{y}_j - \bar{\mathbf{y}}) = \operatorname{tr}\left[\boldsymbol{\Sigma}_0^{-1}\left\{\sum_{j=1}^{n}(\mathbf{y}_j - \bar{\mathbf{y}})(\mathbf{y}_j - \bar{\mathbf{y}})'\right\}\right]$$

Hence

$$\sum_{j=1}^{n}(\mathbf{Y}_j - \bar{\mathbf{Y}})(\mathbf{Y}_j - \bar{\mathbf{Y}})' \qquad \bar{\mathbf{Y}} \qquad \sum_{j=1}^{n}\mathbf{V}_j'\mathbf{V}_j$$

is a set of sufficient statistics, and we have the following theorem.

THEOREM 12.4.2

Consider the model in Equation (12.4.1) *and Equation* (12.4.2). $\hat{\boldsymbol{\beta}}, \hat{\boldsymbol{\Sigma}}_0, \hat{\sigma}^2$ *is a set of sufficient statistics, where we have the following:*

(1) $\hat{\boldsymbol{\beta}} = \mathbf{T}^{-}\bar{\boldsymbol{\chi}}$

$$\hat{\boldsymbol{\Sigma}}_0 = \left(\frac{1}{n-1}\right)\mathbf{T}^- \sum_{j=1}^{n} (\boldsymbol{\chi}_j - \bar{\boldsymbol{\chi}})(\boldsymbol{\chi}_j - \bar{\boldsymbol{\chi}})'\mathbf{T}'^- = \left(\frac{1}{n-1}\right)\mathbf{T}^-\mathscr{A}\mathbf{T}'^-$$
$$= \left(\frac{1}{n-1}\right)\mathscr{A}_0$$
$$\hat{\sigma}^2 = \left[\frac{1}{n(K-M)}\right] \sum_{j=1}^{n} \boldsymbol{\chi}_j'(\mathbf{I} - \mathbf{TT}^-)\boldsymbol{\chi}_j$$

(2) $\mathscr{E}[\hat{\boldsymbol{\beta}}] = \boldsymbol{\beta}$, $\mathscr{E}[\hat{\boldsymbol{\Sigma}}_0] = \boldsymbol{\Sigma}_0$, *and* $\mathscr{E}[\hat{\sigma}^2] = \sigma^2$;

(3) *the set of statistics* $\hat{\boldsymbol{\beta}}, \hat{\boldsymbol{\Sigma}}_0, \hat{\sigma}^2$ *is complete*;

(4) $\hat{\boldsymbol{\beta}}, \hat{\boldsymbol{\Sigma}}_0$, *and* $\hat{\sigma}^2$ *are UMVU estimators of* $\boldsymbol{\beta}, \boldsymbol{\Sigma}_0$, *and* σ^2, *respectively*;

(5) $\ell'\hat{\boldsymbol{\beta}}$ *is the UMVU estimator of* $\ell'\boldsymbol{\beta}$ *for any specified* $M \times 1$ *vector* ℓ *of constants*;

(6) $\hat{\boldsymbol{\Sigma}}_{\mathbf{b}} = \hat{\boldsymbol{\Sigma}}_0 - \hat{\sigma}^2(\mathbf{T}'\mathbf{T})^{-1}$ *is the UMVU estimator of* $\boldsymbol{\Sigma}_{\mathbf{b}}$;

(7) $\hat{\boldsymbol{\Sigma}} = \mathscr{A}/(n-1)$ *is the UMVU estimator of* $\boldsymbol{\Sigma}$.

Proof

Substitute for the quantities $\mathbf{y}_j$, $\bar{\mathbf{y}}$, and $\mathbf{v}_j$ in Equation (12.4.7) and use the factorization theorem to show the statistics are sufficient. The unbiasedness can be shown by simply taking expectations. We will omit the proof that the statistics are complete. The proofs of (4), (5), (6), and (7) follow from Theorem 2.7.7, after showing that the estimators are unbiased for their respective parameters.

THEOREM 12.4.3

Let the model be given by Equation (12.4.1) *and Equation* (12.4.2).

(1) $U_1 = \mathbf{c}'\mathscr{A}_0\mathbf{c}/\mathbf{c}'\boldsymbol{\Sigma}_0\mathbf{c}$ *is distributed* $\chi^2(u_1 : n-1)$ *for any nonzero constant* $M \times 1$ *vector* $\mathbf{c}$, *where*

$$\mathscr{A}_0 = \mathbf{T}^- \sum_{i=1}^{n} (\boldsymbol{\chi}_j - \bar{\boldsymbol{\chi}})(\boldsymbol{\chi}_j - \bar{\boldsymbol{\chi}})'\mathbf{T}'^-$$

(2) $U_2 = n(K-M)\hat{\sigma}^2/\sigma^2$ *is distributed* $\chi^2(u_2 : nK - nM)$;

(3) $\hat{\boldsymbol{\beta}}$ *is distributed* $\mathbf{N}(\hat{\boldsymbol{\beta}} : \boldsymbol{\beta}, (1/n)\boldsymbol{\Sigma}_0)$;

(4) U_1 *and* U_2 *are independent of* $\hat{\boldsymbol{\beta}}$.

Proof

The proof of (1) follows from (4) of Theorem 9.3.2. To prove (2) we note that U_2 is equal to

$$U_2 = \frac{n(K - M)\hat{\sigma}^2}{\sigma^2} = \sum_{j=1}^{n} \frac{\boldsymbol{\chi}_j'(\mathbf{I} - \mathbf{TT}^-)\boldsymbol{\chi}_j}{\sigma^2}$$

and if we define Q_j by

$$Q_j = \frac{\boldsymbol{\chi}_j'(\mathbf{I} - \mathbf{TT}^-)\boldsymbol{\chi}_j}{\sigma^2}$$

then the Q_j are independent for each j. Also, by Theorem 4.4.3, Q_j is distributed as a chi-square random variable since $[(\mathbf{I} - \mathbf{TT}^-)/\sigma^2]\boldsymbol{\Sigma} = \mathbf{I} - \mathbf{TT}^-$ is idempotent; also, $\text{tr}[\mathbf{I} - \mathbf{TT}^-] = K - M$, the degrees of freedom for Q_j. Thus Q_j, $j = 1, 2, \ldots, n$, are independent chi-square random variables each with $K - M$ degrees of freedom, and hence $U_2 = \sum_{j=1}^{n} Q_j$ is distributed $\chi^2(u_2 : nK - nM)$. We leave the proof of (3) and (4) for the reader.

THEOREM 12.4.4

Let the model be given by Equation (12.4.2). *Then a* $1 - \alpha$ *confidence interval on* $\boldsymbol{\ell}'\boldsymbol{\beta}$, *where* $\boldsymbol{\ell}$ *is any constant* $M \times 1$ *vector, is given by*

$$\boldsymbol{\ell}'\hat{\boldsymbol{\beta}} \mp t_{\alpha/2:n-1}\sqrt{\left(\frac{1}{n}\right)\boldsymbol{\ell}'\hat{\boldsymbol{\Sigma}}_0\boldsymbol{\ell}}$$

Proof

The proof is a direct application of Theorem 12.4.3 and will be left to the reader.

Example 12.4.5

To establish a growth curve of the ramus bone in young boys, a random sample of 20 boys was selected and the ramus height measured in millimeters at 8, $8\frac{1}{2}$, 9, and $9\frac{1}{2}$ years of age. The data are from [G-10] and are given in the table below.

Assume the growth curve for each boy (and for the population) is linear in the range from 8 to 10 years of age. We want to estimate the growth curve and set 95 percent one-at-a-time confidence intervals on the intercept β_0 and the slope β_1. We assume the twenty boys constitute a random sample from a well-defined population of boys in this age group. Since measurements are made on *each* boy at times 8, $8\frac{1}{2}$, 9, and $9\frac{1}{2}$ years, we use the "random coefficient" growth model with the assumptions in Equation (12.4.2). We get $K = 4$, $M = 2$,

Ramus Height of 20 Boys

Individual	*Age in years*			
	8	$8\frac{1}{2}$	9	$9\frac{1}{2}$
1	47.8	48.8	49.0	49.7
2	46.4	47.3	47.7	48.4
3	46.3	46.8	47.8	48.5
4	45.1	45.3	46.1	47.2
5	47.6	48.5	48.9	49.3
6	52.5	53.2	53.3	53.7
7	51.2	53.0	54.3	54.5
8	49.8	50.0	50.3	52.7
9	48.1	50.8	52.3	54.4
10	45.0	47.0	47.3	48.3
11	51.2	51.4	51.6	51.9
12	48.5	49.2	53.0	55.5
13	52.1	52.8	53.7	55.0
14	48.2	48.9	49.3	49.8
15	49.6	50.4	51.2	51.8
16	50.7	51.7	52.7	53.3
17	47.2	47.7	48.4	49.5
18	53.3	54.6	55.1	55.3
19	46.2	47.5	48.1	48.4
20	46.3	47.6	51.3	51.8
Mean	48.66	49.63	50.57	51.45
S.D.	2.52	2.54	2.63	2.73

$n = 20$; the population growth curve is $\mu(t) = \beta_0 + \beta_1 t$, $8 \leq t \leq 10$. The quantities $\bar{\mathbf{x}}$ and $\mathbf{A} = \sum_{j=1}^{20} (\mathbf{x}_j - \bar{\mathbf{x}})(\mathbf{x}_j - \bar{\mathbf{x}})'$ are computed below.

$$\bar{\mathbf{x}} = \begin{bmatrix} 48.66 \\ 49.62 \\ 50.57 \\ 51.45 \end{bmatrix} \qquad \mathbf{A} = \begin{bmatrix} 120.2695 & 117.5925 & 109.7630 & 105.4150 \\ 117.5925 & 122.5375 & 116.9150 & 112.5450 \\ 109.7630 & 116.9150 & 131.4420 & 131.9800 \\ 105.4150 & 112.5450 & 131.9800 & 141.8300 \end{bmatrix}$$

Also, $\mathbf{T}$ and $\mathbf{T}^-$ are computed to be

$$\mathbf{T} = \begin{bmatrix} 1 & 8.0 \\ 1 & 8.5 \\ 1 & 9.0 \\ 1 & 9.5 \end{bmatrix} \qquad \mathbf{T}^- = (\mathbf{T}'\mathbf{T})^{-1}\mathbf{T}' = \begin{bmatrix} 5.5 & 2.0 & -1.5 & -5.0 \\ -0.6 & -0.2 & 0.2 & 0.6 \end{bmatrix}$$

Hence we have the following:

$$\hat{\boldsymbol{\Sigma}}_0 = \begin{bmatrix} 103.9593355 & -11.5248263 \\ -11.5248263 & 1.3582358 \end{bmatrix}$$

$$\hat{\boldsymbol{\beta}} = \begin{bmatrix} 33.747 \\ 1.866 \end{bmatrix} \qquad \widehat{\mu(t)} = 33.747 + 1.866t \qquad 8 \le t \le 10$$

The 95 percent one-at-a-time confidence intervals on β_0 and β_1 are

$$\beta_0 : 33.747 \mp 2.093\sqrt{5.1980} \qquad \text{or} \qquad 28.852 \le \beta_0 \le 38.643$$

$$\beta_1 : \ 1.866 \mp 2.093\sqrt{0.0679} \qquad \text{or} \qquad 1.306 \le \beta_1 \le 2.426$$

Note 2. As we stated above, the function $\mu(t)$ can be any linear function where the functional *form* is known and it is the same functional *form* for each individual in the population. For example, $\mu(t)$ could be a polynomial of specified degree, a trigonometric function, or a combination of the two.

12.4.2 Multivariate Growth Model

In this growth model it is assumed that at each of K *specified* time points, $t_1, t_2, \ldots, t_K$, observations are made on n individuals drawn at random from a population of individuals. The observation on the jth individual is denoted by the $K \times 1$ random vector $\boldsymbol{\chi}_j$, where $\boldsymbol{\chi}_j' = [X_{1j}, X_{2j}, \ldots, X_{Kj}]$, and $\boldsymbol{\chi}_j$, for $j = 1, 2, \ldots, n$, are distributed $\mathbf{NID}(\mathbf{x} : \boldsymbol{\mu}, \boldsymbol{\Sigma})$, where $\boldsymbol{\Sigma}$ is a $K \times K$ positive definite covariance matrix with no specific structure such as in Equation (12.4.3). The mean of $\boldsymbol{\chi}_j$, namely $\boldsymbol{\mu}$, has a certain structure that determines the population growth model.

We assume the population growth model is a polynomial of degree $M - 1$ (specified) with unknown coefficients. For example, if $M = 2$, the growth curve is linear and $\boldsymbol{\mu}$ is defined by $\boldsymbol{\mu}' = [\beta_0 + \beta_1 t_1, \beta_0 + \beta_1 t_2, \ldots, \beta_0 + \beta_1 t_K]$. If $M = 3$, the growth curve is quadratic and defined by

$$\boldsymbol{\mu}' = [\beta_0 + \beta_1 t_1 + \beta_2 t_1^2, \beta_0 + \beta_1 t_2 + \beta_2 t_2^2, \ldots, \beta_0 + \beta_1 t_K + \beta_2 t_K^2]$$

If the population growth curve is cubic, the ith element of $\boldsymbol{\mu}$ is $\beta_0 + \beta_1 t_i + \beta_2 t_i^2 + \beta_3 t_i^3$. If it is quartic, the ith element of $\boldsymbol{\mu}$ is $\beta_0 + \beta_1 t_i + \beta_2 t_i^2 + \beta_3 t_i^3 + \beta_4 t_i^4$. Thus $\boldsymbol{\mu}$ can be written as $\boldsymbol{\mu} = \mathbf{T}\boldsymbol{\beta}$, where $\mathbf{T}$ is a $K \times p$ matrix, and where $\mathbf{T} = [t_{km}]$ and $t_{km} = t_k^{m-1}$ (we also require $\mathbf{T}$ to have rank p), and $p = M - 1$ if the polynomial has no constant term β_0 and $p = M$ if β_0 is present (in which case the first column of $\mathbf{T}$ has each element equal to 1).

A random sample of size n, denoted by $\boldsymbol{\chi}_1, \boldsymbol{\chi}_2, \ldots, \boldsymbol{\chi}_n$, is selected from the p.d.f. above and inferences are made about $\boldsymbol{\beta}$. We shall not discuss this model further, but the interested reader can consult [G-10] and [R-2].

12.5 Discrimination (Classification)

An investigator is sometimes faced with the following problem: It is known that an individual belongs to one of several known populations; p attributes are observed on this individual, and on the basis of these measurements, the investigator decides which of the populations the individual belongs to. We illustrate with some simple examples.

Example 12.5.1

In Example 12.2.1 suppose the director of admissions is not particularly interested in what a prospective student's grade point will be at the end of the freshman year, but instead he is interested in determining whether the prospective student will *complete* the freshman year. Thus the model the director uses is this: There are two populations of prospective students; one population consists of those who *will* finish the freshman year, and the other population consists of those who *will not*. On the basis of p observations on a prospective student, the director of admissions classifies a prospective student as belonging to one of the two populations. The p observations might be high school grade point average X_1, I.Q. X_2, the grade on a special entrance examination $X_3, \ldots$, the grade on a personality test X_p.

Example 12.5.2

An oil company drilled a wildcat well in a certain area and it turned out to be a dry hole. The company must now decide whether to drill another well or abandon the area. If another well is drilled, it will belong to one of two populations; it will be a dry well, or it will be a producer. On the basis of available information, such as depth of sand X_1, sand/shale ratio X_2, porosity X_3, and so on, the prospective well (before it is drilled) is *classified* into one of the two populations, and a decision on whether or not to drill is made.

Example 12.5.3

A doctor must decide whether a patient should undergo a series of treatments for a certain disease. The patient belongs to one of *three* populations: The population of patients for which (1) the treatments will be useful, (2) the treatments will have no effect, (3) the treatments will be harmful. On the basis of several observations, the doctor must decide to which population the patient belongs and thus decide if he should administer the treatments.

The problem will now be formally stated. There are M populations with densities denoted by $f_1(\cdot), f_2(\cdot), \ldots, f_M(\cdot)$, where each is a density of a p-variate random variable. A random observation, denoted by χ, is selected from *one* of the p.d.f.'s (it is not known from which p.d.f. the observation is selected), and on the basis of the value of the random observation, one decides which of the p.d.f.'s the observation came from. In other words, the observation is classified as having come from *one* of the specified p.d.f.'s.

In this book we discuss only the case of two populations ($M = 2$). Thus a $p \times 1$ vector sample value $\mathbf{x}_0$ is observed to have come from either $f_1(\cdot)$ or $f_2(\cdot)$. The observation space S is partitioned into two sets C_1 and C_2 (that is, $C_1 \cup C_2 = S$ and $C_1 \cap C_2 = \varnothing$) such that if $\mathbf{x}_0$ is observed to be in C_1, it is decided that it came from (will be classified into) $f_1(\cdot)$; if $\mathbf{x}_0$ is observed to be in C_2, it is decided that it came from (will be classified into) $f_2(\cdot)$.

A mistake is made if $\mathbf{x}_0$ actually came from $f_i(\cdot)$ and it is classified into $f_j(\cdot)$, where $i \neq j = 1, 2$. The conditional probabilities of misclassification are $P_{1|2}$ and $P_{2|1}$, where

$$
\begin{aligned}
P_{1|2} &= \int_{C_1} f_2(\mathbf{x})\, d\mathbf{x} \qquad \text{the probability of classifying } \mathbf{x}_0 \text{ into } f_1(\mathbf{x}) \text{ when it actually came from } f_2(\mathbf{x}) \\
P_{2|1} &= \int_{C_2} f_1(\mathbf{x})\, d\mathbf{x} \qquad \text{the probability of classifying } \mathbf{x}_0 \text{ into } f_2(\mathbf{x}) \text{ when it actually came from } f_1(\mathbf{x})
\end{aligned}
\tag{12.5.1}
$$

If p_i is the probability that an individual to be classified came from the ith p.d.f. $f_i(\cdot)$ for $i = 1, 2$, the probability of misclassification is

$$P = p_1 P_{2|1} + p_2 P_{1|2}$$

The problem is to find the sets C_1 and C_2 such that P, the probability of misclassification, is a minimum.

THEOREM 12.5.1

Let $f_1(\cdot)$ and $f_2(\cdot)$ be p.d.f.'s of p-variate continuous random variables. The probability of misclassification P is minimized if C_1 and C_2 are defined by

$$C_1 = \left\{\mathbf{x} : \frac{f_1(\mathbf{x})}{f_2(\mathbf{x})} > \frac{p_2}{p_1}\right\} \qquad C_2 = \left\{\mathbf{x} : \frac{f_1(\mathbf{x})}{f_2(\mathbf{x})} < \frac{p_2}{p_1}\right\}$$

Proof

$$P = p_1 P_{2|1} + p_2 P_{1|2} = p_1 \int_{C_2} f_1(\mathbf{x})\, d\mathbf{x} + p_2 \int_{C_1} f_2(\mathbf{x})\, d\mathbf{x}$$
$$= p_1\left(1 - \int_{C_1} f_1(\mathbf{x})\, d\mathbf{x}\right) + p_2 \int_{C_1} f_2(\mathbf{x})\, d\mathbf{x}$$
$$= p_1 + \int_{C_1} [p_2 f_2(\mathbf{x}) - p_1 f_1(\mathbf{x})]\, d\mathbf{x}$$

Thus P is minimized if C_1 is chosen so that $p_2 f_2(\mathbf{x}) - p_1 f_1(\mathbf{x}) < 0$ and C_2 is chosen so that $p_2 f_2(\mathbf{x}) - p_1 f_1(\mathbf{x}) > 0$.

For the remainder of this section, we set $p_1 = p_2$. So C_1 and C_2 are

$$C_1 = \left\{\mathbf{x} : \frac{f_1(\mathbf{x})}{f_2(\mathbf{x})} > 1\right\} \qquad C_2 = \left\{\mathbf{x} : \frac{f_2(\mathbf{x})}{f_1(\mathbf{x})} > 1\right\}$$

All formulas can be easily modified if the reader wants to consider the case where $p_2/p_1 = \rho$, where ρ is known.

Note 1. The values of $\mathbf{x}$ such that $f_1(\mathbf{x})/f_2(\mathbf{x}) = 1$ can be put into either C_1 or C_2 and the probabilities $P_{1|2}$ and $P_{2|1}$ will be unchanged, since we assume that $f_1(\cdot)$ and $f_2(\cdot)$ are p.d.f.'s of continuous random variables.

In general to determine the sets C_1 and C_2, the investigator must know $f_1(\cdot)$ and $f_2(\cdot)$. In the next theorem we discuss how to construct C_1 and C_2 when the p.d.f.'s are p-variate normals.

THEOREM 12.5.2

Let $f_1(\cdot)$ and $f_2(\cdot)$ be p-variate normal p.d.f.'s with vector means $\boldsymbol{\mu}_1$ and $\boldsymbol{\mu}_2$, respectively, and covariance matrices $\boldsymbol{\Sigma}$. Then C_1 and C_2 are defined by

$$\begin{aligned} C_1 &= \{\mathbf{x} : (\boldsymbol{\mu}_1 - \boldsymbol{\mu}_2)'\boldsymbol{\Sigma}^{-1}\mathbf{x} > \tfrac{1}{2}(\boldsymbol{\mu}_1 + \boldsymbol{\mu}_2)'\boldsymbol{\Sigma}^{-1}(\boldsymbol{\mu}_1 - \boldsymbol{\mu}_2)\} \\ C_2 &= \{\mathbf{x} : (\boldsymbol{\mu}_1 - \boldsymbol{\mu}_2)'\boldsymbol{\Sigma}^{-1}\mathbf{x} < \tfrac{1}{2}(\boldsymbol{\mu}_1 + \boldsymbol{\mu}_2)'\boldsymbol{\Sigma}^{-1}(\boldsymbol{\mu}_1 - \boldsymbol{\mu}_2)\} \end{aligned} \tag{12.5.2}$$

Proof

By Theorem 12.5.1, C_1 is defined by $C_1 = \{\mathbf{x} : f_1(\mathbf{x})/f_2(\mathbf{x}) > 1\}$. Hence

$$1 < \frac{f_1(\mathbf{x})}{f_2(\mathbf{x})} = \frac{(2\pi)^{-p/2}|\boldsymbol{\Sigma}|^{-1/2}\exp\{-\frac{1}{2}(\mathbf{x} - \boldsymbol{\mu}_1)'\boldsymbol{\Sigma}^{-1}(\mathbf{x} - \boldsymbol{\mu}_1)\}}{(2\pi)^{-p/2}|\boldsymbol{\Sigma}|^{-1/2}\exp\{-\frac{1}{2}(\mathbf{x} - \boldsymbol{\mu}_2)'\boldsymbol{\Sigma}^{-1}(\mathbf{x} - \boldsymbol{\mu}_2)\}}$$

Simplifying gives the result for C_1. Reversing the inequality gives C_2.

The regions in Equation (12.5.2) are not usable in an applied problem since a knowledge of the unknown parameters $\boldsymbol{\mu}$ and $\boldsymbol{\Sigma}$ is required. A procedure that is often used in this case is to select a random sample that is known to have come from $f_1(\cdot)$ and a random sample that is known to have come from $f_2(\cdot)$, and from these observations estimates of $\boldsymbol{\mu}_1$, $\boldsymbol{\mu}_2$, and $\boldsymbol{\Sigma}^{-1}$ are computed. The resulting "estimated" C_1 and C_2 are used for classification. These ideas are formalized in the following classification procedure.

CLASSIFICATION PROCEDURE

Let $\mathbf{y}_1, \mathbf{y}_2, \ldots, \mathbf{y}_{n_1}$ $(n_1 > p)$ *be a random sample of* $p \times 1$ *vectors from the distribution* $\mathrm{N}(\mathbf{y} : \boldsymbol{\mu}_1, \boldsymbol{\Sigma})$; *let* $\mathbf{z}_1, \mathbf{z}_2, \ldots, \mathbf{z}_{n_2}$ $(n_2 > p)$ *be a random sample of* $p \times 1$ *vectors from the distribution* $\mathrm{N}(\mathbf{z} : \boldsymbol{\mu}_2, \boldsymbol{\Sigma})$. *Then*

$$\hat{\boldsymbol{\mu}}_1 = \bar{\mathbf{y}} \qquad \hat{\boldsymbol{\mu}}_2 = \bar{\mathbf{z}}$$

$$\hat{\boldsymbol{\Sigma}} = (n_1 + n_2 - 2)^{-1}\left[\sum_{i=1}^{n_1} (\mathbf{y}_i - \bar{\mathbf{y}})(\mathbf{y}_i - \bar{\mathbf{y}})' + \sum_{j=1}^{n_2} (\mathbf{z}_j - \bar{\mathbf{z}})(\mathbf{z}_j - \bar{\mathbf{z}})'\right]$$

are M.L. estimates of $\boldsymbol{\mu}_1, \boldsymbol{\mu}_2$, *and* $\boldsymbol{\Sigma}$ *(corrected for bias), respectively. An observation* $\mathbf{x}_0$ *which is known to come from one of the two normal p.d.f.'s (but it is not known from which of the two it came) is classified by the following rule:*

$$\begin{aligned} &\mathbf{x}_0 \text{ is classified into } \mathrm{N}(\mathbf{y} : \boldsymbol{\mu}_1, \boldsymbol{\Sigma}) \text{ if } (\bar{\mathbf{y}} - \bar{\mathbf{z}})'\hat{\boldsymbol{\Sigma}}^{-1}\mathbf{x}_0 > \tfrac{1}{2}(\bar{\mathbf{y}} + \bar{\mathbf{z}})'\hat{\boldsymbol{\Sigma}}^{-1}(\bar{\mathbf{y}} - \bar{\mathbf{z}}) \\ &\mathbf{x}_0 \text{ is classified into } \mathrm{N}(\mathbf{z} : \boldsymbol{\mu}_2, \boldsymbol{\Sigma}) \text{ if } (\bar{\mathbf{y}} - \bar{\mathbf{z}})'\hat{\boldsymbol{\Sigma}}^{-1}\mathbf{x}_0 < \tfrac{1}{2}(\bar{\mathbf{y}} + \bar{\mathbf{z}})'\hat{\boldsymbol{\Sigma}}^{-1}(\bar{\mathbf{y}} - \bar{\mathbf{z}}) \end{aligned} \tag{12.5.3}$$

> ***Note 2.*** This method is sometimes referred to as "the plug in" method, that is, the estimates are merely "plugged in" or substituted for the unknown parameters in Equation (12.5.2).

> ***Note 3.*** The operating characteristics of the classification procedure in Equation (12.5.3) are not known for finite size samples.

A classification procedure proposed by R. A. Fisher is to calculate a sample *linear* function $\ell(\mathbf{x}) = \boldsymbol{\lambda}'\mathbf{x}$ and a number d_0 such that if $\boldsymbol{\lambda}'\mathbf{x}_0 > d_0$, the observation $\mathbf{x}_0$ is classified as belonging to $f_1(\cdot)$, and if $\boldsymbol{\lambda}'\mathbf{x}_0 < d_0$, the observation $\mathbf{x}_0$ is classified as belonging to $f_2(\cdot)$. The coefficient vector $\boldsymbol{\lambda}$ and the number d_0 are computed from data that are known to have come from $f_1(\cdot)$ and $f_2(\cdot)$, respectively. The function $\boldsymbol{\lambda}'\mathbf{x}$ is generally referred to as a "linear" discriminant function. The procedure for calculating $\boldsymbol{\lambda}$ is as follows:

1. A random sample (of size n_1) of $p \times 1$ vectors is selected from $f_1(\cdot)$ and denoted by $\mathbf{y}_1, \mathbf{y}_2, \ldots, \mathbf{y}_{n_1}$; let $\bar{\mathbf{y}}$ denote the sample mean and let $\mathbf{A}_y = \sum_{i=1}^{n_1} (\mathbf{y}_i - \bar{\mathbf{y}})(\mathbf{y}_i - \bar{\mathbf{y}})'$.

2. A random sample (of size n_2) of $p \times 1$ vectors is selected from $f_2(\cdot)$ and denoted by $\mathbf{z}_1, \mathbf{z}_2, \ldots, \mathbf{z}_{n_2}$; let $\bar{\mathbf{z}}$ denote the sample mean and let $\mathbf{A}_z = \sum_{i=1}^{n_2} (\mathbf{z}_i - \bar{\mathbf{z}})(\mathbf{z}_i - \bar{\mathbf{z}})'$.

3. On the basis of these $n_1 + n_2$ observations, the vector $\boldsymbol{\lambda}$ is determined such that $q(\boldsymbol{\lambda}) = (\boldsymbol{\lambda}'\bar{\mathbf{y}} - \boldsymbol{\lambda}'\bar{\mathbf{z}})^2/\boldsymbol{\lambda}'\mathbf{S}\boldsymbol{\lambda}$ is a maximum, where $\mathbf{S} = (n_1 + n_2 - 2)^{-1}(\mathbf{A}_y + \mathbf{A}_z) = \hat{\boldsymbol{\Sigma}}$. (12.5.4)

THEOREM 12.5.3

Under the conditions of Equation (12.5.4), *the value of* $\boldsymbol{\lambda}$ *that maximizes* $q(\boldsymbol{\lambda})$ *is* $\hat{\boldsymbol{\lambda}} = k\mathbf{S}^{-1}(\bar{\mathbf{y}} - \bar{\mathbf{z}})$, *where k can be any nonzero constant* (*so we let* $k = 1$).

Proof

We can write $q(\boldsymbol{\lambda})$ as $\boldsymbol{\lambda}'[(\bar{\mathbf{y}} - \bar{\mathbf{z}})(\bar{\mathbf{y}} - \bar{\mathbf{z}})']\boldsymbol{\lambda}/\boldsymbol{\lambda}'\mathbf{S}\boldsymbol{\lambda} = \boldsymbol{\lambda}'\mathbf{B}\boldsymbol{\lambda}/\boldsymbol{\lambda}'\mathbf{S}\boldsymbol{\lambda}$, say, where S is a positive definite matrix, and the result is a direct application of Theorem 6.11.1.

Note 4. The fact that we set k equal to $+1$ implies $\hat{\boldsymbol{\lambda}}'\bar{\mathbf{y}} \geq \hat{\boldsymbol{\lambda}}'\bar{\mathbf{z}}$, otherwise $(\bar{\mathbf{y}} - \bar{\mathbf{z}})'\mathbf{S}^{-1}(\bar{\mathbf{y}} - \bar{\mathbf{z}}) < 0$, which is impossible since $\mathbf{S}^{-1}$ is p.d.

Note 5. The rationale for using the value of $\boldsymbol{\lambda}$ that maximizes $q(\boldsymbol{\lambda})$ for the coefficient vector in the linear discriminant function can be argued by noting that since $\bar{\mathbf{y}}$ is the mean of the sample vectors from $f_1(\cdot)$ and $\bar{\mathbf{z}}$ is the mean of the sample vectors from $f_2(\cdot)$, then $(\boldsymbol{\lambda}'\bar{\mathbf{y}} - \boldsymbol{\lambda}'\bar{\mathbf{z}})^2$ should be as large as possible if $\boldsymbol{\lambda}'\mathbf{x}$ is a "good" function for deciding whether $\mathbf{x}$ came from $f_1(\cdot)$ or from $f_2(\cdot)$, that is, for discriminating between the two p.d.f.'s. But the quantity $(\boldsymbol{\lambda}'\bar{\mathbf{y}} - \boldsymbol{\lambda}'\bar{\mathbf{z}})^2$ must be normalized or else its maximum value is $+\infty$. A logical normalizing factor is the variance of $\boldsymbol{\lambda}'\boldsymbol{\chi}$, which is $\boldsymbol{\lambda}'\boldsymbol{\Sigma}\boldsymbol{\lambda}$. We substitute an estimate of $\boldsymbol{\Sigma}$, namely S, and use $\boldsymbol{\lambda}'\mathbf{S}\boldsymbol{\lambda}$ as the normalizing factor.

Note 6. For d_0 we use the number $\frac{1}{2}(\bar{\mathbf{y}} + \bar{\mathbf{z}})'\mathbf{S}^{-1}(\bar{\mathbf{y}} - \bar{\mathbf{z}})$.

Note 7. The rationale for the number d_0 is as follows: Let $\mathbf{x}_0$ be the observed value of a sample (or the mean of a sample of size n) from either $f_1(\cdot)$ or $f_2(\cdot)$, but it is not known from which p.d.f. it came. Recall that $\boldsymbol{\lambda}'\bar{\mathbf{y}} \geq \boldsymbol{\lambda}'\bar{\mathbf{z}}$, and note that $M = \frac{1}{2}(\boldsymbol{\lambda}'\bar{\mathbf{y}} + \boldsymbol{\lambda}'\bar{\mathbf{z}})$ is the point halfway between $\boldsymbol{\lambda}'\bar{\mathbf{y}}$ and $\boldsymbol{\lambda}'\bar{\mathbf{z}}$.

1. If $\boldsymbol{\lambda}'\mathbf{x}_0 > \frac{1}{2}\boldsymbol{\lambda}'(\bar{\mathbf{y}} + \bar{\mathbf{z}})$, the observation $\mathbf{x}_0$ is classified into $f_1(\cdot)$.
2. If $\boldsymbol{\lambda}'\mathbf{x}_0 < \frac{1}{2}\boldsymbol{\lambda}'(\bar{\mathbf{y}} + \bar{\mathbf{z}})$, the observation $\mathbf{x}_0$ is classified into $f_2(\cdot)$.

The inequality in 1 implies that $\mathbf{x}_0$ is "closer" to $\bar{\mathbf{y}}$ than it is to $\bar{\mathbf{z}}$ and hence we should classify $\mathbf{x}_0$ as being from the same p.d.f. as $\bar{\mathbf{y}}$, that is, from $f_1(\cdot)$. In 2 $\mathbf{x}_0$ is "closer" to $\bar{\mathbf{z}}$ than it is to $\bar{\mathbf{y}}$ so we should classify $\mathbf{x}_0$ as being from the same p.d.f. as $\bar{\mathbf{z}}$, namely $f_2(\cdot)$. If we substitute $\hat{\boldsymbol{\lambda}}$ from Theorem 12.5.3 into 1 and 2, we get

1. If $(\bar{\mathbf{y}} - \bar{\mathbf{z}})'\mathbf{S}^{-1}\mathbf{x}_0 > \frac{1}{2}(\bar{\mathbf{y}} + \bar{\mathbf{z}})'\mathbf{S}^{-1}(\bar{\mathbf{y}} - \bar{\mathbf{z}})$, classify $\mathbf{x}_0$ into $f_1(\cdot)$.
2. If $(\bar{\mathbf{y}} - \bar{\mathbf{z}})'\mathbf{S}^{-1}\mathbf{x}_0 < \frac{1}{2}(\bar{\mathbf{y}} + \bar{\mathbf{z}})'\mathbf{S}^{-1}(\bar{\mathbf{y}} - \bar{\mathbf{z}})$, classify $\mathbf{x}_0$ into $f_2(\cdot)$. (12.5.5)

Hence $d_0 = \frac{1}{2}(\bar{\mathbf{y}} + \bar{\mathbf{z}})'\mathbf{S}^{-1}(\bar{\mathbf{y}} - \bar{\mathbf{z}})$.

Note 8. $\hat{\boldsymbol{\lambda}}'\mathbf{x}$ is called Fisher's sample linear discriminant function.

Note 9. Classification by Fisher's sample linear discriminant function is the same as the more general procedure discussed in Theorem 12.5.2 and stated in Equation (12.5.3) when $f_1(\cdot)$ and $f_2(\cdot)$ are p-variate normal p.d.f.'s with the same covariance matrix.

To compute the quantities needed for the sample linear discriminant function, the square root procedure can be used. First compute the $p \times 1$ mean vectors $\bar{\mathbf{y}}$ and $\bar{\mathbf{z}}$ and the $p \times p$ matrix $\mathbf{S}$ by 1, 2, and 3 of Equation (12.5.4). Also compute the observed vector $\mathbf{x}_0$ that is to be classified into population 1 or 2. Use the format below, where $\mathbf{S}$ is reduced to an upper triangular matrix by the square root procedure.

$$\left[\begin{array}{c|c|c|c} \mathbf{S} & \bar{\mathbf{y}} - \bar{\mathbf{z}} & \bar{\mathbf{y}} + \bar{\mathbf{z}} & \mathbf{x}_0 \\ \hline \mathbf{T} & \mathbf{t}_1 & \mathbf{t}_2 & \mathbf{t}_3 \end{array}\right] \tag{12.5.6}$$

$\hat{\boldsymbol{\lambda}}$ in Theorem 12.5.3 is the backward solution to $[\mathbf{T} \mid \mathbf{t}_1]$. The linear discriminant function is

$$\ell(\mathbf{x}) = \sum_{i=1}^{p} \hat{\lambda}_i x_i = \hat{\boldsymbol{\lambda}}'\mathbf{x} \tag{12.5.7}$$

The number d_0 is computed by

$$d_0 = \tfrac{1}{2}\mathbf{t}_1'\mathbf{t}_2 \tag{12.5.8}$$

Also, $\mathbf{x}_0$ is classified by Equation (12.5.5) into $f_1(\cdot)$ if and only if $\mathbf{t}_1'\mathbf{t}_3 > d_0$, that is, if and only if $\mathbf{t}_1'\mathbf{t}_3 > \frac{1}{2}\mathbf{t}_1'\mathbf{t}_2$. Otherwise $\mathbf{x}_0$ is classified into $f_2(\cdot)$. If one wanted to obtain the linear discriminant function and d_0 but not classify an observed mean vector $\mathbf{x}_0$, one would omit the last column in Equation (12.5.6).

Example 12.5.4

Link [L-13] used four factors, denoted by G_1, G_2, G_3, G_4, to see if they could be used effectively to discriminate between two types of water (clear water or water abundant in algae). We will present no subject matter details here; we use the example only for illustrative purposes.

It is assumed that a random sample of size 15 was selected from the 4-variate distribution $N(\mathbf{y} : \boldsymbol{\mu}_1, \Sigma)$, and a random sample of size 15 was selected from the 4-variate distribution $N(\mathbf{z} : \boldsymbol{\mu}_2, \Sigma)$. The observed samples are shown in the table below.

The following were computed from the data.

$$\bar{\mathbf{y}} = \begin{bmatrix} -63.93 \\ 5.94 \\ 1.68 \\ 1.12 \end{bmatrix} \qquad \mathbf{A}_y = \begin{bmatrix} 263{,}988.9333 & -654.5860 & -184.2947 & -19.3300 \\ -654.5860 & 21.6146 & -7.6842 & 1.3910 \\ -184.2947 & -7.6842 & 7.1656 & -2.5842 \\ -19.3300 & 1.3910 & -2.5842 & 2.3406 \end{bmatrix}$$

$$\bar{\mathbf{z}} = \begin{bmatrix} -169.67 \\ 6.02 \\ 2.54 \\ 2.13 \end{bmatrix} \qquad \mathbf{A}_z = \begin{bmatrix} 144{,}565.3333 & 1341.2267 & -335.7000 & -301.0467 \\ 1341.2267 & 27.6211 & -4.9088 & -5.9925 \\ -335.7000 & -4.9088 & 14.7540 & 8.2246 \\ -301.0467 & -5.9925 & 8.2246 & 7.7878 \end{bmatrix}$$

Samples from Population 1	*Samples from Population* 2
$\mathbf{y}_1' = [-261, 7.56, 0.82, 1.30]$	$\mathbf{z}_1' = [48, 7.92, 1.68, 1.08]$
$\mathbf{y}_2' = [110, 4.44, 2.31, 0.94]$	$\mathbf{z}_2' = [-76, 7.97, 2.17, 0.97]$
$\mathbf{y}_3' = [83, 4.30, 2.51, 0.56]$	$\mathbf{z}_3' = [-383, 5.42, 2.12, 1.51]$
$\mathbf{y}_4' = [-45, 4.28, 2.14, 0.79]$	$\mathbf{z}_4' = [-225, 4.89, 1.37, 1.78]$
$\mathbf{y}_5' = [-214, 6.56, 2.41, 0.10]$	$\mathbf{z}_5' = [-193, 4.60, 1.70, 1.60]$
$\mathbf{y}_6' = [0, 7.08, 0.13, 1.57]$	$\mathbf{z}_6' = [-224, 4.34, 2.01, 1.64]$
$\mathbf{y}_7' = [-158, 5.53, 2.38, 1.01]$	$\mathbf{z}_7' = [-214, 4.74, 3.14, 2.79]$
$\mathbf{y}_8' = [-107, 5.86, 1.93, 1.13]$	$\mathbf{z}_8' = [-235, 4.80, 3.16, 2.84]$
$\mathbf{y}_9' = [-264, 7.22, 1.90, 1.20]$	$\mathbf{z}_9' = [-170, 6.92, 2.85, 2.86]$
$\mathbf{y}_{10}' = [43, 6.29, 1.91, 1.21]$	$\mathbf{z}_{10}' = [-213, 6.10, 3.52, 2.72]$
$\mathbf{y}_{11}' = [104, 5.65, 0.78, 1.41]$	$\mathbf{z}_{11}' = [-157, 5.86, 2.90, 2.22]$
$\mathbf{y}_{12}' = [74, 5.86, 1.52, 1.13]$	$\mathbf{z}_{12}' = [-79, 5.42, 2.31, 2.91]$
$\mathbf{y}_{13}' = [34, 8.36, 0.88, 1.23]$	$\mathbf{z}_{13}' = [-36, 8.93, 1.22, 1.33]$
$\mathbf{y}_{14}' = [-200, 4.86, 1.93, 1.55]$	$\mathbf{z}_{14}' = [-214, 6.86, 2.59, 2.43]$
$\mathbf{y}_{15}' = [-158, 5.19, 1.72, 1.67]$	$\mathbf{z}_{15}' = [-174, 5.54, 5.30, 3.20]$

From these quantities we compute $\mathbf{S}$, $\bar{\mathbf{y}} - \bar{\mathbf{z}}$, and $\bar{\mathbf{y}} + \bar{\mathbf{z}}$, and evaluate the necessary quantities by the square root method described by the setup in Equation (12.5.6). We get

$$\left[\frac{\mathbf{S} \mid \bar{\mathbf{y}} - \bar{\mathbf{z}} \mid \bar{\mathbf{y}} \times \bar{\mathbf{z}}}{\mathbf{T} \mid \quad \mathbf{t}_1 \quad \mid \quad \mathbf{t}_2}\right] =$$

14591.22381000	24.52288095	−18.5712381000	−11.44202381	105.73333333	−233.60000000
24.52288095	1.758416190	−0.4497492857	−0.164337619	−0.08466667	11.95666667
−18.57123810	−0.4497492857	0.7828404762	0.2014435714	−0.85133333	4.22066667
−11.44202381	−0.1643376190	0.2014435714	0.3617276190	−1.00533333	3.24533333
120.79413814	0.20301383	−0.15374288	−0.09472334	0.87531841	−1.93386868
	1.31042038	−0.31939167	−0.11073353	−0.20021698	9.42389858
		0.81067414	0.18689774	−0.96303429	8.55246577
			0.55277702	−1.38320160	4.53574545

From $[\mathbf{T} \mid \mathbf{t}_1]$ we perform the backward solution to obtain $\hat{\lambda}_i$, the coefficients of the linear discriminant function. The solution yields

$$\hat{\lambda}_1 = 0.0054 \qquad \hat{\lambda}_2 = -0.5132 \qquad \hat{\lambda}_3 = -0.6111 \qquad \hat{\lambda}_4 = -2.5023$$

and the discriminant function is

$$\ell(\mathbf{x}) = 0.0054x_1 - 0.5132x_2 - 0.6111x_3 - 2.5023x_4$$

and

$$d_0 = \tfrac{1}{2}\mathbf{t}_1'\mathbf{t}_2 = -9.0449$$

It would be useful to be able to determine if the discrimination procedure is effective. If we assume normal p.d.f.'s, we want to determine whether the quantity $(\boldsymbol{\mu}_1 - \boldsymbol{\mu}_2)'\boldsymbol{\Sigma}^{-1}\mathbf{x}$ is quite different when $\bar{\mathbf{y}}$, the mean of a sample from $f_1(\cdot)$, is substituted for $\mathbf{x}$ than when $\bar{\mathbf{z}}$, the mean of a random sample from $f_2(\cdot)$, is substituted for $\mathbf{x}$. Thus the procedure will be considered effective if "on the average" $(\boldsymbol{\mu}_1 - \boldsymbol{\mu}_2)'\boldsymbol{\Sigma}^{-1}\bar{\mathbf{Y}}$ is different from $(\boldsymbol{\mu}_1 - \boldsymbol{\mu}_2)\boldsymbol{\Sigma}^{-1}\bar{\mathbf{Z}}$; that is, if

$$\mathscr{E}[(\boldsymbol{\mu}_1 - \boldsymbol{\mu}_2)'\boldsymbol{\Sigma}^{-1}\bar{\mathbf{Y}} - (\boldsymbol{\mu}_1 - \boldsymbol{\mu}_2)\boldsymbol{\Sigma}^{-1}\bar{\mathbf{Z}}]$$

is not zero, or, in other words, if

$$(\boldsymbol{\mu}_1 - \boldsymbol{\mu}_2)'\boldsymbol{\Sigma}^{-1}(\boldsymbol{\mu}_1 - \boldsymbol{\mu}_2) \neq 0$$

But this quantity is different from zero if and only if $\boldsymbol{\mu}_1 - \boldsymbol{\mu}_2 \neq \mathbf{0}$ since $\boldsymbol{\Sigma}$ and hence $\boldsymbol{\Sigma}^{-1}$ are p.d.

A test that could be used to determine if the discrimination procedure in Theorem 12.5.2 is useful is a test of $H_0 : \boldsymbol{\mu}_1 = \boldsymbol{\mu}_2$ *vs.* $H_a : \boldsymbol{\mu}_1 \neq \boldsymbol{\mu}_2$, based on a random sample $\mathbf{Y}_1, \mathbf{Y}_2, \ldots, \mathbf{Y}_{n_1}$ from the p.d.f. $\mathbf{N}(\mathbf{y} : \boldsymbol{\mu}_1, \boldsymbol{\Sigma})$ and a random sample

$\mathbf{Z}_1, \mathbf{Z}_2, \ldots, \mathbf{Z}_{n_2}$ from the p.d.f. $N(\mathbf{z} : \boldsymbol{\mu}_2, \Sigma)$. This test is described in Theorem 9.4.3. If the test rejects H_0 and hence suggests that the classifying function is effective, then an investigator may want to determine whether *certain* factors are important in classifying.

For additional information on this topic, see [L-2] and [R-3].

Another topic of interest in classification problems is that of estimating, on the basis of the data from the investigation, the probabilities of *misclassification*. A crude but simple way of estimating these probabilities is to evaluate $\hat{\boldsymbol{\lambda}}'\mathbf{y}_i$ for $i = 1, 2, \ldots, n_1$ for the observed sample and estimate $P_{2|1}$ as $\hat{P}_{2|1} =$ (number of the $\boldsymbol{\lambda}'\mathbf{y}_i$ less than $d_0)/n_1$ = the proportion of the observed sample from population 1 that is classified into population 2. To estimate $P_{1|2}$ one could use $\hat{P}_{1|2} =$ (number of the $\boldsymbol{\lambda}'\mathbf{z}_i$ greater than $d_0)/n_2$ = the proportion of the observed sample from population 2 that is classified into population 1. For the data in Example 12.5.4, we get $\hat{P}_{2|1} = \frac{1}{15}$ and $\hat{P}_{1|2} = \frac{6}{15}$. For additional information on the probabilities of misclassification, the interested reader can consult [B-10], [L-2], [L-3], and the references listed therein.

Problems

12.1. Prove Corollary 12.2.1.2.

12.2. Prove Theorem 12.2.2.

12.3. Prove Corollary 12.2.3.

12.4. A random sample of size 20 is selected from the p.d.f. $N(\mathbf{x}^* : \boldsymbol{\mu}^*, \Sigma^*)$, where $\mathbf{x}^* = [x_0, x_1, x_2, x_3]'$. $\mathbf{A}^*$ and $\bar{\mathbf{x}}^*$ were computed and are given below.

$$\mathbf{A}^* = \begin{bmatrix} 4.41 & 3.36 & 2.73 & 0.42 \\ 3.36 & 3.56 & 2.48 & 0.42 \\ 2.73 & 2.48 & 1.94 & 0.54 \\ 0.42 & 0.42 & 0.54 & 1.50 \end{bmatrix} \qquad \bar{\mathbf{x}}^* = \begin{bmatrix} 6.1 \\ 2.0 \\ 0.8 \\ 1.3 \end{bmatrix}$$

Find the UMVU estimate of the best prediction function of X_0 based on X_1, X_2, and X_3.

12.5. In Problem 12.4 find the UMVU estimate of the error of the best prediction function.

12.6. In Problem 12.4 find the M.L. estimate of the relative error of the best prediction function.

12.7. Let the 4×1 vector $\boldsymbol{\chi}'^* = [X_0, X_1, X_2, X_3]$ be distributed $N(\mathbf{x}^* : \boldsymbol{\mu}^*, \Sigma^*)$. A random sample of size 30 is selected from this distribution and the sample values are denoted by $\mathbf{x}_1^*, \mathbf{x}_2^*, \ldots, \mathbf{x}_{30}^*$. The following is computed.

$$\hat{\boldsymbol{\Sigma}}^* = \begin{bmatrix} 16.81 & 13.12 & 4.51 & 5.74 \\ 13.12 & 14.24 & 5.92 & 9.08 \\ 4.51 & 5.92 & 14.21 & 14.16 \\ 5.74 & 9.08 & 14.16 & 17.91 \end{bmatrix} = \left(\frac{1}{29}\right) \sum_{i=1}^{30} (\mathbf{x}_i^* - \bar{\mathbf{x}}^*)(\mathbf{x}_i^* - \bar{\mathbf{x}}^*)'$$

Compute estimates of the squares of the multiple correlation coefficients of X_0 with all possible subsets of the variables X_1, X_2, and X_3.

12.8. In Problem 12.7 compute C_{ij} for $i = 1, 2, 3, 4$ and each j.

12.9. In Problem 12.7 arrange the factors 1, 2, and 3 in order of importance by the forward selection procedure.

12.10. In Problem 12.7 arrange the factors 1, 2, and 3 in order of importance by the backward elimination procedure.

12.11. In Problem 12.4 arrange the factors in order of importance by the backward elimination procedure. Exhibit all correlation coefficients that are used.

12.12. In Problem 12.4 arrange the factors in order of importance by the forward selection procedure. Exhibit all correlation coefficients that are used.

12.13. In Problem 12.4 compute the C_{ij} and plot them.

12.14. In Problem 12.11 use an appropriate test at each step to decide the important factors, and then compute the resulting "best" prediction function.

12.15. In Problem 12.12 use an appropriate test at each step to decide the important factors, and then compute the resulting "best" prediction function.

12.16. Prove the statements in Equation (12.4.3).

12.17. Prove parts (3) and (4) of Theorem 12.4.3.

12.18. In Example 12.4.5 use only the first 15 individuals and compute $\mathbf{A}$ and $\bar{\mathbf{x}}$.

12.19. In Problem 12.18 compute $\hat{\boldsymbol{\beta}}$, $\hat{\boldsymbol{\Sigma}}_0$, and $\hat{\mu}(t)$.

12.20. In Problem 12.18 set 90 percent one-at-a-time confidence limits on β_0 and β_1.

12.21. Work through the details of the proof of Theorem 12.5.1.

12.22. Prove that $\hat{\boldsymbol{\lambda}}$ in Equation (12.5.7) is indeed the backward solution of $[\mathbf{T} | \mathbf{t}_1]$ in Equation (12.5.6).

12.23. Prove that d_0 in Equation (12.5.5) is given by $d_0 = \frac{1}{2}\mathbf{t}_1'\mathbf{t}_2$.

12.24. In Example 12.5.4 use the first 12 observations in population 1 and all 15 observations in population 2 to compute $\bar{\mathbf{y}}$, $\mathbf{A}_\mathbf{y}$, and $\mathbf{S}$.

12.25. In Problem 12.24 find the best linear discriminant function.

12.26. In Problem 12.24 test whether the discriminant function is effective.

12.27. In Problem 12.24 estimate the probabilities of misclassification $P_{2|1}$ and $P_{1|2}$.

CHAPTER 13

Design Models

13.1 Introduction

The design model has been discussed and defined in Section 5.4. Here we shall restate the definition but the examples in Section 5.4 can be consulted for additional details. In this chapter we discuss the general theory of design models and a special case—the one-factor design model. We shall also use a two-factor model for illustrative purposes, but Chapter 14 is devoted to a detailed discussion of that model.

DEFINITION 13.1.1

Design Model. *Consider the general linear model* $\mathbf{Y} = \mathbf{X}\boldsymbol{\beta} + \boldsymbol{\varepsilon}$, *where* $\mathbf{Y}$ *is an observable* $n \times 1$ *random vector,* $\mathbf{X}$ *is an* $n \times p$ *matrix of rank* K *of observable nonrandom variables (where* $n > p \geq K$*),* $\boldsymbol{\beta}$ *is a* $p \times 1$ *vector of unknown parameters, and* $\boldsymbol{\varepsilon}$ *is an* $n \times 1$ *nonobservable random vector. This model is defined to be a design model if and only if the elements of* $\mathbf{X}$ *consist of the numbers* 0 *and* 1 *and* $\mathbf{X}$ *has a certain pattern that will be defined later (in Definition* 13.5.1).

> ***Note 1.*** If $p = K$, this model is the general linear model and all the theory in Chapter 6 applies. However, K will be less than p for most cases that we consider, and this presents new problems. Even when $K = p$, some special computing formulas can be derived by taking advantage of the pattern of $\mathbf{X}$ and the fact that its elements consist of only the numbers 0 and 1.

We discuss this model for two sets of assumptions about the distribution of the error term $\boldsymbol{\varepsilon}$.

Case I: $\boldsymbol{\varepsilon}$ is distributed $N(\boldsymbol{\varepsilon} : \mathbf{0}, \sigma^2\mathbf{I})$.

Case II: $\boldsymbol{\varepsilon}$ is distributed $(\boldsymbol{\varepsilon} : \mathbf{0}, \sigma^2\mathbf{I})$.

Some special cases of I and II will also be discussed.

We are interested in point and interval estimators of the elements of $\boldsymbol{\beta}$ and σ^2, and in tests of hypotheses about these parameters. In Sections 13.2 and 13.3, respectively, we discuss point estimation for Cases I and II. Section 13.4 is devoted to confidence intervals and tests of hypotheses for Case I; Section 13.5 is devoted to computing for the design model; Section 13.6 is devoted to the one-factor design model; and the final section is devoted to additional comments about inference for Case I.

13.2 Point Estimation for the Design Model; Case I

The assumptions for the design model to be discussed in this section are summarized below.

1. $\mathbf{Y} = \mathbf{X}\boldsymbol{\beta} + \boldsymbol{\varepsilon}$, $\boldsymbol{\varepsilon}$ is distributed $N(\boldsymbol{\varepsilon} : \mathbf{0}, \sigma^2\mathbf{I})$.
2. $\mathbf{X}$ has size $n \times p$ and rank K, where $n > p > K$.
3. The parameter space is $\Omega = \{(\boldsymbol{\beta}, \sigma^2) : \boldsymbol{\beta} \in E_p, \sigma^2 > 0\}$. (13.2.1)

This model is sometimes referred to as a general linear model of less than full rank (since $K < p$).

For point estimation we shall attempt to find M.L. estimators of $\boldsymbol{\beta}$ and σ^2. The likelihood function is

$$L(\boldsymbol{\beta}, \sigma^2 : \mathbf{y}; \mathbf{X}) = n(\mathbf{y} : \mathbf{X}\boldsymbol{\beta}, \sigma^2\mathbf{I}) = (2\pi\sigma^2)^{-n/2} \exp\left[-\frac{1}{2\sigma^2}(\mathbf{y} - \mathbf{X}\boldsymbol{\beta})'(\mathbf{y} - \mathbf{X}\boldsymbol{\beta})\right]$$

If we set to zero the derivatives of $\log[L(\boldsymbol{\beta}, \sigma^2 : \mathbf{y}; \mathbf{X})]$ with respect to $\boldsymbol{\beta}$ and σ^2, we get

$$\frac{\partial}{\partial \boldsymbol{\beta}} \log[L(\boldsymbol{\beta}, \sigma^2 : \mathbf{y}; \mathbf{X})] = -\frac{1}{2\sigma^2}[2\mathbf{X}'\mathbf{X}\boldsymbol{\beta} - 2\mathbf{X}'\mathbf{y}] = \mathbf{0}$$

$$\frac{\partial}{\partial \sigma^2} \log[L(\boldsymbol{\beta}, \sigma^2 : \mathbf{y}; \mathbf{X})] = -\frac{n}{2\sigma^2} + \frac{1}{2\sigma^4}(\mathbf{y} - \mathbf{X}\boldsymbol{\beta})'(\mathbf{y} - \mathbf{X}\boldsymbol{\beta}) = 0$$

If we let $\tilde{\boldsymbol{\beta}}$ and $\tilde{\sigma}^2$ denote the values of the parameters that are solutions to these equations, we get

$$\mathbf{X}'\mathbf{X}\tilde{\boldsymbol{\beta}} = \mathbf{X}'\mathbf{y} \qquad \tilde{\sigma}^2 = \frac{1}{n}(\mathbf{y}'\mathbf{y} - \tilde{\boldsymbol{\beta}}'\mathbf{X}'\mathbf{y}) \tag{13.2.2}$$

Here we encounter a problem. The $p \times p$ matrix $\mathbf{X}'\mathbf{X}$ has rank $K < p$, and hence the inverse of $\mathbf{X}'\mathbf{X}$ does not exist. The normal equations are consistent if and only if $(\mathbf{X}'\mathbf{X})(\mathbf{X}'\mathbf{X})^c\mathbf{X}'\mathbf{y} = \mathbf{X}'\mathbf{y}$ (see Theorem 1.6.3). But by Theorem 1.5.25, $\mathbf{X}'[\mathbf{X}(\mathbf{X}'\mathbf{X})^c\mathbf{X}'] = \mathbf{X}'$, and hence the normal equations are indeed consistent. Thus the general solutions for $\tilde{\boldsymbol{\beta}}$ and $\tilde{\sigma}^2$ are

$$\begin{aligned} \tilde{\boldsymbol{\beta}} &= (\mathbf{X}'\mathbf{X})^c\mathbf{X}'\mathbf{y} + [\mathbf{I} - (\mathbf{X}'\mathbf{X})^c(\mathbf{X}'\mathbf{X})]\mathbf{b} \qquad \text{for all } \mathbf{b} \text{ in } E_p \\ \tilde{\sigma}^2 &= \frac{1}{n}[\mathbf{y}'\mathbf{y} - \mathbf{y}'\mathbf{X}(\mathbf{X}'\mathbf{X})^c\mathbf{X}'\mathbf{y}] = \left(\frac{1}{n}\right)\mathbf{y}'[\mathbf{I} - \mathbf{X}(\mathbf{X}'\mathbf{X})^c\mathbf{X}']\mathbf{y} \end{aligned} \tag{13.2.3}$$

Thus there are an infinite number of solutions to Equation (13.2.2), and it can be shown, by a method very similar to the one used in the proof of Theorem 9.3.1, that each solution does indeed maximize the likelihood function. This implies that there is no *unique* maximum likelihood estimator for all of the parameters $\beta_1, \beta_2, \ldots, \beta_p$ and σ^2 in the design model (since $K < p$).

However, there may be unique M.L. estimators for *some* of the parameters or for certain *functions* of the parameters. In fact, it is clear that any solution for $\tilde{\boldsymbol{\beta}}$ in Equation (13.2.2) leads to a unique solution for $\tilde{\sigma}^2$ given in Equation (13.2.3). Hence $\tilde{\sigma}^2 = n^{-1}\mathbf{Y}'[\mathbf{I} - \mathbf{X}(\mathbf{X}'\mathbf{X})^c\mathbf{X}']\mathbf{Y}$ is the M.L. estimator for σ^2, but there is no unique M.L. estimator for *all* elements in $\boldsymbol{\beta}$. It may be of interest to determine if there exists any "reasonable" estimator of each element in $\boldsymbol{\beta}$.

In a crude sense, point estimation can be described as follows: $\mathbf{y}$ is the observed value of a random vector with p.d.f. $f_{\mathbf{Y}}(\mathbf{y} : \boldsymbol{\theta}_0)$, where $\boldsymbol{\theta}_0$ is a fixed but unknown vector in Ω. Using the vector $\mathbf{y}$ one wants to determine $\boldsymbol{\theta}_0$, and also the p.d.f., from which $\mathbf{y}$ was selected. However, if two (or more) distinct values of $\boldsymbol{\theta}$ in the parameter space determine the *same* p.d.f., then in a sense the observed sample cannot help "identify" or distinguish the two (or more) values of $\boldsymbol{\theta}$. For a simple example, suppose a sample is selected from the p.d.f. $n(y : \mu_1 + \mu_2, 1)$, where $\Omega = \{(\mu_1, \mu_2) : \mu_1 + \mu_2 = 0,\ -\infty < \mu_1 < \infty,\ -\infty < \mu_2 < \infty\}$; this implies that it is *known* that the sample was obtained from the p.d.f. $n(y : 0, 1)$. Since an infinite number of points in the parameter space Ω determine the *same* p.d.f. (that is, if $\mu_1 = -\mu_2$, then $\mu_1 + \mu_2 = 0$), the sample values *can* help identify the p.d.f. (that the mean is zero), but it *cannot* identify which one of the infinite number of points μ_1, μ_2 in Ω gave rise to the zero mean. So we say, "the parameters μ_1 and μ_2 are not identifiable." We now state the formal definition.

DEFINITION 13.2.1

Identifiable Parameters. *Let* $\mathbf{Y}$ *be an observable random vector with p.d.f.* $f_{\mathbf{Y}}(\mathbf{y} : \boldsymbol{\theta})$ *and* $\boldsymbol{\theta} \in \Omega$. *The parameter* $\boldsymbol{\theta}$ *is defined to be identifiable if and only if each distinct value of* $\boldsymbol{\theta}$ *in* Ω *defines a distinct p.d.f.*

Example 13.2.1

In the illustration above, if $\mu_1 = 6$ and $\mu_2 = -6$, the sample is selected from $n(y : 0, 1)$. Also, if $\mu_1 = 8$ and $\mu_2 = -8$, the sample is from $n(y : 0, 1)$. So two values of $\boldsymbol{\theta} = [\mu_1, \mu_2]'$ give the same p.d.f., and the sample can only help determine the p.d.f. In this case two (or more) distinct values of $\boldsymbol{\theta}$ give the same p.d.f., so μ_1 and μ_2 are not identifiable.

If a parameter is not identifiable, it seems reasonable to assume that no estimator of the parameter exists that has acceptable optimum properties. It can indeed be shown that if a parameter $\boldsymbol{\theta}$ is nonidentifiable, then no mean-squared-error (and no simple) consistent estimator of $\boldsymbol{\theta}$ exists.

Note 1. A parameter $\boldsymbol{\theta}$ may not be identifiable and yet some function of the parameter may be identifiable. For instance, in the example above, $\boldsymbol{\theta}' = [\mu_1, \mu_2]$ is not identifiable, but $\mu_1 + \mu_2$, the mean of the normal distribution, *is* identifiable.

In the design model ($K < p$), a problem is encountered due to the fact that the parameter $\boldsymbol{\theta}' = [\beta_1, \beta_2, \ldots, \beta_p, \sigma^2]$ is not identifiable. This can be demonstrated as follows: If $\mathbf{X}\boldsymbol{\beta}$ is denoted by $\boldsymbol{\mu}$, then $\mathbf{Y}$ is distributed $\mathbf{N}(\mathbf{y} : \boldsymbol{\mu}, \sigma^2\mathbf{I})$. Let $\boldsymbol{\mu}_0$ be a vector for which the set of equations $\mathbf{X}\boldsymbol{\beta} = \boldsymbol{\mu}_0$ has a solution. Since $\mathbf{X}$ is $n \times p$ of rank $K < p < n$, we know that there are an infinite number of values of $\boldsymbol{\beta}$ for which $\mathbf{X}\boldsymbol{\beta} = \boldsymbol{\mu}_0$. This says that $\mathbf{Y}$ has the same p.d.f., namely, normal with mean $\boldsymbol{\mu}_0$ and variance $\sigma^2\mathbf{I}$, for an infinite number of different values of $\boldsymbol{\theta}$ in Ω (actually for an infinite number of different values of $\boldsymbol{\beta}$), and hence $\boldsymbol{\theta}$ is not identifiable.

Since the parameter $\boldsymbol{\theta}' = [\boldsymbol{\beta}', \sigma^2]$ is not identifiable, we attempt to determine what *functions*, if any, of $\boldsymbol{\beta}$ and σ^2 *are* identifiable. In the design model the main interest is in estimating σ^2 and *linear* functions of $\boldsymbol{\beta}$, so most of our discussion will concern these.

One of the main optimum properties of point estimation that we have been considering is that of UMVU. To be UMVU an estimator must, of course, be unbiased, and we later show that there is indeed an unbiased (and, in fact, an UMVU) estimator of σ^2. Our main concentration will be on determining which, if any, *linear* functions of $\boldsymbol{\beta}$ have unbiased estimators and UMVU estimators.

In the literature on design models, the words "estimable function" are often used to denote a function of unknown parameters for which an unbiased estimator exists. We will find it convenient to use these words, so we formally define them and then state and prove several theorems relating to estimable functions.

DEFINITION 13.2.2

Estimable Function. *Consider the design model defined in Equation* (13.2.1). *A linear function of the parameter* $\boldsymbol{\beta}$, *say* $\ell'\boldsymbol{\beta}$, *is defined to be an estimable function if and only if there exists an unbiased estimator of* $\ell'\boldsymbol{\beta}$, *which is a linear function of the* Y_i *in* $\mathbf{Y}$.

We now state a fundamental theorem relating to estimable functions of $\boldsymbol{\beta}$.

THEOREM 13.2.1

Consider the design model given in Equation (13.2.1). *Let* $\ell'\boldsymbol{\beta}$ *be a specified linear function of* $\boldsymbol{\beta}$. *Then*:

(1) $\ell'\boldsymbol{\beta}$ *is an estimable function if and only if there exists an* $n \times 1$ *vector* $\mathbf{a}$ *such that* $\ell = \mathbf{X}'\mathbf{a}$;

(2) $\ell'\boldsymbol{\beta}$ *is identifiable if and only if* $\ell'\boldsymbol{\beta}$ *is an estimable function.*

Proof

To prove (1) we note that if there exists a constant vector $\mathbf{a}$ such that $\mathbf{X}'\mathbf{a} = \ell$, then clearly $\mathscr{E}[\mathbf{a}'\mathbf{Y}] = \mathbf{a}'\mathbf{X}\boldsymbol{\beta} = \ell'\boldsymbol{\beta}$, and hence $\ell'\boldsymbol{\beta}$ is an estimable function.

To prove "only if" we must show that if a linear function $\mathbf{c}'\mathbf{Y}$ of the observations $\mathbf{Y}$ exists such that $\mathscr{E}[\mathbf{c}'\mathbf{Y}] = \ell'\boldsymbol{\beta}$, then there also exists a constant vector $\mathbf{a}$ such that $\ell = \mathbf{X}'\mathbf{a}$. Of course, $\mathbf{c}'\mathbf{Y}$ must be a statistic and hence $\mathbf{c}$ can involve $\mathbf{X}$ but not $\boldsymbol{\beta}$ or σ^2. We get $\ell'\boldsymbol{\beta} = \mathscr{E}[\mathbf{c}'\mathbf{Y}] = \mathbf{c}'\mathbf{X}\boldsymbol{\beta}$, and the result follows from this.

We omit the proof of (2), but a proof and further discussion of estimable functions and identifiability can be found in [R-7].

In the next theorem we state several necessary and sufficient conditions for $\ell'\boldsymbol{\beta}$ to be an estimable function.

THEOREM 13.2.2

Consider the design model given in Equation (13.2.1). *A specified linear function of* $\boldsymbol{\beta}$, *namely* $\ell'\boldsymbol{\beta}$, *where* ℓ *is a given* $p \times 1$ *constant vector, is an estimable function if and only if any of the conditions below are satisfied.*

(1) ℓ *is a linear combination of the columns of* $\mathbf{X}'$ (*other ways of stating this are as follows*: ℓ *is in the column space of* $\mathbf{X}'$; *or,* ℓ' *is a linear combination of the rows of* $\mathbf{X}$; *or,* ℓ' *is in the row space of* $\mathbf{X}$).

(2) *rank*$[\mathbf{X}', \ell] =$ *rank*$[\mathbf{X}']$.

(3) *rank*$[\mathbf{X}'\mathbf{X}] =$ *rank*$[\mathbf{X}'\mathbf{X}, \ell]$.

(4) *A solution vector* $\mathbf{r}$ *exists for the equations* $\mathbf{X}'\mathbf{X}\mathbf{r} = \ell$.

(5) $\ell'\mathbf{X}^c\mathbf{X} = \ell'$ *for any c-inverse of* $\mathbf{X}$.

(6) $\mathbf{X}'(\mathbf{X}')^c\ell = \ell$ *for any c-inverse of* $\mathbf{X}'$.

(7) $(\mathbf{X}'\mathbf{X})(\mathbf{X}'\mathbf{X})^c\ell = \ell$ *for any c-inverse of* $\mathbf{X}'\mathbf{X}$.

(8) $\ell'(\mathbf{X}'\mathbf{X})^c(\mathbf{X}'\mathbf{X}) = \ell'$ *for any c-inverse of* $\mathbf{X}'\mathbf{X}$.

Proof

By Theorem 13.2.1, $\ell'\boldsymbol{\beta}$ is an estimable function if and only if there is a solution vector $\mathbf{a}$ to the set of equations $\mathbf{X}'\mathbf{a} = \ell$. Each condition in this theorem is simply a necessary and sufficient condition for the set of equations $\mathbf{X}'\mathbf{a} = \ell$ to be a consistent set for a given $\mathbf{X}$ and ℓ. The proof for each part is therefore a direct application of results in Section 1.6 and will be left for the reader.

Now we state and prove some results that will be useful in determining "all" of the estimable functions of $\boldsymbol{\beta}$ and in finding optimum estimators of all of these functions. First we define "linearly independent estimable functions of $\boldsymbol{\beta}$."

DEFINITION 13.2.3

Linearly Independent Estimable Functions of $\boldsymbol{\beta}$. *A set of M linear functions of* $\boldsymbol{\beta}$, *say* $\ell'_1\boldsymbol{\beta}, \ell'_2\boldsymbol{\beta}, \ldots, \ell'_M\boldsymbol{\beta}$, *is defined to be a set of M linearly independent estimable functions of* $\boldsymbol{\beta}$ *if and only if* (1) *each* $\ell'_m\boldsymbol{\beta}$ *is an estimable function for* $m = 1, 2, \ldots, M$; (2) *the* $p \times 1$ *vectors* $\ell_1, \ell_2, \ldots, \ell_M$ *are linearly independent* (*or the rank of* $\mathbf{L}$ *is* M, *where* $\mathbf{L} = [\ell_1, \ell_2, \ldots, \ell_M]$).

We now prove a theorem stating the number of linearly independent estimable functions of $\boldsymbol{\beta}$.

THEOREM 13.2.3

The number of linearly independent estimable functions of $\boldsymbol{\beta}$ *is equal to the rank of* $\mathbf{X}$, *which is* K.

Proof

We first show that there exist at least K linearly independent $p \times 1$ vectors $\ell_1, \ell_2, \ldots, \ell_K$ such that $\ell'_k\boldsymbol{\beta}$ is estimable for each $k = 1, 2, \ldots, K$. We then show that if $\ell'_m\boldsymbol{\beta}$ are linearly independent estimable functions for $m = 1, 2, \ldots, M$, then M must be no larger than K; these two results imply $M = K$.

Let the ith row of $\mathbf{X}$ be denoted by ℓ_i'; then since $\mathscr{E}[\mathbf{Y}] = \mathbf{X}\boldsymbol{\beta}$, it follows that $\mathscr{E}[Y_i] = \ell_i'\boldsymbol{\beta}$. But since $\mathbf{X}$ has rank K, the matrix $\mathbf{X}$ has K linearly independent rows; in other words, K of the $\ell_i'\boldsymbol{\beta}$ are linearly independent estimable functions. Thus we know that there are at least K linearly independent estimable functions, namely K rows of $\mathbf{X}\boldsymbol{\beta}$. We now show that there can be no more than K.

Let $\ell_1'\boldsymbol{\beta}, \ell_2'\boldsymbol{\beta}, \ldots, \ell_M'\boldsymbol{\beta}$ be *any* set of M estimable functions, where $M \geq K$. By Theorem 13.2.1 there must exist a constant vector, say $\mathbf{a}_m$, such that $\mathbf{X}'\mathbf{a}_m = \ell_m$ for each function $\ell_m'\boldsymbol{\beta}$, $m = 1, 2, \ldots, M$. We can write these M equations in one matrix equation as $\mathbf{X}'[\mathbf{a}_1, \mathbf{a}_2, \ldots, \mathbf{a}_M] = [\ell_1, \ell_2, \ldots, \ell_M]$, or $\mathbf{X}'\mathbf{A} = \mathbf{L}$. Thus the rank of $\mathbf{L}$ must be less than or equal to the rank of $\mathbf{X}'$, which is K; but the rank of $\mathbf{L}$ is the number of linearly independent vectors in the set $\ell_1, \ell_2, \ldots, \ell_M$; hence M must be less than or equal to K, and this completes the proof.

DEFINITION 13.2.4

Set, Full Set, and Basis Set of Estimable Functions. *Consider the* $p \times M$ *matrix of constants* $\mathbf{L} = [\ell_1, \ell_2, \ldots, \ell_M]$, *where* $\ell_m'\boldsymbol{\beta}$ *is an estimable function for each* $m = 1, 2, \ldots, M$. *Then* $\mathbf{L}'\boldsymbol{\beta}$ *is defined to be the following*:

(1) *a set of* M *estimable functions*;

(2) *a full set of estimable functions if* $\mathbf{L}$ *has rank* K;

(3) *a basis set of estimable functions if* $M = K$ *and* $\mathbf{L}$ *has rank* K. (13.2.4)

The next theorem explains how the normal equations can be used to obtain UMVU estimators of estimable functions.

THEOREM 13.2.4

Consider the design model in Equation (13.2.1) *and the normal equations*

$$\mathbf{X}'\mathbf{X}\hat{\boldsymbol{\beta}} = \mathbf{X}'\mathbf{Y} \tag{13.2.5}$$

(1) *If* $\ell'\boldsymbol{\beta}$ *is an estimable function, then* $\ell'\hat{\boldsymbol{\beta}}$ *is invariant for "any" solution* $\hat{\boldsymbol{\beta}}$ *of the normal equations, and* $\ell'\hat{\boldsymbol{\beta}} = \ell'\mathbf{X}^{-}\mathbf{Y}$.

(2) *If* $\ell'\boldsymbol{\beta}$ *is an estimable function, then* $\ell'\hat{\boldsymbol{\beta}}$ *is the UMVU estimator of* $\ell'\boldsymbol{\beta}$, *where* $\hat{\boldsymbol{\beta}}$ *is any solution to the normal equations.*

(3) $\hat{\sigma}^2 = (n - K)^{-1}(\mathbf{Y}'\mathbf{Y} - \hat{\boldsymbol{\beta}}'\mathbf{X}'\mathbf{Y})$ *is invariant for any solution* $\hat{\boldsymbol{\beta}}$ *of the normal equations.*

(4) $\hat{\sigma}^2$ *is the UMVU estimator of* σ^2.

(5) *Every row of* $\mathbf{X\beta}$ *is an estimable function.*

(6) *The UMVU estimator of any estimable function* $\ell'\boldsymbol{\beta}$ *must be a linear combination of the UMVU estimators of every basis set of estimable functions (and also of every full set of estimable functions).*

Proof

To prove (1) we note that the general solution to the normal equation is

$$\hat{\boldsymbol{\beta}} = (\mathbf{X'X})^{c_1}\mathbf{X'Y} + [\mathbf{I} - (\mathbf{X'X})^{c_2}(\mathbf{X'X})]\mathbf{b} \qquad (13.2.6)$$

where $\mathbf{b}$ is any $p \times 1$ vector and $(\mathbf{X'X})^{c_1}$ and $(\mathbf{X'X})^{c_2}$ are any c-inverses of $\mathbf{X'X}$. Since $\ell'\boldsymbol{\beta}$ is an estimable function of $\boldsymbol{\beta}$, we know by Theorem 13.2.1 that ℓ' can be written as $\mathbf{a'X}$ for some vector $\mathbf{a}$. Hence

$$\ell'\hat{\boldsymbol{\beta}} = \mathbf{a'X}\hat{\boldsymbol{\beta}} = \mathbf{a'XX^-Y} = \ell'\mathbf{X^-Y} \qquad (13.2.7)$$

since by Theorem 1.5.25, $\mathbf{X(X'X)}^c\mathbf{X'} = \mathbf{XX^-}$, and by Definition 1.5.1, $\mathbf{XX^-X} = \mathbf{X}$. So $\ell'\hat{\boldsymbol{\beta}} = \ell'\mathbf{X^-Y}$ for any solution to the normal equations given in Equation (13.2.6). This proves (1).

To prove (2) we could find a set of complete sufficient statistics and use the Lehmann-Scheffé theorem (which we will indeed do later), but here we demonstrate Theorem 2.7.4. We define $\hat{\alpha}$ by $\hat{\alpha} = \ell'\hat{\boldsymbol{\beta}} + q(\mathbf{Y})$, and since $\ell'\hat{\boldsymbol{\beta}}$ is a *known* function of $\mathbf{Y}$, we want to determine $q(\mathbf{Y})$ so that $\hat{\alpha}$ is the UMVU estimator of $\ell'\boldsymbol{\beta}$. For $\hat{\alpha}$ to be an unbiased estimator of $\ell'\boldsymbol{\beta}$, we have

$$\ell'\boldsymbol{\beta} = \mathscr{E}[\ell'\hat{\boldsymbol{\beta}} + q(\mathbf{Y})] = \mathscr{E}[\ell'\mathbf{X^-Y} + q(\mathbf{Y})] = \ell'\boldsymbol{\beta} + \mathscr{E}[q(\mathbf{Y})]$$

and this requires $\mathscr{E}[q(\mathbf{Y})]$ to be zero. For var$[\hat{\alpha}]$ we get

$$\begin{aligned}\text{var}[\hat{\alpha}] &= \text{var}[\ell'\mathbf{X^-Y} + q(\mathbf{Y})]\\ &= \text{var}[\ell'\mathbf{X^-Y}] + \text{var}[q(\mathbf{Y})] + 2\,\text{cov}[\ell'\mathbf{X^-Y}, q(\mathbf{Y})] \qquad (13.2.8)\end{aligned}$$

We show that $\text{cov}[\ell'\mathbf{X}^-\mathbf{Y}, q(\mathbf{Y})] = 0$, and to do so we use the fact that $\mathscr{E}[q(\mathbf{Y})] = 0$ and differentiate with respect to $\boldsymbol{\beta}$. We get

$$0 = \mathscr{E}[q(\mathbf{Y})] = (2\pi\sigma^2)^{-n/2} \int_{-\infty}^{\infty} \cdots \int_{-\infty}^{\infty} q(\mathbf{y}) \times \exp\left[-\left(\frac{1}{2\sigma^2}\right) \sum_{i=1}^{n} \left(y_i - \sum_{j=1}^{p} x_{ij}\beta_j\right)^2\right] dy_1\, dy_2 \cdots dy_n$$

$$0 = \frac{\partial\{\mathscr{E}[q(\mathbf{Y})]\}}{\partial\beta_k} = (2\pi\sigma^2)^{-n/2} \int_{-\infty}^{\infty} \cdots \int_{-\infty}^{\infty} q(\mathbf{y}) \times \exp\left[-\left(\frac{1}{2\sigma^2}\right) \sum_{i=1}^{n} \left(y_i - \sum_{j=1}^{p} x_{ij}\beta_j\right)^2\right] \times \left[\left(-\frac{1}{2\sigma^2}\right)(2) \sum_{t=1}^{n} \left(y_t - \sum_{m=1}^{p} x_{tm}\beta_m\right)(-x_{tk})\right] d\mathbf{y}$$

which simplifies to

$$\left(\frac{1}{\sigma^2}\right) \sum_{t=1}^{n} x_{tk}\{\mathscr{E}[q(\mathbf{Y})Y_t]\} - \left(\frac{1}{\sigma^2}\right) \sum_{t=1}^{n} \sum_{m=1}^{p} x_{tm}x_{tk}\beta_m\{\mathscr{E}[q(\mathbf{Y})]\} = 0$$

Since $\mathscr{E}[q(\mathbf{Y})] = 0$, the second term vanishes, and this further simplifies to

$$\mathscr{E}\left[\sum_{t=1}^{n} x_{tk} Y_t\, q(\mathbf{Y})\right] = 0 \qquad \text{for } k = 1, 2, \ldots, p$$

We write this in vector and matrix form and get

$$\mathscr{E}[\mathbf{X}'\mathbf{Y} \cdot q(\mathbf{Y})] = \mathbf{0} = \mathbf{X}'\,\mathscr{E}[\mathbf{Y} \cdot q(\mathbf{Y})] = \mathbf{0}$$

If we multiply both sides of this equation by $\mathbf{a}'\mathbf{X}(\mathbf{X}'\mathbf{X})^c$, where $\mathbf{a}$ is any vector such that $\ell' = \mathbf{a}'\mathbf{X}$ and $(\mathbf{X}'\mathbf{X})^c$ is *any* c-inverse of $\mathbf{X}'\mathbf{X}$, we get

$$\begin{aligned} 0 &= \mathbf{a}'\mathbf{X}(\mathbf{X}'\mathbf{X})^c\mathbf{X}'\,\mathscr{E}[\mathbf{Y} \cdot q(\mathbf{Y})] = \mathbf{a}'\mathbf{X}\mathbf{X}^-\,\mathscr{E}[\mathbf{Y} \cdot q(\mathbf{Y})] \\ &= \ell'\mathbf{X}^-\,\mathscr{E}[\mathbf{Y} \cdot q(\mathbf{Y})] = \mathscr{E}[\ell'\mathbf{X}^-\mathbf{Y} \cdot q(\mathbf{Y})] \end{aligned}$$

which implies that $\text{cov}[\ell'\mathbf{X}^-\mathbf{Y}, q(\mathbf{Y})] = 0$ (since $\mathscr{E}[q(\mathbf{Y})] = 0$), and hence we can write Equation (13.2.8) as

$$\text{var}[\hat{\alpha}] = \text{var}[\ell'\hat{\boldsymbol{\beta}}] + \text{var}[q(\mathbf{Y})] \geq \text{var}[\ell'\hat{\boldsymbol{\beta}}]$$

Equality holds if and only if $q(\mathbf{Y})$ is a constant (with probability one), but since $\mathscr{E}[q(\mathbf{Y})] = 0$, the constant is zero. Hence a lower bound on the variance of $\hat{\alpha}$ (an unbiased estimator of the estimable function $\ell'\boldsymbol{\beta}$) is var$[\ell'\hat{\boldsymbol{\beta}}]$. This lower bound is, of course, attained if $q(\mathbf{Y}) = 0$ (with probability one), and hence $\ell'\hat{\boldsymbol{\beta}}$ (which is $\ell'\mathbf{X}^-\mathbf{Y}$) is the UMVU estimator of $\ell'\boldsymbol{\beta}$. This proves (2).

To prove (3) we note by Equation (13.2.6) that $\mathbf{X}\hat{\boldsymbol{\beta}} = \mathbf{X}\mathbf{X}^-\mathbf{Y}$, and hence $\mathbf{X}\hat{\boldsymbol{\beta}}$ is invariant for *any* solution to the normal equations. Thus we can write $\hat{\sigma}^2 = (n - K)^{-1}(\mathbf{Y}'\mathbf{Y} - \mathbf{Y}'\mathbf{X}\mathbf{X}^-\mathbf{Y})$, and each term depends only on $\mathbf{Y}$ and $\mathbf{X}$ in the model and not on a particular solution to the normal equations. This proves (3).

We leave the proofs of (4), (5), and (6) for the reader.

COROLLARY 13.2.4

In the design model in Equation (13.2.1), *every row of* $\mathbf{X}'\mathbf{X}\boldsymbol{\beta}$ *is estimable, and the UMVU estimator is the corresponding row in* $\mathbf{X}'\mathbf{X}\hat{\boldsymbol{\beta}}$ (*the corresponding element in* $\mathbf{X}'\mathbf{Y}$). *Any estimable function* (*say* $\ell'\boldsymbol{\beta}$) *of* $\boldsymbol{\beta}$ *can be obtained by taking the appropriate linear combination of the rows of* $\mathbf{X}'\mathbf{X}\boldsymbol{\beta}$; *the UMVU estimator of this particular* $\ell'\boldsymbol{\beta}$ *is obtained by taking the same linear combination of the rows of* $\mathbf{X}'\mathbf{X}\hat{\boldsymbol{\beta}}$ (*of* $\mathbf{X}'\mathbf{Y}$).

Proof

Since $\mathscr{E}[\mathbf{X}'\mathbf{Y}] = \mathbf{X}'\mathbf{X}\boldsymbol{\beta}$, each of the p rows of $\mathbf{X}'\mathbf{X}\boldsymbol{\beta}$ is estimable, and since $\mathbf{X}'\mathbf{X}$ has rank K, the p rows of $\mathbf{X}'\mathbf{X}\boldsymbol{\beta}$ are a "full set" of estimable functions. By (4) of Theorem 13.2.2 there exists a $p \times 1$ vector $\mathbf{r}$ such that $\mathbf{r}'\mathbf{X}'\mathbf{X} = \ell'$ for any ℓ, where $\ell'\boldsymbol{\beta}$ is an estimable function. But $\mathscr{E}[\mathbf{r}'\mathbf{X}'\mathbf{Y}] = \mathbf{r}'\mathbf{X}'\mathbf{X}\boldsymbol{\beta} = \ell'\boldsymbol{\beta}$. Also, if we multiply both sides of the normal equations by $\mathbf{r}'$, we get $\mathbf{r}'\mathbf{X}'\mathbf{X}\hat{\boldsymbol{\beta}} = \mathbf{r}'\mathbf{X}'\mathbf{Y}$, which is $\ell'\hat{\boldsymbol{\beta}} = \mathbf{r}'\mathbf{X}'\mathbf{Y}$. Thus if we take the linear combination of $\mathbf{X}'\mathbf{X}\boldsymbol{\beta}$, which is the same as multiplying by $\mathbf{r}'$, and get $\ell'\boldsymbol{\beta}$, then the same linear combination of the right-hand side of the normal equations gives $\mathbf{r}'\mathbf{X}'\mathbf{Y}$, which is $\ell'\hat{\boldsymbol{\beta}}$, the UMVU estimator of $\ell'\boldsymbol{\beta}$.

Note 2. To summarize, the following are equivalent: (1) $\ell'\boldsymbol{\beta}$ is an estimable function; (2) $\ell'\boldsymbol{\beta}$ is identifiable; (3) $\ell'\boldsymbol{\beta}$ has an unbiased estimator; (4) $\ell'\boldsymbol{\beta}$ has an UMVU estimator; (5) $\ell'\boldsymbol{\beta}$ has a *unique* M.L. estimator.

Let $\ell'\boldsymbol{\beta}$ be an estimable function and let $\hat{\boldsymbol{\beta}}$ be *any* solution to the normal equations; the following are equivalent: (1) $\ell'\hat{\boldsymbol{\beta}}$ is the same for *any* solution $\hat{\boldsymbol{\beta}}$ of the normal equations; (2) $\ell'\hat{\boldsymbol{\beta}}$ is the UMVU estimator of $\ell'\boldsymbol{\beta}$; (3) $\ell'\hat{\boldsymbol{\beta}}$ is the unique M.L. estimator of $\ell'\boldsymbol{\beta}$.

Note 3. Below are some equivalent expressions for $\hat{\sigma}^2$, where $\hat{\boldsymbol{\beta}}$ is *any* solution to the normal equations.

$$(n - K)\hat{\sigma}^2 = \mathbf{Y}'\mathbf{Y} - \hat{\boldsymbol{\beta}}'\mathbf{X}'\mathbf{Y} = \mathbf{Y}'(\mathbf{I} - \mathbf{X}\mathbf{X}^-)\mathbf{Y}$$
$$= \mathbf{Y}'[\mathbf{I} - \mathbf{X}(\mathbf{X}'\mathbf{X})^c\mathbf{X}']\mathbf{Y} \tag{13.2.9}$$

where $(\mathbf{X}'\mathbf{X})^c$ is any c-inverse of $\mathbf{X}'\mathbf{X}$.

Notation. In the previous sections of the book, we have used $\tilde{\boldsymbol{\theta}}$ for M.L. estimators and $\hat{\boldsymbol{\theta}}$ when the M.L. estimators (or modified M.L. estimators) are unbiased. Strictly speaking, if $\ell'\boldsymbol{\beta}$ is an estimable function, we should use $\widehat{\ell'\boldsymbol{\beta}}$ for the M.L. estimator of $\ell'\boldsymbol{\beta}$ (since it is unbiased). However, instead we shall write $\ell'\hat{\boldsymbol{\beta}}$ for $\widehat{\ell'\boldsymbol{\beta}}$, where $\hat{\boldsymbol{\beta}}$ will denote *any* solution to the normal equations.

Procedure. To determine if $\ell'\boldsymbol{\beta}$ is estimable, one can take linear combinations of $\mathbf{X}\boldsymbol{\beta}$ in the model, say $\mathbf{a}'\mathbf{X}\boldsymbol{\beta}$, or linear combinations of the normal equations, say $\mathbf{r}'\mathbf{X}'\mathbf{X}\hat{\boldsymbol{\beta}}$. If the linear combination of $\mathbf{X}\boldsymbol{\beta}$ is $\ell'\boldsymbol{\beta}$, or if the linear combination of $\mathbf{X}'\mathbf{X}\hat{\boldsymbol{\beta}}$ is $\ell'\hat{\boldsymbol{\beta}}$, then $\ell'\boldsymbol{\beta}$ is estimable. Moreover, this linear combination of the *normal equations* gives the UMVU estimator of $\ell'\boldsymbol{\beta}$, but the linear combination of the elements of $\mathbf{Y}$ that corresponds to the linear combination of the elements $\mathscr{E}[\mathbf{Y}] = \mathbf{X}\boldsymbol{\beta}$ in the model may *not* be the UMVU estimator of $\ell'\boldsymbol{\beta}$.

The next theorem states the distributions of $\ell'\hat{\boldsymbol{\beta}}$ and $\hat{\sigma}^2$.

THEOREM 13.2.5

Consider the design model in Equation (13.2.1). *Let* $\mathbf{L}'\boldsymbol{\beta}$ *be any set of estimable functions (where* $\mathbf{L}'$ *is* $q \times p$ *of rank* M*) and let* $\hat{\boldsymbol{\beta}}$ *denote any solution to the normal equations* $\mathbf{X}'\mathbf{X}\hat{\boldsymbol{\beta}} = \mathbf{X}'\mathbf{Y}$.

(1) $\mathbf{L}'\hat{\boldsymbol{\beta}}$ *is distributed as the q-variate normal distribution of rank* M *with mean* $\mathbf{L}'\boldsymbol{\beta}$ *and covariance matrix* $\sigma^2\mathbf{L}'(\mathbf{X}'\mathbf{X})^c\mathbf{L}$, *where* $(\mathbf{X}'\mathbf{X})^c$ *is any c-inverse of* $\mathbf{X}'\mathbf{X}$.

(2) $U = (n - K)\hat{\sigma}^2/\sigma^2$ *is distributed* $\chi^2(u : n - K)$.

(3) *The random vector* $\mathbf{L}'\hat{\boldsymbol{\beta}}$ *is independent of* U.

Proof

The proof can easily be obtained by using the procedures employed in Theorem 6.2.1, adding the modifications necessary since $\mathbf{X}'\mathbf{X}$ is singular. The details will be asked for in the problems.

As an aid to finding UMVU estimators of specified functions of $\boldsymbol{\beta}$ and σ^2, we state a theorem on complete sufficient statistics for the design model, and then use an example to help explain the concepts we have discussed so far.

THEOREM 13.2.6

Consider the design model in Equation (13.2.1), *and let* $\mathbf{L}'\boldsymbol{\beta}$ *be a basis set of estimable functions. The statistic* $\hat{\sigma}^2$ *and the vector* $\mathbf{L}'\hat{\boldsymbol{\beta}}$ *are a set of* $K + 1$ *complete sufficient statistics.*

Proof

Theorem 2.7.8 can be used for the proof. We leave the details for the reader.

Note 4. By this theorem and the Lehmann-Scheffé theorem, any unbiased estimator of a specified function of $\boldsymbol{\beta}$ and σ^2 is the UMVU estimator of that function if the estimator is a function of $\mathbf{L}'\hat{\boldsymbol{\beta}}$ and $\hat{\sigma}^2$ only.

Example 13.2.2

Consider the design model given in Equation (5.4.6), which is written in the matrix form $\mathbf{Y} = \mathbf{X}\boldsymbol{\beta} + \boldsymbol{\varepsilon}$ in Equation (5.4.7). Clearly $\mathbf{X}$ has size 6×3 and rank 2; hence $n = 6$, $p = 3$, and $K = 2$. A basis set of estimable functions will consist of two linearly independent estimable functions. Since $\mathscr{E}[\mathbf{Y}] = \mathbf{X}\boldsymbol{\beta}$ is a "full set" of estimable functions, it contains a "basis set," and it is easy to determine that the third and fourth rows of $\mathbf{X}$ are linearly independent; that is, $\ell_1' = [1, 1, 0]$ and $\ell_2' = [1, 0, 1]$ are linearly independent. To find the UMVU estimators of $\ell_1'\boldsymbol{\beta}$ and $\ell_2'\boldsymbol{\beta}$, we find the normal equations, which are

$$\begin{aligned} 6\hat{\mu} + 3\hat{\tau}_1 + 3\hat{\tau}_2 &= Y_{..} \\ 3\hat{\mu} + 3\hat{\tau}_1 &= Y_{1.} \\ 3\hat{\mu} + 3\hat{\tau}_2 &= Y_{2.} \end{aligned}$$

where we define the Y_{ij} with a subscript replaced by a dot to be the total when summed over the subscript that has been replaced by a dot. Thus $Y_{i.} = \sum_{j=1}^{3} Y_{ij}$; $Y_{..} = \sum_{i=1}^{2}\sum_{j=1}^{3} Y_{ij}$. A letter with a bar over it will indicate the *mean* of the variable when summed over the subscript replaced by a dot. Thus $\overline{Y}_{i.} = (\frac{1}{3})Y_{i.}$, and so on. The same notation will apply when the random variable, capital Y, is replaced by the observation, lowercase y.

By Theorem 13.2.4 every row of $\mathbf{X}\boldsymbol{\beta}$ is estimable, so $\mu + \tau_1$ and $\mu + \tau_2$ are estimable; by Corollary 13.2.4 every row of the right-hand side of the normal equations gives the UMVU estimator of the corresponding left-hand side (with the ^ removed). If the second row of both sides of the normal equations is multiplied by $\frac{1}{3}$ (this is a linear combination of the rows of $\mathbf{X}'\mathbf{X}\hat{\boldsymbol{\beta}}$), we get $\hat{\mu} + \hat{\tau}_1 = \overline{Y}_{1.}$, so $\overline{Y}_{1.}$ is the UMVU estimator of $\mu + \tau_1$. Similarly, for the third row we get $\hat{\mu} + \hat{\tau}_2 = \overline{Y}_{2.}$, so $\overline{Y}_{2.}$ is the UMVU estimator of $\mu + \tau_2$.

Thus $\mu + \tau_1$, $\mu + \tau_2$ is a basis set of estimable functions; every estimable function $\ell'\boldsymbol{\beta}$ must be a linear combination of these; and the UMVU estimator of the resulting function is the same linear combination of the UMVU estimators (of $\bar{Y}_{1.}, \bar{Y}_{2.}$). For example, $\tau_1 - \tau_2$ can be obtained by $(\mu + \tau_1) - (\mu + \tau_2)$, so the UMVU estimator of $\tau_1 - \tau_2$ is $(\hat{\mu} + \hat{\tau}_1) - (\hat{\mu} + \hat{\tau}_2) = \bar{Y}_{1.} - \bar{Y}_{2.}$. We can also obtain the UMVU estimator of $\tau_1 - \tau_2$ by subtracting $\frac{1}{3}$ times the third row of the normal equations from $\frac{1}{3}$ times the second row. We get $\hat{\tau}_1 - \hat{\tau}_2 = \frac{1}{3}(Y_{1.} - Y_{2.}) = \bar{Y}_{1.} - \bar{Y}_{2.}$.

To evaluate $\hat{\sigma}^2$ we first find *any* solution to the normal equations and use Equation (13.2.9). It is easy to demonstrate that $\hat{\boldsymbol{\beta}}' = [\hat{\mu}, \hat{\tau}_1, \hat{\tau}_2] = [\bar{Y}_{..}, \bar{Y}_{1.} - \bar{Y}_{..}, \bar{Y}_{2.} - \bar{Y}_{..}]$ is a solution. Multiply this by the right-hand side of the normal equations and get

$$\hat{\boldsymbol{\beta}}'\mathbf{X}'\mathbf{Y} = \bar{Y}_{..}(Y_{..}) + (\bar{Y}_{1.} - \bar{Y}_{..})Y_{1.} + (\bar{Y}_{2.} - \bar{Y}_{..})Y_{2.} = \frac{Y_{1.}^2 + Y_{2.}^2}{3}$$

Another solution to the normal equations is $\hat{\boldsymbol{\beta}}' = [0, \bar{Y}_{1.}, \bar{Y}_{2.}]$, and

$$\hat{\boldsymbol{\beta}}'\mathbf{X}'\mathbf{Y} = Y_{..}(0) + \bar{Y}_{1.}(Y_{1.}) + \bar{Y}_{2.}(Y_{2.}) = \frac{Y_{1.}^2 + Y_{2.}^2}{3}$$

the same as before. Then

$$\hat{\sigma}^2 = (6 - 2)^{-1}\left(\mathbf{Y}'\mathbf{Y} - \frac{Y_{1.}^2}{3} - \frac{Y_{2.}^2}{3}\right) = \sum_{i=1}^{2}\sum_{j=1}^{3}\frac{(Y_{ij} - \bar{Y}_{i.})^2}{4}$$

We note in the example above that the model could be written as $Y_{ij} = \mu_i + \varepsilon_{ij}$, where $\mu_i = \mu + \tau_i$. This is illustrated in Equation (5.4.4), and the $\mathbf{X}$ matrix is given in Equation (5.4.5). In the latter equation the $\mathbf{X}$ matrix is full rank and hence *all* the theory in Chapter 6 applies, but the parameter vector $\boldsymbol{\beta}$ has been changed from one containing the three parameters μ, τ_1, and τ_2 to one that contains only two parameters μ_1 and μ_2. However, there is a relationship between the two sets of parameters, namely, $\mu_1 = \mu + \tau_1$ and $\mu_2 = \mu + \tau_2$. By the theory in Chapter 6, where $\mathbf{X}$ in the model has full (column) rank, all parameters are estimable (that is, μ_1 and μ_2 are estimable). The normal equations are

$$3\hat{\mu}_1 = Y_{1.}$$
$$3\hat{\mu}_2 = Y_{2.}$$

Thus the UMVU estimator of μ_1 is $\hat{\mu}_1 = \bar{Y}_{1.}$, and of μ_2 is $\hat{\mu}_2 = \bar{Y}_{2.}$. But $\mu_1 = \mu + \tau_1$ and $\mu_2 = \mu + \tau_2$, so the UMVU estimator of $\mu + \tau_1$ is $\bar{Y}_{1.}$, and of $\mu + \tau_2$ is $\bar{Y}_{2.}$, the same as we obtained by using the model in Equation (5.4.7) where $\mathbf{X}$ is not full rank.

The question that presents itself from this simple example is this: Can the matrix $\mathbf{X}$, whose rank is *less* than the number of its columns, be "changed" to a matrix $\mathbf{U}$ whose rank is *equal* to the number of its columns? If this can be done it may be advantageous for two reasons: (1) the normal equations would have a unique solution and hence may be easier to work with; (2) *all* the theory in Chapter 6 would become available and directly applicable to the new model. This problem will be discussed next, and the result is that the design model, where $\text{rank}[\mathbf{X}] = K < p$, *can* indeed be "changed" to a general linear model (of full rank). The procedure will be to change (or transform) the $\boldsymbol{\beta}$ vector and the $\mathbf{X}$ matrix to a new vector $\boldsymbol{\theta}$ and a new matrix $\mathbf{U}$ of size $n \times M$ such that $\mathbf{X}\boldsymbol{\beta} = \mathbf{U}\boldsymbol{\theta}$. If $\mathbf{U}$ is $n \times K$ of rank K, then the transformed model $\mathbf{Y} = \mathbf{U}\boldsymbol{\theta} + \boldsymbol{\varepsilon}$ satisfies *all* conditions of the *general linear model* (of full rank). In this case the change from $\mathbf{X}\boldsymbol{\beta}$ to $\mathbf{U}\boldsymbol{\theta}$ will be accomplished by transforming the parameter $\boldsymbol{\beta}$ to a new parameter $\boldsymbol{\theta}$ by a $K \times p$ matrix $\mathbf{L}'$ of rank K, where each row of $\mathbf{L}'\boldsymbol{\beta}$ is a linearly independent estimable function. This transformation $\boldsymbol{\theta} = \mathbf{L}'\boldsymbol{\beta}$ of the parameter $\boldsymbol{\beta}$ to the parameter $\boldsymbol{\theta}$ is called *reparameterization* of $\boldsymbol{\beta}$ to a basis set of estimable functions. These ideas are formally stated in the following definition.

DEFINITION 13.2.5

Transformation and Reparameterization. *Consider the design model* $\mathbf{Y} = \mathbf{X}\boldsymbol{\beta} + \boldsymbol{\varepsilon}$ *in Equation* (13.2.1), *where* $\mathbf{X}$ *is* $n \times p$ *of rank* K. *Let* $\mathbf{L}$ *be any* $p \times M$ *known matrix and let* $\boldsymbol{\theta} = \mathbf{L}'\boldsymbol{\beta}$. *Denote the ith column of* $\mathbf{L}$ *by* ℓ_i *so that* $\mathbf{L} = [\ell_1, \ell_2, \ldots, \ell_M]$. *Then*:

(1) $\mathbf{L}'\boldsymbol{\beta}$ *is defined to be a "transformation" of the vector* $\boldsymbol{\beta}$ *to the vector* $\boldsymbol{\theta}$.

(2) $\mathbf{L}'\boldsymbol{\beta}$ *is defined to be an "estimable transformation" of the vector* $\boldsymbol{\beta}$ *to the vector* $\boldsymbol{\theta}$ *if and only if each* θ_i *(each* $\ell_i'\boldsymbol{\beta}$*) is estimable for* $i = 1, 2, \ldots, M$.

(3) $\mathbf{L}'\boldsymbol{\beta}$ *is defined to be a "reparameterization" of the vector* $\boldsymbol{\beta}$ *to the vector* $\boldsymbol{\theta}$ *if and only if each* θ_i *(each* $\ell_i'\boldsymbol{\beta}$*) is estimable for* $i = 1, 2, \ldots, M$, *where* $\mathbf{L}$ *has rank* K, *and* $K = M$; *that is,* $\boldsymbol{\theta}$ *is a basis set of estimable functions of* $\boldsymbol{\beta}$.

Before we discuss how reparameterization can be used in the design model, we state some matrix results that will be needed.

THEOREM 13.2.7

In the design model in Equation (13.2.1), *let* $\boldsymbol{\theta} = \mathbf{L}'\boldsymbol{\beta}$ *be a reparameterization from* $\boldsymbol{\beta}$ *to* $\boldsymbol{\theta}$. *Then*:

(1) *There exists a* $K \times n$ *matrix* $\mathbf{A}'$ *of rank* K *such that* $\mathbf{L}' = \mathbf{A}'\mathbf{X}$.

(2) *The equation* $\mathbf{X}(\mathbf{L}')^c\mathbf{L}' = \mathbf{X}$ *holds for any c-inverse of* $\mathbf{L}'$; *also,* $\mathbf{X}(\mathbf{L}')^c$ *has rank* K.

(3) *If* $\boldsymbol{\theta}_1 = \mathbf{L}_1'\boldsymbol{\beta}$ *is another reparameterization of* $\boldsymbol{\beta}$, *then there exists a* $K \times K$ *nonsingular matrix* $\mathbf{B}$ *such that* $\mathbf{L}_1' = \mathbf{B}\mathbf{L}'$.

(4) $\mathbf{L}'(\mathbf{L}')^c = \mathbf{I}$ *for any c-inverse of* $\mathbf{L}'$.

Proof

The proof of (1) follows from the fact that if $\mathbf{L}'$ has rows consisting of the vectors $\ell_1', \ell_2', \ldots, \ell_K'$, and since each $\ell_i'\boldsymbol{\beta}$ is an estimable function, there must exist an $n \times 1$ vector $\mathbf{a}_i$ such that $\ell_i' = \mathbf{a}_i'\mathbf{X}$. Put these K equations into a matrix equation and get $\mathbf{L}' = \mathbf{A}'\mathbf{X}$, where $\mathbf{A} = [\mathbf{a}_1, \mathbf{a}_2, \ldots, \mathbf{a}_K]$. Since by hypothesis $\mathbf{L}'$ has rank K, it follows that rank$[\mathbf{A}] \geq K$; but since $\mathbf{A}$ is $n \times K$, we know that rank$[\mathbf{A}] \leq K$; so rank$[\mathbf{A}] = K$. This proves (1).

To prove (2) we know that $\mathbf{L}' = \mathbf{A}'\mathbf{X}$ for some matrix $\mathbf{A}$ of rank K; so write

$$(\mathbf{L}')(\mathbf{L}')^c(\mathbf{L}') = \mathbf{L}' \qquad \text{or} \qquad (\mathbf{A}'\mathbf{X})(\mathbf{A}'\mathbf{X})^c(\mathbf{A}'\mathbf{X}) = \mathbf{A}'\mathbf{X}$$

which can be written as

$$(\mathbf{A}'\mathbf{X}_L\mathbf{X}_R)(\mathbf{A}'\mathbf{X})^c(\mathbf{A}'\mathbf{X}) = \mathbf{A}'\mathbf{X}_L\mathbf{X}_R$$

where $\mathbf{X}_L\mathbf{X}_R$ is a full rank factorization of $\mathbf{X}$ (see Corollary 1.2.12). So $\mathbf{A}'\mathbf{X}_L$ is a $K \times K$ matrix of rank K, since $\mathbf{A}'\mathbf{X}_L\mathbf{X}_R = \mathbf{L}'$, and $\mathbf{L}'$ has rank K, since $\mathbf{L}'\boldsymbol{\beta}$ is a reparameterization of $\boldsymbol{\beta}$.

Multiply both sides of the equation $\mathbf{A}'\mathbf{X}_L\mathbf{X}_R(\mathbf{A}'\mathbf{X})^c(\mathbf{A}'\mathbf{X}) = \mathbf{A}'\mathbf{X}_L\mathbf{X}_R$ by $\mathbf{X}_L(\mathbf{A}'\mathbf{X}_L)^{-1}$, and the result is $\mathbf{X}(\mathbf{A}'\mathbf{X})^c(\mathbf{A}'\mathbf{X}) = \mathbf{X}$, which is $\mathbf{X}(\mathbf{L}')^c\mathbf{L}' = \mathbf{X}$, and (2) is proved.

To prove (3) we use the fact that there exist $K \times n$ matrices $\mathbf{A}'$ and $\mathbf{A}_1'$ each of rank K such that $\mathbf{L}_1' = \mathbf{A}_1'\mathbf{X}$ and $\mathbf{L}' = \mathbf{A}'\mathbf{X}$. But we can write $\mathbf{L}_1' = \mathbf{A}_1'\mathbf{X}_L\mathbf{X}_R$ and $\mathbf{L}' = \mathbf{A}'\mathbf{X}_L\mathbf{X}_R$. Multiply the equations on the left by $(\mathbf{A}_1'\mathbf{X}_L)^{-1}$ and $(\mathbf{A}'\mathbf{X}_L)^{-1}$, respectively. We get

$$(\mathbf{A}_1'\mathbf{X}_L)^{-1}\mathbf{L}_1' = \mathbf{X}_R = (\mathbf{A}'\mathbf{X}_L)^{-1}\mathbf{L}'$$

so

$$\mathbf{L}_1' = (\mathbf{A}_1'\mathbf{X}_L)(\mathbf{A}'\mathbf{X}_L)^{-1}\mathbf{L}' = \mathbf{B}\mathbf{L}'$$

where $\mathbf{B}$ is $K \times K$ of rank K, since both $\mathbf{A}_1'\mathbf{X}_L$ and $(\mathbf{A}'\mathbf{X}_L)^{-1}$ are $K \times K$ matrices of rank K.

Part (4) will be left for the reader to prove.

As a consequence of this theorem, the design model $\mathbf{Y} = \mathbf{X}\boldsymbol{\beta} + \boldsymbol{\varepsilon}$, where $\mathbf{X}$ is $n \times p$ of rank K, can be written as $\mathbf{Y} = \mathbf{X}(\mathbf{L}')^c\mathbf{L}'\boldsymbol{\beta} + \boldsymbol{\varepsilon}$, which we write as $\mathbf{Y} = \mathbf{U}\boldsymbol{\theta} + \boldsymbol{\varepsilon}$, where $\boldsymbol{\theta} = \mathbf{L}'\boldsymbol{\beta}$ is a reparameterization of $\boldsymbol{\beta}$. Hence $\mathbf{U}$, which is $\mathbf{X}(\mathbf{L}')^c$, has size $n \times K$ and rank K. We have transformed (in fact reparameterized) the model $\mathbf{Y} = \mathbf{X}\boldsymbol{\beta} + \boldsymbol{\varepsilon}$ of less-than-full rank to the model $\mathbf{Y} = \mathbf{U}\boldsymbol{\theta} + \boldsymbol{\varepsilon}$ which is full rank, and all the results of Chapter 6 are valid for the reparameterized model. For example, the UMVU estimator of $\boldsymbol{\theta}$, using the model $\mathbf{Y} = \mathbf{U}\boldsymbol{\theta} + \boldsymbol{\varepsilon}$, is $\hat{\boldsymbol{\theta}} = (\mathbf{U}'\mathbf{U})^{-1}\mathbf{U}'\mathbf{Y}$, which we can write as $\mathbf{U}'\mathbf{U}\hat{\boldsymbol{\theta}} = \mathbf{U}'\mathbf{Y}$. Replace $\mathbf{U}$ with $\mathbf{X}(\mathbf{L}')^c$ to get $[\mathbf{X}(\mathbf{L}')^c]'[\mathbf{X}(\mathbf{L}')^c]\hat{\boldsymbol{\theta}} = [\mathbf{X}(\mathbf{L}')^c]'\mathbf{Y}$ or $[(\mathbf{L}')^c]'\mathbf{X}'\mathbf{X}(\mathbf{L}')^c\hat{\boldsymbol{\theta}} = [(\mathbf{L}')^c]'\mathbf{X}'\mathbf{Y}$. Multiply on the left by $\mathbf{L}$ and simplify to obtain $\mathbf{X}'\mathbf{X}(\mathbf{L}')^c\hat{\boldsymbol{\theta}} = \mathbf{X}'\mathbf{Y}$, since $\{\mathbf{L}[(\mathbf{L}')^c]'\mathbf{X}'\}' = \mathbf{X}(\mathbf{L}')^c\mathbf{L}' = \mathbf{X}$ by (2) of Theorem 13.2.7.

The general solution of $\mathbf{X}'\mathbf{X}(\mathbf{L}')^c\hat{\boldsymbol{\theta}} = \mathbf{X}'\mathbf{Y}$ for $(\mathbf{L}')^c\hat{\boldsymbol{\theta}}$ is

$$(\mathbf{L}')^c\hat{\boldsymbol{\theta}} = (\mathbf{X}'\mathbf{X})^c\mathbf{X}'\mathbf{Y} + [\mathbf{I} - (\mathbf{X}'\mathbf{X})^c(\mathbf{X}'\mathbf{X})]\mathbf{b}$$

for any $p \times 1$ vector $\mathbf{b}$. Now multiply the result on the left by $\mathbf{L}'$ and by (4) of Theorem 13.2.7 we get

$$\hat{\boldsymbol{\theta}} = \mathbf{L}'(\mathbf{X}'\mathbf{X})^c\mathbf{X}'\mathbf{Y} \qquad \text{since} \qquad \mathbf{L}'(\mathbf{X}'\mathbf{X})^c\mathbf{X}'\mathbf{X} = \mathbf{A}'\mathbf{X}(\mathbf{X}'\mathbf{X})^c\mathbf{X}'\mathbf{X} = \mathbf{A}'\mathbf{X} = \mathbf{L}'$$

If we use the model $\mathbf{Y} = \mathbf{X}\boldsymbol{\beta} + \boldsymbol{\varepsilon}$, the estimator of the basis set of estimable functions $\mathbf{L}'\boldsymbol{\beta}$ can be obtained by multiplying the normal equations $\mathbf{X}'\mathbf{X}\hat{\boldsymbol{\beta}} = \mathbf{X}'\mathbf{Y}$ on the left by $\mathbf{L}'(\mathbf{X}'\mathbf{X})^c$. Use (8) of Theorem 13.2.2 and get

$$\mathbf{L}'(\mathbf{X}'\mathbf{X})^c\mathbf{X}'\mathbf{X}\hat{\boldsymbol{\beta}} = \mathbf{L}'\hat{\boldsymbol{\beta}} = \mathbf{L}'(\mathbf{X}'\mathbf{X})^c\mathbf{X}'\mathbf{Y}$$

Thus $\hat{\boldsymbol{\theta}}$, using the reparameterized model $\mathbf{Y} = \mathbf{U}\boldsymbol{\theta} + \boldsymbol{\varepsilon}$, is identical to $\mathbf{L}'\hat{\boldsymbol{\beta}}$ when the model $\mathbf{Y} = \mathbf{X}\boldsymbol{\beta} + \boldsymbol{\varepsilon}$ is used, that is, $\mathbf{L}'\hat{\boldsymbol{\beta}} = \hat{\boldsymbol{\theta}}$. Clearly $\hat{\sigma}^2$ is also the same for each model. We have proved the following theorem.

THEOREM 13.2.8

Let $\mathbf{Y} = \mathbf{X}\boldsymbol{\beta} + \boldsymbol{\varepsilon}$ *be the design model in Equation* (13.2.1), *and let* $\mathbf{Y} = \mathbf{U}\boldsymbol{\theta} + \boldsymbol{\varepsilon}$ *be any reparameterization of the design model. The UMVU estimator of any estimable function of* $\boldsymbol{\beta}$ *is the same for both models. This estimator can be obtained from the normal equations of either model. The UMVU estimator of* σ^2 *is also the same for both models.*

This result will be used when we discuss confidence intervals and testing hypotheses in the design model in Section 13.4. Next we illustrate some of the material presented in this section.

Example 13.2.3

To illustrate some of the foregoing theory, we consider the design model in Example 5.4.3, where $n = 8, p = 7$, and $\boldsymbol{\beta}' = [\mu, \alpha_1, \alpha_2, \tau_1, \tau_2, \tau_3, \tau_4]$.

Find (1) the normal equations; (2) K, the number of linearly independent estimable functions; (3) a basis set of estimable functions; (4) the UMVU estimators in part (3); (5) $\hat{\sigma}^2$.

For part (1) the normal equations are as follows:

$$\begin{aligned}
8\hat{\mu} + 4\hat{\alpha}_1 + 4\hat{\alpha}_2 + 2\hat{\tau}_1 + 2\hat{\tau}_2 + 2\hat{\tau}_3 + 2\hat{\tau}_4 &= Y_{..} \\
4\hat{\mu} + 4\hat{\alpha}_1 \qquad\quad + \hat{\tau}_1 + \hat{\tau}_2 + \hat{\tau}_3 + \hat{\tau}_4 &= Y_{1.} \\
4\hat{\mu} \qquad\quad + 4\hat{\alpha}_2 + \hat{\tau}_1 + \hat{\tau}_2 + \hat{\tau}_3 + \hat{\tau}_4 &= Y_{2.} \\
2\hat{\mu} + \hat{\alpha}_1 + \hat{\alpha}_2 + 2\hat{\tau}_1 &= Y_{.1} \\
2\hat{\mu} + \hat{\alpha}_1 + \hat{\alpha}_2 \qquad + 2\hat{\tau}_2 &= Y_{.2} \\
2\hat{\mu} + \hat{\alpha}_1 + \hat{\alpha}_2 \qquad\qquad + 2\hat{\tau}_3 &= Y_{.3} \\
2\hat{\mu} + \hat{\alpha}_1 + \hat{\alpha}_2 \qquad\qquad\qquad + 2\hat{\tau}_4 &= Y_{.4}
\end{aligned} \tag{13.2.10}$$

In this model $\boldsymbol{\beta}$ consists of three subvectors $\boldsymbol{\mu}' = [\mu]$, $\boldsymbol{\alpha}' = [\alpha_1, \alpha_2]$, and $\boldsymbol{\tau}' = [\tau_1, \tau_2, \tau_3, \tau_4]$. We can write an abbreviated form of the normal equations by displaying one equation for each of the subvectors in $\boldsymbol{\beta}$. We get

$$\begin{aligned}
&\text{for } \mu: && 8\hat{\mu} + 4\hat{\alpha}_1 + 4\hat{\alpha}_2 + 2\hat{\tau}_1 + 2\hat{\tau}_2 + 2\hat{\tau}_3 + 2\hat{\tau}_4 = Y_{..} \\
&\text{for } \boldsymbol{\alpha}: && 4\hat{\mu} + 4\hat{\alpha}_i + \hat{\tau}_1 + \hat{\tau}_2 + \hat{\tau}_3 + \hat{\tau}_4 = Y_{i.} \qquad i = 1, 2 \\
&\text{for } \boldsymbol{\tau}: && 2\hat{\mu} + \hat{\alpha}_1 + \hat{\alpha}_2 + 2\hat{\tau}_j = Y_{.j} \\
& && j = 1, 2, 3, 4
\end{aligned} \tag{13.2.11}$$

In Section 13.5 we will give a method whereby this abbreviated set of normal equations can easily be obtained from the model $Y_{ij} = \mu + \alpha_i + \tau_j + \varepsilon_{ij}$.

We now show that the answers to parts (2), (3), (4), and (5) can be obtained from the normal equations. We use the abbreviated set but the reader can check the procedure by using the full set. To find K we note that if we add the equations in the $\boldsymbol{\alpha}$ set and subtract this sum from the μ equation, we get $0 = 0$, so the μ equation is a linear combination of the $\boldsymbol{\alpha}$ equations. This produces one linear restriction among the rows of the normal equations (among the rows of $\mathbf{X}'\mathbf{X}$). Next we note that the sum of the $\boldsymbol{\alpha}$ equations minus the sum of the $\boldsymbol{\tau}$ equations gives $0 = 0$; so there is at least one linear restriction among the $\boldsymbol{\alpha}$ and $\boldsymbol{\tau}$ equations. This produces two (there may be more) linear restrictions among the rows of the normal equations (among the rows of $\mathbf{X}'\mathbf{X}$). Thus $K = \text{rank}[\mathbf{X}] = \text{rank}[\mathbf{X}'\mathbf{X}] \le p - 2 = 7 - 2 = 5$.

Since no other linear restriction among the normal equations is immediately apparent, we next attempt to find as many linearly *independent* estimable functions as we can. We use the left side of the normal equations with the ^ removed and have $\mathbf{X}'\mathbf{X}\boldsymbol{\beta}$, which is a full set of estimable functions and contains a basis set. We know that every row of $\mathbf{X}'\mathbf{X}\boldsymbol{\beta}$ and every linear combination of the rows of $\mathbf{X}'\mathbf{X}\boldsymbol{\beta}$ is an estimable function. Consider the following:

1. the first row: $8\mu + 4\alpha_1 + 4\alpha_2 + 2\tau_1 + 2\tau_2 + 2\tau_3 + 2\tau_4$
2. row 2 minus row 3: $4\alpha_1 - 4\alpha_2$
3. row 4 minus row 5: $2\tau_1 - 2\tau_2$
4. row 4 minus row 6: $2\tau_1 - 2\tau_3$
5. row 4 minus row 7: $2\tau_1 - 2\tau_4$

We have displayed five estimable functions and they are linearly independent.

We show they are linearly independent by the following argument: The first function is the only one that contains μ, so it must be linearly independent of the last four functions; but the last four functions are linearly independent since each contains a parameter that is not contained in any of the other three. So these five functions are linearly independent estimable functions and $K \geq 5$ (we include $K > 5$ since we have actually exhibited five linearly independent estimable functions, but there may be some that we have not found). However, by the number of constraints among the normal equations we showed that $K \leq 5$, and the two results, $K \leq 5$ and $K \geq 5$, imply that $K = 5$; this is the answer to part (2). We have already answered part (3) since we have found a basis set consisting of five linearly independent estimable functions.

We use Corollary 13.2.4 to answer part (4). We get

$$8\hat{\mu} + 4\hat{\alpha}_1 + 4\hat{\alpha}_2 + 2\hat{\tau}_1 + 2\hat{\tau}_2 + 2\hat{\tau}_3 + 2\hat{\tau}_4 = Y_{..}$$

$$4\hat{\alpha}_1 - 4\hat{\alpha}_2 = Y_{1.} - Y_{2.} \qquad 2\hat{\tau}_1 - 2\hat{\tau}_2 = Y_{.1} - Y_{.2}$$

$$2\hat{\tau}_1 - 2\hat{\tau}_3 = Y_{.1} - Y_{.3} \qquad 2\hat{\tau}_1 - 2\hat{\tau}_4 = Y_{.1} - Y_{.4}$$

To answer part (5) we must find *any* solution $\hat{\boldsymbol{\beta}}$ of the normal equations and find $\hat{\boldsymbol{\beta}}'\mathbf{X}'\mathbf{Y}$. One solution is $\hat{\mu} = \bar{Y}_{..}$; $\hat{\alpha}_1 = \bar{Y}_{1.} - \bar{Y}_{..}$; $\hat{\alpha}_2 = \bar{Y}_{2.} - \bar{Y}_{..}$; $\hat{\tau}_1 = \bar{Y}_{.1} - \bar{Y}_{..}$; $\hat{\tau}_2 = \bar{Y}_{.2} - \bar{Y}_{..}$; $\hat{\tau}_3 = \bar{Y}_{.3} - \bar{Y}_{..}$; $\hat{\tau}_4 = \bar{Y}_{.4} - \bar{Y}_{..}$. The reader can readily check that these values are actually a solution to the normal equations.

An easy method for finding solutions for many design models will be discussed later. We obtain $\hat{\boldsymbol{\beta}}'\mathbf{X}'\mathbf{Y}$ by multiplying the solution vector by the right-hand side of the normal equations. We get

$$\hat{\boldsymbol{\beta}}'\mathbf{X}'\mathbf{Y} = \bar{Y}_{..}(Y_{..}) + (\bar{Y}_{1.} - \bar{Y}_{..})Y_{1.} + (\bar{Y}_{2.} - \bar{Y}_{..})Y_{2.} + (\bar{Y}_{.1} - \bar{Y}_{..})Y_{.1} + (\bar{Y}_{.2} - \bar{Y}_{..})Y_{.2} + (\bar{Y}_{.3} - \bar{Y}_{..})Y_{.3} + (\bar{Y}_{.4} - \bar{Y}_{..})Y_{.4}$$

$$= \frac{Y_{..}^2}{8} + \left(\sum_{i=1}^{2} \frac{Y_{i.}^2}{4} - \frac{Y_{..}^2}{8}\right) + \left(\sum_{j=1}^{4} \frac{Y_{.j}^2}{2} - \frac{Y_{..}^2}{8}\right)$$

$$= \frac{Y_{..}^2}{8} + \sum_{i=1}^{2}\sum_{j=1}^{4} (\bar{Y}_{i.} - \bar{Y}_{..})^2 + \sum_{i=1}^{2}\sum_{j=1}^{4} (\bar{Y}_{.j} - \bar{Y}_{..})^2 \tag{13.2.12}$$

Hence

$$\hat{\sigma}^2 = \frac{1}{n-K}[\mathbf{Y}'\mathbf{Y} - \hat{\boldsymbol{\beta}}'\mathbf{X}'\mathbf{Y}]$$

$$= \frac{1}{3}\left[\left(\sum_{i=1}^{2}\sum_{j=1}^{4} Y_{ij}^2 - \frac{Y_{..}^2}{8}\right) - \left(\sum_{i=1}^{2} \frac{Y_{i.}^2}{4} - \frac{Y_{..}^2}{8}\right) - \left(\sum_{j=1}^{4} \frac{Y_{.j}^2}{2} - \frac{Y_{..}^2}{8}\right)\right]$$

$$= \left(\frac{1}{3}\right) \sum_{i=1}^{2}\sum_{j=1}^{4} (Y_{ij} - \bar{Y}_{i.} - \bar{Y}_{.j} + \bar{Y}_{..})^2 \tag{13.2.13}$$

13.3 Point Estimation for the Design Model; Case II

The design model for Case II has been defined as follows:

1. $\mathbf{Y} = \mathbf{X}\boldsymbol{\beta} + \boldsymbol{\varepsilon}$, $\boldsymbol{\varepsilon}$ is distributed $(\boldsymbol{\varepsilon} : \mathbf{0}, \sigma^2\mathbf{I})$.
2. $\mathbf{X}$ has size $n \times p$ and rank K, where $n > p > K$.
3. The parameter space Ω is defined by $\Omega = \{(\boldsymbol{\beta}, \sigma^2) : \boldsymbol{\beta} \in E_p, \sigma^2 > 0\}$.

(13.3.1)

For this case the form of the p.d.f. is not specified and, of course, M.L. estimators cannot be obtained. In Section 6.10 a similar situation was discussed for the general linear model, and many of the computation formulas for point estimation for Case 2 were the same as for Case 1. We will find that the same situation obtains for the design model.

Since M.L. estimators cannot be found, we use least squares to obtain an estimator of the elements of $\boldsymbol{\beta}$. We must find the value of $\boldsymbol{\beta}$, say $\tilde{\boldsymbol{\beta}}$, that minimizes $\boldsymbol{\varepsilon}'\boldsymbol{\varepsilon} = (\mathbf{y} - \mathbf{X}\boldsymbol{\beta})'(\mathbf{y} - \mathbf{X}\boldsymbol{\beta})$. If we let $\tilde{\boldsymbol{\beta}}$ be the value of $\boldsymbol{\beta}$ that satisfies $\partial(\boldsymbol{\varepsilon}'\boldsymbol{\varepsilon})/\partial\boldsymbol{\beta} = \mathbf{0}$, we get $-2\mathbf{X}'\mathbf{y} + 2\mathbf{X}'\mathbf{X}\tilde{\boldsymbol{\beta}} = \mathbf{0}$, or $\mathbf{X}'\mathbf{X}\tilde{\boldsymbol{\beta}} = \mathbf{X}'\mathbf{y}$, the same normal equations we obtained when trying to find the M.L. estimator of $\boldsymbol{\beta}$ for Case I. But this system of equations has an infinite number of solutions since $K < p$; so as for Case I there is no *unique* solution for $\tilde{\boldsymbol{\beta}}$.

The question of identifiability cannot be examined as it was for Case I since the p.d.f of $\mathbf{Y}$ is not specified. However, we will determine whether an unbiased estimator exists for each element of $\boldsymbol{\beta}$. To do this we determine for what vectors ℓ an unbiased estimator of $\ell'\boldsymbol{\beta}$ exists. We use the same logic for Case II of the design model as we did for Case 2 of the general linear model and restrict estimators of $\ell'\boldsymbol{\beta}$ to *linear* functions of $\mathbf{Y}$.

DEFINITION 13.3.1

Estimability of $\ell'\boldsymbol{\beta}$. *For the design model in Equation* (13.3.1), *the linear function of* $\boldsymbol{\beta}$, *namely* $\ell'\boldsymbol{\beta}$, *is defined to be estimable if and only if there esists a linear function of* $\mathbf{Y}$, *say* $\mathbf{a}'\mathbf{Y}$, *such that* $\mathscr{E}[\mathbf{a}'\mathbf{Y}] = \ell'\boldsymbol{\beta}$.

THEOREM 13.3.1

For the design model in Equation (13.3.1), *the linear function of* $\boldsymbol{\beta}$, *namely* $\ell'\boldsymbol{\beta}$, *is estimable if and only if there exists a vector* $\mathbf{a}$ *such that* $\ell = \mathbf{X}'\mathbf{a}$.

Proof

A general linear function of the observations is $\ell(\mathbf{Y}) = \mathbf{a}'\mathbf{Y}$. By Definition 13.3.1, $\ell'\boldsymbol{\beta}$ is estimable if and only if there exists a vector $\mathbf{a}$ such that $\mathscr{E}[\mathbf{a}'\mathbf{Y}] = \ell'\boldsymbol{\beta}$, which implies $\mathbf{a}'\mathbf{X}\boldsymbol{\beta} = \ell'\boldsymbol{\beta}$, which implies $\mathbf{a}'\mathbf{X} = \ell'$ (or $\ell = \mathbf{X}'\mathbf{a}$).

Note 1. The conditions for the estimability of $\ell'\boldsymbol{\beta}$ are the same for both Cases I and II of the design model.

THEOREM 13.3.2

For the design model in Equation (13.3.1), $\ell'\boldsymbol{\beta}$ *is estimable if and only if the eight conditions of Theorem* 13.2.2 *obtain.*

Proof

The eight conditions in Theorem 13.2.2 are necessary and sufficient conditions for a solution for $\mathbf{a}'$ to exist for the set of equations $\mathbf{X}\mathbf{a}' = \ell'$, the necessary and sufficient condition for $\ell'\boldsymbol{\beta}$ to be estimable.

Definitions 13.2.3 and 13.2.4 of linearly independent estimable functions, set, full set, and basis set of estimable functions are applicable to Case II of the design model.

THEOREM 13.3.3

For the design model in Equation (13.3.1), *the number of linearly independent estimable functions is equal to* K, *the rank of* $\mathbf{X}$.

Proof

The proof is the same as the proof for Theorem 13.2.3.

Properties of $\ell'\hat{\boldsymbol{\beta}}$ for Case I were stated in Theorem 13.2.4. We now state similar properties for $\ell'\hat{\boldsymbol{\beta}}$ for Case II of the design model, but since the p.d.f. of $\mathbf{Y}$ is not known, we replace the optimum property of UMVU with BLU.

THEOREM 13.3.4

Consider the design model given in Equation (13.3.1) *and the normal equations* $\mathbf{X}'\mathbf{X}\hat{\boldsymbol{\beta}} = \mathbf{X}'\mathbf{Y}$.

(1) *If $\ell'\boldsymbol{\beta}$ is an estimable function, then $\ell'\hat{\boldsymbol{\beta}}$ is invariant for any solution $\hat{\boldsymbol{\beta}}$ of the normal equations, and $\ell'\hat{\boldsymbol{\beta}} = \ell'\mathbf{X}^-\mathbf{Y}$.*

(2) *If $\ell'\boldsymbol{\beta}$ is an estimable function, then $\ell'\hat{\boldsymbol{\beta}}$ is the BLU estimator of $\ell'\boldsymbol{\beta}$.*

(3) $\hat{\sigma}^2 = (n - K)^{-1}(\mathbf{Y}'\mathbf{Y} - \hat{\boldsymbol{\beta}}'\mathbf{X}'\mathbf{Y})$ *is invariant for any solution $\hat{\boldsymbol{\beta}}$ of the normal equations.*

(4) $\hat{\sigma}^2$ *is an unbiased estimator of σ^2.*

Proof

The proofs of (1) and (3) are the same as the proofs of (1) and (3) for Theorem 13.2.4. We shall prove (2) and leave (4) for the reader to prove.

To prove (2) assume the linear function $\ell(\mathbf{Y}) = \ell'\mathbf{X}^-\mathbf{Y} + \mathbf{b}'\mathbf{Y}$ is the BLU estimator of $\ell'\boldsymbol{\beta}$, where $\mathbf{b}'$ is to be determined. The unbiased condition requires $\mathscr{E}[\ell(\mathbf{Y})] = \ell'\boldsymbol{\beta}$, which gives $\ell'\boldsymbol{\beta} = \ell'\boldsymbol{\beta} + \mathbf{b}'\mathbf{X}\boldsymbol{\beta}$, or $\mathbf{b}'\mathbf{X}\boldsymbol{\beta} = 0$ for all $\boldsymbol{\beta}$ in E_p. This implies $\mathbf{b}'\mathbf{X} = \mathbf{0}$.

Now

$$\begin{aligned}\text{var}[\ell(\mathbf{Y})] &= \text{var}[\ell'\mathbf{X}^-\mathbf{Y} + \mathbf{b}'\mathbf{Y}] \\ &= \text{var}[\ell'\mathbf{X}^-\mathbf{Y}] + \text{var}[\mathbf{b}'\mathbf{Y}] + 2\,\text{cov}[\ell'\mathbf{X}^-\mathbf{Y}, \mathbf{b}'\mathbf{Y}]\end{aligned}$$

We show that the covariance is zero. We get

$$\begin{aligned}\text{cov}[\ell'\mathbf{X}^-\mathbf{Y}, \mathbf{b}'\mathbf{Y}] &= \mathscr{E}[(\ell'\mathbf{X}^-\mathbf{Y})(\mathbf{b}'\mathbf{Y})] - (\ell'\boldsymbol{\beta})(\mathbf{b}'\mathbf{X}\boldsymbol{\beta}) \\ &= \mathscr{E}[(\ell'\mathbf{X}^-)(\mathbf{X}\boldsymbol{\beta} + \boldsymbol{\varepsilon})(\mathbf{b}'\mathbf{X}\boldsymbol{\beta} + \mathbf{b}'\boldsymbol{\varepsilon})'] = \mathscr{E}[\ell'\mathbf{X}^-\boldsymbol{\varepsilon}\boldsymbol{\varepsilon}'\mathbf{b}]\end{aligned}$$

by using the unbiased condition $\mathbf{b}'\mathbf{X} = \mathbf{0}$. We get $\mathscr{E}[\ell'\mathbf{X}^-\boldsymbol{\varepsilon}\boldsymbol{\varepsilon}'\mathbf{b}] = \sigma^2[\ell'\mathbf{X}^-\mathbf{b}] = 0$, since if $\mathbf{b}'\mathbf{X} = \mathbf{0}$, then $\mathbf{X}'\mathbf{b} = \mathbf{0}$ and $\mathbf{X}^-\mathbf{b} = \mathbf{0}$.

We then have

$$\text{var}[\ell(\mathbf{Y})] = \text{var}[\ell'\mathbf{X}^-\mathbf{Y}] + \text{var}[\mathbf{b}'\mathbf{Y}] \geq \text{var}[\ell'\mathbf{X}^-\mathbf{Y}]$$

Thus var[$\ell'\mathbf{X}^-\mathbf{Y}$] is a lower bound for the variance of the linear unbiased estimator, $\ell(\mathbf{Y})$, of $\ell'\boldsymbol{\beta}$. But the lower bound is attained if and only if var[$\mathbf{b}'\mathbf{Y}$] = 0. This implies $\mathbf{b}'\mathbf{Y}$ is a constant (with probability one). But since the unbiased property implies $\mathscr{E}[\mathbf{b}'\mathbf{Y}] = 0$, it follows that $\mathbf{b}'\mathbf{Y} = 0$ (with probability one) and $\ell(\mathbf{Y}) = \ell'\mathbf{X}^-\mathbf{Y} = \ell'\hat{\boldsymbol{\beta}}$ is the BLU estimator of $\ell'\boldsymbol{\beta}$.

THEOREM 13.3.5

Consider the design model in Equation (13.3.1).

(1) *The results of Corollary* 13.2.4 *obtain if UMVU is replaced by BLU.*

(2) *The procedure note following Corollary* 13.2.4 *applies if UMVU is replaced by BLU.*

(3) *The results of Example* 13.2.2 *are valid if UMVU is replaced by BLU.*

Proof

The proof will be left for the reader.

Terminology. The estimator of an estimable function of $\boldsymbol{\beta}$, say $\ell'\boldsymbol{\beta}$, will be called the best unbiased estimator of $\ell'\boldsymbol{\beta}$ if it is an UMVU estimator for Case I or a BLU estimator for Case II.

We now turn our attention to confidence intervals and tests of hypotheses for Case I of the design model.

13.4 Confidence Intervals and Tests of Hypotheses for Case I of the Design Model

The model is given in Equation (13.2.1) and only the hypothesis $H_0 : \mathbf{H}\boldsymbol{\beta} = \mathbf{0}$ *vs.* $H_a : \mathbf{H}\boldsymbol{\beta} \neq \mathbf{0}$ will be tested, where $\mathbf{H}\boldsymbol{\beta}$ is a set of *linearly independent estimable functions* (a subset of a basis set). This will be called an *estimable* hypothesis (often referred to as a *testable* hypothesis).

It seems intuitively plausible that a reasonable test statistic would be a function of "estimators" of the parameters being tested, and if a hypothesis includes nonidentifiable linear functions of $\boldsymbol{\beta}$, then estimators with reasonable optimum properties do not exist, and it would seem that perhaps no test statistic with reasonably good properties would exist either. So we shall discuss only those hypotheses which are equivalent to a hypothesis that a set of linearly independent estimable functions of $\boldsymbol{\beta}$ is equal to zero.

THEOREM 13.4.1

In the design model in Equation (13.2.1), *let* $\mathbf{H}\boldsymbol{\beta}$ ($\mathbf{H}$ *known*) *be a set of q linearly independent estimable functions of* $\boldsymbol{\beta}$. *W is a generalized likelihood ratio test statistic for* $H_0 : \mathbf{H}\boldsymbol{\beta} = \mathbf{0}$ *vs.* $H_a : \mathbf{H}\boldsymbol{\beta} \neq \mathbf{0}$ *and is given in two forms below.*

$$W = \frac{(\mathbf{H}\hat{\boldsymbol{\beta}})'[\mathbf{H}(\mathbf{X}'\mathbf{X})^c\mathbf{H}']^{-1}(\mathbf{H}\hat{\boldsymbol{\beta}})}{q\hat{\sigma}^2} \tag{13.4.1}$$

where $\hat{\boldsymbol{\beta}}$ *is any solution of the normal equations* $\mathbf{X}'\mathbf{X}\hat{\boldsymbol{\beta}} = \mathbf{X}'\mathbf{Y}$ *and* $\hat{\sigma}^2 = (n - K)^{-1}(\mathbf{Y}'\mathbf{Y} - \hat{\boldsymbol{\beta}}'\mathbf{X}'\mathbf{Y})$, *and* $(\mathbf{X}'\mathbf{X})^c$ *is any c-inverse of* $\mathbf{X}'\mathbf{X}$.

$$W = \left(\frac{\hat{\sigma}^2_\omega - \hat{\sigma}^2_\Omega}{\hat{\sigma}^2_\Omega}\right)\left(\frac{n - K}{q}\right) \tag{13.4.2}$$

where $\hat{\sigma}^2_\Omega = (1/n)(\mathbf{Y}'\mathbf{Y} - \hat{\boldsymbol{\beta}}'\mathbf{X}'\mathbf{Y})$ *is the M.L. estimator of* σ^2 *in the full model* $\mathbf{Y} = \mathbf{X}\boldsymbol{\beta} + \boldsymbol{\varepsilon}$, *and* $\hat{\sigma}^2_\omega = (1/n)(\mathbf{Y}'\mathbf{Y} - \hat{\boldsymbol{\gamma}}'\mathbf{B}'\mathbf{Y})$ *is the M.L. estimator of* σ^2 *in the reduced model* $\mathbf{Y} = \mathbf{B}\boldsymbol{\gamma} + \boldsymbol{\varepsilon}$ (*where* $\mathbf{Y} = \mathbf{B}\boldsymbol{\gamma} + \boldsymbol{\varepsilon}$ *is the full model reduced by the hypothesis* H_0). *W is distributed* $F(w : q, n - K; \lambda)$, *where*

$$\lambda = (2\sigma^2)^{-1}(\mathbf{H}\boldsymbol{\beta})'[\mathbf{H}(\mathbf{X}'\mathbf{X})^c\mathbf{H}']^{-1}(\mathbf{H}\boldsymbol{\beta})$$

H_0 *is rejected if and only if w, the computed value of W, satisfies*

$$w \geq F_{\alpha:q,n-K} \tag{13.4.3}$$

The power of the test is $\Pi(\lambda)$, *where*

$$\Pi(\lambda) = \int_{F_{\alpha:q,n-K}}^{\infty} F(w : q, n - K; \lambda)\, dw \tag{13.4.4}$$

Proof

This test statistic is very similar to the one given in Theorem 6.3.1. In fact, we shall derive it from that test by reparameterizing the design model (where $K < p$) to a full rank model so that the theory of the general linear model is applicable.

Let $\mathbf{L}'\boldsymbol{\beta}$ be a basis set of estimable functions, where $\mathbf{L} = [\mathbf{H}', \mathbf{H}_1']$; thus $\mathbf{H}$ is the first q rows of the matrix $\mathbf{L}'$ and $\mathbf{H}_1$ is the last $K - q$ rows (if $q = K$, then $\mathbf{L} = \mathbf{H}'$).

The design model $\mathbf{Y} = \mathbf{X}\boldsymbol{\beta} + \boldsymbol{\varepsilon}$ can be written $\mathbf{Y} = \mathbf{X}(\mathbf{L}')^c\mathbf{L}'\boldsymbol{\beta} + \boldsymbol{\varepsilon}$, which is $\mathbf{Y} = \mathbf{U}\boldsymbol{\theta} + \boldsymbol{\varepsilon}$, where $\mathbf{U} = \mathbf{X}(\mathbf{L}')^c$ and $\boldsymbol{\theta} = \mathbf{L}'\boldsymbol{\beta}$. If we partition $\mathbf{U} = [\mathbf{B}_1, \mathbf{B}]$ and $\boldsymbol{\theta}' = [\boldsymbol{\gamma}_1', \boldsymbol{\gamma}']$, we can write the model as $\mathbf{Y} = \mathbf{B}_1\boldsymbol{\gamma}_1 + \mathbf{B}\boldsymbol{\gamma} + \boldsymbol{\varepsilon}$, where $\boldsymbol{\gamma}_1 = \mathbf{H}\boldsymbol{\beta}$. The reduced model is $\mathbf{Y} = \mathbf{B}\boldsymbol{\gamma} + \boldsymbol{\varepsilon}$ and is full rank; the full model is $\mathbf{Y} = \mathbf{U}\boldsymbol{\theta} + \boldsymbol{\varepsilon}$ (or $\mathbf{Y} = \mathbf{X}\boldsymbol{\beta} + \boldsymbol{\varepsilon}$). From these we can obtain the normal equations for the full model $\mathbf{X}'\mathbf{X}\hat{\boldsymbol{\beta}} = \mathbf{X}'\mathbf{Y}$ or as $\mathbf{U}'\mathbf{U}\hat{\boldsymbol{\theta}} = \mathbf{U}'\mathbf{Y}$. Then

$$\begin{aligned}\hat{\sigma}^2_\Omega &= \frac{1}{n}(\mathbf{Y}'\mathbf{Y} - \hat{\boldsymbol{\beta}}'\mathbf{X}'\mathbf{Y}) = \frac{1}{n}(\mathbf{Y}'\mathbf{Y} - \hat{\boldsymbol{\theta}}'\mathbf{U}'\mathbf{Y})\\ &= \frac{1}{n}(\mathbf{Y}'\mathbf{Y} - \mathbf{Y}'\mathbf{X}\mathbf{X}^-\mathbf{Y}) = \frac{1}{n}(\mathbf{Y}'\mathbf{Y} - \mathbf{Y}'\mathbf{U}\mathbf{U}^-\mathbf{Y})\\ &= \frac{1}{n}[\mathbf{Y}'\mathbf{Y} - \mathbf{Y}'\mathbf{X}(\mathbf{X}'\mathbf{X})^c\mathbf{X}'\mathbf{Y}] = \frac{1}{n}[\mathbf{Y}'\mathbf{Y} - \mathbf{Y}'\mathbf{U}(\mathbf{U}'\mathbf{U})^{-1}\mathbf{U}'\mathbf{Y}]\end{aligned}$$

The reduced normal equations are

$$\mathbf{B}'\mathbf{B}\hat{\boldsymbol{\gamma}} = \mathbf{B}'\mathbf{Y} \tag{13.4.5}$$

and

$$\hat{\sigma}^2_\omega = \frac{1}{n}(\mathbf{Y}'\mathbf{Y} - \hat{\boldsymbol{\gamma}}'\mathbf{B}'\mathbf{Y}) = \frac{1}{n}(\mathbf{Y}'\mathbf{Y} - \mathbf{Y}'\mathbf{B}\mathbf{B}^-\mathbf{Y}) = \frac{1}{n}[\mathbf{Y}'\mathbf{Y} - \mathbf{Y}'\mathbf{B}(\mathbf{B}'\mathbf{B})^{-1}\mathbf{B}'\mathbf{Y}]$$

From this we get for the generalized likelihood ratio:

$$W = \left(\frac{\hat{\boldsymbol{\beta}}'\mathbf{X}'\mathbf{Y} - \hat{\boldsymbol{\gamma}}'\mathbf{B}'\mathbf{Y}}{\mathbf{Y}'\mathbf{Y} - \hat{\boldsymbol{\beta}}'\mathbf{X}'\mathbf{Y}}\right)\left(\frac{n-K}{q}\right) = \left(\frac{\mathbf{Y}'[\mathbf{U}\mathbf{U}^- - \mathbf{B}\mathbf{B}^-]\mathbf{Y}}{\mathbf{Y}'\mathbf{Y} - \hat{\boldsymbol{\beta}}'\mathbf{X}'\mathbf{Y}}\right)\left(\frac{n-K}{q}\right) \tag{13.4.6}$$

In Chapter 6 we showed that W is distributed as $F(w : q, n - K; \lambda)$, and by the method used to prove Theorem 6.3.1, it can be shown that W in Equation (13.4.6) is equal to $\{(\mathbf{H}\hat{\boldsymbol{\beta}})'[\mathbf{H}(\mathbf{X}'\mathbf{X})^c\mathbf{H}']^{-1}(\mathbf{H}\hat{\boldsymbol{\beta}})\}/q\hat{\sigma}^2$.

All the theorems and procedures in Chapter 6 concerning one-at-a-time and multiple confidence intervals on estimable functions of $\boldsymbol{\beta}$ apply to the design model if $(\mathbf{X}'\mathbf{X})^{-1}$ is replaced by $(\mathbf{X}'\mathbf{X})^c$. We state a theorem here for one-at-a-time confidence intervals.

THEOREM 13.4.2

Consider the design model for Case I given in Equation (13.2.1), *and let $\boldsymbol{\ell}'\boldsymbol{\beta}$ be any estimable function of $\boldsymbol{\beta}$. A $1 - \alpha$ confidence interval on $\boldsymbol{\ell}'\boldsymbol{\beta}$ is*

$$\boldsymbol{\ell}'\hat{\boldsymbol{\beta}} \mp t_{\alpha/2:n-K}\sqrt{\widehat{\text{var}}[\boldsymbol{\ell}'\hat{\boldsymbol{\beta}}]}$$

which can be written as

$$\boldsymbol{\ell}'\mathbf{X}^-\mathbf{Y} \mp t_{\alpha/2:n-K}\hat{\sigma}[\boldsymbol{\ell}'(\mathbf{X}'\mathbf{X})^c\boldsymbol{\ell}]^{1/2}$$

Proof

$Z = (\ell'\hat{\beta} - \ell'\beta)/\sqrt{\sigma^2\ell'(\mathbf{X}'\mathbf{X})^c\ell}$ is distributed $N(z:0,1)$; $U = (n-K)\hat{\sigma}^2/\sigma^2$ is distributed $\chi^2(u:n-K)$, Z and U are independent, so $T = (Z/\hat{\sigma})/\sigma$ is distributed $s(t:n-K)$. The results follow from these facts.

COROLLARY 13.4.2

Consider the design model for Case I given in Equation (13.2.1), *and let* $\ell_1'\beta$, $\ell_2'\beta, \ldots, \ell_M'\beta$ *be a set of M linearly independent estimable functions of* β. *Simultaneous confidence intervals on* $\ell_m'\beta$, $m = 1, 2, \ldots, M$, *with a confidence coefficient greater than or equal to* $1-\alpha$, *are given by*

$$\ell_m'\hat{\beta} \mp t_{\alpha/2:M,n-K}\sqrt{\widehat{\text{var}}[\ell_m'\hat{\beta}]} \qquad m = 1, 2, \ldots, M$$

which can be written

$$\ell_m'\mathbf{X}^-\mathbf{Y} \mp t_{\alpha/2:M,n-K}\hat{\sigma}[\ell_m'(\mathbf{X}'\mathbf{X})^c\ell_m]^{1/2} \qquad m = 1, 2, \ldots, M$$

Proof

The proof is a direct application of Equation (6.6.8).

In the next section we discuss some computing procedures for the design model.

13.5 Computations

To perform the computations for obtaining point estimates, confidence intervals, and test statistics for the general design model, one could reparameterize to a full rank model and use all the results in Chapter 7 that apply to the general linear model. Often, however, the computations needed to effect the reparameterization can be quite troublesome and can require considerable computations; so that approach will not generally be utilized. Fortunately, in many cases, the design matrix $\mathbf{X}$ has a structure such that the computations are simple.

To demonstrate general procedures for calculating the quantities needed in the design model, we partition the parameter vector β into subvectors such that each subvector represents a *factor* being studied and each element of a subvector represents a *level* of the factor. A factor is difficult to define explicitly; it is sometimes referred as a "treatment" under study, but we shall reserve the word "treatment" for a special kind of factor. Roughly speaking, a factor is anything an investigator wants to study. For example, all of the following could be factors: fertilizer; temperature; time; psychological (or other kinds of) tests; size (of anything, such as rocks or cities); and so forth.

The numbers in the vector **y** are measurements of a factor, called the *response factor*, but unless we specifically write *response factor*, we will mean the factors concerned with the **X** matrix. The *response factor* is also sometimes referred to as the *response variable* and sometimes called the *yield*. The *levels* of a factor refer to the quantity, or amounts, or different types, and so on, of the factor. For example, if the factor is variety of corn, and there are 10 varieties under study, the 10 varieties are referred to as 10 *levels* of the factor corn variety. If the factor is nitrogen fertilizer, and the fertilizer is applied at the rates of 10 pounds, 20 pounds, and 32 pounds per experimental unit, then 10 pounds, 20 pounds, and 32 pounds are the levels of the factor nitrogen fertilizer. If the factor is time in weeks (for instance time between administering a certain drug), then 1 week, 2 weeks, 3 weeks, and 4 weeks are the levels.

An investigation for which a design model is appropriate is one in which it is desired to determine how various levels of different factors affect the response factor. In the vector $\boldsymbol{\beta}$ are subvectors, one subvector for each factor; in addition, there are often subvectors that allow for the effect of various combinations of factors (such as the interaction of two or more factors); also, most models include μ, a general location parameter, in the $\boldsymbol{\beta}$ vector. The design matrix **X** consists of the numbers 0 and 1 and is an indicator matrix. For example, if a specified (say the qth) equation of the model contains certain levels of various factors, then there will be a 1 in the appropriate places in the qth row of the **X** matrix. This will be illustrated in detail later.

We return to the $\boldsymbol{\beta}$ vector and partition it into subvectors, one for each factor or combination of factors in the model and one for μ. We denote μ by β_0 and the other subvectors by $\boldsymbol{\beta}_i$, $i = 1, 2, \ldots, q$. We write $\boldsymbol{\beta}' = [\beta_0, \boldsymbol{\beta}_1', \ldots, \boldsymbol{\beta}_q']$, where there are $q + 1$ subvectors. The reader can refer to the model in Equation (5.4.6) where $\beta_0 = \mu$, $\boldsymbol{\beta}_1 = [\tau_1, \tau_2]'$, and so $\boldsymbol{\beta}' = [\mu, \boldsymbol{\beta}_1']$. In Example 5.4.3 we note that

$$\boldsymbol{\beta}' = [\beta_0, \boldsymbol{\beta}_1', \boldsymbol{\beta}_2'] = [\mu, \boldsymbol{\alpha}', \boldsymbol{\tau}'] \qquad \text{where} \qquad \boldsymbol{\alpha}' = [\alpha_1, \alpha_2] \qquad \boldsymbol{\tau}' = [\tau_1, \tau_2, \tau_3, \tau_4]$$

In the design model we can partition the columns of the **X** matrix to be compatible with the subvectors in $\boldsymbol{\beta}$ and get for $\mathbf{X}\boldsymbol{\beta}$

$$\mathbf{X}\boldsymbol{\beta} = [\mathbf{X}_0, \mathbf{X}_1, \ldots, \mathbf{X}_q]\begin{bmatrix} \beta_0 \\ \boldsymbol{\beta}_1 \\ \vdots \\ \boldsymbol{\beta}_q \end{bmatrix} = \sum_{i=0}^{q} \mathbf{X}_i\boldsymbol{\beta}_i \qquad \text{where} \qquad \mathbf{X}_0 = \mathbf{1} \qquad \boldsymbol{\beta}_0 = \mu \tag{13.5.1}$$

If the model does not contain the general mean μ, then μ and the vector $\mathbf{X}_0$ can be omitted, and $\mathbf{X}\boldsymbol{\beta}$ could be written $\sum_{i=1}^{q} \mathbf{X}_i\boldsymbol{\beta}_i$; see Equation (5.4.4). We will, however, always include the parameter μ in the basic model in this book. We now define a matrix that will be used in this book for a *design* matrix.

DEFINITION 13.5.1

Design Matrix. *An $n \times p$ matrix $\mathbf{X}$ is defined to be a design matrix if and only if $\mathbf{X}$ can be partitioned as $[\mathbf{X}_0, \mathbf{X}_1, \ldots, \mathbf{X}_q]$, where $\mathbf{X}_i$ is an $n \times q_i$ matrix and satisfies the following:*

(1) *the elements of the matrix are the numbers* 0 *or* 1;

(2) *for each submatrix $\mathbf{X}_i$, $i = 0, 1, \ldots, q$, every row contains exactly one element equal to* 1 (*the remaining elements in each row are zeros*);

(3) *for each $\mathbf{X}_i$, $i = 0, 1, \ldots, q$, every column contains at least one nonzero element.*

Example 13.5.1

The $\mathbf{X}$ matrix in Equation (5.4.3) is a design matrix if we view the entire matrix as a single partition, that is, $\mathbf{X} = [\mathbf{X}_1]$. The $\mathbf{X}$ matrix in Equation (5.4.7) is a design matrix with the first column $\mathbf{X}_0$, the second and third column $\mathbf{X}_1$. The $\mathbf{X}$ matrix in Equation (5.4.10) is a design matrix, and $\mathbf{X}_0$ is column 1, $\mathbf{X}_1$ contains columns 2 and 3, $\mathbf{X}_2$ contains columns 4, 5, 6, and 7.

Note 1. We notice that a matrix with the particular structure given in Definition 13.5.1 requires each equation in the model $\mathbf{Y} = \mathbf{X}\boldsymbol{\beta} + \boldsymbol{\varepsilon}$ to contain exactly one element from each of the subvectors $\boldsymbol{\beta}_0, \boldsymbol{\beta}_1, \ldots, \boldsymbol{\beta}_q$ of $\boldsymbol{\beta}$, and therefore, a parameter representing each factor under study is contained in each equation in the model.

Note 2. If $\mathbf{Y} = \mathbf{X}\boldsymbol{\beta} + \boldsymbol{\varepsilon}$ is a design model ($\mathbf{X}$ is a design matrix), this does not necessarily imply that $\mathbf{U}$ is a design matrix in the reparameterized model $\mathbf{Y} = \mathbf{U}\boldsymbol{\theta} + \boldsymbol{\varepsilon}$.

Most of the results for the design model concerning point and interval estimation and hypotheses tests have been derived from the normal equations. In order to compute the quantities needed, one must first compile these equations. There are two ways to write the model, namely, exhibit *each* equation in the model $\mathbf{Y} = \mathbf{X}\boldsymbol{\beta} + \boldsymbol{\varepsilon}$ (this requires writing n equations); or write a single representative equation of the model from which all n equations can be implied. For example, examine Equation (5.4.1), where all n equations of the model are displayed, and Equation (5.4.3), where the corresponding matrix and vectors are shown. The single representative equation for the model is exhibited in Equation (5.4.4).

For another illustration, note that the full model is written in Equation (5.4.7), and in Equation (5.4.6) a single representative equation is displayed from which the full model can easily be obtained. Also see Equations (5.4.8) and (5.4.9).

We now show how an abbreviated set of *normal* equations can be constructed. By an abbreviated set we mean one representative equation for each subvector in $\boldsymbol{\beta}$. If the entire set of normal equations is written, there are p equations, one for each element in $\boldsymbol{\beta}$, while in the abbreviated set of normal equations, only $q + 1$ instead of p equations are written. To obtain the abbreviated normal equations, we note that the full set, $\mathbf{X}'\mathbf{X}\hat{\boldsymbol{\beta}} = \mathbf{X}'\mathbf{y}$, could be obtained by taking the expectation of the $p \times 1$ vector $\mathbf{X}'\mathbf{Y}$, namely $\mathscr{E}[\mathbf{X}'\mathbf{Y}]$; we would get $\mathscr{E}[\mathbf{X}'\mathbf{Y}] = \mathbf{X}'\mathbf{X}\boldsymbol{\beta}$. Then the symbol $\boldsymbol{\beta}$ is replaced by the symbol $\hat{\boldsymbol{\beta}}$, $\mathbf{X}'\mathbf{y}$ is computed, and we have $\mathbf{X}'\mathbf{X}\hat{\boldsymbol{\beta}} = \mathbf{X}'\mathbf{y}$, the full normal equations.

We illustrate with Example 13.2.2 where $n = 6$, $p = 3$, and $K = 2$. $\mathbf{X}'\mathbf{Y}$ is $[Y_{..}, Y_{1.}, Y_{2.}]'$, and clearly,

$$\mathscr{E}[Y_{..}] = \mathscr{E}\left[\sum_{i=1}^{2}\sum_{j=1}^{3} Y_{ij}\right] = \sum_{i=1}^{2}\sum_{j=1}^{3}(\mu + \tau_i) = 6\mu + 3\tau_1 + 3\tau_2$$

and the left-hand side of the first normal equation is $6\hat{\mu} + 3\hat{\tau}_1 + 3\hat{\tau}_2$, the right-hand side is $y_{..}$, where $y_{..}$ is a number obtained from the data vector $\mathbf{y}$. Then the second and third equations are obtained from

$$\mathscr{E}[Y_{i.}] = \mathscr{E}\left[\sum_{j=1}^{3} Y_{ij}\right] = \sum_{j=1}^{3}(\mu + \tau_i) = 3\mu + 3\tau_i \qquad i = 1, 2$$

Thus the second and third equations are obtained by putting the symbol $\hat{}$ on μ, τ_1, and τ_2 and replacing the notation for the random variables $Y_{1.}$ and $Y_{2.}$ with the notation for the observed values. We get $3\hat{\mu} + 3\hat{\tau}_1 = y_{1.}$ and $3\hat{\mu} + 3\hat{\tau}_2 = y_{2.}$.

For the abbreviated normal equations for this model, we get

$$\begin{aligned} \mu:&\quad 6\hat{\mu} + 3\hat{\tau}_1 + 3\hat{\tau}_2 = y_{..} \\ \tau_i:&\quad 3\hat{\mu} + 3\hat{\tau}_i = y_{i.} \qquad i = 1, 2 \end{aligned}$$

Since $p = 3$ and $q = 1$, not much is saved by using the abbreviated normal equations in the example. But if the index j went from 1 to 100, then $p = 101$ and $q = 1$, and the *two* equations could represent the 101 equations of the full normal equations, and the savings by using the abbreviated method would be tremendous.

Since the left-hand sides of the normal equations are obtained by evaluating the expectation of the right-hand side $\mathbf{X}'\mathbf{Y}$, we will determine a method for finding an abbreviated set for the vector $\mathbf{X}'\mathbf{Y}$. Write $\mathbf{X}'\mathbf{Y}$ as $[\mathbf{X}_0, \mathbf{X}_1, \ldots, \mathbf{X}_q]'\mathbf{Y}$, and since each $\mathbf{X}_i$ refers to a subvector of parameters in $\boldsymbol{\beta}$, we find that a representative equation for each $\mathbf{X}_i'\mathbf{Y}$ is a sum of appropriate elements in $\mathbf{Y}$. Also, $\mathbf{X}\boldsymbol{\beta}$ in the model can be written $[\mathbf{X}_0, \mathbf{X}_1, \ldots, \mathbf{X}_q]\boldsymbol{\beta}$, and the jth element of the ith subvector $\boldsymbol{\beta}_i$ appears in a given equation, say the tth, of the model if and only if the tth row of $\mathbf{X}_i$ contains a 1 in the jth column. So the jth element in the subvector $\boldsymbol{\beta}_i$ appears in every equation in the model in which a 1 occurs in the corresponding row of the jth column of the matrix $\mathbf{X}_i$. But these 1's correspond exactly with the elements in $\mathbf{Y}$ that are summed. Thus to obtain the value of the jth element in $\mathbf{X}_i'\mathbf{Y}$, sum $\mathbf{Y}$ over those equations in the model that contain the jth element of the subvector $\boldsymbol{\beta}_i$. Do this for each subvector. Then $q + 1$ elements of $\mathbf{X}'\mathbf{Y}$ are obtained which are representative elements of the right-hand side of the normal equations—one for each subvector $\boldsymbol{\beta}_i$. We illustrate the procedure with an example.

Example 13.5.2

Consider the model $Y_{ij} = \mu + \alpha_i + \tau_j + \varepsilon_{ij}$, $i = 1, 2$, and $j = 1, 2, 3, 4$. The $\boldsymbol{\beta}$ vector has three subvectors: $\boldsymbol{\mu} = [\mu]$, $\boldsymbol{\alpha}' = [\alpha_1, \alpha_2]$, and $\boldsymbol{\tau}' = [\tau_1, \tau_2, \tau_3, \tau_4]$; so $n = 8$, $p = 7$, and $q = 2$. The $\mathbf{X}$ matrix is partitioned as $\mathbf{X} = [\mathbf{X}_0, \mathbf{X}_1, \mathbf{X}_2]$ corresponding to $\boldsymbol{\beta}' = [\mu, \boldsymbol{\alpha}', \boldsymbol{\tau}']$. We write the $\mathbf{X}$ matrix, which is given in Equation (5.4.10), in partitioned form and get

$$\mathbf{X}\boldsymbol{\beta} = [\mathbf{X}_0 \mid \mathbf{X}_1 \mid \mathbf{X}_2]\begin{bmatrix} \mu \\ \hline \boldsymbol{\alpha} \\ \hline \boldsymbol{\tau} \end{bmatrix} = \left[\begin{array}{c|cc|cccc} 1 & 1 & 0 & 1 & 0 & 0 & 0 \\ 1 & 1 & 0 & 0 & 1 & 0 & 0 \\ 1 & 1 & 0 & 0 & 0 & 1 & 0 \\ 1 & 1 & 0 & 0 & 0 & 0 & 1 \\ 1 & 0 & 1 & 1 & 0 & 0 & 0 \\ 1 & 0 & 1 & 0 & 1 & 0 & 0 \\ 1 & 0 & 1 & 0 & 0 & 1 & 0 \\ 1 & 0 & 1 & 0 & 0 & 0 & 1 \end{array}\right]\begin{bmatrix} \mu \\ \hline \alpha_1 \\ \alpha_2 \\ \hline \tau_1 \\ \tau_2 \\ \tau_3 \\ \tau_4 \end{bmatrix}$$

For the abbreviated normal equations, we find a representative equation for each subvector $\boldsymbol{\mu}$, $\boldsymbol{\alpha}$, and $\boldsymbol{\tau}$. The jth element in $\boldsymbol{\mu}$ is, of course, μ itself, and $\mathbf{X}_0'\mathbf{Y}$ is obtained by summing the elements in $\mathbf{Y}$ over all equations in the model that contain μ. Clearly, every equation in the model $Y_{ij} = \mu + \alpha_i + \tau_j + \varepsilon_{ij}$ contains μ, so $\mathbf{X}_0'\mathbf{Y} = \sum_{i=1}^{2} \sum_{j=1}^{4} Y_{ij} = Y_{..}$.

Next we obtain a representative equation for $\boldsymbol{\alpha}$. We note that α_r appears in every equation of the model in which the first subscript of Y_{ij}, namely i, is equal to r, so the representative element in $\mathbf{X}_1'\mathbf{Y}$ is $\sum_{j=1}^{4} Y_{rj} = Y_{r.}$ (that is, sum Y_{ij} over those equations in the model that contain α_r).

To obtain a representative equation for $\boldsymbol{\tau}$, say the sth, we sum $\mathbf{Y}$ over those equations in the model that contain τ_s, namely $\sum_{i=1}^{2} Y_{is} = Y_{.s}$. So the abbreviated form of $\mathbf{X}'\mathbf{Y}$, the right-hand side of the normal equations, is $Y_{..}$; $Y_{r.}$, $r = 1, 2$; $Y_{.s}$, $s = 1, 2, 3, 4$.

To obtain the left-hand side we find the expected value of each of these random variables and replace each parameter by the parameter with a $\hat{}$. For example,

$$\mathscr{E}[Y_{..}] = \mathscr{E}\left[\sum_{i=1}^{2}\sum_{j=1}^{4} Y_{ij}\right] = \sum_{i=1}^{2}\sum_{j=1}^{4} (\mu + \alpha_i + \tau_j)$$
$$= 8\mu + 4\alpha_1 + 4\alpha_2 + 2\tau_1 + 2\tau_2 + 2\tau_3 + 2\tau_4$$

We then find the expectations of $Y_{r.}$ and $Y_{.s}$ and get

$$\mu: \quad 8\hat{\mu} + 4\hat{\alpha}_1 + 4\hat{\alpha}_2 + 2\hat{\tau}_1 + 2\hat{\tau}_2 + 2\hat{\tau}_3 + 2\hat{\tau}_4 = y_{..}$$
$$\alpha_r: \quad 4\hat{\mu} + 4\hat{\alpha}_r + \hat{\tau}_1 + \hat{\tau}_2 + \hat{\tau}_3 + \hat{\tau}_4 = y_{r.} \quad r = 1, 2$$
$$\tau_s: \quad 2\hat{\mu} + \hat{\alpha}_1 + \hat{\alpha}_2 + 2\hat{\tau}_s = y_{.s} \quad s = 1, 2, 3, 4$$

These are the $q + 1 = 3$ abbreviated normal equations. From this abbreviated set we can determine K, the number of linearly independent estimable functions and exhibit such a set. We can also find a solution $\hat{\boldsymbol{\beta}}$ to the normal equations and thus find $\hat{\boldsymbol{\beta}}'\mathbf{X}'\mathbf{y}$ and hence compute $\hat{\sigma}^2$.

We have been discussing how to derive the normal equations from a knowledge of the model. We now turn our attention to computing the necessary quantities for point and interval estimation and hypotheses tests. The quantities needed are listed below.

1. Point estimation: $\hat{\sigma}^2$ and $\ell_i'\hat{\boldsymbol{\beta}}$ for all estimable functions $\ell_i'\boldsymbol{\beta}$ that one wants to estimate.
2. Confidence intervals: $\hat{\sigma}^2$, $\ell_i'(\mathbf{X}'\mathbf{X})^c\ell_i$, and $\ell_i'\hat{\boldsymbol{\beta}}$ for all estimable functions $\ell_i'\boldsymbol{\beta}$ for which one wants to obtain confidence intervals.
3. Hypotheses tests: $\hat{\sigma}^2$ and $(\mathbf{H}\hat{\boldsymbol{\beta}})'[\mathbf{H}(\mathbf{X}'\mathbf{X})^c\mathbf{H}']^{-1}(\mathbf{H}\hat{\boldsymbol{\beta}})$, from which w can be computed to test $\mathbf{H}\boldsymbol{\beta} = \mathbf{0}$ by Equation (13.4.1); or $\hat{\sigma}_\omega^2$ and $\hat{\sigma}_\Omega^2$ can be computed and Equation (13.4.2) used. (13.5.2)

For a certain class of design models which includes "the balanced design models" to be defined and discussed later, the procedure is to find the abbreviated normal equations, and, from these, to obtain explicit, and generally quite simple, formulas for computing all quantities needed in Equation (13.5.2).

However, for many types of design models, the *abbreviated* normal equations are of limited help in reducing the amount of the computation. For these models the *full* normal equations can be constructed and the computations performed using them. We discuss three methods that can be used to solve the normal equations.

Method 1

Find a set of $p - K$ vectors $\mathbf{v}_i$, each of size $p \times 1$, and define $\mathbf{V}$ by $\mathbf{V} = [\mathbf{v}_1, \mathbf{v}_2, \ldots, \mathbf{v}_{p-K}]$ such that the matrix

$$\begin{bmatrix} \mathbf{X}'\mathbf{X} \\ \mathbf{V}' \end{bmatrix}$$

has rank p. By Corollary 1.6.6.4 the set of equations

$$\begin{bmatrix} \mathbf{X}'\mathbf{X} \\ \mathbf{V}' \end{bmatrix} \hat{\boldsymbol{\beta}} = \begin{bmatrix} \mathbf{X}'\mathbf{y} \\ \mathbf{0} \end{bmatrix} \tag{13.5.3}$$

has a unique solution for $\hat{\boldsymbol{\beta}}$. But this set of equations is equivalent to the two sets $\mathbf{X}'\mathbf{X}\hat{\boldsymbol{\beta}} = \mathbf{X}'\mathbf{y}$ and $\mathbf{V}'\hat{\boldsymbol{\beta}} = \mathbf{0}$.

Often the set $\mathbf{V}'\boldsymbol{\beta}$ is such that the matrix equation

$$\begin{bmatrix} \mathbf{X}'\mathbf{X} \\ \mathbf{V}' \end{bmatrix} \hat{\boldsymbol{\beta}} = \begin{bmatrix} \mathbf{X}'\mathbf{y} \\ \mathbf{0} \end{bmatrix}$$

is very easily solved for $\hat{\boldsymbol{\beta}}$. Since this is a solution to the normal equations, the desired estimate of $\ell'\boldsymbol{\beta}$ can be obtained as $\ell'\hat{\boldsymbol{\beta}}$ for any ℓ, where $\ell'\boldsymbol{\beta}$ is an estimable function.

Also, since

$$\begin{bmatrix} \mathbf{X}'\mathbf{X} \\ \mathbf{V}' \end{bmatrix}$$

must have rank p, it follows that $\mathbf{V}'\boldsymbol{\beta}$ must be a set of $p - K$ nonestimable functions of $\boldsymbol{\beta}$ and no linear combination of $\mathbf{V}'\boldsymbol{\beta}$ can be estimable; otherwise $\mathbf{V}'\boldsymbol{\beta}$ would be some linear combination of $\mathbf{X}'\mathbf{X}\boldsymbol{\beta}$ (which contains a basis set of estimable functions), and hence

$$\begin{bmatrix} \mathbf{X}'\mathbf{X} \\ \mathbf{V}' \end{bmatrix}$$

could not have rank p. In many models it is easy to find this set of nonestimable functions $\mathbf{V}'\boldsymbol{\beta}$ and to solve for $\hat{\boldsymbol{\beta}}$.

Method 2

The set of equations in Equation (13.5.3), which is equivalent to the two sets of equations $\mathbf{X}'\mathbf{X}\hat{\boldsymbol{\beta}} = \mathbf{X}'\mathbf{y}$ and $\mathbf{V}'\hat{\boldsymbol{\beta}} = \mathbf{0}$, is also equivalent to the system shown below:

$$\begin{bmatrix} \mathbf{X'X} & \mathbf{V} \\ \mathbf{V'} & \mathbf{0} \end{bmatrix} \begin{bmatrix} \hat{\boldsymbol{\beta}} \\ \mathbf{0} \end{bmatrix} = \begin{bmatrix} \mathbf{X'y} \\ \mathbf{0} \end{bmatrix} \tag{13.5.4}$$

which we write as $\mathbf{S}_V\hat{\boldsymbol{\beta}}_V = \mathbf{s}_V$. Although the coefficient matrix for this system is symmetric and nonsingular, it is *not* nonnegative so the square root procedures discussed in Chapter 7 cannot be used. However, various methods are available that can be used to solve for $\hat{\boldsymbol{\beta}}_V$, and from this one can compute $\boldsymbol{\ell}'\hat{\boldsymbol{\beta}}$, the best unbiased estimate of any estimable function $\boldsymbol{\ell}'\boldsymbol{\beta}$.

If $\mathbf{S}_V\hat{\boldsymbol{\beta}}_V = \mathbf{s}_V$ is used to find $\hat{\boldsymbol{\beta}}$, a solution to the normal equations, it requires solving a system of $2p - K$ equations. Since $2p - K > p$, this is a larger system than the original normal equations; so, in general, this method should not be used.

However, in many cases a modification of this method (one that reduces the system to a set of K equations) is a very good procedure. For this modified procedure a set of the β_i are used for the $p - K$ nonestimable functions $\mathbf{V}'\boldsymbol{\beta}$. In this case the system $\mathbf{V}'\hat{\boldsymbol{\beta}} = \mathbf{0}$ is simply $\hat{\beta}_{i_1} = \hat{\beta}_{i_2} = \cdots = \hat{\beta}_{i_{p-K}} = 0$, that is, $p - K$ of the $\hat{\beta}_i$ are set equal to zero. Of course, one must select certain β_i so that the rank of

$$\begin{bmatrix} \mathbf{X'X} \\ \mathbf{V'} \end{bmatrix}$$

is p. When this is the case, the corresponding rows and columns of $\mathbf{X'X}$ can be omitted, and $\mathbf{S}_0$, the symbol we shall use for the resulting submatrix, is positive definite.

Let $\hat{\boldsymbol{\beta}}_0$ denote the subvector that remains after omitting the elements $\hat{\beta}_{i_1}, \hat{\beta}_{i_2}, \ldots, \hat{\beta}_{i_{p-K}}$ from $\hat{\boldsymbol{\beta}}$, and let $\mathbf{s}_0$ denote the subvector that remains after omitting the $i_1, i_2, \ldots, i_{p-K}$ elements from $\mathbf{X'y}$. The resulting system is

$$\mathbf{S}_0\hat{\boldsymbol{\beta}}_0 = \mathbf{s}_0 \tag{13.5.5}$$

and $\mathbf{S}_0$ is a positive definite $K \times K$ matrix. The techniques of Chapter 7 can be used on this system to solve for $\hat{\boldsymbol{\beta}}_0$ and $\mathbf{S}_0^{-1}$.

If the zeros are replaced in $\hat{\boldsymbol{\beta}}_0$ for the $i_1, i_2, \ldots, i_{p-K}$ elements, then the resulting vector $\hat{\boldsymbol{\beta}}$ is a solution to the normal equations, and $\boldsymbol{\ell}'\hat{\boldsymbol{\beta}}$ is the best unbiased estimate of the estimable function $\boldsymbol{\ell}'\boldsymbol{\beta}$. If rows and columns of zeros are replaced in the $i_1, i_2, \ldots, i_{p-K}$ rows and columns of $\mathbf{S}_0^{-1}$, then the resulting matrix is a c-inverse of $\mathbf{X'X}$, and $\sigma^2\boldsymbol{\ell}'(\mathbf{X'X})^c\boldsymbol{\ell}$ is the variance of $\boldsymbol{\ell}'\hat{\boldsymbol{\beta}}$. Since Method 2 will be used extensively, we will illustrate it with an example.

Example 13.5.3

Suppose a set of normal equations is given by the following:

$$
\begin{aligned}
18\hat{\beta}_0 + 9\hat{\beta}_1 + 9\hat{\beta}_2 + 6\hat{\beta}_3 + 6\hat{\beta}_4 + 6\hat{\beta}_5 &= 57\\
9\hat{\beta}_0 + 9\hat{\beta}_1 + 3\hat{\beta}_3 + 3\hat{\beta}_4 + 3\hat{\beta}_5 &= 15\\
9\hat{\beta}_0 + 9\hat{\beta}_2 + 3\hat{\beta}_3 + 3\hat{\beta}_4 + 3\hat{\beta}_5 &= 42\\
6\hat{\beta}_0 + 3\hat{\beta}_1 + 3\hat{\beta}_2 + 6\hat{\beta}_3 &= 27\\
6\hat{\beta}_0 + 3\hat{\beta}_1 + 3\hat{\beta}_2 + 6\hat{\beta}_4 &= -3\\
6\hat{\beta}_0 + 3\hat{\beta}_1 + 3\hat{\beta}_2 + 6\hat{\beta}_5 &= 33
\end{aligned}
$$

It can easily be shown that $p = 6$ and $K = 4$, so we can use $p - K = 2$ linearly independent estimable functions. Also, it can be shown that if we use $\hat{\beta}_0 = \hat{\beta}_5 = 0$ for $\mathbf{V}'\hat{\boldsymbol{\beta}} = \mathbf{0}$, then the coefficient matrix in Equation (13.5.3) has rank $p = 6$.

The system $\mathbf{S}_0\hat{\boldsymbol{\beta}}_0 = \mathbf{s}_0$ in Equation (13.5.5) is (eliminate rows and columns 1 and 6 that correspond to $\hat{\beta}_0$ and $\hat{\beta}_5$)

$$
\begin{bmatrix} 9 & 0 & 3 & 3\\ 0 & 9 & 3 & 3\\ 3 & 3 & 6 & 0\\ 3 & 3 & 0 & 6 \end{bmatrix}
\begin{bmatrix} \hat{\beta}_1\\ \hat{\beta}_2\\ \hat{\beta}_3\\ \hat{\beta}_4 \end{bmatrix}
=
\begin{bmatrix} 15\\ 42\\ 27\\ -3 \end{bmatrix}
$$

If we reduce this by the square root prodedure, we get

$$
\left[\begin{array}{c|c|c} \mathbf{S}_0 & \mathbf{s}_0 & \mathbf{I}\\ \hline \mathbf{T}_0 & \mathbf{t}_0 & \mathbf{T}_0'^{-1} \end{array}\right]
=
\left[\begin{array}{cccc|c|cccc}
9 & 0 & 3 & 3 & 15 & 1 & 0 & 0 & 0\\
0 & 9 & 3 & 3 & 42 & 0 & 1 & 0 & 0\\
3 & 3 & 6 & 0 & 27 & 0 & 0 & 1 & 0\\
3 & 3 & 0 & 6 & -3 & 0 & 0 & 0 & 1\\ \hline
3 & 0 & 1 & 1 & 5 & \frac{1}{3} & 0 & 0 & 0\\
 & 3 & 1 & 1 & 14 & 0 & \frac{1}{3} & 0 & 0\\
 & & 2 & -1 & 4 & -\frac{1}{6} & -\frac{1}{6} & \frac{1}{2} & 0\\
 & & & \sqrt{3} & \frac{-18}{\sqrt{3}} & \frac{-1}{2\sqrt{3}} & \frac{-1}{2\sqrt{3}} & \frac{1}{2\sqrt{3}} & \frac{1}{\sqrt{3}}
\end{array}\right] \tag{13.5.6}
$$

The backward solution gives $\hat{\beta}_4 = -6$, $\hat{\beta}_3 = -1$, $\hat{\beta}_2 = 7$, and $\hat{\beta}_1 = 4$. If we use these values with $\hat{\beta}_0 = \hat{\beta}_5 = 0$, we get $\hat{\boldsymbol{\beta}}' = [0, 4, 7, -1, -6, 0]$, which is a solution to the normal equations.

Next we compute $\mathbf{T}_0^{-1}\mathbf{T}_0'^{-1}$ and $(\mathbf{X}'\mathbf{X})^c$.

$$\mathbf{T}_0^{-1}\mathbf{T}_0'^{-1} = \left(\frac{1}{36}\right)\begin{bmatrix} 8 & 4 & -6 & -6 \\ 4 & 8 & -6 & -6 \\ -6 & -6 & 12 & 6 \\ -6 & -6 & 6 & 12 \end{bmatrix}$$

$$(\mathbf{X}'\mathbf{X})^c = \left(\frac{1}{36}\right)\begin{bmatrix} 0 & 0 & 0 & 0 & 0 & 0 \\ 0 & 8 & 4 & -6 & -6 & 0 \\ 0 & 4 & 8 & -6 & -6 & 0 \\ 0 & -6 & -6 & 12 & 6 & 0 \\ 0 & -6 & -6 & 6 & 12 & 0 \\ 0 & 0 & 0 & 0 & 0 & 0 \end{bmatrix}$$

By Theorem 13.2.4 if $\boldsymbol{\ell}'\boldsymbol{\beta}$ is any estimable function, then $\boldsymbol{\ell}'\hat{\boldsymbol{\beta}}$ is the best unbiased estimate, $\hat{\sigma}^2\boldsymbol{\ell}'(\mathbf{X}'\mathbf{X})^c\boldsymbol{\ell}$ is the estimated variance of $\boldsymbol{\ell}'\hat{\boldsymbol{\beta}}$, and $\hat{\sigma}^2$ is given by

$$\hat{\sigma}^2 = \frac{1}{n-K}[\mathbf{y}'\mathbf{y} - \hat{\boldsymbol{\beta}}'\mathbf{X}'\mathbf{y}] = \frac{1}{n-K}[\mathbf{y}'\mathbf{y} - \mathbf{t}_0'\mathbf{t}_0]$$

Of course, one does not need to use $\mathbf{I}$ in Equation (13.5.6) since $\mathbf{T}_0^{-1}$ can be computed directly from $\mathbf{T}_0$. Also, it is not necessary to compute $(\mathbf{X}'\mathbf{X})^c$ since $\boldsymbol{\ell}'(\mathbf{X}'\mathbf{X})^c\boldsymbol{\ell} = \boldsymbol{\ell}_0'(\mathbf{T}_0^{-1}\mathbf{T}_0'^{-1})\boldsymbol{\ell}_0$, where $\boldsymbol{\ell}_0$ is obtained from $\boldsymbol{\ell}$ by omitting the elements corresponding to the $\hat{\beta}_i$ that are set equal to zero to obtain $\mathbf{V}'\boldsymbol{\beta}$. Clearly, $\boldsymbol{\ell}'\hat{\boldsymbol{\beta}} = \boldsymbol{\ell}_0'\hat{\boldsymbol{\beta}}_0$.

Method 3

Use the format in Equation (7.3.4) and reduce $\mathbf{X}'\mathbf{X}$ by the square root method to the format in Equation (7.3.5) for estimating $\boldsymbol{\ell}_i'\boldsymbol{\beta}$, setting confidence limits on $\boldsymbol{\ell}_i'\boldsymbol{\beta}$, or testing the hypothesis that $\boldsymbol{\ell}_i'\boldsymbol{\beta} = 0$. Use the format in Equation (7.3.8) and reduce $\mathbf{X}'\mathbf{X}$ by the square root method explained there to test the hypothesis $\mathbf{H}\boldsymbol{\beta} = \mathbf{0}$.

The square root method must be modified slightly when the matrix $\mathbf{X}'\mathbf{X}$ is positive semidefinite instead of positive definite. The modification is required since, as one proceeds with the square root method, zeros will appear on the diagonal. When a zero is encountered, replace that entire row with zeros and proceed to the next row. We demonstrate the details in the next chapter.

Note 3. The matrix $\mathbf{T}$ can be computed directly from the $\mathbf{X}$ matrix without using the normal equations $\mathbf{X}'\mathbf{X}\hat{\boldsymbol{\beta}} = \mathbf{X}'\mathbf{y}$ by the method discussed in Section 7.7. From the matrix $\mathbf{T}$ one can then compute $\hat{\boldsymbol{\beta}}$, $\ell'\hat{\boldsymbol{\beta}}$, $\hat{\sigma}^2$, and $\widehat{\text{var}}[\ell'\hat{\boldsymbol{\beta}}]$.

13.6 The One-Factor Design Model

In this section we discuss in detail the design model that is defined as the *one-factor design model.* It is discussed here because it illustrates the theory in this chapter and because it is an important model for investigating certain real-world situations.

DEFINITION 13.6.1

One-Factor Design Model. *Below are the specifications that define a one-factor design model.*

(1) $Y_{ij} = \mu + \alpha_i + \varepsilon_{ij}$; $j = 1, 2, \ldots, J_i$; $i = 1, 2, \ldots, I$; $J_i \geq 1$ *for all* i, *and* $J_i > 1$ *for at least one value of* i; $I > 1$.

(2) *The* Y_{ij} *are observable random variables.*

(3) *The* ε_{ij} *are nonobservable random variables; for Case I they are distributed* $NID(\varepsilon_{ij} : 0, \sigma^2)$; *for Case II they are uncorrelated with means zero and variances* σ^2.

(4) $\sigma^2, \mu, \alpha_1, \alpha_2, \ldots, \alpha_I$ *are unknown parameters, and the parameter space is* Ω, *where*

$$\Omega = \{(\sigma^2, \mu, \alpha_1, \alpha_2, \ldots, \alpha_I) : \sigma^2 > 0, -\infty < \mu < \infty,$$
$$-\infty < \alpha_i < \infty \text{ for } i = 1, 2, \ldots, I\}$$

In addition to the preceding specifications, the following definitions will be used.

1. The *factor* under study will be denoted by A.
2. The ith *level* of the factor under study will be denoted by A_i.
3. The *parameter* of the ith level of factor A is defined as α_i.
4. The *mean* of the ith level of factor A is defined as $\mu + \alpha_i$.

5. The *main effect* of the ith level of factor A is defined as $\alpha_i - \bar{\alpha}_.$, where $\bar{\alpha}_. = I^{-1} \sum_{i=1}^{I} \alpha_i$. (13.6.1)

Thus the *main effect* of the ith level of factor A is the excess of the value of α_i over the average of all the α_i's.

To analyze this model we shall first determine the estimable functions of $\mu, \alpha_1, \alpha_2, \ldots, \alpha_I$ and the best unbiased estimates. The abbreviated normal equations are

$$\begin{aligned} \mu: &\quad \sum_{i=1}^{I} J_i\hat{\mu} + \sum_{i=1}^{I} J_i\hat{\alpha}_i = y_{..} \\ \alpha_i: &\quad J_i\hat{\mu} + J_i\hat{\alpha}_i = y_{i.} \qquad i = 1, 2, \ldots, I \end{aligned} \tag{13.6.2}$$

Clearly, $p = I + 1$, and since each equation on the left-hand side (with the $\hat{}$ removed) of the normal equations is estimable, it follows that $\mu + \alpha_i$, $i = 1, 2, \ldots, I$, are I linearly independent estimable functions (they are linearly independent since each contains a different parameter). Thus there are at least I linearly independent estimable functions (that is, $K \geq I$). The sum of the last I equations is equal to the first equation, so we know that there are no more than I linearly independent estimable functions (that is, $K \leq I$). Thus $K = I$ and a basis set of estimable functions is $\mu + \alpha_i$, $i = 1, 2, \ldots, I$. The BLU (or UMVU) estimates are

$$\hat{\mu} + \hat{\alpha}_i = \bar{y}_{i.} \qquad i = 1, 2, \ldots, I \tag{13.6.3}$$

All estimable functions must be linear combinations of this basis set, so to determine what types of linear functions of the α_i are estimable, we note that $\sum_{i=1}^{I} c_i(\mu + \alpha_i)$ is estimable for any set of constants c_i. But from this we get $\mu \sum_{i=1}^{I} c_i = \sum_{i=1}^{I} c_i\alpha_i$, so the only linear combinations of the α_i *only* that are estimable must be such that $\sum_{i=1}^{I} c_i = 0$ (this is the only way to eliminate the parameter μ from the estimable function). This leads to an important definition.

DEFINITION 13.6.2

Contrast. *A linear combination of the parameters in* $\boldsymbol{\beta}$ *(or in any subvector of* $\boldsymbol{\beta}$*) is called a contrast of the parameters if and only if the sum of the coefficients of the linear combination is zero.*

In the discussion above we have proved the following.

THEOREM 13.6.1

In the one-factor design model, all contrasts of the parameters α_i *are estimable, and contrasts are the only linear combinations of the* α_i *that are estimable. Also, the best unbiased estimate of* $\sum_{i=1}^{I} c_i\alpha_i$ *(where* $\sum_{i=1}^{I} c_i = 0$*) is* $\sum_{i=1}^{I} c_i\bar{y}_{i.}$. *The best unbiased estimates of the mean and main effect, respectively, of the ith level of A are* $\hat{\mu} + \hat{\alpha}_i = \bar{y}_{i.}$ *and* $\hat{\alpha}_i - \hat{\bar{\alpha}}_. = \bar{y}_{i.} - I^{-1}\sum_{i=1}^{I} \bar{y}_{i.}$.

> ***Reminder.*** By best unbiased estimate we mean UMVU estimate for Case I and BLU estimate for Case II.

We find a solution $\hat{\boldsymbol{\beta}}$ to the normal equations in order to compute $\hat{\sigma}^2$. To use Method 1 of Section 13.5, we note that $p - K = 1$, so we determine one nonestimable function that can be used to solve the system of normal equations. Clearly, $\sum J_i\alpha_i$ is not estimable since $J_i > 0$ for all i, and hence this cannot be a contrast among the α_i. So we use $\sum J_i\hat{\alpha}_i = 0$ in Equation (13.6.2); we get (let $\sum J_i = n$)

$$\hat{\mu} = \frac{y_{..}}{n} = \bar{y}_{..} \qquad \hat{\alpha}_i = \frac{y_{i.}}{J_i} - \frac{y_{..}}{n} = \bar{y}_{i.} - \bar{y}_{..} \qquad \text{for } i = 1, 2, \ldots, I$$

and

$$\hat{\boldsymbol{\beta}}'\mathbf{X}'\mathbf{y} = (\bar{y}_{..})(y_{..}) + \sum_{i=1}^{I} (\bar{y}_{i.} - \bar{y}_{..})(y_{i.}) = \sum_{i=1}^{I} \frac{y_{i.}^2}{J_i} - \frac{y_{..}^2}{n} + \frac{y_{..}^2}{n} = \sum_{i=1}^{I} \frac{y_{i.}^2}{J_i}$$

We should remember that the $\hat{\alpha}_i$ above is not a BLU or UMVU estimate of α_i (actually, of course, α_i is not estimable) but is only the value of $\hat{\alpha}_i$ that is a solution to the normal equations with the (nonestimable) condition $\sum J_i\hat{\alpha}_i = 0$.

THEOREM 13.6.2

For Case I of the one-factor model, the UMVU estimate of σ^2 *is*

$$\hat{\sigma}^2 = \frac{1}{n - I}\left[\sum_{i=1}^{I}\sum_{j=1}^{J_i} y_{ij}^2 - \sum_{i=1}^{I}\frac{y_{i.}^2}{J_i}\right] = \frac{1}{n - I}\sum_{i=1}^{I}\sum_{j=1}^{J_i}(y_{ij} - \bar{y}_{i.})^2$$

A hypothesis test that is usually of interest is this: the main effects of all levels of factor A are equal. This is the hypothesis $\alpha_i - \bar{\alpha}_. = 0$ for all i, which is equivalent to $\alpha_1 - \bar{\alpha}_. = \alpha_2 - \bar{\alpha}_. = \cdots = \alpha_I - \bar{\alpha}_.$, which is equivalent to $\alpha_1 = \alpha_2 = \cdots = \alpha_I$. The alternate hypothesis is that at least one equality is an inequality. Since $\alpha_i - \bar{\alpha}_.$ is estimable for $i = 1, 2, \ldots, I$, this is an estimable hypothesis.

We shall use the test function in Equation (13.4.2). From $\hat{\sigma}^2$ above we obtain $\hat{\sigma}_\Omega^2$ as

$$\hat{\sigma}_\Omega^2 = \frac{1}{n}\left[\sum_{i=1}^{I}\sum_{j=1}^{J_i} y_{ij}^2 - \sum_{i=1}^{I}\left(\frac{y_{i.}^2}{J_i}\right)\right]$$

To get $\hat{\sigma}^2_\omega$ we use the reduced model. If we let $\alpha_1 = \alpha_2 = \cdots = \alpha_I = \alpha$, say, where α is unknown, the reduced model is

$$Y_{ij} = \mu + \alpha + \varepsilon_{ij} = \mu_0 + \varepsilon_{ij} \qquad j = 1, 2, \ldots, J_i, \quad i = 1, 2, \ldots, I$$
$$\varepsilon_{ij} \text{ are distributed } NID(\varepsilon_{ij}: 0, \sigma^2), \quad \omega = \{\mu_0 : -\infty < \mu_0 < \infty\}$$

There is one unknown parameter and hence $p = 1$ in the reduced model. The normal equation is

$$\mu_0 : \quad n\tilde{\mu}_0 = y_{..}$$

The solution is $\tilde{\mu}_0 = \bar{y}_{..}$ and $\hat{\boldsymbol{\gamma}}'\mathbf{B}'\mathbf{y} = (\bar{y}_{..})y_{..} = y_{..}^2/n$. So

$$\hat{\sigma}^2_\omega = \frac{1}{n}\left(\sum_{i=1}^{I}\sum_{j=1}^{J_i} y_{ij}^2 - \frac{y_{..}^2}{n}\right) = \frac{1}{n}\sum_{i=1}^{I}\sum_{j=1}^{J_i}(y_{ij} - \bar{y}_{..})^2$$

and

$$w = \left(\frac{\sum_{i=1}^{I}(y_{i.}^2/J_i) - y_{..}^2/n}{\sum_{i=1}^{I}\sum_{j=1}^{J_i} y_{ij}^2 - \sum_{i=1}^{I}(y_{i.}^2/J_i)}\right)\left(\frac{n-I}{I-1}\right) = \frac{\sum_{i=1}^{I}\sum_{j=1}^{J_i}(\bar{y}_{i.} - \bar{y}_{..})^2/(I-1)}{\sum_{i=1}^{I}\sum_{j=1}^{J_i}(y_{ij} - \bar{y}_{i.})^2/(n-I)} \tag{13.6.4}$$

These results can be exhibited in a table such as Table 13.6.1. Some authors use a slightly different table (different source column). For a discussion of the various entries, see Section 7.4.

Table 13.6.1

ANOVA for Testing $H_0: \alpha_1 = \alpha_2 = \cdots \alpha_I$ in One-Factor Model

Source	*d.f.*	*S.S.*	*M.S.*	*E.M.S.*
Total	n	$\sum_{i=1}^{I}\sum_{j=1}^{J_i} y_{ij}^2$		
$R(\mu, \alpha)$	I	$\sum_{i=1}^{I}\left(\frac{y_{i.}^2}{J_i}\right)$		
$R(\mu)$	1	$\frac{y_{..}^2}{n}$		
$R(H_0)$	$I - 1$	$\sum_{i=1}^{I}\left(\frac{y_{i.}^2}{J_i}\right) - \frac{y_{..}^2}{n} = A_{ss}$	$A_{ms} = \frac{A_{ss}}{I-1}$	$\sigma^2 + (I-1)^{-1}\sum_{i=1}^{I} J_i(\alpha_i - \bar{\alpha}^*_.)^2$
Error	$n - I$	$\sum_{i=1}^{I}\sum_{j=1}^{J_i} y_{ij}^2 - \sum_{i=1}^{I}\left(\frac{y_{i.}^2}{J_i}\right) = E_{ss}$	$E_{ms} = \frac{E_{ss}}{n-I}$	σ^2

In Section 13.7 we discuss the quantities in the E.M.S. column of Table 13.6.1 and show that

$$\lambda = \frac{1}{2\sigma^2}\sum_{i=1}^{I} J_i(\alpha_i - \bar{\alpha}^*)^2 \qquad \text{where} \qquad \bar{\alpha}^* = \frac{1}{n}\sum_{i=1}^{I}\sum_{j=1}^{J_i}\alpha_i = \frac{1}{n}\sum_{i=1}^{I} J_i\alpha_i$$

If the J_i are all equal, say $J_i = J$ for $i = 1, 2, \ldots, I$, then the expressions simplify slightly.

We examine $\mathscr{E}[A_{ss}]$ in more detail and obtain

$$\begin{aligned}
\mathscr{E}[A_{ss}] &= \mathscr{E}\left[\sum_{i=1}^{I}\sum_{j=1}^{J_i}(\bar{Y}_{i.} - \bar{Y}_{..})^2\right] \\
&= \mathscr{E}\left[\sum_{i=1}^{I}\sum_{j=1}^{J_i}\left\{\left(\mu + \alpha_i + \left(\frac{1}{J_i}\right)\sum_{m=1}^{J_i}\varepsilon_{im}\right) - \left(\mu + \bar{\alpha}^* + \left(\frac{1}{n}\right)\sum_{r=1}^{I}\sum_{s=1}^{J_r}\varepsilon_{rs}\right)\right\}^2\right] \\
&= \sum_{i=1}^{I}\sum_{j=1}^{J_i}(\alpha_1 - \bar{\alpha}^*)^2 + \sum_{i=1}^{I}\sum_{j=1}^{J_i}\mathscr{E}\left[\left(\frac{1}{J_i}\sum_{m=1}^{J_i}\varepsilon_{im}\right)^2\right] \\
&\quad + \sum_{i=1}^{I}\sum_{j=1}^{J_i}\mathscr{E}\left[\left(\frac{1}{n}\sum_{r=1}^{I}\sum_{s=1}^{J_r}\varepsilon_{rs}\right)^2\right] \\
&\quad - 2\sum_{i=1}^{I}\sum_{j=1}^{J_i}\mathscr{E}\left[\left(\frac{1}{J_i}\sum_{m=1}^{J_i}\varepsilon_{im}\right)\left(\sum_{r=1}^{I}\sum_{s=1}^{J_r}\left(\frac{1}{n}\right)\varepsilon_{rs}\right)\right] \\
&= \sum_{i=1}^{I}\sum_{j=1}^{J_i}(\alpha_i - \bar{\alpha}^*)^2 + \sum_{i=1}^{I}\sum_{j=1}^{J_i}\left(\frac{\sigma^2}{J_i}\right) + \sum_{i=1}^{I}\sum_{j=1}^{J_i}\left(\frac{\sigma^2}{n}\right) - 2\sum_{i=1}^{I}\sum_{j=1}^{J_i}\left(\frac{\sigma^2}{n}\right) \\
&= \sum_{i=1}^{I}\sum_{j=1}^{J_i}(\alpha_i - \bar{\alpha}^*)^2 + I\sigma^2 + \sigma^2 - 2\sigma^2 \\
&= (I - 1)\sigma^2 + \sum_{i=1}^{I}\sum_{j=1}^{J_i}(\alpha_i - \bar{\alpha}^*)^2
\end{aligned}$$

From this the quantity $\mathscr{E}[A_{ms}]$ can be found.

One-at-a-time confidence intervals (with confidence coefficient $1 - \alpha$) on $\mu + \alpha_i$ and on $\sum_{i=1}^{I} c_i\alpha_i$, where $\sum c_i = 0$, are, respectively,

$$\mu + \alpha_i\colon\ \hat{\mu} + \hat{\alpha}_i \mp t_{\alpha/2:n-I}\sqrt{\widehat{\text{var}}[\hat{\mu} + \hat{\alpha}_i]} \qquad \text{or } \bar{y}_{i.} \mp t_{\alpha/2:n-I}\left(\frac{E_{ms}}{J_i}\right)^{1/2}$$

$$i = 1, 2, \ldots, I$$

$$\sum_{i=1}^{I} c_i\alpha_i\colon\ \sum_{i=1}^{I} c_i\hat{\alpha}_i \mp t_{\alpha/2:n-I}\sqrt{\widehat{\text{var}}\left[\sum_{i=1}^{I} c_i\hat{\alpha}_i\right]} \quad \text{or } \sum_{i=1}^{I} c_i\bar{y}_{i.} \mp t_{\alpha/2:n-I}\left(E_{ms}\sum_{i=1}^{I}\frac{c_i^2}{J_i}\right)^{1/2}$$

$$\sum_{i=1}^{I} c_i = 0 \qquad (13.6.5)$$

Example 13.6.1

The model for the data in Table 13.6.2 is assumed to be Case I of a

Table 13.6.2
Data for a One-Factor Design Model

	Levels of Factor A 1	2	3	4	5
	19.33	19.51	17.50	17.67	19.95
	18.41	19.37	18.79	13.83	16.25
	20.71	16.45	19.81	15.35	16.11
	19.73	18.83	18.36	18.62	20.69
	21.67	19.46		19.34	15.22
	20.38	16.98		14.96	16.54
		16.16		17.54	17.49
		17.59		14.37	15.04
				15.77	18.28
				16.49	18.74
				15.51	
				18.18	
Total	120.23	144.35	74.46	197.63	174.31
J_i	6	8	4	12	10
$\hat{\mu} + \hat{\alpha}_i$	20.04	18.04	18.62	16.47	17.43
$\frac{\hat{\sigma}}{\sqrt{J_i}}$	0.661	0.573	0.810	0.468	0.512

one-factor design model. Find the ANOVA table. Find UMVU estimates for σ^2; $\mu + \alpha_i$, $i = 1, 2, \ldots, 5$; $\alpha_1 - \alpha_2$, and $\alpha_1 - (\alpha_2 + \alpha_3)/2$. For $\alpha = 0.05$ test $H_0 : \alpha_1 = \alpha_2 = \cdots = \alpha_5$ *vs.* H_a : at least one equality is an inequality. Set a 95 percent confidence interval on $\alpha_1 - \alpha_2$ and on $\mu + \alpha_1$.

Clearly $I = 5$, $\sum_{i=1}^{5} J_i = 40$, and by computing the quantities in Table 13.6.1, we obtain Table 13.6.3 and $\hat{\sigma}^2 = 2.624$; $\hat{\sigma} = 1.620$ (computations for Table 13.6.3 are performed by using nine significant

Table 13.6.3
ANOVA Table for Data in Table 13.6.2

Source	*d.f.*	*S.S.*	*M.S.*	*E.M.S.*
Total	40	12,784.9380		
$R(\mu, \alpha)$	5	12,693.0961		
$R(\mu)$	1	12,637.3140		
$R(H_0)$	4	55.7821	13.9455	$\sigma^2 + \frac{\sum_{i=1}^{I}\sum_{j=1}^{J_i}(\alpha_i - \bar{\alpha}_.^*)^2}{4}$
Error	35	91.8419	2.6241	σ^2

figures and the final answers are rounded to four decimals). By Equation (13.6.3) we get $\hat{\mu} + \hat{\alpha}_i = \bar{y}_{i.}$, which are entered at the bottom of Table 13.6.2.

Also, $\hat{\alpha}_1 - \hat{\alpha}_2 = \bar{y}_{1.} - \bar{y}_{2.} = 1.995$; $\hat{\alpha}_1 - (\hat{\alpha}_2 + \hat{\alpha}_3)/2 = 1.709$. We have answered the first two problems.

To answer the third problem, we compute w in Equation (13.6.4). From the ANOVA table we get $w = A_{ms}/E_{ms} = 5.31$, and since $F_{0.05:4,35} = 2.64$, the hypothesis H_0 *vs.* H_a is rejected.

To set a 95 percent confidence interval on $\alpha_1 - \alpha_2$ and $\mu + \alpha_1$, we use the data at the bottom of Table 13.6.2 and Equation (13.6.5). We get (for $t_{0.025:35} = 2.03$)

$$\mu + \alpha_1: \quad 20.04 \mp 2.03(0.661) \quad \text{or} \quad 18.70 \le \mu + \alpha_1 \le 21.38$$

$$\alpha_1 - \alpha_2: \quad 1.995 \mp 2.03(1.62)(\tfrac{1}{6} + \tfrac{1}{8})^{1/2} \quad \text{or} \quad 0.219 \le \alpha_1 - \alpha_2 \le 3.771$$

13.7 Further Discussion of Tests and Confidence Intervals for Design Models

In this section we state several theorems that will be useful in applying design models. The first can be used to determine whether certain hypotheses that are used extensively in applied work are estimable; the second theorem can often be used to find the form of the noncentrality for the power of tests; the remaining theorems discuss simultaneous confidence intervals that are often used in design models.

THEOREM 13.7.1

Let the model be given by Equation (13.2.1), *and let* $\boldsymbol{\alpha}$ *be an* $m \times 1$ *subvector of* $\boldsymbol{\beta}$. *The hypothesis* $\alpha_1 = \alpha_2 = \cdots = \alpha_m$ *is an estimable hypothesis if and only if every contrast of* $\boldsymbol{\alpha}$ *is estimable.*

Proof

The proof will be left for the reader.

THEOREM 13.7.2

Let the model be given by Equation (13.2.1). *The noncentrality parameter* λ *in the power of the test of* $\mathbf{H}\boldsymbol{\beta} = \mathbf{0}$ *vs.* $\mathbf{H}\boldsymbol{\beta} \ne \mathbf{0}$, *where* $\mathbf{H}$ *has size* $q \times p$, *is given by*

$$\lambda = \frac{\mathscr{E}[\text{S.S. due to } H_0]}{2\sigma^2} - \frac{q}{2} \tag{13.7.1}$$

Proof

The proof is obtained by noting that the random variable U, defined by $U = (\text{S.S. due to } H_0)/\sigma^2$, is distributed $\chi^2(u : q; \lambda)$, and $\mathscr{E}[U] = q + 2\lambda$. The result follows from this.

In many applications of the one-way design model, the investigator is interested in *comparing* the main effects of two levels of a factor under study. This, of course, means estimating and setting confidence intervals on $(\alpha_i - \bar{\alpha}_.) - (\alpha_j - \bar{\alpha}_.)$, which is the same as $\alpha_i - \alpha_j$ for various $i \neq j$. One-at-a-time confidence intervals on $\alpha_i - \alpha_j$ are given in Equation (13.6.5), where $\mathbf{c}'$ has the ith element equal to $+1$, the jth element equal to -1, and the remaining elements equal to 0.

If the investigator desires confidence intervals on *several* comparisons of levels of factor A, so that the probability is $1 - \alpha$ that all confidence intervals are simultaneously correct, the several methods discussed in Chapter 6 are candidates for procedures to use.

However, an investigator may want confidence intervals on *all* differences $\alpha_i - \alpha_j$, $i \neq j = 1, 2, \ldots, m$, such that the probability is $1 - \alpha$ that all intervals are correct. The multivariate t method cannot be used since the parameters $\alpha_i - \alpha_j$ are not linearly independent. The extended multivariate t method could be used with any m linearly independent set of $\alpha_i - \alpha_j$ as the fundamental set, but there is a problem in deciding which set should be the fundamental set. Scheffé's method could be used but it includes all estimable functions of $\boldsymbol{\alpha}$, so the confidence coefficient is greater than $1 - \alpha$ for only the set of all *differences*. We discuss a method of simultaneous confidence intervals that applies specifically to this situation, and the probability is exactly $1 - \alpha$ that the intervals for $\alpha_i - \alpha_j$, for all $i \neq j$, are simultaneously correct. The procedure, since it was first proposed by Tukey, is referred to as Tukey's method of simultaneous confidence intervals. It involves the "studentized range" and is the context of the next theorem.

THEOREM 13.7.3

Let Z_i be distributed $N(z_i : \mu_i, \sigma^2)$, $i = 1, 2, \ldots, m$; let $U = n\hat{\sigma}^2/\sigma^2$ be distributed as $\chi^2(u : n)$; and let $U, Z_1, Z_2, \ldots, Z_m$ be mutually independent. Define the random variable Q by $Q = (max[Z_i - \mu_i] - min[Z_i - \mu_i])/\hat{\sigma}$, where max and min are over $i = 1, 2, \ldots, m$. Let $f_Q(q)$ denote the p.d.f. of Q, and let $q_{\alpha:m,n}$ denote the upper α probability point of $f_Q(q)$. The probability is $1 - \alpha$ that the following confidence intervals are simultaneously correct.

$$Z_i - Z_j - q_{\alpha:m,n}\hat{\sigma} \leq \mu_i - \mu_j \leq Z_i - Z_j + q_{\alpha:m,n}\hat{\sigma}$$
$$i = 1, 2, \ldots, m, \quad j = 1, 2, \ldots, m, \quad i \neq j \quad (13.7.2)$$

Proof

We will merely sketch a proof. Define the $m \times 1$ vectors $\hat{\boldsymbol{\theta}}$ and $\boldsymbol{t}$ by

$$\hat{\boldsymbol{\theta}}' = [Z_1 - \mu_1, Z_2 - \mu_2, \ldots, Z_m - \mu_m] \qquad \boldsymbol{t}' = [T_1, T_2, \ldots, T_m]$$

where $T_i = \hat{\theta}_i/\hat{\sigma}$. The joint p.d.f. of the T_i is $\mathbf{S}(\mathbf{t} : m, n; \mathbf{I})$. The p.d.f. is given in Equation (6.6.2); see Theorem 6.6.1.

From the joint p.d.f. of the $T_i = (Z_i - \mu_i)/\hat{\sigma}$, the p.d.f. $f_Q(q)$ of $\max[T_i] - \min[T_i] = Q$ can be obtained. Since the joint p.d.f. of the T_i contains no unknown parameters, the p.d.f. of Q contains no unknown parameters. Thus the number $q_{\alpha:m,n}$ can be found which satisfies the following:

$$\int_{q_{\alpha:m,n}}^{\infty} f_Q(q)\,dq = \alpha \tag{13.7.3}$$

The p.d.f. $f_Q(q)$ is quite complicated and we will not attempt to find it. However, in Table T.7 are values of $q_{\alpha:m,n}$ for various values of α, m, and n.

To demonstrate further we note that the following statements are equivalent and the probability of the first one, and hence of each, is $1 - \alpha$ (max and min are over $i = 1, 2, \ldots, m$).

$$Q \leq q_{\alpha:m,n} \tag{13.7.4}$$

$$\max[T_i] - \min[T_i] \leq q_{\alpha:m,n}$$

$$\frac{\max[Z_i - \mu_i] - \min[Z_i - \mu_i]}{\hat{\sigma}} \leq q_{\alpha:m,n}$$

$$\max[Z_i - \mu_i] - \min[Z_i - \mu_i] \leq \hat{\sigma} q_{\alpha:m,n}$$

$$|(Z_i - \mu_i) - (Z_j - \mu_j)| \leq \hat{\sigma} q_{\alpha:m,n} \quad i = 1, 2, \ldots, m, \quad j = 1, 2, \ldots, m$$

$$-\hat{\sigma} q_{\alpha:m,n} \leq (Z_i - Z_j) - (\mu_i - \mu_j) \leq \hat{\sigma} q_{\alpha:m,n} \qquad i = 1, 2, \ldots, m, \quad j = 1, 2, \ldots, m$$

$$Z_i - Z_j - \hat{\sigma} q_{\alpha:m,n} \leq \mu_i - \mu_j \leq Z_i - Z_j + \hat{\sigma} q_{\alpha:m,n} \qquad i = 1, 2, \ldots, m, \quad j = 1, 2, \ldots, m$$

This concludes the proof.

Two slight extensions of Theorem 13.7.3 are contained in the next two theorems. The proofs will be left for the reader.

THEOREM 13.7.4

Let Y_i be distributed $N(y_i : \mu_i, d^2\sigma^2)$, $i = 1, 2, \ldots, m$, where d^2 is a known constant; let $U = n\hat{\sigma}^2/\sigma^2$ be distributed $\chi^2(u : n)$; and let U and $Y_1, Y_2, \ldots, Y_m$ be jointly independent. Simultaneous $1 - \alpha$ confidence intervals on all differences $\mu_i - \mu_j$ are given by

$$Y_i - Y_j \mp q_{\alpha:m,n}\hat{\sigma}d \qquad \text{for } i = 1, 2, \ldots, m, \quad j = 1, 2, \ldots, m \tag{13.7.5}$$

The principal use of this theorem is when the Y_i are sample means, and in that case $d = 1/\sqrt{k}$, where k is the number of observations in each mean.

The next theorem considers the situation when the Y_i are not independent but each Y_i and Y_j $(i \neq j)$ is required to have the same covariance.

THEOREM 13.7.5

Let Y_i be distributed $N(y_i : \mu_i, d^2\sigma^2)$, $i = 1, 2, \ldots, m$, where d^2 is a known constant; let $U = n\hat{\sigma}^2/\sigma^2$ be distributed $\chi^2(u : n)$; let U be independent of the random variables $Y_1, Y_2, \ldots, Y_m$; and let $\text{cov}[Y_i, Y_j] = c\sigma^2$ for all $i \neq j = 1, 2, \ldots, m$, where c is a known nonpositive constant. Simultaneous $1 - \alpha$ confidence intervals on all differences $\mu_i - \mu_j$ are given by

$$Y_i - Y_j \mp q_{\alpha:m,n}\hat{\sigma}\sqrt{d^2 - c} \qquad \text{for } i = 1, 2, \ldots, m, \quad j = 1, 2, \ldots, m \tag{13.7.6}$$

This theorem will be useful for setting simultaneous $1 - \alpha$ confidence intervals on all differences for certain design models to be discussed in the next chapter. The constant c must be less than or equal to zero for the theorem to be true. However, there is another restriction on c, namely $c \geq -d^2/(m - 1)$, to insure that the covariance matrix of the Y_i is a nonnegative matrix. The restriction $c \leq 0$ is generally the case in most applied problems where this procedure is used.

In some design models the investigator does not want to set simultaneous confidence intervals on the differences of *all* pairs of means, but he may want to compare the means of all levels of a factor with *one* level, say a control level. For example, in a one-factor design model, suppose the factors are varieties of rice, and the investigator wants to compare, say, six new varieties with a standard variety. He may want to set simultaneous confidence intervals on $\mu_0 - \mu_i$, $i = 1, 2, \ldots, 6$, where $\mu_0 - \mu_i$ is the difference between the standard variety and the ith new variety. He may not be interested in comparisons between any two *new* varieties.

As another example, suppose a certain drug is being examined for its effect in reducing the pain of headache. The drug is the factor and different amounts of the drug are the levels. In order to have a standard to check the effectiveness against, the investigator may choose one of the levels to be "no drug." He may then be interested in confidence intervals on all differences of the various levels with the "no drug" level.

As a last example, consider a fertilizer experiment concerning the effect of various levels of nitrogen on the yield of wheat. The investigator may be principally interested in the increase in yield when using various amounts of nitrogen versus when no nitrogen is used. So one of the levels of the nitrogen factor will be no nitrogen (zero pounds per acre) and confidence intervals on all differences of the mean effect of each level with the zero level is what the investigator will compute.

These types of confidence intervals are referred to in the literature as "comparing treatments with a control," and exact simultaneous confidence interval procedures are available for many situations; the multivariate t method can often be used. No further discussion of this topic will be presented in this book, but the interested reader can consult [D-10] and [D-11].

Example 13.7.1

The artificial data in Table 13.7.1 are assumed to satisfy the one-factor design model $Y_{ij} = \mu + \alpha_i + \varepsilon_{ij}$, where the ε_{ij} are distributed $NID(\varepsilon : 0, \sigma^2)$. Find the ANOVA table for testing $\alpha_1 = \alpha_2 = \alpha_3 = \alpha_4$. Find the UMVU estimator of σ^2. Find the UMVU estimators of the mean effects and main effects of the four levels of A. Set 95 percent simultaneous confidence intervals on the differences of all pairs of mean effects.

The answer to the first problem is given in Table 13.7.2. The answer to the second problem is $\hat{\sigma}^2 = 3.1300$, obtained from the Error Mean Square in Table 13.7.2. The answer to the third problem is given in Table 13.7.3.

Table 13.7.1

Artificial Data for One-Factor Model

	Levels of Factor A		
1	2	3	4
32.72	32.95	33.01	36.41
29.15	35.96	29.30	37.58
29.73	32.26	35.98	39.86
27.10	33.11	34.70	36.86
32.14	34.65	33.51	35.99
31.53	34.79	31.71	33.47
31.41	31.83	33.98	35.79
32.73	35.22	33.13	38.89
29.97	37.01	31.67	35.68
30.67	33.46	33.07	35.93

Table 13.7.2

ANOVA Table for Data in Table 13.7.1

Source	*d.f.*	*S.S.*	*M.S.*
Total	40	45,514.5185	
$R(\mu, \boldsymbol{\alpha})$	4	45,401.8395	
$R(\mu)$	1	45,219.5727	
$R(\boldsymbol{\alpha} \mid \mu) = R(H_0)$	3	182.2668	60.7556
Error	36	112.6790	3.1300

Table 13.7.3

Table of Means and Main Effects for Data in Table 13.7.1

i	1	2	3	4
$\hat{\mu} + \hat{\alpha}_i$	30.715	34.124	33.006	36.646
$\hat{\alpha}_i - \hat{\bar{\alpha}}_.$	−2.90775	0.50125	−0.61675	3.02325

Table 13.7.4

Simultaneous Confidence Intervals* on $\alpha_i - \alpha_j$ for All $i \neq j$

	α_2	α_3	α_4
α_1	(−5.541, −1.277)	(−4.423, −0.159)	(−8.063, −3.799)
α_2		(−1.014, 3.250)	(−4.654, −0.390)
α_3			(−5.772, −1.508)

* The confidence interval on $\alpha_i - \alpha_j$ is the interval that is the entry of α_i in the row and α_j in the column; for example, the confidence interval on $\alpha_2 - \alpha_3$ is (−1.014, 3.250); the confidence interval on $\alpha_4 - \alpha_1$ is (3.799, 8.063), which is the negative of the interval on $\alpha_1 - \alpha_4$.

To answer the fourth problem, Theorem 13.7.4 can be used with Y_i, μ_i, and d^2 in the theorem corresponding, respectively, to $\bar{y}_{i.}$, $\mu + \alpha_i$, and $\frac{1}{10}$ in this example. Also, we obtain $q_{\alpha:m,n} = q_{0.05:4,36} = 3.81$ from Table T.7. The results are displayed in Table 13.7.4.

Problems

13.1. In Equation (13.2.3) show that for any solution of $\tilde{\boldsymbol\beta}$ (for any $p \times 1$ vector $\mathbf{b}$), the solution for $\tilde{\sigma}^2$ is the same.

13.2. Work through the details of the proof of part (4) of Theorem 13.2.2.

13.3. Prove (4), (5), and (6) of Theorem 13.2.4.

13.4. Supply the details for the proof of Theorem 13.2.5.

13.5. In the design model in Equation (13.2.1), let $\mathbf{G}'$ be any $q \times n$ matrix of rank q such that $\mathscr{E}[\mathbf{G}'\mathbf{Y}] = \mathbf{0}$ for all values of $\boldsymbol\beta$ and σ^2 in Ω. Show that $q \le n - K$.

13.6. If $\boldsymbol\ell'\boldsymbol\beta$ is any estimable function, show that $\text{cov}[\boldsymbol\ell'\hat{\boldsymbol\beta}, \mathbf{g}_i'\mathbf{Y}] = 0$, where $\mathbf{g}_i$ is the ith column of $\mathbf{G}$ in Problem 13.5.

13.7. In Example 13.2.2 prove that $\tau_1 + \tau_2$ is not estimable.

13.8. In Example 13.2.2 show that $\tilde{\boldsymbol\beta}' = [\bar{Y}_{1.}, 0, \bar{Y}_{2.} - \bar{Y}_{1.}]$ is a solution to the normal equations.

13.9. Find the UMVU estimator of $\tau_1 - \tau_2$ by using for $\tilde{\boldsymbol\beta}$ the solution to the normal equations given in Problem 13.8.

13.10. In Problem 13.8 find $\tilde{\boldsymbol\beta}'\mathbf{X}'\mathbf{Y}$ and demonstrate it is the same as $\hat{\boldsymbol\beta}'\mathbf{X}'\mathbf{Y}$, where $\hat{\boldsymbol\beta}$ is the solution to the normal equations $\hat{\boldsymbol\beta}' = [0, \bar{Y}_{1.}, \bar{Y}_{2.}]$.

13.11. Prove part (4) of Theorem 13.2.7.

13.12. In Example 13.2.3 show that

$$\hat{\boldsymbol\beta}' = \tfrac{1}{2}[0, 0, 2\bar{Y}_{2.} - 2\bar{Y}_{1.}, Y_{.1} - \bar{Y}_{2.} + \bar{Y}_{1.}, Y_{.2} - \bar{Y}_{2.} + \bar{Y}_{1.}, Y_{.3} - \bar{Y}_{2.} + \bar{Y}_{1.}, \\ Y_{.4} - \bar{Y}_{2.} + \bar{Y}_{1.}]$$

is a solution to the normal equations.

13.13. In Example 13.2.3 demonstrate that $\tilde{\boldsymbol\beta}'\mathbf{X}'\mathbf{Y} = \hat{\boldsymbol\beta}'\mathbf{X}'\mathbf{Y}$, where $\tilde{\boldsymbol\beta}$ is the solution in Problem 13.12 and $\hat{\boldsymbol\beta}$ is given by

$$\hat{\boldsymbol\beta}' = [\bar{Y}_{..}, \bar{Y}_{1.} - \bar{Y}_{..}, \bar{Y}_{2.} - \bar{Y}_{..}, \bar{Y}_{.1} - \bar{Y}_{..}, \bar{Y}_{.2} - \bar{Y}_{..}, \bar{Y}_{.3} - \bar{Y}_{..}, \bar{Y}_{.4} - \bar{Y}_{..}]$$

13.14. Prove part (4) of Theorem 13.3.4.

13.15. Prove Theorem 13.3.5.

13.16. In Theorem 13.4.1 show that $\mathbf{H}(\mathbf{X}'\mathbf{X})^c\mathbf{H}'$ is invariant for any c-inverse of $\mathbf{X}'\mathbf{X}$ if $\mathbf{H}\boldsymbol{\beta}$ is a set of q linearly independent estimable functions.

13.17. In Problem 13.16 show that $\mathbf{H}(\mathbf{X}'\mathbf{X})^c\mathbf{H}'$ is nonsingular.

13.18. In Example 13.5.3 show that $\hat{\boldsymbol{\beta}}' = [1, -1, 2, 3, -2, 4]$ is a solution to the normal equations. Use this solution to find $\hat{\sigma}^2$. Assume $\mathbf{y}'\mathbf{y} = 409$ and $n = 18$.

13.19. In Example 13.5.3 show that $\theta = \beta_3 + 2\beta_4 - 3\beta_5$ is an estimable function.

13.20. In Problem 13.19 find $\hat{\theta}$, the UMVU estimate of θ. Assume the model is $\mathbf{Y} = \mathbf{X}\boldsymbol{\beta} + \boldsymbol{\varepsilon}$, $\boldsymbol{\varepsilon}$ is distributed $N(\boldsymbol{\varepsilon} : \mathbf{0}, \sigma^2\mathbf{I})$.

13.21. In Problem 13.20 find $\widehat{\text{var}}[\hat{\theta}]$. Use $\mathbf{y}'\mathbf{y} = 409$ and $n = 18$.

13.22. In Problem 13.20 find a 95 percent confidence interval on θ. Use $\mathbf{y}'\mathbf{y} = 409$ and $n = 18$.

13.23. In Example 13.5.3 use the nonestimable conditions $\beta_1 + \beta_2 = 0$ and $\beta_3 + \beta_4 + \beta_5 = 0$ for $\mathbf{V}'\boldsymbol{\beta} = \mathbf{0}$. Exhibit

$$\begin{bmatrix} \mathbf{X}'\mathbf{X} & \mathbf{V} \\ \mathbf{V}' & \mathbf{0} \end{bmatrix} = \mathbf{S}_V$$

13.24. Solve the system $\mathbf{S}_V\hat{\boldsymbol{\beta}}_V = \mathbf{s}_V$ in Example 13.5.3 using the nonestimable conditions in Problem 13.23.

13.25. Use the results of Problem 13.24 to find $\hat{\theta}$, where θ is given in Problem 13.19.

13.26. Use the results of Problem 13.24 to find $\widehat{\text{var}}[\hat{\theta}]$, where θ is given in Problem 13.19.

13.27. In Example 13.5.3 use all six of the normal equations and reduce $[\mathbf{X}'\mathbf{X} \mid \mathbf{X}'\mathbf{y}]$ to $[\mathbf{T} \mid \mathbf{t}]$ by the square root procedure. Find $\hat{\boldsymbol{\beta}}$ from the backward solution to $[\mathbf{T} \mid \mathbf{t}]$.

13.28. In Problem 13.27 show that $\mathbf{t}'\mathbf{t} = \hat{\boldsymbol{\beta}}'\mathbf{X}'\mathbf{y}$, where $\hat{\boldsymbol{\beta}}$ is the solution given in Problem 13.18.

13.29. In Table 13.6.1 show $\mathscr{E}[E_{ms}] = \sigma^2$.

13.30. The data in the table on the next page are from the one-factor model given in Definition 13.6.1, Case I. Find the ANOVA table for testing equality of the main effects of the four levels of factor A.

Levels of Factor A			
1	2	3	4
103.72	103.95	104.01	107.41
100.15	106.96	100.30	108.58
100.73	103.26	106.98	110.86
98.10	104.11	105.70	107.86
103.14	105.65	104.51	106.99
102.53	105.79	102.71	104.47
102.41	102.83	104.98	106.79
103.73	106.22	104.13	109.89
100.97	108.01	102.67	106.68
101.67	104.46	104.07	106.93

13.31. In Problem 13.30 find the UMVU estimates of the means of the four levels of factor A.

13.32. In Problem 13.30 find the UMVU estimates of the main effects of the four levels of factor A.

13.33. In Problem 13.30 find 95 percent one-at-a-time confidence intervals on the main effects of the four levels of factor A.

13.34. In Problem 13.30 find 95 percent simultaneous confidence intervals on all differences of the four levels of factor A.

13.35. In Problem 13.30 find 95 percent simultaneous confidence intervals on all differences of the first, second, and third levels of factor A.

13.36. In Problem 13.30 find 95 percent simultaneous confidence intervals on $\alpha_1 - \alpha_2$, $\alpha_1 - \alpha_3$, and $\alpha_1 - \alpha_4$.

13.37. In Problem 13.30 find 95 percent simultaneous confidence intervals on $\alpha_1 - \alpha_2$, $\alpha_1 - \alpha_3$, $\alpha_1 - \alpha_4$, and $\alpha_2 - \alpha_4$. Use the extended multivariate t method.

CHAPTER 14

Two-Factor Design Model

14.1 Introduction

In this chapter we shall discuss an extension of the one-factor design model that was discussed in some detail in Sections 13.6 and 13.7. It is probably the most useful and most used of all design models. It is often referred to as the "two-way classification model," or the "row by column model," or the "two-way layout model," or a "randomized block model." There are many special cases of this model depending on whether or not interaction is present and whether or not an equal number of observations is available for each combination of the levels of each factor.

In this section we define the special two-factor design models that will be discussed, and we briefly outline the contents of the other sections.

Suppose two factors denoted by A and T are to be investigated; factor A is to be examined at a different levels and factor T at t different levels. The two-factor design model applies to a physical situation where various levels of factor A are associated with various levels of factor T. The parameter μ_{ij} represents the "true" or "average" effect of the ith level of factor A with the jth level of factor T. There are, conceptually, ta populations, and the ijth population (ith level of factor A is associated with the jth level of factor T) has mean μ_{ij} and variance σ^2. A random sample of size n_{ij} is selected from the ijth population, where n_{ij} can be any nonnegative integer (if $n_{ij} = 0$, this means the ijth population was not sampled). We denote the mth observation that will be obtained from the ijth population by Y_{ijm} and write the model as follows:

$$Y_{ijm} = \mu_{ij} + \varepsilon_{ijm} \qquad \mathscr{E}[\varepsilon_{ijm}] = 0 \qquad \text{var}[\varepsilon_{ijm}] = \sigma^2$$
$$m = 0, 1, \ldots, n_{ij}, \quad i = 1, 2, \ldots, a, \quad j = 1, 2, \ldots, t \qquad (14.1.1)$$

μ_{ij} and σ^2 are unobservable constant parameters defined in a specified parameter space Ω; the ε_{ijm} are unobservable random variables; the Y_{ijm} are observable random variables.

Of course, the model could allow for the variance of ε_{ijm} to depend on ijm. In many cases additional assumptions will be made on the random variables ε_{ijm}, such as independence, normality, and so forth.

Note 1. When the subscript m is zero, this means that the corresponding observable random variable Y_{ij0} is not in the model. Hence $Y_{ij0} = \mu_{ij} + \varepsilon_{ij0}$ is not a term in the model.

The problem here is to assume a certain structure for μ_{ij}; for example, assume that μ_{ij} is a *specified* function of unknown parameters α_i, τ_j, and so on, and obtain estimates and hypotheses tests about these unknown parameters on the basis of the observable random variables Y_{ijm}. Several examples will be given to illustrate some models of interest.

Example 14.1.1

An animal nutritionist wants to investigate five different kinds of diet for cattle to determine how the different diets affect the growth of the cattle. The investigator decides to select 20 one-year old calves at random from herds in a large geographical area. Most of the cattle in the area are either Angus or Herefords, and the investigator wants to determine not only the effect of the diets, but the effect of the diets on each breed. So a two-factor design model is used and 10 cattle from breed 1 (Angus) and 10 cattle from breed 2 (Hereford) are used. Each diet is fed to two Angus and two Hereford animals for a year and the gain in pounds of each animal is measured. The observable data could appear as shown in the table, where Y_{ijm} denotes the observable weight gain of the mth animal of breed i which was fed the jth diet.

Conceptually, there are 10 populations, and Y_{ij1}, Y_{ij2} is a random sample of size two from the population of the ith breed fed the jth diet.

Levels of Factor T (Different Diets)

Levels of Factor A (Different Breeds)		1	2	3	4	5
	1	Y_{111} Y_{112}	Y_{121} Y_{122}	Y_{131} Y_{132}	Y_{141} Y_{142}	Y_{151} Y_{152}
	2	Y_{211} Y_{212}	Y_{221} Y_{222}	Y_{231} Y_{232}	Y_{241} Y_{242}	Y_{251} Y_{252}

(14.1.2)

The mean of Y_{ijm} is μ_{ij} and it might be assumed that the structure of μ_{ij} is

$$\mu_{ij} = \mu + \alpha_i + \tau_j \tag{14.1.3}$$

where μ is a general location parameter, α_i is the parameter due to the ith level of factor A, and τ_j is the parameter due to the jth level of factor T.

The model for this investigation is then

$$Y_{ijm} = \mu + \alpha_i + \tau_j + \varepsilon_{ijm} \qquad n_{ij} = 2, \quad a = 2, \quad t = 5 \tag{14.1.4}$$

Actually the model means that an observation y_{ijm} is made up of a general constant μ, often called the general mean, plus a constant α_i which is added to the weight gain of the cattle due to the fact they are of the ith breed, plus a constant τ_j which is added to the weight gain of the cattle due to the fact they are fed the jth diet, plus a random error ε_{ijm} which is due to all other factors that affect the weight gain, such as different initial weights of the animals, individual differences of animals, and measurement errors. If the diets and the breeds did not affect weight gain, then α_i and τ_j would be zero and μ would be the mean weight gain of all Angus and Hereford cattle in the population when fed any of the diets.

Suppose all animals survived the experiment except one animal of breed 1 which was fed diet 3. Then the observation y_{131} (or y_{132}) would be missing, and n_{ij} would equal 2 for all i and j except n_{13} which would equal 1. If only one animal was used in each breed for each diet, then $n_{ij} = 1$ for all i and j, and the third subscript on Y and ε would not be needed.

From the arrangement in the table in Equation (14.1.2), it is easy to see why the model is sometimes referred to as a "two-way classification model," a "row by column model," or a "two-way layout."

The objectives for this model are to estimate and test σ^2, various functions of the α_i, and various functions of the τ_j. The reader can easily exhibit the vectors and matrices relating this model to the general design model $\mathbf{Y} = \mathbf{X}\boldsymbol{\beta} + \boldsymbol{\varepsilon}$.

Example 14.1.2

An economist wants to study the starting salaries of employees who operate cash registers in large grocery stores with respect to the locations of the grocery stores and the sex of the employees. Factor A is the location, and the levels of factor A are the various locations such as the East Coast, Great Lakes region, Midwest, Southeast, South, Rocky Mountains, and West Coast, which are locations in the United States that are of interest. Factor T is sex and, of course, there are only two levels, male and female. So this is a 2×7 two-factor design model, where the observations y_{ijm} are starting salaries in dollars per week.

Example 14.1.3

A medical experiment is to be run to determine the side effects on people of different ages when they take various dosages of a medicine used to control a certain allergy. Factor A could be ages, and the investigator might decide to use people classified into the following age groups for levels: 6 to 10 years old for level 1; 11 to 25 years old for level 2; 25 to 40 years old for level 3; 40 to 60 years old for level 4. Factor T could be dosage, and the levels could be 0.5 milligrams, 1 milligram, 1.5 milligrams, 2 milligrams. The observation y_{ijm} might be the amount of a certain substance in the blood 24 hours after taking the drug.

Example 14.1.4

A petroleum engineer wants to study how the speed of the drill bit and the pressure on the bit affect the drilling rate through granite rock when drilling an oil well. He examines the records of wells that were drilled in a certain geographical area. If he finds that different pressures and different speeds were used when various wells were drilled, and if, in addition to this information, the records reveal the drilling rate in, say, feet per hour, he may decide to use a two-factor model with factor A being the speed of the bit in revolutions per minute, factor T being pressure on the bit in pounds, and the observations being feet per hour.

Example 14.1.5

An educational psychologist wants to determine the effect of four different methods of teaching mathematics to students of three different races. Factor A could be methods of teaching (4 levels), factor T could be races (3 levels), and the observations could be the grades on a test at the end of the period of instruction.

Example 14.1.6

An agronomist is interested in how different amounts of a fertilizer affect the heights of new seedlings of a certain flower three weeks after emergence. The experiment is conducted in a greenhouse, and the investigator knows that the *location* on the greenhouse bench will affect the height since there is a temperature and humidity gradient that runs perpendicular to the greenhouse wall. He is not interested in the effect of this temperature and humidity differential, but he does not want it to influence or mask the effect of the fertilizer. Thus he could choose factor A to be distance from the wall and factor T to be the fertilizer. If there are three benches parallel to the wall, then there are three distances from the wall and hence three levels of factor A. If he wants to investigate ten different concentrations of the fertilizer, then factor T has ten levels. The observation y_{ijm} is the height of seedlings on bench i that received the jth level of the fertilizer.

These examples should serve to illustrate the usefulness of two-factor designs. Now we define the various special cases that will be discussed in this chapter. Actually, the special cases of this model depend on the structure of μ_{ij}, the values that n_{ij} can assume, and the distributional properties of the random error ε_{ijm}. These cases are listed below along with the section in which each is discussed.

$$Y_{ijm} = \mu + \alpha_i + \tau_j + \varepsilon_{ijm}$$
$$m = 1, \quad i = 1, 2, \ldots, a > 1, \quad j = 1, 2, \ldots, t > 1$$
$$\Omega = \{\mu, \alpha_i, \tau_j, \sigma^2) : \sigma^2 > 0, \mu, \alpha_i, \tau_j \text{ are each in the interval } (-\infty, \infty)\}$$

This model is called a two-factor design model with no interaction and with one observation per cell (population). It is discussed in Section 14.2. (14.1.5)

The same model as in Equation (14.1.5) except $m = 1, 2, \ldots, M > 1$. This model is called a two-factor design model with no interaction and with $M > 1$ observations per cell (population). It is discussed in Section 14.3. (14.1.6)

The same model as defined in Equation (14.1.5) except $m = 0, 1, \ldots, n_{ij}$ and the n_{ij} are not all equal and can be any set of nonnegative integers subject to mild restrictions. This model is called a two-factor design model with no interaction and with unequal numbers of observations in the cells (populations). It is discussed in Section 14.4. (14.1.7)

$$Y_{ijm} = \mu + \alpha_i + \tau_j + \gamma_{ij} + \varepsilon_{ijm}$$
$$m = 1, 2, \ldots, M > 1, \quad i = 1, 2, \ldots, a > 1, \quad j = 1, 2, \ldots, t > 1$$
$$\Omega = \{(\mu, \alpha_i, \tau_j, \gamma_{ij}, \sigma^2) : \sigma^2 > 0, \mu, \alpha_i, \tau_j, \gamma_{ij} \text{ are each in the interval } (-\infty, \infty)\}$$

This model is called a two-factor design model with interaction and with an equal number M ($M > 1$) observations per cell. It is discussed in Section 14.6. (14.1.8)

The same model as defined in Equation (14.1.8) except $M = 1$. This model is called a two-factor design model with interaction and with one observation per cell. It is discussed in Section 14.7. (14.1.9)

The same model as defined in Equation (14.1.8) except $m = 1, 2, \ldots, n_{ij}$ and the n_{ij} are not all equal and can be any set of positive integers subject to mild restrictions. This model is called a two-factor design model with interaction and with unequal numbers of observations in the cells. It is discussed in Section 14.8. (14.1.10)

Two sets of assumptions on the errors ε_{ijm} will be discussed for all the models above.

Case I: ε_{ijm} are distributed $NID(\varepsilon : 0, \sigma^2)$ for all allowable values of i, j, and m;

Case II: ε_{ijm} are distributed $(\varepsilon : 0, \sigma^2)$ for all allowable values of i, j, and m; also, ε_{ijm} and $\varepsilon_{i'j'm'}$ are uncorrelated if $i \neq i'$, $j \neq j'$, or $m \neq m'$.

Point estimation will be discussed for both Cases I and II; confidence intervals and tests will be discussed only for Case I.

All these models are special cases of the design model discussed in Chapter 13 and all the theory developed there applies. However, some specialized results can be obtained and that will be the content of succeeding sections. The literature on the two-factor design model is huge and only an introduction to the available material will be discussed.

14.2 Two-Factor Design Model, No Interaction, One Observation Per Cell

The model is stated in Equation (14.1.5) but it will be given here also. Since $M = 1$, the third subscript will not be needed. The model is

$$Y_{ij} = \mu + \alpha_i + \tau_j + \varepsilon_{ij} \qquad i = 1, 2, \ldots, a > 1, \quad j = 1, 2, \ldots, t > 1 \quad (14.2.1)$$

If this model is written as $\mathbf{Y} = \mathbf{X}\boldsymbol{\beta} + \boldsymbol{\varepsilon}$, then $\boldsymbol{\beta}$ consists of three subvectors, namely, $\boldsymbol{\mu} = [\mu]$, $\boldsymbol{\alpha}' = [\alpha_1, \alpha_2, \ldots, \alpha_a]$, and $\boldsymbol{\tau}' = [\tau_1, \tau_2, \ldots, \tau_t]$; so $\boldsymbol{\beta}' = [\mu, \boldsymbol{\alpha}', \boldsymbol{\tau}']$. Clearly, an element from each subvector appears in each of the ta equations in the model, so $\mathbf{X} = [\mathbf{x}_0, \mathbf{X}_1, \mathbf{X}_2]$ is a design matrix by Definition 13.5.1. We shall write the normal equations in abbreviated form as discussed in Section (13.5). We get

$$\begin{aligned}
\mu:&\quad at\hat{\mu} + t\sum \hat{\alpha}_i + a\sum \hat{\tau}_j = Y_{..} \\
\alpha_i:&\quad t\hat{\mu} + t\hat{\alpha}_i + \sum \hat{\tau}_j = Y_{i.} \qquad i = 1, 2, \ldots, a \\
\tau_j:&\quad a\hat{\mu} + \sum \hat{\alpha}_i + a\hat{\tau}_j = Y_{.j} \qquad j = 1, 2, \ldots, t
\end{aligned} \quad (14.2.2)$$

There are $a + t + 1$ parameters in $\boldsymbol{\beta}$, so p, the number of normal equations, which is also the size of $\mathbf{X}'\mathbf{X}$, is $(a + t + 1)$. We want to find K, the number of linearly independent estimable functions and then find a *basis* set of estimable functions.

To find K we note that the sum of the α_i equations is the μ equation, and also that the sum of the α_i equations is equal to the sum of the τ_j equations. So by row operations we can obtain two zero rows in the normal equations. Thus we know that K, the rank of $\mathbf{X}'\mathbf{X}$, is less than or equal to $p - 2$ (in other words, $K \leq a + t - 1$). There may be more linear dependencies, but since they are not readily apparent, we next look for linearly *independent* estimable functions.

Perform the following row operations on the normal equations in Equation (14.2.2):

1. divide the first row by ta;
2. subtract the α_i row from the α_1 row and divide by t for $i = 2, 3, \ldots, a$;
3. subtract the τ_j row from the τ_1 row and divide by a for $j = 2, 3, \ldots, t$.

If we ignore the α_1 and τ_1 rows, the resulting rows are as follows:

$$\begin{aligned} \hat{\mu} + a^{-1}\sum \hat{\alpha}_i + t^{-1}\sum \hat{\tau}_j &= \bar{Y}_{..} \\ \hat{\alpha}_1 - \hat{\alpha}_i &= \bar{Y}_{1.} - \bar{Y}_{i.} \qquad \text{for } i = 2, 3, \ldots, a \\ \hat{\tau}_1 - \hat{\tau}_j &= \bar{Y}_{.1} - \bar{Y}_{.j} \qquad \text{for } j = 2, 3, \ldots, t \end{aligned} \tag{14.2.3}$$

Since the expected value of any and of every linear function of the right-hand side of the normal equations is the same linear function of the left-hand side with the ^ removed, we observe that the following are estimable functions:

$$\begin{aligned} &\mu + \bar{\alpha}_. + \bar{\tau}_. \qquad \alpha_1 - \alpha_i \qquad \text{for } i = 2, 3, \ldots, a, \\ &\qquad\qquad\qquad\;\; \tau_1 - \tau_j \qquad \text{for } j = 2, 3, \ldots, t \end{aligned} \tag{14.2.4}$$

We have thus exhibited $1 + (a - 1) + (t - 1) = (a + t - 1)$ linearly independent estimable functions in Equation (14.2.4). They are linearly independent because (1) the first equation contains μ and μ is in no other equation, so it is independent of the remaining equations; and (2) each of the last $(a + t - 2)$ equations contains a distinct parameter and hence those $(a + t - 2)$ equations are linearly independent. So we know that $K \geq a + t - 1$, and this inequality, with the inequality $K \leq a + t - 1$ proved earlier, leaves us with $K = a + t - 1$ for the rank of $\mathbf{X}'\mathbf{X}$.

A basis of estimable functions and the corresponding best unbiased estimators are as follows:

$$\begin{aligned} \hat{\mu} + \hat{\bar{\alpha}}_. + \hat{\bar{\tau}}_. &= \bar{Y}_{..} \\ \hat{\alpha}_1 - \hat{\alpha}_i &= \bar{Y}_{1.} - \bar{Y}_{i.} \qquad i = 2, 3, \ldots, a \\ \hat{\tau}_1 - \hat{\tau}_j &= \bar{Y}_{.1} - \bar{Y}_{.j} \qquad j = 2, 3, \ldots, t \end{aligned} \tag{14.2.5}$$

By Corollary 13.2.4 and Theorem 13.3.5, these are the best unbiased estimators of their respective parameters, and the best unbiased estimator of any estimable function $\ell'\boldsymbol{\beta}$ must be a linear combination of this (actually of every) basis set. So every linear combination of $\alpha_1 - \alpha_i$, $i = 1, 2, \ldots, a$, is estimable, and every estimable function of the α_i's only must come from these linear combinations. Thus $\sum_{i=1}^a \ell_i(\alpha_1 - \alpha_i)$ is estimable for every set of constants $\ell_1, \ell_2, \ldots, \ell_a$, and the best unbiased estimator is $\sum_{i=1}^a \ell_i(\hat{\alpha}_1 - \hat{\alpha}_i) = \sum_{i=1}^a \ell_i(\bar{Y}_{1.} - \bar{Y}_{i.})$.

From this it is easy to see that the only linear combinations of the α_i's that are estimable are contrasts, that is, $\sum c_i\alpha_i$ is estimable if and only if $\sum c_i = 0$. This is easy to see since if $\sum c_i\alpha_i$ is estimable, it must be some linear combination of the $\alpha_1 - \alpha_i$, that is, $\sum_{i=1}^a \ell_i(\alpha_1 - \alpha_i)$. We get

$$\alpha_1 \sum_{i=1}^a \ell_i - \sum_{i=1}^a \ell_i\alpha_i = \left(\sum_{i=1}^a \ell_i - \ell_1\right)\alpha_1 - \ell_2\alpha_2 - \cdots - \ell_a\alpha_a$$

Thus $c_1 = \sum_{i=2}^a \ell_i$, $c_2 = -\ell_2, \ldots, c_a = -\ell_a$, so $\sum_{i=1}^a c_i = 0$.

The best unbiased estimator of any contrast of the α_i's, say $\sum c_i\alpha_i$ (or $\mathbf{c}'\boldsymbol{\alpha}$) is $\sum c_i\bar{Y}_{i.}$, since we can write $\sum c_i\alpha_i = \sum c_i(\alpha_i - \alpha_1)$, and the best unbiased estimator of $\alpha_i - \alpha_1$ is $\hat{\alpha}_i - \hat{\alpha}_1 = \bar{Y}_{i.} - \bar{Y}_{1.}$. So the best unbiased estimator of

$$\sum c_i\alpha_i \quad \text{is} \quad \sum c_i(\hat{\alpha}_i - \hat{\alpha}_1) = \sum c_i(\bar{Y}_{i.} - \bar{Y}_{1.}) = \sum c_i\bar{Y}_{i.} - \bar{Y}_{1.}\sum c_i = \sum c_i\bar{Y}_{i.}$$

Due to the symmetry of the α_i's and the τ_j's, all statements made above for the α_i's also apply to the τ_j's. These results and others on point estimation are summarized in the following theorem.

THEOREM 14.2.1

Consider the two-factor design model with no interaction and one observation per cell given in Equation (14.2.1). *The linear combination $\sum c_i\alpha_i$ is estimable if and only if $\sum c_i\alpha_i$ is a contrast of the α_i's. The best unbiased estimator (the UMVU and BLU estimator of $\sum c_i\alpha_i$ when the ε_{ij} satisfy Case I and Case II, respectively) is $\sum c_i\hat{\alpha}_i = \sum c_i\bar{Y}_{i.}$. The same results apply to the τ_j's, and the best unbiased estimator of a contrast $\sum d_j\tau_j$ is $\sum d_j\hat{\tau}_j = \sum d_j\bar{Y}_{.j}$. In particular, the best unbiased estimator of*

$$\begin{aligned} \alpha_i^* = \alpha_i - \bar{\alpha}_. \quad &\textit{is} \quad \hat{\alpha}_i^* = \widehat{\alpha_i - \bar{\alpha}_.} = \bar{Y}_{i.} - \bar{Y}_{..} \quad \textit{for each } i = 1, 2, \ldots, a \\ &\textit{and of} \\ \tau_j^* = \tau_j - \bar{\tau}_. \quad &\textit{is} \quad \hat{\tau}_j^* = \widehat{\tau_j - \bar{\tau}_.} = \bar{Y}_{.j} - \bar{Y}_{..} \quad \textit{for each } j = 1, 2, \ldots, t \end{aligned} \tag{14.2.6}$$

The best unbiased estimator of

$$\begin{array}{lll} \mu + \alpha_i + \bar{\tau}_. & \textit{is} & \bar{Y}_{i.} \quad \textit{for each } i = 1, 2, \ldots, a \\ & & \textit{and of} \\ \mu + \bar{\alpha}_. + \tau_j & \textit{is} & \bar{Y}_{.j} \quad \textit{for each } j = 1, 2, \ldots, t \end{array} \tag{14.2.7}$$

Next we state a theorem about the estimator of σ^2 and then a theorem about the distributional properties of the estimators of $\sum c_i\alpha_i$, $\sum d_j\tau_j$, and σ^2.

THEOREM 14.2.2

Consider the model given in Equation (14.2.1) *for Case I. The UMVU estimator of* σ^2 *is*

$$\hat{\sigma}^2 = \sum_{j=1}^{t} \sum_{i=1}^{a} \frac{(Y_{ij} - \bar{Y}_{i.} - \bar{Y}_{.j} + \bar{Y}_{..})^2}{(a-1)(t-1)} \tag{14.2.8}$$

Proof

By Theorem 13.2.4 the UMVU estimator of σ^2 is

$$(at - K)^{-1}(\mathbf{Y}'\mathbf{Y} - \hat{\boldsymbol{\beta}}'\mathbf{X}'\mathbf{Y})$$

where $K = a + t - 1$, the number of linearly independent estimable functions of $\boldsymbol{\beta}$, and $\hat{\boldsymbol{\beta}}$ is any solution to the normal equations in Equation (14.2.2). Clearly, $(at - K) = at - a - t + 1 = (a-1)(t-1)$ and $\mathbf{Y}'\mathbf{Y} = \sum_{j=1}^{t} \sum_{i=1}^{a} Y_{ij}^2$. It is easy to demonstrate that the following is a solution to the normal equations: $\tilde{\mu} = \bar{Y}_{..}$; $\tilde{\alpha}_i = \bar{Y}_{i.} - \bar{Y}_{..}$ for $i = 1, 2, \ldots, a$; $\tilde{\tau}_j = \bar{Y}_{.j} - \bar{Y}_{..}$ for $j = 1, 2, \ldots, t$. Thus

$$\begin{aligned} \hat{\boldsymbol{\beta}}'\mathbf{X}'\mathbf{Y} &= \tilde{\mu}(Y_{..}) + \sum_{i=1}^{a} \tilde{\alpha}_i(Y_{i.}) + \sum_{j=1}^{t} \tilde{\tau}_j(Y_{.j}) \\ &= \frac{Y_{..}^2}{ta} + \left(\sum_{i=1}^{a} \frac{Y_{i.}^2}{t} - \frac{Y_{..}^2}{ta}\right) + \left(\sum_{j=1}^{t} \frac{Y_{.j}^2}{a} - \frac{Y_{..}^2}{ta}\right) \end{aligned}$$

and

$$\begin{aligned} \mathbf{Y}'\mathbf{Y} - \hat{\boldsymbol{\beta}}'\mathbf{X}'\mathbf{Y} &= \left(\sum_{j=1}^{t} \sum_{i=1}^{a} Y_{ij}^2 - \frac{Y_{..}^2}{ta}\right) - \left(\sum_{i=1}^{a} \frac{Y_{i.}^2}{t} - \frac{Y_{..}^2}{ta}\right) - \left(\sum_{j=1}^{t} \frac{Y_{.j}^2}{a} - \frac{Y_{..}^2}{ta}\right) \\ &= \sum_{i=1}^{a} \sum_{j=1}^{t} (Y_{ij} - \bar{Y}_{i.} - \bar{Y}_{.j} + \bar{Y}_{..})^2 = (a-1)(t-1)\hat{\sigma}^2 \end{aligned} \tag{14.2.9}$$

This completes the proof of the theorem.

THEOREM 14.2.3

Consider the model given in Equation (14.2.1) *for Case I. The results below follow.*

(1) $Z_1 = \sum c_i\hat{\alpha}_i = \sum c_i\bar{Y}_{i}$ *is distributed* $N(z_1 : c_i\alpha_i, \sigma^2 \sum c_i^2/t)$ *if* $\sum c_i = 0$;

(2) $Z_2 = \sum d_j\hat{\tau}_j = \sum d_j\bar{Y}_j$ *is distributed* $N(z_2 : \sum d_j\tau_j, \sigma^2 \sum d_j^2/a)$ *if* $\sum d_j = 0$;

(3) $U = (a-1)(t-1)\hat{\sigma}^2/\sigma^2$ *is distributed* $\chi^2(u : (a-1)(t-1))$;

(4) $U, Z_1,$ *and* Z_2 *are mutually independent*;

(5) $cov[\sum c_i\hat{\alpha}_i, \sum c_i^*\hat{\alpha}_i] = \sigma^2 \sum c_i c_i^*/t$ *if* $\sum c_i = \sum c_i^* = 0$;

(6) $cov[\sum d_j\hat{\tau}_j, \sum d_j^*\hat{\tau}_j] = \sigma^2 \sum d_j d_j^*/a$ *if* $\sum d_j = \sum d_j^* = 0$.

Proof

The proof is straightforward by using the appropriate theorems in Chapters 3 and 4 and will be left for the reader.

From these results we can obtain confidence intervals on various contrasts of interest among the α_i's and among the τ_j's.

THEOREM 14.2.4

Consider the model given in Equation (14.2.1) *for Case I. The results below follow.*

(1) *A one-at-a-time* $1-\alpha$ *confidence interval on* $\sum c_i\alpha_i$, *where* $\sum c_i = 0$, *is* $\sum c_i\bar{Y}_{i.} \mp t_{\alpha/2:(a-1)(t-1)}\hat{\sigma}\sqrt{\sum c_i^2/t}$.

(2) *A one-at-a-time* $1-\alpha$ *confidence interval on* $\sum d_j\tau_j$, *where* $\sum d_j = 0$, *is* $\sum d_j\bar{Y}_{.j} \mp t_{\alpha/2:(a-1)(t-1)}\hat{\sigma}\sqrt{\sum d_j^2/a}$.

(3) *Simultaneous* $1-\alpha$ *confidence intervals on* $\alpha_i - \alpha_{i'}$, *for* $i = 1, 2, \ldots, a$, $i' = 1, 2, \ldots, a$, *and* $i \neq i'$, *are* $\bar{Y}_{i.} - \bar{Y}_{i'.} \mp q_{\alpha:a,(a-1)(t-1)}\hat{\sigma}/\sqrt{t}$.

(4) *Simultaneous* $1-\alpha$ *confidence intervals on* $\tau_j - \tau_{j'}$, *for* $j = 1, 2, \ldots, t$, $j' = 1, 2, \ldots, t$ *and* $j \neq j'$, *are* $\bar{Y}_{.j} - \bar{Y}_{.j'} \mp q_{\alpha:t,(a-1)(t-1)}\hat{\sigma}/\sqrt{a}$.

Proof

The proofs for (1) and (2) follow from Theorem 13.4.2, and the proofs for (3) and (4) follow from Theorem 13.7.4.

If one-at-a-time or simultaneous confidence intervals are wanted on other linear functions of the α_i's or the τ_j's, the appropriate theory in Chapters 6, 9, and 13 can be used.

We now turn our attention to tests of hypotheses. The hypotheses that are generally of interest in this model are $H_0 : \alpha_1 = \alpha_2 = \cdots = \alpha_a$ and $H_0 : \tau_1 = \tau_2 = \cdots = \tau_t$. We shall discuss these two tests, but only the first will be discussed in detail since the second one is the same with the α_i's and τ_j's and a and t interchanged.

THEOREM 14.2.5

Consider the model given in Equation (14.2.1) *for Case I.*

(1) *The hypothesis* $H_0 : \alpha_1 = \alpha_2 = \cdots = \alpha_a$ *vs.* H_a: *at least one equality is an inequality is an estimable hypothesis.*

(2) *A generalized likelihood ratio test statistic for the hypothesis in* (1) *is* W_A, *where*

$$W_A = \frac{\dfrac{\sum\sum(\bar{Y}_{i.} - \bar{Y}_{..})^2}{(a-1)}}{\dfrac{\sum\sum(Y_{ij} - \bar{Y}_{i.} - \bar{Y}_{.j} + \bar{Y}_{..})^2}{(a-1)(t-1)}}$$

(3) *For a size* α *test of* H_0 *vs.* H_a *in* (1), *reject* H_0 *if and only if* $w_A \geq F_{\alpha:a-1,(a-1)(t-1)}$; w_A *is the computed value of* W_A.

(4) *The power of the test is*

$$\Pi(\lambda) = \int_{F_{\alpha:a-1,(a-1)(t-1)}}^{\infty} F(w : a-1, (a-1)(t-1); \lambda)\, dw$$

where $\lambda = (2\sigma^2)^{-1} t \sum_{i=1}^{a} (\alpha_i - \bar{\alpha}_.)^2$.

(5) *The hypothesis* $H_0 : \tau_1 = \tau_2 = \cdots = \tau_t$ *vs.* H_a: *at least one equality is an inequality is an estimable hypothesis.*

(6) *A generalized likelihood ratio test statistic for the hypothesis in* (5) *is* W_T, *where*

$$W_T = \frac{\dfrac{\sum\sum(\bar{Y}_{.j} - \bar{Y}_{..})^2}{t-1}}{\dfrac{\sum\sum(Y_{ij} - \bar{Y}_{i.} - \bar{Y}_{.j} + \bar{Y}_{..})^2}{(a-1)(t-1)}}$$

(7) *For a size* α *test of* H_0 *vs.* H_a *in* (5), *reject* H_0 *if and only if* $w_T \geq F_{\alpha:t-1,(a-1)(t-1)}$; w_T *is the computed value of* W_T.

(8) *The power of the test is*

$$\Pi(\lambda) = \int_{F_{\alpha:t-1,(a-1)(t-1)}}^{\infty} F(w : t-1, (a-1)(t-1); \lambda)\, dw$$

where $\lambda = (2\sigma^2)^{-1} a \sum_{j=1}^{t} (\tau_j - \bar{\tau}_.)^2$.

Proof

We shall prove (1), (2), (3), and (4). The proofs of (5), (6), (7), and (8) are identical, with the α_i's and the τ_j's interchanged and t and a interchanged. The proof of (1) follows immediately from Theorem 13.7.1 since we have proved that every contrast of the α_i is estimable.

To prove (2) we use Theorem 13.4.1 and the form of W given in Equation (13.4.2). We can easily calculate $\hat{\sigma}_\Omega^2$ since $\hat{\sigma}^2 = n\hat{\sigma}_\Omega^2/(n-K)$; so by Equation (14.2.8) we get $\hat{\sigma}_\Omega^2 = (at)^{-1} \sum\sum (Y_{ij} - \bar{Y}_{i.} - \bar{Y}_{.j} + \bar{Y}_{..})^2$. To obtain $\hat{\sigma}_\omega^2$ we must examine the model $Y_{ij} = \mu + \alpha_i + \tau_j + \varepsilon_{ij}$ when reduced by $H_0 : \alpha_1 = \alpha_2 = \cdots = \alpha_a = \gamma$, say, where γ is unknown. The reduced model is $Y_{ij} = \mu + \gamma + \tau_j + \varepsilon_{ij}$, or $Y_{ij} = \mu_0 + \tau_j + \varepsilon_{ij}$, where we have set $\mu_0 = \mu + \gamma$. This is the one-factor model (with i and j interchanged), so by Theorem 13.6.2 we get $\hat{\sigma}_\omega^2 = (at)^{-1} \sum\sum (Y_{ij} - \bar{Y}_{.j})^2$, and we substitute these quantities into Equation (13.4.2). Note that $at - K = (a-1)(t-1)$ and $q = a - 1$. Simplifying the result gives the formula for W_A in (2).

To prove (3) and (4) we use the results of Theorem 13.4.1, except we use Equation (13.7.1) to obtain λ. We must evaluate $\mathscr{E}$[S.S. due to H_0], which is the expected value of the sum of squares in the numerator of W_A in (2). We get

$$\begin{aligned}
\mathscr{E}\left[\sum_{j=1}^{t}\sum_{i=1}^{a}(\bar{Y}_{i.} - \bar{Y}_{..})^2\right] &= \mathscr{E}\left[\sum_{j=1}^{t}\sum_{i=1}^{a}(\mu + \alpha_i + \bar{\tau}_. + \bar{\varepsilon}_{i.} - \mu - \bar{\alpha}_. - \bar{\tau}_. - \bar{\varepsilon}_{..})^2\right] \\
&= \mathscr{E}\left[\sum_{j=1}^{t}\sum_{i=1}^{a}(\alpha_i - \bar{\alpha}_.)^2\right] + \sum_{j=1}^{t}\left\{\mathscr{E}\left[\sum_{i=1}^{a}(\bar{\varepsilon}_{i.} - \bar{\varepsilon}_{..})^2\right]\right\} \\
&= t\sum_{i=1}^{a}(\alpha_i - \bar{\alpha}_.)^2 + (a-1)\sigma^2
\end{aligned}$$

Substitute into Equation (13.7.1) and the value of λ in (4) is obtained.

Identical methods can be used to prove (5), (6), (7), and (8). Thus the proof of the theorem is complete.

These two test procedures can be exhibited in an ANOVA table such as in Section 7.4. They are given in Tables 14.2.2 and 14.2.3. Table 14.2.1 exhibits the data.

Table 14.2.1

Data for Two-Factor Design Model, No Interaction, One Observation Per Cell

Levels of Factor A	*Levels of Factor T* 1	2	3	...	*t*	*Total*	*Mean*
1	y_{11}	y_{12}	y_{13}	...	y_{1t}	$y_{1.}$	$\bar{y}_{1.}$
2	y_{21}	y_{22}	y_{23}	...	y_{2t}	$y_{2.}$	$\bar{y}_{2.}$
3	y_{31}	y_{32}	y_{33}	...	y_{3t}	$y_{3.}$	$\bar{y}_{3.}$
$\vdots$	$\vdots$	$\vdots$	$\vdots$		$\vdots$	$\vdots$	$\vdots$
a	y_{a1}	y_{a2}	y_{a3}	...	y_{at}	$y_{a.}$	$\bar{y}_{a.}$
Total	$y_{.1}$	$y_{.2}$	$y_{.3}$	...	$y_{.t}$	$y_{..}$	
Mean	$\bar{y}_{.1}$	$\bar{y}_{.2}$	$\bar{y}_{.3}$	...	$\bar{y}_{.t}$		$\bar{y}_{..}$

Reminder. Generally, but not always, we use capital letters for random variables and lowercase letters for the observed values of the random variables. Also, we use an overbar to denote a mean, that is, $\bar{Y}_{i..}$, $\bar{y}_{i..}$.

In Table 14.2.2 we use A_{ss} and A_{ms} as symbols for the sum of squares and the mean square, respectively, due to H_0 for factor A. We use E_{ss} and E_{ms} as symbols

Table 14.2.2

ANOVA for Testing H_0: $\alpha_1 = \alpha_2 = \cdots = \alpha_a$ in Two-Factor Design Model

Source	*d.f.*	*S.S.*	*M.S.*
Total	ta	$\sum_{j=1}^{t}\sum_{i=1}^{a} y_{ij}^2$	
$R(\mu, \alpha, \tau)$	$a + t - 1$	$\frac{y_{..}^2}{ta} + \left(\sum_{i=1}^{a}\frac{y_{i.}^2}{t} - \frac{y_{..}^2}{ta}\right) + \left(\sum_{j=1}^{t}\frac{y_{.j}^2}{a} - \frac{y_{..}^2}{ta}\right)$	
$R(\mu, \tau)$	t	$\sum_{j=1}^{t}\frac{y_{.j}^2}{a}$	
$R(H_0)$	$a - 1$	$\sum_{i=1}^{a}\frac{y_{i.}^2}{t} - \frac{y_{..}^2}{ta} = A_{ss}$	$A_{ms} = \frac{A_{ss}}{a-1}$
Error	$(a-1)(t-1)$	$\left(\sum_{i=1}^{a}\sum_{j=1}^{t} y_{ij}^2 - \frac{y_{..}^2}{at}\right) - \left(\sum_{i=1}^{a}\frac{y_{i.}^2}{t} - \frac{y_{..}^2}{ta}\right) - \left(\sum_{j=1}^{t}\frac{y_{.j}^2}{a} - \frac{y_{..}^2}{ta}\right) = E_{ss}$	$E_{ms} = \frac{E_{ss}}{(a-1)(t-1)}$

Table 14.2.3

ANOVA for Testing H_0: $\tau_1 = \tau_2 = \cdots = \tau_t$ in Two-Factor Design Model

Source	*d.f.*	*S.S.*	*M.S.*
Total	ta	$\sum_{i=1}^{a}\sum_{j=1}^{t} y_{ij}^2$	
$R(\mu, \alpha, \tau)$	$a + t - 1$	$\frac{y_{..}^2}{ta} + \left(\sum_{i=1}^{a}\frac{y_{i.}^2}{t} - \frac{y_{..}^2}{ta}\right) + \left(\sum_{j=1}^{t}\frac{y_{.j}^2}{a} - \frac{y_{..}^2}{ta}\right)$	
$R(\mu, \alpha)$	a	$\sum_{i=1}^{a}\frac{y_{i.}^2}{t}$	
$R(H_0)$	$t - 1$	$\sum_{j=1}^{t}\frac{y_{.j}^2}{a} - \frac{y_{..}^2}{ta} = T_{ss}$	$T_{ms} = \frac{T_{ss}}{t-1}$
Error	$(a-1)(t-1)$	$\left(\sum_{i=1}^{a}\sum_{j=1}^{t} y_{ij}^2 - \frac{y_{..}^2}{ta}\right) - \left(\sum_{i=1}^{a}\frac{y_{i.}^2}{t} - \frac{y_{..}^2}{ta}\right) - \left(\sum_{j=1}^{t}\frac{y_{.j}^2}{a} - \frac{y_{..}^2}{ta}\right) = E_{ss}$	$E_{ms} = \frac{E_{ss}}{(a-1)(t-1)}$

for the error sum of squares and the mean square, respectively. In Table 14.2.3 we use T_{ss} and T_{ms} to denote the sum of squares and the mean square, respectively, due to H_0 for factor T.

The computation of the quantities needed in Tables 14.2.2 and 14.2.3 are very easily obtained from the data in Table 14.2.1 and its rows and columns totals. There is no need to compile the normal equations or use the square root

Table 14.2.4

ANOVA for Testing H_0: $\alpha_1 = \alpha_2 = \cdots = \alpha_a$ and for Testing H_0: $\tau_1 = \tau_2 = \cdots = \tau_t$

Source	*d.f.*	*S.S.*	*M.S.*	*F*
Total	ta	$\sum_{i=1}^{a}\sum_{j=1}^{t} y_{ij}^2$		
Mean	1	$\frac{y_{..}^2}{ta}$		
$R(H_0)$ for α	$a - 1$	$\sum_{i=1}^{a}\frac{y_{i.}^2}{t} - \frac{y_{..}^2}{at} = A_{ss}$	A_{ms}	$\frac{A_{ms}}{E_{ms}}$
$R(H_0)$ for τ	$t - 1$	$\sum_{j=1}^{t}\frac{y_{.j}^2}{a} - \frac{y_{..}^2}{at} = T_{ss}$	T_{ms}	$\frac{T_{ms}}{E_{ms}}$
Error	$(a-1)(t-1)$	$\sum_{i=1}^{a}\sum_{j=1}^{t}(y_{ij} - \bar{y}_{i.} - \bar{y}_{.j} + \bar{y}_{..})^2 = E_{ss}$	E_{ms}	

procedure, and so on. Also, note that many of the quantities in Table 14.2.3 are the same quantities that were computed in Table 14.2.2.

To test the desired hypotheses, T_{ss}, A_{ss}, and E_{ss} are all that are needed to compute the test statistics in (2) and (6) of Theorem 14.2.5. These are generally put into a single table, as exhibited in Table 14.2.4.

There are several things to note in Table 14.2.4. The quantity E_{ss} can be computed by subtraction; E_{ms} is the UMVU estimate of σ^2; A_{ms}/E_{ms} is w_A in (2) and T_{ms}/E_{ms} is w_T in (6) of Theorem 14.2.5.

14.3 Two-Factor Design Model, No Interaction, $M > 1$ Observations Per Cell

The model is stated in Equation (14.1.6) but it will be repeated here.

$$\begin{aligned} &Y_{ijm} = \mu + \alpha_i + \tau_j + \varepsilon_{ijm} \\ &\qquad m = 1, 2, \ldots, M > 1, \quad i = 1, 2, \ldots, a > 1, \quad j = 1, 2, \ldots, t > 1 \end{aligned} \qquad (14.3.1)$$

There are the same number of parameters in this model as there are in the model discussed in Section 14.2. The normal equations are given below in abbreviated form by using the procedure discussed in Section 13.5.

$$\begin{aligned} \mu:&\quad atM\hat{\mu} + tM\sum\hat{\alpha}_i + aM\sum\hat{\tau}_j = Y_{...} \\ \alpha_i:&\quad tM\hat{\mu} + tM\hat{\alpha}_i + M\sum\hat{\tau}_j = Y_{i..} \qquad i = 1, 2, \ldots, a \\ \tau_j:&\quad aM\hat{\mu} + M\sum\hat{\alpha}_i + aM\hat{\tau}_j = Y_{.j.} \qquad j = 1, 2, \ldots, t \end{aligned} \qquad (14.3.2)$$

By procedures very similar to those used to solve the normal equations in Section 14.2, the following theorem can be proved.

THEOREM 14.3.1

Let the model be given by Equation (14.3.1).

(1) *There are* $(a + t - 1)$ *linearly independent estimable functions, that is,* $K = a + t - 1$.

(2) $\sum c_i\alpha_i$ *is estimable if and only if* $\sum c_i = 0$; *the best unbiased estimator of* $\sum c_i\alpha_i$ *is* $\sum c_i\hat{\alpha}_i = \sum c_i\bar{Y}_{i..}$.

(3) $\sum d_j\tau_j$ *is estimable if and only if* $\sum d_j = 0$; *the best unbiased estimator of* $\sum d_j\tau_j$ *is* $\sum d_j\hat{\tau}_j = \sum d_j\bar{Y}_{.j.}$.

Case I is assumed for (4), (5), (6), (7), *and* (8). *Define n by* $n = atM - a - t + 1$.

(4) *The UMVU estimator of* σ^2 *is*

$$\hat{\sigma}^2 = n^{-1}\left[\sum_{i=1}^{a}\sum_{j=1}^{t} M(\bar{Y}_{ij.} - \bar{Y}_{i..} - \bar{Y}_{.j.} + \bar{Y}_{...})^2 + \sum_{i=1}^{a}\sum_{j=1}^{t}\sum_{m=1}^{M}(Y_{ijm} - \bar{Y}_{ij.})^2\right]$$

(5) $Z_1 = \sum c_i\bar{Y}_{i..} = \sum c_i\hat{\alpha}_i$ *is distributed* $N(z_1 : \sum c_i\alpha_i,\ \sigma^2 \sum c_i^2/Mt)$ *if* $\sum c_i = 0$.

(6) $Z_2 = \sum d_j\bar{Y}_{.j.} = \sum d_j\hat{\tau}_j$ *is distributed* $N(z_2 : \sum d_j\tau_j,\ \sigma^2 \sum d_j^2/Ma)$ *if* $\sum d_j = 0$.

(7) $U = n\hat{\sigma}^2/\sigma^2$ *is distributed* $\chi^2(u : n)$.

(8) U, Z_1, *and* Z_2 *are jointly independent.*

Next we state a theorem that can be used to test various hypotheses and compute confidence intervals for the model in Equation (14.3.1).

THEOREM 14.3.2

Let the model be given by Equation (14.3.1) *for Case I.*

(1) *One-at-a-time* $1 - \alpha$ *confidence intervals on* $\sum c_i\alpha_i$ *and* $\sum d_j\tau_j$ *(where* $\sum c_i = \sum d_j = 0$*) are, respectively,*

$$\sum_{i=1}^{a} c_i\bar{Y}_{i..} \mp t_{\alpha/2:n}\hat{\sigma}\sqrt{\sum c_i^2/Mt} \qquad \sum_{j=1}^{t} d_j\bar{Y}_{.j.} \mp t_{\alpha/2:n}\hat{\sigma}\sqrt{\sum d_j^2/Ma}$$

(2) *Simultaneous* $1 - \alpha$ *confidence intervals on* $\alpha_i - \alpha_{i'}$, *for all* $i = 1, 2, \ldots, a$ *and* $i' = 1, 2, \ldots, a$, *and on* $\tau_j - \tau_{j'}$, *for all* $j = 1, 2, \ldots, t$ *and* $j' = 1, 2, \ldots, t$, *are, respectively,*

$$\bar{Y}_{i..} - \bar{Y}_{i'..} \mp \frac{q_{\alpha:a,n}\hat{\sigma}}{\sqrt{tM}} \qquad \bar{Y}_{.j.} - \bar{Y}_{.j'.} \mp \frac{q_{\alpha:t,n}\hat{\sigma}}{\sqrt{aM}}$$

(3) *The hypothesis* $H_0 : \alpha_1 = \alpha_2 = \cdots = \alpha_a$ *vs.* H_a: *at least one equality is an inequality, is an estimable hypothesis, and the generalized likelihood ratio test of size* α *is as follows: Reject* H_0 *if and only if* $w_A \geq F_{\alpha:a-1,n}$, *where* w_A *is the computed value of* W_A *and*

$$W_A = tM \sum_{i=1}^{a} \frac{(\bar{Y}_{i..} - \bar{Y}_{...})^2}{(a-1)\hat{\sigma}^2}$$

The power of the test is

$$\Pi(\lambda) = \int_{F_{\alpha:a-1,n}}^{\infty} F(w : a - 1, n; \lambda)\, dw$$

where $\lambda = (2\sigma^2)^{-1} tM \sum_{i=1}^{a} (\alpha_i - \bar{\alpha}_.)^2$.

(4) *The hypothesis* $H_0 : \tau_1 = \tau_2 = \cdots = \tau_t$ *vs.* H_a: *at least one equality is an inequality, is an estimable hypothesis, and the generalized likelihood ratio test of size* α *is as follows: Reject* H_0 *if and only if* $w_T \geq F_{\alpha:t-1,n}$, *where* w_T *is the computed value of* W_T *and*

$$W_T = aM \sum_{j=1}^{t} \frac{(\bar{Y}_{.j.} - \bar{Y}_{...})^2}{(t - 1)\hat{\sigma}^2}$$

The power of the test is

$$\Pi(\lambda) = \int_{F_{\alpha:t-1,n}}^{\infty} F(w : t - 1, n; \lambda)\, dw$$

where $\lambda = (2\sigma^2)^{-1} aM \sum_{j=1}^{t} (\tau_j - \bar{\tau}_.)^2$.

Proof

The proof is very similar to the proofs of Theorems 14.2.4 and 14.2.5 and will be left for the reader.

An ANOVA table is useful for exhibiting the various quantities needed for computing statistics for this model. Table 14.3.1 is the data table and Table 14.3.2 is the ANOVA table, a combination of two tables that could be exhibited to test the hypotheses in (3) and (4) in Theorem 14.3.2 (see the next page).

In Table 14.3.2 all the quantities in the S.S. column can be obtained directly from the data table by squaring and summing the appropriate numbers. The S.S. for error can be obtained by subtracting from the total sum of squares the following sums of squares: mean, $R(H_0)$ for $\boldsymbol{\alpha}$, $R(H_0)$ for $\boldsymbol{\tau}$. The number E_{ms} is $\hat{\sigma}^2$, and w_A and w_T are the values of the test statistics described in Theorem 14.3.2.

14.4 Two-Factor Design Model, No Interaction, Unequal Numbers of Observations in Cells

This model is defined in Equation (14.1.7) but it will be defined here in more detail. In Sections 14.2 and 14.3, models were discussed that possessed a great deal of symmetry; also, computations were very easy to perform to obtain the

Table 14.3.1

Data for a Two-Factor Design Model, No Interaction, $M > 1$ Observations Per Cell

Levels of Factor A	Levels of Factor T: 1	2	$\cdots$	t	Total	Mean
1	y_{111} y_{112} $\vdots$ y_{11M}	y_{121} y_{122} $\vdots$ y_{12M}	$\cdots$	y_{1t1} y_{1t2} $\vdots$ y_{1tM}	$y_{1..}$	$\bar{y}_{1..}$
2	y_{211} y_{212} $\vdots$ y_{21M}	y_{221} y_{222} $\vdots$ y_{22M}	$\cdots$	y_{2t1} y_{2t2} $\vdots$ y_{2tM}	$y_{2..}$	$\bar{y}_{2..}$
$\vdots$	$\vdots$	$\vdots$		$\vdots$	$\vdots$	$\vdots$
a	y_{a11} y_{a12} $\vdots$ y_{a1M}	y_{a21} y_{a22} $\vdots$ y_{a2M}	$\cdots$	y_{at1} y_{at2} $\vdots$ y_{atM}	$y_{a..}$	$\bar{y}_{a..}$
Total	$y_{.1.}$	$y_{.2.}$	$\cdots$	$y_{.t.}$	$y_{...}$	
Mean	$\bar{y}_{.1.}$	$\bar{y}_{.2.}$	$\cdots$	$\bar{y}_{.t.}$		$\bar{y}_{...}$

Table 14.3.2

ANOVA for Testing $H_0: \alpha_1 = \alpha_2 = \cdots = \alpha_a$ and for Testing $H_0: \tau_1 = \tau_2 = \cdots = \tau_t$

Source	*d.f.*	*S.S.*	*M.S.*	*F*
Total	atM	$\sum\sum\sum y_{ijm}^2$		
Mean	1	$\frac{y_{...}^2}{atM}$		
$R(H_0)$ for α	$a - 1$	$\sum \frac{y_{i..}^2}{tM} - \frac{y_{...}^2}{atM} = A_{ss}$	A_{ms}	$\frac{A_{ms}}{E_{ms}} = w_A$
$R(H_0)$ for τ	$t - 1$	$\sum \frac{y_{.j.}^2}{aM} - \frac{y_{...}^2}{atM} = T_{ss}$	T_{ms}	$\frac{T_{ms}}{E_{ms}} = w_T$
Error	n	[subtract] $= E_{ss}$	E_{ms}	

quantities needed for estimation and hypothesis testing. This is not generally the case for the model to be discussed in this section. This model is a generalization of the models discussed in the two previous sections, or, in other words, they are special cases of the model to be discussed here. Sometimes the unequal numbers of observations in the cells are due to accidents, such as animals dying or wrong measurements recorded, but this model also applies when the unequal numbers of observations are intentional, such as for the incomplete block designs. These ideas will be discussed later; first we define the model in detail and show how to get the desired statistics.

The model is

$$Y_{ijm} = \mu + \alpha_i + \tau_j + \varepsilon_{ijm}$$
$$m = 0, 1, \ldots, n_{ij}, \quad i = 1, 2, \ldots, a > 1, \quad j = 1, 2, \ldots, t > 1 \quad (14.4.1)$$

where each n_{ij} can be any nonnegative integer with the restriction that the design is connected (this term will be defined below). Not all n_{ij} are the same.

> ***Note 1.*** The restriction that not all n_{ij} are the same is not an essential part of the model, but if it is not the case, then this model is either the model in Equation (14.3.1) or in Equation (14.2.1).

By Section 13.5 the abbreviated set of normal equations can be obtained. They are as follows:

$$\mu: \quad n_{..}\hat{\mu} + \sum_{i=1}^{a} n_{i.}\hat{\alpha}_i + \sum_{j=1}^{t} n_{.j}\hat{\tau}_j = Y_{...}$$

$$\alpha_i: \quad n_{i.}\hat{\mu} + n_{i.}\hat{\alpha}_i + \sum_{j=1}^{t} n_{ij}\hat{\tau}_j = Y_{i..} \qquad \text{for } i = 1, 2, \ldots, a \qquad (14.4.2)$$

$$\tau_j: \quad n_{.j}\hat{\mu} + \sum_{i=1}^{a} n_{ij}\hat{\alpha}_i + n_{.j}\hat{\tau}_j = Y_{.j.} \qquad \text{for } j = 1, 2, \ldots, t$$

where

$$n_{..} = \sum_{i=1}^{a}\sum_{j=1}^{t} n_{ij} \qquad n_{i.} = \sum_{j=1}^{t} n_{ij} \qquad n_{.j} = \sum_{i=1}^{a} n_{ij}$$

Since the models in Equation (14.2.1) and Equation (14.3.1) are special cases of the model in this section, the normal equations in Equation (14.2.2) and Equation (14.3.2) are special cases of the normal equations in Equation (14.4.2). The normal equations for the models in the two previous sections were easily solved, but that may not be the case for the normal equations in Equation (14.4.2). We know, however, that the equations are consistent since this was proved in Section 13.2.

An approach for solving these equations is to consider them as a general system $\mathbf{X'X\hat{\beta}} = \mathbf{X'y}$ and use the square root method and the procedures described in Chapter 7 when $\mathbf{X'X}$ is positive semidefinite. However, we will not take that approach since there is sometimes a pattern to the numbers n_{ij} that will enable easier and "better" computing methods to be used. If a or t is large, and since $\mathbf{X}'\mathbf{X}$ is an $(a + t + 1) \times (a + t + 1)$ matrix, this may be a large system of equations to solve; so easier and better methods for solving them are important considerations. We note that in the two previous sections the system was the same size as in this section, and even though the normal equations could have been solved by procedures similar to those used in Chapter 7, we found instead a very easy and virtually exact method for computing estimates, confidence intervals, and test statistics by using only sums of squares of the observations, of row totals, and of column totals of the data matrix.

The first thing we shall do is determine K, the number of linearly independent estimable functions, and exhibit a basis set. In the model in Equation (14.4.1), as was the case for the models in Equations (14.2.1) and (14.3.1), the interest in applied work is generally in linear combinations of the α_i's and in linear combinations of the τ_j's. There is generally not much interest in linear combinations of the α_i's and τ_j's together. For the models in the two previous sections, we proved that $\sum c_i\alpha_i$ and $\sum d_j\tau_j$ were estimable if and only if $\sum c_i = \sum d_j = 0$. This is not always true for the model to be discussed in this section, but it depends on which of the n_{ij}'s are zero. In exhibiting the data for this model, two tables will be presented: one table of the observations y_{ijm} and one table of the n_{ij}. See Table 14.4.1.

The notation we shall use is given in detail below.

$$
\begin{aligned}
&n_{i.} = \sum_{j=1}^{t} n_{ij} \qquad n_{.j} = \sum_{i=1}^{a} n_{ij} \qquad n_{..} = \sum_{i=1}^{a} n_{i.} = \sum_{j=1}^{t} n_{.j} = \sum_{i=1}^{a}\sum_{j=1}^{t} n_{ij} \\
&Y_{ij.} = \sum_{m=1}^{n_{ij}} Y_{ijm} \qquad \bar{Y}_{ij.} = n_{ij}^{-1} \sum_{m=1}^{n_{ij}} Y_{ijm} \qquad \text{if } n_{ij} \neq 0 \\
&Y_{i..} = \sum_{j=1}^{t}\sum_{m=1}^{n_{ij}} Y_{ijm} \qquad \bar{Y}_{i..} = n_{i.}^{-1} \sum_{j=1}^{t}\sum_{m=1}^{n_{ij}} Y_{ijm} \\
&Y_{.j.} = \sum_{i=1}^{a}\sum_{m=1}^{n_{ij}} Y_{ijm} \qquad \bar{Y}_{.j.} = n_{.j}^{-1} \sum_{i=1}^{a}\sum_{m=1}^{n_{ij}} Y_{ijm} \\
&Y_{...} = \sum_{i=1}^{a}\sum_{j=1}^{t}\sum_{m=1}^{n_{ij}} Y_{ijm} \qquad \bar{Y}_{...} = n_{..}^{-1} \sum_{i=1}^{a}\sum_{j=1}^{t}\sum_{m=1}^{n_{ij}} Y_{ijm}
\end{aligned}
\tag{14.4.3}
$$

If $n_{ij} = 0$ for any i and j combination, then there are no observations in that cell and Y_{ij0} is not observed, so $Y_{ij.}$ and $\bar{Y}_{ij.}$ do not exist. We assume that $n_{i.} > 0$ and $n_{.j} > 0$ for all i and j; if we allowed, say, $n_{i.}$ to be zero for a value of i, then there would be no observations for the ith level of factor A and that level would not be in the investigation; a similar situation obtains if $n_{.j} = 0$ for a value of j. If too many of the n_{ij} are zero, or if certain ones are zero, then this may mean that certain linear combinations of the α_i's (or the τ_j's) are not estimable. This leads to the definitions of A-connected and T-connected models.

Table 14.4.1

Table (*a*) of Observations y_{ijm} and Table (*b*) of n_{ij} for the Model in Equation (14.4.1)

(*a*)

Levels of Factor A	*Levels of Factor T* 1	2	$\cdots$	*t*	*Total*	*Mean*
	y_{111}	y_{121}	$\cdots$	y_{1t1}		
1	$\vdots$	$\vdots$		$\vdots$		
	$y_{11n_{11}}$	$y_{12n_{12}}$	$\cdots$	$y_{1tn_{1t}}$		
	$y_{11.}$	$y_{12.}$	$\cdots$	$y_{1t.}$	$y_{1..}$	$\bar{y}_{1..}$
	y_{211}	y_{221}	$\cdots$	y_{2t1}		
2	$\vdots$	$\vdots$		$\vdots$		
	$y_{21n_{21}}$	$y_{22n_{22}}$	$\cdots$	$y_{2tn_{2t}}$		
	$y_{21.}$	$y_{22.}$	$\cdots$	$y_{2t.}$	$y_{2..}$	$\bar{y}_{2..}$
$\vdots$	$\vdots$	$\vdots$		$\vdots$	$\vdots$	$\vdots$
	y_{a11}	y_{a21}	$\cdots$	y_{at1}		
a	$\vdots$	$\vdots$		$\vdots$		
	$y_{a1n_{a1}}$	$y_{a2n_{a2}}$	$\cdots$	$y_{atn_{at}}$		
	$y_{a1.}$	$y_{a2.}$	$\cdots$	$y_{at.}$	$y_{a..}$	$\bar{y}_{a..}$
Total	$y_{.1.}$	$y_{.2.}$	$\cdots$	$y_{.t.}$	$y_{...}$	
Mean	$\bar{y}_{.1.}$	$\bar{y}_{.2.}$	$\cdots$	$\bar{y}_{.t.}$		$\bar{y}_{...}$

(*b*)

Levels of Factor A	*Levels of Factor T* 1	2	$\cdots$	*t*	*Total*
1	n_{11}	n_{12}	$\cdots$	n_{1t}	$n_{1.}$
2	n_{21}	n_{22}	$\cdots$	n_{2t}	$n_{2.}$
$\vdots$	$\vdots$	$\vdots$		$\vdots$	$\vdots$
a	n_{a1}	n_{a2}	$\cdots$	n_{at}	$n_{a.}$
Total	$n_{.1}$	$n_{.2}$	$\cdots$	$n_{.t}$	$n_{..}$

DEFINITION 14.4.1

***A*-Connected and *T*-Connected Models.** *Let the model be given by Equation* (14.4.1). *If the set of n_{ij} is such that $\alpha_i - \alpha_{i'}$ is estimable for $i = 1, 2, \ldots, a$ and $i' = 1, 2, \ldots, a$, the model is defined to be an A-connected model. If $\tau_j - \tau_{j'}$ is estimable for $j = 1, 2, \ldots, t$ and $j' = 1, 2, \ldots, t$, the model is defined to be a T-connected model.*

> ***Note 2.*** Whether a model is *A*-connected (or *T*-connected) is determined by *which* n_{ij} are zero and *which* n_{ij} are nonzero; the *values* of the nonzero n_{ij} have no bearing on whether the model is *A*- or *T*-connected.

It can be shown that if a model is A-connected, it is also T-connected, and if it is T-connected, it is also A-connected. Hence if a design is T- or A-connected, we shall refer to it as a connected design (or a connected model).

> ***Note 3.*** All models to be discussed in this section are assumed to be connected. See [W-4] for further information on this subject.

We now prove a theorem to demonstrate various consequences of this definition.

THEOREM 14.4.1

Let the model be given in Equation (14.4.1) *for Case I or II. The only linear combinations of the α_i's that are estimable are contrasts, and "all" contrasts of the α_i's are estimable if and only if the design is connected. The only linear combinations of the τ_j's that are estimable are contrasts, and "all" contrasts of the τ_j's are estimable if and only if the design is connected.*

Proof

The proof is straightforward and will be asked for in the problems.

THEOREM 14.4.2

Let the model be given in Equation (14.4.1) *for Case I or II. The number K of linearly independent estimable functions is equal to $a + t - 1$. A basis set of estimable functions is*

$$\begin{aligned} &\alpha_1 - \alpha_i && \text{for } i = 2, 3, \ldots, a \\ &\tau_1 - \tau_j && \text{for } j = 2, 3, \ldots, t \\ &\mu + \sum_{i=1}^{a} \left(\frac{n_{i.}}{n_{..}}\right)\alpha_i + \sum_{j=1}^{t} \left(\frac{n_{.j}}{n_{..}}\right)\tau_j \end{aligned} \tag{14.4.4}$$

Proof

$\alpha_1 - \alpha_i$ for $i = 2, 3, \ldots, a$ are estimable by the definition of an A-connected model; $\tau_1 - \tau_j$ for $j = 2, 3, \ldots, t$ are estimable by the definition of a T-connected model; divide the first equation of the normal equations by $n_{..}$ and get $\hat{\mu} + \sum_{i=1}^{a} (n_{i.}/n_{..})\hat{\alpha}_i + \sum_{j=1}^{t} (n_{.j}/n_{..})\hat{\tau}_j = \bar{Y}_{...}$. The expected value of $\bar{Y}_{...}$ is the linear function in the third line of Equation (14.4.4) and is estimable.

If we examine the $(a + t - 1)$ functions in Equation (14.4.4) in the order presented, we see that each function contains a distinct parameter, and hence they are linearly independent. Thus we have exhibited $(a - 1) + (t - 1) + 1 = (a + t - 1)$ linearly independent estimable functions. By examining the normal equations it is easy to see that the rank of $\mathbf{X}'\mathbf{X}$ can be no greater than $a + t - 1$ (the sum of the α equations equals the sum of the τ equations and equals the μ equation). Hence the number of linearly independent estimable functions is $K = a + t - 1$, and those in Equation (14.4.4) form a basis set. This completes the proof of the theorem.

COROLLARY 14.4.2

The following are estimable functions for the model defined in Equation (14.4.1): $\alpha_i - \bar{\alpha}_.$ *for* $i = 1, 2, \ldots, a$; $\tau_j - \bar{\tau}_.$ *for* $j = 1, 2, \ldots, t$; $\sum_{i=1}^{a} c_i\alpha_i$ *for any set of* c_i*'s such that* $\sum_{i=1}^{a} c_i = 0$; $\sum_{j=1}^{t} d_j\tau_j$ *for any set of* d_j*'s such that* $\sum_{j=1}^{t} d_j = 0$.

We have found the number of linearly independent functions of μ, $\boldsymbol{\alpha}$, and $\boldsymbol{\tau}$ that are estimable and have exhibited several sets of estimable functions. We now discuss some computational techniques that will be useful for solving the normal equations of the model in this section. First we demonstrate how the square root procedure can be used to solve the normal equations to obtain point and interval estimates and test statistics.

To obtain the format for the normal equations $[\mathbf{X}'\mathbf{X} \mid \mathbf{X}'\mathbf{Y}]$, we notice from the abbreviated normal equations in Equation (14.4.2) that we can use Table 14.4.1 to obtain $\mathbf{X}'\mathbf{X}$. However, instead of the format $[\mathbf{X}'\mathbf{X} \mid \mathbf{X}'\mathbf{Y}]$, where $\mathbf{X}'\mathbf{X}$ is not full rank, we shall obtain a modified normal equations format—modified by two nonestimable functions so the resulting matrix will be full rank—and use Method 2 in Section 13.5. We have proved that we can use two nonestimable functions for the model in this section (since $p - K = 2$) and the two we shall use are $\hat{\mu} = 0$ and $\hat{\tau}_t = 0$.

We use the notation $\mathbf{n}_{i.} = [n_{1.}, n_{2.}, \ldots, n_{a.}]'$ and $\mathbf{n}_{.j} = [n_{.1}, n_{.2}, \ldots, n_{.t-1}]'$; observe that the elements of the two vectors $\mathbf{n}_{i.}$ and $\mathbf{n}_{.j}$ are the elements of the row and column totals, respectively, in Table 14.4.1(b) except that the tth column total has not been included in $\mathbf{n}_{.j}$. We will remark further on this point later. We let $\mathbf{y}_{i.} = [Y_{1..}, Y_{2..}, \ldots, Y_{a..}]'$ be the vector of row totals of Table 14.4.1(a) and $\mathbf{y}_{.j} = [Y_{.1.}, Y_{.2.}, \ldots, Y_{.t-1.}]'$ be the vector of the first $t - 1$ column totals. We denote by $\mathbf{D}_{i.}$ a diagonal matrix whose diagonal is the vector $\mathbf{n}_{i.}$ and by $\mathbf{D}_{.j}$ a diagonal matrix whose diagonal is the vector $\mathbf{n}_{.j}$. We denote by $\mathbf{N}$ the $a \times (t - 1)$ matrix of the n_{ij} in Table 14.4.1(b) with the last column omitted, that is, $\mathbf{N} = [n_{ij}]$, $i = 1, 2, \ldots, a$, and $j = 1, 2, \ldots, t - 1$.

The resulting normal equations can be written in matrix form as (denote $\hat{\boldsymbol{\tau}}_t'$ by $[\hat{\tau}_1, \hat{\tau}_2, \ldots, \hat{\tau}_{t-1}]$)

$$\begin{bmatrix} \mathbf{D}_{i.} & \mathbf{N} \\ \mathbf{N}' & \mathbf{D}_{.j} \end{bmatrix} \begin{bmatrix} \hat{\boldsymbol{\alpha}} \\ \hat{\boldsymbol{\tau}}_t \end{bmatrix} = \begin{bmatrix} \mathbf{y}_{i.} \\ \mathbf{y}_{.j} \end{bmatrix}. \tag{14.4.5}$$

If the format in Equation (14.4.6) is reduced by the square root method, the result is Equation (14.4.7).

$$[\mathbf{W} \mid \mathbf{w} \mid \mathbf{I}] = \left[\begin{array}{cc|c|cc} \mathbf{D}_{i.} & \mathbf{N} & \mathbf{y}_{i.} & \mathbf{I} & \mathbf{0} \\ \mathbf{N}' & \mathbf{D}_{.j} & \mathbf{y}_{.j} & \mathbf{0} & \mathbf{I} \end{array}\right] \tag{14.4.6}$$

$$[\mathbf{T} \mid \mathbf{t} \mid \mathbf{T}'^{-1}] = \left[\begin{array}{cc|c|cc} \mathbf{T}_{11} & \mathbf{T}_{12} & \mathbf{t}_1 & \mathbf{T}^*_{11} & \mathbf{0} \\ \mathbf{0} & \mathbf{T}_{22} & \mathbf{t}_2 & \mathbf{T}^*_{21} & \mathbf{T}^*_{22} \end{array}\right] \tag{14.4.7}$$

where $\mathbf{T}_{11}$ and $\mathbf{T}^*_{11}$ are $a \times a$ matrices, and the sizes of the other matrices are easily determined.

Note 4. Several things can be inferred from the format in Equation (14.4.7).

1. $\mathbf{T}_{11}$ is a diagonal matrix whose kth diagonal element is the square root of the kth diagonal element of $\mathbf{D}_{i.}$, that is, $\sqrt{n_{k.}}$.
2. The sth element of $\mathbf{t}_1$ is the sth element of $\mathbf{y}_{i.}$ divided by the square root of the sth diagonal element of $\mathbf{D}_{i.}$, that is, $Y_{s..}/\sqrt{n_{s.}}$.
3. Denote the backward solution of Equation (14.4.7) by $\tilde{\tau}_{t-1}, \tilde{\tau}_{t-2}, \ldots, \tilde{\tau}_1$ and $\tilde{\alpha}_a, \tilde{\alpha}_{a-1}, \ldots, \tilde{\alpha}_1$, and define $\tilde{\boldsymbol{\beta}}$ by $\tilde{\boldsymbol{\beta}}' = [0, \tilde{\alpha}_1, \tilde{\alpha}_2, \ldots, \tilde{\alpha}_a, \tilde{\tau}_1, \ldots, \tilde{\tau}_{t-1}, 0] = [\tilde{\mu}, \tilde{\boldsymbol{\alpha}}', \tilde{\boldsymbol{\tau}}']$. Thus $\tilde{\boldsymbol{\beta}}$ is a solution to the normal equations and, in fact, $\tilde{\boldsymbol{\beta}}$ is the solution to the normal equations with the nonestimable constraints $\hat{\mu} = \hat{\tau}_t = 0$.
   If $\sum_{j=1}^t d_j = 0$, then $\sum_{j=1}^t d_j\tilde{\tau}_j$ is the best unbiased estimator of $\sum_{j=1}^t d_j\tau_j$, where we define $\tilde{\tau}_t = 0$. If $\sum_{i=1}^a c_i = 0$, then $\sum_{i=1}^a c_i\tilde{\alpha}_i$ is the best unbiased estimator of $\sum_{i=1}^a c_i\alpha_i$.
4. For Case I of the model, $\tilde{\boldsymbol{\beta}}$ in part 3 is distributed $N(\tilde{\boldsymbol{\beta}} : \boldsymbol{\beta}_0, \mathbf{V}_0\sigma^2)$, where

   $$\boldsymbol{\beta}_0' = [0, \mu + \alpha_1 + \tau_t, \ldots, \mu + \alpha_a + \tau_t, \tau_1 - \tau_t, \ldots, \tau_{t-1} - \tau_t, 0]$$

   and $\mathbf{V}_0$ is given by

   $$\mathbf{V}_0 = \begin{bmatrix} 0 & \mathbf{0} & 0 \\ \mathbf{0} & \mathbf{V}^* & \mathbf{0} \\ 0 & \mathbf{0} & 0 \end{bmatrix}$$

   where

   $$\mathbf{V}^* = \begin{bmatrix} \mathbf{T}^{*\prime}_{11} & \mathbf{T}^{*\prime}_{21} \\ \mathbf{0} & \mathbf{T}^{*\prime}_{22} \end{bmatrix} \begin{bmatrix} \mathbf{T}^*_{11} & \mathbf{0} \\ \mathbf{T}^*_{21} & \mathbf{T}^*_{22} \end{bmatrix}$$
   $$= \begin{bmatrix} \mathbf{T}^{*\prime}_{11}\mathbf{T}^*_{11} + \mathbf{T}^{*\prime}_{21}\mathbf{T}^*_{21} & \mathbf{T}^{*\prime}_{21}\mathbf{T}^*_{22} \\ \mathbf{T}^{*\prime}_{22}\mathbf{T}^*_{21} & \mathbf{T}^{*\prime}_{22}\mathbf{T}^*_{22} \end{bmatrix} = \begin{bmatrix} \mathbf{V}^*_{11} & \mathbf{V}^*_{12} \\ \mathbf{V}^*_{21} & \mathbf{V}^*_{22} \end{bmatrix}$$

   say, and where $\mathbf{T}^*_{ij}$ is given in Equation (14.4.7).

5. Let $\mathbf{c} = [c_i]$ be any $a \times 1$ vector of constants such that $\mathbf{1}'\mathbf{c} = 0$; for Case I of the model, the estimator $\mathbf{c}'\tilde{\boldsymbol{\alpha}}$ is distributed $N(\mathbf{c}'\tilde{\boldsymbol{\alpha}} : \sum c_i\alpha_i, \mathbf{c}'\mathbf{V}_{11}^*\mathbf{c}\sigma^2)$, where $\tilde{\boldsymbol{\alpha}}$ is defined in part 3.

6. Let $\mathbf{d} = [d_j]$ be any $t \times 1$ vector of constants such that $\mathbf{1}'\mathbf{d} = 0$; for Case I of the model, the estimator $\mathbf{d}'\tilde{\boldsymbol{\tau}}$ is distributed $N(\mathbf{d}'\tilde{\boldsymbol{\tau}} : \sum d_j\tau_j, \mathbf{d}'\mathbf{V}_{22}\mathbf{d}\sigma^2)$, where $\tilde{\boldsymbol{\tau}}$ is defined in part 3 and

$$\mathbf{V}_{22} = \begin{bmatrix} \mathbf{V}_{22}^* & \mathbf{0} \\ \mathbf{0} & 0 \end{bmatrix}$$

7. For Case I of the model, the UMVU estimator of σ^2 is $\hat{\sigma}^2$, where

$$\hat{\sigma}^2 = (n_{..} - a - t + 1)^{-1}\left(\sum_{i=1}^{a} \sum_{j=1}^{t} \sum_{m=1}^{n_{ij}} Y_{ijm}^2 - \mathbf{t}_1'\mathbf{t}_1 - \mathbf{t}_2'\mathbf{t}_2 \right)$$

and $\hat{\sigma}^2$ is independent of the elements in $\tilde{\boldsymbol{\beta}}$.

8. One-at-a-time $1 - \alpha$ confidence intervals on contrasts $\sum c_i\alpha_i = \mathbf{c}'\boldsymbol{\alpha}$ and on contrasts $\sum d_j\tau_j = \mathbf{d}'\boldsymbol{\tau}$ are, respectively,

$$\sum c_i\tilde{\alpha}_i \mp t_{\alpha/2:n}\sqrt{\hat{\sigma}^2\mathbf{c}'\mathbf{V}_{11}^*\mathbf{c}}$$
$$\sum d_j\tilde{\tau}_j \mp t_{\alpha/2:n}\sqrt{\hat{\sigma}^2\mathbf{d}'\mathbf{V}_{22}\mathbf{d}}$$

where $n = n_{..} - a - t + 1$, and $\tilde{\boldsymbol{\alpha}}$ and $\tilde{\boldsymbol{\tau}}$ are defined in part 3.

9. Simultaneous confidence intervals on contrasts $\mathbf{c}_1'\boldsymbol{\alpha}, \mathbf{c}_2'\boldsymbol{\alpha}, \ldots, \mathbf{c}_m'\boldsymbol{\alpha}$, with confidence coefficient greater than or equal to $1 - \alpha$, are

$$\mathbf{c}_i'\tilde{\boldsymbol{\alpha}} \mp t_0\sqrt{\hat{\sigma}^2\mathbf{c}_i'\mathbf{V}_{11}^*\mathbf{c}_i} \qquad \text{for } i = 1, 2, \ldots, m$$

where (define n by $n = n_{..} - a - t + 1$)

(a) $t_0 = t_{\alpha/2:m,n}$ if $\mathbf{c}_1, \mathbf{c}_2, \ldots, \mathbf{c}_m$ are linearly independent,

(b) $t_0 = \min[t_{\alpha/2m:n}, \sqrt{qF_{\alpha:q,n}}]$ if $\mathbf{c}_1, \mathbf{c}_2, \ldots, \mathbf{c}_m$ are not linearly independent where q is the rank of $[\mathbf{c}_1, \mathbf{c}_2, \ldots, \mathbf{c}_m]$.

Simultaneous confidence intervals on $\mathbf{d}_1'\boldsymbol{\tau}, \mathbf{d}_2'\boldsymbol{\tau}, \ldots, \mathbf{d}_m'\boldsymbol{\tau}$, with confidence coefficient greater than or equal to $1 - \alpha$, are

$$\mathbf{d}_j'\tilde{\boldsymbol{\tau}} \mp t_0\sqrt{\hat{\sigma}^2\mathbf{d}_j'\mathbf{V}_{22}\mathbf{d}_j} \qquad \text{for } j = 1, 2, \ldots, m$$

where

(a) $t_0 = t_{\alpha/2:m,n}$ if $\mathbf{d}_1, \mathbf{d}_2, \ldots, \mathbf{d}_m$ are linearly independent,

(b) $t_0 = \min[t_{\alpha/2m:n}, \sqrt{qF_{\alpha:q,n}}]$ if $\mathbf{d}_1, \mathbf{d}_2, \ldots, \mathbf{d}_m$ are not linearly independent where q is the rank of $[\mathbf{d}_1, \mathbf{d}_2, \ldots, \mathbf{d}_m]$.

10. A size α test of $H_0 : \tau_1 = \tau_2 = \cdots = \tau_t$ *vs.* H_a : at least one equality is an inequality is this: Reject H_0 if and only if $w \geq F_{\alpha:t-1,n}$, where w is the computed value of W and $W = \mathbf{t}_2'\mathbf{t}_2/(t-1)\hat{\sigma}^2$, .

11. A size α test of $H_0 : \alpha_1 = \alpha_2 = \cdots = \alpha_a$ *vs.* H_a : at least one equality is an equality is this: Reject H_0 if and only if $w \geq F_{\alpha:a-1,n}$, where where w is the computed value of W and

$$W = \frac{\mathbf{t}_1'\mathbf{t}_1 + \mathbf{t}_2'\mathbf{t}_2 - \sum_{j=1}^{t} (Y_{.j.}^2/n_{.j})}{(a-1)\hat{\sigma}^2}$$

12. In the format in Equation (14.4.6), we assume $a \geq t$. The format should always be constructed so that the size of the diagonal matrix $\mathbf{D}_{i.}$ in the upper left-hand corner is larger than the size of the matrix $\mathbf{D}_{.j}$ in the lower right-hand corner.

13. The matrix equations represented by those in the format in Equation (14.4.6) with the identity matrix omitted are

$$\mathbf{D}_{i.}\tilde{\boldsymbol{\alpha}} + \mathbf{N}\tilde{\boldsymbol{\tau}}_t = \mathbf{y}_{i.}$$
$$\mathbf{N}'\tilde{\boldsymbol{\alpha}} + \mathbf{D}_{.j}\tilde{\boldsymbol{\tau}}_t = \mathbf{y}_{.j}$$

If we solve these for $\tilde{\boldsymbol{\tau}}_t$ we get $(\mathbf{D}_{.j} - \mathbf{N}'\mathbf{D}_{i.}^{-1}\mathbf{N})\tilde{\boldsymbol{\tau}}_t = \mathbf{y}_{.j} - \mathbf{N}'\mathbf{D}_{i.}^{-1}\mathbf{y}_{i.}$, or $\mathbf{A}\tilde{\boldsymbol{\tau}}_t = \mathbf{q}$, say.

If a is much larger than t, and if the computer being used does not have sufficient storage to handle the entire format in Equation (14.4.6), then an alternative is to compile $\mathbf{A}$ and $\mathbf{q}$ directly from Table 14.4.1 and obtain $\mathbf{A}\tilde{\boldsymbol{\tau}}_t = \mathbf{q}$; then solve this set of $(t-1) \times (t-1)$ equations for $\tilde{\boldsymbol{\tau}}_t$, and use $\tilde{\boldsymbol{\alpha}} = \mathbf{D}_{i.}^{-1}\mathbf{y}_{i.} - \mathbf{D}_{i.}^{-1}\mathbf{N}\tilde{\boldsymbol{\tau}}_t$ to solve for $\tilde{\boldsymbol{\alpha}}$.

Some of the previous theory will be illustrated with a simple artificial example.

Example 14.4.1

Consider the data in Table 14.4.2 where (a) is the table of observations y_{ijm} and (b) is the table of n_{ij}. It is assumed that the model from which the data were selected is given in Equation (14.4.1). Compute the following: the best unbiased estimates of $\alpha_i - \bar{\alpha}_.$ for $i = 1, 2, 3$; the best unbiased estimates of $\tau_j - \bar{\tau}_.$ for $j = 1, 2, 3$; the UMVU estimate of σ^2; one-at-a-time 95 percent confidence intervals for $\alpha_i - \bar{\alpha}_.$, $i = 1, 2, 3$, and $\tau_j - \bar{\tau}_.$, $j = 1, 2, 3$; an ANOVA table for testing $H_0 : \alpha_1 = \alpha_2 = \alpha_3$ and $H_0 : \tau_1 = \tau_2 = \tau_3$.

Table 14.4.2

Table (*a*) of Observations y_{ijm} and Table (*b*) of Number n_{ij} of Observations in the Cells

(*a*)					(*b*)				
Levels of Factor A	*Levels of Factor T* 1	2	3	*Total*	*Levels of Factor A*	*Levels of Factor T* 1	2	3	*Total*
1	2, 6		3, 1	12	1	2	0	2	4
2	3	4	2, 5	14	2	1	1	2	4
3	1	3		4	3	1	1	0	2
Total	12	7	11	30	Total	4	2	4	10

By using Equation (14.4.2) we obtain the following normal equations:

$$\begin{aligned}
10\hat{\mu} + 4\hat{\alpha}_1 + 4\hat{\alpha}_2 + 2\hat{\alpha}_3 + 4\hat{\tau}_1 + 2\hat{\tau}_2 + 4\hat{\tau}_3 &= 30 \\
4\hat{\mu} + 4\hat{\alpha}_1 + 2\hat{\tau}_1 + 2\hat{\tau}_3 &= 12 \\
4\hat{\mu} + 4\hat{\alpha}_2 + \hat{\tau}_1 + \hat{\tau}_2 + 2\hat{\tau}_3 &= 14 \\
2\hat{\mu} + 2\hat{\alpha}_3 + \hat{\tau}_1 + \hat{\tau}_2 &= 4 \\
4\hat{\mu} + 2\hat{\alpha}_1 + \hat{\alpha}_2 + \hat{\alpha}_3 + 4\hat{\tau}_1 &= 12 \\
2\hat{\mu} + \hat{\alpha}_2 + \hat{\alpha}_3 + 2\hat{\tau}_2 &= 7 \\
4\hat{\mu} + 2\hat{\alpha}_1 + 2\hat{\alpha}_2 + 4\hat{\tau}_3 &= 11
\end{aligned}$$

Actually there is no need to compute the normal equations, but we do so for illustrative purposes. By examining Table 14.4.2(a), it is easily determined that the design is connected. For if we examine column one of Table 14.4.2(a), we note that $y_{111} - y_{211}$, $y_{111} - y_{311}$, and $y_{211} - y_{311}$ are, respectively, unbiased estimates of $\alpha_1 - \alpha_2$, $\alpha_1 - \alpha_3$, and $\alpha_2 - \alpha_3$. Also, by examining the second row of the table, we note that $y_{211} - y_{221}$, $y_{211} - y_{231}$, and $y_{221} - y_{231}$ are, respectively, unbiased estimates of $\tau_1 - \tau_2$, $\tau_1 - \tau_3$, and $\tau_2 - \tau_3$. These unbiased estimates may not, however, be "best" unbiased estimates. Also $p = 7$ and by Theorem 14.4.2, $K = a + t - 1 = 3 + 3 - 1 = 5$.

We can use Method 2 in Section 13.5 with the $p - K = 2$ nonestimable conditions $\hat{\mu} = \hat{\tau}_3 = 0$ to compute the desired quantities. From Table 14.4.2 we obtain the quantities $\mathbf{S}_0$ and $\mathbf{s}_0$, and we use the square root method. These results follow.

$$
\left[\begin{array}{c|c|c} \mathbf{S}_0 & \mathbf{s}_0 & \mathbf{I} \\ \hline \mathbf{T}_0 & \mathbf{t}_0 & \mathbf{T}_0^{\prime -1} \end{array}\right] = \left[\begin{array}{cc|c|cc} \mathbf{D}_{i.} & \mathbf{N} & \mathbf{y}_{i.} & \mathbf{I} & \mathbf{0} \\ \mathbf{N}' & \mathbf{D}_{.j} & \mathbf{y}_{.j} & \mathbf{0} & \mathbf{I} \\ \hline \mathbf{T}_{11} & \mathbf{T}_{12} & \mathbf{t}_1 & \mathbf{T}_{11}^* & \mathbf{0} \\ \mathbf{0} & \mathbf{T}_{22} & \mathbf{t}_2 & \mathbf{T}_{21}^* & \mathbf{T}_{22}^* \end{array}\right]
$$

$$
= \left[\begin{array}{ccccc|c|ccccc}
4 & 0 & 0 & 2 & 0 & 12 & 1 & 0 & 0 & 0 & 0 \\
0 & 4 & 0 & 1 & 1 & 14 & 0 & 1 & 0 & 0 & 0 \\
0 & 0 & 2 & 1 & 1 & 4 & 0 & 0 & 1 & 0 & 0 \\
2 & 1 & 1 & 4 & 0 & 12 & 0 & 0 & 0 & 1 & 0 \\
0 & 1 & 1 & 0 & 2 & 7 & 0 & 0 & 0 & 0 & 1 \\
\hline
2 & 0 & 0 & 1 & 0 & 6 & \frac{1}{2} & 0 & 0 & 0 & 0 \\
 & 2 & 0 & \frac{1}{2} & \frac{1}{2} & 7 & 0 & \frac{1}{2} & 0 & 0 & 0 \\
 & & \sqrt{2} & \frac{1}{\sqrt{2}} & \frac{1}{\sqrt{2}} & \frac{4}{\sqrt{2}} & 0 & 0 & \frac{1}{\sqrt{2}} & 0 & 0 \\
 & & & \frac{3}{2} & -\frac{1}{2} & \frac{1}{3} & -\frac{1}{3} & -\frac{1}{6} & -\frac{1}{3} & \frac{2}{3} & 0 \\
 & & & & 1 & \frac{5}{3} & -\frac{1}{6} & -\frac{1}{3} & -\frac{2}{3} & \frac{1}{3} & 1
\end{array}\right]
\tag{14.4.8}
$$

We use $[\mathbf{T}_0 \mid \mathbf{t}_0]$ and perform the backward solution to obtain a solution to the normal equations. We get (after inserting $\tilde{\mu} = 0$ and $\tilde{\tau}_3 = 0$)

$$
\tilde{\boldsymbol{\beta}}' = \left[0, \frac{47}{18}, \frac{52}{18}, \frac{14}{18}, \frac{14}{18}, \frac{30}{18}, 0\right]
$$

and the best unbiased estimate of any estimable function $\ell'\boldsymbol{\beta}$ is $\ell'\tilde{\boldsymbol{\beta}}$.

For confidence intervals on $\ell'\boldsymbol{\beta}$, we need $\widehat{\text{var}}[\ell'\tilde{\boldsymbol{\beta}}]$, which is $\hat{\sigma}^2\ell'(\mathbf{X}'\mathbf{X})^c\ell$, but in applications the interest is almost always in obtaining confidence intervals on $\mathbf{c}'\boldsymbol{\alpha}$ and $\mathbf{d}'\boldsymbol{\tau}$, contrasts of $\boldsymbol{\alpha}$ and $\boldsymbol{\tau}$. To obtain these we need $\widehat{\text{var}}[\mathbf{c}'\tilde{\boldsymbol{\alpha}}]$, which is $\hat{\sigma}^2\mathbf{c}'(\mathbf{T}_{11}^{*\prime}\mathbf{T}_{11}^* + \mathbf{T}_{21}^{*\prime}\mathbf{T}_{21}^*)\mathbf{c}$, and $\widehat{\text{var}}[\mathbf{d}'\tilde{\boldsymbol{\tau}}]$, which is

$$
\hat{\sigma}^2\mathbf{d}'\begin{bmatrix} \mathbf{T}_{22}^{*\prime}\mathbf{T}_{22}^* & \mathbf{0} \\ \mathbf{0}' & 0 \end{bmatrix}\mathbf{d}
$$

We can compute the required matrices from the matrix in the lower right-hand part of the format in Equation (14.4.8). We get

$$\mathbf{T}_{11}^{*\prime}\mathbf{T}_{11}^{*} + \mathbf{T}_{21}^{*\prime}\mathbf{T}_{21}^{*} = \frac{1}{36}\begin{bmatrix} 14 & 4 & 8 \\ 4 & 14 & 10 \\ 8 & 10 & 38 \end{bmatrix} \qquad \begin{bmatrix} \mathbf{T}_{22}^{*\prime}\mathbf{T}_{22}^{*} & \mathbf{0} \\ \mathbf{0}' & 0 \end{bmatrix} = \frac{1}{9}\begin{bmatrix} 5 & 3 & 0 \\ 3 & 9 & 0 \\ 0 & 0 & 0 \end{bmatrix}$$

Also, $\sum_{i=1}^{a}\sum_{j=1}^{t}\sum_{m=1}^{n_{ij}} y_{ijm}^2 = 144$ and $\mathbf{t}_1'\mathbf{t}_1 + \mathbf{t}_2'\mathbf{t}_2 = 863/9$.

To obtain the best unbiased estimates of $\alpha_i - \bar{\alpha}_.$, we use $\mathbf{c}_1' = [2/3, -1/3, -1/3]$, so $\mathbf{c}_1'\tilde{\boldsymbol{\alpha}} = \widehat{\alpha_1 - \bar{\alpha}_.} = 28/54$; $\mathbf{c}_2' = [-1/3, 2/3, -1/3]$, so $\mathbf{c}_2'\tilde{\boldsymbol{\alpha}} = \widehat{\alpha_2 - \bar{\alpha}_.} = 43/54$; and $\mathbf{c}_3' = [-1/3, -1/3, 2/3]$, so $\mathbf{c}_3'\tilde{\boldsymbol{\alpha}} = \widehat{\alpha_3 - \bar{\alpha}_.} = -71/54$. Also, $\widehat{\text{var}}[\widehat{\alpha_1 - \bar{\alpha}_.}] = (80/324)\hat{\sigma}^2$; $\widehat{\text{var}}[\widehat{\alpha_2 - \bar{\alpha}_.}] = (68/324)\hat{\sigma}^2$; and $\widehat{\text{var}}[\widehat{\alpha_3 - \bar{\alpha}_.}] = (116/324)\hat{\sigma}^2$.

To obtain the best unbiased estimates of $\tau_j - \bar{\tau}_.$, we use $\mathbf{d}_1' = [2/3, -1/3, -1/3]$, so $\mathbf{d}_1'\tilde{\boldsymbol{\tau}} = \widehat{\tau_1 - \bar{\tau}_.} = -2/54$; $\mathbf{d}_2' = [-1/3, 2/3, -1/3]$, so $\mathbf{d}_2'\tilde{\boldsymbol{\tau}} = \widehat{\tau_2 - \bar{\tau}_.} = 46/54$; and $\mathbf{d}_3' = [-1/3, -1/3, 2/3]$, so $\mathbf{d}_3'\tilde{\boldsymbol{\tau}} = \widehat{\tau_3 - \bar{\tau}_.} = -44/54$. Also, $\widehat{\text{var}}[\widehat{\tau_1 - \bar{\tau}_.}] = (17/81)\hat{\sigma}^2$; $\widehat{\text{var}}[\widehat{\tau_2 - \bar{\tau}_.}] = (29/81)\hat{\sigma}^2$; and $\widehat{\text{var}}[\widehat{\tau_3 - \bar{\tau}_.}] = (20/81)\hat{\sigma}^2$.

The point estimate of σ^2 is $\hat{\sigma}^2 = (1/5)[114 - (863/9)] = 163/45 = 3.622$.

The 95 percent one-at-a-time confidence intervals are obtained by using the formulas

$$\alpha_i - \bar{\alpha}_. : \widehat{\alpha_i - \bar{\alpha}_.} \mp t_{0.025:5}\sqrt{\widehat{\text{var}}[\widehat{\alpha_i - \bar{\alpha}_.}]} \qquad \text{for } i = 1, 2, 3$$

$$\tau_j - \bar{\tau}_. : \widehat{\tau_j - \bar{\tau}_.} \mp t_{0.025:5}\sqrt{\widehat{\text{var}}[\widehat{\tau_j - \bar{\tau}_.}]} \qquad \text{for } j = 1, 2, 3$$

We illustrate for $\alpha_1 - \bar{\alpha}_.$, which is $28/54 \mp 2.571\sqrt{(3.622)(80/324)}$, or $-1.913 \leq \alpha_1 - \bar{\alpha}_. \leq 2.950$.

The ANOVA table is shown in Table 14.4.3.

Table 14.4.3

ANOVA for Testing $H_0: \alpha_1 = \alpha_2 = \cdots = \alpha_a$ and $H_0: \tau_1 = \tau_2 = \cdots = \tau_t$

Source	*d.f.*	*S.S.*	*M.S.*	*F*
Total	10	$\sum\sum\sum y_{ijm}^2 = 114$		
$R(\mu, \boldsymbol{\alpha}, \boldsymbol{\tau})$	5	$\mathbf{t}_1'\mathbf{t}_1 + \mathbf{t}_2'\mathbf{t}_2 = \frac{863}{9}$		
$R(H_0)$ for τ	2	$\mathbf{t}_2'\mathbf{t}_2 = 2.889 = T_{ss}$	1.445	0.399
$R(H_0)$ for α	2	$\mathbf{t}_1'\mathbf{t}_1 + \mathbf{t}_2'\mathbf{t}_2 - \sum\left(\frac{y_{.j.}^2}{n_{.j}}\right) = \frac{863}{9} - \frac{363}{4} = 5.139 = A_{ss}$	2.569	0.709
Error	5	$\frac{163}{9} = 18.111 = E_{ss}$	3.622	

To illustrate Method 3 of Section 13.5, we reduce the entire normal equations by the square root method. We get

$$
\left[\begin{array}{c|c|c} \mathbf{X}'\mathbf{X} & \mathbf{X}'\mathbf{y} & \mathbf{I} \\ \hline \mathbf{T} & \mathbf{t} & \mathbf{K} \end{array}\right] =
\left[\begin{array}{ccccccc|c|ccccccc}
10 & 4 & 4 & 2 & 4 & 2 & 4 & 30 & 1 & 0 & 0 & 0 & 0 & 0 & 0 \\
4 & 4 & 0 & 0 & 2 & 0 & 2 & 12 & 0 & 1 & 0 & 0 & 0 & 0 & 0 \\
4 & 0 & 4 & 0 & 1 & 1 & 2 & 14 & 0 & 0 & 1 & 0 & 0 & 0 & 0 \\
2 & 0 & 0 & 2 & 1 & 1 & 0 & 4 & 0 & 0 & 0 & 1 & 0 & 0 & 0 \\
4 & 2 & 1 & 1 & 4 & 0 & 0 & 12 & 0 & 0 & 0 & 0 & 1 & 0 & 0 \\
2 & 0 & 1 & 1 & 0 & 2 & 0 & 7 & 0 & 0 & 0 & 0 & 0 & 1 & 0 \\
4 & 2 & 2 & 0 & 0 & 0 & 4 & 11 & 0 & 0 & 0 & 0 & 0 & 0 & 1 \\
\hline
\sqrt{10} & \frac{4}{\sqrt{10}} & \frac{4}{\sqrt{10}} & \frac{2}{\sqrt{10}} & \frac{4}{\sqrt{10}} & \frac{2}{\sqrt{10}} & \frac{4}{\sqrt{10}} & \frac{30}{\sqrt{10}} & \frac{1}{\sqrt{10}} & 0 & 0 & 0 & 0 & 0 & 0 \\
 & \frac{12}{\sqrt{60}} & -\frac{8}{\sqrt{60}} & -\frac{4}{\sqrt{60}} & \frac{2}{\sqrt{60}} & -\frac{4}{\sqrt{60}} & \frac{2}{\sqrt{60}} & 0 & -\frac{2}{\sqrt{60}} & \frac{5}{\sqrt{60}} & 0 & 0 & 0 & 0 & 0 \\
 & & \frac{2}{\sqrt{3}} & -\frac{2}{\sqrt{3}} & -\frac{1}{2\sqrt{3}} & -\frac{1}{2\sqrt{3}} & \frac{1}{\sqrt{3}} & \sqrt{3} & -\frac{1}{\sqrt{3}} & \frac{1}{\sqrt{3}} & \frac{3}{2\sqrt{3}} & 0 & 0 & 0 & 0 \\
 & & & 0 & 0 & 0 & 0 & 0 & 0 & 0 & 0 & 0 & 0 & 0 & 0 \\
 & & & & \frac{3}{2} & -\frac{1}{2} & -1 & \frac{1}{3} & -\frac{1}{3} & 0 & \frac{1}{6} & 0 & \frac{2}{3} & 0 & 0 \\
 & & & & & 1 & -1 & \frac{5}{3} & -\frac{2}{3} & \frac{1}{2} & \frac{1}{3} & 0 & \frac{1}{3} & 1 & 0 \\
 & & & & & & 0 & 0 & 0 & 0 & 0 & 0 & 0 & 0 & 0
\end{array}\right]
$$

The backward solution yields a solution $\hat{\boldsymbol{\beta}}$ to the normal equations $\hat{\boldsymbol{\beta}}' = [14/18, 33/18, 38/18, 0, 14/18, 30/18, 0]$. Also, we compute

$$
(\mathbf{X}'\mathbf{X})^c = \mathbf{K}'\mathbf{K} = \frac{1}{180}
\begin{bmatrix}
190 & -150 & -140 & 0 & -80 & -120 & 0 \\
-150 & 180 & 120 & 0 & 30 & 90 & 0 \\
-140 & 120 & 160 & 0 & 40 & 60 & 0 \\
0 & 0 & 0 & 0 & 0 & 0 & 0 \\
-80 & 30 & 40 & 0 & 100 & 60 & 0 \\
-120 & 90 & 60 & 0 & 60 & 180 & 0 \\
0 & 0 & 0 & 0 & 0 & 0 & 0
\end{bmatrix}
$$

In the problems at the end of the chapter, we will ask for the solutions to the problems posed in this example by using Method 3 of Section 13.5.

14.5 Interaction in the Two-Factor Design Model

The concept of interaction in the two-factor design model will be defined and discussed in this section. In Sections 14.6, 14.7, and 14.8, the models with interaction defined in Equations (14.1.8), (14.1.9), and (14.1.10) will be discussed in detail. To help explain the concept of interaction, our discussion in this section will be about population means μ_{ij}; in the sections referred to above, inference procedures will be discussed.

Consider Example 14.1.1. One of the questions of interest is, "What is the difference between diets 1 and 5?" The answer is $\tau_1 - \tau_5$ pounds if the model for μ_{ij} is the one defined in Equation (14.1.3). However, for that model we note that $\mu_{11} - \mu_{15} = \tau_1 - \tau_5$ and $\mu_{21} - \mu_{25} = \tau_1 - \tau_5$, which means that for breed 1 the difference between diets 1 and 5 is the same as for breed 2.

A similar situation obtains for the difference between *any* two diets j and j' if $j \neq j'$, that is, the difference between diets j and j' is $\tau_j - \tau_{j'}$, and it is the same for breed 1 as it is for breed 2 for the model in Equation (14.1.3). This says that $\mu_{1j} - \mu_{1j'} = \mu_{2j} - \mu_{2j'} = \tau_j - \tau_{j'}$ for all $j \neq j'$. In fact, if c_j, for $j = 1, 2, \ldots, 5$, is any set of constants such that $\sum c_j = 0$, then $\sum c_j\tau_j$, any contrast among the diets, is the same for breed 1 and breed 2 since $\sum c_j\mu_{1j} = \sum c_j\mu_{2j} = \sum c_j\tau_j$. But it may be more realistic to assume that a contrast among the diets for breed 1 is possibly not the same for breed 2, which means that $\sum c_j\mu_{1j} \neq \sum c_j\mu_{2j}$ for some sets of constants $\{c_j\}$ such that $\sum c_j = 0$. For the case of diets 1 and 5 discussed above, if, in fact, $\mu_{11} - \mu_{15} = \mu_{21} - \mu_{25}$, then we say "breeds 1 and 2 do *not* interact with diets 1 and 5"; if $\mu_{11} - \mu_{15} \neq \mu_{21} - \mu_{25}$, we say "breeds 1 and 2 *do* interact with diets 1 and 5." More generally, if $\mu_{1j} - \mu_{2j} = \mu_{1j'} - \mu_{2j'}$, for $j = 1, 2, \ldots, 5$ and $j' = 1, 2, \ldots, 5$, then we say "breeds 1 and 2 do not interact with any two diets."

One of the important consequences of a model when there is no interaction is that the question, "What is the difference between diet 1 and diet 2?" can be answered as "$\tau_1 - \tau_2$ pounds." However, if there *is* interaction, the answer must be, "It depends on the breed, and the difference of the two diets may not be the same for breed 1 and breed 2." In the two-way model *without* interaction discussed in previous sections of this chapter, the "main effect" of, say, the jth diet was defined as $\tau_j - \bar{\tau}_.$, and for the model in Equation (14.1.3) and Example 14.1.1, $\tau_j - \bar{\tau}_. = \bar{\mu}_{.j} - \bar{\mu}_{..}$. This says that since the difference between diets j and j' is the same for each breed, the "main effect" of the jth diet is the excess of the jth average effect over the average of the effects of *all* diets.

Now let us consider the case when both factors have more than two levels. Let μ_{ij} denote the mean of the population that is the combination of the ith level of factor A with the jth level of factor T. The quantity $\mu_{ij} - \mu_{ij'}$ is the difference of the j and j' levels of factor T at the ith level of factor A, and $\mu_{i'j} - \mu_{i'j'}$ is the difference of the j and j' levels of factor T at the i'th level of factor A. If these two quantities are equal, that is, if $\mu_{ij} - \mu_{ij'} = \mu_{i'j} - \mu_{i'j'}$, then we say "the i and i' levels of factor A do *not* interact with the j and j' levels of factor T." If they are *not* equal, we say "the i and i' levels of factor A *do* interact with the j and j' levels of factor T."

We write

$$\gamma(i, j; i', j') = (\mu_{ij} - \mu_{ij'}) - (\mu_{i'j} - \mu_{i'j'}) \tag{14.5.1}$$

and state that levels i and i' of factor A do not interact or do interact with the j

and j' levels of factor T if and only if $\gamma(i,j;i',j')$ is or is not zero. If $\gamma(i,j;i',j') = 0$ for all $i = 1, 2, \ldots, a$, $i' = 1, 2, \ldots, a$, $j = 1, 2, \ldots, t$, and $j' = 1, 2, \ldots, t$, then we say "factors A and T do not interact." If $\gamma(i, i'; j, j') \neq 0$ for at least one set of values i, i', j, j', we say "factors A and T interact," or "there is interaction between factors A and T," or we sometimes express this with the statement "factors A and T are not additive." We now formalize these ideas.

DEFINITION 14.5.1

Interaction in a Two-Factor Design Model. *Let a design model be defined by Equation* (14.1.1), *and define* $\gamma(i,j;i',j') = \mu_{ij} - \mu_{ij'} - \mu_{i'j} + \mu_{i'j'}$ *for all allowable values of* i, i', j, *and* j'. *Then* $\gamma(i,j;i',j')$ *is defined to be the value of the interaction of the* i *and* i' *levels of factor* A *with the* j *and* j' *levels of factor* T. *Factors* A *and* T *are defined to not interact if and only if the interaction is zero between all pairs of the levels of factor* A *and all pairs of the levels of factor* T, *that is, if and only if* $\gamma(i,j;i',j') = 0$ *for "all" allowable values of* i, i', j, *and* j'.

Note 1. When considering interaction of two factors, there is a symmetry present since $(\mu_{ij} - \mu_{ij'}) - (\mu_{i'j} - \mu_{i'j'}) = (\mu_{ij} - \mu_{i'j}) - (\mu_{ij'} - \mu_{i'j'})$. The quantity on the left side of the equality is the difference of the j and j' levels of factor T at the ith level of factor A minus the difference of the j and j' levels of factor T at the i' level of factor A. The quantity on the right side of the equality is the difference of the i and i' levels of factor A at the jth level of factor T minus the difference of the i and i' levels of factor A at the j' level of factor T.

The next theorem contains some consequences of the above discussion.

THEOREM 14.5.1

Consider the interaction $\gamma(i,j;i',j')$ *given in Definition* 14.5.1. *Factors* A *and* T *do not interact if and only if any of the following obtain*:

(1) $\gamma^*_{ij} = 0$ *for all allowable values of* i *and* j, *where*

$$\gamma^*_{ij} = \mu_{ij} - \bar{\mu}_{i.} - \bar{\mu}_{.j} + \bar{\mu}_{..} \tag{14.5.2}$$

and where

$$\bar{\mu}_{i.} = \left(\frac{1}{t}\right) \sum_{j=1}^{t} \mu_{ij} \qquad \bar{\mu}_{.j} = \left(\frac{1}{a}\right) \sum_{i=1}^{a} \mu_{ij} \qquad \bar{\mu}_{..} = \left(\frac{1}{at}\right) \sum_{i=1}^{a} \sum_{j=1}^{t} \mu_{ij}$$

(2) $\sum_{j=1}^{t} d_j \mu_{ij} = \sum_{j=1}^{t} d_j \mu_{i'j}$ *for all sets of the* t *constants* $\{d_j\}$, *where* $\sum_{j=1}^{t} d_j = 0$ *and all allowable values of* i *and* i';

(3) $\sum_{i=1}^{a} c_i \mu_{ij} = \sum_{i=1}^{a} c_i \mu_{ij'}$ *for all sets of* a *constants* $\{c_i\}$, *where* $\sum_{i=1}^{a} c_i = 0$, *and all allowable values of* j *and* j';

(4) $\sum_{i=1}^{a} \sum_{j=1}^{t} \gamma_{ij}^{*2} = 0$, *where* γ_{ij}^* *is defined in Equation* (14.5.2).

Proof

The proof is a direct consequence of Definition 14.5.1, and the details will be left for the reader.

We can write the following identity in μ_{ij}:

$$\mu_{ij} = \bar{\mu}_{..} + (\bar{\mu}_{i.} - \bar{\mu}_{..}) + (\bar{\mu}_{.j} - \bar{\mu}_{..}) + (\mu_{ij} - \bar{\mu}_{i.} - \bar{\mu}_{.j} + \bar{\mu}_{..})$$

or in the alternative notation

$$\mu_{ij} = \mu^* + \alpha_i^* + \tau_j^* + \gamma_{ij}^* \tag{14.5.3}$$

where $\mu^* = \bar{\mu}_{..}$, $\alpha_i^* = \bar{\mu}_{i.} - \bar{\mu}_{..}$, $\tau_j^* = \bar{\mu}_{.j} - \bar{\mu}_{..}$, and $\gamma_{ij}^* = \mu_{ij} - \bar{\mu}_{i.} - \bar{\mu}_{.j} + \bar{\mu}_{..}$.
Clearly

$$\begin{aligned} \sum_{i=1}^{a} \alpha_i^* &= \sum_{j=1}^{t} \tau_j^* = 0 \\ \sum_{i=1}^{a} \gamma_{ij}^* &= 0 \qquad \text{for each } j = 1, 2, \ldots, t \\ \sum_{j=1}^{t} \gamma_{ij}^* &= 0 \qquad \text{for each } i = 1, 2, \ldots, a \end{aligned} \tag{14.5.4}$$

We can write a two-factor design model $Y_{ijm} = \mu_{ij} + \varepsilon_{ijm}$ with interaction in two ways:

$$Y_{ijm} = \mu + \alpha_i + \tau_j + \gamma_{ij} + \varepsilon_{ijm} \quad \text{where} \quad \mu_{ij} = \mu + \alpha_i + \tau_j + \gamma_{ij} \tag{14.5.5}$$

and there are no constraints on α_i, τ_j, and γ_{ij}; or as

$$Y_{ijm} = \mu^* + \alpha_i^* + \tau_j^* + \gamma_{ij}^* + \varepsilon_{ijm} \tag{14.5.6}$$

where μ^*, α_i^*, τ_j^*, and γ_{ij}^* are defined in Equation (14.5.3) and the constraints in Equation (14.5.4) apply. Of course, each model can be obtained from the other and from the μ_{ij}. We will use the model in Equation (14.5.5) for the theoretical development, but the model in Equation (14.5.6) is generally more useful in practical applications.

If the interaction is zero, then $\gamma_{ij}^* = 0$ for all allowable values of i and j, and this implies $\mu_{ij} - \bar{\mu}_{i.} - \bar{\mu}_{.j} + \bar{\mu}_{..} = 0$ and hence $\mu_{ij} = \bar{\mu}_{i.} + \bar{\mu}_{.j} - \bar{\mu}_{..}$. Thus we can write the model with no interaction as $Y_{ijm} = \mu_{ij} + \varepsilon_{ijm} = \bar{\mu}_{i.} + \bar{\mu}_{.j} - \bar{\mu}_{..} + \varepsilon_{ijm}$, or in the notation of Equation (14.5.5), as $Y_{ijm} = \mu + \alpha_i + \tau_j + \varepsilon_{ijm}$. So we obtain $\mu + \alpha_i + \tau_j = \bar{\mu}_{i.} + \bar{\mu}_{.j} - \bar{\mu}_{..}$. If we sum both sides of this equation over i and divide by a, we get $\bar{\mu}_{.j} = \mu + \bar{\alpha}_{.} + \tau_j$. If we sum both sides of the equation over j and divide by t, we get $\bar{\mu}_{i.} = \mu + \alpha_i + \bar{\tau}_{.}$. If we sum both sides of the equation over i and j and divide by ta, we get $\bar{\mu}_{..} = \mu + \bar{\alpha}_{.} + \bar{\tau}_{.}$. We have proved the following theorem.

THEOREM 14.5.2

If the two-factor design model has no interaction and is defined by $Y_{ijm} = \mu_{ij} + \varepsilon_{ijm}$, then μ_{ij} can be written as

$$\mu + \alpha_i + \tau_j = (\mu + \bar{\alpha}_{.} + \bar{\tau}_{.}) + (\alpha_i - \bar{\alpha}_{.}) + (\tau_j - \bar{\tau}_{.})$$

or as

$$\mu^* + \alpha_i^* + \tau_j^* = \bar{\mu}_{..} + (\bar{\mu}_{i.} - \bar{\mu}_{..}) + (\bar{\mu}_{.j} - \bar{\mu}_{..}) = \bar{\mu}_{i.} + \bar{\mu}_{.j} - \bar{\mu}_{..}$$

The following relationships obtain among μ_{ij} and μ, α_i, and τ_j:

(1) $\bar{\mu}_{i.} = \mu + \alpha_i + \bar{\tau}_{.}$;

(2) $\bar{\mu}_{.j} = \mu + \bar{\alpha}_{.} + \tau_j$;

(3) $\bar{\mu}_{..} = \mu + \bar{\alpha}_{.} + \bar{\tau}_{.}$;

(4) $\mu + \alpha_i + \tau_j = \bar{\mu}_{i.} + \bar{\mu}_{.j} - \bar{\mu}_{..}$.

Note 2. The parameters μ, α_i, and τ_j cannot be written individually as linear functions of the μ_{ij} and this is the reason that they are not estimable. If they could be written as linear functions of the μ_{ij}, they would be estimable since μ_{ij} is estimable, that is, $\mathscr{E}[Y_{ijm}] = \mu_{ij}$ if $n_{ij} > 0$ for all i and j.

In the two-factor design model with no interaction, the *main* effect of the ith level of factor A at the jth level of factor T is defined as $\mu_{ij} - \bar{\mu}_{.j}$, which is $\alpha_i - \bar{\alpha}_{.}$ in terms of the model $\mu_{ij} = \mu + \alpha_i + \tau_j$. This, of course, means that the main effect of the ith level of factor A is the same for each level of factor T, but, as stated above, that is not the case for the interaction model. This leads us to the following definition.

DEFINITION 14.5.2

Main Effects for the Two-Factor Model with Interaction. *Let the model be given by Equation* (14.1.1), *where $\mu_{ij} = \mu + \alpha_i + \tau_j + \gamma_{ij}$.*

(1) *The main effect of the ith level of factor A at the jth level of factor T is defined as $\mu_{ij} - \bar{\mu}_{.j}$.*

(2) *The average main effect of the ith level of factor A (averaged over the t levels of factor T) is defined as* $\bar{\mu}_{i.} - \bar{\mu}_{..} = \alpha_i^* = \alpha_i - \bar{\alpha}_. + \bar{\gamma}_{i.} - \bar{\gamma}_{..}$.

(3) *The main effect of the jth level of factor T at the ith level of factor A is defined as* $\mu_{ij} - \bar{\mu}_{i.}$.

(4) *The average main effect of the jth level of factor T (averaged over the a levels of factor A) is defined as* $\bar{\mu}_{.j} - \bar{\mu}_{..} = \tau_j^* = \tau_j - \bar{\tau}_. + \bar{\gamma}_{.j} - \bar{\gamma}_{..}$.

Note 3. The averages referred to in Definition 14.5.2 are "unweighted" averages. In some applications it may be desirable to use "weighted" averages. See [S-4]. For a further discussion of the definition of interaction and main effects, see [E-2], [E-3], and [S-4].

Consider the table in Equation (14.1.2) but with the Y_{ijm} replaced by their expected values μ_{ij}. Then the interaction of the i and i' levels of factor A with the j and j' levels of factor T, defined in Equation (14.5.1), can be evaluated by considering the 2×2 table shown here and $\gamma(i, j; i', j') = (\mu_{ij} + \mu_{i'j'}) - (\mu_{i'j} + \mu_{ij'})$.

Levels of Factor T

		j	j'
Levels of Factor A	i	μ_{ij}	$\mu_{ij'}$
	i'	$\mu_{i'j}$	$\mu_{i'j'}$

(14.5.7)

Thus by Definition 14.5.1, factors A and T do not interact if and only if the interaction is zero for *all* 2×2 tables of the i and i' levels of factor A with the j and j' levels of factor T. For example, consider the table of μ_{ij} shown here.

Levels of Factor T

		1	2	3
Levels of Factor A	1	4	7	15
	2	1	4	12
	3	−4	−1	7

From this table, thirty-six 2×2 tables can be constructed; nine such tables are exhibited below, and three tables can be obtained from each of these by interchanging rows and columns to get the thirty-six tables.

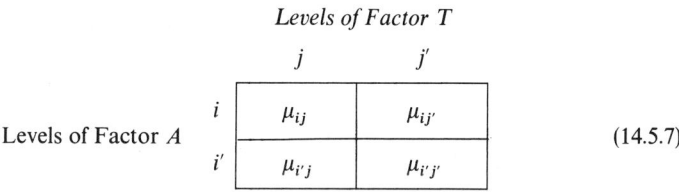

4	7
1	4

4	7
−4	−1

1	4
−4	−1

4	15
1	12

4	15
−4	7

1	12
−4	7

7	15
4	12

7	15
−1	7

4	12
−1	7

Clearly the interaction of each 2×2 table is zero, so factors A and T do not interact. These ideas are formalized in the following definition.

DEFINITION 14.5.3

2×2 ***Tables of Cell Means.*** *Consider a two-factor design model with μ_{ij} as the mean of the combination of the ith level of factor A with the jth level of factor T. The table in Equation* (14.5.7) *is defined as the 2×2 table of cell means of the i and i′ levels of factor A with the j and j′ levels of factor T.*

DEFINITION 14.5.4

2×2 ***Contrasts.*** *Consider the two-factor design model with M observations in each cell, and let $\bar{Y}_{ij.}$ be the mean of the M observations in cell ij. The 2×2 contrast of the i and i′ levels of factor A with the j and j′ levels of factor T is defined to be* $\bar{Y}_{ij.} - \bar{Y}_{ij'.} - \bar{Y}_{i'j.} + \bar{Y}_{i'j'.}$.

14.6 Two-Factor Design Model with Interaction and $M > 1$ Observations Per Cell

The model to be discussed in this section is defined in Equation (14.1.8), but we repeat it below.

$$Y_{ijm} = \mu + \alpha_i + \tau_j + \gamma_{ij} + \varepsilon_{ijm} \qquad m = 1, 2, \ldots, M > 1$$
$$i = 1, 2, \ldots, a > 1, \quad j = 1, 2, \ldots, t > 1 \qquad (14.6.1)$$

The abbreviated normal equations are as follows:

$$
\begin{aligned}
&\mu: && Mat\hat{\mu} + Mt\sum_{i=1}^{a}\hat{\alpha}_i + Ma\sum_{j=1}^{t}\hat{\tau}_j + M\sum_{i=1}^{a}\sum_{j=1}^{t}\hat{\gamma}_{ij} = Y_{...} \\
&\alpha_i: && Mt\hat{\mu} + Mt\hat{\alpha}_i + M\sum_{j=1}^{t}\hat{\tau}_j + M\sum_{j=1}^{t}\hat{\gamma}_{ij} = Y_{i..} \\
& && \qquad i = 1, 2, \ldots, a \\
&\tau_j: && Ma\hat{\mu} + M\sum_{i=1}^{a}\hat{\alpha}_i + Ma\hat{\tau}_j + M\sum_{i=1}^{a}\hat{\gamma}_{ij} = Y_{.j.} \\
& && \qquad j = 1, 2, \ldots, t \\
&\gamma_{ij}: && M\hat{\mu} + M\hat{\alpha}_i + M\hat{\tau}_j + M\hat{\gamma}_{ij} = Y_{ij.} \\
& && \qquad i = 1, 2, \ldots, a, \; j = 1, 2, \ldots, t
\end{aligned}
\tag{14.6.2}
$$

The results below follow from these normal equations.

1. $p = 1 + a + t + at = (a + 1)(t + 1)$, where p is the number of equations.
2. The α_i equation is equal to the sum over j of the γ_{ij} equations for each i.
3. The τ_j equation is equal to the sum over i of the γ_{ij} equations for each j.
4. The μ equation is equal to the sum over i and j of the γ_{ij} equations.
5. The μ equation, each α_i equation, and each τ_j equation is a linear combination of the γ_{ij} equations, so $K \le ta$, the number of γ_{ij} equations.
6. Each of the γ_{ij} equations contains a distinct element, namely, $\hat{\gamma}_{ij}$, so $K \ge ta$.
7. From parts 5 and 6 it follows that $K = ta$.
8. Divide the γ_{ij} equations by M, and clearly $\mathscr{E}[\overline{Y}_{ij.}] = \mu + \alpha_i + \tau_j + \gamma_{ij}$ for $i = 1, 2, \ldots, a$ and $j = 1, 2, \ldots, t$.
9. $\mu + \alpha_i + \tau_j + \gamma_{ij}$, for $i = 1, 2, \ldots, a$, and $j = 1, 2, \ldots, t$, is a basis set of estimable functions.
10. $p - K = a + t + 1$.
11. The following are $(a + t + 1)$ nonestimable functions: $\mu, \alpha_1, \alpha_2, \ldots, \alpha_a, \tau_1, \tau_2, \ldots, \tau_t$. No linear combination of these parameters is estimable since every estimable

function must be a linear combination of every basis set of estimable functions and every linear combination of the basis set in part 9 must contain some of the γ_{ij} parameters.

12. If we let $\mathbf{V}'\boldsymbol{\beta} = \mathbf{0}$ in Section 13.5 be $\mu = \alpha_1 = \alpha_2 = \cdots = \alpha_a = \tau_1 = \tau_2 = \cdots = \tau_t = 0$, a solution to the normal equations is

$$\hat{\mu} = 0 \qquad \hat{\alpha}_1 = 0, \ldots, \hat{\alpha}_a = 0$$

$$\hat{\tau}_1 = 0, \ldots, \hat{\tau}_t = 0 \qquad \hat{\gamma}_{ij} = \bar{Y}_{ij.}$$

for $i = 1, 2, \ldots, a$ and $j = 1, 2, \ldots, t$.

13. $$\hat{\sigma}^2 = \frac{1}{Mat - K}\left[\sum_{i=1}^{a}\sum_{j=1}^{t}\sum_{m=1}^{M} Y_{ijm}^2 - \hat{\boldsymbol{\beta}}'\mathbf{X}'\mathbf{Y}\right]$$
$$= \frac{1}{at(M-1)}\left[\sum_{i=1}^{a}\sum_{j=1}^{t}\sum_{m=1}^{M} Y_{ijm}^2 - \sum_{i=1}^{a}\sum_{j=1}^{t} \bar{Y}_{ij.}Y_{ij.}\right]$$
$$= \frac{1}{at(M-1)}\left[\sum_{i=1}^{a}\sum_{j=1}^{t}\sum_{m=1}^{M} Y_{ijm}^2 - \sum_{i=1}^{a}\sum_{j=1}^{t} \frac{Y_{ij.}^2}{M}\right]$$
$$= \frac{1}{at(M-1)}\left[\sum_{i=1}^{a}\sum_{j=1}^{t}\sum_{m=1}^{M} (Y_{ijm} - \bar{Y}_{ij.})^2\right] \tag{14.6.3}$$

We have proved the following theorem.

THEOREM 14.6.1

Consider the two-factor design model with interaction given in Equation (14.6.1).

(1) $\mu + \alpha_i + \tau_j + \gamma_{ij}$, *for* $i = 1, 2, \ldots, a$ *and* $j = 1, 2, \ldots, t$, *is a basis set of estimable functions.*

(2) *The best unbiased estimator of* $\mu + \alpha_i + \tau_j + \gamma_{ij}$ *is* $\bar{Y}_{ij.}$.

(3) *The UMVU estimator of* σ^2 *is*

$$\hat{\sigma}^2 = \frac{1}{at(M-1)}\sum_{i=1}^{a}\sum_{j=1}^{t}\sum_{m=1}^{M} (Y_{ijm} - \bar{Y}_{ij.})^2$$

for Case I.

COROLLARY 14.6.1

Let the model be given in Theorem 14.6.1. *The best unbiased estimator of* α_i^*, *the average main effect of the ith level of factor A, is* $\bar{Y}_{i..} - \bar{Y}_{...}$; *the best unbiased estimator of* τ_j^*, *the average main effect of the jth level of factor T, is* $\bar{Y}_{.j.} - \bar{Y}_{...}$.

Next we turn our attention to confidence intervals and hypotheses tests.

THEOREM 14.6.2

Consider Case I of the model given in Equation (14.6.1).

(1) *The one-at-a-time* $1-\alpha$ *confidence intervals on* α_i^* *and* τ_j^* *are*

$$\alpha_i^* : \bar{Y}_{i..} - \bar{Y}_{...} \mp t_{\alpha/2:at(M-1)}\sqrt{\frac{\hat{\sigma}^2(a-1)}{atM}} \qquad \text{for } i = 1, 2, \ldots, a$$

$$\tau_j^* : \bar{Y}_{.j.} - \bar{Y}_{...} \mp t_{\alpha/2:at(M-1)}\sqrt{\frac{\hat{\sigma}^2(t-1)}{atM}} \qquad \text{for } j = 1, 2, \ldots, t$$

(2) *A size* α *test of* $H_0 : \sum_{i=1}^a \sum_{j=1}^t \gamma_{ij}^{*2} = 0$ *vs.* $H_a : \sum_{i=1}^a \sum_{j=1}^t \gamma_{ij}^{*2} \neq 0$ *(that is, a test for interaction) is this: Reject* H_0 *if and only if* $w \geq F_{\alpha:(a-1)(t-1),at(M-1)}$, *where* $w = I_{ms}/E_{ms}$.

(3) *A size* α *test of* $H_0 : \alpha_1^* = \alpha_2^* = \cdots = \alpha_a^* = 0$ *vs.* H_a *: at least one* $a_i^* \neq 0$ *is this: Reject* H_0 *if and only if* $w \geq F_{\alpha:a-1,at(M-1)}$, *where* $w = A_{ms}/E_{ms}$.

(4) *A size* α *test of* $H_0 : \tau_1^* = \tau_2^* = \cdots = \tau_t^* = 0$ *vs.* H_a *: at least one* $\tau_j^* \neq 0$ *is this: Reject* H_0 *if and only if* $w \geq F_{\alpha:t-1,at(M-1)}$, *where* $w = T_{ms}/E_{ms}$.

The quantities I_{ms}, A_{ms}, T_{ms}, *and* E_{ms} *are defined in Table* 14.6.1.

Proof

We sketch the proof and ask for the details in the problems. To obtain a confidence interval on $\alpha_i^* = \alpha_i - \bar{\alpha}_. + \bar{\gamma}_{i.} - \bar{\gamma}_{..}$, we examine the distribution of $\bar{Y}_{i..} - \bar{Y}_{...}$. Since we are considering Case I for the errors ε_{ijm}, we know that $\bar{Y}_{i..} - \bar{Y}_{...}$ is normally distributed. From the normal equations in Equation (14.6.2), we obtain

$$\begin{aligned}\mathscr{E}[\bar{Y}_{i..} - \bar{Y}_{...}] &= \left[\mu + \alpha_i + \left(\frac{1}{t}\right)\sum_{j=1}^t \tau_j + \left(\frac{1}{t}\right)\sum_{j=1}^t \gamma_{ij} - \mu \right. \\ &\quad \left. - \left(\frac{1}{a}\right)\sum_{i=1}^a \alpha_i - \left(\frac{1}{t}\right)\sum_{j=1}^t \tau_j - \left(\frac{1}{at}\right)\sum_{i=1}^a\sum_{j=1}^t \gamma_{ij}\right] \\ &= \alpha_i - \bar{\alpha}_. + \bar{\gamma}_{i.} - \bar{\gamma}_{..}\end{aligned}$$

which is the definition of α_i^*. Also,

$$\begin{aligned}\operatorname{var}[\bar{Y}_{i..} - \bar{Y}_{...}] &= \operatorname{var}[\bar{Y}_{i..}] + \operatorname{var}[\bar{Y}_{...}] - 2\operatorname{cov}[\bar{Y}_{i..}, \bar{Y}_{...}] \\ &= \frac{\sigma^2}{tM} + \frac{\sigma^2}{atM} - \frac{2\sigma^2}{atM} = \frac{\sigma^2(a-1)}{atM}\end{aligned}$$

Table 14.6.1

ANOVA for Two-Factor Design Model with Interaction, $M > 1$

Source	*d.f.*	*S.S.*	*M.S.*	*E.M.S.*
Total	atM	$\sum_{i=1}^{a}\sum_{j=1}^{t}\sum_{m=1}^{M} y_{ijm}^2$		
Mean	1	$\frac{y_{...}^2}{atM}$		
$R(H_0)$ for α^*	$a - 1$	$\sum_{i=1}^{a}\sum_{j=1}^{t}\sum_{m=1}^{M} (\bar{y}_{i..} - \bar{y}_{...})^2 = A_{ss}$	A_{ms}	$\sigma^2 + \sum_{i=1}^{a}\sum_{j=1}^{t}\sum_{m=1}^{M} \frac{(\alpha_i^*)^2}{a-1}$
$R(H_0)$ for τ^*	$t - 1$	$\sum_{i=1}^{a}\sum_{j=1}^{t}\sum_{m=1}^{M} (\bar{y}_{.j.} - \bar{y}_{...})^2 = T_{ss}$	T_{ms}	$\sigma^2 + \sum_{i=1}^{a}\sum_{j=1}^{t}\sum_{m=1}^{M} \frac{(\tau_j^*)^2}{t-1}$
$R(H_0)$ for γ^*	$(a - 1)(t - 1)$	$\sum_{i=1}^{a}\sum_{j=1}^{t}\sum_{m=1}^{M} (\bar{y}_{ij.} - \bar{y}_{i..} - \bar{y}_{.j.} + \bar{y}_{...})^2 = I_{ss}$	I_{ms}	$\sigma^2 + \sum_{i=1}^{a}\sum_{j=1}^{t}\sum_{m=1}^{M} \frac{(\gamma_{ij}^*)^2}{(a-1)(t-1)}$
Error	$at(M - 1)$	$\sum_{i=1}^{a}\sum_{j=1}^{t}\sum_{m=1}^{M} (y_{ijm} - \bar{y}_{ij.})^2 = E_{ss}$	E_{ms}	σ^2

So $Z = \bar{Y}_{i..} - \bar{Y}_{...}$ is distributed $N(z : \alpha_i^*, \sigma^2(a-1)/atM)$, $U = at(M - 1)\hat{\sigma}^2/\sigma^2$ is distributed $\chi^2(u : at(M-1))$, and Z and U are independent. The confidence interval on α_i^* follows since these facts imply $T = (Z - \alpha_i^*)/\hat{\sigma}\sqrt{(a-1)/atM}$ is distributed $s(t : at(M-1))$. A similar procedure can be used to obtain a confidence interval on τ_j^*.

Next we discuss the test $H_0 : \sum_{i=1}^{a} \sum_{j=1}^{t} \gamma_{ij}^{*2} = 0$, which can be written $\sum_{i=1}^{a} \sum_{j=1}^{t} (\gamma_{ij} - \bar{\gamma}_{i.} - \bar{\gamma}_{.j} + \bar{\gamma}_{..})^2 = 0$, which obtains if and ~~this obtains if and only if $\mu_{ij} - \bar{\mu}_{i.} - \bar{\mu}_{.j} + \bar{\mu}_{..} = 0$ for all allowable i if and~~ only if $\gamma_{ij} - \gamma_{i'j} - \gamma_{ij'} + \gamma_{i'j'} = 0$ for all allowable i, i', j, and j'; this obtains if and only if $\mu_{ij} - \bar{\mu}_{i.} - \bar{\mu}_{.j} + \bar{\mu}_{..} = 0$ for all allowable i and j. So $\sum_{i=1}^{a} \sum_{j=1}^{t} \gamma_{ij}^{*2} = 0$ if and only if there is no interaction between factors A and T.

In Theorem 14.5.2 we showed that the two-factor design model without interaction can be written as $Y_{ijm} = \mu + \alpha_i + \tau_j + \varepsilon_{ijm}$, and this is exactly the model discussed in Section 14.3. So by (4) of Theorem 14.3.1, we get

$$\hat{\sigma}_\omega^2 = \frac{(atM - a - t + 1)\hat{\sigma}^2}{atM} = \left(\frac{1}{atM}\right)$$
$$\times \left[\sum_{i=1}^{a} \sum_{j=1}^{t} \sum_{m=1}^{M} (\bar{Y}_{ij.} - \bar{Y}_{i..} - \bar{Y}_{.j.} + \bar{Y}_{...})^2 + \sum_{i=1}^{a} \sum_{j=1}^{t} \sum_{m=1}^{M} (Y_{ijm} - \bar{Y}_{ij.})^2 \right]$$

So the generalized likelihood ratio statistic in Equation (13.4.2) is

$$W_I = \frac{\dfrac{\sum_{i=1}^{a} \sum_{j=1}^{t} \sum_{m=1}^{M} (\bar{Y}_{ij.} - \bar{Y}_{i..} - \bar{Y}_{.j.} + \bar{Y}_{...})^2}{(a-1)(t-1)}}{\dfrac{\sum_{i=1}^{a} \sum_{j=1}^{t} \sum_{m=1}^{M} (Y_{ijm} - \bar{Y}_{ij.})^2}{at(M-1)}} = \frac{I_{ms}}{E_{ms}}$$

The result in (2) follows.

The proofs of (3) and (4) can be obtained by a similar procedure. These results are displayed in Table 14.6.1.

The "expected mean square" column (E.M.S.) in Table 14.6.1 can be used with Theorem 13.7.2 to evaluate the noncentrality parameter for the power of each test.

Note 1. The d.f. column and the S.S. column in Table 14.6.1 for the last five entries add to the total entry.

14.7 Two-Factor Design Model with Interaction and with $M = 1$

The model to be discussed in this section is defined in Equation (14.1.9), but it will be redefined in more detail here. Since $n_{ij} = M = 1$, the subscript m will not be needed. The model is

$$Y_{ij} = \mu + \alpha_i + \tau_j + \gamma_{ij} + \varepsilon_{ij} \qquad \varepsilon_{ij} \text{ are distributed } NID(\varepsilon : 0, \sigma^2)$$
$$i = 1, 2, \ldots, a > 1, \quad j = 1, 2, \ldots, t > 1 \qquad (14.7.1)$$

For this model we have assumed that the errors are normally distributed and this is the only case we shall discuss. The normal equations are obtained from Equation (14.6.2) when the third subscript is omitted on Y_{ijm}, $Y_{ij.}$, $Y_{i..}$, $Y_{.j.}$, and $Y_{...}$. All of the results 1 through 12 of Equation (14.6.3) apply to the model in Equation (14.7.1). Note, however, that since the third subscript is omitted, result 13 implies that there is no M.L. estimator of σ^2. These results are summed up in the following theorem.

THEOREM 14.7.1

Let the model be given by Equation (14.7.1). *The UMVU estimator of* $\mu + \alpha_i + \tau_j + \gamma_{ij}$ *is* Y_{ij}. *Other UMVU estimators are given below:*

$$\hat{\alpha}_i^* = \bar{Y}_{i.} - \bar{Y}_{..} \qquad \hat{\tau}_j^* = \bar{Y}_{.j} - \bar{Y}_{..} \qquad \hat{\gamma}_{ij}^* = Y_{ij} - \bar{Y}_{i.} - \bar{Y}_{.j} + \bar{Y}_{..}$$

There exists no M.L. and no unbiased estimator of σ^2.

We will not prove that there exists no unbiased estimator of σ^2, but intuitively one might argue that there are ta observations Y_{ij} and these unbiasedly estimate the ta functionally independent parameters $\mu_{ij} = \mu + \alpha_i + \tau_j + \gamma_{ij}$, so there are no observations "left over" to estimate σ^2. This can be related to the situation when one tries to obtain an unbiased estimator of σ^2 by using Y, a sample of size one, from the distribution $N(y : \mu, \sigma^2)$.

Since no satisfactory estimator of σ^2 exists, there are no exact $1 - \alpha$ confidence intervals on the α_i^*, τ_i^*, and γ_{ij}^*. However, we will discuss a size α test of $H_0 : \sum_{i=1}^{a} \sum_{j=1}^{t} \gamma_{ij}^{*2} = 0$, that is, a test that the interaction is zero. We note that if the interaction term γ_{ij}^* is zero, this implies that $\mu_{ij} - \bar{\mu}_{i.} - \bar{\mu}_{.j} + \bar{\mu}_{..} = 0$, which in turn implies $\mu_{ij} = \bar{\mu}_{i.} + \bar{\mu}_{.j} - \bar{\mu}_{..}$. In this equation μ_{ij} can be viewed as a function of the integer values of i and j, and, in fact, we could write this as $\mu(i, j) = \mu_1(i) + \mu_2(j) + \mu$, where $\mu(i, j)$ is a function of two variables i and j, $\mu_1(i)$ is a function of i only, $\mu_2(j)$ is a function of j only, and μ is a constant.

If we extend these ideas to a function of two real variables x and y on a set, say $a < x < b$ and $c < y < d$, then $\mu(x, y) = \mu + \mu_1(x) + \mu_2(y)$, and $\mu(x, y)$ is sometimes referred to as an *additive* function, that is, a function of x only which is *added* to a function of y only which is *added* to a constant. The functions defined by $3x - 2y$, $6x + 8y + 16$, and $6 \sin x + 2 \log x + 3y^2$ are additive functions of x and y where, for example, in the last function, $\mu_1(x)$ is defined by $\mu_1(x) = 6 \sin x + 2 \log x$ and $\mu_2(y)$ by $\mu_2(y) = 3y^2$. On the other hand, the functions defined by xy, $x + y - 3xy$, and $\sin xy$ are *not* additive functions of x and y.

We now return to the two-factor design model. We assume that γ_{ij}^* is a function of the two parameters α_i^* and τ_j^*, and if $\gamma_{ij}^* \neq 0$ for some i and j, then the model is nonadditive (interaction is not zero). In terms of the model $\mu + \alpha_i + \tau_j + \gamma_{ij}$, this means that $\gamma_{ij} \neq 0$ for some i and j and γ_{ij} is a nonadditive function of the parameters α_i and τ_j. To indicate this, the interaction term γ_{ij}^* is sometimes written as $(\alpha\tau)_{ij}^*$, and γ_{ij} is often written as $(\alpha\tau)_{ij}$.

In one sense the two-factor design model with interaction is not a linear model, but we have seen in the previous section that when $n_{ij} = M > 1$, it can be treated by linear model theory. When $M = 1$, however, some modifications must be made.

The first thing we do is decide on the functional form of γ_{ij}^*. In an applied problem this functional form may not be known, so what we shall do is use a function that "approximates a general function." By the words "approximates a general function," we mean that if we were dealing with a function $\mu(x, y)$ of two real variables x and y, and if the function could be expanded into a Taylor series, an approximation is

$$a_{00} + a_{10}x + a_{01}y + a_{20}x^2 + a_{02}y^2 + a_{11}xy + a_{30}x^3 + a_{03}y^3$$

which can be viewed as a constant term a_{00} plus a function of x only, given by $a_{10}x + a_{20}x^2 + a_{30}x^3$, plus a function of y only, given by $a_{01}y + a_{02}y^2 + a_{03}y^3$, plus a product term given by $a_{11}xy$.

With these ideas as a guide, we write the two-factor interaction model as

$$Y_{ij} = \mu^* + \alpha_i^* + \tau_j^* + \delta\alpha_i^*\tau_j^* + \varepsilon_{ij} \qquad \varepsilon_{ij} \text{ are distributed } NID(\varepsilon : 0, \sigma^2)$$
$$i = 1, 2, \ldots, a > 1, \quad j = 1, 2, \ldots, t > 1, \quad \sum \alpha_i^* = \sum \tau_j^* = 0 \qquad (14.7.2)$$

In the next theorem we give a size α test of $H_0 : \delta = 0$ *vs.* $H_a : \delta \neq 0$, which is a test for interaction (additivity) in the model in Equation (14.7.2).

THEOREM 14.7.2

Let the model be given by Equation (14.7.2). *A size* α *test of* (*no interaction*) $H_0 : \delta = 0$ *vs.* $H_a : \delta \neq 0$ *is this: Reject* H_0 *if and only if* $w \geq F_{\alpha:1,(a-1)(t-1)-1}$, *where* w *is the computed value of* W *and where*

$$W = \frac{N_{ss}}{R_{ss}/[(a-1)(t-1)-1]} = \frac{N_{ms}}{R_{ms}}$$

and where N_{ss} and R_{ss} are

$$N_{ss} = \frac{\left[\sum_{i=1}^{a}\sum_{j=1}^{t}(Y_{ij} - \bar{Y}_{i.} - \bar{Y}_{.j} + \bar{Y}_{..})(\bar{Y}_{i.} - \bar{Y}_{..})(\bar{Y}_{.j} - \bar{Y}_{..})\right]^2}{\sum_{i=1}^{a}(\bar{Y}_{i.} - \bar{Y}_{..})^2 \sum_{j=1}^{t}(\bar{Y}_{.j} - \bar{Y}_{..})^2}$$

$$R_{ss} = \sum_{i=1}^{a}\sum_{j=1}^{t}(Y_{ij} - \bar{Y}_{i.} - \bar{Y}_{.j} + \bar{Y}_{..})^2 - N_{ss}$$

Proof

The proof will be given in Section 14.11.

The quantity N_{ss} is called the nonadditivity sum of squares and it has one degree of freedom, so $N_{ss} = N_{ms}$, the nonadditivity mean square. The quantity R_{ss} is called the residual sum of squares and it has $(a - 1)(t - 1) - 1$ degrees of freedom; hence $R_{ss}/[(a - 1)(t - 1) - 1] = R_{ms}$, the residual mean square. The quantities in W can be obtained from an ANOVA table such as Table 14.7.1.

The quantity R_{ss} can be obtained by subtracting from the total sum of squares the following: $Y_{..}^2/ta$, A_{ss}, T_{ss}, N_{ss}. So N_{ss} is the only new quantity that is not used in a two-factor design model without interaction and $M = 1$. The

Table 14.7.1

ANOVA Table for Testing Interaction in a Two-Factor Design with One Observation Per Cell

Source	*d.f.*	*S.S.*	*M.S.*
Total	ta	$\sum_{i=1}^{a}\sum_{j=1}^{t} Y_{ij}^2$	
Mean	1	$\frac{Y_{..}^2}{ta}$	
Factor A	$a - 1$	$\sum_{i=1}^{a}\frac{Y_{i.}^2}{t} - \frac{Y_{..}^2}{ta} = A_{ss}$	
Factor T	$t - 1$	$\sum_{j=1}^{t}\frac{Y_{.j}^2}{a} - \frac{Y_{..}^2}{ta} = T_{ss}$	
Nonadditivity	1	N_{ss}	N_{ms}
Residual	$(a - 1)(t - 1) - 1$	R_{ss} (by subtraction)	R_{ms}

denominator of N_{ss} is equal to $A_{ss}T_{ss}/ta$, and the numerator can be written as

$$\left[\sum_{i=1}^{a}\sum_{j=1}^{t}(Y_{ij}-\bar{Y}_{i.}-\bar{Y}_{.j}+\bar{Y}_{..})(\bar{Y}_{i.}-\bar{Y}_{..})(\bar{Y}_{.j}-\bar{Y}_{..})\right]^2$$

$$=\left[\sum_{i=1}^{a}\sum_{j=1}^{t}Y_{ij}(\bar{Y}_{i.}-\bar{Y}_{..})(\bar{Y}_{.j}-\bar{Y}_{..})\right]^2$$

$$=\left[\frac{\sum_{i=1}^{a}\sum_{j=1}^{t}Y_{ij}Y_{i.}Y_{.j}}{at}-\left(\frac{Y_{..}}{at}\right)\left\{\left(\frac{\sum_{i=1}^{a}Y_{i.}^2}{t}-\frac{Y_{..}^2}{at}\right)+\left(\frac{\sum_{j=1}^{t}Y_{.j}^2}{a}-\frac{Y_{..}^2}{at}\right)+\frac{Y_{..}^2}{at}\right\}\right]^2$$

$$=\frac{1}{a^2t^2}\left[\sum_{i=1}^{a}\sum_{j=1}^{t}Y_{ij}Y_{i.}Y_{.j}-Y_{..}\left(A_{ss}+T_{ss}+\frac{Y_{..}^2}{at}\right)\right]^2$$

So

$$N_{ss}=\frac{\left[\sum_{i=1}^{a}\sum_{j=1}^{t}Y_{ij}Y_{i.}Y_{.j}-Y_{..}(A_{ss}+T_{ss}+Y_{..}^2/at)\right]^2}{atA_{ss}T_{ss}}$$

To compute the quantities in Table 14.7.1, the only new quantity needed is $\sum_{i=1}^{a}\sum_{j=1}^{t}y_{ij}y_{i.}y_{.j}$, and this is easily computed from the entries in a two-way table and the rows and columns totals. We illustrate with a simple artificial example.

Example 14.7.1

The data in Table 14.7.2 are assumed to have come from the model in Equation (14.7.2). Compute the ANOVA table for testing $H_0: \delta = 0$.

We must compute the column $\sum_{j=1}^{t} y_{ij}y_{.j}$; we get

$$154 = (6)(13) + (2)(4) + (5)(10) + (3)(6)$$
$$42 = (2)(13) + (0)(4) + (1)(10) + (1)(6)$$
$$125 = (5)(13) + (2)(4) + (4)(10) + (2)(6)$$

Table 14.7.2

Artificial Data from Two-Factor Design with Interaction

Levels of Factor A	*Levels of Factor T* 1	2	3	4	*Total* $y_{i.}$	$\sum_{j=1}^{t} y_{ij}y_{.j}$
1	6	2	5	3	16	154
2	2	0	1	1	4	42
3	5	2	4	2	13	125
Total $y_{.j}$	13	4	10	6	33	321

Also, we can compute the following:

$$\sum_{i=1}^{a}\left(\sum_{j=1}^{t} y_{ij}y_{.j}\right)y_{i.} = (154)(16) + (42)(4) + (125)(13) = 4257$$

$$T_{ss} = 16.25 \qquad A_{ss} = 19.50 \qquad \sum_{i=1}^{a}\sum_{j=1}^{t} y_{ij}^2 = 129 \qquad \frac{y_{..}^2}{at} = 90.75$$

$$E_{ss} = 129 - 90.75 - 16.25 - 19.50 = 2.50$$

$$N_{ss} = \frac{[4257 - 33(16.25 + 19.50 + 90.75)]^2}{(3)(4)(16.25)(19.50)} = 1.790$$

These quantities are exhibited in Table 14.7.3. The data indicate the model has an interaction term (the interaction is not zero).

In addition to testing for interaction, one may wish to set confidence intervals on α_i^*, the main effects of factor A, and on τ_j^*, the main effects of factor T. However, if $\gamma_{ij}^* \neq 0$ for all i and j, there is no estimator of σ^2 that is available to use for exact confidence intervals on the α_i^* or the τ_j^*.

In the two-factor model with interaction discussed in the previous section, an estimator of σ^2 was obtained from the "within cell" sum of squares, even when $\gamma_{ij}^* \neq 0$ for each i and j. For the model in Equation (14.7.2), if the hypothesis $H_0 : \delta = 0$ is accepted, then a procedure that can be used is to assume that the model is given by Equation (14.2.1), and inference procedures in Section 14.2 can be used. However, one must keep in mind that the model being used is based on an examination of the data (a hypothesis test); of course, if the test implies that $\gamma_{ij}^* = 0$ for all i and j, but if, in fact, $\gamma_{ij}^* \neq 0$ for some i and j, then the inference procedures using the methods in Section 14.2 are not exact.

If t or a is fairly large, it seems reasonable that $\gamma_{ij}^* = 0$ for *some* values of i and j (even though the test $H_0 : \gamma_{ij}^* = 0$ for *all* i and j is rejected), and this implies

Table 14.7.3

ANOVA Table for Testing Interaction in a Two-Factor Design with One Observation Per Cell

Source	*d.f.*	*S.S.*	*M.S.*	*F*
Total	12	129.00		
Mean	1	90.75		
Factor T	3	16.25		
Factor A	2	19.50		
Nonadditivity	1	1.790	1.790	12.61
Residual	5	0.710	0.142	

$\mu_{ij} - \bar{\mu}_{i.} - \bar{\mu}_{.j} + \bar{\mu}_{..} = 0$ for those values of i and j. The corresponding statistics $Y_{ij} - \bar{Y}_{i.} - \bar{Y}_{.j} + \bar{Y}_{..}$ can be used to obtain an estimator of σ^2 that can be used for hypotheses tests and confidence intervals on the α_i^* and the τ_j^*. For a full discussion of the present state of knowledge for this problem, see [J-4], [J-5], and references given in these papers.

14.8 Two-Factor Model with Interaction and Unequal Number of Observations in the Cells

The model is given in Equation (14.1.10) and is repeated here in detail.

$$Y_{ijm} = \mu_{ij} + \varepsilon_{ijm} = \mu + \alpha_i + \tau_j + \gamma_{ij} + \varepsilon_{ijm}$$

$$m = 1, 2, \ldots, n_{ij} > 0 \text{ for all } i \text{ and } j$$

$$i = 1, 2, \ldots, a > 1, \quad j = 1, 2, \ldots, t > 1 \qquad (14.8.1)$$

and at least two n_{ij} are distinct.

> *Note 1.* The restriction "at least two n_{ij} are distinct" is not an essential part of the model, but if it does not obtain, then $n_{ij} = M$ for all i and j, and this model has been discussed for $M > 1$ and $M = 1$ in previous sections.

> *Note 2.* The restriction "$n_{ij} > 0$ for all i and j" is required for the methods that will be presented to be valid. A discussion of this model without this restriction can be found in [B-1].

Throughout this section the following notation will be used.

$$h_{ij} = n_{ij}^{-1} \qquad h_{i.} = \sum_{j=1}^{t} n_{ij}^{-1} \qquad \bar{h}_{i.} = \left(\frac{1}{t}\right) \sum_{j=1}^{t} n_{ij}^{-1}$$

$$h_{.j} = \sum_{i=1}^{a} n_{ij}^{-1} \qquad \bar{h}_{.j} = \left(\frac{1}{a}\right) \sum_{i=1}^{a} n_{ij}^{-1} \qquad \bar{h}_{..} = \left(\frac{1}{at}\right) \sum_{i=1}^{a} \sum_{j=1}^{t} n_{ij}^{-1}$$

$$Z_{ij} = \bar{Y}_{ij.} = n_{ij}^{-1} \sum_{m=1}^{n_{ij}} Y_{ijm} \qquad Z_{i.} = \sum_{j=1}^{t} Z_{ij} \qquad \bar{Z}_{i.} = \left(\frac{1}{t}\right) \sum_{j=1}^{t} Z_{ij}$$

$$Z_{.j} = \sum_{i=1}^{a} Z_{ij} \qquad \bar{Z}_{.j} = \left(\frac{1}{a}\right) \sum_{i=1}^{a} Z_{ij}$$

$$Z_{..} = \sum_{i=1}^{a} \sum_{j=1}^{t} Z_{ij} \qquad \bar{Z}_{..} = \left(\frac{1}{at}\right) \sum_{i=1}^{a} \sum_{j=1}^{t} Z_{ij}$$

$$\mu_{ij} = \mu + \alpha_i + \tau_j + \gamma_{ij} \qquad \bar{\mu}_{i.} = \mu + \alpha_i + \bar{\tau}_{.} + \bar{\gamma}_{i.}$$

$$\bar{\mu}_{.j} = \mu + \bar{\alpha}_{.} + \tau_j + \bar{\gamma}_{.j} \qquad \bar{\mu}_{..} = \mu + \bar{\alpha}_{.} + \bar{\tau}_{.} + \bar{\gamma}_{..}$$

The abbreviated normal equations for this model are given below.

$$\mu: \quad n_{..}\hat{\mu} + \sum_{i=1}^{a} n_{i.}\hat{\alpha}_i + \sum_{j=1}^{t} n_{.j}\hat{\tau}_j + \sum_{i=1}^{a}\sum_{j=1}^{t} n_{ij}\hat{\gamma}_{ij} = Y_{...}$$

$$\alpha_i: \quad n_{i.}\hat{\mu} + n_{i.}\hat{\alpha}_i + \sum_{j=1}^{t} n_{ij}\hat{\tau}_j + \sum_{j=1}^{t} n_{ij}\hat{\gamma}_{ij} = Y_{i..} \quad \text{for } i = 1, 2, \ldots, a$$

$$\tau_j: \quad n_{.j}\hat{\mu} + \sum_{i=1}^{a} n_{ij}\hat{\alpha}_i + n_{.j}\hat{\tau}_j + \sum_{i=1}^{a} n_{ij}\hat{\gamma}_{ij} = Y_{.j.} \quad \text{for } j = 1, 2, \ldots, t$$

$$\gamma_{ij}: \quad n_{ij}\hat{\mu} + n_{ij}\hat{\alpha}_i + n_{ij}\hat{\tau}_j + n_{ij}\hat{\gamma}_{ij} = Y_{ij.} \quad \text{for } i = 1, 2, \ldots, a, \; j = 1, 2, \ldots, t$$

The ta equations for γ_{ij} are linearly independent since the expected value of each equation contains a distinct parameter γ_{ij}; all other equations are linear functions of these ta equations, so $K = at$ and $p = at + a + t + 1$. Also, $\mu_{ij} = \mu + \alpha_i + \tau_j + \gamma_{ij}$, for $i = 1, 2, \ldots, a$ and $j = 1, 2, \ldots, t$, is a basis set of estimable functions, and the best unbiased estimator μ_{ij} is $\bar{Y}_{ij.}$.

These results and some additional ones are summarized in the following theorem.

THEOREM 14.8.1

Let the model be given by Equation (14.8.1). *The best unbiased estimators of various parameters are displayed below.*

(1) $\hat{\mu}_{ij} = \hat{\mu} + \hat{\alpha}_i + \hat{\tau}_j + \hat{\gamma}_{ij} = Z_{ij} = \bar{Y}_{ij.}$ *for* $i = 1, 2, \ldots, a$, $j = 1, 2, \ldots, t$.

(2) $\hat{\hat{\mu}}_{i.} = \hat{\mu} + \hat{\alpha}_i + \hat{\hat{\tau}}_{.} + \hat{\hat{\gamma}}_{i.} = \bar{Z}_{i.}$ *for* $i = 1, 2, \ldots, a$.

(3) $\hat{\hat{\mu}}_{.j} = \hat{\mu} + \hat{\hat{\alpha}}_{.} + \hat{\tau}_j + \hat{\hat{\gamma}}_{.j} = \bar{Z}_{.j}$ *for* $j = 1, 2, \ldots, t$.

(4) $\hat{\hat{\mu}}_{..} = \hat{\mu} + \hat{\hat{\alpha}}_{.} + \hat{\hat{\tau}}_{.} + \hat{\hat{\gamma}}_{..} = \bar{Z}_{..}$.

(5) $\hat{\alpha}_i^* = \hat{\hat{\mu}}_{i.} - \hat{\hat{\mu}}_{..} = \hat{\alpha}_i - \hat{\hat{\alpha}}_{.} + \hat{\hat{\gamma}}_{i.} - \hat{\hat{\gamma}}_{..} = \bar{Z}_{i.} - \bar{Z}_{..}$ *for* $i = 1, 2, \ldots, a$.

(6) $\hat{\tau}_j^* = \hat{\hat{\mu}}_{.j} - \hat{\hat{\mu}}_{..} = \hat{\tau}_j - \hat{\hat{\tau}}_{.} + \hat{\hat{\gamma}}_{.j} - \hat{\hat{\gamma}}_{..} = \bar{Z}_{.j} - \bar{Z}_{..}$ *for* $j = 1, 2, \ldots, t$.

(7) $\hat{\gamma}_{ij}^* = \hat{\mu}_{ij} - \hat{\hat{\mu}}_{i.} - \hat{\hat{\mu}}_{.j} + \hat{\hat{\mu}}_{..} = \hat{\gamma}_{ij} - \hat{\hat{\gamma}}_{i.} - \hat{\hat{\gamma}}_{.j} + \hat{\hat{\gamma}}_{..}$
$= Z_{ij} - \bar{Z}_{i.} - \bar{Z}_{.j} + \bar{Z}_{..}$ *for* $i = 1, 2, \ldots, a$, $j - 1, 2, \ldots, t$.

In the next theorem we state some additional results for the model in Equation (14.8.1).

THEOREM 14.8.2

Let the model be given by Equation (14.8.1), *and let* ε_{ijm} *be distributed* $NID(\varepsilon : 0, \sigma^2)$. *The results below follow.*

(1) $\hat{\sigma}^2$ *and* $\bar{Y}_{ij.}$, *for* $i = 1, 2, \ldots, a$ *and* $j = 1, 2, \ldots, t$, *are* $ta + 1$ *complete sufficient statistics, where* $\hat{\sigma}^2 = (n_{..} - at)^{-1} \sum_{i=1}^{a} \sum_{j=1}^{t} \sum_{m=1}^{n_{ij}} (Y_{ijm} - \bar{Y}_{ij.})^2$.

(2) $\hat{\sigma}^2, \bar{Y}_{11.}, \ldots, \bar{Y}_{at.}$ *are jointly independent statistics.*

(3) $U = (n_{..} - at)\hat{\sigma}^2/\sigma^2$ *is distributed* $\chi^2(u : n_{..} - at)$.

(4) $Z_{ij} = \bar{Y}_{ij.}$ *are distributed* $NID(\bar{y}_{ij.} : \mu + \alpha_i + \tau_j + \gamma_{ij}, \sigma^2/n_{ij})$ *for* $i = 1, 2, \ldots, a$ *and* $j = 1, 2, \ldots, t$.

(5) $\hat{\alpha} = \sum_{i=1}^{a} \ell_i \hat{\bar{\mu}}_{i.}$ *is distributed* $N(\hat{\alpha} : \sum_{i=1}^{a} \ell_i \bar{\mu}_{i.}, \sigma_{\hat{\alpha}}^2)$, *where* $\sigma_{\hat{\alpha}}^2 = \sigma^2(\sum_{i=1}^{a} \ell_i^2 \bar{h}_{i.})/t$.

(6) $\hat{\tau} = \sum_{j=1}^{t} \ell_j \hat{\bar{\mu}}_{.j}$ *is distributed* $N(\hat{\tau} : \sum_{j=1}^{t} \ell_j \bar{\mu}_{.j}, \sigma_{\hat{\tau}}^2)$, *where* $\sigma_{\hat{\tau}}^2 = \sigma^2(\sum_{j=1}^{t} \ell_j^2 \bar{h}_{.j})/a$.

Proof

The proof of this theorem is a straightforward application of the previous theorem and the appropriate theorems in Chapters 2, 3, and 4. The details will be omitted.

In the next theorem a test for interaction is discussed.

THEOREM 14.8.3

Let the model be given by Equation (14.8.1), *and let* ε_{ijm} *be distributed* $NID(\varepsilon : 0, \sigma^2)$. *To test* $H_0 : \gamma_{ij}^* = 0$ *for all allowable i and j vs.* $H_a : \gamma_{ij}^* \neq 0$ *for at least one value of i and j, the generalized likelihood ratio test of size* α *is this: Reject* H_0 *if and only if* $w_I \geq F_{\alpha:(a-1)(t-1),n}$; w_I *is the computed value of* $W_I = I_{ms}/E_{ms}$; $n = n_{..} - at$. *Also,* I_{ms} *is given by*

$$I_{ms} = \frac{I_{ss}}{(a-1)(t-1)} = \frac{1}{(a-1)(t-1)} \left[\sum_{i=1}^{a} \sum_{j=1}^{t} \frac{Y_{ij.}^2}{n_{ij}} - \mathbf{t}'\mathbf{t} \right]$$

and **t** *is given in Equation* (14.4.7). E_{ms} *is given by*

$$E_{ms} = \frac{E_{ss}}{(n_{..} - at)} = \frac{1}{(n_{..} - at)} \left[\sum_{i=1}^{a} \sum_{j=1}^{t} \sum_{m=1}^{n_{ij}} (Y_{ijm} - \bar{Y}_{ij.})^2 \right]$$

$$= \frac{1}{(n_{..} - at)} \left[\sum_{i=1}^{a} \sum_{j=1}^{t} \sum_{m=1}^{n_{ij}} Y_{ijm}^2 - \sum_{i=1}^{a} \sum_{j=1}^{t} \frac{Y_{ij.}^2}{n_{ij}} \right]$$

When H_0 *is true,* W_I *is distributed as* $F(w : (a-1)(t-1), n)$.

Proof

We evaluate $\hat{\sigma}^2_\Omega$ and $\hat{\sigma}^2_\omega$ and use Theorem 13.4.1. By using (1) of Theorem 14.8.2, $\hat{\sigma}^2_\Omega = (n_{..} - at)\hat{\sigma}^2/n_{..} = n_{..}^{-1}\sum_{i=1}^a \sum_{j=1}^t \sum_{m=1}^{n_{ij}} (Y_{ijm} - \bar{Y}_{ij.})^2$. We know that the model under H_0 is $Y_{ijm} = \mu^* + \alpha_i^* + \tau_j^* + \varepsilon_{ijm}$, which is the model in Equation (14.4.1), so the M.L. estimator of σ^2 for this model is $\hat{\sigma}^2_\omega$ and is obtained from part 7 of Note 4 in Section 14.4. We get $\hat{\sigma}^2_\omega = n_{..}^{-1}(\sum_{i=1}^a \sum_{j=1}^t \sum_{m=1}^{n_{ij}} Y^2_{ijm} - \mathbf{t}_1'\mathbf{t}_1 - \mathbf{t}_2'\mathbf{t}_2)$, where $\mathbf{t}_1$ and $\mathbf{t}_2$ are given by Equation (14.4.7). The results of the theorem follow by substituting $\hat{\sigma}^2_\Omega$ and $\hat{\sigma}^2_\omega$ into Theorem 13.4.1.

THEOREM 14.8.4

Let the model be given by Equation (14.8.1), *and let* ε_{ijm} *be distributed* $NID(\varepsilon : 0, \sigma^2)$.

(1) *To test* $H_0 : \alpha_i^* = 0$, *for* $i = 1, 2, \ldots, a$, *vs.* $H_a : \alpha_i^* \neq 0$, *for at least one value of i, the generalized likelihood ratio test of size* α *is this: Reject* H_0 *if and only if* $w_A \geq F_{\alpha:a-1,n}$, *where* w_A *is the computed value of* $W_A = A_{ms}/E_{ms}$ *and* A_{ms} *is defined by*

$$A_{ms} = \frac{A_{ss}}{(a-1)} = \frac{1}{(a-1)} \sum_{i=1}^{a} h_{i.}^{-1}\left(\sum_{j=1}^{t} \bar{Y}_{ij.} - \bar{Y}_A\right)^2$$

where

$$\bar{Y}_A = \frac{\sum_{i=1}^{a}\sum_{j=1}^{t} h_{i.}^{-1}\bar{Y}_{ij.}}{\sum_{i'=1}^{a} h_{i'.}^{-1}}$$

E_{ms} *is given in Theorem* 14.8.3. *When* H_0 *is true,* W_A *is distributed as* $F(w : a-1, n)$.

(2) *One-at-a-time* $1-\alpha$ *confidence limits on* $\sum_{i=1}^a \ell_i\bar{\mu}_{i.}$ *for any set of a constants* $\{\ell_i\}$ *are given by* $\sum_{i=1}^a \ell_i\hat{\bar{\mu}}_{i.} \mp t_{\alpha/2:n}\sqrt{\hat{\sigma}^2(\sum_{i=1}^a \ell_i^2\bar{h}_{i.}/t)}$.

(3) *Simultaneous (Scheffé)* $1-\alpha$ *confidence limits on* $\sum_{i=1}^a \ell_i\bar{\mu}_{i.}$ *for all sets of a constants* $\{\ell_i\}$ *are given by*

$$\sum_{i=1}^{a} \ell_i\hat{\bar{\mu}}_{i.} \mp \sqrt{aF_{\alpha:a,n}}\sqrt{\hat{\sigma}^2\left(\sum_{i=1}^{a} \ell_i^2\bar{h}_{i.}/t\right)}$$

where $\hat{\sigma}^2$ *is given in* (1) *of Theorem* 14.8.2.

Proof

The proof for (1) is a straightforward application of Theorem 13.4.1. The proofs for (2) and (3) are obtained by using the distribution theory in Theorem 14.8.2.

Note 3. If we use the notation $Z_{ij} = \bar{Y}_{ij.}$, and so forth, we can write A_{ms} as

$$A_{ms} = \frac{1}{(a-1)}\left[\sum_{i=1}^{a}\left(\frac{Z_{i.}^2}{h_{i.}}\right) - \frac{\left(\sum_{i=1}^{a}\frac{Z_{i.}}{h_{i.}}\right)^2}{\sum_{i'=1}^{a} h_{i'.}^{-1}}\right]$$

or as

$$A_{ms} = \frac{1}{(a-1)}\left[\sum_{i=1}^{a}\left(\frac{Z_{i.}^2}{h_{i.}}\right) - \left(\sum_{i=1}^{a} h_{i.}^{-1}\right)\bar{Y}_A^2\right]$$

THEOREM 14.8.5

Let the model be given by Equation (14.8.1), and let ε_{ijm} be distributed $NID(\varepsilon:0, \sigma^2)$.

(1) *To test $H_0: \tau_j^* = 0$, for $j = 1, 2, \ldots, t$, vs. $H_a: \tau_j^* \neq 0$, for at least one value of j, the generalized likelihood ratio test of size α is this: Reject H_0 if and only if $w_T \geq F_{\alpha:t-1,n}$, where w_T is the computed value of $W_T = T_{ms}/E_{ms}$ and T_{ms} is defined by*

$$T_{ms} = \frac{T_{ss}}{(t-1)} = \frac{1}{(t-1)}\sum_{j=1}^{t} h_{.j}^{-1}\left(\sum_{i=1}^{a}\bar{Y}_{ij.} - \bar{Y}_T\right)^2$$

where

$$\bar{Y}_T = \frac{\sum_{i=1}^{a}\sum_{j=1}^{t} h_{.j}^{-1}\bar{Y}_{ij.}}{\sum_{j'=1}^{t} h_{.j'}^{-1}}$$

E_{ms} is given in Theorem 14.8.3. When H_0 is true, W_T is distributed as $F(w: t-1, n)$.

(2) *One-at-a-time $1-\alpha$ confidence limits on $\sum_{j=1}^{t} \ell_j\bar{\mu}_{.j}$ for any set of t constants $\{\ell_j\}$ are given by $\sum_{j=1}^{t} \ell_j\hat{\bar{\mu}}_{.j} \mp t_{\alpha/2:n}\sqrt{\hat{\sigma}^2(\sum_{j=1}^{t} \ell_j^2\bar{h}_{.j})/a}$.*

(3) *Simultaneous (Scheffé) $1-\alpha$ confidence limits on $\sum_{j=1}^{t} \ell_j\bar{\mu}_{.j}$ for all sets of t constants $\{\ell_j\}$ are given by*

$$\sum_{j=1}^{t} \ell_j\hat{\bar{\mu}}_{.j} \mp \sqrt{tF_{\alpha:t,n}}\sqrt{\hat{\sigma}^2\left(\sum_{j=1}^{t} \ell_j^2\bar{h}_{.j}\right)\Big/ a}$$

Proof

The proof is obtained by the same methods used to prove Theorem 14.8.4.

This model and the theorems in this section will be illustrated by a simple artificial example.

Example 14.8.1

The data in Table 14.8.1 are assumed to have come from the model defined in Equation (14.8.1), where the ε_{ijm} are distributed $NID(\varepsilon : 0, \sigma^2)$, and the n_{ij} are exhibited in Table 14.8.2. For $\alpha = 0.05$, (1) test whether the model is additive (test for interaction); (2) test the hypothesis that the "average main effects" of factor A are equal, that is, test $H_0 : \alpha_1^* = \alpha_2^* = \cdots = \alpha_a^*$; (3) set 95 percent one-at-a-time confidence limits on the "average main effects" of factor A, that is, on $\alpha_i^* = \bar{\mu}_{i.} - \bar{\mu}_{..}$ for $i = 1, 2$.

To answer (1) we use Theorem 14.8.3, and this means we must find $\mathbf{t}$ by methods described in Section 14.4. We use the format in Equation (14.4.6) without the identity matrix and with i and j interchanged since $t > a$. We get

$$\left[\begin{array}{c|c} \mathbf{W} & \mathbf{w} \\ \hline \mathbf{T} & \mathbf{t} \end{array}\right] = \left[\begin{array}{cc|c} \mathbf{D}_{.j} & \mathbf{N}' & \mathbf{y}_{.j} \\ \mathbf{N} & \mathbf{D}_{i.} & \mathbf{y}_{i.} \\ \hline \mathbf{T}_{11} & \mathbf{T}_{12} & \mathbf{t}_1 \\ \mathbf{0} & \mathbf{T}_{22} & \mathbf{t}_2 \end{array}\right] = \left[\begin{array}{cccc|c} 4 & 0 & 0 & 2 & 18 \\ 0 & 2 & 0 & 1 & 8 \\ 0 & 0 & 3 & 1 & 15 \\ 2 & 1 & 1 & 4 & 16 \\ \hline 2 & 0 & 0 & 1 & 9 \\ & \sqrt{2} & 0 & \dfrac{1}{\sqrt{2}} & \dfrac{8}{\sqrt{2}} \\ & & \sqrt{3} & \dfrac{1}{\sqrt{3}} & \dfrac{15}{\sqrt{3}} \\ & & & \sqrt{\dfrac{13}{6}} & -\dfrac{2\sqrt{6}}{\sqrt{13}} \end{array}\right]$$

Table 14.8.1

Artificial Data for Example 14.8.1

Levels of Factor A	*Levels of Factor T* 1	2	3	*Total* $y_{i..}$
1	6 4	3	3	16
2	3 5	5	5 7	25
Total $y_{.j.}$	18	8	15	$41 = y_{...}$

Table 14.8.2

Numbers n_{ij} in Cells for Data in Table 14.8.1

Levels of Factor A	*Levels of Factor T* 1	2	3	*Total* $n_{i.}$
1	2	1	1	4
2	2	1	2	5
Total $n_{.j}$	4	2	3	$9 = n_{..}$

We obtain $\mathbf{t}'\mathbf{t} = (9)^2 + (8/\sqrt{2})^2 + (15/\sqrt{3})^2 + (-2\sqrt{6}/\sqrt{13})^2 = 189.8462$; $\sum\sum y_{ij.}^2/n_{ij} = (10)^2/2 + (3)^2/1 + (3)^2/1 + (8)^2/2 + (5)^2/1 + (12)^2/2 = 197.0000$; $I_{ms} = [(1)(2)]^{-1}[7.1538] = 3.5769$; $\sum\sum\sum y_{ijm}^2 = 203.0000$, so $E_{ms} = [9 - 6]^{-1}[203 - 197] = 6/3 = 2.0000$; $w_I = 3.5769/2.0000 = 1.7885$; and $F_{0.05:2,3} = 9.5521$. So the data do not indicate that the model contains interaction. In a practical situation, from the result of this test, an investigator might assume a model *without* interaction and obtain answers to questions (2) and (3) by using the model in Equation (14.1.7). However, to demonstrate the theory in this section, we shall use the model in Equation (14.8.1) for the remainder of this example.

To answer (2) we use (1) of Theorem 14.8.4. We note that $\alpha_1^* = \alpha_2^* = \cdots = \alpha_a^*$ if and only if $\alpha_i^* = 0$ for $i = 1, 2, \ldots, a$. First we compute Tables 14.8.3 and 14.8.4. These tables are for illustrative purposes only. In a practical situation the formulas in Theorem 14.8.4 would be programmed, and the necessary quantities would be obtained directly from the data in Tables 14.8.1 and 14.8.2. From Tables 14.8.1 and 14.8.2 we compute Tables 14.8.3 and 14.8.4.

Table 14.8.3

Cell Means ($z_{ij} = \bar{y}_{ij.}$) for Data in Table 14.8.1

Levels of Factor A	*Levels of Factor T* 1	2	3	*Total* $z_{i.} = \sum_{j=1}^{t} \bar{y}_{ij.}$
1	5	3	3	11
2	4	5	6	15
Total $z_{.j} = \sum_{i=1}^{a} \bar{y}_{ij.}$	9	8	9	26

Table 14.8.4

Reciprocal (h_{ij}) of n_{ij} in Table 14.8.2

Levels of Factor A	*Levels of Factor T* 1	2	3	*Total* $h_{i.}$
1	0.50	1.00	1.00	2.50
2	0.50	1.00	0.50	2.00
Total $h_{.j}$	1.00	2.00	1.50	4.50

We obtain $\sum_{i=1}^{a} h_{i.}^{-1} = (1/2.50) + (1/2.00) = 0.900$; $\bar{y}_A = [(11/2.50) + (15/2.00)]/0.900 = 11.900/0.900 = 13.2222$; $\sum_{i=1}^{2} z_{i.}^2/h_{i.} = [(11)^2/2.50] + [(15)^2/2.00] = 160.9000$; $A_{ms} = (1)^{-1}[160.900 - (0.900)(13.2222)^2] = 3.5556$; we obtained $E_{ms} = 2.0000$ from part (1). This gives $w_A = 3.5556/2.0000 = 1.7778$; and $F_{0.05:1,3} = 10.128$; so H_0 is not rejected. This answers part (2).

The answer to (3) is obtained by using (2) of Theorem 14.8.4 with $\ell_1 = 1/2, \ell_2 = -1/2$ for confidence limits on α_1^* and then with $\ell_1 = -1/2, \ell_2 = 1/2$ for confidence limits on α_2^*. We get ($t_{0.025:3} = 3.1825$)

$$\alpha_1^* : \frac{11}{6} - \frac{15}{6} \mp 3.1825\sqrt{\frac{(2.0000)[(\frac{1}{2})^2(2.50) + (-\frac{1}{2})^2(2.00)]}{9}}$$

or

$$-2.2579 \le \alpha_1^* \le 0.9246$$

$$\alpha_2^* : \frac{15}{6} - \frac{11}{6} \mp 1.59125 \qquad \text{or} \qquad -0.9246 \le \alpha_2^* \le 2.2579$$

14.9 Some Situations Described by Two-Factor Design Models

In previous sections we have discussed two-factor design models without specific reference to what kind of factors were involved. In this section we briefly discuss the different types of factors that might be modeled by a two-factor design. This section is only a short introduction since the subject is vast and a huge amount of literature is available. We shall illustrate with examples various situations that could be modeled by the two-factor design.

Example 14.9.1

Consider Example 14.1.4. In this investigation suppose that records are available on all oil wells that have been drilled in a certain location.

In each case the records reveal whether granite rock was encountered, the speed of the drill bit (factor A) in revolutions per minute, the pressure on the drill bit (factor T) in pounds per square inch, and rate (observation Y) that the drill bit penetrated the rock. The two factors are actually quantitative in nature, but the investigator might, for simplicity, consider four classes of speeds. For example, the various number of revolutions per minute might be labeled slow, medium, fast, and very fast. Pressure on the bit is also a quantitative factor, but the investigator might like to consider it qualitative by forming, say, five classes with various pressures being placed in the appropriate classes.

The data on the records have been "classified" by two factors: (1) the speed of the drill bit which has four levels; (2) the pressure on the drill bit which has five levels. Several observations (one for each well that was drilled through some solid granite) are recorded for combinations of the levels of the two factors. The model for these data is a two-factor design model, and the investigator would have to decide if the model would be one that includes an interaction term.

Undoubtedly there would be an unequal number of observations in each cell, so perhaps the model in Equation (14.1.10) would be used. Very important considerations in using the data for drawing inferences to a population are the definitions of the sampled and the target populations. If records from all oil wells that were drilled in a certain oil field are examined, then it appears that no sampling was performed and the investigator is studying the entire sampled population. However, if records on hundreds of wells are available and the investigator uses only a few of the records sampled at random from all of the available records, then the sampled population is the entire set of records and the target population would have to be defined, perhaps as the set of all *possible* wells that could have been drilled in the geographical area under consideration. What we wish to point out here is that the investigator should be as careful and precise as possible in his definitions so that his inferences will be valid and useful.

We define these types of two-factor design models as "two-factor observational" models. The investigator had no control over how the investigation was conducted; he merely observed the results, cross-tabulated factors of importance to him, and tried to determine if the factors were important and perhaps decide which levels were "best" in some sense. He should definitely examine the residuals to make a determination as to whether the assumptions on the errors ε_{ijm} are realistic.

Example 14.9.2

Next we discuss Example 14.1.2. In many ways this investigation is very similar to the one discussed in Example 14.9.1. However, it appears that the sampled and target populations are perhaps easier to identify. There are $7 \times 2 = 14$ target populations which are made up of the seven geographical areas and two sexes. Each population consists of the set of starting salaries for employees who started operating cash registers in all stores (of a specified size) within the past year. The sampled and target populations are the same in this example. A sample is obtained from each of these 14 populations and the observations are classified by location of the store (factor A at seven levels) and by sex (factor T at two levels).

So the factors are "classification" factors. Of course, we have greatly oversimplified the problem since there are certainly other factors of interest to study, such as length of time employed and size of store. Also, the sampling problem is somewhat complicated and must be carefully and scientifically accomplished. The main distinction between this investigation and the one described in Example 14.9.1 is that in the present example, the sampling is under the supervision of the investigator and that the study is carried out to see what the state of affairs is at the present time. In the previous example the data were already collected and the investigator could only examine the records. The present two-factor model could, however, be defined as a "two-factor survey" model, and perhaps one of the models in this chapter could be used to draw the desired inferences.

Example 14.9.3

In Example 14.1.1 the situation can be viewed in a different light from the two previous examples. Here there are two main populations that comprise the two levels of factor A: all Hereford cattle in a certain geographical region in a certain time interval comprise level 1 and similarly all Angus cattle comprise level 2.

From these well-defined populations, two animals from each are selected from each breed by some random process and fed level 1 of factor T (diet 1), two more animals are selected from each breed and fed level 2 of factor T (diet 2), and so on. The inference can be made as if there were actually ten populations involved.

All Angus cattle could have been fed level 1 of factor T (diet 1) and a sample of two animals selected at random for the observations Y_{111} and Y_{112}. These comprise a sample of size two from the population of all Angus cattle when fed diet 1. Conceptually, all the Angus cattle could have been fed diet 2 and two animals selected at random to obtain the observations Y_{121} and Y_{122}. These comprise a sample of size two from the population of all Angus cattle when fed diet 2. This could be continued for all five diets and repeated for the Hereford cattle.

So conceptually there are ten populations: (1) the population of all Angus cattle when fed diet 1; (2) the population of all Angus cattle when fed diet 2; . . . ; (10) the population of all Hereford cattle when fed diet 5. Of course, these populations are only conceptual since no animal will be fed more than one diet. However, since the investigator has decided to select and observe only two animals from each population, he might as well select the two animals first and then select the diet to give them.

This is the way the experiment is conducted. Ten Angus and ten Hereford animals are selected at random from the two populations; two Herefords are selected at random from the ten and fed diet 1, two are selected at random and fed diet 2, and so on. This is essentially equivalent to giving each diet to the entire populations and selecting two animals at random from each of the ten populations (obviously this procedure is impossible to perform). The two observations from breed i and diet j can be considered a random sample from the conceptual population of *all* animals of the ith breed if they were fed the jth diet.

In this investigation the sampled populations (although conceptual) are relatively easy to identify and define. Similarly for the target population. One principal difference between this example and the ones discussed in Examples 14.9.1 and 14.9.2 is that the diets (levels of factor T) are actually administered to the animals by the investigator and are not an inherent part of the makeup of the animals. This is not the case for factor A. In other words, any of the 20 animals could receive any one of the five levels of factor T (diets). However, no choice exists for factor A. An animal *cannot* be selected from a herd and randomly assigned by the investigator to be an Angus or a Hereford.

We designate the diets as a "treatment" factor and the breeds as a "classification" factor. Each animal that could receive any of the five treatments (diets) is defined to be an "experimental unit," and a factor is a "treatment" factor if the levels of the factor are applied by the investigator.

Example 14.9.4

Consider Example 14.1.5. Suppose that 480 students in a certain university who must take a course in remedial mathematics are assigned to 24 groups of 20 students each. These 24 groups are considered to be the "experimental units," and each of the 12 treatments (combination of each of the four methods of teaching with each of the three times during the day) is randomly assigned to one of the 24 groups so that each treatment is administered to two groups. This example differs from the previous one in that both factors are under the control of the researcher and are applied at random to the experimental units and hence are treatment factors.

The target population could be all similar classes in all colleges and universities. Since the experiment was conducted at one college during one semester, the sampled populations could be defined as all possible similar classes of size 20 of remedial mathematics for the past ten years at this university. However, strictly speaking, these classes were not randomly selected from these populations.

Perhaps a better way to view this type of problem is to consider the sampled population to be all possible experiments that *could* have been the result of the application of the 12 treatments to *these* 24 classes (experimental units). There are $(24!)/(2!)^{12}$ distinct arrangements. This can be seen by numbering the 24 classes from 1 through 24; so there are (24!) distinct arrangements of the classes. Each of 12 treatments is applied to two classes, and it is not necessary to distinguish between the two classes in any treatment. Hence the total number of distinct arrangements is $N = (24!)/(2!)^{12}$. Thus there are N *possible* outcomes of the randomization procedure, and these *possible* outcomes could be considered as the sampled population.

Actually only 1 of the randomizations resulted, and the experiment was conducted. So this could be considered a sample of size 1 from the N elements in the population, and the inference, in a relative-frequency probability sense, could be to this population. This way of looking at the investigation has many of the features of what are called "randomization models" in the subject called design of experiments. We shall not develop it further in this book but the interested reader can consult [K-2], [K-3], [S-4], and references contained there.

If instead of 24 classes of 20 students each, the experiment consisted of, say, $12r$ classes, and each of the 12 treatments was applied at random to r classes, the setup would be called a completely randomized experiment with r replications and with a 3×4 factorial treatment structure. For further information on completely randomized designs and factorial treatments, consult [C-5], [D-7], [D-8], [K-2], [K-8], [S-4], [S-7], [S-15], and [W-8].

Example 14.9.5

The last example that we discuss is Example 14.1.6. In a study of this kind there appear to be two factors, but actually only one of the factors is of interest. In Example 14.1.6 the agronomist is perhaps only interested in how the various levels of the fertilizer affect the height of the seedlings. The other factor, namely, location on the greenhouse bench, is considered not for its interest but for its influence on the height of the plant; the investigator wants to remove that influence from the result of the investigation.

In a rough sense if the model for the experiment was considered to be a one-factor design model, then the variation due to location on the bench (actually due to temperature and humidity) would be in the error term ε_{ij}, and σ^2 would be larger than if the location was considered to be a factor in the model and hence not included in the error term. Since the width of the confidence interval (actually, expected width) is directly proportional to σ, it is important to decrease σ if possible. Thus one of the so-called factors may not be a factor, that is, it may not be of interest to estimate it, but it is similar to a factor and the purpose is to improve the quality of the investigation (decrease σ) by considering it. This factor is generally referred to as a block and the design is a randomized block design. We would call this factor a "design" factor to distinguish it from a "classification" factor and a "treatment" factor. We shall not discuss this further, but it is very important; further information can be found in [C-6].

In this section we have discussed various situations where the two-factor design model can be useful in real-world investigations. Two additional points will be made about design models.

1. We have discussed two-factor design models in some detail, but extensions to three or more factors are also very useful; these are special cases of the model discussed in Chapter 13.
2. The distribution of the error terms in the design model may not be normally distributed; in this case tests of hypotheses, and sometimes confidence intervals, can be evaluated for very general distributions of the error terms by using the theory of permutation tests, the theory of randomization tests, and the theory of rank tests. The interested reader can consult [K-2], [K-3], [K-8], [S-4], and references contained therein.

14.10 Balanced Incomplete Block Models

A model that is sometimes considered in the theory of the two-factor design model is often referred to as the balanced incomplete block (BIB) model. Consider a two-factor model where one factor will be termed the "block" factor and the other the "treatment" factor. The model is a special case of the one discussed in Section 14.4. The n_{ij} values are only zeros and ones, and appear in a special pattern. We shall illustrate with examples.

Example 14.10.1

Suppose an investigator wants to examine the effect that different makes of washing machines (factor A) and different brands of soap (factor T)

have on the strength of fabric after 20 launderings. He wants to examine 15 brands of soap and he has ten washing machines he can use. The "washing machine" is not a factor of interest, but he feels that the effect of washing machines should be a design factor and eliminated from the error variance σ^2. So he will use the ten washing machines as ten blocks. If a "complete" two-factor design is used, this will require $10 \times 15 = 150$ different combinations of treatments and blocks (washing machines) and $150 \times 20 = 3000$ launderings. The size of this experiment is too large to complete with the time and money restrictions available, so the investigator may decide to use an "incomplete" two-factor design model, that is, each brand of soap will not be used with each make of washing machine. Thus the model will be given by Equation (14.1.7) with $n_{ij} = 0$ or 1 in a certain pattern determined by the investigator.

Example 14.10.2

Consider Example 14.1.6 and suppose that the experimenter wants to examine seven fertilizers, but on each bench in the greenhouse there is enough space for the experimental material of only three treatments. He feels that there is a temperature and humidity differential that will certainly affect the height of the new seedlings, so he decides to design his experiment in a manner that will enable him to eliminate these effects from the error term.

The investigator chooses a randomized block design where benches are blocks. But the benches available for the experiment are large enough for only three treatments each. He is not interested in estimating the differences among blocks but only in eliminating these effects from the error so that σ can be reduced. The layout of the experiment could be as shown below, where the number in each block is the treatment number.

Blocks (benches)

1	1 2 4
2	2 3 5
3	3 4 6
4	4 5 7
5	5 6 1
6	6 7 2
7	7 1 3

Temperature and humidity gradient ↓

Clearly, if blocks are considered as a factor, this appears to be a special case of the model in Equation (14.1.7). However, the particular n_{ij}'s that are zero (the missing observations) are designed to be such by the investigator. In this model there is the belief on the part of the investigator that an experiment with blocks that contain only three treatments will have smaller error variance than an experiment with blocks that contain seven treatments or an experiment that utilizes a *completely* randomized design.

Example 14.10.3

For another example consider an animal experiment where four different diets will be fed to lambs to determine what effect the diets have on the quality of the wool. The investigator knows that the differences among lambs will be a big factor in the quality of the wool, so he would like to eliminate as much of this difference as possible. He believes that twin lambs are very similar so he decides on a randomized block design where each block contains two units (twin lambs). The layout for this experiment is given below, where 6 sets of twins were used and the numbers in each block are the treatment (diet) numbers.

Sets of twin lambs		
1	1	2
2	1	3
3	1	4
4	2	3
5	2	4
6	3	4

The interest here is not in the differences among lambs but only in the differences among treatments (diets). This model can be viewed as a two-factor design model with unequal numbers (determined by the investigator) of observations in the cells. Restrictions may be required on the n_{ij} values in certain cases so that the "incomplete" two-factor model will have desired properties.

The restrictions that we discuss in this section are those that are required for what is generally referred to as a "balanced incomplete block" model. We refer to the α_i constants as blocks and the τ_j constants as treatments. We assume the investigation consists of b blocks and t treatments.

DEFINITION 14.10.1

Balanced Incomplete Block Models. *Let the model be defined by Equation* (14.1.7) *with the following restrictions on the* n_{ij}:

(1) *Each block contains k experimental units;*

(2) $k < t$, *that is, there are more treatments than there are experimental units per block;*

(3) *each treatment appears in r blocks and no more than once in any block;*

(4) *each pair of treatments appears together in exactly* λ *blocks.*

If these conditions are satisfied, the model in Equation (14.1.7) *is defined to be a balanced incomplete block model with b blocks, t treatments, r replications, and k treatments per block.*

From this definition it is easy to determine the following, since n_{ij} is the number (0 or 1) of times that treatment j appears in block i.

$$n_{i.} = \sum_{j=1}^{t} n_{ij} = k = \text{number of treatments (experimental units) in the } i\text{th block}$$

$$n_{.j} = \sum_{i=1}^{b} n_{ij} = r = \text{number of blocks in which the } j\text{th treatment appears (number of times } j\text{th treatment is replicated)}$$

$$n_{..} = rt = bk = \text{total number of observations}$$

$$\sum_{i=1}^{b} n_{ij}n_{ij'} = \lambda \text{ if } j \neq j'\text{; this is the number of blocks in which treatment } j \text{ and treatment } j' \text{ occur together.} \quad (14.10.1)$$

The following relationship exists among the numbers r, k, b, t, and λ:

$$\lambda = \frac{r(k-1)}{t-1} \tag{14.10.2}$$

This can be shown by considering any one treatment (say treatment 1). This treatment appears in exactly r blocks. The number of experimental units in *these* r blocks not occupied by treatment 1 is $r(k-1)$. But in these r blocks, treatment 1 appears with each of the remaining $t-1$ treatments in λ blocks; hence the number of experimental units involved is equal to $\lambda(t-1)$. Equate these two numbers and solve for λ to get the relationship in Equation (14.10.2).

We also note the following:

$$Y_{i..} = \text{total of the observations of the } i\text{th block}$$

$$Y_{.j.} = \text{total of the observations of the } j\text{th treatment}$$

$$Y_{...} = \text{total of all observations}$$

$$\sum_{i=1}^{b} n_{ij} Y_{i..} = B_j, \text{ say, } = \text{total of the observations in all the blocks that contain treatment } j \quad (14.10.3)$$

The normal equations are given in Equation (14.4.2), but if the relationships in Equation (14.10.1) are used, they simplify to:

$$\mu : bk\hat{\mu} + k\sum_{i=1}^{b}\hat{\alpha}_i + r\sum_{j=1}^{t}\hat{\tau}_j = Y_{...}$$

$$\alpha_i : \quad k\hat{\mu} + k\hat{\alpha}_i + \sum_{j=1}^{t} n_{ij}\hat{\tau}_j = Y_{i..} \qquad \text{for } i = 1, 2, \ldots, b$$

$$\tau_j : \quad r\hat{\mu} + \sum_{i=1}^{b} n_{ij}\hat{\alpha}_i + r\hat{\tau}_j = Y_{.j.} \qquad \text{for } j = 1, 2, \ldots, t \quad (14.10.4)$$

For this set of normal equations it is easily seen that $p = b + t + 1$ and $K = b + t - 1$; so to solve the system we can use the two nonestimable conditions $\sum \tau_j = \sum \alpha_i = 0$. If we solve the α equations for $\hat{\mu} + \hat{\alpha}_i$, we get $\hat{\mu} + \hat{\alpha}_i = (1/k)[Y_{i..} - \sum_{j=1}^{t} n_{ij}\hat{\tau}_j]$ for $i = 1, 2, \ldots, b$. If we substitute these into the τ equations we get

$$r\hat{\tau}_j + \sum_{i=1}^{b} n_{ij}(\hat{\mu} + \hat{\alpha}_i) = Y_{.j.}$$

or

$$r\hat{\tau}_j + \sum_{i=1}^{b} n_{ij}\left[\left(\frac{1}{k}\right)\left(Y_{i..} - \sum_{j'=1}^{t} n_{ij'}\hat{\tau}_{j'}\right)\right] = Y_{.j.} \qquad \text{for } j = 1, 2, \ldots, t$$

Simplifying gives us

$$\left[r - \left(\frac{1}{k}\right)\sum_{i=1}^{b} n_{ij}^2\right]\hat{\tau}_j - \left(\frac{1}{k}\right)\left(\sum_{\substack{j'=1 \\ j' \neq j}}^{t}\sum_{i=1}^{b} n_{ij}n_{ij'}\hat{\tau}_{j'}\right) = Y_{.j.} - \left(\frac{1}{k}\right)\left(\sum_{i=1}^{b} n_{ij}Y_{i..}\right)$$

$$= Y_{.j.} - \left(\frac{1}{k}\right)B_j = G_j \text{ say.}$$

But $\sum_{i=1}^{b} n_{ij}n_{ij'} = \lambda$ if $j \neq j'$, and $n_{ij}^2 = n_{ij}$, so by using these and

$\sum_{j'=1,j'\neq j}^{t} \hat{\tau}_{j'} = -\hat{\tau}_j$, we get $[r - (r/k) + (\lambda/k)]\hat{\tau}_j = G_j$ for $j = 1, 2, \ldots, t$. Note $\sum_{j'=1,j'\neq j}^{t} \hat{\tau}_{j'} = -\hat{\tau}_j$ comes from the nonestimable condition $\sum_{j=1}^{t} \hat{\tau}_j = 0$.

If we use the relationships in Equations (14.10.1) and (14.10.2), we get

$$\left(\frac{\lambda t}{k}\right)\hat{\tau}_j = G_j \qquad \text{for } j = 1, 2, \ldots, t \tag{14.10.5}$$

It is straightforward to show $\mathscr{E}[G_j] = (\lambda t/k)(\tau_j - \bar{\tau}_.)$, $\text{var}[G_j] = [r(k-1)/k]\sigma^2$, and $\text{cov}[G_j, G_{j'}] = -\lambda\sigma^2/k$ for $j \neq j'$. From these results we get the following theorem.

THEOREM 14.10.1

Let the model be given by Definition 14.10.1.

(1) *All contrasts of the* τ_j *are estimable, and the best unbiased estimator of* $\delta = \sum_{j=1}^{t} c_j\tau_j$ *is* $\hat{\delta} = (k/\lambda t)\sum_{j=1}^{t} c_j G_j$ *if* $\sum_{j=1}^{t} c_j = 0$, *where* $G_j = Y_{.j.} - (1/k)B_j$. *Assume the errors* ε_{ijm} *satisfy Case I in* (2) *through* (8); $N = bk - b - t + 1$.

(2) *The UMVU estimator of* σ^2 *is*

$$\hat{\sigma}^2 = \left(\frac{1}{N}\right)\left[\sum_{i=1}^{b}\sum_{j=1}^{t}\sum_{m=1}^{n_{ij}} Y_{ijm}^2 - \left(\frac{1}{k}\right)\sum_{i=1}^{b} Y_{i..}^2 - \left(\frac{k}{\lambda t}\right)\sum_{j=1}^{t} G_j^2\right]$$

(3) G_j *is distributed* $N(g_j : (\lambda t/k)(\tau_j - \bar{\tau}_.), r(k-1)\sigma^2/k)$, *and* $\text{cov}[G_j, G_{j'}] = -\lambda\sigma^2/k$ *for* $j \neq j'$.

(4) *The UMVU estimator of* δ *in* (1) *is* $\hat{\delta}$, *which is distributed* $N(\hat{\delta} : \sum_{j=1}^{t} c_j\tau_j, \sigma^2 k \sum_{j=1}^{t} c_j^2/\lambda t)$.

(5) $U = N\hat{\sigma}^2/\sigma^2$ *is distributed* $\chi^2(u : N)$ *and is independent of* $G_1, G_2, \ldots, G_t$ *and* $\hat{\delta}$.

(6) *One-at-a-time* $1 - \alpha$ *confidence limits on* δ *are given by*

$$\hat{\delta} \mp t_{\alpha/2:N}\sqrt{\frac{\hat{\sigma}^2 k \sum_{j=1}^{t} c_j^2}{\lambda t}}$$

(7) W *is distributed* $F(w : t-1, N; \gamma)$; $\gamma = (2\sigma^2)^{-1}(\lambda t/k)\sum_{j=1}^{t}(\tau_j - \bar{\tau})^2$, *where* $W = (k/\lambda t)\sum_{j=1}^{t} G_j^2/(t-1)\hat{\sigma}^2$.

(8) *The generalized likelihood ratio test of size* α *of* $H_0 : \tau_1 = \tau_2 = \cdots = \tau_t$ *vs.* H_a *: at least one equality is an inequality is this: Reject*

H_0 if and only if $w \geq F_{\alpha:t-1,N}$. The power of the test is

$$\Pi(\gamma) = \int_{F_{\alpha:t-1,N}}^{\infty} F(w : t-1, N; \gamma)\, dw$$

Note 1. We have used γ for the noncentrality parameter in this theorem since we have used λ (which is conventional) as the number of blocks in which every pair of treatments appear together.

An ANOVA table for the balanced incomplete block model is given in Table 14.10.1.

The computation of the quantities necessary for estimation and tests in the balanced incomplete block model is quite easy. The format exhibited in Table 14.10.2 may prove useful. From this table the quantities for total, $R(\mu, \boldsymbol{\alpha}, \boldsymbol{\tau})$, and

Table 14.10.1

ANOVA Table for Incomplete Block Model

Source	*d.f.*	*S.S.*
Total	bk	$\sum_{i=1}^{b}\sum_{j=1}^{t}\sum_{m=1}^{n_{ij}} y_{ijm}^2$
$R(\mu, \boldsymbol{\alpha}, \boldsymbol{\tau})$	$b + t - 1$	$\left(\frac{1}{k}\right)\sum_{i=1}^{b} y_{i..}^2 + \left(\frac{k}{\lambda t}\right)\sum_{j=1}^{t} g_j^2$
$R(\mu, \boldsymbol{\alpha})$	b	$\left(\frac{1}{k}\right)\sum_{i=1}^{b} y_{i..}^2$
$R(H_0)$	$t - 1$	$\left(\frac{k}{\lambda t}\right)\sum_{j=1}^{t} g_j^2$
Error	$N = bk - b - t + 1$	$\sum_{i=1}^{b}\sum_{j=1}^{t}\sum_{m=1}^{n_{ij}} y_{ijm}^2 - R(\mu, \boldsymbol{\alpha}, \boldsymbol{\tau})$

Table 14.10.2

Format for Computations in Balanced Incomplete Block Model

Treatment Number	*Treatment Total*	*Total of Blocks Containing Treatment j; b_j Is Computed Value of B_j*	$g_j = y_{.j.} - \left(\frac{1}{k}\right)b_j$	$\left(\frac{k}{\lambda t}\right)g_j$ *Estimates* $\tau_j - \bar{\tau}_.$
1	$y_{.1.}$	b_1	g_1	$\tau_1 - \bar{\tau}_.$
2	$y_{.2.}$	b_2	g_2	$\tau_2 - \bar{\tau}_.$
⋮	⋮	⋮	⋮	⋮
t	$y_{.t.}$	b_t	g_t	$\tau_t - \bar{\tau}_.$

$R(H_0)$ in Table 14.10.1 can be easily computed. Also, $\hat{\sigma}^2$, w, and the quantities needed for estimation and tests can also be easily computed.

Note 2. For a check on the computations, one should note

$$\sum_{j=1}^{t} g_j = 0 \qquad \sum_{j=1}^{t} y_{.j.} = y_{...} \qquad \sum_{j=1}^{t} b_j = ky_{...}$$

Example 14.10.4

The data given in Table 14.10.3 were artificially constructed [M-5] and we assume a balanced incomplete block model. The numbers in parentheses are the treatment numbers. Find the ANOVA table; find the best unbiased estimates of $\tau_j - \bar{\tau}$ for $j = 1, 2, \ldots, t$. We note that $t = 7$, $b = 7$, $k = 3$, $r = 3$, $\lambda = 1$, and $k/\lambda t = 3/7$.

The computations in Table 14.10.2 are displayed in Table 14.10.4.

The ANOVA table is given in Table 14.10.5.

From these results confidence intervals can be computed on $\sum c_j\tau_j$ when $\sum c_j = 0$.

Table 14.10.3

Data for Example 14.10.4

Block	*Data*			*Block Total*
1	1.54 (1)	2.45 (2)	1.97 (4)	5.96
2	5.02 (2)	7.11 (3)	5.98 (5)	18.11
3	8.75 (3)	5.00 (4)	2.52 (6)	16.27
4	6.07 (4)	9.01 (5)	14.95 (7)	30.03
5	4.52 (5)	1.50 (6)	2.25 (1)	8.27
6	0.51 (6)	2.46 (7)	1.25 (2)	4.22
7	17.41 (7)	4.25 (1)	12.25 (3)	33.91
				total 116.77

Table 14.10.4

Computations for Table 14.10.2

Treatment Number	*Treatment Total*	b_j	g_j	$(k/\lambda t)g_j = \widehat{\tau_j - \bar{\tau}_.}$
1	8.04	48.14	−8.0067	−3.4314
2	8.72	28.29	−0.7100	−0.3043
3	28.11	68.29	5.3467	2.2914
4	13.04	52.26	−4.3800	−1.8771
5	19.51	56.41	0.7067	0.3029
6	4.53	28.76	−5.0567	−2.1671
7	34.82	68.16	12.1000	5.1857
Total	116.77	350.31	0.0000	0.0000

Table 14.10.5

ANOVA Table for Example 14.10.4

Source	*d.f.*	*S.S.*	*M.S.*	*F*
Total	21	1080.0585		
$R(\mu, \alpha, \tau)$	13	1044.0924		
$R(\mu, \alpha)$	7	922.0323		
$R(H_0)$	6	122.0601	20.3434	4.5250
Error	8	35.9661	4.4958	

14.11 Test for Interaction

In this section a test for interaction is derived for the model in Equation (14.7.2). We shall actually derive a test for interaction for a more general model and then discuss various special cases.

Let the model without interaction be Case I of the design model $\mathbf{Y} = \mathbf{X}\boldsymbol{\beta} + \boldsymbol{\varepsilon}$ given in Definition 13.1.1; a special case of this is the two-factor design model in Equation (14.1.4).

There may be experimental situations when an investigator wants to examine a more complete model. He may feel that the factors, and the levels of these factors, represented by the elements in $\boldsymbol{\beta}$ are the only factors of major importance for the situation under investigation, but one of his aims is to determine how these factors interact. So he may want to make a preliminary examination of a more complete model that includes nonlinear functions of the elements in $\boldsymbol{\beta}$.

A more complete model is written as

$$\mathbf{Y} = \mathbf{X}\boldsymbol{\beta} + \mathbf{F}\boldsymbol{\delta} + \boldsymbol{\varepsilon}$$

where $\mathbf{F} = [f_{ij}(\cdot)]$ is an $n \times m$ matrix and the elements of $\mathbf{F}$, namely $f_{ij}(\cdot)$, are *known* nonadditive functions of estimable functions of $\boldsymbol{\beta}$; hence we can write the *ij*th element as $f_{ij}(\mathbf{X}\boldsymbol{\beta})$. Also, $\boldsymbol{\delta}$ is an unknown $m \times 1$ vector.

The objective is to test the hypothesis $\boldsymbol{\delta} = \mathbf{0}$ and thus determine if, in fact, $\mathbf{Y} = \mathbf{X}\boldsymbol{\beta} + \boldsymbol{\varepsilon}$ is the correct model or whether a more complete model should be used that includes nonlinear functions of the elements in $\boldsymbol{\beta}$. If we relate this to the model in Equation (14.7.2), then $\mathbf{Y} = \mathbf{X}\boldsymbol{\beta} + \boldsymbol{\varepsilon}$ is $Y_{ij} = \mu^* + \alpha_i^* + \tau_j^* + \varepsilon_{ij}$, and $\mathbf{Y} = \mathbf{X}\boldsymbol{\beta} + \mathbf{F}\boldsymbol{\delta} + \boldsymbol{\varepsilon}$ is $Y_{ij} = \mu^* + \alpha_i^* + \tau_j^* + \delta\alpha_i^*\tau_j^* + \varepsilon_{ij}$. Hence $\boldsymbol{\delta}$ is a 1×1 vector and $\mathbf{F}$ is an $at \times 1$ vector with elements $\alpha_i^*\tau_j^*$.

To derive the test $H_0 : \boldsymbol{\delta} = \mathbf{0}$ *vs.* $H_a : \boldsymbol{\delta} \neq \mathbf{0}$ in the model $\mathbf{Y} = \mathbf{X}\boldsymbol{\beta} + \mathbf{F}\boldsymbol{\delta} + \boldsymbol{\varepsilon}$, when $\boldsymbol{\varepsilon}$ is distributed $N(\boldsymbol{\varepsilon} : \mathbf{0}, \sigma^2\mathbf{I})$, we assume for the present that $\mathbf{F}$ is a matrix of *known* numbers and the rank of $[\mathbf{X}, \mathbf{F}]$ is r, where $K < r < n$ and K is the rank of $\mathbf{X}$. We use Equation (6.3.11) to derive the test statistic.

We must obtain $\hat{\sigma}_\Omega^2$ from the full model, which is

$$\mathbf{Y} = [\mathbf{X}, \mathbf{F}]\begin{bmatrix}\boldsymbol{\beta}\\ \boldsymbol{\delta}\end{bmatrix} + \boldsymbol{\varepsilon}$$

and we must obtain $\hat{\sigma}_\omega^2$ from the model reduced by the hypothesis $H_0 : \boldsymbol{\delta} = \mathbf{0}$. The reduced model is $\mathbf{Y} = \mathbf{X}\boldsymbol{\beta} + \boldsymbol{\varepsilon}$. We get

$$\begin{aligned}\hat{\sigma}_\Omega^2 &= n^{-1}\mathbf{Y}'(\mathbf{I} - [\mathbf{X}, \mathbf{F}][\mathbf{X}, \mathbf{F}]^-)\mathbf{Y}\\ &= \mathbf{Y}'\{\mathbf{I} - \mathbf{X}\mathbf{X}^- - [(\mathbf{I} - \mathbf{X}\mathbf{X}^-)\mathbf{F}][(\mathbf{I} - \mathbf{X}\mathbf{X}^-)\mathbf{F}]^-\}\mathbf{Y}\end{aligned}$$

since by Theorem 1.5.19

$$[\mathbf{X}, \mathbf{F}][\mathbf{X}, \mathbf{F}]^- = \mathbf{X}\mathbf{X}^- + [(\mathbf{I} - \mathbf{X}\mathbf{X}^-)\mathbf{F}][(\mathbf{I} - \mathbf{X}\mathbf{X}^-)\mathbf{F}]^-$$

For $\hat{\sigma}_\omega^2$ we obtain

$$\hat{\sigma}_\omega^2 = n^{-1}\mathbf{Y}'(\mathbf{I} - \mathbf{X}\mathbf{X}^-)\mathbf{Y}$$

and for W we get

$$\begin{aligned}W &= \left(\frac{\hat{\sigma}_\omega^2 - \hat{\sigma}_\Omega^2}{\hat{\sigma}_\Omega^2}\right)\left(\frac{n - p}{q}\right)\\ &= \left(\frac{\mathbf{Y}'\{[(\mathbf{I} - \mathbf{X}\mathbf{X}^-)\mathbf{F}][(\mathbf{I} - \mathbf{X}\mathbf{X}^-)\mathbf{F}]^-\}\mathbf{Y}}{\mathbf{Y}'\{(\mathbf{I} - \mathbf{X}\mathbf{X}^-) - [(\mathbf{I} - \mathbf{X}\mathbf{X}^-)\mathbf{F}][(\mathbf{I} - \mathbf{X}\mathbf{X}^-)\mathbf{F}]^-\}\mathbf{Y}}\right)\left(\frac{n - r}{r - K}\right)\end{aligned}$$

and $n - r$ is the rank of the matrix

$$\mathbf{I} - \mathbf{X}\mathbf{X}^- - [(\mathbf{I} - \mathbf{X}\mathbf{X}^-)\mathbf{F}][(\mathbf{I} - \mathbf{X}\mathbf{X}^-)\mathbf{F}]^- = \mathbf{I} - [\mathbf{X}, \mathbf{F}][\mathbf{X}, \mathbf{F}]^-$$

since the matrix is idempotent and the rank is equal to its trace. We get

$$\text{tr}[\mathbf{I} - [\mathbf{X}, \mathbf{F}][\mathbf{X}, \mathbf{F}]^-] = \text{tr}[\mathbf{I}] - \text{tr}[[\mathbf{X}, \mathbf{F}][\mathbf{X}, \mathbf{F}]^-] = n - \text{rank}[\mathbf{X}, \mathbf{F}] = n - r$$

The rank of the matrix $[(\mathbf{I} - \mathbf{X}\mathbf{X}^-)\mathbf{F}][(\mathbf{I} - \mathbf{X}\mathbf{X}^-)\mathbf{F}]^-$ is clearly $r - K$. Also, W is distributed as $F(w : r - K, n - r)$ when H_0 is true, and a size α test is this: Reject H_0 if and only if $w \geq F_{\alpha:r-K,n-r}$. However, w, the computed value of W, contains the matrix $\mathbf{F}$ of parameters and is not observable.

We recall that the functional *form* of the elements $f_{ij}(\mathbf{X}\boldsymbol{\beta})$ in $\mathbf{F}$ was assumed known, but $\mathbf{X}\boldsymbol{\beta}$ is not known since $\boldsymbol{\beta}$ is not known. We shall replace $\mathbf{X}\boldsymbol{\beta}$ by $\mathbf{X}\hat{\boldsymbol{\beta}}$ in $f_{ij}(\mathbf{X}\boldsymbol{\beta})$, where $\mathbf{X}\hat{\boldsymbol{\beta}}$ is the UMVU estimator of $\mathbf{X}\boldsymbol{\beta}$ in the reduced model $\mathbf{Y} = \mathbf{X}\boldsymbol{\beta} + \boldsymbol{\varepsilon}$. We get $\mathbf{X}\hat{\boldsymbol{\beta}} = \mathbf{X}\mathbf{X}^-\mathbf{Y}$ and $f_{ij}(\mathbf{X}\boldsymbol{\beta})$ is replaced by $f_{ij}(\mathbf{X}\hat{\boldsymbol{\beta}}) = f_{ij}(\mathbf{X}\mathbf{X}^-\mathbf{Y})$.

When these estimators are substituted into $\mathbf{F}$, we denote the resulting matrix by $\hat{\mathbf{F}}$; when $\hat{\mathbf{F}}$ is substituted for $\mathbf{F}$ into W, we denote the resulting random variable by $\hat{W}$. We can write $\hat{W}$ as

$$\hat{W} = \left(\frac{\{(\mathbf{I} - \mathbf{X}\mathbf{X}^-)\mathbf{Y}\}'\hat{\mathbf{F}}\{[(\mathbf{I} - \mathbf{X}\mathbf{X}^-)\hat{\mathbf{F}}]'[(\mathbf{I} - \mathbf{X}\mathbf{X}^-)\hat{\mathbf{F}}]\}^-\hat{\mathbf{F}}'(\mathbf{I} - \mathbf{X}\mathbf{X}^-)\mathbf{Y}}{\{(\mathbf{I} - \mathbf{X}\mathbf{X}^-)\mathbf{Y}\}'[\mathbf{I} - \hat{\mathbf{F}}\{[(\mathbf{I} - \mathbf{X}\mathbf{X}^-)\hat{\mathbf{F}}]'[(\mathbf{I} - \mathbf{X}\mathbf{X}^-)\hat{\mathbf{F}}]\}^-\hat{\mathbf{F}}']\{(\mathbf{I} - \mathbf{X}\mathbf{X}^-)\mathbf{Y}\}} \right)$$
$$\times \left(\frac{n - r}{r - K} \right) = \left(\frac{\mathbf{Z}'\hat{\mathbf{A}}\mathbf{Z}}{\mathbf{Z}'(\mathbf{I} - \hat{\mathbf{A}})\mathbf{Z}} \right) \left(\frac{n - r}{r - K} \right)$$

where

$$\hat{\mathbf{A}} = (\mathbf{I} - \mathbf{X}\mathbf{X}^-)\hat{\mathbf{F}}\{[(\mathbf{I} - \mathbf{X}\mathbf{X}^-)\hat{\mathbf{F}}]'[(\mathbf{I} - \mathbf{X}\mathbf{X}^-)\hat{\mathbf{F}}]\}^-\hat{\mathbf{F}}'(\mathbf{I} - \mathbf{X}\mathbf{X}^-)$$

and

$$\mathbf{Z} = (\mathbf{I} - \mathbf{X}\mathbf{X}^-)\mathbf{Y}$$

When H_0 is true, $\mathbf{Y}$ is distributed $N(\mathbf{y} : \mathbf{X}\boldsymbol{\beta}, \sigma^2\mathbf{I})$ and $\mathbf{Z}$ is distributed $N(\mathbf{z} : \mathbf{0}, \sigma^2(\mathbf{I} - \mathbf{X}\mathbf{X}^-))$. To find the distribution of $\hat{W}$ when H_0 is true, we first find the distribution of $(\hat{W} \mid \hat{\mathbf{F}} = \mathbf{F}_0)$, where $\mathbf{F}_0$ is any fixed matrix such that the distribution of $(\hat{W} \mid \hat{\mathbf{F}} = \mathbf{F}_0)$ is defined.

Since any element in $\hat{\mathbf{F}}$ is a function of $\mathbf{X}\hat{\boldsymbol{\beta}}$ (which is $\mathbf{X}\mathbf{X}^-\mathbf{Y}$), and since $\mathbf{X}\hat{\boldsymbol{\beta}}$ is independent of $(\mathbf{I} - \mathbf{X}\mathbf{X}^-)\mathbf{Y}$, this means that $\hat{\mathbf{F}}$ is independent of $(\mathbf{I} - \mathbf{X}\mathbf{X}^-)\mathbf{Y}$; that is, $\hat{\mathbf{F}}$ is independent of $\mathbf{Z}$. So $\mathbf{Z}_0 = (\mathbf{Z} \mid \hat{\mathbf{F}} = \mathbf{F}_0)$ is distributed $N(\mathbf{z}_0 : \mathbf{0}, \sigma^2(\mathbf{I} - \mathbf{X}\mathbf{X}^-))$; that is, $\mathbf{Z}$ and $\mathbf{Z}_0$ have the same distribution. Thus

$$W_0 = (\hat{W} \mid \hat{\mathbf{F}} = \mathbf{F}_0) = \left(\frac{\mathbf{Z}_0'\mathbf{A}_0\mathbf{Z}_0}{\mathbf{Z}_0'(\mathbf{I} - \mathbf{A}_0)\mathbf{Z}_0} \right) \left(\frac{n - r}{r - K} \right)$$

is distributed $F(w_0 : r - K, n - r)$ when H_0 is true, where

$$\mathbf{A}_0 = (\mathbf{I} - \mathbf{XX}^-)\mathbf{F}_0\{[(\mathbf{I} - \mathbf{XX}^-)\mathbf{F}_0]'[(\mathbf{I} - \mathbf{XX}^-)\mathbf{F}_0]\}^-\mathbf{F}_0'(\mathbf{I} - \mathbf{XX}^-)$$

That this is the distribution of $(\hat{W} \mid \hat{\mathbf{F}} = \mathbf{F}_0)$ is proved by using the appropriate theorems in Chapter 4 and showing that $(\mathbf{A}_0/\sigma^2)\sigma^2(\mathbf{I} - \mathbf{XX}^-)$ is idempotent of rank $r - K$; that $[(\mathbf{I} - \mathbf{A}_0)/\sigma^2](\mathbf{I} - \mathbf{XX}^-)\sigma^2$ is idempotent of rank $n - r$; and that $(\mathbf{A}_0/\sigma^2)[\sigma^2(\mathbf{I} - \mathbf{XX}^-)](\mathbf{I} - \mathbf{A}_0)/\sigma^2 = \mathbf{0}$.

Since the distribution of $(\hat{W} \mid \hat{\mathbf{F}} = \mathbf{F}_0)$ does not depend on the conditioned value $\mathbf{F}_0$ of the random matrix $\hat{\mathbf{F}}$, the marginal distribution of $\hat{W}$ is the same as the distribution of $(\hat{W} \mid \hat{\mathbf{F}} = \mathbf{F}_0)$; that is, $\hat{W}$ is distributed as $F(w : r - K, n - r)$ when H_0 is true. Thus a size α test of $H_0 : \boldsymbol{\delta} = \mathbf{0}$ *vs.* $H_a : \boldsymbol{\delta} \neq \mathbf{0}$ is this: Reject H_0 if and only if $\hat{w} \geq F_{\alpha:r-K,n-r}$ ($\hat{w}$ is the computed value of $\hat{W}$).

We have proved the following theorem.

THEOREM 14.11.1

Let the model be Case I of the design model $\mathbf{Y} = \mathbf{X}\boldsymbol{\beta} + \boldsymbol{\varepsilon}$ *given in Definition 13.1.1. Consider the extended model* $\mathbf{Y} = \mathbf{X}\boldsymbol{\beta} + \mathbf{F}\boldsymbol{\delta} + \boldsymbol{\varepsilon}$, *where* $\boldsymbol{\varepsilon}$ *is distributed* $N(\boldsymbol{\varepsilon} : \mathbf{0}, \sigma^2\mathbf{I})$; $\mathbf{F} = [f_{ij}(\mathbf{X}\boldsymbol{\beta})]$, *where each* $f_{ij}(\mathbf{X}\boldsymbol{\beta})$ *is a nonadditive known function of* $\mathbf{X}\boldsymbol{\beta}$; $\mathbf{F}$ *has size* $n \times m$; $[\mathbf{X}, \mathbf{F}]$ *has rank* r, *where* $K < r < n$ *(generally* $r = K + m$); $\boldsymbol{\delta}$ *is an* $m \times 1$ *vector of unknown parameters; and* $\hat{\mathbf{F}} = [f_{ij}(\mathbf{XX}^-\mathbf{Y})]$. *A size* α *test of* $H_0 : \boldsymbol{\delta} = \mathbf{0}$ *vs.* $H_a : \boldsymbol{\delta} \neq \mathbf{0}$ *is this: Reject* H_0 *if and only if* $\hat{w} \geq F_{\alpha:r-K,n-r}$, *where* $\hat{w}$ *is the computed value of* $\hat{W}$, *and* $\hat{W}$ *is*

$$\hat{W} = \left(\frac{\mathbf{Y}'\{[(\mathbf{I} - \mathbf{XX}^-)\hat{\mathbf{F}}][(\mathbf{I} - \mathbf{XX}^-)\hat{\mathbf{F}}]^-\}\mathbf{Y}}{\mathbf{Y}'(\mathbf{I} - \mathbf{XX}^-)\mathbf{Y} - \mathbf{Y}'\{[(\mathbf{I} - \mathbf{XX}^-)\hat{\mathbf{F}}][(\mathbf{I} - \mathbf{XX}^-)\hat{\mathbf{F}}]^-\}\mathbf{Y}}\right)\left(\frac{n - r}{r - K}\right)$$

$\hat{W}$ is obtained by using *known* nonadditive functions $f_{ij}(\mathbf{X}\hat{\boldsymbol{\beta}})$; however, *any* nonadditive functions of $\mathbf{X}\hat{\boldsymbol{\beta}}$ can be used and Theorem 14.11.1 is still valid but the power will be affected; see [M-5], [M-6], and [S-4].

In 1 through 10 below we show that Theorem 14.7.2 is a special case of Theorem 14.11.1.

1. The model $\mathbf{Y} = \mathbf{X}\boldsymbol{\beta} + \boldsymbol{\varepsilon}$ is $Y_{ij} = \mu + \alpha_i + \tau_j + \varepsilon_{ij}$, or in reparameterized form, $Y_{ij} = \mu^* + \alpha_i^* + \tau_j^* + \varepsilon_{ij}$.
2. The model $\mathbf{Y} = \mathbf{X}\boldsymbol{\beta} + \mathbf{F}\boldsymbol{\delta} + \boldsymbol{\varepsilon}$ is

$$Y_{ij} = \mu + \alpha_i + \tau_j + \delta(\alpha_i - \bar{\alpha}_.)(\tau_j - \bar{\tau}_.) + \varepsilon_{ij}$$

   or in reparameterized form, $Y_{ij} = \mu^* + \alpha_i^* + \tau_j^* + \delta\alpha_i^*\tau_j^* + \varepsilon_{ij}$, where $\alpha_i^* = \alpha_i - \bar{\alpha}_.$, $\tau_j^* = \tau_j - \bar{\tau}_.$, and $\mu^* = \mu + \bar{\alpha}_. + \bar{\tau}_.$.
3. $\mathbf{F}$ is an $at \times 1$ vector whose elements are $f_{ij}(\mathbf{X}\boldsymbol{\beta}) = f_{ij}(\alpha_i^*, \tau_j^*) = \alpha_i^*\tau_j^*$.

4. $\boldsymbol{\delta}$ is a scalar.

5. By Theorem 14.2.1, $\hat{\alpha}_i^* = \bar{Y}_{i.} - \bar{Y}_{..}$ and $\hat{\tau}_j^* = \bar{Y}_{.j} - \bar{Y}_{..}$, so the general element in $\hat{\mathbf{F}}$ is

$$\hat{f}_{ij} = f_{ij}(\hat{\alpha}_i^*, \hat{\tau}_j^*) = \hat{\alpha}_i^* \hat{\tau}_j^* = (\bar{Y}_{i.} - \bar{Y}_{..})(\bar{Y}_{.j} - \bar{Y}_{..})$$

6. The general element in $(\mathbf{I} - \mathbf{XX}^-)\mathbf{Y}$ is $Y_{ij} - \bar{Y}_{i.} - \bar{Y}_{.j} + \bar{Y}_{..}$, so

$$\mathbf{Y}'(\mathbf{I} - \mathbf{XX}^-)\hat{\mathbf{F}} = \sum_{i=1}^{a} \sum_{j=1}^{t} (Y_{ij} - \bar{Y}_{i.} - \bar{Y}_{.j} + \bar{Y}_{..})(\bar{Y}_{i.} - \bar{Y}_{..})(\bar{Y}_{.j} - \bar{Y}_{..})$$

7. Since $\mathbf{F}$ is an $at \times 1$ vector, $(\mathbf{I} - \mathbf{XX}^-)\hat{\mathbf{F}} = \mathbf{b}$, say, is an $at \times 1$ vector, and by Problem 1.12, $\mathbf{b}^- = \mathbf{b}'/\mathbf{b}'\mathbf{b}$, so

$$\mathbf{Y}'\{[(\mathbf{I} - \mathbf{XX}^-)\hat{\mathbf{F}}][(\mathbf{I} - \mathbf{XX}^-)\hat{\mathbf{F}}]^-\}\mathbf{Y} = \mathbf{Y}'\mathbf{bb}^-\mathbf{Y} = \frac{\mathbf{Y}'\mathbf{bb}'\mathbf{Y}}{(\mathbf{b}'\mathbf{b})}$$

8. To compute $(\mathbf{I} - \mathbf{XX}^-)\hat{\mathbf{F}}$, replace $\mathbf{Y}$ by $\hat{\mathbf{F}}$ (that is, Y_{ij} by $\hat{f}_{ij}$) in $(\mathbf{I} - \mathbf{XX}^-)\mathbf{Y}$. The ijth element of $(\mathbf{I} - \mathbf{XX}^-)\hat{\mathbf{F}}$ is

$$\hat{f}_{ij} - \hat{\bar{f}}_{i.} - \hat{\bar{f}}_{.j} + \hat{\bar{f}}_{..} = \hat{f}_{ij} = (\bar{Y}_{i.} - \bar{Y}_{..})(\bar{Y}_{.j} - \bar{Y}_{..})$$

since $\sum_{i=1}^{a} \hat{f}_{ij} = \sum_{j=1}^{t} \hat{f}_{ij} = 0$; so $\mathbf{b} = \hat{\mathbf{F}}$.

9. $$\mathbf{Y}'\{[(\mathbf{I} - \mathbf{XX}^-)\hat{\mathbf{F}}][(\mathbf{I} - \mathbf{XX}^-)\hat{\mathbf{F}}]^-\}\mathbf{Y} = \frac{\mathbf{Y}'\mathbf{bb}'\mathbf{Y}}{(\mathbf{b}'\mathbf{b})}$$

$$= \frac{\left[\sum_{i=1}^{a} \sum_{j=1}^{t} (Y_{ij} - \bar{Y}_{i.} - \bar{Y}_{.j} + \bar{Y}_{..})(\bar{Y}_{i.} - \bar{Y}_{..})(\bar{Y}_{.j} - \bar{Y}_{..})\right]^2}{\sum_{i=1}^{a} (\bar{Y}_{i.} - \bar{Y}_{..})^2 \sum_{j=1}^{t} (\bar{Y}_{.j} - \bar{Y}_{..})^2} = N_{SS}$$

defined in Theorem 14.7.2.

10. Also,

$$\mathbf{Y}'(\mathbf{I} - \mathbf{XX}^-)\mathbf{Y} = \sum_{i=1}^{a} \sum_{j=1}^{t} (Y_{ij} - \bar{Y}_{i.} - \bar{Y}_{.j} + \bar{Y}_{..})^2$$

$n = at$, $K = a + t - 1$, and $r = a + t$; if these are substituted into the formula for $\hat{W}$ in Theorem 14.11.1, the result is the formula for W in Theorem 14.7.2. This proves Theorem 14.7.2.

From the above discussion we can obtain a result that shows how $\hat{W}$ is simplified when $\mathbf{F}$ is a vector. This is stated in the next theorem.

THEOREM 14.11.2

Let the model be given in Theorem 14.11.1, *except* $\mathbf{F}$ *is an* $n \times 1$ *vector* (*hence* $m = 1$ *and* $r = K + 1$) *denoted by* $\hat{\mathbf{f}} = [f_i(\cdot)]$. *The formula for* $\hat{W}$ *is*

$$\hat{W} = \left(\frac{(\mathbf{Y}'\mathbf{b})^2/\mathbf{b}'\mathbf{b}}{\mathbf{Y}'(\mathbf{I} - \mathbf{X}\mathbf{X}^-)\mathbf{Y} - [(\mathbf{Y}'\mathbf{b})^2/\mathbf{b}'\mathbf{b}]}\right)(n - K - 1)$$

where $\mathbf{b} = (\mathbf{I} - \mathbf{X}\mathbf{X}^-)\hat{\mathbf{f}}$ *and* $\hat{\mathbf{f}} = [f_i(\mathbf{X}\mathbf{X}^-\mathbf{Y})]$.

The models in this chapter for which Theorem 14.11.2 can be used to test for interaction is the two-factor design model with no more than one observation per cell. This includes the model in Section 14.8 with $\gamma_{ij}^* = \delta\alpha_i^*\tau_j^*$ and with the added restriction on the n_{ij} that $n_{ij} = 0$ or $n_{ij} = 1$ and not all $n_{ij} = 1$. Of course, the restriction of connectedness (when $\delta = 0$) is also essential.

For this model two applications of the square root method discussed in Section 7.3 can be used to compute the quantities needed to compute $\hat{w}$ in Theorem 14.11.2. Use the format below:

$$\left[\begin{array}{c|c} \mathbf{X}'\mathbf{X} & \mathbf{X}'\mathbf{y} \\ \hline \mathbf{T} & \mathbf{t} \end{array}\right]$$

and compute $\hat{\boldsymbol{\beta}}$ by the backward procedure (actually by solving the triangular system $\mathbf{T}\hat{\boldsymbol{\beta}} = \mathbf{t}$); then compute $\mathbf{X}\hat{\boldsymbol{\beta}} = \mathbf{X}\mathbf{X}^-\mathbf{y}$, $f_i(\mathbf{X}\mathbf{X}^-\mathbf{y}) = \hat{f}_i$, $\hat{\mathbf{f}}$, and $\mathbf{X}'\hat{\mathbf{f}}$. Use the format below:

$$\left[\begin{array}{c|c} \mathbf{X}'\mathbf{X} & \mathbf{X}'\hat{\mathbf{f}} \\ \hline \mathbf{T} & \mathbf{t}_0 \end{array}\right]$$

From these results one can compute $\mathbf{t}_0'\mathbf{t}_0 = \hat{\mathbf{f}}'\mathbf{X}\mathbf{X}^-\hat{\mathbf{f}}$, $\mathbf{b}'\mathbf{b} = \hat{\mathbf{f}}'\hat{\mathbf{f}} - \mathbf{t}_0'\mathbf{t}_0$, $\mathbf{t}'\mathbf{t}_0 = \mathbf{y}'\mathbf{X}\mathbf{X}^-\hat{\mathbf{f}}$, $\mathbf{y}'\mathbf{b} = \mathbf{y}'\hat{\mathbf{f}} - \mathbf{t}'\mathbf{t}_0$, and $\mathbf{y}'\mathbf{y} - \mathbf{t}'\mathbf{t} = \mathbf{y}'(\mathbf{I} - \mathbf{X}\mathbf{X}^-)\mathbf{y}$. These are the quantities needed for $\hat{w}$ in Theorem 14.11.2.

If the model is given in Equation (14.7.2), the computations given in Section 14.7 and exhibited in Table 14.7.1 should be used.

Problems

14.1. The data in the table below are assumed to be the result of an investigation of four drugs for controlling pain. Each drug is administered by three different methods. The model is assumed to be a two-factor design with no interaction and one observation per cell. The observation y_{ij} is the amount of a certain substance in the blood of a person two hours after receiving the drug. The model for the data is assumed to be Case I of Equation (14.1.5). Write out the normal equations for these data.

		Drug			
		A	*B*	*C*	*D*
Method of Administering	1	12.6	14.1	10.4	11.4
	2	11.3	12.2	21.0	11.8
	3	15.1	16.0	21.1	14.1

14.2. In Problem 14.1 find the UMVU estimate of σ^2.

14.3. In Problem 14.1 find the best unbiased estimates of the main effects of the four drugs.

14.4. In Problem 14.1 set 95 percent one-at-a-time confidence intervals on the main effects of the three methods of administering the drugs.

14.5. In Problem 14.1 set 90 percent simultaneous confidence intervals on the differences of all pairs of the main effects of the four drugs.

14.6. In Problem 14.1 exhibit an ANOVA table.

14.7. Prove Theorem 14.2.3.

14.8. Exhibit the details for the proof of Theorem 14.2.4.

14.9. An investigation was made to determine how the speed of drill bits and the viscosities of a lubricant affect the speed with which a drill can penetrate granite rock. Records were examined for wells that had been drilled using four viscosities of a lubricant and three bit speeds. Information on three wells for each speed-viscosity combination was recorded and the data are given in the table below.

		Viscosity of Lubricant (Factor T)			
		1	2	3	4
Speed of Drill (Factor *A*)	1	16.1 15.8 15.1	12.7 15.3 11.2	8.1 9.3 6.2	14.4 15.8 17.3
	2	20.2 18.7 16.3	11.2 14.6 13.0	10.7 12.1 15.4	16.2 17.3 19.1
	3	12.1 18.1 15.9	16.1 14.2 13.9	13.5 12.7 10.1	12.8 14.1 15.5

The model for these data is assumed to be Case I of Equation (14.1.6). Write out the normal equations for these data.

14.10. Find the UMVU estimate of σ^2 for the data in Problem 14.9.

14.11. In Problem 14.9 find the best unbiased estimates of the main effects of the viscosities of the lubricant.

14.12. In Problem 14.9 find 90 percent one-at-a-time confidence intervals on the main effects of the speeds of the drill.

14.13. In Problem 14.9 find 90 percent simultaneous confidence intervals on the differences of all pairs of viscosities of the lubricant.

14.14. In Problem 14.9 exhibit an ANOVA table.

14.15. Prove Theorem 14.3.1.

14.16. Prove Theorem 14.3.2.

14.17. A simple example of Case I of the model in Equation (14.1.7) is given in the table below. Exhibit the table of n_{ij}.

		Levels of Factor T			
		1	2	3	4
Levels of Factor A	1	6 4 3	4 2	3	4 6
	2	2	3	1 2	6 5

14.18. In Problem 14.17 exhibit the normal equations.

14.19. In Problem 14.17 exhibit the format in Equation (14.4.6) by using the two non-estimable conditions $\mu = 0$ and $\alpha_2 = 0$.

14.20. In Problem 14.19 reduce the format by the square root procedure and obtain the format in Equation (14.4.7).

14.21. In Problem 14.17 find the UMVU estimate of σ^2.

14.22. In Problem 14.17 find the UMVU estimates of $\tau_j - \tau_{j'}$ for all $j \neq j'$.

14.23. In Problem 14.17 find 95 percent one-at-a-time confidence limits on $\tau_1 - \tau_2$, $\tau_1 + \tau_2 - 2\tau_3$, and $\tau_1 - \tau_4$.

14.24. In Problem 14.17 test $H_0 : \tau_1 = \tau_2 = \tau_3 = \tau_4$ *vs.* H_a : at least one equality is an inequality.

14.25. In Problem 14.17 set a 90 percent confidence interval on σ.

14.26. In Problem 14.17 exhibit the ANOVA table given in Table 14.4.3.

14.27. Prove Theorem 14.4.1.

14.28. Use all the normal equations in Problem 14.17 and reduce the entire set by the square root procedure to exhibit Method 3 of Section 13.5.

14.29. In Problem 14.28 solve for $\tilde{\boldsymbol{\beta}}$.

14.30. From the result of Problem 14.28, find the UMVU estimate of σ^2 and demonstrate that the answer is the same as the answer to Problem 14.21.

14.31. From the result of Problem 14.28, find the best unbiased estimate of $\tau_j - \tau_{j'}$ for all $j \neq j'$ and demonstrate that the estimates are the same as obtained in Problem 14.22.

14.32. Exhibit all distinct 2×2 tables that can be derived from the two-way table of μ_{ij}'s below.

		Levels of Factor T			
		1	2	3	4
Levels of Factor *A*	1	3	1	4	9
	2	−1	−3	0	4
	3	5	3	6	11

14.33. In Problem 14.32 find the interaction of all 2×2 tables.

14.34. In Problem 14.32 do factors A and T interact?

14.35. In a two-way design model, with observations y_{ij} for $i = 1, 2, \ldots, a$ and $j = 1, 2, \ldots, t$, show that

$$[4at(a-1)(t-1)]^{-1} \sum_{i=1}^{a} \sum_{i'=1}^{a} \sum_{j=1}^{t} \sum_{j'=1}^{t} (y_{ij} - y_{i'j} - y_{ij'} + y_{i'j'})^2$$

$$= [(a-1)(t-1)]^{-1} \sum_{i=1}^{a} \sum_{j=1}^{t} (y_{ij} - \bar{y}_{i.} - \bar{y}_{.j} + \bar{y}_{..})^2$$

and thus demonstrate that $\hat{\sigma}^2$ in a two-way model without interaction and with one observation per cell can be evaluated as a constant times the sum of squares of all 2×2 contrasts.

14.36. Suppose that the table below is a table of observations y_{ij}.
(a) Evaluate all 2 × 2 contrasts..
(b) Evaluate $\sum_{i=1}^{a} \sum_{j=1}^{t} (y_{ij} - \bar{y}_{i.} - \bar{y}_{.j} + \bar{y}_{..})^2$.
(c) For this example demonstrate the formula in Problem 14.35.

		Levels of Factor T			
		1	2	3	4
Levels of Factor A	1	3	5	2	2
	2	6	8	6	4
	3	0	2	1	9

14.37. Use Case I of Equation (14.1.8) for the model for the data in Problem 14.9 and write out the normal equations.

14.38. In Problem 14.37 test the hypothesis of no interaction.

14.39. In Problem 14.37 exhibit the UMVU estimate of the main effect of the first level of factor A at the third level of factor T.

14.40. In Problem 14.37 find the UMVU estimate of the average main effect of the first level of factor A (averaged over the four levels of factor T). Repeat for the second level of factor A (averaged over the four levels of factor T).

14.41. In Problem 14.37 set 95 percent one-at-a-time confidence intervals on α_1^*, α_2^*, and α_3^*.

14.42. In Problem 14.37 exhibit the ANOVA table given in Table 14.6.1.

14.43. From the results of Problem 14.42, test $H_0 : \alpha_1^* = \alpha_2^* = \alpha_3^*$.

14.44. From the results of Problem 14.42, test $H_0 : \tau_1^* = \tau_2^* = \tau_3^* = \tau_4^*$.

14.45. Supply the details for the proof of Theorem 14.6.2.

14.46. In Problem 14.1 exhibit the table of residuals.

14.47. In Problem 14.1 write out all distinct 2 × 2 tables and compute the interaction of each.

14.48. Use the results of Problems 14.46 and 14.47 and compute $\hat{\sigma}^2$ from each.

14.49. Prove Theorem 14.5.1.

14.50. The data in the table below are assumed to fit Case I of the model in Equation (14.1.9). Test the hypothesis of additivity. Exhibit the ANOVA table similar to Table 14.7.1.

		Levels of Factor T			
		1	2	3	4
Levels of Factor A	1	5.3	4.8	11.0	8.1
	2	11.2	1.1	7.4	4.5
	3	18.2	7.3	12.2	9.7

14.51. In Problem 14.50 exhibit the table of residuals. Exhibit all distinct 2×2 tables and compute the interaction for each.

14.52. In Problem 14.50 eliminate the (1, 1) observation, that is, the observation 5.3, and test the resulting data for additivity.

14.53. In Problem 14.52 find the best unbiased estimates of the average main effects of the three levels of factor A.

14.54. Assume the data in Problem 14.17 are from Case I of the model in Equation (14.1.10). Exhibit the normal equations.

14.55. In Problem 14.54 exhibit the table of z_{ij} with column and row totals and means; exhibit the table of h_{ij} with column and row totals and means.

14.56. In Problem 14.54 find the best unbiased estimate of the average main effects $\hat{\alpha}_1^*, \hat{\alpha}_2^*; \hat{\tau}_1^*, \hat{\tau}_2^*, \hat{\tau}_3^*, \hat{\tau}_4^*$.

14.57. In Problem 14.54 test for interaction.

14.58. Assume interaction is present and test the hypothesis $\tau_1^* = \cdots = \tau_4^*$ for the data in Problem 14.54.

14.59. In Problem 14.54 assume the model is nonadditive and set 95 percent one-at-a-time confidence intervals on $\tau_1^*, \tau_2^*, \tau_3^*, \tau_4^*; \alpha_1^*, \alpha_2^*$.

14.60. Prove part 11, page 554; that is, show

$$R(\mu, \tau) = \sum_{j=1}^{t} \frac{Y_{.j.}^2}{n_{.j}}$$

14.61. In Example 14.4.1 show that $\mathbf{t}_1'\mathbf{t}_1 = \sum_{i=1}^{a} (y_{i..}^2/n_{i.})$.

CHAPTER 15

Components-of-Variance Models

15.1 Introduction

The model to be discussed in this chapter is defined in Section 5.5. In Section 15.2 we discuss point estimation, interval estimation, and hypotheses tests for a special case of this model, the one-factor model, and in Section 15.3 we give some information that may be used in more general situations. Section 15.4 is devoted to the two-factor model with equal numbers; Section 15.5 contains a summary of the three-factor and four-factor models with equal numbers. In Section 15.6 we give an approximation that can often be used in components-of-variance models. Finally in Section 15.7 is a proof of the general theory for balanced complete models.

Before proceeding with a discussion of special cases, the general components-of-variance model is defined along with the notation to be used.

DEFINITION 15.1.1

Components-of-Variance Model. *Consider the model*

$$\mathbf{Y} = \mathbf{XB} + \boldsymbol{\varepsilon}$$

where $\mathbf{Y}$ *is an* $n \times 1$ *observable random vector;* $\mathbf{X}$ *is an* $n \times p$ *observable non-random design matrix, as given in Definition* 13.5.1, *which can be written as* $\mathbf{X} = [\mathbf{X}_0, \mathbf{X}_1, \ldots, \mathbf{X}_q]$ *where* $\mathbf{X}_0 = \mathbf{1}$ *and* $\mathbf{X}_i$ *is an* $n \times p_i$ *matrix for* $i = 0, 1, \ldots, q$ *(hence* $p_0 = 1$ *and* $\sum_{i=0}^{q} p_i = p$); and $\boldsymbol{\varepsilon}$ *is an* $n \times 1$ *unobservable random vector.* $\mathbf{B}$ *is a* $p \times 1$ *unobservable vector that can be written* $\mathbf{B}' = [\mu, \mathbf{B}_1', \ldots, \mathbf{B}_q']$ *where*

μ is a scalar parameter and $\mathbf{B}_i$ is a $p_i \times 1$ random vector. The following distributional properties are assumed:

(1) *The vectors $\mathbf{B}_1, \mathbf{B}_2, \ldots, \mathbf{B}_q$, and $\boldsymbol{\varepsilon}$ are pairwise uncorrelated;*

(2) $\mathscr{E}[\mathbf{B}_i] = \mathbf{0}$, $\mathbf{cov}[\mathbf{B}_i] = \sigma_i^2\mathbf{I}$, *and* $\sigma_i^2 > 0$ *for* $i = 1, 2, \ldots, q$;

(3) $\boldsymbol{\varepsilon}$ *is an* $n \times 1$ *unobservable random vector with mean vector* $\mathbf{0}$ *and covariance matrix* $\sigma_\varepsilon^2\mathbf{I}$. (15.1.1)

The parameter space is $\Omega = \{(\mu, \sigma_1^2, \ldots, \sigma_q^2, \sigma_\varepsilon^2): -\infty < \mu < \infty,\ \sigma_i^2 > 0$ *for* $i = 1, 2, \ldots, q;\ \sigma_\varepsilon^2 > 0\}$. *These specifications define a components-of-variance model.*

Note 1. Two special cases will be considered for the distribution of the random vectors $\mathbf{B}_1, \mathbf{B}_2, \ldots, \mathbf{B}_q$, and $\boldsymbol{\varepsilon}$. Case I: The random vectors $\mathbf{B}_1, \mathbf{B}_2, \ldots, \mathbf{B}_q$, and $\boldsymbol{\varepsilon}$ are jointly normally distributed. Case II: All random variables contained in the vectors $\mathbf{B}_1, \mathbf{B}_2, \ldots, \mathbf{B}_q$, and $\boldsymbol{\varepsilon}$ are mutually independent; the third and fourth moments of each random variable in $\mathbf{B}_i$ are ξ_i^3 and ξ_i^4, respectively, for $i = 1, 2, \ldots, q + 1$, where the third and fourth moments of each random variable in $\boldsymbol{\varepsilon}$ are denoted by ξ_{q+1}^3 and ξ_{q+1}^4, respectively.

Notation 1. We have used capital $\mathbf{B}$ and $\mathbf{B}_i$ for random vectors, which is a departure from the custom of using capital boldface letters for matrices (except $\mathbf{Y}$, $\mathbf{Z}$, and so on). When it simplifies notation, we sometimes use the symbol $\mathbf{B}_{q+1}$ for $\boldsymbol{\varepsilon}$.

Notation 2. Throughout this chapter we use the following notation:

$$\boldsymbol{\Sigma} = \mathbf{cov}[\mathbf{Y}] \qquad \mathscr{E}[\mathbf{YY}'] = \boldsymbol{\Sigma}_0 \qquad \mathbf{X}_i\mathbf{X}_i' = \mathbf{V}_i$$

for $i = 0, 1, \ldots, q, q + 1$. Note that

$$\mathbf{V}_0 = \mathbf{J} \quad \text{and} \quad \mathbf{V}_{q+1} = \mathbf{I}$$

THEOREM 15.1.1

Let the model be given by Definition 15.1.1. *Then:*

(1) $\mathbf{Y} = \mathbf{XB} + \boldsymbol{\varepsilon}$ *can be written* $\mathbf{Y} = \mathbf{1}\mu + \sum_{i=1}^q \mathbf{X}_i\mathbf{B}_i + \boldsymbol{\varepsilon}$.

(2) $\mathscr{E}[\mathbf{Y}] = \boldsymbol{\mu} = \mathbf{1}\mu$, $\mathbf{cov}[\mathbf{Y}] = \sum_{i=1}^{q+1} \mathbf{X}_i\mathbf{X}_i'\sigma_i^2 = \sum_{i=1}^q \mathbf{V}_i\sigma_i^2 + \sigma_\varepsilon^2\mathbf{I} = \boldsymbol{\Sigma}$, *and* $\mathscr{E}[\mathbf{YY}'] = \boldsymbol{\Sigma}_0 = \mathbf{J}\mu^2 + \boldsymbol{\Sigma}$.

(3) *For Case I the $n \times 1$ vector* $\mathbf{Y}$ *is distributed* $N(\mathbf{y} : \boldsymbol{\mu}, \boldsymbol{\Sigma})$, *where* $\boldsymbol{\mu}$ *and* $\boldsymbol{\Sigma}$ *are defined in* (2).

Proof

By Definition 15.1.1 we can substitute $[\mathbf{1}, \mathbf{X}_1, \ldots, \mathbf{X}_q]$ for $\mathbf{X}$, $[\mu, \mathbf{B}_1', \ldots, \mathbf{B}_q']$ for $\mathbf{B}$ and get

$$\mathbf{XB} = [\mathbf{1}, \mathbf{X}_1, \ldots, \mathbf{X}_q] \begin{bmatrix} \mu \\ \mathbf{B}_1 \\ \vdots \\ \mathbf{B}_q \end{bmatrix} = \mathbf{1}\mu + \sum_{i=1}^{q} \mathbf{X}_i \mathbf{B}_i$$

The result (1) follows from this.

To prove (2) we use (1) and get

$$\mathscr{E}[\mathbf{Y}] = \mathscr{E}\left[\mu\mathbf{1} + \sum_{i=1}^{q} \mathbf{X}_i\mathbf{B}_i + \boldsymbol{\varepsilon}\right] = \mu\mathbf{1}$$

since $\mathscr{E}[\mathbf{B}_i] = \mathbf{0}$ for $i = 1, 2, \ldots, q$ and $\mathscr{E}[\boldsymbol{\varepsilon}] = \mathbf{0}$; also,

$$\begin{aligned} \boldsymbol{\Sigma} = \mathbf{cov}[\mathbf{Y}] &= \mathscr{E}[\mathbf{Y} - \mathscr{E}[\mathbf{Y}]][\mathbf{Y} - \mathscr{E}[\mathbf{Y}]]' \\ &= \mathscr{E}\left[\left(\sum_{i=1}^{q} \mathbf{X}_i\mathbf{B}_i + \boldsymbol{\varepsilon}\right)\left(\sum_{j=1}^{q} \mathbf{X}_j\mathbf{B}_j + \boldsymbol{\varepsilon}\right)'\right] \\ &= \mathscr{E}\left[\sum_{i=1}^{q} \mathbf{X}_i\mathbf{B}_i\mathbf{B}_i'\mathbf{X}_i' + \boldsymbol{\varepsilon}\boldsymbol{\varepsilon}'\right] = \sum_{i=1}^{q} \mathbf{X}_i\mathbf{X}_i'\sigma_i^2 + \sigma_\varepsilon^2\mathbf{I} \end{aligned}$$

since

$$\mathscr{E}[\mathbf{B}_i\mathbf{B}_i'] = \sigma_i^2\mathbf{I} \qquad \mathscr{E}[\mathbf{B}_i\mathbf{B}_j'] = \mathbf{0} \qquad \text{for } i \neq j$$

$$\mathscr{E}[\boldsymbol{\varepsilon}\boldsymbol{\varepsilon}'] = \sigma_\varepsilon^2\mathbf{I} \qquad \mathscr{E}[\mathbf{B}_i\boldsymbol{\varepsilon}'] = \mathbf{0}$$

Clearly $\mathscr{E}[\mathbf{YY}'] = \mu^2\mathbf{X}_0\mathbf{X}_0' + \boldsymbol{\Sigma}$ and (2) is proved. Part (3) follows directly from (1) and (2).

15.2 One-Factor Components-of-Variance Model; Point Estimation, Confidence Intervals, and Tests

The model to be discussed in this section is sometimes referred to as a "one-fold nested model" or a "one-way classification model." The model will be defined and best unbiased estimators of the parameters will be exhibited.

DEFINITION 15.2.1

One-Factor Components-of-Variance Model. *Consider the model* $Y_{ij} = \mu + A_i + \varepsilon_{ij}$ *for* $i = 1, 2, \ldots, I > 1$ *and* $j = 1, 2, \ldots, J > 1$, *where* $\mathscr{E}[A_i] = 0$, $var[A_i] = \sigma_A^2$, $\mathscr{E}[\varepsilon_{ij}] = 0$, *and* $var[\varepsilon_{ij}] = \sigma_\varepsilon^2$. *The random variables* Y_{ij} *are observable; the random variables* $A_1, A_2, \ldots, A_I, \varepsilon_{11}, \varepsilon_{12}, \ldots, \varepsilon_{IJ}$ *are pairwise uncorrelated and unobservable;* μ, σ_A^2, *and* σ_ε^2 *are unobservable parameters. The parameter space* Ω *is defined by* $\Omega = \{(\mu, \sigma_A^2, \sigma_\varepsilon^2) : -\infty < \mu < \infty, \sigma_A^2 > 0, \sigma_\varepsilon^2 > 0\}$. *These specifications define a one-factor components-of-variance model with equal numbers in the subclasses.*

Note 1. Two special cases of this model will be discussed. Case I: The random variables $A_1, A_2, \ldots, A_I, \varepsilon_{11}, \varepsilon_{12}, \ldots, \varepsilon_{IJ}$ are jointly normally distributed. Case II: The random variables $A_1, A_2, \ldots, A_I$, ε_{11}, $\varepsilon_{12}, \ldots, \varepsilon_{IJ}$ are mutually independent and $\mathscr{E}[A_i^3] = \xi_A^3$, $\mathscr{E}[A_i^4] = \xi_A^4$, $\mathscr{E}[\varepsilon_{ij}^3] = \xi_\varepsilon^3$, $\mathscr{E}[\varepsilon_{ij}^4] = \xi_\varepsilon^4$. This model can be related to the general model in Definition 15.1.1. We see that $q = 1$, $\mathbf{B}_1' = [A_1, A_2, \ldots, A_I]$, $\sigma_1^2 = \sigma_A^2$, $p_1 = I$, and $n = IJ$.

To find point estimators of the parameters in this model, we do not resort to the maximum likelihood procedure directly since this is a tedious task. Instead, we proceed by examining the same partition of the total sum of squares that was used for the one-factor *design* model. The next theorem states the results.

THEOREM 15.2.1

Let the model be given in Definition 15.2.1 *for Case I. Then:*

(1) $U_1 = IJ\bar{Y}_{..}^2/(\sigma_\varepsilon^2 + J\sigma_A^2)$ *is distributed* $\chi^2(u_1 : 1; \lambda)$, *where* $\lambda = IJ\mu^2/2(\sigma_\varepsilon^2 + J\sigma_A^2)$.

(2) $U_2 = \sum_{i=1}^I \sum_{j=1}^J (\bar{Y}_{i.} - \bar{Y}_{..})^2/(\sigma_\varepsilon^2 + J\sigma_A^2)$ *is distributed* $\chi^2(u_2 : I - 1)$.

(3) $U_3 = \sum_{i=1}^I \sum_{j=1}^J (Y_{ij} - \bar{Y}_{i.})^2/\sigma_\varepsilon^2$ *is distributed* $\chi^2(u_3 : I(J - 1))$.

(4) U_1, U_2, *and* U_3 *are jointly independent.*

Proof

Since the Y_{ij} are distributed normally, it follows that $\bar{Y}_{..}$ is also distributed normally. But $\bar{Y}_{..} = \mu + \bar{A}_. + \bar{\varepsilon}_{..}$, so $\mathscr{E}[\bar{Y}_{..}] = \mu$, $\text{var}[\bar{Y}_{..}] = (\sigma_A^2/I) + (\sigma_\varepsilon^2/IJ)$, and by Corollary 4.2.1.3, $\bar{Y}_{..}^2/[(\sigma_A^2/I) + (\sigma_\varepsilon^2/IJ)] = IJ\bar{Y}_{..}^2/(\sigma_\varepsilon^2 + J\sigma_A^2) = U_1$ is distributed $\chi^2(u_1 : 1; \lambda)$, where $\lambda = IJ\mu^2/2(\sigma_\varepsilon^2 + J\sigma_A^2)$; this proves (1).

To prove (2) we note that the $\bar{Y}_{i.} = \mu + A_i + \bar{\varepsilon}_{i.}$ are distributed $NID(\bar{y}_{i.} : \mu, \sigma_A^2 + \sigma_\varepsilon^2/J)$. If we define the $I \times 1$ vector $\mathbf{Y}_0$ by $\mathbf{Y}_0' = [\bar{Y}_{1.}, \ldots, \bar{Y}_{I.}]$, it follows that $\mathbf{Y}_0$ is distributed $\mathbf{N}(\mathbf{y}_0 : \mu\mathbf{1}, \sigma^2\mathbf{I})$, where

$\sigma^2 = \sigma_A^2 + \sigma_\varepsilon^2/J$. Also,

$$U_2 = \sum_{i=1}^{I} \frac{(\bar{Y}_{i.} - \bar{Y}_{..})^2}{\sigma^2} = \frac{\mathbf{Y}_0'(\mathbf{I} - [1/I]\mathbf{J})\mathbf{Y}_0}{\sigma^2}$$

is distributed $\chi^2(u_2 : I - 1)$ since $[(\mathbf{I} - [1/I]\mathbf{J})/\sigma^2](\sigma^2\mathbf{I}) = \mathbf{I} - (1/I)\mathbf{J}$ is idempotent of rank $I - 1$ and $\lambda = (\mathbf{1}\mu)'(\mathbf{I} - [1/I]\mathbf{J})\mathbf{1}\mu/2\sigma^2 = 0$. This proves (2).

To prove (3) we examine

$$W_i = \sum_{j=1}^{J} \frac{(Y_{ij} - \bar{Y}_{i.})^2}{\sigma_\varepsilon^2} = \sum_{j=1}^{J} \frac{(\mu + A_i + \varepsilon_{ij} - \mu - A_i - \bar{\varepsilon}_{i.})^2}{\sigma_\varepsilon^2}$$
$$= \sum_{j=1}^{J} \frac{(\varepsilon_{ij} - \bar{\varepsilon}_{i.})^2}{\sigma_\varepsilon^2}$$

For each i the random variables ε_{ij} are distributed $NID(\varepsilon_{ij} : 0, \sigma_\varepsilon^2)$, so $W_i = \sum_{j=1}^{J} (\varepsilon_{ij} - \bar{\varepsilon}_{i.})^2/\sigma_\varepsilon^2$ is distributed $\chi^2(w : J - 1)$. The W_i for $i = 1, 2, \ldots, I$ are jointly independent since the ε_{ij} are jointly independent, so $U_3 = \sum_{i=1}^{I} W_i$ is distributed $\chi^2(u_3 : I(J - 1))$ and $\sum_{i=1}^{I} W_i = \sum_{i=1}^{I} \sum_{j=1}^{J} (Y_{ij} - \bar{Y}_{i.})^2/\sigma_\varepsilon^2$. This proves (3).

To prove (4) we use the identity

$$Y_{ij} = \bar{Y}_{..} + (\bar{Y}_{i.} - \bar{Y}_{..}) + (Y_{ij} - \bar{Y}_{i.}) = Z + Z_i + W_{ij} \quad (15.2.1)$$

say. First we show that the three sets of random variables $\{Z\}$, $\{Z_i\}$, and $\{W_{ij}\}$ are jointly independent. Since Y_{ij} is distributed normally, we have only to show $\text{cov}[Z, Z_i] = 0$, $\text{cov}[Z, W_{ij}] = 0$, and $\text{cov}[Z_i, W_{i'j}] = 0$. We note that $\mathscr{E}[\bar{Y}_{..}] = \mu$, and $\mathscr{E}[Z_i] = \mathscr{E}[W_{ij}] = 0$ for all i and j; so we have the following:

$$\begin{aligned}
\text{cov}[Z, Z_i] &= \mathscr{E}[ZZ_i] = \mathscr{E}[\bar{Y}_{..}(\bar{Y}_{i.} - \bar{Y}_{..})] \\
&= \mathscr{E}[(\mu + \bar{A}_{.} + \bar{\varepsilon}_{..})(\mu + A_i + \bar{\varepsilon}_{i.} - \mu - \bar{A}_{.} - \bar{\varepsilon}_{..})] \\
&= \mathscr{E}[(\bar{A}_{.} + \bar{\varepsilon}_{..})(A_i - \bar{A}_{.} + \bar{\varepsilon}_{i.} - \bar{\varepsilon}_{..})] \\
&= \mathscr{E}[\bar{A}_{.}(A_i - \bar{A}_{.})] + \mathscr{E}[\bar{\varepsilon}_{..}(\bar{\varepsilon}_{i.} - \bar{\varepsilon}_{..})] \\
&= \mathscr{E}[A_i\bar{A}_{.}] - \mathscr{E}[\bar{A}_{.}^2] + \mathscr{E}[\bar{\varepsilon}_{..}\bar{\varepsilon}_{i.}] - \mathscr{E}[\bar{\varepsilon}_{..}^2] \\
&= \frac{\sigma_A^2}{I} - \frac{\sigma_A^2}{I} + \frac{\sigma_\varepsilon^2}{IJ} - \frac{\sigma_\varepsilon^2}{IJ} = 0
\end{aligned}$$

By a similar procedure it is easy to show the remaining two covariances are also zero. The proof of the theorem is now complete.

If we square both sides of the identity in Equation (15.2.1) and sum over i and j, all cross products vanish, and we obtain (i is summed from 1 to I and

j is summed from 1 to J)

$$\sum_{j=1}^{J}\sum_{i=1}^{I} Y_{ij}^2 = IJ\bar{Y}_{..}^2 + \sum_{i=1}^{I}\sum_{j=1}^{J}(\bar{Y}_{i.} - \bar{Y}_{..})^2 + \sum_{i=1}^{I}\sum_{j=1}^{J}(Y_{ij} - \bar{Y}_{i.})^2 \tag{15.2.2}$$

Each term is a quadratic form in the random variables Y_{ij}, so if we define $\mathbf{Y}$ by $\mathbf{Y} = [Y_{11}, \ldots, Y_{1J}, Y_{21}, \ldots, Y_{IJ}]'$, we can write Equation (15.2.2) as

$$\mathbf{Y}'\mathbf{Y} = \mathbf{Y}'\mathbf{A}_0\mathbf{Y} + \mathbf{Y}'\mathbf{A}_1\mathbf{Y} + \mathbf{Y}'\mathbf{A}_2\mathbf{Y} \tag{15.2.3}$$

Since $\mathbf{Y}$ is distributed $\mathbf{N}(\mathbf{y} : \mathbf{1}\mu, \boldsymbol{\Sigma})$, where $\mathscr{E}[\mathbf{Y}] = \mathbf{1}\mu$ and $\mathbf{cov}[\mathbf{Y}] = \boldsymbol{\Sigma}$, we use Theorems 4.4.3 and 4.5.3 to prove the following.

THEOREM 15.2.2

In Theorem 15.2.1 *the results below follow where the* $\mathbf{A}_i$ *are defined by Equations* (15.2.2) *and* (15.2.3).

(1) $\boldsymbol{\Sigma}\mathbf{A}_0/(\sigma_\varepsilon^2 + J\sigma_A^2)$ *is an idempotent matrix of rank* 1.

(2) $\boldsymbol{\Sigma}\mathbf{A}_1/(\sigma_\varepsilon^2 + J\sigma_A^2)$ *is an idempotent matrix of rank* $I - 1$.

(3) $\boldsymbol{\Sigma}\mathbf{A}_2/\sigma_\varepsilon^2$ *is an idempotent matrix of rank* $I(J - 1)$.

(4) $\mathbf{A}_0\boldsymbol{\Sigma}\mathbf{A}_1 = \mathbf{A}_0\boldsymbol{\Sigma}\mathbf{A}_2 = \mathbf{A}_1\boldsymbol{\Sigma}\mathbf{A}_2 = \mathbf{0}$.

From these results we prove a theorem about the matrices $\mathbf{A}_0$, $\mathbf{A}_1$, $\mathbf{A}_2$, and $\boldsymbol{\Sigma}$ that will enable us to find UMVU estimators of μ, σ_A^2, and σ_ε^2.

THEOREM 15.2.3

Let the model be given by Definition 15.2.1; *let the matrices* $\mathbf{A}_0$, $\mathbf{A}_1$, *and* $\mathbf{A}_2$ *be given in Equations* (15.2.2) *and* (15.2.3); *and let* $\boldsymbol{\Sigma}$ *be the covariance matrix of* $\mathbf{Y}$.

(1) $\boldsymbol{\Sigma}$ *commutes with* $\mathbf{A}_0$, $\mathbf{A}_1$, *and* $\mathbf{A}_2$, *that is,* $\mathbf{A}_0\boldsymbol{\Sigma} = \boldsymbol{\Sigma}\mathbf{A}_0$, $\mathbf{A}_1\boldsymbol{\Sigma} = \boldsymbol{\Sigma}\mathbf{A}_1$, *and* $\mathbf{A}_2\boldsymbol{\Sigma} = \boldsymbol{\Sigma}\mathbf{A}_2$.

(2) $\mathbf{A}_i$ *is an idempotent matrix of rank* n_i *for* $i = 0, 1, 2$, *where* $n_0 = 1$, $n_1 = I - 1$, *and* $n_2 = I(J - 1)$.

(3) $\mathbf{A}_i\mathbf{A}_j = \mathbf{0}$ *for* $i = 0, 1, 2$; $j = 0, 1, 2$, *and* $i \neq j$.

(4) σ_ε^2, $\sigma_\varepsilon^2 + J\sigma_A^2$, *and* $IJ\mu^2 + \sigma_\varepsilon^2 + J\sigma_A^2$ *are the distinct characteristic roots of* $\mathscr{E}[\mathbf{YY}']$ *with multiplicity* $I(J - 1)$, $I - 1$, *and* 1, *respectively.*

Proof

For (1) we shall only prove $\mathbf{A}_2\boldsymbol{\Sigma} = \boldsymbol{\Sigma}\mathbf{A}_2$ since the other two results can be proved by a similar procedure. By Equation (15.2.3) we obtain

$\mathbf{I} = \mathbf{A}_0 + \mathbf{A}_1 + \mathbf{A}_2$, so

$$\mathbf{A}_2\mathbf{\Sigma} = \mathbf{A}_2\mathbf{\Sigma}\mathbf{I} = \mathbf{A}_2\mathbf{\Sigma}(\mathbf{A}_0 + \mathbf{A}_1 + \mathbf{A}_2) = \mathbf{A}_2\mathbf{\Sigma}\mathbf{A}_2$$

by using (4) of Theorem 15.2.2. Also,

$$\mathbf{\Sigma}\mathbf{A}_2 = \mathbf{I}\mathbf{\Sigma}\mathbf{A}_2 = (\mathbf{A}_0 + \mathbf{A}_1 + \mathbf{A}_2)\mathbf{\Sigma}\mathbf{A}_2 = \mathbf{A}_2\mathbf{\Sigma}\mathbf{A}_2$$

Thus $\mathbf{\Sigma}\mathbf{A}_2 = \mathbf{A}_2\mathbf{\Sigma}$, and similarly it can be shown that $\mathbf{A}_1\mathbf{\Sigma} = \mathbf{\Sigma}\mathbf{A}_1$ and $\mathbf{A}_0\mathbf{\Sigma} = \mathbf{\Sigma}\mathbf{A}_0$.

To prove (2) we note that $\mathbf{A}_i\mathbf{\Sigma} = \mathbf{A}_i\mathbf{\Sigma}\mathbf{A}_i = \mathbf{A}_i\mathbf{A}_i\mathbf{\Sigma}$; multiply on the right by $\mathbf{\Sigma}^{-1}$ and get $\mathbf{A}_i = \mathbf{A}_i^2$ for $i = 0, 1, 2$. The rank of each $\mathbf{A}_i$ can be obtained by examining the sums of squares in Equation (15.2.1) that each $\mathbf{A}_i$ represents.

To prove (3) use (4) of Theorem 15.2.2 to get, for $i \neq j$, $\mathbf{0} = \mathbf{A}_i\mathbf{\Sigma}\mathbf{A}_j = \mathbf{A}_i\mathbf{A}_j\mathbf{\Sigma}$; multiply on the right by $\mathbf{\Sigma}^{-1}$ and the result is $\mathbf{A}_i\mathbf{A}_j = \mathbf{0}$ for $i \neq j$.

To prove (4) we use the fact that since $\mathbf{A}_i$ is symmetric idempotent, it can be written as $\mathbf{A}_i = \mathbf{P}_i\mathbf{P}_i'$, where $\mathbf{P}_i$ has size $IJ \times n_i$, where n_i is the rank of $\mathbf{A}_i$, and where $n_0 + n_1 + n_2 = IJ$. Also, since $\mathbf{P}_i'\mathbf{P}_j = \mathbf{0}$ if $i \neq j$, and $\mathbf{P}_i'\mathbf{P}_i = \mathbf{I}$, it follows that $\mathbf{P} = [\mathbf{P}_0, \mathbf{P}_1, \mathbf{P}_2]$ is an orthogonal $IJ \times IJ$ matrix. If we examine $\mathbf{P}'\mathbf{\Sigma}\mathbf{P}$, we get

$$\begin{bmatrix} \mathbf{P}_0' \\ \mathbf{P}_1' \\ \mathbf{P}_2' \end{bmatrix} \mathbf{\Sigma}[\mathbf{P}_0, \mathbf{P}_1, \mathbf{P}_2] = \begin{bmatrix} \sigma_\varepsilon^2 + J\sigma_A^2 & \mathbf{0} & \mathbf{0} \\ \mathbf{0} & (\sigma_\varepsilon^2 + J\sigma_A^2)\mathbf{I}_{n_1} & \mathbf{0} \\ \mathbf{0} & \mathbf{0} & \sigma_\varepsilon^2\mathbf{I}_{n_2} \end{bmatrix} = \mathbf{\Delta} \tag{15.2.4}$$

say, since for $i \neq j$ we have $\mathbf{0} = \mathbf{A}_i\mathbf{\Sigma}\mathbf{A}_j = \mathbf{P}_i\mathbf{P}_i'\mathbf{\Sigma}\mathbf{P}_j\mathbf{P}_j'$. Multiply on the left and right by $\mathbf{P}_i'$ and $\mathbf{P}_j$, respectively, and the result is $\mathbf{P}_i'\mathbf{\Sigma}\mathbf{P}_j = \mathbf{0}$ for $i \neq j$.

Next we examine $\mathbf{P}_2'\mathbf{\Sigma}\mathbf{P}_2$. From (3) of Theorem 15.2.2 we get $(\mathbf{\Sigma}\mathbf{A}_2/\sigma_\varepsilon^2) \times (\mathbf{\Sigma}\mathbf{A}_2/\sigma_\varepsilon^2) = \mathbf{\Sigma}\mathbf{A}_2/\sigma_\varepsilon^2$, which implies $\mathbf{A}_2\mathbf{\Sigma}\mathbf{A}_2 = \mathbf{A}_2\sigma_\varepsilon^2$, or $\mathbf{P}_2\mathbf{P}_2'\mathbf{\Sigma}\mathbf{P}_2\mathbf{P}_2' = \mathbf{P}_2\mathbf{P}_2'\sigma_\varepsilon^2$; and finally (since $\mathbf{P}_2'\mathbf{P}_2 = \mathbf{I}$), $\mathbf{P}_2'\mathbf{\Sigma}\mathbf{P}_2 = \mathbf{I}_{n_2}\sigma_\varepsilon^2$. By (3) of Theorem 15.2.1 the rank of $\mathbf{A}_2$ is $I(J-1)$, so $n_2 = I(J-1)$. By a similar procedure it can be shown that $\mathbf{P}_1'\mathbf{\Sigma}\mathbf{P}_1 = (\sigma_\varepsilon^2 + J\sigma_A^2)\mathbf{I}_{n_1}$, where $n_1 = I - 1$, and that $\mathbf{P}_0'\mathbf{\Sigma}\mathbf{P}_0 = (\sigma_\varepsilon^2 + J\sigma_A^2)\mathbf{I}_{n_0}$, where $n_0 = 1$.

We have shown that $\mathbf{P}'\mathbf{\Sigma}\mathbf{P} = \mathbf{\Delta}$, where $\mathbf{\Delta}$ is the diagonal matrix displayed in Equation (15.2.4); so the diagonal elements are the characteristic roots of $\mathbf{\Sigma}$. Now $\mathscr{E}[\mathbf{Y}\mathbf{Y}'] = \mathbf{\Sigma} + \mu^2\mathbf{J} = \mathbf{\Sigma}_0$. If we examine $\mathbf{P}'\mathbf{\Sigma}\mathbf{P}$ we get $\mathbf{P}'\mathbf{\Sigma}_0\mathbf{P} = \mathbf{P}'(\mathbf{\Sigma} + \mu^2\mathbf{J})\mathbf{P} = \mathbf{\Delta} + \mu^2\mathbf{P}'\mathbf{J}\mathbf{P}$; but $\mathbf{P}_0 = \mathbf{1}(IJ)^{-1/2}$, so $\mathbf{P}_1'\mathbf{1} = \mathbf{0}$ and $\mathbf{P}_2'\mathbf{1} = \mathbf{0}$. Thus

$$\mathbf{P}'\mathbf{J}\mathbf{P} = \begin{bmatrix} IJ & \mathbf{0} \\ \mathbf{0} & \mathbf{0} \end{bmatrix}$$

and (4) follows. This completes the proof of the theorem.

In the next theorem we exhibit a set of complete sufficient statistics for the model in this section, and from this set we obtain UMVU estimators of the parameters μ, σ_A^2, and σ_ε^2.

THEOREM 15.2.4

Let the model be given by Definition 15.2.1 *for Case I. The three statistics*

$$\bar{Y}_{..} \qquad S_1^2 = \sum_{i=1}^{I}\sum_{j=1}^{J}(\bar{Y}_{i.} - \bar{Y}_{..})^2 \qquad S_2^2 = \sum_{i=1}^{I}\sum_{j=1}^{J}(Y_{ij} - \bar{Y}_{i.})^2$$

are complete sufficient statistics for this model. If $\mathscr{E}[t(\bar{Y}_{..}, S_1, S_2)] = q(\mu, \sigma_A^2, \sigma_\varepsilon^2)$, *then* $t(\bar{Y}_{..}, S_1, S_2)$ *is the UMVU estimator of* $q(\mu, \sigma_A^2, \sigma_\varepsilon^2)$. *In particular,* $\bar{Y}_{..}$, $\hat{\sigma}_\varepsilon^2 = S_2^2/I(J-1)$, *and* $\hat{\sigma}_A^2 = [S_1^2/J(I-1)] - [S_2^2/IJ(J-1)]$ *are, respectively, the UMVU estimators of* μ, σ_ε^2, *and* σ_A^2. *Also,* $a\hat{\sigma}_\varepsilon^2 + b\hat{\sigma}_A^2$ *is the UMVU estimator of* $a\sigma_\varepsilon^2 + b\sigma_A^2$ *for any specified constants a and b.*

Proof

We use the factorization criterion in Theorem 2.6.1 to demonstrate that $\bar{Y}_{..}$, S_1^2, and S_2^2 are sufficient statistics. We omit the proof that they are complete, but Theorem 2.7.8 can be used. The remaining parts of the theorem then follow by the Lehmann-Scheffé result given in Theorem 2.7.7.

To demonstrate that $\bar{Y}_{..}$, S_1^2, and S_2^2 are sufficient statistics, we obtain the p.d.f. of the Y_{ij} as (let $n = IJ$)

$$\begin{aligned} f_{\mathbf{Y}}(\mathbf{y} : \mu, \sigma_A^2, \sigma_\varepsilon^2) &= (2\pi)^{-n/2}|\mathbf{\Sigma}|^{-1/2}\exp\{-\tfrac{1}{2}(\mathbf{y} - \mathbf{1}\mu)'\mathbf{\Sigma}^{-1}(\mathbf{y} - \mathbf{1}\mu)\} \\ &= (2\pi)^{-n/2}|\mathbf{P}'\mathbf{\Sigma}\mathbf{P}|^{-1/2}\exp\{-\tfrac{1}{2}(\mathbf{y} - \mathbf{1}\mu)'\mathbf{P}(\mathbf{P}'\mathbf{\Sigma}^{-1}\mathbf{P})\mathbf{P}'(\mathbf{y} - \mathbf{1}\mu)\} \end{aligned}$$

since $|\mathbf{P}'\mathbf{\Sigma}\mathbf{P}| = |\mathbf{\Sigma}|$, where $\mathbf{P}$ is the orthogonal matrix defined in the proof of Theorem 15.2.3. Clearly, by Equation (15.2.4), we get $|\mathbf{\Sigma}| = (\sigma_\varepsilon^2 + J\sigma_A^2)^I(\sigma_\varepsilon^2)^{I(J-1)}$.

If we examine the exponent of the p.d.f., we get (omit the $-1/2$)

$$\begin{aligned} &(\mathbf{y} - \mathbf{1}\mu)'\mathbf{\Sigma}^{-1}(\mathbf{y} - \mathbf{1}\mu) \\ &\quad = (\mathbf{y} - \mathbf{1}\mu)'\mathbf{P}\mathbf{P}'\mathbf{\Sigma}^{-1}\mathbf{P}\mathbf{P}'(\mathbf{y} - \mathbf{1}\mu) \\ &\quad = (\mathbf{P}'\mathbf{y} - \mathbf{P}'\mathbf{1}\mu)'\mathbf{P}'\mathbf{\Sigma}^{-1}\mathbf{P}(\mathbf{P}'\mathbf{y} - \mathbf{P}'\mathbf{1}\mu) \\ &\quad = [n^{1/2}(\bar{y}_{..} - \mu), \mathbf{y}'\mathbf{P}_1, \mathbf{y}'\mathbf{P}_2]\mathbf{\Delta}^{-1}[n^{1/2}(\bar{y}_{..} - \mu), \mathbf{y}'\mathbf{P}_1, \mathbf{y}'\mathbf{P}_2]' \\ &\quad = \frac{n(\bar{y}_{..} - \mu)^2}{\sigma_\varepsilon^2 + J\sigma_A^2} + \frac{\mathbf{y}'\mathbf{P}_1\mathbf{P}_1'\mathbf{y}}{\sigma_\varepsilon^2 + J\sigma_A^2} + \frac{\mathbf{y}'\mathbf{P}_2\mathbf{P}_2'\mathbf{y}}{\sigma_\varepsilon^2} \end{aligned}$$

Substitute this into the exponent of the p.d.f. of **Y**, and by the factorization theorem, it follows that

$$\bar{Y}_{..} \qquad \mathbf{Y}'\mathbf{P}_1\mathbf{P}_1'\mathbf{Y} = \mathbf{Y}'\mathbf{A}_1\mathbf{Y} = \sum_{i=1}^{I}\sum_{j=1}^{J}(\bar{Y}_{i.} - \bar{Y}_{..})^2$$

$$\mathbf{Y}'\mathbf{P}_2\mathbf{P}_2'\mathbf{Y} = \mathbf{Y}'\mathbf{A}_2\mathbf{Y} = \sum_{i=1}^{I}\sum_{j=1}^{J}(Y_{ij} - \bar{Y}_{i.})^2$$

are sufficient statistics.

Next we state a result on point estimation when the random variables A_i and ε_{ij} are not necessarily normally distributed.

THEOREM 15.2.5

Let the model be given by Definition 15.2.1. *Then*:

(1) $\hat{\sigma}_\varepsilon^2 = S_2^2/I(J-1)$ *is an unbiased estimator of* σ_ε^2.

(2) $\hat{\sigma}_\varepsilon^2$ *is the BQU estimator of* σ_ε^2 *for Case II.*

(3) $\hat{\sigma}_A^2 = [S_1^2/J(I-1)] - [S_2^2/IJ(J-1)]$ *is an unbiased estimator of* σ_A^2.

(4) $\hat{\sigma}_A^2$ *is the BQU estimator of* σ_A^2 *for Case II.*

(5) *For any constants a and b,* $a\hat{\sigma}_\varepsilon^2 + b\hat{\sigma}_A^2$ *is an unbiased estimator of* $a\sigma_\varepsilon^2 + b\sigma_A^2$.

(6) *For any constants a and b,* $a\hat{\sigma}_\varepsilon^2 + b\hat{\sigma}_A^2$ *is the BQU estimator of* $a\sigma_\varepsilon^2 + b\sigma_A^2$ *for Case II.*

Proof

The proofs for (1), (3), and (5) are obtained by straightforward application of expectations and the use of the fact that the random variables $A_1, A_2, \ldots, A_I, \varepsilon_{11}, \varepsilon_{12}, \ldots, \varepsilon_{IJ}$ are pairwise uncorrelated. We sketch the proof for (2) and leave the details and the proofs for (4) and (6) for the reader.

Let a general quadratic form estimator of σ_ε^2 be given by $\hat{\sigma}_\varepsilon^2$, where $\hat{\sigma}_\varepsilon^2 = \mathbf{Y}'\mathbf{B}\mathbf{Y} + \mathbf{Y}'\mathbf{C}\mathbf{Y}$ and $\mathbf{Y}'\mathbf{B}\mathbf{Y} = S_2^2/I(J-1)$. We want to show that $\mathbf{Y}'\mathbf{C}\mathbf{Y} = 0$, which will imply that $\hat{\sigma}_\varepsilon^2$ is the BQU estimator of σ_ε^2. Unbiasedness implies $\mathscr{E}[\hat{\sigma}_\varepsilon^2] = \sigma_\varepsilon^2$, and since $\mathscr{E}[S_2^2/I(J-1)] = \sigma_\varepsilon^2$, this implies $\mathscr{E}[\mathbf{Y}'\mathbf{C}\mathbf{Y}] = 0$.

Minimum variance implies

$$\mathscr{E}[(\mathbf{Y}'\mathbf{B}\mathbf{Y} + \mathbf{Y}'\mathbf{C}\mathbf{Y})^2] = \mathscr{E}[(\mathbf{Y}'\mathbf{B}\mathbf{Y})^2] + \mathscr{E}[2(\mathbf{Y}'\mathbf{B}\mathbf{Y})(\mathbf{Y}'\mathbf{C}\mathbf{Y})] + \mathscr{E}[(\mathbf{Y}'\mathbf{C}\mathbf{Y})^2]$$

is a minimum. By straightforward evaluation of the expected values involved, it can be shown that if $\mathscr{E}[\mathbf{Y}'\mathbf{C}\mathbf{Y}] = 0$, then $\mathscr{E}[(\mathbf{Y}'\mathbf{C}\mathbf{Y})(\mathbf{Y}'\mathbf{B}\mathbf{Y})] =$

0, and this results in

$$\text{var}[\hat{\sigma}_\varepsilon^2] = \mathscr{E}[(\mathbf{Y}'\mathbf{BY})^2] + \mathscr{E}[(\mathbf{Y}'\mathbf{CY})^2] - \sigma_\varepsilon^4 \geq \mathscr{E}[(\mathbf{Y}'\mathbf{BY})^2] - \sigma_\varepsilon^4$$

So $\mathscr{E}[(\mathbf{Y}'\mathbf{BY})^2] - \sigma_\varepsilon^4$ is a lower bound for the variance of any quadratic form of the observations Y_{ij} which is also unbiased for σ_ε^2. This lower bound is attained if $\mathscr{E}[(\mathbf{Y}'\mathbf{CY})^2] = 0$.

The two conditions $\mathscr{E}[\mathbf{Y}'\mathbf{CY}] = \mathscr{E}[(\mathbf{Y}'\mathbf{CY})^2] = 0$ imply $\mathbf{Y}'\mathbf{CY} = 0$ (with probability one), which in turn implies $\mathbf{C} = \mathbf{0}$. So the best quadratic unbiased estimator of σ_ε^2 is $\mathbf{Y}'\mathbf{BY}$, which is $\sum_{i=1}^I \sum_{j=1}^J (Y_{ij} - \bar{Y}_{i.})^2/I(J-1)$. This proves (2).

The proofs for (4) and (6) are similar. For details see [G-6] and [H-20].

Next we discuss hypotheses tests and confidence intervals for Case I of the model in Definition 15.2.1. For a discussion of optimum properties of tests and confidence intervals for this problem, see [L-8], Chapter 7.

First we discuss σ_ε^2.

THEOREM 15.2.6

Let the model be given in Definition 15.2.1 *for Case I. A size α test of (d_0 is known)*

(1) *$H_0 : \sigma_\varepsilon^2 = d_0$ vs. $H_a : \sigma_\varepsilon^2 \neq d_0$ is this: Reject H_0 if and only if s_2^2, the computed value of S_2^2, does not satisfy $d_0\chi^2_{1-\alpha_2:n_2} \leq s_2^2 \leq d_0\chi^2_{\alpha_1:n_2}$, where $\alpha_1 + \alpha_2 = \alpha$; α_1 and α_2 can be chosen so the test is UMPU, or α_1 and α_2 can be chosen to minimize the length of the interval. Often $\alpha_1 = \alpha_2 = \alpha/2$ is used (see* [P-1]);

(2) *$H_0 : \sigma_\varepsilon^2 = d_0$ (or $\sigma_\varepsilon^2 \leq d_0$) vs. $H_a : \sigma_\varepsilon^2 > d_0$ is this: Reject H_0 if and only if $d_0\chi^2_{\alpha:n_2} \leq s_2^2$; this test is UMP;*

(3) *$H_0 : \sigma_\varepsilon^2 = d_0$ (or $\sigma_\varepsilon^2 \geq d_0$) vs. $H_a : \sigma_\varepsilon^2 < d_0$ is this: Reject H_0 if and only if $d_0\chi^2_{1-\alpha:n_2} \geq s_2^2$; this test is UMPU.*

Proof

The rejection regions are obtained by using the fact that $U_2 = S_2^2/\sigma_\varepsilon^2$ is distributed $\chi^2(u_2 : n_2)$. For proofs of *UMP* and *UMPU* see [L-8].

Notation. We use $n_2 = I(J-1)$ and $n_1 = I - 1$ when convenient.

Next we state a theorem concerning tests on θ, where $\theta = \sigma_A^2/\sigma_\varepsilon^2$.

THEOREM 15.2.7

Let the model be given by Definition 15.2.1 *for Case I. Define W by*

$$W = \frac{S_1^2/(I-1)}{S_2^2/I(J-1)}$$

A size α test of (g_0 known)

(1) $H_0 : \theta = g_0$ *vs.* $H_a : \theta \neq g_0$ *is this: Reject* H_0 *if and only if* w*, the computed value of* W*, does not satisfy* $(1 + Jg_0)F_{1-\alpha_2:n_1,n_2} \leq w \leq (1 + Jg_0)F_{\alpha_1:n_1,n_2}$*, where* $\alpha_1 + \alpha_2 = \alpha$*; often one uses* $\alpha_1 = \alpha_2 = \alpha/2$*; see* [R-1] *for values of* α_1 *and* α_2 *so that the test is UMPU;*

(2) $H_0 : \theta = g_0$ *(or* $\theta \leq g_0$*) vs.* $H_a : \theta > g_0$ *is this: Reject* H_0 *if and only if* $w \geq (1 + Jg_0)F_{\alpha:n_1,n_2}$*; this test is UMPU;*

(3) $H_0 : \theta = g_0$ *(or* $\theta \geq g_0$*) vs.* $H_a : \theta < g_0$ *is this: Reject* H_0 *if and only if* $w \leq (1 + Jg_0)F_{1-\alpha:n_1,n_2}$*; this test is UMPU.*

The powers of the tests are, respectively,

(1) $\Pi(\theta) = 1 - \int_{\gamma F_{1-\alpha_2:n_1,n_2}}^{\gamma F_{\alpha_1:n_1,n_2}} F(w^* : n_1, n_2)\, dw^*$;

(2) $\Pi(\theta) = \int_{\gamma F_{\alpha:n_1,n_2}}^{\infty} F(w^* : n_1, n_2)\, dw^*$;

(3) $\Pi(\theta) = \int_{0}^{\gamma F_{1-\alpha:n_1,n_2}} F(w^* : n_1, n_2)\, dw^*$;

where $F(w^* : n_1, n_2)$ *is Snedecor's F distribution with* n_1 *and* n_2 *degrees of freedom, and where* $\gamma = (1 + Jg_0)/(1 + J\theta)$ *and* θ *varies over its allowable values for each test.*

Proof

We demonstrate the proof for (2). The proofs for (1) and (3) are similar. Consider $H_0 : \theta \leq g_0$ *vs.* $H_a : \theta > g_0$. Clearly the random variable $W^* = W\sigma_\varepsilon^2/(\sigma_\varepsilon^2 + J\sigma_A^2) = W/(1 + J\theta)$ is distributed $F(w^* : n_1, n_2)$, and since H_0 is rejected if and only if $w \geq (1 + Jg_0)F_{\alpha:n_1,n_2}$, we obtain for the power of the test

$$\Pi(\theta) = P[W \geq (1 + Jg_0)F_{\alpha:n_1,n_2}] = P\left[\frac{W}{1 + J\theta} \geq \frac{(1 + Jg_0)F_{\alpha:n_1,n_2}}{1 + J\theta}\right]$$

$$= P[W^* \geq \gamma F_{\alpha:n_1,n_2}] = \int_{\gamma F_{\alpha:n_1,n_2}}^{\infty} F(w^* : n_1, n_2)\, dw^*$$

Also, when H_0 is true (when $\theta \leq g_0$), it follows that $\gamma \geq 1$, that $\Pi(\theta) \leq \alpha$, and that $\Pi(\theta) = \alpha$ when $\theta = g_0$. The *UMPU* proofs are in [L-8].

Next we discuss confidence intervals on σ_ε^2, θ, and σ_A^2. In fact, exact $1 - \alpha$ confidence intervals can be obtained for σ_ε^2 and θ, but no procedure exists for setting exact $1 - \alpha$ confidence intervals on σ_A^2, except an artificial method that uses a set of random numbers which is of little use in applied work [H-9].

THEOREM 15.2.8

Let the model be defined by Definition 15.2.1 for Case I. Below are $1 - \alpha$ confidence limits on σ_ε^2, $\sigma_A^2/\sigma_\varepsilon^2$, $\sigma_A^2/(\sigma_A^2 + \sigma_\varepsilon^2)$, and $\sigma_\varepsilon^2/(\sigma_A^2 + \sigma_\varepsilon^2)$.

(1) $\sigma_\varepsilon^2 : S_2^2/\chi^2_{\alpha_1:n_2} \le \sigma_\varepsilon^2 \le S_2^2/\chi^2_{1-\alpha_2:n_2}$, *where* $\alpha_1 + \alpha_2 = \alpha$; *often* $\alpha_1 = \alpha_2 = \alpha/2$ *is used; if* α_1 *and* α_2 *are chosen correctly, the confidence interval is UMAU and has smallest expected width of all unbiased* $1 - \alpha$ *confidence intervals; see* [P-6];

(2) $\sigma_A^2/\sigma_\varepsilon^2 = \theta : L \le \theta \le U$;

(3) $\sigma_A^2/(\sigma_A^2 + \sigma_\varepsilon^2) = \theta/(1 + \theta) : L/(1 + L) \le \sigma_A^2/(\sigma_A^2 + \sigma_\varepsilon^2) \le U/(1 + U)$;

(4) $\sigma_\varepsilon^2/(\sigma_\varepsilon^2 + \sigma_A^2) = 1/(1 + \theta) : 1/(1 + U) \le \sigma_\varepsilon^2/(\sigma_\varepsilon^2 + \sigma_A^2) \le 1/(1 + L)$; *where*

$$L = \frac{(W/F_{\alpha_1:n_1,n_2}) - 1}{J} \qquad U = \frac{(W/F_{1-\alpha_2:n_1,n_2}) - 1}{J} \tag{15.2.5}$$

W is defined in Theorem 15.2.7, and $\alpha_1 + \alpha_2 = \alpha$; *often* $\alpha_1 = \alpha_2 = \alpha/2$ *is used.*

Proof

The confidence interval in (1) is a result of the fact that $U_2 = S_2^2/\sigma_\varepsilon^2$ is distributed $\chi^2(u_2 : n_2)$. For a proof of *UMAU* see [L-8].

To prove (2) we note that $W^* = W\sigma_\varepsilon^2/(\sigma_\varepsilon^2 + J\sigma_A^2)$ is distributed $F(w^* : n_1, n_2)$. So $P[F_{1-\alpha_2:n_1,n_2} \le W^* \le F_{\alpha_1:n_1,n_2}] = 1 - \alpha$ where $\alpha_1 + \alpha_2 = \alpha$. If we substitute for W^*, we get the equivalent inequalities (so the probability of each is $1 - \alpha$):

$$F_{1-\alpha_2:n_1,n_2} \le \frac{W\sigma_\varepsilon^2}{\sigma_\varepsilon^2 + J\sigma_A^2} \le F_{\alpha_1:n_1,n_2}$$

$$\frac{W}{F_{\alpha_1:n_1,n_2}} \le 1 + J\theta \le \frac{W}{F_{1-\alpha_2:n_1,n_2}}$$

$$\frac{(W/F_{\alpha_1:n_1,n_2}) - 1}{J} \le \theta \le \frac{(W/F_{1-\alpha_2:n_1,n_2}) - 1}{J}$$

which is $L \le \theta \le U$, and this proves (2).

To prove (3) we start with $P[L \le \theta \le U] = 1 - \alpha$ and get the following inequalities (so the probability of each is $1 - \alpha$):

$$L \le \theta \le U \qquad \frac{1}{U} \le \frac{1}{\theta} \le \frac{1}{L} \qquad 1 + \frac{1}{U} \le 1 + \frac{1}{\theta} \le 1 + \frac{1}{L}$$

$$\left(1 + \frac{1}{L}\right)^{-1} \le \left(1 + \frac{1}{\theta}\right)^{-1} \le \left(1 + \frac{1}{U}\right)^{-1}$$

$$\frac{L}{1 + L} \le \frac{\theta}{1 + \theta} \le \frac{U}{1 + U}$$

which proves (3).

The statement in (4) is proved by a similar procedure. If the value of U or L is negative that limit is replaced with zero.

Next we obtain a confidence interval for σ_A^2. As we stated above, no exact $1 - \alpha$ confidence limits exist for σ_A^2 for practical situations. Several approximate procedures are available and [B-6] contains comparative evaluations of the important ones. The method proposed by Williams [W-10] will be presented since it appears to be one of the best methods.

THEOREM 15.2.9

Let the model be given by Definition 15.2.1 *for Case I. A confidence interval on* σ_A^2 *with confidence coefficient greater than or equal to* $1 - 2\alpha$ *is*

$$\frac{1}{J\chi^2_{\alpha_1:n_1}}\left[S_1^2 - \left(\frac{n_1}{n_2}\right)S_2^2 F_{\alpha_1:n_1,n_2}\right] \le \sigma_A^2 \le \frac{1}{J\chi^2_{1-\alpha_2:n_1}}\left[S_1^2 - \left(\frac{n_1}{n_2}\right)S_2^2 F_{1-\alpha_2:n_1,n_2}\right] \tag{15.2.6}$$

where $\alpha_1 + \alpha_2 = \alpha$; *often* $\alpha_1 = \alpha_2 = \alpha/2$ *is used*; $n_1 = I - 1$ *and* $n_2 = I(J - 1)$.

Proof

Consider $1 - \alpha$ confidence intervals on $\sigma_\varepsilon^2 + J\sigma_A^2$ and $\sigma_A^2/\sigma_\varepsilon^2$, respectively, denoted by I_1 and I, where

$$I_1 = [L_1, U_1] = \left[\frac{S_1^2}{\chi^2_{\alpha_1:n_1}}, \frac{S_1^2}{\chi^2_{1-\alpha_2:n_2}}\right]$$

and $1 - \alpha = P[I_1 \text{ contains } \sigma_\varepsilon^2 + J\sigma_A^2] = P[A_1]$ say. $I = [L, U]$, and $1 - \alpha = P[I \text{ contains } \sigma_A^2/\sigma_\varepsilon^2] = P[A]$, say, by (2) of Theorem 15.2.8, where U and L are defined in Equation (15.2.5). Also,

$$P[L_1 \le \sigma_\varepsilon^2 + J\sigma_A^2 \le U_1 \quad \text{and} \quad L \le \sigma_A^2/\sigma_\varepsilon^2 \le U] = P[A_1 A] \ge 1 - 2\alpha \tag{15.2.7}$$

The inequality $1 - 2\alpha \le P[A_1 A]$ can be justified by the Bonferroni inequality in Section 9.5.

By examining the inequalities inside the brackets in Equation (15.2.7), we get the four bounding lines in the parameter space of σ_ε^2 and σ_A^2, where ℓ, u, ℓ_1, u_1, ℓ_2, u_2 are respective values of the random variables L, U, L_1, U_1, L_2, U_2:

$$\ell_1 = \sigma_\varepsilon^2 + J\sigma_A^2 \qquad u_1 = \sigma_\varepsilon^2 + J\sigma_A^2 \qquad \sigma_A^2 = \ell\sigma_\varepsilon^2 \qquad \sigma_A^2 = u\sigma_\varepsilon^2$$

The lines are shown in Figure 15.2.1, and, clearly, the intersection points u_2 and ℓ_2 are given by the following:

1. u_2: where u_2 is the solution for σ_A^2 of the two equations $u_1 = \sigma_\varepsilon^2 + J\sigma_A^2$ and $u\sigma_\varepsilon^2 = \sigma_A^2$; the solution is $u_2 = u_1 u/(uJ + 1)$;
2. ℓ_2: where ℓ_2 is the solution for σ_A^2 of the two equations $\ell_1 = \sigma_\varepsilon^2 + J\sigma_A^2$ and $\ell\sigma_\varepsilon^2 = \sigma_A^2$; the solution is $\ell_2 = \ell_1 \ell/(\ell J + 1)$. (15.2.8)

Finally, we know that

$$P[L_2 \le \sigma_A^2 \le U_2] \ge P[A_1 A] \ge 1 - 2\alpha \tag{15.2.9}$$

where $P[A_1 A]$ is given in Equation (15.2.7). If we substitute for u_1, u_2, ℓ_1, and ℓ, we get Equation (15.2.6) for a confidence interval on σ_A^2 with confidence coefficient greater than or equal to $1 - 2\alpha$, and the theorem is proved.

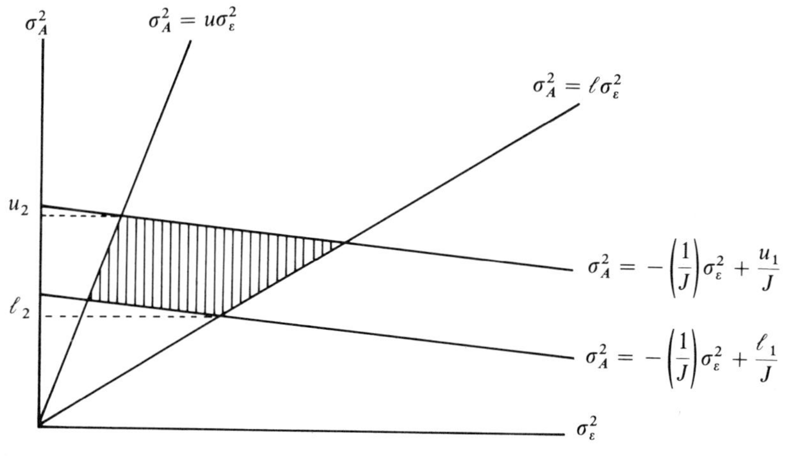

Figure 15.2.1

Note 2. If $\ell_2 \leq 0$, replace it by 0; if $u_2 \leq 0$, replace ℓ_2 and u_2 both with zero.

Note 3. The confidence interval on σ_A^2 can be used to test $H_0 : \sigma_A^2 = A_0^2$ (specified) *vs.* $H_a : \sigma_A^2 \neq A_0^2$. A test of size less than 2α is this: Reject H_0 if and only if A_0^2 is *not* in the $1 - 2\alpha$ confidence interval on σ_A^2.

Note 4. Empirical evidence indicates that for the confidence interval in Equation (15.2.6), the probability $1 - 2\alpha$ can be replaced by $1 - \alpha$, and we shall do so in the remainder of this chapter. See [B-6].

Example 15.2.1

Data were obtained that were assumed to satisfy the model in Definition 15.2.1, where $I = 10$ and $J = 4$; the sums of squares were computed and are exhibited in (an ANOVA) Table 15.2.1.

1. Find UMVU estimates of σ_ε^2, σ_A^2, and $\sigma_\varepsilon^2 + \sigma_A^2$.
2. Test $H_0 : \sigma_\varepsilon^2 = 1$ *vs.* $H_a : \sigma_\varepsilon^2 \neq 1$ with $\alpha = 0.05$.
3. Find 0.95 confidence limits on $\theta = \sigma_A^2/\sigma_\varepsilon^2$.
4. Find confidence limits on σ_A^2 with confidence coefficient greater than or equal to 0.095.
5. Test $H_0 : \sigma_A^2 = 0.61$ *vs.* $H_a : \sigma_A^2 \neq 0.61$ with size $\alpha \leq 0.05$.

1. From the table we obtain UMVU estimates $\hat{\sigma}_\varepsilon^2 = 1.02$, $\hat{\sigma}_A^2 = 2.00$, and $\hat{\sigma}_\varepsilon^2 + \hat{\sigma}_A^2 = 3.02$.
2. A 0.05 size test of $H_0 : \sigma_\varepsilon^2 = 1$ *vs.* $H_a : \sigma_\varepsilon^2 \neq 1$ is obtained by using (1) of Theorem 15.2.6; we get (using $\alpha_1 = \alpha_2 = \alpha/2 = 0.025$) $\chi_{0.025:30}^2 = 46.979$, $\chi_{0.975:30}^2 = 16.791$, $d_0 = 1$, and the interval is [16.791, 46.979]; $s_2^2 = 30.60$ is contained within it, so H_0 is not rejected.

Table 15.2.1

ANOVA for Components-of-Variance Data in Example 15.2.1

Source	*d.f.*	*S.S.*	*M.S.*	*E.M.S.*
Total	40	117.99		
$R(\mu)$	1	$6.12 = s_0^2$		
$R(\boldsymbol{\alpha} \mid \mu)$	$9 = n_1$	$81.27 = s_1^2$	9.03	$\sigma_\varepsilon^2 + 4\sigma_A^2$
Error	$30 = n_2$	$30.60 = s_2^2$	1.02	σ_ε^2

3. We use (2) of Theorem 15.2.8, where $w = 9.03/1.02 = 8.8529$, $F_{0.025:9,30} = 2.5746$, and $F_{0.975:9,30} = 0.2809$. We get $\ell = 0.6096$, $u = 7.6291$, and the 0.95 interval is $0.6096 \le \sigma_A^2/\sigma_\varepsilon^2 \le 7.6291$.

4. We use Equation (15.2.6). Set $1 - 2\alpha = 0.90$ and by Note 4 we state, "the confidence coefficient is $\ge 1 - \alpha = 0.95$." So $1 - 2\alpha = 0.90$, $\alpha = 0.05$, $\chi^2_{0.025:9} = 19.023$, $\chi^2_{0.975:9} = 2.700$, $F_{0.025:9,30} = 2.5746$, and $F_{0.975:9,30} = 0.2809$. Substituting into Equation (15.2.6) we obtain $0.7574 \le \sigma_A^2 \le 7.2862$.

   To use Equation (15.2.8) directly to solve part 4, we use the computed 0.95 confidence limits on $\sigma_A^2/\sigma_\varepsilon^2$, denoted by ℓ and u; also, $[\ell_1, u_1]$ in Equation (15.2.7) can be used to compute 0.95 confidence limits on $\sigma_\varepsilon^2 + 4\sigma_A^2$. They are obtained by the formula $s_1^2/\chi^2_{\alpha/2:n_1} \le \sigma_\varepsilon^2 + J\sigma_A^2 \le s_1^2/\chi^2_{1-\alpha/2:n_1}$. For these data we get the limits $81.27/19.023 = 4.2722 = \ell_1$ and $81.27/2.700 = 30.1000 = u_1$. From the answer to part 3 we obtained $\ell = 0.6096$ and $u = 7.6291$. Substituting these values of ℓ, u, ℓ_1, and u_1 into Equation (15.2.8), we get $\ell_2 = 0.7574$ and $u_2 = 7.2862$, and the confidence interval is $[0.7574, 7.2862]$, which, of course, is the same as was obtained by substituting into Equation (15.2.6).

5. We note that 0.61 is not in the interval, so H_0 is rejected.

In the next section we derive complete sufficient statistics for the *general* components-of-variance model defined in Section 15.1. In subsequent sections we examine various special cases.

15.3 A General Components-of-Variance Model

The model we analyze in this section is Case I of the model given in Definition 15.1.1. The procedure is to partition the observable sum of squares $\mathbf{Y}'\mathbf{Y}$ into $q + 2$ quadratic forms.

$$\mathbf{Y}'\mathbf{Y} = \mathbf{Y}'\mathbf{A}_0\mathbf{Y} + \mathbf{Y}'\mathbf{A}_1\mathbf{Y} + \cdots + \mathbf{Y}'\mathbf{A}_{q+1}\mathbf{Y} \quad \text{where} \quad \mathbf{A}_0 = (1/n)\mathbf{J} \qquad (15.3.1)$$

(which implies $\mathbf{Y}'\mathbf{A}_0\mathbf{Y} = n\bar{Y}^2$). If these quadratic forms have certain distributional properties, it is then very easy to obtain complete sufficient statistics, and these can be used to obtain point estimators, interval estimators, and test statistics.

Note 1. In many models that are useful in applied statistics, namely the balanced complete models, the quadratic forms in Equation (15.3.1) can be obtained by using an identity in the observable random variables $Y_{ij\ldots m}$. Many times this identity is the same one that was used for the corresponding *design* model. This was the situation in the preceding section where the identity in Equation (15.2.1) is the same as the identity in Equation (15.2.3) for the one-factor *design* model.

Note 2. The number of quadratic forms into which $\mathbf{Y}'\mathbf{Y}$ is partitioned is $q + 2$, the number of partitions of the $\mathbf{X}$ matrix in Definition 15.1.1 plus one additional quadratic form for the error vector $\boldsymbol{\varepsilon}$.

THEOREM 15.3.1

Let the model be given in Definition 15.1.1 *for Case I and let* $\mathbf{Y}'\mathbf{Y}$ *be partitioned into quadratic forms as in Equation* 15.3.1. (*See Table* 15.3.1, *page* 627.) *Suppose*

(1) $U_j = S_j^2/\gamma_j^2 = \mathbf{Y}'\mathbf{A}_j\mathbf{Y}/\gamma_j^2$ *is distributed* $\chi^2(u_j : n_j)$ *for* $j = 1, 2, \ldots, q + 1$ *where the* γ_j^2 *are linearly independent linear functions of the* σ_i^2;

(2) $U_0 = S_0^2/\gamma_0^2 = \mathbf{Y}'\mathbf{A}_0\mathbf{Y}/\gamma_0^2$ *is distributed* $\chi^2(u_0 : n_0 ; \lambda)$, *where* $\mathbf{Y}'\mathbf{A}_0\mathbf{Y} = n\bar{Y}^2$;

(3) $U_0, U_1, \ldots, U_{q+1}$ *are jointly independent.*

Then

(a) *there exist constants* ℓ_{ij} *such that* $\sigma_i^2 = \sum_{j=1}^{q+1} \ell_{ij}\gamma_j^2$ *for* $i = 1, 2, \ldots, q + 1$;

(b) $\bar{Y}, S_1^2, S_2^2, \ldots, S_{q+1}^2$ *are complete sufficient statistics for the model.*

Proof

This theorem will be proved in Section 15.7; the proof can be omitted by those readers who are not interested in it and are interested only in its applications.

As a consequence of this theorem, we now state several results about point estimation, interval estimation, and hypotheses tests for the components-of-variance model.

THEOREM 15.3.2

Let the model be Case I of Definition 15.1.1 *and let* (1), (2), *and* (3) *of Theorem* 15.3.1 *hold. Then*:

(1) $\hat{\sigma}_i^2 = \sum_{j=1}^{q+1} \ell_{ij}\mathbf{Y}'\mathbf{A}_j\mathbf{Y}/n_j$ *is the UMVU estimator of* σ_i^2 *for* $i = 1, 2, \ldots, q + 1$.

(2) $\hat{\sigma}^2 = \sum_{i=1}^{q+1} c_i\hat{\sigma}_i^2$ *is the UMVU estimator of* $\sigma^2 = \sum_{i=1}^{q+1} c_i\sigma_i^2$ *for any set of* $q + 1$ *constants* $c_1, c_2, \ldots, c_{q+1}$.

(3) *$\bar{Y}$ is the UMVU estimator of μ.*

Proof

By (a) of Theorem 15.3.1, σ_i^2 and σ_ε^2 have unbiased estimators which are functions of the complete sufficient statistics. The Lehmann-Scheffé theorem can be used to obtain UMVU estimators.

THEOREM 15.3.3

Let the model be given in Definition 15.1.1. *If conditions* (1), (2), *and* (3) *of Theorem* 15.3.1 *hold when the model satisfies Case I, then* (1) *below obtains when the model does not necessarily satisfy Case I, and result* (2) *below obtains when the model satisfies Case II.*

(1) *$\hat{\sigma}_i^2$ in Theorem* 15.3.1 *is an unbiased estimator of σ_i^2 for $i = 1, 2, \ldots, q + 1$.*

(2) *$\hat{\sigma}_i^2$ in Theorem* 15.3.1 *is a BQU estimator of σ_i^2 for $i = 1, 2, \ldots, q + 1$.*

Proof

The proof of (1) is easily obtained by simply taking expectations of $\hat{\sigma}_i^2$. The proof for (2) can be found in [G-6].

THEOREM 15.3.4

Let the model be Case I of Definition 15.1.1, *and let* (1), (2), *and* (3) *of Theorem* 15.3.1 *hold. For any $\gamma_j^2 \geq \gamma_k^2$, $j \neq k$, $j \neq 0$, and $k \neq 0$, a size α generalized likelihood ratio test statistic of $H_0 : \gamma_j^2 = \gamma_k^2$ vs. $H_a : \gamma_j^2 > \gamma_k^2$ is W, where*

$$W = \frac{\mathbf{Y}'\mathbf{A}_j\mathbf{Y}/n_j}{\mathbf{Y}'\mathbf{A}_k\mathbf{Y}/n_k}$$

The test is this: Reject H_0 if and only if $w \geq F_{\alpha:n_j,n_k}$. When H_0 is true, W is distributed $F(w : n_j, n_k)$. The power of the test is (let $\theta = \gamma_k^2/\gamma_j^2$, so $0 < \theta \leq 1$, H_0 is $\theta = 1$, and H_a is $0 < \theta < 1$)

$$\Pi(\theta) = \int_{\theta F_{\alpha:n_j,n_k}}^{\infty} F(w : n_j, n_k)\, dw \qquad \text{for } 0 < \theta \leq 1$$

This test is UMPU of size α.

Proof

The joint p.d.f. of $\bar{Y}$ and $\mathbf{Y}'\mathbf{A}_i\mathbf{Y}$ for $i = 1, 2, \ldots, q + 1$ can be easily obtained, and since they are sufficient statistics, this p.d.f. can be used as the likelihood function. It is

$$L(\mu, \gamma_0^2, \gamma_1^2, \ldots, \gamma_{q+1}^2)$$
$$= \left(\frac{2\pi\gamma_0^2}{n}\right)^{-1/2} e^{-n(\bar{y}-\mu)^2/2\gamma_0^2} \prod_{i=1}^{q+1} \left[\Gamma\left(\frac{n_i}{2}\right)2^{n_i/2}\right]^{-1} \left(\frac{\mathbf{y}'\mathbf{A}_i\mathbf{y}}{\gamma_i^2}\right)^{(n_i-2)/2} e^{-\mathbf{y}'\mathbf{A}_i\mathbf{y}/2\gamma_i^2}$$

It is straightforward to show that the likelihood ratio statistic for testing H_0 *vs.* H_a is a (monotonic) function of $W = (\mathbf{Y}'\mathbf{A}_j\mathbf{Y}/n_j)/(\mathbf{Y}'\mathbf{A}_k\mathbf{Y}/n_k)$, and the rejection region is the interval $(F_{\alpha:n_j,n_k}, \infty)$. The power of the test is

$$\begin{aligned}
\Pi(\theta) &= P[\text{rejecting } H_0 \text{ for } 0 < \theta \le 1] \\
&= P\left[\frac{\mathbf{Y}'\mathbf{A}_j\mathbf{Y}/n_j}{\mathbf{Y}'\mathbf{A}_k\mathbf{Y}/n_k} \ge F_{\alpha:n_j,n_k} \text{ for } 0 < \theta \le 1\right] \\
&= P\left[\frac{\theta(\mathbf{Y}'\mathbf{A}_j\mathbf{Y}/n_j)}{\mathbf{Y}'\mathbf{A}_k\mathbf{Y}/n_k} \ge \theta F_{\alpha:n_j,n_k} \text{ for } 0 < \theta \le 1\right] \\
&= \int_{\theta F_{\alpha:n_j,n_k}}^{\infty} F(w : n_j, n_k)\, dw
\end{aligned}$$

since $\theta(\mathbf{Y}'\mathbf{A}_j\mathbf{Y}/n_j)/(\mathbf{Y}'\mathbf{A}_k\mathbf{Y}/n_k)$ is distributed $F(w : n_j, n_k)$ for each value of θ that satisfies $0 < \theta \le 1$. Proof that the test is *UMPU* is in [L-8].

THEOREM 15.3.5

Let the model be Case I of Definition 15.1.1, *and let* (1), (2), *and* (3) *of Theorem* 15.3.1 *hold. For any* $\gamma_j^2 \ge \gamma_k^2$, *where* $\gamma_j^2 = \gamma_k^2 + \gamma^2$ *obtains, a confidence interval on* γ^2 *with confidence coefficient greater than or equal to* $1 - 2\alpha$ *(actually greater than or equal to* $1 - \alpha$ *by Note* 4 *in Section* 15.2) *is*

$$(\chi^2_{\alpha_1:n_j})^{-1}\left[S_j^2 - \left(\frac{n_j}{n_k}\right)S_k^2 F_{\alpha_1:n_j,n_k}\right] \le \gamma^2 \le (\chi^2_{1-\alpha_2:n_j})^{-1}\left[S_j^2 - \left(\frac{n_j}{n_k}\right)S_k^2 F_{1-\alpha_2:n_j,n_k}\right]$$

where $\alpha_1 + \alpha_2 = \alpha$, *and, often,* $\alpha_1 = \alpha_2 = \alpha/2$ *is used;* γ^2 *is assumed to be a linear combination of the* σ_i^2 *with nonnegative coefficients. See Table* 15.3.1.

Proof

The proof is almost identical to the proof of Theorem 15.2.9 and will be omitted.

COROLLARY 15.3.5

In Theorem 15.3.5 *a test of size less than* 2α *of* $H_0 : \gamma^2 = g^2$ *(specified) vs.* $H_a : \gamma^2 \ne g^2$ *is this: Reject* H_0 *if and only if* g^2 *is not in the confidence interval on* γ^2 *in Theorem* 15.3.5. *(By Note* 4 *in Section* 15.2, *the size is* $\le \alpha$.)

THEOREM 15.3.6

One-at-a-time $1 - \alpha$ *confidence intervals on* γ_j^2 *and on* $\theta = \gamma_j^2/\gamma_k^2$ *are given by*

$$\frac{S_j^2}{\chi^2_{\alpha_1:n_j}} \leq \gamma_j^2 \leq \frac{S_j^2}{\chi^2_{1-\alpha_2:n_j}} \qquad \textit{for } j = 1, 2, \ldots, q + 1$$

and by

$$\left(\frac{S_j^2/n_j}{S_k^2/n_k}\right) F_{1-\alpha_2:n_k,n_j} \leq \frac{\gamma_j^2}{\gamma_k^2} \leq \left(\frac{S_j^2/n_j}{S_k^2/n_k}\right) F_{\alpha_1:n_k,n_j}$$

where $\alpha_1 + \alpha_2 = \alpha$. α_1 *and* α_2 *can be chosen so that the confidence interval is UMAU; see* [R-1]. *Often* $\alpha_1 = \alpha_2 = \alpha/2$ *is used.*

Proof

This proof is a direct result of the fact that $U_j = S_j^2/\gamma_j^2$ is distributed $\chi^2(u_j : n_j)$; $U_k = S_k^2/\gamma_k^2$ is distributed $\chi^2(u_k : n_k)$; and U_j and U_k are independent.

To conclude this section we summarize the results and indicate how they will be used for *special* components-of-variance models that will be discussed in succeeding sections of this chapter.

The general components-of-variance model is assumed to be given by Definition 15.1.1. The technique described in this section that often leads to best unbiased estimators of the variances σ_i^2 and linear functions of the variances is listed below. Also see Table 15.3.1.

1. Write an identity for the general element in the random vector $\mathbf{Y}$ so that one element in the identity is $\bar{Y}$; for example, for the one-factor model with equal numbers in the subclasses the identity is given in Equation (15.2.1).

2. Square and sum both sides of the identity to obtain a partition of $\mathbf{Y}'\mathbf{Y}$, the total sum of squares, represented by $\mathbf{Y}'\mathbf{Y} = \mathbf{Y}'\mathbf{A}_0\mathbf{Y} + \mathbf{Y}'\mathbf{A}_1\mathbf{Y} + \cdots + \mathbf{Y}'\mathbf{A}_{q+1}\mathbf{Y}$; it follows that $\mathbf{Y}'\mathbf{A}_0\mathbf{Y} = n\bar{Y}^2$ since one element in the identity is $\bar{Y}$. For the one-factor model, this partition of $\mathbf{Y}'\mathbf{Y}$ is exhibited in Equation (15.2.2).

3. For Case I demonstrate that $\mathbf{Y}'\mathbf{A}_i\mathbf{Y}$, for $i = 0, 1, \ldots, q + 1$, are jointly independent. This can often be accomplished quite easily by showing that the elements in the identity in part 1 are pairwise uncorrelated; for the one-factor model, this method is demonstrated in the proof of Theorem 15.2.1.

4. For Case I show that $U_j = \mathbf{Y}'\mathbf{A}_j\mathbf{Y}/\gamma_j^2$ is distributed $\chi^2(u_j : n_j)$ for $j = 1, 2, \ldots, q + 1$, where the γ_j^2, which are linear functions of the variances σ_i^2, are distinct.

5. For Case I show that $U_0 = \mathbf{Y}'\mathbf{A}_0\mathbf{Y}/\gamma_0^2 = n\bar{Y}^2/\gamma_0^2$ is distributed $\chi^2(u_0 : n_0; \lambda)$. (15.3.2)

If steps 1, 2, 3, 4, and 5 can be demonstrated, the results are as listed below.

1. $\bar{Y}$ and $S_i^2 = \mathbf{Y}'\mathbf{A}_i\mathbf{Y}$, for $i = 1, 2, \ldots, q + 1$, are complete sufficient statistics for Case I.

2. $\mathbf{Y}'\mathbf{A}_i\mathbf{Y}/n_i$ is the UMVU estimator of γ_i^2 for $i = 1, 2, \ldots, q + 1$ for Case I, and $\bar{Y}$ is the UMVU estimator of μ.

3. $\mathbf{Y}'\mathbf{A}_i\mathbf{Y}/n_i$ is the BQU estimator of γ_i^2 for $i = 1, 2, \ldots, q + 1$ for Case II.

4. For Case I, if $\gamma_j^2 \geq \gamma_k^2$, the size α likelihood ratio test (which is UMPU) of $H_0 : \gamma_j^2 - \gamma_k^2 = 0$ *vs.* $H_a : \gamma_j^2 - \gamma_k^2 > 0$ is this: Reject H_0 if and only if $w \geq F_{\alpha:n_j,n_k}$. For many models $\gamma_j^2 = \gamma_k^2 + \gamma^2$ obtains, and the test above is a test of $\gamma^2 = 0$ *vs.* $\gamma^2 > 0$.

5. For Case I if $\gamma_j^2 = \gamma_k^2 + \gamma^2$ obtains, then a confidence interval on γ^2 with confidence coefficient $\geq 1 - 2\alpha$ (actually $\geq 1 - \alpha$ by Note 4 in Section 5.2) is given in Theorem 15.3.5 as

$$(\chi^2_{\alpha_1:n_j})^{-1}\left[S_j^2 - \left(\frac{n_j}{n_k}\right)S_k^2 F_{\alpha_1:n_j,n_k}\right] \leq \gamma^2$$
$$\leq (\chi^2_{1-\alpha_2:n_j})^{-1}\left[S_j^2 - \left(\frac{n_j}{n_k}\right)S_k^2 F_{1-\alpha_2:n_j,n_k}\right]$$

where $\alpha_1 + \alpha_2 = \alpha$; often $\alpha_1 = \alpha_2 = \alpha/2$ is used.

6. A best unbiased estimator for $\sigma^2 = \sum_{i=1}^{q+1} c_i\sigma_i^2$ can be obtained.

7. For Case I a UMVU estimator of any function of $\sigma_1^2, \sigma_2^2, \ldots, \sigma_{q+1}^2$ can be obtained if an unbiased estimator of that function exists.

8. For Case I, $1 - \alpha$ confidence intervals on γ_j^2 and on $\theta = \gamma_j^2/\gamma_k^2$ are given in Theorem 15.3.6. (15.3.3)

The partitioning of $\mathbf{Y}'\mathbf{Y}$ into appropriate quadratic forms often can be usefully exhibited in an ANOVA table, such as Table 15.3.1.

We now turn our attention to various special cases of the components-of-variance models.

Table 15.3.1

ANOVA Table for Components-of-Variance Models

Source	*d.f.*	*S.S.*	*M.S.*	*E.M.S.*
Total	n	$\mathbf{Y'Y}$		
Mean	1	S_0^2		
1	n_1	S_1^2	MS_1	γ_1^2
2	n_2	S_2^2	MS_2	γ_2^2
⋮	⋮	⋮	⋮	⋮
q	n_q	S_q^2	MS_q	γ_q^2
Error	n_{q+1}	S_{q+1}^2	MS_{q+1}	γ_{q+1}^2

15.4 Two-Factor Components-of-Variance Model

In Chapter 14 the two-factor design model was defined and variations of it were discussed. The variations depended on whether or not interaction was present and how many observations were in each subcell. For the components-of-variance model, two quite distinct models with two factors, and variations within each, can be defined. The two principal models are (1) the two-factor *crossed* model, and (2) the two-factor *nested* model.

The model

$$Y_{ijm} = \mu + A_i + T_j + (AT)_{ij} + \varepsilon_{ijm} \tag{15.4.1}$$

resembles the two-factor design model with interaction. But if A_i, T_j, $(AT)_{ij}$, and ε_{ijm} are *all* considered to be random variables, this is a components-of-variance model.

However, the two-factor model

$$Y_{ijm} = \mu + A_i + B_{ij} + \varepsilon_{ijm} \tag{15.4.2}$$

is clearly different than the model in Equation (15.4.1). These two models are very useful for distinct situations when studying components-of-variance.

The model in Equation (15.4.1) is defined to be a two-factor *crossed* components-of-variance model with or without interaction depending on whether the term $(AT)_{ij}$ is present or absent. The model in Equation (15.4.2) is defined to be a two-factor *nested* components-of-variance model. The *crossed* models will be discussed in Sections 15.4.1, 15.4.2, 15.4.3, and 15.5.3; the *nested* model will be discussed in Sections 15.4.4, 15.5.1, and 15.5.2.

15.4.1 Two-Factor Crossed Components-of-Variance Model

In this section two models will be defined, a two-factor *crossed* components-of-variance model, *with* interaction and *without* interaction. First we discuss a practical situation where these two models could be used, then we define each model and discuss appropriate inference techniques.

Example 15.4.1

An investigator wants to examine the effects of drivers and automobiles on gas mileage. One type of automobile is used and 20 are selected at random from one month's production. Ten people are selected at random from a large city and are asked to drive each car for two weeks and record the number of miles per gallon of gas used for each car for the two-week period. Clearly there are two populations involved: the population of drivers and the population of one month's production of this type of automobile.

Let Y_{ij} be the miles per gallon of gas used by the ith auto that was driven by the jth driver, where Y_{ij} is assumed to be structured by

$$Y_{ij} = \mu + A_i + D_j + \varepsilon_{ij}$$

where A_i is the contribution of the ith auto, D_j is the contribution of the jth driver, and ε_{ij} is the contribution of all uncontrollable factors not accounted for in A_i and D_j.

Assume $A_1^*, A_2^*, \ldots, A_{20}^*$, where A_i^* is the effect of the ith auto on miles per gallon, represent an unobservable random sample from a population that has a mean μ_{A^*} and a variance $\sigma_{A^*}^2$. Assume $D_1^*, D_2^*, \ldots, D_{10}^*$, where D_j^* is the effect of the jth driver on miles per gallon, represent an unobservable random sample from a population that has a mean μ_{D^*} and a variance $\sigma_{D^*}^2$. Finally, assume $\varepsilon_{11}^*, \varepsilon_{12}^*, \ldots, \varepsilon_{20,10}^*$ is an unobservable random sample selected from a population that has a mean μ_{ε^*} and a variance $\sigma_{\varepsilon^*}^2$.

Then the model assumes that Y_{ij} is an observable random variable that represents the miles per gallon that will be recorded by the jth driver for the ith auto, and Y_{ij} has the structure

$$Y_{ij} = A_i^* + D_j^* + \varepsilon_{ij}^* = \mu_{A^*} + A_i + \mu_{D^*} + D_j + \mu_{\varepsilon^*} + \varepsilon_{ij} \quad (15.4.3)$$

$$Y_{ij} = \mu + A_i + D_j + \varepsilon_{ij}$$

where $A_i = A_i^* - \mu_{A^*}$, $D_j = D_j^* - \mu_{D^*}$, and $\varepsilon_{ij} = \varepsilon_{ij}^* - \mu_{\varepsilon^*}$ so that A_i, D_j, and ε_{ij} are deviations from their respective population means.

Thus $\mathscr{E}[A_i] = 0$, $\text{var}[A_i] = \sigma_A^2 = \sigma_{A*}^2$, $\mathscr{E}[D_j] = 0$, $\text{var}[D_j] = \sigma_D^2 = \sigma_{D*}^2$, $\mathscr{E}[\varepsilon_{ij}] = 0$, and $\text{var}[\varepsilon_{ij}] = \sigma_\varepsilon^2 = \sigma_{\varepsilon*}^2$. Also, $\mu = \mu_{A*} + \mu_{D*} + \mu_{\varepsilon*}$.

The objective is to observe values of the Y_{ij} and make inferences about σ_A^2, σ_D^2, and σ_ε^2. In this investigation one is not interested in the performance of each car with each driver, but rather in the evaluation of the variance of the population of cars σ_A^2, and in the variance of the population of drivers σ_D^2. If σ_A^2 is large, the investigator knows that his cars differ widely with respect to gas mileage, and this could be important information to him in designing or advertising his product. Of course, there also may be interest in μ, the average gas mileage.

The model fits the definition of a two-factor crossed model since *each* driver in the investigation is associated with *each* car in the investigation. The interaction term will be included in the model if the investigator thinks it appropriate.

We now define a two-factor crossed components-of-variance model.

DEFINITION 15.4.1

Two-Factor Crossed Components-of-Variance Model. *Consider the model* $Y_{ijm} = \mu + A_i + T_j + G_{ij} + \varepsilon_{ijm}$; $m = 0, 1, \ldots, n_{ij}$; $i = 1, 2, \ldots, I > 1$; *and* $j = 1, 2, \ldots, J > 1$. Y_{ijm} *are observable random variables;* μ *is an unobservable constant;* $A_1, A_2, \ldots, A_I, T_1, T_2, \ldots, T_J, G_{11}, G_{12}, \ldots, G_{IJ}, \varepsilon_{111}, \varepsilon_{112}, \ldots, \varepsilon_{IJn_{IJ}}$ *are unobservable random variables that are pairwise uncorrelated, have zero means, and* $\text{var}[A_i] = \sigma_A^2$, $\text{var}[T_j] = \sigma_T^2$, $\text{var}[G_{ij}] = \sigma_G^2$, *and* $\text{var}[\varepsilon_{ijm}] = \sigma_\varepsilon^2$. *For Case I the random variables* A_i, T_j, G_{ij}, *and* ε_{ijm} *are jointly normally distributed (other cases will be defined when they are used). These specifications define a two-factor crossed components-of-variance model.*

We shall discuss only the two models stated in Equations (15.4.4) and (15.4.5).

$$n_{ij} = M > 1 \qquad \text{and} \qquad Y_{ijm} = \mu + A_i + T_j + G_{ij} + \varepsilon_{ijm} \qquad (15.4.4)$$

This model is defined to be a "balanced, complete," two-factor crossed components-of-variance model with interaction and is discussed in Section 15.4.2.

$$n_{ij} = M = 1 \qquad \text{and} \qquad Y_{ij} = \mu + A_i + T_j + \varepsilon_{ij} \qquad (15.4.5)$$

that is, there is no interaction term and there is only one observation per cell. This model, called a "balanced, complete," two-factor crossed components-of-variance model without interaction, is discussed in Section 15.4.3.

For various inference procedures we shall require some additional assumptions on the distributions of the unobservable random variables.

15.4.2 Two-Factor Crossed Components-of-Variance Model, $n_{ij} = M > 1$

This model is given in Definition 15.4.1 and Equation (15.4.4). First we assume (Case I) that the joint distribution of the unobservable random variables A_i, T_j, G_{ij}, and ε_{ijm} is normal. This model appears to be quite similar to the model in Equation (14.1.8), so we attempt to find a set of sufficient statistics by using the identity

$$Y_{ijm} = \bar{Y}_{...} + (\bar{Y}_{i..} - \bar{Y}_{...}) + (\bar{Y}_{.j.} - \bar{Y}_{...}) + (\bar{Y}_{ij.} - \bar{Y}_{i..} - \bar{Y}_{.j.} + \bar{Y}_{...}) + (Y_{ijm} - \bar{Y}_{ij.}) \quad (15.4.6)$$

It is straightforward but tedious to show that the following five *sets* of random variables are jointly independent:

$$\{\bar{Y}_{...}\}$$
$$\{\bar{Y}_{i..} - \bar{Y}_{...}; i = 1, 2, \ldots, I\}$$
$$\{\bar{Y}_{.j.} - \bar{Y}_{...}; j = 1, 2, \ldots, J\}$$
$$\{\bar{Y}_{ij.} - \bar{Y}_{i..} - \bar{Y}_{.j.} + \bar{Y}_{...}; i = 1, 2, \ldots, I; j = 1, 2, \ldots, J\}$$
$$\{Y_{ijm} - \bar{Y}_{ij.}; i = 1, 2, \ldots, I; j = 1, 2, \ldots, J; m = 1, 2, \ldots, M\}$$

Since the Y_{ijm} are jointly normal random variables, the above statement is proved if we can show that the covariance is zero between a general element in each pair of the five sets. We illustrate for one such pair, say $\{\bar{Y}_{i..} - \bar{Y}_{...}; i = 1, 2, \ldots, I\}$ and $\{Y_{ijm} - \bar{Y}_{ij.}; i = 1, 2, \ldots, I; j = 1, 2, \ldots, J; m = 1, 2, \ldots, M\}$. We get

$$\begin{aligned}
\operatorname{cov}[(\bar{Y}_{i..} - \bar{Y}_{...}), (Y_{i'jm} - \bar{Y}_{i'j.})] &= \mathscr{E}[(\mu + A_i + \bar{T}_. + \bar{G}_{i.} + \bar{\varepsilon}_{i..} - \mu - \bar{A}_. - \bar{T}_. - \bar{G}_{..} - \bar{\varepsilon}_{...}) \\
&\quad \times (\mu + A_{i'} + T_j + G_{i'j} + \varepsilon_{i'jm} - \mu - A_{i'} - T_j - G_{i'j} - \bar{\varepsilon}_{i'j.})] \\
&= \mathscr{E}[\{(A_i - \bar{A}_.) + (\bar{G}_{i.} - \bar{G}_{..}) + (\bar{\varepsilon}_{i..} - \bar{\varepsilon}_{...})\}\{(\varepsilon_{i'jm} - \bar{\varepsilon}_{i'j.})\}] \\
&= \mathscr{E}[\bar{\varepsilon}_{i..}\varepsilon_{i'jm} - \bar{\varepsilon}_{i..}\bar{\varepsilon}_{i'j.} - \bar{\varepsilon}_{...}\varepsilon_{i'jm} + \bar{\varepsilon}_{...}\bar{\varepsilon}_{i'j.}] \\
&= \frac{\delta_{ii'}\sigma_\varepsilon^2}{JM} - \frac{\delta_{ii'}\sigma_\varepsilon^2}{JM} - \frac{\sigma_\varepsilon^2}{IJM} + \frac{\sigma_\varepsilon^2}{IJM} = 0
\end{aligned}$$

The proofs for the remaining pairs are similar.

If we square the left and right sides of Equation (15.4.6) and sum over i, j, and m, we note that all cross products vanish, and the result is

$$\begin{aligned}
\sum_{i=1}^{I}\sum_{j=1}^{J}\sum_{m=1}^{M} Y_{ijm}^2 &= \frac{Y_{...}^2}{IJM} + \sum_{i=1}^{I}\sum_{j=1}^{J}\sum_{m=1}^{M} (\bar{Y}_{i..} - \bar{Y}_{...})^2 + \sum_{i=1}^{I}\sum_{j=1}^{J}\sum_{m=1}^{M} (\bar{Y}_{.j.} - \bar{Y}_{...})^2 \\
&\quad + \sum_{i=1}^{I}\sum_{j=1}^{J}\sum_{m=1}^{M} (\bar{Y}_{ij.} - \bar{Y}_{i..} - \bar{Y}_{.j.} + \bar{Y}_{...})^2 + \sum_{i=1}^{I}\sum_{j=1}^{J}\sum_{m=1}^{M} (Y_{ijm} - \bar{Y}_{ij.})^2 \\
&= \mathbf{Y}'\mathbf{A}_0\mathbf{Y} + \mathbf{Y}'\mathbf{A}_1\mathbf{Y} + \mathbf{Y}'\mathbf{A}_2\mathbf{Y} + \mathbf{Y}'\mathbf{A}_3\mathbf{Y} + \mathbf{Y}'\mathbf{A}_4\mathbf{Y} \quad (15.4.7)
\end{aligned}$$

where $\mathbf{Y} = [Y_{111}, Y_{112}, \ldots, Y_{IJM}]'$. These computed sums of squares appear in Table 15.4.1 (page 633) for the two-factor *design* model.

We now state a theorem about distributional properties of these five quadratic forms.

THEOREM 15.4.1

Let the model be given by Definition 15.4.1 and Equation (15.4.4) for Case I. The results below follow.

(1) $U_0 = IJM\bar{Y}_{...}^2/(\sigma_\varepsilon^2 + M\sigma_G^2 + IM\sigma_T^2 + JM\sigma_A^2)$ *is distributed* $\chi^2(u_0 : 1; \lambda)$, *where* $\lambda = IJM\mu^2/2(\sigma_\varepsilon^2 + M\sigma_G^2 + IM\sigma_T^2 + JM\sigma_A^2)$.

(2) $U_1 = \sum_{i=1}^I \sum_{j=1}^J \sum_{m=1}^M (\bar{Y}_{i..} - \bar{Y}_{...})^2/(\sigma_\varepsilon^2 + M\sigma_G^2 + JM\sigma_A^2)$ *is distributed* $\chi^2(u_1 : I - 1)$.

(3) $U_2 = \sum_{i=1}^I \sum_{j=1}^J \sum_{m=1}^M (\bar{Y}_{.j.} - \bar{Y}_{...})^2/(\sigma_\varepsilon^2 + M\sigma_G^2 + IM\sigma_T^2)$ *is distributed* $\chi^2(u_2 : J - 1)$.

(4) $U_3 = \sum_{i=1}^I \sum_{j=1}^J \sum_{m=1}^M (\bar{Y}_{ij.} - \bar{Y}_{i..} - \bar{Y}_{.j.} + \bar{Y}_{...})^2/(\sigma_\varepsilon^2 + M\sigma_G^2)$ *is distributed* $\chi^2(u_3 : (I - 1)(J - 1))$.

(5) $U_4 = \sum_{i=1}^I \sum_{j=1}^J \sum_{m=1}^M (Y_{ijm} - \bar{Y}_{ij.})^2/\sigma_\varepsilon^2$ *is distributed* $\chi^2(u_4 : (M - 1)IJ)$.

(6) U_0, U_1, U_2, U_3, *and* U_4 *are jointly independent.*

Proof

The numerators in the random variables $U_0, U_1, \ldots, U_4$ are the quadratic forms in Equation (15.4.7). The proofs for (1) through (5) are all similar and we shall demonstrate for (4).

If we substitute the model into U_3 and simplify, we get

$$U_3 = \sum_{m=1}^M \left\{ \sum_{i=1}^I \sum_{j=1}^J \frac{[(G_{ij} + \bar{\varepsilon}_{ij.}) - (\bar{G}_{i.} + \bar{\varepsilon}_{i..}) - (\bar{G}_{.j} + \bar{\varepsilon}_{.j.}) + (\bar{G}_{...} + \bar{\varepsilon}_{...})]^2}{\sigma_\varepsilon^2 + M\sigma_G^2} \right\}$$

$$= M\left\{ \sum_{i=1}^I \sum_{j=1}^J \frac{[W_{ij} - \bar{W}_{i.} - \bar{W}_{.j} + \bar{W}_{..}]^2}{\sigma_\varepsilon^2 + M\sigma_G^2} \right\}$$

where we have set $W_{ij} = G_{ij} + \bar{\varepsilon}_{ij.}$. But the W_{ij} are distributed $NID(w : 0, \sigma_G^2 + \sigma_\varepsilon^2/M)$, so the random variable

$$\sum_{i=1}^I \sum_{j=1}^J \frac{(W_{ij} - \bar{W}_{i.} - \bar{W}_{.j} + \bar{W}_{..})^2}{\sigma_G^2 + \sigma_\varepsilon^2/M}$$

is distributed as a chi-square random variable with $(I - 1)(J - 1)$

degrees of freedom. This completes the proof for (4). Proofs of the remaining parts are similar. We have already given the method for proof of (6).

From these results we can proceed in a fashion similar to the procedure following Theorem 15.2.3 and establish results for the model in this section similar to the results in Theorem 15.2.4 for the one-way components-of-variance model. The results are stated in the following theorem; the proof will be left for the reader.

THEOREM 15.4.2

Let the model be given in Definition 15.4.1 *and in Equation* (15.4.4) *for Case I. The five statistics* $\bar{Y}_{...}$, $\mathbf{Y}'\mathbf{A}_1\mathbf{Y}$, $\mathbf{Y}'\mathbf{A}_2\mathbf{Y}$, $\mathbf{Y}'\mathbf{A}_3\mathbf{Y}$, *and* $\mathbf{Y}'\mathbf{A}_4\mathbf{Y}$ *are complete sufficient statistics. From these statistics UMVU estimators of* σ_ε^2, σ_G^2, σ_T^2, σ_A^2, μ, *and any linear function of these parameters can be obtained* (*see Table* 15.4.1 *for computations*).

The next result concerns BQU estimators of variance components.

THEOREM 15.4.3

Let the model be given in Definition 15.4.1 *and in Equation* (15.4.4), *but instead of Case I we use the following assumptions*:

$$\mathscr{E}[\varepsilon_{ijm}^3] = \xi_\varepsilon^3 \qquad \mathscr{E}[\varepsilon_{ijm}^4] = \xi_\varepsilon^4 \qquad \mathscr{E}[G_{ij}^3] = \xi_G^3$$
$$\mathscr{E}[G_{ij}^4] = \xi_G^4 \qquad \mathscr{E}[T_j^3] = \xi_T^3 \qquad \mathscr{E}[T_j^4] = \xi_T^4$$
$$\mathscr{E}[A_i^3] = \xi_A^3 \qquad \mathscr{E}[A_i^4] = \xi_A^4$$

the random variables $A_1, A_2, \ldots, A_I$, $T_1, T_2, \ldots, T_J$, $G_{11}, G_{12}, \ldots, G_{IJ}$, ε_{111}, $\varepsilon_{112}, \ldots, \varepsilon_{IJM}$ *are jointly independent.* (*These assumptions are Case II of the general model given in Definition* 15.1.1.) *The results below follow.*

(1) $\mathbf{Y}'\mathbf{A}_i\mathbf{Y}$ *is the BQU estimator of* $\mathscr{E}[\mathbf{Y}'\mathbf{A}_i\mathbf{Y}]$ *for* $i = 1, 2, 3, 4$.

(2) $\sum_{i=1}^4 c_i\mathbf{Y}'\mathbf{A}_i\mathbf{Y}$ *is the BQU estimator of* $\mathscr{E}[\sum_{i=1}^4 c_i\mathbf{Y}'\mathbf{A}_i\mathbf{Y}]$, *where the* c_i *are specified constants.*

Proof

The proof is similar to the proof for Theorem 15.2.5 and will be left for the reader. See [G-6].

An ANOVA table is often useful for displaying the computations, and from the table the best unbiased estimates can be easily obtained. This is demonstrated in Table 15.4.1. For point estimation and hypotheses tests, Table 15.3.1 and the results of Equations (15.3.2) and (15.3.3) can be used.

Table 15.4.1

Computations for Two-Factor Crossed Components-of-Variance Model with Interaction and $M > 1$ Observations Per Cell

Source	*d.f.*	*S.S.*	*M.S.*	*E.M.S.*
Total	IJM	$\sum_{i=1}^{I}\sum_{j=1}^{J}\sum_{m=1}^{M} y_{ijm}^2$		
Mean	1	$\frac{y_{\ldots}^2}{IJM} = s_0^2$		
Factor A	$I - 1$	$\sum_{i=1}^{I}\sum_{j=1}^{J}\sum_{m=1}^{M} (\bar{y}_{i..} - \bar{y}_{\ldots})^2 = s_1^2$	MS_1	$\gamma_1^2 = \sigma_\varepsilon^2 + M\sigma_G^2 + JM\sigma_A^2$
Factor T	$J - 1$	$\sum_{i=1}^{I}\sum_{j=1}^{J}\sum_{m=1}^{M} (\bar{y}_{.j.} - \bar{y}_{\ldots})^2 = s_2^2$	MS_2	$\gamma_2^2 = \sigma_\varepsilon^2 + M\sigma_G^2 + IM\sigma_T^2$
Interaction	$(I - 1)(J - 1)$	$\sum_{i=1}^{I}\sum_{j=1}^{J}\sum_{m=1}^{M} (\bar{y}_{ij.} - \bar{y}_{i..} - \bar{y}_{.j.} + \bar{y}_{\ldots})^2 = s_3^2$	MS_3	$\gamma_3^2 = \sigma_\varepsilon^2 + M\sigma_G^2$
Error	$IJ(M - 1)$	$\sum_{i=1}^{I}\sum_{j=1}^{J}\sum_{m=1}^{M} (y_{ijm} - \bar{y}_{ij.})^2 = s_4^2$	MS_4	$\gamma_4^2 = \sigma_\varepsilon^2$

Table 15.4.2

Computations for Two-Factor Crossed Components-of-Variance Model without Interaction and $M = 1$ Observations Per Cell

Source	*d.f.*	*S.S.*	*M.S.*	*E.M.S.*
Total	IJ	$\sum_{i=1}^{I}\sum_{j=1}^{J} y_{ij}^2$		
Mean	1	$\frac{y_{..}^2}{IJ} = s_0^2$		
Factor A	$n_1 = I - 1$	$\sum_{i=1}^{I}\sum_{j=1}^{J} (\bar{y}_{i.} - \bar{y}_{..})^2 = s_1^2$	MS_1	$\gamma_1^2 = \sigma_\varepsilon^2 + J\sigma_A^2$
Factor T	$n_2 = J - 1$	$\sum_{i=1}^{I}\sum_{j=1}^{J} (\bar{y}_{.j} - \bar{y}_{..})^2 = s_2^2$	MS_2	$\gamma_2^2 = \sigma_\varepsilon^2 + I\sigma_T^2$
Error	$n_3 = (I - 1)(J - 1)$	$\sum_{i=1}^{I}\sum_{j=1}^{J} (y_{ij} - \bar{y}_{i.} - \bar{y}_{.j} + \bar{y}_{..})^2 = s_3^2$	MS_3	$\gamma_3^2 = \sigma_\varepsilon^2$

15.4.3 Two-Factor Crossed Model with $n_{ij} = M = 1$ and No Interaction

The model is given in Equation (15.4.5). The computations are displayed in Table 15.4.2.

Inference procedures for σ_ε^2, σ_A^2, and σ_T^2 can be obtained by the methods described in Table 15.3.1 and Equations (15.3.2) and (15.3.3).

15.4.4 Two-Factor Nested Components-of-Variance Model with Equal Numbers in the Subclasses

The model to be discussed in this section is given by $Y_{ijm} = \mu + A_i + B_{ij} + \varepsilon_{ijm}$; $i = 1, 2, \ldots, I > 1$; $j = 1, 2, \ldots, J > 1$; $m = 1, 2, \ldots, M > 1$; $\mathscr{E}[A_i] = \mathscr{E}[B_{ij}] = \mathscr{E}[\varepsilon_{ijm}] = 0$; $\text{var}[A_i] = \sigma_A^2$; $\text{var}[B_{ij}] = \sigma_B^2$; and $\text{var}[\varepsilon_{ijm}] = \sigma_\varepsilon^2$. The computations are displayed in Table 15.4.3.

The identity in Y_{ijm} is

$$Y_{ijm} = \bar{Y}_{...} + (\bar{Y}_{i..} - \bar{Y}_{...}) + (\bar{Y}_{ij.} - \bar{Y}_{i..}) + (Y_{ijm} - \bar{Y}_{ij.})$$

The identity in $\sum_{i=1}^{I}\sum_{j=1}^{J}\sum_{m=1}^{M} Y_{ijm}^2$ is

$$\sum_{i=1}^{I}\sum_{j=1}^{J}\sum_{m=1}^{M} Y_{ijm}^2 = S_0^2 + S_1^2 + S_2^2 + S_3^2 = \mathbf{Y'A_0Y} + \mathbf{Y'A_1Y} + \mathbf{Y'A_2Y} + \mathbf{Y'A_3Y}$$

Table 15.4.3

Computations for Two-Factor Nested Components-of-Variance Model with Equal Numbers in the Subclasses

Source	*d.f.*	*S.S.*	*M.S.*	*E.M.S.*
Total	IJM	$\sum_{i=1}^{I}\sum_{j=1}^{J}\sum_{m=1}^{M} y_{ijm}^2$		
Mean	1	$\frac{y_{...}^2}{IJM} = s_0^2$		
Factor A	$I - 1 = n_1$	$\sum_{i=1}^{I}\sum_{j=1}^{J}\sum_{m=1}^{M} (\bar{y}_{i..} - \bar{y}_{...})^2 = s_1^2$	MS_1	$\gamma_1^2 = \sigma_\varepsilon^2 + M\sigma_B^2 + JM\sigma_A^2$
B within A	$I(J - 1) = n_2$	$\sum_{i=1}^{I}\sum_{j=1}^{J}\sum_{m=1}^{M} (\bar{y}_{ij.} - \bar{y}_{i..})^2 = s_2^2$	MS_2	$\gamma_2^2 = \sigma_\varepsilon^2 + M\sigma_B^2$
Error	$IJ(M - 1) = n_3$	$\sum_{i=1}^{I}\sum_{j=1}^{J}\sum_{m=1}^{M} (y_{ijm} - \bar{y}_{ij.})^2 = s_3^2$	MS_3	$\gamma_3^2 = \sigma_\varepsilon^2$

The best unbiased estimates are

$$\hat{\sigma}_\varepsilon^2 = MS_3 \qquad \hat{\sigma}_B^2 = \frac{MS_2 - MS_3}{M} \qquad \hat{\sigma}_A^2 = \frac{MS_1 - MS_2}{JM}$$

By using the procedures outlined in Table 15.3.1 and Equations (15.3.2) and (15.3.3), one can compute confidence intervals (and tests) on σ_ε^2, σ_B^2, and σ_A^2.

Next we shall give a simple artificial example to illustrate some of the formulas.

Example 15.4.2

Suppose that data are collected as the result of an investigation, and the data are assumed to satisfy Case I of the two-factor nested components-of-variance model with $M = 3$, $J = 4$, and $I = 6$. The quantities needed in Table 15.4.3 are computed and are displayed in Table 15.4.4.

Table 15.4.4

Computations for Two-Factor Nested Components-of-Variance Model

Source	*d.f.*	*S.S.*	*M.S.*	*E.M.S.*
Total	72			
Mean	1			
Factor A	$5 = n_1$	$1927.0 = s_1^2$	385.4	$\gamma_1^2 = \sigma_\varepsilon^2 + 3\sigma_B^2 + 12\sigma_A^2$
B Within A	$18 = n_2$	$1537.2 = s_2^2$	85.4	$\gamma_2^2 = \sigma_\varepsilon^2 + 3\sigma_B^2$
Error	$48 = n_3$	$585.6 = s_3^2$	12.2	$\gamma_3^2 = \sigma_\varepsilon^2$

We want the following: (1) UMVU estimates of σ_ε^2, σ_B^2, σ_A^2, and $\sigma_A^2 + \sigma_B^2$; (2) a 95 percent confidence interval on σ_A^2.

The answer to (1) is obtained by equating the computed mean squares to the respective expected mean squares and solving for σ_ε^2, σ_B^2, and σ_A^2. We get $\hat{\sigma}_\varepsilon^2 = 12.2$, $\hat{\sigma}_B^2 = 24.4$, and $\hat{\sigma}_A^2 = 25.0$; hence $\hat{\sigma}_A^2 + \hat{\sigma}_B^2 = 49.4$.

To answer (2) we can use the formula in Theorem 15.3.5; $1 - 2\alpha = 0.90$, $\alpha/2 = 0.025$, $j = 1$, and $k = 2$. Also $\gamma^2 = \gamma_1^2 - \gamma_2^2 = 12\sigma_A^2$, $n_j = n_1 = 5$, and $n_k = n_2 = 18$. We get $\chi^2_{\alpha_1:n_1} = \chi^2_{0.025:5} = 12.832$, $\chi^2_{1-\alpha_2:n_1} = \chi^2_{0.975:5} = 0.831$, $F_{\alpha_1:n_1,n_2} = F_{0.025:5,18} = 3.403$, and $F_{1-\alpha_2:n_1,n_2} = F_{0.975:5,18} = 0.157$. Substituting gives us

$$[12(12.832)]^{-1}[1927.0 - (5/18)(1537.2)(3.403)] \le \sigma_A^2 \le [12(0.831)]^{-1}[1927.0 - (5/18)(1537.2)(0.157)]$$

which simplifies to $3.078 \le \sigma_A^2 \le 186.518$.

15.5 Other Components-of-Variance Models

In this section we present several models, exhibit the ANOVA tables, relate them to Table 15.3.1, and display the appropriate statistics that can be used for inference about the variance components.

15.5.1 Three-Factor Nested Components-of-Variance Model

The model is

$$Y_{ijkm} = \mu + A_i + B_{ij} + C_{ijk} + \varepsilon_{ijkm} \qquad i = 1, 2, \ldots, I > 1$$
$$j = 1, 2, \ldots, J > 1, \quad k = 1, 2, \ldots, K > 1, \quad m = 1, 2, \ldots, M > 1$$
$$\mathscr{E}[A_i] = \mathscr{E}[B_{ij}] = \mathscr{E}[C_{ijk}] = \mathscr{E}[\varepsilon_{ijkm}] = 0$$
$$\text{var}[A_i] = \sigma_A^2 \qquad \text{var}[B_{ij}] = \sigma_B^2 \qquad \text{var}[C_{ijk}] = \sigma_C^2 \qquad \text{var}[\varepsilon_{ijkm}] = \sigma_\varepsilon^2$$

This is a special case of the model in Definition 15.1.1.

The computations are displayed in Table 15.5.1, where the sums are over i, j, k, and m as specified in the model.

The identity in Y_{ijkm} is

$$Y_{ijkm} = \bar{Y}_{....} + (\bar{Y}_{i...} - \bar{Y}_{....}) + (\bar{Y}_{ij..} - \bar{Y}_{i...}) + (\bar{Y}_{ijk.} - \bar{Y}_{ij..}) + (Y_{ijkm} - \bar{Y}_{ijk.})$$

Table 15.5.1

Computations for Three-Factor Nested Components-of-Variance Model with Equal Numbers in the Subclasses

Source	*d.f.*	*S.S.*	*M.S.*	*E.M.S.*
Total	$IJKM$	$\sum\sum\sum\sum y_{ijkm}^2$		
Mean	1	$\frac{y_{....}^2}{IJKM} = s_0^2$		
Factor A	$I - 1$	$\sum\sum\sum\sum(\bar{y}_{i...} - \bar{y}_{....})^2 = s_1^2$	MS_1	$\gamma_1^2 = \sigma_\varepsilon^2 + M\sigma_C^2 + KM\sigma_B^2 + JKM\sigma_A^2$
B within A	$I(J - 1)$	$\sum\sum\sum\sum(\bar{y}_{ij..} - \bar{y}_{i...})^2 = s_2^2$	MS_2	$\gamma_2^2 = \sigma_\varepsilon^2 + M\sigma_C^2 + KM\sigma_B^2$
C within B within A	$IJ(K - 1)$	$\sum\sum\sum\sum(\bar{y}_{ijk.} - \bar{y}_{ij..})^2 = s_3^2$	MS_3	$\gamma_3^2 = \sigma_\varepsilon^2 + M\sigma_C^2$
Error	$IJK(M - 1)$	$\sum\sum\sum\sum(y_{ijkm} - \bar{y}_{ijk.})^2 = s_4^2$	MS_4	$\gamma_4^2 = \sigma_\varepsilon^2$

The identity in $\sum\sum\sum\sum Y_{ijkm}^2$ is

$$\sum\sum\sum\sum Y_{ijkm}^2 = S_0^2 + S_1^2 + S_2^2 + S_3^2 + S_4^2 = \sum_{i=0}^{4} \mathbf{Y}'\mathbf{A}_i\mathbf{Y}$$

The best unbiased estimates are

$$\hat{\sigma}_\varepsilon^2 = MS_4 \qquad \hat{\sigma}_C^2 = \frac{MS_3 - MS_4}{M}$$

$$\hat{\sigma}_B^2 = \frac{MS_2 - MS_3}{KM} \qquad \hat{\sigma}_A^2 = \frac{MS_1 - MS_2}{JKM}$$

By using the procedures outlined in Table 15.3.1 and Equations (15.3.2) and (15.3.3), confidence intervals and tests on σ_ε^2, σ_C^2, σ_B^2, and σ_A^2 can be computed.

15.5.2 Four-Factor Nested Components-of-Variance Model

The model is

$$Y_{ijkmn} = \mu + A_i + B_{ij} + C_{ijk} + D_{ijkm} + \varepsilon_{ijkmn} \qquad i = 1, 2, \ldots, I > 1,$$
$$j = 1, 2, \ldots, J > 1, \quad k = 1, 2, \ldots, K > 1, \quad m = 1, 2, \ldots, M > 1,$$
$$n = 1, 2, \ldots, N > 1$$

$$\mathscr{E}[A_i] = \mathscr{E}[B_{ij}] = \mathscr{E}[C_{ijk}] = \mathscr{E}[D_{ijkm}] = \mathscr{E}[\varepsilon_{ijkmn}] = 0$$
$$\text{var}[A_i] = \sigma_A^2 \qquad \text{var}[B_{ij}] = \sigma_B^2 \qquad \text{var}[C_{ijk}] = \sigma_C^2$$
$$\text{var}[D_{ijkm}] = \sigma_D^2 \qquad \text{var}[\varepsilon_{ijkmn}] = \sigma_\varepsilon^2$$

This is a special case of the model in Definition 15.1.1.

The computations are displayed in Table 15.5.2, where the sums are over i, j, k, m, and n as specified in the model.

The identity in Y_{ijkmn} is

$$Y_{ijkmn} = (Y_{ijkmn} - \bar{Y}_{ijkm.}) + (\bar{Y}_{ijkm.} - \bar{Y}_{ijk..}) + (\bar{Y}_{ijk..} - \bar{Y}_{ij...})$$
$$+ (\bar{Y}_{ij...} - \bar{Y}_{i....}) + (\bar{Y}_{i....} - \bar{Y}_{.....}) + \bar{Y}_{.....}$$

The identity in $\sum\sum\sum\sum\sum Y_{ijkmn}^2$ is

$$\sum\sum\sum\sum\sum Y_{ijkmn}^2 = S_0^2 + S_1^2 + S_2^2 + S_4^2 + S_5^2 = \sum_{i=0}^{5} \mathbf{Y}'\mathbf{A}_i\mathbf{Y}$$

Table 15.5.2

Computations for Four-Factor Nested Components-of-Variance Model with Equal Numbers in the Subclasses

Source	*d.f.*	*S.S.*	*M.S.*	*E.M.S.*
Total	$IJKMN$	$\sum\sum\sum\sum\sum y_{ijkmn}^2$		
Mean	1	$\frac{y_{.....}^2}{IJKMN} = s_0^2$		
Factor A	$I - 1$	$\sum\sum\sum\sum\sum (\bar{y}_{i....} - \bar{y}_{.....})^2 = s_1^2$	MS_1	$\gamma_1^2 = \sigma_\varepsilon^2 + N\sigma_D^2 + MN\sigma_C^2 + KMN\sigma_B^2 + JKMN\sigma_A^2$
B within A	$I(J - 1)$	$\sum\sum\sum\sum\sum (\bar{y}_{ij...} - \bar{y}_{i....})^2 = s_2^2$	MS_2	$\gamma_2^2 = \sigma_\varepsilon^2 + N\sigma_D^2 + MN\sigma_C^2 + KMN\sigma_B^2$
C within B within A	$IJ(K - 1)$	$\sum\sum\sum\sum\sum (\bar{y}_{ijk..} - \bar{y}_{ij...})^2 = s_3^2$	MS_3	$\gamma_3^2 = \sigma_\varepsilon^2 + N\sigma_D^2 + MN\sigma_C^2$
D within C within B within A	$IJK(M - 1)$	$\sum\sum\sum\sum\sum (\bar{y}_{ijkm.} - \bar{y}_{ijk..})^2 = s_4^2$	MS_4	$\gamma_4^2 = \sigma_\varepsilon^2 + N\sigma_D^2$
Error	$IJKM(N - 1)$	$\sum\sum\sum\sum\sum (y_{ijkmn} - \bar{y}_{ijkm.})^2 = s_5^2$	MS_5	$\gamma_5^2 = \sigma_\varepsilon^2$

The best unbiased estimates are

$$\hat{\sigma}_\varepsilon^2 = MS_5 \qquad \hat{\sigma}_D^2 = \frac{MS_4 - MS_5}{N} \qquad \hat{\sigma}_C^2 = \frac{MS_3 - MS_4}{MN}$$

$$\hat{\sigma}_B^2 = \frac{MS_2 - MS_3}{KMN} \qquad \hat{\sigma}_A^2 = \frac{MS_1 - MS_2}{JKMN}$$

By using the procedures outlined in Table 15.3.1 and Equations (15.3.2) and (15.3.3), confidence intervals and tests on $\sigma_\varepsilon^2, \sigma_D^2, \sigma_C^2, \sigma_B^2$, and σ_A^2 can be computed.

15.5.3 Three-Factor Crossed Components-of-Variance Model with Interaction

The model is

$$Y_{ijkm} = \mu + A_i + B_j + F_{ij} + C_k + G_{ik} + H_{jk} + P_{ijk} + \varepsilon_{ijkm}$$

$$i = 1, 2, \ldots, I > 1, \quad j = 1, 2, \ldots, J > 1, \quad k = 1, 2, \ldots, K > 1, \quad m = 1, 2, \ldots, M > 1$$

$$\mathscr{E}[A_i] = \mathscr{E}[B_j] = \mathscr{E}[F_{ij}] = \mathscr{E}[C_k] = \mathscr{E}[G_{ik}] = \mathscr{E}[H_{jk}] = \mathscr{E}[P_{ijk}] = \mathscr{E}[\varepsilon_{ijkm}] = 0$$

$$\text{var}[A_i] = \sigma_A^2 \quad \text{var}[B_j] = \sigma_B^2 \quad \text{var}[F_{ij}] = \sigma_F^2 \quad \text{var}[C_k] = \sigma_C^2$$

$$\text{var}[G_{ik}] = \sigma_G^2 \quad \text{var}[H_{jk}] = \sigma_H^2 \quad \text{var}[P_{ijk}] = \sigma_P^2 \quad \text{var}[\varepsilon_{ijkm}] = \sigma_\varepsilon^2$$

This is a special case of the model in Definition 15.1.1.

The computations are displayed in Table 15.5.3, where the sums are over i, j, k, and m as specified in the model.

The identity in Y_{ijkm} is

$$\begin{aligned} Y_{ijkm} = {} & \bar{Y}_{....} + (\bar{Y}_{i...} - \bar{Y}_{....}) + (\bar{Y}_{.j..} - \bar{Y}_{....}) + (\bar{Y}_{ij..} - \bar{Y}_{i...} - \bar{Y}_{.j..} + \bar{Y}_{....}) \\ & + (\bar{Y}_{..k.} - \bar{Y}_{....}) + (\bar{Y}_{i.k.} - \bar{Y}_{i...} - \bar{Y}_{..k.} + \bar{Y}_{....}) + (\bar{Y}_{.jk.} - \bar{Y}_{.j..} - \bar{Y}_{..k.} + \bar{Y}_{....}) \\ & + (\bar{Y}_{ijk.} - \bar{Y}_{ij..} - \bar{Y}_{i.k.} - \bar{Y}_{.jk.} + \bar{Y}_{i...} + \bar{Y}_{.j..} + \bar{Y}_{..k.} - \bar{Y}_{....}) + (Y_{ijkm} - \bar{Y}_{ijk.}) \end{aligned}$$

The identity in $\sum\sum\sum\sum Y_{ijkm}^2$ is $\sum\sum\sum\sum Y_{ijkm}^2 = \sum_{i=0}^{8} S_i^2$. The best unbiased estimate of any σ^2 is obtained by setting $MS_i = \hat{\gamma}_i^2$ and solving for the desired $\hat{\sigma}^2$. By using the procedures outlined in Table 15.3.1 and Equations (15.3.2) and (15.3.3), confidence intervals and tests can be computed for σ_P^2, σ_H^2, σ_G^2, σ_F^2 (these are the results of confidence intervals and tests on $\gamma_k^2 - \gamma_j^2$) and σ_ε^2. This procedure will not work for confidence intervals on σ_A^2, σ_B^2, and σ_C^2. An approximate procedure that can be used for this case is described in the next section.

Table 15.5.3

Computations for Three-Factor Crossed Components-of-Variance Model with Interaction and Equal Numbers in the Subclasses

Source	*d.f.*	*S.S.*	*M.S.*	*E.M.S.*
Total	$IJKM$	$\sum\sum\sum\sum y_{ijkm}^2$		
Mean	1	$\frac{y_{....}^2}{IJKM} = s_0^2$		
Factor A	$I - 1$	$\sum\sum\sum\sum (\bar{y}_{i...} - \bar{y}_{....})^2 = s_1^2$	MS_1	$\gamma_1^2 = \sigma_\varepsilon^2 + M\sigma_P^2 + MK\sigma_F^2 + MJ\sigma_G^2 + MJK\sigma_A^2$
Factor B	$J - 1$	$\sum\sum\sum\sum (\bar{y}_{.j..} - \bar{y}_{....})^2 = s_2^2$	MS_2	$\gamma_2^2 = \sigma_\varepsilon^2 + M\sigma_P^2 + MK\sigma_F^2 + MI\sigma_H^2 + MIK\sigma_B^2$
AB Interaction (F)	$(I - 1)(J - 1)$	$\sum\sum\sum\sum (\bar{y}_{ij..} - \bar{y}_{i...} - \bar{y}_{.j..} + \bar{y}_{....})^2 = s_3^2$	MS_3	$\gamma_3^2 = \sigma_\varepsilon^2 + M\sigma_P^2 + MK\sigma_F^2$
Factor C	$K - 1$	$\sum\sum\sum\sum (\bar{y}_{..k.} - \bar{y}_{....})^2 = s_4^2$	MS_4	$\gamma_4^2 = \sigma_\varepsilon^2 + M\sigma_P^2 + MJ\sigma_G^2 + MI\sigma_H^2 + MIJ\sigma_C^2$
AC Interaction (G)	$(I - 1)(K - 1)$	$\sum\sum\sum\sum (\bar{y}_{i.k.} - \bar{y}_{i...} - \bar{y}_{..k.} + \bar{y}_{....})^2 = s_5^2$	MS_5	$\gamma_5^2 = \sigma_\varepsilon^2 + M\sigma_P^2 + MJ\sigma_G^2$
BC Interaction (H)	$(J - 1)(K - 1)$	$\sum\sum\sum\sum (\bar{y}_{.jk.} - \bar{y}_{.j..} - \bar{y}_{..k.} + \bar{y}_{....})^2 = s_6^2$	MS_6	$\gamma_6^2 = \sigma_\varepsilon^2 + M\sigma_P^2 + MI\sigma_H^2$
ABC Interaction (P)	$(I - 1)(J - 1)(K - 1)$	$\sum\sum\sum\sum (\bar{y}_{ijk.} - \bar{y}_{ij..} - \bar{y}_{i.k.} - \bar{y}_{.jk.} + \bar{y}_{i...} + \bar{y}_{.j..} + \bar{y}_{..k.} - \bar{y}_{....})^2 = s_7^2$	MS_7	$\gamma_7^2 = \sigma_\varepsilon^2 + M\sigma_P^2$
Error	$IJK(M - 1)$	$\sum\sum\sum\sum (y_{ijkm} - \bar{y}_{ijk.})^2 = s_8^2$	MS_8	$\gamma_8^2 = \sigma_\varepsilon^2$

15.6 Additional Results on Components-of-Variance Models

In previous sections of this chapter we have proved that for Case I of the model, defined in Equation (15.1.1), confidence intervals (with exact confidence coefficient) exist for γ_i^2 in Table 15.3.1 and with confidence coefficient greater than or equal to $1 - 2\alpha$ for $\gamma_k^2 - \gamma_j^2$ (where $\gamma_k^2 \geq \gamma_j^2$). However, there are many models for which confidence intervals are desired on variances which are not γ_i^2 nor $\gamma_k^2 - \gamma_j^2$. For example, in Table 15.5.3, σ_A^2 (or σ_B^2, or σ_C^2) is not equal to $\gamma_k^2 - \gamma_j^2$ but is a more general linear combination of the γ_i^2, and no confidence interval with exact confidence coefficient exists.

A somewhat general method for finding approximate confidence intervals for these situations was proposed by Satterthwaite; see [D-5], [H-18], [H-21], and [S-2]. We shall outline the procedure and refer the reader to some recent literature on the subject. The central idea is this: If the $U_i = S_i^2/\gamma_i^2$ are independent chi-square random variables with n_i degrees of freedom, for $i = 1, 2, \ldots, q + 1$ (see Table 15.3.1), and a confidence interval is desired on $\gamma^2 = \sum_{i=1}^{q+1} c_i\gamma_i^2$, where the c_i are specified constants, then clearly $\mathscr{E}[\sum_{i=1}^{q+1} c_i n_i^{-1} S_i^2] = \gamma^2$, and it may seem reasonable to consider $U = n(\sum c_i n_i^{-1} S_i^2)/\gamma^2$ to be approximately distributed as a chi-square random variable with n degrees of freedom. If this were indeed true, then a $1 - \alpha$ confidence interval on $\gamma^2 = \sum c_i\gamma_i^2$ would be

$$\frac{n\sum c_i n_i^{-1} S_i^2}{\chi^2_{\alpha/2:n}} \leq \gamma^2 \leq \frac{n\sum c_i n_i^{-1} S_i^2}{\chi^2_{1-\alpha/2:n}} \tag{15.6.1}$$

To determine the degrees of freedom n, one might assume that U is (approximately) distributed as $\chi^2(u:n)$, so $\mathscr{E}[U] = n$ and $\text{var}[U] = 2n$. If we consider $\mathscr{E}[U] = n$, we get $n = \mathscr{E}[U] = (n/\gamma^2)\mathscr{E}\sum[c_i n_i^{-1} S_i^2] = (n/\gamma^2)\gamma^2 = n$. This does not lead to a formula for n. However, when we consider $\text{var}[U] = 2n$, we get

$$2n = \text{var}[U] = \text{var}\left[\frac{n\sum c_i n_i^{-1} S_i^2}{\gamma^2}\right] = \left(\frac{n^2}{\gamma^4}\right)\sum c_i^2 n_i^{-2}\,\text{var}[S_i^2]$$

$$= \left(\frac{n^2}{\gamma^4}\right)\sum\left(\frac{c_i^2 2\gamma_i^4}{n_i}\right)$$

Solving for n gives us

$$n = \frac{(\sum c_i\gamma_i^2)^2}{\sum c_i^2\gamma_i^4/n_i}$$

This equation contains the unknown parameters γ_i^2 and γ_i^4, so one can substitute $s_i^2/n_i = \hat{\gamma}_i^2$ (the UMVU estimate of γ_i^2) for γ_i^2 and substitute $(\hat{\gamma}_i^2)^2$ for γ_i^4. This gives the value

$$\hat{n} = \frac{(\sum c_i \hat{\gamma}_i^2)^2}{\sum c_i^2 (\hat{\gamma}_i^2)^2 / n_i} \tag{15.6.2}$$

to use in the approximate confidence interval in Equation (15.6.1). This procedure should be used with care but is generally sufficiently accurate if all $c_i > 0$.

All of the components-of-variance models that we have discussed have been models with equal numbers in all cells and subcells and are called balanced complete models. When the model contains an unequal number of observations in the cells, very few inference procedures with optimum properties are available. A good account of these models is contained in [S-7]. The reader should also consult [R-2] and [R-5]. All the methods described in this chapter for Case I are very sensitive to departures from the normality assumption. For information on the subject, see [G-1], [M-10], and [S-4].

15.7 Proof of Theorem 15.3.1

In this section a proof of Theorem 15.3.1 is presented. For those readers who are not interested in this proof, this section can be omitted.

Theorem 15.3.1 derives its usefulness from many facts: (1) an identity in $Y_{ij\ldots m}$, such as in Equations (15.2.1), (15.4.6), and so on, can often be surmised from the similar *design* model; (2) the identity in $\mathbf{Y}'\mathbf{Y}$ can often be easily obtained from the identity in the $Y_{ij\ldots m}$ or from the similar design model; (3) it is often easy, but sometimes tedious, to show that the various components in the identity in $Y_{ij\ldots m}$ are pairwise uncorrelated; (4) it is often straightforward, but again sometimes tedious, to show that the distribution of each quadratic form in the identity in $\mathbf{Y}'\mathbf{Y}$ is that of a constant times a chi-square random variable. From these facts complete sufficient statistics (if they exist) can be easily obtained, and from these one can construct best unbiased estimators, tests, and confidence intervals.

Of course, this procedure will not always work since complete sufficient statistics do not exist for all models. But it will always work for the balanced complete models for Case I.

We now give the proof for Theorem 15.3.1. We note that part (a) of the result essentially states that a solution exists for each variance component σ_i^2 in terms of linear functions of the γ_j^2. By the hypothesis of the theorem, an unbiased estimator of each γ_j^2 exists (it is equal to S_j^2/n_j), so by (a) an unbiased estimator of each σ_i^2 also exists.

First we prove lemmas that concern the matrices involved in the theorem.

LEMMA 15.7.1

If conditions (1), (2), *and* (3) *in Theorem* 15.3.1 *hold, then*

(1) $\mathbf{I} = \sum_{i=0}^{q+1} \mathbf{A}_i$;

(2) $\mathbf{A}_i\mathbf{\Sigma}\mathbf{A}_i = \mathbf{A}_i\gamma_i^2$ *for* $i = 0, 1, \ldots, q+1$;

(3) $\mathbf{A}_i\mathbf{\Sigma}\mathbf{A}_j = \mathbf{0}$ *for* $i = 0, 1, \ldots, q+1, j = 0, 1, \ldots, q+1, i \neq j$;

(4) $\mathbf{\Sigma}\mathbf{A}_i = \mathbf{A}_i\mathbf{\Sigma}$ *for* $i = 0, 1, \ldots, q+1$.

Proof

Part (1) is a direct result of the fact that $\mathbf{Y}'\mathbf{Y} = \sum_{i=0}^{q+1} \mathbf{Y}'\mathbf{A}_i\mathbf{Y}$ for the $n \times 1$ random vector $\mathbf{Y}$.

To prove (2) we use Theorem 4.4.3, which implies that $(\mathbf{A}_i/\gamma_i^2)\mathbf{\Sigma}$ is idempotent of rank n_i, so $(\mathbf{A}_i/\gamma_i^2)\mathbf{\Sigma}(\mathbf{A}_i/\gamma_i^2)\mathbf{\Sigma} = (\mathbf{A}_i/\gamma_i^2)\mathbf{\Sigma}$. Since $\mathbf{\Sigma}$ is nonsingular (actually p.d.), multiply both sides on the right by $\mathbf{\Sigma}^{-1}\gamma_i^4$ and (2) is proved.

To prove (3) we use Theorem 4.5.3, which implies that $(\mathbf{A}_i/\gamma_i^2)\mathbf{\Sigma}(\mathbf{A}_j/\gamma_j^2) = \mathbf{0}$, and hence $\mathbf{A}_i\mathbf{\Sigma}\mathbf{A}_j = \mathbf{0}$ for all $i \neq j$ since $U_0, U_1, \ldots, U_{q+1}$ are jointly independent and hence U_i and U_j are pairwise independent.

To prove (4) we use (for any $i = 0, 1, \ldots, q+1$)

$$\mathbf{\Sigma}\mathbf{A}_i = \mathbf{I}\mathbf{\Sigma}\mathbf{A}_i = (\mathbf{A}_0 + \mathbf{A}_1 + \cdots + \mathbf{A}_{q+1})\mathbf{\Sigma}\mathbf{A}_i = \mathbf{A}_i\mathbf{\Sigma}\mathbf{A}_i$$

by (3); also,

$$\mathbf{A}_i\mathbf{\Sigma} = \mathbf{A}_i\mathbf{\Sigma}\mathbf{I} = \mathbf{A}_i\mathbf{\Sigma}(\mathbf{A}_0 + \mathbf{A}_1 + \cdots + \mathbf{A}_{q+1}) = \mathbf{A}_i\mathbf{\Sigma}\mathbf{A}_i$$

and hence $\mathbf{\Sigma}\mathbf{A}_i = \mathbf{A}_i\mathbf{\Sigma}$ for $i = 0, 1, \ldots, q+1$. This proves the lemma.

LEMMA 15.7.2

If conditions (1), (2), *and* (3) *in Theorem* 15.3.1 *hold, then the following result.*

(1) $\mathbf{A}_i$ *is symmetric idempotent of rank* n_i *for* $i = 0, 1, \ldots, q+1$ *and* $\sum_{i=0}^{q+1} n_i = n$.

(2) $\mathbf{A}_i\mathbf{A}_j = \mathbf{0}$ *for* $i = 0, 1, \ldots, q+1, j = 0, 1, \ldots, q+1, i \neq j$.

(3) *Let* $\mathbf{A}_i = \mathbf{P}_i\mathbf{P}_i'$ *be a factorization of* $\mathbf{A}_i$, *where* $\mathbf{P}_i'\mathbf{P}_i = \mathbf{I}_{n_i}$ *for* $i = 0, 1, \ldots, q+1$, *and form the matrix* $\mathbf{P} = [\mathbf{P}_0, \mathbf{P}_1, \ldots, \mathbf{P}_{q+1}]$. *Then* $\mathbf{P}\mathbf{P}' = \mathbf{P}'\mathbf{P} = \mathbf{I}$.

(4) $\mathbf{P}'\mathbf{\Sigma}\mathbf{P} = \mathbf{\Delta}$, *where* $\mathbf{\Delta}$ *is a diagonal matrix.*

(5) $\mathbf{P}'\mathbf{\Sigma}_0\mathbf{P} = \mathbf{\Delta}_0$, *where* $\mathbf{\Delta}_0$ *is a diagonal matrix.*

(6) *The characteristic roots of* $\mathbf{\Sigma}_0$ *are* $n\mu^2 + \gamma_0^2, \gamma_1^2, \ldots, \gamma_{q+1}^2$ *with multiplicities* $n_0, n_1, \ldots, n_{q+1}$, *respectively.*

(7) $(\mathbf{Y} - \mu\mathbf{1})'\mathbf{\Sigma}^{-1}(\mathbf{Y} - \mu\mathbf{1}) = n(\bar{Y} - \mu)^2/\gamma_0^2 + \sum_{i=1}^{q+1} \mathbf{Y}'\mathbf{A}_i\mathbf{Y}/\gamma_i^2$.

Proof

To prove (1) we note that $\mathbf{A}_i\mathbf{\Sigma} = \mathbf{A}_i\gamma_i^2 = \mathbf{A}_i\mathbf{\Sigma}\mathbf{A}_i = \mathbf{A}_i\mathbf{A}_i\mathbf{\Sigma}$, so $\mathbf{A}_i\mathbf{A}_i = \mathbf{A}_i$. By Theorem 4.4.3 if $\mathbf{Y}'(\mathbf{A}_i/\gamma_i^2)\mathbf{Y}$ is distributed as chi-square with n_i degrees of freedom, then $\text{rank}[\mathbf{A}_i/\gamma_i^2] = n_i$, but $\text{rank}[\mathbf{A}_i/\gamma_i^2] = \text{rank}[\mathbf{A}_i]$, and the proof for (1) is complete.

Since for all $i \neq j$ we have $\mathbf{0} = \mathbf{A}_i\mathbf{\Sigma}\mathbf{A}_j = \mathbf{A}_i\mathbf{A}_j\mathbf{\Sigma}$, it follows that $\mathbf{A}_i\mathbf{A}_j = \mathbf{0}$ for all $i \neq j$, and this proves (2).

If $\mathbf{A}_i = \mathbf{P}_i\mathbf{P}_i'$, and since $\mathbf{A}_i$ is idempotent of rank n_i, it follows that $\mathbf{P}_i$ has size $n \times n_i$ and $\mathbf{P}_i'\mathbf{P}_i = \mathbf{I}_{n_i}$; thus $\mathbf{P}$ has size $n \times n$ and $\mathbf{P}'\mathbf{P} = \mathbf{I}$ since, for $i \neq j$, we get $\mathbf{0} = \mathbf{A}_i\mathbf{A}_j = \mathbf{P}_i\mathbf{P}_i'\mathbf{P}_j\mathbf{P}_j'$ implies $\mathbf{P}_i'\mathbf{P}_j = \mathbf{0}$. This proves (3).

To prove (4) we note that $\mathbf{P}'\mathbf{\Sigma}\mathbf{P} = \mathbf{\Delta}$ (say) can be written

$$\begin{bmatrix} \mathbf{P}_0' \\ \mathbf{P}_1' \\ \vdots \\ \mathbf{P}_{q+1}' \end{bmatrix} \mathbf{\Sigma}[\mathbf{P}_0, \mathbf{P}_1, \ldots, \mathbf{P}_{q+1}]$$

$$= \begin{bmatrix} \mathbf{P}_0'\mathbf{\Sigma}\mathbf{P}_0 & \mathbf{P}_0'\mathbf{\Sigma}\mathbf{P}_1 & \cdots & \mathbf{P}_0'\mathbf{\Sigma}\mathbf{P}_{q+1} \\ \mathbf{P}_1'\mathbf{\Sigma}\mathbf{P}_0 & \mathbf{P}_1'\mathbf{\Sigma}\mathbf{P}_1 & \cdots & \mathbf{P}_1'\mathbf{\Sigma}\mathbf{P}_{q+1} \\ \vdots & \vdots & & \vdots \\ \mathbf{P}_{q+1}'\mathbf{\Sigma}\mathbf{P}_0 & \mathbf{P}_{q+1}'\mathbf{\Sigma}\mathbf{P}_1 & \cdots & \mathbf{P}_{q+1}'\mathbf{\Sigma}\mathbf{P}_{q+1} \end{bmatrix}$$

$$= \begin{bmatrix} \gamma_0^2\mathbf{I}_{n_0} & \mathbf{0} & \cdots & \mathbf{0} \\ \mathbf{0} & \gamma_1^2\mathbf{I}_{n_1} & \cdots & \mathbf{0} \\ \vdots & \vdots & & \vdots \\ \mathbf{0} & \mathbf{0} & \cdots & \gamma_{q+1}^2\mathbf{I}_{n_{q+1}} \end{bmatrix} \qquad (15.7.1)$$

since, for $i \neq j$, we get $\mathbf{0} = \mathbf{A}_i\mathbf{\Sigma}\mathbf{A}_j = \mathbf{P}_i\mathbf{P}_i'\mathbf{\Sigma}\mathbf{P}_j\mathbf{P}_j'$, which implies $\mathbf{P}_i'\mathbf{\Sigma}\mathbf{P}_j = \mathbf{0}$; and $\mathbf{A}_i\mathbf{\Sigma}\mathbf{A}_i = \mathbf{A}_i\gamma_i^2$ implies $\mathbf{P}_i\mathbf{P}_i'\mathbf{\Sigma}\mathbf{P}_i\mathbf{P}_i' = \mathbf{P}_i\mathbf{P}_i'\gamma_i^2$, which in turn implies $\mathbf{P}_i'\mathbf{\Sigma}\mathbf{P}_i = \gamma_i^2\mathbf{I}_{n_i}$. Thus $\mathbf{P}'\mathbf{\Sigma}\mathbf{P}$ is a diagonal matrix.

To prove (5) note that

$$\mathbf{P}'\mathbf{\Sigma}_0\mathbf{P} = \mathbf{P}'(\mu^2\mathbf{X}_0\mathbf{X}_0' + \mathbf{\Sigma})\mathbf{P} = \mu^2\mathbf{P}'\mathbf{X}_0\mathbf{X}_0'\mathbf{P} + \mathbf{\Delta}$$

but since $\mathbf{A}_0 = (1/n)\mathbf{J}$, it follows that $\mathbf{P}_0 = (\sqrt{1/n})\mathbf{1}$, and since $\mathbf{P}_0'\mathbf{P}_j = \mathbf{0}$

for $j \neq 0$, this implies $\mathbf{1}'\mathbf{P}_j = \mathbf{0}$. But $\mathbf{X}_0 = \mathbf{1}$, so

$$\mu^2\mathbf{P}'\mathbf{X}_0\mathbf{X}_0'\mathbf{P} = \begin{bmatrix} n\mu^2 & \mathbf{0} \\ \mathbf{0} & \mathbf{0} \end{bmatrix} \quad \text{and} \quad \mathbf{P}'\mathbf{\Sigma}_0\mathbf{P} = \begin{bmatrix} n\mu^2 & \mathbf{0} \\ \mathbf{0} & \mathbf{0} \end{bmatrix} + \mathbf{\Delta} = \mathbf{\Delta}_0$$

and this proves (5).

The proof of (6) is immediate since $\mathbf{P}$ is an orthogonal matrix, and we have proven $\mathbf{P}'\mathbf{\Sigma}_0\mathbf{P}$ is the diagonal matrix in Equation (15.7.1), except the first diagonal element is $\gamma_0^2 + n\mu^2$ instead of γ_0^2. By Theorem 1.2.50 these diagonal elements are the characteristic roots of $\mathbf{\Sigma}_0$.

We leave the proof of (7) for the reader. This completes the proof of the lemma.

LEMMA 15.7.3

If conditions (1), (2), *and* (3) *of Theorem* 15.3.1 *hold, then the p.d.f. of* $\mathbf{Y}$ *can be written as*

$$f_{\mathbf{Y}}(\mathbf{y} : \mu, \mathbf{\Sigma}) = (2\pi)^{-n/2}(\gamma_0^2)^{-1/2} \prod_{j=1}^{q+1} (\gamma_j^2)^{-n_j/2} \exp\left\{-\left(\frac{1}{2}\right)\left[\frac{n(\bar{y} - \mu)^2}{\gamma_0^2} + \sum_{i=1}^{q+1} \frac{\mathbf{y}'\mathbf{A}_i\mathbf{y}}{\gamma_i^2}\right]\right\} \tag{15.7.2}$$

and a set of complete sufficient statistics for this model is $\{\bar{\mathbf{Y}}, \mathbf{Y}'\mathbf{A}_1\mathbf{Y}, \ldots, \mathbf{Y}'\mathbf{A}_{q+1}\mathbf{Y}\}$.

Proof

The p.d.f. of $\mathbf{Y}$ is

$$\begin{aligned} f_{\mathbf{Y}}(\mathbf{y} : \mu, \mathbf{\Sigma}) &= (2\pi)^{-n/2}|\mathbf{\Sigma}|^{-1/2} \exp\{-\tfrac{1}{2}(\mathbf{y} - \mathbf{1}\mu)'\mathbf{\Sigma}^{-1}(\mathbf{y} - \mathbf{1}\mu)\} \\ &= (2\pi)^{-n/2}|\mathbf{P}'\mathbf{\Sigma}\mathbf{P}|^{-1/2} \exp\{-\tfrac{1}{2}(\mathbf{y} - \mathbf{1}\mu)'\mathbf{P}(\mathbf{P}'\mathbf{\Sigma}^{-1}\mathbf{P})\mathbf{P}'(\mathbf{y} - \mathbf{1}\mu)\} \end{aligned}$$

But

$$|\mathbf{P}'\mathbf{\Sigma}\mathbf{P}| = \prod_{j=0}^{q+1} (\gamma_j^2)^{n_j} \quad \text{and} \quad \mathbf{P}'\mathbf{\Sigma}^{-1}\mathbf{P} = (\mathbf{P}'\mathbf{\Sigma}\mathbf{P})^{-1} = \mathbf{\Delta}^{-1}$$

by Equation (15.7.1). Also, $\mathbf{Y}'\mathbf{P}_i\mathbf{P}_i'\mathbf{Y} = \mathbf{Y}'\mathbf{A}_i\mathbf{Y}$, and $\mathbf{1}'\mathbf{P} = [\sqrt{n}, 0, \ldots, 0]$. Substitute these into the p.d.f., simplify, and the result is given in Equation (15.7.2). By the factorization criterion in Theorem 2.6.1, the statistics $\bar{\mathbf{Y}}$, $\mathbf{Y}'\mathbf{A}_i\mathbf{Y}$ for $i = 1, 2, \ldots, q + 1$ are clearly a sufficient set. We omit the proof that they are complete but Theorem 2.7.8 can be used. The above results prove (b) of Theorem 15.3.1.

To prove (a) we note that hypothesis (1) of the theorem states that the γ_j^2 are linearly independent linear functions of the σ_i^2. This statement, of course, means that we can write $\gamma^2 = \mathbf{L}^{-1}\boldsymbol{\sigma}^2$, where $\gamma^2 = [\gamma_1^2, \gamma_2^2, \ldots, \gamma_{q+1}^2]'$, $\boldsymbol{\sigma}^2 = [\sigma_1^2, \sigma_2^2, \ldots, \sigma_{q+1}^2]'$, and $\mathbf{L}^{-1}$ is nonsingular. Hence $\boldsymbol{\sigma}^2 = \mathbf{L}\gamma^2$ and this proves (a).

Note in Tables 15.4.1, 15.4.2, 15.4.3, and 15.5.1 the σ_A^2, σ_T^2, σ_ε^2, and so on can indeed be written as linear combinations of the γ_j^2.

Problems

15.1. In the proof of Theorem 15.2.1, demonstrate that the two sets of random variables $\{Z\}$ and $\{W_{ij}\}$ are uncorrelated. Do the same for $\{Z_i\}$ and $\{W_{ij}\}$.

15.2. Work out the details for the proof of Theorem 15.2.2.

15.3. In Theorem 15.2.3 prove $\mathbf{A}_0\boldsymbol{\Sigma} = \boldsymbol{\Sigma}\mathbf{A}_0$ and $\mathbf{A}_1\boldsymbol{\Sigma} = \boldsymbol{\Sigma}\mathbf{A}_1$.

15.4. Work out the details for the proof of (2) of Theorem 15.2.5.

15.5. An investigation is made and data are collected that are assumed to satisfy Case I of the one-factor components-of-variance model $Y_{ij} = \mu + A_i + \varepsilon_{ij}$ for $j = 1, 2, \ldots, 5$ and $i = 1, 2, \ldots, 8$. The ANOVA table is computed and is given below. Find the best unbiased estimates of (a) σ_ε^2; (b) σ_A^2; (c) σ_ε; (d) $2\sigma_\varepsilon^2 - 4\sigma_A^2$.

Source	*d.f.*	*S.S.*	*M.S.*	*E.M.S.*
Total	40	120		
Mean	1	35		
Factor *A*	7	21	3.0	$\sigma_\varepsilon^2 + 5\sigma_A^2$
Error	32	64	2.0	σ_ε^2

15.6. In Problem 15.5 compute 90 percent confidence limits on (a) σ_ε^2; (b) σ_A^2; (c) $\sigma_A^2/\sigma_\varepsilon^2$; (d) $\sigma_\varepsilon^2/(\sigma_A^2 + \sigma_\varepsilon^2)$.

15.7. In Problem 15.5 test $H_0: \sigma_A^2 = 0.4$ *vs.* $H_a: \sigma_A^2 \neq 0.4$. Use $\alpha = 0.20$.

15.8. In Problem 15.5 test $H_0: \sigma_A^2/\sigma_\varepsilon^2 = 0.6$ *vs.* $H_a: \sigma_A^2/\sigma_\varepsilon^2 \neq 0.6$. Use $\alpha = 0.10$.

15.9. In Problem 15.8 find the power of the test when $\sigma_A^2/\sigma_\varepsilon^2 = 0.5$.

15.10. In Theorem 15.4.1 prove (1), (2), and (3).

15.11. In Table 15.4.1 prove $\mathscr{E}[S_1^2/(I-1)] = \sigma_\varepsilon^2 + M\sigma_G^2 + JM\sigma_A^2$.

15.12. In Table 15.4.3 prove the identity

$$\sum_{i=1}^{I}\sum_{j=1}^{J}\sum_{m=1}^{M} y_{ijm}^2 = \sum_{i=0}^{3} s_i^2$$

15.13. Use the procedure in Section 15.6 to set 90 percent confidence limits on $2\sigma_\varepsilon^2 + 5\sigma_A^2$ for the data in Problem 15.5.

15.14. Work part (b) of Problem 15.6 by the procedure discussed in Section 15.6.

15.15. Set a 90 percent confidence interval on $\sigma_A^2 + \sigma_B^2$ in Example 15.4.2 by the procedure discussed in Section 15.6.

Tables

T.1 Ordinates of the Standard Normal p.d.f.

T.2 Cumulative Standard Normal p.d.f.

T.3 Upper α Probability Points of Student's t Distribution

T.4 Upper α Probability Points of Chi-Square Distribution

T.5 Upper α Probability Points of Central F Distribution with n_1 d.f. in Numerator and n_2 d.f. in Denominator

T.6 Probability Points for Multivariate t Distribution

T.7 Upper α Probability Points of Studentized Range ($\alpha = .01$, $\alpha = .05$, $\alpha = .10$)

T.8 Confidence Curves for Simple Correlation Coefficient ($1 - \alpha = .90$, $1 - \alpha = .95$, $1 - \alpha = .98$, $1 - \alpha = .99$)

T.9 Fisher's z Transformation for the Correlation Coefficient

T.10 Upper α Probability Points of Multiple Correlation Coefficient ($\alpha = .01$, $\alpha = .05$, $\alpha = .95$, $\alpha = .99$)

T.11 Upper α Probability Points of the Noncentral F Distribution ($\alpha = .005$, $\alpha = .01$, $\alpha = .025$, $\alpha = .05$, $\alpha = .10$)

Table T.1
Ordinates of the Standard Normal p.d.f.

Entries are $n(z:0,1) = (2\pi)^{-1/2}\, e^{-z^2/2}$.

z	.00	.01	.02	.03	.04	.05	.06	.07	.08	.09
.0	.3989	.3989	.3989	.3988	.3986	.3984	.3982	.3980	.3977	.3973
.1	.3970	.3965	.3961	.3956	.3951	.3945	.3939	.3932	.3925	.3918
.2	.3910	.3902	.3894	.3885	.3876	.3867	.3857	.3847	.3836	.3825
.3	.3814	.3802	.3790	.3778	.3765	.3752	.3739	.3725	.3712	.3697
.4	.3683	.3668	.3653	.3637	.3621	.3605	.3589	.3572	.3555	.3538
.5	.3521	.3503	.3485	.3467	.3448	.3429	.3410	.3391	.3372	.3352
.6	.3332	.3312	.3292	.3271	.3251	.3230	.3209	.3187	.3166	.3144
.7	.3123	.3101	.3079	.3056	.3034	.3011	.2989	.2966	.2943	.2920
.8	.2897	.2874	.2850	.2827	.2803	.2780	.2756	.2732	.2709	.2685
.9	.2661	.2637	.2613	.2589	.2565	.2541	.2516	.2492	.2468	.2444
1.0	.2420	.2396	.2371	.2347	.2323	.2299	.2275	.2251	.2227	.2203
1.1	.2179	.2155	.2131	.2107	.2083	.2059	.2036	.2012	.1989	.1965
1.2	.1942	.1919	.1895	.1872	.1849	.1826	.1804	.1781	.1758	.1736
1.3	.1714	.1691	.1669	.1647	.1626	.1604	.1582	.1561	.1539	.1518
1.4	.1497	.1476	.1456	.1435	.1415	.1394	.1374	.1354	.1334	.1315
1.5	.1295	.1276	.1257	.1238	.1219	.1200	.1182	.1163	.1145	.1127
1.6	.1109	.1092	.1074	.1057	.1040	.1023	.1006	.0989	.0973	.0957
1.7	.0940	.0925	.0909	.0893	.0878	.0863	.0848	.0833	.0818	.0804
1.8	.0790	.0775	.0761	.0748	.0734	.0721	.0707	.0694	.0681	.0669
1.9	.0656	.0644	.0632	.0620	.0608	.0596	.0584	.0573	.0562	.0551
2.0	.0540	.0529	.0519	.0508	.0498	.0488	.0478	.0468	.0459	.0449
2.1	.0440	.0431	.0422	.0413	.0404	.0396	.0387	.0379	.0371	.0363
2.2	.0355	.0347	.0339	.0332	.0325	.0317	.0310	.0303	.0297	.0290
2.3	.0283	.0277	.0270	.0264	.0258	.0252	.0246	.0241	.0235	.0229
2.4	.0224	.0219	.0213	.0208	.0203	.0198	.0194	.0189	.0184	.0180
2.5	.0175	.0171	.0167	.0163	.0158	.0154	.0151	.0147	.0143	.0139
2.6	.0136	.0132	.0129	.0126	.0122	.0119	.0116	.0113	.0110	.0107
2.7	.0104	.0101	.0099	.0096	.0093	.0091	.0088	.0086	.0084	.0081
2.8	.0079	.0077	.0075	.0073	.0071	.0069	.0067	.0065	.0063	.0061
2.9	.0060	.0058	.0056	.0055	.0053	.0051	.0050	.0048	.0047	.0046
3.0	.0044	.0043	.0042	.0040	.0039	.0038	.0037	.0036	.0035	.0034
3.1	.0033	.0032	.0031	.0030	.0029	.0028	.0027	.0026	.0025	.0025
3.2	.0024	.0023	.0022	.0022	.0021	.0020	.0020	.0019	.0018	.0018
3.3	.0017	.0017	.0016	.0016	.0015	.0015	.0014	.0014	.0013	.0013
3.4	.0012	.0012	.0012	.0011	.0011	.0010	.0010	.0010	.0009	.0009
3.5	.0009	.0008	.0008	.0008	.0008	.0007	.0007	.0007	.0007	.0006
3.6	.0006	.0006	.0006	.0005	.0005	.0005	.0005	.0005	.0005	.0004
3.7	.0004	.0004	.0004	.0004	.0004	.0004	.0003	.0003	.0003	.0003
3.8	.0003	.0003	.0003	.0003	.0003	.0002	.0002	.0002	.0002	.0002
3.9	.0002	.0002	.0002	.0002	.0002	.0002	.0002	.0002	.0001	.0001

Table T.2
Cumulative Standard Normal p.d.f.

Entries are $\int_{-\infty}^{N_\alpha} n(z:0,1)\,dz = 1 - \alpha$.

N_α	.00	.01	.02	.03	.04	.05	.06	.07	.08	.09
.0	.5000	.5040	.5080	.5120	.5160	.5199	.5239	.5279	.5319	.5359
.1	.5398	.5438	.5478	.5517	.5557	.5596	.5636	.5675	.5714	.5753
.2	.5793	.5832	.5871	.5910	.5948	.5987	.6026	.6064	.6103	.6141
.3	.6179	.6217	.6255	.6293	.6331	.6368	.6406	.6443	.6480	.6517
.4	.6554	.6591	.6628	.6664	.6700	.6736	.6772	.6808	.6844	.6879
.5	.6915	.6950	.6985	.7019	.7054	.7088	.7123	.7157	.7190	.7224
.6	.7257	.7291	.7324	.7357	.7389	.7422	.7454	.7486	.7517	.7549
.7	.7580	.7611	.7642	.7673	.7704	.7734	.7764	.7794	.7823	.7852
.8	.7881	.7910	.7939	.7967	.7995	.8023	.8051	.8078	.8106	.8133
.9	.8159	.8186	.8212	.8238	.8264	.8289	.8315	.8340	.8365	.8389
1.0	.8413	.8438	.8461	.8485	.8508	.8531	.8554	.8577	.8599	.8621
1.1	.8643	.8665	.8686	.8708	.8729	.8749	.8770	.8790	.8810	.8830
1.2	.8849	.8869	.8888	.8907	.8925	.8944	.8962	.8980	.8997	.9015
1.3	.9032	.9049	.9066	.9082	.9099	.9115	.9131	.9147	.9162	.9177
1.4	.9192	.9207	.9222	.9236	.9251	.9265	.9279	.9292	.9306	.9319
1.5	.9332	.9345	.9357	.9370	.9382	.9394	.9406	.9418	.9429	.9441
1.6	.9452	.9463	.9474	.9484	.9495	.9505	.9515	.9525	.9535	.9545
1.7	.9554	.9564	.9573	.9582	.9591	.9599	.9608	.9616	.9625	.9633
1.8	.9641	.9649	.9656	.9664	.9671	.9678	.9686	.9693	.9699	.9706
1.9	.9713	.9719	.9726	.9732	.9738	.9744	.9750	.9756	.9761	.9767
2.0	.9772	.9778	.9783	.9788	.9793	.9798	.9803	.9808	.9812	.9817
2.1	.9821	.9826	.9830	.9834	.9838	.9842	.9846	.9850	.9854	.9857
2.2	.9861	.9864	.9868	.9871	.9875	.9878	.9881	.9884	.9887	.9890
2.3	.9893	.9896	.9898	.9901	.9904	.9906	.9909	.9911	.9913	.9916
2.4	.9918	.9920	.9922	.9925	.9927	.9929	.9931	.9932	.9934	.9936
2.5	.9938	.9940	.9941	.9943	.9945	.9946	.9948	.9949	.9951	.9952
2.6	.9953	.9955	.9956	.9957	.9959	.9960	.9961	.9962	.9963	.9964
2.7	.9965	.9966	.9967	.9968	.9969	.9970	.9971	.9972	.9973	.9974
2.8	.9974	.9975	.9976	.9977	.9977	.9978	.9979	.9979	.9980	.9981
2.9	.9981	.9982	.9982	.9983	.9984	.9984	.9985	.9985	.9986	.9986
3.0	.9987	.9987	.9987	.9988	.9988	.9989	.9989	.9989	.9990	.9990
3.1	.9990	.9991	.9991	.9991	.9992	.9992	.9992	.9992	.9993	.9993
3.2	.9993	.9993	.9994	.9994	.9994	.9994	.9994	.9995	.9995	.9995
3.3	.9995	.9995	.9995	.9996	.9996	.9996	.9996	.9996	.9996	.9997
3.4	.9997	.9997	.9997	.9997	.9997	.9997	.9997	.9997	.9997	.9998

N_α	1.282	1.645	1.960	2.326	2.576	3.090	3.291	3.891	4.417
$1 - \alpha$	.90	.95	.975	.99	.995	.999	.9995	.99995	.999995

Table T.3
Upper α Probability Points of Student's *t* Distribution

Entries are $t_{\alpha:n}$.

n \ α	.25	.10	.05	.025	.01	.005	.0005
1	1.000	3.078	6.314	12.706	31.821	63.657	636.619
2	.816	1.886	2.920	4.303	6.965	9.925	31.598
3	.765	1.638	2.353	3.182	4.541	5.841	12.941
4	.741	1.533	2.132	2.776	3.747	4.604	8.610
5	.727	1.476	2.015	2.571	3.365	4.032	6.859
6	.718	1.440	1.943	2.447	3.143	3.707	5.959
7	.711	1.415	1.895	2.365	2.998	3.499	5.405
8	.706	1.397	1.860	2.306	2.896	3.355	5.041
9	.703	1.383	1.833	2.262	2.821	3.250	4.781
10	.700	1.372	1.812	2.228	2.764	3.169	4.587
11	.697	1.363	1.796	2.201	2.718	3.106	4.437
12	.695	1.356	1.782	2.179	2.681	3.055	4.318
13	.694	1.350	1.771	2.160	2.650	3.012	4.221
14	.692	1.345	1.761	2.145	2.624	2.977	4.140
15	.691	1.341	1.753	2.131	2.602	2.947	4.073
16	.690	1.337	1.746	2.120	2.583	2.921	4.015
17	.689	1.333	1.740	2.110	2.567	2.898	3.965
18	.688	1.330	1.734	2.101	2.552	2.878	3.922
19	.688	1.328	1.729	2.093	2.539	2.861	3.883
20	.687	1.325	1.725	2.086	2.528	2.845	3.850
21	.686	1.323	1.721	2.080	2.518	2.831	3.819
22	.686	1.321	1.717	2.074	2.508	2.819	3.792
23	.685	1.319	1.714	2.069	2.500	2.807	3.767
24	.685	1.318	1.711	2.064	2.492	2.797	3.745
25	.684	1.316	1.708	2.060	2.485	2.787	3.725
26	.684	1.315	1.706	2.056	2.479	2.779	3.707
27	.684	1.314	1.703	2.052	2.473	2.771	3.690
28	.683	1.313	1.701	2.048	2.467	2.763	3.674
29	.683	1.311	1.699	2.045	2.462	2.756	3.659
30	.683	1.310	1.697	2.042	2.457	2.750	3.646
40	.681	1.303	1.684	2.021	2.423	2.704	3.551
60	.679	1.296	1.671	2.000	2.390	2.660	3.460
120	.677	1.289	1.658	1.980	2.358	2.617	3.373
∞	.674	1.282	1.645	1.960	2.326	2.576	3.291

This table is abridged from Table III of Fisher and Yates: *Statistical Tables for Biological, Agricultural and Medical Research*, published by Longman Group Ltd., London. (Previously published by Oliver and Boyd, Edinburgh), and by permission of the authors and publishers.

Table T.4
Upper α Probability Points of Chi-Square Distribution

Entries are $\chi^2_{\alpha:n}$.

n \ α	.995	.990	.975	.950	.900	.750	.500	.250	.100	.050	.025	.010	.005
1	$.0^4393$	$.0^3157$	$.0^3982$	$.0^2393$	.0158	.102	.455	1.32	2.71	3.84	5.02	6.63	7.88
2	.0100	.0201	.0506	.103	.211	.575	1.39	2.77	4.61	5.99	7.38	9.21	10.6
3	.0717	.115	.216	.352	.584	1.21	2.37	4.11	6.25	7.81	9.35	11.3	12.8
4	.207	.297	.484	.711	1.06	1.92	3.36	5.39	7.78	9.49	11.1	13.3	14.9
5	.412	.554	.831	1.15	1.61	2.67	4.35	6.63	9.24	11.1	12.8	15.1	16.7
6	.676	.872	1.24	1.64	2.20	3.45	5.35	7.84	10.6	12.6	14.4	16.8	18.5
7	.989	1.24	1.69	2.17	2.83	4.25	6.35	9.04	12.0	14.1	16.0	18.5	20.3
8	1.34	1.65	2.18	2.73	3.49	5.07	7.34	10.2	13.4	15.5	17.5	20.1	22.0
9	1.73	2.09	2.70	3.33	4.17	5.90	8.34	11.4	14.7	16.9	19.0	21.7	23.6
10	2.16	2.56	3.25	3.94	4.87	6.74	9.34	12.5	16.0	18.3	20.5	23.2	25.2
11	2.60	3.05	3.82	4.57	5.58	7.58	10.3	13.7	17.3	19.7	21.9	24.7	26.8
12	3.07	3.57	4.40	5.23	6.30	8.44	11.3	14.8	18.5	21.0	23.3	26.2	28.3
13	3.57	4.11	5.01	5.89	7.04	9.30	12.3	16.0	19.8	22.4	24.7	27.7	29.8
14	4.07	4.66	5.63	6.57	7.79	10.2	13.3	17.1	21.1	23.7	26.1	29.1	31.3
15	4.60	5.23	6.26	7.26	8.55	11.0	14.3	18.2	22.3	25.0	27.5	30.6	32.8
16	5.14	5.81	6.91	7.96	9.31	11.9	15.3	19.4	23.5	26.3	28.8	32.0	34.3
17	5.70	6.41	7.56	8.67	10.1	12.8	16.3	20.5	24.8	27.6	30.2	33.4	35.7
18	6.26	7.01	8.23	9.39	10.9	13.7	17.3	21.6	26.0	28.9	31.5	34.8	37.2
19	6.84	7.63	8.91	10.1	11.7	14.6	18.3	22.7	27.2	30.1	32.9	36.2	38.6
20	7.43	8.26	9.59	10.9	12.4	15.5	19.3	23.8	28.4	31.4	34.2	37.6	40.0
21	8.03	8.90	10.3	11.6	13.2	16.3	20.3	24.9	29.6	32.7	35.5	38.9	41.4
22	8.64	9.54	11.0	12.3	14.0	17.2	21.3	26.0	30.8	33.9	36.8	40.3	42.8
23	9.26	10.2	11.7	13.1	14.8	18.1	22.3	27.1	32.0	35.2	38.1	41.6	44.2
24	9.89	10.9	12.4	13.8	15.7	19.0	23.3	28.2	33.2	36.4	39.4	43.0	45.6
25	10.5	11.5	13.1	14.6	16.5	19.9	24.3	29.3	34.4	37.7	40.6	44.3	46.9
26	11.2	12.2	13.8	15.4	17.3	20.8	25.3	30.4	35.6	38.9	41.9	45.6	48.3
27	11.8	12.9	14.6	16.2	18.1	21.7	26.3	31.5	36.7	40.1	43.2	47.0	49.6
28	12.5	13.6	15.3	16.9	18.9	22.7	27.3	32.6	37.9	41.3	44.5	48.3	51.0
29	13.1	14.3	16.0	17.7	19.8	23.6	28.3	33.7	39.1	42.6	45.7	49.6	52.3
30	13.8	15.0	16.8	18.5	20.6	24.5	29.3	34.8	40.3	43.8	47.0	50.9	53.7

This table is abridged from "Tables of percentage points of the incomplete beta function and of the chi-square distribution," *Biometrika*, Vol. 32 (1941). It is here published with the kind permission of the editor of *Biometrika*.

Table T.5

Upper α Probability Points of Central F Distribution with n_1 d.f. in Numerator and n_2 d.f. in Denominator

Entries are $F_{\alpha:n_1,n_2}$.

α	n_2 \ n_1	1	2	3	4	5	6	7	8	9	10	12	15	20	30	60	120	∞
.10	1	39.9	49.5	53.6	55.8	57.2	58.2	58.9	59.4	59.9	60.2	60.7	61.2	61.7	62.3	62.8	63.1	63.3
.05		161	200	216	225	230	234	237	239	241	242	244	246	248	250	252	253	254
.025		648	800	864	900	922	937	948	957	963	969	977	985	993	1000	1010	1010	1020
.01		4,050	5,000	5,400	5,620	5,760	5,860	5,930	5,980	6,020	6,060	6,110	6,160	6,210	6,260	6,310	6,340	6,370
.005		16,200	20,000	21,600	22,500	23,100	23,400	23,700	23,900	24,100	24,200	24,400	24,600	24,800	25,000	25,200	25,400	25,500
.10	2	8.53	9.00	9.16	9.24	9.29	9.33	9.35	9.37	9.38	9.39	9.41	9.42	9.44	9.46	9.47	9.48	9.49
.05		18.5	19.0	19.2	19.2	19.3	19.3	19.4	19.4	19.4	19.4	19.4	19.4	19.5	19.5	19.5	19.5	19.5
.025		38.5	39.0	39.2	39.2	39.3	39.3	39.4	39.4	39.4	39.4	39.4	39.4	39.4	39.5	39.5	39.5	39.5
.01		98.5	99.0	99.2	99.2	99.3	99.3	99.4	99.4	99.4	99.4	99.4	99.4	99.4	99.5	99.5	99.5	99.5
.005		199	199	199	199	199	199	199	199	199	199	199	199	199	199	199	199	199
.10	3	5.54	5.46	5.39	5.34	5.31	5.28	5.27	5.25	5.24	5.23	5.22	5.20	5.18	5.17	5.15	5.14	5.13
.05		10.1	9.55	9.28	9.12	9.01	8.94	8.89	8.85	8.81	8.79	8.74	8.70	8.66	8.62	8.57	8.55	8.53
.025		17.4	16.0	15.4	15.1	14.9	14.7	14.6	14.5	14.5	14.4	14.3	14.3	14.2	14.1	14.0	13.9	13.9
.01		34.1	30.8	29.5	28.7	28.2	27.9	27.7	27.5	27.3	27.2	27.1	26.9	26.7	26.5	26.3	26.2	26.1
.005		55.6	49.8	47.5	46.2	45.4	44.8	44.4	44.1	43.9	43.7	43.4	43.1	42.8	42.5	42.1	42.0	41.8
.10	4	4.54	4.32	4.19	4.11	4.05	4.01	3.98	3.95	3.93	3.92	3.90	3.87	3.84	3.82	3.79	3.78	3.76
.05		7.71	6.94	6.59	6.39	6.26	6.16	6.09	6.04	6.00	5.96	5.91	5.86	5.80	5.75	5.69	5.66	5.63
.025		12.2	10.6	9.98	9.60	9.36	9.20	9.07	8.98	8.90	8.84	8.75	8.66	8.56	8.46	8.36	8.31	8.26
.01		21.2	18.0	16.7	16.0	15.5	15.2	15.0	14.8	14.7	14.5	14.4	14.2	14.0	13.8	13.7	13.6	13.5
.005		31.3	26.3	24.3	23.2	22.5	22.0	21.6	21.4	21.1	21.0	20.7	20.4	20.2	19.9	19.6	19.5	19.3
.10	5	4.06	3.78	3.62	3.52	3.45	3.40	3.37	3.34	3.32	3.30	3.27	3.24	3.21	3.17	3.14	3.12	3.11
.05		6.61	5.79	5.41	5.19	5.05	4.95	4.88	4.82	4.77	4.74	4.68	4.62	4.56	4.50	4.43	4.40	4.37
.025		10.0	8.43	7.76	7.39	7.15	6.98	6.85	6.76	6.68	6.62	6.52	6.43	6.33	6.23	6.12	6.07	6.02
.01		16.3	13.3	12.1	11.4	11.0	10.7	10.5	10.3	10.2	10.1	9.89	9.72	9.55	9.38	9.20	9.11	9.02
.005		22.8	18.3	16.5	15.6	14.9	14.5	14.2	14.0	13.8	13.6	13.4	13.1	12.9	12.7	12.4	12.3	12.1
.10	6	3.78	3.46	3.29	3.18	3.11	3.05	3.01	2.98	2.96	2.94	2.90	2.87	2.84	2.80	2.76	2.74	2.72
.05		5.99	5.14	4.76	4.53	4.39	4.28	4.21	4.15	4.10	4.06	4.00	3.94	3.87	3.81	3.74	3.70	3.67
.025		8.81	7.26	6.60	6.23	5.99	5.82	5.70	5.60	5.52	5.46	5.37	5.27	5.17	5.07	4.96	4.90	4.85
.01		13.7	10.9	9.78	9.15	8.75	8.47	8.26	8.10	7.98	7.87	7.72	7.56	7.40	7.23	7.06	6.97	6.88
.005		18.6	14.5	12.9	12.0	11.5	11.1	10.8	10.6	10.4	10.2	10.0	9.81	9.59	9.36	9.12	9.00	8.88
.10	7	3.59	3.26	3.07	2.96	2.88	2.83	2.78	2.75	2.72	2.70	2.67	2.63	2.59	2.56	2.51	2.49	2.47
.05		5.59	4.74	4.35	4.12	3.97	3.87	3.79	3.73	3.68	3.64	3.57	3.51	3.44	3.38	3.30	3.27	3.23
.025		8.07	6.54	5.89	5.52	5.29	5.12	4.99	4.90	4.82	4.76	4.67	4.57	4.47	4.36	4.25	4.20	4.14
.01		12.2	9.55	8.45	7.85	7.46	7.19	6.99	6.84	6.72	6.62	6.47	6.31	6.16	5.99	5.82	5.74	5.65
.005		16.2	12.4	10.9	10.1	9.52	9.16	8.89	8.68	8.51	8.38	8.18	7.97	7.75	7.53	7.31	7.19	7.08
.10	8	3.46	3.11	2.92	2.81	2.73	2.67	2.62	2.59	2.56	2.54	2.50	2.46	2.42	2.38	2.34	2.31	2.29
.05		5.32	4.46	4.07	3.84	3.69	3.58	3.50	3.44	3.39	3.35	3.28	3.22	3.15	3.08	3.01	2.97	2.93
.025		7.57	6.06	5.42	5.05	4.82	4.65	4.53	4.43	4.36	4.30	4.20	4.10	4.00	3.89	3.78	3.73	3.67
.01		11.3	8.65	7.59	7.01	6.63	6.37	6.18	6.03	5.91	5.81	5.67	5.52	5.36	5.20	5.03	4.95	4.86
.005		14.7	11.0	9.60	8.81	8.30	7.95	7.69	7.50	7.34	7.21	7.01	6.81	6.61	6.40	6.18	6.06	5.95

.10		3.36	3.01	2.81	2.69	2.61	2.55	2.51	2.47	2.44	2.42	2.38	2.34	2.30	2.25	2.21	2.18	2.16
.05		5.12	4.26	3.86	3.63	3.48	3.37	3.29	3.23	3.18	3.14	3.07	3.01	2.94	2.86	2.79	2.75	2.71
.025	9	7.21	5.71	5.08	4.72	4.48	4.32	4.20	4.10	4.03	3.96	3.87	3.77	3.67	3.56	3.45	3.39	3.33
.01		10.6	8.02	6.99	6.42	6.06	5.80	5.61	5.47	5.35	5.26	5.11	4.96	4.81	4.65	4.48	4.40	4.31
.005		13.6	10.1	8.72	7.96	7.47	7.13	6.88	6.69	6.54	6.42	6.23	6.03	5.83	5.62	5.41	5.30	5.19
.10		3.29	2.92	2.73	2.61	2.52	2.46	2.41	2.38	2.35	2.32	2.28	2.24	2.20	2.15	2.11	2.08	2.06
.05		4.96	4.10	3.71	3.48	3.33	3.22	3.14	3.07	3.02	2.98	2.91	2.84	2.77	2.70	2.62	2.58	2.54
.025	10	6.94	5.46	4.83	4.47	4.24	4.07	3.95	3.85	3.78	3.72	3.62	3.52	3.42	3.31	3.20	3.14	3.08
.01		10.0	7.56	6.55	5.99	5.64	5.39	5.20	5.06	4.94	4.85	4.71	4.56	4.41	4.25	4.08	4.00	3.91
.005		12.8	9.43	8.08	7.34	6.87	6.54	6.30	6.12	5.97	5.85	5.66	5.47	5.27	5.07	4.86	4.75	4.64
.10		3.18	2.81	2.61	2.48	2.39	2.33	2.28	2.24	2.21	2.19	2.15	2.10	2.06	2.01	1.96	1.93	1.90
.05		4.75	3.89	3.49	3.26	3.11	3.00	2.91	2.85	2.80	2.75	2.69	2.62	2.54	2.47	2.38	2.34	2.30
.025	12	6.55	5.10	4.47	4.12	3.89	3.73	3.61	3.51	3.44	3.37	3.28	3.18	3.07	2.96	2.85	2.79	2.72
.01		9.33	6.93	5.95	5.41	5.06	4.82	4.64	4.50	4.39	4.30	4.16	4.01	3.86	3.70	3.54	3.45	3.36
.005		11.8	8.51	7.23	6.52	6.07	5.76	5.52	5.35	5.20	5.09	4.91	4.72	4.53	4.33	4.12	4.01	3.90
.10		3.07	2.70	2.49	2.36	2.27	2.21	2.16	2.12	2.09	2.06	2.02	1.97	1.92	1.87	1.82	1.79	1.76
.05		4.54	3.68	3.29	3.06	2.90	2.79	2.71	2.64	2.59	2.54	2.48	2.40	2.33	2.25	2.16	2.11	2.07
.025	15	6.20	4.77	4.15	3.80	3.58	3.41	3.29	3.20	3.12	3.06	2.96	2.86	2.76	2.64	2.52	2.46	2.40
.01		8.68	6.36	5.42	4.89	4.56	4.32	4.14	4.00	3.89	3.80	3.67	3.52	3.37	3.21	3.05	2.96	2.87
.005		10.8	7.70	6.48	5.80	5.37	5.07	4.85	4.67	4.54	4.42	4.25	4.07	3.88	3.69	3.48	3.37	3.26
.10		2.97	2.59	2.38	2.25	2.16	2.09	2.04	2.00	1.96	1.94	1.89	1.84	1.79	1.74	1.68	1.64	1.61
.05		4.35	3.49	3.10	2.87	2.71	2.60	2.51	2.45	2.39	2.35	2.28	2.20	2.12	2.04	1.95	1.90	1.84
.025	20	5.87	4.46	3.86	3.51	3.29	3.13	3.01	2.91	2.84	2.77	2.68	2.57	2.46	2.35	2.22	2.16	2.09
.01		8.10	5.85	4.94	4.43	4.10	3.87	3.70	3.56	3.46	3.37	3.23	3.09	2.94	2.78	2.61	2.52	2.42
.005		9.94	6.99	5.82	5.17	4.76	4.47	4.26	4.09	3.96	3.85	3.68	3.50	3.32	3.12	2.92	2.81	2.69
.10		2.88	2.49	2.28	2.14	2.05	1.98	1.93	1.88	1.85	1.82	1.77	1.72	1.67	1.61	1.54	1.50	1.46
.05		4.17	3.32	2.92	2.69	2.53	2.42	2.33	2.27	2.21	2.16	2.09	2.01	1.93	1.84	1.74	1.68	1.62
.025	30	5.57	4.18	3.59	3.25	3.03	2.87	2.75	2.65	2.57	2.51	2.41	2.31	2.20	2.07	1.94	1.87	1.79
.01		7.56	5.39	4.51	4.02	3.70	3.47	3.30	3.17	3.07	2.98	2.84	2.70	2.55	2.39	2.21	2.11	2.01
.005		9.18	6.35	5.24	4.62	4.23	3.95	3.74	3.58	3.45	3.34	3.18	3.01	2.82	2.63	2.42	2.30	2.18
.10		2.79	2.39	2.18	2.04	1.95	1.87	1.82	1.77	1.74	1.71	1.66	1.60	1.54	1.48	1.40	1.35	1.29
.05		4.00	3.15	2.76	2.53	2.37	2.25	2.17	2.10	2.04	1.99	1.92	1.84	1.75	1.65	1.53	1.47	1.39
.025	60	5.29	3.93	3.34	3.01	2.79	2.63	2.51	2.41	2.33	2.27	2.17	2.06	1.94	1.82	1.67	1.58	1.48
.01		7.08	4.98	4.13	3.65	3.34	3.12	2.95	2.82	2.72	2.63	2.50	2.35	2.20	2.03	1.84	1.73	1.60
.005		8.49	5.80	4.73	4.14	3.76	3.49	3.29	3.13	3.01	2.90	2.74	2.57	2.39	2.19	1.96	1.83	1.69
.10		2.75	2.35	2.13	1.99	1.90	1.82	1.77	1.72	1.68	1.65	1.60	1.54	1.48	1.41	1.32	1.26	1.19
.05		3.92	3.07	2.68	2.45	2.29	2.18	2.09	2.02	1.96	1.91	1.83	1.75	1.66	1.55	1.43	1.35	1.25
.025	120	5.15	3.80	3.23	2.89	2.67	2.52	2.39	2.30	2.22	2.16	2.05	1.94	1.82	1.69	1.53	1.43	1.31
.01		6.85	4.79	3.95	3.48	3.17	2.96	2.79	2.66	2.56	2.47	2.34	2.19	2.03	1.86	1.66	1.53	1.38
.005		8.18	5.54	4.50	3.92	3.55	3.28	3.09	2.93	2.81	2.71	2.54	2.37	2.19	1.98	1.75	1.61	1.43
.10		2.71	2.30	2.08	1.94	1.85	1.77	1.72	1.67	1.63	1.60	1.55	1.49	1.42	1.34	1.24	1.17	1.00
.05		3.84	3.00	2.60	2.37	2.21	2.10	2.01	1.94	1.88	1.83	1.75	1.67	1.57	1.46	1.32	1.22	1.00
.025	∞	5.02	3.69	3.12	2.79	2.57	2.41	2.29	2.19	2.11	2.05	1.94	1.83	1.71	1.57	1.39	1.27	1.00
.01		6.63	4.61	3.78	3.32	3.02	2.80	2.64	2.51	2.41	2.32	2.18	2.04	1.88	1.70	1.47	1.32	1.00
.005		7.88	5.30	4.28	3.72	3.35	3.09	2.90	2.74	2.62	2.52	2.36	2.19	2.00	1.79	1.53	1.36	1.00

This table is abridged from "Tables of percentage points of the inverted beta distribution," *Biometrika*, Vol. 33 (1943). It is here published with the kind permission of the editor of *Biometrika*.

Table T.6
Probability Points for Multivariate **t** Distribution

Entries are $t_{\alpha/2:q,m}$, where $P[\max|T_i| \le t_{\alpha/2:q,m}$ for $i = 1, 2, \ldots, q] = 1 - \alpha$ and $t = [T_1, T_2, \ldots, T_q]'$ is distributed $\mathbf{S}(\mathbf{t}: q, m; \mathbf{I})$.

$m \backslash q$	1	2	3	4	5	6	8	10	12	15	20
						$1 - \alpha = .90$					
3	2·353	2·989	3·369	3·637	3·844	4·011	4·272	4·471	4·631	4·823	5·066
4	2·132	2·662	2·976	3·197	3·368	3·506	3·722	3·887	4·020	4·180	4·383
5	2·015	2·491	2·769	2·965	3·116	3·239	3·430	3·576	3·694	3·837	4·018
6	1·943	2·385	2·642	2·822	2·961	3·074	3·249	3·384	3·493	3·624	3·790
7	1·895	2·314	2·556	2·725	2·856	2·962	3·127	3·253	3·355	3·478	3·635
8	1·860	2·262	2·494	2·656	2·780	2·881	3·038	3·158	3·255	3·373	3·522
9	1·833	2·224	2·447	2·603	2·723	2·819	2·970	3·086	3·179	3·292	3·436
10	1·813	2·193	2·410	2·562	2·678	2·771	2·918	3·029	3·120	3·229	3·368
11	1·796	2·169	2·381	2·529	2·642	2·733	2·875	2·984	3·072	3·178	3·313
12	1·782	2·149	2·357	2·501	2·612	2·701	2·840	2·946	3·032	3·136	3·268
15	1·753	2·107	2·305	2·443	2·548	2·633	2·765	2·865	2·947	3·045	3·170
20	1·725	2·065	2·255	2·386	2·486	2·567	2·691	2·786	2·863	2·956	3·073
25	1·708	2·041	2·226	2·353	2·450	2·528	2·648	2·740	2·814	2·903	3·016
30	1·697	2·025	2·207	2·331	2·426	2·502	2·620	2·709	2·781	2·868	2·978
40	1·684	2·006	2·183	2·305	2·397	2·470	2·585	2·671	2·741	2·825	2·931
60	1·671	1·986	2·160	2·278	2·368	2·439	2·550	2·634	2·701	2·782	2·884
						$1 - \alpha = .95$					
3	3·183	3·960	4·430	4·764	5·023	5·233	5·562	5·812	6·015	6·259	6·567
4	2·777	3·382	3·745	4·003	4·203	4·366	4·621	4·817	4·975	5·166	5·409
5	2·571	3·091	3·399	3·619	3·789	3·928	4·145	4·312	4·447	4·611	4·819
6	2·447	2·916	3·193	3·389	3·541	3·664	3·858	4·008	4·129	4·275	4·462
7	2·365	2·800	3·056	3·236	3·376	3·489	3·668	3·805	3·916	4·051	4·223
8	2·306	2·718	2·958	3·128	3·258	3·365	3·532	3·660	3·764	3·891	4·052
9	2·262	2·657	2·885	3·046	3·171	3·272	3·430	3·552	3·651	3·770	3·923
10	2·228	2·609	2·829	2·984	3·103	3·199	3·351	3·468	3·562	3·677	3·823
11	2·201	2·571	2·784	2·933	3·048	3·142	3·288	3·400	3·491	3·602	3·743
12	2·179	2·540	2·747	2·892	3·004	3·095	3·236	3·345	3·433	3·541	3·677
15	2·132	2·474	2·669	2·805	2·910	2·994	3·126	3·227	3·309	3·409	3·536
20	2·086	2·411	2·594	2·722	2·819	2·898	3·020	3·114	3·190	3·282	3·399
25	2·060	2·374	2·551	2·673	2·766	2·842	2·959	3·048	3·121	3·208	3·320
30	2·042	2·350	2·522	2·641	2·732	2·805	2·918	3·005	3·075	3·160	3·267
40	2·021	2·321	2·488	2·603	2·690	2·760	2·869	2·952	3·019	3·100	3·203
60	2·000	2·292	2·454	2·564	2·649	2·716	2·821	2·900	2·964	3·041	3·139
						$1 - \alpha = .99$					
3	5·841	7·127	7·914	8·479	8·919	9·277	9·838	10·269	10·616	11·034	11·559
4	4·604	5·462	5·985	6·362	6·656	6·897	7·274	7·565	7·801	8·087	8·451
5	4·032	4·700	5·106	5·398	5·625	5·812	6·106	6·333	6·519	6·744	7·050
6	3·707	4·271	4·611	4·855	5·046	5·202	5·449	5·640	5·796	5·985	6·250
7	3·500	3·998	4·296	4·510	4·677	4·814	5·031	5·198	5·335	5·502	5·716
8	3·355	3·809	4·080	4·273	4·424	4·547	4·742	4·894	5·017	5·168	5·361
9	3·250	3·672	3·922	4·100	4·239	4·353	4·532	4·672	4·785	4·924	5·103
10	3·169	3·567	3·801	3·969	4·098	4·205	4.373	4·503	4·609	4·739	4·905
11	3·106	3·485	3·707	3·865	3·988	4·087	4·247	4·370	4·470	4·593	4·750
12	3·055	3·418	3·631	3·782	3·899	3·995	4·146	4·263	4·359	4·475	4·625
15	2·947	3·279	3·472	3·608	3·714	3·800	3·935	4·040	4·125	4·229	4·363
20	2·845	3·149	3·323	3·446	3·541	3·617	3·738	3·831	3·907	3·999	4·117
25	2·788	3·075	3·239	3·354	3·442	3·514	3·626	3·713	3·783	3·869	3·978
30	2·750	3·027	3·185	3·295	3·379	3·448	3·555	3·637	3·704	3·785	3·889
40	2·705	2·969	3·119	3·223	3·303	3·367	3·468	3·545	3·607	3·683	3·780
60	2·660	2·913	3·055	3·154	3·229	3·290	3·384	3·456	3·515	3·586	3·676

Table T.6 is reprinted from "A Table of Percentage Points of the Distribution of the Largest Absolute Value of q Student t Variates and Its Applications," *Biometrika*, Vol. 58. It is reprinted here with the kind permission of the authors, G. J. Hahn and R. W. Hendrickson, and the Trustees of *Biometrika*.

Table T.7

Upper 1 Percent Points of the Studentized Range

The entries are $q_{.01:m,n}$, where $P[Q < q_{.01:m,n}] = .99$.

n \ m	2	3	4	5	6	7	8	9	10	11	12	13	14	15	16	17	18	19	20
1	90.03	135.0	164.3	185.6	202.2	215.8	227.2	237.0	245.6	253.2	260.0	266.2	271.8	277.0	281.8	286.3	290.4	294.3	298.0
2	14.04	19.02	22.29	24.72	26.63	28.20	29.53	30.68	31.69	32.59	33.40	34.13	34.81	35.43	36.00	36.53	37.03	37.50	37.95
3	8.26	10.62	12.17	13.33	14.24	15.00	15.64	16.20	16.69	17.13	17.53	17.89	18.22	18.52	18.81	19.07	19.32	19.55	19.77
4	6.51	8.12	9.17	9.96	10.58	11.10	11.55	11.93	12.27	12.57	12.84	13.09	13.32	13.53	13.73	13.91	14.08	14.24	14.40
5	5.70	6.98	7.80	8.42	8.91	9.32	9.67	9.97	10.24	10.48	10.70	10.89	11.08	11.24	11.40	11.55	11.68	11.81	11.93
6	5.24	6.33	7.03	7.56	7.97	8.32	8.61	8.87	9.10	9.30	9.48	9.65	9.81	9.95	10.08	10.21	10.32	10.43	10.54
7	4.95	5.92	6.54	7.01	7.37	7.68	7.94	8.17	8.36	8.55	8.71	8.86	9.00	9.12	9.24	9.35	9.46	9.55	9.65
8	4.75	5.64	6.20	6.62	6.96	7.24	7.47	7.68	7.86	8.03	8.18	8.31	8.44	8.55	8.66	8.76	8.85	8.94	9.03
9	4.60	5.43	5.96	6.35	6.66	6.91	7.13	7.33	7.49	7.65	7.78	7.91	8.03	8.13	8.23	8.33	8.41	8.49	8.57
10	4.48	5.27	5.77	6.14	6.43	6.67	6.87	7.05	7.21	7.36	7.49	7.60	7.71	7.81	7.91	7.99	8.08	8.15	8.23
11	4.39	5.15	5.62	5.97	6.25	6.48	6.67	6.84	6.99	7.13	7.25	7.36	7.46	7.56	7.65	7.73	7.81	7.88	7.95
12	4.32	5.05	5.50	5.84	6.10	6.32	6.51	6.67	6.81	6.94	7.06	7.17	7.26	7.36	7.44	7.52	7.59	7.66	7.73
13	4.26	4.96	5.40	5.73	5.98	6.19	6.37	6.53	6.67	6.79	6.90	7.01	7.10	7.19	7.27	7.35	7.42	7.48	7.55
14	4.21	4.89	5.32	5.63	5.88	6.08	6.26	6.41	6.54	6.66	6.77	6.87	6.96	7.05	7.13	7.20	7.27	7.33	7.39
15	4.17	4.84	5.25	5.56	5.80	5.99	6.16	6.31	6.44	6.55	6.66	6.76	6.84	6.93	7.00	7.07	7.14	7.20	7.26
16	4.13	4.79	5.19	5.49	5.72	5.92	6.08	6.22	6.35	6.46	6.56	6.66	6.74	6.82	6.90	6.97	7.03	7.09	7.15
17	4.10	4.74	5.14	5.43	5.66	5.85	6.01	6.15	6.27	6.38	6.48	6.57	6.66	6.73	6.81	6.87	6.94	7.00	7.05
18	4.07	4.70	5.09	5.38	5.60	5.79	5.94	6.08	6.20	6.31	6.41	6.50	6.58	6.65	6.73	6.79	6.85	6.91	6.97
19	4.05	4.67	5.05	5.33	5.55	5.73	5.89	6.02	6.14	6.25	6.34	6.43	6.51	6.58	6.65	6.72	6.78	6.84	6.89
20	4.02	4.64	5.02	5.29	5.51	5.69	5.84	5.97	6.09	6.19	6.28	6.37	6.45	6.52	6.59	6.65	6.71	6.77	6.82
24	3.96	4.55	4.91	5.17	5.37	5.54	5.69	5.81	5.92	6.02	6.11	6.19	6.26	6.33	6.39	6.45	6.51	6.56	6.61
30	3.89	4.45	4.80	5.05	5.24	5.40	5.54	5.65	5.76	5.85	5.93	6.01	6.08	6.14	6.20	6.26	6.31	6.36	6.41
40	3.82	4.37	4.70	4.93	5.11	5.26	5.39	5.50	5.60	5.69	5.76	5.83	5.90	5.96	6.02	6.07	6.12	6.16	6.21
60	3.76	4.28	4.59	4.82	4.99	5.13	5.25	5.36	5.45	5.53	5.60	5.67	5.73	5.78	5.84	5.89	5.93	5.97	6.01
120	3.70	4.20	4.50	4.71	4.87	5.01	5.12	5.21	5.30	5.37	5.44	5.50	5.56	5.61	5.66	5.71	5.75	5.79	5.83
∞	3.64	4.12	4.40	4.60	4.76	4.88	4.99	5.08	5.16	5.23	5.29	5.35	5.40	5.45	5.49	5.54	5.57	5.61	5.65

From E. S. Pearson and H. O. Hartley, "Biometrika Tables for Statisticians," Vol. 1, pp. 176–177, published by the Biometrika Trustees, Cambridge University Press, London, 1954. Reproduced with the permission of the authors and publishers. Corrections of ±1 in the last figure, supplied by Dr. Leon Harter, have been incorporated in some entries.

Table T.7
Upper 5 Percent Points of the Studentized Range

The entries are $q_{.05:m,n}$, where $P[Q < q_{.05:m,n}] = .95$.

n \ m	2	3	4	5	6	7	8	9	10	11	12	13	14	15	16	17	18	19	20
1	17.97	26.98	32.82	37.08	40.41	43.12	45.40	47.36	49.07	50.59	51.96	53.20	54.33	55.36	56.32	57.22	58.04	58.83	59.56
2	6.08	8.33	9.80	10.88	11.74	12.44	13.03	13.54	13.99	14.39	14.75	15.08	15.38	15.65	15.91	16.14	16.37	16.57	16.77
3	4.50	5.91	6.82	7.50	8.04	8.48	8.85	9.18	9.46	9.72	9.95	10.15	10.35	10.52	10.69	10.84	10.98	11.11	11.24
4	3.93	5.04	5.76	6.29	6.71	7.05	7.35	7.60	7.83	8.03	8.21	8.37	8.52	8.66	8.79	8.91	9.03	9.13	9.23
5	3.64	4.60	5.22	5.67	6.03	6.33	6.58	6.80	6.99	7.17	7.32	7.47	7.60	7.72	7.83	7.93	8.03	8.12	8.21
6	3.46	4.34	4.90	5.30	5.63	5.90	6.12	6.32	6.49	6.65	6.79	6.92	7.03	7.14	7.24	7.34	7.43	7.51	7.59
7	3.34	4.16	4.68	5.06	5.36	5.61	5.82	6.00	6.16	6.30	6.43	6.55	6.66	6.76	6.85	6.94	7.02	7.10	7.17
8	3.26	4.04	4.53	4.89	5.17	5.40	5.60	5.77	5.92	6.05	6.18	6.29	6.39	6.48	6.57	6.65	6.73	6.80	6.87
9	3.20	3.95	4.41	4.76	5.02	5.24	5.43	5.59	5.74	5.87	5.98	6.09	6.19	6.28	6.36	6.44	6.51	6.58	6.64
10	3.15	3.88	4.33	4.65	4.91	5.12	5.30	5.46	5.60	5.72	5.83	5.93	6.03	6.11	6.19	6.27	6.34	6.40	6.47
11	3.11	3.82	4.26	4.57	4.82	5.03	5.20	5.35	5.49	5.61	5.71	5.81	5.90	5.98	6.06	6.13	6.20	6.27	6.33
12	3.08	3.77	4.20	4.51	4.75	4.95	5.12	5.27	5.39	5.51	5.61	5.71	5.80	5.88	5.95	6.02	6.09	6.15	6.21
13	3.06	3.73	4.15	4.45	4.69	4.88	5.05	5.19	5.32	5.43	5.53	5.63	5.71	5.79	5.86	5.93	5.99	6.05	6.11
14	3.03	3.70	4.11	4.41	4.64	4.83	4.99	5.13	5.25	5.36	5.46	5.55	5.64	5.71	5.79	5.85	5.91	5.97	6.03
15	3.01	3.67	4.08	4.37	4.59	4.78	4.94	5.08	5.20	5.31	5.40	5.49	5.57	5.65	5.72	5.78	5.85	5.90	5.96
16	3.00	3.65	4.05	4.33	4.56	4.74	4.90	5.03	5.15	5.26	5.35	5.44	5.52	5.59	5.66	5.73	5.79	5.84	5.90
17	2.98	3.63	4.02	4.30	4.52	4.70	4.86	4.99	5.11	5.21	5.31	5.39	5.47	5.54	5.61	5.67	5.73	5.79	5.84
18	2.97	3.61	4.00	4.28	4.49	4.67	4.82	4.96	5.07	5.17	5.27	5.35	5.43	5.50	5.57	5.63	5.69	5.74	5.79
19	2 96	3.59	3.98	4.25	4.47	4.65	4.79	4.92	5.04	5.14	5.23	5.31	5.39	5.46	5.53	5.59	5.65	5.70	5.75
20	2.95	3.58	3.96	4.23	4.45	4.62	4.77	4.90	5.01	5.11	5.20	5.28	5.36	5.43	5.49	5.55	5.61	5.66	5.71
24	2.92	3.53	3.90	4.17	4.37	4.54	4.68	4.81	4.92	5.01	5.10	5.18	5.25	5.32	5.38	5.44	5.49	5.55	5.59
30	2.89	3.49	3.85	4.10	4.30	4.46	4.60	4.72	4.82	4.92	5.00	5.08	5.15	5.21	5.27	5.33	5.38	5.43	5.47
40	2.86	3.44	3.79	4.04	4.23	4.39	4.52	4.63	4.73	4.82	4.90	4.98	5.04	5.11	5.16	5.22	5.27	5.31	5.36
60	2.83	3.40	3.74	3.98	4.16	4.31	4.44	4.55	4.65	4.73	4.81	4.88	4.94	5.00	5.06	5.11	5.15	5.20	5.24
120	2.80	3.36	3.68	3.92	4.10	4.24	4.36	4.47	4.56	4.64	4.71	4.78	4.84	4.90	4.95	5.00	5.04	5.09	5.13
∞	2.77	3.31	3.63	3.86	4.03	4.17	4.29	4.39	4.47	4.55	4.62	4.68	4.74	4.80	4.85	4.89	4.93	4.97	5.01

From E. S. Pearson and H. O. Hartley, "Biometrika Tables for Statisticians," Vol. 1, pp. 176–177, published by the Biometrika Trustees, Cambridge University Press, London, 1954. Reproduced with the permission of the authors and the publisher. Corrections of ± 1 in the last figure, supplied by Dr. James Pachares, have been incorporated in some entries.

Table T.7

Upper 10 Percent Points of the Studentized Range

The entries are $q_{.10:m,n}$, where $P[Q < q_{.10:m,n}] = .90$.

n \ m	2	3	4	5	6	7	8	9	10	11	12	13	14	15	16	17	18	19	20
1	8.93	13.44	16.36	18.49	20.15	21.51	22.64	23.62	24.48	25.24	25.92	26.54	27.10	27.62	28.10	28.54	28.96	29.35	29.71
2	4.13	5.73	6.77	7.54	8.14	8.63	9.05	9.41	9.72	10.01	10.26	10.49	10.70	10.89	11.07	11.24	11.39	11.54	11.68
3	3.33	4.47	5.20	5.74	6.16	6.51	6.81	7.06	7.29	7.49	7.67	7.83	7.98	8.12	8.25	8.37	8.48	8.58	8.68
4	3.01	3.98	4.59	5.03	5.39	5.68	5.93	6.14	6.33	6.49	6.65	6.78	6.91	7.02	7.13	7.23	7.33	7.41	7.50
5	2.85	3.72	4.26	4.66	4.98	5.24	5.46	5.65	5.82	5.97	6.10	6.22	6.34	6.44	6.54	6.63	6.71	6.79	6.86
6	2.75	3.56	4.07	4.44	4.73	4.97	5.17	5.34	5.50	5.64	5.76	5.87	5.98	6.07	6.16	6.25	6.32	6.40	6.47
7	2.68	3.45	3.93	4.28	4.55	4.78	4.97	5.14	5.28	5.41	5.53	5.64	5.74	5.83	5.91	5.99	6.06	6.13	6.19
8	2.63	3.37	3.83	4.17	4.43	4.65	4.83	4.99	5.13	5.25	5.36	5.46	5.56	5.64	5.72	5.80	5.87	5.93	6.00
9	2.59	3.32	3.76	4.08	4.34	4.54	4.72	4.87	5.01	5.13	5.23	5.33	5.42	5.51	5.58	5.66	5.72	5.79	5.85
10	2.56	3.27	3.70	4.02	4.26	4.47	4.64	4.78	4.91	5.03	5.13	5.23	5.32	5.40	5.47	5.54	5.61	5.67	5.73
11	2.54	3.23	3.66	3.96	4.20	4.40	4.57	4.71	4.84	4.95	5.05	5.15	5.23	5.31	5.38	5.45	5.51	5.57	5.63
12	2.52	3.20	3.62	3.92	4.16	4.35	4.51	4.65	4.78	4.89	4.99	5.08	5.16	5.24	5.31	5.37	5.44	5.49	5.55
13	2.50	3.18	3.59	3.88	4.12	4.30	4.46	4.60	4.72	4.83	4.93	5.02	5.10	5.18	5.25	5.31	5.37	5.43	5.48
14	2.49	3.16	3.56	3.85	4.08	4.27	4.42	4.56	4.68	4.79	4.88	4.97	5.05	5.12	5.19	5.26	5.32	5.37	5.43
15	2.48	3.14	3.54	3.83	4.05	4.23	4.39	4.52	4.64	4.75	4.84	4.93	5.01	5.08	5.15	5.21	5.27	5.32	5.38
16	2.47	3.12	3.52	3.80	4.03	4.21	4.36	4.49	4.61	4.71	4.81	4.89	4.97	5.04	5.11	5.17	5.23	5.28	5.33
17	2.46	3.11	3.50	3.78	4.00	4.18	4.33	4.46	4.58	4.68	4.77	4.86	4.93	5.01	5.07	5.13	5.19	5.24	5.30
18	2.45	3.10	3.49	3.77	3.98	4.16	4.31	4.44	4.55	4.65	4.75	4.83	4.90	4.98	5.04	5.10	5.16	5.21	5.26
19	2.45	3.09	3.47	3.75	3.97	4.14	4.29	4.42	4.53	4.63	4.72	4.80	4.88	4.95	5.01	5.07	5.13	5.18	5.23
20	2.44	3.08	3.46	3.74	3.95	4.12	4.27	4.40	4.51	4.61	4.70	4.78	4.85	4.92	4.99	5.05	5.10	5.16	5.20
24	2.42	3.05	3.42	3.69	3.90	4.07	4.21	4.34	4.44	4.54	4.63	4.71	4.78	4.85	4.91	4.97	5.02	5.07	5.12
30	2.40	3.02	3.39	3.65	3.85	4.02	4.16	4.28	4.38	4.47	4.56	4.64	4.71	4.77	4.83	4.89	4.94	4.99	5.03
40	2.38	2.99	3.35	3.60	3.80	3.96	4.10	4.21	4.32	4.41	4.49	4.56	4.63	4.69	4.75	4.81	4.86	4.90	4.95
60	2.36	2.96	3.31	3.56	3.75	3.91	4.04	4.16	4.25	4.34	4.42	4.49	4.56	4.62	4.67	4.73	4.78	4.82	4.86
120	2.34	2.93	3.28	3.52	3.71	3.86	3.99	4.10	4.19	4.28	4.35	4.42	4.48	4.54	4.60	4.65	4.69	4.74	4.78
∞	2.33	2.90	3.24	3.48	3.66	3.81	3.93	4.04	4.13	4.21	4.28	4.35	4.41	4.47	4.52	4.57	4.61	4.65	4.69

From James Pachares, "Table of the upper 10% points of the Studentized range," *Biometrika*, Vol. 46, Pts. 3 and 4 (1959), pp. 461–466. Reproduced with the permission of the author and the Biometrika Trustees.

Table T.8

Confidence Curves for Simple Correlation Coefficient

The curves are for $1 - \alpha = .90$.

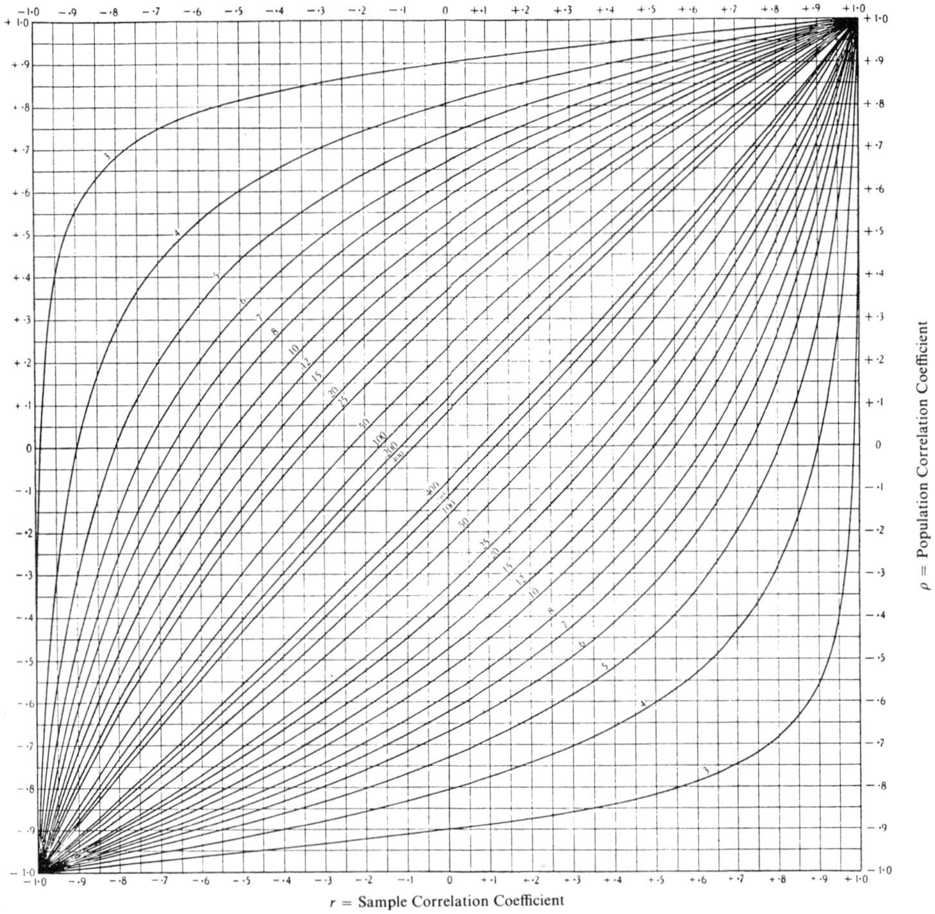

This graph is from "Tables of the Correlation Coefficient" by F. N. David. It is here published with the kind permission of its author, F. N. David, and the trustees of *Biometrika*.

Table T.8
Confidence Curves for Simple Correlation Coefficient

The curves are for $1 - \alpha = .95$.

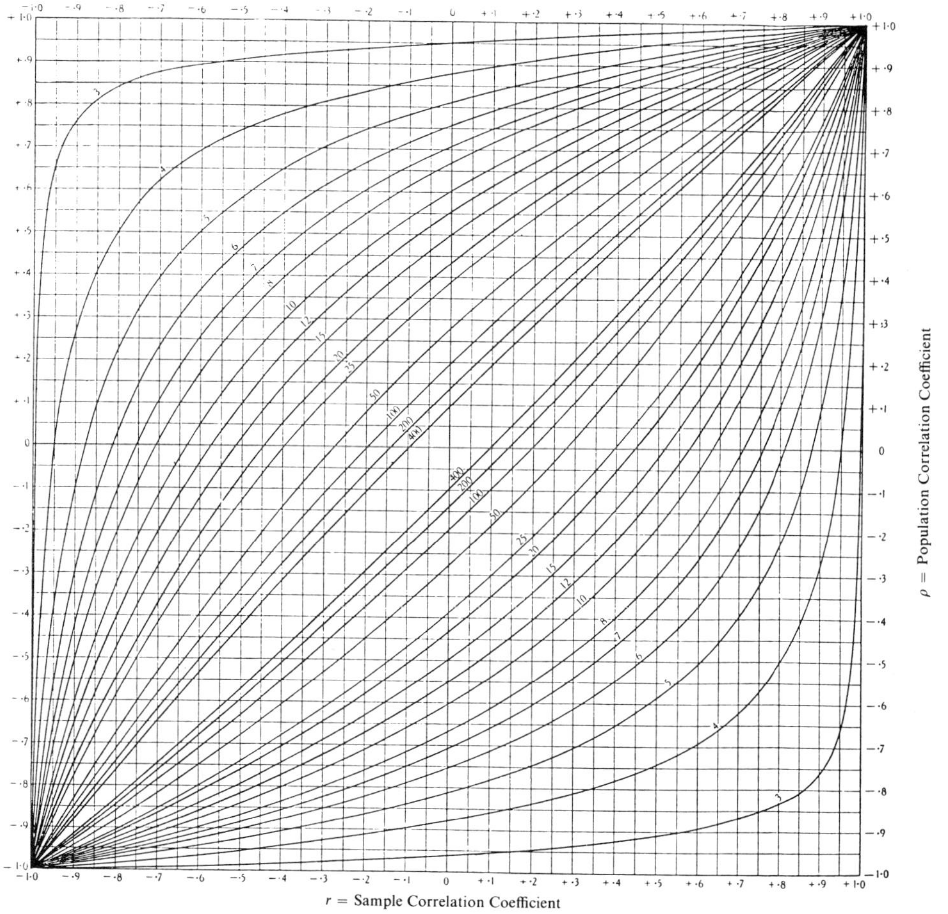

This graph is from "Tables of the Correlation Coefficient" by F. N. David. It is here published with the kind permission of its author, F. N. David, and the trustees of *Biometrika*.

Table T.8

Confidence Curves for Simple Correlation Coefficient

The curves are for $1 - \alpha = .98$.

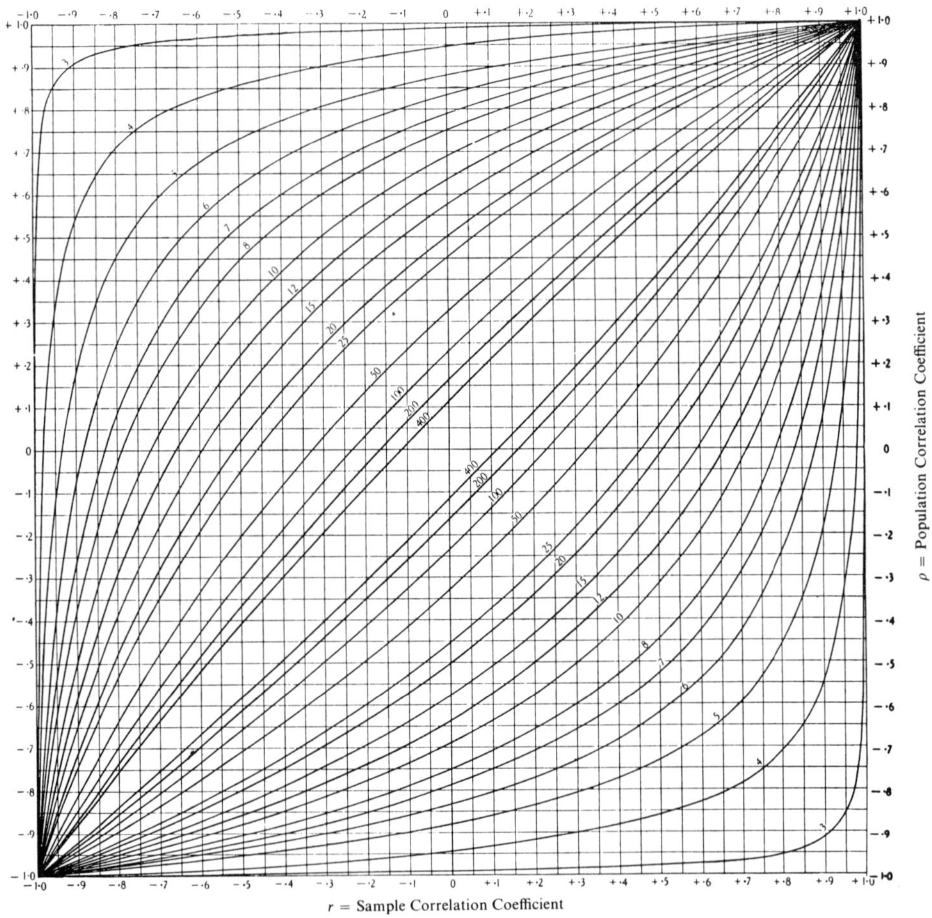

This graph is from "Tables of the Correlation Coefficient" by F. N. David. It is here published with the kind permission of its author, F. N. David, and the trustees of *Biometrika*.

Table T.8
Confidence Curves for Simple Correlation Coefficient

The curves are for $1 - \alpha = .99$.

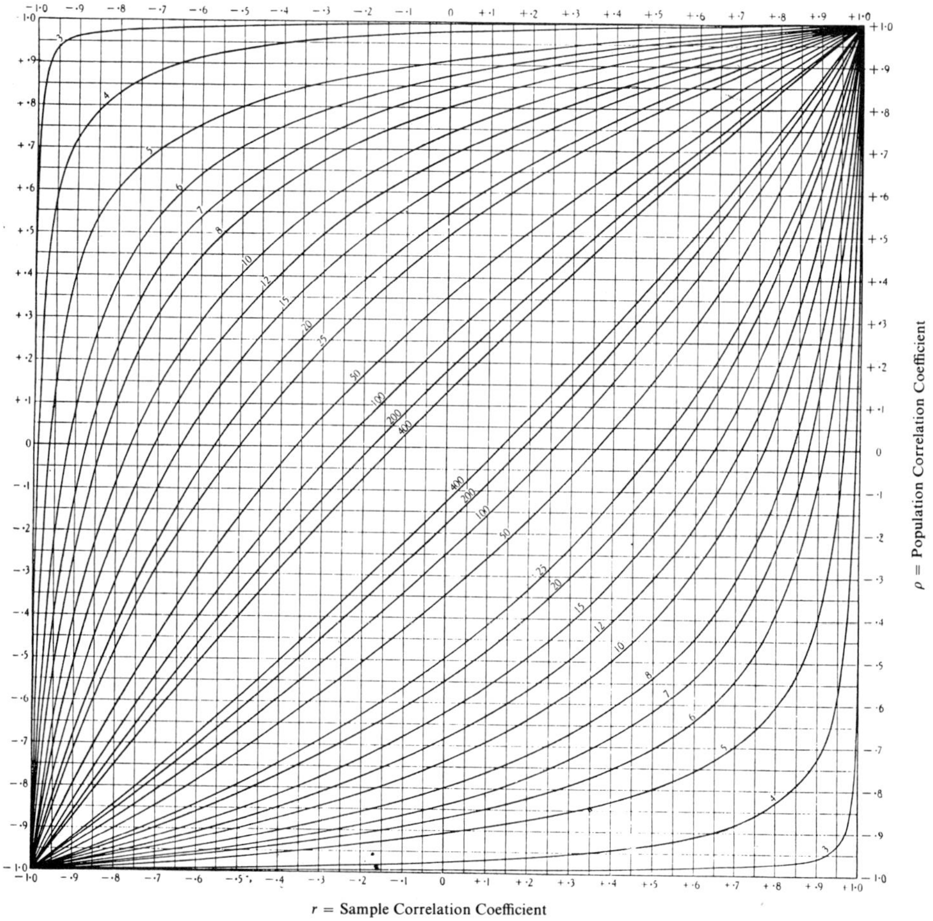

This graph is from "Tables of the Correlation Coefficient" by F. N. David. It is here published with the kind permission of its author, F. N. David, and the trustees of *Biometrika*.

Table T.9

Fisher's z Transformation for the Correlation Coefficient

Entry in the table is z, where $z = (1/2) \log_e[(1 + r)/(1 - r)]$.

r	.000	.001	.002	.003	.004	.005	.006	.007	.008	.009
0.00	0.00000	0.00100	0.00200	0.00300	0.00400	0.00500	0.00600	0.00700	0.00800	0.00900
0.01	0.01000	0.01100	0.01200	0.01300	0.01400	0.01500	0.01600	0.01700	0.01800	0.01900
0.02	0.02000	0.02100	0.02200	0.02300	0.02400	0.02501	0.02601	0.02701	0.02801	0.02901
0.03	0.03001	0.03101	0.03201	0.03301	0.03401	0.03501	0.03602	0.03702	0.03802	0.03902
0.04	0.04002	0.04102	0.04202	0.04303	0.04403	0.04503	0.04603	0.04703	0.04804	0.04904
0.05	0.05004	0.05104	0.05205	0.05305	0.05405	0.05506	0.05606	0.05706	0.05807	0.05907
0.06	0.06007	0.06108	0.06208	0.06308	0.06409	0.06509	0.06610	0.06710	0.06811	0.06911
0.07	0.07011	0.07112	0.07212	0.07313	0.07414	0.07514	0.07615	0.07715	0.07816	0.07916
0.08	0.08017	0.08118	0.08218	0.08319	0.08420	0.08521	0.08621	0.08722	0.08823	0.08924
0.09	0.09024	0.09125	0.09226	0.09327	0.09428	0.09529	0.09630	0.09731	0.09832	0.09933
0.10	0.10034	0.10135	0.10236	0.10337	0.10438	0.10539	0.10640	0.10741	0.10842	0.10943
0.11	0.11045	0.11146	0.11247	0.11348	0.11450	0.11551	0.11652	0.11754	0.11855	0.11957
0.12	0.12058	0.12160	0.12261	0.12363	0.12464	0.12566	0.12667	0.12769	0.12871	0.12972
0.13	0.13074	0.13176	0.13277	0.13379	0.13481	0.13583	0.13685	0.13787	0.13889	0.13991
0.14	0.14093	0.14195	0.14297	0.14399	0.14501	0.14603	0.14705	0.14807	0.14910	0.15012
0.15	0.15114	0.15216	0.15319	0.15421	0.15524	0.15626	0.15728	0.15831	0.15933	0.16036
0.16	0.16139	0.16241	0.16344	0.16447	0.16549	0.16652	0.16755	0.16858	0.16961	0.17064
0.17	0.17167	0.17270	0.17373	0.17476	0.17579	0.17682	0.17785	0.17888	0.17992	0.18095
0.18	0.18198	0.18302	0.18405	0.18508	0.18612	0.18715	0.18819	0.18923	0.19026	0.19130
0.19	0.19234	0.19337	0.19441	0.19545	0.19649	0.19753	0.19857	0.19961	0.20065	0.20169
0.20	0.20273	0.20377	0.20482	0.20586	0.20690	0.20795	0.20899	0.21003	0.21108	0.21213
0.21	0.21317	0.21422	0.21526	0.21631	0.21736	0.21841	0.21946	0.22051	0.22156	0.22261
0.22	0.22366	0.22471	0.22576	0.22681	0.22786	0.22892	0.22997	0.23102	0.23208	0.23313
0.23	0.23419	0.23525	0.23630	0.23736	0.23842	0.23948	0.24053	0.24159	0.24265	0.24371
0.24	0.24477	0.24584	0.24690	0.24796	0.24902	0.25009	0.25115	0.25222	0.25328	0.25435
0.25	0.25541	0.25648	0.25755	0.25862	0.25968	0.26075	0.26182	0.26289	0.26396	0.26504
0.26	0.26611	0.26718	0.26825	0.26933	0.27040	0.27148	0.27255	0.27363	0.27471	0.27579
0.27	0.27686	0.27794	0.27902	0.28010	0.28118	0.28226	0.28335	0.28443	0.28551	0.28660
0.28	0.28768	0.28877	0.28985	0.29094	0.29203	0.29312	0.29420	0.29529	0.29638	0.29747
0.29	0.29857	0.29966	0.30075	0.30184	0.30294	0.30403	0.30513	0.30623	0.30732	0.30842

0.30	0.30952	0.31062	0.31172	0.31282	0.31392	0.31502	0.31613	0.31723	0.31833	0.31944
0.31	0.32055	0.32165	0.32276	0.32387	0.32498	0.32609	0.32720	0.32831	0.32942	0.33053
0.32	0.33165	0.33276	0.33388	0.33499	0.33611	0.33723	0.33835	0.33947	0.34059	0.34171
0.33	0.34283	0.34395	0.34507	0.34620	0.34732	0.34845	0.34958	0.35070	0.35183	0.35296
0.34	0.35409	0.35522	0.35636	0.35749	0.35862	0.35976	0.36089	0.36203	0.36317	0.36430
0.35	0.36544	0.36658	0.36772	0.36887	0.37001	0.37115	0.37230	0.37344	0.37459	0.37574
0.36	0.37689	0.37804	0.37919	0.38034	0.38149	0.38264	0.38380	0.38495	0.38611	0.38726
0.37	0.38842	0.38958	0.39074	0.39190	0.39307	0.39423	0.39539	0.39656	0.39772	0.39889
0.38	0.40006	0.40123	0.40240	0.40357	0.40474	0.40592	0.40709	0.40827	0.40944	0.41062
0.39	0.41180	0.41298	0.41416	0.41534	0.41653	0.41771	0.41890	0.42008	0.42127	0.42246
0.40	0.42365	0.42484	0.42603	0.42723	0.42842	0.42962	0.43081	0.43201	0.43321	0.43441
0.41	0.43561	0.43681	0.43802	0.43922	0.44043	0.44164	0.44285	0.44406	0.44527	0.44648
0.42	0.44769	0.44891	0.45012	0.45134	0.45256	0.45378	0.45500	0.45622	0.45745	0.45867
0.43	0.45990	0.46112	0.46235	0.46358	0.46481	0.46605	0.46728	0.46852	0.46975	0.47099
0.44	0.47223	0.47347	0.47471	0.47596	0.47720	0.47845	0.47970	0.48094	0.48220	0.48345
0.45	0.48470	0.48595	0.48721	0.48847	0.48973	0.49099	0.49225	0.49351	0.49478	0.49604
0.46	0.49731	0.49858	0.49985	0.50112	0.50240	0.50367	0.50495	0.50623	0.50751	0.50879
0.47	0.51007	0.51135	0.51264	0.51393	0.51522	0.51651	0.51780	0.51909	0.52039	0.52169
0.48	0.52298	0.52428	0.52559	0.52689	0.52819	0.52950	0.53081	0.53212	0.53343	0.53475
0.49	0.53606	0.53738	0.53870	0.54002	0.54134	0.54266	0.54399	0.54531	0.54664	0.54797
0.50	0.54931	0.55064	0.55198	0.55331	0.55465	0.55600	0.55734	0.55868	0.56003	0.56138
0.51	0.56273	0.56408	0.56544	0.56679	0.56815	0.56951	0.57087	0.57224	0.57360	0.57497
0.52	0.57634	0.57771	0.57908	0.58046	0.58184	0.58322	0.58460	0.58598	0.58737	0.58876
0.53	0.59015	0.59154	0.59293	0.59433	0.59572	0.59712	0.59853	0.59993	0.60134	0.60275
0.54	0.60416	0.60557	0.60698	0.60840	0.60982	0.61124	0.61266	0.61409	0.61552	0.61695
0.55	0.61838	0.61982	0.62125	0.62269	0.62413	0.62558	0.62702	0.62847	0.62992	0.63138
0.56	0.63283	0.63429	0.63575	0.63721	0.63868	0.64015	0.64162	0.64309	0.64457	0.64604
0.57	0.64752	0.64901	0.65049	0.65198	0.65347	0.65496	0.65646	0.65795	0.65945	0.66096
0.58	0.66246	0.66397	0.66548	0.66700	0.66851	0.67003	0.67155	0.67308	0.67460	0.67613
0.59	0.67767	0.67920	0.68074	0.68228	0.68382	0.68537	0.68692	0.68847	0.69003	0.69159
0.60	0.69315	0.69471	0.69628	0.69785	0.69942	0.70100	0.70258	0.70416	0.70574	0.70733
0.61	0.70892	0.71052	0.71211	0.71371	0.71532	0.71692	0.71853	0.72015	0.72176	0.72338
0.62	0.72501	0.72663	0.72826	0.72989	0.73153	0.73317	0.73481	0.73646	0.73811	0.73976
0.63	0.74142	0.74308	0.74474	0.74641	0.74808	0.74975	0.75143	0.75311	0.75479	0.75648
0.64	0.75817	0.75987	0.76157	0.76327	0.76498	0.76669	0.76840	0.77012	0.77184	0.77357
0.65	0.77530	0.77703	0.77877	0.78051	0.78226	0.78401	0.78576	0.78752	0.78928	0.79104
0.66	0.79281	0.79459	0.79637	0.79815	0.79993	0.80172	0.80352	0.80532	0.80712	0.80893

Table T.9 (continued)

r	.000	.001	.002	.003	.004	.005	.006	.007	.008	.009
0.67	0.81074	0.81256	0.81438	0.81621	0.81804	0.81987	0.82171	0.82355	0.82540	0.82726
0.68	0.82911	0.83098	0.83284	0.83472	0.83659	0.83847	0.84036	0.84225	0.84415	0.84605
0.69	0.84796	0.84987	0.85178	0.85370	0.85563	0.85756	0.85950	0.86144	0.86339	0.86534
0.70	0.86730	0.86926	0.87123	0.87321	0.87519	0.87717	0.87916	0.88116	0.88316	0.88517
0.71	0.88718	0.88920	0.89123	0.89326	0.89530	0.89734	0.89939	0.90144	0.90350	0.90557
0.72	0.90764	0.90972	0.91181	0.91390	0.91600	0.91811	0.92022	0.92233	0.92446	0.92659
0.73	0.92873	0.93087	0.93302	0.93518	0.93734	0.93952	0.94169	0.94388	0.94607	0.94827
0.74	0.95048	0.95269	0.95491	0.95714	0.95938	0.96162	0.96387	0.96613	0.96840	0.97067
0.75	0.97296	0.97524	0.97754	0.97985	0.98216	0.98448	0.98681	0.98915	0.99150	0.99385
0.76	0.99622	0.99859	1.00097	1.00336	1.00575	1.00816	1.01058	1.01300	1.01543	1.01788
0.77	1.02033	1.02279	1.02526	1.02774	1.03023	1.03273	1.03524	1.03776	1.04028	1.04282
0.78	1.04537	1.04793	1.05050	1.05308	1.05567	1.05827	1.06088	1.06350	1.06613	1.06878
0.79	1.07143	1.07410	1.07677	1.07946	1.08216	1.08488	1.08760	1.09033	1.09308	1.09584
0.80	1.09861	1.10140	1.10419	1.10700	1.10982	1.11266	1.11551	1.11837	1.12124	1.12413
0.81	1.12703	1.12994	1.13287	1.13581	1.13877	1.14174	1.14473	1.14773	1.15074	1.15377
0.82	1.15682	1.15988	1.16295	1.16604	1.16915	1.17227	1.17541	1.17857	1.18174	1.18493
0.83	1.18814	1.19136	1.19460	1.19786	1.20113	1.20443	1.20774	1.21107	1.21442	1.21779
0.84	1.22117	1.22458	1.22801	1.23145	1.23492	1.23840	1.24191	1.24544	1.24899	1.25256
0.85	1.25615	1.25977	1.26340	1.26706	1.27075	1.27445	1.27818	1.28194	1.28571	1.28952
0.86	1.29334	1.29720	1.30108	1.30498	1.30891	1.31287	1.31686	1.32087	1.32491	1.32898
0.87	1.33308	1.33721	1.34137	1.34555	1.34977	1.35403	1.35831	1.36262	1.36697	1.37135
0.88	1.37577	1.38022	1.38470	1.38922	1.39378	1.39838	1.40301	1.40768	1.41239	1.41714
0.89	1.42193	1.42676	1.43163	1.43654	1.44150	1.44651	1.45156	1.45665	1.46179	1.46698
0.90	1.47222	1.47751	1.48285	1.48824	1.49368	1.49918	1.50473	1.51034	1.51601	1.52174
0.91	1.52752	1.53337	1.53928	1.54526	1.55130	1.55741	1.56359	1.56984	1.57616	1.58256
0.92	1.58903	1.59558	1.60221	1.60892	1.61571	1.62260	1.62957	1.63663	1.64379	1.65104
0.93	1.65839	1.66584	1.67340	1.68107	1.68885	1.69674	1.70475	1.71288	1.72114	1.72953
0.94	1.73805	1.74671	1.75552	1.76447	1.77358	1.78284	1.79227	1.80188	1.81166	1.82162
0.95	1.83178	1.84214	1.85270	1.86349	1.87450	1.88574	1.89723	1.90898	1.92100	1.93331
0.96	1.94591	1.95882	1.97207	1.98566	1.99961	2.01395	2.02870	2.04388	2.05952	2.07565
0.97	2.09230	2.10950	2.12730	2.14574	2.16486	2.18472	2.20539	2.22692	2.24940	2.27291
0.98	2.29756	2.32346	2.35074	2.37958	2.41014	2.44266	2.47741	2.51472	2.55499	2.59875
0.99	2.64665	2.69958	2.75873	2.82574	2.90307	2.99448	3.10630	3.25039	3.45338	3.80020

Table T.10

Upper .01 Probability Points of Multiple Correlation Coefficient

Entries are $r_{.01:K,n-K-1;(\rho_0)}$, where $\int_{r_{.01:K,n-K-1;(\rho_0)}}^{1} f_R(r : K, n - K - 1; \rho_0)\, dr = .01$.

$n-K-1$	K	0·0	0·1	0·2	0·3	0·4 $\rho_0 = \rho_{0(1,2,\ldots,K)}$	0·5	0·6	0·7	0·8	0·9
10	2	0·776	0·785	0·807	0·835	0·863	0·890	0·916	0·940	0·961	0·982
	4	·840	·844	·856	·872	·891	·911	·930	·949	·967	·984
	6	·874	·877	·884	·896	·909	·925	·940	·956	·971	·986
	8	·895	·897	·903	·912	·923	·935	·948	·961	·974	·987
	10	·911	·912	·917	·923	·932	·943	·954	·965	·977	·989
	12	·922	·923	·927	·932	·940	·949	·958	·969	·979	·990
	16	0·937	0·938	0·941	0·945	0·951	0·958	0·965	0·974	0·982	0·991
	20	·948	·948	·951	·954	·959	·964	·970	·977	·985	·992
	24	·955	·956	·957	·960	·964	·969	·974	·980	·986	·993
	30	·963	·963	·965	·967	·970	·974	·978	·983	·988	·994
	34	·967	·967	·968	·970	·973	·976	·980	·985	·990	·995
	40	·971	·972	·973	·974	·977	·979	·983	·987	·991	·995
20	2	0·607	0·627	0·670	0·719	0·767	0·812	0·855	0·895	0·933	0·968
	4	·685	·696	·723	·757	·795	·833	·869	·905	·938	·970
	6	·733	·740	·759	·786	·817	·849	·881	·913	·943	·972
	8	·767	·772	·787	·809	·835	·862	·891	·919	·947	·974
	10	·792	·797	·809	·827	·849	·874	·899	·925	·951	·976
	12	·812	·816	·826	·842	·861	·883	·906	·930	·954	·977
	16	0·842	0·845	0·853	0·865	0·881	0·898	0·918	0·938	0·959	0·979
	20	·864	·866	·872	·882	·895	·910	·927	·945	·963	·981
	24	·880	·882	·887	·896	·907	·920	·934	·950	·966	·983
	30	·898	·900	·904	·911	·920	·930	·943	·956	·970	·985
	34	·907	·909	·912	·918	·926	·936	·947	·959	·972	·986
	40	·918	·920	·923	·928	·935	·943	·953	·964	·975	·987
30	2	0·514	0·541	0·596	0·655	0·713	0·768	0·820	0·870	0·916	0·959
	4	·591	·606	·643	·689	·738	·786	·833	·878	·921	·961
	6	·640	·651	·679	·717	·759	·801	·844	·885	·925	·963
	8	·677	·685	·708	·740	·776	·815	·853	·892	·929	·965
	10	·706	·713	·732	·759	·791	·826	·862	·897	·933	·967
	12	·729	·735	·752	·776	·805	·836	·869	·903	·936	·968
	16	0·766	0·771	0·783	0·803	0·827	0·854	0·882	0·912	0·941	0·971
	20	·793	·797	·808	·824	·844	·867	·893	·919	·946	·973
	24	·815	·818	·827	·841	·858	·879	·902	·925	·950	·975
	30	·839	·842	·849	·861	·875	·893	·912	·933	·955	·977
	34	·852	·855	·861	·871	·885	·900	·918	·938	·958	·979
	40	·868	·870	·876	·884	·896	·910	·926	·943	·961	·981
40	2	0·454	0·486	0·548	0·614	0·678	0·739	0·797	0·852	0·904	0·953
	4	·526	·545	·590	·644	·700	·755	·808	·859	·909	·955
	6	·575	·589	·624	·669	·718	·769	·818	·866	·913	·957
	8	·612	·623	·652	·691	·735	·781	·827	·872	·916	·959
	10	·642	·651	·676	·710	·750	·792	·835	·878	·920	·960
	12	·667	·674	·696	·727	·763	·802	·842	·883	·923	·962
	16	0·706	0·712	0·729	0·755	0·785	0·819	0·855	0·892	0·928	0·964
	20	·736	·741	·756	·777	·804	·834	·866	·899	·933	·967
	24	·761	·765	·777	·796	·819	·846	·876	·906	·937	·969
	30	·789	·793	·803	·818	·838	·862	·887	·915	·943	·971
	34	·805	·808	·817	·831	·849	·870	·894	·919	·946	·973
	40	·824	·827	·834	·846	·863	·882	·903	·926	·950	·975
50	2	0·410	0·447	0·514	0·584	0·652	0·718	0·780	0·839	0·896	0·949
	4	·479	·502	·552	·611	·672	·732	·790	·846	·900	·951
	6	·526	·543	·583	·634	·689	·744	·799	·852	·903	·953
	8	·562	·576	·610	·655	·704	·756	·807	·858	·907	·954
	10	·592	·603	·633	·673	·718	·766	·815	·863	·910	·956
	12	·617	·627	·653	·689	·731	·776	·822	·867	·913	·957
	16	0·658	0·665	0·686	0·716	0·753	0·793	0·834	0·876	0·918	0·959
	20	·689	·696	·713	·739	772	·807	·845	·884	·923	·962
	24	·715	·721	·736	·759	·787	·820	·854	·890	·927	·964
	30	·746	·751	·763	·783	·808	·836	·867	·899	·933	·966
	34	·764	·767	·779	·796	·819	·845	·874	·904	·936	·968
	40	·785	·788	·798	·814	·834	·857	·883	·911	·940	·970

Table T.10 is from "Biometrika Tables for Statisticians," Vol. 2, edited by E. S. Pearson and H. O. Hartley. It is reprinted here with the kind permission of the editors, the author of the tables, K. H. Kramer, and the trustees of *Biometrika*.

Table T.10

Upper .05 Probability Points of Multiple Correlation Coefficient

Entries are $r_{.05:K,n-K-1;(\rho_0)}$, where $\int_{r_{.05:K,n-K-1;(\rho_0)}}^{1} f_R(r:K, n-K-1; \rho_0)\,dr = .05$.

$n-K-1$	K	0·0	0·1	0·2	0·3	0·4	0·5	0·6	0·7	0·8	0·9
						$\rho_0 = \rho_{0(1,2,\ldots,K)}$					
10	2	0·671	0·682	0·710	0·748	0·789	0·829	0·868	0·904	0·939	0·970
	4	·763	·768	·784	·806	·833	·862	·891	·920	·948	·974
	6	·812	·815	·826	·842	·861	·884	·907	·931	·954	·978
	8	·843	·846	·854	·866	·881	·899	·919	·939	·960	·980
	10	·865	·867	·874	·884	·896	·912	·928	·946	·964	·982
	12	·882	·884	·889	·897	·908	·921	·935	·951	·967	·983
	16	0·905	0·906	0·910	0·916	0·925	0·935	0·946	0·959	0·972	0·986
	20	·920	·922	·925	·930	·936	·945	·954	·965	·976	·988
	24	·932	·932	·935	·939	·945	·952	·960	·969	·979	·989
	30	·943	·944	·946	·950	·954	·960	·966	·974	·982	·991
	34	·949	·950	·952	·955	·959	·964	·970	·976	·984	·992
	40	·956	·957	·958	·961	·964	·968	·973	·979	·986	·993
20	2	0·509	0·528	0·576	0·634	0·693	0·751	0·806	0·859	0·908	0·955
	4	·604	·615	·645	·685	·731	·778	·826	·872	·916	·959
	6	·662	·670	·692	·723	·760	·801	·842	·883	·923	·962
	8	·703	·709	·727	·752	·784	·819	·855	·892	·929	·965
	10	·735	·740	·754	·776	·803	·834	·866	·900	·933	·967
	12	·760	·764	·776	·795	·819	·846	·876	·906	·938	·969
	16	0·797	0·801	0·810	0·825	0·844	0·867	0·891	0·918	0·945	0·972
	20	·825	·827	·835	·847	·863	·882	·903	·926	·950	·975
	24	·845	·847	·854	·864	·878	·894	·913	·933	·955	·977
	30	·868	·870	·875	·884	·895	·909	·924	·942	·960	·980
	34	·880	·882	·886	·894	·904	·916	·930	·946	·963	·981
	40	·895	·896	·899	·906	·915	·925	·938	·952	·967	·983
30	2	0·425	0·451	0·510	0·577	0·645	0·710	0·774	0·834	0·892	0·947
	4	·514	·529	·569	·620	·676	·733	·790	·845	·899	·950
	6	·571	·582	·612	·654	·702	·753	·804	·855	·905	·953
	8	·614	·623	·647	·683	·724	·770	·816	·863	·910	·956
	10	·647	·655	·675	·706	·743	·784	·827	·871	·914	·958
	12	·675	·681	·699	·726	·760	·797	·837	·878	·919	·960
	16	0·718	0·723	0·737	0·759	0·787	0·819	0·853	0·889	0·926	0·963
	20	·750	·754	·766	·785	·808	·836	·866	·899	·932	·966
	24	·776	·779	·789	·805	·826	·850	·877	·907	·937	·968
	30	·805	·808	·816	·829	·847	·868	·891	·917	·944	·971
	34	·821	·823	·830	·842	·858	·877	·899	·922	·947	·973
	40	·840	·842	·848	·858	·872	·889	·908	·929	·952	·975
40	2	0·373	0·403	0·469	0·541	0·614	0·685	0·753	0·819	0·882	0·942
	4	·455	·473	·520	·578	·641	·704	·767	·828	·888	·945
	6	·509	·523	·560	·609	·664	·722	·779	·837	·893	·947
	8	·551	·562	·592	·635	·684	·737	·790	·844	·897	·949
	10	·585	·594	·620	·657	·702	·750	·800	·851	·901	·951
	12	·613	·621	·644	·677	·718	·762	·809	·857	·905	·953
	16	0·657	0·664	0·682	0·710	0·745	0·784	0·825	0·868	0·912	0·956
	20	·692	·697	·713	·737	·767	·801	·839	·878	·918	·959
	24	·720	·724	·738	·758	·785	·816	·850	·886	·924	·962
	30	·753	·757	·768	·785	·808	·835	·865	·897	·930	·965
	34	·771	·774	·784	·800	·820	·845	·873	·903	·934	·967
	40	·793	·796	·804	·818	·836	·858	·883	·910	·939	·969
50	2	0·336	0·370	0·440	0·517	0·593	0·667	0·739	0·808	0·874	0·938
	4	·412	·434	·485	·549	·616	·684	·751	·816	·879	·941
	6	·464	·480	·522	·576	·637	·699	·762	·823	·884	·943
	8	·504	·517	·552	·600	·655	·713	·771	·830	·888	·945
	10	·537	·548	·578	·621	·671	·725	·781	·836	·892	·946
	12	·565	·575	·601	·640	·686	·737	·789	·842	·896	·948
	16	0·610	0·618	0·639	0·672	0·712	0·757	0·804	0·853	0·902	0·951
	20	·645	·652	·670	·699	·734	·774	·817	·862	·908	·954
	24	·674	·680	·696	·721	·753	·789	·828	·870	·913	·956
	30	·709	·714	·727	·749	·776	·808	·843	·881	·920	·960
	34	·728	·733	·745	·764	·789	·819	·852	·887	·924	·962
	40	·753	·756	·767	·784	·806	·833	·863	·895	·929	·964

Table T.10

Upper .95 Probability Points of Multiple Correlation Coefficient

Entries are $r_{.95:K,n-K-1;(\rho_0)}$, where $\int_{r_{.95:K,n-K-1;(\rho_0)}}^{1} f_R(r:K, n-K-1;\rho_0)\,dr = .95$.

$n-K-1$	K	0·0	0·1	0·2	0·3	0·4	0·5	0·6	0·7	0·8	0·9
						$\rho_0 = \rho_{0(1,2,\ldots,K)}$					
10	2	0·101	0·104	0·114	0·133	0·167	0·224	0·314	0·441	0·599	0·785
	4	·251	·255	·268	·291	·328	·382	·457	·555	·679	·827
	6	·359	·363	·376	·399	·433	·481	·546	·629	·731	·855
	8	·439	·443	·455	·477	·508	·552	·608	·681	·769	·875
	10	·501	·505	·517	·536	·565	·605	·656	·719	·798	·891
	12	·551	·554	·565	·584	·610	·646	·692	·750	·820	·903
	16	0·625	0·628	0·638	0·654	0·677	0·707	0·746	0·794	0·852	0·920
	20	·678	·681	·689	·703	·724	·750	·784	·825	·875	·933
	24	·718	·721	·728	·741	·759	·782	·812	·848	·891	·942
	30	·762	·764	·771	·782	·797	·817	·842	·873	·909	·951
	34	·785	·787	·792	·802	·816	·835	·858	·885	·918	·956
	40	·811	·813	·818	·827	·839	·856	·876	·900	·929	·962
20	2	0·072	0·076	0·089	0·118	0·172	0·260	0·374	0·507	0·656	0·820
	4	·183	·188	·205	·237	·287	·359	·452	·565	·694	·839
	6	·268	·274	·290	·321	·366	·430	·511	·609	·724	·854
	8	·336	·341	·357	·385	·427	·484	·557	·645	·749	·867
	10	·391	·396	·411	·437	·476	·528	·594	·675	·770	·878
	12	·437	·442	·456	·481	·517	·565	·626	·700	·787	·887
	16	0·510	0·514	0·527	0·549	0·581	0·623	0·676	0·740	0·815	0·902
	20	·566	·570	·581	·601	·629	·667	·713	·770	·836	·913
	24	·610	·613	·624	·642	·668	·701	·743	·794	·853	·922
	30	·661	·664	·674	·689	·712	·741	·778	·822	·873	·933
	34	·688	·691	·700	·715	·735	·762	·796	·836	·884	·938
	40	·722	·724	·732	·745	·764	·788	·818	·854	·896	·945
30	2	0·058	0·063	0·081	0·119	0·191	0·292	0·410	0·541	0·683	0·836
	4	·151	·157	·178	·216	·278	·361	·462	·578	·707	·848
	6	·223	·230	·250	·286	·341	·414	·504	·609	·727	·858
	8	·282	·289	·308	·342	·391	·458	·540	·636	·745	·867
	10	·332	·337	·356	·387	·433	·494	·570	·659	·761	·875
	12	·374	·379	·396	·426	·469	·526	·596	·679	·775	·882
	16	0·442	0·447	0·463	0·489	0·527	0·577	0·639	0·713	0·798	0·894
	20	·496	·501	·515	·539	·574	·618	·674	·740	·817	·904
	24	·540	·545	·558	·580	·611	·652	·702	·763	·833	·912
	30	·593	·597	·609	·628	·656	·692	·737	·790	·852	·922
	34	·622	·626	·637	·655	·680	·714	·755	·805	·862	·927
	40	·658	·661	·671	·688	·711	·741	·779	·823	·875	·934
40	2	0·051	0·056	0·077	0·125	0·210	0·316	0·434	0·562	0·699	0·845
	4	·131	·138	·162	·208	·277	·367	·472	·589	·716	·853
	6	·196	·203	·226	·267	·329	·409	·504	·613	·732	·861
	8	·248	·255	·277	·316	·372	·445	·533	·634	·746	·868
	10	·293	·300	·321	·356	·408	·476	·558	·652	·758	·874
	12	·332	·338	·358	·392	·440	·503	·580	·669	·769	·880
	16	0·396	0·402	0·420	0·450	0·493	0·549	0·618	0·698	0·789	0·890
	20	·448	·453	·469	·497	·536	·587	·649	·722	·805	·898
	24	·491	·496	·511	·536	·572	·618	·676	·743	·819	·905
	30	·543	·548	·561	·584	·616	·657	·708	·768	·837	·914
	34	·572	·577	·589	·610	·640	·679	·726	·783	·847	·920
	40	·609	·613	·625	·644	·671	·707	·750	·801	·860	·926
50	2	0·045	0·052	0·076	0·133	0·225	0·333	0·451	0·576	0·710	0·851
	4	·118	·126	·153	·204	·279	·373	·480	·598	·723	·858
	6	·176	·184	·210	·256	·323	·408	·507	·616	·736	·864
	8	·224	·232	·256	·299	·360	·438	·530	·634	·747	·869
	10	·266	·273	·296	·336	·392	·465	·551	·649	·757	·874
	12	·301	·309	·330	·368	·421	·489	·570	·663	·767	·879
	16	0·362	0·368	0·388	0·422	0·469	0·530	0·604	0·689	0·783	0·887
	20	·411	·417	·435	·466	·509	·565	·632	·710	·798	·895
	24	·453	·458	·475	·503	·543	·594	·656	·729	·811	·901
	30	·504	·509	·524	·550	·585	·631	·687	·753	·827	·910
	34	·533	·538	·552	·576	·609	·652	·705	·766	·836	·914
	40	·570	·575	·588	·609	·640	·680	·728	·784	·849	·921

Table T.10

Upper .99 Probability Points of Multiple Correlation Coefficient

Entries are $r_{.99:K,n-K-1;(\rho_0)}$, where $\int_{r_{.99:K,n-K-1;(\rho_0)}}^{1} f_R(r : K, n-K-1; \rho_0)\, dr = .99$.

$n-K-1$	K	0·0	0·1	0·2	0·3	0·4 $\rho_0 = \rho_{0(1,2,\ldots,K)}$	0·5	0·6	0·7	0·8	0·9
10	2	0·015	0·046	0·051	0·059	0·075	0·105	0·161	0·269	0·444	0·685
	4	·161	·166	·175	·192	·218	·260	·325	·422	·562	·752
	6	·266	·269	·280	·298	·327	·370	·432	·519	·637	·795
	8	·348	·351	·362	·381	·410	·451	·508	·586	·691	·826
	10	·413	·417	·428	·446	·474	·513	·566	·637	·730	·849
	12	·467	·471	·481	·499	·525	·562	·612	·677	·761	·867
	16	0·550	0·553	0·563	0·579	0·603	0·636	0·679	0·735	0·805	0·892
	20	·610	·613	·622	·637	·659	·688	·727	·775	·835	·910
	24	·657	·659	·667	·681	·701	·727	·762	·805	·858	·922
	30	·708	·711	·718	·730	·747	·771	·800	·837	·882	·936
	34	·735	·737	·744	·755	·771	·792	·820	·853	·894	·942
	40	·767	·769	·775	·785	·799	·818	·843	·872	·908	·950
20	2	0·032	0·033	0·040	0·053	0·081	0·140	0·244	0·386	0·559	0·762
	4	·119	·122	·134	·156	·193	·254	·343	·462	·611	·789
	6	·197	·202	·215	·239	·277	·334	·414	·520	·651	·811
	8	·264	·268	·281	·306	·343	·397	·470	·565	·684	·829
	10	·319	·324	·337	·361	·397	·447	·515	·602	·711	·843
	12	·367	·371	·384	·407	·441	·489	·553	·634	·734	·856
	16	0·444	0·448	0·460	0·482	0·513	0·556	0·612	0·683	0·770	0·875
	20	·504	·508	·519	·539	·568	·607	·657	·720	·798	·890
	24	·552	·556	·566	·585	·611	·647	·693	·750	·819	·902
	30	·609	·612	·622	·638	·662	·694	·734	·784	·844	·916
	34	·639	·642	·651	·667	·689	·718	·756	·802	·857	·923
	40	·677	·679	·688	·702	·722	·749	·782	·824	·873	·932
30	2	0·026	0·028	0·036	0·055	0·098	0·184	0·304	0·447	0·610	0·793
	4	·098	·102	·116	·143	·192	·267	·369	·494	·641	·809
	6	·164	·169	·184	·213	·260	·328	·420	·533	·667	·823
	8	·221	·226	·242	·270	·315	·378	·462	·566	·690	·835
	10	·270	·275	·291	·318	·361	·420	·498	·594	·710	·845
	12	·312	·317	·333	·360	·400	·456	·529	·619	·727	·854
	16	0·383	0·388	0·402	0·427	0·464	0·515	0·580	0·660	0·757	0·870
	20	·440	·444	·458	·481	·515	·561	·620	·693	·780	·882
	24	·487	·491	·504	·525	·557	·599	·653	·720	·799	·893
	30	·543	·547	·559	·579	·607	·645	·693	·752	·823	·905
	34	·575	·578	·589	·608	·635	·670	·715	·770	·835	·912
	40	·614	·617	·627	·645	·669	·702	·743	·792	·851	·921
40	2	0·022	0·025	0·034	0·059	0·119	0·220	0·343	0·483	0·639	0·811
	4	·085	·090	·106	·139	·196	·282	·390	·517	·661	·822
	6	·143	·149	·167	·200	·254	·331	·429	·546	·680	·831
	8	·194	·200	·218	·250	·301	·372	·462	·571	·697	·840
	10	·238	·244	·261	·293	·341	·407	·492	·594	·713	·848
	12	·277	·282	·300	·330	·376	·438	·518	·614	·727	·855
	16	0·342	0·347	0·364	0·392	0·434	0·490	0·562	0·648	0·751	0·868
	20	·396	·401	·416	·442	·481	·533	·598	·677	·771	·878
	24	·440	·445	·460	·484	·520	·568	·628	·701	·788	·887
	30	·496	·500	·514	·536	·569	·612	·666	·732	·809	·898
	34	·527	·531	·544	·565	·596	·636	·687	·748	·821	·905
	40	·567	·571	·582	·602	·630	·667	·714	·770	·836	·913
50	2	0·020	0·023	0·034	0·066	0·139	0·247	0·371	0·508	0·658	0·822
	4	·075	·082	·100	·138	·204	·295	·407	·534	·675	·830
	6	·129	·135	·155	·193	·253	·336	·438	·557	·690	·838
	8	·175	·181	·201	·238	·294	·370	·466	·577	·704	·845
	10	·215	·222	·241	·276	·329	·401	·490	·596	·716	·851
	12	·251	·257	·276	·310	·360	·428	·512	·613	·728	·857
	16	0·312	0·318	0·336	0·367	0·413	0·474	0·551	0·642	0·748	0·867
	20	·363	·368	·385	·414	·457	·513	·583	·667	·765	·876
	24	·405	·411	·427	·454	·493	·546	·611	·689	·780	·884
	30	·459	·464	·479	·504	·540	·587	·646	·717	·800	·894
	34	·490	·494	·508	·532	·566	·610	·666	·733	·811	·900
	40	·529	·533	·545	·568	·600	·641	·692	·754	·825	·907

Table T.11 for $\alpha = .005, .025, .01, .05$ is from "Tables of the Power of the F-Test," *Journal of the American Statistical Association*, Vol. 62; Table T.11 for $\alpha = .10$ is from "More Tables of the Power of the F-Test," *Journal of the American Statistical Association*, Vol. 67. They are reprinted here with the kind permission of the author, M. L. Tiku, and the American Statistical Association. In Table T.11 for $\alpha = .005, .025, .05$, some corrected values are listed below.

n_1	α	n_2	ϕ	$1 - \Pi(\lambda)$
1	0.005	60	1.0	0.9249
12	.005	10	1.0	.9439
10	.005	∞	2.2	.0013
12	.005	∞	2.0	.0027
6	0.025	22	2.0	.0943
6	.025	∞	2.0	.0202
7	.025	10	1.8	.3565
9	0.05	28	1.6	.1100
10	.05	∞	1.0	.4074

Table T.11
Upper α Probability Points of the Noncentral *F* Distribution

Entries are $1 - \pi(\lambda) = 1 - \int_{F_{\alpha:n_1,n_2}}^{\infty} F(w : n_1, n_2; \lambda)\, dw$, $\phi = \sqrt{2\lambda/(n_1 + 1)}$.

n_2	$\phi = .5$	1.0	1.2	1.4	1.6	1.8	2.0	2.2	2.6	3.0
					$n_1 = 1, \alpha = 0.005$					
2	.9925	.9851	.9808	.9757	.9699	.9634	.9561	.9481	.9301	.9096
4	.9902	.9729	.9610	.9454	.9258	.9017	.8731	.8398	.7602	.6663
6	.9886	.9630	.9441	.9185	.8855	.8443	.7951	.7382	.6068	.4646
8	.9874	.9557	.9314	.8983	.8551	.8014	.7377	.6653	.5052	.3460
10	.9866	.9502	.9220	.8832	.8326	.7700	.6965	.6144	.4390	.2762
12	.9860	.9461	.9149	.8718	.8157	.7467	.6663	.5778	.3942	.2325
14	.9855	.9429	.9093	.8629	.8026	.7288	.6436	.5507	.3623	.2033
16	.9851	.9404	.9048	.8558	.7923	.7149	.6258	.5298	.3387	.1827
18	.9848	.9383	.9012	.8501	.7839	.7035	.6117	.5134	.3206	.1676
20	.9846	.9365	.8982	.8453	.7770	.6942	.6002	.5001	.3064	.1560
22	.9843	.9351	.8957	.8413	.7712	.6865	.5907	.4892	.2950	.1469
24	.9842	.9338	.8935	.8379	.7663	.6800	.5827	.4801	.2856	.1396
26	.9840	.9327	.8916	.8350	.7620	.6744	.5758	.4724	.2777	.1336
28	.9839	.9318	.8900	.8324	.7584	.6695	.5699	.4658	.2710	.1286
30	.9838	.9310	.8886	.8302	.7552	.6653	.5648	.4600	.2653	.1244
40	.9833	.9280	.8834	.8221	.7437	.6502	.5467	.4899	.2458	.1104
60	.9829	.9240	.8780	.8137	.7318	.6348	.5284	.4199	.2270	.0976
120	.9824	.9216	.8724	.8050	.7195	.6191	.5100	.4001	.2092	.0860
∞	.9819	.9182	.8665	.7959	.7069	.6031	.4915	.3805	.1922	.0756
					$n_1 = 2, \alpha = 0.005$					
2	.9931	.9876	.9843	.9805	.9761	.9711	.9656	.9595	.9458	.9301
4	.9913	.9772	.9673	.9541	.9371	.9161	.8907	.8608	.7881	.7004
6	.9898	.9674	.9500	.9259	.8938	.8530	.8033	.7452	.6093	.4615
8	.9886	.9593	.9354	.9015	.8562	.7986	.7293	.6503	.4764	.3089
10	.9878	.9528	.9235	.8818	.8258	.7553	.6720	.5793	.3866	.2199
12	.9871	.9475	.9139	.8658	.8015	.7214	.6280	.5265	.3256	.1664
14	.9865	.9432	.9061	.8529	.7820	.6945	.5939	.4867	.2828	.1326
16	.9861	.9397	.8996	.8423	.7662	.6728	.5670	.4560	.2517	.1099
18	.9857	.9368	.8942	.8334	.7530	.6552	.5453	.4317	.2284	.0941
20	.9854	.9343	.8897	.8259	.7421	.6405	.5276	.4121	.2104	.0825
22	.9852	.9321	.8858	.8196	.7327	.6282	.5128	.3961	.1961	.0738
24	.9849	.9302	.8824	.8141	.7247	.6177	.5003	.3827	.1846	.0670
26	.9847	.9286	.8794	.8093	.7178	.6086	.4897	.3714	.1751	.0617
28	.9846	.9272	.8768	.8051	.7117	.6008	.4805	.3617	.1672	.0573
30	.9844	.9259	.8745	.8014	.7064	.5989	.4725	.3534	.1605	.0537
40	.9839	.9212	.8661	.7878	.6870	.5692	.4443	.3244	.1383	.0425
60	.9833	.9162	.8570	.7734	.6667	.5438	.4159	.2961	.1181	.0332
120	.9826	.9108	.8472	.7581	.6455	.5177	.3876	.2686	.0999	.0256
∞	.9819	.9049	.8368	.7419	.6234	.4912	.3594	.2422	.0838	.0196
					$n_1 = 3, \alpha = 0.005$					
2	.9933	.9884	.9855	.9821	.9781	.9737	.9688	.9634	.9511	.9370
4	.9916	.9787	.9693	.9569	.9408	.9206	.8962	.8673	.7966	.7107
6	.9902	.9686	.9514	.9271	.8944	.8525	.8012	.7409	.6000	.4478
8	.9890	.9597	.9349	.8992	.8506	.7886	.7138	.6289	.4449	.2742
10	.9881	.9521	.9207	.8751	.8132	.7349	.6428	.5417	.3389	.1758
12	.9873	.9458	.9088	.8549	.7821	.6914	.5870	.4760	.2680	.1201
14	.9867	.9404	.8988	.8379	.7564	.6561	.5431	.4263	.2196	.0870
16	.9862	.9359	.8903	.8237	.7351	.6274	.5082	.3881	.1854	.0662
18	.9858	.9320	.8830	.8117	.7172	.6037	.4801	.3581	.1605	.0525
20	.9854	.9287	.8768	.8014	.7021	.5840	.4571	.3341	.1419	.0431
22	.9851	.9258	.8714	.7925	.6892	.5673	.4380	.3146	.1275	.0363
24	.9848	.9233	.8867	.7847	.6780	.5531	.4219	.2985	.1162	.0313
26	.9846	.9211	.8825	.7780	.6683	.5408	.4082	.2850	.1070	.0275
28	.9844	.9191	.8588	.7720	.6597	.5301	.3964	.2735	.0996	.0245
30	.9842	.9173	.8555	.7666	.6522	.5207	.3862	.2637	.0934	.0222
40	.9835	.9107	.8433	.7470	.6247	.4872	.3504	.2302	.0736	.0153
60	.9827	.9034	.8298	.7257	.5957	.4528	.3149	.1985	.0570	.0102
120	.9819	.8953	.8151	.7029	.5652	.4177	.2803	.1690	.0432	.0067
∞	.9809	.8863	.7990	.6783	.5333	.3824	.2469	.1420	.0322	.0042
					$n_1 = 4, \alpha = 0.005$					
2	.9934	.9888	.9861	.9829	.9792	.9750	.9704	.9653	.9538	.9405
4	.9918	.9794	.9703	.9582	.9425	.9228	.8988	.8703	.8004	.7153
6	.9903	.9691	.9518	.9271	.8937	.8506	.7978	.7357	.5907	.4354
8	.9892	.9595	.9337	.8961	.8448	.7788	.6995	.6099	.4189	.2477
10	.9882	.9510	.9175	.8683	.8011	.7163	.6171	.5097	.3016	.1448
12	.9874	.9436	.9034	.8441	.7638	.6642	.5512	.4338	.2248	.0897
14	.9867	.9372	.8912	.8234	.7323	.6215	.4990	.3765	.1739	.0592
16	.9861	.9318	.8807	.8057	.7059	.5863	.4576	.3328	.1392	.0414
18	.9856	.9270	.8716	.7904	.6834	.5572	.4242	.2989	.1148	.0304
20	.9852	.9228	.8637	.7773	.6643	.5329	.3970	.2722	.0971	.0232
22	.9848	.9192	.8568	.7658	.6479	.5123	.3745	.2507	.0839	.0184
24	.9845	.9159	.8506	.7558	.6336	.4948	.3557	.2331	.0737	.0150
26	.9842	.9131	.8452	.7470	.6212	.4797	.3398	.2186	.0658	.0125
28	.9840	.9105	.8404	.7391	.6103	.4665	.3261	.2064	.0594	.0106
30	.9838	.9082	.8360	.7321	.6006	.4550	.3144	.1960	.0543	.0092
40	.9829	.8994	.8197	.7061	.5653	.4140	.2737	.1615	.0387	.0054
60	.9820	.8896	.8014	.6776	.5278	.3723	.2345	.1303	.0267	.0030
120	.9809	.8784	.7810	.6467	.4885	.3306	.1973	.1027	.0177	.0016
∞	.9797	.8658	.7585	.6133	.4477	.2895	.1631	.0791	.0114	.0008

Table T.11 (continued)

n_2	$\phi = .5$	1.0	1.2	1.4	1.6	1.8	2.0	2.2	2.6	3.0
					$n_1 = 5, \alpha = 0.005$					
2	.9935	.9890	.9864	.9834	.9798	.9758	.9714	.9665	.9554	.9426
4	.9919	.9798	.9709	.9590	.9435	.9240	.9002	.8720	.8025	.7177
6	.9905	.9693	.9518	.9267	.8927	.8486	.7944	.7308	.5826	.4251
8	.9892	.9591	.9325	.8933	.8394	.7703	.6873	.5940	.3981	.2275
10	.9882	.9498	.9145	.8621	.7903	.7000	.5952	.4832	.2726	.1225
12	.9873	.9415	.8984	.8343	.7474	.6404	.5207	.3991	.1923	.0695
14	.9866	.9342	.8842	.8100	.7107	.5911	.4617	.3361	.1407	.0420
16	.9860	.9278	.8718	.7890	.6794	.5503	.4148	.2886	.1069	.0269
18	.9854	.9221	.8609	.7707	.6527	.5164	.3773	.2522	.0839	.0183
20	.9850	.9172	.8513	.7547	.6299	.4881	.3469	.2239	.0678	.0130
22	.9846	.9127	.8428	.7408	.6102	.4642	.3220	.2015	.0562	.0097
24	.9842	.9088	.8353	.7285	.5931	.4438	.3013	.1835	.0476	.0074
26	.9839	.9053	.8285	.7176	.5781	.4263	.2838	.1687	.0410	.0059
28	.9836	.9021	.8225	.7079	.5649	.4111	.2690	.1565	.0360	.0047
30	.9833	.8992	.8170	.6992	.5532	.3979	.2563	.1462	.0319	.0039
40	.9823	.8882	.7963	.6667	.5106	.3510	.2132	.1130	.0203	.0019
60	.9812	.8755	.7729	.6309	.4655	.3041	.1730	.0845	.0123	.0009
120	.9798	.8609	.7464	.5918	.4185	.2581	.1364	.0609	.0070	.0004
∞	.9783	.8441	.7167	.5496	.3704	.2143	.1045	.0423	.0039	.0002
					$n_1 = 6, \alpha = 0.005$					
2	.9935	.9892	.9867	.9837	.9802	.9763	.9720	.9673	.9565	.9440
4	.9920	.9801	.9713	.9595	.9441	.9247	.9011	.8730	.8037	.7191
6	.9905	.9694	.9517	.9263	.8917	.8468	.7915	.7266	.5759	.4167
8	.9893	.9587	.9313	.8907	.8348	.7630	.6769	.5807	.3812	.2117
10	.9882	.9486	.9117	.8566	.7810	.6860	.5766	.4612	.2497	.1061
12	.9873	.9395	.8939	.8255	.7330	.6198	.4949	.3705	.1674	.0555
14	.9865	.9314	.8778	.7980	.6914	.5646	.4301	.3032	.1163	.0308
16	.9858	.9241	.8635	.7738	.6557	.5188	.3789	.2530	.0840	.0182
18	.9852	.9176	.8509	.7525	.6251	.4808	.3381	.2152	.0628	.0115
20	.9847	.9118	.8396	.7339	.5988	.4491	.3054	.1863	.0485	.0076
22	.9843	.9066	.8296	.7175	.5761	.4223	.2787	.1637	.0386	.0053
24	.9838	.9020	.8206	.7030	.5563	.3996	.2568	.1458	.0314	.0038
26	.9835	.8978	.8126	.6901	.5390	.3802	.2385	.1314	.0261	.0028
28	.9831	.8940	.8054	.6786	.5237	.3634	.2230	.1196	.0221	.0022
30	.9828	.8905	.7988	.6682	.5102	.3487	.2099	.1099	.0191	.0017
40	.9817	.8771	.7737	.6294	.4610	.2975	.1662	.0793	.0108	.0007
60	.9804	.8615	.7448	.5865	.4093	.2473	.1269	.0545	.0057	.0003
120	.9788	.8431	.7119	.5395	.3561	.1996	.0931	.0356	.0027	.0001
∞	.9770	.8216	.6745	.4888	.3026	.1558	.0653	.0219	.0012	.0000
					$n_1 = 7. \alpha = 0.005$					
2	.9936	.9893	.9868	.9839	.9805	.9767	.9725	.9678	.9572	.9450
4	.9920	.9802	.9716	.9598	.9445	.9252	.9017	.8737	.8046	.7200
6	.9906	.9694	.9516	.9259	.8907	.8451	.7889	.7230	.5703	.4098
8	.9893	.9583	.9302	.8885	.8308	.7567	.6681	.5695	.3674	.1992
10	.9882	.9476	.9093	.8517	.7727	.6738	.5608	.4428	.2314	.0937
12	.9872	.9378	.8898	.8177	.7202	.6019	.4729	.3467	.1481	.0455
14	.9864	.9288	.8720	.7871	.6743	.5415	.4033	.2761	.0980	.0234
16	.9857	.9207	.8560	.7599	.6346	.4914	.3485	.2242	.0673	.0128
18	.9850	.9134	.8416	.7359	.6004	.4497	.3053	.1857	.0480	.0075
20	.9845	.9068	.8288	.7148	.5709	.4151	.2708	.1567	.0355	.0046
22	.9840	.9009	.8173	.6960	.5454	.3860	.2430	.1345	.0270	.0030
24	.9835	.8955	.8069	.6794	.5231	.3614	.2204	.1171	.0212	.0020
26	.9831	.8906	.7976	.6645	.5037	.3404	.2017	.1034	.0170	.0014
28	.9827	.8862	.7891	.6513	.4866	.3223	.1860	.0923	.0139	.0010
30	.9824	.8822	.7814	.6394	.4715	.3067	.1729	.0833	.0116	.0008
40	.9811	.8664	.7518	.5944	.4166	.2526	.1300	.0559	.0058	.0003
60	.9796	.8476	.7175	.5446	.3594	.2007	.0930	.0351	.0026	.0001
120	.9778	.8252	.6778	.4901	.3013	.1531	.0629	.0205	.0010	.0000
∞	.9756	.7985	.6326	.4317	.2445	.1114	.0400	.0111	.0004	.0000
					$n_1 = 8, \alpha = 0.005$					
2	.9936	.9894	.9870	.9841	.9807	.9770	.9728	.9682	.9578	.9458
4	.9921	.9804	.9718	.9601	.9448	.9256	.9021	.8742	.8052	.7206
6	.9906	.9694	.9515	.9255	.8899	.8437	.7867	.7199	.5655	.4041
8	.9893	.9579	.9293	.8865	.8273	.7512	.6606	.5601	.3560	.1891
10	.9882	.9467	.9071	.8474	.7655	.6633	.5471	.4271	.2164	.0840
12	.9872	.9362	.8861	.8107	.7089	.5862	.4539	.3267	.1327	.0381
14	.9863	.9264	.8667	.7773	.6590	.5212	.3803	.2535	.0838	.0182
16	.9855	.9175	.8491	.7474	.6156	.4673	.3226	.2006	.0550	.0093
18	.9849	.9095	.8331	.7208	.5781	.4226	.2775	.1619	.0375	.0050
20	.9843	.9021	.8187	.6972	.5457	.3855	.2419	.1333	.0265	.0029
22	.9837	.8955	.8057	.6762	.5177	.3544	.2134	.1117	.0194	.0018
24	.9832	.8894	.7940	.6575	.4933	.3283	.1905	.0951	.0146	.0011
26	.9828	.8839	.7834	.6408	.4720	.3061	.1717	.0822	.0113	.0008
28	.9824	.8788	.7737	.6259	.4532	.2871	.1562	.0720	.0089	.0005
30	.9820	.8742	.7650	.6125	.4367	.2708	.1433	.0637	.0072	.0004
40	.9806	.8559	.7308	.5617	.3768	.2149	.1020	.0397	.0032	.0001
60	.9788	.8338	.6909	.5054	.3152	.1628	.0681	.0227	.0012	.0000
120	.9767	.8072	.6446	.4441	.2540	.1168	.0422	.0117	.0004	.0000
∞	.9742	.7750	.5913	.3790	.1956	.0786	.0240	.0055	.0001	.0000

Table T.11 (continued)

n_2	$\phi = .5$	1.0	1.2	1.4	1.6	1.8	2.0	2.2	2.6	3.0
					$n_1 = 9, \alpha = 0.005$					
2	.9936	.9895	.9871	.9842	.9809	.9772	.9731	.9686	.9583	.9464
4	.9921	.9805	.9719	.9603	.9451	.9259	.9024	.8745	.8056	.7211
6	.9906	.9694	.9514	.9252	.8892	.8424	.7848	.7173	.5615	.3992
8	.9893	.9576	.9284	.8847	.8242	.7465	.6540	.5519	.3463	.1807
10	.9882	.9459	.9051	.8436	.7591	.6540	.5353	.4136	.2039	.0763
12	.9871	.9347	.8828	.8044	.6989	.5724	.4375	.3096	.1203	.0325
14	.9862	.9243	.8619	.7684	.6453	.5034	.3604	.2347	.0728	.0145
16	.9854	.9147	.8427	.7359	.5985	.4461	.3005	.1811	.0457	.0069
18	.9847	.9059	.8252	.7069	.5580	.3987	.2539	.1425	.0298	.0035
20	.9840	.8978	.8094	.6810	.5230	.3595	.2176	.1145	.0202	.0019
22	.9835	.8904	.7950	.6579	.4927	.3269	.1888	.0937	.0141	.0011
24	.9829	.8837	.7819	.6373	.4664	.2996	.1659	.0781	.0102	.0006
26	.9825	.8775	.7700	.6189	.4434	.2765	.1473	.0660	.0076	.0004
28	.9820	.8718	.7592	.6024	.4232	.2568	.1321	.0567	.0058	.0003
30	.9816	.8666	.7493	.5875	.4054	.2400	.1195	.0493	.0046	.0002
40	.9800	.8458	.7108	.5313	.3414	.1833	.0804	.0284	.0018	.0000
60	.9781	.8204	.6653	.4689	.2764	.1321	.0499	.0147	.0006	.0000
120	.9757	.7893	.6122	.4015	.2133	.0887	.0281	.0067	.0001	.0000
∞	.9727	.7512	.5510	.3309	.1552	.0548	.0142	.0027	.0000	.0000
					$n_1 = 10, \alpha = 0.005$					
2	.9936	.9895	.9871	.9843	.9811	.9774	.9733	.9688	.9586	.9469
4	.9921	.9806	.9720	.9604	.9453	.9261	.9027	.8748	.8059	.7214
6	.9907	.9694	.9513	.9248	.8885	.8413	.7832	.7150	.5580	.3951
8	.9893	.9573	.9277	.8832	.8215	.7423	.6483	.5448	.3380	.1737
10	.9882	.9451	.9034	.8402	.7534	.6458	.5249	.4020	.1935	.0701
12	.9871	.9334	.8798	.7987	.6899	.5601	.4232	.2950	.1101	.0282
14	.9861	.9223	.8575	.7604	.6330	.4875	.3432	.2186	.0640	.0118
16	.9853	.9120	.8369	.7255	.5831	.4273	.2814	.1647	.0385	.0053
18	.9845	.9025	.8180	.6941	.5399	.3776	.2338	.1266	.0241	.0025
20	.9839	.8937	.8007	.6661	.5025	.3366	.1969	.0993	.0156	.0013
22	.9832	.8857	.7849	.6410	.4702	.3028	.1681	.0794	.0105	.0007
24	.9827	.8783	.7706	.6186	.4421	.2745	.1454	.0647	.0073	.0004
26	.9822	.8714	.7575	.5986	.4176	.2508	.1272	.0536	.0053	.0002
28	.9817	.8651	.7455	.5805	.3962	.2308	.1124	.0451	.0039	.0001
30	.9812	.8593	.7346	.5643	.3773	.2137	.1003	.0385	.0030	.0001
40	.9795	.8360	.6916	.5030	.3099	.1569	.0638	.0205	.0010	.0000
60	.9774	.8072	.6407	.4352	.2426	.1073	.0367	.0095	.0003	.0000
120	.9747	.7715	.5809	.3624	.1787	.0671	.0187	.0038	.0001	.0000
∞	.9713	.7273	.5120	.2874	.1221	.0378	.0083	.0015	.0000	.0000
					$n_1 = 12, \alpha = 0.005$					
2	.9937	.9896	.9873	.9845	.9813	.9777	.9736	.9692	.9592	.9476
4	.9921	.9807	.9722	.9606	.9455	.9264	.9030	.8752	.8063	.7219
6	.9907	.9694	.9510	.9243	.8875	.8395	.7804	.7112	.5523	.3884
8	.9893	.9568	.9264	.8806	.8169	.7354	.6388	.5332	.3247	.1627
10	.9881	.9430	.9004	.8344	.7438	.6321	.5077	.3830	.1770	.0607
12	.9870	.9311	.8746	.7890	.6745	.5395	.3994	.2713	.0945	.0221
14	.9860	.9189	.8498	.7463	.6117	.4607	.3147	.1930	.0511	.0083
16	.9851	.9073	.8265	.7071	.5565	.3956	.2501	.1391	.0285	.0033
18	.9843	.8965	.8049	.6716	.5085	.3422	.2013	.1022	.0164	.0014
20	.9835	.8864	.7850	.6396	.4670	.2986	.1642	.0766	.0099	.0006
22	.9828	.8770	.7667	.6109	.4311	.2628	.1358	.0586	.0061	.0003
24	.9822	.8683	.7499	.5852	.4001	.2334	.1138	.0457	.0040	.0001
26	.9816	.8603	.7345	.5622	.3732	.2090	.0967	.0364	.0027	.0001
28	.9811	.8528	.7203	.5414	.3497	.1886	.0831	.0294	.0018	.0000
30	.9806	.8458	.7073	.5227	.3292	.1714	.0721	.0241	.0013	.0000
40	.9786	.8175	.6559	.4523	.2569	.1162	.0408	.0109	.0003	.0000
60	.9760	.7818	.5944	.3750	.1871	.0711	.0200	.0041	.0001	.0000
120	.9728	.7365	.5218	.2939	.1246	.0382	.0082	.0012	.0000	.0000
∞	.9684	.6792	.4386	.2157	.0740	.0174	.0031	.0003	.0000	.0000
					$n_1 = 1, \alpha = 0.01$					
2	.9851	.9705	.9620	.9521	.9408	.9282	.9143	.8991	.8654	.8277
4	.9809	.9492	.9280	.9012	.8682	.8292	.7843	.7341	.6216	.5014
6	.9782	.9340	.9030	.8629	.8131	.7541	.6870	.6136	.4589	.3125
8	.9764	.9236	.8859	.8367	.7759	.7043	.6242	.5387	.3678	.2211
10	.9752	.9163	.8738	.8184	.7501	.6704	.5824	.4904	.3136	.1725
12	.9743	.9109	.8650	.8050	.7314	.6462	.5532	.4574	.2787	.1437
14	.9736	.9068	.8582	.7949	.7174	.6283	.5318	.4336	.2547	.1250
16	.9730	.9036	.8529	.7870	.7066	.6145	.5156	.4158	.2374	.1121
18	.9726	.9010	.8487	.7807	.6979	.6036	.5028	.4020	.2243	.1027
20	.9723	.8989	.8452	.7755	.6908	.5947	.4925	.3910	.2141	.0957
22	.9720	.8971	.8423	.7712	.6850	.5874	.4841	.3820	.2060	.0902
24	.9717	.8956	.8398	.7675	.6801	.5813	.4771	.3746	.1994	.0858
26	.9715	.8943	.8377	.7644	.6758	.5760	.4712	.3683	.1938	.0822
28	.9713	.8931	.8359	.7617	.6722	.5716	.4661	.3630	.1892	.0792
30	.9711	.8922	.8343	.7593	.6690	.5677	.4617	.3584	.1852	.0767
40	.9705	.8886	.8285	.7509	.6578	.5539	.4462	.3424	.1718	.0683
60	.9699	.8850	.8226	.7423	.6463	.5401	.4308	.3267	.1590	.0608
120	.9693	.8812	.8165	.7335	.6347	.5261	.4155	.3113	.1468	.0539
∞	.9687	.8773	.8102	.7244	.6229	.5120	.4003	.2962	.1354	.0478

Table T.11 (continued)

n_2	$\phi = .5$	1.0	1.2	1.4	1.6	1.8	2.0	2.2	2.6	3.0
					$n_1 = 2, \alpha = 0.01$					
2	.9863	.9753	.9688	.9613	.9527	.9430	.9323	.9207	.8945	.8650
4	.9828	.9567	.9386	.9153	.8862	.8511	.8100	.7635	.6571	.5401
6	.9803	.9409	.9118	.8730	.8237	.7640	.6951	.6191	.4576	.3052
8	.9784	.9288	.8910	.8401	.7754	.6982	.6110	.5182	.3358	.1869
10	.9770	.9196	.8751	.8150	.7393	.6500	.5515	.4498	.2626	.1268
12	.9760	.9124	.8627	.7957	.7118	.6142	.5085	.4022	.2163	.0934
14	.9752	.9067	.8529	.7806	.6905	.5869	.4765	.3678	.1854	.0733
16	.9745	.9021	.8450	.7684	.6736	.5655	.4519	.3420	.1636	.0603
18	.9740	.8983	.8386	.7585	.6600	.5485	.4326	.3221	.1476	.0513
20	.9735	.8951	.8331	.7502	.6486	.5345	.4170	.3063	.1354	.0449
22	.9731	.8924	.8285	.7433	.6392	.5229	.4042	.2936	.1260	.0401
24	.9728	.8901	.8246	.7373	.6312	.5132	.3936	.2830	.1184	.0364
26	.9725	.8881	.8212	.7322	.6243	.5048	.3845	.2742	.1122	.0335
28	.9723	.8863	.8182	.7277	.6182	.4976	.3768	.2667	.1070	.0312
30	.9721	.8848	.8156	.7238	.6130	.4914	.3701	.2603	.1027	.0293
40	.9713	.8791	.8060	.7096	.5943	.4693	.3468	.2382	.0885	.0233
60	.9704	.8731	.7960	.6948	.5749	.4469	.3237	.2170	.0757	.0183
120	.9695	.8668	.7854	.6794	.5551	.4244	.3011	.1968	.0643	.0143
∞	.9686	.8600	.7743	.6634	.5349	.4019	.2789	.1776	.0543	.0111
					$n_1 = 3, \alpha = 0.01$					
2	.9867	.9769	.9711	.9644	.9567	.9481	.9385	.9280	.9045	.8779
4	.9835	.9592	.9421	.9199	.8919	.8580	.8181	.7726	.6678	.5517
6	.9809	.9427	.9136	.8742	.8237	.7620	.6906	.6117	.4448	.2899
8	.9790	.9291	.8896	.8357	.7665	.6835	.5902	.4917	.3032	.1576
10	.9775	.9181	.8703	.8047	.7214	.5234	.5166	.4085	.2191	.0941
12	.9763	.9093	.8547	.7800	.6861	.5776	.4625	.3504	.1675	.0615
14	.9753	.9021	.8419	.7600	.6580	.5421	.4220	.3086	.1343	.0434
16	.9746	.8961	.8314	.7437	.6354	.5142	.3910	.2776	.1118	.0325
18	.9739	.8910	.8227	.7302	.6169	.4917	.3666	.2540	.0958	.0256
20	.9734	.8868	.8152	.7188	.6016	.4733	.3471	.2355	.0841	.0209
22	.9729	.8831	.8089	.7092	.5886	.4580	.3311	.2207	.0752	.0175
24	.9725	.8799	.8034	.7008	.5776	.4451	.3178	.2087	.0683	.0151
26	.9721	.8772	.7986	.6936	.5681	.4341	.3066	.1987	.0628	.0132
28	.9718	.8747	.7944	.6873	.5599	.4247	.2971	.1903	.0584	.0118
30	.9716	.8725	.7906	.6817	.5526	.4164	.2889	.1831	.0547	.0107
40	.9705	.8645	.7769	.6614	.5266	.3873	.2606	.1590	.0430	.0074
60	.9694	.8558	.7622	.6400	.4997	.3582	.2332	.1367	.0334	.0050
120	.9682	.8464	.7464	.6175	.4721	.3292	.2070	.1163	.0255	.0033
∞	.9669	.8361	.7295	.5938	.4439	.3005	.1821	.0978	.0192	.0022
					$n_1 = 4, \alpha = 0.01$					
2	.9869	.9777	.9723	.9660	.9587	.9506	.9416	.9317	.9096	.8844
4	.9838	.9604	.9438	.9221	.8946	.8612	.8217	.7767	.6725	.5566
6	.9812	.9433	.9139	.8738	.8219	.7585	.6848	.6036	.4330	.2767
8	.9792	.9284	.8873	.8306	.7575	.6697	.5716	.4691	.2776	.1363
10	.9776	.9160	.8650	.7944	.7047	.5996	.4865	.3745	.1867	.0726
12	.9763	.9056	.8464	.7647	.6622	.5452	.4236	.3087	.1330	.0424
14	.9752	.8969	.8309	.7403	.6281	.5027	.3765	.2620	.0998	.0270
16	.9743	.8896	.8178	.7200	.6003	.4691	.3405	.2279	.0783	.0184
18	.9736	.8834	.8068	.7030	.5774	.4420	.3124	.2023	.0636	.0133
20	.9730	.8780	.7974	.6886	.5583	.4199	.2901	.1825	.0533	.0101
22	.9724	.8734	.7892	.6763	.5421	.4015	.2719	.1670	.0457	.0079
24	.9719	.8693	.7821	.6656	.5283	.3861	.2570	.1545	.0400	.0064
26	.9715	.8657	.7759	.6563	.5164	.3730	.2445	.1442	.0355	.0054
28	.9711	.8625	.7704	.6482	.5060	.3617	.2340	.1357	.0320	.0046
30	.9708	.8597	.7655	.6409	.4969	.3519	.2249	.1286	.0292	.0040
40	.9695	.8491	.7473	.6145	.4643	.3176	.1942	.1051	.0207	.0023
60	.9682	.8374	.7275	.5864	.4306	.2836	.1653	.0844	.0143	.0013
120	.9666	.8245	.7060	.5566	.3962	.2504	.1386	.0665	.0096	.0007
∞	.9649	.8103	.6828	.5253	.3614	.2185	.1144	.0513	.0063	.0004
					$n_1 = 5, \alpha = 0.01$					
2	.9870	.9782	.9730	.9669	.9600	.9521	.9435	.9340	.9126	.8884
4	.9840	.9611	.9448	.9233	.8961	.8629	.8237	.7789	.6749	.5591
6	.9814	.9435	.9138	.8729	.8199	.7550	.6795	.5965	.4231	.2663
8	.9793	.9276	.8850	.8258	.7494	.6578	.5559	.4504	.2575	.1207
10	.9776	.9138	.8600	.7852	.6899	.5792	.4615	.3471	.1625	.0581
12	.9762	.9021	.8387	.7510	.6413	.5174	.3914	.2757	.1084	.0306
14	.9750	.8920	.8206	.7224	.6017	.4690	.3391	.2257	.0763	.0176
16	.9740	.8835	.8052	.6984	.5692	.4306	.2994	.1898	.0564	.0109
18	.9732	.8761	.7920	.6782	.5423	.3998	.2688	.1633	.0435	.0073
20	.9725	.8696	.7806	.6609	.5198	.3746	.2446	.1433	.0347	.0051
22	.9718	.8640	.7706	.6460	.5007	.3538	.2252	.1278	.0284	.0037
24	.9713	.8590	.7619	.6330	.4844	.3363	.2093	.1156	.0239	.0029
26	.9708	.8546	.7543	.6217	.4704	.3216	.1962	.1057	.0205	.0023
28	.9704	.8507	.7474	.6118	.4581	.3089	.1851	.0976	.0179	.0018
30	.9700	.8472	.7413	.6029	.4474	.2980	.1758	.0909	.0158	.0015
40	.9685	.8339	.7186	.5705	.4090	.2601	.1446	.0695	.0100	.0007
60	.9668	.8189	.6935	.5359	.3696	.2232	.1163	.0516	.0061	.0003
120	.9650	.8023	.6660	.4992	.3298	.1882	.0913	.0372	.0035	.0002
∞	.9628	.7835	.6360	.4606	.2901	.1556	.0699	.0259	.0020	.0000

Table T.11 (continued)

n_2	$\phi = .5$	1.0	1.2	1.4	1.6	1.8	2.0	2.2	2.6	3.0
					$n_1 = 6, \alpha = 0.01$					
2	.9871	.9785	.9735	.9675	.9608	.9532	.9447	.9355	.9147	.8910
4	.9841	.9616	.9454	.9241	.8971	.8640	.8250	.7802	.6764	.5605
6	.9815	.9435	.9135	.8720	.8180	.7518	.6749	.5905	.4149	.2578
8	.9794	.9267	.8829	.8216	.7424	.6477	.5428	.4351	.2417	.1090
10	.9776	.9118	.8556	.7770	.6772	.5618	.4406	.3248	.1442	.0480
12	.9761	.8988	.8318	.7388	.6230	.4938	.3647	.2492	.0905	.0230
14	.9748	.8876	.8113	.7064	.5785	.4402	.3083	.1971	.0600	.0120
16	.9737	.8778	.7936	.6790	.5418	.3978	.2659	.1604	.0419	.0068
18	.9728	.8692	.7783	.6556	.5113	.3639	.2335	.1339	.0306	.0042
20	.9720	.8617	.7650	.6356	.4857	.3363	.2082	.1142	.0232	.0027
22	.9713	.8551	.7533	.6183	.4641	.3136	.1881	.0992	.0182	.0019
24	.9707	.8493	.7430	.6032	.4456	.2946	.1719	.0876	.0147	.0013
26	.9701	.8441	.7339	.5900	.4297	.2787	.1586	.0784	.0121	.0010
28	.9696	.8394	.7258	.5783	.4158	.2651	.1476	.0710	.0102	.0008
30	.9692	.8351	.7185	.5679	.4037	.2533	.1383	.0649	.0088	.0006
40	.9675	.8191	.6911	.5299	.3605	.2133	.1080	.0462	.0049	.0002
60	.9655	.8008	.6607	.4891	.3166	.1753	.0816	.0315	.0026	.0001
120	.9633	.7800	.6271	.4459	.2728	.1402	.0595	.0205	.0013	.0000
∞	.9607	.7563	.5901	.4009	.2301	.1089	.0417	.0128	.0006	.0000
					$n_1 = 7, \alpha = 0.01$					
2	.9872	.9787	.9738	.9680	.9614	.9539	.9456	.9365	.9161	.8929
4	.9842	.9619	.9459	.9247	.8977	.8648	.8258	.7811	.6773	.5613
6	.9816	.9435	.9132	.8711	.8163	.7490	.6710	.5854	.4082	.2510
8	.9794	.9260	.8810	.8179	.7363	.6390	.5317	.4224	.2290	.1000
10	.9775	.9100	.8516	.7699	.6661	.5469	.4231	.3065	.1299	.0407
12	.9760	.8959	.8256	.7280	.6070	.4735	.3423	.2278	.0770	.0178
14	.9746	.8835	.8029	.6922	.5581	.4156	.2828	.1744	.0482	.0085
16	.9735	.8726	.7831	.6615	.5176	.3698	.2385	.1375	.0319	.0044
18	.9724	.8629	.7658	.6353	.4840	.3333	.2049	.1113	.0221	.0025
20	.9716	.8544	.7506	.6127	.4558	.3038	.1791	.0923	.0160	.0015
22	.9708	.8469	.7373	.5931	.4319	.2796	.1587	.0781	.0120	.0010
24	.9701	.8401	.7254	.5760	.4115	.2596	.1425	.0673	.0093	.0006
26	.9695	.8341	.7149	.5610	.3940	.2429	.1294	.0589	.0074	.0005
28	.9689	.8287	.7055	.5477	.3787	.2286	.1186	.0522	.0060	.0003
30	.9684	.8237	.6971	.5359	.3654	.2165	.1096	.0469	.0050	.0002
40	.9665	.8048	.6651	.4926	.3182	.1754	.0810	.0309	.0025	.0001
60	.9642	.7830	.6294	.4462	.2709	.1375	.0572	.0193	.0011	.0000
120	.9616	.7580	.5896	.3973	.2246	.1038	.0384	.0112	.0005	.0000
∞	.9585	.7290	.5456	.3467	.1807	.0751	.0244	.0062	.0002	.0000
					$n_1 = 8, \alpha = 0.01$					
2	.9872	.9789	.9740	.9683	.9618	.9544	.9463	.9373	.9172	.8943
4	.9843	.9621	.9462	.9251	.8982	.8653	.8264	.7817	.6779	.5619
6	.9817	.9435	.9128	.8703	.8148	.7467	.6676	.5811	.4026	.2454
8	.9794	.9252	.8793	.8147	.7311	.6315	.5223	.4117	.2186	.0928
10	.9775	.9084	.8481	.7635	.6564	.5341	.4082	.2912	.1185	.0352
12	.9758	.8933	.8201	.7184	.5930	.4559	.3234	.2101	.0668	.0142
14	.9744	.8798	.7953	.6794	.5401	.3943	.2614	.1560	.0396	.0063
16	.9732	.8678	.7735	.6458	.4963	.3458	.2157	.1193	.0248	.0030
18	.9721	.8571	.7543	.6169	.4598	.3072	.1815	.0938	.0163	.0016
20	.9711	.8477	.7374	.5919	.4292	.2762	.1554	.0756	.0113	.0009
22	.9703	.8392	.7224	.5702	.4034	.2510	.1352	.0624	.0081	.0005
24	.9695	.8316	.7091	.5512	.3814	.2302	.1193	.0524	.0060	.0003
26	.9689	.8247	.6972	.5345	.3625	.2129	.1065	.0449	.0046	.0002
28	.9682	.8185	.6866	.5198	.3461	.1983	.0962	.0389	.0036	.0001
30	.9677	.8129	.6770	.5067	.3318	.1859	.0876	.0343	.0029	.0001
40	.9655	.7911	.6406	.4584	.2815	.1447	.0611	.0209	.0012	.0000
60	.9630	.7658	.5995	.4070	.2318	.1079	.0402	.0118	.0005	.0000
120	.9600	.7362	.5536	.3531	.1843	.0765	.0247	.0061	.0002	.0000
∞	.9563	.7016	.5028	.2981	.1406	.0512	.0141	.0029	.0000	.0000
					$n_1 = 9, \alpha = 0.01$					
2	.9872	.9790	.9742	.9686	.9621	.9549	.9468	.9380	.9181	.8954
4	.9843	.9623	.9464	.9254	.8986	.8657	.8268	.7821	.6783	.5623
6	.9817	.9434	.9125	.8696	.8135	.7446	.6647	.5774	.3978	.2407
8	.9794	.9246	.8778	.8119	.7265	.6251	.5142	.4025	.2099	.0871
10	.9774	.9070	.8450	.7579	.6479	.5229	.3953	.2782	.1093	.0310
12	.9757	.8909	.8151	.7098	.5806	.4407	.3073	.1955	.0587	.0116
14	.9742	.8764	.7884	.6679	.5242	.3759	.2433	.1410	.0331	.0047
16	.9729	.8634	.7647	.6316	.4774	.3249	.1966	.1047	.0197	.0021
18	.9718	.8518	.7438	.6002	.4384	.2847	.1621	.0800	.0124	.0010
20	.9708	.8414	.7252	.5730	.4057	.2525	.1361	.0628	.0081	.0005
22	.9698	.8320	.7086	.5493	.3782	.2265	.1162	.0504	.0056	.0003
24	.9690	.8235	.6939	.5286	.3548	.2053	.1007	.0414	.0040	.0002
26	.9683	.8159	.6807	.5104	.3347	.1877	.0885	.0346	.0029	.0001
28	.9676	.8090	.6689	.4943	.3174	.1730	.0786	.0294	.0022	.0001
30	.9670	.8026	.6581	.4799	.3023	.1606	.0706	.0254	.0017	.0000
40	.9646	.7780	.6174	.4273	.2497	.1199	.0464	.0143	.0006	.0000
60	.9618	.7490	.5712	.3714	.1986	.0848	.0283	.0073	.0002	.0000
120	.9583	.7148	.5194	.3133	.1508	.0562	.0158	.0033	.0001	.0000
∞	.9542	.6745	.4620	.2549	.1085	.0345	.0080	.0014	.0000	.0000

Table T.11 (continued)

n_2	$\phi = .5$	1.0	1.2	1.4	1.6	1.8	2.0	2.2	2.6	3.0
					$n_1 = 10, a = 0.01$					
2	.9873	.9791	.9744	.9688	.9624	.9552	.9472	.9385	.9188	.8963
4	.9844	.9625	.9466	.9256	.8989	.8660	.8271	.7825	.6786	.5625
6	.9817	.9433	.9123	.8690	.8124	.7428	.6622	.5742	.3938	.2367
8	.9794	.9240	.8765	.8094	.7225	.6195	.5072	.3947	.2026	.0823
10	.9774	.9057	.8422	.7529	.6404	.5131	.3842	.2672	.1017	.0277
12	.9756	.8888	.8106	.7022	.5696	.4273	.2935	.1831	.0523	.0097
14	.9741	.8734	.7822	.6575	.5101	.3597	.2279	.1285	.0282	.0037
16	.9727	.8594	.7567	.6187	.4605	.3068	.1805	.0928	.0160	.0015
18	.9715	.8469	.7341	.5850	.4193	.2652	.1459	.0690	.0096	.0007
20	.9704	.8355	.7139	.5558	.3848	.2322	.1201	.0527	.0060	.0003
22	.9694	.8253	.6959	.5303	.3558	.2057	.1007	.0413	.0039	.0002
24	.9685	.8160	.6798	.5080	.3312	.1841	.0858	.0331	.0027	.0001
26	.9677	.8076	.6653	.4883	.3102	.1665	.0741	.0270	.0019	.0001
28	.9670	.7999	.6523	.4709	.2921	.1518	.0649	.0225	.0014	.0000
30	.9664	.7929	.6405	.4555	.2764	.1395	.0574	.0190	.0010	.0000
40	.9638	.7655	.5955	.3989	.2220	.0998	.0355	.0098	.0003	.0000
60	.9606	.7328	.5443	.3390	.1702	.0668	.0200	.0045	.0001	.0000
120	.9568	.6939	.4869	.2776	.1232	.0411	.0101	.0018	.0000	.0000
∞	.9520	.6475	.4234	.2170	.0832	.0230	.0045	.0007	.0000	.0000
					$n_1 = 12, \alpha = 0.01$					
2	.9873	.9793	.9746	.9691	.9628	.9557	.9478	.9392	.9198	.8977
4	.9844	.9627	.9469	.9260	.8993	.8665	.8276	.7829	.6790	.5628
6	.9818	.9432	.9118	.8679	.8104	.7398	.6581	.5689	.3872	.2304
8	.9794	.9231	.8743	.8052	.7158	.6101	.4956	.3819	.1910	.0750
10	.9773	.9035	.8375	.7445	.6277	.4968	.3661	.2494	.0900	.0228
12	.9754	.8850	.8029	.6890	.5509	.4050	.2708	.1635	.0429	.0071
14	.9738	.8680	.7713	.6396	.4860	.3329	.2030	.1092	.0212	.0024
16	.9723	.8523	.7426	.5963	.4318	.2768	.1549	.0749	.0110	.0009
18	.9710	.8380	.7169	.5585	.3868	.2333	.1206	.0529	.0060	.0003
20	.9698	.8250	.6938	.5256	.3493	.1991	.0958	.0384	.0035	.0001
22	.9687	.8131	.6730	.4969	.3179	.1721	.0775	.0286	.0021	.0001
24	.9677	.8023	.6543	.4717	.2914	.1505	.0638	.0219	.0013	.0000
26	.9668	.7924	.6376	.4496	.2690	.1330	.0533	.0171	.0009	.0000
28	.9659	.7833	.6223	.4300	.2438	.1187	.0452	.0136	.0006	.0000
30	.9652	.7750	.6086	.4127	.2333	.1069	.0389	.0110	.0004	.0000
40	.9622	.7419	.5556	.3492	.1770	.0701	.0212	.0048	.0001	.0000
60	.9584	.7019	.4951	.2833	.1256	.0417	.0101	.0018	.0000	.0000
120	.9537	.6534	.4271	.2173	.0819	.0220	.0041	.0005	.0000	.0000
∞	.9476	.5948	.3530	.1552	.0479	.0100	.0015	.0001	.0000	.0000
					$n_1 = 1, \alpha = 0.025$					
2	.9630	.9280	.9081	.8851	.8592	.8309	.8003	.7677	.6983	.6252
4	.9546	.8879	.8463	.7962	.7381	.6735	.6041	.5321	.3898	.2636
6	.9499	.8645	.8102	.7444	.6689	.5864	.5003	.4148	.2600	.1430
8	.9470	.8502	.7882	.7135	.6284	.5369	.4438	.3539	.2008	.0969
10	.9451	.8407	.7737	.6933	.6025	.5060	.4094	.3182	.1689	.0747
12	.9437	.8340	.7636	.6793	.5847	.4850	.3865	.2949	.1495	.0622
14	.9427	.8290	.7560	.6690	.5717	.4700	.3703	.2788	.1365	.0543
16	.9419	.8251	.7503	.6611	.5619	.4587	.3583	.2670	.1273	.0489
18	.9413	.8221	.7457	.6549	.5542	.4499	.3490	.2579	.1205	.0451
20	.9408	.8196	.7420	.6499	.5480	.4428	.3417	.2508	.1152	.0422
22	.9404	.8176	.7389	.6457	.5429	.4371	.3357	.2451	.1110	.0399
24	.9401	.8158	.7364	.6423	.5386	.4323	.3307	.2404	.1076	.0381
26	.9398	.8144	.7342	.6393	.5350	.4283	.3266	.2364	.1048	.0367
28	.9395	.8131	.7323	.6368	.5319	.4248	.3230	.2330	.1024	.0354
30	.9393	.8120	.7306	.6346	.5292	.4218	.3199	.2301	.1004	.0344
40	.9385	.8081	.7248	.6268	.5198	.4114	.3093	.2202	.0937	.0310
60	.9376	.8040	.7189	.6190	.5104	.4010	.2989	.2106	.0872	.0280
120	.9368	.8000	.7129	.6111	.5010	.3907	.2887	.2012	.0812	.0252
∞	.9359	.7958	.7069	.6031	.4915	.3805	.2786	.1922	.0756	.0227
					$n_1 = 2, \alpha = 0.025$					
2	.9659	.9391	.9237	.9059	.8858	.8635	.8392	.8132	.7567	.6957
4	.9585	.9017	.8650	.8195	.7658	.7047	.6380	.5675	.4249	.2943
6	.9536	.8753	.8225	.7569	.6798	.5941	.5039	.4139	.2519	.1326
8	.9504	.8570	.7935	.7146	.6232	.5241	.4234	.3277	.1708	.0732
10	.9481	.8441	.7729	.6851	.5847	.4780	.3726	.2761	.1285	.0474
12	.9464	.8344	.7578	.6637	.5573	.4460	.3385	.2427	.1038	.0342
14	.9451	.8270	.7462	.6476	.5369	.4226	.3142	.2197	.0881	.0267
16	.9440	.8212	.7371	.6350	.5211	.4049	.2962	.2030	.0773	.0219
18	.9432	.8165	.7298	.6249	.5087	.3911	.2823	.1904	.0696	.0187
20	.9425	.8126	.7238	.6166	.4986	.3800	.2713	.1806	.0639	.0164
22	.9419	.8093	.7187	.6098	.4903	.3709	.2624	.1728	.0594	.0147
24	.9414	.8065	.7145	.6040	.4833	.3634	.2551	.1664	.0559	.0134
26	.9410	.8041	.7108	.5990	.4773	.3570	.2490	.1611	.0530	.0124
28	.9406	.8021	.7077	.5948	.4722	.3515	.2438	.1566	.0506	.0116
30	.9403	.8002	.7049	.5911	.4678	.3468	.2393	.1528	.0486	.0109
40	.9391	.7937	.6949	.5778	.4521	.3303	.2238	.1399	.0422	.0088
60	.9379	.7868	.6847	.5642	.4363	.3140	.2088	.1277	.0364	.0071
120	.9366	.7798	.6741	.5504	.4204	.2979	.1944	.1161	.0313	.0056
∞	.9353	.7724	.6632	.5364	.4045	.2820	.1804	.1053	.0268	.0045

Table T.11 (continued)

n_2	$\phi = .5$	1.0	1.2	1.4	1.6	1.8	2.0	2.2	2.6	3.0
					$n_1 = 3, \alpha = 0.025$					
2	.9669	.9429	.9291	.9131	.8949	.8748	.8528	.8292	.7776	.7214
4	.9598	.9064	.8710	.8270	.7745	.7144	.6482	.5780	.4348	.3027
6	.9548	.8776	.8241	.7568	.6770	.5880	.4945	.4015	.2369	.1195
8	.9512	.8563	.7895	.7057	.6081	.5028	.3971	.2985	.1441	.0556
10	.9486	.8403	.7637	.6684	.5594	.4449	.3346	.2368	.0977	.0307
12	.9466	.8281	.7441	.6405	.5238	.4042	.2925	.1975	.0721	.0193
14	.9451	.8184	.7288	.6189	.4970	.3743	.2627	.1709	.0566	.0133
16	.9438	.8107	.7165	.6020	.4761	.3516	.2408	.1520	.0466	.0099
18	.9428	.8043	.7065	.5882	.4595	.3339	.2240	.1379	.0397	.0077
20	.9419	.7989	.6982	.5769	.4461	.3198	.2169	.1272	.0347	.0063
22	.9411	.7944	.6912	.5675	.4349	.3082	.2004	.1188	.0310	.0053
24	.9405	.7906	.6852	.5595	.4255	.2986	.1918	.1120	.0281	.0046
26	.9400	.7872	.6801	.5526	.4175	.2905	.1846	.1064	.0259	.0041
28	.9395	.7843	.6756	.5466	.4107	.2836	.1786	.1018	.0241	.0036
30	.9390	.7817	.6716	.5414	.4047	.2777	.1734	.0979	.0226	.0033
40	.9375	.7723	.6574	.5227	.3836	.2570	.1559	.0849	.0179	.0023
60	.9358	.7624	.6424	.5035	.3624	.2368	.1392	.0730	.0140	.0016
120	.9341	.7519	.6269	.4839	.3411	.2171	.1236	.0624	.0109	.0011
∞	.9322	.7408	.6107	.4638	.3199	.1981	.1090	.0529	.0083	.0008
					$n_1 = 4, \alpha = 0.025$					
2	.9674	.9448	.9318	.9167	.8996	.8806	.8598	.8373	.7883	.7347
4	.9605	.9086	.8740	.8305	.7784	.7186	.6526	.5823	.4387	.3057
6	.9553	.8781	.8237	.7546	.6725	.5808	:4848	.3899	.2242	.1092
8	.9515	.8543	.7844	.6963	.5938	.4837	.3747	.2749	.1244	.0442
10	.9487	.8357	.7542	.6523	.5364	.4164	.3034	.2064	.0768	.0210
12	.9464	.8211	.7305	.6186	.4939	.3687	.2556	.1636	.0519	.0115
14	.9446	.8094	.7117	.5923	.4615	.3337	.2221	.1353	.0378	.0071
16	.9431	.7998	.6964	.5713	.4363	.3072	.1978	.1156	.0291	.0047
18	.9419	.7918	.6838	.5541	.4162	.2866	.1794	.1014	.0234	.0034
20	.9408	.7850	.6733	.5400	.3998	.2702	.1652	.0907	.0194	.0026
22	.9399	.7792	.6643	.5281	.3862	.2569	.1540	.0825	.0166	.0020
24	.9392	.7743	.6567	.5180	.3748	.2459	.1448	.0760	.0145	.0016
26	.9385	.7699	.6500	.5093	.3651	.2366	.1373	.0707	.0128	.0014
28	.9379	.7661	.6442	.5017	.3568	.2288	.1310	.0664	.0116	.0012
30	.9374	.7627	.6390	.4951	.3495	.2220	.1256	.0628	.0106	.0010
40	.9354	.7504	.6204	.4714	.3240	.1989	.1078	.0512	.0076	.0006
60	.9334	.7371	.6007	.4469	.2985	.1766	.0915	.0411	.0053	.0004
120	.9311	.7229	.5799	.4218	.2733	.1554	.0767	.0325	.0036	.0002
∞	.9286	.7077	.5581	.3961	.2483	.1355	.0636	.0254	.0024	.0001
					$n_1 = 5, \alpha = 0.025$					
2	.9677	.9460	.9335	.9189	.9024	.8840	.8640	.8423	.7948	.7428
4	.9609	.9099	.8756	.8325	.7806	.7209	.6548	.5845	.4404	.3069
6	.9556	.8780	.8227	.7522	.6681	.5744	.4764	.3802	.2141	.1015
8	.9516	.8521	.7796	.6879	.5813	.4676	.3564	.2562	.1100	.0364
10	.9485	.8314	.7455	.6381	.5167	.3928	.2784	.1831	.0624	.0152
12	.9460	.8146	.7182	.5993	.4683	.3394	.2265	.1383	.0389	.0074
14	.9440	.8009	.6961	.5686	.4312	.3004	.1906	.1094	.0262	.0040
16	.9423	.7895	.6780	.5439	.4022	.2710	.1649	.0899	.0189	.0024
18	.9409	.7800	.6630	.5238	.3791	.2483	.1458	.0761	.0143	.0016
20	.9397	.7718	.6503	.5070	.3602	.2303	.1311	.0660	.0112	.0011
22	.9387	.7648	.6395	.4929	.3447	.2158	.1197	.0583	.0092	.0008
24	.9378	.7587	.6301	.4808	.3316	.2039	.1105	.0524	.0077	.0006
26	.9370	.7534	.6220	.4704	.3205	.1940	.1031	.0477	.0066	.0005
28	.9363	.7487	.6149	.4614	.3110	.1856	.0969	.0439	.0057	.0004
30	.9357	.7446	.6086	.4535	.3027	.1784	.0917	.0407	.0051	.0003
40	.9334	.7291	.5856	.4252	.2739	.1541	.0748	.0310	.0032	.0002
60	.9308	.7124	.5611	.3959	.2453	.1312	.0598	.0230	.0020	.0001
120	.9280	.6942	.5351	.3659	.2173	.1101	.0470	.0167	.0012	.0000
∞	.9249	.6745	.5077	.3355	.1903	.0910	.0361	.0118	.0007	.0000
					$n_1 = 6, \alpha = 0.025$					
2	.9679	.9467	.9346	.9204	.9043	.8864	.8668	.8456	.7992	.7482
4	.9611	.9107	.8767	.8337	.7819	.7222	.6562	.5857	.4413	.3074
6	.9558	.8778	.8216	.7498	.6642	.5688	.4693	.3721	.2061	.0956
8	.9517	.8501	.7754	.6806	.5707	.4542	.3414	.2413	.0990	.0310
10	.9483	.8274	.7377	.6258	.4999	.3731	.2582	.1649	.0521	.0115
12	.9457	.8087	.7072	.5824	.4464	.3152	.2033	.1191	.0301	.0050
14	.9434	.7932	.6822	.5478	.4053	.2730	.1659	.0903	.0189	.0024
16	.9416	.7802	.6615	.5199	.3731	.2414	.1395	.0713	.0127	.0013
18	.9400	.7691	.6441	.4969	.3474	.2172	.1201	.0583	.0091	.0008
20	.9378	.7596	.6294	.4777	.3266	.1982	.1056	.0489	.0068	.0005
22	.9375	.7514	.6167	.4616	.3094	.1830	.0932	.0420	.0052	.0003
24	.9365	.7443	.6058	.4478	.2950	.1706	.0855	.0368	.0042	.0002
26	.9355	.7380	.5963	.4359	.2828	.1603	.0783	.0327	.0035	.0002
28	.9347	.7324	.5879	.4256	.2724	.1516	.0725	.0295	.0029	.0001
30	.9340	.7274	.5805	.4165	.2634	.1443	.0676	.0268	.0025	.0001
40	.9313	.7089	.5532	.3840	.2320	.1198	.0522	.0189	.0014	.0000
60	.9283	.6886	.5240	.3506	.2014	.0975	.0392	.0129	.0008	.0000
120	.9249	.6662	.4930	.3166	.1720	.0775	.0285	.0085	.0004	.0000
∞	.9211	.6418	.4601	.2823	.1443	.0602	.0022	.0053	.0002	.0000

Table T.11 (continued)

n_2	$\phi = .5$	1.0	1.2	1.4	1.6	1.8	2.0	2.2	2.6	3.0
					$n_1 = 7, \alpha = 0.025$					
2	.9680	.9473	.9354	.9214	.9056	.8880	.8688	.8480	.8023	.7522
4	.9613	.9113	.8774	.8345	.7828	.7231	.6570	.5864	.4417	.3076
6	.9559	.8774	.8206	.7477	.6608	.5640	.4634	.3654	.1996	.0909
8	.9516	.8483	.7716	.6743	.5617	.4430	.3290	.2292	.0906	.0270
10	.9482	.8238	.7310	.6150	.4856	.3655	.2417	.1505	.0445	.0090
12	.9453	.8034	.6974	.5677	.4276	.2949	.1846	.1042	.0239	.0035
14	.9429	.7862	.6697	.5296	.3831	.2503	.1463	.0759	.0140	.0015
16	.9409	.7716	.6465	.4986	.3481	.2171	.1196	.0577	.0089	.0008
18	.9392	.7592	.6270	.4731	.3204	.1918	.1004	.0455	.0059	.0004
20	.9377	.7484	.6104	.4518	.2979	.1722	.0862	.0370	.0042	.0002
22	.9364	.7391	.5961	.4339	.2794	.1566	.0754	.0309	.0031	.0002
24	.9352	.7308	.5836	.4185	.2640	.1439	.0670	.0263	.0024	.0001
26	.9342	.7236	.5727	.4053	.2509	.1336	.0603	.0228	.0019	.0001
28	.9333	.7171	.5631	.3938	.2398	.1249	.0549	.0201	.0015	.0001
30	.9325	.7114	.5546	.3837	.2302	.1176	.0504	.0180	.0013	.0000
40	.9294	.6897	.5233	.3476	.1972	.0937	.0367	.0117	.0006	.0000
60	.9259	.6657	.4896	.3106	.1655	.0725	.0257	.0073	.0003	.0000
120	.9219	.6391	.4537	.2733	.1357	.0543	.0172	.0043	.0001	.0000
∞	.9173	.6098	.4157	.2361	.1084	.0393	.0111	.0024	.0000	.0000
					$n_1 = 8, \alpha = 0.025$					
2	.9681	.9477	.9359	.9222	.9066	.8893	.8703	.8498	.8047	.7551
4	.9615	.9118	.8779	.8351	.7834	.7237	.6575	.5869	.4419	.3076
6	.9560	.8771	.8197	.7459	.6578	.5599	.4583	.3599	.1942	.0871
8	.9516	.8467	.7683	.6688	.5539	.4334	.3187	.2192	.0839	.0240
10	.9480	.8207	.7250	.6057	.4732	.3425	.2280	.1388	.0387	.0073
12	.9449	.7986	.6888	.5547	.4114	.2779	.1693	.0925	.0195	.0026
14	.9424	.7799	.6586	.5135	.3638	.2312	.1304	.0648	.0107	.0010
16	.9402	.7639	.6331	.4798	.3266	.1968	.1038	.0475	.0064	.0005
18	.9384	.7501	.6116	.4521	.2971	.1709	.0850	.0362	.0040	.0002
20	.9367	.7381	.5931	.4288	.2732	.1509	.0713	.0285	.0027	.0001
22	.9353	.7276	.5772	.4092	.2537	.1351	.0610	.0231	.0019	.0001
24	.9340	.7184	.5633	.3925	.2375	.1225	.0531	.0192	.0014	.0000
26	.9329	.7102	.5512	.3781	.2238	.1122	.0470	.0162	.0011	.0000
28	.9319	.7029	.5404	.3655	.2122	.1037	.0420	.0140	.0008	.0000
30	.9310	.6963	.5309	.3545	.2023	.0966	.0380	.0122	.0007	.0000
40	.9275	.6716	.4957	.3154	.1683	.0737	.0260	.0073	.0003	.0000
60	.9236	.6440	.4578	.2755	.1362	.0541	.0169	.0041	.0001	.0000
120	.9190	.6131	.4173	.2356	.1069	.0380	.0104	.0022	.0000	.0000
∞	.9136	.5786	.3745	.1966	.0809	.0254	.0060	.0010	.0000	.0000
					$n_1 = 9, \alpha = 0.025$					
2	.9682	.9480	.9364	.9228	.9074	.8903	.8715	.8512	.8066	.7575
4	.9616	.9121	.8783	.8356	.7839	.7241	.6579	.5871	.4420	.3075
6	.9561	.8768	.8188	.7443	.6553	.5564	.4541	.3551	.1898	.0840
8	.9516	.8452	.7654	.6640	.5471	.4252	.3098	.2108	.0785	.0216
10	.9478	.8178	.7196	.5974	.4624	.3305	.2165	.1292	.0343	.0061
12	.9446	.7944	.6811	.5433	.3974	.2633	.1567	.0831	.0163	.0019
14	.9420	.7742	.6485	.4992	.3472	.2151	.1175	.0562	.0084	.0007
16	.9396	.7568	.6210	.4631	.3080	.1799	.0911	.0397	.0047	.0003
18	.9376	.7418	.5976	.4333	.2770	.1535	.0728	.0293	.0028	.0001
20	.9359	.7286	.5774	.4083	.2520	.1133	.0597	.0224	.0018	.0001
22	.9343	.7170	.5600	.3873	.2317	.1176	.0500	.0176	.0012	.0000
24	.9330	.7068	.5448	.3693	.2148	.1052	.0427	.0142	.0008	.0000
26	.9317	.6977	.5314	.3538	.2008	.0951	.0370	.0117	.0006	.0000
28	.9306	.6896	.5196	.3404	.1888	.0868	.0326	.0099	.0005	.0000
30	.9296	.6822	.5091	.3286	.1786	.0800	.0290	.0084	.0004	.0000
40	.9258	.6545	.4702	.2868	.1441	.0583	.0186	.0047	.0001	.0000
60	.9213	.6233	.4284	.2446	.1123	.0404	.0112	.0024	.0000	.0000
120	.9161	.5880	.3836	.2029	.0840	.0265	.0062	.0011	.0000	.0000
∞	.9099	.5485	.3366	.1630	.0600	.0163	.0032	.0004	.0000	.0000
					$n_1 = 10, \alpha = 0.025$					
2	.9683	.9483	.9368	.9233	.9081	.8911	.8725	.8523	.8081	.7593
4	.9617	.9124	.8787	.8359	.7842	.7244	.6581	.5873	.4420	.3074
6	.9561	.8765	.8181	.7429	.6531	.5534	.4504	.3511	.1860	.0815
8	.9515	.8439	.7628	.6598	.5413	.4181	.3023	.2038	.0741	.0198
10	.9476	.8153	.7149	.5901	.4530	.3202	.2067	.1212	.0308	.0051
12	.9444	.7905	.6741	.5331	.3850	.2508	.1460	.0754	.0138	.0015
14	.9415	.7691	.6395	.4865	.3326	.2014	.1068	.0492	.0067	.0005
16	.9391	.7504	.6100	.4482	.2917	.1654	.0808	.0337	.0036	.0002
18	.9370	.7341	.5848	.4165	.2594	.1389	.0630	.0240	.0020	.0001
20	.9351	.7199	.5631	.3900	.2336	.1188	.0505	.0178	.0012	.0000
22	.9334	.7072	.5442	.3676	.2126	.1032	.0414	.0136	.0008	.0000
24	.9319	.6961	.5277	.3486	.1953	.0910	.0347	.0107	.0005	.0000
26	.9306	.6861	.5132	.3322	.1809	.0812	.0295	.0086	.0004	.0000
28	.9294	.6771	.5004	.3179	.1688	.0732	.0255	.0071	.0003	.0000
30	.9283	.6690	.4890	.3055	.1585	.0667	.0224	.0059	.0002	.0000
40	.9241	.6384	.4467	.2615	.1240	.0464	.0135	.0030	.0001	.0000
60	.9192	.6035	.4011	.2175	.0928	.0304	.0075	.0014	.0000	.0000
120	.9133	.5639	.3526	.1747	.0660	.0185	.0038	.0005	.0000	.0000
∞	.9062	.5193	.3018	.1345	.0442	.0104	.0017	.0002	.0000	.0000

Table T.11 (continued)

n_2	$\phi = .5$	1.0	1.2	1.4	1.6	1.8	2.0	2.2	2.6	3.0
					$n_1 = 12, \alpha = 0.025$					
2	.9684	.9487	.9373	.9241	.9090	.8923	.8739	.8540	.8103	.7621
4	.9618	.9127	.8791	.8364	.7847	.7249	.6584	.5875	.4420	.3071
6	.9562	.8760	.8168	.7405	.6494	.5484	.4444	.3446	.1801	.0775
8	.9514	.8417	.7585	.6527	.5315	.4064	.2901	.1924	.0672	.0170
10	.9474	.8110	.7069	.5778	.4373	.3032	.1910	.1087	.0256	.0039
12	.9439	.7839	.6622	.5158	.3644	.2305	.1292	.0637	.0104	.0010
14	.9408	.7600	.6238	.4647	.3082	.1792	.0903	.0391	.0046	.0003
16	.9381	.7391	.5909	.4227	.2647	.1426	.0652	.0251	.0022	.0001
18	.9358	.7206	.5625	.3878	.2305	.1159	.0486	.0168	.0011	.0000
20	.9337	.7042	.5379	.3587	.2034	.0961	.0373	.0118	.0006	.0000
22	.9318	.6897	.5165	.3341	.1816	.0812	.0293	.0085	.0004	.0000
24	.9301	.6767	.4977	.3132	.1638	.0696	.0236	.0063	.0002	.0000
26	.9286	.6651	.4811	.2953	.1491	.0605	.0194	.0048	.0001	.0000
28	.9272	.6546	.4665	.2798	.1369	.0533	.0162	.0038	.0001	.0000
30	.9260	.6451	.4534	.2664	.1266	.0474	.0138	.0031	.0001	.0000
40	.9210	.6087	.4050	.2192	.0929	.0300	.0072	.0013	.0000	.0000
60	.9151	.5668	.3528	.1728	.0640	.0173	.0034	.0005	.0000	.0000
120	.9079	.5188	.2977	.1294	.0407	.0090	.0014	.0001	.0000	.0000
∞	.8989	.4642	.2410	.0907	.0236	.0041	.0005	.0000	.0000	.0000
					$n_1 = 1, \alpha = 0.05$					
2	.9271	.8617	.8256	.7847	.7402	.6927	.6432	.5926	.4915	.3950
4	.9141	.8048	.7415	.6694	.5910	.5095	.4284	.3509	.2169	.1198
6	.9077	.7768	.7010	.6153	.5238	.4315	.3431	.2629	.1374	.0611
8	.9040	.7610	.6784	.5858	.4883	.3916	.3015	.2223	.1054	.0413
10	.9017	.7510	.6642	.5675	.4666	.3680	.2775	.1997	.0890	.0322
12	.9000	.7440	.6544	.5551	.4521	.3524	.2620	.1854	.0793	.0272
14	.8988	.7390	.6474	.5462	.4418	.3414	.2513	.1756	.0728	.0240
16	.8979	.7351	.6420	.5394	.4341	.3333	.2433	.1685	.0683	.0219
18	.8972	.7321	.6379	.5342	.4281	.3270	.2373	.1631	.0649	.0203
20	.8966	.7297	.6345	.5300	.4233	.3220	.2325	.1589	.0623	.0192
22	.8961	.7277	.6317	.5265	.4194	.3180	.2287	.1555	.0603	.0183
24	.8957	.7260	.6294	.5236	.4161	.3146	.2255	.1527	.0586	.0175
26	.8954	.7246	.6274	.5212	.4134	.3118	.2228	.1504	.0573	.0169
28	.8951	.7233	.6258	.5192	.4111	.3094	.2206	.1485	.0561	.0165
30	.8948	.7223	.6243	.5173	.4090	.3073	.2186	.1468	.0551	.0160
40	.8939	.7185	.6192	.5110	.4020	.3001	.2119	.1410	.0518	.0147
60	.8930	.7147	.6140	.5047	.3949	.2930	.2053	.1354	.0487	.0134
120	.8920	.7108	.6087	.4983	.3879	.2859	.1988	.1300	.0457	.0123
∞	.8910	.7070	.6036	.4920	.3810	.2791	.1926	.1248	.0430	.0112
					$n_1 = 2, \alpha = 0.05$					
2	.9324	.8814	.8527	.8201	.7840	.7451	.7038	.6608	.5722	.4837
4	.9201	.8239	.7657	.6976	.6219	.5414	.4598	.3804	.2400	.1353
6	.9129	.7891	.7135	.6257	.5303	.4330	.3396	.2554	.1264	.0520
8	.9083	.7672	.6810	.5821	.4769	.3729	.2773	.1955	.0821	.0273
10	.9052	.7523	.6592	.5536	.4430	.3361	.2408	.1624	.0609	.0175
12	.9030	.7417	.6438	.5336	.4197	.3115	.2173	.1419	.0490	.0126
14	.9013	.7337	.6323	.5189	.4028	.2941	.2010	.1281	.0416	.0099
16	.9000	.7274	.6234	.5077	.3901	.2812	.1892	.1183	.0367	.0082
18	.8989	.7225	.6164	.4988	.3802	.2713	.1802	.1110	.0331	.0071
20	.8980	.7184	.6107	.4917	.3723	.2634	.1732	.1054	.0305	.0063
22	.8973	.7150	.6059	.4858	.3658	.2570	.1675	.1009	.0285	.0057
24	.8967	.7122	.6019	.4808	.3603	.2517	.1629	.0973	.0269	.0052
26	.8961	.7097	.5985	.4767	.3558	.2472	.1590	.0943	.0256	.0048
28	.8957	.7076	.5956	.4730	.3518	.2434	.1558	.0918	.0245	.0045
30	.8953	.7058	.5930	.4699	.3484	.2401	.1530	.0896	.0236	.0043
40	.8938	.6992	.5839	.4588	.3365	.2288	.1434	.0824	.0207	.0035
60	.8923	.6924	.5746	.4476	.3247	.2177	.1341	.0756	.0181	.0029
120	.8908	.6855	.5651	.4364	.3129	.2069	.1253	.0692	.0157	.0024
∞	.8892	.6785	.5556	.4251	.3013	.1963	.1168	.0632	.0137	.0019
					$n_1 = 3, \alpha = 0.05$					
2	.9342	.8882	.8623	.8327	.7998	.7640	.7260	.6861	.6030	.5187
4	.9221	.8302	.7735	.7064	.6311	.5505	.4683	.3880	.2453	.1384
6	.9144	.7909	.7134	.6226	.5235	.4225	.3264	.2407	.1132	.0435
8	.9092	.7643	.6733	.5683	.4570	.3482	.2504	.1694	.0639	.0184
10	.9056	.7454	.6453	.5314	.4134	.3019	.2059	.1307	.0419	.0098
12	.9028	.7314	.6249	.5050	.3831	.2709	.1776	.1074	.0305	.0061
14	.9007	.7207	.6093	.4853	.3611	.2490	.1583	.0922	.0238	.0042
16	.8990	.7122	.5972	.4701	.3443	.2328	.1444	.0817	.0196	.0031
18	.8976	.7054	.5874	.4581	.3313	.2204	.1340	.0740	.0167	.0025
20	.8965	.6997	.5794	.4483	.3208	.2106	.1259	.0682	.0146	.0020
22	.8955	.6950	.5728	.4402	.3122	.2026	.1195	.0637	.0131	.0017
24	.8947	.6909	.5671	.4333	.3051	.1961	.1143	.0601	.0119	.0015
26	.8940	.6875	.5623	.4275	.2990	.1907	.1100	.0571	.0110	.0013
28	.8934	.6845	.5581	.4225	.2938	.1860	.1064	.0547	.0103	.0012
30	.8928	.6818	.5544	.4182	.2894	.1820	.1033	.0526	.0097	.0011
40	.8909	.6723	.5414	.4028	.2738	.1684	.0930	.0458	.0078	.0008
60	.8888	.6624	.5279	.3872	.2583	.1552	.0833	.0397	.0062	.0006
120	.8866	.6522	.5142	.3716	.2431	.1425	.0743	.0342	.0049	.0004
∞	.8843	.6415	.5000	.3557	.2280	.1304	.0659	.0293	.0038	.0003

Table T.11 (continued)

n_2	$\phi = .5$	1.0	1.2	1.4	1.6	1.8	2.0	2.2	2.6	3.0
					$n_1 = 4, \alpha = 0.05$					
2	.9351	.8917	.8672	.8391	.8079	.7738	.7375	.6993	.6193	.5374
4	.9232	.8332	.7771	.7103	.6350	.5542	.4714	.3905	.2466	.1389
6	.9151	.7906	.7112	.6178	.5158	.4122	.3143	.2282	.1030	.0375
8	.9094	.7602	.6649	.5549	.4389	.3271	.2286	.1493	.0515	.0132
10	.9052	.7378	.6315	.5110	.3876	.2736	.1788	.1076	.0301	.0059
12	.9020	.7208	.6066	.4791	.3516	.2380	.1475	.0833	.0199	.0032
14	.8995	.7076	.5875	.4550	.3253	.2129	.1266	.0680	.0143	.0019
16	.8975	.6970	.5723	.4363	.3054	.1945	.1118	.0577	.0109	.0013
18	.8958	.6883	.5600	.4214	.2898	.1804	.1009	.0503	.0087	.0009
20	.8945	.6811	.5498	.4092	.2774	.1695	.0926	.0449	.0073	.0007
22	.8933	.6750	.5413	.3991	.2672	.1607	.0861	.0408	.0062	.0006
24	.8923	.6698	.5341	.3907	.2587	.1535	.0808	.0376	.0054	.0005
26	.8914	.6653	.5279	.3834	.2516	.1475	.0765	.0349	.0049	.0004
28	.8906	.6614	.5225	.3772	.2455	.1424	.0730	.0328	.0044	.0003
30	.8899	.6579	.5178	.3718	.2402	.1381	.0700	.0311	.0040	.0003
40	.8874	.6454	.5009	.3526	.2219	.1234	.0601	.0254	.0029	.0002
60	.8848	.6322	.4833	.3332	.2040	.1095	.0511	.0206	.0021	.0001
120	.8819	.6183	.4652	.3136	.1865	.0965	.0431	.0164	.0015	.0001
∞	.8789	.6038	.4466	.2940	.1695	.0844	.0360	.0130	.0011	.0000
					$n_1 = 5, \alpha = 0.05$					
2	.9356	.8939	.8702	.8431	.8128	.7798	.7445	.7074	.6293	.5490
4	.9238	.8349	.7791	.7124	.6369	.5558	.4727	.3914	.2467	.1386
6	.9154	.7897	.7087	.6131	.5088	.4033	.3044	.2181	.0952	.0333
8	.9093	.7561	.6573	.5432	.4237	.3099	.2115	.1342	.0430	.0100
10	.9048	.7308	.6193	.4933	.3660	.2509	.1579	.0909	.0227	.0038
12	.9012	.7111	.5904	.4566	.3254	.2118	.1249	.0665	.0136	.0018
14	.8983	.6956	.5679	.4287	.2957	.1845	.1033	.0516	.0090	.0010
16	.8960	.6829	.5499	.4069	.2732	.1646	.0883	.0418	.0064	.0006
18	.8941	.6725	.5352	.3895	.2557	.1496	.0774	.0351	.0048	.0004
20	.8924	.6638	.5231	.3753	.2417	.1380	.0693	.0303	.0038	.0003
22	.8910	.6564	.5129	.3635	.2303	.1288	.0630	.0267	.0031	.0002
24	.8898	.6501	.5042	.3536	.2209	.1213	.0580	.0240	.0026	.0001
26	.8888	.6445	.4967	.3451	.2129	.1151	.0540	.0218	.0022	.0001
28	.8878	.6397	.4901	.3379	.2062	.1099	.0507	.0201	.0019	.0001
30	.8870	.6354	.4844	.3315	.2003	.1055	.0479	.0186	.0017	.0001
40	.8840	.6198	.4638	.3091	.1803	.0908	.0390	.0142	.0011	.0000
60	.8807	.6033	.4423	.2864	.1609	.0772	.0313	.0106	.0007	.0000
120	.8771	.5857	.4201	.2638	.1422	.0649	.0247	.0078	.0004	.0000
∞	.8733	.5671	.3971	.2412	.1245	.0538	.0192	.0056	.0003	.0000
					$n_1 = 6, \alpha = 0.05$					
2	.9360	.8953	.8722	.8457	.8161	.7839	.7493	.7129	.6361	.5569
4	.9242	.8361	.7803	.7136	.6380	.5567	.4733	.3916	.2464	.1381
6	.9156	.7887	.7063	.6090	.5028	.3959	.2962	.2100	.0893	.0301
8	.9092	.7525	.6506	.5332	.4109	.2958	.1978	.1225	.0369	.0080
10	.9042	.7245	.6086	.4782	.3480	.2325	.1417	.0784	.0177	.0026
12	.9003	.7024	.5761	.4373	.3036	.1908	.1077	.0544	.0097	.0011
14	.8972	.6847	.5506	.4061	.2711	.1619	.0859	.0401	.0059	.0005
16	.8946	.6702	.5301	.3816	.2465	.1412	.0710	.0312	.0039	.0003
18	.8924	.6582	.5132	.3621	.2275	.1257	.0605	.0252	.0028	.0002
20	.8905	.6480	.4992	.3461	.2124	.1139	.0528	.0210	.0021	.0001
22	.8889	.6394	.4874	.3328	.2001	.1045	.0469	.0179	.0016	.0001
24	.8875	.6319	.4773	.3216	.1900	.0970	.0423	.0157	.0013	.0001
26	.8863	.6253	.4686	.3121	.1815	.0908	.0387	.0139	.0011	.0000
28	.8852	.6196	.4610	.3039	.1744	.0857	.0357	.0125	.0009	.0000
30	.8843	.6145	.4543	.2968	.1682	.0814	.0333	.0114	.0008	.0000
40	.8807	.5960	.4302	.2717	.1471	.0672	.0256	.0081	.0004	.0000
60	.8768	.5760	.4050	.2464	.1270	.0545	.0193	.0055	.0002	.0000
120	.8724	.5547	.3789	.2214	.1082	.0434	.0141	.0037	.0001	.0000
∞	.8677	.5319	.3520	.1967	.0907	.0339	.0101	.0024	.0000	.0000
					$n_1 = 7, \alpha = 0.05$					
2	.9363	.8963	.8736	.8476	.8185	.7868	.7527	.7168	.6410	.5627
4	.9245	.8368	.7811	.7144	.6387	.5571	.4735	.3916	.2460	.1376
6	.9157	.7878	.7042	.6054	.4978	.3897	.2895	.2035	.0846	.0278
8	.9090	.7492	.6449	.5247	.4002	.2841	.1868	.1133	.0323	.0065
10	.9038	.7189	.5992	.4652	.3328	.2174	.1288	.0689	.0143	.0019
12	.8996	.6947	.5636	.4207	.2852	.1738	.0944	.0454	.0072	.0007
14	.8961	.6750	.5353	.3866	.2505	.1439	.0726	.0320	.0041	.0003
16	.8933	.6588	.5125	.3598	.2243	.1226	.0582	.0238	.0025	.0001
18	.8908	.6452	.4936	.3383	.2041	.1070	.0482	.0185	.0017	.0001
20	.8888	.6336	.4779	.3208	.1882	.0951	.0409	.0149	.0012	.0000
22	.8870	.6238	.4646	.3062	.1753	.0858	.0355	.0123	.0009	.0000
24	.8854	.6152	.4532	.2940	.1647	.0785	.0314	.0105	.0007	.0000
26	.8840	.6077	.4433	.2836	.1559	.0725	.0282	.0091	.0005	.0000
28	.8828	.6011	.4347	.2747	.1485	.0676	.0256	.0080	.0004	.0000
30	.8817	.5952	.4272	.2669	.1421	.0634	.0234	.0071	.0003	.0000
40	.8776	.5737	.3998	.2396	.1206	.0501	.0170	.0046	.0002	.0000
60	.8730	.5504	.3713	.2124	.1005	.0387	.0119	.0029	.0001	.0000
120	.8679	.5253	.3417	.1857	.0821	.0290	.0080	.0017	.0000	.0000
∞	.8622	.4983	.3112	.1597	.0656	.0211	.0052	.0010	.0000	.0000

Table T.11 (continued)

n_2	$\phi = .5$	1.0	1.2	1.4	1.6	1.8	2.0	2.2	2.6	3.0
					$n_1 = 8, \alpha = 0.05$					
2	.9365	.8971	.8747	.8490	.8203	.7889	.7553	.7198	.6448	.5671
4	.9274	.8374	.7817	.7149	.6391	.5574	.4735	.3914	.2456	.1371
6	.9158	.7869	.7024	.6023	.4935	.3845	.2839	.1981	.0809	.0259
8	.9088	.7464	.6398	.5173	.3910	.2744	.1777	.1059	.0289	.0055
10	.9033	.7140	.5910	.4540	.3200	.2049	.1184	.0615	.0118	.0014
12	.8989	.6878	.5526	.4063	.2697	.1598	.0838	.0387	.0055	.0005
14	.8951	.6663	.5218	.3696	.2330	.1292	.0624	.0260	.0029	.0002
16	.8920	.6484	.4968	.3407	.2056	.1077	.0485	.0186	.0017	.0001
18	.8894	.6334	.4761	.3176	.1846	.0921	.0390	.0139	.0010	.0000
20	.8871	.6205	.4588	.2988	.1680	.0804	.0323	.0108	.0007	.0000
22	.8851	.6095	.4441	.2832	.1548	.0713	.0274	.0087	.0005	.0000
24	.8834	.5999	.4315	.2700	.1439	.0642	.0237	.0072	.0003	.0000
26	.8819	.5915	.4206	.2589	.1349	.0585	.0208	.0060	.0003	.0000
28	.8805	.5840	.4111	.2493	.1274	.0538	.0186	.0052	.0002	.0000
30	.8793	.5774	.4027	.2410	.1209	.0499	.0168	.0045	.0002	.0000
40	.8746	.5530	.3725	.2120	.0995	.0377	.0114	.0027	.0001	.0000
60	.8694	.5264	.3408	.1834	.0798	.0275	.0074	.0015	.0000	.0000
120	.8635	.4975	.3081	.1556	.0623	.0193	.0046	.0008	.0000	.0000
∞	.8568	.4663	.2745	.1292	.0472	.0130	.0027	.0004	.0000	.0000
					$n_1 = 9, \alpha = 0.05$					
2	.9366	.8977	.8756	.8501	.8217	.7906	.7573	.7221	.6477	.5705
4	.9249	.8378	.7821	.7153	.6394	.5575	.4735	.3912	.2452	.1366
6	.9158	.7861	.7007	.5996	.4898	.3800	.2792	.1936	.0778	.0245
8	.9087	.7439	.6354	.5109	.3832	.2661	.1702	.0998	.0262	.0048
10	.9029	.7096	.5838	.4442	.3089	.1944	.1099	.0555	.0100	.0011
12	.8982	.6816	.5428	.3937	.2564	.1481	.0753	.0334	.0043	.0003
14	.8943	.6584	.5097	.3547	.2182	.1171	.0543	.0216	.0021	.0001
16	.8909	.6390	.4827	.3241	.1898	.0956	.0409	.0148	.0011	.0000
18	.8881	.6226	.4604	.2996	.1681	.0801	.0320	.0107	.0007	.0000
20	.8856	.6086	.4416	.2796	.1511	.0686	.0259	.0080	.0004	.0000
22	.8835	.5964	.4257	.2630	.1376	.0599	.0214	.0062	.0003	.0000
24	.8816	.5858	.4120	.2492	.1266	.0531	.0181	.0050	.0002	.0000
26	.8799	.5765	.4002	.2374	.1176	.0477	.0156	.0041	.0001	.0000
28	.8784	.5683	.3898	.2274	.1110	.0433	.0137	.0034	.0001	.0000
30	.8770	.5609	.3807	.2186	.1036	.0397	.0121	.0029	.0001	.0000
40	.8718	.5337	.3477	.1883	.0825	.0286	.0077	.0016	.0000	.0000
60	.8660	.5038	.3133	.1587	.0636	.0197	.0046	.0008	.0000	.0000
120	.8592	.4713	.2778	.1304	.0473	.0129	.0026	.0004	.0000	.0000
∞	.8514	.4361	.2417	.1041	.0337	.0080	.0014	.0002	.0000	.0000
					$n_1 = 10, \alpha = 0.05$					
2	.9368	.8981	.8762	.8510	.8228	.7920	.7589	.7240	.6500	.5732
4	.9250	.8381	.7825	.7156	.6395	.5575	.4734	.3910	.2448	.1362
6	.9158	.7854	.6992	.5972	.4865	.3762	.2751	.1898	.0752	.0233
8	.9085	.7417	.6315	.5053	.3764	.2591	.1638	.0948	.0241	.0042
10	.9026	.7057	.5774	.4357	.2993	.1854	.1028	.0508	.0086	.0009
12	.8976	.6761	.5340	.3826	.2448	.1383	.0683	.0293	.0035	.0002
14	.8935	.6514	.4990	.3417	.2055	.1070	.0478	.0182	.0016	.0001
16	.8899	.6305	.4702	.3094	.1763	.0856	.0350	.0120	.0008	.0000
18	.8869	.6128	.4463	.2836	.1541	.0704	.0267	.0083	.0004	.0000
20	.8843	.5976	.4262	.2627	.1368	.0592	.0210	.0061	.0003	.0000
22	.8819	.5844	.4091	.2454	.1232	.0508	.0170	.0046	.0002	.0000
24	.8799	.5729	.3944	.2309	.1122	.0443	.0141	.0035	.0001	.0000
26	.8780	.5627	.3817	.2186	.1031	.0393	.0119	.0028	.0001	.0000
28	.8764	.5537	.3705	.2082	.0956	.0352	.0102	.0023	.0001	.0000
30	.8749	.5456	.3607	.1991	.0893	.0319	.0089	.0019	.0000	.0000
40	.8692	.5157	.3253	.1678	.0687	.0218	.0053	.0010	.0000	.0000
60	.8627	.4827	.2884	.1377	.0508	.0142	.0029	.0004	.0000	.0000
120	.8551	.4467	.2506	.1094	.0359	.0086	.0015	.0002	.0000	.0000
∞	.8462	.4047	.2124	.0836	.0240	.0049	.0007	.0000	.0000	.0000
					$n_1 = 12, \alpha = 0.05$					
2	.9369	.8989	.8772	.8524	.8245	.7941	.7614	.7268	.6536	.5774
4	.9252	.8385	.7829	.7159	.6397	.5575	.4731	.3905	.2441	.1355
6	.9159	.7842	.6968	.5934	.4813	.3700	.2686	.1837	.0713	.0214
8	.9082	.7379	.6250	.4960	.3653	.2476	.1536	.0869	.0208	.0034
10	.9019	.6991	.5666	.4213	.2836	.1711	.0917	.0435	.0067	.0006
12	.8966	.6666	.5192	.3641	.2260	.1227	.0577	.0234	.0024	.0001
14	.8921	.6391	.4805	.3197	.1847	.0913	.0382	.0135	.0010	.0000
16	.8882	.6157	.4485	.2849	.1544	.0703	.0265	.0083	.0004	.0000
18	.8848	.5956	.4219	.2571	.1316	.0557	.0192	.0053	.0002	.0000
20	.8818	.5783	.3994	.2345	.1142	.0452	.0144	.0036	.0001	.0000
22	.8792	.5631	.3803	.2160	.1005	.0376	.0111	.0026	.0001	.0000
24	.8768	.5498	.3638	.2006	.0896	.0318	.0088	.0019	.0000	.0000
26	.8747	.5381	.3496	.1876	.0808	.0274	.0072	.0014	.0000	.0000
28	.8728	.5276	.3371	.1766	.0736	.0239	.0059	.0011	.0000	.0000
30	.8710	.5182	.3261	.1671	.0676	.0211	.0050	.0009	.0000	.9000
40	.8643	.4831	.2865	.1347	.0485	.0131	.0026	.0004	.0000	.0000
60	.8565	.4443	.2456	.1044	.0329	.0075	.0012	.0001	.0000	.0000
120	.8472	.4016	.2042	.0770	.0207	.0039	.0005	.0000	.0000	.0000
∞	.8359	.3548	.1632	.0535	.0120	.0018	.0002	.0000	.0000	.0000

Table T.11 (continued)

n_2	$\phi = .5$	1.0	1.2	1.4	1.6	1.8	2.0	2.2	2.6	3.0
					$n_1 = 1, \alpha = 0.10$					
2	.8582	.7443	.6846	.6202	.5534	.4863	.4209	.3588	.2491	.1628
4	.8410	.6773	.5919	.5017	.4118	.3266	.2500	.1846	.0899	.0375
6	.8336	.6498	.5552	.4570	.3613	.2738	.1985	.1373	.0570	.0194
8	.8296	.6353	.5363	.4344	.3367	.2490	.1753	.1172	.0447	.0137
10	.8271	.6265	.5248	.4209	.3223	.2348	.1623	.1063	.0385	.0110
12	.8254	.6205	.5171	.4120	.3128	.2256	.1541	.0996	.0348	.0096
14	.8242	.6162	.5116	.4057	.3062	.2192	.1485	.0949	.0324	.0086
16	.8232	.6130	.5075	.4010	.3012	.2145	.1444	.0916	.0307	.0080
18	.8225	.6104	.5043	.3973	.2974	.2109	.1412	.0891	.0294	.0075
20	.8219	.6084	.5017	.3944	.2944	.2081	.1388	.0871	.0285	.0072
22	.8214	.6068	.4996	.3920	.2920	.2058	.1368	.0856	.0277	.0069
24	.8210	.6054	.4979	.3900	.2900	.2038	.1351	.0843	.0271	.0067
26	.8207	.6042	.4964	.3884	.2882	.2022	.1338	.0832	.0266	.0065
28	.8204	.6032	.4951	.3869	.2868	.2009	.1326	.0823	.0261	.0063
30	.8201	.6023	.4940	.3857	.2855	.1997	.1316	.0815	.0257	.0062
40	.8192	.5993	.4902	.3814	.2811	.1956	.1281	.0788	.0245	.0058
60	.8183	.5962	.4864	.3771	.2768	.1916	.1248	.0762	.0233	.0054
120	.8174	.5932	.4826	.3729	.2726	.1877	.1215	.0737	.0222	.0050
∞	.8165	.5901	.4788	.3686	.2683	.1838	.1183	.0713	.0211	.0047
					$n_1 = 2, \alpha = 0.10$					
2	.8669	.7746	.7252	.6707	.6130	.5536	.4939	.4355	.3265	.2333
4	.8486	.6981	.6159	.5268	.4358	.3481	.2680	.1987	.0972	.0405
6	.8392	.6593	.5623	.4595	.3586	.2662	.1876	.1252	.0471	.0140
8	.8335	.6369	.5319	.4228	.3183	.2260	.1508	.0944	.0302	.0073
10	.8298	.6223	.5126	.4000	.2940	.2027	.1305	.0783	.0226	.0048
12	.8272	.6122	.4994	.3846	.2780	.1877	.1179	.0686	.0184	.0035
14	.8252	.6047	.4897	.3734	.2666	.1772	.1093	.0622	.0158	.0028
16	.8237	.5990	.4823	.3651	.2581	.1696	.1031	.0578	.0140	.0024
18	.8225	.5945	.4765	.3586	.2516	.1638	.0984	.0544	.0128	.0021
20	.8215	.5908	.4719	.3533	.2464	.1592	.0948	.0519	.0119	.0019
22	.8207	.5878	.4680	.3490	.2422	.1555	.0919	.0498	.0112	.0017
24	.8200	.5853	.4648	.3455	.2387	.1524	.0895	.0482	.0106	.0016
26	.8194	.5831	.4621	.3425	.2357	.1498	.0875	.0468	.0102	.0015
28	.8190	.5812	.4598	.3399	.2332	.1477	.0859	.0457	.0098	.0014
30	.8185	.5796	.4577	.3376	.2310	.1458	.0844	.0447	.0095	.0014
40	.8169	.5739	.4506	.3298	.2235	.1394	.0796	.0415	.0084	.0011
60	.8153	.5681	.4433	.3220	.2160	.1331	.0749	.0384	.0075	.0010
120	.8137	.5622	.4361	.3142	.2087	.1270	.0705	.0355	.0067	.0008
∞	.8120	.5562	.4288	.3064	.2015	.1211	.0662	.0328	.0059	.0007
					$n_1 = 3, \alpha = 0.10$					
2	.8700	.7858	.7403	.6899	.6359	.5799	.5231	.4668	.3597	.2655
4	.8513	.7047	.6230	.5336	.4416	.3525	.2709	.2002	.0970	.0399
6	.8406	.6585	.5581	.4514	.3468	.2521	.1729	.1117	.0386	.0103
8	.8338	.6298	.5190	.4040	.2953	.2016	.1281	.0755	.0208	.0041
10	.8291	.6106	.4933	.3738	.2638	.1724	.1038	.0574	.0135	.0022
12	.8257	.5968	.4752	.3531	.2429	.1537	.0890	.0470	.0098	.0014
14	.8232	.5864	.4618	.3380	.2280	.1408	.0792	.0404	.0077	.0010
16	.8211	.5784	.4516	.3266	.2170	.1315	.0723	.0359	.0064	.0007
18	.8195	.5720	.4434	.3177	.2085	.1244	.0671	.0326	.0055	.0006
20	.8182	.5668	.4369	.3105	.2017	.1189	.0632	.0301	.0049	.0005
22	.8170	.5624	.4314	.3047	.1963	.1145	.0601	.0282	.0044	.0004
24	.8161	.5588	.4268	.2998	.1917	.1108	.0576	.0267	.0040	.0004
26	.8153	.5556	.4230	.2956	.1879	.1078	.0555	.0255	.0038	.0003
28	.8145	.5529	.4196	.2921	.1847	.1053	.0537	.0244	.0035	.0003
30	.8139	.5506	.4167	.2890	.1819	.1031	.0523	.0236	.0033	.0003
40	.8117	.5421	.4063	.2782	.1722	.0956	.0473	.0207	.0027	.0002
60	.8093	.5335	.3959	.2674	.1627	.0885	.0427	.0182	.0022	.0002
120	.8069	.5246	.3853	.2567	.1535	.0817	.0384	.0159	.0018	.0001
∞	.8044	.5156	.3745	.2460	.1444	.0752	.0344	.0138	.0015	.0001

Table T.11 (continued)

n_2	$\phi = .5$	1.0	1.2	1.4	1.6	1.8	2.0	2.2	2.6	3.0
					$n_1 = 4, \alpha = 0.10$					
2	.8716	.7916	.7482	.6999	.6480	.5939	.5387	.4837	.3781	.2836
4	.8527	.7077	.6259	.5360	.4432	.3532	.2708	.1995	.0958	.0390
6	.8410	.6559	.5527	.4429	.3358	.2399	.1610	.1012	.0327	.0080
8	.8333	.6223	.5066	.3871	.2758	.1821	.1110	.0622	.0151	.0026
10	.8279	.5989	.4754	.3509	.2388	.1489	.0846	.0436	.0086	.0011
12	.8238	.5818	.4531	.3257	.2142	.1279	.0689	.0333	.0056	.0006
14	.8207	.5689	.4365	.3074	.1968	.1136	.0587	.0271	.0040	.0004
16	.8182	.5587	.4236	.2935	.1839	.1033	.0517	.0229	.0031	.0002
18	.8161	.5505	.4133	.2826	.1740	.0957	.0467	.0201	.0025	.0002
20	.8144	.5438	.4050	.2738	.1662	.0898	.0428	.0179	.0021	.0001
22	.8130	.5382	.3981	.2666	.1599	.0851	.0398	.0163	.0018	.0001
24	.8118	.5334	.3922	.2606	.1547	.0812	.0375	.0151	.0016	.0001
26	.8107	.5293	.3872	.2555	.1503	.0781	.0355	.0141	.0014	.0001
28	.8098	.5258	.3829	.2512	.1466	.0754	.0339	.0133	.0013	.0001
30	.8090	.5226	.3792	.2474	.1434	.0732	.0326	.0126	.0012	.0001
40	.8061	.5115	.3659	.2343	.1325	.0655	.0281	.0104	.0009	.0000
60	.8030	.5000	.3524	.2211	.1219	.0584	.0241	.0085	.0007	.0000
120	.7997	.4881	.3387	.2081	.1117	.0518	.0206	.0069	.0005	.0000
∞	.7963	.4758	.3248	.1952	.1019	.0457	.0174	.0056	.0003	.0000
					$n_1 = 5, \alpha = 0.10$					
2	.8726	.7952	.7530	.7061	.6555	.6026	.5485	.4943	.3897	.2953
4	.8534	.7093	.6273	.5369	.4435	.3528	.2699	.1983	.0945	.0381
6	.8412	.6532	.5477	.4354	.3266	.2300	.1516	.0933	.0286	.0066
8	.8327	.6154	.4957	.3728	.2599	.1668	.0982	.0528	.0115	.0017
10	.8266	.5885	.4599	.3316	.2187	.1308	.0707	.0343	.0058	.0006
12	.8219	.5685	.4339	.3029	.1913	.1084	.0548	.0245	.0034	.0003
14	.8183	.5532	.4144	.2818	.1720	.0934	.0448	.0188	.0022	.0002
16	.8153	.5410	.3991	.2658	.1578	.0827	.0380	.0152	.0016	.0001
18	.8129	.5311	.3869	.2532	.1470	.0749	.0332	.0128	.0012	.0001
20	.8109	.5229	.3770	.2432	.1385	.0689	.0297	.0110	.0010	.0000
22	.8092	.5161	.3687	.2349	.1316	.0642	.0270	.0097	.0008	.0000
24	.8077	.5103	.3618	.2280	.1260	.0604	.0249	.0087	.0007	.0000
26	.8064	.5053	.3558	.2222	.1213	.0573	.0232	.0080	.0006	.0000
28	.8053	.5009	.3507	.2173	.1174	.0547	.0218	.0074	.0005	.0000
30	.8043	.4971	.3462	.2129	.1140	.0525	.0206	.0068	.0004	.0000
40	.8007	.4833	.3302	.1979	.1024	.0452	.0169	.0053	.0003	.0000
60	.7968	.4689	.3140	.1830	.0914	.0386	.0137	.0040	.0002	.0000
120	.7927	.4539	.2974	.1684	.0810	.0327	.0109	.0030	.0001	.0000
∞	.7883	.4384	.2807	.1540	.0712	.0274	.0086	.0022	.0001	.0000
					$n_1 = 6, \alpha = 0.10$					
2	.8732	.7976	.7563	.7103	.6606	.6085	.5552	.5016	.3978	.3035
4	.8540	.7102	.6281	.5373	.4434	.3522	.2689	.1971	.0934	.0373
6	.8411	.6507	.5432	.4291	.3189	.2220	.1442	.0872	.0256	.0056
8	.8321	.6094	.4864	.3609	.2469	.1548	.0884	.0459	.0092	.0012
10	.8254	.5794	.4465	.3155	.2023	.1168	.0604	.0278	.0041	.0004
12	.8202	.5568	.4174	.2837	.1728	.0935	.0446	.0187	.0022	.0001
14	.8161	.5392	.3952	.2603	.1522	.0781	.0350	.0136	.0013	.0001
16	.8127	.5252	.3779	.2426	.1371	.0674	.0286	.0104	.0009	.0000
18	.8100	.5137	.3640	.2287	.1257	.0596	.0243	.0084	.0006	.0000
20	.8076	.5042	.3526	.2176	.1167	.0538	.0211	.0070	.0005	.0000
22	.8056	.4962	.3432	.2085	.1096	.0492	.0187	.0060	.0004	.0000
24	.8039	.4894	.3352	.2009	.1038	.0456	.0169	.0052	.0003	.0000
26	.8024	.4835	.3283	.1945	.0989	.0426	.0154	.0046	.0002	.0000
28	.8011	.4783	.3224	.1891	.0949	.0402	.0142	.0042	.0002	.0000
30	.7999	.4738	.3172	.1844	.0914	.0382	.0133	.0038	.0002	.0000
40	.7956	.4574	.2989	.1680	.0797	.0315	.0103	.0027	.0001	.0000
60	.7910	.4403	.2802	.1519	.0688	.0257	.0078	.0019	.0001	.0000
120	.7859	.4223	.2612	.1362	.0587	.0206	.0058	.0013	.0000	.0000
∞	.7805	.4035	.2420	.1210	.0494	.0162	.0042	.0009	.0000	.0000

Table T.11 (continued)

n_2	$\phi = .5$	1.0	1.2	1.4	1.6	1.8	2.0	2.2	2.6	3.0
					$n_1 = 7, \alpha = 0.10$					
2	.8737	.7994	.7587	.7133	.6643	.6129	.5600	.5069	.4037	.3095
4	.8543	.7108	.6285	.5373	.4431	.3515	.2680	.1960	.0924	.0367
6	.8411	.6485	.5394	.4238	.3126	.2154	.1383	.0825	.0234	.0049
8	.8315	.6042	.4784	.3509	.2362	.1451	.0808	.0407	.0076	.0009
10	.8243	.5714	.4351	.3020	.1890	.1057	.0525	.0231	.0031	.0002
12	.8186	.5465	.4030	.2675	.1578	.0819	.0371	.0146	.0015	.0001
14	.8141	.5269	.3786	.2423	.1362	.0665	.0279	.0101	.0008	.0000
16	.8103	.5111	.3594	.2231	.1204	.0559	.0221	.0074	.0005	.0000
18	.8072	.4982	.3440	.2081	.1086	.0483	.0181	.0057	.0003	.0000
20	.8046	.4874	.3313	.1962	.0995	.0427	.0153	.0046	.0002	.0000
22	.8024	.4784	.3208	.1864	.0922	.0383	.0132	.0038	.0002	.0000
24	.8004	.4705	.3119	.1783	.0863	.0349	.0117	.0032	.0001	.0000
26	.7987	.4638	.3043	.1715	.0815	.0322	.0105	.0028	.0001	.0000
28	.7972	.4579	.2977	.1657	.0774	.0300	.0095	.0024	.0001	.0000
30	.7958	.4527	.2919	.1606	.0740	.0281	.0087	.0022	.0001	.0000
40	.7908	.4339	.2715	.1433	.0625	.0222	.0063	.0014	.0000	.0000
60	.7854	.4140	.2507	.1264	.0520	.0172	.0045	.0009	.0000	.0000
120	.7794	.3932	.2296	.1102	.0426	.0130	.0031	.0006	.0000	.0000
∞	.7728	.3712	.2083	.0948	.0342	.0096	.0021	.0003	.0000	.0000
					$n_1 = 8, \alpha = 0.10$					
2	.8740	.8006	.7604	.7156	.6670	.6160	.5636	.5109	.4081	.3140
4	.8546	.7112	.6287	.5373	.4427	.3509	.2671	.1950	.0915	.0362
6	.8410	.6466	.5361	.4192	.3072	.2100	.1334	.0786	.0216	.0043
8	.8310	.5996	.4716	.3423	.2273	.1371	.0747	.0367	.0064	.0007
10	.8233	.5645	.4251	.2904	.1778	.0968	.0465	.0196	.0023	.0002
12	.8172	.5373	.3906	.2538	.1454	.0727	.0315	.0117	.0010	.0000
14	.8123	.5159	.3641	.2269	.1230	.0574	.0228	.0077	.0005	.0000
16	.8082	.4986	.3432	.2066	.1069	.0470	.0174	.0054	.0003	.0000
18	.8048	.4843	.3264	.1907	.0949	.0397	.0138	.0040	.0002	.0000
20	.8019	.4724	.3126	.1781	.0857	.0344	.0114	.0031	.0001	.0000
22	.7994	.4622	.3012	.1678	.0784	.0303	.0096	.0025	.0001	.0000
24	.7972	.4535	.2914	.1593	.0726	.0272	.0083	.0020	.0001	.0000
26	.7952	.4460	.2831	.1521	.0678	.0247	.0072	.0017	.0000	.0000
28	.7935	.4394	.2759	.1460	.0638	.0226	.0065	.0015	.0000	.0000
30	.7920	.4335	.2696	.1408	.0604	.0210	.0058	.0013	.0000	.0000
40	.7863	.4123	.2473	.1228	.0494	.0158	.0040	.0008	.0000	.0000
60	.7801	.3899	.2247	.1056	.0395	.0116	.0026	.0004	.0000	.0000
120	.7731	.3663	.2019	.0893	.0309	.0082	.0016	.0002	.0000	.0000
∞	.7653	.3414	.1791	.0740	.0235	.0056	.0010	.0001	.0000	.0000
					$n_1 = 9, \alpha = 0.10$					
2	.8743	.8017	.7619	.7174	.6693	.6186	.5666	.5141	.4117	.3177
4	.8548	.7115	.6288	.5372	.4423	.3503	.2663	.1942	.0908	.0357
6	.8409	.6449	.5333	.4153	.3027	.2055	.1294	.0755	.0202	.0039
8	.8305	.5956	.4656	.3350	.2198	.1305	.0698	.0335	.0055	.0006
10	.8224	.5583	.4165	.2805	.1685	.0894	.0417	.0170	.0019	.0001
12	.8160	.5293	.3797	.2420	.1350	.0653	.0271	.0096	.0007	.0000
14	.8107	.5061	.3513	.2137	.1121	.0501	.0189	.0060	.0003	.0000
16	.8063	.4873	.3290	.1924	.0958	.0401	.0139	.0040	.0002	.0000
18	.8025	.4718	.3109	.1758	.0837	.0331	.0107	.0028	.0001	.0000
20	.7994	.4588	.2962	.1627	.0745	.0281	.0086	.0021	.0001	.0000
22	.7966	.4476	.2838	.1520	.0673	.0243	.0071	.0016	.0000	.0000
24	.7942	.4381	.2734	.1432	.0616	.0214	.0059	.0013	.0000	.0000
26	.7921	.4298	.2644	.1358	.0569	.0191	.0051	.0011	.0000	.0000
28	.7902	.4225	.2567	.1295	.0530	.0173	.0045	.0009	.0000	.0000
30	.7885	.4161	.2500	.1241	.0498	.0159	.0040	.0008	.0000	.0000
40	.7821	.3927	.2261	.1058	.0393	.0114	.0025	.0004	.0000	.0000
60	.7750	.3678	.2019	.0885	.0302	.0078	.0015	.0002	.0000	.0000
120	.7671	.3415	.1777	.0724	.0224	.0052	.0009	.0001	.0000	.0000
∞	.7581	.3138	.1537	.0577	.0161	.0033	.0005	.0000	.0000	.0000

Table T.11 (continued)

n_2	$\phi = .5$	1.0	1.2	1.4	1.6	1.8	2.0	2.2	2.6	3.0
					$n_1 = 10, \alpha = 0.10$					
2	.8746	.8025	.7630	.7188	.6710	.6207	.5689	.5167	.4146	.3206
4	.8550	.7117	.6289	.5370	.4419	.3497	.2656	.1935	.0902	.0353
6	.8408	.6434	.5308	.4119	.2988	.2016	.1260	.0728	.0191	.0036
8	.8301	.5921	.4604	.3287	.2133	.1250	.0657	.0309	.0049	.0005
10	.8216	.5528	.4088	.2719	.1605	.0834	.0378	.0149	.0015	.0001
12	.8148	.5220	.3700	.2317	.1263	.0592	.0237	.0081	.0006	.0000
14	.8092	.4974	.3401	.2023	.1030	.0443	.0160	.0048	.0002	.0000
16	.8045	.4772	.3164	.1802	.0866	.0346	.0114	.0031	.0001	.0000
18	.8005	.4605	.2972	.1630	.0745	.0279	.0085	.0021	.0001	.0000
20	.7971	.4464	.2815	.1494	.0654	.0232	.0066	00.15	.0000	.0000
22	.7941	.4344	.2684	.1384	.0583	.0197	.0053	.0011	.0000	.0000
24	.7914	.4240	.2573	.1294	.0527	.0171	.0044	.0009	.0000	.0000
26	.7891	.4150	.2479	.1219	.0482	.0151	.0037	.0007	.0000	.0000
28	.7870	.4071	.2397	.1155	.0445	.0134	.0031	.0006	.0000	.0000
30	.7852	.4001	.2326	.1101	.0414	.0121	.0027	.0005	.0000	.0000
40	.7782	.3746	.2073	.0916	.0315	.0083	.0016	.0002	.0000	.0000
60	.7703	.3475	.1819	.0745	.0232	.0054	.0009	.0001	.0000	.0000
120	.7613	.3186	.1566	.0588	.0163	.0033	.0005	.0000	.0000	.0000
∞	.7510	.2883	.1319	.0449	.0110	.0019	.0002	.0000	.0000	.0000
					$n_1 = 12, \alpha = 0.10$					
2	.8749	.8037	.7646	.7210	.6736	.6237	.5723	.5204	.4188	.3250
4	.8552	.7120	.6289	.5368	.4413	.3488	.2645	.1923	.0893	.0348
6	.8406	.6409	.5267	.4064	.2925	.1954	.1207	.0688	.0174	.0032
8	.8293	.5862	.4517	.3182	.2029	.1161	.0594	.0270	.0039	.0003
10	.8203	.5436	.3961	.2577	.1477	.0739	.0320	.0120	.0011	.0001
12	.8129	.5097	.3538	.2149	.1123	.0500	.0187	.0059	.0003	.0000
14	.3067	.4823	.3210	.1836	.0887	.0356	.0118	.0032	.0001	.0000
16	.8014	.4597	.2950	.1603	.0722	.0266	.0079	.0019	.0001	.0000
18	.7969	.4409	.2740	.1423	.0603	.0206	.0056	.0012	.0000	.0000
20	.7930	.4249	.2568	.1281	.0515	.0164	.0041	.0008	.0000	.0000
22	.7896	.4113	.2424	.1167	.0448	.0135	.0031	.0006	.0000	.0000
24	.7865	.3994	.2303	.1074	.0396	.0113	.0025	.0004	.0000	.0000
26	.7838	.3892	.2199	.0998	.0354	.0096	.0020	.0003	.0000	.0000
28	.7814	.3801	.2110	.0933	.0320	.0083	.0016	.0002	.0000	.0000
30	.7792	.3721	.2032	.0879	.0292	.0073	.0014	.0002	.0000	.0000
40	.7709	.3427	.1759	.0697	.0207	.0045	.0007	.0001	.0000	.0000
60	.7614	.3114	.1486	.0532	.0139	.0026	.0003	.0000	.0000	.0000
120	.7503	.2781	.1220	.0389	.0087	.0013	.0001	.0000	.0000	.0000
∞	.7373	.2431	.0967	.0270	.0051	.0006	.0000	.0000	.0000	.0000

References and Further Reading

A–1 Aitken, A. C. On the statistical independence of quadratic forms in normal variates. *Biometrika* 37: 93–96; 1950.

A–2 Aitken, M. A. Simultaneous inference and the choice of variable subsets in multiple regression. *Technometrics*, vol. 16, no. 2: 221–227; 1974.

A–3 Anderson, T. W. *An introduction to multivariate statistical analysis*. New York: Wiley; 1958.

A–4 Anderson, T. W. *The statistical analysis of time series*. New York: Wiley; 1971.

A–5 Anscombe, F. J. Regression analysis in the computer age. Proceedings of the Thirteenth Conference on the Design of Experiments in Army Research Development and Testing.

B–1 Bancroft, T. A. *Topics in intermediate statistical methods*. Vol. 1. Ames, Iowa: Iowa State Univ. Press; 1968.

B–2 Beale, E. M. L.; Kendall, M. G.; and Mann, D. W. The discarding of variables in multivariate analysis. *Biometrika* 54: 357–365; 1967.

B–3 Behnken, D. W., and Draper, N. R. Residuals and their variance patterns. *Technometrics*, vol. 14, no. 1: 101–111; 1972.

B–4 Bement, T. R., and Williams, J. S. Variance of weighted regression estimators when sampling errors are independent and heteroscedastic. *J. Amer. Statist. Assoc.* 64: 1369–1382; 1969.

B–5 Birnbaum, A. Confidence curves: an omnibus technique for estimation and testing statistical hypotheses. *J. Amer. Statist. Assoc.* 56: 246–249; 1961.

B–6 Boardman, T. J. Confidence intervals for variance components—a comparative Monte Carlo study. *Biometrics*, vol. 30, no. 2: 251–262; 1974.

B–7 Box, G. E. P. Use and abuse of regression. *Technometrics*, vol. 8, no 4: 625–629; 1966.

B–8 Box, G. E. P., and Watson, G. S. Robustness to non-normality of regression tests. *Biometrika* 49: 93–106; 1962.

B–9 Breaux, H. J. A modification of Efroymson's technique for stepwise regression analysis. *Commun. of the ACM* 11: 556–557; 1968.

B–10 Broffitt, J. D., and Williams, J. S. Minimum variance estimators for misclassification probabilities in discriminant analysis. *J. Multivariate Analysis*, vol. 3, no. 3: 311–327; 1973.

B–11 Brooks, R. J. The choice of variables for prediction in curvilinear multiple regression. *Ann. of Statist.* 1: 506–516; 1973.

C–1 Chan, L. S., and Dunn, O. J. The treatment of missing values in discriminant analysis—1. The sampling experiment. *J. Amer. Statist. Assoc.* 67: 473–477; 1972.

C–2 Chew, V. Covariance matrix estimation in linear models. *J. Amer. Statist. Assoc.* 65: 173–181; 1970.

C–3 Christensen, L. R. Simultaneous statistical inference in the normal multiple linear regression model. *J. Amer. Statist. Assoc.* 68: 457–461; 1973.

C–4 Cochran, W. G. The distribution of quadratic forms in a normal system. *Proc. Cambridge Phil. Soc.* 30: 178; 1934.

C–5 Cochran, W. G., and Cox, G. M. *Experimental designs*. New York: Wiley; 1957.

C–6 Cox, D. R. *Planning of experiments*. New York: Wiley; 1958.

C–7 Cox, D. R. Regression methods, notes on some aspects of regression analysis. *J. R. Statist. Soc.*, vol. 131, no. 3: 265–279; 1968.

C–8 Cox, D. R., and Snell, E. J. A general definition of residuals. *J. R. Statist. Soc.* 30: 248–275; 1968.

C–9 Cox, D. R., and Snell, E. J. On test statistics calculated from residuals. *Biometrika*, vol. 58, no. 3: 589–594; 1971.

D–1 D'Agostino, R. B. Monte Carlo power comparison of the W' and D test of normality for $n = 100$. *Commun. in Statist.* 1: 545–551; 1973.

D–2 Daniel, C., and Wood, F. *Fitting equations to data; computer analysis of multifactor data for scientists and engineers.* New York: Wiley, Interscience Publishers; 1971.

D–3 Davenport, J. M. *Comparisons in a class of approximate F-tests*. Technical Report No. 101. Dallas, Texas: Southern Methodist Univ., Dept. of Statist.; 1971.

D–4 Davenport, J. M., and Webster, J. T. A comparison of some approximate F-tests. *Technometrics*, vol. 15, no. 4: 779–789; 1973.

D–5 Davenport, J. M., and Webster, J. T. Type-I error and power of a test involving a Satterthwaite's approximate *F*-statistic. *Technometrics* 14: 555–569; 1972.

D–6 David, F. N. *Tables of the correlation coefficient*. London: Cambridge Univ. Press, issued by *Biometrika* office; 1954.

D–7 Davies, O. L. *Design and analysis of industrial experiments*. London: Oliver & Boyd; 1954.

D–8 Dixon, W. J., and Massey, F. J., Jr. *Introduction to statistical analysis*. New York: McGraw-Hill; 1969.

D–9 Draper, N., and Smith, H. *Applied regression analysis*. New York: Wiley; 1966.

D–10 Dunnett, C. W. New tables for multiple comparisons with a control. *Biometrics*, vol. 20, no. 3: 482–491; 1964.

D–11 Dunnett, C. W. A multiple comparison procedure for comparing several treatments with a control. *J. Amer. Statist. Assoc.* 50: 1096–1121; 1955.

D–12 Durand, D. A note on matrix inversion by the square root method. *J. Amer. Statist. Assoc.*, vol. 51, no. 274: 288–292; 1956.

D–13 Dwass, M. *Probability and statistics*. New York: W. A. Benjamin; 1970.

D–14 Dwyer, P. S. *Linear computations*. New York: Wiley; 1951.

D–15 Dwyer, P. S. Matrix inversion with the square root method. *Technometrics*, vol. 6, no. 2: 197–213; 1964.

E–1 Eicker, F. Asymptotic normality and consistency of the least squares estimators for families of linear regressions. *Ann. Math. Statist.* 34: 447–456: 1963.

E–2 Elston, R. C. On additivity in the analysis of variance. *Biometrics*, vol. 17, no. 2: 209–219; 1961.

E–3 Elston, R. C., and Bush, N. The hypotheses that can be tested when there are interactions in an analysis of variance model. *Biometrics*, vol. 20, no. 4: 681–698; 1964.

E–4 Elston, R. C., and Grizzle, J. E. Estimation of time-response curves and their confidence bands. *Biometrics*, vol. 18, no. 2: 148–159; 1962.

F–1 Faddeev, D. K., and Faddeeva, V. N. *Computational methods of linear algebra*. San Francisco: Freeman; 1963.

F–2 Ferguson, T. S. *Mathematical statistics, a decision theoretic approach*. New York and London: Academic Press; 1967.

F–3 Fletcher, R. H. On the iterative refinement of least squares solutions. *J. Amer. Statist. Assoc.*, vol. 70, no. 349: 109–112; 1975.

F–4 Freund, J., *Mathematical statistics*. 2d ed. Englewood Cliffs, New Jersey: Prentice-Hall; 1971.

F–5 Furnival, G. M. All possible regressions with less computations. *Technometrics* 13: 403–408; 1971.

G–1 Gartside, P. S. A study of methods for comparing several variances. *J. Amer. Statist. Assoc.* 67: 342–346; 1972.

G–2 Ghosh, B. K. Some monotonicity theorems for χ^2, F and t distributions with applications. *J. R. Statist. Soc.* 35: 480–492; 1973.

G–3 Ghosh, M. N., and Sharma, D. Power of Tukey's test for non-additivity. *J. R. Statist. Soc.*, vol. 25–26: 213–219; 1963.

G–4 Golub, G. H. Numerical methods for solving linear least squares problems. *Numerische Mathematik* 7: 206–216; 1965.

G–5 Golub, G. H., and Wilkinson, J. H. Note on the iterative refinement of least squares solution. *Numerische Mathematik* 9: 139–148; 1966.

G–6 Graybill, F. A. On quadratic estimates of variance components. *Ann. Math. Statist.*, vol. 25, no. 2: 367–372; 1954.

G–7 Graybill, F. A. *An introduction to linear statistical models*. Vol. 1. New York: McGraw-Hill; 1961.

G–8 Graybill, F. A. *Introduction to matrices with applications in statistics*. Belmont, Calif.: Wadsworth; 1969.

G–9 Graybill, F. A., and Marsaglia, G. Idempotent matrices and quadratic forms in the general linear hypothesis. *Ann. Math. Statist.* 28: 678–686; 1957.

G–10 Grizzle, J. E., and Allen, D. M. Analysis of growth and dose response curves. *Biometrics*, vol. 25, no. 2: 357–381; 1969.

G–11 Guenther, W. C. Shortest confidence intervals. *Amer. Statist.*, vol. 23, no. 1: 22–25; 1969.

G–12 Guenther, W. C. On the use of best tests to obtain best β-content tolerance intervals. *Statistics Laboratory Mimeographed Series*, unsponsored research, no. 511; 1970.

G–13 Guenther, W. C. Unbiased confidence intervals. *Amer. Statist.*, vol. 25, no. 1: 51–53; 1971.

G–14 Guenther, W. C. Tolerance intervals for univariate distributions. *Naval Research Logistics Quarterly*, vol. 19, no. 2: 309–333; 1972.

G–15 Guenther, W. C. On the use of the incomplete gamma table to obtain unbiased tests and unbiased confidence intervals for the variance of a normal distribution. *Amer. Statist.*, vol. 26, no. 1: 31–34; 1972.

G–16 Guenther, W. C. *Evaluation of shortest confidence intervals for the variance and standard deviation from the incomplete gamma table*. Research paper no. 37, Coll. of Commerce and Industry, Univ. of Wyoming, Laramie; 1974.

G–17 Guenther, W. C., and Whitcomb, M. G. Critical regions for tests of interval hypotheses about the variance. *J. Amer. Statist. Assoc.* 61: 204–219; 1966.

G–18 Gurland, J. A relatively simple form of the distribution of the multiple correlation coefficient. *J. R. Statist. Soc.* 30: 276–283; 1968.

G–19 Guttman, I. *Tolerance regions, a survey of its literature; I. Introduction and discussion of distribution-free tolerance regions.* Technical report no. 123, Dept. of Statist., Univ. of Wisconsin, Madison; 1967.

G–20 Guttman, I. *Tolerance regions, a survey of its literature; II. Discussion of β-expectation tolerance regions.* Technical report no. 124, Dept. of Statist., Univ. of Wisconsin, Madison; 1967.

G–21 Guttman, I. *Tolerance regions, a survey of its literature; III. Discussion of β-content tolerance regions.* Technical report no. 125, Dept. of Statist., Univ. of Wisconsin, Madison; 1967.

G–22 Guttman, I. *Tolerance regions, a survey of its literature; IV. Best population problems and tolerance regions.* Technical report no. 126, Dept. of Statist., Univ. of Wisconsin, Madison; 1967.

H–1 Hager, H., and Antle, C. The choice of the degree of a polynomial model. *J. R. Statist. Soc.* 30: 469–471; 1968.

H–2 Hahn, G. J. Simultaneous prediction intervals for a regression model. *Technometrics*, vol. 14, no. 1: 203–214; 1972.

H–3 Hahn, G. J., and Hendrickson, R. W. A table of percentage points of the distribution of the largest absolute value of k student t variates and its applications. *Biometrika*, vol. 58, no. 2: 323–332; 1971.

H–4 Halperin, M. On inverse estimation in linear regression. *Technometrics*, vol. 12, no. 4: 727–736; 1970.

H–5 Han, C. P. Testing the homogeneity of variances in a two-way classification. *Biometrics*, vol. 22, no. 1: 153–158; 1969.

H–6 Hartley, H. O. Some recent developments in analysis of variance. *Commun. Pure and Appl. Math.* 8: 47–72; 1955.

H–7 Hartley, H. O. Tests of significance in harmonic analysis. *Biometrika* 36: 194–201; 1949.

H–8 Hartwell, T. D., and Gaylor, D. W. Estimating variance components for two-way disproportionate data with missing cells by the method of unweighted means. *J. Amer. Statist. Assoc.* 68: 379–383; 1973.

H–9 Healey, W. C., Jr. Limits for a variance component with an exact confidence coefficient. *Ann. Math. Statist.*, vol. 32, no. 2: 466–476; 1961.

H–10 Hemmerle, W. J. Nonorthogonal analysis of variance using iterative improvement and balanced residuals. *J. Amer. Statist. Assoc.* 69: 772–778; 1974.

H–11 Hocking, R. R. Criteria for selection of a subset regression: which one should be used? *Technometrics* 14: 967–970; 1972.

H–12 Hocking, R. R., and Leslie, R. N. Selection of the best subset in regression analysis. *Technometrics* 9: 531–540; 1967.

H–13 Hoel, P. *Introduction to mathematical statistics.* 3d ed. New York: Wiley; 1971.

H–14 Hogg, R. V., and Craig, A. T. Sufficient statistics in elementary distribution theory. *Sankhyā* 17: 209–216; 1956.

H–15 Hogg, R. V., and Craig, A. T. On the decomposition of certain χ^2 variables. *Ann. Math. Statist.* 29: 608–610; 1958.

H–16 Hogg, R. V., and Craig, A. T. *Introduction to mathematical statistics.* 3d ed. Toronto, Canada: Macmillan Co. of Canada; 1970.

H–17 Householder, A. S. A survey of some closed methods for inverting matrices. *J. Soc. Indust. Appl. Math.*, vol. 5, no. 3: 155–169; 1957.

H–18 Howe, R. B., and Myers, R. H. An alternative to Satterthwaite's test involving positive linear combinations of variance components. *J. Amer. Statist. Assoc.* 65: 404–412; 1970.

H–19 Howe, W. G. Approximate confidence limits on the mean of $X + Y$ where X and Y are two tabled independent random variables. *J. Amer. Statist. Assoc.* 69: 789–794; 1974.

H–20 Hsu, P. L. On the best unbiased quadratic estimate of the variance. *Statistical Research Memoirs, Volume II.* J. Neyman and E. S. Pearson, eds. London: Univ. College, Dept. of Statist., pp. 91–104; 1938.

H–21 Hudson, J. D., Jr., and Krutchkoff, R. G. A Monte Carlo investigation of the size and power of tests employing Satterthwaite's synthetic mean squares. *Biometrika* 55: 431–433; 1968.

J–1 Jacquez, J. A.; Mather, F. J.; and Crawford, C. R. Linear regression with non-constant, unknown error variances: sampling experiments with least squares, weighted least squares, and maximum-likelihood estimators. *Biometrics*, vol. 24, no. 3: 607–626; 1968.

J–2 John, S. Critical values for inference about normal dispersion. *Aust. J. Statist.*, vol. 15, no. 2: 71–79; 1973.

J–3 Johnson, A. F. Design of experiments: the single cycle sine wave model. *Biometrics*, vol. 27, no. 3: 730–735; 1971.

J–4 Johnson, D. E., and Graybill, F. A. An analysis of a two-way model with interaction and no replication. *J. Amer. Statist. Assoc.* 67: 862–868; 1972.

J–5 Johnson, D. E., and Graybill, F. A. Estimation of σ^2 in a two-way classification model with interaction. *J. Amer. Statist. Assoc.* 67: 388–394; 1972.

J–6 Johnson, N. L., and Welch, B. L. Applications of the noncentral t-distribution. *Biometrika* 31: 362–389; 1940.

K–1 Kabe, D. G. Stepwise multivariate linear regression. *J. Amer. Statist. Assoc.* 58: 770–773; 1963.

K–2 Kempthorne, O. *Design and analysis of experiments*. New York: Wiley; 1952.

K–3 Kempthorne, O., and Doerfler, T. E. The behaviour of some significance tests under experimental randomization. *Biometrika* 56: 231–248; 1969.

K–4 Kempthorne, O., and Folks, L. *Probability, statistics, and data analysis*. Ames, Iowa: Iowa State Univ. Press; 1971.

K–5 Kendall, M. G. *Rank correlation methods*. New York: Hafner; 1962.

K–6 Kendall, M. G., and Stuart, A. *The advanced theory of statistics, vol. 1, distribution theory*. 2d ed. New York: Hafner; 1963.

K–7 Kendall, M. G., and Stuart, A. *The advanced theory of statistics, vol. 2, inference and relationship*. New York: Hafner; 1961.

K–8 Kendall, M. G., and Stuart, A. *The advanced theory of statistics, vol. 3, design and analysis, and time series*. New York: Hafner; 1966.

K–9 Kopitzke, R.; Boardman, T. J.; and Graybill, F. A. Least squares programs—a look at the square root procedure. *Amer. Statist.*, vol. 29, no. 1: 64–66; 1975.

K–10 Kraemer, H. C. Improved approximation to the non-null distribution of the correlation coefficient. *J. Amer. Statist. Assoc.* 68: 1004–1008; 1973.

K–11 Kramer, K. H. Tables for constructing confidence limits on the multiple correlation coefficient. *J. Amer. Statist. Assoc.* 58: 1082–1085; 1963.

K–12 Krumbein, W. C., and Graybill, F. A. *An introduction to statistical models in geology*. New York: McGraw-Hill; 1965.

K–13 Kruskal, W. K. Significance, tests of. *International encyclopedia of the social sciences*, vol. 14: 238–250; 1968.

K–14 Kshirsagar, A. M., and Arseven, E. A note on the equivalency of two discrimination procedures. *Amer. Statist.*, vol. 29, no. 1: 38–39; 1975.

L–1 Lachenbruch, P. A. An almost unbiased method of obtaining confidence intervals for the probability of misclassification in discriminant analysis. *Biometrics*, vol. 23, no. 4: 639–645; 1967.

L–2 Lachenbruch, P. A. *Discriminant analysis*. New York: Hafner; 1975.

L–3 Lachenbruch, P. A., and Mickey, M. R. Estimation of error rates in discriminant analysis. *Technometrics*, vol. 10, no. 1: 1–11; 1968.

L–4 LaMotte, L. R. On non-negative quadratic unbiased estimation of variance components. *J. Amer. Statist. Assoc.* 68: 728–730; 1973.

L–5 LaMotte, L. R., and Hocking, R. R. Computational efficiency in the selection of regression variables. *Technometrics* 12: 83–93; 1970.

L–6 Laubscher, N. F. Note on Fisher's transformation of the correlation coefficient. *J. R. Statist. Soc.* 21: 409–410; 1959.

L–7 Lee, Y. S. Tables of upper percentage points of the multiple correlation coefficient. *Biometrika* 59: 175–189; 1972.

L–8 Lehmann, E. L. *Testing statistical hypotheses*. New York: Wiley; 1959.

L–9 Lieberman, G. J. Prediction regions for several predictions from a single regression line. *Technometrics*, vol. 3, no. 1: 21–27; 1961.

L–10 Lindgren, B. *Statistical theory*. 2d ed. New York: Macmillan; 1968.

L–11 Lindley, D. V. The choice of variables in multiple regression. *J. R. Statist. Soc.* 131: 31–53; 1968.

L–12 Lindley, D. V.; East, D. A.; and Hamilton, P. A. Tables for making inferences about the variance of a normal distribution. *Biometrika*, vol. 47, no. 3: 433–436; 1960.

L–13 Link, A. J. A physico-chemical and textural study of carbonate sedimentation in a lagoonal environment. Unpublished M.S. thesis, Northwestern University, 1964.

M–1 Madansky, A. More on length of confidence intervals. *J. Amer. Statist. Assoc.* 57: 586–589; 1962.

M–2 Mallows, C. L. Some comments on C_p. *Technometrics* 15: 661–675; 1973.

M–3 Mantel, N. Why stepdown procedures in variable selection. *Technometrics* 12: 621–625; 1970.

M–4 Miller, R. G., Jr. *Simultaneous statistical inference*. New York: McGraw-Hill; 1966.

M–5 Milliken, G. A., and Graybill, F. A. Extensions of the general linear hypothesis model. *J. Amer. Statist. Assoc.* 65: 797–807; 1970.

M–6 Milliken, G. A., and Graybill, F. A. Tests for interaction in the two-way model with missing data. *Biometrics*, vol. 27, no. 4: 1079–1083; 1971.

M–7 Mood, A. M.; Graybill, F. A.; and Boes, D. C. *Introduction to the theory of statistics*. 3d ed. New York: McGraw-Hill; 1974.

M–8 Morgan, J. A., and Tatar, J. F. Calculation of the residual sum of squares for all possible regressions. *Technometrics* 14: 317–325; 1972.

M–9 Morrison, D. *Multivariate statistical methods*. New York: McGraw-Hill; 1967.

M–10 Myers, R. H., and Howe, R. B. On alternative approximate *F*-tests for hypotheses involving variance components. *Biometrika*, vol. 58, no. 2: 393–396; 1971.

N–1 Naik, U. D. On tests of main effects and interactions in higher-way layouts in the analysis of variance random effects model. *Technometrics* 16: 17–25; 1974.

O–1 Olkin, I., and Pratt, J. W. Unbiased estimation of certain correlation coefficients. *Ann. Math. Statist.* 29: 201–211; 1958.

O–2 Owen, D. B. Factors for one-sided tolerance limits and for variables sampling plans. *Sandia Corporation Monograph*, SCR-607; 1963.

O–3 Owen, D. B. A survey of properties and applications of the noncentral t-distribution. *Technometrics* 10: 445–478; 1968.

P–1 Pachares, J. Tables for unbiased tests on the variance of a normal population. *Ann. Math. Statist.* 32: 84–87; 1961.

P–2 Patnaik, P. B. The non-central χ^2 and F distributions and their applications. *Biometrika* 36: 202–232; 1949.

P–3 Pearson, E. S., and Hartley, H. O., eds. *Biometrika tables for statisticians, vol. 1.* 3d ed. London: Cambridge Univ. Press; 1966.

P–4 Pearson, E. S., and Hartley, H. O., eds. *Biometrika tables for statisticians, vol. 2.* London: Cambridge Univ. Press; 1972.

P–5 Pope, P. T., and Webster, J. T. The use of an F-statistic in stepwise regression procedures. *Technometrics* 14: 327–340; 1972.

P–6 Pratt, J. W. Length of confidence intervals. *J. Amer. Statist. Assoc.* 56: 549–567; 1961.

R–1 Ramachandran, K. V. A test of variances. *J. Amer. Statist. Assoc.* 53: 741–747; 1958.

R–2 Rao, C. R. *Linear statistical inference and its applications.* New York: Wiley; 1973.

R–3 Rao, C. R. Inference on discriminant function coefficients. *Essays in probability and statistics.* R. C. Bose et al., eds. Chapel Hill, N. Carolina: Univ. of N. Carolina and Statist. Pub. Soc.; 1970.

R–4 Rao, C. R. Estimation of heteroscedastic variances in linear models. *J. Amer. Statist. Assoc.* 65: 161–172; 1970.

R–5 Rao, C. R. Estimation of variance and covariance components in linear models. *J. Amer. Statist. Assoc.* 67: 112–115; 1972.

R–6 Rao, J. N. K., and Subrahmaniam, K. Combining independent estimators and estimation in linear regression with unequal variances. *Biometrics*, vol. 27, no. 4: 971–990; 1971.

R–7 Reiersøl, O. Identifiability, estimability, pheno-restricting specifications, and zero lagrange multipliers in the analysis of variance. *Skand. Aktuarietidskr.*, pp. 131–142; 1963.

R–8 Resnikoff, G. J., and Lieberman, G. J. *Tables of the noncentral t-distribution.* Stanford, Calif.: Stanford Univ. Press; 1957.

R–9 Rizvi, M. H., and Solomon, H. Selection of largest multiple correlation coefficients: asymptotic case. *J. Amer. Statist. Assoc.* 68: 184–188; 1973.

S–1 Sampson, A. R. A tale of two regressions. *J. Amer. Statist. Assoc.* 69: 682–689; 1974.

S–2 Satterthwaite, F. E. An approximate distribution of estimates of variance components. *Biometrics Bulletin* 2: 110–114; 1946.

S–3 Saw, J. G. A conservative test for the concurrence of several regression lines and related problems. *Biometrika*, vol. 53, nos. 1 and 2: 272–275; 1966.

S–4 Scheffé, H. *The analysis of variance*. New York: Wiley; 1959.

S–5 Scheffé, H. A statistical theory of calibration. *Ann. Statist.*, vol. 1, no. 1: 1–37; 1973.

S–6 Scott, A. A note on conservative confidence regions for the mean of a multivariate normal. *Ann. Math. Statist.* 38: 278–280; 1967.

S–7 Searle, S. R. *Linear models*. New York: Wiley; 1971.

S–8 Sen, P. K. Estimates of the regression coefficient based on Kendall's Tau. *J. Amer. Statist. Assoc.* 63: 1379–1389; 1968.

S–9 Shapiro, S. S., and Francia, R. S. An approximate analysis of variance test for normality. *J. Amer. Statist. Assoc.* 67: 215–216; 1972.

S–10 Shapiro, S. S., and Wilk, M. B. An analysis of variance test for normality (complete samples). *Biometrika* 52: 591–611; 1965.

S–11 Shukla, G. K. On the problem of calibration. *Technometrics*, vol. 14, no. 3: 547–553; 1972.

S–12 Šidák, Z. On multivariate normal probabilities of rectangles. *Ann. Math. Statist.* 39: 1425–1434; 1968.

S–13 Šidák, Z. Rectangular confidence regions for the means of multivariate normal distributions. *J. Amer. Statist. Assoc.* 62: 626–633; 1967.

S–14 Siotani, M. Interval estimation for linear combinations of means. *J. Amer. Statist. Assoc.* 59: 1141–1152; 1964.

S–15 Snedecor, G. W., and Cochran, W. G. *Statistical methods*. Ames, Iowa: Iowa State Coll. Press; 1969.

S–16 Spjøtvoll, E. Confidence intervals and tests for variance ratios in unbalanced variance components models. *Rev. Int. Statist. Inst.* 36: 37–42; 1968.

S–17 Spjøtvoll, E., and Stoline, M. R. An extension of the *T*-method of multiple comparison to include the cases with unequal sample sizes. *J. Amer. Statist. Assoc.* 68: 975–978; 1973.

S–18 Srivastava, A. B. L. Effect of non-normality on the power of the analysis of variance test. *Biometrika* 46: 114–122; 1959.

S–19 Srivastava, J. N., and Anderson, D. A. A comparison of the determinant, maximum root, and trace optimality criteria. *Commun. in Statist.* 3: 933–940; 1974.

T–1 Tang, P. C. The power function of the analysis of variance tests with tables and illustrations for their use. *Statistical Research Memoirs, Volume II*. J. Neyman and E. S. Pearson, eds. London: Univ. College, Dept. of Statist. pp. 126–146; 1938.

T–2 Tate, R. F. Conditional-normal regression models. *J. Amer. Statist. Assoc.* 61: 477–489; 1966.

T–3 Tate, R. F., and Klett, G. W. Optimal confidence intervals for the variance of a normal distribution. *J. Amer. Statist. Assoc.* 54: 674–682; 1959.

T–4 Tietjen, G. L., and Beckman, R. J. Tables for use of the maximum *F*-ratio in multiple comparison procedures. *J. Amer. Statist. Assoc.* 67: 581–583; 1972.

T–5 Tiku, M. L. A note on approximating to the noncentral *F* distribution. *Biometrika* 53: 606–610; 1966.

T–6 Tiku, M. L. Tables of the power of the *F*-test. *J. Amer. Statist. Assoc.* 62: 525–539; 1967.

T–7 Tiku, M. L. More tables of the power of the *F*-test. *J. Amer. Statist. Assoc.* 67: 709–710; 1972.

T–8 Tiku, M. L. Power function of the *F*-test under non-normal situations. *J. Amer. Statist. Assoc.* 66: 913–916; 1971.

W–1 Walker, A. M. *Large-sample properties of least-squares estimators of harmonic components in a time series with stationary residuals; I. Independent residuals.* Technical report. Dept. of Statist., Stanford Univ., Stanford, Calif.; 1968.

W–2 Wallis, W. A. Tolerance intervals for linear regression. Proceedings of the Second Berkeley Symposium; 1951.

W–3 Wang, Y. Y. A comparison of several variance component estimators. *Biometrika* 54: 301–305; 1967.

W–4 Weeks, D. L., and Williams, D. R. A note on the determination of connectedness in a *N*-way cross classification. *Technometrics*, vol. 6, no. 3: 319–324; 1964. Errata, *Technometrics*, vol. 7, no. 2: 281; 1965.

W–5 Weisberg, S. An empirical comparison of the percentage points of *W* and *W'*. *Biometrika*, vol. 61, no. 3: 644–646; 1974.

W–6 Weisberg, S., and Bingham, C. An approximate analysis of variance test for non-normality suitable for machine calculation. *Technometrics*, vol. 17, no. 1: 133–134; 1975.

W–7 Whittle, P. The simultaneous estimation of a time series harmonic components and covariance structure. *Trabajos Estadist.* 3: 43–57; 1952.

W–8 Williams, E. J. *Regression analysis*. New York: Wiley; 1959.

W–9 Williams, E. J. A note on regression methods in calibration. *Technometrics*, vol. 11, no. 1: 189–192; 1969.

W–10 Williams, J. S. A confidence interval for variance components. *Biometrika* 49. 278–281; 1962.

W–11 Williams, J. S. Lower bounds on convergence rates of weighted least squares to best linear unbiased estimators. *A survey of statistical design and linear models.* J. N. Srivastava, ed. North-Holland: pp. 555–570; 1975.

W–12 Wilkinson, J. H. *The algebraic eigenvalue problem.* Oxford: Clarendon Press; 1965.

W–13 Wilson, A. L. An approach to simultaneous tolerance intervals in regression. *Ann. Math. Statist.* 38: 1536–1540; 1967.

W–14 Wilson, P. D., and Tonascia, J. Tables for shortest confidence intervals on the standard deviation and variance ratio from normal distributions. *J. Amer. Statist. Assoc.* 66: 909–912; 1971.

W–15 Wiorkowski, J. J. Estimation of the proportion of the variance explained by regression, when the number of parameters in the model may depend on the sample size. *Technometrics*, vol. 12, no. 4: 915–919; 1970.

W–16 Wood, F. S. The use of individual effects and residuals in fitting equations to data. *Technometrics*, vol. 15, no. 4: 677–695; 1973.

Z–1 Zacks, S. *The theory of statistical inference.* New York: Wiley; 1971.

Z–2 Zyskind, G., and Martin, F. B. On best linear estimation and a general Gauss–Markov theorem in linear models with arbitrary non-negative covariance structure. *SIAM, J. Appl. Math.* 17: 1190–1202; 1969.

Index